The Bowker Family in America

DESCENDANTS
OF
Edmund-1 Bowker

AND

DESCENDANTS
OF
James-1 Bowker

Frances Sterling Drisko

HERITAGE BOOKS
2015

HERITAGE BOOKS
AN IMPRINT OF HERITAGE BOOKS, INC.

Books, CDs, and more—Worldwide

For our listing of thousands of titles see our website
at
www.HeritageBooks.com

Published 2015 by
HERITAGE BOOKS, INC.
Publishing Division
5810 Ruatan Street
Berwyn Heights, Md. 20740

International Standard Book Numbers
Paperbound: 978-0-7884-5601-5
Clothbound: 978-0-7884-6078-4

BOWKER

Introduction

The BOWKER surname can be found in America as early as the 1640's when Edmund[-1] BOWKER
is known to have settled in Massachusetts. Prior to that time the name had numerous spellings in England
and Wales. It had been spelled BOKER, BOOKER, BUCAR, BUKER, BOUCKER, BOUCHER. In France
it was BOUCHIER – which denoted that the persons occupation was that of a " butcher ".

Folklore, when repeated generation after generation, becomes accepted as the true fact. However,
it can be erroneous and propagate false infomation – which I believe is what happened in this family.

In this instance, the folklore repeated a story that there were three brothers, Edmund, John and James,
who came to America, supposedly around the same period of time and settled in the same area of
Massachusetts. Reportedly their father, who was in service to the English Royal family, had been accused
of " stealing some royal jewels ". It caused his family great shame. This is given as the reason for Edmund
to leave England and come to America. It was also reported that the father was later found innocent.

When I began my research, I endeavored to find all three, but seemed to be hitting a brick wall as far as
John and James were concerned.

I pursued the Edmund BOWKER line and found ample evidence of his existence. He had two wives,
was a farmer as most immigrants were, and was a member of the Boston Artillery Company. He was
a " fence viewer " and was involved in the town politics. His descendants are covered in Section 1 of
this work and cover through the 13th generation in some instances.

John BOWKER, as a brother of Edmund, is an enigma. There is no evidence, that I have been able to find,
that shows that he ever resided in America. There were no marriage records or children recorded.

Edmund BOWKER had a son John born 1647 MA. Numerous records referred to John as " son of Edmund
BOWKER ".

Regarding James BOWKER, he was supposedly born ca 1645, which would have been shortly before Edmund
came to America, and he certainly was not a brother. The folklore tale said that he was taken to Sweden by an
older sister or some other adult female, and so he has been often referred to as Swedish, which is erroneous. He
may have been a son of Edmund, but did not come to America until around 1680. There is ample evidence of his
existence, but I cannot state with certainty that they were father and son. Therefore, I have treated the James
BOWKER line separately. James' descendants are covered in Section 2 of this work and cover to the 10th generation.

There are a number of well-known early families that are related to the BOWKER family. Names such as
DOTEN / DOTY, and others of the MAYFLOWER. The distinguished names of BIGELOW, BRIGHAM,
BRUCE, CLAPP, FAIRCHILD, FORBUSH, GATES, HAPGOOD, HOLBROOK, HOWE, LUND, METCALF,
SHATTUCK, SPAULDING, and many more are in this genealogy.

The BOWKER families started out in Massachusetts, and have moved to every state in the USA, and the Canadian
Provinces. They represent almost every occupation. The BOWKER line has had university chancellors, professors,
scientists, actors, clergymen, and many others including doctors and lawyers. Like most other families there are some
who " marched to a different drummer " . Those people add a little spice to the line.

This researcher had made every effort to verify the information in this work. However, no genealogy is ever complete
or 100% accurate.

Frances STERLING Drisko

BOWKER – TABLE OF CONTENTS

Part One
Descendants of Edmund[-1] BOWKER of Massachusetts

Part Two
Descendants of James-1 BOWKER

BOWKER

KEY TO ABBREVIATIONS

bapt	baptized
ca	around or about
ch	children
dau/o	daughter of
dec'd	deceased
EOL	end of line
gs	info from gravestone
int pub	marriage intentions published
marr	marriage
gs	gravestone
s/o	son of
Twsp	Township
wid/o	widow of

PART ONE

Descendants of Edmund-1 BOWKER

BOWKER
The First American Generation

BOWKER is the more familiar present day spelling of the family name which was variably spelled as BOKER, BOOKER; BOUKER; BUCAR; BUKER; BOUCKER; BOUCHER; and BOUCHIER. Both BOWKER and BOOKER are given as a description of the occupation " butcher ", which in French is "boucher".

BURKE'S " Colonial Gentry " said that this family is identical with that of BOURCHIER/ BOWKER families in England, and claim that according to tradition their ancestors lost their estates through adherence to the "Pretender" Charles STUART and were compelled to change the spelling of their name . It does seem reasonable to believe that many spelling changes have been made through the centuries.

There has been much speculation concerning the parents of Edmund[-1] BOWKER, and there have been many stories which seem to carry some validity – BUT – the fact remains that no one, as far as I know, has been able to prove their exact identity. Therefore, in this genealogy, I will cover the descendants of Edmund-[1] – proposing two possibilities as to his lineage in England and continuing on with the succeeding American generations..

In the Dictionary of English and Welsh Surnames " by HARDSLEY, there is mention of a BOWKER in Lancashire County England as early as 1332, and a BOUKER in Norfolk County, England in 1273.

1. EDMUND/ EDMOND[-1] BOWKER, the immigrant, was possibly the son of a Sir William BOURCHIER (BOWKER) and his wife Lady Elizabeth RUSSELL , OR , the son of James /John[A] BOWKER (John[-B]) and _____. It has been fairly well established that he was born between 1610 and 1617, and was baptized on 6 Jan 1619 at Manchester, Lancashire County, England.. He married first to Ellen SMYTH/ SMITH/SMYTHE . She was the daughter of Thomas SMYTH (Richard) and Ann ____. She was born ____ England; died 21 Jan 1659 Dorchester, MA.

Edmund-[1] BOWKER reportedly came to America ca 1646._ Edmund-[1] was a member of the Ancient and Honorable Artillery of Boston (MA) in 1647. Sources state that he died 14 March 1666 at Sudbury, Middlesex County, MA. When Edmund-[1] BOWKER died, notices were published in Boston, Roxbury, Dorchester and Sudbury for a hearing, which took place on 1 October 1667, regarding a petition submitted by his widow asking for an allowance to support herself and her children. The inventory of Edmund's estate was signed by John BOWKER (his mark) (possibly his son) and Mary POTAR (possibly POTTER) of Middlesex County, MA.
The Probate was registered in Volume 2, page 336.

Edmund-[1] married 2nd to Mary Margaret POTTER 3 July 1658/59. She was the daughter of John POTTER and Elizabeth WOOD, and was born ca 1625 Dorchester MA , died ca 1674 Sherborn, Middlesex, MA.

1

BOWKER
The First American Generation

Source: Middlesex Probate Court Records – First Series, Miscellaneous Index, Page 21.
First BOWKERS in New England by Edgar M. BOWKER 1915
BURKE'S Colonial Gentry
HARDESTY , Dictionary of English and Welsh Surnames

Child of Edmund[-1] BOWKER and Ellen SMYTH/ SMITH:
Surname **BOWKER**

2. ENSIGN JOHN   born ca 1647 Dorchester, MA; died 27 Aug 1721 Marlborough, MA (age 74)
married Mary HOWE 8 March 1678 Marlborough, MA
(she dau/o Abraham HOWE and Hannah WARD)
(she born 30 June 1659 Watertown, MA; died 29 Sep 1723)
Source. NEH& GR Page 156

3. Asa   born ca 1649 Marlborough, MA; died ____   (no further info)

Children of Edmund[-1] BOWKER and Mary Margaret POTTER:
Surname **BOWKER**

+   **4. ELIZABETH /**   born 3 May 1659 Dorchester, MA; died ca 1700 Dunstable, Hillsborough, NH
ELEANOR   married Thomas LUND 28 March 1679 Cambridge, Middlesex, MA
(he s/o Thomas LUND and French Walloon)
(he born ca 1660 Dunstable, Hillsborough, NH; died 1721)

5. EDMUND   born 13 Oct 1661 Sudbury, Middlesex, MA; died 6 March 1706 Sudbury, MA
married Sarah PARMENTER 29 March 1688 Sudbury, MA
(she dau/o John PARMENTER and Elizabeth CUTLER)
(she born 20 Aug 1668 Sudbury, MA; died 5 Sep 1724)

6. Daniel   born ca 1663; died 1664   EOL

+   **7. MARY**   born 15 Apr 1665 Sudbury, MA; died _____
married Thomas E. HOLBROOK 20 Feb 1684 Sherborn, Middlesex Co., MA
(he son of Thomas HOLBROOKE and Hannah SHEPHERD)
(he born 2 Sept 1659; died 24 March 1718 Sherborn, MA)

BOWKER
The Second American Generation

2. ENSIGN JOHN-² BOWKER, son of Edmund-¹ BOWKER and Ellen SMYTH/SMITH was born ca 1647 at Dorchester, MA. He married Mary HOWE on 11 Aug 1678 at Marlborough, Middlesex, MA. She was the daughter of Abraham HOWE and Hannah WARD (William) ; and was born 30 June 1659 at Watertown, Middlesex, MA; died 29 Sep 1723 at Marlborough. John-² BOWKER died 27 Aug 1721 at Marlborough.

Children of John-² BOWKER and Mary HOWE:
Surname **BOWKER**

+	**8. JOHN**	born Sep 1679 MA.; died ca 1710; married Ruth HOWE ca ____	
		(she dau/o Josiah HOWE and Mary HAYNES)	
	9. Ezra	born ca 1681; died ca 1690	EOL
+	**10. MARTHA** (**twin**)	born 6 Mar 1685; died ca 1735 Marlborough, MA	
		married John FORBUSH 30 Nov 1704	
		(he s/o Daniel FORBUSH and Deborah-² REDIAT (John-¹ and Ann DOLT))	
		(he born ca 1681 Marlborough; died 7 Feb 1731 Marlborough, MA)	
+	**11. MARY** (**twin**)	born 6 Mar 1685; died 24 Apr 1752 Stow, Middlesex, MA	
		married John GATES ca 1703	
		(he born 9 Apr 1678 Sudbury, MA; died 19 Sep 1747 Stow, MA)	
+	**12. ASA**	born 22 Nov 1691; died 1763; married Martha EAGER 28 Feb 1718	
		(she dau/o Abraham EAGER and Lydia WOODS)	
		(she born 15 Aug 1693; died _____)	
+	**13. EZEKIEL**	born 5 Nov 1693; died 1744; married Abigail RICE 24 June 1733	
		(she dau/o Peter RICE and Rebecca HOWE) (sister of Ruth)	
	14. Un-named male	born 19 Dec 1695; stillborn	EOL
	15. Un-named male	born 25 Mar 1698; died at birth	EOL
+	**16. HANNAH**	born 21 Sep 1699; died 1750; married Gershom HOWE 6 Dec 1721	
	17. Rachel	born 9 Sep 1702; died 1754 unmarried	EOL

4. ELIZABETH-² BOWKER, daughter of Edmund-¹ (John-^A, ^B) and Mary Margaret POTTER, was born 3 May 1659 at Dorchester, MA. She married Thomas LUND on 28 March 1679 at Cambridge, Middlesex, MA. He was the son of Thomas LUND and French Walloon , and was born ca 1660 Dunstable, Hillsborough, NH, died ca 1721.

Children of Elizabeth-² BOWKER and Thomas LUND:
Surname **LUND**

+	**18. THOMAS**	born 9 Sept 1682 Dunstable, NH; died 5 Sept 1724 NH (killed by Indians)
		married Elizabeth TAYLOR 16 Jan 1711 Dunstable, NH
		Gravestone reads: " Here lies the body of Thomas LUND departed this life in the 42nd year of his age.
		This man and 7 more that lies in this grave was slew all in a day by the Indians"
+	**19. ELIZABETH**	born 29 Sep 1684 NH ; died 15 Apr 1781 Groton, MA;
		married Henry SPAULDING ca 1703+++
		(he born 2 Nov 1680, died 5 Apr 1720)
		2 married Samuel SCRIPTURE, Jr. 6 Feb 1724
+	**20. WILLIAM**	born 19/25 Jan 1686; died ca 1768
		married Rachel HOLDEN 20 Dec 1716 Groton, MA
+	**21. MARGARET**	born 26 May 1687 Dunstable ; died 13 June 1764 Groton, MA
		1 married Jonathan ROBBINS 16 Jan 1712 Concord, MA
		(he s/o George ROBBINS and Mary BARRETT)
		(he born 19 Nov 1686; died 8 May 1725)
		2 married William SHATTUCK ca 1729 Groton, MA
		(he s/o William SHATTUCK and Hannah UNDERWOOD)
		(he born ca 1689 Watertown, MA; died Aug 1757 Groton, MA))

+++ Edward[-1] SPAULDING, possibly born ca 1596 in England, first married Margaret ELLIOTT / ELYOT(she was born _____, died Aug 1640) and second Rachel _____ ca 1642. She was born _____, died around 1670. It is believed that he came to the "New World" around 1619, with his first wife, and is said to have settled in Barbados for a period of time. Later, around 1634, he went to Braintree, MA. He was one of the early proprietors of Chelmsford MA. Edward[-1] SPAULDING was made a freeman on 13 May 1640 at Braintree, which is the earliest recorded history about him. He removed from there ca 1645-7 to Wenham, MA and was one of the founders of Chelmsford in 1655, where he died 26 Feb 1670. He was the father of 7 children, the youngest being Andrew[-2] SPAULDING , born 19 Nov 1652 at Chelmsford, MA; died 5 May 1713 In Chelmsford. He married Hannah [-2] JEFES/JEFTS, daughter of Henry[-1] JEFTS of Billerica, MA. She was born 14 Feb 1654; died 21 Jan 1730. Although he was the youngest son, he received his father's home. Henry[-3] SPAULDING, born 2 Nov 1680 Chelmsford, was one of ten children of Andrew[-2] SPAULDING.

5. EDMUND [2] BOWKER, son of Edmund[-1] BOWKER (John-[A,B]), and Mary Margaret POTTER, was born 13 October 1661 at Sudbury, Middlesex Co., MA. He married Sarah PARMENTER on 29 March 1688 at Sudbury. She was the daughter of John PARMENTER (John) and Elizabeth CUTLER (James), and was born 20 August 1668 Sudbury, MA.; died _____. Edmund[-2] BOWKER died by drowning at Sudbury, in March 1706, prior to the birth of his daughter Sara. Guardianship of his son Daniel was given to John BRIGHAM in 1717. Mr. BRIGHAM married Sarah PARMENTER Bowker, widow of Edmund[-2], on 12 May 1717 at Sudbury, Middlesex, MA.

Children of Edmund John[-2] BOWKER and Sarah PARMENTER:
Surname **BOWKER**

+	**22. EDMUND**	born 5 Aug 1689 Sudbury; died ca 1740; married Elizabeth _____ ca 1722	
+	**23. ELIZABETH**	born ca 1691 Sudbury, MA; died ca 1740	
		married Thomas BRIGHAM 24 Dec 1714 Sudbury	
		(he s/o Dr. John BRIGHAM (Thomas) and Sarah DAVIS (Robert)	
		(he born 6 May 1687; died ca 1738 Exeter, NH)	
	24. Joseph	born ca 1693/ died 1694	EOL
+	**25. JOHN**	born ca 1693-96 Sudbury, MA; died ca 1740	
		1 married Sarah CLAPP 21 Feb 1720 Sudbury	
		(she dau/o Noah CLAPP and Mary WRIGHT)	
		(she born 30 April 1693 Dorchester, MA; died ca 1726 Hopkinton, MA)	
		2 married Hannah _____ ca _____	
		(she born ca _____; died after 1740)	
	26 Arabella	born 6 March 1701 Sudbury, MA; died 1702	EOL
	27. Daniel	born 17 Jan 1703/04 Sudbury, MA; died 4 April 1719	EOL
	28. Sara	born 6 Oct 1706; died 1707	EOL

7. MARY[-2] BOWKER, sister of above, was born 15 April 1665 at Sudbury, Middlesex, MA. She married Thomas HOLBROOK/HOLBROOK on 20 Feb 1684 at Sherborn, Middlesex, MA. He was the son of Thomas HOLBROOKE/ HOLBROOK and Hannah SHEPHERD, and was born 2 Sept 1659; died 24 March 1718 Sherborn, MA. Mary[-2] BOWKER died _____.

Children of Mary [2] BOWKER and Thomas HOLBROOKE/HOLBROOK:
Surname **HOLBROOK**

+	**29. MARY**	born 26 Feb 1685 Sherborn, MA; died 18 June 1706 Sherborn, MA (childbirth)
		married Eleazer PERRY 19 June 1705
+	**30. LYDIA**	born 6 Sept 1694; died 1724 Sherborn, Middlesex, MA
		married Jonathan FAIRBANKS ca 1713
+	**31. SAMUEL**	born 23 Aug 1699; died 1763
		married Keziah MORSE 4 Sept 1718
		(she born 30 June 1700; died 18 Feb 1754)
		(she dau/o Capt. Joseph MORSE and Hannah BABCOCK)
+	**32. THANKFUL**	born 21 June 1705; died 12 Sept 1746 Sherborn, MA
		married Uriah GLEASON ca 1736
		(he s/o Thomas GLEASON and Mary MELLEN)
		(he born 28 Dec 1706 Sherborn, MA; died ca 1776 Charlton, Worcester, MA)
		(he 2 married Abigail TUFTS)

8. JOHN-³ BOWKER, son of John-² BOWKER (Edmund⁻¹) and Mary HOWE, was born Sep 1679 Marlborough, MA. He married Ruth HOWE ca 1700. She was the daughter of Josiah HOWE and Mary HAYNES; and was born ca 1684; died ca 1710. John-³ BOWKER died ca 1710.

Children of John-³ BOWKER and Ruth HOWE:
Surname **BOWKER**

+	**33. BATHSHEBA**	born ca 1701 Marlborough, MA; died after 1752 MA
		married Daniel BRUCE 1 Dec 1732 Marlborough, MA
		(he s/o Roger BRUCE (John) and Elizabeth FORBUSH)
		(he born 22 Feb 1701 Marlborough; died 1775 Berlin, MA)
	34. Antipierce	born ca 1703; died young EOL
+	**35. JOHN ANTIPIERCE**	born ca 1705; died ca 1797 Petersham, Worcester, MA
		married Freedom BIGELOW 7 June 1732 Marlborough, MA
		(she dau/o John BIGELOW and Jerusha GARFIELD)
		(she born 14 Feb 1710; died ca 1793 Petersham, MA)
	36. LT. JOSIAH	born 6 July 1707 Marlborough; died 27 Apr 1781
		married Hazadiah EAGER 29 Mar 1733 Westboro, MA (later Northboro)

10. MARTHA-³ BOWKER, sister of above, was born 6 March 1685 Marlborough, MA. She married John FORBUSH on 30 Nov 1705. He was the son of Daniel FORBUSH and Deborah REDIAT , and was born ca 1681 Marlborough, MA; died 7 Feb 1731 Marlborough. Martha-³ BOWKER died 28 May 1735 Marlborough, MA.

Children of Martha-³ BOWKER and John FORBUSH:
Surname **FORBUSH**

	37. John, Jr.	born 5 Nov 1710; died ____; married Eunice HOUGHTON 27 Oct 1732
		Child: Hannah-⁵ FORBUSH born 23 Jan 1734; married Joseph WETHERBEE ca ____; and
		Martha-⁵ FORBUSH born 12 Nov 1735
	38. Martha	born 25 May 1714; died ____; married John GOULD/GOLD 23 Jan 1734
		Children: Anna-⁵ born 16 April 1734 and Martha-⁵ GOULD born 25 Jan 1736
+	**39. DAVID**	born 5 Jan 1718; died 9 May 1803 MA
		married Ruth WOOD 14 May 1737
		(she dau/o Abraham WOOD and ____)

Reference: Forbes/Forbush Genealogy by Frederick Clifton Pierce, pub. 1892; page 23

11. MARY⁻³ BOWKER, twin sister of above, was born 6 March 1685 at Marlorough, MA. She married John-³ GATES ca 1703. He was the son of Thomas⁻² GATES (Stephen⁻¹) and Elizabeth FREEMAN; and was born 9 Apr 1678 Sudbury, MA; died 19 Sep 1747 at Stow, Middlesex, MA. Mary⁻³ BOWKER died 24 Apr 1752 at Stow, MA.

Children of Mary⁻³ BOWKER and John GATES:
Surname **GATES**   (children born Stow, MA)

+	**40. HEZEKIAH**	born ca 1704 Lancaster, MA; died 27 June 1777
		1 married Mary SAWYER 17 Feb 1729 Lancaster, Worcester, MA
		(she dau/o Nathaniel SAWYER and Mary ____)
		(she born 16 Mar 1717 Lancaster, MA; died 3 Apr 1733 Lancaster, MA)
		2 married Anna AUSTIN 28 Oct 1735 CT
		(she dau/o Richard AUSTIN and Dorothy ADAMS)
		(she born 16 Jan 1708 CT; died 23 Apr 1779 Lancaster, MA)
+	**41. EPHRAIM**	born ca 1707; died 27 May 1773 Palmer, MA
		1 married Dorothy GRAVES ca 1731
		(she born 10 June 1710; died 5 Apr 1748)
		2 married Mary HALE 26 Jan 1749 Stow, Middlesex, MA
		(she born 2 Apr 1719 Stow; died ____)

Children of Mary-³ BOWKER and John GATES, continued:.
Surname **GATES**

+	**42. SAMUEL** (twin)	born 15 Oct 1713 Stow, MA; died 24 May 1790 Stow, MA
		married Margaret GATES ca 1741
		(she dau/o Daniel GATES and Anna EVELETH)
		(she born 23 Mar 1721; died 2 Mar 1792 Stow, MA)
+	**43. JOHN** (twin)	born 15 Oct 1713 Stow, MA; died 24 May 1790 Stow, MA)
		married Mary WHITNEY ca 1736 (she born ca 1715; died ____)
+	**44. MARY**	born 13 Mar 1716/17 Stow, MA; died 20 Aug 1762 Stow, MA
		married Elisha GATES ca 1735
		(he s/o Simon GATES (Stephen) and Hannah BENJAMIN)
		(he born ca 1706; died 1762)

12 . ASA-³ BOWKER, brother of above, was born 22 Nov 1691 at Marlborough, MA. He married Martha EAGER 28 Feb 1718. She was the daughter of Abraham EAGER and Lydia WOODS; and was born 15 Aug 1693 Marlborough, MA; died 6 March 1747 Shrewsbury, MA. Asa-³ BOWKER died ca 1763 Shrewsbury.

Children of Asa-³ BOWKER and Martha EAGER:
Surname **BOWKER**

	45. Hezekiah	born 25 June 1718 Shrewsbury, MA; died ____
	46. Hazadiah	born 25 Jan 1720; died ____
+	**47. MARTHA**	born 21 Jan 1722 Shrewsbury, MA ; died 9 Aug 1789 Princeton, MA
		married Robert KEYES 24 Dec 1740
		(he s/o Stephen KEYES and Anna ROBBINS)
		(he born 21 Sep 1711Chelmsford, MA ; died 1 Mar 1795 Princeton
	48. Mary	born 27 Feb 1723; died 2 Aug 1800
+	**49. CHARLES**	born 17 Aug 1725 Marlborough; died 11 Mar 1781 Shrewsbury, MA
		married Eunice STONE 2 May 1748 Shrewsbury, Worcester, MA
		(she dau/o Isaac STONE and Elizabeth BROWN)
		(she born 21 Nov 1722 Shrewsbury, MA; died 31 Oct 1782 Shrewsbury)
+	**50. ANNA D.**	born 4 Sep 1728, bapt 10 Sep 1728; died 4 June 1795
		married Asa-⁴ HAPGOOD 6 Dec 1750 (he born 6 Dec 1728; died ____)
		(he s/o Thomas-³ HAPGOOD (Thomas-²; Shadrach-¹) and _____)
	51. Sibbilla	born 25 Sep 1729; died ___
+	**52. LUCY**	born 30 Dec 1731; died ____
		married Ebenezer FORBUSH 8 Mar 1753 Westboro, Worcester, MA
		(he s/o Deacon Thomas FORBUSH and Hannah BELLOWS)
		(he born 29 Ap 731 MA; died 12 Oct 1806)
+	**53. LYDIA**	born 6 Dec 1733 Shrewsbury, MA; died 9 Oct 1813 Petersham, Worcester, MA
		married Seth HAPGOOD 31 May 1757 Petersham
		(he s/o Captain Thomas HAPGOOD and Damaris HUTCHINS)
		(he born 20 Oct 1732 Shrewsbury; died 23 Apr 1804 Petersham, MA)
	54. Solomon Goddard	born 23 June 1736; died 25 Feb 1810
	55. Martha	born 24 Dec 1740; died ____

13. EZEKIEL-³ BOWKER, brother of above, was born 5 Nov 1693 at Marlborough, MA. He married Abigail RICE on 24 Jan/June 1733. She was the daughter of Peter RICE and Rebecca HOWE; and was born 5 Aug 1702; died ____ . Ezekiel-³ BOWKER died 24 Nov 1744 Marlborough, MA.

Children of Ezekiel-³ BOWKER and Abigail RICE:
Surname **BOWKER**

	56. Mary (1)	born 13 Oct 1733; died 14 Oct 1733	EOL
+	**57. ABIGAIL**	born born 30 Aug 1734 Marlborough, MA; died ____	
		married Silas WHEELER 27 July 1758	
		(he s/o Joseph WHEELER and his 2nd wife Deborah WHITNEY)	
		(he born 23 Oct 1732; died 25 Apr 1802)	
	58. Mary (2)	born 27 Jan 1736; died ____	
	59. Anna	born 10 Aug 1737; died ____	

16. HANNAH⁻³ BOWKER, sister of above, was born 21 Sep 1699 at Marlborough, MA. She married Ensign Gershom HOWE on 6 Dec 1721. He was the son of Captain Ebenezer HOWE and Hannah ____; and was born 8 Sep 1694 Marlborough; died 28 Oct 1738 Marlborough, MA. Hannah⁻³ BOWKER died 12 Mar 1751 Marlborough.

Children of Hannah-³ BOWKER and Gershom HOWE:
Surname **HOWE**   (children all born Marlborough, Worcester, MA)

+	**60. MIRIAM**	born 27 Nov 1722; died 9 May 1801 Northboro, MA
		married Jotham BARTLETT 17 May 1744
		(he born 5 Apr 1717 Marlborough, MA; died 9 May 1790 Marlborough)
+	**61. MOSES**	born 6 Mar 1725; died 8 July 1771 Marlborough
		married Hannah FELTON 4 Sep 1746
		(she dau/o Samuel FELTON and Sarah GOODALE)
		(she born 24 Oct 1716; died 22 Nov 1789
+	**62. SILAS**	born 5 Feb 1727; died ____ Shrewsbury, MA
		married Beulah LELAND 20 Nov 1749
		(she dau/o Isaac LELAND and Mary ____)
+	**63. ZERUIAH**	born 9 Oct 1729; died 28 June 1773 Petersham, MA
		married David FELTON 28 Oct 1747 Marlborough
		(he s/o Samuel FELTON and Sarah GOODALE)
		(he born ____; died Feb 1777)
+	**64. PERSIS**	born 2 March 1736; died 18 July 1820
		married John GLEASON 18 Dec 1755
		(he born 7 Dec 1724; died 13 Nov 1816)
		(he s/o James GLEASON and Mary BARRETT)
+	**65. HANNAH**	born 9 Nov 1737; died ___
		married Eli KEYES, Jr. 12 Feb/1 Apr 1762 Shrewsbury, MA
		(he born 4 Mar 1738 Shrewsury; died 1805 NH)
		(he s/o Eli KEYES and Mary WHEELOCK)

18. THOMAS⁻³ LUND, son of Elizabeth⁻² BOWKER (Edmund-¹; John-^{A,B}) and Thomas LUND, was born 2 Sept 1682 at Dunstable, MA. He married Elizabeth TAYLOR 16 Jan 1712. She was the daughter of Abraham TAYLOR and Mary WHIT-TAKER, and was born 7 Aug 1690 Dunstable, MA; died 23 Aug 1763 Dunstable, NH. Thomas⁻³ LUND served with Lt. Jabez FAIRBANKS, and was killed in the French and Indian War on 5 Sept 1724.

Children of Thomas-³ LUND and Elizabeth TAYLOR:
Surname **LUND**

+	**66. THOMAS**	born 31 Oct 1712 Hillsborough, NH; died 4/ 24 Feb 1790 Hillsborough
		1 married Mary TAYLOR ca 1736 (she born ca 1715; died 1748)
		2 married Sarah CHANDLER ca 1749 (she born 20 Oct 1724; died 16 Apr 1801 NH)
+	**67. ELIZABETH**	born 14 May 1715 Dunstable, MA; died Aug 1766 Nottingham, Rockingham, NH
		married Edward SPAULDING ca 1735
		(he born ca 1707; died ca 1750)
+	**68. JONATHAN**	born 12 Oct 1717 NY; died 29 Nov 1801 MA
		1 married Jean VARNUM 2/9 April 1741
		(she dau/o Thomas VARNUM and Joanna JEWETT)
		(she born 3 April 1743; died 14 Sept 1764)
		2 married Mrs. Olive _____ Sargent 22 Oct 1765
+	**69. EPHRAIM**	born 3 Dec 1720; died 1781 (during the battle with Cornwallis)
		married Rachel PIERCE ca 1742
		(she dau/o Stephen PIERCE and Rachel HARWOOD)
		(she born 21 Oct 1723; died _____)
+	**70. PHINEAS**	3 April 1723 MA; died 2 Dec 1818
		married Rachel FRENCH ca 1744 (she born ca 1726; died 1818)

19. ELIZABETH⁻³ LUND, sister of above, was born 29 Sep 1684 NH. She married first to Henry SPAULDING ca 1703. He was the son of Andrew SPAULDING and Hannah JEFES/JEFTS, and was born 2 Nov 1680; died 5 April 1720. Elizabeth⁻³ LUND married second to Samuel SCRIPTURE, Jr. on 6 Feb 1724. He was the son of Samuel SCRIPTURE and Elizabeth KNAPP, and was born 4 Nov 1675; died 6 Nov 1755 Nelson, NH. Elizabeth⁻³ LUND died ca 1740.

Children of Elizabeth[3] LUND and Henry SPAULDING:
Surname **SPAULDING**   (all children born Chelmsford, Middlesex, MA)

+	**71. HENRY**	born 22 Nov 1704 ; died 29 April 1792 Chelmsford, Middlesex, MA
		1 married Lucy PROCTOR Feb 1727
		(she born 19 Aug 1708; died 1 Jan 1742 Chelmsford, MA)
		(she dau/o Samuel PROCTOR and Sarah _____)
		2 married Marah ADAMS 27 Apr 1743 Chelmsford , MA
		(she born15 Dec 1715; died 29 Apr 1807 Chelmsford, MA)
		(she dau/o Benjamin ADAMS and Mary PARKER
	72. Thomas	born 30 July 1707; died 13 Aug 1795 Carlisle, MA
		married Mary ADAMS 13 March 1731 Chelmsford, MA
		(she dau/ Joseph ADAMS and Mary JONES)
		(she born 1 July 1707 Chelmsford; died 17 Oct 1788 Carlisle, MA)

Child: Zebulon[5] SPAULDING born 12 Nov 1741; died 11 April 1829 Chelmsford; married Mary FLETCHER

+	**73. WILLIAM**	born 7 Mar 1711; died 21 June 1790
		married Hepzibah BLOOD 6 Jan 1731
+	**74. LEONARD**	born 1 Dec 1713; died Feb 1758; married Elizabeth DYRANT 18 Dec 1737
		(she dau/o John DYRANT and Elizabeth JAQUITH)
		(she born ca1717 Chelmsford, MA; died 1799 ME)
	75. Eleazer	born 29 May 1717; died same day EOL

Child of Elizabeth[3] LUND and Samuel SCRIPTURE:
Surname **SCRIPTURE**

+	**76. SAMUEL 3rd**	born 27 Apr 1727 Hillsborough, NH; died ca 1817 Cheshire, NH
		married Mary GREEN 9 Oct 1746 Chelmsford, MA.
		(she born 22 June 1731 Groton, MA; died May 1817)

20. WILLIAM[3] LUND, brother of above, was born 19 Jan 1685/86 Hillsborough, NH. He married Rachel HOLDEN 20 Dec 1716 Groton, MA. She was the daughter of Stephen HOLDEN and Hannah LAWRENCE, and was bornca 1694 Groton, Middlesex, MA , died _____. William[3] LUND died 19 Nov 1758 Dunstable, MA.

Children of William[3] LUND and Rachel HOLDEN:
Surname **LUND**

+	**77. WILLIAM**	born 18 July 1717 Dunstable, MA; died 20 March 1782 Dunstable
		married Sarah A. BECK ca 1742
+	**78. RACHEL**	born 28 Aug 1719; died 2 July 1762 Dunstable, MA
		married John LOVEWELL 2 Nov 1739 Hampton Falls, NH
		(he s/o Captain John LOVEWELL and Hannah MOODY)
		(he born 30 June 1718 Dunstable; died 2 July 1763)
	79. James	born ca 1722; died 1750 Merrimack, Hillsborough, NH
+	**80. LIEUT. CHARITY**	born 16 Feb 1730/ 31 Dunstable, MA; died 11 June 1793 Merrimack, NH
		married Lucy COLBURN ca 1754 NH
+	**81. MARY**	born 28 Nov 1733 Dunstable; died 7 Aug 1809 Hillsborough, NH
		married James UNDERWOOD ca 1752 NH
	82. Lucy	born 26 May 1736 Dunsworth, MA; died 1759

21. MARGARET[3] LUND, sister of above, was born 26 May 1687 Dunstable. She married first to Jonathan ROBBINS on 16 Jan 1712 at Concord, MA. He was the son of George ROBBINS and Mary BARRETT, and was born 19 Nov 1686; died 8 May 1725 at Fryeburg, Maine. She married second to William SHATTUCK ca 1729. He was the son of William SHATTUCK and Hannah UNDERWOOD, and was born 11 Sept 1670 Watertown, MA; died Aug 1757 Groton, MA. He married first to Abigail SHATTUCK on 15 March 1711. She was the daughter of his great uncle Samuel SHATTUCK and ____, and was born 17 Oct 1686; died ca 1717. Margaret[3] LUND died 13 June 1764.

Children of Margaret[3] LUND and Jonathan ROBBINS:
Surname **ROBBINS**

+	**83. JANE**	born 26 Dec 1712; died 25 Feb 1820 Dublin, NH
		married Ensign Stephen John AMES 14 April 1731 Groton, MA
	84. Margaret	born 29 Feb 1715; died ca 1724 EOL

Children of Margaret⁻³ LUND and Jonathan ROBBINS, continued:
Surname **ROBBINS**

	85. Jonathan (Jr)	born 4 Nov 1718 Dunstable; died 1746 DunstableEOL
		married Elizabeth GOULD ca 1745
+	**86. ELLENOR/**	(twin) born 18 June 1721, died 1755 Hillsborough Co., NH
	ELEANOR	married James WHITNEY ca 1738
		(he s/o Joseph WHITNEY and Mary ADAMS)(he born ca 1714; died 1755)
	87. Elvira (twin)	born 18 June 1721 Dunstable; died ___
+	**88. ELIZABETH**	born 26 Sept 1723 Dunstable; died 12 July 1792
		married Stephen SHATTUCK 21 Sept 1754 Charlestown, Suffolk, MA
		born 10 Sep 1710; died 1801 Templeton, MA)
		(he s/o Benjamin SHATTUCK and Martha SHERMAN)
	89. Elisha	born ca 1725; died _____

Children of Margaret⁻³ LUND and William SHATTUCK:
Surname **SHATTUCK**

	90. Ezekiel	born 12 June 1730 Groton, MA; died ca 1758 in the French War; unmarried
+	**91. MARGARET**	born 4 July 1732 Groton; died 19 Jan 1802 Groton, MA
		1 married Joseph BENNETT 26 May 1752
		2 married Joseph METCALF 24 Jan 1759 Groton (he born __died 19 March 1793)
+	**92. CAPT. JOB ***	born 11 Feb 1736 Groton; died 13 Jan 1819 Groton
		1 married Sarah HARTWELL 25 May 1758
		(she dau/o Samuel HARTWELL and 2nd wife Sarah HOLDEN)
		(she born 19 March 1738; died 5 May 1798)
		2 married Elizabeth LAKIN Gragg 2 May 1800
		(she dau/o William LAKIN and Miriam ____)(widow of John GRAGG)

*** Job ⁻⁴ SHATTUCK enlisted as a Private in Capt. Ephraim JONES' company, serving in an expedition to Nova Scotia under Capt. John WINSLOW in 1755 to help bring back the poor French families of that province. He was a 1st Lt. in a militia company that left from Groton on 19 Apr 1775. His name was on the muster roll of Capt. Henry HASKELL's company at Cambridge on 13 Jan 1776. Throughout the Rev War he was honorable and patriotic soldier, and became a Capt. Later he was a participant in what became known as "SHAY'S Rebellion ". The rebellion was basically an uprising of farmers ca 1786 (MA). It grew out of the restless dissatisfaction caused by high taxes, heavy indebtedness and declining farm prices. Job SHATTUCK was arrested for his part in the rebellion. He was convicted in May 1787, of the charges against him, and was sent to prison. He was sentenced to be hanged but was granted a reprieve, and later was given a full pardon.

22. EDMUND⁻³ BOWKER, son of Edmund⁻² BOWKER (Edmund⁻¹) and Sarah PARMENTER, was born 5 Aug 1689 at Sudbury, Middlesex, MA. He married Elizabeth _____ ca 1722.She was the daughter of _____ and ____; and was born ca 1700; died ____. Edmund-3 BOWKER died ca 1740 MA.

Children of Edmund⁻³ BOWKER and Elizabeth _____:
Surname **BOWKER**

	93. Sybil	born March 1723 Sudbury, MA; died ____
+	**94. JOSIAH**	born 19 March 1724 Sudbury; died 11 Aug 1766 Hopkinton, MA
		1 married Mary ANDREWS 5 June 1747
		2 married Mary CROMPTON 24 Aug 1749
	95. Edmund	born 19 Sept 1727 Hopkinton, MA; died ____
+	**96. MICAH**	born 10 June 1729 Hopkinton; died ____
		married Persis MAYNARD 27 June 1749
		(she dau/o Joseph MAYNARD and Miriam WILLARD
		Child: Hannah⁻⁵ BOWKER born ca 1750; died ca 1827
+	**97. SAMUEL**	born 9 Apr 1731 Hopkinton; died 11 Oct 1799 Hopkinton, MA
		1 married Martha STONE 8 Oct 1749 (she born 1733; died ____)
		2 married Lydia WHITNEY 12 Dec 1754 Mendon Worcester, MA
		(she dau/o Jonathan WHITNEY and Lydia JONES)
		(she born ca 1732; died 1765)
		3 married Lois HARROD 3 Sep 1767 Farmington, Middlesex, MA
+	**98. URIAH**	born 9 Jan 1735; died 7 May 1804 Hopkinton, MA
		married Sarah HAYDEN 5 Dec 1759 Hopkinton
+	**99. ELIZABETH**	born 28 June 1738; died ____ ; married James WILSON 16 Aug 1754
+	**100. ABIGAIL**	born 23 Sep 1740; died Feb 1816; married Thornton BARRETT 14 Oct 1758

23. ELIZABETH[3] **BOWKER,** daughter of Edmund[2] BOWKER (Edmund[1]; John [A,B]) and Sarah PARMENTER, was born ca 1691 at Sudbury, Middlesex, MA. She married Thomas BRIGHAM on 24 December 1724 at Sudbury. He was the son of Dr. John BRIGHAM and Sarah DAVIS (Robert), and was born 6 May 1687 Marlborough, MA; died ca 1738 at Exeter, NH. Elizabeth[3] BOWKER died ca 1740.

Children of Elizabeth [3] BOWKER and Thomas BRIGHAM:
Surname **BRIGHAM**

	101. JOHN	born 1 April 1726 Sudbury, MA; died 12 Jan 1802 Alford, MA
		married Abigail JOHNSON 12 March 1750 Sudbury
		(she born 6 Feb 1732 Concord, MA; died ca 1782)
		(she dau/o William JOHNSON and Ruth RUGG)
+	**102. SARAH**	born 10 March 1735 Sudbury; died 28 June 1813
		married Capt. Daniel[4] BOWKER 19 Apr 1755 Leicester, MA (# 108)
		(he s/o John[3] BOWKER and his 2nd wife Hannah _____)
		(he born 23 Nov 1731 Hopkinton, MA; died 31 Jan 1822 Sudbury, MA
+	**103. ABIJAH** ++	born 26 Aug 1737 Sudbury, MA; died ____
		married Eunice WILLIS 5 June 1759 Sudbury
		(she dau/o Joseph WILLIS and Thankful CLAPP)
		(she born 16 Jan 1739/40 Sudbury; died 9 March 1826 Sudbury)

++ Note: Reference to Abijah BRIGHAM'S Revolutionary War service:
" Abijah BRIGHAM, Sudbury, Sergeant, Capt Aaron HAYNES Co. which marched on the alarm of 19 April 1775, via Concord to Cambridge: service 4 days; also Lieutenant, Captain Asahel WHEELER'S 7th (3rd Sudbury) Co., Colonel Ezekiel HOWE'S (4th Middlesex) Regiment; List of officers of Massachusetts Militia commissioned 5 July 1776; also Captain CRANSTON'S Co., Colonel Samuel DENNY'S Regiment; enlisted 20 Oct 1779; discharged 23 Nov 1779, service 1 month 14 days at Claverack, enlisted 3 months "

25. JOHN [3] **BOWKER** , brother of above, was born ca 1693-96 at Sudbury, Middlesex, MA. He married first to Sarah CLAPP on 21 February 1720 at Dorchester, MA. She was the daughter of Noah CLAPP and Mary WRIGHT, and was born 30 Apr 1693 at Dorchester.; died ca 1726 at Hopkinton, MA. He married second to Hannah _____ ca 1730. She was born ____; died after 1740. John[3] BOWKER died ca 1740.

Children of John [3] BOWKER and Sarah CLAPP:
Surname **BOWKER**

+	**104. HANNAH**	born 4 April 1721 Sudbury, MA; died _____ Walpole, Cheshire, NH
		married William JOYNER 18 March 1745 Middlesex Co., MA
		(he s/o Edward JOYNER and Susannah CLAPP)
		(he born ca 1719 Sudbury; died _____ Walpole, NH)
+	**105. MARY**	born 21 Sept 1722 Hopkinton, MA; died _____
		married Reuben MOORE 24 March 1743/44
		(he s/o Uriah MOORE (Benjamin) and Abigail HAYNES) (he born ca 1724)
+	**106. NOAH**	born 16 May 1724 Hopkinton, MA; died _____
		married Hepzibah WILLARD 22 Feb 1753 Grafton, Worcester, MA
		(she dau/o Simon/Simeon WILLARD and Phoebe NEWTON)
		(she born 7 Oct 1731 Grafton, MA)
+	**107. JOSEPH**	born 28 Dec 1725 Hopkinton; died 11 July 1784 Grafton, MA
		married Sarah TAINTER 21 Nov 1749
		(she dau/o Simon TAINTER and Rebecca HARRINGTON)
		(she born 1 Aug 1727 Westborough, MA; died _____)

Children of John [3] BOWKER and Hannah _____;
Surname **BOWKER**

+	**108. CAPT. DANIEL**	born 23 Nov 1731 Hopkinton, MA; died 31 Jan 1822 Sudbury, MA
		married Sarah BRIGHAM 19 April 1755 Leicester, MA.
		(she dau/o Thomas BRIGHAM and Elizabeth[3] BOWKER)
		(she born 10 March 1735 Hopkinton; died 28 June 1813)
+	**109. ELIAS**	born 6 Apr 1733 Hopkinton; died 29 Feb 1816 Georgia , VT
		1 married Sarah HARWOOD 13 Sept 1757
		(she dau/o John HARWOOD and Mary _)(she born 26 Feb 1730; died ca 1760
		2 married Deborah GOODSPEED 3 Nov 1760 Leicester, MA

Children of John[-3] BOWKER and Hannah _____, continued:

+   **109. ELIAS cont'd:**   (she dau/o Nathaniel GOODSPEED and Deborah BRIGGS)
                                           (she born ca 1736 MA; died 11 Sep 1817 Rutland VT)

         110. John   born 4 Oct 1735 Hopkinton; died 21 May 1765 Westboro, MA; no issue EOL
                                            married Tryphena KENDALL 12 Oct 1760 Worcester Co., MA
                                            (she dau/o Joshua KENDALL and Hannah / Theoda BEMENT)
                                            (she born 22 Dec 1738; died 30 Nov 1828 Suffield, Hartford, CT)
                                            (she 2 married Joseph KING III on 12 Sept 1769 (had 4 ch)

+   **111. SILAS (Sr.)**   born 3 May 1739 Westboro, MA; died 15 Oct 1789 Conklin Ctr. Broome, NY
                                            married Esther HOBBS 3 Sept 1761 Weston, MA
                                            (she dau/o Ebenezer HOBBS and Eunice GARFIELD)
                                            (she born 3 April 1739 Concord, MA; died 7 March 1824 NY

                                References: Vital Records of Hopkinton, MA; US and International Marriage records; Early MA
                                Marriages; Early Families of Rutland, VT.; Founders and Patriots of America, page 130

29. MARY[-3] HOLBROOK, daughter of Mary[-2] BOWKER (Edmund[-1]) and Thomas HOLBROOK, was born 26 Feb 1685 at Sudbury, MA. She married Eleazer PERRY on 19 June 1705. He was the son of ____ PERRY and ___, and was born ___, died ___. Mary[-3] HOLBROOK died 18 June 1706 as a result of childbirth at Sherborn, MA.

Child of Mary[-3] HOLBROOK and Eleazer PERRY:
Surname **PERRY**
+   **112. ELEAZER**   born 2 June 1706; died ____, married Mary JOHNSON 14 June 1732.

30. LYDIA[-3] HOLBROOK, daughter of Mary[-2] BOWKER (Edmund[-1]; John[-A,B]) and Thomas HOLBROOK, was born 6 Sept 1694 Sudbury, MA. She married Dr. Jonathan FAIRBANKS ca 1713. He was the son of Dr. Jonathan FAIRBANKS and Sarah _____; and was born 21 March 1689, MA; died 26 Nov 1754 Sherborn, Middlesex, MA. Lydia[-6] HOLBROOK died ca 1724. Jonathan FAIRBANKS married second ca 1726 , to Hannah COOLIDGE, and had 5 more children: Joshua; John. Hannah, Grace and Abner FAIRBANKS.

Children of Lydia[-3] HOLBROOK and Dr. Jonathan FAIRBANKS:
Surname **FAIRBANKS**   (all children born Sherborn, Middlesex, MA)

         113. Jonathan   born 18 Feb 1714; died 31 July 1772 Worcester, MA
                                            married Esther CREATON 5 Aug 1741 Uxbridge, MA (she born ca 1720 Uxbridge)

         114. Benjamin   born 16 Aug 1715; died 1715   EOL

         115. Mary   born 5 Feb 1716; died _; married Samuel WHITE, Jr. 1 Apr 1748 Uxbridge, MA
                                            (he born ca 1712 Worcester, MA; died (poss.) 17 Jan 1785

+   **116. LYDIA**   born 1 Oct 1718; died 9 Oct 1751 Sherborn
                                            1 married Abijah MORSE 10 Oct 1751 Uxbridge, MA
                                            (he s/o Samuel MORSE and Bethia HOLBROOK) (he born ca 1718; died ____)
                                            2 poss. married _____ BOYNTON ca ____

         117. Comfort   born 8 Feb 1720; died 20 Oct 1741 CT.; married Zebulon PALMER, Sr. 25 May 1737
                             Children: Lydia[-5] born ca 1738; Hannah[-5] born ca 1739, died 1832; and Zebulon[-5] PALMER, Jr.
                             born ca 1741, died 1760

+   **118. MOSES**   born 1 March 1722; died ca 1822 MA; married Hannah _____ ca _____

+   **119. DANIEL**   born 5 Nov 1723; died 10 May 1759 MA
                                            married Submit FAIRBANKS ca _____
                                            (she dau/o George FAIRBANKS and Rachel _____) (she born 18 Sept 1729)

31. SAMUEL[-3] HOLBROOK, brother of above, was born 23 Aug 1699 at Sudbury, MA. He married Keziah MORSE on 4 Sept 1718. She was the daughter of Capt. Joseph MORSE and Hannah BABCOCK, and was born 30 June 1700; died 18 Feb 1754. Samuel[-3] HOLBROOK died ca 1763.

Children of Samuel[-3] HOLBROOK and Keziah MORSE:
Surname **HOLBROOK**

         120. Hannah   born 11 Sep 1720; died 27 June 1744 Sherborn, MA   EOL
                                            married Ephraim PERRY on 4 Nov 1742 Sherborn
                                            (he s/o Josiah PERRY and Bethia CUTTER)
                                            (he born 11 Nov 1715 Watertown, MA; died 6 Jan 1781)

Children of Samuel[-3] HOLBROOK and Keziah MORSE, continued:
Surname **HOLBROOK**

	121.Thomas	born 21 April 1723 Sherborn MA; died _____
+	**122. KEZIAH**	born 23 Aug 1729 Sherborn; died ca 1758 Medway, Middlesex, MA
		married Daniel TWITCHELL on 12 July 1742
		(he s/o Benjamin TWITCHELL and Mary WALLIS)
		(he born 22 Feb 1714 Sherborn; died 1754 – killed by Indians)
	123. Lydia	born 12 Aug 1734 Sherborn; died 21 May 1761 Weymouth, MA
		married Gen. Solomon LOVELL 19 Jan 1758 Weymouth, Norfolk, MA)

Child: Lydia[-5] LOVELL born ca 1761; died ca 1830)

32. THANKFUL[-3] HOLBROOK, sister of above, was born 21 June 1705 at Sherborn, MA. She married Uriah GLEASON ca 1736. He was the son of Thomas GLEASON and Mery MELLEN, and was born 28 Dec 1706 Sherborn, died 1776 Charlton, Worcester, MA. Thankful[-3] HOLBROOK died 12 Sept 1746. Uriah GLEASON married second to Abigail TUFTS.

Children of Thankful[-3] HOLBROOK and Uriah GLEASON:
Surname **GLEASON**

	124. John	born 16 Aug 1739 Oxford, Worcester, MA; died Oct 1761 Oxford
+	**125. LUCY**	born 27 Feb 1742 Oxford, MA; died 21 June 1832 Warwick, Franklin, MA
		married William BURNETT 22 Jan 1766 Oxford MA.
		(he s/o Robert BURNETT and Anna WILKINS)
		(he born 28 Jan 1744; died 24 March 1835)

33. BATHSHEBA-⁴ BOWKER, daughter of John-³ BOWKER (John-²; Edmund-¹) and Ruth HOWE, was born ca 1701 at Marlborough, MA. She married Daniel BRUCE on 1 Dec 1732 at Marlborough. He was the son of Roger BRUCE and Elizabeth FORBUSH/ANGIN, and was born 22 Feb 1701 Marlborough, MA; died 13 Feb 1790 Berlin, MA. Bathsheba-⁴ BOWKER died after 1752, MA.

Children of Bathsheba-⁴ BOWKER and Daniel BRUCE:
Surname **BRUCE**   (children born Marlborough, Middlesex, MA)

+	**126. RUTH**	born 22 May 1733; died ca 1820 Templeton, MA
		married Cyrus GATES 8 Jan 1752
		(he born 11 Apr 1731; died 8 July 1813 MA)
		(he s/o Ephraim GATES and Dorothy GRAVES)
	127. Hannah	born ____; died ____; married Solomon JONES
		Child: Peletiah-⁶ JONES born ca ____
	128. Abraham	born 23 Dec 1735; died 1759 Quebec, Canada
		(he was in the expedition against Crown Point in 1755; and was killed in the fall of Quebec)
	129. Lucy	born 6 May 1737; died 8 May 1832 Berlin, Worcester, MA; unmarried EOL
+	**130. BENJAMIN**	born 24 Dec 1739; died ca 1831
		married Nancy Mc BRIDE Dec 1768
		(she dau/o Alexander Mc BRIDE and Mary ____)
	131. JOHN	born 9 May 1744; died 13 Feb 1843; married Martha MOORE 9 July 1771
		(she dau/o Isaac MOORE and Mary FAIRBANKS)
		(she born 14 July 1752 Bolton, MA; died 27 Oct 1735 Berlin, MA)
	132. Betty	born 22 Jan 1746; died ____; married John BROWN ca 1764
	133. Mary	born 9 Aug 1748; died 1786 NH; married Nathan JONES
+	**134. DANIEL**	born 21 Sep 1752; died 1805 Berlin, MA
		married Mary Polly BRUCE ca ____
		(she dau/o Timothy BRUCE, Sr. (John) and Susanna JOSLIN)

Reference: History of the Town of Berlin, Worcester County, MA from 1784 to 1895 Pages 298-300 ; 303

35. JOHN ANTIPIERCE-⁴ BOWKER, brother of above, was born ca 1705 at Marlborough, MA. He married Freedom BIGELOW on 7 June 1732 at Marlborough. She was the daughter of John BIGELOW and Jerusha GARFIELD, and was born 13 Feb 1709/10 Marlborough; died 1793. John A-⁴ BOWKER died ca 1797 at Petersham, Worcester, MA.

Children of John A-⁴ BOWKER and Freedom BIGELOW:
Surname **BOWKER**

+	**135. SILAS**	born 29 May 1733; died 1 April 1820 Royalston, MA
		married Bethia(h) WARD on 29 Nov 1759
+	**136. ELIZABETH/ BETTY**	born 9 Feb 1735; died 1815; married Joshua-⁶ TURNER 23 June 1761
		(he s/o Joshua-⁵ TURNER and Sarah WINSLOW)
		(he born 6 Mar 1738/39 Pembroke, MA; died 3 Jan 1816 Scituate, MA)
	137. John	born 26 Aug/Oct 1736; died ____; married Elizabeth WILDER 27 Apr 1768
		Child: Freedom-⁶ BOWKER born 1769; married Moses LOVETT ca ____
	138. Sarah	born 5 Aug 1738; died 5 Aug 1742 EOL
	139. Benjamin	born 26 Dec 1740; died ca 1742 EOL
+	**140. SOLOMON**	born 25 Mar 1743; died ca 1834
		1 married Mary Eunice WEEKS 21 Apr 1770
		(she born 20 Mar 1749; died 1 Feb 1771)
		2 married Dorothy BARNES 29 Aug 1771
		(she dau/o Jonathan BARNES and Rachel HOSMER)
		(she born 18 Dec 1747; died ca 1841)

Children of John-[4] BOWKER and Freedom BIGELOW, continued:
Surname **BOWKER**

	141. Ezekiel	born 13 Oct 1744; died ____	
	142. Persis	born 24 Oct 1745; died 17 Aug 1833	
		married Jabez FAIRBANKS 28 Feb 1792 (as his 2nd wife) no issue EOL	
		(he born 2 Mar 1738 Lancaster, MA; died 18 Oct 1822 Lancaster)	
		(he s/o Jonathan FAIRBANKS and ____)	
+	**143. JOTHAM**	born ca 1751; died ____; married Patty WHITNEY ca 1791	
		(she born ca 1765; died ____)	

36. LT. JOSIAH-[4] BOWKER, brother of above, was born 6 July 1707 Marlborough, MA. He married Hazadiah EAGER on 29 Mar 1733. She was the daughter of Captain James EAGER and Tabitha HOWE, and was born 1 Dec 1715; died 29 Jan 1800 Marlborough, MA. Josiah-[4] BOWKER died 27 Apr 1781.

Children of Lt. Josiah-[4] BOWKER and Hazadiah EAGER:
Surname **BOWKER** (all children born Westboro, MA (later called Northborough, MA)

+	**144. ANTIPAS**	born 3 Oct 1733; died 14 Nov 1803 Northborough, MA	
		married Esther RICE 6 Oct 1757 Marlborough, MA	
		(she dau/o Gideon RICE and Esther ____)	
	145. Hazadiah	born 12 Nov 1734; died 26 Oct 1750 Westboro	EOL
	146. Josiah, Jr.	born March 1735; died 15 Aug 1811	
		married Sarah NURSE/ NOURSE/MUZZEY 23 May 1765 Shrewsbury, MA	
		(she born ca 1737; died 25 Mar 1806)	
	147. Dorothy	born 25 Nov 1737; died 19 Nov 1745	EOL
+	**148. EPHRAIM**	born 7 June 1740; died ____; married Sarah FARRAR ca 1759	
		(she dau/o John FARRAR and Mary ____)	
	149. Damaris	born 11 Apr 1742; died ____	
	150. Prudence	born 28 Oct 1743; 2 Nov 1745 Westboro, MA	EOL
	151. Phebe	born 19 Sep 1745; died ____	
	152. Comfort	born 18 Apr/May 1747; died ____	
		married Daniel MILES, Jr. 30 Nov 1791 Petersham, MA	
+	**153. TABITHA**	born 18 Apr 1749; died 5 Mar 1827 Princeton, Worcester, MA	
		married Charles NEWTON 4 Oct 1765 Westborough, MA	
		(he born 28 Aug 1742 Shrewsbury, MA; died 10 Dec 1831 Princeton, MA)	
		(he s/o Elisha NEWTON and Sarah TOMLIN)	
+	**154. ITHAMAR**	born 27 Nov 1750; died 14 Apr 1803	
		1 married Miriam BARTLETT 1 May 1775 Brookfield, MA	
		(she dau/o Elijah BARTLETT and Bathsheba GILBERT)	
		(she born 1 Aug 1754 Brookfield, MA; died ____)	
		2 married Sarah RICE 1 May 1793	
+	**155. HAZADIAH (2)**	born 2 Sep 1752; died 9 Oct 1826 Northborough, MA	
		married John WYMAN 30 Aug 1771 Northborough	
		(he s/o Nathaniel WYMAN and Elizabeth EVANS)	
		(he born 19 Oct 1745 Hopkinton, MA; died 18 Sep 1813 Marlborough, MA)	
+	**156. ASA**	born 8 Nov 1754; died 5 Oct 1825	
		married Susanna BRYANT 2/8 June 1781 Petersham, MA	
+	**157. JONATHAN**	born 23 June 1756; died ____	
		married Abigail WHITEHEAD 12 Oct 1791 Phillipston, MA	
	158. Eber	born 6 May 1759; died ____	

39. DAVID-[4] FORBUSH, son of Martha-[3] BOWKER (John-[2]; Edmund-[1]) and John FORBUSH, was born 5 Nov 1710 Marlborough, MA. He married Ruth WOOD on 14 May 1737. She was the daughter of Abraham WOOD and ____; and was born ____; died ____. David[4] FORBUSH was an Orderly Sergeant in the Revolutionary War, and fought in the Battles of Lexington and Concord. He died 19 May 1803 Marlborough, MA.

BOWKER
The Fourth American Generation

Children of David-4 FORBUSH and Ruth WOOD:
Surname **FORBUSH**

	159. Sarah	born 15 June 1738; died ____
+	**160. DAVID**	born 24 Dec 1739 Acton, Middlesex. MA; died 11 Apr 181 Petersborough, NH
		married Sarah HAYWARD 4 Nov 1762 Sudbury, Middlesex, MA
		(she dau/o Josiah Hartwell HAYWARD and Mary HOSMER)
		(she born 17 June 1742 Acton, MA; died 11 Jan 1826 Sudbury, MA)
	161. Molly	born 23 Nov 1741; died ____
	162. Miriam	born 15 Dec 1743; died ____
	163. Abraham	born 11 Mar 1746; died 4 Apr 1817; married Mary WHITNEY 17 Mar 1768

Children: Abraham, Jr.-6 born 1781, died 15 Dec 1863, married Mary JEWETT 20 Aug 1808 Stow, MA.;
and Rebecca-6 FORBUSH born ca 1789, died 1 Mar 1855 Stow, MA

	164. Daniel	born 6 Feb 1747; died 5 Sep 1779
		married Lucy FORBUSH 22 Jan 1770
		(she dau/o Phineas FORBUSH/FORBES and Sarah BELLOWS)
		(she born 10 Oct 1743 Westborough, MA; died 8 Apr 1812)

Child: Lucy-6 FORBUSH born ca 1772

	165. Ruth	born 19 Jan 1749; died ____
	166. Lucy	born 15 Jan 1753; died 23 Feb 1759 EOL
+	**167. EPHRAIM**	born 18 Oct 1756; died 17 Sep 1828
		1 married Mary BUTTRICK 25 Mar 1784
		(she dau/o Samuel BUTTRICK and Lucy WHEELER)
		(she born 8 Dec 1754; died 10 Feb 1805)
		2 married Abigail ROGERS 1 Apr 1806 (int pub 12 Mar 1806)
		(she dau/o Deacon John ROGERS and Ann CHURCHMAN)
+	**168. JAMES**	born 8 Jan 1758; died 1827 Dummer, Coos, NH
		married Eunice BROWN 25 Oct 1775 Boston, Suffolk, MA
		(she dau/o Abishai BROWN and Mary FARRAR)
		(she born 7 Feb 1758 Concord, MA; died 15 July 1837 Stark, Coos, NH)

40. CAPTAIN HEZEKIAH-4 GATES, son of Mary-3 BOWKER (John-2; Edmund-1) and John-3 GATES
(Thomas-2; Stephen-1), was born ca 1704 Stow, Middlesex, MA. He married first to Mary SAWYER on 17 Feb 1729 at
Lancaster, Worcester, MA. She was the daughter of Nathaniel SAWYER and ____; and was born16 Mar 1717; died 3 Apr 1733
Lancaster, MA. Hezekiah-4 GATES married second to Anna AUSTIN on 28 Oct 1735 CT. She was the daughter of Richard
AUSTIN and Dorothy ADAMS, an d was born 16 Jan 1708 CT; died 23 Apr 1779 Lancaster, MA. Hezekiah-4 GATES died 27
June 1777 at Lancaster.

An epitaph on his burial site in the Old Burying Ground, Lancaster , reads:
My flesh shall slumber in ye ground,Til ye last trumpets joyful sound,
Then shall awake with sweet surprise, And in my Saviours image rise.

Children of Captain Hezekiah-4 GATES and Mary SAWYER:
Surname **GATES**   (all children born Lancaster, MA)

	169. Mary	born 15 Jan 1730; died 15 Oct 1763 Colchester, New London, CT
	170. Elizabeth	born 21 Feb 1732; died 18 Apr 1818 Lancaster

Children of Hezekiah-4 GATES and Anna AUSTIN:
Surname **GATES**

	171. Thomas	born 29 Apr 1736; died 27 Dec 1814; married Abigail WILDER 23 Apr 1761
		(she dau/o Oliver WILDER and Mary FAIRBANKS)
		(she born 16 Dec 1740 Lancaster, MA; died 5 Sep 1810 Lancaster)
	172. Dorothy	born 6 Sep 1738; died 16 Feb 1831 Lancaster, MA
		married Peter THURSTON 3 Dec 1761 Lancater, MA
	173. Rebecca	born 31 July 1740; died 15 Feb 1765 Lancaster
		married Philemon HOUGHTON 23 Feb 1740
	174. Sarah	born 1 July 1744; died ca 1791; married James ELDER 16 Jan 1770 Worcester
	175. Anna	born 27 Aug 1748; died ____; married John MOOR 4 Mar 1767 Lancaster, MA

41. EPHRAIM⁻⁴ GATES, brother of above, was born ca 1707 at Stow, MA. He married first to Dorothy GRAVES ca 1731. She was the daughter of ____ GRAVES and ____; and was born 10 June 1710 Stow, MA; died 5 Apr 1748 Stow. Ephraim⁻⁴ GATES married second to Mary HALE on 26 Jan 1749. She was the daughter of ____ HALE and ____; and was born 2 Apr 1719; died _____, Stow, MA. Ephraim⁻⁴ GATES served on a scouting party in July 1745 in King George's War. He died 27 May 1773 at Palmer, Hampden, MA.

Children of Ephraim⁻⁴ GATES and Dorothy GRAVES:
Surname **GATES**   (children all born Stow, MA)
+   **176. CYRUS**   born 11 Apr 1732; died 8 July 1813 Bolton, MA (Rev War soldier)
                                 married Ruth BRUCE 22 May 1733   (she born 22 May 1733; died 1820)
+   **177. MICAH**   born 1 May 1734; died ____; (Rev War soldier)
                                 married Phebe WHITCOMB Feb 1757
+   **178. ELIZABETH**   born 3 May 1737; died 5 May 1833/38
                                 married William POWERS 8 June 1764 Stow, Middlesex, MA
                                 (he s/o Gideon POWERS and Lydia RUSSELL)
                                 (he born 10 Dec 1740 Middlesex, MA; died 13 Mar 1829 Groton, MA)
Children of Ephram⁻⁴ GATES and Mary HALE:
Surname **GATES**
     179. Ephraim   born 25 June 1750; died _____ Palmer, MA

42. SAMUEL⁻⁴ GATES, brother of above, was born 15 Oct 1713 at Stow, Middlesex, MA. He married Margaret GATES ca 1741. She was the daughter of Daniel GATES and Anna EVELETH, and was born 23 Mar 1721; died 2 Mar 1792 Stow, MA. Samuel⁻⁴ GATES died ____.

Children of Samuel⁻⁴ GATES and Margaret GATES:
Surname **GATES**   (children all born Stow, MA)
     180. Thomas   born 24 May 1742; died 20 Oct 1753   EOL
     181. Olive   (1)   born 25 Aug 1744; died 14 Oct 1753   EOL
     182. Dorcas   born 17 Jan 1747; died 7 Sep 1829 Rindge, Cheshire, NH
                                  married Edward JEWETT of Bolton, MA 20 July 1765 Stow, MA
                                  (he born 29 Nov 1741; died 12 Jan 1825 Rindge, NH)
                                  (he s/o Edward JEWETT, Sr. and Sarah FARMER)
                                  Children: Dorcas-⁶ born 135 Jan 1772, died 19 Feb 1773; and Mersylvia-⁶ JEWETT born 4 Nov 1786;
                                  died 2 June 1855, married Ezra SCOLLAY 31 Dec 1807 Rindge, NH; he born 8 Mar 1786;
                                  died 10 Nov 1874 New Ipswich, NH
     183. Samuel   (1)   born 25 May 1750; died 4 Oct 1753   EOL
     184. Lois   born 26 May 1752; died ____; married Elijah PRIEST 25 Oct 1784 Stow,MA
     185. Olive   (2)   born 29 Sep 1754; died 22 Nov 1836 Stow, MA
                                  married Ephraim WETHERBEE 1772
     186. Samuel (2)   (twin)   born 29 Aug 1756; died 11 Nov 1834 (Rev War soldier)
                                  1 married Mary RAND Feb 1779 Stow, MA
                                  (she dau/o David RAND and Mary ROBBINS)
                                  (she born 28 Nov 1752 Stow; died ____ Stow, MA)
                                  Children: Samuel-⁶ born ca 1774, died 1856; Daniel-⁶ born ca 1780, died 1805; and Lucy-⁶ GATES born ca 1787
                                  2 married Sarah LAWRENCE 18 Apr 1797
+   **187. LEVI**   (twin) born 29 Aug 1756; died ____ (Rev War soldier)
                                  married Betty BROOKS 7 Oct 1779
     188. Josiah   born 9 March 1760; died ____

43. JOHN⁻⁴ GATES, twin brother of above, was born 15 Oct 1713 at Stow, Middlesex, MA. He married Mary WHITNEY ca 1736. She was the daughter of _____ WHITNEY and ____, and was born ca 1715; died ____. John⁻⁴ GATES died 24 May 1790 at Stow, Middlesex, MA.

Children of John⁻⁴ GATES and Mary WHITNEY:
Surname **GATES**   (children born Stow, Middlesex, MA) **16**
     189. Hannah   born 6 Sep 1737; died 19 Nov 1814
     190. Josiah   born 24 Mar 1738; died 30 Mar 1757
     191. Dorothy   born 11 Dec 1740; died Aug 1813

Children of John⁻⁴ GATES and Mary WHITNEY, continued:
Surname **GATES**

	192. Damaris	born 9 Jan 1745; died ca 1803
		married Asa FARNSWORTH 6 Aug 1777 (he of Templeton, MA)
		(he s/o Jonathan FARNSWORTH and Rachel NUTTING)
		(he born 12 May 1754; died 22 June 1830 Westborough, MA)

Child: Asa-⁶ Jr. born 31 Oct 1786, died I July 1838 MI; and Polly-⁶ FARNSWORTH born ca 1789, died 22 July 1873 Westborough, MA; married Joel MERRIAM 31 Mar 1808

+	**193. JOHN**	born 12 Sep 1748; died 25 Nov 1814
		married Catherine WETHERBEE 19 Feb 1778
		(she born 15 Mar 1753; died 13 June 1834)
		(she dau/o Thomas WETHERBEE and Elizabeth HEALD)
+	**194. CALEB**	born 14 July 1751; died 14 Aug 1827
		married Mindwell OAK 10 Mar 1776
		(she born 23 Mar 1746; died 26 Nov 1826)
+	**195. MARY**	born 25 Apr 1753; died ____; married Thomas WETHERBEE 19 Jan 1779
		(he born 1 Aug 1750 Stow, MA; died 29 May 1801 Westminster, MA)
	196. Thomas	born 3/5 June 1755; died 14 Feb 1833 (Rev War soldier)
		married Lydia HALE 4 June 1778
		(she born 6 Jan 1759; died 17 June 1817)

Children: Levi-⁶ born 26 Oct 1781 Stow, MA; and Betsey-⁶ GATES born 13 Apr 1783 Stow, MA

44. MARY⁻⁴ GATES, sister of above, was born 13 March 1716 at Stow, Middlesex, MA. She married Elisha GATES ca 1735. He was the son of Simon-² GATES (Stephen-¹) and Hannah BENJAMIN, and was born ca 1706; died 1762. Mary⁻⁴ GATES died 20 Aug 1762.

Children of Mary⁻⁴ GATES and Elisha GATES:
Surname **GATES**

	197. Elisha	born 19 Jan 1735; died ___; married Lucy CHASE 30 Jan 1759
	198. Lucy	born ca ____; died ____
	199. Mary	born ca ____; died ____
	200. Lydia	born 20 Jan 1742 Stow, MA; died ____
	201. Israel	born 11 Mar 1744; died 16 Dec 1809; married Jane WHITMAN ca ____
+	**202. SUSANNAH**	born 15 May 1748; died 27 Mar 1832
		married Ephraim MORRILL 8 May 1773

47. MARTHA⁻⁴ BOWKER, daughter of Asa-³ BOWKER (John-²; Edmund-¹) and Martha EAGER, was born 21 Jan 1722 at Shrewsbury, MA. She married Robert KEYES on 24 Dec 1740. He was the son of Stephen KEYES and Anna ROBBINS, and was born 21 Sep 1711 Chelmsford, MA; died 1 Mar 1795 Princeton. Martha⁻⁴ BOWKER died 9 Aug 1789 at Princeton.

Children of Martha-⁴ BOWKER and Robert KEYES:
Surname **KEYES**

	203. Stephen		born 19 Jan 1741 Shrewsbury, MA; died 20 Dec 1748 Shrewsbury EOL
	204. Jonas		born 24 Dec 1743; died 21 July 1822 Princeton, MA
	205. Martha Patty		born 6 Dec 1745 Shrewsbury; died 30 Mar 1823 Princeton
			married John GLEASON 24 Nov 1799 (as his 2nd wife)
			(he s/o Phinehas GLEASON and Elizabeth PIERCE)
			(he born 12 Oct 1742 Framingham, MA; died 30 Mar 1823 Princeton, MA)
+	**206. ANNA**		born 21 June 1748; died 22 Sep 1840 Westminster, MA
			married Samuel MOSMAN 30 Oct 1769
			(he born 27 Feb 1739/40 Sudbury, MA; died 29 Dec 1828 Westminster, MA)
	207. Lucy	**	born 15 Aug 1750 Shrewsbury; died 14 Apr 1755 Wachusett, MA

** Note: Lucy (5), and 2 of her sisters, went into the woods near Lake Wachusett on 14 Apr 1755. Her sisters returned home, but she did not. An expansive search for her was done immediately, even to the dragging of the lake – but no trace of her was ever found. It is related that every day her mother went into the woods and called her name – LUCY – LUCY – with no response. Her mother never recovered from grieving. There was TV movie, done in 2006, based on Lucy's story . It was called the Legend of Lucy KEYES.

Children of Martha-[4] BOWKER and Robert KEYES, continued:
Surname **KEYES**

	208. Phebe	born 31 June 1752; died 4 July 1837 Gardner, Worcester, MA
		married Jude SAWYER 26 Nov 1776
		(he s/o Darius SAWYER and Deborah _____)
		(he born 8 May 1751 Lancaster, MA; died 18 Dec 1843 Gardner, MA)
	209. Abraham	born 10 Mar 1755; died 25 Oct 1828
	210. Mary	born 10 July 1757; died 22 Sep 1840 Westminster, MA
+	**211. SOLOMON**	born 28 June 1762 Wachusett, MA; died 29 Feb 1808 Princeton
		married Elizabeth HEMENWAY/HEMINGWAY 2 Oct 1796 Weston, MA
		(she born 22 June 1766 Framingham, MA; died 25 Dec 1808 Princeton)
	212. Lucretia	born 6 Sept 1764; died ____

49. LT. CHARLES-[4] BOWKER, brother of above, was born 17 Aug 1725 at Shrewsbury, MA. He married Eunice STONE on 2 May 1748 at Shrewsbury, Worcester, MA. She was the daughter of Isaac STONE and Elizabeth BROWN, and was born 2 Nov 1722 Shrewsbury; died 31 Oct 1782 Shrewsbury. Charles-[4] BOWKER died 11 March 1781 Shrewsbury, MA.

Children of Charles-[4] BOWKER and Eunice STONE:
Surname **BOWKER**   (children all born Shrewsbury, MA)

	213. Ezra	born 9 Sep 1748; died 4 Jan 1782 Shrewsbury, MA	
	214. Noyes	born 18 Feb 1750; died 26 Oct 1764	EOL
	215. Prudence	born 25 Sep 1751; died 14 May 1795 Shrewsbury, MA	
+	**216. ELIZABETH/**	born 21 Aug 1753; died 12 Dec 1846 Leominster, MA	
	BETSEY	1 married William DEXTER, MD 17 Feb 1775 Shrewsbury	
		(he born 17 Apr 1755 Marlborough, MA; died 4 Dec 1785 Marlborough	
		2 married Edward LOW 13 Oct 1795	
		(he born 22 Feb 1744; died 14 Feb 1823	
	217. Sarah Daniels	born 1 Aug 1754; died ____	
	218. Asa	born 2 Oct 1756; died 31 Jan 1787 Shrewsbury, MA	EOL
+	**219. JENNIE**	born 26 May 1761; died 16 Feb 1822 Rushford, Allegany, NY	
		married Asa-[5] HAPGOOD ca 1785 (# 225)	

50. ANNA D-[4] BOWKER, sister of above, was born 4 Sep 1728 at Shrewsbury, Worcester, MA. She married Asa-[4] HAPGOOD on 6 Dec 1750. He was the son of Thomas-[3] HAPGOOD (Thomas-[2]; Shadrach-[1]) and _____ ; and was born 6 Dec 1728; died ____ . Anna D-[4] BOWKER died 4 June 1795.

Children of Anna D-[4] BOWKER and Asa-[4] HAPGOOD:
Surname **HAPGOOD**

	220. Levinah	born 16 Feb 1752; died ____ ; never married	EOL
	221. Thomas	born 22 Mar 1753; died ____ ; married Hannah SAWYER no issue	EOL
	222. Betsey	born 6 May 1754; died Mar 1833; married John JONES 19 Oct 1769	
	223. Sophia	born 6 Apr 1756; died ____ ; married John WILDER, Jr.17 June 1779	
		(he s/o John WILDER and Prudence _____)	
		(he born 12 July 1744 Petersham, MA; died 24 Sep 1799) (4 ch)	
		Child: Prudence-[6] WILDER born 22 Aug 1782; died 29 June 1835; married John GROUT 1 Mar 1803	
+	**224. DAVID**	born 10 May 1757; died 3 July 1829; married Sally MYRICK 29 Dec 1781	
+	**225. ASA**	born 25 Nov 1759; died ____ ; married Jennie-[5] BOWKER ca 1785 (# 219)	
	226. John	born 10 May 1761; died 23 July 1778	EOL
	227. Anna	born 27 Oct 1764; died 17 Apr 1766	EOL
	228. Windsor	born 10 Dec 1767; died 24 Dec 1829 (killed)	EOL
+	**229. ARTEMUS**	born 15 Mar 1769; died 3 Oct 1846	
		married Polly RICE 16 June 1799 Barre, MA	
		(she dau/o Martin RICE and Ruth HASTINGS) (she born 1779; died 1861)	

52. LUCY-[4] BOWKER, sister of above, was born 20 Dec 1731 at Shrewsbury, MA. She married Ebenezer FORBUSH on 8 Mar 1753 at Westboro, Worcester, MA. He was the son of Deacon Thomas FORBUSH and Hannah BELLOWS; and was born 9 Apr 1731 Westboro; died 12 Oct 1806. Lucy-[4] BOWKER died ____ .

Children of Lucy-4 BOWKER and Ebenezer FORBUSH:

Surname **FORBUSH**　　　　(children born at Westboro, Worcester, MA)

230. Ebenezer, Jr.	born 19 Dec 1753; died 8 Oct 1756			EOL
231. Hannah	born 30 May 1755; died ____			
232. Elizabeth	born 29 Jan 1757; died ____			
233. Abel	born 11 July 1759; died 29 July 1759			EOL
234. Asa	born 16 July 1760; died 31 Aug 1818			

234. Asa — married Mehitable FAY ca ____

Child: Benjamin Franklin-6 FORBUSH born ca 1801; died ____

+　**235. MARTHA**　　　born 23 Sep 1762; died 22 Sep 1824 Sutton, MA
　　　　　　　　　　　married Benjamin RICHARDSON 14 Oct 1784 Westboro, MA
　　　　　　　　　　　(he s/o Jeremiah RICHARDSON and Abigail GOWING)
　　　　　　　　　　　(he born 28 July 1760 Sutton, MA; died ____)

236. Lucy	born 19 Aug 1764; died ____			
237. Abner	born 26 Aug 1766; died ____	239. Chloe	born 7 Sep 1770	
238. Catey	born 23 June 1768; died ____	240. Anna	born 25 Sep 1772	

53.　LYDIA-4 BOWKER, sister of above, was born 6 Dec 1733 at Shrewsbury, Worcester, MNA. She married Seth HAPGOOD on 31 May 1757 at Petersham, Worcester, MA. He was the son of Captain Thomas HAPGOOD and Damaris HUTCHINS, and was born 20 Oct 1732 at Shrewsbury, MA; died 23 Apr 1804 at Petersham, MA. Lydia-4 BOWKER died 9 Oct 1813 at Petersham.

Children of Lydia-4 BOWKER and Seth HAPGOOD:

Surname **HAPGOOD**　　　　(children all born Petersham, Worecester, MA)

241. Damaris	born 15 May 1758; died 9 May 1846 Bainbridge, NY	
242. Catharine	born 22 Oct 1759; died 21 Oct 1843 Petersham, MA	
243. Lydia	born 14 May 1761; died 29 Mar 1829 Maine	

+　**244. HUTCHINS**　　born 4 Apr 1763; died 4 Sep 1837 Petersham, MA
　　　　　　　　　　　married Betsey/Elizabeth GROUT 20 Oct 1789 MA
　　　　　　　　　　　(she dau/o Honorable Jonathan GROUT and Sarah PAGE)

245. Lucinda　　　　born 16 Jan 1765; died 18 July 1820 Hinsdale, NH

+　**246. SOLOMON**　　born 30 Dec 1766; died 5 Mar 1856 Bellows Falls, VT
　　　　　　　　　　　married Azubah BURT 10 Aug 1790
　　　　　　　　　　　(she born ca 1771; died 10 Feb 1858 Bellows Falls, VT)
　　　　　　　　　　　(she dau/o Judge Benjamin BURT and Mary ROOT)

247. Lucretia　　　　born 9 Sep 1768; died 11 May 1789　　　　　　　EOL

+　**248. EBER**　　　　born 5 Aug 1770; died 6 July 1851 Petersham, MA
　　　　　　　　　　　married Dolly GROUT 13 July 1803 Petersham, MA
　　　　　　　　　　　(she born 1 May 1772; died 16 July 1822 Petersham, MA)
　　　　　　　　　　　(she sister of Betsey (above)(wife of Hutchins # 244)

249. Oliver　　　　　born 28 Sep 1772; died 7 Jan 1813
　　　　　　　　　　　1 married Lucy SMITH 10 Nov 1799
　　　　　　　　　　　2 married Anna CHAPMAN ca 1810

+　**250. EUNICE**　　　born 22 July 1774; died 22 Aug 1862 Kendall, Orleans, NY
　　　　　　　　　　　married Guy BRIDGMAN 17 Feb 1797

251. Levi　　　　　　born 6 Dec 1778; died 15 June 1864 Sheldon, VT
　　　　　　　　　　　married Anna CHAPMAN Hapgood Sept 1823 (wid/o Oliver (above)

57.　ABIGAIL-4 BOWKER, daughter of Ezekiel-3 BOWKER (John-2; Edmund-1) and Abigail RICE, was born 30 Aug 1734 at Marlborough, MA. She married Silas WHEELER on 27 July 1758. He was the son of Joseph WHEELER and his 2nd wife Deborah WHITNEY, and was born 23 Oct 1732; died 25 Apr 1802. Abigail-4 BOWKER died ____.

Children of Abigail-4 BOWKER and Silas WHEELER:

Surname **WHEELER**

+　**252. ANNA**　　　　born 11 Aug 1760; died 1 May 1810
　　　　　　　　　　　married William BARNARD 23 Apr 1783 Stow, Middlesex, MA
　　　　　　　　　　　(he s/o Joel BARNARD and Lucy STEVENS)
　　　　　　　　　　　(he born 31 Jan 1759 Marlborough; died 1 May 1810 Dixfield, ME)

Children of Abigail-4 BOWKER and Silas WHEELER, continued:
Surname **WHEELER**

	253. Lucy	born 17 Nov 1762; died ___
+	**254. ASA**	born 16 Oct 1764; died Jan 1834
		married Sarah THOMPSON 27 Jan 1792
		(she born ca 1765 Marlborough; died 5 Dec 1833)
	255. Dexter	born ca 1767; died ____
	256. Catherine	born ca 1770; died 4 Jan 1851Marlborough, MA
		married Jonah HOWE 15 June 1806 (as his 2nd wife)
		(he s/o Thaddeus HOWE and Lavina BRIGHAM)
		(he born 22 Feb 1762; died 8 Dec 1834 Marlborough, MA)

Children: Dexter-5 born 18 June 1807; and Freeman-5 HOWE born 16 AUG 1809

60. MIRIAM-4 HOWE, daughter of Hannah-3 BOWKER (John-2; Edmund-1) and Captain Gershom HOWE, was born 27 Nov 1722 Marlborough, MA. She married Jotham BARTLETT on 17 May 1744 at Marlborough. He was the son of _____ BARTLETT and ____, and was born 5 Apr 1717 Marlborough; died 9 May 1790 Marlborough. Miriam-4 HOWE died 9 May 1801.

Children of Miriam-4 HOWE and Jotham BARTLETT:
Surname **BARTLETT**   (all children born Northboro, MA)

257. Antipas	born 3 Mar 1746; died 25 Sep 1817 Northboro
258. Lucy	born 8 Oct 1747; died 5 Aug 1828 Shrewsbvury, MA
259. Ezekiel	born 18 Feb 1750; died Aug 1824 Townsend, Middlesex, MA
260. Abraham	born 27 Feb 1754; died ____

61. MOSES-4 HOWE, brother of above, was born 6 March 1725 at Marlborough, MA. He married Hannah FELTON ca 1746. She was the daughter of Samuel FELTON and Sarah GOODALE, and was born 24 Oct 1716; died 22 Nov 1789. Moses-4 HOWE died 8 July 1771 Marlborough, MA.

Children of Moses-4 HOWE and Hannah FELTON:
Surname **HOWE**

261. Gershom	(1)	born 26 Sep 1747; died 20 May 1752	EOL
262. Samuel		born 12 Jan 1748/49 ; died 31 July 1820 no issue EOL	
		married Hannah BURNAP ca _____ (she born 16 Jan 1745;died 5 Nov 1835)	
		(she dau of David BURNAP and Hannah ____)	
263. Jonathan		born 15 Aug 1751; died ____	
264. Sarah		born 20 Aug 1753; died 23 July 1829 no issue EOL	
		married John GASSETT 3 Dec 1772	
		(he s/o Daniel GASSETT and Hannah WALKER of Hopkinton, MA)	
		(he born ca 1746; died 7 July 1834 Northboro, MA)	
265. Gershom	(2)	born 13 Jan 1756; died 16 Feb 1801 no issue EOL	
		1 married Levinah BARTLETT 24 Sep 1781 (she born ____; died 16 Aug 1790)	
		2 married Abigail HALL 23 Feb 1791	

62. SILAS-4 HOWE, brother of above, was born 5 Feb 1727 Marlborough, MA. He married Beulah LELAND on 20 Nov 1749. She was the daughter of Isaac LELAND and Mary ____, and was born____; died ____. Silas-4 HOWE died ____.

Children of Silas-4 HOWE and Beulah LELAND:
Surname **HOWE**

	266. Hannah	born 10 Dec 1750 Shrewsbury, MA; died 30 May 1778 Northboro, MA
		Note: She was a nurse, and while tending smallpox patients, became ill with the disease herself and died .
	267. Isaac	born 28 Feb 1753 Shrewsbury; died ____
	268. Esther	born 31 Aug 1755 Brookfield, MA; died ____; married Demon SHEFFIELD 5 Mar 1773
	269. Lucy	born 16 Jan 1757 Brookfield; died ___; married Moses TENNEY (int pub 16 Aug 1786)
	270. John	born 9 Feb 1761 Brookfield; died ____
+	**271. LYDIA**	born 30 Oct 1764 Brookfield; died ____; married William PEESO 16 Dec 1784
		(he s/o John PEESO and Hannah RANGER)(he born 30 June 1758; died 25 Mat 1831)
	272. Benjamin	born 28 Apr 1767 Leicester, MA

63. ZERUIAH-[4] HOWE, sister of above, was born 9 Oct 1729 at Marlborough, MA. She married David FELTON on 28 Oct 1747at Marlborough. He was the son of Samuel FELTON and Sarah GOODALE, and the brother of Hannah (above), and was born ca 1720; died 1777. Zerviah-[4] HOWE died 28 June 1773 at Petersham, Worcester, MA.

Children of Zerviah-[4] HOWE and David FELTON:
Surname **FELTON**

273. Zeruiah	(1)	born 24 Nov 1748; died 22 Oct 1755 EOL
274. Nancy		born 28 Nov 1750; died 25 Jan 1820; married David STONE of Petersham ca __
275. Daniel		born 19 Sep 1752; died Sep 1823 Salisbury, Addison, VT
		married Lois WILDER 20 Mar 1774 Petersham, MA
276. Rachel		born 23 Sep 1754; died ____; married Jonathan JOHNSON ca ____
277. Zeruiah	(2)	born 15 Nov 1756; died ____
278. Tamasin		born 28 Nov 1758; died 31 Mar 1843 Ashburnham, Worcester, MA
279. George Webber		born 20 Apr 1761; died 5 July 1817 Petersham; married Hannah OLIVER ca __
280. Phebe		born 12 Sep 1763; died 17 Sep 1830 Ashburnham, MA
281. Amos		born 18 Sep 1765; died 29 Oct 1829 Tunbridge, Orange, VT
282. Abigail		born 26 July 1767; died ____
283. Lydia		born 10 Feb 1770; died ____; married Jedidiah HOWE
		(he son of Abraham HOWE and Rachel RICE)
284. David		born 30 Sep 1772; died ____

64. PERSIS-[4] HOWE, sister of above, was born 2 Mar 1736 at Marlborough, MA. She married John GLEASON on 18 Dec 1755 Marlborough. He was the son of James GLEASON and Mary BARRETT; and was born 7 Dec 1724, died 13 Nov 1816. Persis-[4] HOWE died 18 July 1820.

Children of Persis-[4] HOWE and John GLEASON:
Surname **GLEASON**   (all children born Marlborough, MA)

+	**285. JOHN, Jr.**	born 19 Feb 1758 MA; died 8 Nov 1828
		married Experience STOW 17 Apr 1781
		(she dau/o John STOW and Ruth HOWE)
		(she born 19 Mar 1761 Marlborough, MA; died 27 Feb 1835 Marlborough)
	286. Mary	born 18 Jan 1763; died 3 Dec 1835
		married Zaccheus GLEASON 8 Sep 1789 Marlborough, MA
		(s/o Joseph GLEASON and Persis ALLEN) (he born 23 Dec 1762; died _____)
	287. Anne/ Anna	born 11 Oct 1770; died ____
		married Matthias Rice BRIGHAM 15 Sep 1791
		(he s/o Noah BRIGHAM and Miriam ALLEN) (he born 4 Jan 1765; died _____)

65. HANNAH-[4] HOWE, sister of above, was born 9 Nov 1737 Marlborough, MA. She married Eli KEYES, Jr. on 12 Feb/ 1 Apr 1762 at Shrewsbury, MA. He was the son of Eli KEYES and Mary WHEELOCK, and was born 4 Mar 1738 Shrewsbury; died 1805 NH. Hannah-[4] HOWE died ____.

Children of Hannah-[4] HOWE and Eli KEYES, Jr.:
Surname **KEYES**

+	**288. EZRA**	born 27 Jan/Apr 1763; died 29 Dec 1841 VT
		married Hannah KNOWLTON Dec 1792
		(she born ca 1770; died _____)
+	**289. DANIEL**	born 19 Nov 1764 MA; died 4 Dec 1826 Princeton, MA
		married Jedidiah SAWYER 8 Nov 1792 Lancaster, MA
		(she dau/o Josiah SAWYER and Abigail _____)
		(she born ca 1767 Lancaster, MA; died 14 Feb 1850 Princeton, MA)
+	**290. AZUBAH**	born 5 June 1767; died 3 June 1825 Shrewsbury, MA
		married Hananiah WHITNEY 10 Oct 1787
		(he s/o Lt. Samuel WHITNEY and Abigail FLETCHER)
		(he born 18 Dec 1762 Westminster, MA; died Oct 1835 Ashburnham, MA)
		married Capt. Thomas ROBY 18 Dec 1781
		(he s/o Samuel ROBY and Hannah ROSS)
		(he born 24 Aug 1760 Middlesex, MA; died 1 May 1833 Nashua, NH (gs)

66. DEACON THOMAS-4 LUND, son of Thomas-3 LUND (Elizabeth-2 BOWKER; Edmund-1; John A,B) and Elizabeth TAYLOR, was born 16 Jan 1712 Concord, MA. He married first to Mary TAYLOR ca 1736. She was the daughter of _____ TAYLOR and ____, and was born ca 1715; died 1748. His second marriage was to Sarah CHANDLER ca 1749. She was the daughter of ____ CHANDLER and ____, and was born 20 Oct 1724 Chelmsford, MA; died 16 April 1801 Hillsborough, NH. Thomas-4 LUND died 24 Feb 1790 at Hillsborough, NH.

Children of Thomas-4 LUND and Mary TAYLOR:
Surname **LUND**

291. Jesse	born ca 1737; died 1738		EOL
292. Thomas	born 12 March 1739; died ca 1821		

Children of Thomas-4 LUND and Sarah CHANDLER:
Surname **LUND**

293. Ensign Joel	born 27 Nov 1752 Dunstable, MA; died ca 1800 Dunstable, NH		
294. Sarah	born 24 Feb 1755 Dunstable; died ____		
295. Phebe	born 15 Apr 1757; died 2 Sept 1849 Nashua, NH (gs)		
+	**296. NOAH**	born 31 March 1759; died 8 Aug 1825 Orange , VT	
		married Betsey HALE 6 Dec 1786	
		(she born ca 1763; died ca 1843)	
	297. Mary	born ca 1760; died young	EOL
	298. Daniel	born 31 Oct 1762; died ____	
		1 married Elizabeth EMERSON ca ___; 2 married Hepsibah HUNT ca ____	
	299. Mary (2)	born 8 Jan 1764 Litchfield, MA; died 15 Sept 1846 Nelson, NH	
	300. Betty	born 15 Oct 1766 Dunstable; died ____	
	301. Dolly	born 8 July 1768 Dunstable; died 5 Sep 1838 Marbletown , NY	
		mrried John REED 15 Sept 1794	

67. ELIZABETH-4 LUND, sister of above, was born 14 May 1715 at Dunstable, MA. She married Edward SPAULDING ca 1735. He was the son of _____ SPAULDING and _____; and was born ca 1707; died ca 1750. Elizabeth-4 LUND died ca 1766 at Nottingham, Rockingham, NH.

Children of Elizabeth-4 LUND and Edward SPAULDING:
Surname **SPAULDING**

302. Levi	born ca 1737; died 1825	305. Esther	born ca 1747; died ____
303. Elizabeth	born ca 1741; died ____	306. Sarah	born ca 1754; died ____
304. Lucy	born ca 744; died ____		

68. JONATHAN-4 LUND, brother of above, was born 12 Oct 1717 at Dunstable, MA/NH. He married first to Jean VARNUM on 2/9 April 1741. She was the daughter of Thomas VARNUM and Joanna JEWETT, and was born 3 April 1713; died 14 Sept 1764. His second marriage was to Mrs. Olive _____ Sargent on 22 Oct 1765. Jonathan-4 LUND died 29 Nov 1801 at Dunstable, MA/NH.

Children of Jonathan-4 LUND and Jean VARNUM:
Surname **LUND**   (children all born Dunstable, MA)

	307. Olive	born 15 March 1742; died 22 Oct 1820 Nottingham, NH	
		married Nathaniel MERRILL 25 Feb 1767	
	308. Johannah	born 16 Sept 1743; died 21 Aug 1814	
		married Deacon Benjamin SMITH 6 Oct 1762 Dunstable, MA	
+	**309. CAPT. JONATHAN**	born 24 July 1747; died 11 June 1828 (gs)	
		married Priscilla CUMMINGS ca 1770	
		(she born ca 1748; died 22 Jan 1824 (gs)	
	310. Mary	born 24 Aug 1749; died 8 Sept 1758 Amherst, MA/NH	EOL
	311. Oliver	born 29 July 1752; died 18 March 1776 Dunstable, MA	
		married Elizabeth EMERSON 12 Jan 1775	
		(she born 28 Sept 1751; died 1804 Litchfield, MA/NH)	
		Child: Oliver-6 LUND born 25 Feb 1776 Hillsborough, NH; died ___; married Thankful WILCOX 13 Nov 1800	
	312. Mehitabel	born 19 June 1755; died 22 Nov 1758	EOL
	313. Nathaniel	born 27 Aug 1756; died ____	

Child of Jonathan-[4] LUND and Mrs. Olive ____ Sargent:
Surname **LUND**

314. Joseph	born 24 Dec 1767; died 21 Aug 1835 Hillsborough, NH	
315. Elizabeth	born 10 Jan 1772; died ____	
316. James Tyng	born 24 Jan 1776; died ____; married Sally LUND ca ____	
	(she dau/o Ensign Joel LUND and Sarah _____)	

69. EPHRAIM-[4] LUND, brother of above, was born 3 Aug/Dec 1720 at Dunstable, Hillsborough, NH. He married Rachel PIERCE ca 1741. She was the daughter of Stephen PIERCE and Rachel HARWOOD, and was born 21 Oct 1723; died ____. Ephraim-[4] LUND died 30 March 1788, while participating in the Battle with Cornwallis.

Children of Ephraim-[4] LUND and Rachel PIERCE:
Surname **LUND**

317. Rachel	born 29 Aug 1743; died ____
318. Ephraim	born 25 Aug 1745; died 28 Aug 1820; married Alice WHEELER 12 May 1772 NH
319. Elizabeth	born 23 Oct 1748; died ____
320. Stephen	born 1 July 1851; died ____
321. Joseph	born 28 April 1754; died ca 1843 Grafton, NH
322. Noadiah	born 20 Mar 1757; died 29 Nov 1801
323. Susannah	born 17 Sept 1759; died ____
324. Silas	born 12 Sept 1762; died ca 1840 Grafton, NH

70. PHINEAS-[4] LUND, brother of above, was born 3 April 1723 at Dunstable, Middlesex, MA/NH. He married Rachel FRENCH ca 1744. She was the daughter of Samuel FRENCH and Mary ____, and was born ca 1726; died 1763. Phineas-[4] LUND died 2 Dec 1818 at Amherst, Hillsborough, NH.

Children of Phineas-[4] LUND and Rachel FRENCH:
Surname **LUND**   (all children born Dunstable, MA/NH)

325. Lucy	born 31 Jan 1745; died 6 Nov 1822 Amherst, NH
	married Benjamin SHEPARD (he born ca 1744; died ca 1810
	Children: James-[6] born ___; William Levi-[6] born ca ____; John-[6] born ca ____; Benjamin-[6] SHEPARD born ca ____)
326. Rhoda	born 30 Aug 1748; died ____
327. Samuel French	born 26 July 1751; died 24 June 1827 Tyngsboro, MA
	married Dorcas SNOW 27 April 1790 Tyngsboro
	(she dau/o Jonathan SNOW and Sarah PERHAM)
	(she born 20 Nov 1746 MA; died 7 Feb 1818 Tyngsboro, MA)
	Child: Lucy-[6] LUND born ca ___; died 1 May 1798 EOL
328. Jesse	born 20 March 1757; died 1820 MA
	married Katy PARKER 25 July 1803 Bolton, MA
329. Bridget	born 30 Aug 1759; died ____; married Isaac PARKHURST 24 Feb 1791
	(he s/o Jonathan PARKHURST and Bridget BUTTERFIELD)
	(he born 23 Aug 1767 Chelmsford, MA; died _____)
+ **330. WILLARD**	born 21 Feb 1762; died 29 Dec 1855 Weston, VT
	married Sarah TOWNE ca 1789 (she born ca 1769; died ca 1848)
331. Katherine	born 22 July 1764; died ____
332. Sarah	born 19 Feb 1768; died _____
333. Rachel	born 21 May 1771; died 25 Sept 1863
	married Jacob DUNCKLEE 7/20 Feb 1819 NH
	(he s/o David DUNCKLEE and Phebe ODELL) (he 1m. Abigail HILL – 9 ch)
	(he born 26 Mar 1769 Hillsborough, NH; died Aug 1842 Hillsborough, NH)

71. HENRY-[4] SPAULDING, son of Elizabeth-[3] LUND (Edmund-[2;1] BOWKER) and Henry-[3] SPAULDING (Andrew-[2]; Edward-[1]), was born 22 Nov 1704 Chelmsford, MA.. He married first to Lucy PROCTOR Feb 1727. She was the daughter of Samuel PROCTOR and Sarah ____, and was born 22 Nov 1704 Chelmsford, MA ; died 1 Jan 1742 Chelmsford, MA. Henry-[4] SPAULDING married second to Marah ADAMS on 27 April 1743. She was the daughter of Benjamin ADAMS and Mary PARKER, and was born 15 Dec 1715; died 29 April 1807 Chelmsford. Henry-[4] SPAULDING died 29 April 1792 Chelmsford, Middlesex, MA.

Children of Henry-4 SPAULDING and Lucy PROCTOR:
Surname **SPAULDING**

+	**334. SAMUEL**	born 31 Jan 1727 Chelmsford, MA; died 11 Sept 1797 Merrimack, NH
		married Sarah WOODS 3 May 1753 MA
		(she born 8 Mar 1730 Chelmsford; died 10 April 1815 Merrimack, NH)
+	**335. LUCY**	born 1 Feb 1728 Chelmsford; died _____
		married William REED/READE ca 1759 Litchfield , MA
		(he born 25 Feb 1724 Chelmsford; died Jan 1769 Litchfield, MA
+	**336. SARAH PROCTOR**	born 10 June 1734; died 1758 ; married Henry FLETCHER 12 Apr 1753
	337. Henry III	born 11 Feb 1735/36; died _____; married Mary FLETCHER

Child: Thankful-6 SPAULDING born 3 Dec 1761 Chelmsford, MA

Child of Henry-4 SPAULDING and Mar(i)ah ADAMS:
Surname **SPAULDING**

	338. Abel	born Feb 1739/40; died 1 March 1740
+	**339. ZEBULON**	born 13 March 1744 ; died 26 Feb 1816
		married Lydia WRIGHT 12 Feb 1767 (she born 9 Sep 1745; died _____)
+	**340. DANIEL**	born 21 June 1746 Merrimack, NH; died _____
		1 married Hannah PUTNAM ca ____; 2 married Mary BUTTERFIELD
	341. Thomas	born 24 Nov 1750; died _____
	342. Thankful	born 3 Dec 761 Chelmsford, MA; died Sept 1778 EOL
	343. Mary	born 10 Feb 1789; died ____; married _____ PARKHURST ca _____

73. WILLIAM-4 SPAULDING, brother of above, was born 17 March 1711 at Chelmsford, MA. He married Hepzibah BLOOD on 6 Jan 1731. She was the daughter of Joseph BLOOD and Hannah SAWYER, and was born 26 June 1711 Groton, MA; died 1 Feb 1787 at Pepperell, MA. William-4 SPAULDING died 21 June 1790 at Groton, MA.

Children of William-4 SPAULDING and Hepzibah BLOOD:
Surname **SPAULDING**   (all children born Pepperell, MA)

344. William	born 4 April 1732 ; died May 1817 Norridgewock, MA
345. Eleazer	born 26 May 1733; died 26 June 1813
346. Elizabeth	born 11 March 1737; died 1790 Temple , Hillsborough, NH
347. Joseph	born 26 Apr 1738; died 17 June 1775 Boston, MA
348. Hannah	born 7 Oct 1739; died 30 Aug 1800 Pepperell, MA
	1 married Ephraiim HALL 10 Sept 1755
	2 married Isaac SHATTUCK 15 Jan 1761
349. Thomas	born 7 Oct 1743; died 17 Dec 1802 Pepperell, MA
350. Henry	born Apr 1746; died 12 March 1775 Groton, MA
351. Abel	born 12 June 1749; died 24 Sept 1750 EOL
352. Seth	born 22 Sept 1751; died 24 May 1753 EOL
353. Abel (2)	born 12 May 1755; died 29 May 1849 Pepperell, MA

74. LEONARD-4 SPAULDING, brother of above, was born 11 Dec 1713 at Chelmsford, MA. He married Elizabeth DURANT on 18 Dec 1737. She was the daughter of John DURANT and Elizabeth JAQUITH, and was born ca 1717 Chelmsford, MA; died ca 1799 Oxford County, Maine. Leonard-4 SPAULDING died 7 Feb 1758.

Children of Leonard-4 SPAULDING and Elizabeth DURANT:
Surname **SPAULDING**   (all children born Chelmsford, MA)

354. Benjamin	born 5 Feb 1738; died 14 Oct 1811 ME
	1 married Sarah CHANDLER on 3 Feb 1759
	2 married Patty BARRETT 29 Nov 1764 (she born 31 Jan 1740; died 4 Oct 1819)
355. Elizabeth	born 29 Dec 1740 ; died ____
356. Rachel	born 14 Nov 1742; died ____; married James PEMBERTON ca ____
	Child: Leonard-6 PEMBERTON born ca ____
357. Thankful	born 21 Oct 1744; died _____
358. Sarah	born Oct 1746; died 1828
359. Abel	born ca 1748; died ____
360. Esther	born 1755; died 1772

BOWKER
The Fourth American Generation

Children of Leonard-4 SPAULDING and Elizabeth DURANT, continued:
Surname **SPAULDING**

361. Lucy	born 21 June 1757; died 15 April 1821 Chelmsford, MA
	married William SPAULDING 6 Apr 1779 (he born ____; died 27 Sep 1825)

76. SAMUEL-4 SCRIPTURE, Jr., son of Elizabeth-3 LUND (Elizabeth-2 BOWKER; Edmund-1) and her 2nd husband, Samuel SCRIPTURE, was born 27 Apr 1727 at Hillsborough, NH. He married Mary GREEN on 9 Oct 1746 at Chelmsford, NH. She was the daughter of _____ GREEN and ____; and was born 22 June 1731 Groton, MA; died May 1817. Samuel-4 SCRIPTURE, Jr. died ca 1817 Cheshire, NH.

Children of Samuel-4 SCRIPTURE, Jr. and Mary GREEN:
Surname **SCRIPTURE**

362. Mary	born 5 May 1747 Groton, MA; died 11 May 1797 Cambridge, MA
363. James	born 11 Jan 1748 Groton; died 19 June 1810 Mason, NH
364. Oliver	born 9/19 Dec 1750 Groton; died 27 Jul 1821 New Ipswich, NH
365. Sarah	born 1753 Mason, NH; died 1835
366. Jemima Fay	born ca 1758; died 1796
367. Samuel IV	born 9 Dec 1760 Mason, NH; died 20 Jan 1852 Nelson, NH
368. Hannah	born 1 June 1763 Groton; died ____
369. John	born 18 Sep 1765 Groton; died ____ NY
	married Molly WINSHIP ca _____ (she born ca 1766; died ____)

Child: Elijah-6 SCRIPTURE born 7 Aug 1794 NY; died 6 Feb 1865 IN

77. WILLIAM-4 LUND, son of William-3 LUND (Elizabeth-2 BOWKER; Edmund-1) and Rachel HOLDEN, was born 18 July 1717 MA. He married Sarah A. BECK ca 1742. She was the daughter of _____ BECK and ____; and was born ca 1720; died ____. William-4 LUND died 20 March 1782 at Dunstable, MA.

Children of William-4 LUND and Sarah BECK:
Surname **LUND**   (children all born Dunstable, MA)

370. Hannah	born 18 June 1743; died 11 June 1838 Dunstable
	married William ROBY ca ____
371. William	born 11 May 1745; died 1758 EOL
372. Sarah	born 4 April 1747; died ____; 1 married James WHITNEY ca ____
	2 married Isaac PIKE ca ____
373. John	born 22 Feb 1749; died 11 May 1822
374. Mary Adelaide	born 17 Apr 1762; died Sept 1846 NH; married Nehemiah WRIGHT 8 Jan 1784
375. Levi	born 12 Dec 1754; died 23 Dec 1814 Dunstable
	1 married Sarah CUTLER ca ___; 2 married Naomi GIBSON ca ___
376. Rebecca	born 15 Mar 1757; died 23 Mar 1830 Corinth, VT.
	married Daniel WOODS 30 July 1782
	(he s/o Oliver WOODS and Sarah _____)
	(he born 15 Feb 1760 Dunstable; died ____)
377. William (2)	born 1 July 1758; died 1776 MA EOL
	(he killed in the Revolutionary War)
378. Augustus	born 17 Dec 1764; died ____; married Joanna SMITH 10 Apr 1787
	(she dau/o Deacon Benjamin SMITH and Joanna LUND)
	(she born 31 Oct 1763; died ____)

78. RACHEL-4 LUND, sister of above, was born 28 Aug 1719 at Dunstable, Middlesex, MA. She married John LOVEWELL on 2 Nov 1739 at Hampton Falls, Rockingham, NH. He was the son of Captain John LOVEWELL and Hannah MOODY; and was born ca 1718; died 2 July 1763. Rachel-4 LUND died 2 July 1762 at Dunstable.

Children of Rachel-4 LUND and John LOVEWELL:
Surname **LOVEWELL**   (children all born Dunstable, MA)

379. Rachel	born 18 May 1740; died ca 1813
380. Anna/Hannah	born 29 Feb 1742; died Aug 1758 EOL
+ **381. JOHN**	born 16 Nov 1744; died 18 Apr 1815 Corinth, VT
	married Vodica LOVEWELL ca 1790 Corinth (a cousin)

Children of Rachel-⁴ LUND and John LOVEWELL, continued:
Surname **LOVEWELL**

382. Jonathan	born 20 Aug 1747; died 15 Mar 1788	
383. Mary	born 10 Mar 1749; died ____	
384. James	born 15 Oct 1752; died 27 Nov 1753	EOL
385. Hannah	born 5 Jan 1754; died ____	
386. Zaccheus	born 22 May 1756; died 8 Oct 1758	EOL

80. LIEUTENANT CHARITY-⁴ LUND, son of William-³ LUND (Elizabeth-² BOWKER; Edmund-¹; John-^A,B) and Rachel HOLDEN, was born 16 Feb 1730 MA. He married Lucy COLBURN ca 1754 NH. She was the daughter of Oliver COLBURN and Lucy BOWERS, and was born ca 1735; died 2 Sept 1805 NH. Charity-⁴ LUND died 11 June 1793 NH.

Children of Lt. Charity-⁴ LUND and Lucy COLBURN:
Surname **LUND**

387. Stephen	born 14 May 1754; died 20 May 1821; married Lucy DANFORTH 23 July 1785 MA
388. Lucy	born 24 Sept 1756; died 4 Jan 1833; married Gordon HUTCHINS ca 1780
389. Elizabeth	born 14 Feb 1758; died ____
390. Rachel	born 14 Jan 1760; died 3 July 1849; married James DUNN, Jr.
391. Charity, Jr.	born 17 Nov 1761; died 13 June 1813
392. Sarah	born 6 July 1763; died ____
393. John	born 6 Sep 1765; died ____; married Mary ____ ca ____
394. Hannah	born 6 Feb 1767; died ____
395. James	born 29 May 1768; died ____
396. Cosmo	born 6 Nov 1769; died 15 July 1834 MA
397. Jerahmeel	born 2 May 1771; died 11 Sep 1818; married Sarah Swallow THOMPSON ca ____
398. William	born 17 Nov 1776; died 30 Apr 1845; married Esther ____ ca ____
399. Rebekah	born 6 July 1778; died 13 Feb 1812 NH

Reference: Colonial Gravestones of the State of New Hampshire

81. MARY-⁴ LUND, sister of above, was born 28 Nov 1733. She married James UNDERWOOD ca 1752 NH. He was the son of Joseph UNDERWOOD and Susanna PARKER, and was born 5 Dec 1731 Castleton, VT, died ca 1808 Litchfield, Hillsborough, NH. Mary-⁴ LUND died 7 Aug 1809 Hillsborough, NH.

Children of Mary-⁴ LUND and James UNDERWOOD:
Surname **UNDERWOOD**

	400. James	born 10 June 1753 Hillsborough, NH; died ____
	401. Mary	born 22 Nov 1755; died 4 April 1789
		married William Webb PATTERSON 12 Feb 1782 (he born ca 1752)
+	**402. THOMAS**	born 8 Apr 1759; died 18 Nov 1838 Hillsborough, NH
		married Mehitable GAGE 12 Apr 1778 (she born 9 Sept 1760; died 14 June 1829)
	403. Susannah	born 16 Nov 1761; died 20 Nov 1777 EOL
+	**404. CHARLOTTE**	born 23 Feb 1764 Hillsborough, NH; died 31 Jan 1849 Litchfield, NH
		married Moses TOWNE 28 Feb 1784
	405.Sarah / Sally	born 25 July 1766; died ca 1857
		married Mathew PARKER 5 July 1792 Merrimack, NH
		(he s/o Mathew PARKER and Elizabeth JONES)
		(he born 25 July 1765; died 26 Nov 1826 Litchfield, NH)
		Children: Betsey-⁶ born ca ___; James Underwood-⁶ born ca 1797; and Nathan-⁶ PARKER born 1808, died 1894
+	**406. JOHN**	born 17 Feb 1769 Litchfield, NH; died 5 May 1815
		married Elizabeth/ Betsey PARKER 5 July 1792 Merrimack, NH
		(she born ca 1770; died 1821)
+	**407. RACHEL**	born 15 Aug 1771; died 11 Sept 1838
		1 married Royal BLOOD ca _____ (he born 5 Dec 1765; died ca 1811 NH)
		(he s/o Francis BLOOD and Elizabeth SPAULDING)
		2 married William WRIGHT ca _____ (he born ca 1793; died 1843)
	408. Elizabeth	born ca 1774; died _____

83. JANE-[4] ROBBINS, daughter of Margaret-[3] LUND (Elizabeth-[2] BOWKER; Edmund-[1]) and her first husband, Jonathan ROBBINS, was born 26 Dec 1712 Groton, MA. She married Ensign Stephen John AMES on 14 April 1731 at Groton, Middlesex, MA. He was the son of John AMES and Priscilla KIMBALL, and was born 1 Sept 1712 Boxford, MA; died 19 Feb 1801 at Dublin, Cheshire, NH. Ens. Stephen AMES served in the French War, later operated an iron foundry in Grafton County, NH. Jane -[4] ROBBINS died 25 Feb 1800 at Dublin, NH.

Children of Jane-[4] ROBBINS and Stephen John AMES:
Surname **AMES**

	409. Jane	born 6 Dec 1733 Groton, MA; died ____
	410. Hannah	born 28 April 1736 Groton; died young
+	**411. STEPHEN**	born 14 Mar 1739 Groton; died 17 May 1776; married Abigail FOSTER 26 Sep 1761
	412. Elizabeth	born 10 Feb 1742 Hollis, Hillsborough, NH; died ____
	413. Rachel	born 12 Dec 1744 Hollis, NH ; died 6 April 1841 Monkton, VT
	414. Jonathan Robbins	born 11 April 1747 Hollis, NH; died ca 1813 Dublin, NH; served in Revolutionary War
	415. David	born 30 May 1749 Hollis, NH; died ca 1799 Monkton, VT; served in Rev War
	416. Charles	born 28 Feb 1750 Hollis, NH; died _____
	417. Benjamin	born 14 May 1753 Hollis, NH; died ____
	418. Hannah (2)	born 3 June 1759 Hollis, NH; died 6 Nov 1834 Nelson, NH

86. ELEANOR / ELLENOR-[4] ROBBINS, sister of above, was born 18 June 1721 at ____, MA. She married James WHITNEY ca 1738. He was the son of _____ WHITNEY and ____; and was born ca 1714; died 1755. Eleanor-[4] ROBBINS died ca 1815.

Child of Eleanor-[4] ROBBINS and James WHITNEY:
Surname **WHITNEY**

419. JONATHAN	born 15 Aug 1745 Dunstable, Middlesex, MA; died 1834.
	married Abigail HEMMINWAY/HEMINGWAY 7 May 1772 Fitzwilliam, Cheshre, NH
	(she dau/o Joseph HEMMINWAY/HEMINGWAY and Mary ADAMS)
	(she born 26 Apr 1749; died 1844)

88. ELIZABETH-[4] ROBBINS, sister of above, was born 26 Sep 1722/23 at Dunstable, Middlesex, MA. She married Stephen SHATTUCK, as his second wife, on 21 Sep 1745 at Charlestown, MA. He was the son of Benjamin SHATTUCK and Martha SHERMAN, and was born 10 Sep 1710; died 1801 Templeton, MA. He had been previously married to Mercy WHEELER. Elizabeth-[4] ROBBINS died 12 July 1792.

Children of Elizabeth-[4] ROBBINS and Stephen SHATTUCK:
Surname **SHATTUCK**

+	**420. ELIZABETH**	born ca 1745 Littleton; died 15 June 1798
		married Nathan KINSMAN 6 Sep 1772

91. MARGARET-[4] SHATTUCK , half-sister of above, daughter of Margaret-[3] LUND (Elizabeth-[2] BOWKER; Edmund-[1]; John-[A, B]) and her second husband, William SHATTUCK , was born 4 July 1732 at Groton, MA. She married first to Joseph BENNETT on 26 May 1752. He was the son of Benjamin BENNETT and Mary LAKIN, and was born 15 Dec 1725 Groton, MA, died 1759 Groton.. Her second marriage, 24 Jan 1759, was to Joseph METCALF. He was the son of Samuel METCALF and Rebecca DICKINSON, and was born 3 April 1734 Ipswich, MA , died from injuries sustained by falling from an apple tree on 19 March 1793 Ashburnham, MA. Margaret-[4] died suddenly, while visiting her brother Job , on 20 June 1802 at Groton, MA.

Note: These are said to be the ancestors of all the METCALFS who resided in Ashburnham, MA. The family moved from Groton in 1770, and settled east of Lake Naukeag. Their descendants include many bearing the surnames of RICE, TOWNSEND, LAWS and MERRIAM.. Joseph METCALF served in the Indian War .

Children of Margaret-[4] SHATTUCK and Joseph METCALF:
Surname **METCALF**

+	**421. EZEKIEL SHATTUCK**	born 13 Oct 1759 Groton, MA; died 31 May 1831 Ashburnham
		married Eunice BROOKS 10 Jan 1780
		(she born ca ____; died 12 Jan 1811)
+	**422. SAMUEL**	born 15 Mar 1761 Groton; died 25 Dec 1822 Groton,NH (killed by a falling barn door)
		1 married Phebe FLETCHER 3 Nov 1786 (she born ca ____; died 7 April 1802)
		2 married Betsey KEMP 10 June 1802

Children of Margaret-[4] SHATTUCK and Joseph METCALF, continued:
Surname **METCALF**

+	**423. MARGARET**	born 19 Mar 1763 Groton; died 20 March 1847 married Reuben TOWNSEND 5 Nov 1782 Ashburnham, MA (he born 23 Aug 1758; died 1837 Ashburnham)	
+	**424. SARAH**	born 7 Sept 1765 Ashburnham; died 16 Feb 1814 Ashburnham married Reuben RICE 5 Jan 1784	
+	**425. REBECCA**	born 14 Aug 1767 Ashburnham; died _____ married William MERRIAM 30 Oct 1788 (he a blacksmith)	
	426. Thankful (1)	born 18 Aug1769; died young	EOL
	427. Joseph	born 25 Aug 1771 Ashburnham; died 29 Mar 1791	EOL
	428. Jeremiah	born 20 Dec 1773 Ashburnham, MA; died 8 Mar 1774	EOL
+	**429. THANKFUL (2)**	born 18 May 1775 Ashburnham; died 5 Jan 1852 Westminster, MA married James LAWS , Jr. 21 March 1797 (he born 13 Dec 1772; died 14 Aug 1860 Westminster, Worcester, MA	

92.   CAPTAIN JOB-[4] SHATTUCK, brother of above, was born 11 Feb 1736 Groton, MA. He married first to Sarah HARTWELL on 25 May 1758. She was the daughter of Samuel HARTWELL and Sarah HOLDEN, and was born 19 Mar 1738 Groton, died 5 May 1798 Groton. He married his second wife, Elizabeth LAKIN Gragg, on 2 May 1800. She was the daughter of William LAKIN and Miriam ____, and was born ca 1743, died 1 June 1824. Elizabeth was the widow of John GRAGG. Captain Job-[4] SHATTUCK died 13 Jan 1819 at Groton, MA.

Children of Captain Job-[4] SHATTUCK and Sarah HARTWELL:
Surname **SHATTUCK**   (all children born at Groton, MA)

+	**430. JOB, JR.**	born 10 Dec 1758; died 4 May 1827 Groton married Elizabeth BLOOD ca 1781 (she born 14 July 1762; died 26 April 1840) (she dau/o Simon BLOOD and _____)
+	**431. SARAH**	born 27 Dec 1760; died 20 Sept 1849 Winslow, Kennebec, ME married Benjamin SIMPSON 28 Mar 1781 Boston, MA (he born ca 1745 ; died 1839)
+	**432. EZEKIEL**	born 12 Sept 1763; died 1 April 1813 Boston, Suffolk, MA (typhoid fever) married Prudence BLOOD 25 Sept 1788 Groton, MA (she born 30 Oct 1770 Groton; died 2 Sept 1819 Groton, MA (she dau/o Levi BLOOD (James, Jr.) and Sarah COLBURN)
+	**433. WILLIAM**	born 8 Mar 1765; died 30 Aug 1806 married Eunice BLOOD ca _____ (she sister of Elizabeth BLOOD, above) (she born 25 Feb 1766; died 10 Feb 1807 Groton)
+	**434. RACHEL**	born 12 July 1767; died 12 July 1816 Dunstable married Oliver HARTWELL 27 Mar 1789 (he born 7 Sept 1761 Groton; died ____) (he s/o Oliver HARTWELL (Ebenezer) and Ruth FARNSWORTH)
+	**435. CAPT. DANIEL**	born 11 Feb 1770; died 8 April 1831 (consumption) 1 married Abigail SHEPLE 28 March 1799 (she dau/o Jonathan SHEPLE and Anna BLOOD) (she born15 Jan 1776; died 8 April 1814) 2 married Catharine SHEPLE 7 July 1815 (she born 30 Nov 1795; died 30 May 1825; sister to his first wife) 3 married Hannah DAVIS White 30 April 1826 (she dau/o Josiah DAVIS and _____; and widow of Joel WHITE) (she born 23 April 1789; died _____)
+	**436. NOAH, Esq.**	born 30 Aug 1772; died 28 Sept 1858; married Anna SHEPLE 25 Nov 1798 (she born 22 April 1778; died _____; sister of Abigail SHEPLE, above)
+	**437. MARGARET**	born 13 Mar 1774; died 29 Nov 1852 Amherst, Hillsborough, NH married Jonathan BENNETT, Esq. 11 May 1800 (he born 28 Nov 1775; died 20 Feb 1829 Amherst) (he s/p James B. BENNETT and _____)
+	**438. ANNA**	born 6 Feb 1779; died 7 Feb 1843 Brookline, Hillsborough, NH. married Thomas BENNETT 25 Nov 1798 (he s/o Stephen BENNETT and _____)

BOWKER
The Fourth American Generation

94. JOSIAH-[4] BOWKER, son of Edmund-[3] BOWKER (John-[2]; Edmund-[1]) and Elizabeth ____, was born 19 March 1724 Sudbury, MA. He married first to Mary CROMPTON on 5 June 1747. She was the daughter of ____ CROMPTON and ____, and was born ___; died before 1749. He married second to Mary ANDREWS on 24 Aug 1749. She was the daughter of _____ ANDREWS and ____, and was born ____, died ____. Josiah-[4] BOWKER died 11 Aug 1766 Hopkinton, MA.

Children of Josiah-[4] BOWKER and Mary ANDREWS:
Surname **BOWKER**

	439. Hannah	born 2 Feb 1750; died ____		
+	**440. ELIZABETH/ Betsey**	born 22 Oct 1752; died died 1816 NY; married John WATKINS 3 Dec 1772		
	441. Mary	born 21 May 1755; died ____	442. Josiah, Jr.	born 22 Feb 1757; died ____

96. MICAH-[4] BOWKER, brother of above, was born 10 June 1729 at Hopkinton, MA. He married Persis MAYNARD 27 June 1749. She was the daughter of Joseph MAYNARD and Miriam WILLARD; and was born ____; died ____. Micah-[4] BOWKER died ____.

Children of Micah-[4] BOWKER and Persis MAYNARD:
Surname **BOWKER**

	443. Hannah	born ca 1750; died 1827
+	**444. DEA. EDMUND**	born 9 Sept 1757; died 20 Jan 1841 Milford, MA.
		married Hannah STEARNS 27 Aug 1778
		(she dau/o Jonathan STEARNS and Beulah ____)
		(she born 30 Jan 1755 Hopkinton, MA; died 1824 Hopkinton)

97. SAMUEL-[4] BOWKER, brother of above, was born 9 April 1731 at Hopkinton, Middlesex, MA. He married first to Martha STONE on 5 Oct 1749. She was the daughter of ____ STONE and ____; and was born ca 1733; died before 1754. He married second to Lydia WHITNEY on 12 Dec 1754 at Mendon, Worcester, MA. She was the daughter of Jonathan WHITNEY and Lydia JONES, and was born 18 Nov 1732; died ca 1765. He married third to Lois HARROD on 2 Sept 1767 at Framingham, Middlesex, MA. She was the daughter of ____ HARROD and ____, and was born___; died ____. Samuel-[4] BOWKER died 11 Oct 1799 at Hopkinton, MA.

Children of Samuel-[4] BOWKER and Martha STONE:
Surname **BOWKER**   (born Hopkinton, MA)

445. Mary	born 11 Oct 1750; died ____	446. Martha	born 8 July 1752; died ca 1848

Children of Samuel-[4] BOWKER and Lydia WHITNEY:
Surname **BOWKER**

+	**447. SENATOR ASA**	born 12 Nov 1755 Hopkinton, MA; died 5 Oct 1825 Boston, MA ; Rev War veteran
		married Hannah HARWOOD 8 Dec 1777
		(she dau/o James HARWOOD and Martha ____)
		(she born 31 July 1759 Worcester, MA; died 3 Dec 1842
	448. Abigail	born 13 June 1757; died 1759 EOL
	449. Abigail (2)	born 9 April 1759; died ____
+	**450. ABIATHER**	born 25 Feb 1763; died 5 Jan 1838
		married Lydia FUZZE/FEZZE 12 Feb 1789 Hopkinton, MA
+	**451. RUTH**	born 9 Feb 1765; died 23 Apr 1812 Chester, Windsor, VT
		1 married Daniel WHEATON 30 Aug 1787; 2 married Hezekiah JOHNSON 5 Nov 1789

Children of Samuel-[4] BOWKER and Lois HARROD:
Surname **BOWKER**

	452. Daniel	born 16 Feb 1769; died ____	454. Betsey	born ____; died ____
	453. Samuel	born ____; died ____		

98. URIAH-[4] BOWKER, brother of above, was born 9 Feb 1735 at Hopkinton, Middlesex, MA. He married Sarah HAYDEN on 5 Dec 1759 at Hopkinton. She was the daughter of Edmund HAYDEN and _____; and was born ___; died ____. Uriah-[4] BOWKER died 7 May 1804 Hopkinton, MA.

Children of Uriah-[4] BOWKER and Sarah HAYDEN:
Surname **BOWKER**

+	**455. JOHN**	born 19 Nov 1761 Hopkinton; died ____; married Esther WEDGE 7 March 1782
		(she dau/o Jepthah WEDGE and Esther MARSHALL)(she born ca 1761; died ca 1842)

Children of Uriah-[4] BOWKER and Sarah HAYDEN, continued:
Surname **BOWKER**

	456. Sarah	born 5 Oct 1762; died ____
	457. Lucy	born 21 Mar 1765; died ____
	458. Lois	born 22 Apr 1768 ; died 14 Dec 1841
		married Eli WEDGE 1 Aug 1784 (bro/o Esther (above)
		(he s/o Jepthah WEDGE and Esther MARSHALL)
+	**459. ELIJAH**	born 27 Nov 1773 Hopkinton; died 19 May 1827 after a fall from a beam in his barn
		1 married Patience GAGE 8 Jan 1799
		(she dau/o Moses GAGE, Jr. and Mary BOYNTON)
		(she born 1 Jan 1775 Hopkinton, MA; died 9 Oct 1811)
		2 married Polly BRIGHAM 23 Sep 1812 Hopkinton,MA

99. ELIZABETH-[4] BOWKER, sister of above, was born 28 June 1738 at Hopkinton, MA. She married James WILSON on 16 Aug 1754. He was the son of _____ WILSON and ____, and was born ___; died ____. Elizabeth-[4] BOWKER died ____.

Child of Elizabeth-[4] BOWKER and James WILSON:
Surname **WILSON**

+	**460. ELIZABETH**	born ca 1762 MA; died 2 Aug 1855
		married Peter CLARK ca 1784 (he born 8 June 1762 MA)

100. ABIGAIL-[4] BOWKER, daughter of Edmund John-[3] BOWKER (Edmund-[2,1]) and Elizabeth _____, was born 23 Sept 1740 at Hopkinton, MA. She married Cpl. Thornton-[3] BARRETT on 14 Oct 1758 at Hopkinton. He was the son of George-[2] BARRETT (William-[1]) and Mary BARNARD, and was born 2 May 1740; died June 1806. Abigail-[4] BOWKER died Feb 1816 at Bethlehem, Grafton, NH.

Note: Thornton BARRETT was a Cpl. in 1775, in Capt. Abel WILDER's Company, Lexington Alarm; probably served in the French and Indian War, and was wounded at Fort Edward

Children of Abigail-[4] BOWKER and Thornton BARRETT:
Surname **BARRETT**   (1st three children born Hopkinton, MA; rest born Winchendon, MA)

	461. Elizabeth	born 30 Oct 1761; died ____; married Henry CROOKS ca ____
	462. Sarah	born _____; bapt. 1766; died ____
+	**463. ABIGAIL**	born 25 May 1766; died 30 Sep 1829;
		married Josiah HOSMER, Jr. 27 Jan 1783 (as his 2nd wife)
		(he born 28 Nov 1740; died ca 1837)
	464. Hannah	born 4 May 1768; died ____
	465. John	born 26 Apr 1773; died ____
	466. Jerusha	born 20 Mar 1775; died 3 Feb 1833; married Levi WHEELER ca ____
+	**467. THORNTON II**	born 27 Mar 1777; died 24 Mar 1861 PA; 1 married Betsey REYNOLDS 1 Jan 1800
		2 married Abigail BEAN 24 Jan 1823
		(she born 23 May 1797; died 23 Apr 1859)
	468. Samuel	born 9 Aug 1781; died ____
+	**469. JOSEPH**	born 1 July 1783; died ca 1858; married Mary KENNEY ca ____
	470. Henry	born 1 Dec 1784; died 20 Mar 1866
	471. Nathaniel	born 15 July 1785; died ____; married Lydia BATCHELLER ca ____
		(she dau/o Nehemiah BATCHELLER and Lucy HAYWARD)

101. JOHN-[4] BRIGHAM, son of Elizabeth-[3] BOWKER (Edmund-[2;1]; John-[A,B]) and Thomas BRIGHAM, was born 1 April 1726 Sudbury, MA. He married Abigail JOHNSON 12 May 1750 at Sudbury. She was the daughter of William JOHNSON and Ruth RUGG, and was born 6 Feb 1732; died ca 1782.

Child of John-[4] BRIGHAM and Abigail JOHNSON:
Surname **BRIGHAM**

+	**472. ABIGAIL**	born 5 Dec 1751 Coventry, Tolland, CT; died 24 Nov 1806 Alford. MA
		married Jeremiah SCRIPTURE ca 1765
		(he s/o Simeon SCRIPTURE and Anna SLAFTER)
		(he born 8 Aug 1746/49 CT; died before Oct 1810)

102. SARAH⁻⁴ BRIGHAM, sister of above   (for children see # 108 Daniel⁻⁴ BOWKER (below)

103. ABIJAH⁻⁴ BRIGHAM, brother of above, son of Elizabeth⁻³ BOWKER (Edmund⁻²;¹; John⁻ᴬ,ᴮ) and Thomas BRIGHAM, was born 26 August 1737 at Sudbury, Middlesex, MA. He married Eunice WILLIS 5 June 1759 at Sudbury, MA. She was the daughter of Joseph WILLIS (Samuel) and Thankful CLAPP (John), and was born 16 Jan 1740/41 at Sudbury; died 9 March 1826 Sudbury , MA. Abijah⁻⁴ BRIGHAM, who served as a Lt. in the MA Militia during the Revolutionary War, died 2 April 1814 at Sudbury.

Children of Abijah⁻⁴ BRIGHAM and   Eunice WILLIS:
Surname **BRIGHAM**

	473. Abel	born 25 March 1760; died _____ ; served in the Rev War	
		married Lydia MELVIN 13 Nov 1783 (she from Concord, MA)	
		Children: Abel⁻⁶ Jr. born 1 Oct 1784; Lucy Melvin⁻⁶ born 31 Jan 1787; and Rebecca⁻⁶	
		BRIGHAM born 12 Feb 1789	
+	**474. JOHN**	born 19 May 1762; died _____	
		married Ann Eunice MOORE 20 May 1787 Sudbury, MA	
		(she dau/o Israel MOORE and Susanna WOODWARD)	
		(she born 10 Apr 1868 Sudbury; died 20 May 1862)	
+	**475. JOSEPH**	born 26 Sept 1764; died 17 Jan 1842 Sudbury, MA	
		married Rebecca HAYNES 5 March 1795 Sudbury, MA	
		(she dau/o Charles HAYNES (Daniel) and Elizabeth WINN)	
		(she born 29 Jan 1770; died 12 Jan 1853 Sudbury, MA)	
	476. Eunice	born 27 Feb 1767; died 27 Feb 1767	EOL
	477. Reuben	born 21 Sept 1769; died ____; married _____	
		Children: Reuben, Jr-⁶ born ca ___; and George⁻⁶ BRIGHAM born ca ____	
	478. Elizabeth/Betsey	born 14 April 1772; died 1781	EOL
	479. Abner	born 31 Oct 1774; died 16 Aug 1807; married Persis BOWKER (# 501) 20 April 1797	
		Children: Sophia-⁶ bpt. 6 Jan 1799 Sudbury; and Louisa-⁶ BRIGHAM born ca ___	
	480. Eunice (2)	born 5 July 1779; died ____; married Loring WHEELER 11 Fec 1798	
		(he born ca 1776; died _____	

104. HANNAH⁻⁴ BOWKER, daughter of John⁻³ BOWKER (Edmund⁻²,¹; John ᴬ,ᴮ) and Sarah CLAPP, was born 4 April 1721 Sudbury, Middlesex, MA. She married William JOYNER on 18 March 1745 at Middlesex Co., MA. He was the son of Edward JOYNER and Susannah CLAPP, and was born ca 1719 Sudbury; died _____ Walpole, NH. Hannah-⁴ BOWKER died ____ .

Children of Hannah⁻⁴ BOWKER and William JOYNER:
Surname **JOYNER**

+	**481. JOHN**	born ca 1746 Sudbury, MA; died ca 1790 Windham, VT
		married Jerusha Sarah BIXBY 10 July 1770 Winchendon , Worcester, MA
		(she dau/o Nathaniel BIXBY and Jerusha HOUGHTON) (she born ca 1747)
+	**482. SARAH**	born 3 March 1749 Sudbury; died _____
		married Caleb FLETCHER 14 Sept 1775 Templeton, MA
		(he s/o William FLETCHER, Jr. and Elizabeth REMINGTON)
		(he born 7 Nov 1735 MA; died 21 May 1807 Templeton, MA)
	483. Edward	born ca 1750 Sudbury; died ____; served in the Revolutionary War
	484. Michael	born ca 1752 Hopkinton, MA; died ____; served in the Revolutionary War
	485. Robert	born ca 1753 Hopkinton, MA; died _____; Sudbury, MA
		served in the Revolutionary War
+	**486. FRANCIS**	born ca 1754/55 Bolton, Chittenden, VT; died there 9 Jan 1811
		married Lydia LESTER ca 1780 Bolton, VT.
		(she dau/o Benjamin LESTER and Hannah __)
		(she born 11 Mar 1754 CT; died 1811 VT)
+	**487. MARY**	born 5 April 1760 Bolton, VT; died 5 Jan 1844 Saratoga Co., NY
		married David JOHNSON 14 Nov 1783 Bolton, VT.
		(he s/o Zebadiah JOHNSON and Esther RICHARDSON)
		(he born 16 Feb 1756 MA; died 22 Feb 1839 NY)

BOWKER
The Fourth American Generation

105. MARY[-4] BOWKER, daughter of John Edmund-[3] BOWKER (Edmund-[2,1]) and Sarah CLAPP, was born 21 Sept 1722 at Hopkinton, MA. She married Reuben MOORE 24 March 1747. He was the son of Uriah MOORE and Abigail HAYNES and was born ca 1724; died ____. Mary-[4] BOWKER died ____.

Child of Mary-[4] BOWKER and Reuben MOORE:
Surname **MOORE**

488. Isaac	born 8 Sept 1748; died ____	
	married Elizabeth BRYANT 21 April 1768 Sudbury, Middlesex, MA	
	(she dau/o William BRYANT and Sarah HUGHES)	
	(she born ca 1749 Reading, Middlesex, MA; died ____)	

Children: Elizabeth-[6] born ca 1771; Lucy-[6] born ca 1773; Isaac-[6] born ca 1778;
Catharine-[6] born ca 1781; and William-[6] MOORE born ca 1786

106. NOAH[-4] BOWKER, brother of above, was born 16 May 1724 at Hopkinton, MA. He married Hepzibah WILLARD 22 Feb 1753 at Grafton, Worcester, MA. She was the daughter of Simon/Simeon WILLARD and Phoebe NEWTON, and was born 7 Oct 1731 at Grafton, MA; died _____. Noah-[4] BOWKER died _____.

Child of Noah-[4] BOWKER and Hepzibah WILLARD:
Surname **BOWKER**

+	**489. NOAH**	born 24 Jan 1754 Hopkinton, MA; died Apr 1794 W. Springfield, MA
		married Catherine _____ ca ____

107. JUDGE JOSEPH[-4] BOWKER, brother of above, was born 28 Dec 1725 at Hopkinton, MA. He married Sarah TAINTER on 21 Nov 1749 at Watertown, MA. She was the daughter of Simon TAINTER and Rebecca HARRINGTON, and was born 1 Aug 1727 Westboro, MA; died ____. Joseph-[4] BOWKER served as a Captain in the Vermont Militia in the Revolutionary War. He was a prominent citizen of Rutland, VT and was sometimes referred to as the " John HANCOCK of VT " (Appleton's "New American Cyclopedia") He died 11 July 1784 at Rutland, VT.

Children of Joseph-[4] BOWKER and Sarah TAINTER:
Surname **BOWKER**

+	**490. REBECCA**	born ca 1750-55 CT; died ca 1797 Rutland, VT
		married Solomon BEEBE ca 1775 Rutland, VT
		(he s/o Ezekiel BEEBE and Mary MC MULLEN)
	491. Simon	born 25 Sept 1752 Somers , CT; died ca 1852
+	**492. SARAH**	born 29 Aug 1764 Simsbury, CT; died 16 Nov 1850 Mexico, NY
		married Alexander BEEBE 31 July 1780 Rutland, VT
		(he brother of Solomon BEEBE, above)

108. DANIEL[-4] BOWKER, half- brother of above, son of John-[3] BOWKER (Edmund-[2,1]; John-[A,B]) and his 2nd wife Hannah _____, was born 23 Nov 1731 at Hopkinton, Middlesex County, MA. He married Sarah BRIGHAM **(# 102)** on 19 April 1775 at Leicester, Worcester County, MA. She was the daughter of Thomas BRIGHAM and Elizabeth-[3] BOWKER, and was born 10 March 1735 at Sudbury, MA; died 28 June 1813 at Sudbury, MA. Daniel-[4] BOWKER died 3 Jan 1822 at Sudbury.

Children of Daniel-[4] BOWKER and Sarah BRIGHAM:
Surname **BOWKER**

493. Betty	born 12 Jan 1756 Sudbury, MA; died 11 Jan 1837 Greenfield, MI	
	married Josiah CARRUTH 4 Aug 1779 Sudbury	
	(he s/o John CARRUTH (John) and Jemima RUSSELL (James)	
	(he born ca 1749 Northborough, MA; died 17 May 1836 Greenfield)	
	(he served in the Revolutionary War)	

Child: Daniel-[6] CARRUTH born ca 1784; married Betsey DAVIS (Child: Darius-[7] CARRUTH born 19 Nov 1824 VT)

494. John S.	born Oct 1758 Sudbury, MA; died _____	
+	**495. SARAH**	born 9 April 1760 Sudbury, MA; died _____ (resided Chester, VT)
		married Amos SARGENT 29 Dec 1785
		(he s/o Jabez SARGENT and Abigail MOWER)
		(he born 7 Apr 1753 Worcester, MA; died 12 Sep 1804)

Children of Daniel[4] BOWKER and Sarah BRIGHAM, continued:
Surname **BOWKER**

	496. Hannah	born 27 Sept 1763 Sudbury ; died 1852
		married John JACOBS 19 Aug 1784 Sudbury, MA
		(he s/o John JACOBS and Hannah _____)
		(he born 13 Jan 1761 Merrimack, NH; died 4 Apr 1828 Chester, VT)

Child: Amos S.-[6] JACOBS born ca 1810 Chester, VT; married Barbara ARNOLD ca 1833 Peru, NY

+	**497. EUNICE**	born 9 Feb 1766 Sudbury; died ca 1848; married Nathaniel WHITNEY 1786-88
		(he s/o Micah WHITNEY and Hannah HARWOOD)
		(he born ca 1760; died 27 Aug 1801 Rutland, VT)
	498. Ruth	born 9 March 1768 Sudbury, MA; died 20 Feb 1848
+	**499. LOIS**	born 19 April 1770 Sudbury; died _____
		married Stephen CHAMBERLAIN, Jr. 13 April 1793 Sudbury, MA
		(he s/o Stephen CHAMBERLAIN and Sarah WELD)
		(he born 20 May 1764 Roxbury, Suffolk, MA; died 12 Jan 1803)
+	**500. DANIEL, Jr.**	born 13 Sept 1772 Sudbury; died 18 Oct 1853 Sudbury
		married Ruth Holden BROWN 30 March 1797 Sudbury, MA
		(she dau/o Asa BROWN and Elizabeth _____)
		(she born 23 Aug 1774; died 15 Jan 1846)
	501. Persis	born 23 Jan 1775 Sudbury; died _____; married Abner BRIGHAM 20 April 1797
		(he s/o John BRIGHAM and Mary _____)(# 479)
		(he born 31 Oct 1774 Sudbury; died 16 Aug 1807)

Children: Sophia-[6] BRIGHAM born 6 Jan 1799 Sudbury; and Louisa -[6] BRIGHAM born ca ___

+	**502. JOSEPH**	born 15 July 1777 Sudbury; died 3 Sept 1848 Westboro, MA
		1 married Mary BROWN ca 1802; 2 married Patty PROCTOR 22 Feb 1804 Sudbury
		(she dau/o Nathan PROCTOR and Lydia ROBBINS)
		(she born ca 1780 Stoddard, NH; died 10 Sep 1841 Middlesex Co., MA)

109. ELIAS[-4] BOWKER, brother of above, was born 6 April 1733 at Hopkinton, MA . He married first to Sarah HARWOOD on13 Sept 1757. She was the daughter of John HARWOOD and Mary ____, and was born 26 Feb 1730, died ca 1760. He married second to Deborah GOODSPEED on 3 Nov 1760. She was the daughter of Nathaniel GOODSPEED and Deborah BRIGGS, and was born ca 1736 MA; died 11Sept 1817. Elias[-4] BOWKER died 29 Feb 1816 at Georgia, Franklin County, VT

Children of Elias[-4] BOWKER and Deborah GOODSPEED:
Surname **BOWKER**

+	**503. DEBORAH** (twin)	born 19 March 1763 CT; died ca 1837 VT; married Sheldon SEELEY ca ____
+	**504. NATHANIEL** (twin)	born 19 March 1763 CT; died ca 1853 Bombay, NY; married Alice LOVELAND
+	**505. JOHN**	born ca 1772; died 25 Aug 1812 Georgia, VT
		married Sybill LOOMIS ca 1795 (she born 25 June1770 CT; died 23 Jan 1861 VT)
	506. Persis	born May 1777; died _____

111. SILAS[-4] BOWKER, son of John[-3] BOWKER (Edmund[-2,1]; John[-A,B]) and Sarah CLAPP, was born 3 May 1739 at Hopkinton, Middlesex, MA. He married Esther HOBBS on 9 March 1761 at Weston, Middlesex, MA. She was the daughter of Ebenezer HOBBS (Josiah HOBBS, Jr) and Eunice GARFIELD (Thomas) , and was born 13 April 1739 at Concord, Middlesex, MA; died 7 March 1824 at Lansing, Tompkins County, NY. She was the grand-daughter of Josiah HOBBS and Esther DAVENPORT; and Thomas GARFIELD and Mary BIGELOW. In 1774, Silas[-4] BOWKER was among the early settlers of Colchester, Delaware County, NY; and one of the early settlers of Conklin Center, Broome County, NY.

Silas[-4] BOWKER, Sr. died at Conklin Center, Broome, NY on 15 Oct 1789. He was reported to be the first death occurring there (French's Gazetteer of NY). Marriage and death info is also included in the Revolutionary War file (# W4578) of his son-in-law Jacob ROSE. Sometime before the 1790 Census, the BOWKERS and the ROSE families, along with the younger Silas, moved to Chemung County, NY. Esther was listed there in 1790, as a widow of Silas BOWKER, Sr.

Both Silas-[4] BOWKER, Sr. and Jr. served in the Revolutionary War and were " Indian scouts ". Pat Clinton, Librarian in the Town of Warwarsing (Ulster County, NY) related the story of " Silas, Sr. and a man by the name of Philip HINE, were taken prisoner at the Battle of Warwarsing. They were captured by the Indians, on 22 August 1781, who reportedly were working under orders by the British Tories. BOWKER and HINE were tied hand and foot, apart from each other, and were left for three days while the Indians made raids on the Town of Warwarsing where the families of the two "scouts" lived."

BOWKER
The Fourth American Generation

Silas[4] BOWKER was offered liberty, by the Indians, if he would act as the guide of a group of about 100 of them, across the Delaware River to Newton (MA), for a raid. Reportedly, Silas refused stating that " they could but kill him " and " he would rather die on the spot than be an accessory to the death of his countryman."

During the raids, the Indians did more looting than killing. The BOWKER family was among those spared. After the raids, the Indians deserted the area with their British commander COLWELL. Needing a guide, COLWELL, told Silas BOWKER that if he would pilot him through to Niagara, he would do everything in his power to save him when they came to the fort there. Silas consented, but upon their arrival at Niagara, Philip HINE gave his allegiance to the British crown and went with the British Troops to Troy (NY).

Silas[4] BOWKER was taken to Montreal and imprisoned with two other men in a log hut. There were few provisions and the living conditions were bad. However, they managed to escape by digging under the floor, working only with a knife they had found in the building. The night they escaped, they entered the St. Lawrence River to swim across to the American side. Unfortunately, Silas was the only one to make it successfully. He went into the wilderness, and survived by eating raw food, including a rattlesnake he had killed, and bread he had stolen from a home. He hid in the hollow of a tree when the Indians were searching for him. Fourteen months after his capture, he finally arrived at Catskill, along the Hudson River, during an assembly for a public meeting. He was greeted with open arms and carried into the house where the meeting was being held. An historic marker in Accord, NY memorializes the spot where Silas BOWKER returned.

Children of Silas[4] BOWKER and Esther HOBBS:
Surname **BOWKER**

+	**507. ESTHER**	born 10 March 1762 Concord, Middlesex, MA; died _____
		married William WILLISON ca 1781 Marbletown, Ulster, NY
		(he s/o _____ WILLISON and _____)
		(he born 15 Jan 1762 Scotland; died 2 Jan 1836 Genoa, Cayuga, NY)
+	**508. SILAS DAY, Jr.**	born 26 Apr 1763 Concord; died 14 Oct 1834 Genoa, NY
		married Amy HARDING 6 Nov 1786 Pataukunck, Ulster, NY
		(she dau/o James HARDING and Mary _____)
		(she born 2 May 1769; died 25 Nov 1843)
+	**509. LISA**	born 15 June 1765 Willington, Tolland, CT; died 10 Feb 1846 Trenton, Delaware, OH
		married Jacob ROSE 5 Aug 1784 Marbletown, Ulster, NY
		(he s/o Wilhelm/William ROSE and Elizabeth SCHOOLCRAFT)
		(he born 11 Apr 1761; died 20 Aug 1839 Delaware Co., NY/OH)

Reference: BARBOUR Collection, Vol. B; page 18

+	**510. DANIEL**	born 22 Feb 1767 Willington, CT; died 1 May 1829 Hancock, NY
		1 married Azubah GREGORY ca ____
		(she born ca 1769; died 1 Jan 1813 Hancock, Delaware, NY)
		2 married Margaret _____ ca ____ (she born ca 1762; died _____
	511. Cynthia	born 25 Sep 1768 Willington, CT; died 1769 EOL
	512. Orsimas	born 9 March 1770 Willington; died ca 1795
+	**513. JOHN**	born 10 Sept 1771 Marbletown, Ulster, NY; died 16 Sept 1855 Lansing, NY
		1 married _____?_____
		2 married Jerusha ROBINSON ca _____
		(she born 20 Aug 1771 Brookhaven, LI,NY; died 16 Feb 1866 Lansing, NY)
+	**514. MARY POLLY**	born ca 1771/72 Ulster Co., NY; died 16 Aug 1854 (aged 83) Cayuga County, NY
		married Andrew ARMSTRONG ca ____
		(he born 23 May 1763; died ca 1822 Genoa, Cayuga, NY)
+	**515. JOSEPH**	born 4 May 1773 Marbleton, Ulster, NY; died 25 Aug 1827 Lansing, NY
		1 married Silva RUDI ca _____
		(she dau/o _____ RUDI and _____)
		(she born ca ____; died before 1812)
		2 married Peninah RUDI ca 1812 NY (she 1 married Moses LAWRENCE)
		(she born ca 1787; died 1 June 1868, MI)
+	**516. NOAH**	born ca 1780 Ulster Co., NY; died 17 Oct 1866 Barry Twsp., MI
		married Mary BECKWITH 19 Mar 1895 Milton, Cayuga, NY
		(she dau/o _____ BECKWITH and _____)
		(she born 3 Nov 1787 VT; died 12 July 1880 Barry, Barry, MI)
		(they are buried at North Cemetery, Barry County, MI)

112. ELEAZER[-4] **PERRY,** son of Mary[-3] HOLBROOK (Mary[-2] BOWKER; Edmund[-1]) and Thomas HOLBROOK, was born 2 June 1706 MA. He married Mary JOHNSON on 14 June 1732. She was the daughter of _____ JOHNSON and ____; and was born ca 1710; died ____. Eleazer-[4] PERRY died ____.

Children of Eleazer[-4] PERRY and Mary JOHNSON:
Surname **PERRY**   (Children all born Holliston, Middlesex, MA)

517. Eleazer	born 12 April 1733; died ___	519. Lois	born 9 Sept 1737
518. Asa	born 1 Aug 1735; died ____	520. Reuben	born 26 Oct 1739

116. LYDIA-[4] **FAIRBANKS,** daughter of Lydia-[3] HOLBROOK (Mary[-2] BOWKER; Edmund-[1]) and Dr. Jonathan FAIRBANKS, as born 1 Oct 1718 at Sherborn, MA. She married first to Abijah MORSE on 10 Oct 1751. He was the son of Samuel MORSE and Bethia HOLBROOK, and was born Oct 1718; died 1754. She married second to _____ BOYNTON ca ____. Lydia[-4] FAIRBANKS died 9 Oct 1751 at Sherborn.

Children of Lydia[-4] FAIRBANKS and Abijah MORSE:
Surname **MORSE**

521. Comfort	(twin)	born 31 July 1755 Medway, MA; died 9 May 1819 Holliston, MA
522. Joel	(twin)	born 31 July 1755; _____; married Abigail FORCE ca _____
		(he born ca 1760; died ca 1861)
		Child: Polly[-6] MORSE born ca 1789; died 1872
523. Samuel		born ca 1758; died ____

118. MOSES-[4] **FAIRBANKS,** brother of above, was born 1 March 1722 at Sherborn, MA. He married Hannah ____ ca 1767. She was born ca 1746; died 1846. He was a soldier in the Colonial Wars. Not much else is known about him.

Children of Moses-[4] FAIRBANKS and Hannah _____:
Surname **FAIRBANKS**   (all children born Shutesbury, MA)

+	**524. MOSES**	born 9 Aug 1768 ; died 20 July 1845; married Betsey MATTHEWS ca _____
		(she born 10 Feb 1771 Ticonderoga, NY; died _____
+	**525. DANIEL**	born 1 June 1769 /70; died 14 March 1854 Colrain, Franklin, MA
		1 married I. Keziah CLARK ca _____
		(she born ca _____; died 12 Aug 1817, aged 43)
		2 married Ruth FAULKNER 22 Feb 1818
		(she born 11 Apr 1782; died 21 May 1872)
+	**526. JONATHAN**	born 3 April 1772; died 1858 Antwerp, Jefferson, NY
		1 married Sally AYERS ca ____ (she born 9 Feb 1778; died _____
		2 married Nabby AYERS ca _____ (sister of Sally)
+	**527. ASA**	born 1 May 1774; died 24 Feb 1828 VT
		married Lucy SAUNDERS ca ____ (she born ca ____; died 20 July 1843)
	528. Joshua	born 17 Oct 1775

119. DANIEL-[4] **FAIRBANKS,** brother of above, was born 5 Nov 1723 at ____. He married Submit FAIRBANKS ca ___. She was the daughter of George FAIRBANKS and Rachel ____, and was born 18 Sep 1729; died ____. Daniel-[4] FAIRBANKS died before March 1771. An inventory of his estate was filed 3 May 1771 (Middlesex Probate Records). He was a soldier in the Colonial Wars. Submit FAIRBANKS married second to a James DIX on 19 Mar 1771 at Mendon, MA

Children of Daniel-[4] FAIRBANKS and Submit FAIRBANKS:
Surname **FAIRBANKS**

+	**529. RACHEL**	born 13 May 1748; died _____ (6 ch)
		married Jethro PETERS ca ____ (int pub 8 Oct 1769) ; he from Northborough, MA
+	**530. COMFORT**	born 4 July 1750; died _____ married Joseph SEAVER ca ___ (int pub 1 June 1771)
	531. George	born 30 July 1752; died 18 July 1759 EOL
+	**532. JONATHAN**	born 29 Mar 1755 Holliston, MA ; died 28 Feb 1840 Sudbury, MA
		1 married Hannah MORSE 28 Feb 1781
		(she born ca 1763; died 7 Dec 1783 , probably as a result of childbirth)
		2 married Bridget PARMENTER 3 Dec 1784
		(she born ca 1764; died 29 Sept 1828)

Children of Daniel[4] FAIRBANKS and Submit FAIRBANKS:
Surname **FAIRBANKS**

533. Drury	born 6 Aug 1757; died ___; married Lucy BIGELOW 16 Aug 1779
	(she dau/o Cornelius BIGELOW and Sarah MILLER)
	(she born 4 Sept 1757; died _____)
	Child: Jonathan-[6] FAIRBANKS born 12 May 1780
534. Submit	born 5 Nov 1759; died 30 Jan 1804 Sudbury, MA
	married William PARMENTER 25 May 1780 Sudbury
	(he s/o William PARMENTER and Mary PEPPER) (he born ca 1755; died ____)

123. KEZIAH[4] HOLBROOK, sister of above, was born 23 Aug 1729 Sherborn, MA. She married Daniel TWITCHELL ca ____. He was the son of Benjamin TWITCHELL and Mary WALLIS, and was born 22 Feb 1714; died 1754. He served as a Private in the Expedition against Lewisburg in 1745. In 1753, along with his brother Benjamin and 21 others, he signed a petition which was sent to the Governor of New Hampshire, asking for a grant of lands at Upper Ashuelot. In the following year he was massacred by Indians near his home at Walpole, MA. Keziah[4] HOLBROOK died ____.

Children of Keziah[4] HOLBROOK and Daniel TWITCHELL:
Surname **TWITCHELL**

+ **535. NATHAN**	born 12 Jan 1742; died _____
	married Hannah KEMPTON / KIMPTON 18 Dec 1766 MN
	(she born 27 July 1748; died 1787)
536. Joanna	born 16 Feb 1744; died ____
537. Jonas	born 4 Feb 1745 Walpole, MA; died 29 May 1829 Walpole
	1 married Joanna ALDRICH 1 Feb 1768
	(she born 16 Feb 1744; died ca 1820)
	2 married Elizabeth BENNETT 6 Sept 1822
538. Abner	born 23 Dec 1753; died ____

125. LUCY[4] GLEASON, daughter of Thankful-[3] HOLBROOK (Mary-[2] BOWKER; Edmund-[1]) and Uriah GLEASON, was born 27 Feb 1742 Oxford, MA. She married William BURNETT on 22 Jan 1766 at Oxford. He was the son of Robert BURNETT and Anna WILKINS, and was born 28 Jan 1744; died 24 March 1835.

Children of Lucy-[4] GLEASON and William BURNETT:
Surname **BURNETT**

539. Lucy	born 6 July 1767 Oxford, MA; died ____
+ **540. REUBEN**	born 4 Aug 1782; died 14 July 1817 Canton, St. Lawrence, NY
	married Polly BENJAMIN 25 Feb 1804 Bridgeport, VT
	(she dau/o Samuel Clark BENJAMIN and Phoebe MINOR)
	(she born ca 1783; died 1854)

126. RUTH⁻⁵ BRUCE, daughter of Bathsheba⁻⁴ BOWKER (John ³,²; Edmund⁻¹) and Daniel BRUCE, was born 22 May 1733 at Marlborough, Middlesex, MA. She married Cyrus Lovewell⁻⁵ GATES (# 176) on 22 May 1753 at Bolton, Worcester, MA. He was the son of Ephraim⁻⁴ GATES (Mary⁻³ BOWKER; John⁻²; Edmund⁻¹) and Dorothy GRAVES, and was born 11 April 1731; died 8 July 1813 Bolton, MA. Ruth⁻⁵ BRUCE died ca 1820 at Templeton, Worcester, MA.

Children of Ruth⁻⁵ BRUCE and Cyrus GATES:
Surname **GATES**   (all children born at Bolton, MA)

541. Cyrus Lovewell	born 30 Aug 1754; died 22 Oct 1770 Bolton, MA	EOL
542. Ruth	born 5 May 1757; died 1 Oct 1819 Nelson, NH	
	married Philip ATWOOD 30 Sep 1782	
543. Eunice	born 12 Aug 1759; died 14 May 1762 Bolton	EOL
544. Hannah/ Ruhama	born 22 Feb 1762; died ____	
545. Laban	born 16 Sep 1764; died 7 Jan 1837 Chester, VT	
	1 married Elizabeth TAFT 30 May 1796 (she born ____; died 1812)	
	2 married ____ SCOTT 1 April 1813 (she born ____, died 1827)	
	3 married Lucy HILL Smith Mack 30 Dec 1829 (she born ____; died 1869)	
546. Ebenezer	born 14 Mar 1767; died ____	
547. Abiathar	born 20 Aug 1769; died 16 June 1841/42 Morrisville, Madison, NY	
	married Lois HOLT 24 Oct 1793 (she dau/o Daniel HOLT and Alice ___)	
548. Lovell	born 19 Sep 1772; died ____	
549. Luther	born 17 Mar 1775; died 19 Aug 1777	EOL
550. Ephraim	born ca 1777; died 1778	EOL

130. BENJAMIN⁻⁵ BRUCE, brother of above, was born ca 1739 at Marlborough, MA. He married Nancy Mc BRIDE Dec 1768. She was the daughter of Alexander Mc BRIDE and Mary ____; and was born ____; died __ Nov 1824. A widow, she was " burned to death while alone on a Sunday". Benjamin⁻⁵ BRUCE , a cooper, died 1786. He served in the French and Indian War in 1757, and was a minute man in 1775, and was at the surrender of Burgoyne in 1777.

Children of Benjamin⁻⁵ BRUCE and Nancy Mc BRIDE:
Surname **BRUCE**

551. Mary	born 29 April 1769; died ____; married Jonathan BAKER ca ____	
552. Katy	born 6 Mar 1771; died _____	
553. Otis	born 17 Apr 1773; died ____	
554. Calvin	born 2 May 1775; died 30 Nov 1857 Berlin, MA ; married Ruth PRIEST ca ____	
555. Anna	born 6 Sep 1777; died ____ unmarried	EOL
556. William	born ca 1780; died ____	
557. Oliver	born 6 May 1782; died ____; married Sally BURNAM 2 Oct 1809 Bolton, MA	
558. Franklin	born 21 June 1784; died _____; resided VT	
559. Amos	born 16 Oct 1786; died _____	

131. JOHN⁻⁵ BRUCE, brother of above , was born 9 May 1744 at Berlin, Worcester, MA. He married Martha MOORE on 9 July 1771 at Bolton, Worcester, MA. She was the daughter of Israel MOORE and Mary FAIRBANKS, and was born 14 July 1752 Bolton, MA; died 27 Oct 1835 Berlin, MA. John-⁵ BRUCE was at the Battle of Lexington, and died 13 Feb 1843, from a fall, at Berlin, Worcester, MA.

Children of John-⁵ BRUCE and Martha MOORE:
Surname **BRUCE**   (1ˢᵗ two children born Bolton, MA; the others born Berlin, MA)

+	**560. HUGH**	born 5 Aug 1770; died 14 Sept 1821 Boston, MA	
		married Sally MOORE 25 May 1796	
		(she dau/o Jacob MOORE and ____)	
	561. Dorcas (1)	born 25 Apr 1772; died young	
	562. Nancy (1) (twin)	born 30 June 1774; died young	EOL

Children of John-⁵ BRUCE and Martha MOORE, continued:
Surname **BRUCE**

	563. Eunice (1) (twin)	born 30 June 1774; died young
	564. Asenath	born 16 Apr 1776; died 30 Aug 1862; married Luther PRIEST ca ____
	565. Anna	born 6 Sep 1777; died 1850 Peru, Clinton, NY
+	**566. EUNICE (2)**	born 1779; died ca ____ Brimfield, OH
		married Asa SAWYER 19 June 1800
		(he s/o William SAWYER and ____)
+	**567. JOHN, Jr.**	born 15 May 1781; died 29 Apr 1865 MA
		married Prudence PRIEST ca ____
	568. Nancy Ann (2)	born June 1783; died 10 Feb 1850 Windham, VT; married ____ LAWRENCE ca ____
	569. Dorcas (2)	born 18 Dec 1785; died 1852; married John BREWER 1 Feb 1810
	570. Parnell	born 30 May 1788; died ____; 1 married Josiah BENNETT ca ____
		Child: Josiah-⁷ BENNETT, Jr. born ____; died ____; resided Marlborough, MA
		2 married Solomon GREENE ca ____
+	**571. SEWELL**	born 15 July 1790; died 3 Nov 1846 Berlin, MA
		married Eunice BENNETT 8 Nov 1813
		(she dau/o Ephraim BENNETT and Priscilla WELLINGTON)
		(she born ____; died 11 Feb 1873)
+	**572. SYLVANUS**	born 15 Dec 1792; died 30 July 1879 Berlin, MA
		married Hannah READ ca _____ (she born ca 1798 Providence, RI)
	573. Sophia	born 10 Apr 1795; died 1884

134. DANIEL-⁵ BRUCE, brother of above, was born 21 Sep 1752 at Berlin, Worcester, MA. He married Mary BRUCE ca 1790. She was the daughter of Timothy BRUCE and Susanna JOSLIN, and was born ___; died ___. Daniel-⁵ BRUCE died ____.

Children of Daniel-⁵ BRUCE and Mary BRUCE:
Surname **BRUCE**

+	**574. ABRAHAM**	born 1791 MA; died 1878 NY; married Mary Polly BRIGGS ca 1817 NY
		(she born ca 1801 Burlington, Otsego, NY; died 1873)
	575. Linda Mira	born 1798; died ____; married David KEYES ca 1826
		(he born 19 Apr 1794; died ____) Child: Addison-⁷ KEYES born ca 1827
	576. Lydia	born 1801; died ____; married Timothy AUSTIN 3 June 1826; resided VT
		(he born 17 Mar 1791 Methuen, MA; died _____)
		Children: Matilda-⁷ born 1827, died 1907; Maria-⁷ born ca 1836; Lydia-⁷ born ca 1837;
		and Jeremy-⁷ AUSTIN born ca 1843
+	**577. LOIS / LOUISA**	born 30 Oct 1802; died ____; married Ziba KEYES 17 Aug 1828
		(he born 9 Dec 1796; died 29 Nov 1851)
		(he s/o Thomas KEYES and Eunice WRIGHT) (bro/o David KEYES above)
	578. Sally	born ca ____; died ____; married James RICH, Jr. ca ____

135. SILAS-⁵ BOWKER, son of John-⁴ BOWKER (John-³,²; Edmund-¹) and Freedom BIGELOW, was born 29 May 1733 at Westborough, Worcester, MA. He married Bethia WARD on 29 Nov 1759 at Marlborough, MA. She was the daughter of Daniel WARD and Mary BIGELOW, and was born 26 Feb 1735/36; died 6 Nov 1815 Royalston, MA. Silas-⁵ BOWKER died 1 Apr 1820 Royalston, MA.

Children of Silas-⁵ BOWKER and Bethia WARD:
Surname **BOWKER**

+	**579. SAMUEL WARD**	born 16 Dec 1760 Royalston, MA; died _____; 1 married Sarah LOCKE 31 July 1794
		(she born 19 Nov 1768; died 13 Jan 1799)
(		(she dau/o John LOCKE and Beulah NEWTON)
		2 married Charlotte LOCKE 30 June 1803 Royalston, MA (sister of Sarah (above)
		(she born 17 Dec 1771; died after 1852)
	580. Sarah	born 28 Dec 1762; died 16 Aug 1776 EOL
+	**581. STEPHEN BIGELOW**	born 25 Dec 1772 Worcester, MA; died 30 Oct 1833 Royalston, MA
		married Submit GROVER 12 Sep 1799
		(she dau/o Nathaniel GROVER and Sarah HARRINGTON)
		(she born 2 Dec 1777 Fitzwilliam, NH; died 17 Feb 1857 Royalston, MA)

136. ELIZABETH/BETTY⁻⁵ BOWKER, sister of above, was born 9 Feb 1735 at Marlborough, MA. She married Joshua TURNER, Jr. on 23 June 1761. He was the son of Joshua TURNER, Sr. and Sarah WINSLOW, and was born 6 Mar 1738/38 Pembroke, Plymouth, MA; died 3 Jan 1816 Pembroke, MA. Betty⁻⁵ BOWKER died 7 Aug 1815.

Children of Betty⁻⁵ BOWKER and Joshua TURNER:

Surname **TURNER**	(children all born Pembroke, MA)
582. Betty/Betsey	born 15 Feb 1763; died ____
583. Winslow	born 7 June 1764; died ____
584. Joshua III	born 24 Nov 1765; died 1795 RI
585. Deborah	born 7 Sep 1767; died ____
586. Celia	born ca 1771; died young
587. Joseph	born 2 Nov 1773; died ____
588. Ezekiel	born 7 Dec 1776; died ____; lost at sea
589. Thomas	born 24 Aug 1778; died ____
+ **590. CELIA WINSLOW**	born 14 Feb 1781; died 20 Feb 1856 Pembroke, MA
	married Laban LEAVITT 13 Feb 1806

140. SOLOMON-⁵ BOWKER, brother of above, was born 25 March 1743 at Marlborough, MA. He married first to Mary Eunice WEEKS on 21 April 1770. She was the daughter of ____ WEEKS and ____; and was born 20 Mar 1749; died 11 Feb 1771. He married second to Dorothy BARNES on 29 Aug 1771. She was the daughter of Jonathan BARNES and Rachel HOSMER, and was born 18 Dec 1747; died ca 1841. Solomon-⁵ BOWKER died ca 1834.

Children of Solomon⁻⁵ BOWKER and Dorothy BARNES:

Surname **BOWKER**	(all but last child born Marlborough, MA)	
591. Infant son	born 16 Sep 1772; died 17 Sep 1772	EOL
+ **592. JONATHAN**	born 9 Aug 1774; died 16 June 1852 Canada	
	married Abigail BEAMAN ca 1808	
	(she dau/o Nathaniel BEAMAN and Thankful FARNSWORTH)	
	(she born 12 Feb 1787 Lancaster, MA; died ca 1851)	
593. Abraham Morrs	born 29 Apr 1778; died ____	
	married Maria SIMMONS 19 Mar 1797 (she born 16 Sep 1772 NH; died ____)	
594. Dorcas	born 1/21 July 1780; poss. died young	
595. Betsey	born 5 Nov 1782; died ____ 596. Dolly born 30 Jan 1786 Berlin, MA	

143. JOTHAM-⁵ BOWKER, brother of above, was born ca 1751. He married Patty WHITNEY ca 1791 at Petersham, Worchester, MA. She was the daughter of ____ WHITNEY and ____, and was born 29 Dec 1765 Worcester, MA; died ____. Jotham⁻⁵ BOWKER died ____.

Children of Jotham-⁵ BOWKER and Patty WHITNEY:

Surname **BOWKER**	
+ **597. GEORGE**	born 6 Nov 1791/92; died ___
	married Betsey UNDERWOOD ca 1820
598. Nathaniel	born 16 May 1793; died 20 June 1869; married Sarah SMITH Dec 1821 Barre, MA.
	(she born 14 Feb 1800; died 10 May 1870 Burlington, VT
599. Nancy	born 20 Jan 1795; died ____
600. Luke	born 2 Feb 1797; died ____
601. Betsey	born 19 June 1799; died ____
+ **602. FREEMAN**	born 26 Sep 1801; died 1893; married Sarah B. KNOWLES 28 Sep 1837
603. Huldah	born 8 Oct 1803; died ____

144. ANTIPAS-⁵ BOWKER, son of Josiah-⁴ BOWKER (John-³,²; Edmund-¹) and Hazadiah EAGER, was born 3 Oct 1733 MA. He married Esther RICE on 6 Oct 1757 at Marlborough,, MA. She was the daughter of Gideon RICE and Esther ____; and was born 6 March 1742; died 1792. Antipas-⁵ BOWKER died 14 Nov 1803 at Northborough, Worcester, MA.

Children of Antipas-⁵ BOWKER and Esther RICE:

Surname **BOWKER**	
604. Antipas II	born 18 Oct 1758; died ____
	married Miriam NEWTON 28 June 1779 Northborough, MA

Children of Antipas-[5] BOWKER and Hazadiah EAGER, continued:
Surname **BOWKER**

+	**605. GIDEON**		born 9 Mar 1760; died 3 June 1815 Lunenburg, VT
			married Hannah FLETCHER ca ____ (she born 12 Sep 1762; died 1842)
	606. Esther		born 3 Nov 1761; died 19 Sep 1851 Gill, Franklin, MA
			married Asa HOWE 8 May 1786
	607. Sapphira	(twin)	born 24 Oct 1763; died ____
	608. Zeppelin	(twin)	born 24 Oct 1763; died ____
	609. Lucena		born 15 June 1766; died ____
	610. Eber		born 24 Mar 1768; died 3 June 1769 EOL
	611. Anne		born 12 May 1770; died 20 May 1771 EOL
	612. Anne (2)		born 6 Mar 1772; died ____
	613. Sarah		born 24 Nov 1774; died ____
	614. James	(twin)	born 14 Feb 1777; died 22 Dec 1856 Waterville, NY
	615. Lydia	(twin)	born 14 Feb 1777; died ____

148. EPHRAIM-[5] BOWKER, brother of above, was born 7 June 1740 MA. He married Sarah FARRAR ca 1759. She was the daughter of John FARRAR and Mary ____, and was born 9 Jan 1737 Lancaster, Worcester, MA; died ____. Ephraim -[5] BOWKER died ____.

Children of Ephraim-[5] BOWKER and Sarah FARRAR:
Surname **BOWKER**

+	**616. OLIVER**	born 22 Jan 1760 Westborough, MA; died ____
		married Hannah PIERSON/PEARSON 12 Dec 1779
	617. Prudence	born 8 May 1763; died 2 Feb 1764 EOL

153. TABITHA-[5] BOWKER, sister of above, was born 18 April 1749 . She married Charles NEWTON on 4 Oct 1765 . He was the son of Elisha NEWTON and Sarah TOMLIN, and was born 28 Aug 1742 Shrewsbury, Ma; died 10 Dec 1831 Princeton, MA. Tabitha-[5] BOWKER died 5 March 1827.

Children of Tabitha-[5] BOWKER and Charles NEWTON:
Surname **NEWTON**   (children born Shrewsbury, MA)

+	**618. DOLLY**	born 7 Aug 1766; died 11 Feb 1786; married Abraham HAGER ca 1781 (age 15)
		(he s/o William HAGER and Mary WARREN) (he born 11 Mar 1755; died ____)
	619. Azubah	born 27 Apr 1769; died 3 July 1836 Princeton, MA
		1 married Samuel COBB 31 Oct 1787 Princeton; 2 married Samuel RICE 6 Oct 1813
		(he s/o Seth RICE and Rachel COOLIDGE) (he born 11 Apr 1762; died 14 Jan 1832)
		Child: Lucy-[7] RICE born 14 June 1814; married Elijah PACKARD of Worcester, MA
+	**620. EZRA**	born 22 Nov 1774 ; died 9 Apr 1863
		1 married Ruth HASTINGS ca ____ (she of Weston, MA)
		2 married Lucy HOWE 27 Jan 1812 (she dau/o Adonijah HOWE and Lydia ____)
		(she born 24 Oct 1779; died 28 July 1826)
		3 married Mrs. Candace ALLEN Howe ca ____
	621. Mary	born/bapt 31 Mar 1777; died ____
+	**622. TABITHA**	born 25 July 1781; died 25 July 1835 Holden, MA
		married Jonathan STEARNS, Jr. 17 Feb 1803 Princeton, MA
		(he s/o Jonathan STEARNS and Abigail MOORE)
		(he born 2 May 1771 Rutland, MA; died 8 May 1844 Rutland)

154. ITHAMAR-[5] BOWKER, brother of above, was born 27 Nov 1750 MA. He married first to Miriam BARTLETT on 1 May 1775 Brookfield, MA. She was the daughter of Elijah BARTLETT and Bathsheba GILBERT, and was born ____; died ____. He married second to Sarah RICE / DANIELS on 1 May 1793. She was the daughter of ____ RICE and ____; and was born 1 Aug 1754 Brookfield; died ____. Ithamar-[5] BOWKER died.

Child of Ithamar-[5] BOWKER and Miriam BARTLETT:
Surname **BOWKER**

623. Josiah	born 18 July 1783; died ____

Child of Ithamar-[5] BOWKER and Sarah RICE:
Surname **BOWKER**

+   **624. OBADIAH**   born 27 Oct 1799 MA; 24 Nov 1861 Bergen, Hudson, NJ.
                                      married Catherine Ann ANDERSON 4 Apr 1824 (she born ca 1810 NJ; died ca 1850)

155. HAZADIAH-[5] BOWKER, sister of above, was born 2 Sep 1752 MA. She married John WYMAN on 30 Aug 1771 at Northborough, MA. he was the son of Nathaniel WYMAN and Elizabeth EVANS, and was born 19 Oct 1745 Hopkinton, MA; died 18 Sep 1813 Marlborough, MA. Hazadiah-[5] BOWKER died ca 1826.

Children of Hazadiah-[5] BOWKER and John WYMAN:
Surname **WYMAN**   (all children born Northborough, MA)

625. Polly	born 16 Sep 1771; died 28 Oct 1854 Northborough	
626. Persis	born 5 July 1774; died ____	
627. Jonas	born 18 June 1776; died ____	
628. Lovisa	born 28 July 1778; died 22 Sep 1860; married James PATTERSON 13 Sep 1798	
	(he s/o David PATTERSON and Beulah CLARK) (he born ca 1767)	
629. John, Jr.	born 18 May 1782; died young	EOL
630. Hazadiah	born 28 Sep 1783; died ____	
631. Azubah	born 0 Aug 1785; died ____	
632. Lucy	born 4 Aug 1787; died ____	
633. Abraham	born 14 July 1790; died ____; poss. married Sarah CRAWFORD ca 1815	
	Children: George Edward-[7] born 29 Aug 1816; Nancy Crawford-[7] born 13 Apr 1819;	
	and John Crawford-[7] WYMAN born 13 Sep 1822	
634. John	born 21 Oct 1794; died 1795	EOL

156. ASA-[5] BOWKER, brother of above, was born 8 Nov 1754 MA. He married Susanna BRYANT on 2/8 June 1781 at Petersham, MA. She was the daughter of _____ BRYANT and ____; and was born poss. ca 1759; died 3 Nov 1842. Asa-[5] BOWKER died 5 Oct 1825 at Winchendon, MA.

Children of Asa-[5] BOWKER and Susanna BRYANT:
Surname **BOWKER**

635. John	born 3 Jan 1782; died ____	
636. Betsey	born 24 June 1784; died ____	
637. Asa (twin) (1)	born 20 May 1786; poss. died young	
638. Susan (twin)	born 20 May 1786; died ____	
639. Sally	born 14 Nov 1789; died ____	
+ **640. ASA, Jr.** (twin) (2)	born 9 June 1794; died ____; married Joanna WALKER 3 Apr 1817	
641. Lydia (twin)	born 9 June 1794; died ____	
+ **642. WINDSOR**	born 25 June 1796; died 23 Aug 1851 (killed by a runaway animal)	
	married Sarah OSGOOD ca 1824	
	(she dau/o Joseph OSGOOD and _____)(she born ___; died _____ aged 49 years old)	
643. Lucy	born 7 Aug 1800; died ____	

157. JONATHAN-[5] BOWKER, brother of above, was born 23 July 1756 at Westborough, MA. He married Abigail WHITEHEAD on 10 Oct 1791 at Phillipston, MA. She was the daughter of John WHITEHEAD and Abigail ____; and was born 27 Feb 1763; died ____. Jonathan-[5] BOWKER died 24 May 1838 at Phillipston, MA.

Children of Jonathan-[5] BOWKER and Abigail WHITEHEAD:
Surname **BOWKER**

644. George B.	born ca 1792; died ____
645. Almira	born ca 1794; died ____
646. Polly	born ca 1797; died ____
647. Jonathan	born ca 1799; died ____
648. Horace	born ca 1800; died ____; married Anna MAYNARD Smith 18 May 1824
	Children: Eunice A-[7] born ca 1839; Sarah S-[7] BOWKER born ca 1840
649. Eunice	born ca 1802; died ____
650. Lysander	born ca 1804/5; died 4 Apr 1806 Phillipston, MA

160. DAVID-⁵ FORBUSH, son of David-⁴ FORBUSH (Martha-³ BOWKER (John-²; Edmund-¹) and Ruth WOOD, was born 24 Dec 1739 at Acton, Middlesex, MA. He married Sarah HAYWARD on 4 Nov 1762 at Sudbury, MA. She was the daughter of Josiah Hartwell HAYWARD and Mary HOSMER; and was born 17 June 1742 Acton; died 11 Jan 1826 at Sudbury, MA. David-⁵ FORBUSH died 11 April 1819 at Petersborough, NH.

Children of David-⁵ FORBUSH and Sarah HAYWARD:
Surname **FORBUSH**   (children born Acton, Middlesex, MA)

	651. Lucy	born 1 Sep 1763; died 10 Sep 1829 Sudbury, MA
	652. Sally	born 12 Jan 1865; died 3 Mar 1826 Sudbury
	653. Lois	born 13 Apr 1766; died 10 Sep 1829 Sudbury
	654. Rebecca	born 26 Mar 1768; died 1 May 1813
	655. Simeon	born 22 Feb 1770; died 12 Feb 1860
	656. Paul	born 30 Jan 1772; died 24 Sep 1830 Carlisle, MA
	657. Silas	born ca 1772; died 1 Aug 1841 Rutland, MA
	658. Daniel	born 4 Mar 1774; died 11 May 1834 Chautauqua, NY
	659. Ruth	born 31 Dec 1776; died Mar 1836 Chautauqua, Ny
	660. David, Jr.	born 16 Nov 1778; died 9 Feb 1865 Clarendon, Orleans, NY
	661. Betsey	born ca 1780; died 30 Aug 1831
+	**662. MARY HOSMER**	born 3 Jan 1781; died 20 Mar 1834 Concord, MA

167. EPHRAIM-⁵ FORBUSH, brother of above, was born 18 Oct 1756 MA. He married first to Mary BUTTRICK on 25 March 1784 MA. She was the daughter of Samuel BUTTRICK and Lucy WHEELER, and was born 8 Dec 1754; died 10 Feb 1805. He married second to Abigail ROGERS 1 Apr 1806 (int pub 12 March 1806). She was the daughter of Deacon John ROGERS and Ann CHURCHMAN; and was born 1761; died 25 Apr 1832 Harvard, MA . Ephraim-⁵ FORBUSH died 17 Sept 1828.

Children of Ephraim-⁵ FORBUSH and Mary BUTTRICK:
Surname **FORBUSH**

663. Lucy	born 7 Aug 1785; died ____
664. Dolly/Polly	born 17 Oct 1787; died ____
665. Sally	born1 May 1790; died _____
666. Miriam	born 25 Apr 1792; died ____
667. Abel	born 28 Nov 1795; died 4 Aug 1881
	married Susan ROBBINS 3 Sep 1820 Acton, MA
668. Samuel	born 4 Sep 1799; died ____

168. JAMES-⁵ FORBUSH, brother of above, was born 8 Jan 1758 at Acton, MA. He married Eunice BROWN on 25 Oct 1775 at Acton, MA. She was the daughter of Abishai BROWN and Mary FARRAR, and was born 7 Feb 1758 Concord, MA; died 15 July 1837 at Stark, Coos, NH. James-⁵ FORBUSH died ca 1827 at Dummer, Coos, NH.

Children of James-⁵ FORBUSH and Eunice BROWN:
Surname **FORBUSH**

	669. Eunice (twin)	born 24 Aug 1777; died ____; married Joel BRIDGES 30 Nov 1797
		(he s/o Edmund BRIDGES and Lucy BARTLETT)
		(he born 11 Sep 1766 Worcester, MA; died Whiting, Addison, VT)
+	**670. MARY/MOLLY**	born 24 Aug 1777; died 2 Aug 1849; married Elihu DAVIS 3 Feb 1794
	(twin)	(he born Sep 1769; died 30 May 1838 Bennington, VT)
		(he s/o Nathan DAVIS and Abigail ROGERS)
+	**671. BETSEY**	born 15 Aug 1778 MA; died 6 June 1839 Bennington, VT
		married John HARWOOD 18 Oct 1798
		(he born 26 Oct 1772 Weare, Hampshire, MA; died 25 Sep 1853 Bennington, VT.
		(he s/o Andrew HARWOOD and Rachel D. HIGGINS)

Note: Unknown as to why there is a 13 year gap in this family

+	**672. DANIEL**	born 26 July 1791 Chelsea, Hampshire, NH; died 26 July 1859
		1 married Nancy GRAPES 20 June 1814 VT.
		(she dau/o Jacob GRAPES and Patience CLIFFORD)(she born ca 1800 ; died 1831)
		2 married Elizabeth/Betsey LEIGHTON ca 1835
		(she born ca 1799; died 1861)
	673. James, Jr.	born ca 1795 Weare, MA; died ____

Children of James-[5] FORBUSH and Eunice BROWN, continued:
Surname **FORBUSH**

674. Anna	born 17 Apr 1797 NH; died 27 Nov 1848 Littleton, Grafton, NH	
675. Lucy Ann	born 9 Nov 1798 MA; died 10 Oct 1877 Stark, Coos, NH	
	married Captain Moses JACKSON 26 May 1818	
	(he s/o Sgt. Aaron JACKSON and Sarah COLE)(he born 1 May 1800; died 9 May 1887)	

+ **676. CHEBAR** born 4 May 1801; died Dec 1874 Minneapolis, MN
married Elizabeth GRAPES 25 July 1820
(she born 5 May 1805; died 1 Sept 1890 MN) (sister of Nancy, above)

677. Roxey   born ca 1802 NH; died ____   678. Almira   born ca 1808; died ____

176. CYRUS-[5] GATES, son of Ephraim-[4] GATES (Mary-[3] BOWKER; John-[2]-; Edmund-1) and Dorothy GRAVES, was born 11 Apr 1732 at Stow, MA. He married Ruth-[5] BRUCE (# 126) on 22 May 1753. She was the daughter of Daniel BRUCE and Bathsheba-[4] BOWKER, and was born 22 May 1783; died 1820. Cyrus-[5] GATES, who served in the Revolutionary War; died 8 July 1813 at Bolton, MA

Children of Cyrus-[5] GATES and Ruth BRUCE:
Surname **GATES**   (all children born at Bolton, MA)

679. Cyrus Lovell	born 31 Aug 1754; died 22 Oct 1770 Bolton, MA	EOL
680. Ruth	born 5 May 1757; died ____; married Philip ATWOOD 30 Sep 1782	
681. Eunice	born12 Aug 1759; died 14 May 1762	EOL
682. Ruhama/ Hannah	born 25 Feb 1762; died ____	
683. Laban	born 16 Sep 1761; died 7 Jan 1837 Chester, VT	
	1 married Elizabeth TUFT 30 May 1796 (she born ____; died 1812)	
	2 married ____SCOTT 1 Apr 1813 (she born ____; died 1827)	
	3 married Lucy HILL Smith Mack 30 Dec 1829	
684. Ebenezer	born March 1767; died ____	
685. Abiathar	born 20 Aug 1769; died 16 June 1842; married Lois HOLT 24 Oct 1793	
686. Lovell	born 19 Sep 1772; died ____	
687. Luther	born 17 Mar 1775; died 19 Aug 1777	EOL
688. Ephraim	born 1777; died 1778	EOL

177. MICAH-[5] GATES, brother of above, was born 1 May 1734 at Stow, MA. he married Phebe WHITCOMB 21 Feb 1757. She was the daughter of_____WHITCOMB and ____; and was born ____; died ____. Micah-[5] GATES served In Col. PRESCOTT's regiment at the siege of Boston in 1775; also is on the rolls of Col. MOULTON's company at King Ferry, NY.

Children of Micah-[5] GATES and Phebe WHITCOMB:
Surname **GATES**   (all children born Stow, MA)

689. William	born 5 Jan 1758; died ____; married Dorcas HALE 5 July 1786	
690. Ephraim	born 20 Jan 1760; died ____	
691. Lois	born 6 July 1762; died ____; married William TAYLOR 16 Dec 1784	
692. Micah, Jr.	born 7 Aug 1764; died 15 Dec 1855 Palmer, MA	
693. Phebe	born 18 Jan 1767; died ____	
694. Ebenezer	born 1 June 1769; died ____; married Eunice JEWELL 20 May 1797	
695. John	born 16 June 1771; died ____ 696. Daniel born 14 May 1777; died ____	

Reference: Genealogy of the Stephen GATES Family of Hingham, Lancaster and Cmbridge, MA

178. ELIZABETH-[5] GATES, sister of above, was born 3 May 1737 at Stow, Middlesex, MA. She married William POWERS on 5 Apr/ 8 June 1764 at Stow. He was the son of Gideon POWERS and Lydia RUSSELL, and was born 10 Dec 1740 Middlesex, MA; died 13 Mar 1829 Groton, MA. Elizabeth-[5] GATES died 9 Nov 1833/38.

Child of Elizabeth-[5] GATES and William POWERS:
Surname **POWERS**

+ **697. WILLIAM II**   born 11 Feb 1767 Dunbarton, NH; died 2 Nov 1834 Groton, NH
married Mary THOMPSON 22 Sep 1787
(she dau/o Seth THOMPSON and Elizabeth ____)
(she born 11 Sep 1769 Groton, NH; died 4 Dec 1857)

BOWKER
The Fifth American Generation

187.   LEVI-⁵ GATES, son of Samuel⁻⁴ GATES (Mary⁻³ BOWKER; John⁻²; Edmund⁻¹) and Margaret GATES, was born 29 Aug 1756 at Stow, MA. He married Betty BROOKS on 7 Oct 1779. She was the daughter of _____ BROOKS and ____; and was born ____; died ____. Levi-⁵ GATES died ____.

Children of Levi-⁵ GATES and Betty BROOKS:
Surname **GATES**   (all children born Stow, MA)

698. Betsey	born 12 Jan 1781; died ____	
699. Reuben	born 29 July 1783; died ____; married Polly SCOTT 19 Dec 1808	
700. Margaret	born 19 Feb 1791; died young	EOL
701. Lois	born 28 Dec 1793; died ____	
702. Samuel (twin)	born 19 Feb 1797; died 20 Feb 1797 703. Levi (twin) born 19 Feb 1797	

193. JOHN-⁵ GATES, son of (John-⁴ GATES; Mary-³ BOWKER; John-²; Edmund-¹) and Mary WHITNEY, was born 12 Sept 1748 at Stow, MA. He married Catherine WETHERBEE on 19 Feb 1778. She was the daughter of Thomas WETHERBEE and Elizabeth HEALD, and was born 15 Mar 1753 Stow; died 13 June 1834. John-⁵ GATES died 25 Nov 1814.

Children of John-⁵ GATES and Catherine WETHERBEE:
Surname **GATES**   (children all born Stow, MA.

704. Olive		born 11 Mar 1786; died 26 Aug 1877; married Abel GATES ca 1805
705. Hezekiah		born 2 Mar 1790; died 20 Dec 1861; married Mary HOUGHTON ca 1825
706. John		born 21 Mar 1791; died 6 June 1866; married Susan W. GATES Putnam ca 1838
707. Elizabeth	(twin)	born 17 Nov 1792; died ____; married Jacob WHITNEY ca ___ (no issue) EOL
708. Mary	(twin)	born 17 Nov 1792; died ____; married Arna WETHERBEE ca ; he from Harvard, MA

194. CALEB-⁵ GATES, brother of above, was born 14 July 1751 Stow, MA. He married Mindwell OAK on 10 Mar 1776. She was the daughter of _____ OAK and _____; and was born 23 Mar 1746; died 22 Nov 1826. Caleb-⁵ GATES died ___ Acton, MA.

Children of Caleb-⁵ GATES and Mindwell OAK:
Surname **GATES**   (children all born Stow, MA)

709. Achsah	born 8 Mar 1777; died July 1854 Townsend, VT
	married Dennis HOLDEN 19 Mar 1807 (he born 6 Dec 1784; died 15 July 1872)
710. Artemus	born 25 Apr 1780; died young
711. Josiah	born 9 Oct 1783; died 10 Mar 1812; married Sabra HOLDEN 8 Jan 1803
	(she born 23 Dec 1782; died 13 Dec 1815) (sister to Dennis HOLDEN, above)

195. MARY-⁵ GATES, sister of above , was born 25 April 1753 at Stow, Middlesex, MA. She married Thomas WETHERBEE on 19 Jan 1779 at Westminster, MA. He was the son of _____ WETHERBEE and _____; and was born ca 1750; died 1801. Mary-⁵ GATES died 1 May 1831 at Westminster.

Children of Mary-⁵ GATES and Thomas WETHERBEE:
Surname **WETHERBEE**

712. Mary	born 28 Mar 1780; died 6 May 1843; married Jonathan SAWTELL 14 Apr 1807
713. Josiah	born 19 Mar 1783; died 5 Oct 1873; married Clarissa SAWTELL 28 Nov 1805
714. Sarah	born 14 Mar 1786; died 7 Mar 1850; married Solomon WETHERBEE 14 Apr 1807
715. Dolly	born 22 Mar 1789; died ____; married Joel HAYWARD 22 Mar 1824
	Child: Joel Augustus-⁷ HAYWARD born ca 1836; died ca 1927
716. Arni	born 21 Feb 1793; died 23 Mar 1862 Harvard, MA
717. Elizabeth/ Betsey	born 2 Apr 1796; died 22 Nov 1873; married William WASHBURNE ca ____

202. SUSANNAH-⁵ GATES, daughter of Mary-⁴ GATES (Mary-³ BOWKER; John-²; Edmund-¹) and Elisha GATES, was born 15 May 1748 at Stow, MA. She married Ephraim MORRILL on 8 May 1773. He was the son of _____ MORRILL and _____, and was born ____; died ____. Susannah-⁵ GATES died ____.

Child of Susannah-⁵ GATES and Ephraim MORRILL:
Surname **MORRILL**

+ **718. SUSANNAH**	born 22 July 1778 Henniker, Merrimack, NH; died 25 Oct 1829 Peoria, IL
	married Nathaniel AIKEN on 30 May 1807
	(he born 5 Mar 1774 Deering, Hillsboro, NH; died _____)

206. ANNA D-[5] KEYES, daughter of Martha-[4] BOWKER (Asa-[3]; John-[2;] Edmund-[1]) and Robert KEYES, was born 21 June 1748 at Shrewsbury, MA. She married Samuel MOSMAN on 30 Oct 1769 at Princeton, Worcester, MA. He was the son of _____ MOSMAN and ____, and was born 27 Feb 1739/40 at Sudbury, Middlesex, MA; died 29 Dec 1828 at Westminster, Worcester, MA. Anna D-[5] KEYES died 22 Set 1840 at Westminster, MA.

Children of Anna D-[5] KEYES and Samuel MOSMAN :
Surname **MOSMAN**

+	**719. ABRAHAM**	born 27 Oct 1770; died 30 Sep 1847
		married Achsah Whitney SEAVER 19 Apr 1802 Westminster, Worcester, MA
		(she dau/o Benjamin SEAVER and Martha WHITNEY)
		(she born 30 Dec 1784 MA; died 16 Mar 1865 Westminster, Worcester, MA)
	720. Samuel, Jr.	born 23 Mar 1772; died 1 Jan 1852
		married Elizabeth / Betsey BRIGHAM 8 Mar 1801
		(she dau/o Artemus BRIGHAM and Keziah RICE) (she born 1771; died 1851)
	721. Asaph	born 12 Jan 1774; died 26 Jan 1847
	722. Lucy	born 16 Dec 1775; died 19 June 1830
	723. Eunice	born 20 Nov 1778; died 31 Mar 1829
		married Samuel GARFIELD 3 June 1810 Ashburnham, MA
		Child: Asaph Mosman-[7] GARFIELD born 17 Apr 1820; died 21 Sep 1886 Waltham, MA; married Phebe Submit SMITH 20 Aug 1847 Waltham, MA (she born 29 Nov 1818 Waltham, died 4 Dec 1899 Waltham)
	724. Mary	born 20 Nov 1780 Greenfield, MA; died 28 July 1861
		married John MILES 29 Nov 1804 (he born ca 1775; died 1863)
+	**725. ANNA**	born 3 Apr 1782; died 30 Sep 1850; married Reuben GATES 12 Feb 1806
		(brother of Daniel GATES, below)
		(he born 211 Apr 1786; died 16 Dec 1873 Gardner, MA)
+	**726. PHOEBE**	born 31 Oct 1785 Westminster, MA; died 1 Aug 1850
		married Daniel GATES 27 May 1805 Gardner, MA
		(he s/o Simon GATES and Susannah REED)
		(he born 23 July 1782; died 17 Sep 1847 Gardner, MA)
	727. Moses	born 20 Jan 1792; died 9 July 1829 Fitchburg, Worcester, MA

211. SOLOMON-[5] KEYES, brother of above, was born 28 June 1762 at Wachusett, MA. He married Elizabeth HEMENWAY/ HEMINGWAY on 2 Oct 1796. She was the daughter of _____ HEMENWAY/ HEMINGWAY and ____; and was born 22 June 1766 at Framingham, Middlesex, MA; died 25 Dec 1808 Princeton, MA. Solomon-[5] KEYES died 29 Feb 1808 Princeton.

Children of Solomon-[5] KEYES and Elizabeth HEMENWAY / HEMINGWAY:
Surname **KEYES**

728. Stephen	born 20 Feb 1797; died 1869 Norwich, Chenango, NY	
	married Eunice JENNISON 26 Nov 1821	
	Child: Rosena Elizabeth-[7] KEYES born ca 1822	
729. Lucinda	born 14 Sep 1798; died 9 Jan 1868; married Samuel EVERETT 9 Feb 1825	
730. Phoebe	born 11 Dec 1800 Princeton, MA; died _____	
	married Hezekiah KEYES 14 Feb 1823	
731. Lucretia	born 19 Oct 1802 Princeton; died _____	
	married Jubal HARRINGTON ca _____ Worcester, MA	
732. Elizabeth	born 26 May 1805 Princeton; died 15 Oct 1810 Princeton	EOL
733. Martha Bowker	born 26 Aug 1807; died 23 Feb 1808 Princeton	EOL

216. ELIZABETH / BETSEY-[5] BOWKER, daughter of Lt. Charles-[4] BOWKER (Asa-[3]; John-[2]; Edmund-[1]) and Eunice STONE, was born 21 Aug 1753 at Shrewsbury, MA. She married first to William DEXTER, MD on 17 Feb 1775 at Shrewsbury. He was the son of Ebenezer DEXTER and Lydia WOODS; and was born 17 April 1755 Marlborough, MA; died 4 Dec 1785 at Marlborough. Elizabeth/ Betsey-[5] BOWKER married second to Edward LOW on 13 Oct 1795. He was the son of ____ LOW and ____; and was born 22 Feb 1744; died 14 Feb 1823. Elizabeth/Betsey-[5] BOWKER died 12 Dec 1846 at Leominster, MA.

Children of Betsey-[5] BOWKER and William DEXTER, MD:
Surname **DEXTER** (all children born Marlborough, MA)

734. Ebenezer	born 30 Oct 1775 ; died 22 Jan 1850 Leominster, MA
735. Lydia	born 28 Feb 1777; died 8 Aug 1808 Portland, ME

Children of Elizabeth/ Betsey-[5] BOWKER and William DEXTER, MD, continued:
Surname **DEXTER**

736. Sarah	born 14 Oct 1778; died 28 Mar 1846 Leominster	
737. William, Jr.	born 29 Dec 1779; died 14 June 1804 Leominster (single) EOL	
	Reference: Dexter Genealogy, pages 90-92	

219.   JENNIE-[5] BOWKER, sister of above, was born 26 May 1761 Shrewsbury; married Asa-[5] HAPGOOD ca 1785. For children see Asa-[5] HAPGOOD (# 225 below)

224. DAVID-[5] HAPGOOD, son of Anna D-[4] BOWKER (Asa-[3]; John-[2]; Edmund-[1]) and Asa-[4] HAPGOOD (Thomas-[3,2]; Shadrach-[1]), was born 10 May 1757. He married Sally MYRICK on 29 Dec 1781. She was the daughter of Caleb MYRICK and Eunice JONES, and was born 6 Apr 1762 at Hubbardstown, MA; died 7 Aug 1826. David-[5] HAPGOOD died 3 July 1829 MA.

Children of David-[5] HAPGOOD and Sally MYRICK:
Surname **HAPGOOD**

	738. John	born 11 Dec 1782; died 23 Jan 1854 Como, Italy
+	**739. LUCINDA**	born 28 June 1790 Princeton, MA; died 21 Oct 1835 Reading, Windsor, VT
		married Jared BIGELOW 2 Feb 1812 Reading, VT
	740. Fidelia	born ca 1798; died 1866
	741. Bridgman	born ca 1799; died 1877

225. ASA-[5] HAPGOOD, brother of above, was born 25 Nov 1759. He married Jennie-[5] BOWKER (above) ca 1785. She was the daughter of Charles-[4] BOWKER and Eunice STONE, and was born 26 May 1761 Shrewsbury, MA; died 16 Feb 1822 Rushford, Allegany, NY. Asa-[5] HAPGOOD died ____ .

Children of Asa-[5] HAPGOOD and Jennie-[5] BOWKER:
Surname **HAPGOOD**

742. Elmore	born 29 Oct 1787 Reading, MA; died ____
	married Rheuanna SMITH 14 Mar 1813
	(she dau/o William SMITH and Ruth WOOD)
743. Sylvia	born 2 July 1788; died 10 Nov 1826 Milton, VT; married John BOOTH ca ____
744. Charles	born 18 Nov 1790; died ____; married Lucy KENDALL ca ____
745. Tillison	born 13 Apr 1792; died ____; married Cynthia BLISS 13 Feb 1823
746. Lucy	born 2 June 1794; died 20 Mar 1865 VT; married Eben WOODWORTH ca ____
747. Asa	born 18 Dec 1795; died 2 April 1829
	(drowned in Lake Correnango, near Maysville, NY)
748. Elmira	born 26 June 1797 Fairfax, VT; died 28 Dec 1805 Jericho, VT EOL
749. Jane	born 21 Mar 1799 Fairfax, VT; died 25 Jan 1883 Asheville, NY
	married James WELLS 10 Dec 1826 Ripley, NY (he born ____; died 28 Mar 1854)
750. Bates Turner	born 6 Nov 1800; died ____; married Alzina TAYLOR 25 Jan 1826
751. Joel Wilson	born 21 Apr 1802; died ____; married Susan HARRINGTON 1 Sep 1830 Whitehall, NY
752. Martha	born 16 Nov 1805 Jericho, VT; died 24 Jan 1826

229. ARTEMUS-[5] HAPGOOD, brother of above, was born 15 Mar 1769 MA. He married Polly RICE on 16 June 1799 at Barre, Worcester, MA. She was the daughter of Martin RICE and Ruth HASTINGS, and was born 21 Sep 1779 at Petersham, Worcester, MA; died 7 Oct 1861 at Barre, MA. Artemus-[5] HAPGOOD died 3 Oct 1846.

Children of Artemus-[5] HAPGOOD and Polly RICE:
Surname **HAPGOOD**   (all children born Barre, Worcester, MA)

	753. Horace	born 25 May 1800; died 26 June 1877 Athol, MA
	754. Sylvia	born 4 July 1801; died 6 Jan 1867 Kenwood, NY
+	**755. CHAUNCEY**	born ca 1804; died 3 Apr 1887 Petersham, MA
		married Lucy F. RICE 2 May 1833 Barre, MA
		(she dau/o James RICE and Hannah HAMMOND) (she born 1808; died 1897)
	756. Direxa	born 15 June 1805; died 4 Feb 1890 Cornwall, VT
	757. Mary Ann	born 28 Feb 1807; died 29 Jan 1864
	758. Betsey	born 17 Jul 1808; died 19 Jan 1882 Barre, MA; married Samuel KINSMAN 8 Dec 1842
		(he s/o Samuel KINSMAN and Kezia NEWTON) (he born 24 Jan 1808; died 14 Mar 1888 Philadelphia, PA

Children of Artemus-[5] HAPGOOD and Polly RICE, continued:
Surname **HAPGOOD**

759. Harriet	born 27 Feb 1810; died 23 Nov 1878	
760. Lyman Wilder	born 27 Nov 1811; died 18 oct 1874	
761. Asa	born 1 Jul 1813; died 10 June 1868	
762. Anson	born 21 Feb 1815; died 30 Apr 1839 Petersham, MA	
763. Fidelia	born 27 May 1818; died 9 Apr 1894	

235. MARTHA-[5] FORBUSH, daughter of Lucy-[4] BOWKER (Asa-[3] BOWKER; John-[2]; Edmund-[1]) and Ebenezer FORBUSH, was born 23 Sep 1762 at Westborough, MA. She married Benjamin RICHARDSON on 14 Oct 1784 at Westborough. He was the son of Jeremiah RICHARDSON and Abigail GOWING, and was born 28 July 1760, Sutton, MA; died ____. Martha-[5] FORBUSH died 22 Sep 1824 at Sutton, MA.

Children of Martha-[5] FORBUSH and Benjamin RICHARDSON:
Surname **RICHARDSON**

+	**764. EDWARD**	born 3 Sep 1785; died 24 Mar 1872; married Charlotte ELLIS 27 Sep 1812 Sutton, MA	
		(she born 30 July 1791 Sutton, MA; died ____	
+	**765. EBENEZER**	born 7 March 1787; died ____; married Cynthia ____ ca 1827 (she born ca 1794)	
	766. Chloe	born ca _____ Sutton, MA; died ____; married Ebenezer CARPENTER 3 Oct 1816	
		(he born 15 June 1781; died 19 Mar 1823 Norton, MA)	
		(he s/o William CARPENTER and Sarah FULLER)	
		Children: Moses-[7] born 1817 Sutton, MA, died ca 1860, OH; and Lucy-[7] CARPENTER	
		born ca 1823, died 1827 EOL	
	767. Jeremiah	born 30 Sep 1797; died ___	
	768. Pliny	born 6 Apr 1800; died _____	770. Abner
	769. Patty	born 27 Apr 1802; died _____	771. Catherine

770. Abner   born 22 Apr 1804; died ____
771. Catherine   born 1 July 1806; died _____

244. HUTCHINS-[5] HAPGOOD, son of Lydia-[4] BOWKER (Asa-[3]; John-[2]; Edmund-[1]) and Seth HAPGOOD, was born 4 Apr 1763 at Petersham, Worcester, MA. He married Betsey/Elizabeth GROUT on 20 Oct 1789. She was the daughter of Honorable Jonathan GROUT and ____, and was born ____; died ____. Hutchins-[5] HAPGOOD died 4 Sept 1837.

Children of Hutchins-[5] HAPGOOD and Betsey GROUT:
Surname **HAPGOOD**   (all children born Petersham, MA)

772. Thomas	born 20 Jan 1790; died 10 Oct 1820
	married Betsey HOPKINS 3 Feb 1818 Petersham, MA
	(she dau/o Samuel HOPKINS and Elizabeth HASTINGS)
773. Hutchins, Jr.	born 2 Sept 1792; died 2 June 1828

Children of Hutchins-[5] HAPGOOD AND Betsey GROUT:
Surname **HAPGOOD**

774. Eliza	born 9 Oct 1796; died 24 Sep 1835; married Aaron ARMS, Esq. ca ____	
775. Maria	born 15 July 1798; died 28 Jan 1842	
776. Lydia	born 5 Sep 1802; died 6 June 1807	EOL
777. Seth	born 10 June 1805; died ____	
778. Charles	born 2 Apr 1811; died 17 Sep 1828	EOL

246. SOLOMON-[5] HAPGOOD, brother of above, was born 30 Dec 1766 at Petersham, Worcester, MA. He married Azubah BURT on 10 Aug 1790. She was the daughter of Judge Benjamin BURT and Mary ROOT, and was born ca 1771; died 10 Feb 1858 Bellows Falls, VT. Solomon-[5] HAPGOOD died 5 March 1856 Bellows Falls, VT.

Children of Solomon-[5] HAPGOOD and Azubah BURT:
Surname **HAPGOOD**

+	**779. LUCRETIA**	born 12 Jan 1792; died 19 March 1791 Brooklyn, NY
		married Daniel TUTTLE ca 1808
		(he s/o Titus TUTTLE and Lois ATWATER) (he born ca 1788; died 1861)

248. EBER-[5] HAPGOOD, brother of above, was born 5 Aug 1770 Petersham, Worcester, MA. He married Dolly GROUT on 13 July 1803. She was the daughter of Jonathan GROUT and Sarah PAGE, and was born 1 May 1772 Petersham, died 16 July 1822 Petersham. Eber-[5] HAPGOOD died 6 July 1851 at Petersham.

Children of Eber-[5] HAPGOOD and Dolly GROUT:
Surname **HAPGOOD**   (children born Petersham, MA)

780. George Grout	born 11 Feb 1804; died 17 May 1876 Apulia Station, Onondaga, NY	
	married Marcia Mc GRAW ca ____	
781. Dolly	born 14 Oct 1805; died 27 July 1871	
	married Joel BORDWELL, Jr. 8 Sep 1840 Cazenovia, Madison, NY	
	(he s/o Rev Joel BORDWELL and _____) (he born 4 Feb 1808; died 12 May 1882)	
782. Charles	born 11 Oct 1807; died 25 Aug 1886 Red Bluff, CA	
	married Rebecca HIBBARD ca ____ ; she from Waterford, VT	
783. Lyman Wilder	born 7 Feb 1810; died 19 Apr 1871 Grafton, VT	
	married Nancy PINKERTON 5 Mar 1840	
	(she dau/o James PINKERTON and Eliza Mc KENZIE)	
	(she born 6 July 1813; died 3 May 1864 Petersham, MA)	
784. Mary Frances	born 19 May 1812; died 1 Aug 1874	
	1 married Elijah KIMBALL ca ____ (he born ____; died 17 Dec 1867)	
	2 married Joel BORDWELL, Jr. 3 Apr 1872 (he wid/o her sister Dolly (above)	
785. Levi	born 2 Apr 1814; died 31 Dec 1839 Bedford, OH single	EOL
786. Susan	born 17 June 1818; died 8 Apr 1855 Petersham, MA	
	married Joseph Warren UPTON 17 May 1842 (he born 26 Apr 1818; died 25 Oct 1889)	

250. EUNICE-[5] HAPGOOD, sister of above, was born 22 July 1774 at Petersham, Worcester, MA. She married Guy-[5] BRIDGMAN on 10 Feb 1797. He was the son of Judge John-[4] BRIDGMAN (Orlando-[3]; John-[2]; James-[1]) and ____, and was born 15 March 1774 at Vernon, VT; died 21 Feb 1853 at Kendall, Orleans, NY. Eunice-[5] HAPGOOD died 22 Aug 1862 at Kendall, NY.

Children of Eunice-[5] HAPGOOD and Guy BRIDGMAN:
Surname **BRIDGMAN**   (children born Guilford, VT)

787. Nancy	born 2 Dec 1797; died 11 April 1843 Greece, NY	
	married Daniel BARNES (her cousin) ca ____	
	(he s/o Timothy T. BARNES and Matilda BRIDGMAN)	
788. Lydia	born 25 Feb 1799; died 22 April 1882 Parma, NY	
	married Humphrey Dennis TABER 20 Jan 1831 Parma, NY	(5 ch)
789. George	born 28 Dec 1800; died 6 Jan 1883 Medina, NY	
790. Levi	born 22 Jan 1802; died 29 Sep 1804 Greece, NY	
791. Thomas	born 20 Mar 1803; died 13 Sep 1803 Guilford, VT	EOL
792. Miranda	born 11 July 1804; died 1 May 1845 Pembroke, NY	
	married Jabez SMITH of Guilford ca ____	
793. Eunice	born 2 May 1806; died 25 Aug 1808	EOL
794. Horatio Nelson	born 28 Feb 1808; died 4 May 1874 Galena, IL	
795. Electa	born born 24 July 1809; died ___	
	1 married Shubael BASCOM 27 May 1827 Guilford, VT	
	(he born____; died 19 Dec 1853; he from Hinsdale, NH)	
	2 married Dennis P. BROWN 6 June 1856 Greece, NY	
796. Guy Carleton	born 13 Apr 1811; died 25 Apr 1872	
797. Oliver Hapgood	born 3 March 1813; died ____	
798. John Fitch	born 23 Apr 1815; died 14 Nov 1815	
+ **799. LUCRETIA**	born 11 Dec 1816; died ____	
SAMANTHA	1 married Varnum CURTIS on 16 Apr 1836 (he born ____; died 5 July 1837)	
	2 married Amasa Dwight WALKER 1 June 1841 (he of Byron, NY)	
	(he born 18 Jan 1814; died 7 Sep 1872 Hamlin, Monroe, NY)	

252. ANNA-[5] WHEELER, daughter of Abigail-[4] BOWKER (Ezekiel-[3]; John-[2]; Edmund-[1]) and Silas WHEELER, was born 17 Aug 1760 MA. She married William BARNARD on 23 April 1783 at Stow, MA. he was the son of Joel BARNARD and Lucy STEVENS , and was born ca 1760 Marlborough; died 1 May 1810 Dixfield, Maine. Anna-[5] WHEELER died ____.

Children of Anna-[5] WHEELER and William BARNARD:
Surnamne **BARNARD**

800. Abigail	born Oct 1785 Marlborough, MA; died ____

Children of Anna[-5] WHEELER and William BARNARD, continued:
Surname **BARNARD**

	801. Joel	born 20 June 1790 Marlborough; died ____
	802. Eliza	born ca 1791 Marlborough, MA; died ____
+	**803. SIMON**	born ca 1792 Dixfield, ME; died 12 Feb 1872 Woburn, MA
		1 married Lucy SIMONDS 12 Feb 1818 Woburn, MA
		(she born 10 Nov 1787 Woburn; died 13 Aug 1842 Woburn)
		(she dau/o Jonathan SIMONDS and Phebe CUMMINGS)
		2 married Elizabeth Julia Ann BEERS 23 May 1843)
		(she dau/o William BEERS and Elizabeth _____) (she born 22 Dec 1822; died ___)
	804. Nancy	born ca 1794; died ____; married Walter CARPENTER ca ____
	805. Silas	born 16 Sep 1795; died ____
	806. Harriet	born ca 1796; died ____; married Baldwin MARBLE ca ____

254. ASA[-5] WHEELER, brother of above, was born 16 Oct 1764 MA. He married Sarah THOMPSON on 27 Jan 1792. She was the daughter of _____ THOMPSON and ____; and was born ca 1765 Marlborough, MA; died 5 Dec 1833. Asa[-5] WHEELER died Jan 1834.

Children of Asa[-5] WHEELER and Sarah THOMPSON:
Surname **WHEELER**

	807. Mary V.	born 17 May 1793; died ____
+	**808. LUMAN**	born 19 May 1795; died ____; resided Madison Lake, OH
		1 married Sarah SEAVER 22 Nov 1818 Swanzey, NH
		(she born 11 Oct 1802; died 26 Mar 1831)
		2 married Ann M. ____ ca 1832 (she born ca 1812; died ____)
	809. Dexter	born 26 June 1797; died Sept 1853 Marlborough, MA
		married Jane Mc CLINTOCK ca 1820
		(she dau/o Thomas Mc CLINTOCK and Mary SMITH) (she born ca 1799 PA)
+	**810. ASA BOWKER**	born 24 Mar 1799; died 28 Mar 1864; married Persis BURKE ca 1821
		(she born 30 July 1802 NH; died ____ VT)
+	**811. LORENZO DOW**	born 24 Nov 1800; died ____
		married Finetta LEWIS 12 Aug 1824 NY (she born ca 1805; died 1892)

271. LYDIA[-5] HOWE, daughter of Silas[-4] HOWE (Hannah[-3] BOWKER; John[-2]; Edmund[-1]) and Beulah LELAND, was born 30 Oct 1764 Brookfield, MA. She married William PEESO on 16 Dec 1784 at Brookfield. He was the son of John PEESO and Hannah RANGER, and was born 30 June 1758; died 25 May 1831 at Cherry Valley, NY. Lydia[-5] HOWE died ____.

Children of Lydia[-5] HOWE and William PEESO:
Surname **PEESO**

	812. Sally	born 5 Aug 1785 NY; died Feb 1850 Florence, Williams, OH
		1 married Joseph PALMER ca 1804; 2 married Joseph RANDELL 3 Jan 1819
+	**813. SYDNEY W.**	born 26 Mar 1793 MA; died 3 July 1853 Wyandot Co., OH
	814. Theodore	born ca 1794; died after 1880 Cherry Valley, NY
	815. Maria	born ca 1801 NY; died ____
	816. Austin Elifilet	born 28 May 1806 Roseboom, Otsego, NY; died 16 Oct 1883

285. JOHN[-5] GLEASON, JR., son of Persis[-4] HOWE (Hannah[-3] BOWKER; John[-2]; Edmund[-1]) and John GLEASON, was born 19 Feb 758. He married Experience STOW on 17 April 1781. She was the daughter of John STOW and Ruth HOWE, and was born 19 Mar 1761 Marlborough, MA; died 27 Feb 1835 Marlboro. John[-5] GLEASON, Jr. died 8 Nov 1828.

Children of John[-5] GLEASON, Jr. and Experience STOW:
Surname **GLEASON**   (children all born Marlborough, MA)

817. Samuel	born	819. Elizabeth	born ____
818. Francis	born		

288. EZRA[-5] KEYES, son of Hannah[-4] HOWE (Hannah[-3] BOWKER; John[-2]; Edmund[-1]) and Eli KEYES, was born 27 Jan 1763 at Holden, MA. He married Hannah KNOWLTON Dec 1792. She was the daughter of _____ KNOWLTON and ____, and was born ca 1770; died ____. Ezra[-5] KEYES died 29 Dec 1841 at Readsboro, VT.

Children of Ezra[5] KEYES and Hannah KNOWLTON:
Surname **KEYES**　　　　(children all born Readsboro, VT)

820. Eli	born 19 Aug 1794; died ____; married Mary CHAPMAN ca _____
821. Sally	born 2 Nov 1795; died ____
822. Ruel	born 22 June 1797; died 22 Dec 1870 NY; married Hannah BOTTUM ca 1823
823. Hannah	born 17 Feb 1799; died ____
824. Polly	born 4 Jan 1801; died ____; married _____ WILCOX ca ____
825. Ezra, Jr.	born 14 Oct 1802; died ____; married Elizabeth P. COLBURN 1 Apr 1830
826. Herman	born 11 Dec 1804; died ____
827. Daniel	born 28 Mar 1807; died ____
828. Nathan	born 8 Oct 1809; died ____
829. Azubah	born 28 July 1813; died 29 May 1898 VT married Henry CAMP 7 May 1838 Marlborough, MA
830. Lawton	born 19 July 1816; married Sarah SAMMRER ca _____ (she born 17 Jul 1814 CAN/VT; died 4 Sep 1860 VT)

289. DANIEL[5] KEYES, brother of above, was born 17 Nov 1764 MA. He married Jedidiah SAWYER on 8 Nov 1792 at Lancaster, Worcester, MA. She was the daughter of Josiah SAWYER and Abigail _____, and was born ca 1767; died 14 Feb 1850 Princeton, MA. Daniel[5] KEYES died 4 Dec 1826 Princeton.

Children of Daniel[5] KEYES and Jedidiah SAWYER:
Surname **KEYES**　　　　(children all born Lancaster, Worcester, MA)

831. un-named infant	born 21 Jan 1794; died 22 Jan 1794
832. Sarah	born 17 July 1795; died 22 Jan 1856 Princeton　(never married)　EOL
833. John	born 4 Dec 1797; died ____
834. Mary	born 8 July 1801; died 22 Feb 1879 Sterling, Worcester, MA married Elisha N. HAGER ca ____
835. Lucinda	born 16 June 1804; died 28 Jan 1859 Princeton　(never married)　EOL
836. Martha	born 13 July 1808; died 27 May 1873 East Princeton, MA married Silas KEYES ca ____
837. Charles Howe	born 7 May 1811; died 24 May 1839 Princeton

290. AZUBAH[5] KEYES, sister of above, was born 13 May 1760 at Shrewsbury, MA. She married Hananiah WHITNEY on 10 Oct 1787 at Shrewsbury. He was the son of Lt. Samuel WHITNEY and Abigail FLETCHER, and was born 18 Dec 1762 at Westminster, MA; died Oct 1835 at Ashburnham, MA. Azubah[5] WHITNEY died 3 June 1825 at Shrewsbury, MA.

Children of Azubah[5] KEYES and Hananiah WHITNEY:
Surname **WHITNEY**　　　　(children all born Winchendon, MA)

	838. Stacy	born ca 1788; died ____
	839. Moses	born 28 Nov 1789; died 16 May 1831
+	**840. CAPT. HANANIAH**	born 29 May 1792; died 2 Mar 1867 Lowell, MA married Sally T. BEAMAN 19 Oct 1820 Winchendon
	841. Alpheus B.	born 6 Mar 1794; died ____
	842. Azubah B.	born 25 Aug 1796; died ____
	843. Artemus B.	born 5 Sep 1798; died ____
	844. Barsina	born 4 Feb 1801; died 22 Jan 1802 Winchendon, MA　　EOL
	845. Esther B	born 13 June 1803; died ____
	846. Silas Stacy	born 27 June 1805; died 5 Aug 1873
	847. Levi Pilsbury	born 19 Aug 1807; died ____
	848. Samuel Austin	born 10 Nov 1809; died June 1886 Fitzwilliam, NH 1 married Hannah BLACKMER Johnson 5 June 1881 (she dau/o Willard BLACKMER and Hannah ____) (she born ca 1826; died ____) 2 married Harriet M. BOSWORTH 27 Apr 1883
	849. Abigail Fletcher	born 27 Dec 1812; died ____

296. NOAH[5] LUND, son of Thomas[4] LUND (Thomas[3]; Elizabeth[2] BOWKER; Edmund[1]) and Sarah CHANDLER, was born 3 March 1759 at _____. He married Betty/Betsey HALE on 6 Dec 1786 at Dunstable, MA. She was the daughter of ____ HALE and ____, and was born ca 1763; died ca 1843. Noah[5] LUND died 8 Aug 1825.

Children of Noah[-5] LUND and Betsey HALE:

Surname **LUND**   (all children born Orange County, CT/VT)

850. Noah	born 13 Sept 1787; died 6 Nov 1800	EOL
851. Betsey	born 7 Dec 1788; died 22 July 1847	
852. Sophia	born 15 Aug 1790; died 26 Nov 1872	
853. Thomas (1)	born 7 July 1792; died 8 July 1793	EOL
854. Thomas (2)	born 29 April 1794; died 8 July 1869	
855. Sally Chandler	born 5 Feb 1796; died 21 June 1860	
856. Joel	born 3 Nov 1798; died 9 Sep 1848; married Sarah HATCH	
857. Noah Hale	born 29 Nov 1801; died 10 Jan 1872	

                                      1 married Marinda C. PARKER 11 Dec 1833 VT

                                        2 married Mary Louisa GALE   (she born ca 1816, died ca 1850)

        Children: Sidney Nelson-[7] born 6 July 1840; Stillman Gale-[7] born Oct 1842, married Lois SCRIPTURE;
and Mary E.-[7] LUND born ca 1847

                                        3 married Jane _____ ca____ (after 1850 and before 1860)

        858. Joseph   born 4 Dec 1804; died ____

309. CAPT. JONATHAN WILLIAM[-5] **LUND**, son of Jonathan[-4] LUND (Thomas[-3]; Elizabeth[-2] BOWKER; Edmund[-1]) and Jean VARNUM, was born 24 July 1747 at ____. He married Priscilla CUMMINGS ca 1770. She was the daughter of _____ CUMMINGS and ____, and was born ca 1748; died 22 Jan 1824. Capt. Jonathan[-5] LUND died 11 June 1828.

Children: of Jonathan[-5] LUND and Priscilla CUMMINGS:

Surname **LUND**   (all children born Amherst, Hillsborough, NH)

859. Jonathan	born 5 July 1771; died 30 Mar 1778	EOL
860. David	born 10 June 1773; died ____	
861. Isaac	born 17 Mar 1775; died ca 1837 Amherst, NH; married Abigail TAYLOR 17 Mar 1805	

                              Child: Susan-[7] LUND born ca 1815; died 1844; married ____ GIBBS

862. Hannah	born 3 Jan 1777; died ____	
863. Oliver	born 25 Jan 1781; died ____	
864. Mary	born 6 Aug 1783; died ____	
865. Elizabeth	born 15 April 1785; died ____	
866. Samuel	born 11 Dec 1785/86; died 14 Nov 1793	EOL
867. Ephraim	born 17 March 1788; died 30/31 March 1788	EOL

330. WILLARD[-5] **LUND**, son of Phineas[-4] LUND (Thomas[-3]; Elizabeth-[2] BOWKER; Edmund[-1]) and Rachel FRENCH, was born 21 Feb 1762. He married Sarah TOWNE ca 1789. She was the daughter of Rev. Thomas TOWNE and Sarah BENTON, and was born 18 Oct 1769 MA; died 5 July 1848 VT. Willard[-4] LUND died 29 Dec 1855 VT.

Children of Willard[-5] LUND and Sarah TOWNE:

Surname **LUND**

+ **868. ALVA**	born 8 Oct 1799 VT; died 31 Jan 1882 Martville, Cayuga Co., NY
	married Andrea GODFREY ca ____ (she born ca 1811 NY)
+ **869. LUCINDA**	born 24/28 May 1802; died 18 Jan 1895/96 Calmar, Iowa
	married Ira GARFIELD 2 Sept 1826
	(he s/o Enoch GARFIELD and Martha Patty POWERS)
	(he born 19 Feb 1802; died 21 Aug 1891)
+ **870. HENRY**	born 11 March 1811 VT; died 10 Feb 1894 Hannibal, Cayuga, NY
	married Mary L. EDDY ca 1846 (she born ca 1813; died 1865)

334. SAMUEL[-5] **SPAULDING**, son of Henry[-4] SPAULDING (Elizabeth[-3] LUND: Edmund[-2,1] BOWKER; John[-A,B]) and Lucy PROCTOR, was born 31 Jan 1726/ 27 Chelmsford, MA. He married Sarah WOODS ca 3 May 1753 Chelmsford , MA. She was the daughter of Samuel WOODS and Mary PARKER , and was born 8 March 1730; died 10 April 1815 at Merrimack. Samuel[-5] SPAULDING, who was a Lt. in the Battle of White Plains during the Revolutioary War, died 11 Sept 1797 at Merrimack, NH, and is buried at the Turkey Hill Cemetery.

Children of Samuel-[5] SPAULDING and Sarah WOODS:
Surname **SPAULDING**

+	**871. SAMUEL, JR.**	born 23 Aug 1754 Merrimack; died 1 March 1825
		married Sarah HEALD 28 Nov 1782 (she born ca 1759; died ca 1823)
		(she dau/o Ephraim HEALD and Sarah CONANT)
+	**872. ABIJAH**	born 18 June 1756 Merrimack; died 12 April 1828 Wilton, Hillsborough, NH
		1 married Polly WYMAN ca _____ ; 2 married Sarah HEALD ca _____
	873. Sarah	born 14 Oct 1758; died 8 Feb 1774 EOL
	874. Henry	born 3 Nov 1760; died ____
+	**875. OLIVER**	born 6 Feb 1763; died 21 Aug 1841 NH
+	**876. ISAAC**	born 20 Aug 1765; died 2 June 1830
		1 married Mary RITTER ca _____ ; 2 married Mary FLYNN Colburn ca ____
+	**877. SILAS**	born 11 June 1767 Merrimack; died ca 1827 NH
+	**878. ASA**	born 5 Apr 1769; died 9 Apr 1815
	879. Ephraim	born ca 1783; died 1790 EOL

335 . LUCY-[5] SPAULDING, sister of above, was born 1 Feb 1728 at Chelmsford, MA. She married William REED /READ / READE ca 1759 at Litchfield, MA. He was the son of William REED/READE and Hannah BATES, and was born 25 Feb 1724; died Jan 1769. He was killed at Litchfield, MA while working on the raising of a building. Lucy-[5] SPAULDING died _____.

Children of Lucy-[5] SPAULDING and William READE:
Surname **READE**

880. Zadoc	born 6 Oct 1761 NH; died _____
	married Lucy Mc LEAN ca _____ (Child: Dudley-[7] READE born ca 1790; died 1863)
881. William	born ca 1763; died _____ ; married Lydia _____ ca ____
882. Henry	born 25 July 1766; died 6 Aug 1833 Quebec, Canada
883. Hannah	born 18 May 1768 Litchfield; died 21 Jan 1848 Windham, NH
	married Samuel CENTER ca _____
884. Lucy	born ca 1770; died _____ ; married Jonathan LYON ca _____
	Children: Read-[7] LYON and Sally-[7] LYON born ca ____, married Roger COLBURN
885. Sally	born ca 1772; died ____

336. SARAH-[5] SPAULDING, sister of above, was born 10 June 1734 at Chelmsford, MA. She married Henry FLETCHER on 12 April 1753. He was the son of Josiah Cornet FLETCHER and Joanna SPAULDING, and was born 4 May 1729 Chelmsford; died 1 June 1764 Chelmsford. Sarah-[5] SPAULDING died _____.

Children of Sarah-[5] SPAULDING and Henry FLETCHER:
SAurname **FLETCHER**   (children all born Chelmsford, MA)

	886. Henry	born 17 Jan 1754; died 3 Feb 1780 White Plains, NY
	887. Josiah	born 27 June 1758; died ca 1832 Dunstable, MA
+	**888. SHEREBIAH**	born 4 Nov 1760; died 15 Apr 1844 Belpre, Washington, OH
		1 married Martha ELLENWOOD 26 Nov 1785
		(she born 31 July 1761; died 5 Sept 1823)
		(she dau/o Joseph ELLENWOOD and Sarah _____)
		2 married Mary Ann BELLOWS 9 Dec 1832
		(she born 4 April 1807- died 29 Apr 1882 OH)
		(she dau/o James BELLOWS and Anna CULVER)
	889. Sarah	born 11 Jan 1763; died _____

339. ZEBULON-[5] SPAULDING, half-brother of above, son of Henry-[4] SPAULDING and his second wife Marah ADAMS, and was born 13 March 1744 at _____,MA. He married Lydia WRIGHT on 12 Feb 1767. She was the daughter of Ebenezer WRIGHT and Deliverance STEVENS, and was born 9 Sept 1745; died _____. Zebulon-[5] SPAULDING died 26 Feb 1816.

Children of Zebulon-[5] SPAULDING and Lydia WRIGHT:
Surname **SPAULDING**

890. Lydia	born 31 Jan 1768 MA.; died _____
891. Zebulon	born 9 April 1769 MA; died 25 Sept 1855 VT; married Dorcas PARKER 5 June 1806
892. Sarah	born ca 1771 Chelmsford, MA; died 31 March 1856 Lunenburg, MA

Children of Zebulon[-5] SPAULDING and Lydia WRIGHT, continued:
Surname **SPAULDING**

893. Dolly	born 12 Oct 1771; died 12 March 1846 NH	
894. Olive	born 6 Jan 1776; died 30 Aug 1778	EOL

340. DANIEL[-5] SPAULDING, brother of above, was born 21 June 1746 at Chelmsford, MA. He married first to Hannah PUTNAM on 8 June 1769. She was the daughter of Jonathan PUTNAM and Hannah MELVIN, and was born 31 Oct 1745, died 17 July 1814. His second marriage was to Mary BUTTERFIELD on 15 May 1777. She was the daughter of _____ BUTTER-FIELD of Pelham, NY and ____, and was born 1 Nov 1746, died ____. Daniel[-5] SPAULDING settled early in Merrimack, NH. He served in the Revolutionary War, was a Surveyor of Highways in Merrimack, and served in several other capacities.

Children of Daniel[-5] SPAULDING and Hannah PUTNAM:
Surname **SPAULDING**   (all children born Merrimack, NH)

895. Daniel	born 19 Dec 1769; died young	EOL
896. Sarah	born ca 1769; died young	EOL
+ **897. JONATHAN**	born 4 July 1771; died ca 1814	
	married Taomis YOUNG ca 1796 (she born ca 1773; died 1815)	
	(she dau/o David YOUNG and Rachel GRANT)	
898. Willard	born 10 Feb 1773; died ____ ; married Deborah DAGGETT 22 March 1795 ME.	
899. Hannah	born 25 July 1776; died ____	

Children of Daniel[-5] SPAULDING and Mary BUTTERFIELD:
Surname **SPAULDING**

900. Benjamin	born 28 Aug 1780; died 13 Dec 1839; married Betsey Mc CLURE
	(she dau/o William Mc CLURE and Rebecca DANFORTH)
	(she born 23 Nov 1791; died 30 Aug 1863)
+ **901. SOLOMON**	born 31 March 1783; died 23 Feb 1864
	married Martha Mc CLURE 7 Sep 1806 (sister of Betsey)
	(she born 13 Apr 1784 Merrimack, NH ; died 21 Aug 1867
902. Henry	born 9 Oct 1785; died ____
+ **903. DANIEL**	born 18 Aug 1787; died ____; married Abigail BROWN 2 Jan 1812
904. Mary	born 24 Jan 1790, bapt 16 Oct 1793; married William Mc KEAN ca ____
905. David	born 24 March 1795, bapr. 5 Nov 1807; died ____
906. Sarah/ Sally	born 18 Feb 1798, bapt 5 Nov 1807; died ____; married Simeon BACHELDER

381. JOHN[-5] LOVEWELL, son of Rachel[-4] LUND (William[-3]; Elizabeth[-2] BOWKER; Edmund[-1]) and John LOVEWELL, was born 16 Nov 2744 at Dunstable, Middlesex, MA. He married his cousin Vodica LOVEWELL ca 1790 at Corinth, VT.. She was the daughter of Colonel Nehemiah LOVEWELL and Rachel FARWELL, and was born 18 Jan 1764; died Jan 1840. John[-5] LOVEWWELL died 18 April 1815 at Corinth, Orange, Vermont.

Children of John[-5] LOVEWELL and Vodica LOVEWELL:
Surname **LOVEWELL**   (children all born Corinth, VT)

907. Hannah		born 3 April 1791; died ca 1832
908. Sophia	(twin)	born 3 May 1792; died ____; married Jacob MILLS 28 Aug 1815
+ **909. HEPHZIBAH**	(twin)	born 3 May 1792; died 23 Sep 1878 Canton, St. Lawrence, NY
		married Laban LASELL/LAZELL 28 Aug 1815 (he born ca 1793; died 1857)
910. John		born 3 Mar 1797; died ca 1823
911. Louisa		born 8 Apr 1800; died ca 1875
912. Nehemiah		born ca 1803; died 1883; married Martha MILLS ca ____
		Children: John[-7] born ____; and Joseph Taplin[-7] LOVEWELL born ca ____

Reference: 30 Dunstable Families; Dunstable VR

402. THOMAS[-5] UNDERWOOD, son of Mary[-4] LUND (William[-3]; Elizabeth[-2] BOWKER; Edmund[-1]) and James UNDERWOOD, was born 8 April 1759 NH. He married Mehitable GAGE on 12 April 1778. She was the daughter of Aaron GAGE and Sarah ____, and was born 9 Sept 1760; died 14 June 1829. Thomas[-5] died 18 Nov 1838 Hillsborough, NH.

Children of Thomas-5 UNDERWOOD and Mehitable GAGE:
Surname **UNDERWOOD**

913. Susannah Lucinda	born 29 July 1779; died ____; married John MUSSEY 15 July 1798	
	(he s/o Reuben Diamond MUSSEY and Sarah SHAW)	
	(he born 19 Sept 1775 Hillsborough, NH; died 18 Dec 1866 Coventry, VT)	
914. Thomas Gage	born 24 Feb 1781 NH; died 3 May 1808 NH	
+ **915. JOSEPH HALL**	born 13 June 1783 NH; died 8 Nov 1867 ME	
	1 married Mary AIKEN 16 Oct 1809; 2 married Jane AIKEN 25 Dec 1822	
916. Parker L.	born 30 April 1785 ; died 26 Jan 1812 Kennebec, ME	
+ **917. SALLY H.**	born 8 July 1787 Hillsborough, NH; died 7 Sept 1860 Hillsborough	
	married Isaac GAGE 19 March 1816	
	(he born 6 Oct 1788 Merrimack, NH; died 13 April 1866 Hillsborough, NH)	
918. John	born 19 Aug 1789; died ____	
919.Peter	born 16 July 1792 Hillsborough; died ____	
	married Ann GAGE 19 June 1817 (she born 12 Mar 1798; died ____)	

Child: Anna Elizabeth-7 UNDERWOOD born 22 Jan 1819; died 12 Oct 1895 RI

920. Charles	born 21 May 1795; died ca 1863	
921. James	born 3 May 1800; died 9 July 1832	
	married Esther KENDALL ca ____ (she born ___, died 24 Oct 1885 NH)	
922. William	born 30 Oct 1806; died ____	

404. CHARLOTTE-5 UNDERWOOD, sister of above, was born 23 Feb 1764 Hillsborough, NH. She married Moses TOWNE on 28 Feb 1784. He was the son of Jabez TOWNE and Lydia PERKINS, and was born 6 Sept 1757; died 24 Jan 1828. Charlotte-5 UNDERWOOD died 31 Jan 1849 at Litchfield, NH.

Children of Charlotte-5 UNDERWOOD and Moses TOWNE:
Surname **TOWNE**   (all children born Londonderry, Rockingham, NH)

923. Jabez	born 22 Dec 1784; died 18 Dec 1849	
	1 married Mary CAMPBELL; 2 married Elizabeth CHASE	
924. James W.	born 22 Sept 1786; died ____; married Elizabeth ANDERSON	
925. Lydia	born 5 Nov 1788; died 12 Aug 1872 Londonderry, NH	
926. Mary Lund	born 23 April 1791; died 10 May 1888; married Robert BOYD 24 Dec 1812	
927. John	born 13 July 1793; died 1873 Londonderry, NH	
928. Moses	born 22 Aug 1795; died ca 1804 Londonderry, NH	EOL
929. Foster	born 3 Nov 1797; died 1 July 1842 Londonderry, NH	
930. Charlotte	born 16 Jan 1800; died ca 1893 Londonderry	
931. Susannah	born 23 May 1802; died ca 1804	EOL
932. Moody Bridges	born 3 Oct 1805; died Jan 1888	

406. JOHN-5 UNDERWOOD, brother of above, was born 17 Feb 1769 Litchfield, NH. He married Elizabeth PARKER on 5 July 1792 at Merrimack, NH. It appears that he and his sister Sally participated in a double wedding ceremony that day. Sally married Mathew PARKER,JR . Mathew PARKER and, presumably, Elizabeth PARKER were brother and sister, and children of Mathew PARKER and Elizabeth JONES. John-5 UNDERWOOD died 5 May 1815 Litchfield.

Children of John-5 UNDERWOOD and Elizabeth PARKER:
Surname **UNDERWOOD**

933. Mathew Parker	born ca 1794; died 28 Apr 1795 Litchfield, NH	EOL
934. Mary Lund	born 3 July 1797; died ____	
935. John	born ca 1802; died ca 1866	

407. RACHEL-5 UNDERWOOD, sister of above , was born 15 Aug 1771. She married first to Royal BLOOD ca ____. He was the son of Francis BLOOD and Elizabeth SPAULDING, and was born 5 Dec 1765 NH; died 1811 NH . Rachel-5 died 11 Sept 1838.

Children of Rachel-5 UNDERWOOD and Royal BLOOD:
Surname **BLOOD**

936. Francis	born 6 June 1793; died 8 Dec 1838 NH; married Margaret PATTERSON 2 May 1822	

Children of Rachel⁻⁵ UNDERWOOD and Royal BLOOD, continued:
Surname **BLOOD**

+	**937. GRAND ROYAL**	born 21 Dec 1794 NH; died 26 Jan 1861 Peru, Indiana
		married Mary Polly STILES 29 Apr 1821 Wilton, NH
		(she dau/o Asa STILES and Ruth ___) (she born 7 June 1800 NH; died 11 Apr 1896 IN
	938. Joseph Underwood	born ca 1801 NH; died 19 Oct 1871 Saginaw, MI
		married Anna MILLS 2 Sept 1822 Deering, NH

411. STEPHEN⁻⁵ AMES, Jr., son of Jane⁻⁴ ROBBINS (Margaret⁻³ LUND; Elizabeth⁻² BOWKER; Edmund⁻¹) and Stephen AMES, Sr. , was born 14 March 1739 at Groton, MA. He married Abigail FOSTER on 26 Sept 1761. She was the daughter of ____ FOSTER and ____, and was born ca 1741; died 1812.

Children of Stephen-⁵ AMES and Abigail FOSTER:
Surname **AMES**

939. Stephen III	born 16 Oct 1762; died 2 Nov 1825
940. Abigail	born 20 Dec 1766 NH; died 13 June 1835 NH; marred Asahel BUELL 1 Jan 1787
941. Peter	born 5 Feb 1778; died _____
942. Abel	born ca 1780; died 7 Feb 1838

419. JONATHAN⁻⁵ WHITNEY, son of Eleanor⁻⁴ ROBBINS (Margaret⁻³ LUND ; Elizabeth-² BOWKER; Edmund-¹) and _____ WHITNEY was born 15 Aug 1745 at Dunstable, Middlesex, MA. He married Abigail HEMMINWAY / HEMING-WAY on 7 May 1772 at Fitzwilliam, Cheshire, NH. She was the daughter of Joseph HEMMINWAY / HEMINGWAY and Mary ADAMS; and was bornn26 Apr 1849; died ca 1844. Jonathan⁻⁵ WHITNEY died ca 1834.

Children of Jonathan⁻⁵ WHITNEY and Abigail HEMMINWAY/HEMINGWAY:
Surname **WHITNEY**   (children all born Fitzwilliam, NH)

943. James.	born 3 Nov 1772; died 1862
944. Joseph	born 17 Jan 1774; died 5 Jan 1860 Wilson, NY
945. Francis	born 17 June 1776; died ____
946. Benjamin	born 6 Aug 1781; died ____; married Amelia MEAD 15 May 1825
947. Jonathan, Jr.	born 6 Apr 1783; died ____
948. Charles	born June 1786; died 31 Dec 1866
949. Calvin	born 25 May 1788; died 24 Feb 1870 Port Hope, Columbia, Wisconsin
950. Abigail	born ca 1792; died 1875

420. ELIZABETH⁻⁵ SHATTUCK, daughter of Elizabeth⁻⁴ ROBBINS (Mary⁻³ LUND; Elizabeth⁻² BOWKER; Edmund⁻¹) and Jonathan ROBBINS, was born ca 1745 Littleton, MA. She married Nathan KINSMAN on 6 Sep 1772 . He was the son of _____ KINSMAN and ___; and was born ____; died ____. Elizabeth⁻⁵ SHATTUCAK died 15 June 1798.

Children of Elizabeth⁻⁵ SHATTUCK and Nathan KINSMAN:
Surname **KINSMAN**   (1ˢᵗ 4 children all born Concord, Merrimack, NH)

951. Stephen	born 14 Aug 1773; died 30 Sep 1866
952. Nathan	born 14 Nov 1777; died 26 Feb 1829 Portland, ME
953. Peter	born 23 Nov 1779; died 24 Dec 1838 Landaff, NH
954. Martha	born 9 Oct 1781; died 1831
955. Timothy	born 17 Aug 1783 Landaff, NH; died 26 Feb 1826 Bedford, MA

421. EZEKIEL SHATTUCK⁻⁵ METCALF, son of Margaret⁻⁴ SHATTUCK (Margaret⁻³ LUND; Elizabeth² BOWKER; Edmund⁻¹; John⁻ᴬ·ᴮ) and Joseph METCALF, was born 13 Oct 1759 at Ashburnham, MA. He married Eunice BROOKS 10 Jan 1782. She was the daughter of Joseph BROOKS and Ruth RUSSELL of Ashburnham, and was born ca ____, died 12 Jan1811. Ezekiel⁻⁵ METCALF died 31 May 1831

Children of Ezekiel⁻⁵ METCALF and Eunice BROOKS:
Surname **METCALF**

956. Eunice	born ca ____; died ____; married Jonas ROBBINS
957. Ezekiel	born ca ____; died ____
958. Joseph	born ca ____; died ____; married Lucy ADAMS of Westminster, MA
959. Jeremiah	born ca 1789; died ____

Children of Ezekiel[-5] METCALF and Eunice BROOKS, continued:
Surname **METCALF**

960. Lucy	born ca ____ ; died ____ ; married Samuel MARBLE	
961. Asa	born 8 June 1793; died 10 Sep 1794	EOL
962. Dinah	born ca ____ ; died ca 1830; married Daniel ADAMS of Gardner, MA	
963. Rhoda	born 4 May 1799; died ____ ; married Phinehas STIMSON	

422. SAMUEL[-5] **METCALF**, brother of above, was born 15 March 1761 Ashburnham , MA. He married first to Phebe FLETCHER on 3 Nov 1786. She was the daughter of Oliver FLETCHER and Olive LAWRENCE, and was born 28 Jan 1764; died 7 April 1802, shortly after the birth of her 8th child. He married second to Betsey KEMP on 10 June 1802. She was the daughter of ____ KEMP and ____, and was born 1776; died ____ . Samuel[-5] METCALF died 25 Dec 1822 Groton, NH.

Children of Samuel[-5] METCALF and Phebe FLETCHER:
Surname **METCALF**   (all born Groton, NH)

964. Samuel	born 3 Aug 1787; died _____	
	married Mary BALL 26 Dec 1815 ; moved to Kirtland, OH	
965. Reuben	born 3 Aug 1789; died ca 1823; never married	EOL
966. Aaron	born 3 Aug 1789; died _____	
	married Sally AMES ca _____ (she born ca 1788 Groton, NH)	
967. Joseph	born 12 Aug 1792; died _____	
	married Lucy AMES ca ____ (sister of Sally, above)	
	(she born ca 1794; died 1843); moved to Kirtland, OH	
968. Levi	born 7 Nov 1794; died 1848; married Betsey WHIPPLE ca _____ ; moved to MI	
969. Moses	born 5 May 1797; died ____	
	married Sally OVERROCKER ca ; moved to Jackson Co., MI	
970. David (1)	born 10 Feb 1799; died March 1799	EOL
971. Nehemiah	born 24 March 1802; died 11 Nov 1842; never married	

Children of Samuel[-5] METCALF and 2nd wife Betsey KEMP:
Surname **METCALF**

972. William	born 31 Dec 1804; died _____ ; a ship carpenter; resided MA
973. Betsey	born 15 June 1808; died _____ ; married _____ KIDDER ca ___
974. Infant	born 29 April 1811; died young
975. Phebe	born 28 May 1815; died _____ ; married Ezra AMES ca _____ ; moved to Minnesota
976. David (2)	born 31 July 1819; died _____ ; moved to CA.

423. MARGARET [-5] **METCALF,** sister of above, was born 19 March 1763 at Groton, MA. She married Reuben TOWNSEND on 5 Nov 1782. He was the son of Joshua TOWNSEND and Mary ____ , and was born 23 Aug 1758 Shrewsbury, MA; died 11 Feb 1837. Margaret[-5] METCALF died 20 March 1847.

Children of Margaret[-5] METCALF and Reuben TOWNSEND:
Surname **TOWNSEND**

	977. Dolly	born 12 Jan 1784; died _____ ; married John WARD, Jr. ca ____
	978. Eunice	born 16 Jan 1786; died _____ ; married Joshua SMITH, Jr. ca ____
+	**979. REUBEN**	born 15 Jan 1788; died 1867 (paralysis)
		1 married Sultina HILL 18 July 1815 (she dau/o Isaac HILL and _____)
		(she born _____ ; died 18 June 1860)
		2 married Matilda BOLTON Shumway ca ____
		(she dau/o Capt. BOLTON of Westminster, MA and _____)
+	**980. JOSHUA**	born 22 Oct 1790; died 20 June 1855; 1 married Betsey KIMBALL 17 July 1823
		(she born 25 Sep 1796; died 15 Nov 1849)
		(she dau/o William KIMBALL and Abigail HAMLET)
		2 married Esther EATON ca 1852 (she born _____ ; died 27 June 1855)
	981. Joseph	born 23 June1793; died _____ ; married Mary SMITH ca _____
	982. Lucy	born 8 July1800; died 20 July 1803 EOL

424. SARAH[-5] **METCALF**, sister of above, was born 7 Sept 1765 at Ashburnham, MA. She married Reuben RICE on 8 June 1784 at Ashburnham. He was the son of Zebulon RICE (Elisha) and Susanna ALLEN (Zebediah), and was born 10 Aug 1757 in Lancaster, Worcester, MA; died 22 March 1837 at Ashburnham. Sarah[-5] METCALF died 16 Feb 1814 Ashburnham.

Children of Sarah[-5] METCALF and Reuben RICE:
Surname **RICE**   (all children born Ashburnham, MA)

983. Un-named infant	born 20 May 1785; died same day
984. Sarah	born 25 Nov 1786; died 17 Jan 1840; married Benjamin GIBBS 19 Dec 1813
985. Reuben	born 20 Jan 1789; died 21 Mar 1858 Fitchburg, MA;
	married Charlotte STEARNS 12 July 1820
986. Anna	born 15 Sep 1794 ; died 24 Feb 1891 Ashburnham
	married Ephraim TAYLOR 3 Nov 1815
987. Eunice	born 19 June 1797; died 26 June 1828 (after childbirth)
	married John CONN 26 Sept 1816 Ashburnham
988. Amos	born 23 June 1799; died 4 April 1841 Cambridge, MA
	married Eunice ROBBINS 14 Sept 1824
989. Zebulon	born 6 May 1801; died 14 Jan 1888 Ashburnham; married Susan WHITING 1 June 1826
990. Lucy	born 20 Dec 1803; died 29 Dec 1885; married Benjamin GIBBS 22 July 1841(2nd wife)
991. Matilda	born ca 1805; died 7 April 1881 Fitchburg, MA
	married John CONN 26 Sept 1828 (widower of her sister Eunice, above)
992. Emma	born 6 Mar 1811; died ca 1843 MA; married Benjamin ADAMS
	(he s/o Jonathan ADAMS and Elizabeth GARY)
	(he born 21 July 1805 Lunenburg, MA; died 880 Worcester, MA)

425. REBECCA-[5] METCALF, sister of above, was born 13 Aug 1769 at Ashburnham, MA. She married William MERRIAM 30 Oct 1788. He was the son of Ignatius MERRIAM / MARION (Isaac) and Rebecca KNIGHT, and was born ca ____, died 11 June 1834. He was a blacksmith. Rebecca[-5] METCALF died 9 Dec 1831.

Children of Rebecca[-5] METCALF and William MERRIAM:
Surname **MERRIAM**

993. William S.	born 14 Feb 1789; died _____		
994. Ezekiel	born 17 May 1792; died ____		
995. Moses B.	born 19 March 1794; died 24 Dec 1876 Northboro, MA		
	married Abigail SIMONDS 14 March 1824	(she born ca ____; died 17 Dec 1870)	
996. Rebecca	born 12 Dec 1796; died 1 April 1819		
997. Margaret	born 26 April 1800; died 10 June 1830		
998. Joel	born 28 Jan 1802; died _____	1000. Asa	born 2 Feb 1810; died ____
999. James	born 16 Oct 1803; died ____	1001. Sarah R.	born 20 Sept 1816; died 15 Jan 1817

429. THANKFUL[5] METCALF, sister of above, was born 18 May 1775 at Ashburnham, MA. She married James M. LAWS on 21 March 1797. He was the son of James LAWS and Anna DANFORTH , and was born 13 Dec 1772; died ___. Thankful [-5] METCALF died 5 Jan 1852 Worcester, MA.

Children of Thankful[-5] METCALF and James LAWS:
Surname **LAWS**

1002. James	born 9 Sep 1797; died 10 May 1803	EOL
+ **1003. DAVID**	born 16 March 1799; died 22 March 1875; married Nancy WILDER 24 April 1828	
	(she dau/o Caleb WILDER and Sarah WHITNEY)	
1004. Joseph	born 3 March 1801; died 10 July 1803	EOL
1005. Hosea	born 13 Aug 1803; died 8 Feb 1887; resided Boston, MA	
1006. Thankful	born 30 May 1805; died Oct 1849/52	
	married Ruel/Rouel/Russell LAWRENCE 30 Jan 1827 Westminster, MA	
1007. Anna Danforth	born 4 July 1807; died 8 April 1885	
	married John ROGERS/RODGERS ca ____; resided Roxbury, MA	
+ **1008. JAMES HERVEY**	born 8 Sept 1809; died 11 March 1891	
	married Julia Augusta HASTINGS 24 March 1836	
	(she dau/o John HASTINGS and Sarah GREEN)(she b. 3 Sept 1811; d. 19 Nov 1885)	
1009. Sylvia	born 3 Sep 1811; died ____; married _____ MORTON ca ____	
1010. Mary	born 2 Nov 1815; died 24 Nov 1815	EOL
1011. Samuel Newell	born 23 July 1817; died 8 June 1896 Gardner, MA	
	married Fidelia WHITNEY ca ____; resided Groton, MA	

Child: Frederick A[-7] LAWS born ca 1850

430. **JOB[-5] SHATTUCK, JR.,** son of Job[-4] SHATTUCK (Margaret-[3] LUND; Edmund-[2,1] BOWKER) and Sarah HARTWELL, was born 10 Dec 1759 Groton, MA. He married Elizabeth BLOOD ca 1781 Groton, MA.. She was the daughter of Simon BLOOD and Anna SHATTUCK, and was born 14 July 1762; died 26 April 1840 Groton. Job-[5] died 4 May 1827.

Children of Job[-5] SHATTUCK, Jr. and Elizabeth BLOOD:
Surname **SHATTUCK**

1012. Job	born 22 Jan 1782 Groton, MA; died 20 Feb 1813	
	married Polly Prescott SAWTELLE 19 April 1803	
1013. Anna	born 31 Mar 1784 ; died _____; married James BENNETT ca _____	
1014. Samson	born 17 Nov 1787; died 11 May 1837 Groton; married Joanna SAWTELLE	
1015. Sarah	born 8 May 1790; died 19 Sep 1840; married Nathaniel LAWRENCE ca ____	
1016. Luther	born 1 Feb 1794; died ____	
	married Polly Prescott SAWTELLE 15 April 1821 (widow of his brother Job)	
1017. George	born 11 April 1796 Groton; died 22 Aug 1797	EOL
1018. Rachel	born 28 Aug 1799; died 3 Jan 1844; married James Mc LAIN	
1019. Eliza	born 11 Dec 1801/ died 12 Jan 1849 Groton; married Isaac WOOD ca _____	
1020. Warren	born 16 Feb 1803 ; died ____; married Olive PROCTOR 29 March 1825	
1021. Merrick	born 7 June 1805; died 12 Sept 1867	
	married Almira SHATTUCK 16 Oct 1828 (she born Sept 1809; died July 1832)	

431. SARAH[-5] SHATTUCK, sister of above, was born 27 Dec 1760 at Groton, MA. She married Benjamin SIMPSON on 28 March 1781 Boston, MA. He was the son of _____ SIMPSON and _____, and was born 2 Jan 1755; died Sept 1839 Winslow, Maine. Sarah-[5] SHATTUCK died 20 Sept 1849 Winslow, Maine.

Children of Sarah[-5] SHATTUCK and Benjamin SIMPSON:
Surname **SIMPSON**

+	**1022. ROXANNA**	born ca 1784 Groton, MA; died 18 Jan 1878 Clinton, Kennebec, Maine
		1 married John WITHERELL 15 May 1799; 2 married Joseph FOSS, Jr. 15 Feb 1819
+	**1023. DANIEL**	born 29 Sept 1790; died 1875; married Harriet STIMPSON 29 Sept 1816
	1024. Tufton	born 20 May 1793; died 1865 Winslow, ME
+	**1025. EZEKIEL**	born ca 1795 Groton, MA; died 1863; married Roxanna SIMPSON 29 Jan 1825
	1026. Sarah	born 9 June 1798 Groton; died ____; married Simon SHATTUCK 5 Aug 1819
	1027. Harriet	born 10 May 1801; died ____; married Noah CHASE 10 May 1821 Boston, MA
	1028. Sophronia	born 4 Sept 1803; died _____; married Jonathan STANLEY Nov 1825

432. EZEKIEL[-5] SHATTUCK, brother of above, was born 12 Sept 1763 Groton, Middlesex, MA. He married Prudence BLOOD on 25 Sept 1788 at Groton. She was the daughter of Levi BLOOD (James BLOOD, Jr) and Sarah COLBURN, and was born 30 Oct 1770 Groton; died 2 Sept 1819 Groton. Ezekiel-[5] SHATTUCK died 1 April 1813 Boston, MA.

Children of Ezekiel[-5] SHATTUCK and Prudence BLOOD:
Surname **SHATTUCK**

1029. Prudence	born 8 May 1789 Groton; died 7 Sept 1802 Groton, MA	EOL
1030. Amelia Hepsibeth	born 6 Sept 1791 Groton; died 20 Aug 1844 Groton, MA	
	married Stephen SHEPLE 9 April 1818	
	(he s/o John SHEPLE and Mary _____)(he born 1 Aug 1791; died 17 Oct 1836 Groton)	
	Child: Stephen-[7] SHATTUCK born ca 1818	
1031. Sarah	born 29 Sept 1794 Groton; died _____	
	1 married Samuel BENNETT ca ____; 2 married Jonas MERRIAM ca _____	
1032. Ezekiel	born 3 June 1796 Groton; died _____	
1033. Rufus	born 16 June 1798 Groton; died ____; married Elizabeth MARTIN ca ____	

+	**1034. HARRIET**	born 2 May 1800 Groton; died 22 Jan 1847 Dunstable, MA
		married William Shattuck BENNETT 2 April 1828; (he born ca 1804; died _____)

433. WILLIAM[-5] SHATTUCK, brother of above, was born 8 March 1765 at Groton, MA. He married Eunice BLOOD before 1789. She was the daughter of Simon BLOOD and ____, and was born 25 Feb 1766; and died 10 Feb 1807 Groton. William-[5] SHATTUCK died 9 Oct 1806 (aged 41-7-1) from a complication / infection of a knee.

Children of William-⁵ SHATTUCK and Eunice BLOOD:
Surname **SHATTUCK**   (all children born at Groton, MA)

1035. William	born 12 Dec 1789; died ____; married Sarah PARKER	
1036. Alexander (1)	born ca 1791; died 14 Aug 1793	EOL
1037. Simon	born 25 Feb 1793; died ____; married Sarah SIMPSON	
1038. Margaret	born 9 Sept 1795; died ____; married George BRIGHAM	
1039. Alexander (2)	born 9 Sept 1797; died ____; married Flora ANDREWS	
1040. Sarah	born 6 Aug 1799; died 7 Nov 1806 (7-3-1)	
1041. Anna	born 3 Oct 1802; died 10 Nov 1823 Dunstable, MA.; married Stephen BATES	

Child: Emily -⁷ BATES born ____

1042. Mary	born 27 Aug 1804; died ____; married Sumner BOYNTON 16 Dec 1830	EOL

434. RACHEL -⁵ SHATTUCK, sister of above, was born 12 July 1767 at Groton, MA. She married Oliver HARTWELL on 27 March 1789. He was the son of Oliver (Ebenezer H) HARTWELL and Ruth FARNSWORTH, and was born 7 Sept 1761 at Groton, MA; died ____. Rachel-⁵ SHATTUCK died on her birthday 12 July 1816 (49). Oliver HARTWELL was still living in 1854 (93) at Stetson, Penobscot, Maine. Note: His mother lived to be over 100 years old.

Children of Rachel-⁵ SHATTUCK and Oliver HARTWELL:
Surname **HARTWELL**

	1043. Sarah	born 8 Nov 1791; died _____; married David LAKIN 6 June 1809	
		(he born 2 Jan 1785; died ____; resided at Stetson, Maine)	

Children: Elizabeth-⁷ born 26 Aug 1810; Sarah-⁷ born 7 July 1812; John-⁷ born 12 Aug 1814; and George Washington -⁷ LAKIN born 22 Oct 1824

+	**1044. RACHEL**	born 28 Feb 1793; died _____; married Jonathan LAWRENCE ca 1812	
		(he born 11 Sept 1788 Groton, MA; died 26 Sept 1842)	
	1045. Asahel	born ____; died young	EOL
	1046. Nancy	born ____; died young	EOL
	1047. Margaret	born ____; died young	EOL
+	**1048. CLARISSA**	born 2 June 1800; died _____; married Samuel WILLIAMS 3 Aug 1827	
	1049. Oliver	born 22 Nov 1822; died 7 March 1833; married Louisa BENNETT	

Children: Jacob-⁷ born ___; Ira-⁷ born ____; James D-⁷ born ____; Belinda-⁷ HARTWELL born ___

+	**1050. MARGARET**	born 9 March 1805; died ____	
		married Rufus WILLIAMS 4 May 1834 (he born 6 Sept 1804 Groton, MA; died ____)	
	1051. Elizabeth	born 15 Jan 1807; died 11 Feb 1850 Groton; married Robert SHAW of Nashua, NH	

Child: Elizabeth-⁷ SHAW born ca 1829; died ca 1847

	1052. Ruth Farnsworth	born ___; died young	EOL

435. CAPTAIN DANIEL-⁵ SHATTUCK, brother of above, was born 11 Feb 1770 at Groton. He was a farmer and tavern owner , and accumulated a "considerable estate". He married first to Abigail " Nabby " SHEPLE on 28 March 1799. She was the daughter of Jonathan SHEPLE and ____, and was born 15 Jan 1776; died 8 April 1814. His second marriage was to her sister Catherine SHEPLE on 7 July 1815. She was born 30 Nov 1795; died 20 May 1825. He married third to Hannah DAVIS White on 30 April 1826. She was the daughter of Josiah DAVIS and _____; and the widow of Joel WHITE ; and was born 23 April 1789; died _____. Captain Daniel-⁵ SHATTUCK died of consumption on 8 April 1831 (age 61).

Children of Captain Daniel-⁵ SHATTUCK and Abigail SHEPLE:
Surname **SHATTUCK**   (all children born Groton, MA)

+	**1053. ROSILLA**	born 10 Nov 1799; died 15 Dec 1845; married James M. COLBURN 17 May 1821	
	1054. Daniel	born 10 Feb 1802; died 28 July 1850; married Maria RICHARDSON 10 May 1827	

Note: He was a prominent man, having commanded a military company; and served as a legislator. He left a large estate to his brothers and sisters as he had no children.

	1055. Charles	born 28 June 1804; died ____; never married	EOL
	1056. James	born 30 Aug 1806; died ____ at sea; never married	EOL
	1057. Francis	born 30 Nov 1808; died ____; resided Groton; never married	EOL
	1058. Otis	born 28 Nov 1810; died ____; resided Groton; never married	EOL
	1059. Abigail	born 9 Sept 1812; died 8 Oct 1818	EOL

Children of Captain Daniel-⁵ SHATTUCK and Catherine SHEPLE:
Surname **SHATTUCK**

	1060. Cortlandt Wilkins	born 23 Sept 1816; died 13 Oct 1847 of consumption	EOL

Note: graduated Dartmouth College, Class of 1840

Children of Captain Daniel[-5] SHATTUCK and Catherine SHEPLE, continued:
Surname **SHATTUCK**

1061. Jerome Marshall	born 12 Sep 1817; died 12 Aug 1845		EOL
1062. Abby Rosalinda	born 7 March 1820; died 4 Dec 1854; married Albert SPAULTER Nov 1838		

Children: Henry Albert Clarence-[7] born ___; Catharine Elizabeth-[7] born ____; and Abby Maria[-7] SPAULTER born _____.

1063. Alvin French	born ____; died young EOL
1064. Catherine (1)	born ____; died young EOL 1065. Catharine (2) born ____; died young

Children of Captain Daniel[-5] SHATTUCK and Hannah DAVIS White:
Surname **SHATTUCK**

1066. Sarah Elizabeth	born 16 Nov 1826; died 9 Sept 1827	EOL
1067. Hannah Maria	born 29 Feb 1828; died ___; married John S P WHEELER I Jan 1849	

Child: Lizzie Lincoln-[7] WHEELER born 2 March 1851

1068. Bigelow (twin)	born 23 Dec 1829; died 20 Jan 1830	EOL
1069. Bancroft (twin)	born 23 Dec 1829; died 28 Jan 1830	EOL

436. NOAH[-5] SHATTUCK, Jr., brother of above, was born 30 Aug 1772 Groton, MA. He married first to Anna SHEPLE on 25 Nov 1798 Groton, MA.. She was the daughter of Jonathan SHEPLE and Anna BLOOD, and was born 22 Apr 1778, died ____. His second marriage was to Elizabeth LAKIN Gragg on 2 May 1800. She was the daughter of William LAKIN and Miriam ____, and the widow of John GRAGG. Noah[-5] SHATTUCK died 28 Sept 1858 at Groton, MA.

Children of Noah[-5] SHATTUCK and Anna SHEPLE:
Surname **SHATTUCK**

+	**1070. NOAH**	born 14 Sept 1799; died 5 Dec 1883; married Prudence WRIGHT ca _____ (she dau/o Artemus WRIGHT and Prudence COREY) (she born 2 Feb 1806; died ___)
+	**1071. WALTER**	born 9 Aug 1801 Groton, MA; died ___; married Roxanna FLETCHER 9 May 1827 (she dau/o David FLETCHER and Mary ALLEN) (she born ca 1804; died _____)
	1072. Anna	born 2 Dec 1803; died 19 Sept 1813 EOL
+	**1073. ANDREW**	born 28 Dec 1805; died 1879; married Cynthia STONE 24 April 1832 Groton, MA (she dau/o Joseph STONE and Rachel GREEN) (she born ca 1804; died April 1869)
	1074 Susanna	born 3 May 1807 Groton

1075. George	born 1 May 1809 Groton	1077. William	born 5 June 1816 Groton
1076. Caroline	born 14 Oct 1811 Groton; died _____	1078. Norman	born 6 Sept 1818 Groton

437. MARGARET[-5] SHATTUCK, sister of above, was born 13 March 1774 at Groton. She married Jonathan BENNETT, Esq. on 11 May 1800. He was the son of James BENNETT and ____, and was born 28 Nov 1775; and died 20 Feb 1829 at Amherst, NH. Margaret-[5] SHATTUCK died 13 March 1774 at Amherst, NH.

Children of Margaret[-5] SHATTUCK and Jonathan BENNETT:
Surname **BENNETT**

1079. Sarah	born 13 Oct 1800; died 6 April 1846; married Dr. Hezekiah ELDRIDGE ca 1826

Children: Lucius Owen-[7] born Apr 1827; Erastus Darwin-[7] born Dec 1829; and Frederick Augustus-[7] ELDRIDGE born Nov 1836.

1080. Jonathan	born 1 Sept 1802; died ____; married Mary TAYLOR Dec 1831

Child: John Owen-[7] BENNETT born Nov 1838

1081. William Shattuck	born 28 Sept 1804; died ____; married his 1st cousin Harriet-[6] SHATTUCK 2 Apr 1828 (she dau/o Ezekiel[-5] SHATTUCK and Prudence BLOOD) (she born 2 May 1800; died Feb 1847 Dunstable, MA)

Children: Harriet Josephine -[7] born Mar 1829; Rufus Shattuck -[7] born Feb 1831, died Aug 1832; William-[7] born Jan 1834; and George-[7] BENNETT born Nov 1837

+	**1082. MARGARET**	born 2 Sept 1806; died ____; married Jefferson TAYLOR Nov 1825
+	**1083. LOUISA**	born 13 July 1808; died ____; married Joel Fletcher OSGOOD June 1830
	1084. James	born 2 Sep 1811; died ____; married Rebecca SWALLOW May 1834

Child: Rebecca E-[7] BENNETT born Feb 1835

+	**1085. WILDER**	born 17 Apr 1813; died ____; married Mary Ann DAVIS Nov 1840
+	**1086. ALDEN BRADFORD**	born 18 Apr 1816; died ____; married Elizabeth STEBBINS Nov 1836

438. ANNA/ NANCY⁻⁵ SHATTUCK, sister of above, was born 6 Feb 1779 at Groton. She married Thomas BENETT on 25 Nov 1798. He was the son of Stephen BENNETT and _____, and was born ____, died ____. They settled in Brookline, NH and Anna⁻⁵ SHATTUCK died there on 7 Feb 1843.

Children of Anna-⁵ SHATTUCK and Thomas BENNETT:
Surname **BENNETT**

+	**1087. ASHER**	born 2 Apr 1799; died 13 Nov 1881 NH; married Sally/Sarah H. HALL ca 1825
	1088. Nancy	born 22 June 1801; died ____
	1089. Almira	born 11 Jan 1804; died ____; married Leonard FRENCH ca 1828
	1090. Philiahasse	born 16 Aug 1806; died ____; married John BURGE 12 Apr 1832
+	**1091. BERI**	born 19 Sep 1808; died ____; married Margaret RUSSELL 12 June 1828
	1092. Thirza	born 14 Jan 1811; died ____; married Calvin R. SHED 23 June 1835
	1093. Thomas	born 9 Jan 1814; died 10 Aug 1818 EOL
+	**1094. RODOLPHUS D.**	born Feb 1817 NH; died 19 Feb 1885; married Mary WOODWARD 14 May 1840
+	**1095. ROSILLA**	born 10 Feb 1819; died ____; married Alpheus MELENDY 1/8 March 1838
	1096. Mary C.	born 27 Oct 1820; died 19 Jan 1847; married Jeremiah BALDWIN 6 Apr 1843

440. ELIZABETH / BETSEY⁻⁵ BOWKER, daughter of Josiah⁻⁴ BOWKER (Edmund⁻³; John-²; Edmund-¹) and Mary CROMPTON, was born 22 Oct 1752 Hopkinton, MA. She married John WATKINS on 3 Dec 1772. He was the son of _____ WATKINS and ____, and was born ____; died _____. Elizabeth⁻⁵ died ca 1816 NY

Children of Elizabeth⁻⁵ BOWKER and John WATKINS:
Surname **WATKINS**

	1097. Arenith	born _____; died ____
	1098. Betsey (1)	born ____; died ____
	1099. John	born____; died _____
	1100. Polly	born ____; died ____; married Oliver WHITMORE 17 Jan 177 Peru, MA
	1101. Betsey (2)	born 11 Nov 1781; died 1864; married Elijah GILBERT ca ____
		(he s/o Elijah GILBERT and Mary DUNBAR)
		(he born ca 1780; died 1843)
	1102. Artemus	born 25 Aug 1786; died 20 May 1865; married Phoebe GILBERT 11 Sep 1808
		(she born ___; died 3 May 1840; sister of Elijah, Jr. above)
	1103. Aaron	born 25 Dec 1788

444. DEACON EDMUND⁻⁵ BOWKER, son of Micah⁻⁴ BOWKER (Edmund⁻³; John-²; Edmund⁻¹) and Persis MAYNARD, was born 9 Sep 1757 at Hopkinton, MA. He married Hannah STEARNS on 27 Aug 1778. She was the daughter of Jonathan STEARNS and Beulah ____; and was born ____; died ____. Deacon Edmund-⁵ BOWKER died 20 Jan 1841 Milford, Worcester, MA. He was a veteran of the Revolutionary War, and in his later years was a pensioner.

Children of Edmund⁻⁵ BOWKER and Hannah STEARNS:
Surname **BOWKER**

+	**1104. LOVICE**	born 22 March 1779; died 7 March 1824
		married Alexander CHENEY 2 Aug 1801
		(he s/o Wales CHENEY and _____) (he born 8 Oct 1780; died ____)
+	**1105. JONATHAN**	born 6 July 1781; died ____; married Penelope DEWING ca ____
		(she dau/o John DEWING and Patience SUMNER)
	1106. Lydia	born 24 Sep 1788; died ____
		married David STEARNS , 2ⁿᵈ 23 June 1811 (a cousin)
	1107. Polly	born 7 Sep 1791; died ____
		married Samuel Mc FARLAND 12 April 1812 Hopkinton, MA
+	**1108. IRA**	born 26 Aug 1793; died 25 Aug 1830
		married Julia EVERETT 27 Nov 1817 Milford, MA
		(she born ___; bpt. 11 Sep 1796; died ____
		(she dau/o Capt. Abel EVERETT and Mary SMITH)

447. SENATOR ASA⁻⁵ BOWKER, son of Samuel⁻⁴ BOWKER (Edmund⁻³,²,¹) and his second wife Lydia WHITNEY, was born 12 Nov 1755 at Hopkinton, MA. He married Hannah HARWOOD on 8 Dec 1777. She was the daughter of James HARWOOD and Martha ____; and was born31 July 1759 Leicester, MA; died 3 Dec 1842 at Winchendon, MA. Asa-⁵ BOWKER died 5 Oct 1825. He was a veteran of the Revolutionary War and is buried at the New Boston Cemetery, Winchendon, MA.

Children of Asa-⁵ BOWKER and Hannah HARWOOD:
Surname **BOWKER**   (all children born at Winchendon, Worcester, MA)

+	**1109. LYDIA**	born 6 May 1780; died ____; 1 married Thomas WYMAN 25 Sep 1798
		2 married Stephen R. SMITH Apr 1819
	1110. Daniel	born 14 Mar 1782; died 1 June 1863 Winchendon, MA
		married Persis ALLEN 30 Nov 1809 Winchendon, MA
		Children: Benjamin-⁷ born ca 1810, died 1833; and Elizabeth-⁷ BOWKER born ca 1818, died 1866
+	**1111. WILLIAM**	born 15 July 1784; died 16 Oct 1847; married Sally HARWOOD
+	**1112. LUTHER**	born 16 Jan 1787; died 18 Jan 1826; married Betsey WALKER 5 Mar 1812
		(she dau/o Samuel WALKER and Elizabeth WYMAN)
	1113. Nancy	born 16 May 1789; died ____
+	**1114. ASA, JR.**	born 13 June 1792; died 20 Dec 1867 Winchendon, MA
		1 married Joanna WALKER 3 Apr 1817
		2 married Abigail CHUBB int pub 5 June 1824
		3 married Louise LATHE Day 7 June 1854
+	**1115. HANNAH**	born 6 Aug 1794; died ____; married Silas WYMAN 5 Mar 1812
		(he s/o Thomas WYMAN and Elizabeth REED)
	1116. Persis	born 3 July 1800; died ____

450. ABIATHER-⁵ **BOWKER,** brother of above, was born 25 Feb 1763 at Hopkinton, MA. He married Polly FUZZE/ FEZZE on 12 Feb 1789 at Hopkinton. She was the daughter of ____ FUZZE/FEZZE and ____, and was born ____; died ____. Abiather-⁵ BOWKER died 5 Jan 1838.

Children of Abiather-⁵ BOWKER and Polly FUZZE:
Surname **BOWKER**

	1117. Lemuel	born 23 July 1789; died 1791	EOL
	1118. Ede	born 22 Feb 1791; died ___	
+	**1119. ABIATHER, Jr.**	born 4 Oct 1793; died 13 June 1848; married Mary GOULD 28 Nov 1816	
		(she born 2 Feb 1796 Greenfield, NH; died 25 June 1848 Hopkinton, MA)	
+	**1120. HARRIET**	born 2 July 1799; died ____; married Lowell FROST 10 Apr 1825	
		(he s/o John FROST and Mary BACON) (he born 6 Jan 1798 Sherborn, MA)	
	1121. John Starkweather	born 14 Apr 1808; died 19 Dec 1810	EOL

451. RUTH-⁵ **BOWKER,** sister of above, was born 9 Feb 1765 at Hopkinton, MA. She married first to Daniel WHEATON on 30 Aug 1787. He was the son of _____ WHEATON and ____, and was born____, died ____. She married second to Hezekiah JOHNSON on 5 Nov 1789 at Chester, Windsor, VT. He was the son of Asahel JOHNSON and Phebe ____, and was born 1769 Chester, VT; died 1810. Ruth-⁵ BOWKER died 23 April 1812 at Chester, VT.

Children of Ruth-⁵ BOWKER and her 2ndd husband Hezekiah JOHNSON:
Surname **JOHNSON**   (children born Chester, Windsor, VT)

1122. Susan/ Sukey	born 17 Apr 1790; died July 1860 VT	
1123. Ira (1)	born 10 Mar 1792; died 6 July 1794	EOL
1124. Hezekiah, Jr.	born 15 May 1794; died 13 Sep 1874; married Susannah DODGE ca ____	
1125. Phebe	born 28 June 1796; died ____	
1126. Sarah	born 4 Sep 1798; died _____	
1127. Ira (2)	born 3 Sep 1800; died 26 Mar 1813	EOL
1128. Jane	born 27 Nov 1804; died 19 June 1808	EOL
1129. Moranda	born 20 Aug 1807; died 16 Oct 1818	EOL
1130. Mary H.	born 5 Apr 1810; died ____	

456. JOHN-⁵ **BOWKER,** son of Uriah-⁴ BOWKER (Edmund-³; John-²; Edmund-¹) and _____, was born 19 Nov 1761 Hopkinton, MA. He married Esther WEDGE 7 Mar 1782. She was the daughter of Jepthah WEDGE and Esther MARSHALL; and was born 1 Jan 1761 Worcester, MA; died 5 Oct 1842 Hopkinton, MA . John-⁵ BOWKER died ____.

Children of John-[5] BOWKER and Esther WEDGE:
Surname **BOWKER**

1131. Meletiah	born 31 Mar 1782; Hopkinton, MA; died _____
	married Daniel M. UNDERWOOD 18 May 1818
	Children: John Bowker-[7] UNDERWOOD born ca 1818; and James-[7] UNDERWOOD born ca 1821
1132. James	born ____; died ____; married Izanna EAMES of Milford, MA on 16 Aug 1815
	(she dau/o Phinehas EAMES and Izanna JONES)
1133. Ralph	born 8 Apr 1784 Hopkinton; died 17 Aug 1811 (drowned in the Charles River)
	married Mitta HAYWARD 4 Oct 1807 Milford, Worcester, MA
	(she dau/o Adam HAYWARD and Judith _____)
1134. Eli	born 11 Nov 1786 Hopkinton; died ____
+ **1135. ETHAN**	born 6 Dec 1789; died 24 Apr 1817; married Alpha WHEELOCK 8 Nov 1814
	(she dau/o Obadiah WHEELOCK and Lydia THURBER)
	(she born 28 Nov 1798 Milford, MA; died 15 Nov 1875)
+ **1136. CHARLOTTE**	born ca 1794 Hopkinton; died 20 Nov 1877 Charlton, MA
	married Ephraim WHEELOCK 21 Sep 1816
	(he s/o Paul WHEELOCK, Jr. and Beulah JOHNSON)
	(he born 4 Nov 1791 Charlton, MA; died 2 Oct 1873 Spencer, MA)
1137. Nahum	born ca 1798 Hopkinton; died 14 Mar 1855 Hopkinton, MA
	1 married Sally/Sarah MORSE 5 May 1817
	(she born 9 Apr 1797; died 17 June 1848)(she dau/o Elisha MORSE and Betsey ____)

Child: Charlotte-[7] BOWKER born 23 Mar 1818 Hopkinton; died 16 May 1848 (typhoid fever); married Daniel WHEELOCK

2 married Eliza BROAD Parkhurst 3 May 1849
(she born 24 Feb 1803; died 18 May 1862)
(she dau/o Joseph BROAD and Sibbel ___) (wid/o Ephraim PARKHURST)

461. ELIJAH-[5] **BOWKER,** brother of above, was born ca 1733 at Hopkinton, MA. He married first to Patience GAGE 8 Jan 1799. She was the daughter of Moses GAGE, Jr. and Mary BOYNTON, and was born 1 Jan 1775 Hopkinton; died 9 Oct 1811. He married second to Polly BRIGHAM 23 Sep 1812 Hopkinton. She was the daughter of _____ BRIGHAM and ____; and was born 1774; died 12 Oct 1819. Elijah-[5] BOWKER carried the US Mail from Boston to Hartford in saddle-bags, for several years, before the introduction of the stage coach. Elijah-[5] BOWKER died suddenly after a fall from a high beam in his barn on 19 May 1827 (age 54).

Children of Elijah-[5] BOWKER and Patience GAGE:
Surname **BOWKER**   (children all born Hopkinton, MA)

+ **1138. URIAH**	born 3 March 1800; died _____
	married Lois EAMES 24 Dec 1821 (she from Farmington, MA)
	(she dau/o Moses EAMES and Lois ADAMS)
+ **1139. MARY GAGE**	born 30 Nov 1801; died ____; married Dexter L. MAYBRY 8 June 1819
	(he born 22 Apr 1799; died ____)
+ **1140. ELIZA**	born 21 Oct 1803; died ____; married Wetherby CHAMBERLAIN Nov 1830
1141. Abigail Hunting	born 19 June 1805; died 29 Sep 1876 Natick, MA
	married Capt. HILL of Sherborn ca _____ (3 ch)
1142. Lovett Hayden	born 28 June 1807; died 20 Jan 1876 (no issue) EOL
	married Maria SKINNER of Foxboro, MA ca ____
	(she dau/o William SKINNER and Lois _____)
	(she born 20 July 1809; died ____)

Children of Elijah-[5] BOWKER and Polly BRIGHAM:
Surname **BOWKER**

1143. SARAH (twin)	born 19 Oct 1813; died 28 Oct 1870 Hopkinton, MA
	married William Adams. PHIPPS of Hayden Row 22 Oct 1832 Hopkonton, MA
	(he s/o Moses PHIPPS and Hannah ADAMS)
	(he born 19 Sep 1809; died 13 Nov 1890)
+ **1144. PATIENCE** (twin)	born 19 Oct 1813; died ____; married Josiah HAVEN of Hopkinton 21 Nov 1832

462. ELIZABETH-[5] **WILSON,** daughter of Elizabeth-[4] BOWKER (Edmund-[3,2,1]) and James WILSON, was born ca 1762, MA. She married Peter CLARK ca 1784. He was the son of ____ CLARK and ____, and was born 8 June 1762 MA; died ____. Elizabeth-[5] WILSON died 2 Aug 1855.

Children of Elizabeth-5 WILSON and Peter CLARK:
Surname **CLARK**

1145. Henry	born 19 July 1785; died ____	
1146. Elizabeth	born 1 Sep 1787; died ____	
1147. Gilbert	born 10 June 1790; died ____	
1148. George	born 20 Aug 1798; died ____	
1149. James Wilson	born 13 April 1802; died ____	

+   **1150. WILLIAM HENRY** born 4 Aug 1805; died 25 Jan 1887; married Frances MARTIN 27 Apr 1828

465. ABIGAIL-5 BARRETT, daughter of Abigail-4 BOWKER (Edmund-3,2,1) and Thornton BARRETT, was born 25 May 1766 at Hopkinton, MA. She married Josiah HOSMER, Jr. on 27 Jan 1783 (as his second wife). He was the son of Josiah HOSMER (Stephen) and Hannah WESSON; and was born 28 Nov 1740; died 24 Dec 1833 Templeton, MA. Abigail-5 BOWKER died 30 Sep 1829. Note: Josiah HOSMER, Jr. was married first to Eunice WHITCOMB on 28 Apr 1766. She was born ca 1747; died 1779.

Children of Abigail-5 BARRETT and Josiah HOSMER, Jr.
Surname **HOSMER**   (children all born Templeton, Worcester, MA)

1151. Sally	born 11 Feb 1784; died 13 Aug 1863 Waterford, Caledonia, VT
1152. Josiah, III	born 8 April 1786; died 14 Sep 1876 Burlington, VT
+ **1153. LUTHER**	born 31 Oct 1788; died 22 Nov 1875 Springfield, MA
	married Abiah BLISS 4 July 1812
	(she dau/o Gad BLISS and Abiah COLTON)
	(she born 18 Aug 1794; died 4 Feb 1883 Springfield, Hampden, MA)
1154. David Leonard	born 23 Feb 1793; died 7 June 1873 Bangor, Maine
1155. Abigail	born 10 Feb 1799; died May 1842 Whitefield, Coos, NH
1156. Jefferson	born 23 Mar 1801; died 7 Mar 1875 Littleton, Grafton, NH
1157. Julia Maria	born 6 June 1810; died 31 Jan 1881 Brooklyn, NY

469. THORNTON-5 BARRETT II, brother of above, was born 27 Mar 1777 at Winchendon, Worcester, MA. He married first to Betsey REYNOLDS on 1 Jan 1800 at Bethlehem, Grafton, NH. She was the daughter of _____ REYNOLDS and ____; and was born 15 Oct 1773; died 31 Oct 1822 at Bethlehem, NH. He married second to Abigail BEAN on 30 Jan 1823 at Littleton, Grafton, NH. She was the daughter of ____ BEAN and ____; and was born ca 1797; died ca 1859. Thornton-5 BARRETT died 24 March 1862 at Smethport, McKean, PA.

Children of Thornton-5 BARRETT, II and Betsey REYNOLDS:
Surname **BARRETT**

1158. Nancy	born 1 June 1801; died ____ PA
	1 married John Lathrop BEAN; 2 married M. CLIFFORD 31 Jan 1827
1159. Louisa	born ca 1804; died 24 Jan 1890; married Jedediah FARMER ca ____
	(he born 23 Dec 1798; died 15 Aug 1871 Littleton, NH)
+ **1160. THORNTON, III**	born 30 Apr 1807 NH; died 7 Jan 1882 Winona, NH
	married Rebecca Stanton BREWER 24 Apr 1834
1161. Gardner	born ca 1808; died 1886
1162. Clifford B.	born 6 May 1821; died ____; 1870 resided MI

Children of Thornton-5 BARRETT, II and Abigail BEAN:
Surname **BARRETT**

1163. Sarah Abigail	born ca 1825 NH; died ____; married Darius Vernon SHEPARD ca ____
1164. Henry	born ca 1827; died ____
	1 married Betsey HIGGINS ca ___; 2 married Harriet MARBLE ca ____
1165. Laura M.	born 18 Dec 1829; died 23 Apr 1890; married Jason W. BLANCHARD ca ____
1166. George William	born 27 May 1834; died 10 Oct 1880
1167. West B.	born 19 July 1835 NH ; died 29 Jan 1901 Seward, Alaska
	married Anna D. CHASE ca ____
	Children: Arthur West-7 born ca 1870 WI ; Grace-7 born ca 1877; and Ellen C-7 BARRETT born 1879
1168. Adelia	born ca 1839 PA; died ____

471. JOSEPH-5 BARRETT, brother of above, was born 1 July 1783 at Bethlehem, NH. He married Mary KENNEY ca ____. She was the daughter of William KENNEY and _____, and was born ____; died ____. Joseph-5 BARRETT died ca 1858.

Children of Joseph[-5] BARRETT and Mary KENNEY:
Surname **BARRETT**

1169. Thornton	born 7 Mar 1805; died 24 Feb 1812	EOL
1170. Laurecty	born 10 Jan 1807; died 24 Sep 1879; married Caleb BAKER of Bethlehem ca ____	
	(he born ____; died 12 Sep 1870)	
1171. Lorinda	born 9 Aug 1812; died ____; married Allen THOMPSON of Bethlehem ca ____	
1172. Sally Oaks	born 18 Sept 1815; died ____; married Caleb BOWLES ca ____	
1173. Permelia W.	born 16 May 1819; died 17 Aug 1825	EOL
+ **1174. JAMES JOHNSON**	born 6 Feb 1823; died 24 Aug 1885; married Lydia SMITH 3 Jan 1845	
	(she dau/o Isaac SMITH and _____) (she born 8 Aug 1821 ; died ___)	

474. ABIGAIL[-5] BRIGHAM, daughter of John[-4] BRIGHAM (Elizabeth[-3] BOWKER; Edmnd[-2,1]; John[-A,B]) and Abigail JOHNSON, was born 5 Dec 1751 at Sudbury, Middlesex, MA. She married Jeremiah SCRIPTURE ca 1765/66. He was the son of Simeon SCRIPTURE and Anna SLAFTER, and was born 8 Aug 1746 Coventry, Tolland, CT; died 15 Oct 1810, Alford, MA. Abigail[-5] BRIGHAM died 24 Nov 1806 Alford, Berkshire, MA.

Children of Abigail[-5] BRIGHAM and Jeremiah SCRIPTURE:
Surname **SCRIPTURE**

+ **1175. OLIVE**	born ca 1767 Alford, MA; died 12 April 1845 Ontario, Canada	
	(he born 12 Mar 1763 Rutland, VT; died _____)	
	married James KEELER 11 July 1787 Rutland, VT	
+ **1176. SARAH**	born ca 1769 Alford, MA; died 18 Aug 1829 W. Stockbridge, MA	
	married Abisha LEWIS 17 Dec 1791 W. Stockbridge	
	(he born 15 May 1766 Farmington, CT; died 9 July 1852 Stockbridge	
1177. Clarissa	born ca 1769 Alford, MA; died _____; married John FINN/FENN	
+ **1178. LOIS**	born 28 June 1771 Tyringham, MA; died ____	
	married Jonathan TOWNSEND 18 May 1791 Berkshire County, MA	
+ **1179. JEREMIAH**	born 14 July 1773 Tyringham, MA; died 1836; married Submit CURTIS ca 1804 CAN.	
	Children: Fanny Minerva[-7] born 17 Feb 1800; Eliphalet Spencer[-7] born 12 Dec 1801; and Clarissa[-7] born 14 June 1804	
1180. Simeon Liberty	born Oct 1775 Tyringham, MA; died after 1852	
1181. John	born 2 Nov 1777 Tyringham, MA; died 5 Dec 1851 Alford, MA	

476. JOHN[-5] BRIGHAM, son of Lt. Abijah[-4] BRIGHAM (Elizabeth[-3] BOWKER; Edmund[-2,1]) and Eunice WILLIS, was born 19 May 1762 Sudbury, Middlesex, MA. He married Ann Eunice MOORE on 20 May 1787 at Sudbury. She was the daughter of Israel MOORE and Susanna WOODWARD, and was born 10 April 1768 Sudbury, died 20 May 1862. John[-5] BRIGHAM died ____.

Children of John[-5] BRIGHAM and Eunice MOORE:
Surname **BRIGHAM**

1182. Roxey	born 7 Jan 1788; died _____; married Luke ROBINSON ca _____ (from Rutland , MA)	
	(he born ca 1781; died 7 Sept 1870 (aged 89)	
1183. Oreb	born 25 July 1789 Sudbury; died 10 Dec 1868 Sudbury	
+ **1184. ABIJAH**	born 17 March 1791 Sudbury, died 7 Feb 1892	
	married Melissa STRATTON on 19 Oct 1817 Rutland, Worcester, MA	
	(she born 11 Oct 1798 Rutland, died _____)	
1185. Susanna Woodward	born 15 May 1793; died 5 Oct 1879	
+ **1186. JOHN**	born 22 Mar 1795; died 24 May 1874 Watertown, MA	
	1 married Mary LEVERITT of Burke Co., GA	
	2 married Mary CRAFTS Brigham 8 July 1844 Watertown, MA (wid/o brother Wm.)	
	(she dau/o Joseph CRAFTS and Eunice DOWSE)	
	(she born 7 June 1813 Cambridge, MA; died 25 Feb 1847 Watertown, MA)	
1187. Sewall	born 2 Mar 1797; died 12 May 1869 Watertown, MA; a blacksmith	
1188. Horatio	born 16 Sep 1801; died 20 Sep 1835 GA	
1189. James Moore	born 4 Jan 1807; died 8 Jan 1855	
+ **1190. WILLIAM**	born 11 Aug 1810; died 23 Apr 1843 MA; 1 married Adeline COLE 17 April 1834	
	(she dau/o Thaddeus COLE and ____ of Waterown, MA)(she born ca 1813; died 1836)	
	2 married Mary CRAFTS 16 Mar 1837	
	(she dau/o Joseph CRAFTS and Eunice DOWSE) (she married 2nd to his brother John)	

477. JOSEPH[5] **BRIGHAM,** brother of above, was born 26 Sep 1764 at Sudbury, MA. He married Rebecca HAYNES on 5 March 1795 at Sudbury. She was the daughter of Charles HAYNES and Elizabeth WINN, and was born 9 Jan 1770; died 12 Jan 1853 at Sudbury. Joseph[5] BRIGHAM died 17 Jan 1842 at Sudbury, MA.

Children of Joseph[5] BRIGHAM and Rebecca HAYNES:
Surname **BRIGHAM**

+	**1191. NANCY**	born 1 March 1796 Sudbury, MA; died 14 June 1878 Russellville, Alabama
		1 married Daniel CROCKER ca _____ (he born ca ____, died 1829)
		2 married Benjamin HARRIS 14 July 1833 at Russellville, Alabama
		(he born 12 Jan 1786 Cranger Co., AL; died 28 June 1858 Russellville)
+	**1192. LEWIS**	born 27 Oct 1797 Sudbury; died 8 Sep 1875 Sudbury , MA
		married Almira -[6] BOWKER 27 May 1838 (she born 12 Aug 1810; #1265)
		(she dau/o Joseph-[5] BOWKER (Daniel-[4]; John-[3]; Edmund-[2,1]) and Patty PROCTOR)
+	**1193. EUNICE**	born 19 Dec 1798 Sudbury; died 13 March 1856 Springfield, MA
		married Rev. Addison PARKER 16 Oct 1834 (as his 2nd wife)
	1194. Rev. Alanson	born 11 Oct 1802 Sudbury; died 24 Sep 1833 PA
	1195. Esther H.	born 30 Mar 1805 Sudbury; died ____
+	**1196. REBECCA**	born 28 Aug 1807 Sudbury, MA ; died 1856
		married Lawrence THOMPSON 9 Jan 1834 (a wealthy planter of Prides Station, AL
+	**1197. CHARLES**	born 16 July 1811 Sudbury; died _____
		married Eunice Hagar GARFIELD ca _____ (she dau/o Francis GARFIELD and ____)

483. JOHN[5] **JOYNER,** son of Hannah-[4] BOWKER (John-[3]; Edmund-[2,1]; John-[A,B]) and William JOYNER, was born 20 Jan 1746 at Sudbury, Middlesex County, MA. He married Jerusha Sarah BIXBY on 10 July 1770 at Winchendon, Worcester, MA. She was the daughter of Nathaniel BIXBY and Jerusha HOUGHTON, and was born ca 1747 __; died ____. John[5] JOYNER died ca 1790 at Windham, VT.

Children of John[5] JOYNER and Jerusha BIXBY:
Surname **JOYNER**

+	**1198. NAHUM NATHAN**	born 19 May 1771 Winchendon, MA; died _____
		married Hulda SPENCER ca 1791 Rumney, Grafton, NH
+	**1199. ANNA EMMA**	born ca 1774 MA; died ____; married David CANEDY ca 1791 Halifax, VT
+	**1200. JOHN**	born ca 1780 MA; died _____; married Bathsheba CANEDY ca _____
+	**1201. JAMES (twin)**	born 1 Jan 1787 Lynn, Essex, MA; died ca 1883 Harford, Cortland, NY
		1 married Mary BROWN ca _____; 2 married Maria NESBITT ca _____
	1202. Samuel (twin)	born 1 Jan 1787 Lynn, MA; died 20 Dec 1867 Lapeer, Cortland, NY
		married Hannah _____ ca 1807 Cortland, NY
		(she born 1 Feb 1877; died 29 Jan 1850; buried Virgil, Cortland, NY)

484. SARAH[5] **JOYNER,** sister of above, was born 3 March 1749 at Sudbury, Middlesex, MA. She married Caleb FLETCHER on 14 Sept 1775 at Templeton, Worcester, MA. He was the son of William FLETCHER, Jr. and Elizabeth REMINGTON, and was born 7 Nov 1735 MA; died 21 May 1807 at Templeton, MA. Sarah[5] JOYNER died ____.

Children of Sarah[5] JOYNER and Caleb FLETCHER:
Surname **FLETCHER**

	1203. William	born ca 1776-77; died _____
	1204. Sally	born 8 Aug 1778; died _____
	1205. Francis	born 19 May 1783; died ____
+	**1206. CALEB**	born 5 Apr 1785 Chelmsford, MA; died _____
	REMINGTON	married Eliza STOWELL ca ____
	1207. Oliver	born 13 Oct 1787 MA; died ___; married Laura HENSHAW 26 Feb 1822 Leicester, MA
		(she dau/o David HENSHAW and Mary S. ___)
		(she born 3 Mar 1795 ENG; died 23 Feb 1875 Somerville, MA)
		Child: Catherine S-[7] FLETCHER born ca 1825; married Henry W. ALLEN 29 Sep 1847

488. FRANCIS[5] **JOYNER,** brother of above, was born ca 1753 at Sudbury, Middlesex, MA. He married Lydia LESTER ca 1780 at ____ VT. She was the daughter of Benjamin LESTER and Hannah ____, and was born ca 1759 CT; died ca 1811 VT. Francis[5] JOYNER died 9 Jan 1811 at Bolton, Chittenden, VT.

Children of Francis-[5] JOYNER and Lydia LESTER:
Surname **JOYNER**

	1208. Fanny	born 12 Dec 1784 VT; died ca 1811 VT.
+	**1209. BENJAMIN**	born 4 June 1786 Bradford, Orange,VT; died 8 June 1846 Ontario Co., NY
	LESTER	1 married Caroline ALGER ca 1810
		(she born 24 May 1786 NY; died 22 Aug 1828 NY)
		2 married Hepzibah SUTLIEFF ca ____
		(she dau/o ____ SUTLIEFF and _____) (she born ca 1801; died 1876)
	1210. John	born 14 Dec 1787 VT; died 16 Nov 1811 VT
	1211. Francis	born 18 Aug 1790 VT; died 1791 EOL
	1212. Hannah	born 10 Nov 1793 VT; died 1829 Chittenango, Madison, NY
	1213. Nancy (twin)	born 19 Nov 1797 VT; died 1884 VT; married David RIDDLE ca _____
		(he s/o Robert RIDDLE; he born 28 Jan 1794; died 27 Dec 1881 NY)
	1214. William (twin)	born 19 Nov 1797 VT; died 1797 VT EOL
	1215. Polly	born 22 Oct 1799 VT; died 1893
+	**1216. WILLIAM (2)**	married Polly RANDALL 20 June 1825 Lorraine, NY(she born ca 1799; died ca 1868)

489. MARY-[5] JOYNER, sister of above, was born 5 April 1760 at Bolton, Chittenden, VT. She married David JOHNSON on 14 Nov 1783 at Bolton. He was the son of Zebadiah JOHNSON and Esther RICHARDSON, and was born 16 Feb 1756 MA; died 22 Feb 1839, NY. Mary-[5] JOYNER died 5 Jan 1844 at Saratoga County, NY.

Child of Mary-[5] JOYNER and David JOHNSON:
Surname **JOHNSON**

	1217. Sally	born 3 Sept 1791 VT; died 29 Dec 1844 NY
		married Abner WAITE ca _____; (he born ca 1784; died ca 1850)
		Child: Abner Day-[7] WAITE born ca 1826; died ca 1903

491. NOAH-[5] BOWKER, son of Noah-[4] BOWKER (John-[3]; Edmund-[2,1]) and Hepzibah WILLARD , was born ca Jan 1754 at Somers, Tolland, CT. He married Catherine COPPS. She was born ca _____; died ____. Noah-[5] BOWKER died Apr 1794 at West Springfield, MA

Child of Noah-[5] BOWKER and Catherine COPPS:
Surname **BOWKER**

+	**1218. WILLARD**	born 15 July 1784 West Springfield, MA; died 27 June 1852 NY
		married Sally GREEN 11 Nov 1805 W. Springfield, 8MA
		(she dau/o Amos GREEN and Mary NELSON)
		(she born 22 Dec 1780 VT; died 31 Dec 1871 PA)

492. REBECCA-[5] BOWKER, daughter of Joseph-[4] BOWKER (John-[3] ; Edmund-[2,1]; John-[A,B]) and Sarah TAINTER, was born ca 1755 at ____. She married Solomon BEEBE ca 1775. He was the son of Ezekiel BEEBE and Mary Mc MULLEN, and was born ca 1755 New London, CT; died 16 May 1835 at Salisbury, VT. Rebecca-[5] BOWKER died ca 1797 at Rutland, VT.

Children of Rebecca-[5] BOWKER and Solomon BEEBE:
Surname **BEEBE**

	1219. Olive	born 14 Dec 1781 Rutland, VT; died 3 April 1854 Addison, VT
		married Abiathar BENTLEY 14 Mar 1808 VT
+	**1220. ROXANNA**	born ca 1787 VT; died 5 July 1856 Brunswick, OH
		married Heman STEPHENSON
+	**1221. SIMEON**	born 1 May 1789 VT; died Dec 1870 Isabella, MI; married Hester BUCK
	1222. Nancy	born ca 1792 VT; died ____
		married Abel HOLMAN 6 Apr 1814 Salisbury, Addison, VT
		Child: Sally-[7] HOLMAN born ca _____
+	**1223. LATHROP/**	born 23 July 1795 VT; died 4 Feb 1891 Machias, Cattaraugus, NY
	LOTHROP	married Sally BEMIS 11 Feb 1820 Carthage, Jefferson, NY

494. SARAH-[5] BOWKER, sister of above, was born 29 Aug 1764 at Simsbury, Fairfield County, CT. She married Alexander-8 BEEBE +++ on 31 July 1780 at Rutland, Rutland, VT. He was the son of Ezekiel-[7] BEEBE, Jr. (Ezekiel-[6]; William-[5]; Samuel-

[4]: John-[3], Jr; John-[2]; Thomas-[1]) and Mary Mc MULLEN, and was born 29 Oct 1759 at New London, CT.; died 30 Jan 1841 at Mexico, Oswego County, NY. They moved from Rutland, VT to New York State , and in 1808 resided at Mexico, NY. Sarah-[5] BOWKER died 16 Nov 1850 at Mexico.

Children of Sarah-[5] BOWKER and Alexander-[8] BEEBE:
Surname **BEEBE**

+	**1224. SALLY**	born 23 July 1781 VT; died ca 1863 Onondaga County, NY
		married Cornelius HALSTEAD 20 Mar 1800 Rutland, VT
+	**1225. LUNA**	born 15 Aug 1783 VT; died 1850 MI
		married Asa MORTON Oct 1805 Rutland, VT
		(he s/o Martin MORTON and Jerusha TWITCHELL)
		(he born 28 May 1782 Athol, MA; died 1 June 1850 Homer, MI)
	1226. Joseph Bowker	born 4 July 1785 Rutland, VT; died 9 June 1826/28 Mexico, NY
		married Asenath SAVAGE 4 Nov 1810
		(she dau/o Joel SAVAGE and Abigail SMITH) (she born ca 1788; died ca 1852)
+	**1227. AURORA (m)**	born 8 July 1787 VT; died 3 Jan 1814 VT
		married Sarah/Sally COLTON/ COTTON
	1228. Cynthia	born 18 July 1789 VT; died 30 Oct 1870 Franklin, MI
+	**1229. ASA**	born 7 Nov 1792 NY; died 10 June 1878
		married Mary WHIPPLE 1 May 1814 Mexico, Oswego, NY
		(she dau Joseph S. WHIPPLE and _____)
		(she born 23 Sep 1793 Cooperstown, Otsego, NY; died 21 Sep 1878 Mexico, NY)

Note: He served in the War of 1812, along with his brothers Curtis and Clark, in PARKHURST'S Battalion of NY Militia.
At one time he had a foundry (he was a blacksmith) and he had a blind and sash factory in Mexico, NY

	1230. Curtis	born 14 April 1795; died _____
		married Sophia GREEN ca 1816 (She born VT)

Child: Amanda B. -[7] BEEBE born ca _____

+	**1231. CLARK(E)**	born 25 Nov 1797 Brandon, VT; died 12 Mar 1882 MI
		1 married Sarah SAVAGE Oct 1823; 2 married Dolly SAVAGE Nov 1833
+	**1232. CATHERINE**	born 2 June 1800 Westmoreland, NY; died 27 June 1841 Winfield, NY
		married Chester HOLCOMB 3 Nov 1824 Rutland VT.
+	**1233. ALLEN**	born 27 Apr 1803 Westmoreland, NY; died 21 July 1862 MI
		married Abigail/Abby MATHEWS 26 April 1823
+	**1234. ADAH**	born 2 Feb 1806 Verona, NY; died 3 July 1845 Franklin, MI
		married James CARPENTER 16 Mar 1829 First Presbyterian Church, Mexico, NY
	1235. Ann Sophia	born 5 Sep 1809 Mexico, Oswego, NY; died 10 Apr 1874
		married Ara FENN ca Feb 1826

Children: Melvina-[7] FENN born 11 Feb 1829; and Ruhama -[7] FENN born 25 Nov 1831, died 4 July 1834

+++ Alexander-[8] BEEBE, husband of Sarah-[5] BOWKER, enlisted 8 Dec 1775 in the Rev War and served as a Private in Capt. Levi WELLS and Henry CHAMPION'S Co., Col. Samuel WYLLYS' CT. regiment. He was discharged 1 Jan 1777. During his service he engaged in the skirmish up the Hudson River. He enlisted again on 8 May 1777, and served 4 months as a Cpl. in Capt. Ephraim CHAPINN'S Co., Col Ruggles WOOD-BRIDGE'S Regt. In March 1778 he served in Capt. CUMSTON'S Co., Col. Joh GREATOR'S Regt. Length of that service was 8 months. March 1779 he served as a marine on board the "BOSTON" under Capt. Samuel TUCKER. Service 7 months. After the Revolution he resided in Rutland and Brandon, VT. until ca 1801, when he removed to Westmoreland, Oneida County, NY. for a period of 2 years. He and his family then moved to Verona, NY and finally to Mexico, Oswego County, NY. Around 1830 several members of his family moved to Franklin, Lenawee, Michigan. They were Asa and Luna (BEEBE) MORTON; Benjamin and Cynthia (BEEBE) KNIGHT; Clark and Dolly (SAVAGE) BEEBE; Allen and Abby (MATTHEWS) BEEBE; and James and Ada (BEEBE) CARPENTER.

497. SARAH-[5] BOWKER, daughter of Daniel-[4] BOWKER (John-[3]; Edmund-[2,1]; John-[A,B]) and Sarah BRIGHAM, was born 14 April 1760 at Sudbury, Middlesex, MA. She married Amos SARGENT on 29 Dec 1785. He was the son of Jabez SARGENT and Abigail MOWER, and was born 7 April 1753 Worcester, MA; died 12 April 1804. They resided at Chester, VT.

Children of Sarah-[5] BOWKER and Amos SARGENT:
Surname **SARGENT**

	1236. Mary	born 13 Jan 1787; died 29 Mar 1870
	1237. Sarah	born 13 Dec 1788; died 3 July 1877
+	**1238. AMOS, Jr.**	born 12 Feb 1791; died ___;
		married Rebecca ANDREWS 3 Feb 1823; res. Warrensburg. NY

Children of Sarah-5 BOWKER and Amos SARGENT, continued:
Surname **SARGENT**

1239. Nahum	born 16 Feb 1793; died _____	
	married Susan RICE 23 June 1826	(resided Chester, VT; later moved to CA)
	Child: Susan-7 SARGENT born 30 Apr 1827	
+ **1240. SILAS**	born 1 Oct 1795; died _____	
	married Roxanna MEAD 12 Sep 1831; resided Chester, VT	
1241. John	born 10 Jan 1798; died Sep 1852	
	married Lydia BARKER ca ____; resided Sherwood, MI	
	Children: Nahum-7 SARGENT born ca 1834; Lucia-7 SARGENT born ca 1837	
1242. Lucia	born 2 Apr 1801; died 28 Apr 1833	

499. EUNICE-5 BOWKER, sister of above, was born 9 Feb 1766 at Sudbury, Middlesex, MA. She married Nathaniel WHITNEY ca 1786. He was the son of Micah WHITNEY and Hannah HARWOOD, and was born ca 1760; died 27 Aug 1801 Rutland. Eunice-5 BOWKER died 20 Feb 1848 at Pittsford, VT.

Children of Eunice-5 BOWKER and Nathaniel WHITNEY:
Surname **WHITNEY**

1243. Eunice	born 12 Dec 1787; died 27 Feb 1812	
1244. Hannah	born ca 1787; died 18 Dec 1801	EOL
1245. Sarah/Sally	born ca 1791; died 22 Feb 1851 Pittsford, VT	
+ **1246. POLLY/MARY**	born ca 1793; died 17 Jan 1878 Pittsford; married Ezra F. SPENCER 24 Jan 1815, VT	
	(he s/o William SPENCER and Margaret OSGOOD) (he born ca 1790; died 19 Mar 1881)	
1247. Merinda	born ca 1800 VT; married Pardon DERBY ca 1822	
+ **1248. AZUBAH**	born ca 1803 VT; died ca 1874 Hyde Park, Norfolk, MA	
	married Thomas BUDLONG ca 1820 (he born ca 1792 RI; died _____)	
1249. Lucy	born ca _____; died 1857	

501. LOIS-5 BOWKER, sister of above, was born April 1770 at Sudbury, MA. She married Stephen CHAMBERLAIN, Jr. on 13 April 1793. He was the son of Stephen CHAMBERLAIN, Sr. and Sarah WELD, and was born ca 1764; died _____. Lois-5 BOWKER died ca 1823.

Child of Lois-5 BOWKER and Stephen CHAMBERLAIN, Jr.:
Surname **CHAMBERLAIN**

+ **1250. DANIEL BOWKER**	born ca 1800 Roxbury, MA; died 15 Jan 1888 Roxbury
	1 married Marie BALADE/BALLARD 20 June 1825 (she born ca 1807; died 1877)
	2 married Martha LORD
Note: possibly three other children of Lois and Stephen , 2 females and 1 male, no further info	

502. DANIEL-5 BOWKER, Jr., brother of above, was born 13 Sep 1772 at Sudbury, Middlesex, MA. He married Ruth Holden BROWN on 30 March 1797 at Sudbury. She was the daughter of Asa BROWN and Elizabeth ____, and was born 24 Aug 1777 Holden, MA; died 15 June 1846 at Sudbury, MA. Daniel-5 BOWKER, Jr. died 18 Oct 1853 at Sudbury, MA.

Children of Daniel-5 BOWKER, Jr. and Ruth BROWN:
Surname **BOWKER**

+ **1251. SUSAN/SUKEY**	born 16 Oct 1797 Sudbury, MA; died 14 July 1832	
	married John HAYNES, Jr. 21 Sep 1817 Sudbury	
	(he s/o JOHN HAYNES and _____) (he born _____; died _____)	
+ **1252. SAMUEL NOYES**	born 16 June 1799 Sudbury, MA; died 9 Oct 1782;	
	married Mary EARLE 5 Nov 1826 MA	
	(she dau/o Stephen EARLE and Mary/Lucy WEYMOUTH)	
	(she born Apr 1804 Maine; died 1 Feb 1881 Sudbury, MA)	
1253. Daniel Brigham	born 12 March 1801; died 1803	EOL
1254. Daniel	born 29 June 1803; died _____; married Lucretia _____ ca ____ (she born ca 1818 NH)	
+ **1255. SARAH**	born 5 Apr 1807; died 12 July 1888 Sudbury, MA	
	married John HAYNES, Jr. 29 Nov 1832 (as his 2nd wife)	
	(he was the widower of her sister Susan (# 1251 above)	
+ **1256. MATILDA**	born 20 July 1809; died ___; married John FLETCHER 4 July 1839 Sudbury, MA	

Children of Daniel-5 BOWKER, Jr. and Ruth BROWN:
Surname **BOWKER**

1257. Elias	born 2 Jan 1811 Sudbury; died _____	
1258. Ruth	born 6 Apr 1812 Sudbury; died ____	
1259. Stillman	born 23 Sep 1813 Sudbury; died 16 May 1827 New Jersey (NJ Deaths 1798-1977) EOL	
1260. Charles	born 25 Feb 1816; died 31 Oct 1820 Sudbury	EOL
+ **1261. HARRIET N.**	born 30 Sep 1818 Sudbury; died 6 Feb 1868 St. Johnsbury, VT.	
	married John Franklin-6 MURDOCK 22 Sep 1841 Westminster, MA	
+ **1262. ELIZABETH**	born 19 Mar 1821 Sudbury; died _____	
	married David Crawford MAYBIN 1 May 1840 Sudbury, MA (he born ca 1814 PA)	

504. JOSEPH-5 BOWKER, brother of above, was born 15 July 1777 at Sudbury, Middlesex, MA. He married first to Mary BROWN 9 June 1802. She was the daughter of _____ BROWN and ____, and was born ca ____, died 12 Jan 1803, after giving birth to her daughter. He married second to Patty PROCTOR on 22 Feb 1804 at Sudbury, MA. She was the daughter of Nathan PROCTOR and Lydia ROBBINS, and was born ca 1780 at Stoddard, NH; died 10 Sept 1841 at ____, Middlesex, MA. Joseph-5 BOWKER died 3 Sept 1846/48 at Westboro, MA.

Child of Joseph-5 BOWKER and Mary BROWN:
Surname **BOWKER**

+ **1263. MARY R.**	born 8 Jan 1803 MA; died 9 Dec 1827 Spencer, MA
	married Avery BUSH 15 June 1823 Spencer. MA

Children of Joseph-5 BOWKER and Patty PROCTOR:
Surname **BOWKER**

+ **1264. LYDIA**	born 11 Apr 1807 Sudbury, MA; died _____
	married Avery BUSH (as his 2nd wife) 2 Oct 1828 Spencer, MA
	(he s/o Josiah BUSH and Mary KNOWLTON)
+ **1265. ALMIRA**	born 25 Aug 1810 North Sudbury, MA; died _____
	married Lewis-6 BRIGHAM 27 May 1837 (he # 1192)
	(he s/o Joseph-5 BRIGHAM and Rebecca HAYNES)
	(he born 27 Oct 1797 Sudbury; died 8 Sep 1875 Sudbury, MA)
+ **1266. AMOS G.**	born 5 Aug 1812 North Sudbury, MA; died _____
	1 married Lucy SNOW 15 Apr 1834
	(she dau/o ____ SNOW and _____) (she born ca ____; died ca 1845)
	2 married Lucinda HASKINS 1 Sep 1847
	(she dau/o _____ HASKINS and _____) (she born ca ____; died 2 Aug 1868)
+ **1267. JOSEPH PROCTOR**	born 4 Apr 1814 North Sudbury, MA; died _____
	married Catherine WILSON 19 May 1847 Metropolis, IL
1268. David	born 11 Mar 1817 North Brookfield, MA

505. DEBORAH-5 BOWKER, daughter of Elias-4 BOWKER (John-3; Edmund-2,1) and Deborah GOODSPEED, was born 19 March 1763 CT. She married Sheldon SEELEY ca 1782 VT. He was the son of Joseph SEELEY and Thankful BARTLETT, and was born 22 Nov 1760 at Litchfield, MA; died 7 Feb 1823 at Sandusky, Erie, OH. Deborah-5 BOWKER died ca 1837 VT.

Children of Deborah-5 BOWKER and Sheldon SEELEY:
Surname **SEELEY**   (all children born Thetford, Orange, VT)

1269. Sheldon Owen	born ca 1782; died 1796	EOL
+ **1270. HANNAH**	born 25 Dec 1783; died 1850 Camden, IL; married Ethan OWEN ca ____	
1271. Mathew	born 27 Oct 1786 ; died 1829	
1272. Mark	born 22 Feb 1789; died ca 1829 VT	
+ **1273. LUKE**	born 15 Nov 1791; died 15 Oct 1856 IL	
	1 married Electa OWEN ca 1810; 2 married _____ 10 Aug 1834	
1274. Caroline	born 8 Feb 1796 ; died 18 Aug 1881 VT	
1275. John Bowker	born 8 Feb 1796	

506. NATHANIEL-5 BOWKER, twin brother of above, was born 19 March 1763 CT. He married Alice LOVELAND ca ____. She was the daughter of ____ LOVELAND and _____, and was born ca 1762; died ca 1845. Nathaniel-5 BOWKER died ca 1853 at Bombay, Franklin County, NY.

Children of Nathaniel-[5] BOWKER and Alice LOVELAND:
Surname **BOWKER**

+	**1276. ELIAS**	born 28 Feb 1790; died 22 Oct 1868 Hogansburg, Franklin, NY
	NATHANIEL	married Asenath HOTCHKISS 18 Apr 1825 Georgia , VT
	1277. Joseph	born 30 Jan 1791; died 26 Oct 1868 Brattleboro, VT
	1278. Comely	born 16 Oct 1794 Springfield, VT; died _____
	1279. Betsey	born 11 Sep 1796; died _____
	1280. Emily	born ca 1797; died _____; married Lewis FAIRBANKS ca ____
		(he born ca 1788; died 1826) Child: Lewis Levi-[7] FAIRBANBKS born ca 1820; died 1897
	1281. Deborah	born 1 Apr 1798; died 22 Jan 1813 Georgia, VT

507 JOHN-[5] BOWKER, brother of above, was born ca 1772 VT. He married Sybil LOOMIS ca 1795 VT. She was the daughter of Ichabod LOOMIS and Mindwell LEWIS, and was born 25 June 1770 CT; died 23 Jan 1861 VT. John-[5] BOWKER died 25 Aug 1812 VT.

Child of John-[5] BOWKER and Sybill LOOMIS:
Surname **BOWKER**

+	**1282. JOHN**	born Aug 1805 VT; died 26 Nov 1853 Georgia, VT.
		1 married Elvira WHITE 29 Jan 1828 VT.
		(she born 1 Jan 1804; died 29 July 1842 Georgia, VT)
		2 married Sarah M. LEACH 19 Oct 1842 (she born ca 1819; died ca 1856)

509. ESTHER-[5] BOWKER, daughter of Silas Day-[4] BOWKER, Sr. (John-[3]; Edmund-[2,1]; John-[A,B]) and Esther HOBBS, was born 10 March 1762 at Concord, Middlesex, MA. She married William WILLISON +++ ca 1781 at Marbletown, Ulster County, NY. He was the son of ____ WILLISON and _____, and was born 15 Jan 1852 in Scotland; died 24 Jan 1836 at Genoa, Cayuga County, NY. Esther-5 BOWKER died 23 April 1836 at Genoa, NY. William WILLISON and Esther-[5] BOWKER, along with their son Silas, are buried at Wilcox Cemetery, Town of Genoa, Cayuga, NY

Children of Esther-[5] BOWKER and William WILLISON:
Surname **WILLISON**

	1283. Silas	born ca 1785 Marbletown, NY; died before 1800 EOL
+	**1284. MARY**	born 23 June 1787 NY; died 19 Apr 1844 Barry Twsp, MI
		married Jesse HAMPTON 19 Dec 1809 Genoa, Cayuga, NY
		(he s/o John HAMPTON and Martha BENEDICT)
		(he born 23 Apr 1789 Orange Co., NY; died 11 Nov 1871 Barry Co., MI)
+	**1285. JAMES**	born 10 Nov 1790 Chemung , NY; died 9 Sep 1866
		1 married Betsey WILLIAMS ca 1810 Genoa, NY (she born ca ____; died 1821 OH)
		2 married Margaret BORTHWICK 5 June 1825 Allen Twsp, Allegany, NY
		(she dau/o John M. BORTHWICK and Rebecca BRICE)
		(she born 20 Jan 1798 Schoharie Co., NY; died 5 Feb 1885 Barry, MI
+	**1286. ESTHER**	born ca 1794; died ca 1843 Coshocton, OH
		married John G. COY ca 1815 (he s/o Elisha COY and Mary GRAY)
		(he born 7 Aug 1793; died 23 Apr 1877 Dresden, OH)
	1287. Samuel	born 15 Oct 1797 Genoa, Cayuga, NY; died _____
		married Elizabeth BANKS ca 1824 Cayuga County, NY
		(she dau/o Joshua BANKS and Ruth SMITH)
		(she born 29 June 1800 Greenwich, CT; died 21 Sep 1850 Barry, MI)
		Children: Elias Banks-[7] WILLISON born 22 Aug 1825, died 10 Mar 1908 Kalamazoo, MI; and Samuel Riley-[7] WILLISON born 12 July 1835, died ca 1906
	1288. Hannah	born ca 1805 Genoa, NY; died before 1847
		married Jesse W. MILLER ca _____ (he born ca 1805; died _____)
		Children: Mary A-[7] MILLER born 11 Aug 1834 Tompkins Co., NY; and Charles-[7] MILLER born ca 1844; and Amos-[7] MILLER born ca 1848 MI
+	**1289. CYNTHIA**	born 24 Aug 1807 Genoa, NY; died 19 Jan 1873 Genoa
		married Isaac ARMSTRONG 28 Jan 1829 Genoa
		(he born 2 Dec 1801 Genoa; died 2 March 1883 Genoa, NY)
+	**1290. ORSEMUS**	born 8 Dec 1810 Genoa; died 2 Nov 1867 Johnstown, Barry, MI
		married Eunice PETTEE ca 1830 Genoa, NY
		(she born 1815; died 15 Sep 1881 Barry Co., MI)

BOWKER
The Fifth American Generation

" William (WILLISON) emigrated from Scotland to the Port of Baltimore in 1768. He eventually settled in Chamberstown, PA. (After the Palatine Germans moved into that area, it was called Chambersburg). In 1775, the whole town attended a church service, given by the Reverend CHAMBERS, on the need for able bodied young men to fight for their country.

One old lady stood up and stated that she had six sons and she didn't think it was fair that they should (all) march off and be killed while the Reverend CHAMBERS remained safely at home. At that point the Reverend dramatically threw off his gown and revealed the uniform of a chaplain in the Continental Army. He again asked the town's young men to march off, with him, and join the Continental Army. About a 100 men, including William WILLISON, marched to New York City and there they met with General George WASHINGTON and were led to a long table where they signed into the Army."

The following is a letter from the National Archives regarding the service of William WILLISON:
" – advise you that from the papers in the Revolutionary War pension claim (# B1812), it appears that William WILLISON, while living in Chamberstown, PA, enlisted in the winter of 1775 for one year and nine months, served as a Private in Captain William PEOPLE'S Company, Colonel MILES' Pa. Regiment; was taken prisoner at the Battle of Flatbush and held until the following January. At the end of his term he re-enlisted and served for three years in Colonel Walter STEWART'S PA Regiment, and was in the Battle of Brandywine and Monmouth. He also served in Colonel CANTINE'S NY Regiment, dates as stated. He was allowed a pension on his application executed 16 July 1832 while living in Genoa, Cayuga County, NY, aged 82 years ."

510. SILAS DAY^{-5} BOWKER, Jr., brother of above, was born 26 April 1763 at Concord, MA. He married Amy HARDING 6 Nov 1786 at Pataukunck, Ulster County, NY. She was the daughter of James HARDING and Mary ____; and was born 2 May 1769; died 25 Nov 1843.

Silas Day^{-5} BOWKER, Jr. served with his father in the Revolutionary War. He was a Private in the 3rd Regulars of the Ulster County (NY) Militia under Captain ____ Da PUE. He served during the entire campaign until the surrender at Yorktown. Following this service he again " signed up " and served with General SULLIVAN in his raid against the Indians at the Battle of Newtown (Now Elmira, NY) in Chemung County.

After his military service, he and his wife resided for a time in the Chemung Valley and later purchased property, in the Town of Milton, Cayuga County, NY, from a Solomon HUBBARD in 1797. The town was later renamed Genoa.

In January 1798 he purchased and settled on Lot 44 which was about 2 miles southeast of Milan, in the Town of Locke, which became the family homestead. According to the History of Cayuga County, NY 1789-1879, Silas Day^{-5} BOWKER, Jr. " came in from the eastern part of the state previous to 1802, in which year he was elected Supervisor of the Town of Locke. " In May 1827 he would sell part of the property in Locke , to his son Archilbald^{-6} BOWKER, and his wife Rebecca DRAKE.

In 1814, Silas Day BOWKER, Jr. was elected to the New York State Assembly, and again in 1824. He also served as a State Senator from the 7th District in 1823-24. He was in attendance at the 46th and 47th sessions of the State Legislature. In 1831, at the age of 69, he was placed on the pension roles for his service in the Revolutionary War. He was granted an allowance of $80. per year. He died 14 Oct 1834 at Locke, and is buried at the Greenleaf Farm Cemetery there.

Children of Silas Day^{-5} BOWKER and Amy HARDING:
Surname **BOWKER**

+	**1291. MEHITABLE**	born Sept 1787 Big Flats, Chemung Co., NY; died 27 Nov 1864 Moravia, NY
		married Wing TABER ca 1807 Cayuga County, NY
		(he s/o Amaziah TABER and Silence BABCOCK)
		(he born 13 Feb 1782 MA; died 19 Jan 1865 Moravia, NY)
	1292. Mary	born 24 Mar 1789 Big Flats, married Eber / Elias CURTIS; died 18 July 1831
+	**1293. ARCHIBALD, Esq.**	born 16 Mar 1790 Big Flats, Chemung, NY; died 8 June 1832 Summerhill, Cayuga, NY)
		married Rebecca DRAKE ca 1810 Cayuga County, NY
		(she dau/o Jasper DRAKE and Mary _____)
		(she born 7 Dec 1784, NY; died 2 Feb 1872 Summerhill)
+	**1294. LISA/LIZA/ELIZA**	born 30 May 1794 Locke, Cayuga, NY; died 14 Aug 1859 Boston, Summit, OH
		married Nathan DRAKE ca ____
	1295. Joseph	born 9 Oct 1797 Locke, NY; died 26 Mar 1856 Delevan, WI
		married Eliza MAYNARD ca ____
		(she dau/o ____ MAYNARD and ____) (she born ca 1800; died after 1860 WI)
		Child: Silas W.$^{-7}$ BOWKER born 19 Sep 1827 NY; died 19 July 1903 WI
+	**1296. AURELIA**	born ca 1804 Cayuga Co., NY; died _____
		married Levi HENRY ca 1825 Cayuga County, NY
		(he s/o _____ HENRY and _____)(he born 11 Apr 1800 NY; died 11 Oct 1860 NY)

BOWKER
The Fifth American Generation

511. LISA-⁵ BOWKER, sister of above, was born 15 June 1765 at Willington, Tolland, CT. She married Jacob ROSE on 5 Aug 1784 at Marbletown, Ulster County, NY. He was the son of Wilhelm (William) ROSE (ROOS) and Elizabeth SCHOOLCRAFT (SCHULCRAFT), and was born 11 April 1761 at Schoharie, NY; died 20 Aug 1839 at Trenton Township, Delaware, Ohio. Lisa-⁵ BOWKER died 10 Feb 1846 at Delaware County, Ohio. (William ROSE/ROOS, father of Jacob, moved to Marbletown, NY ca 1776. The family became acquainted with the BOWKER family before the Revolutionary War, in which they both served.

According to the Pension affidavit for Jacob ROSE (National Archives Rev War file # W4578), he enlisted in the latter part of 1778 at the Town of Rochester, Ulster Co., NY. His Company was commanded by Captain Jonathan HALLETT in Colonel VAN CORTLANDT'S Regiment of the Continental line. He was discharged at Sneekhill, NY in 1783 and returned to Marbletown. Sometime before the 1790 Census Jacob ROSE and his family, along with the Silas BOWKER family, moved to the Town of Chemung, Montgomery County, NY.

In 1794 Jacob ROSE, then residing in Locke, Cayuga County, NY, purchased 190 acres of land (Lot 91) in Onondaga County, NY. Later, that lot became part of Cayuga County. (Cayuga County Deed Book Vol. F., page 405) . Note: The Town of Locke, Onondaga County , and then Cayuga County, was again changed , and in 1817 became part of a new town known as Groton, Tompkins County, NY. On 14 April 1827, Jacob ROSE and his wife Lisa, deeded to their son-in-law Stephen Decatur CARPENTER, 4 acres in Lot 91 for 40#. Stephen was married to their daughter Jerusha.

Jacob ROSE died at Trenton Township, Delaware County, Ohio on 20 Aug 1839. The following is part of his obituary from a newspaper called The Statesman: ------ " Mr. ROSE entered the Army of the Revolution when he was quite young, and remained until it was disbanded. He was in several important engagements with the Indians in the State of New York. He was with General SULLIVAN in his expedition against the Six Nations in 1779, when they were completely subdued. He was at the capture of CORNWALLIS in 1781 which important event put an end to the British oppression. He also took part in the last war with Great Britain, which terminated so gloriously or American Liberty.

Mr. ROSE was distinguished through life for his exemplary and retiring habits, as well as his gentlemanly deportment. A great lover of his country and her republican institutions, and a devoted and ardent Christian, always ready to lend his aid to the afflicted. In a word he was a Christian in whom there was no guile, and he died as he lived, respected and esteemed by all who knew him. He has been gathered to his father, after having lived long enough to see the fruits of his early toil, in behalf of the liberties of his country, crowned by the smiles of Heaven in its abundant prosperity."

Children of Lisa-⁵ BOWKER and Jacob ROSE:
Surname **ROSE**

+	**1297. WILLIAM**	born 27 April 1785 Marbletown, Ulster, NY; died ca 1861
		1 married Sally CURTIS 12 Jan 1806 Locke, NY
		(she dau/o Joseph CURTIS and _____) (she born ca 1786; died _____)
		2 married Hannah WATERS 19 Feb 1849 Delaware County, NY
+	**1298. CYNTHIA**	born 9 July 1786 Colchester, Delaware, NY
		married Eber A. HOWE 17 Oct 1802 Milton (Lansing), Cayuga (later Tompkins), NY
	1299. Jerusha	born 25 Feb 1788 Colchester, NY; died 25 May 1859 Delaware Co., OH
		married Stephen Decatur CARPENTER Nov 1810 Genoa, Cayuga, NY
		(he s/o Elisha CARPENTER and Mary DAVIS)
		(he born 8 Sept 1788 IL; died 19 Aug 1841 Genoa, NY)
		Child: Julia Ann-⁷ CARPENTER born ca ___ ; married Dabney C. BRAGG
+	**1300. ISAAC HOBBS**	born 31Mar 1790 Chenango, Tioga, NY; died 25 Sept 1874 St. Mary's, IN
		married Anna YOUNG 10 Aug 1813 Genoa, NY
		(she dau/o Christian YOUNG and Sarah LINDERMAN)
		(she born 12 Jan 1795 NY; died 26 Jan 1876 IN)
+	**1301. SAMUEL HOBBS**	born 5 Mar 1792 Chenango, Tioga, NY; died 10 May 1877 Otisco Twsp, Ionia, MI
		married Delany COLLINS ca 1817 Groton, Tompkins, NY
		(she dau/o Joseph L. COLLINS and Tamesin RICE)
		(she born ca Mar 1799 Groton, NY; died _____)
+	**1302. SILAS**	born 2 Sep 1794 Chenango; died _____
		married Nancy YOUNG 18 June 1818 (sister of above) Genoa, NY
		(she born ca 1799 ; died 4 Dec 1882)
+	**1303. JOHN**	born 24 Oct 1796 Locke/Groton, NY; died 18 Aug 1865 Trenton, OH
		married Mary Eliza CRANS ca ____
		(she dau/o Andrew CRANS and Rebecca JOHNSON)
		(she born 6 Nov 1811 PA; died 3 Mar 1884 OH)

Children of Lisa-[5] BOWKER and Jacob ROSE, continued:
Surname **ROSE**

1304.	Matthew H.	born 22 July 1798 Locke, NY; died 17 July 1822 Groton, NY	EOL
1305.	Sarah/Sally	born 30 Mar 1800 Locke; died 28 July 1825 Tompkins Co., NY	
		married John MILLER 17 Oct 1822 Groton, Tompkins, NY	

Children: Lovina-[7] MILLER born Sept 1823, died 8 Nov 1824 and Sally Lovina-[7] MILLER born 6 May 1825, died 11 July 1825 Groton, NY

+	**1306. JACOB S.**	born 17 Feb 1802 Locke, NY; died _____
		married Deborah Ann HEAD 8 Jan 1824 Lansing, Tompkins, NY
		(she born ca 1802; died _____ (living 1880)
	1307. Orsamus B.	born 5 Feb 1805 Locke, NY; died ca 1831
		married Phebe BILES/BILOT 3 Dec 1825 Lansing, NY

512. DANIEL-[5] **BOWKER**, brother of above, was born 22 Feb 1767 at Willington, Tolland, CT. His first marriage was to Azubah GREGORY on ____ at ____. She was the daughter of Timothy GREGORY and Susanna OAKLEY, and was born ca 1769; died 1 Jan 1813 at Hancock, Delaware, NY. He married second to Margaret ____ ca ____. She was born ca 1762; died 24 July 1868 at Delaware County, NY. Daniel-[5] BOWKER died 1 May 1829 at Hancock.

Children of Daniel-[5] BOWKER and Azubah GREGORY:
Surname **BOWKER**

	1308. Elisha	born 11 May 1792 Hancock, NY; died _____
+	**1309. ORSIMAS**	born ca 1800 Delaware Co., NY; died ca 1877; married Sally BOGART ca ____
+	**1310. CYNTHIA**	born 17 Aug 1804 Harvard, Delaware, NY; died 6 March 1880 Grahamsville,, NY
		married Samuel B. CURREY ca _____
+	**1311. ANSON A.**	born Apr 1810 Colchester, Del., NY; died 1898; married Elizabeth JONES ca _____

515. JOHN-[5] **BOWKER**, brother of above, was born 10 Sept 1771 at Marbletown, Ulster, New York. " Landmarks of Tompkins County – Lansing " stated " John BOWKER came in 1791 from Ulster County by way of Owego and Ithaca (NY) and settled in North Lansing, where his son James afterwards lived. He was a Justice of the Peace, Constable and Supervisor in the Town of Milton. His brothers Joseph and Noah came in 1792. John BOWKER had 12 children, all of whom reared families, and at the time of his death in 1855, was father, grandfather and great grandfather to 130 children."

He married first to _____, prior to 1791. She is unknown except for the fact that a first wife is referred to in " Landmarks of Tompkins County – Part III ", where it states " that John BOWKER, grandfather of Mrs. French (Sarah BOWKER French), daughter of his son Madison BOWKER) was born in Ulster County (NY) in 1771, and came to Lansing with his two brothers, Joseph and Noah, bringing their provisions on their backs from Owego. They cut and cleared away on the land where they settled, building themselves a log cabin, and when their stock of provisions were exhausted they had to walk to Owego for more. John bought 100 acres from the State – where he spent the remainder of his days, growing into prominence in this town -------
He was twice married. By his second wife , Jerusha ROBINSON, he had twelve children ------- . " This researcher believes that there were 12 children total, one having been born of his first wife.

He married Jerusha ROBINSON before 1797, probably at Lansing. She was the daughter of David ROBINSON, Jr. and Polly/Mary RAYNOR, and was born 20 Aug 1781 Brookhaven, Long Island, NY.; died 16 Feb 1866 at Lansing, Tompkins County, NY. John-[5] BOWKER was a Baptist; and was elected Pound Keeper of Genoa, NY on 1 April 1794. In 1817 he was Justice of the Peace of Tompkins County; and died 16 Sep 1855 at Lansing. He and members of his family are buried at the Miller Cemetery, Lansing, NY

Child of John-[5] BOWKER and his first wife:
Surname **BOWKER**

	1312. Sally	born 14 April 1791 Tompkins Co., NY; died _____

Children of John-[5] BOWKER and Jerusha ROBINSON:
Surname **BOWKER**

+	**1313. JONATHAN**	born 18 Nov 1797 Tompkins Co., NY; died 23 Feb 1891 Groton, Tompkins, NY
		1 married Nancy FOOTE ca 1816; 2 married Emeline POWERS ca 1823/24
		(she dau/o William Cale POWERS and Ruth PENNOYER)
		(she born 5 Feb 1806 Dutchess Co., NY; died 21 Nov 1888 Groton, NY)
+	**1314. ESTHER**	born ca 1800 NY; died 21 Nov 1888 Groton
		married Robert BOTHWELL before 1825

Children of John[-5] BOWKER and Jerusha ROBINSON, continued:
Surname **BOWKER**

+	**1315. HANNAH**	born 11 May 1802 NY; died 14 June 1871 ; married William WALKER ca _____
+	**1316. JEFFERSON T.**	born 18 Mar 1804 Lansing; died 24 May 1856
		married Sophronia HENDERSON 21 Apr 1824
		(she dau/o _____ HENDERSON and _____) (she born ca 30 Apr 1809; died _____)
+	**1317. MADISON**	born 23 March 1808; died 4 March 1836; married Sarah / Sally DAVIS
	1318. Daniel	born ca 1810 NY; died _____; 1 married Deborah ARMSTRONG ca _____
		(she born 25 Feb 1801; died 26 March 1838)
		Child: Eunice[-7] BOWKER born 18 Mar 1831 Gtroton, married Theron SHAW 26 Sep 1852 Groton
		2 married Mary ROBBINS after 1838
	1319. Susannah Margaret	born 23 May 1814; died 20 Mar 1850
+	**1320. JAMES M.**	born 30 May 1816 Tompkins Co., NY; died 24 Mar 1904
		married Elizabeth MILLER ca _____
		(she born 18 Feb 1817 Tompkins Co., NY; died 1 Apr 1884)
+	**1321. POLLY**	born ca 1818; died ca 1898
		married John GOWER ca _____ (he born ca 1816; died ca 1885)
+	**1322. JOHN**	born 26 April 1822; died 19 July 1879 Tompkins Co., NY
		married Eliza LEARN 31 Oct 1838 (she dau/o John LEARN and Elizabeth _____)
		(she born 21 Sep 1821; died 14 Sep 1888)
	1323. Jerusha	born ca 1825; died Feb 1882 Genoa, Cayuga, NY; married _____ HERRON

516. MARY POLLY[-5] BOWKER, daughter of Silas Day[-4] BOWKER (John[-3]; Edmund[-2,1]) and Esther HOBBS, was born ca 1771/72 at Milton, Ulster, NY. She married Andrew ARMSTRONG ca _____. He was the son of _____ ARMSTRONG and ____, and was born 23 May 1763; died ca 1822. Mary Polly[-5] BOWKER died 16 August 1854 at Cayuga, Cayuga County, NY. Gravestone reads : Polly, wife of Andrew ARMSTRONG, died 16 Aug 1854, 83 years old.

Child of Polly[-5] BOWKER and Andrew ARMSTRONG:
Surname **ARMSTRONG**

1324. Susanna A.	born 28 April 1800 Genoa, NY; died 28 Oct 1895 Shelby County, IL
	1 married Matthias PARKER ca ____; (he born ca ___ CA; died 1830 Cayuga, NY)
	Child: Lemuel[-7] PARKER born 6 Sept 1827 Cayuga, NY ; died 3 Mar 1909 Shelby Co., IL;
	married Cena A. ____ (she born ca 1834 NY)
	2 married Owen Oliver DEWITT ca 1833; (he born ca 1789; died ca 1866)
	Child: Daniel D-[7] DEWITT born ca 1838; died 1921

517 JOSEPH[-5] BOWKER, brother of above, was born 4 May 1773 at Marbletown, Ulster County, NY. His first marriage was to Silva RUDI ca _____. She was the daughter of _____ RUDI and ____, and was born ca ____, died before 1812. His second marriage was to her sister Peninah RUDI. They married ca 1812 at Tompkins County, NY. She was born ca 1787; died 1 June 1868, MI. Peninah RUDI was married first to Moses LAWRENCE. Joseph[-5] BOWKER died 25 Aug 1827 at Lansing, NY.

Children of Joseph[-5] BOWKER and Silva RUDI:
Surname **BOWKER**   *** Source: Nebraska Probate Records, Lancaster County

	1325. Anna	born ca ___; married _____ NEILL
		Child: Amelia-[7] NEILL born ca ____, married ____ WOOD
+	**1326. LUCINDA**	born 24 June 1801 Milton, Cayuga, NY; died _____
		married Derrick SNEDEKER/SNEDAKER ca 1817
	1327. Candace	born ca 1804/05 NY; married _____ MILLER
+	**1328. CHESTER**	born ca 1807 NY; married Louisa _____; died ca 1871 OH
	1329. Clinton ***	born ca 1808 NY; married Mary J. ___ Jacobs ; died 6 May 1872 NE
		(she born _____; died 21 Mar 1882)
+	**1330. IRA**	born 23 July 1810 NY; died ca 1852 Green County, WI
		married Rebecca BORTHWICK ca 1830

Children of Joseph-[5] BOWKER and Peninah RUDI:
Surname **BOWKER**

	1331. Peninah	born 18 Feb 1813 Lansing, Tompkins, NY; died _____; married _____ PARSON
+	**1332. ASA**	born 28 Apr 1818 Tompkins Co., ; died _____; married Hester PIPER 14 Apr 1842
		(she dau/o George PIPER and Sarah Ann SPRATT)
		(she born 29 Dec 1824 Exeter, ENG; died 11 Apr 1867 Alamo Twsp, MI)

Clinton BOWKER of Lincoln, late of Tompkins County, NY, died 6 May 1872. Will: Widow Mary J. appointed administratrix; removed to NY, died 21 Mar 1882. Stepsons R. Wilson JACOBS, Clinton B. JACOBS; brothers and sisters Chester BOWKER, Lucinda Snedaker, Peninah Parson, Anna NEILL (dec'd), Candace Miller; Ira BOWKER, half-brother Asa BOWKER, Amelia WOOD (dau/o Anna NEILL (dec'd). Final decree 15 Dec 1923.

518. NOAH-5 BOWKER, brother of above, was born ca 1780 at Ulster County, NY. He married Mary BECKWITH on 19 Mar 1805 at Milton, Cayuga County, NY. She was the daughter of David BECKWITH and Abigail WHITNEY, and was born 3 Nov 1787/ 22 Mar 1788 VT; died 12 July 1880 at Barry Township, Barry County, MI. Noah-5 BOWKER died 17 Oct 1866 at Barry. They are buried at the North Cemetery, Barry County, MI.

Children of Noah-5 BOWKER and Mary BECKWITH:
Surname **BOWKER**

+ **1333. VIOLETTA** — born 23 Aug 1806; died ca 1839 Allegany, NY; married Augustus WOODWORTH ca 1835 (he s/o Asa WOODWORTH and Sally BOYNTON) (he born 11 Nov 1812 NY; died April 1893 NE)

+ **1334. SILAS** — born 1 Apr 1808 Genoa, Cayuga, NY; died 27 Sept 1858 Hope, Barry, MI; married Margaret ARDREY ca _____

+ **1335. ESTHER** — born ca 1810 NY; died _____; married Joseph MUNSON ca 1831 Genoa, Cayuga, NY (he s/o Caleb T. MUNSON and Sally COSTON) (he born 28 Oct 1809 Locke, Cayuga, NY; died _____)

1336. Abigail — born ca 1812 NY; died 18 June 1853 MI; married John LAWRENCE 25 April 1847 MI
Child: Esther Ann-7 LAWRENCE born ca _____

1337. David A. — born 16 Jan 1815 NY; died 23 Nov 1889 MI
1 married Susan _____ ca ___ (she born 8 Dec 1819 NY; died 1 Dec 1851)
Child: Mary L-7 BOWKER born 1 Jan 1848 MI
2 married Sarah A. KELLEY 18 April 1853 Barry, MI
3 married Almira ___ (she born ca 1818 NY; died 1896 MI)
Note: David-6 BOWKER served in Co. L, 11th Michigan Cavalry Regiment from 11 Nov 1863 – 16 May 1865. He entered as a Private and rose to the rank of Sgt.

1338. Noah Warren — born ca 1818 NY; died before 1900 MI (poss. 1882); married Harriet FARMER 1 May 1843 Kalamazoo, MI (she born ca 1827; died 1906)
Children: Emma-7 BOWKER born ca ___, and Edwin Edgar-7 BOWKER born ca ___

1339. Elijah B. — born 23 Feb 1820 Lansing, NY; died 12 Aug 1896 Ross Twsp., MI
1 married Jane King HARKNESS; 2 married Hannah CADWALLADER
Children: James-7 BOWKER, Charles-7 BOWKER, Alonzo-7 BOWKER and Harry-7 BOWKER

+ **1340. WELLINGTON** — born ca 1827 NY; died 3 Dec 1880 Kalamazoo, MI; married Lucy S. _____ ca 1859

+ **1341. CANDACE** — born 31 Aug 1829 NY; died 16 Oct 1902 Caldwell Twsp. MI; married John Borthwick WILLISON 26 March 1848 Barry Twsp, Barry, MI (he born 1 Apr 1826 Allen Twsp, Allegany, NY; died_____)

526. MOSES-5 FAIRBANKS, son of Jonathan-4 FAIRBANKS (Lydia-3 HOLBROOK, Mary-2 BOWKER, Edmund-1) and Dr. Jonathan FAIRBANKS, was born 9 Aug 1768 at Shutesbury, MA. He married Betsey MATTHEWS ca _____ at Ticonderoga, NY. She was the daughter of ____ MATTHEWS and _____, and was born 10 Feb 1771; died ____. Moses-5 died _____.

Children of Moses-5 FAIRBANKS and Betsey MATTHEWS:
Surname **FAIRBANKS**

+ **1342. ADAM** — born 30 May 1790 Colrain, MA; died Sept 1873 Cass, Jones, Iowa
1 married Cynthia WILBOR ca 1818 (she born 26 Dec 1801; died 25 May 1844)
2 married Gracia MILLS ca 1844/45 (she born ca 1791 NH; died _____) 1860 resided Hyde Park, VT.

1343. Fanny — born 18 March 1792; died _____
1344. Betsey — born 2 March 1795; died _____
1345. Mary — born 20 May 1799; died _____
1346. Sarah — born 13 Dec 1801; died _____
1347. Truman — born 24 July 1804; died ca 1831 Hyde Park; married Betsey BOYCE ca _____

Children of Moses[-5] FAIRBANKS and Betsey MATTHEWS, continued:
Surname **FAIRBANKS**

1348. Emily	born 13 Feb 1806	**1350. RICHMOND**	born 9 May 1814
1349. Clarissa	born 5 May 1813; died _____		

527. DANIEL[-5] FAIRBANKS, brother of above, was born 1 June 1769/70 at Shutesbury, MA. He married first to I. Keziah CLARK ca _____. She was the daughter of ____ CLARK and ____, and was born ca 1774; died 19 Aug 1817 (aged 43). He married second to Ruth FAULKNER on 22 Feb 1818. She was the daughter of ____ FAULKNER and ____, and was born 11 April 1782; died 21 May 1872 (90-1-10) Daniel[-5] FAIRBANKS died 14 March 1854 Colerain, MA

Children of Daniel[-5] FAIRBANKS and Keziah CLARK:
Surname **FAIRBANKS**

	1351. Arena	born ca _____
	1352. Daniel	born ca ____
+	**1353. JOHN**	born 3 Feb 1796; died 11 Dec 1853 Heath, MA; married Sally BURRINGTON ca _____

Children of Daniel[-5] FAIRBANKS and Ruth FAULKNER:
Surname **FAIRBANKS**

+	**1354. KEZIAH**	born 22 Sept 1818; died ____
		married Green NICHOLS 10 May 1837 (he born ca ____; died 19 Feb 1888)
	1355. Jeremiah	born 22 Sept 1818; died 16 April 1847 EOL
+	**1356. MARY**	born 22 Feb 1821; died ____
		married Arad NICHOLS of Colerain on 2 Dec 1840
		(he born ____; died 2 Sept 1891)
+	**1357. ROMINOR SMITH**	born 2 July 1822; died 18 Sept 1892 Colerain, MA
+	**1358. RUTH**	born 2 Jan 1824; died 24 Feb 1852; married John HAGAR ca _____
		(he born ____; died 7 Feb 1852, just 17 days apart from his wife)

528. JONATHAN[-5] FAIRBANKS, brother of above, was born 3 April 1772 at Shutesbury, MA. He married first to Sally AYERS ca ____. She was the daughter of ____ AYERS and ____, and was born 9 Feb 1778; died ____. His second marriage was to Nabby AYERS, the sister of his first wife, on ____. Jonathan-[5] FAIRBANKS died ca 1858 Heath, MA

Children of Jonathan-[5] FAIRBANKS and Sally AYERS:
Surname **FAIRBANKS**   (all children born at Heath, MA)

	1359. Sally	born 3 Nov 1796; died ____; married Leonard BRIGGS
	1360. Betsey	born 9 Nov 1797; died ____; married Walter BURT
	1361. John	born 30 Apr 1799; died ____; married Anna SLACK
	1362. Polly	born 24 Aug 1800; died ____; married Whiting TUTTLE ca ____
		(he s/o Jude TUTTLE and Lovice SMITH)
		(he born ca 1796 Franklin Co., MA; died 12 Feb 1883)
		Children: Cynthia-[7] born 31 July 1825; Sarah Adaline-[7] born 11 Oct 1826; and Henry Whiting-[7] TUTTLE born 3 Feb 1828
+	**1363. HIRAM**	born 6 Nov 1801; died 2 Mar 1885 Newburg, WI
		married Effie CASWELL 4 June 1826
+	**1364. ROYAL**	born 18 Aug 1803; died Oct 1852 St. Lawrence Co., NY
		1 married Miranda WILLIAMS ca 1823; (she born ca 1804; died 1845)
		2 married Jane F. KINNE 26 Oct 1845
+	**1365. ANNA**	born 15 Nov 1804; died ____; married John BARBER ca ___
		(he born ca 1797; died 1843)
	1366. Emeline	born 2 Nov 1807; died _____; married John HOWE
	1367. Robert	born 3 Oct 1808; died ____
+	**1368. DAVID**	born 2 July 1811 Ashfield, MA; died 25 Jan 1853 Antwerp, NY
		married Sybil SMITH ca _____
	1369. Wilkins	born 13 Sept 1814; died _____
	1370. Laura	born 18 April 1818; died ____; married John MITCHELL

529. ASA[-5] FAIRBANKS, brother of above, was born 1 May 1774 Shutesbury, MA. He married Lucy SAUNDERS ca ____. She was the daughter of ____ SAUNDERS and ____, and was born ca 1779; died 20 July 1843. Asa-[5] FAIRBANKS died 24 Feb 1828 Whitingham, VT.

Children of Asa-[5] FAIRBANKS and Lucy SAUNDERS:
Surname **FAIRBANKS**

+	**1371. ASA**	born 27 June 1800; died 21 Jan 1861; married Sally STACY ca _____
	1372. Amos	born 18 Feb 1802; died 24 Sept 1824; married Jemima FULLER
		(she born ca 1805; died 6 Dec 1824 , age 19) EOL
+	**1373. EZRA**	born 4 Feb 1804 Whitingham VT.; died 11 Oct 1874
		married Cynthia STACY 23 Sept 1830
	1374. Phebe	born 16 March 1806; died 9 Sept 1806 EOL
+	**1375. ABRAHAM**	born 3 May 1808 Whitingham ; died 20 Dec 1891; married Olivia COOK ca ____
+	**1376. LUCY**	born 11 July 1810; died ____; married Levi LAMB
+	**1377. ANNA**	born 2 Feb 1813; died 23 Dec 1858; married Warren CHASE
		(he born 30 Nov 1805; died ____)
	1378. Samuel	born 26 June 1815; died _____
		married Clarissa C. PARKER 30 Oct 1847 (she born 23 July 1830 Whitingham, VT
		(she dau/o Flavel PARKER and Almo FIELD)
		Children: Frank S-[7] born 21 May 1848; and Almo A-[7] FAIRBANKS born 6 Aug 1852; married Alfred P.
		DUDLEY 16 Jan 1876; resided Northampton, MA
	1379. Louisa	born 10 Jan 1817; died ca _____ Hoosick Falls, NY; married Joel STACY
	1380. Leafy	born 18 May 1820; died 5 April 1846; single EOL

531. RACHEL-[5] FAIRBANKS, daughter of Daniel-[4] FAIRBANKS (Lydia-[3] HOLBROOK; Mary-[2] BOWKER; Edmund-[1]) and Submit FAIRBANKS, was born 13 May 1748. She married Jethro PETERS 8/31 Oct 1769 at Holliston, MA. He was the son of William PETERS and Hannah CHENERY, and was born 13 June 1744 Norfolk, MA; died 16 Feb 1826 at Bolton, MA. Rachel-[5] FAIRBANKS died ca 1792.

Children of Rachel-[5] FAIRBANKS and Jethro PETERS:
Surname **PETERS**

1381. William	born 13 Sept 1770; died ____			
1382. Rachel	born 20 July 1772; died ____		1386. Peter	born 15 April 1781
1383. George	born 9 Aug 1774; died ____			
1384. Hannah	born 12 April 1777; died 22 Apr 1871; married James MOORE ca ____			
1385. Julia	born 13 April 1779; died ____		1387. Peace	born 25 March 1783

532. COMFORT-[5] FAIRBANKS, sister of above, was born 4 July 1750. She married Joseph SEAVER 1 June 1771. He was the son of ___ SEAVER and __, and was born ca 1750; died 1829. Comfort-[5] FAIRBANKS died 27 June 1789 Northborough, MA.

Children of Comfort-[5] FAIRBANKS and Joseph SEAVER:
Surname **SEAVER**   (all children born Northborough, MA)

1388. Sarah	born 18 Apr 1771; died ____; married Ephraim CARRUTH
1389. Abigail	born 21 Apr 1773; died ____; married Nathan HENDERSON
1390. Joseph	born 7 Sept 1775; died 19 Sep 1776 EOL
1391. Sabra	born 15 Sept 1777; died ____; married Nahum RICE
1392. Mary	born 19 Feb 1780; died 28 March 1832; married Asa ANDREWS (1782-1844)
1393. Caroline	born 7 Nov 1784; died ____; married Joshua BLOOD
1394. Lois	born 13 July 1787; died ____

534. JONATHAN-[5] FAIRBANKS, brother of above, was born 29 March 1755 at Holliston, MA. He married first to Hannah MORSE of Northborough, MA on 28 Feb 1781. She was the daughter of ____ MORSE and ____, and was born ca 1763; died 7 Dec 1783 (aged 20). He married second to Bridget PARMENTER on 3 Dec 1784. She was the daughter of ____ PARMENTER and ___ of Sudbury, and was born ca 1764; died 29 Sept 1828. Jonathan-[5] FAIRBANKS died 28 Feb 1840. He was a Revolutionary War veteran.

Children of Jonathan-[5] FAIRBANKS and Hannah MORSE:
Surname **FAIRBANKS**

+	**1395. DANIEL**	born 28 Oct 1781 Holliston, MA; died 5 Aug 1821 Boston, MA
		married Elizabeth BLACKMAN 8 Apr 1812
+	**1396. HANNAH**	born 13 Nov 1783; died ____; married Martin HAGAR

Children of Jonathan-[5] FAIRBANKS and Bridget PARMENTER:
Surname **FAIRBANKS**

+	**1397. ELIZABETH**	born 16 Sep 1785; died ____; married John CUTLER
+	**1398. JONATHAN**	born 7 April 1787; died 30 Dec 1865 Cochituate, MA
		married Augusta HADDEN ca _____
	1399. Zana	born 29 July 1790; died ____; married James QUINN ca _____ EOL
+	**1400. Col. DRURY**	born 17 July 1793 Sudbury, MA ; died 25 May 1864
		married Mary SPRING 26 Oct 1817 Hubbardston, MA
+	**1401. Capt. EDDY**	born ca 1795; died 31 July 1862 North Reading, MA
		married Nancy SIMMS 30 April 1822 Boston, MA
+	**1402. GEORGE**	born 15 Sep 1797 Sudbury, MA ; died 31 Aug 1873
		married Susan SMITH ca 1819
+	**1403. DR. DEXTER**	born 19 July 1799; died 11 Aug 1879 New York
		married Lucretia WHEELER ca _____
+	**1404. MARY**	born 5 March 1803; died 13 Mar 1879; married Jonas PIERCE ca _____
+	**1405. JOSEPH BRADLEY VARNUM**	born 3 Oct 1804 Sudbury, MA ; died 20 May 1833
		married Margaret HADDEN ca _____
+	**1406. ELBRIDGE**	born 9 Jan 1809 Sudbury, MA ; died 10 July 1842 Cambridge, MA
		married Annie C. REMIE, of Cambridge, MA ca _____

537. NATHAN-[5] **TWITCHELL,** son of Keziah-[4] HOLBROOK (Samuel-[3]; Mary-[2] BOWKER: Edmund-[1]; John-[A,B]) and Daniel TWITCHELL, was born 12 Jan 1742/43 at ____. He married Hannah KEMPTON / KIMPTON 18 Dec 1766 MA. She was the daughter of _____ KEMPTON/KIMPTON and ____, and was born 27 July 1748; died ca 1787.

Children of Nathan-[5] TWITCHELL and Hannah KEMPTON/KIMPTON:
Surname **TWITCHELL**

	1407. Keziah	born ca 1767/68; died ____
		married Silas TAFT 26 April 1771 Uxbridge, MA
+	**1408. DANIEL**	born 30 Sep 1769 ; died 22 Dec 1811; married Eunice WRIGHT ca _____

542. REUBEN-[5] **BURNETT,** son of Lucy-[4] GLEASON (Thankful-[3] HOLBROOK; Mary-[2] BOWKER; Edmund-[1]) and William BURNETT, was born 4 Aug 1782 Oxford, MA. He married Polly BENJAMIN on 25 February 1804 at Bridgeport, VT. She was the daughter of Samuel Clark BENJAMIN and Phoebe MINOR , and was born ca 1783; died 1854. Reuben-[5] BURNETT died 14 July 1817 at Canton, St. Lawrence, NY.

Children of Reuben-[5] BURNETT and Polly BENJAMIN:
Surname **BURNETT**   (children born St Lawrence County, NY)

	1409. Harriet	born 8 April 1806; died ____
	1410. Lois S.	born 4 May 1808 St. Lawrence Co., NY; died 6 Feb 1886 IL
		married Oliver CARVER 25 March 1824 (12 children)
		(he born ca 1801; died ca 1853)
+	**1411. LUCY G.**	born 23 Jan 1814 Ogdensburg, NY; died 1842
		married John HULETT, Sr. ca _____
		(s/o Samuel HEWLITT/ HULETT and Sarah CLARK
		(he born 23 Feb 1808 NY; died 11 Sep 1906 Kingsley, WI)
+	**1412. EVALINE F..**	born 29 Oct 1814; died 29 July 1856 Rossie, St. Lawrence, NY
		married Philander George TAYLOR 27 Oct 1829 St. Lawrence County, NY
		(he s/o Noah TAYLOR and Polly HEWLITT / HULETT)
		(he born 17 Jan 1810 Grand Isle, VT; died 16 Feb 1877 Plainfield, IA)
		(he born 17 Jan 1810 VT; died 16 Feb 1877 Plainfield, IA)
	1413. Elizabeth B.	born 24 Nov 1816; died ____

BOWKER

560.   HUGH-⁶ BRUCE, son of John-⁵ BRUCE (Bathsheba-⁴ BOWKER; John-³,²; Edmund-¹) and Martha MOORE, was born 5 Aug 1770 Berlin, MA. He married Sally MOORE on 23 May 1796. She was the daughter of Jacob MOORE and ____; and was born ____; died 10 May 1840. High-⁶ BRUCE died 14 Sep 1821 at Boston, MA.

Children of Hugh⁻⁶ BRUCE and Sally MOORE:
Surname **BRUCE**

1414. Chandler	born 9 Nov 1797; died ____	
1415. Roxana	born 23 Feb 1800; died 7 Aug 1804	EOL
1416. Louise	born 12 Jan 1802; died ____	
1417. Levi	born 7 Mar 1804; died ____; resided Clinton, MA; unmarried	EOL
1418. Ira	born 23 Jan 1808; died 4 Aug 1876; married Lucy WHITE 13 Sep 1835	
1419. Ezra T.	born 18 Jan 1811; died 26 Nov 1897	
1420. Sarah Ann	born 6 Aug 1813; died ____ 1421. John born 20 Nov 1816; died ____	

566.   EUNICE-⁶ BRUCE, sister of above, was born 30 June 1774 at Berlin, Worcester, MA. She married Asa SAWYYER on 19 June 1800 at Berlin, MA. He was the son of William SAWYER and Hannah BARRETT, and was born 2 Aug 1775; died 7 Aug 1845 OH. Eunice-⁶ BRUCE died 11 Oct 1861 at Brimfield, Portage, OH.

Children of Eunice-⁶ BRUCE and Asa SAWYER:
Surname **SAWYER**   (all children born Berlin, Worcester, MA)

1422. Levi	born 28 June 1801; died 2 Feb 1836 Berlin, MA
1423. Asa, Jr.	born 10 Oct 1802; died 4 Nov 1881 Brimfield, OH
	married Caroline Augusta LINCOLN 5 Apr 1830
	(she dau/o Luke A. LINCOLN and Mary THORNDIKE)
	Children: Francis L-⁸ born ca 1831, died 1905; Mary D-⁸ born ca 1833, died 1885; Ellen A-⁸
	born ca 1834; and Henry D-⁸ SAWYER born ca 1838, died 1921
1424. William	born 15 Feb 1805; died 18 Nov 1845
1425. Sophia	born Jan 1806; died 21 Mar 1861 Brimfield, OH
1426. Infant	born ca 1808; died 1811 EOL
1427. Alvin	born 22 Dec 1809; died 1885
1428. Lucy	born 1 Feb 1815; died 6 Apr 1886; married William Richie KELSO 16 Oct 1834
1429. Mary Ann	born 12 Jan 1821; died 1885
1430. Sarah	born ca 1822; died Sep 1899
1431. Luke E.	born 12 July 1825; died 1 Dec 1851

567.   JOHN⁻⁶ BRUCE, Jr., brother of above, was born 15 May 1781 at Berlin, Worcester, MA. He married Prudence PRIEST ca 1805. She was the daughter of Holman PRIEST and Prudence SAWYER; and was born ____; died ____. John⁻⁶ BRUCE, Jr. died ____.

Children of John⁻⁶ BRUCE, Jr. and Prudence PRIEST:
Surname **BRUCE**

	1432. Eusebia	born 29 Dec 1806; died ____; married William JONES 16 May 1827 Berlin, MA
	1433. Persis	born 11 Oct 1808; died 1872
	1434. Olive M.	born 4 April 1810; died ____; married Daniel FARNSWORTH 2 Apr 1833
	1435. Silas	born 11 Dec 1811; died 1880
+	**1436. IRA**	born 30 Mar 1814; died ____; married Phebe SAWIN 7 Dec 1836; res. W. Boylston, MA
	1437. Zilpah	born 11 Mar 1815; died 1893; 1 married Ephraim Merrick HOLT 28 Sep 1836
		2 married Jason KNOWLTON 24 Apr 1845; 3 married David WHITE 17 Oct 1855

571. SEWELL⁻⁶ BRUCE, brother of above, was born 10 April 1795 at Berlin, MA. He married Eunice BENNETT on 8 Nov 1812. She was the daughter of Ephraim BENNETT and Priscilla WELLINGTON, and was born____; died 11 Feb 1873. Sewell⁻⁶ BRUCE died 3 Nov 1846.

Children of Sewell⁻⁶ BRUCE and Eunice BENNETT:
Surname **BRUCE**

1438. Martha M.	born 24 May 1813; died 7 July 1850; married Anthony S. STARKEY 22 Mar 1835	
	Child: Charles-⁷ STARKEY born ca 1839	
1439. Roxana	born 9 Dec 1815; died 27 Mar 1890; married Ebenezer S. SAWTELL 5 Mar 1834	
	(he born ca 1811; died 15 Feb 1901 Berlin, MA)	
1440. Joanna	born 11 Dec 1818; died ____; married William H. HORTON ca ____	
1441. Lorenzo	born 3 June 1820; died ____	
	Child: John L.-⁸ BRUCE born ____; married Mary Ann STONE; dau/o Isaac S. STONE	
1442. Horatio	born 23 June 1822; died ____	
1443. Simeon	born 6 Feb 1824; died ____; resided Worcester, MA	
1444. Philo	born 1 May 1826; died ____ 1445. Phidelia born 21 Sept 1830; died 1832 EOL	

572. SYLVANUS⁻⁶ BRUCE, brother of above, was born 15 Dec 1792 at Berlion, MA. He married Hannah READ/ REED ca ____. She was the daughter of ____ READ/ REED and ____; and was born 1798 Providence, RI; died 22 Mar 1880 Berlin, MA.. Sylvanus ⁻⁶ BRUCE, a farmer, died ____.

Children of Sylvanus-⁶ BRUCE and Hannah READ:
Surname **BRUCE**

1446. Christiana R.	born 23 Feb 1824; died ____; married Samuel MASON, Jr. 28 Apr 1842	
	(he s/o Samuel MASON, Sr. and Ruth JONES of Boston, MA) (he a hat manufacturer	
	(he born 28 Apr 1822 Providence, RI; died 9 Feb 1908 Boston, MA)	
	Child: Christiana-⁸ MASON born ca 1850 MA; died ____	
1447. Lyman	born 31 Jan 1826; died 7 Aug 1843 Berlin, MA	EOL
1448. Lewis B.	born ca 1833; died 5 July 1853 Berlin, MA	EOL
1449. Leverett W.	born ____; died ____; 1 married Emeline BROWN 12 Jan 1874	
	(she born ca 1843 ME; died ____) 2 married Emma ____	
	Child: Abby Molly-⁸ BRUCE born 19 Jan 1876; died 5 May 1898 Brunswick, ME	
+ **1450. GEORGE HENRY**	born 7 Aug 1837; died 11 Jan 1919 Berlin, MA	
	married Vilena Augusta GODDARD 4 Oct 1862	
	(she dau/o Ephraim GODDARD and ____) (she born ca 1844; died 1885)	
1451. Willard G.	born Oct 1839; died ____; married Rachel HOLDER Fry 23 Sep 1867	
	(she married 1ˢᵗ to Charles FRY/FRYE 12 June 1859)	
	(she dau/o Joseph HOLDER and Rachel ____) (she born ca 1842; died ____)	

574. ABRAHAM⁻⁶ BRUCE, son of Daniel⁻⁵ BRUCE (Bathsheba-⁴ BOWKER; John-³,²; Edmund-¹) and Mary BRUCE, was born ca 1791 Middlesex County, MA. He married Mary Polly BRIGGS ca 1817. She was the daughter of ____ BRIGGS and ____, and was born ca 1801 Burlington, Otsego, NY; died ca 1873. Abraham-⁶ BRUCE died 1878 NY.

Children of Abraham-⁶ BRUCE and Mary Polly BRIGGS:
Surname **BRUCE**   (all children born Burlington, Otsego, NY)

+ **1452. DANFORD**	born ca 1818; died 14 Mar 1863 Washington, DC (smallpox)	
+ **1453. JANE**	born ca 1822; died 16 Feb 1852 Otsego, NY	
	married David Fairchild GOODRICH ca 1841	
1454. Harriett	born June 1823; died ____ Pittsfield, NY; married Truman SPAFFORD ca 1850	
	(he born Mar 1832 NY; died ____) (he s/o Asa SPAFFORD and ____)	
1455. Maryette	born 19 May 1828; died 27 June 1863 Plymouth, NY; married Bradford A. BOYDEN	
+ **1456. DIANA A.**	born 6 Nov 1830; died 7 Dec 1885 Emporia, KS	
	married David Fairchild GOODRICH ca 1852 (widower of her sister Jane)	
1457. Emeline	born 9 Sep 1833; died 13 Mar 1920 NY	
1458. Albert	born 12 Oct 1842; died 29 Oct 1919 Rome, Oneida, NY	
	married Cornelia PADDOCK ca 1878 (she born ca 1843 IN)	
	Children: Giles William-⁸ BRUCE born 1867 NY; died 26 Dec 1946 OK	
1459. Elba	(twin) born 2 Mar 1845 ; died ____; married La Fayette PORTER 24 Sep 1873 Milwaukee, WI	
1460. Helena	(twin) born 2 Mar 1845; died 12 Nov 1915; married Alpheus GOODRICH 17 Oct 1866	

577. LOIS/LOUISA⁻⁶ BRUCE, sister of above, was born 30 Oct 1802 MA. She married Ziba KEYES 17 Aug 1828. He was the son of Thomas KEYES and Eunice KNIGHT, and was born 9 Dec 1796; died 29 Nov 1851. Lois/Louisa⁻⁶ BRUCE died ____

Children of Lois/Louisa⁻⁶ BRUCE and Ziba KEYES:
Surname **KEYES**

1461. Charles G.	born ____; died ____; married Juliet A. WHIPPLE 6 Nov 1860
1462. Henry F.	born ca 1833; died 3 Apr 1899; married Jane M. WINCH 22 Sep 1859

579. SAMUEL WARD⁻⁶ BOWKER, son of Silas⁻⁵ BOWKER (John⁻⁴·³·²; Edmund⁻¹) and Bethia WARD, was born 16 Dec 1760 at Petersham, Worcester, MA. He married first to Sarah LOCKE on 31 July 1794. She was the daughter of John LOCKE and Beulah NORTON, and was born 19 Nov 1768; died 13 Jan 1799. He married her sister Charlotte LOCKE on 30 June 1803. She was born 17 Dec 1771; died 30 Dec 1858 Fitchburg, MA. Samuel Ward⁻⁶ BOWKER died 29 May 1835 MA.

Children of Samuel Ward⁻⁶ BOWKER and Sarah LOCKE:
Surname **BOWKER**

+	**1463. STEPHEN**	born 15 Oct 1794 Royalston, MA; died ____
		married Prudence RAND Dec 1814 (she born 14 Jan 1795; died _____)
	1464. Samuel (1)	born 7 June 1796 Royalston, MA; died 1798
+	**1465. SAMUEL (2)**	born 28 Dec 1798 Royalston, MA; died 5 Nov 1861 Ashby, MA
		married Mary GIBSON 21 Dec 1826 / int pub 5 Nov 1826
		(she born 8 Feb 1800 Ashburnham, MA ; died 20 Jan 1890)
		(she dau/o Joseph Barker GIBSON and Submit WARREN)

Children of Samuel Ward⁻⁶ BOWKER and Charlotte LOCKE:
Surname **BOWKER**

	1466. Sally/Sarah	born 9 Nov 1803 Royalston, MA; died ____
+	**1467. ELIZABETH /**	born 25 Feb 1805 Royalston, MA; died 18 June 1892 Westford, MA
	BETSEY	married Benjamin BOSWORTH 1 Nov 1828
	1468. Alfred	born 6 Feb 1807 Royalston; died 10 Sep 1841
		married Caroline L. DAMON ca ____ (she born 5 Apr 1808; died 1 July 1905)
		(she dau/o William DAMON and Abigail WILLARD)
		Child: James Alfred⁻⁸ BOWKER born 12 Jan 1840; died 4 Nov 1893 NH; married
		Ella M. COLBY ca ____ (she born ca 1842; died 1870)
	1469. John	born 5 Aug 1810; died 17 Mar 1894 Keene, NH
		married Hannah Electa STUART 2 Apr 1840 (she born ca 1810; died 1892)

581. STEPHEN BIGELOW⁻⁶ BOWKER, brother of above, was born 25 Dec 1772 at Royalston, MA. He married Submit GROVER on 12 Sep 1799. She was the daughter of Nathaniel GROVER and Sarah HARRINGTON, and was born 2 Dec 1777 Fitzwilliam, NH; died 17 Feb 1857 Royalston, MA. Stephen⁻⁶ BOWKER died 30 Oct 1833 Royalston.

Children of Stephen⁻⁶ BOWKER and Submit GROVER:
Surname **BOWKER**

	1470. Silas	born 17 Jan 1800 Royalston, MA; died ____;
+	**1471. NATHANIEL**	born 26 July 1808 Worcester, MA; died ____; married Philena WHEELER 9 Nov 1830

590. CELIA WINSLOW⁻⁶ TURNER, daughter of Elizabeth/ Betty⁻⁵ BOWKER (John⁻⁴·³·²; Edmund⁻¹) and Joshua TURNER, was born 2 Sep 1781 at Pembroke, Plymouth, MA. She married Laban LEAVITT on 13 Feb 1806 at Pembroke. He was the son of _____ LEAVITT and ____; and was born ____; died 6 Dec 1819 Pembroke, MA. She lived all her life on her father's farm, and died there 26 Feb 1856.

Children of Celia⁻⁶ TURNER and Laban LEAVITT:
Surname **LEAVITT**   (children all born Pembroke, Plymouth, MA)

+	**1472. LIBERTY**	born 20 Oct 1806; died 29 June 1841
		married Chloe BELCHER 18 Nov 1824 (she of Foxboro, MA)
		(she born 10 Sep 1808; died ____)
+	**1473. SUMNER**	born 3 Jan 1808; died ____
		married Betsey WITHERELL 23 Oct 1831 Pembroke
+	**1474. QUINCY**	born 8 Feb 1809; died 12 Dec 1851
		married Clymenia/Climenia SOPER 22 Dec 1839 (she of Hanson, MA)

BOWKER
The Sixth American Generation

Children of Celia-[6] TURNER and Laban LEAVITT:
Surname **LEAVITT**

+	**1475. WINSLOW**	born 17 May 1811; died 1895 Whitman, MA
		married Mehitable KEENE 4 July 1841 (she of Hanson, MA)
+	**1476. NAHUM** (twin)	born 21 Dec 1815; died ____ Pembroke, MA
		married Eunice S. EVERSON Sept 1837 (she of Hanson, MA
	1477. Hiram (twin)	21 Dec 1815; died March 1817 EOL

Sources: The TILSON Genealogy; Genealogy of the BIGELOW Family of America, p.37; Pub 1890

592. JONATHAN-[6] BOWKER, son of Solomon-[5] BOWKER (John-[4, 3, 2]; Edmund-[1]) and Dorothy BARNES, was born 9 Aug 1774 at Marlborough , Middlesex, MA. He married Abigail BEAMAN ca 1808. She was the daughter of Capt. Nathaniel BEAMAN and Thankful FARNSWORTH, and was born 12 Feb 1787 Lancaster, NH; died 1851. Jonathan-[6] BOWKER died 16 June 1852 Canada.

Children of Jonathan-[6] BOWKER and Abigail BEAMAN:
Surname **BOWKER**

	1478. Thankful	born 8 Jan 1809 Canada; died 23 Jan 1891 Bloomfield, VT
+	**1479. ALEXANDER**	born Mar 1810 Canada; died 14 Aug 1881 Quebec, Canada
		married Louisa WHEELER 2 Apr 1832 Stanstead, Quebec, Canada
	1480. Solomon	born 12 Feb 1812 Quebec, Canada; died 20 May 1886
	1481. Jonathan	born ca 1817 VT; died ____
+	**1482. NATHANIEL BEAMAN**	born 9 Feb 1821 Dalton, NH; died 26 Mar 1889 Bloomfield, VT. married Mary Ann PARNELL 9 May 1853 Melbourne, Quebec, Canada (she dau/o Lawrence PARNELL and _____) (she born ca 1827; died 28 Aug 1902 Lancaster, NH

597. GEORGE-[6] BOWKER, son of Jotham-[5] BOWKER (John-[4]; John-[3;2]; Edmund-[1]) and Patty WHITNEY, was born ca Nov 1791/92 MA. He married Betsey UNDERWOOD ca 1820. She was the daughter of ____ UNDERWOOD and ____; and was born ca 1792 Worcester, MA; died 1844 Barre, MA. George-[6] BOWKER died ____.

Children of George-[6] BOWKER and Betsey UNDERWOOD:
Surname **BOWKER**

	1483. Edward Brigham	born 16 Jan 1821; died 11 June 1854 Barre, MA
		married Mary C. HAYNES 4 May 1848 Sudbury, MA
		(she born ca 1827; died _____) (she dau/o David HAYNES and Rachel Newell CUTTER)
+	**1484 MARY B.**	born 2 June 1823; died _____; 1 married William W. HINCKLEY 4 Dec 1849
		(he s/o Timothy HINCKLEY and Roxana __) (he born ca 1826; died 13 Feb 1864)
		2 married Ebenezer FOSTER 7 Mar 1872
	1485. Elvira J.	born 22 Sep 1825; died ____
	1486. George Franklin	born 4 Jan 1827; died ____
		married Eliza J. Mc STODDARD 1 May 1853 Boston, MA
		(she dau/o Simon J. Mc STODDARD and ____)
		Children: Georgianna-[8] born ca 1854; and Edward W.-[8] BOWKER born ca 1866
+	**1487. LUKE FREEMAN**	born 22 May 1828; died 17 July 1864 Dinwiddie, VA ** (killed in the Civil War)
		married Eliza Jane WILSON 31 Mar 1855 Athol, MA
		(she born ca 1832 NY; died _____) (she dau/o Charles WILSON and _____)
	1488. Jotham Liberty	born 4 July 1830; died ___ ;married Abigail B. LEIGHTON 26 Aug 1850 Harmony, ME
		Child: Clara A-[8] BOWKER born ca 1855; married Orlando Alfred WALLACE 18 Oct 1878 Phippsburg, ME

602. FREEMAN-[6] BOWKER, brother of above, was born 23 Sep 1801 MA. He married Sarah B. KNOWLES on 28 Sep 1837. She was the daughter of David KNOWLES and Sally BATCHELDER; and was born 23 Oct 1814 Northwood, Rockingham, NH; died ____. Freeman-[6] BOWKER died ca 1893.

Children of Freeman-[6] BOWKER and Sarah KNOWLES:
Surname **BOWKER**

	1489. Edwin Freeman	born 17 Apr 1840; died 11 June 1924 Cambridge, MA; a Civil Engineer
		married Jennie/Jane HOWARTH Wellington 24 Dec 1872 MA
		(she dau/o Joseph HOWARTH and Mary C. _____)
	1490. Henrietta Florence	born 1 Sep 1852; died 8 Feb 1853 1491. Charles A. born 20 Jan 1854; died 1865

605. GIDEON-⁶ BOWKER, son of Antipas⁻⁵ BOWKER (Josiah⁻⁴; John⁻³,²; Edmund⁻¹) and Esther RICE, was born 9 March 1760 at Northborough, MA. He married Hannah FLETCHER ca 1780. She was the daughter of ____ FLETCHER and ____ ; and was born 12 Sep 1762 MA; died ____ . Gideon-⁶ BOWKER died 3 June 1815 at Lunenburg, Essex, VT.

Children of Gideon-⁶ BOWKER and Hannah FLETCHER:
Surname **BOWKER**

	1492. Phoebe	born 21 Dec 1781 Chesterfield, NH; died ____
+	**1493. LEVI**	born 14 Mar 1783 Chesterfield; died 23 March 1863 VT
		married Betsey SILSBY Nov 1806 Lunenburg, VT
		(she dau/o Mitchell SILSBY and _____) (she born 16 Apr 1783; died 15 Feb 1832)
	1494. Lucy	born 15 Apr 1786 Guilford, Windham, VT; died ___
+	**1495. RICE**	born 3 Feb 1789 Guilford; died 15 Nov 1843 Sullivan, Ashland, OH
		married Elizabeth/ Betsey CLARK 3 July 1814 (she born ca 1792 VT; died 1861)
	1496. Betsey	born 23 Sep 1791 Guilford; died ____
+	**1497. LYMAN JAMES**	born 12 Jan 1794 Guilford; died 1 Dec 1867 Newport, Quebec, Canada
		married Betsey MERRIAM Nov 1818 Quebec, Canada
		(she dau/ Isaac MERRIAM and Betsey WAITE) (she born ca 1794; died 1867)
	1498. Zimri	born 17 May 1796 Guilford; died ____
+	**1499. LEONARD**	born 20 Feb 1799; died 27 Sep 1869 MI; married Phoebe CURTISS ca 1821
	1500. Gilman	born 25 Jan 1804 Guilford; died ____

616. OLIVER-⁶ BOWKER, son of Ephrain⁻⁵ BOWKER (Josiah⁻⁴; John⁻³,²; Edmund⁻¹) and _____ ; and was born 22 Jan 1760 Westborough, MA. He married Hannah/ Anna PIERSON/PEARSON on 12 Dec 1779. She was the daughter of _____ PIERSON/PEARSON and ____ , and was born ____ ; died ____ . Oliver⁻⁶ BOWKER died ____ .

Children of Oliver-⁶ BOWKER and Hannah/Anna PIERSON/PEARSON:
Surname **BOWKER**

	1501. Sally	born ca 1785; died ____		
+	**1502. JOHN PIERSON**	born 9 Sep 1787 Rutland, MA; died 24 Jan 1862 Walpole, MA		
		1 married Polly BAKER 18 July 1812 Rutland		
		(she dau/o Ziba BAKER and Mildred CLEVELAND) (she born 2 June 1794; died 19 Dec 1820)		
		2 married Patty BELCHER 24 July 1822		
	1503. Fannie	born ca 1790; died ____		
	1504. Tyler	born 7 June 1792; died 12 Nov 1839	1505. Almira	born ca 1801

618. DOLLY-⁶ NEWTON, daughter of Tabitha⁻⁵ BOWKER (Josiah⁻⁴; John⁻³,²; Edmund⁻¹) and Charles NEWTON, was born 7 Aug 1766 at Shrewsbury, MA.. She married Abraham HAGER ca 1781 at age 15. He was the son of William HAGER and Mary WARREN, and was born 11 Mar 1755;died ____ . Dolly-⁶ NEWTON died 11 Feb 1786, 8 days after giving birth to her 3ʳᵈ child.

Children of Dolly-⁶ NEWTON and Abraham HAGER:
Surname **HAGER**

	1506. William	born 28 Dec 1782; died 15 Mar 1783	EOL
+	**1507. AZUBAH**	born 22 Mar 1784; died ____ ; married Ichabod FARRER (int pub 4 Aug 1804)	
	1508. Dolly	born 3 Feb 1786; died 4 Feb 1786	EOL

620. EZRA-⁶ NEWTON, brother of above, was born 22 Nov 1774 Shrewsbury, MA. He married first to (unknown) born ___ ; died 1811 (possibly due to childbirth). He married second to Lucy HOWE on 27 Jan 1812. She was the daughter of Adonijah HOWE and Lydia ____ ; and was born 24 Oct 1779; died 28 July 1826. His third wife was Mrs. Candace ALLEN Howe whom he married ca ___ . She was the daughter of Simeon ALLEN and Candace HOWE, and was born ca 1780; died 21 June 1850. He married lastly to Ruth HASTINGS Leonard of Weston , MA on 31 Aug 1851. She was the daughter of John HASTINGS and Esther____ , and was born ____ ; died ____ . Ezra-⁶ NEWTON died 19 Apr 1863 Princeton, MA

Child of Ezra-⁶ NEWTON and his 1ˢᵗ wife:
Surname **NEWTON**

1509. Sally Hastings	born 25 March 1811; died 9 July 1887 Taunton, Bristol, MA
	married Benjamin F. DEAN 3 Feb 1842
	(he born 13 July 1805 Taunton, MA; died 25 Apr 1882 Taunton)

Children of Ezra-6 NEWTON and his 2nd wife, Lucy HOWE:
Surname **NEWTON**

	1510. Ezekiel	born 16 Aug 1812; died 27 May 1905 Westborough, MA
		married Eliza Ann PRIEST 24 Nov 1835 (she born ca 1811; died ____)
	1511. Charles	born 3 Mar 1814; died 23 Oct 1887 Milbury, MA; married Jane BOYDEN ca ____
+	**1512. LYDIA CHURCH**	born 8 July 1816; died 31 May 1869; married Elbridge T. CLARK 12 Sep 1835
		(he born 11 Sep 1812 Medway, Norfolk, MA; died 6 Feb 1896 Millis, MA.
+	**1513. EZRA, Jr.**	born 30 Sep 1818; died 4 Nov 1897 Seattle, King, WA
		married Martha Brown PATTEN 20 Aug 1846 Medway, MA
	1514. Lucy Howe	born 17 Sep 1820; died 7 Oct 1854 Worcester, MA
		married Charles Cotesworth GREENWOOD 22 Feb 1844
	1515. Abraham Howe	born 24 Mar 1823; died 16 Nov 1903 Worcester, MA
		married Sarah B. KENDRICK 21 Apr 1846 Enfield, Hampshire, MA
		(she born ca 1819; died 1903) (she dau/o Jaziel KENDRICK and Hannah FELTON)

Children: Lucy A.-8 born 26 Mar 1848, married Walter H. SEARS (1851-1943) and Genevieve Alleta-8
NEWTON born 15 Jan 1850, died 2 July 1934; married Clarence W. GOULD (1847-1899)

622. TABITHA-6 NEWTON, sister of above, was born 25 July 1781 at Shrewsbury, MA. She married Jonathan STEARNS, Jr. on 17 Feb 1803 at Princeton, MA. He was the son of Jonathan STEARNS, Sr. and Abigail MOORE of Billerica, Lancaster, MA, and was born 2 May 1771 at Rutland, MA; died 8 May 1844 ar Rutland. Tabitha-6 NEWTON died 25 July 1835 Holden, MA

Children of Tabitha-6 NEWTON and Jonathan STEARNS, Jr.:
Surname **STEARNS**   (children born Rutland, MA)

1516. Charles		born 9 Aug 1803; died 23 Dec 1853; unmarried	EOL
1517. Abigail		born 21 Nov 1804; died 27 June 1840 Grafton, MA; unmarried	EOL
1518. Alice		born 23 Oct 1806; died Apr 1858 Templeton, MA; unmarried	EOL
1519. Ruth		born 22 Mar 1808; died 1 Feb 1841 Uxbridge, MA; married Charles ELLIS ca ____	
		(he born ____; died 28 Oct 1866 Uxbridge, MA)	

Children: Mary-8 ELLIS born ca ____, Principal of Holyoke Female Seminary and later Mills College,
Alameda, CA; and Albert-8 ELLIS born ___, died 1863 unmarried

1520. Mary		born 7 Jan 1811; died 25 Sep 1831 Holden, MA	
1521. Azubah Newton		born 24 July 1813; died 27 Aug 1831 Holden, MA	
1522. John		born 11 Apr 1815; died 21 Sep 1885 Benona, MI	
1523. Dolly	(1)	born 22 Feb 1817; died 14 Aug 1819 Rutland, MA	EOL
1524. Dolly	(2)	born 6 Oct 1819; died Mar 1852; married _____ MILLER ca ____	
		Child: Lizzie-8 MILLER born ca ____; died young	EOL
1525. Martha Ann		born 28 Feb 1821; died ____; married Joseph SNOW 15 Aug 1849	

Children: Mary-8 born ca ___, died young; John H.-8 SNOW born ca 1856; Fred-8 born ca ___;
and Eliza-8 SNOW born ca 1860

1526. William		born 8 May 1823; died 15 Nov 1844	
1527. Dana		born 6 Sep 1827; died 9 Oct 1831 Holden, MA	EOL

Information source: NEWTON Genealogy, a record of the descendants of Richard Newton of Sudbury, and The Genealogy and Memoirs of Isaac STEARNS and his Descendants , pages 205-6

624. OBADIAH-6 BOWKER, son of Ithamar-5 BOWKER (Josiah-4; John-3,2; Edmund-1) and Sarah RICE/DANIELS; and was born 27 Oct 1799 MA. He married Catherine Ann ANDERSON 4 Apr 1824 . She was the daughter of ____ ANDERSON and ____; and was born ca 1810 NJ; died 1850. Obadiah-6 BOWKER died 24 Nov 1861 Bergen, Hudson, NJ.

Children of Obadiah-6 BOWKER and Catherine ANDERSON:
Surname **BOWKER**   (children all born NJ)

	1528.Obadiah, Jr.	born ca 1827; died ____; married Susan M. _____ ca ____
	1529. John Anderson	born ca 1829; died ____
	1530. Andrew	born ca 1832; died ____
	1531. George	born ca 1834; died ____; married Elizabeth ____ ca 1857
		Children: Nathaniel-8 born ca 1857; DeWitt-8 born ca 1860; George, Jr-8 born 1864; and Benjamin-8 BOWKER
		born ca 1868
+	**1532. DEWITT CLINTON**	born Aug 1836; died 20 Apr 1906 Kings Co., NY
		married Sarah Gertrude DRAKE ca ____ (she born ca 1847 NJ ; died 26 July 1933)

Children of Obadiah-6 BOWKER and Catherine ANDERSON, continued:
Surname **BOWKER**

1533. Martha J.	born ca 1839; died ____	1536. Samuel	born ca 1845; died ____
1534. Charles	born ca 1841; died ____	1537. Elizabeth	born ca 1846; died ____
1535. Lorena	born ca 1841; died ____	1538. Margaret	born ca 1853; died ____

640. ASA-6 BOWKER, Jr., son of Asa-5 BOWKER (Josiah-4; John-3;2; Edmund-1) and Susanna BRYANT, was born 9 June 1798 Winchendon, MA. He married first to Joanna WALKER on 3 April 1817. She was the daughter of Samuel WALKER and ____; and was born ca ____; died poss. 21 Sep 1823. He married second to Abigail CHUBB , int pub 5 June 1824. She was the daughter of ____ CHUBB and ____; and was born ____; died ____. Asa-6 BOWKER, Jr. died ____

Children of Asa-6 BOWKER, Jr. and Joanna WALKER:
Surname **BOWKER**

1539. Esther	born 9 Sep 1817; died ____
1540. Abigail	born 16 Jan 1819; died ____
1541. Levi	born 4 Feb 1821; died 8 June 1851

Children of Asa-6 BOWKER and Abigail CHUBB:
Surname **BOWKER**

1542. Ephraim	born 25 Jan 1825; died 15 Mar 1870		
1543. Joanna	born 26 Mar 1828; died ____	1544. Abigail	born 4 July 1830; died ____

642. WINDSOR-6 BOWKER, brother of above, was born 25 June 1796 Phillipston, Worcester, MA. He married Sarah OSGOOD ca 1822. She was the daughter of Joseph OSGOOD and ____; and was born ca 1811 Wendell, MA; died ca 1860. Windsor-6 BOWKER died 23 Aug 1851- killed by a runaway animal.

Children of Windsor-6 BOWKER and Sarah OSGOOD:
Surname **BOWKER**

1545. Angelina	born ca 1823; died 7 Mar 1865 NH
1546. Judge John S.	born ca 1825; died ____ after being assaulted by a criminal whom he had judged against
+ **1547. JANNETTE C.**	born ca 1828 NH; died 31 Mar 1876 Hinsdale, Cheshire, NH
	married Rev. William H. MARBLE ca 1851 Hinsdale
1548. Harrison M.	born 31 July 1835 Hinsdale, NH; died 19 Feb 1920 Los Angeles, CA.
	1 married Ellen Sanger CURRIER 13 Oct 1874 Chicago, IL
	(she born Dec 1833 VT; did 25 Nov 1906)
	(she dau/o John Wenneck CURRIER and Mary Butterfield ELKINS)
	2 married Elizabeth H. _____ ca ____
1549. George	born ca 1839 NH; died 5 Jan 1860 Hinsdale, NH

662. MARY HOSMER-6 FORBUSH, daughter of David-5 FORBUSH (David-4; Martha-3 BOWKER; John-2; Edmund-1) and Sarah HAYWARD, was born 3 Jan 1781 at Acton, Middlesex, MA. She married Daniel WHEELER, as his second wife, on 2 April 1801 at Concord, Middlesex, MA. He was the son of Francis WHEELER and Mary HAYWARD, and was born 27 Apr 1774; died 7 Nov 1810.

Children of Mary Hosmer-6 FORBUSH and Daniel WHEELER:
Surname **WHEELER**

1550. Amos	born 21/23 Oct 1801 Concord, MA; died 1862	
1551. Francis	born 1801; died 1896; married Jane Roxalana FOLLETT ca ____ (she born ca 1808)	
	Child: William-8 WHEELER born ca 1843; res. Stillwater, MN; a river pilot	
1552. Mary	born ca 1802; died 1811	EOL
+ **1553. OLIVE**	born 16 Jan 1803; died 27 Apr 1858; married Bryant KAY ca 1836	
1554. Francis	born 1804; died 1805	EOL
1555. Josiah H.	born 1807; died 1807 EOL	
1556. Jonas Lee	born 1808; died 1809 EOL	

670. MARY / MOLLY-6 FORBUSH, daughter of James-5 FORBUSH (David-4; Martha-3 BOWKER; John-2; Edmund-1) and Eunice BROWN, was born 24 Aug 1777 at Weare, Hampshire, MA. She married Elihu DAVIS on 3 Feb 174. He was the son of Nathan DAVIS and Abigail ROGERS, and was born Sep 1769; died 30 May 1838 Bennington, VT. Mary/Molly-6 FORBUSH died 2 Aug 1849.

Children of Mary/ Molly-[6] FORBUSH and Elihu DAVIS:
Surname **DAVIS**

+	**1557. PARTHENIA**	born 12 May 1795; died 30 July 1880 Readsboro, VT
		married Benjamin GREENSLET 24 Oct 1813 Bennington, VT
	1558. Amos	born 15 Dec 1799; died 20 Dec 1884
+	**1559. POLLY / MARY**	born 22 Mar 1802; died ____; married Almon/Almeron CRAWFORD ca ____
		(he born ca 1799; died 1871)
+	**1560. ALMIRA**	born 2 July 1806; died 24 Dec 1891 Union Settlement, Oswego Co., NY
		married Almon/Almeron POTTER 19 Oct 1834
		(he s/o William POTTER and Cynthia BURGESS)
		(he born 30 Mar 1811; died 10 Mar 1848)
	1561. Hinkley	born 23 March 1809; died ____; married Rhoda WEEKS 1 Jan 1834 Bennington, VT

Children: Helen M-[8]born ca 1835; Lydia-[8]born ca 1838; George F-[8] born ca 1841; and William H-[8] DAVIS born ca 1843

	1562. Franklin S.	born 22 Jan 1815; died ____

671. BETSEY-[6] FORBUSH, sister of above, was born was born 15 Aug 1778 at Weare, Hampshire, MA. She married John HARWOOD on 18 Oct 1798 at Weare, MA. He was the son of Andrew HARWOOD and Rachel D. HIGGINS, and was born 26 Oct 1772 Weare, MA; died 25 Sep 1853 at Bennington, VT. Betsey-[6] FORBUSH died 6 June 1839 at Bennington.

Children of Betsey-[6] FORBUSH and John HARWOOD:
Surname **HARWOOD**

1563. Asahel	born 1 Aug 1799 Weare, MA; died 12 Dec 1862 Bennington, VT
	1 married Temperance PARMALEE 9 Mar 1824
	(she born 3 July 1802; died 19 May 1829)
	2 married Barbara PARMALEE 27 Nov 1829
1564. Clarissa	born 19 July 1801 Weare; died 2 Nov 1820 Cortland, NY
1565. James F.	born 1 July 1803 Weare, MA; died 25 July 1869 Bennington, VT
1566. Betsey Eliza	born 1 Sept 1805 Weare, MA; died 4 Aug 1869 Bennington
1567. John, Jr.	born 20 July 1809 Greenwich, MA; died 29 Apr 1813 Bennington
1568. William	born 18 Oct 1812 Bennington, VT; died Feb 1813 Bennington EOL
1569. Un-named	born 20 July 1814 Bennington; died 20 Sep 1815 Bennington EOL
1570. Eunice	born 1 Aug 1815 Bennington; died 15 Mar 1816 Bennington EOL
1571. Martha	born 11 June 1817; died 13 Sep 1817 Bennington
1572. Mary	born 6 May 1820 ; died 28 Feb 1894 Canandaigua, NY

672. DANIEL-[6] FORBUSH, brother of above, was born 26 July 1791 at Weare, Hampshire, MA. He married first to Nancy GRAPES on 20 June 1814 at Brunswick, VT. She was the daughter of Jacob GRAPES and Patience CLIFFORD, and was born ca 1800; died 1831. He married second to Elizabeth/Betsey LEIGHTON ca 1833. She was the daughter of ____ LEIGHTON and ____; and was born ca 1799; died 1861. Daniel-[6] FORBUSH died 26 July 1859 at Dummer, Coos, NH.

Children of Daniel-[6] FORBUSH and Nancy GRAPES:
Surname **FORBUSH**

	1573. Daniel, Jr.	born ca 1817; died ____; married ____ LOVEJOY ca ____
		(she dau/o William LOVEJOY and Rebecca ____)
+	**1574. GEORGE W.**	born 19 May 1820; died 13 June 1899
		1 married Marion Marina WHEELER 3 July 1843
		(she born 13 Oct 1825; died ca 1869 Dummer, NH)
		2 married Phebe LEAVITT ca ____
		(she dau/o Marden LEAVITT and Louisa BURNS)
		(she born 2 Nov 1829 Stratford, NH; died 21 Nov 1898 Stark, Coos, NH)
+	**1575. CATHERINE**	born 12 Apr 1822; died 21 Aug 1900
		married John M. BICKFORD 13 Oct 1839 Dummer, NH
		(he s/o Charles BICKFORD and Elizabeth/ Betsey DURGIN)
		(he born ca 1818; died 1887)
+	**1576. CAROLINE** A.	born 2 Apr 1824; died 1905; married George Hubbard LEAVITT 24 July 1849
		(he s/o Peter LEAVITT and Sarah SPAULDING)
		(he born 30 Mar 1824; died 1905 Nebraska)

Children of Daniel-₆ FORBUSH and Nancy GRAPES, continued;
Surname **FORBUSH**

+	**1577. JERUSHA**	born 1826; died _____; married John L. BICKFORD ca _____
+	**1578. LEVI**	born 1828; died 13 June 1899 Winnebago, WI
		married Mary A. JACKSON ca 1862 (she born 24 Mar 1839; died 1923 WI)
+	**1579. EPHRAIM R.**	born 17 Mar 1831; died 14 June 1917; married Louisa P MILES ca 1859
		(she born ca 1834 Stark, Coos, NH; died ____)
		(she dau/o Josiah MILES and Abigail _____)

Children of Daniel-⁶ FORBUSH and Elizabeth LEIGHTON:
Surname **FORBUSH**

+	**1580. JAMES HENRY**	born 9 Oct 1836; died 14 Feb 1910 Dummer, Coos, NH
		1 married Betsey De Merritt NICHOLS ca 1852
		(she dau/o Jonathan NICHOLS and Fanny LEAVITT)
		(she born 16 Sep 1836; died Jan 1855)
+	**1581. NANCY A.**	born 25 May 1837 Crystal, Coos, NH; died 9 Apr 1920 Berlin, Coos, NH
		married John N. HOWLAND 11 May 1859 Coos, NH
		(s/o _____ HOWLAND and Dorcas SPOONER)
		(he born 12 Oct 1820 Benton, NH; died 2 Jan 1882 Whitefield, Coos, NH)
	1582. William Harrison	born 1841; died ____; married Alva A. ELLIOTT 27 Sep 1883 Stark, Coos, NH
	1583. Chuen/Chebar (?)	born 1846; died ____

676. CHEBAR-⁶ FORBUSH, brother of above, was born 4 May 1801 at Roxbury, Suffolk, MA. He married Elizabeth GRAPES on 25 July 1820 at Coos, NH. She was the daughter of Jacob GRAPES and Patience CLIFFORD, and the sister of Nancy (above), and was born 5 May 1805 NH; died 1 Sep 1890 at Minneapolis, MN. Chebar-⁶ FORBUSH died Dec 1874 at Minneapolis, Hennepin, MN.

Children of Chebar-⁶ FORBUSH and Elizabeth GRAPES:
Surname **FORBUSH**

1584. Eunice	born 4 June 1822 ; died 1852 North Adams, MA		
1585. Miranda	born 1824; died 1897	1591. Lavina	born 1836; died 1922
1586. Emily	born 1826;	1592. George Henry	born 1838; died 1904
1587. Betsey	born 1829; died 1920	1593. Harriet Ann	born ____
1588. Patience	born 1830;	1594. Adaline	born ___
1589. James	born 1832; died 1843 EOL	1595. Evaline	born ____
1590. Chebar, Jr.	born 1834; died 1914		

697. WILLIAM-⁶ POWERS, II, son of Elizabeth-⁵ GATES (Ephraim-⁴; Mary-³ BOWKER; John-²; Edmund-¹) and William POWERS, was born 11 Feb 1767 at Dunbarton, Merrimack, NH. He married Mary THOMPSON on 22 Sept 1787. She was the daughter of Seth THOMPSON and Elizabeth _____, and was born 11 Sep 1769 Groton, Grafton, NH; died 4 Dec 1857. William-⁶ POWERS died 2 Nov 1834 at Groton, NH.

Children of William⁶ POWERS II and Mary THOMPSON:
Surname **POWERS**   (all children born at Groton, Grafton, NH)

	1596. Gideon	born 20 Oct 1791 ; died 7 Jan 1840 Hebron, NH
		married Hannah CROSBY 3 Oct 1816 (she born ca 1796; died 1868)
	1597. Mary	born 1 July 1793; died ____
+	**1598. JACOB**	born May 1798; died ca 1882 Brandon, Rutland, VT
		married Amelia CONANT ca 1833
	1599. Joseph	born 19 May 1802; died 19 Mar 1879 North Haverhill, Grafton, NH
		married Betsey BLOOD 17 Mar 1825 (she born 15 Nov 1898; died _____)
		Child: Caroline W-⁸ POWERS born ca 1837 NH

718. SUSANNAH-⁶ MORRILL, daughter of Susannah-⁵ GATES (Mary-⁴; Mary-³ BOWKER; John-²; Edmund-¹) and Ephraim MORRILL, and was born 22 July 1778 at Henniker, NH. She married Nathaniel AIKEN on 30 May 1807. He was the son of _____ AIKEN and ____; and was born 5 Mar 1774 at Deering, Hillsboro, NH; died ____. Susannah-⁶ MORRILL died 25 Oct 1829 at Peoria, IL.

Children of Susannah[6] MORRILL and Nathaniel AIKEN:
Surname **AIKEN**

1600. Mark M.	born 21 June 1808; died ____	
1601. Eliza Woodburn	born 28 Apr 1810; died ____	
1602. James R.	born 3 May 1813; died ____; married Hannah AIKEN (she born ca 1818 MA)	
1603. Louella	born 6 Dec 1816; died ____	
1604. John	born 21 June 1819; died ____	

719. ABRAHAM[6] MOSMAN, son of Anna D[5] KEYES (Martha[4] BOWKER; Asa[3]; John[2]; Edmund[1]) and Samuel MOSMAN, was born 27 Oct 1770 at Westminster, Worcester, MA. He married Achsah Whitney SEAVER on 19 Apr 1802 at Westminster. She was the daughter of Benjamin SEAVER and Martha WHITNEY, and was born 30 Dec 1784 MA; died 16 Mar 1865 at Westminster, MA. Abraham[6] MOSMAN died 30 Sep 1847 Westminster.

Children of Abraham[6] MOSMAN and Achsah SEAVER:
Surname **MOSMAN**   (all children born Westminster, Worcester, MA)

1605. Abijah	born 19 Feb 1802; died 1 Oct 1810	EOL
1606. Abel	born 31 July 1803; died 6 May 1872 Westminster	
1607. John	born 12 Mar 1806; died ____; married Susan PRATT 14 Apr 1835	
1608. Abigail (1)	born 19 Nov 1807; died 1810	EOL
1609. Daniel	born 30 Dec 1809; died 18 Mar 1889; married Delana DAVIS 28 Oct 1852 Westminster	
1610. Abigail (2)	born 19 Sep 1812; died ____; married Ezekiel GATES 16 Aug 1836 Gardner, MA (he s/o Reuben GATES and Anna MOSMAN) (he born 21 Sep 1809; died 12 Nov 1892 Worcester, MA)	
1611. James	born 7 Nov 1813; died ____	
1612. Phebe	born ca 1815; died ____	
1613. Benjamin Seaver	born 12 Dec 1817; died ____; married Ann B. DAVIS 20 Apr 1842	
1614. Silas	born 14 May 1822; died ____	
1615. Charles	born 12 Feb 1825; died ____	

725. ANNA [6] MOSMAN, sister of above, was born 3 April 1782 at Westminster, MA. She married Reuben[6] GATES on 12 Feb 1806 at Westminster. He was the son of Simon[5] GATES and Susannah REED, and was born 21 April 1786 Gardner, Worcester, MA; died 16 Dec 1873 at Gardner. Anna[6] MOSMAN died 30 Sept 1850.

Children of Anna[6] MOSMAN and Reuben GATES:
Surname **GATES**   (1st three children born Gardner, MA; last 4 born Westminster, MA))

1616. Samantha Keyes	born 23 July 1806; died 23 Nov 1820 Gardner, MA
1617. Anna Mosman	born 16 Oct 1807; died ____
1618. Ezekiel	born 21 Sep 1809; died 12 Nov 1892 married Abigail[7] (2) MOSMAN (above) (# 1610)
1619. Pliny	born ca 1811; died ____
1620. Charles Wesley	born ca 1813; died ____
1621. Derwin R.	born ca 1815; died ____
1622. Abiel	born May 1817; died 10 Oct 1900 Templeton, MA; 1 married Ann T. GATES bef. 1860 2 married Emily A. ABBOTT Hoyt 23 Feb 1895

726. PHOEBE[6] MOSMAN, sister of above, was born 31 Oct 1785 at Westminster, Worcester, MA. She married Daniel[6] GATES on 27 May 1805 at Gardner, MA. He was the son of Simon[5] GATES (Amos[4]; Simon[3]; Stephen[2,1]) and Susannah REED, and was born 23 July 1782 Gardner, MA ; died 17 Sep 1847 Gardner, MA. Phoebe[6] MOSMAN died 1 Aug 1850.

Children of Phoebe[6] MOSMAN and Daniel GATES:
Surname **GATES**   (all children born Gardner, MA)

1623. Daniel Merrick	born 22 Apr 1806; died 31 Oct 1861 Northboro, MA married Arvilli LAWRENCE ca 1832 (she born ____; died 1871)
	Child: George Henry[8] GATES born ca 1833 Cambridge, MA; married Sarah A BUTLER
1624. Sophronia	born 18 Apr 1808; died ____; married John STICKNEY ca ____
	Children: Lyman[8] born ____; married Helen JOHNSON ; and Alvin[8] STICKNEY born ____, married Sylvia HUNTLEY

Children of Phoebe-6 MOSMAN and Daniel GATES, continued:
Surname **GATES**

+ **1625. LEONARD MOSMAN** born 28 July 1810; died ____
        1 married Martha J. LELAND 24 Dec 1837 Gardner, MA
        (she dau/o Amasa LELAND and Martha SEAVER)(she born ____; died 2 Jan 1852)
        2 married Eliza Ann PEABODY 26 Oct 1854 (she of Nashua, NH)
   1626. Lucy   born 5 Feb 1813; died ____; married George SMITH ca ____
      Child: Abbott-8 SMITH born ca ____; married Ella SMITH of Leominster, MA
+ **1627. PHEBE DIANTHA**   born 23 Aug 1815; died ____; married Gamaliel Sawyer BEAMAN ca ____
        (he born ca 1809; died July 1883 Fitcchburg, MA
   1628. Charlotte   born 11 Aug 1818; died 30 Aug 1842; married Stillman SAWYER ca ____
   1629. Solomon Keyes   born 16 May 1820; died 2 Jan 1891
      Child: Solomon Keyes-8 GATES born ca _____
      Reference: The Genealogy of the GATES Family, published 1898; pages 53; 117; 199-201

739. LUCINDA-6 HAPGOOD, daughter of David-5 HAPGOOD (Anna D-4 BOWKER; Asa-3; John-2; Edmund-1) and Sally MYRICK, was born 28 June 1790 at Princeton, Worcester, MA. She married Jared BIGELOW on 2 Feb 1812 at Reading, VT. He was the son of Elisha BIGELOW and Wealthea GORTON, and was born 26 Apr 1786 Colchester, CT; died 8 Aug 1856 at Reading, VT. Lucinda-6 HAPGOOD died 21 Oct 1835 at Reading, VT.

Children of Lucinda-6 HAPGOOD and Jared BIGELOW:
Surname **BIGELOW**   (all children born Reading, VT)

1630. Addison Clinton	born 28 Sep 1812; died 21 May 1813	EOL
1631. Fidelia Hapgood	born ca 1814; died 1870 Belchertown, MA	
1632. Mary Ann	born 25 Jan 1816; died 11 Nov 1873 Short Tract, Allegany. NY	
1633. Norman Curtis	born 16 Jan 1819; died 8 Oct 1882 Cavendish, VT	
1634. Jared Addison	(twin) born 24 Aug 1821; died 16 Mar 1822	EOL
1635. Lucinda Adeline (twin)	born 24 Aug 1821; died 31 May 1856	
1636. Laura Durrin	born 25 Oct 1824; died 3 Jan 1889 Belchertown, MA	
	married Benjamin Burr SNOW 3 Oct 1842 (4 ch)	
1637. Sarah	born 14 Aug 1827; died _____	

755. CHAUNCEY-6 HAPGOOD, son of Artemus-5 HAPGOOD (Anna D-4 BOWKER; Asa-3; John-2; Edmund-1) and Polly RICE, was born ca 1804 MA. He married Lucy F. RICE on 2 May 1833 at Barre, Worcester, MA. She was the daughter of James RICE and Hannah HAMMOND, and was born 15 June 1808 Barre,MA; died 15 Mar 1897 at Petersham, Worcester, MA. Chauncey-6 HAPGOOD died 3 Apr 1887 at Petersham.

Children of Chauncey-6 HAPGOOD and Lucy RICE:
Surname **HAPGOOD**

1638. Mary A.	born ca 1836; died ____; married Frederick C. BRYANT 23 June 1858		
1639. Charles F.	born 20 Feb 1838; died 8 Aug 1863		
1640. George A.	born 29 Dec 1839; died 13 Mar 1860		
1641. Harriet	born 17 May 1842; died 5 July 1873		
1642. Lyman Wilder	born 26 June 1845; died _____	1644. Ellen Eliza	born 25 May 1850; died ___
1643. Stella	born 2 July 1847; died ____	1645. Henry Edgar	born 7 Dec 1855; died ____

764. EDWARD-6 RICHARDSON, son of Martha-5 FORBUSH (Lucy-4 BOWKER; Asa-3; John-2; Edmund-1) and Benjamin RICHARDSON, was born 3 Sep 1785 MA. He married Charlotte ELLIS on 27 Sep 1812 at Sutton, Worcester, MA. She was the daughter of ____ELLIS and ____; and was born 30 July 1791 Sutton, MA; died ____. Edward-6 RICHARD-SON died 24 March 1872.

Children of Edward-6 RICHARDSON and Charlotte ELLIS:
Surname **RICHARDSON**

1646. Abel Ellis	born 23 June 1813; died 26 July 1878; married Ann EVANS ca ____, ME
1647. Asa Forbush	born 1 May 1817; died 8 May 1876; married Sarah Elliott ABBOTT ca ____
1648. Martha Maria	born 4 Oct 1819 NH; died 11 Apr 1882 Boston, MA
1649. Silence Leland	born 24 Sep 1821 NH; died ____
1650. Pliny Warren	born 8 Mar 1824 NH; died 18 Jan 1890; married Apphia H. OSGOOD ca ____

Children of Edward-[6] RICHARDSON and Charlotte ELLIS, continued:
Surname **RICHARDSON**

1651. Lucy Twitchell	born 23 Aug 1826 Coos, NH; died 19 Aug 1888; married William P. WHEELER ca ___	
1652. Ebenezer Andrus	born 29 Apr 1829 Milan, Coos, NH; died 1 Mar 1865; married Emeline COLE ca ____	
1653. Louise Cole	born 23 Dec 1831 Milan, NH; died 10 Dec 1908 Milan	
	married James C. BRADBURY ca ____	

765. EBENEZER-[6] RICHARDSON, brother of above, was born 7 March 1787. He married Cynthia ____ ca 1827 Maine.

Children of Ebenezer-[6] RICHARDSON and Cynthia ____:
Surname **RICHARDSON** (children born Gilead, Oxford, Maine)

1654. Edward L.	(twin) born ca 1828; died 2 Dec 1890 Gorham, NH		
1655. Rhoda Emeline.	(twin) born ca 1828; died ____		
+ **1656. ELI T.**	born ca 1831; died 9 Feb 1892 Oxford, ME		
	married Hannah Abbott TWITCHELL ca 1855		
	(she dau/o Andrew TWITCHELL and Lydia LITTLEHALE) (she born 12 July 1829 Gilead, ME; died ____)		
1657. Moses	born ca 1833; died _____		
1658. Albert B.	born ca 1838; died ____	1659. John A.	born June 1851; died ____

779. LUCRETIA-[6] HAPGOOD, daughter of Solomon-[5] HAPGOOD (Lydia-[4] BOWKER; Asa-[3]; John-[2]; Edmund-[1]) and Azubah BURT, was born 12 June 1792. She married Daniel TUTTLE ca 1808. He was the son of Titus TUTTLE and Lois ATWATER, and was born 5 June 1788; died 6 June 1861. Lucretia-[6] HAPGOOD died 19 March 1871 at Brooklyn, NY .

Reference: HAPGOOD Genealogy by Warren HAPGOOD (1816- ____)

Children of Lucretia-[6] HAPGOOD and Daniel TUTTLE:
Surname **TUTTLE**

1660. Quarters Morgan	born 28 Aug 1809; died 19 March 1877, single	EOL
+ **1661. FRANCES ADELINE**	born 15 March 1811 Grafton, VT; died 11 Feb 1905	
	1 married Holland WHEELER 27 Nov 1834 Bellows Falls, VT	
	(he born 3 Apr 1796 Westmoreland, NH; died 10 Oct 1842)	
	2 married Edward HALL 12 May 1846 (as his 2nd wife)	
	(he s/o Atherton HALL and Olive HALLETT)	
	(he born 20 Dec 1795; died 13 Mar 1889)	
1662. Adeline	born Oct 1813; died 3 Oct 1818	EOL
1663. Daniel Atwater	born 3 July 1815; died 17 July 1882; married Harriet LOMBARD 27 July 1842	
1664. Caroline Matilda	born 18 Aug 1817; died ___; married Solon Foster GOODRIDGE 21 Sep 1841	
1665. Lyman Hapgood	born 28 Oct 1819; died 3 Oct 1841 (lost at sea)	EOL

799. LUCRETIA SAMANTHA-[6] BRIDGMAN, daughter of Eunice-[5] HAPGOOD (Lydia-[4] BOWKER; Asa-[3]; John-[2]; Edmund-[1]) and Guy BRIDGMAN, was born 1 Dec 1816 at Guilford, VT. She married first to Varnum CURTIS on 16 Apr 1836 at Kendall, NY. He was the son of ____ CURTIS and ____; and was born ____; died 5 July 1837. She married second to Amasa Dwight WALKER on 1 June 1841. He was the son of ____ WALKER and ____; and was born 18 June 1814; died 7 Sep 1872. Lucretia S-[6] BRIDGMAN died ____.

Child of Lucretia-[6] BRIDGMAN and Varnum CURTIS:
Surname **CURTIS**

1666. child	born ca 1836/37; died ____	EOL

Children of Lucretia-[6] BRIDGMAN and Amasa WALKER:
Surname **WALKER**

1667. George Winfield	born 2 Jan 1843; died 5 Jan 1870 Hamlin, NY
	Note: He died as a result of wounds suffered in June 1864 at the Battle of Cold Harbor in the Civil War
1668. Marietta Elizabeth	born 12 Jan 1845; died ____
1669. Eleanor Lucretia	born 12 May 1847; died ____
1670. Augustus Dwight	born 6 Apr 1850; died ____
1671. Nettie	born 20 Oct 1854; died ____

803. SIMON-[6] BARNARD, son of Anna-[5] WHEELER (Abigail-[4] BOWKER; Ezekiel-[3]; John-[2]; Edmund-[1]) and William BARNARD, and was born ca 1792 at _____ . He married first to Lucy SIMONDS on 12 Feb 1818 at Woburn, Middlesex,

MA. She was the daughter of Jonathan SIMONDS and Phebe CUMMINGS, and was born 10 Nov 1787 Woburn; died 13 Aug 1842 Woburn. He married second to Elizabeth BEERS on 23 May 1843. She was the daughter of William BEERS and Elizabeth _____; and was born 22 Dec 1822; died _____. Simon[-6] BARNARD died 12 Feb 1872 Woburn, MA.

Children of Simon[-6] BARNARD and Lucy SIMONDS:
Surname **BARNARD**   (children all born Woburn, Middlesex, MA)

1672. Lucy	born 25 July 1819; died ____; married Benjaamin PAGE 28 Nov 1844	
1673. William	born 1 July 1821; died 19 Jan 1844 Woburn	
1674. Nathan Simonds	born 2 June 1823; died ____; married Emma LOVERING 3 Apr 1857	
1675. Silas (1)	born May 1825; died Mar 1827	EOL
1676. Silas (2)	born 4 April 1827; died 3 Mar 1828	EOL
1677. Susan Simonds	born 30 July 1829; died ____; 1 married Ignatius SARGENT ca ____ 2 married Cyrus MONROE 18 Sep 1862	
1678. Julia Ann	born 8 May 1831; died ____; married Joseph STEVENS 24 Mar 1859	
1679. Mary Elizabeth	born 26 Nov 1834; died 9 Sep 1920 San Diego, CA married Lyman Simon WHEELER on 16 Feb 1864 (he born 11 Feb 1837; died 18 Feb 1929)	

Child: Frederick Harlan[-8] WHEELER born 2 Oct 1871 NE; died 19 May 1903 AZ

808. LUMAN[-6] WHEELER, son of Asa[-5] WHEELER (Abigail[-4] BOWKER; Ezekiel[-3]; John[-2]; Edmund[-1]) and Sarah Thompson, was born 19 May 1795 at Marlborough, MA. He married first to Sarah SEAVER on 22 Nov 1818 at Swanzey, NH. She was the daughter of Shubael SEAVER and Mary PIERCE; and was born 11 Oct 1802; died 26 Mar 1831. He married 2nd to Anna M. SHERER 9 Jan 1871. She was the daughter of _____ SHERER and _____; and was born 11 July 1812 MA; died 20 Aug 1889. Luman[-6] WHEELER died ____.

Children of Luman[-6] WHEELER and Sarah SEAVER:
Surname **WHEELER**   (children all born Marlborough, MA)

1680. Luman, Jr.	born ca 1820; died ____	1682. Eliza	born ca 1827; died ____
1681. Alfred	born ca 1824; died ____	1683. Alonzo	born ca 1830; died ____

Children of Luman[-6] WHEELER and Anna M. SHERER:
Surname **WHEELER**

1684. Cynthia	born 6 Nov 1833; died ____	1685. Samuel (twin)	born Aug 1836; died ca 1902
1686. Sarah Maria (twin) "Sally"	born Aug 1836; died 1927 OH married Edward GRISWOLD ca ____	(he born ca 1832; died 1909)	
1687. Maria	born ca 1839; died ____		
1688. Jonathan (twin)	born June 1842; died ____		
1689. Josephine (twin)	born June 1842; died 20 May 1842		
1690. Hannah	born May 1845; died 29 Aug 1865		
1691. Edward (twin)	born May 1848; died 24 Dec 1895		
1692. Edgar(twin)	born May 1848; died 14 Oct 1901		
1693. Charles A.	born Aug 1850; died 1 Apr 1852		

810. ASA BOWKER[-6] WHEELER, brother of above, was born 24 Mar 1799 at Marlboro, Middlesex, MA. He married Persis BURKE ca 1821. She was the daughter of Philip Eastman BURKE and Sarah SWAN; and was born 30 July 1802 NH; died _____ Saxtons River, VT. Asa Bowker[-6] WHEELER died 28 Mar 1864.

Children of Asa Bowker[-6] WHEELER and Persis BURKE:
Surname **WHEELER**   (children all born VT)

1694. Mary	born 11 Sep 1822 Rockingham, Windham, VT; died ____ married Daniel George NOURSE 23 Sep 1841 (he born ca 1819; died 1882)
1695. Lucius Burke	born 3 Feb 1824; died ____
1696. Sarah	born 17 Dec 1825; died 30 Sep 1884; married Edward WALKER ca ___ (he born ca 1822; died 1898)
1697. George Persis	born 29 Mar 1827; died 8 Nov 1910 MI married Lucy Ann WILLISTON 12 Oct 1852

Child: Dr. Charles Salter[-8] WHEELER born 27 Aug 1856; died 10 Mar 1911; married Catherine Agnes FENTON 27 Dec 1880 Brattleboro, VT   (she dau/o Joseph FENTON and Eileen FITZGERALD)(she born ca 1855)

1698. Eliza W.	born 9 Dec 1829 VT; died 27 Mar 1895 NH; married David G. NOURSE ca ____
1699. Martha Jane	born 23 Dec 1831; died 9 Feb 1835

Children of Asa Bowker⁻⁶ WHEELER and Persis BURKE, continued:
Surname **WHEELER**

+	**1700. HENRY ASA**	born 8 Feb 1834; died 22 Apr 1915 Bennington, VT
		married Harriet Eliza WILLISTON ca 1856
		(she born 13 Dec 1835; died 1910; she d/o Josiah WILLISTON and Eliza FARNHAM)
	1701. Laura Ann	born 19 July 1837; died ____ Green Oak, MI (no issue) EOL
		married Lucas Hammond COGSWELL 17 Mar 1866 Rockingham, VT
		(he born 10 Dec 1834 NH; died 10 Jan 1917 MI)
		(he s/o William COGSWELL and Mary FISKE/FISH

811. LORENZO DOW⁻⁶ WHEELER, brother of above, was born 24 Nov 1800. He married Finetta LEWIS on 12 Aug 1824 NY. She was the daughter of____LEWIS and _____; and was born 18 Aug 1805; died 30 May 1892. Lorenzo-⁶ WHEELER died 28 March 1864.

Children of Lorenzo-⁶ WHEELER and Finetta LEWIS:
Surname **WHEELER**

	1702. James Asa	born 10 May 1825; died 13 Apr 1892; married Elizabeth LUCAS 25 Nov 1865
	1703. Sarah Adelia	born 4 Aug 1826; died 23 Sep 1827 EOL
	1704. Edward Mortimer	born 1 Oct 1828; died ____; married Mary Martha BROWN 11 Feb 1855
+	**1705. FINETTA LOUISE**	born 29 Dec 1835; died 26 Aug 1917 (aged 81)
		married Enoch WOOD 12 Feb 1856 (he was a potter)(a Capt. in the Civil War)
		(he born ca 1832 England; died 27 July 1903)
		(poss. s/o William WOOD and Rebecca BRADBURY)

Children: Enoch Lorenzo-⁸ born 17 Mar 1862; and Annie Estella-⁸ WOOD born 18 Jan 1866

	1706. Julia Estella	born 14 Apr 1840; died ____; married Robert Miller HOYT 24 Feb 1859
	1707. Mary A	born 7 Nov 1842; died ____; married Smith KEELER 7 Nov 1867
		(he s/o Harry KEELER and Emeline ___; he born Feb 1845 NY)

Children: Frederick-⁸ born ca 1869 and Florence-⁸ KEELER born ca 1870, married Charles PRATT

813. SYDNEY W-⁶ PEESO, son of Laura-⁵ HOWE (Silas-⁴; Hannah-³ BOWKER; John-²; Edmund-¹) and William PEESO, was born 26 March 1793. He married Pamela PRATT on 24 June 1824 at Greece, Monroe, NY. She was the daughter of ____ PRATT and ____, and was born 14 June 1803; died 6 June 1873.

Children of Sydney-⁶ PEESO and Pamela PRATT:
Surname **PEESO**

	1708. Theodore Austin	born 4 Oct 1825 MI; died 25 July 1864
	1709. Mary Maria	born 21 Jan 1833 MI; died 28 Jan 1912 Sycamore, OH

840. CAPT. HANANIAH⁻⁶ WHITNEY, Jr., son of Azubah-⁵ KEYES (Hannah-⁴ HOWE; Hannah-³ BOWKER; John-²; Edmund-¹) and Hananiah WHITNEY, and was born 18 Dec 1762 Winchendon, MA. He married Sally T. BEAMAN on 19 Oct 1820 at Winchendon. She was the daughter of _____ BEAMAN and _____, and was born ____; died ____. Hananiah-⁶ WHITNEY died 2 Mar 1887 Lowell, MA.

Children of Capt. Hananiah-⁶ WHITNEY and Sally BEAMAN:
Surname **WHITNEY**

1710. Mary Beal	born 17 July 1821	1713. William Melos	born 15 May 1826
1711. Martha Beaman	born 8 Nov 1822	1714. George Leavitt	born 21 Aug 1828
1712. John Milton	born 21 Sep 1824		
1715. Henry M.	born ca 1829; died ____; married Harriet BAGLEY 25 Apr 1854		
1716. Sarah A.	born ca 1833; died ____; 1 married _____ SMITH		
	2 married William H. FLAGG 18 Nov 1869 Lowell, MA		
	(he born ca 1828; died ____) (he s/o William FLAGG and Martha B _____)		
1717. Elizabeth	born ca ____; died _____; married Joseph A. BAILEY 11 Jul 1860		
1718. Abby A.	born 20 Aug 1843/44 Lowell, MA 1719. Charles Edwards born 15 May 1846;		

868. ALVA⁻⁶ LUND, son of Willard-⁵ LUND (Phineas-⁴; Thomas-³; Elizabeth-² BOWKER; Edmund-¹) and Sarah TOWNE, was born 8 Oct 1799 at ____ VT. He married Andrea GODFREY ca 1833 . She was the daughter of ____ GODFREY and _____; and was born ca 1811 NY; died _____. Alva-⁶ LUND died 31 Jan 1882 Martville, Cayuga County, NY.

Children of Alva-[6] LUND and Andrea GODFREY:
Surname **LUND**

1720. Alvira	born ca 1835 NY; died ____	
1721. Emerett	born 14 July 1837 NY; died 17 June 1859 Martville, NY	
1722. Anna	born ca 1840 NY; died ____	
1723. Harvey E.	born ca 1846	
1724. Elwood/Elmore/Elmer	born Aug 1852 NY; died 3 Mar 1930 Hannibal, Cayuga, NY; married _____?	

Children: Nellie E-[8] born 1874 Hannibal, NY, and Percy-[8] LUND born ca 1878 Hannibal

869. LUCINDA-[6] LUND, sister of above, was born 24/28 May 1802 . She married Ira GARFIELD 25 Sept 1826. He was the son of Enoch GARFIELD and Martha Patty POWERS, and was born 19 Feb 1802; died 21 Aug 1891. Lucinda-[6] LUND died 18 Jan 1895/96 at Calmar, Iowa.

Children of Lucinda-[6] LUND and Ira GARFIELD:
Surname **GARFIELD**

1725. Sarah C.	born Dec 1826; died _____	1729. Henry Washington	born ca 1844
1726. Augusta Jane	born ca 1831 VT; died ca 1860		
1727. Daniel W.	born ca 1834 Mechanicsville, VT; died ____		
+ **1728. LUCY JANETTE**	born 5 May 1841 VT; died 15 Nov 1901 Kent , OR married John L. MC CULLOCH 21 Dec 1858		

870. HENRY-[6] LUND, brother of above, was born 1 March 1811 VT. He married Mary L. EDDY ca 1846. She was the daughter of ____ EDDY and ____; and was born ca 1813 VT; died 5 Jan 1865 . Henry-[6] LUND died 10 Feb 1894.

Children of Henry-[6] LUND and Mary EDDY:
Surname **LUND**

1730. Angeline P.	born 15 June 1847 Grafton, NY; died 22 May 1901 NY
1731. Caleb Foster	born 4 July 1849 Grafton, Rennselaer, NY; died ____ married Margaret BONNIE 2 Sept 1889 (she born 10 Dec 1865; died 11 May 1895)
1732. William Ward Volney	born 29 Dec 1851 Grafton, NY; died _____ married Emma Melora PULCIPHER ca ___ (she born 24 Feb 1852; died _____)

Children: Lela F-[8] born Jan 1875; and Cora-[8] LUND born ca 1880 Hannibal, Cayuga, NY

871. SAMUEL-[6] SPAULDING , son of Samuel-[5] SPAULDING (Henry-[4]; Elizabeth-[3] LUND; Edmund-[2,1] BOWKER) and Sarah WOODS, was born 22/23 August 1754 at Merrimack, NH. He married on 28 Nov 1782 to Sarah/Sally HEALD . She was the daughter of Ephraim HEALD and Sarah CONANT, and was born 4 Sept 1759 Temple, NH; died 26 March 1823. Samuel-[6] SPAULDING died 1 March 1825 at Merrimack. He had seen military service in the Revolutionary War as a Private (MA) in Captain Daniel EMERSON'S Co., Col. Hercules MOONEY'S Regiment which had been raised for the defense of RI. He was also a surveyor of Highways in Merrimack.

Children of Samuel-[6] SPAULDING and Sarah HEALD:
Surname **SPAULDING** (all children born Merrimack, NH)

1733. Ephraim	born 19 April 1783 ; died 7 June 1790	EOL
1734. Sarah	born 29 March 1785; died ____; married Luther ABBOTT of Andover, VT	
+ **1735. ABIJAH**	born 18 March 1787; died 21 Sep 1867 Nashua, NH married Hannah Goodrich EASTMAN Sept 1814 (she dau/o Nicholas EASTMAN and Olive BARNES) (she born 4 Sept 1792 Francestown, NH; died 6 April 1877 Nashua, NH)	
1736. Betsey	born 7 Jan 1789; died ____; married Isaac BLOOD	
1737. Luther	born 29 Apr 1790; died ____; removed to Baltimore, MD	
1738. Muriel	born 25 Dec 1792; died ____; married John THOMAS ca	

Child: Elizabeth B-[8] THOMAS ca ___; married Cyrus CASS; Resided Andover, VT and WI

+ **1739. IRA**	born 30 Nov 1794; died 1855 married Eliza Jane ATWOOD ca 1829 (she born ca 1805 Merrimack; died _____)
1740. Capt.Josiah	born 15 Feb 1797; died 4 April 1868 Salem, Essex, MA married Rebecca CHAPMAN 10 April 1825 Salem, MA (she born 5 Feb 1800 Salem, MA ; died _____ MA

Children: Josiah Chapman-[8] SPAULDING; and George Henry[8] SPAULDING

1741. Elenor/ Eleanor	born 30 Nov 1799; died ____; married Leonard BLANCHARD of Andover

872. ABIJAH-⁶ SPAULDING, brother of above, was born 18 June 1756 at Merrimack, NH. He married Polly WYMAN of Billerica, MA ca ____. She was the daughter of ___ WYMAN and ___, and was born ca 1760; died 1 Feb 1817. Abijah⁻⁶ SPAULDING died 12 April 1828 at Wilton, NH

Children of Abijah⁻⁶ SPAULDING and Polly WYMAN:
Surname **SPAULDING**

1742. Mary	born 11 Feb 1789 Wilton, NH; died 26 Dec 1852; married Joseph GRAY April 1815	
1743. Samuel	born 20 Sept 1791; died 7 Oct 1859; married Nancy PHELPS 31 Dec 1824	
	Children: Mary-⁸; John Henry-⁸; and Mary Ann-⁸ SPAULDING	
1744. Abijah	born 11 Jan 1804; died ____; married Olive HUTCHINSON 1 Dec 1831 Milford, NH	
	Children: Horatio Augustus-⁸; Theresa Augusta-⁸; and Henry Erastus-⁸ SPAULDING	

875. OLIVER-⁶ SPAULDING, brother of above, was born 6 Feb 1763 at Merrimack, NH. He married first to Abigail NOURSE ca ____. She was the daughter of Francis NOURSE and Eunice PUTNAM, and was born 13 Jan 1762; died 17 March 1793. His 2ⁿᵈ marriage was to Lucy DAVIS on 24 April 1800. She was the daughter of ____ DAVIS and ____, and was born ca 1767; died 5 May 1823. He married 3ʳᵈ to Sally CALDWELL ca ____. She was the daughter of ___ CALDWELL and ____, and was born ca 1781; died 21 April 1860. Oliver⁻⁶ SPAULDING died 21 Aug 1841. He resided in Merrimack, on his fathers' farm.

Children of Oliver⁻⁶ SPAULDING and Abigail NOURSE:
Surname **SPAULDING**

1745. Abigail	born 25 Sep 1789; died 26 July 1795		EOL
+ **1746. OLIVER, JR.**	born 23 May 1791; died ____; married Asenath DANFORTH 28 Dec 1817		
	(she dau/o Solomon DANFORTH and _____)		

876. ISAAC-⁶ SPAULDING, brother of above, was born 20 Aug 1765 at Merrimack, NH. He married first to Mary RITTER on 9 April 1795. She was the daughter of ____ RITTER and ____, and was born ___; died 27 April 1808. His second marriage was to Mrs. Mary FLYNN Colburn of Milford, NH., on 2 Nov 1809. She was the daughter of ___ FLYNN and ____, and the widow of _____ COLBURN, and was born ca ____, died ____. His occupation was that of a tanner. He removed from Merrimack to , then to Ipswich, NH and finally to Wilton , NH ca 1800. He resided at Wilton the rest of his life, dying there on 2 June 1830.

Children of Isaac⁻⁶ SPAULDING and Mary RITTER:
Surname **SPAULDING**

+ **1747. ISAAC**	born 1 Feb 1796 New Ipswich, NH; died 14 May 1876 Wilton, NH	
	married Lucy KENDALL 1 May 1828	
+ **1748. MOSES**	born 10 March 1797 New Ipswich; died 1879	
	married Anna Hunt KIMBALL 29 May 1823	
+ **1749. CHARLES**	born 4 Nov 1798 New Ipswich, NH; died 15 Feb 1880	
	married Lydia Joyce BURNS 25 Dec 1827	
1750. Harvey	born 8 Oct 1800 Wilton, NH; died ____; never married	EOL
1751. Mary	born ca 1801; died 20 Aug 1848 Milford, NH	
	married Prescott KIMBALL 8 Apr 1828 North Chelmsford, Ma	
1752. Aaron	born 28 Dec 1803; died young	EOL
1753. Lyman	born 6 Dec 1806; died 5 Oct 1854; never married	EOL

Children of Isaac⁻⁶ SPAULDING and Mary FLYNN Colburn:
Surname **SPAULDING**

1754. Emma	born 2 July 1813; died ____; married David WHITING 5 Oct 1830 Wilton, NH
1755. Orpah	born 5 July 1816; died ____
	1 married John MACK 24 Feb 1839 (he born ca ____; died 27 Oct 1840)
	2 married Sewall G. MACK 5 Sept 1844 (her brother –in-law)

877. SILAS-⁶ SPAULDING, brother of above, was born 11 June 1767 at Merrimack, NH. He married first to Rebecca SHEDD on 22 Jan 1797. She was the daughter of ____ SHEDD and ____, and was born ____; died ___. His second marriage was to Elizabeth HILLS on 14 Jan 1798. She was the daughter of Stephen HILLS and ____, and was born 2 June 1779; died 2 July 1841. He married third to Dorcas CHANDLER on 27 Nov 1806. She was the daughter of Daniel CHANDLER and ____, and was born ___, died ____. Silas-⁶ SPAULDING died Oct 1828 at Merrimack, NH

Children of Silas-6 SPAULDING and Elizabeth HILLS:
Surname **SPAULDING**

1756. Rebecca Jane	born 22 May 1798; died ____; married James HOWARD 11 July 1816 Andover, NH	
1757. Leonard Woods	born 26 Nov 1799; died ____; married Emily EATON 19 Dec 1823	

Children: Emily-8 born ca 1824; Harriet E-8 born ca 1834; and Charles-8 SPAULDING born ca 1836

1758. Eldridge	born 4 Jan 1802	1759. Ebenezer	born 2 Aug 1804

Children of Silas-6 SPAULDING and Dorcas CHANDLER:
Surname **SPAULDING**

1760. Alfred	born 10 Oct 1806; died ____; married Amy _____ ca ____

Children: Mary Ann-8 born ca 1838; Emily F-8 born ca 1839; George C-8 born ca 1842;
Henry L-8 born ca 1843; and Charles M-8 SPAULDING born ca 1846

1761. Eliza	born 6 Oct 1808; died 10 Dec 1902; married Benjamin M. HILLS
1762. Lydia	born 16 Dec 1810; died 21 June 1871; never married EOL

878. ASA-6 SPAULDING, brother of above, was born 5 April 1769 at Merrimack, NH. He married Joanne CHANDLER ca ___. She was the daughter of Daniel CHANDLER, and sister of Dorcas above) and ____, and was born Aug 1774 Andover, MA; died ____. Asa-6 SPAULDING died 9 April 1815 of spotted fever.

Children of Asa-6 SPAULDING and Joanne CHANDLER:
Surname **SPAULDING**

+	**1763. ASA**	born 21 April 1794 Merrrimack, NH; died ___; married Sarah GILMORE ca ____
	1764. Ephraim	born 28 March 1796; died 5 Sep 1799 EOL
	1765. Samuel Woods	born 9 Apr 1798; died 11 April 1815 EOL
	1766. Joanna	born 3 Apr 1800; died 11 april 1815 EOL
	1767. Sophia	born 5 March 1802; died ____; married Timothy FRY/FRYE of Lowell, MA
+	**1768. CYNTHIA**	born 31 March 1804; died ___; married Gilbert COLBURN 13 Nov 1828
	1769. Albert Jefferson	born 1 March 1806; died 22 Dec 1879
		married Mary BERRY 30 Nov 1830; (she born15 April 1808; died ____)

Children: Albert-8 born ca 1831; Benjamin Berry-8 born ca 1835; Mary Ellen-8 born ca 1837; Jacob Carlton-8 born ca 1842; Emma-8 born ca 1844; and Albert Jefferson-8 SPAULDING born ca 1847

1770. Lucy Davis	born 5 Apr 1808; died 11 Jan 1832; married Jacob CARLTON 28 July 1830	
1771. Sarah/ Sally	born 26 May 1812; died ____; married Jacob CARLTON 13 Sep 1832	
1772. Dorcas	born 27 June 1814; died ____; married Andrew J. NUTE 6 Sept 1835	

888. SHEREBIAH-6 FLETCHER, son of Sarah-5 SPAULDING (Henry-4; Elizabeth-3 LUND; Edmund-2,1 BOWKER) and Henry FLETCHER, was born 4 Nov 1760 NH. He married first to Martha ELLENWOOD on 26 Nov 1785. She was the daughter of Joseph ELLENWOOD and Sarah ____, and was born 31 July 1761; died 5 Sept 1823. He married second to Mary Ann BELLOWS on 9 Dec 1832. She was the daughter of James BELLOWS and Anna CULVER, and was born 4 April 1807; died 25 April 1882 OH.

Children of Sherebiah-6 FLETCHER and Martha ELLENWOOD:
Surname **FLETCHER**

+	**1773. MARY**	born 1786-9; died 6 June 1846; married David IRWIN 1 Aug 1810
		(he born 1 July 1778 Ireland; died 22 March 1848 OH) (he s/o John IRWIN and ____)
	1774. Charles	born 11 July 1796 VT; died 2 Oct 1866 OH
		married Susanna CANNON Starks 24 Nov 1822
		(she born 25 Feb 1793; died 5 Mar 1869)
	1775. Sally/ Sarah Merrick	born 29 Apr 1798; died 1883; married Abraham BALL 16 Aug 1818
		(s/o Richard BALL and Rachel MOORE) Ch: Simon-8 1831-84; and Rufus-8 1833-1910
	1776. Clarifia	born 19 May 1801; died ____ 1777. Lucinda born 22 Dec 1803; died 1807

Children of Sherebiah-6 FLETCHER and Mary Ann BELLOWS:
Surname **FLETCHER**

1778. Emeline	born 13 Nov 1838; died 6 Seept 1885 NE
	1 married Alexander L. FOSTER 24 Sept 1856; 2 married Allen MILLER 3 Sept 1867
1779. John Vinton	born 12 Jan 1842; died 4 March 1925 NE
1780. Amasa Samuel	born 14 June 1843; died 4 Sept 1905 NE
	married Mary Elizabeth FOSTER ca 1867; resided Mineral IL in 1880

Children: Alberta-8 born ca 1868; Austin-8 born ca 1870; Earnest-8 born ca 1873; Preston-8 born ca 1877; and Nellie Mae-8 FLETCHER born ca 1879

897. JONATHAN^{-6} SPAULDING, son of Daniel^{-5} SPAULDING (Henry^{-4}; Elizabeth^{-3} LUND; Edmund-^{2,1} BOWKER) and Hannah PUTNAM, was born 4 July 1771. He married Taomis/Tamison YOUNG ca 1796. She was the daughter of David YOUNG and Rachel GRANT, and was born ca 1773; died 1815. Jonathan^{-6} SPAULDING died ca 1814.

Children of Jonathan $^{-6}$ SPAULDING and Taomis YOUNG:
Surname **SPAULDING**   (children born Embden, Maine)

1781. Daniel	born 28 Feb 1798 ME; died ____; married Betsey COLBY	
1782. Jesse	born ca 1799 ME; died ____	
1783. Christopher Columbus	born ca 1800 ME; died ca 1850 ME; married Lydia MAPES ca ____	
1784 Thomas Blake	born 7 Jan 1801 ME.; died ____; a Methodist minister	
1785. Benjamin	born 22 March 1803; died 3 Dec 1839 MA	
	Information source: " Embden, Maine, Town of Yore"	
1786. Samuel	born ca 1805; died ca 1825	
1787. William	born ca 1807; died ____	
1788. Louisa	born ca 1809; died ____	
1789. Lavinia	born April 1811 ME; died 16 Oct 1855 ME; married Cyrus Wellington Mc KENNEY	
	Child: Edwin^{-8} Mc KENNEY born ca 1835; died ca 1914	
1790. David	born ca 1813; died _____ 1791. Mary Ann	born ca 1815; died ca 1875

901. SOLOMON^{-6} SPAULDING, half-brother of above, son of Daniel^{-5} SPAULDING (Henry^{-4}; Elizabeth-^{3} LUND; Edmund-^{2,1} BOWKER) and Mary BUTTERFIELD, was born 31 March 1783 at Merrimack, NH. He married Martha MC CLURE on 7 Sept 1806. She was the daughter of William MC CLURE and ___, and was born 13 April 1784 Merrimack, NH ; died 21 Aug 1867. Solomon^{-6} SPAULDING died 23 Feb 1864 at Merrimack, NH.

Children of Solomon^{-6} SPAULDING and Martha MC CLURE:
Surname **SPAULDING**   (all children born Merrimack, NH)

1792. Roxanna	born 29 Oct 1806 ; died ____; married Benjamin MOORE ca ____	
1793. Lucinda	born 22 Feb 1809; died ____; married John REED 9 Dec 1831 Lowell, MA	
+ **1794. SOLOMON**	born 20 July 1811; died 2 June 1902 Nashua, NH	
	married Sarah Darling EDSON 16 Feb 1834	
1795. Daniel	born 18 Oct 1817; died ____ 1796. Mary	born 26 Oct 1824; died ____

903. DANIEL^{-6} SPAULDING, brother of above, was born 18 Aug 1787 at Merrimack, NH. He married Abigail BROWN on 2 Jan 1812. She was the daughter of Captain Daniel Josiah BROWN and Sarah WRIGHT, and was born 22 June 1790 NH; died 24 April 1864 New Ipswich, NH. Daniel^{-6} SPAULDING, a farmer and brick maker, died 9 Jan 1840 NH.

Children of Daniel-^{6} SPAULDING and Abigail BROWN:
Surname **SPAULDING**

1797. Abby Frost	born 6 Nov 1812; died 19 Aug 1840; never married EOL	
1798. Eliza Field	born 20 Aug 1814 NH; died 26 July 1870 MN	
	married Benjamin HALE 19 Jan 1848 (as his 2nd wife)	
	(he s/o Moses HALE and Ruth TOWNE)	
	(he born 18 Aug 1819 NH; died 22 Jan 1887 MN)	
	Children: Abigail^{-8} born ca 1850, and Benjamin^{-8} HALE born ca 1859, died 1908	
1799. Benjamin Daniel	born 25 Apr 1815; died ____; married Sarah F. MARSTON 13 Sept 1846	
1800. Ebenezer Brown	born 26 Oct 1817; died ____; married Samantha FIELD 12 Oct 1845	
1801. Almira Stevens	born 30 Oct 1819; died ____; married Dr. Solomon BLOOD 2 Apr 1851	
1802. Samuel	born 6 March 1821; died ____; married Betsey MARSTON 27 Aug 1848	
1803. James Chandler	born 31 May 1823; died 29 Nov 1887; married Sarah B. RICHARDSON 26 Dec 1846	
1804. Mary Ann	born 16 Apr 1825; died 29 Mar 1847; married Benjamin HALE 15 May 1845	
1805. Charles	born 1 Feb 1827; died ____; married Sarah E. HOLT Greenough 5 Sept 1862	
1806. George Putnam	born 24 Sept 1828; died 8 Feb 1867; married Sarah WHITNEY 29 Jan 1852	
1807. Sarah Jane	born 6 Mar 1830; died 19 Aug 1867; married Edward F. PARKER 11 Nov 1852	

909. HEPHZIBAH^{-6} LOVEWELL, daughter of John^{-5} LOVEWELL (Rachel^{-4} LUND; William-$^{3;}$ Elizabeth-^{2} BOWKER; Edmund-$_{1}$) and Vodica LOVEWELL, was born 3 May 1792 at Corinth, Orange, VT. She married Laban LASELL/LAZELL on 28 Aug 1815 at St. Albans, Franklin, VT. He was the son of ____ LASELL/LAZELL and ____; and was born ca 1793; died ca 1857. Hephzibah^{-6} LOVEWELL died 23 Sep 1878 at Canton, St. Lawrence, NY.

Children of Hephzibah[-6] LOVEWELL and Laban LASELL/LAZELL:
Surname **LASELL/LAZELL**

1808. Myron	born 30 Aug 1816; died 14 Sep 1895 Canton, NY	
1809. Charlotte	born 31 May 1818; died 21 July 1894 IA.	
+ **1810. MORRIS SMITH**	born 5 May 1822 VT; died 4 Nov 1878 Ellenburg, Clinton, NY	
	married Sarah Ann SKINNER 27 Nov 1845 St. Albans, VT	
	(she dau/o Alvah SKINNER and Betsey SANBORN)	
	(she born 16 Jan 1824; died 21 Apr 1901 Ellenburg, NY	

915. JOSEPH HALL[-6] UNDERWOOD, son of Thomas-[5] UNDERWOOD (Mary-[4] LUND; William[-3]; Elizabeth-[2] BOWKER, Edmund-[1]) and Mehitable GAGE, was born 13 June 1783 NH. He married first to Mary McAfee AIKEN on 16 Oct 1809. She was the daughter of ____ AIKEN and Mary MC AFEE, and was born 1784; died 1822. His second marriage was to Jane AIKEN, sister of Mary. Joseph[-6] UNDERWOOD died 8 Nov 1867 ME.

Children of Joseph Hall[-6] UNDERWOOD and Mary AIKEN:
Surname **UNDERWOOD**

1811. Joseph Hall	born ca 1811; died 25 May 1814	EOL
1812. Mary Aiken	born 30 July 1812; died 7 April 1887; married Marshall LANE 1 Feb 1851	
1813. Eliza Hall	born 8 Nov 1814; died 31 July 1896; married Joseph Henry NORTH	
1814. Joseph Hall	born ca 1817; died 12 Feb 1845	
1815. Thomas Parker	born 8 Jun 1818; died 27 Jan 1852	
1816. Sarah Ann	born 17 July 1822; died 9 May 1891; married James FULLER	

Children of Joseph Hall[-6] UNDERWOOD and Jane AIKEN:
Surname **UNDERWOOD**

1817. Jane Aiken	born 29 Sept 1823; died 24 Dec 1884; married Alonzo WING
+ **1818. ALBERT GALLATIN**	born 16 Sept 1831 Fayette , ME; died 21 July 1906; married Eliza TUCK 6 Nov 1856
	(she dau/o Samuel TUCK and Didamia STIMPSON)
	(she born 23 Aug 1834; died _____)
1819. Henry C.	born 29 Apr 1833; died 2 Dec 1853
1820. George	born 20 Sept 1834; died 8 Dec 1906; married Caroline NASH
1821. Gilbert	born 11 Dec 1835; died ____; married Annie E. HOLMES
1822. Helen	born 20 June 1841; died ca 1910; married William H. GOODWIN

917. SALLY H[-6] UNDERWOOD, sister of above, was born 8 July 1787 NH. She married Isaac GAGE on 19 March 1816. He was the son of Isaac GAGE and Mary WEBSTER, and was born 5 Apr 1788 MA , died 13 Apr 1866 Bedford, NH. Sally[-6] UNDERWOOD died 7 Sept 1860.

Children of Sally[-6] UNDERWOOD and Isaac GAGE:
Surname **GAGE**

1823. Sally Jane	born ca 1817; died 1858	
+ **1824. THOMAS UNDERWOOD**	born 30 Sept 1819; died 20 Jan 1867 NH	
	married Dolly Adeline FRENCH 12 June 1845	
	(she dau/o Ebenezer FRENCH and Rhoda COBURN)	
	(she born 26 Jan 1826; died 8 Feb 1896)	
1825. William	born 4 Oct 1822 Bedford, NH; died 26 July 1879 Bedford, NH	
1826. Lydia	born ca 1827; died ____	
1827. Letitia	born ca 1827; died ____	1829. Edward A. born ca 1831; died 19 March 1876 MA.
1828. Lucinda	born ca 1829; died 1849	

937. ROYAL[-6] BLOOD, son of Rachel-[5] UNDERWOOD (Mary-[4] LUND; William-[3;] Elizabeth-[2] BOWKER; Edmund-[1]) and Royal BLOOD, was born 21 Dec 1794 NH. He married Mary Polly STILES 29 Apr 1821 Wilton, NH. She was the daughter of Asa STILES and Ruth ____, and was born 7 June 1800 NH; died 11 April 1896 Miami County, Indiana. Royal[-6] BLOOD died 26 Jan 1861 Peru, Indiana.

Children of Royal[-6] BLOOD and Mary Polly STILES:
Surname **BLOOD**

1830. James Underwood	born 22 Oct 1822 NH; died ____, IN
	1 married Lois Ellen FISHER 28 Mar 1850; 2 married Mary Ann HOPKINS ca 1866

Children of Royal[6] BLOOD and Mary Polly STILES, continued:
Surname **BLOOD**

1831. Frances	born ca 1825; died ca 1896	
1832. Albert P.	born 12 Apr 1823; died 7 May 1908 IN	
1833. Orrin	born ca 1829 Oswego, NY; died ____	
1834. Asa Stiles	born 12 June 1831 NY; died 25 June 1894; married Martha E. SMITH 10 May 1862	
1835. Lucien	born ca 1833 NY; died ____	
1836. Nathan Whitney	born 5 Nov 1835 Auburn, NY; died 5 Aug 1898 Orting, WA	

married Sarah Adelaide BEAUMONT 15 Sep 1873 New London, CT
(she born Nov 1837 England; immigrated 1841; died ____
Children: Mary A-[8] born 18 Nov 1876 MN, died 11 June 1884 MA; and William R-[8] BLOOD
born 27 Sep 1879 MN, died 14 Sep 1957 Los Angeles, CA.

1837. Joseph	born Apr 1837 NY; died 18 Mar 1849 IN	
1838. Sarah A.	born born Aug 1840 NY; died 26 Oct 1916; married Oliver BORDEN 20 Nov 1860	
1839. Mary F.	born 7 Feb 1843 NY; died 27 Oct 1904 Miami Co., IN	

979. REUBEN[6] TOWNSEND, son of Margaret[5] METCALF (Margaret[4] SHATTUCK; Margaret[3] LUND; Edmund[2,1] BOWKER) and Reuben TOWNSEND, and was born 15 Jan 1788. He married first to Sultina HILL on 18 July 1815. She was the daughter of Isaac HILL and ____, and was born ____; died 18 June 1860. His second marriage was to Matilda BOLTON Shumway ca ___. She was the daughter of Captain BOLTON of Westminster, MA and ____, and was born ____; died ____ Reuben[6] TOWNSEND died ca 1867 of paralysis.

Children of Reuben[6] TOWNSEND and Sultina HILL:
Surname **TOWNSEND**

1840. Sultina Cobleigh	born 10 Nov 1816; died 28 July 1824	EOL
+ **1841. LUCY**	born 20 July 1818; died _____	

married Samuel Sawin COOLIDGE 24 Aug 1842
(he son of James COOLIDGE and Annis SAWIN)
(he born 24 Aug 1813 Gardner, MA; died _____ VT)

980. JOSHUA[6] TOWNSEND, brother of above, was born 22 Oct 1790. He married Betsey KIMBALL 17 July 1823. She was the daughter of William KIMBALL and Abigail HAMLET, and was born 25 Sept 1796; died 15 Nov 1849. He married second ca 1852 to Esther EATON of Lancaster. Esther EATON was the daughter of ____ EATON and ___, and was born ____; died 27 June 1855. Joshua[6] TOWNSEND died 20 June 1855.

Children of Joshua[6] TOWNSEND and Betsey KIMBALL:
Surname **TOWNSEND**

1842. Leonard Kimball	born 11 July 1825; died 3 July 1836	EOL
1843. Albert	born 22 Nov 1827; died 23 Nov 1827	EOL
1844. Mary	born 27 April 1830; died ____; married Ivers WELLINGTON 6 Jan 1857	

(he s/o Liberty WELLINGTON and Mary LAWRENCE)(he born 12 Jan 1812 Ashby)

1845. William Kimball	born 10 June 1839; died 21 April 1843	EOL

1003. DAVID[6] LAWS, son of Thankful[5] METCALF (Margaret[4] SHATTUCK; Margaret[3] LUND; Edmund[2,1] BOWKER) and James LAWS, and was born 6 March 1799. He married Nancy WILDER on 24 April 1828. She was the daughter of Caleb WILDER and Sarah WHITNEY, and was born ____; died ____. David[6] LAWS died 22 March 1875.

Children of David [6] LAWS and Nancy WILDER
Surname **LAWS**

1846. Sarah Ann	born 3 Feb 1829; died 14 Aug 1829	EOL
+ **1847. LYMAN**	born 30 Sept 1830; died 16 June 1890	

married Eliza J. FAY ca _____; resided Boston, MA

1848. M. Rebecca	born 29 May 1833; died 2 Nov 1879	

married James H. BANCROFT ca ____; resided Worcester, MA

1008. JAMES HERVEY[6] LAWS, brother of above, was born 8 Sept 1809. He married Julia Augusta HASTINGS on 24 March 1836. She was the daughter of John HASTINGS and Sarah GREEN, and was born 3 Sept 1811; died 19 Nov 1885. James Hervey[6] LAWS died 1 March 1891.

Children of James Hervey [-6] LAWS and Julia HASTINGS:
Surname **LAWS**

1849. Unnamed infant	born 13 June 1837; died in infancy		EOL
1850. Unnamed twins	born 24 April 1838; died in infancy		EOL
1851. Sarah G.	born 7 June 1840; died 15 Aug 1848		EOL
1852. Ellen	born 22 June 1841; died 30 Oct 1905; unmarried		EOL

+   **1853. HIRAM**   born 27 June 1844 Westminster, MA; died 17 May 1913; resided Bedford, MA
married Mary Elizabeth. DUTTON 15 Oct 1871
(she dau/o Hildreth P. DUTTON and Abigail __) (she born 15 Oct 1849; died __)

1854. Julia	born 26 Feb 1846; died 9 June 1849		EOL

1855. Sidney Julius   born 13 May 1848 MA; died 12 March 1913 Framingham, MA
married Emily/ Emma Jane BRAMAN 23 Sept 1874 ; resided Worcester, MA
(she dau/o William A. BRAMAN and Harriet _____) (she born ca 1854 MA)
Children: A. Bertha-[8] born ca 1882; and Marion B-[8] LAWS born ca 1888

1856. Walter H.	born 25 April 1850; died _____ ; unmarried EOL		
1857. Mary E.	born 18 Oct 1852; died 11 Jan 1873	1858. Anna C.	born 24 May 1857

1022. ROXANNA[-6] **SIMPSON**, daughter of Sarah[-5] SHATTUCK (Job[-4]; Margaret[-3] LUND; Edmund[-2;1] BOWKER) and Benjamin SIMPSON, was born ca 1784 Groton, Middlesex, MA. She married first to John Longley WITHERELL on 15 May 1799. He was the son of ____ WITHERELL and ____, and was born Oct 1772 Pepperell, MA; died 31 Dec 1813 at Chateaugay, NY. She married second to Joseph FOSS, Jr. on 15 Feb 1819 at Clinton, ME. He was the son of Joseph FOSS and Hannah CARLL, and was born ca 1789 Pepperell, died 11 Apr 1873. Roxanna[-6] SIMPSON died 18 Jan 1878 at Clinton, Kennebec, ME..

Children of Roxanna[-6] SIMPSON and John WITHERELL:
Surname **WITHERELL**

+   **1859. NANCY**   born 7 Apr 1800 Groton, MA; died 7 Nov 1884
married Alexander BUZZELL 31 Dec 1818 Winslow, Kennebec, ME
(he s/o Ezekiel BUZZELL and Hannah ALLEN)
(he born 11 Jan 1792 Kennebunk, York, ME; died 23 Apr 1880 Benton, Kennebec, ME

1860. Harriett	born ca 1810; died _____
1861. John	born ca 1812/13; died _____

Children of Roxanna[-6] SIMPSON and Joseph FOSS, Jr.
Surname **FOSS**

1862. Joseph Bunker	born ca 1820 Clinton, ME; died 11 Aug 1873; married Mary Sophia SIMPSON ca ___
1863. Harriet	born ca 1821; died _____

+   **1864. LIBERTY**
         SHATTUCK   born May 1823; died 1910 Danforth, ME
1 married Tenny BUTTERFIELD 5 Dec 1842
2 married Abbie FARNHAM on 8 Dec 1868

1023. DANIEL P-[6] **SIMPSON**, brother of above, was born 29 Sep 1790 MA. He married Harriet STIMPSON 29 Sep 1816 at Boston, Suffolk, MA. She was the daughter of Benjamin STIMPSON and Rebecca HILL, and was born 22 Jan 1796 at Boston, died 28 June 1871 Boston, MA. Daniel[-6] SIMPSON died ca 1875.

Children of Daniel[-6] SIMPSON and Harriet STIMPSON:
Surname **SIMPSON**

1865. Daniel P., Jr.	born ca 1819; died _____
1866. William P.	born ca 1822; died _____
1867 Harriet L.	born ca 1824; died _____
1868. Thomas L.	born ca 1824; died _____
1869. Mary H.	born ca 1827; died _____
1870. Samuel A.	born ca 1830; died _____
1871. George W.	born ca 1834; died _____

+   **1872. ANDREW**
         JACKSON   born 20 July 1834; died 23 Apr 1915 OH
1 married Clara A. MASON Holt 24 Apr 1858
(she born ca 1830; died 12 July 1877 Worcester, MA
2 married Zurella Jane RICHARDSON ca _____
(she born 16 June 1843; died 30 Apr 1929 OH)

1025. EZEKIEL-6 SIMPSON, brother of above, was born ca 1795 Groton, MA. He married Roxanna SIMPSON on 29 Jan 1825. She was the daughter of _____ SIMPSON and _____; and was born ca 1798 Boston, Suffolk, MA; died 19 Oct 1891 Winslow, Kennebec, Maine. Ezekiel-6 SIMPSON died ca 1863.

Children of Ezekiel-6 SIMPSON and Roxanna SIMPSON:
Surname **SIMPSON**

1873. LaForest	born 12 Sep 1825; died _____; married Mary J. MOODY ca (she born ca 1827; died ca 1906)	(6 ch)
1874. Sarah Amanda	born 14 Nov 1826 Winslow, ME; died 7 Apr 1905 married John A. HOLBROOK 23 June 1850	(5 ch)
1875. Emeline Phebe	born 4 Apr Winslow, ME; died 28 Jan 1917 married James Preston HILL 2 Feb 1849	(6 ch)
1876. Albert Allen	born 2 Nov 1832 ME; died 27 June 1902; married Esther HALL 2 Feb 1859	
1877. William Wallace	born 7 Sep 1836 ME; died 7 Sep 1859; married Lucinda DOWSE 22 Nov 1855	
1878. Daniel Worcester	born 11 Apr 1838 ME; died 1899; married Minerva Johnson NYE 1863	
1879. Della Arabina	born 25 Dec 1841 ME; died 27 May 1879; married Abijah A. BROWN 5 Oct 1866	

1034. HARRIET-6 SHATTUCK, daughter of Ezekiel-5 SHATTUCK (Capt Job-4; Margaret-3 LUND; Mary-2 BOWKER; Edmund-1) and Prudence BLOOD, was born 2 May 1800 at Groton, MA. She married William Shattuck BENNETT 2 April 1828. He was the son of ___ BENNETT and ____, and was born ca 1804; died __. Harriet-6 SHATTUCK died 22 Jan 1847 at Dunstable, MA.

Children of Harriet-6 SHATTUCK and William Shattuck BENNETT:
Surname **BENNETT**

1880. Harriet Josephine	born Mar 1829; died _____	1882. William	born Jan 1834; died _____
1881. Rufus Shattuck	born ca 1831; died 1832 EOL	1883. George	born Nov 1837; died _____

1044. RACHEL-6 HARTWELL, daughter of Rachel-5 SHATTUCK (Capt. Job-4; Margaret-3 LUND; Mary-2 BOWKER, Edmund-1) and Oliver HARTWELL, was born 28 Feb 1793 Groton, MA. She married Jonathan LAWRENCE 18 Feb 1812. He was the son of Rowland LAWRENCE and Mahala WORCESTER, and was born 11 Sept 1788 at Groton, died 26 Sept 1842 at Groton. Rachel-6 HARTWELL died _____.

Children of Rachel-6 SHATTUCK and Jonathan LAWRENCE:
Surname **LAWRENCE**

1884. Eliza	born ca ___; died in infancy	1889. John H.	born 13 April 1824; died ___
1885. Jonathan (1)	born ca ___; died in infancy	1890. Walter	born 27 Dec 1825; died _____
1886. Ephraim (1)	born ca ___ died in infancy	1891. Sarah	born 26 Aug 1827; died young
1887. Jonathan (2)	born ca ___; died in infancy	1892. Mahala R.	born 6 Jan 1831; died
1888. Ephraim (2)	born 31 May 1821; died Oct 1847	1893. Mary E.	born 11 April 1833; died young

1048. CLARISSA-6 HARTWELL, sister of above, was born 2 June 1800 at Groton, MA. She married Samuel WILLIAMS on 3 Aug 1827. He was the son of _____ WILLIAMS and _____, and was born 3 Nov 1794 at Groton. He was a farmer and died _____. Clarissa-6 HARTWELL died _____.

Children of Clarissa-6 HARTWELL and Samuel WILLIAMS:
Surname **WILLIAMS**

1894. Samuel P.	born 5 Feb 1828; died _____	1902. Sarah A.	born 20 May 1843; died _____
1895. Jacob L.	born 24 Oct 1829; died _____	1903. Ellen M.	born 29 Oct 1844; died _____
1896. Mary S.	born 17 Apr 1832; died _____	1904. Herbert M.	born 5 April 1850; died _____
1897. Clarissa H.	born 29 Oct 1834; died _____		
1898. Charles H. (1)	born 23 Sept 1836; died 17 Oct 1836		
1899. Sarah E.	born 1 Nov 1837; died 3 Nov 1837		
1900. Charles H. (2)	born 12 Dec 1839; died _____		
1901. Asa	born 21 Feb 1842; died 4 Apr 1842		

1050. MARGARET SHATTUCK-6 HARTWELL, sister of above, was born 9 March 1805 at Groton, MA. She married Rufus WILLIAMS on 8 May 1834. He was the son of Josiah Sawtell WILLIAMS and Lydia SIMONDS, and was born 6 Sept 1808 at Groton; died 11 July 1893. Margaret-6 HARTWELL died 16 Sept 1878 Groton, MA.

Children of Margaret-6 HARTWELL and Rufus WILLIAMS:
Surname **WILLIAMS**

1905.. Sarah Margaret	born 8 Aug 1834 Stetson, ME; died 14 April 1852 Groton, MA	
1906. George Henry	born 4 May 1836 Groton, MA ; married Susan Adeline EATON 20 Nov 1861	
	died/killed near Dallas, GA 25 May 1864, member Co. E, 33rd MA. Vol. in Civil War	
1907. Marcelina Phoenicia	born 4 July 1839 Groton; died 11 Jan 1926	
	married Albert Freeman. PARKHURST 15 Apr 1862	
	(he s/o Jacob PARKHURST and Betsey ___)	

Child: Alice Theresa-8 PARKHURST born ca 1863

1908. Adelaide Louise	born 16 Dec 1841Groton; died ____ ; married David H. COCHRAN 26 Nov 1868	
	(he from Brookline, NH) Child: Earl W-8 COCHRAN born ca 1873	

Source: " A Record of Some Groton Families ", page 313 and 314

1909. Frances Adelia	born 28 Aug 1843 Groton; died 27 July 1867 Groton
	married Abbott Lawrence BLOOD 9 Mar 1865
1910. Asa Richard	born 28 Aug 1845 Groton; died 14 March 1936
	married Carrie E. ADAMS of Townsend on 30 Nov 1874
1911. Josiah Sawtell	born 13 Aug 1848 Groton; died 29 July 1932; married Mary E P EATON 28 Sept 1871

1053. ROSILLA-6 SHATTUCK, daughter of Daniel-5 SHATTUCK (Job-4; Margaret-3 LUND; Edmund-2,1 BOWKER) and Abigail SHEPLE, was born 26 Oct 1799. She married James Minot-6 COLBURN 17 May 1821 at Groton, MA. He was the son of Abiel-5 COLBURN (Abiel-4; Moses-3; Joseph-2; Edward-1) and ____. Rosilla-6 SHATTUCK died 15 Dec 1845.

Children of Rosilla-6 SHATTUCK and James COLBURN:
Surname **COLBURN**

1912. Charles Minot	born 20 Feb 1822; died 1856 (he drowned in Lake Erie)
	married Mary Jane ALLEN 24 May 1846 (divorced)
1913. Alfred Hall	born 8 Sept 1823; died 12 March 1847 MA
1914. Martha M.	born 22 Aug 1825; died ca 1828 Groton, MA
1915. James Francis	born 14 Oct 1827 Groton; died ____
1916. Martha Jane	born 20 Apr 1831; died 21 March 1852
1917. Sarah Maria	born 21 Oct 1836 Groton; died 14 June 1860
1918. Sumner Boynton	born 8 Apr 1839 Groton; died ____
	married Josephine Maria HASLEY 8 Nov 1859 (she dau/o Luther HASLEY)

Children: Elmer Harlan-8 born 13 Aug 1865; and Sarah M-8 COLBURN born ca 1860

1919. Eliza A.	born 12 April 1850; died ____

1070. NOAH-6 SHATTUCK, Jr. , son of Noah -5 SHATTUCK (Job-4; Margaret-3 LUND; Edmund-2,1 BOWKER) and Anna SHEPLE, was born 14 Sept 1799 Groton, MA. He married Prudence WRIGHT on ____. She was the daughter of Artemus WRIGHT and Prudence COREY, and was born 2 Feb 1806 Groton, MA; died ____. Noah-6 SHATTUCK, Jr. died 28 Sept 1858.

Children of Noah-6 SHATTUCK and Prudence WRIGHT:
Surname **SHATTUCK**

1920. Augusta P.	born 25 Dec 1824 Groton; died ____ ; married James LEWIS 11 April 1846/47		
	(he born 3 July 1820; died ____)		

Children: Herbert M-8 born 4 Feb 1848; Frederick J-8 born 10 Nov 1852; and Edward A -8 LEWIS born ca 1861

1921. Noah Gilman	born 18 Dec 1828 Groton; died ____ ; married Mary W. HENDERSON		
1922. George H.	born 9 July 1831 Groton; died 12 May 1832	EOL	
1923. Charles A.	born 13 Jan 1834 Groton; died ____		
1924. Henry P.	born 19 Aug 1844 Groton; died ___	1926. Herbert	born ca 1848
1925. Arthur W.	born 6 Oct 1848; died ____	1927. Frederick	born ca 1852

1071. WALTER-6 SHATTUCK, brother of above, was born 9 Aug 1801 at Groton, Middlesex, MA. He married Roxanna FLETCHER on 9 May 1827 at Groton. She was the daughter of David FLETCHER and Mary ALLEN, and was born ca 1804.

Children of Walter-6 SHATTUCK and Roxanna FLETCHER:
Surname **SHATTUCK**   (all children born Groton, MA)

1928. Martha Roxanna	born 1 April 1828; died ____	
1929. David Walker	born 3 Feb 1830; died 3 Jan 1851 Groton	
1930. Mary Allen	born 3 Aug 1831; died 21 Nov 1835	EOL

Children of Walter-6 SHATTUCK and Roxanna FLETCHER, continued:
Surname **SHATTUCK**

1931. Susan French	born 12 June 1833; died ____	
1932. Almira Ann	born 4 Aug 1834; died 20 March 1835	EOL
1933. Noah Fletcher	born 25 March 1836; died 22 April 1842	EOL
1934.George Francis	born 28 July 1838; died ____	
	married Louise HERRICK 26 Oct 1868 (her 2nd marriage)	
	(she dau/o Benjamin Adams HERRICK and Mariah JONES)	
	(she born 28 June 1833 VT; died 15 Jan 1905 Lunenburg, MA)	
1935. Samuel Walker	born 18 Feb 1841; died 13 Feb 1915; married Adelaide WHITE 14 Aug 1866	
1936. Abbott Allen	born 4 May 1843; died ____ 1937. Mary Fletcher born 25 Oct 1845	

1073. ANDREW-6 SHATTUCK, brother of above, was born 28 Dec 1805 Groton, MA. He married Cynthia STONE on 24 April 1832 at Groton, MA. She was the daughter of Joseph STONE and Rachel GREEN, and was born 30 Apr 1804; died 9 March 1869. Andrew-6 SHATTUCK died ca 1879.

Children of Andrew-6 SHATTUCK and Cynthia STONE:
Surname **SHATTUCK**

1938. Cynthia Maria	born 21 March 1833 Groton, MA	
1939. Anna Augusta	born 6 Mar 1835 Groton; died 3 Oct 1848 EOL	
1940. Andrew Payson	born 20 Apr 1837; died _____	
1941. Sarah Baldwin	born 27 April 1839; died ca 1905	
1942. James Fowler Baldwin	born 2 Feb 1845; died 2 Aug 1864	EOL
1943. Henry A. Richards	born 14 Sept 1846; died 30 Sept 1847	EOL
1944. Harriet Newell	born 23 July 1850; died ____	

1082. MARGARET-6 BENNETT, daughter of Margaret-5 SHATTUCK (Job-4; Mary-3 LUND; Edmund-2,1 BOWKER) and Jonathan BENNETT, was born 2 Sept 1806 at ____. She married Jefferson TAYLOR Nov 1825. He was the son of Jonas TAYLOR and Hannah ____, and was born 11 Jan 1802 at Dunstable, died 6 Nov 1873 IL. Margaret-6 BENNETT died 12 Dec 1868 at Moline, IL.

Children of Margaret-6 BENNETT and Jefferson TAYLOR:
Surname **TAYLOR**   Source: Descendants of William SHATTUCK , page 186; A Record of Some Groton Families page 310

1945. Margaret Shattuck	born 18 Jan 1827 Dunstable, MA; died ____
	1 married Nathan RUSS 5 Nov 1851 (he born ca 1822; died 1859)
	2 married Nathan Cram TYRRELL 29 May 1859 (as his 2nd wife)
	(he s/o Samuel TYRRELL and Anna B. CRAM)
	(he born 5 Apr 1814; died 1899)
	Children: Mary Augusta-8 born ca 1861; Nathan Edward-8 born ca 1863; and
	Benjamin Butler-8 TYRRELL born 7 Sept 1864, died 14 April 1944
1946. Hannah Augusta	born 9 June 1828 Groton; died 25 Nov 1905; married Ezra T. BLODGETT May 1851
1947. Sarah Ann Eldridge (1)	born 3 Jan 1831; died 4 March 1831
1948. Sarah Ann Eldridge (2)	born 20 Feb 1832 Groton; died ____
1949. Lucinda/Lucretia Maria	born 30 Aug 1833 Groton; died ____; married C P CURTIS
1950. Mary Frances	born 16 March 1837; died ____
1951. Joseph Jefferson	born 6 Nov 1838; died 1 Oct 1839
1952. Louisa Jane	born 10 May 1840; died ____
1953. Annie Elizabeth	born 23 May 1851; died ____

1083. LOUISA-6 BENNETT, sister of above, was born 13 July 1808. She married Joel Fletcher OSGOOD on __ June 1830. He was the son of _____ OSGOOD and ____, and was born ____, died _____. Louisa-6 BENNETT died ____.

Children of Louisa-6 BENNETT and Joel OSGOOD:
Surname **OSGOOD**

1954. Ann Maria	born Feb 1831; died July 1832
1955. Louisa Jane	born June 1832; died ____; married James PRINCE 1 Nov 1851
1956. George Wilder	born Dec 1836; died ____
1957. Joel Fletcher	born Dec 1845; died ____

1085. WILDER-⁶ BENNETT, brother of above, was born 17 April 1813 at Dunstable, MA. He married Mary Ann DAVIS ca Nov 1840. She was the daughter of ___ DAVIS and ___, and was born ____, died ____. Wilder-⁶ BENNETT died 17 May 1896.

Children of Wilder-⁶ BENNETT and Mary Ann DAVIS:
Surname **BENNETT**   Source: MA. Town VR 1620-1988

1958. Mary Louisa	born Aug 1843; died May 1847
1959. Frank Wilder	born 29 Jan 1846; died Aug 1848
1960. Caroline Delia	born Dec 1848 MA; died 9 Aug 1900
1961. Marion Jane (twin)	born Aug 1851; died ____, married _____ TARBELL
1962. Wilder C. (twin)	born Aug 1851; died 14 Dec 1855

1086. ALDEN BRADFORD-⁶ BENNETT, brother of above, was born 18 April 816 at Dunstable, MA. He married Elizabeth B. STEBBINS on 13 Nov 1836. She was the daughter of ____ STEBBINS and ____, and was born ca 1818, died ____. Alden-⁶ BENNETT died 15 May 1895 at Amherst, NH.

Children of Alden-⁶ BENNETT and Elizabeth STEBBINS:
Surname **BENNETT**

1963. Emily Elizabeth	born Aug 1837 Amherst, NH; died 16 Dec 1861 Lowell, MA married David GOODHUE 2 July 1854
1964. Margaret Adelaide	born March 1843; died ca 1900; married George W D YOUNG
1965. Sarah Louisa	born 7 Aug 1844; 1 married Joseph W. HOWE; 2 married Oscar SHAFFER
1966. Isabel Bradford	born Oct 1845; died 14 Apr 1904 MA; married Eugene V. McLEOD

1087. ASHER-⁶ BENNETT, son of Anna/Nancy-⁵ SHATTUCK (Job-⁴; Mary-³ LUND; Edmund-²;¹ BOWKER) and Thomas BENNETT, was born 2 April 1799 MA. He married Sarah H. ____ ca 1825. She was the daughter of ____ and ____, and was born ca 1798; died ____. Asher-⁶ BENNETT died 13 Nov 1881 NH.

Children of Asher-⁶ BENNETT and Sarah H. ____:
Surname **BENNETT**

1967. Sarah Catharine	born 28 May 1826; died _____ married Dr. Stephen S. MIXER 30 May 1843 (he a magnetic physician) Child: Carrie-⁸ MIXER born ca 1854 NH
1968. Mary Ann	born 28 Oct 1827; died ____
1969. Augusta H.	born ca 1830; died _____
1970. James H.	born ca 1835; died ____ married Mary Eliza DANIELS (Sumner) on 4 Dec 1862
1971. Orlina J.	born ca 1837; died ____

1091. BERI-⁶ BENNETT, son of Anna/Nancy-⁵ SHATTUCK (Job-⁴; Mary-³ LUND; Edmund-²;¹ BOWKER) and Thomas BENNETT, was born 19 Sept 1808. He married first to Margaret RUSSELL on 12 June 1828. She was the daughter of ____ RUSSELL and ____, and was born ca 1812, died ____. His second marriage was to Mrs. Nancy LYNCH Marvell/Marble on 17 April 1867. Beri-⁶ BENNETT died ____.

Children of Beri-⁶ BENNETT and Margaret RUSSELL:
Surname **BENNETT**

1972. Nancy	born 13 Oct 1828; died ____
1973. Thomas D.	born 24 March 1831; died ____
1974. Beri S.	born 9 Dec 1832; died ____
1975. Thirza	born 28 June 1835; died 10 Feb 1914; married David MILLER
1976. John C.	born 13 Mar 1837; died ____; married Ella BIGNALL 13 Dec 1855

1094. RODOLPHUS-⁶ BENNETT, brother of above, was born 7 Feb 1817 NH. He married Mary WOODWARD on 14 May 1840. She was the daughter of Isaac WOODWARD and Mary MELENDY, and was born ___; died 27 Feb 1887 Manchester, NH. Rodolphus-⁶ BENNETT died 19 Feb 1885 at Milford, NH.

Children of Rodolphus-⁶ BENNETT and Mary WOODWARD:
Surname **BENNETT**

1977. Albert Rodolphus	born 27 Sept 1842, Merrimack, NH
1978. William Alphonso	born 9 Dec 1845 Merrimack, NH

Children of Rodolphus[6] BENNETT and Mary WOODWARD, continued:
Surname **BENNETT**

1979. Alfred Allen.	born 30 Nov 1848 Brookline, NH; married Permelia E. CHAPIN 1 July 1878 (he a teacher in Ames, Iowa)	
1980. Mary Emily	born 20 Sep 1851 Milford, NH; died ____; married John F. GILLIS 8 Sept 1874	
1981. Anna Frances	born 24 Oct 1853; died ____; married Louis P. CUMNOCK 24 July 1880	
1982. Clara Louise.	born 5 Dec 1859; died ____; married Frank L. DOWNS 20 Oct 1885	

1095. ROSILLA-[6] BENNETT, sister of above, was born 10 Feb 1819 at Brookline, NH. She married Alpheus MELENDY on 1/8 March 1838. He was the son of Thomas MELENDY and Sally TAY, and was born 12 May 1816 at Brookline, NH; died ____. Rosilla-[6] BENNETT died ____

Children of Rosilla[6] BENNETT and Alpheus MELENDY:
Surname **MELENDY**

1983. Elmira/Almira F.	born ca 1840; died 26 Jan 1894 NH. 1 married Frederick Wells PEACOCK 10 Nov 1860 2 married Charles GILSON 14 Nov 1891
1984. Mary Emeline	born ca 1850; died 20 May 1922; married George B. PETTINGILL
1985. Sarah A.	born ca 1854; died 30 Nov 1926; married Harvey T. DUNKLEE

1104. LOVICE-[6] BOWKER, daughter of Deacon Edmund-[5] BOWKER (Micah-[4]; Edmund-[3]; John-[2]; Edmund-[1]) and Hannah STEARNS, was born 22 Mar 1779 at Hopkinton, MA. She married Alexander-[6] CHENEY on 2 Aug 1801 . He was the son of Wales-[5] CHENEY (William-[4;3;2;1]) and ____; and was born 8 Oct 1780; died ____. She died 7 March 1824.

Children of Lovice-[6] BOWKER and Alexander CHENEY:
Surname **CHENEY**

1986. Penelope	born 7 Sept 1801; died ____; married Dana KNOWLTON 27 Apr 1823 Petersham, MA
1987. Sophia	born 9 Feb 1803; died ____; married Rufus CLAFLIN, Jr. on 24 Oct 1824
1988. Nathan	born 25 July 1804; died ____; married Susan STONE 5 Apr 1827
1989. Jonathan	born 31 Aug 1806; died 22 Aug 1834 unmarried EOL
1990. Emily	born 26 Aug 1808; died 6 Oct 1850; married Amos WALES 21 Apr 1831
1991. Lydia Bowker	born 9 Nov 1810; died ____; married Alfred WARNER ca ____

1105. JONATHAN-[6] BOWKER, brother of above, was born 6 July 1781 at Hopkinton, MA. He married Penelope DEWING ca ____. She was the daughter of John DEWING and Patience SUMNER; and was born ____; died ____. Jonathan-[6] BOWKER died ____.

Child of Jonathan-[6] BOWKER and Penelope DEWING:
Surname **BOWKER**

1992. Miranda	born 29 May 1808; died 24 Feb 1833; res. North Purchase, MA married Eliphalet BAILEY 30 Jan 1825 (he born ____; died 26 Aug 1831 (suicide)

1108. IRA-[6] BOWKER, brother of above, was born 26 Aug 1793 at Hopkinton, MA. He married Julia EVERETT of Dedham, MA on 27 Nov 1817. She was the daughter of ____ EVERETT and ____; and was born ____; died Oct 1840. Ira-[6] BOWKER died 25 Aug 1830.

Children of Ira-[6] BOWKER and Julia EVERETT:
Surname **BOWKER**

+	**1993. GEORGE STEARNS**	born 2 June 1818; died ____ married Chloe Ann SAUNDERS 28 Nov 1838 (she dau/o Nathaniel SAUNDERS and Hannah HAWKS)
	1994. Ann Marie	born 14 July 1820; died ___; married Newell PHIPPS 14 Feb 1838 Milford, MA

1109. LYDIA-[6] BOWKER, daughter of Senator Asa-[5] BOWKER (Samuel-[4]; Edmund-[3,2,1]) and Hannah HARWOOD, was born 6 May 1780 at Hopkinton, MA. She married first to Thomas WYMAN, Jr. on 25 Sep 1798 at Winchendon, Worcester, MA. He was the son of Thomas WYMAN and Elizabeth REED, and was born ca 1774 Woburn, MA; died 14 Oct 1816 Winchendon, MA. She married second to Stephen R. SMITH ca April 1819 at Winchendon. He was the son of ____ SMITH and ____; and was born ____; died ____. Lydia-[6] BOWKER died ____.

Children of Lydia-[6] BOWKER and Thomas WYMAN:
Surname **WYMAN**

1995. Asa		born 2 Oct 1800; died 12 Nov 1811		EOL
1996. Lydia		born 10 Aug 1802; died 10 Sep 1820		
1997. Olive	(1)	born 28 Mar 1804; died 10 Nov 1811		EOL
1998. Franklin		born 17 June 1806; died 7 Nov 1811		EOL
1999. Stillman		born 10 May 1808; died 15 Nov 1811		EOL

Note: Four children died within a span of 8 days. There may have been an epidemic of small pox or another contagious disease

2000. Harvey	born 5 Oct 1810; died 11 July 1879	
	1 married Phebe H. JOHNSON 17 Oct 1835	
	2 married Mariah C. HAYES 12 July 1855	
	3 married Gail C. WHITCOMB 2 Feb 1867	
2001. Newell (1)	born 13 Dec 812; died 15 Sep 1813	EOL
2002. Newell (2)	born 6 Feb 1814; died 10 Jan 1875	
2003. Olive (2)	born 10 Mar 1816; died 10 Oct 1841; married Erastus W. CLARK ca _____	

1111. WILLIAM-[6] BOWKER, brother of above, was born 15 July 1784 at Hopkinton, MA. He married Sally HARWOOD ca ____. She was the daughter of ____ HARWOOD and ____, and was born 27 Nov 1780; died 23 Sep 1867. William-[6] BOWKER died 16 Oct 1847.

Children of William-[6] BOWKER and Sally HARWOOD:
Surname **BOWKER**

+   **2004. SULLIVAN**   born 28 March 1808 Winchendon, MA; died 11 Dec 1870 Winchendon
         married Eunice ADAMS 11 Oct 1835 Winchendon, MA
         (she dau/o Benjamin ADAMS and Chloe ALGER)
         (she born 22 Mar 1818; died 6 Oct 1895 Winchendon)

1112. LUTHER-[6] BOWKER, brother of above, was born 16 Jan 1787 at Hopkinton, MA. He married Betsey WALKER on 5 March 1812. She was the daughter of Samuel WALKER and Elizabeth WYMAN, and was born ___, died ____. Luther-[6] BOWKER died 18 Jan 1826.

Children of Luther-[6] BOWKER and Betsey WALKER:
Surname **BOWKER**

2005. Abraham	born ca 1816; died 27 Dec 1893; 1 married _____ ca ____
	2 married Sarah SPRAGUE West 26 June 1871

+   **2006. LUTHER A.**   born 22 Jan 1826; died 1 Feb 1884 Royalston, MA.
         married Charlotte Newton MAYNARD 2 Sep 1850
         (she dau/o Oren MAYNARD and Huldah ALGER)
         (she born 3 Sept 1834; died 3 July 1888)

1114. ASA-[6] BOWKER, JR., brother of above, was born 13 June 1792 at Winchendon, Worcester, MA. He married first to Joanna WALKER on 3 April 1817. She was the daughter of ____ WALKER and ____; and was born ____; died ____. He married second to Abigail CHUBB ; intentions published 5 June 1824. He married a third time to Louise LATHE Day on 7 June 1854. She was the daughter of ____ LATHE and ____; and the widow of _____ DAY, and was born 30 June 1792; died 21 Dec 1866. Asa-[6] BOWKER, Jr. died ____.

Children of Asa-[6] BOWKER, Jr. and Joanna WALKER:
Surname **BOWKER**

2007. Esther	born 9 Sept 1817; died ____		
2008. Abigail (1)	born 16 Jan 1819; died young		EOL
2009. Levi	born 4 Feb 1821; died 6 Aug 1851; never married		EOL

Children of Asa-[6] BOWKER, Jr. and Abigail CHUBB:
Surname **BOWKER**

2010. Ephraim	born 25 Jan 1825; died ____		
2011. Joanna	born 26 Mar 1828; died ____	2012. Abigail (2)	born 4 July 1830; died ____

1115. HANNAH-[6] BOWKER, sister of above, was born 6 Aug 1794 at Hopkinton, Worcester, MA. She married Silas WYMAN on 5 March 1812 at Winchendon. He was the son of Thomas WYMAN and Elizabeth REED, and was born ca 1788; died ca 1863. Hannah-[6] BOWKER died ____.   **107**

BOWKER
The Sixth American Generation

Children of Hannah[6] BOWKER and Silas WYMAN:
Surname **WYMAN**   (children all born Winchendon, Worcester, MA)

+ **2013. DAVID**	born 14 Nov 1812; died 12 Jan 1883 Winchendon	
	married Lucinda OLIN ca ____ (she born ca 1821 VT; died 1 July 1866 WI)	
2014. Eunice	born 10 July 1814; died 5 Sep 1886; married Joseph ALGER 2 Feb 1836	
2015. Mary Ann	born ca 1816; died ____	
2016. Thomas	born 25 Apr 1821; died 29 Sep 1893	
2017. Louisa	born 31 Aug 1823; died ____	
2018. Julia Ann (1) (twin)	born 1 May 1827; died 15 Apr 1836	EOL
2019. Persis (twin)	born 1 May 1827; died young	EOL
2020. Julia Ann (2)	born ca 1828; died ____	
2021. Silas, Jr. (twin)	born 5 Mar 1831; died ____	
2022. Sylvanus Bowker (twin) born 5 Mar 1831; died Feb 1905 MI	2023. Sarah A. born ca 1832; died 4 Dec 1898	

1119. ABIATHER[6] BOWKER, Jr., son of Abiather[5] BOWKER (Samuel[4;] Edmund[3;2;1]) and Polly FUZZE/FEZZE, was born 4 Oct 1793 Hopkinton, MA. He married Mary GOULD on 28 Nov 1816 Hopkinton. She was the daughter of ____ GOULD and _____, and was born 2 Feb 1796 Greenfield, Hillsborough, NH; died 25 June 1848 Hopkinton, MA . Abiather[6] BOWKER, Jr. died 13 June 1848.

Children of Abiather[6] BOWKER, Jr. and Mary GOULD:
Surname **BOWKER**

2024. Mary	born ca 18__; died 14 Jan 1899; married _____ JENNINGS ca ____
2025. John Starkweather	born 30 Dec 1819; died 10 Dec 1846
2026. Harriet M.	born 27 Nov 1824; died 8 Dec 1907 Everett, MA
	married John BANCROFT 7 Nov 1844
	Children: Mary E[8] born ca 1846, married ___ SMITH; and Clara E.[8] BANCROFT
	born ca 1849; married ____ FISHER
2027. George Washington	born 30 Jan 1827; died 5 July 1892
+ **2028. JAMES MADISON**	born 21 Dec 1829; died 25 Mar 1894; married Martha J. NEWTON 3 July 1862
	(she dau/o Benjamin NEWTON and Lucy ____) (she born ca 1845)

1120. HARRIET[6] BOWKER, sister of above, was born 2 July 1799 at Hopkinton, Middlesex, MA. She married Lowell FROST 10 April 1825 at Hopkinton. He was the son of John FROST and Mary BACON; and was born 6 Jan 1798 Sherborn, MA; died ____.

Children of Harriet[6] BOWKER and Lowell FROST:
Surname **FROST**

+ **2029. LOWELL LELAND**	born 31 Aug 1826 Hopkinton; died 3 Jan 1899 Susanville, Lassen, CA
	1 married Sophrona CHASE 12 May 1850 Bath, NH (she born ca 1825 VT; died ___)
	2 married Anna Maria JACOBS ca ____
	(she born 29 Jan 1839 CA; died 16 Dec 1928 CA)
2030. Martha Ann	born 14 Aug 1828 Hopkinton; died _____
	married Ethan HOMES on 30 Nov 1848 at Hopkinton, MA
	(he s/o Simpson HOMES and Hannah LORING)
	(he born 7 Apr 1814 Hopkinton, died 27 Feb 1889)
	Children: Emma[8] born ca 1852; Charles Ethan[8] born 9 June 1854; and Fred E.[8] HOMES born 3 Mar 1857
2031. Charles A.	born 1834/35; died 21 May 1884 Calhoun County, MI

1135. ETHAN[6] BOWKER, son of John-[5] BOWKER (Uriah[4]; Edmund[3]; John[2]; Edmund[1]) and Esther WEDGE, was born _____ at Hopkinton, MA. He married Alpha WHEELOCK on 8 Nov 1814. She was the daughter of Obadiah WHEELOCK and Lydia THURBER; and was born 28 Nov 1798 Milford, MA; died 15 Nov 1875 Milford. Ethan[6] BOWKER died 26 April 1817. NOTE: His widow married 2nd to Lowell FALES (Aaron) on 9 Feb 1824 and had 6 more children.

Children of Ethan[6] BOWKER and Alpha WHEELOCK:
Surname **BOWKER**

2032. Ralph Wheelock	born ___; bapt. 20 Oct 1815; died 18 Aug 1876
	married Mary Brunson HOWARD 26 Nov 1840
	(she dau/o Abijah HOWARD and Margery __)

Children of Ethan-[6] BOWKER and Alpha WHEELOCK, continued:
Surname **BOWKER**

2033. Ethan Loring	born 2 Aug 1817; died 5 Feb 1855 (age 37)	
	1 married Sarah Sadler HOWARD 9 May 1842 (she sister of Mary, above)	
	(she born 17 June 1821; died 15 June 1843)	
	2 married Adeline Metcalf ALBEE 16 June 1845	

1136. CHARLOTTE-[6] BOWKER, sister of above, was born ca 1794 Hopkinton, MA. She married Ephraim WHEELOCK on 21 Sep 816. He was the son of Paul WHEELOCK, Jr. and Beulah JOHNSON, and was born 4 Nov 1791 Charlton, MA; died 2 Oct 1873 Spencer, MA. Charlotte-[6] BOWKER died 20 Nov 1877 Charlton, Worcester, MA.

Child of Charlotte-[6] BOWKER and Ephraim WHEELOCK:
Surname **WHEELOCK**   Reference: Some of the Ancestors of Samuel CONVERSE, Jr. of Killington, CT

+   **2034. AARON BOWKER**   born 21 Oct 1826 Uxbridge, MA; died 20 Oct 1909 Charlton, MA
                    married Ruth CONVERSE Sibley 17 Nov 1851 (as her 2nd husband)
                    (she born 10 Aug 1824 Spencer, MA; died there 4 Oct 1883)
                    (she dau/o Willard-[7] CONVERSE and Sarah _____)

1138. URIAH-[6] BOWKER, son of Elijah-[5] BOWKER (Uriah-[4]; Edmund-[3]; John-[2]; Edmund-[1]) and his first wife, Patience GAGE, was born 3 March 1800 at Hopkinton, MA. He married Lois EAMES on 24 Dec 1821. She was the daughter of Moses EAMES and Lois ADAMS, and was born ____; died ____. Uriah-[6] BOWKER died 9 Feb 1880.

Children of Uriah-[6] BOWKER and Lois EAMES:
Surname **BOWKER**

+   **2035. ALMIRA E.**   born 19 Dec 1822 Hopkinton, MA; died 23 Apr 1859 Cincinnati, OH
                    married Amasa CHAPIN 30 Aug 1845 Milford, MA
                    (he s/o Capt. Rufus-[7] CHAPIN and Lydia TUFTS) (he born 28 May 1821 Milford MA)
     2036. Eliza M.   born 29 April 1829; died 19 Mar 1862; married Warren CHAPIN 2 Nov 1849
                    (he s/o Leonard CHAPIN and Semira HAYWARD/HOWARD)
                    (he born 19 Dec 1827 Milford, MA; died 29 Nov 1910)
                    (he 2 married Augusta BRIDGES 19 July 1862)
     2037. Martha A.   born 25 April 1831; died 1 Mar 1900 never married   EOL
+   **2038. CHARLES E.**   born 10 Feb 1833; died ____
                    1 married Helen R. STACY 22 Feb 1858; 2 married Elvira PHIPPS 22/28 Feb 1863

1139. MARY GAGE-[6] BOWKER, sister of above, was born 30 Nov 1801 Hopkinton, MA. She married Dexter L. MAYBRY 8 June 1820. He was the son of _____ MAYBRY and _____; and was born 22 Apr 1799; died Dec 1879/Jan 1880.

Children of Mary Gage-[6] BOWKER and Dexter MAYBRY:
Surname **MAYBRY**

     2039. Lowell Bowker   born 28 Aug 1820; died ___; married Sophia Perry WALKER 22 Sep 1847 Hopkinton
                    (she dau/o Lovett WALKER and Sophia ____)
                    2 married Mrs. Mary Matilda BINGHAM Glidden 27 Feb 1889 Claremont, NH
     2040. Susannah L.   born 20 Jul 1822; died _____   EOL
     2041. Sarah L.   born 11 June 1824; died _____
                    married Milton CLAFLIN (as his 2nd wife) on 22 Nov 1849
                    (he born 7 Nov 1815 Framingham, MA; died 6 June 1892 Hopkinton, MA)
                    (he s/o William CLAFLIN and Sally _____)
                    Child: Clarence Edgar-[8] CLAFLIN born 23 Aug 1856 Hopkinton; died Mar 1935
     2042. Samuel D.   born ca 1831; died 7 Jan 1891 Hopkinton, MA
                    married Nancy/Nancie M. COMEY Miller (as her 2nd husband) ca 1861
                    (she dau/o Aaron COMEY and Charlotte _____) (she born ca 1825 Foxborough, MA)
                    Child: Charles Alliston-[8] MAYBRY born 13 Sep 1862 Hopkinton; married Minnie Estelle CARNEY on
                    2 Oct 1884 Milford, MA (she dau/o Samuel J. CARNEY and Laura S. ____)
     2043. Eliza C.   born 8 Sep 1833; died 16 May 1863
                    married Amasa-[8] CHAPIN ca 1860   (as his 2nd wife)
                    (he 1 married Almira E-[7] BOWKER (# 2035 above)) 30 Aug 1845 Hopkinton, MA)
                    (he s/o Capt Rufus-[7] CHAPIN (Adams-[6]; Josiah-[5]; Seth-[4,3]; Josiah-[2]; Samuel-[1]) and Lydia TUFTS)

1140. ELIZA-6 BOWKER, sister of above, was born 21 Oct 1803 at Hopkinton, Middlesex, MA. She married Weatherby CHAMBERLAIN on 6 Nov 1830 at Sherborn, MA. He was the son of Elisha CHAMBERLAIN and Susanna BROWN, and was born ca 1803; died 1878. Eliza-6 BOWKER died July 1860 at North Bridgewater, Plymouth, MA.

Children of Eliza-6 BOWKER and Weatherby CHAMBERLAIN:
Surname **CHAMBERLAIN**

2044. Abigail B.	born ca 1832; died 1 Oct 1884 Natick, MA	
	married George E. RAMSDELL ca ____ (he born 1831; died 1884)	
2045. Perry Dowse	born 8 Jan 1834; died 22 Mar 1895; married Ann Elizabeth MASON ca ____	
2046. William H.	born May 1836; died 1 Mar 1904 Natick, MA	
	married Susan M. WILLOUGHBY 6 Nov 1883	
2047. Frances N.	born ca 1839; died ____	
2048. Edwin B.	born Aug 1842; died ____; married Ellen T. KNIGHT ca 1871	
2049. Eliza J.	born ca 1844; died 1847	EOL

1143. SARAH-6 BOWKER, half-sister of above, daughter of Elijah-5 BOWKER (Uriah-4; Edmund-3; John-2; Edmund-1) and his second wife Polly BRIGHAM, was born 19 Oct 1813 Hopkinton, MA. She married Dr. William Adams PHIPPS, a dentist, on 22 Oct 1832 at Hopkinton. He was the son of Moses PHIPPS and Hannah ADAMS, and was born 19 Sep 1909 Hopkinton; died 13 Nov 1890 Hopkinton, MA. Sarah-6 BOWKER died 28 Oct 1870 Hopkinton.

Children of Sarah-6 BOWKER and Dr. William Adams PHIPPS;
Surname **PHIPPS**

2050. William Henry	born 9 Oct 1833; died ____; married Mary A. LANE 26 Jan 1859	
	(she dau/o Daniel LANE and _____) (she born ca 1833; died 1909)	
	Child: Carrie Estella-8 PHIPPS born ca 1866, died 1957	
+ **2051. MARILLA F.**	born 29 Aug 1835; died 4 July 1874	
	married John Quincy ADAMS 26 Jan 1859 (double wedding with brother)	
	(he born 16 Dec 1826 Norfolk, MA; died 1872 Livingston, NY)	
	(he s/o John ADAMS and Joanna ADAMS)	
+ **2052. WALDO**	born 9 Oct 1836; died 10 Feb 1919	
	married Margaret Hart CLAFLIN 17 Aug 1862 (she born Mar 1842)	
	(she dau/o William H. CLAFLIN and Margaret R. _____)	
+ **2053. FREDERICK S.**	born Aug 1840; died 13 May 1886 Hopkinton, MA	
	married Emma Augusta CROCKER 5 Apr 1863 Milford, MA	
	(she dau/o William CROCKER and Eleanor DARLING) (she born 5 Apr 1843)	
2054. Anna	born 1843; died 1844 EOL	
2055. Isabelle D.	born 1844; died 1844 EOL	
+ **2056. JOSEPH BOWKER**	born 27 June 1848; died 1930	
	married Mary Wheeler WALKER 10 June 1869 Milford, MA	
	(she dau/o William WALKER and Susan WHEELER) (she born ca 1850)	
+ **2057. NORMAN B.**	born Oct 1856; died 1910 Waltham, MA	
	married Nettie B. HANSON 24 Feb 1878 Marlborough, MA	
	(she dau/o Sylvester B. HANSON and Lucretia A. MILES) (she born Feb 1853)	

1144. PATIENCE-6 BOWKER, twin sister of above, was born 19 Oct 1813 at Hopkinton, MA. She married Josiah Stone HAVEN on 21 Nov 1832 at Hopkinton. He was the son of Elisha HAVEN and Sally STONE, and was born 6 Jan 1808; died _____. Patience-6 BOWKER died 25 March 1861 at Milford, MA, of typhoid fever.

Children of Patience-6 BOWKER and Josiah HAVEN:
Surname **HAVEN**

2058. George Edwin.	born 8 Oct 1833; died _____
2059. Ellen Maria	born 24 Sep 1836; died _____
2060. Amelia Caroline	born 24 Jan 1840; died 12 Dec 1895 Haverhill, MA
	married John E. LEIGHTON 23 July 1879 MA (he s/o Geo. LEIGHTON and Phebe __)
2061. Eliza	born 8 Dec 1841; died _____
2062. Margaret Phipps	born 22 Feb 1843; died ____
2063. Josephus Sanford	born 8 Jul 1848; died _____; married Anna Mc FARLAND 5 Aug 1869
	(she dau/o Cromwell Mc FARLAND and Hannah _____)

1150. WILLIAM HENRY[-6] **CLARK,** son of Elizabeth-[5] WILSON (Elizabeth-[4] BOWKER (Edmund-[3,2,1]) and Peter CLARK, was born 4 Aug 1805 MA. He married Frances MARTIN on 27 April 1828. She was the daughter of ____ MARTIN and ____, and was born 16 May 1809 NH; died ____. William Henry-[6] CLARK died 25 Jan 1887.

Children of William Henry-[6] CLARK and Frances MARTIN:
Surname **CLARK**

2064. William Henry, Jr.	born 12 Dec 1828; died ____	2067. George	born 2 July 1833; died ____
2065. Elizabeth Frances	born 23 Dec 1829; died ____		
2066. Mary Ann	born 25 Jan 1831; died ____; married Wesley ARMSTRONG on 1 Jan 1853 Lapeer, MI.		

1153. LUTHER[-6] **HOSMER,** son of Abigail-[5] BARRETT (Abigail-[4] BOWKER; Edmund-[3,2,1]) and Josiah HOSMER, was born 1 Oct 1788 at Templeton, MA. He married Abiah BLISS on 4 July 1812. She was the daughter of Gad BLISS and Abiah COLTON, and was born 18 Aug 1794; died 4 Feb 1883 at Springfield, Hampden, MA. Luther-[6] HOSMER died 22 Nov 1875.

Children of Luther-[6] HOSMER and Abiah BLISS;
Surname **HOSMER**

2068. Charles Bliss	born 8 Feb 1814; died ____		
2069. Caroline	born 2 Jan 1816; died 18 Aug 1895; married Hiram BOOTH 21 Oct 1837		
2070. Abigail	born 24 March 1818; died ____		
2071. Harriet	born 15 Oct 1819; died ____		
+ **2072. LUTHER, Jr.**	born 21 Aug 1821; died 25 Nov 1866; married Nancy Judson HALL 7 July 1846 (she born 26 Nov 1823; died 11 Mar 1878)		
2073. Chester Cooley	born 6 Oct 1823; died ____	2076. Henry J.	born ca 1833
2074. George	born 8 Feb 1826; died ____	2077. William Edward	born 23 Oct 1835
2075. Mary Ann	born 5 Apr 1828; died ____		

1160. THORNTON[-6] **BARRETT, III,** son of Thornton-[5] BARRETT II (Abigail-[4] BOWKER; Edmund-[3,2,1]) and Betsey REYNOLDS, was born 30 Apr 1807 at Bethlehem, Grafton, New Hampshire. He married Rebecca Stanton BREWER on 24 April 1834 at Farmers Valley, McKean, PA. She was the daughter of ____ BREWER and ____; and was born 24 Aug 1814 Stonington, CT; died ____. Thornton-[6] BARRETT, III died 7 Jan 1882 at Winona, Minnesota.

Children of Thornton-[6] BARRETT, III and Rebecca Stanton BREWER:
Surname **BARRETT**   (children all born PA)

+ **2078. STILLMAN SNOW**	born 7 May 1835 Smethport, PA; died ca 1882 married Hannah Elizabeth COOLEY 23 March 1863 (she dau/o Aretus COOLEY and Elvira ____) (she born 20 Sep 1829 Palmer, MA)
2079. Violetta	born ca 1836; died ____
2080. John	born ca 1838; died ____
2081. Mary Jane	born ca 1841; died ____
2082. Ellen	born ca 1842; died ____
2083. Betsey	born ca 1843; died ____
2084. Leander C.	born 25 Mar 1845; died 3 Aug 1920 Spokane, WA married Jennie ____ ca (she born ca 1841 England)
	Child: Maud-[8] BARRETT born July 1882 ND
2085. Isaac	born Oct 1846; 1 married Louisa ____ ca ____; 2 married Eliza COOK ca 1870
2086. Sophronia	born ca 1852; died ____
+ **2087. JULIA MADORA**	born Oct 1853; died 25 Mar 1909; married Rufus Llewellyn WOODARD ca 1873 (he born May 1846 VT; died 14 Apr 1925 Rice, Minnesota)

1174. JAMES JOHNSON[-6] **BARRETT,** son of Joseph-[5] BARRETT (Abigail-[4] BOWKER; Edmund-[3,2,1]) and Mary KENNEY, was born 6 Feb 1823. He married Lydia SMITH on 2/3 Jan 1845. She was the daughter of Isaac SMITH and ____; and was born * Aug 1821/3 VT; died ____. James Johnson-[6] BARRETT died 24 Aug 1885.

Children of James Johnson-[6] BARRETT and Lydia SMITH:
Surname **BARRETT**

+ **2088. GEORGE WARREN**	born 13 July 1846 Bethlehem, NH; died ____ Lakeport, NH married Ella Maria TAYLOR 22 June 1871 (she dau/o Pliny White TAYLOR and ____) (she born 10 July 1850 Springfield, VT

Children of James Johnson-[6] BARRETT and Lydia SMITH, continued:
Surname **BARRETT**

2089. Alice Estelle	born 22 Dec 1851; died 23 Dec 1853 Bethlehem	EOL
2090. Allen	born 17 Sep 1857; died 5 Jan 1927 Littleton, NH	

        1 married Ida May WHITCHER 29 May 1880
        (she dau/o John WHITCHER and ___) (she born 29 Dec 1861; died 21 Jan 1887)
        Children: Amanda Jane-[8] born 8 May 1881, died 25 Sep 1881; and Harry Howard-[8] BARRETT born 9 Mar 1885
        2 married Hattie Belle FOLSOM 2 Apr 1888
        (she dau/o Ira FOLSOM and ____) (she born 25 Sep 1864 Lakeport, NH)
        3 married Grace TILTON Downing 2 May 1908 Boston, MA
        (she dau/o John TILTON and Betsey LEWIS)

1175. OLIVE-[6] SCRIPTURE, daughter of Abigail-[5] BRIGHAM (John-[4]; Elizabeth-[3] BOWKER, Edmund-[2,1]) and Jeremiah SCRIPTURE, was born ca 1767 at Alford, Berkshire, MA. She married James KEELER 11 July 1787 at Rutland, VT. He was the son of ____ KEELER and ___, and was born 12 March 1763 Rutland; died ____. Olive-[6] SCRIPTURE died 12 April 1845 Ontario, Canada.

Children of Olive-[6] SCRIPTURE and James KEELER
Surname **KEELER**

2091. Joseph Abbott	born 20 July 1788 Rutland, VT		
2092. Clarissa	born 9 May 1790	2093. Sophia	born ca 1792

1176. SARAH-[6] SCRIPTURE, sister of above, was born ca 1769 at Alford, MA. She married Abisha LEWIS 17 Dec 1791 at West Stockbridge, MA. He was the son of Benjamin LEWIS, Jr. and Sarah HART, and was born 15 May 1766 at Farmington, CT; died 9 July 1852 Stockbridge, MA. Sarah-[6] SCRIPTURE died 18 Aug 1829 West Stockbridge, MA.

Children of Sarah-[6] SCRIPTURE and Abisha LEWIS:
Surname **LEWIS**   (all children born at West Stockbridge, Hartford, MA)

	2094. Edna	born Apr 1793; died ca 1823; married Sands NILES	(he born ca 1790)
+	**2095. AURELIA**	born 5 Apr 1795; died 5 Feb 1861 Farmington, CT	
		married Lyman HINMAN ca 16 Aug 1819 West Stockbridge ,MA	
	2096. Benjamin Hart	born 25 Aug 1796; died 20 Sep 1856; married Betsey A. ____	
	2097. Beri/ Berry	born 20 Sep 1799; 24 Jan 1809	EOL
	2098. William Brigham	born 8 Feb 1802; died 29 May 1814	EOL
	2099. Sarah Ann	born ca 1803	
	2100. Clarinda	born 18 Feb 1804; died Jan 1880; married John L.TAYLOR	
	2101. Morgan	born 7 Feb 1806; died 6 Apr 1894; married Ruby WAIT Mar 1830 Winsted, CT	
		(she born 7 Feb 1806; died 3 Nov 1883)	

        Child: John L. Avery -[8] LEWIS born ca 1843 MA

+	**2102. NANCY ABIGAIL**	born 1 Mar 1808 MA; died 20 Apr 1881 Alford, Berkshire, MA
		married Frederick FITCH 30 May 1827 MA

1178. LOIS-[6] SCRIPTURE, sister of above, was born 28 June 1771 at Tyringham, Berkshire, MA. She married Jonathan TOWNSEND 18 May 1791 Berkshire County, MA. He was the son of _____ TOWNSEND and _____; and was born ca ____; died ____. Lois-[6] SCRIPTURE died ____.

Children of Lois-[6] SCRIPTURE and Jonathan TOWNSEND:
Surname **TOWNSEND**   (all children born Tyringham, Berkshire, MA)

2103. Gregory	born 19 Jan 1793	2108. Francis	born 25 June 1802
2104. George	born 21 Nov 1794	2109. Jeremiah	born 24 Nov 1804
2105. Simeon	born 29 Sept 1796	2110. Asahel	born 26 Apr 1807
2106. Laura	born 22 Nov 1798	2111. Esther	born 20 Mar 1809
2107. Belinda	born 9 Aug 1800		

1179. JEREMIAH-[6] SCRIPTURE, brother of above, was born 14 July 1773 at Tyringham, Berkshire, MA. He married Submit CURTIS ca 1804 at Ontario, Canada. She was the daughter of _____ CURTIS and ____, and was born 13 Nov 1785 Onondaga County, NY; died ____. Jeremiah-[6] SCRIPTURE died ca 1836. Removed to Ontario, Canada

BOWKER
The Sixth American Generation

Children of Jeremiah[6] SCRIPTURE and Submit CURTIS:
Surname **SCRIPTURE**

2112. Mary Porthema	born ca 1805 Berkshire, MA	2116. Julia Anna	born 12 June 1812 Ontario
2113. Thomas Nelson	born 1 Jan 1808 Berkshire, MA	2117. Simeon Liberty	born 4 Aug 1815 Ontario
2114. Vallonia Eleanor	born 8 Sep 1809 Berkshire, MA	2118. Robert	born ca 1820 Ontario
2115. Sarah Sophia	born 31 Oct 1810 Berkshire, MA	2119. George	born 17 Mar 1826 Ontario

1184. ABIJAH[6] BRIGHAM, son of John-[5] BRIGHAM (Lt. Abijah-[4]; Elizabeth-[3] BOWKER, Edmund-[2,1]) and Eunice MOORE, was born 17 March 1791 at Sudbury, Middlesex, MA. He married Melissa STRATTON on 19 Oct 1817 at Rutland, Middlesex. MA. She was the daughter of _____ STRATTON and ____, and was born 11 Oct 1798 Rutland, MA; died ____. Abijah[6] BRIGHAM died 7 Feb 1892.

Children of Abijah[6] BRIGHAM and Melissa STRATTON:
Surname **BRIGHAM**

+ **2120. CLARISSA**   born 13 March 1818; died ____ ; married Daniel HITCHINGS
  2121. Lucy Keys   born 13 Aug 1819; died ____
+ **2122. LAVINIA MOORE** born 1 Dec 1820; died ____; married Robert Lewis GODDARD ca 1845 Palmer, MA
   (he born 21 May 1822 Petersham, MA; died ____)
+ **2123. JOHN WARREN** born 19 Dec 1822; died _____; married Martha Eliza BRIGHAM ca 1838
   (she dau/o Dr. Luther BRIGHAM and Eunice HAWLEY) (she born 27 July 1818)

1186. JOHN[6] BRIGHAM, brother of above, was born 22 March 1795 at Sudbury, Middlesex, MA. He married first to Mary LEVERITT ca ____. She was the daughter of ___- LEVERITT and ___ of Burke County, GA, and was born ____; died ____. His second marriage was to Mary CRAFTS Brigham, widow of his brother William on 8 July 1844. John-[6] BRIGHAM died 24 May 1874 at Watertown, MA.

Children of John[6] BRIGHAM and Mary LEVERITT:
Surname **BRIGHAM**   (children born in Georgia)

+ **2124. WILLIAM**   born 19 July 1819 GA; died 2 June 1893 Girard, GA
   married Caroline M. T. WHITE 10 April 1844   (she born ____; died 24 Feb 1883)
+ **2125. ELIZABETH ANN** born 15 Jan 1824 Girard, GA; died 20 March 1857 Watertown, MA
   EUNICE   married Artemus B. ROGERS 6 May 1846
   (he born 19 Apr 1817 Newton, MA; died 17 July 1901 Watertown, MA)
+ **2126. JOHN**   born 13 Feb 1827 Burke Co., GA; died 20 Dec 1871 Watertown, MA
   married Mary Elizabeth TAINTER 5 Jan 1852   (she born 3 Jan 1830 Boston)
   (she dau/o Capt. William C. TAINTER and ____ of Boston)
Child of John[6] BRIGHAM and Mary CRAFTS Brigham:
Surname **BRIGHAM**
  2127. Maria   born 25 Feb 1847 Watertown, MA; died _____; never married   EOL

1190. WILLIAM[6] BRIGHAM, brother of above, was born 11 Aug 1810 at Sudbury, MA. He married first to Adeline COLE on 17 April 1834. She was the daughter of Thaddeus COLE of Watertown, MA. and _____, and was born ca 1813; died ca 1836. He married second to Mary CRAFTS on 15 March 1837. She was the daughter of ____ CRAFTS and ____, and was born 7 June 1813 at Cambridge, MA; died 15 Nov 1902 Watertown, MA. William[6] BRIGHAM died 23 April 1843 at Watertown, MA.

Child of William[6] BRIGHAM and Adeline COLE:
Surname **BRIGHAM**
+ **2128. WILLIAM**   born 12 Sep 1835 Watertown, MA; died _____
   THEODORE   married Marion Billings COLE 2 Feb 1864
   (she dau/o Thaddeus COLE of Watertown, MA; and _____)
Children of William[6] BRIGHAM and Mary CRAFTS:
Surname **BRIGHAM**
  2129. George   born 16 March 1838; died young
  2130. Charles   ***   born 21 June 1841; died _____; married Rebecca S. JORDAN 13 Dec 1892
   (she dau/o George V. JORDAN of Saco, ME. and _____)

*** Charles BRIGHAM served in the office of an architect to study for his chosen profession. The Civil War began, and he enlisted in Company K, 5th Regt. of MA Volunteer Infantry for 9 months at New Berne, NC. After he returned to Boston, he completed his studies and formed an

architectural firm called " Sturgis and Brigham ". It later became " Brigham and Spofford ".
There are numerous buildings in Boston, as well as other parts of New England, that were designed by him. Mr. Brigham was awarded the contract to design and build a large extension to the MA state House on Beacon Hill, Boston. He resided in Watertown, MA where he was a highly respected citizen.

1191. NANCY-6 BRIGHAM, daughter of Joseph-5 BRIGHAM (Lt. Abijah-4; Elizabeth-3 BOWKER, Edmund-2,1) and Rebecca HAYNES, was born 11 March 1796 at Sudbury, Middlesex, MA. She married first to Daniel CROCKER ca ____. He was the son of _____ CROCKER and ____, and was born ____, died 1829. Her second marriage was to Benjamin HARRIS on 14 July 1833 at Russellvile, Alabama.. He was the son of _____ HARRIS and ____, and was born 12 June 1786 at Cranger County, TN.; died 28 June 1858 at Russellville, Alabama. Nancy-6 BRIGHAM died 14 June 1878 at Russellville.

Child of Nancy-6 BRIGHAM and Daniel CROCKER;
Surname **CROCKER**

2131. Alphonso	born ca ____; died ____	

Child of Nancy-6 BRIGHAM and Benjamin HARRIS:
Surname **HARRIS**

+ **2132. REBECCA BRIGHAM** — born 17 Jan 1842 Franklinville, AL; died 11 June 1914 Pocahontas, AL.
married Harvey Gholsen SARGENT 7 Apr 1868 Russellville, AL
(he born Jan 1844 AL; died 16 July 1913 AL)

1192. LEWIS-6 BRIGHAM, brother of above, was born 27 Oct 1797 at Sudbury, Middlesex, MA. He married Almira-6 BOWKER on 27 May 1838. She was the daughter of Joseph-5 BOWKER and Patty PROCTOR, and was born 12 Aug 1810 at Sudbury, MA; died ____. They lived on the homestead of Dr. John BRIGHAM until it was taken down to build a new residence in northwestern Sudbury. Lewis-6 BRIGHAM died 8 Sept 1875 at Sudbury.

Children of Lewis-6 BRIGHAM and Almira-6 BOWKER:
Surname **BRIGHAM**

2133. Martha Ann	born 9 March 1839; died _____ Child: Julia H-8 GREENE born ca ____	
	married Hiram GREENE ca ____ (he a merchant, resided Boston, MA)	
2134. Rebecca Haynes	born ca ____; died 12 May 1911; married Thomas Albert BENT ca _____	
	Child: Carrie F-8 BENT born ca ___, married Lucius E. BENT ca ____	
2135. Nancy Elizabeth	born 25 April 1843; died ____; resided Boston, MA	
2136. Esther Louisa	born 16 Dec 1846; died 8 May 1903; never married	EOL
2137. Lewis Alanson	born 25 Feb 1850; died 6 March 1850	EOL
2138. Emma Alvira	born 8 Aug 1851; died _____	
	married Newell D. WHITCOMB 20 Mar 1872 Sudbury, MA	
	(he s/o John WHITCOMB and Mary ____) (he born ca 1843 ME; died _____	
	Child: Alice-8 WHITCOMB born ca 1882; died 1935; married Leverett Whittredge WOODBURY	

1193. EUNICE-6 BRIGHAM, sister of above, was born 19 Dec 1798 at Sudbury, Middlesex, MA. She married the Reverend Addison PARKER, as his 2nd wife, on 16 Oct 1834. He was the son of Aaron PARKER and ____, and was born ____; died ____. Eunice-6 BRIGHAM died 13 March 1856 at Springfield, MA.

Children of Eunice-6 BRIGHAM and Rev. Addison PARKER:
Surname **PARKER**

+ **2139. SARAH FRANCES** — born 26 July 1837 Metheun, MA; died _____
married Elias Cornelius ATKINS 17 Aug 1865 IN (as his 3rd wife)
(he born 28 June 1833; died 18 April 1901 IN)

+ **2140. REV. ADDISON** — born 12 Nov 1839 Danbury, CT; died _____
married Mary L. BOYDEN 18 Sept 1866 Dedham, MA

1196. REBECCA-6 BRIGHAM, sister of above, was born 28 Aug 1807 at Sudbury, Middlesex, MA. She married Lawrence THOMPSON on 9 Jan 1834. He was the son of _____ THOMPSON and _____, and was born ____, died ____. Rebecca-6 BRIGHAM died ca 1856.

Children of Rebecca-6 BRIGHAM and Lawrence THOMPSON:
Surname **THOMPSON**   (children all born in Alabama)

2141. Sarah	born ca ____; died young	2143. Lawrence born ca ____; died young	EOL
2142. Annie S.	born ca ____; died Nov 1866; never married		EOL

Children of Rebecca[6] BRIGHAM and Lawrence THOMPSON, continued:
Surname **THOMPSON**

+	**2144. JOSEPH N.**	born ca 1844 AL; died 14 Nov 1926
		married Lucie Blackwell MALONE ca 1869 ; resided Tuscombia, Alabama
+	**2145. REBECCA**	born ca 1846/48; died ca 1918
		married Capt. William Wilkins BAYLESS Dec 1866 Florence, Alabama
		(he s/o William Barclay BAYLESS and Ann M. TANNEHILL)
		(he born ca 1841; died ca 1889 AL)
	2146. Mary Nancy	born ca ____; died _____; married Dr. Joseph P. PRIDE

Children: Empson T-[8] PRIDE born ca ____; died unmarried; and L. Thompson-[8] PRIDE
born ca ____; married May MAHOON, resided Prides Station, Alabama

1197. CHARLES[6] BRIGHAM, brother of above, was born 16 July 1811 at Sudbury, Middlesex, MA. He married Eunice Hagar GARFIELD 7 Dec 1850. She was the daughter of Francis GARFIELD and Dorcas STRATTON, and was born 11 March 1832; died 24 Dec 1892. Charles[6] died 9 Aug 1897 Greenfield, MA. He was a convert to Christadelphianism.

Children of Charles[6] BRIGHAM and Eunice GARFIELD:
Surname **BRIGHAM**   (all children born Greenfield, MA)

2147. Maria	born 16 July 1852; died Oct 1862	EOL
2148. Dorcas	born 17 April 1855; died 9 April 1856	
2149. Alanson	born 5 July 1859; died 28 Mar 1913; married Stella Genevieve MOORE ca _____	
	(she dau/o Jason MOORE and Emma Frances BLACKHAM) (she born 7 Oct 1863)	

Child Lewis Alanson -[8] BRIGHAM born 14 Aug 1889; graduated Boston University 1913

2150. Jane	born 3 Oct 1862; died _____; 1 married Milton O. DAMON 11 July 1881
	(he born 9 Nov 1859 Leominster; died 20 Mar 1890)
	2 married Levi Tyler COATES ca ____ (he born 2 Oct 1853 E. Charlemont; died ____)

Note: They adopted a Charles GARDNER born 27 July 1899 and Changed his name to Charles Milton COATES

2151. Joseph	born 9 April 1868 Worcester, MA ; resided Greenwich, CT;
	married Elizabeth SAUTER 2 Dec 1897

Child: Eunice Elizabeth-[8] BRIGHAM born 2 Dec 1898 Greenfield, MA; married Roland Leese MORRELL
26 June 1924; he s/o Henry Albert MORRELL and Grace A. DECATUR, born 29 Jan 1898 MA.

1198. NATHAN NAHUM[6] JOYNER, son of John-[5] JOYNER (Hannah-[4] BOWKER; John-[3;] Edmund-[2,1]) and Jerusha Sarah BIXBY, was born 9 May 1771 at Winchendon, Worcester, MA. He married Hulda SPENCER ca 1791 at Rumney, Chittenden, Vermont. She was the daughter of Asahel SPENCER (Caleb) and Mabel CHURCH (Caleb), and was born ca 1768 at Deerfield, Franklin, MA; died 8 Aug 1846 at Bolton, Chittenden, VT. Nahum[6] JOYNER died there ca 1853.

Children of Nathan Nahum[6] JOYNER and Hulda SPENCER:
Surname **JOYNER**

2152. Simeon D.	born ca 1791		
2153. John Laban	born 28 Mar 1792 Bolton, Chittenden, VT; died 1826;		
	married Florus Banker YOUNG ca 1814		
2154. Hulda Eliza	born ca _____	2155. Francis	born ca _____

1199. ANNA[6] JOYNER, sister of above, was born ca 1774 MA. She married David CANEDY ca 1791 at Halifax, VT. He was the son of Hugh CANEDY and Bathsheba BAKER, and was born 10 Oct 1771; died 1826. Anna Emma[6] JOYNER died ____.

Children of Anna Emma[6] JOYNER and David CANEDY:
Surname **CANEDY**

2156. Anna	born ca 1797	2157. Esther	born ca 1798
2158. Wealthy	born ca 1802		
2159. David	born ca 1803; died 1844; married Maria STEVENS		
2160. Barbara	born 8 Aug 1805; died 16 May 1891, married Artemus FAIRBANKS 27 Apr 1819		
	(he s/o Artemus FAIRBANKS and Polly WHITING)		
	(he born 8 Aug 1800 VT; died 28 Nov 1848 WI)		
2161. Alma	born ca 1807		

1200. JOHN[6] JOYNER, brother of above, brother of above, was born ca 1780, MA. He married Bathsheba CANEDY ca ___.
She was the daughter of _____CANEDY and ___, and was born ____, died ____. John[6] JOYNER died ___.

Children of John-[6] JOYNER and Bathsheba CANEDY:
Surname **JOYNER**

2162. William Marvin	born ca 1800 VT; died ____	2164. Horace A.	born ca 1808 VT; died ____
2163. John	born ca 1801 VT; died ____		

1201. JAMES[-6] JOYNER, brother of above and twin to Samuel, was born 1 Jan 1787 at Lynn, Essex, MA. He married first to Mary BROWN ca ___. She was the daughter of ____ BROWN and ____, and was born ____, died ____. His second marriage was to Maria NESBITT on ____. She was the daughter of ____ NESBITT and ____, and was born ___, died ____. James[-6] JOYNER died ca 1884 Harford, Cortland County, NY.

Children of James[-6] JOYNER and Maria NESBITT:
Surname **JOYNER**

2165. JOHN   born ca 1812 MA; died ____ Harford, Cortland , NY
married Mary M. BENTLEY ca 1832 Harford, Cortland, NY

1206. CALEB R[-6] FLETCHER, son of Sarah-[5] JOYNER (Hannah-[4] BOWKER; John-[3]; Edmund-[2,1]) and Caleb FLETCHER, was born 5 April 1785 at Chelmsford, MA, He married Elizabeth STOWELL ca ____.

Children of Caleb R-[6] FLETCHER and Elizabeth STOWELL:
Surname **FLETCHER**

2166. Lorenzo	born 31 Oct 1815 Adams, Jefferson, NY; died _____	
	married Adelia ROBBINS 10 Jan 1840 Wethersfield, CT.; (she born ca 1818 NY)	
	Child: Ella A-[8] FLETCHER born ca 1848 OH	
+ **2167. DAVID**	born 17 July 1817 Champion, Jefferson, NY; died _____	
STOWELL	married Caroline FLEMMING 21 Oct 1857(she born March 1828 OH; living 1910)	
2168. Elizabeth Remington	born 17 Dec 1819 Adams, NY; died 22 July 1858	

1209. BENJAMIN[-6] JOYNER, son of Francis -[5] JOYNER (Hannah-[4] BOWKER; John-[3]; Edmund-[2,1]) and Lydia LESTER, was born 4 June 1876 at Bradford, Orange County, VT. He married first to Caroline ALGER ca 1810. She was the daughter of ____ ALGER and ____, and was born 24 May 1786 NY; died 22 Aug 1828 NY. His second marriage was to Hepzibah SUTLIEFF ca _____. Benjamin-[6] JOYNER died 8 June 1846 at Bristol, Ontario, NY.

Children of Benjamin-[6] JOYNER and Caroline ALGER:
Surname **JOYNER**

2169. Sarah Mariah	born 13 Feb 1812 Madison Co., NY; died 1831 Sacketts Harbor, NY
2170. Irena Lester	born 20 Oct 1814 Madison, NY; died 1866 Ontario County, NY
	married Ward TOTMAN ca _____ (he born ca 1803 ; died ___)
2171. Francis Kneeland	born 23 May 1817 Madison Co., NY; died 1834 Jefferson Co., NY
2172. Caroline Osgood	born 17 Sep 1821 Jefferson Co., NY; died ca 1920 Jefferson Co., NY
2173. Benjamin Lester	born 1 Mar 1824 Jefferson Co., NY; died 11 Apr 1847 Ontario Co., NY
2174. Nancy Janet	born 12 May 1827 Jefferson Co., NY; died 1828 Jefferson Co., NY

1216. WILLIAM[-6] JOYNER, brother of above, was born 29 April 1803 ____, NY. He married Polly RANDALL on 20 June 1825 at Lorraine, Jefferson County, New York. Polly RANDALL was the daughter of Hubbard RANDALL and Mary JENNINGS, and was born ca 1759; died 1811. William-[6] JOYNER died 9 Jan 1875 at Lorraine, NY.

Children of William-[6] JOYNER and Polly RANDALL:
Surname **JOYNER**   (all children born NY)

2175. Ann Eliza	born ca 1825; died 1903	2185. Alonzo W.	born 2 Mar 1840; died 1904
2176. Angeline P.	born 26 Mar 1826; died 1871 Jefferson Co., NY		
2177. Eliza A.	born 15 Aug 1827; died 1921		
2178. Robert Jackson	born 8 Aug 1828; died 11 Apr 1901; married Harriet W. WASHBURN ca 1845		
2179. Albert	born ca 1830; died _____		
2180. Nancy C.	born 2 Sept 1831; died June 1919; married Daniel BALLOU		
2181. Charlotte H.	born ca 1832; died 1926		
2182. Mary O.	born 16 Apr 1834; died 1900		
+ **2183. HUBBARD W.**	born 31 Mar 1836; died 1904; married Olive RITTER ca 1864		
2184. Lewis M.	born 12 May 1838; died 1923 Oswego, NY; married Margaret YERDON 1862 Oswego		

1218. WILLARD[-6] BOWKER, son of Noah-[5] BOWKER (Noah-[4]; John-[3]; Edmund-[2,1]) and Catherine _____, was born 15 July 1784 at West Springfield, MA. He married Sally GREENE 11 Nov 1805 at West Springfield, MA. She was the daughter of Amos GREENE and Mary NELSON; and was born 22 Dec 1780 Whitingham, Windham, VT., died _____. Willard[-6] BOWKER died _____.

Children of Willard[-6] BOWKER and Sally GREENE:
Surname **BOWKER**

	2185. Mary Ann	born 19 Nov 1806 Longmeadow, MA; died 11 Nov 1891 Susquehanna, PA
		married Marsena Hitchcock MC INTYRE (as his 2nd wife) ca 1845
		(he born 29 Dec 1799 Otsego, NY; died 4 Oct 1865 Broome Co., NY)
		(he s/o Oliver MC INTYRE and Mary Miller HITCHCOCK)
+	**2186. FRANKLIN NOAH**	born 22 July 1809 W. Springfield, MA; died 28 Mar 1884 Maine, Broome, NY
		married Jane _____ ca _____ (she born ca 1814; died ____)
+	**2187. AMOS GREEN**	born 20 Nov 1810 West Springfield, MA; died 31 Dec 1871 E. Herrick, Bradford, PA
		1 married Serilla _____; 2 married Lovina Adeline WILBUR 26 Mar 1848 Chester, MA.
+	**2188. WILLIAM MINOR**	born 24 May 1816 Union, Broome, NY; died 17 Feb 1886 Herrick, Bradford, PA
		1 married Betsey BEERS 8 Feb 1844 Litchfield, CT
		(she born ca 1814 Litchfield, CT; died 14 Jan 1848)
		married Melicent Parthenia SKILTON 4 Feb 1850 Owego, NY +++
		(she dau/o James SKILTON and Chloe STEELE)
		(she born 24 Dec 1816 Watertown, CT; died 1 March 1904 Herrrick, PA

+++ Note: Melicent SKILTON married first to Ebenezer Osborne BEERS on 27 Dec 1842. They had 2 sons: James Wesley BEERS born 5 Feb 1845 CT; and George Osborne BEERS born 7 Nov 1846 Middlebury, CT. These children were living with William Minor BOWKER according to the 1860 Census . Reference: Dr. Henry SKILTON and his Descendants (1899) Pages 249, 251

1220. ROXANNA[-6] BEEBE, daughter of Rebecca-[5] BOWKER (Joseph-[4]; John-[3,] Edmund-[2,1]) and Solomon BEEBE, was born ca 1787 VT. She married Heman STEPHENSON ca 1807 . He was the son of Abiathar STEPHENSON and Olive LOMBARD, and was born 3 Nov 1782 MA; died 13 Sept 1858 OH. Roxanna[-6] BEEBE died 5 July 1856 Brunswick, OH.

Children of Roxanna[-6] BEEBE and Heman STEPHENSON:
Surname **STEPHENSON**

2189. Eliza Ann	born ca 1808 Springfield, NY; died ca 1889 KS
	married Stutely STARK ca _____ (he born ca 1809; died 1869)
	Child: Helen-[8] STARK born ca 1832; died 1909
2190. Elvira A.	born 1814 Seneca Co., NY; died IA; married James HARKNESS 17 March 1836
2191. Marvin	born ca 1816 Junius, Seneca, NY; died ca 1910; married Lucina Elvira HANCHETT
2192. Lothrop Anson	born ca 1818 Junius, NY; died Oct 1859 MI; married Chloe WARNER ca ____
2193. Solomon Beebe	born 8 May 1823 Springfield, Otsego, NY; died 25 Mar 1892 MI
	married Harriet M. MIX ca _____
2194. Margaret	born ca 1826 Bloomfield, Ontario, NY; died bet. 1880-90 Sturgis Co., MI
	married Jonas V. HIBBARD ca ____
2195. Hiram	born ca 1827 Bloomfield, NY; died after 1880 IA; married Caroline BRADLEY

1221. SIMEON[-6] BEEBE, brother of above, was born 1 May 1789 VT. He married Hester BUCK ca ___ . She was the daughter of ___ BUCK and ____, and was born 2 Aug 1794; died 29 Nov 1859. Simeon[-6] BEEBE died Dec 1870 at Isabella, MI

Children of Simeon[-6] BEEBE and Hester BUCK:
Surname **BEEBE**

2196. Marvin	born ca _____	2202. Melitta	born ca ____
2197. William	born ca _____ ; died 9 May 1880 Lerned, KS		
2198. Solomon	born ca 1817 NY; died ca 1898 MI		
2199. Edward Hart	born ca 1826 ; died ____		
2200. Samuel Byron	born 5 Oct 1832; died 12 June 1912 El Reno, OK		
2201. Abram Burr	born 27 Sept 1834 Walworth, Wayne, NY; died 11 Sept 1911 Plainwell, Allegan, MI		

1223. LATHROP/LOTHROP W.[-6] BEEBE, brother of above, as born 23 July 1795 VT. He married Sally BEMIS 11 Feb 1820 at Carthage, Jefferson County, NY. She was the daughter of _____ BEMIS and _____, and was born ca 1801 VT; died 1 Mar 1904 Springville, NY. Lathrop-[6] BEEBE died 4 Feb 1891 Machias, Cattaraugus, NY.

Children of Lathrop⁻⁶ BEEBE and Sally BEMIS:
Surname **BEEBE**

2203. Maria B.	born Sept 1826; died Aug 1854 Springfield, Erie, NY		
2204. Edward C.	born ca 1832 Erie Co., NY; died ____		
2205. Norman	born 2 May 1834 Concord, Erie, NY; died 12 Jan 1904 Upland, CA		
	married Susan DAVIS		
2206. Sally	born ca 1837; died ____		

+   **2207. ELVIRA L. .**   born 17 Jan 1840 NY; died ____ Machias, Cattaraugus, NY
                                married Jehiel WHITNEY ca ____

1224. SALLY⁻⁶ BEEBE, daughter of Sarah-⁵ BOWKER (Joseph-⁴; John-³; Edmund^{-2,1}) and Alexander BEEBE, was born 23 July 1781 VT. She married Cornelius HALSTEAD 20 March 1800 at Rutland, VT. He was the son of _____ HALSTEAD and _____, and was born ca 1772; died ca 1863 Onondaga County, NY.

Children of Sally⁻⁶ BEEBE and Cornelius HALSTEAD:
Surname **HALSTEAD**

2208. Catherine	born 15 June 1803 NY		
2209. Luna	born 10 Mar 1804 NY		
+ **2210. EZEKIEL BEEBE**	born 7 June 1806 NY; died 1 Apr 1897 MI; married Sarah Ann BURDICK ca 1829		
2211. Sarah	born 1 Oct 1810 Onondaga Co., NY		
2212. Maria Polly	born 12 Dec 1812 Onon. Co., NY		
2213. Samuel	born May 1815	2215. Adah E.	born 1 June 1821
2214. Phoebe	born 26 Mar 1817	2216. Cornelius H.	born Oct 1827

1225. LUNA⁻⁶ BEEBE, sister of above, was born 15 Aug 1783 VT. She married Asa MORTON Oct 1805 at Rutland, VT. He was the son of Martin MORTON and Jerusha TWITCHELL , and was born 28 May 1782 Athol, MA; died 1 June 1850 Homer, MI. Luna⁻⁶ BEEBE died ca 1850 MI.

Children of Luna⁻⁶ BEEBE and Asa MORTON:
Surname **MORTON**   (all children born Mexico, Oswego County, NY)

2217. William Allen	born ca 1813
+ **2218. AURORA DWIGHT**	born 15 June 1815; died 16 Feb 1877 Evart, Osceola, MI
	married Patricia HARDY ca _____ (she born ca 1822)
2219. Henry Clarke	born 27 Jan 1822; died 18 Mar 1841 MI
2220. Charity	born 25 Sep 1824; married Abraham DAY 1845
	(he born 22 Feb 1821) (he s/o Chauncey DAY and Adah CLEVELAND)

1227. AURORA⁻⁶ BEEBE, son of Sarah-⁵ BOWKER (Joseph-⁴; John-³; Edmund ^{2,1}) and Alexander⁻⁸ BEEBE, was born 8 July 1787 at Rutland, VT. He married Sally/Sarah COLTON/COTTON ca ___. Aurora-⁶ BEEBE died ____.

Children of Aurora⁻⁶ BEEBE and Sarah COLTON/COTTON:
Surname **BEEBE**

2221. Aurora, Jr.	born ca 1808
+ **2222. DANIEL P.**	born 26 Sep 1809 NY; died Dec 1881 Kankakee, IL
	married Eliza Jane GREEN 19 March 1829
	(she born 25 Sept 1814 NY; died 24 June 1887 Obrien Co., IA)

1229. ASA⁻⁶ BEEBE, brother of above, was born 7 Nov 1792 at Brandon, VT. He married Mary WHIPPLE on 1 May 1814 at Mexico, Oswego, New York. She was the daughter of Joseph S. WHIPPLE and ____, and was born 23 Sep 1793 Cooperstown, Otsego, NY; died 21 Sep 1878 Mexico, NY Asa⁻⁶ BEEBE died 10 June 1878 Mexico, NY

Children of Asa⁻⁶ BEEBE and Mary WHIPPLE:
Surname **BEEBE**   (all children born Mexico, Oswego, NY)

2223. Harriet	born 18 Feb 1815; died young
2224. Nancy Jane	born 23 Jan 1816; died 17 Nov 1888
2225. Mary Ann	born 13 Apr 1818; died 22 June 1880; married Edmond WHEELER 27 Sept 1843
2226. Renett	born 7 Jan 1820; died ____
2227. Harriet R.	born 3 Dec 1821; died 14 Apr 1842

Children of Asa[-6] BEEBE and Mary WHIPPLE, continued:
Surname **BEEBE**

    2228. Salem Town   born 9 Dec 1823 ; died 20 Feb 1871 NY; married Harriet _____ ca _____
              Child: Frank[-8] BEEBE born March 1850 Mexico, NY
    2229. Fanny Minerva   born 14 Aug 1827; died 12 Apr 1902 IA

+   **2230. ISAAC WINDSOR**   born 20 May 1830; died 4 Feb 1903;   married Wealthy Arvilla WHEELER ca 1856
                               (she born 12 July 1827; died 1 July 1870)
    2231. Helen Lucretia   born 29 Feb 1832; died 14 Feb 1903
    2232. Emma Naomi   born 12 Jul 1834; died 1919 NY

1231. CLARK(E)[-6] BEEBE, brother of above, was born 28 Nov 1797 at Westmoreland, Oneida, NY. He married Sarah SAVAGE Oct 1823. She was the daughter of Reuben SAVAGE and Lydia ____, and was born ca ____; died 22 Sept 1831. His second marriage was to Dolly SAVAGE, ca Nov 1833. She was the daughter of Joel SAVAGE and Abigail SMITH, and was born 16 Oct 1799; died 26 July1860. She is buried in the Tipton Cemetery at Franklin, Lenawee County, MI. Clark[-6] BEEBE died 12 March 1882 at Bennington, MI.

In 1820, Clark BEEBE was appointed as the second caretaker of the first cemetery in Mexico, NY. It was founded on Lot 54, land which was donated by George SCRIBA. He held title as the original land grant known as Scriba's Patent. It is noted on 1831 church records that Clark BEEBE, and his wife were members of the Presbyterian church in Mexico. Later Clark took his family West to Michigan to join other members of the family.

Children of Clark[-6] BEEBE and Sarah SAVAGE:
Surname **BEEBE**

    2233. Joseph B   born 13 Sept 1824 NY
    2234. Harriet L.   born 10 Aug 1826 NY
    2235. Cynthia B.   born 15 March 1828 NY
    2236. Gardner C.   born 18 Feb 1829 NY; died 9 Apr 1845 Hillsdale Co., MI
    2237. Frederick   born 6 March 1831 NY

Children of Clark-[6] BEEBE and Dolly SAVAGE:
Surname **BEEBE**

    2238. William   born ca 1836 MI; died _____; married Ellen ____
              Children: Zerada-[8] born ca 1861 MI, Charles[-8] born ca 1863 MI; and Clark J[-8] BEEBE born ca 1866 MI

+   **2239. CHARLES**   born 21 Aug 1838 MI; died 9 Feb 1892; married Hannah E. BUNN 4 July 1863
    2240. Sarah Ann   born ca 1841 MI; died ca 1920 MI; married George Washington. SLATER ca _____
                 (he born ca 1839; died 1910)   Child: Perley C[-8] SLATER born ca 1871 MI

1232. CATHERINE[-6] BEEBE, sister of above, was born 2 June 1800 at Westmoreland, Madison County, NY. She married Chester HOLCOMB on 3 Nov 1824/ 25 at Rutland, VT. He was the son of Bethuel HOLCOMB and Deziah / Desire ____, and was born 10 Sept 1804 NY; , died 21 Sep 1865 NJ. Catherine[-6] BEEBE died 27 June 1841 at Winfield, Herkimer, NY. He married second to Lucy TOMPKINS ca ____. She was the daughter of Gilbert TOMPKINS and Mary BROWNELL.

Children of Catherine[-6] BEEBE and Chester HOLCOMB:
Surname **HOLCOMB**

+   **2241. EDWARD**   born July 1827 Oswego County, NY; died ____
          SEYMOUR   married Ann / Anna E. _____ ca 1849 (she born ca Apr 1827; died ____)
    2242. George Wilson   born ca 1829 Oswego, NY; died _____
    2243. Charles W.   born ca 1830 NY; died _____
    2244. Edwin Clarke   born ca 1831 NY; died _____
           Note: He was a grocer and Postmaster at Bethel Corners, Cayuga, NY 1867-68
    2245. Andrew Hart   born ca 1833 NY; died ____
    2246. Henry   born ca 1833
    2247. Julia E.   born ca 1835 NY; died ____
    2248. Harmon W.   born ca 1838 NY; died _____; agent for musical instruments
                  married Imogene O. _____ (she born ca 1842 NY)
           Children: Clarence[-8] HOLCOMB born ca 1866 NY; and Frank[-8] HOLCOMB born ca 1869 MI
           Note: Harmon[8] HOLCOMB enlisted, on 20 Nov 1861, in Company I, NY 6th Cavalry Regiment; promoted
           to Sgt. on 1 Jan 1865; mustered out 27 June 1865 Clouds Mills, VA. !870 resided Grass Lake, Jackson, MI
    2249. Catherine   born ca 1841; died _____

1233. ALLEN⁻⁶ BEEBE, brother of above, was born 27 April 1803 at Westmoreland, NY. He married Abigail/ Abby MATTHEWS on 31 March 1823. She was the daughter of ____ MATTHEWS and ____, and was born ____; died ____. Allen⁻⁶ BEEBE died 21 July 1862 Tipton, Michigan.

Children of Allen⁻⁶ BEEBE and Abigail MATTHEWS:
Surname **BEEBE**

2250. Rhoda Rennet	born 2 Jan 1824 Mexico, NY; died Aug 1849	
	married Seymour Kimball BALL March 1842	
	(he s/o Ebenezer BALL and Elizabeth CLARK)	
	(he born 3 Mar 1820 MA; died 2 Sept 1898 Albany, NY)	
2251. Joseph Bowker	born 27 Oct 1826 Mexico, NY; died 10 Jan 1894 Eugene, OR	
	married Julia HOGAN ca ____	
2252. Pliny Fisk	born 22 Dec 1830 Mexico, NY; died 15 April 1918 Tipton, MI	
	married Sarah Ann WHELAN 7 Srpt 1856 MI	
2253. Levi Mathew	born 3 Aug 1883 Mexico, NY; died 30 June 1912 Eugene, OR	
	married Nancy A. DEYO ca ____	
2254. Rebecca Martha	born 3 Aug 1833 Mexico, NY; died 6 Dec 1892 Columbus, NE	
	married Alexander Thurston SIMMONS ca 1860	
2255. Sarah Orrie	born 9 Oct 1841 Franklin, Lenawee, MI; died May 1924 Council Bluffs, IA	
	married Alonzo HAIGHT ca 1867	
2256. Phoebe M.	born 25 Feb 1844 Franklin, MI; died 18 Nov 1915 Columbus, NE	
	married Erastus Melanethon SPARHAWK 26 Dec 1870	

1234. ADAH⁻⁶ BEEBE, sister of above, was born 2 Feb 1806 at Verona, NY. She married James CARPENTER on 16 March 1829 at the First Presbyterian Church, Mexico, Oswego, NY. He was the son of ____ CARPENTER and ____, and was born ____; died ____. Adah⁻⁶ BEEBE died 3 July 1845 at Franklin, Lenawee, Michigan.

Children of Adah-⁶ BEEBE and James CARPENTER:
Surname **CARPENTER**   (all born Franklin, MI)

2257. Mary A.	born 19 April 1830		2259. Watson	born 31 July 1834
2258. Morris	born 27 Aug 1832			

1238. AMOS ⁻⁶ SARGENT, Jr., son of Sarah-⁵ BOWKER (Joseph⁻⁴; John⁻³; Edmund⁻²,¹) and Amos SARGENT, Sr., was born 12 Feb 1791 at ____. He married Rebecca ANDREWS on 3 Feb 1823. She was the daughter of ____ ANDREWS and ____, and was born 23 Dec 1794; died ____. Amos⁻⁶ SARGENT, Jr. died ____.

Children of Amos⁻⁶ SARGENT, Jr. and Rebecca ANDREWS:
Surname **SARGENT**

2260. Caroline R.	born 30 Mar 1827		2262. John A.	born 13 Apr 1836
2261. Amos Leland	born 12 Aug 1833		2263. Charles F.	born 4 May 1838

1240. SILAS⁻⁶ SARGENT, brother of above, was born 1 Oct 1795 at __, VT.. He married Roxanna MEAD on 12 Sept 1831. She was the daughter of ____ MEAD and __, and was born ca 23 Feb 1800 VT; died 23 Dec 1875 MI.. They res. at Chester, VT.

Children of Silas⁻⁶ SARGENT and Roxanna MEAD:
Surname **SARGENT**

2264. Frederick	born 13 June 1832; died 13 Mar 1834	EOL
2265. Ann Eliza	born 27 May 1834; died 20 June 1836	EOL
2266. Silas G.	born 14 June 1836; died 20 June 1836	EOL
2267. Edmund T.	born 19 Aug 1837; died ____	
	1 married Fidelia BONNELL ca ____ (she born 24 Jan 1847; died 15 Mar 1874)	
	Children : Anna M⁻⁸ born 21 Oct 1870, died 29 Feb 1940; and Jessie⁸ born 18 Aug 1873 NY, died 9 July 1874	
	2 married Ada M. MURDOCK 16 May 1879	
	(she born 9 Feb 1851 MI; died 19 Dec 1922 Sherwood, MI)	
	Children: Carrie Bernice-⁸ born 19 Jan 1880, died Apr 1962 FL ; and Edmund Leland-⁸ SARGENT born 16 Feb 1884 Sherwood, Branch, MI)	
2268. John	born 13 Jan 1841; died 21 Feb 1842 2269. Mary Amelia born 23 Sep 1844	

BOWKER
The Sixth American Generation

1246. POLLY-6 WHITNEY, daughter of Eunice-5 BOWKER (Daniel-4; John-3; Edmund-2,1) and Nathaniel WHITNEY, was born ca 1793 at ____. She married Ezra F. SPENCER on 24 Jan 1815 at Rutland, VT, as his 2nd wife. He was the son of William SPENCER and Margaret OSGOOD , and was born 1790, died 19 March 1881. Polly-6 WHITNEY died 17 Jan 1878 at Pittsford, VT. Ezra SPENCER married first to Nancy SNELL. She died ca 1813.

Child of Polly-6 WHITNEY and Ezra SPENCER:
Surname **SPENCER**

+   **2270. HARRIET**   born 9 Mar1816; died 17 Apr 1859 Pittsford., VT
                    married Junia SARGENT ca _____   (he s/o Junia SARGENT and Sally CLARK)
                    (he born 26 May 1809; died 16 Apr 1896 Pittsford, VT)

1248. AZUBAH-6 WHITNEY, daughter of Eunice-5 BOWKER (Daniel-4; John-3; Edmund-2,1) and Nathaniel WHITNEY, was born ca 1803 VT. She married Thomas BUDLONG ca 1820. He was the son of ____ BUDLONG and ____, and was born ca 1792 RI; died ____. Azubah-6 WHITNEY died ca 1874 Hyde Park, Norfolk, VA.

Children of Azubah-6 WHITNEY and Thomas BUDLONG:
Surname **BUDLONG**

2271. Thomas Russell   born 7 Sep 1822 MA; died 6 Jan 1855 Jacksonville, FL
              Note: Thomas Russell BUDLONG graduated from Brown University 1842; received an MD
                    from Harvard in 1851, and was a Physician in San Francisco, and Providence, RI
2272. James S.   born ca 1824 MA; died ____
2273. Rebecca T.   born ca 1829 MA; died ____

1250. DANIEL BOWKER-6 CHAMBERLAIN, son of Lois-5 BOWKER (Daniel-4; John-3; Edmund-2,1) and Stephen CHAMBERLAIN, JR., was born ca 1800 Roxbury, MA. He married 1st to Marie BALADE/ BALLARD 20 June 1825. She was the daughter of Peter BALADE/BALLARD and Sophia De PROISEY____, and was born ca 1807 France ; died ca 1877. His second marriage was to Martha LORED on ___. Daniel-6 CHAMBERLAIN died 15 Jan 1888 at Roxbury, MA.

Children of Daniel Bowker-6 CHAMBERLAIN and Marie BALADE:
Surname **CHAMBERLAIN**

2274. Watson   born ca 1834
2275. Curtis   born 22 Aug 1838; died 10 July 1904   (13 ch)
                married Anna Augusta WELLINGTON 23 Sept 1858
2276. Warren   born ca 1841 MA   2277. Angeline   born ca 1847 MA

1251. SUSAN / SUKEY-6 BOWKER, daughter of Daniel-5 BOWKER, Jr. (Daniel-4; John-3; Edmund-2,1) and Ruth BROWN, was born 16 Oct 1797 at Sudbury, Middlesex, MA. She married John HAYNES, Jr. (as his 1st wife) on 21 Sept 1817 at Sudbury, MA. He was the son of John HAYNES and Sally FORBUSH, and was born 20 Nov 1793 at Sudbury; died 1 July 1875 at Sudbury. Susan/Sukey-6 BOWKER died 14 July 1832 at Sudbury, MA. John HAYNES married 2nd to her younger sister Sarah-6 BOWKER (# 1255 below).

Children of Susan/Sukey-6 BOWKER and John HAYNES, Jr.:
Surname **HAYNES**   (all children born Sudbury, Middlesex, MA)

2278. Adaline   born 12 Aug 1819; died 2 Jan 1826
2279. Elbridge   born 2 Jan 1922; married Josephine M. PRATT 25 July 1843 Sudbury, MA
              (she born ca 1823 Fitchburg, MA; died 10 Sept 1847)
              (she dau/o Solomon v. PRATT and Sarah C. HARTON)
        Child: Frederick-8 HAYNES born 30 March 1846 Sudbury, MA)
2280. Caroline   born 16 Nov 1824
2281. Susan Emily   born 6 April 1827; died 1874; married Samuel Adams WILLIS 1 June 1848 Sudbury
              (he born 27 Oct 1820; died 29 Mar 1874 Waltham, MA)
        Child: Jesse Gilman-8 WILLIS born 18 Mar 1849 Sudbury, MA
2282. George   born 8 Apr 1829; died 1830
2283. Georgianna   born 16 Aug 1831; died 26 Nov 1862

1252. SAMUEL NOYES-6 BOWKER, brother of above, was born 16 June 1799 at Sudbury, Middlesex, MA. He married Mary EARLE on 5 Nov 1826 MA. She was the daughter of Stephen EARLE and Mary/Lucy WEYMOUTH, and was born April 1804 Maine; died 1 Feb 1881 Sudbury. Samuel Noyes-6 BOWKER died 9 Oct 1872 at ____.

BOWKER
The Sixth American Generation

Children of Samuel Noyes[6] BOWKER and Mary EARLE:
Surname **BOWKER**

	2284. Mary	born ca 1827 MA; married Otis PUFFER ca ____ (he born ca 1825 MA)
+	**2285. ELIZA ANN**	born 15 May 1829; died 22 July 1901 MO
		married Thomas Andrew HUTCHINS (he born ca 1824; died 1893)
	2286. Henrietta	born ca 1831 MA; died _____
	2287. ANGIE/ ANGELINE	born 13 June 1832 Sudbury, MA; died 29 Dec 1912 Springfield, MO
		married Prof. Jonathan FAIRBANKS 3 Sep 1854 Springfield, MO
		(he s/o Joseph Varnum FAIRBANKS and Margaret HADDEN)
		(he born 7 Jan 1828 Andover, MA; died
	2288. Lucy M.	born ca 1835, MA; married Joseph HALL; died ca 1905 Ontario, CA
		Child: George-[8] HALL born ca 1860 MA
+	**2289. HARRIET**	born 11 Jan 1839 MA; died __;1 married Charles Phineas WEBSTER 4 June 1862
	MATILDA	(he s/o James A. WEBSTER and Maria EAYRS/AYRES)
		(he born 28 June 1833 Derry, NH; died 31 Dec 1865 NH)
		2 married Henry Stowe HAPGOOD 23 Sept 1869
		(he s/o John HAPGOOD and Mary Ann HOSMER)
+	**2290. FRANK MAYBIN**	born 31 Jan 1850 Sudbury , MA; died 12 Feb 1904; 1 married Annie /Anna___ ca ____
		2 married Caroline Mary CONLEY ca ___ MA (she born 25 Mar 1853)

1255. SARAH[6] BOWKER, sister of above, was born 5 April 1801 at Sudbury, MA. She married John HAYNES, Jr. (as his 2nd wife) on 29 Nov 1832 at Sudbury, Middlesex, MA. He had been married previously to her sister , Susan-[6] BOWKER (# 533 above) . Sarah[6] BOWKER died 12 July 1888 at Sudbury, MA. John HAYNES born 29 Nov 1793; died 1 July 1875 Sudbury. She resided with her son at Red Oak, IA after her husband died, according to the 1889 Census.

Children of Sarah[6] BOWKER and John HAYNES, Jr.:
Surname **HAYNES**   (all children born Sudbury, MA)

	2291. Elias E.	born ca 1833/34; occupation carpenter; died 25 June 1894
		married Abby E. ____ ca ____ (she born ca 1838 MA)
	Note: He served in the 26th Regiment of MA Infantry (Co. E and D), enlisted as a Private on 18 Oct 1861; promoted to 1st Sgt. on 1 Nov 1861; promoted to 2nd Lt. on 12 Nov 1862; resigned on 21 April 1865	
	Child: Hattie A-[8] HAYNES born ca 1867 MA	
+	**2292. ELLEN L.**	born ca 1836; married Samuel S. WOOD 1 Apr 1860
	Note: residing with her son Shelley WOOD at Carbon County, WY in 1920	
	2293. Harriet E.	born ca 1838; married Samuel BENT 29 Nov 1860
	2294. Addison	born 30 Nov 1841; died 24 Dec 1858 EOL
+	**2295. JOHN NEWTON**	born 7 July 1843; died _____
		married Susan Norton GODING 4 Nov 1870 Sudbury, MA
		(she dau/o Elbrit GODING (Jonas) and Susanna M. NORTON (Jethro)
		(she born 26 Feb 1854 Sudbury; died _____)
	2296. Sarah Frances	born 4 Dec 1846
	2297. Clarence Edwin	born 4 March 1849 Sudbury, MA; living 1922

1256. MATILDA[6] BOWKER, daughter of Daniel[5] BOWKER (Daniel[4]; John-3; Edmund[2,1]) and Ruth BROWN, was born 20 July 1809. She married John FLETCHER 4 July 1839 Sudbury, MA. He was the son of ____ FLETCHER and ____, and was born ____ ; died ____. Matilda[6] BOWKER died 16 May 1872.

Children of Matilda[6] BOWKER and John FLETCHER
Surname **FLETCHER**

2298. Josephine	born ca 1843	2300. John Herbert A	born ca 1845; died 1 Sept 1864
2299. Matilda	born 17 Nov 1845	2301. Edwin	born 21 March 1847; died 11 Sept 1850

1261. HARRIET N-[6] BOWKER, daughter of Daniel-[5] BOWKER (Daniel[4]; John-[3]; Edmund[2,1]) and Ruth BROWN, was born 30 Sep 1818 Sudbury, MA. She married John Franklin-[6] MURDOCK, a railroad engineer, on 22 Sep 1841 (as his 3rd wife) at Westminster, MA. He was the son of John-[5] MURDOCK (William-[4]; Joshua-[3]; Robert-[2,1]) and ____, and was born 28 Oct 1810 Westminster; died 16 July 1886 Lawrence, MA. Harriet-[6] BOWKER died 6 Feb 1868 St. Johnsbury, VT.

Note: His second wife was a Mary M. BOWKER of Fitchburg, MA, on 24 Sep 1840. She born ca 1811; died 19 Apr 1841. No children. Undetermined as to any relationship to Harriet (above)
Reference: The MURDOCK Genealogy: Robert MURDOCK of Roxbury, MA; pages 104-105

Children of Harriet-[6] BOWKER and John Franklin-[6] MURDOCK:
Surname **MURDOCK**

2302. Walter C.	born ca 1843 Westminster, MA; died ___; married Mary A. MARDEN 25 July/Sep 1869 (she dau/o George S. MARDEN and Eliza ____) (she born ca 1848 NH)
2303. Mary L.	born July 1845 Fitchburg, MA; died ____; married Charles P. OSGOOD ca 1876
2304. John F.	born ca 1848 Fitchburg, MA; died 2 Aug 1854 St. Johnsbury, VT EOL
2305. Louis J.	born Nov 1852 St. Johnsbury, VT; died 13 July 1854 VT. EOL

1262. ELIZABETH-[6] BOWKER, sister of above, was born 19 March 1821 at ____. She married David Crawford MAYBIN +++ 13 May 1840 at Sudbury, MA. He was the son of ____ MAYBIN and ____, and was born 7 Sep 1814 Philadelphia, PA; died 2 Feb 1881 Morenci, MI.

Child of Elizabeth-[6] BOWKER and David Crawford MAYBIN.
Surname **MAYBIN**

2306. Mary Hart	born July 1856 KY; died 25 Jan 1932 Morenci, Lenawee, MI
	married Charles Eurotus BLANCHARD, MD, PhD 24 Sep 1879
	(he born ca 1858 MI; died after 1930)
	Children: Ruth-[8] BLANCHARD born ca 1889 MI, married Mortimer FULLER (he born ca 1855 NY);
	and Elizabeth-[8] BLANCHARD born ca 1895 MI

+++ Source: " Biographical Records of Alumni of Amherst College during its First Half-Century (!812-71)"   David Crawford MAYBIN graduated Amherst College 1832-33; Middlebury College 1835-37; 1839 student at Bowdoin College; graduated Castleton Medical College, VT 1845; Episcopal Theological Seminary, Gambia, OH 1852; Physician at Great Falls, NH 1845-48; Episcopal clergyman 52-57; Baptist clergyman 1857-81.

1263. MARY B/R-[6] BOWKER, daughter of Joseph-[5] BOWKER (Daniel-[4]; John-[3]; Edmund-[2,1]) and Mary BROWN, was born 8 Jan 1803 MA. She married Avery BUSH on 15 June 1823 at Spencer, MA. He was the son of Josiah BUSH (Joseph) and Mary KNOWLTON, and was born 18 Aug 1794 MA; died 27 Nov 1846 North Brookfield, MA.. Mary R-[6] BOWKER died 29 Dec 1827 Spencer, MA., a few days after giving birth. A strange coincidence since her mother also died in childbirth..

Child of Mary R-[6] BOWKER and Avery BUSH:
Surname **BUSH**

2307. Elizabeth Thurston	born 11 May 1824; died 10 Mar 1864 Worcester, MA		
	married Addison PALMER 2 Nov 1850 Worcester, MA		
2308. Harvey Fails/ Fales	born 29 Jan 1826	2309. Joseph Bowker	born 24 Dec 1827

1264. LYDIA-[6] BOWKER, half-sister of above, daughter of Joseph-[5] BOWKER (Daniel-[4]; John-[3]; Edmund-[2,1]) and Patty PROCTOR, was born 11 April 1807 at Sudbury, Middlesex, MA. She married Avery BUSH (as his 2nd wife) on 2 Oct 1828 at Spencer, MA. He was the son of Josiah BUSH and Mary KNOWLTON, and was born 18 Aug 1794 North Brookfield, MA; died 27 Nov 1846 North Brtookfield. He was the widower of her half-sister above, Mary R-[6] BOWKER. Lydia-[6] BOWKER died 5 Nov 1881 at Eyota, Olmsted, MN.

Children of Lydia-[6] BOWKER and Avery BUSH:
Surname **BUSH**

	2310. Amos	born 20 May 1830 Spencer, MA, died 10 March 1831
+	**2311. JOHN AVERY**	born 23 June 1832 Spencer, MA; died _____
		married Hannah Matilda CUMMINGS 1 Oct 1868 Orion, MN
		(she dau/o Francis H. CUMMINGS and Hannah Carlton WALDO)
		(she born 28 Aug 1847 Boston, MA; died 17 Dec 1916 Eyota, MN)
	2312. Julia Ann	born 19 July 1834 MA; married Charles C. RUSSELL 5 Mar 1854
	2313. Charles	born 8 Oct 1836; died 21 Oct 1859
	2314. George A.	born 2 Feb 1846; died 11 March 1856 Eyota, MN

1265. ALMIRA-[6] BOWKER, sister of above, was born 25 Aug 1810 at North Sudbury, MA. She married Lewis-[6] BRIGHAM (# 1192) on 27 May 1838. He was the son of Joseph BRIGHAM and Rebecca HAYNES , and was born 27 Oct 1797 Sudbury; died 8 Sept 1875 Sudbury. Almira-[6] BOWKER died ____.

Children of Almira-[6] BOWKER and Lewis BRIGHAM:
Surname **BRIGHAM**

2315. Martha Ann	born ca 1839; died ____; married Hiram GREENE of Boston, MA ca _____

BOWKER
The Sixth American Generation

Children of Almira[6] BOWKER and Lewis BRIGHAM, continued:
Surname **BRIGHAM**

2316. Rebecca Haynes	born ca 1841; died 12 May 1911; married Thomas Albert BENTca	
	(he born ca ____; died Aug 1901)	
	Child: Carrie F[8] BENT born ca ____; married Lucius E. BENT ca _____	
2317. Nancy E.	born ca 1843; died 1906	
2318. Louisa Esther	born ca 1846; died 1903	
2319. Emma Almira	born ca 1852; died ____; married Newell D. WHITCOMB 20 March 1872	
	Children: Alice Emma-[8] born ca ___, died age 15; Ida Louise-[8] WHITCOMB born ca ____	

1266. AMOS[6] BOWKER, brother of above, was born 5 Aug 1812 at North Sudbury, MA. He married first to Lucy SNOW on 15 April 1834. She was the daughter of ____ SNOW and ____, and was born ca ____; died 23 May 1845 Westfield, Hampden, MA. His second marriage was to Lucinda HASKINS on 1 Sep 1847. She was the daughter of ____ HASKINS and _____, and was born ____; died 2 Aug 1868. Amos[6] BOWKER died ____.

Children of Amos[6] BOWKER and Lucy SNOW:
Surname **BOWKER**

	2320. Mary H.	born ca 1838 MA; married William H. BUSH
+	**2321. PROCTOR F.**	born 7 Jul 1840 VT; died 6 Jul 1923 San Antonio, Bexar, TX
		married Emerett "Emma" SHERMAN 18 July 1866 MA.
		Children: Etta-[8] born ca 1867; and Medora-[8] BOWKER born ca 18790

Children of Amos[6] BOWKER and Lucinda HASKINS:
Surname **BOWKER**

2322. Lucy M.	born 22 June 1848; married William A. WILSON
2323. Lucinda Isadore	born 29 July 1849 MA; died 4 May 1932; married John Woodburn ROBERTSON ca ___
	(he born 17 Aug 1847; died 2 Dec 1918)
	Children: Francis Hamilton-[8] ROBERTSON born 1878; died 1965; and
	John Woodburn-[8] ROBERTSON born 1887; died 1959
2324. Sarah Jane	born 9 July 1852 MA; died 18 Apr 1923 KS
	married Henry A. STANLEY 28 May 1879 Leavenworth, KS
2325. Martha A.	born 14 Apr 1854 MA; died 3 Nov 1869 MA

1267. JOSEPH PROCTOR[6] BOWKER, brother of above, was born 4 Apr 1814 at North Salisbury, Middlesex, MA. He married Catherine WILSON on 19 May 1847 at Metropolis, IL. She was the daughter of Thomas WILSON and Molly O'BRIANT, and was born 6 Mar 1827 at Granville, NC; died _____ (after 1910). Joseph[6] BOWKER held a variety of jobs. He was a school teacher, a farmer, a cotton ginner, and a mailman. He died 14 Feb 1891 Metropolis, IL

Children of Joseph Proctor[6] BOWKER and Catherine WILSON:
Surname **BOWKER**

2326. Mary Catherine	born 9 Feb 1848 Metropolis, IL	2333. Maggie F.	born 24 July 1864
2327. Joseph W.	born 25 Sept 1849; died ____	2334. Ellen Ann	born ca 1869
2328. Thomas D.	born 15 Feb 1852; died ____		
2329. Martha R.	born 25 March 1854; died _____		
2330. Charles A.	born 30 Jan 1856; died ____		
2331. Sarah M.	born 12 Oct 1859; died ____		
2332. Lewis Warren	born 25 Nov 1861; died ____		

married Mary Blessing LAMB 23 Jan 1895 Shelby Co., TN
(she born 2 July 1854 Memphis, TN; died 28 Oct ___ Memphis)
Child: Francis-[8] Lamb BOWKER born 7 Jan 1897 Memphis, Shelby, TN

1270. HANNAH[6] SEELEY, daughter of Deborah[5] BOWKER (Elias[4]; John[3]; Edmund[2,1]) and Sheldon SEELEY, was born 25 Dec 1783 VT. She married Ethan OWEN 22 Jan 1801 Milton, Chittenden, VT. He was the son of Elijah OWEN and Olive BEEMAN, and was born 10 June 1774 Poultney, VT; died 21 May 1849 Camden, IL. Hannah[6] SEELEY died ca 1850 IL.

Children of Hannah[6] SEELEY and Ethan OWEN:
Surname **OWEN**

2335. Ann	born ca 1802 Milton, VT; died ca 1827 Blanco, TX
2336. Alva (h)	born 3 Oct 1803 Milton, VT; died 21 Nov 1883 Maysville, Arkansas
	married Sophia KENIKE ca 1831 OH (born ca 1808 DE)

Children of Hannah-[6] SEELEY and Ethan OWEN, continued:

Surname **OWEN**

+	**2337. SEELEY**	born 20 March 1805 Milton, VT; died ca 1881 Flagstaff, AZ; a polygamist	
		1 married Lydia Ann/ Adeline OWEN on 27 Nov 1834 IL	
		(she born 1 July 1811; died 19 Sept 1846)	
		2 married Elizabeth Betsy PICKLE/PICKELL 22 March 1847 OH	
		(she born May 1826 OH; died _____)	
		3 married Helen Louisa FREDERICK Jefferds ca 1853	
		(she dau/o David Ira FREDERICK and Martha INGERSOLL)	
		(she born 19 Jun 1839; adopted out 1845; died ca 1876)	
	2338. Luke	born ca 1810 Milton, VT; died _____	
		married Mrs. Rhoda ____ Owen 27 Nov 1834	
	2339. Hannah	born 8 Nov 1812; died ca 1891 Blanco, TX	
		married William Neil TRAINER 1 Sept 1831	
		(he s/o James TRAINER and Ann BRICE)	
		(he born 28 April 1808 Dalton, GA; died 1 Feb 1866 Blanco, TX)	
		Child: Martha Ann-[8] TRAINER born 15 Nov 1832; died 4 July 1909; married John Lewis TINNEY	
	2340. Clarissa	born ca 1818 Locking, OH; died 1851 Schuyler, IL	
	2341. Rachel	born ca 1822 OH; died 1839	EOL
	2342. Ethan	born ca 1829; died 1836 Locking, OH	EOL

1273. LUKE-[6] SEELEY, brother of above, was born 15 Nov 1791 VT. He married first to Electa/ Electra OWEN ca 1810. She was the daughter of ____ OWEN and ____, and was born ca 1792; died 1834. His second marriage was to Susan WILLOUGHBY ca 1834. She was the daughter of James WILLOUGHBY and Annie COLE, and was born ca 1802; died ca 1846. He married third to Sophronia _____ . She was born ca 1805; died ____. Luke-[6] SEELEY died 15 Oct 1856 IL.

Children of Luke-[6] SEELEY and Electa/Electra OWEN:

Surname **SEELEY**

	2343. Elijah H. Owen	born 15 Dec 1811; died 13 Mar 1906 IL; married Catherine A. HASKELL 26 Dec 1839
		(she born Dec 1820 NY; died _____)
		Children: Charles H-[8] born ca 1840; Albert H-[8] born ca 1842; Frances M-[8] born ca 1844 IL; William L-[8] born ca 1855 IL; and Ella-[8] SEELEY born ca 1859 IL.
	2344. Mathew Malone	born 21 Aug VT 1813: 17 June 1894; married Mary SIMS 29 April 1838 IL
		Children: Sarah-[8] born ca 1840; William Wallace-[8] born ca 1842; and Lewis-[8] SEELEY born ca 1854
	2345. Luke	born ca ____; died 1863
	2346. Mary Eliza	born 18 Nov 1824 Russellville, KY; died 18 Nov 1878 KS
+	**2347. NATHANIEL B.**	born ca 1825; died 1896; married Elizabeth CAMPBELL

Children of Luke-[6] SEELEY and Susan WILLOUGHBY:

Surname **SEELEY**

	2348. James Willoughby	born ca 1835; died 10 Apr 1893 Rushville, IL ; married Henrietta SANFORD
		Children: Carlton-[8] born ca 1857; Clara-[8] born ca 1859; Ida-[8] born ca 1861; Ora-[8] born ca 1866; Frederick-[8] born ca 1869; and Eva-[8] SEELEY born ca 1871
	2349. Ann Willoughby	born ca 1838; died ca 1906
	2350. John Jay	born 2 Apr 1840 Rushville; died 8 Jan 1920
		1 married Mary Elizabeth WELLS 16 Oct 1862
		(she dau/o Edward Durand WELLS and Margaret Elizabeth SNIDER)
		(she born ca 1842 IL; died ____)
		Children: Warren-[8] born ca 1866; Charles W-[8] born ca 1871, died 1940; and Dwight E-[8] SEELEY born ca 1876
		2 married Catherine Ida SCOTT 15 Oct 1885
		Child: Susan Catherine-[8] SEELEY born 1 Feb 1887; died 2 June 1931; married George W. MONTOOTH

1276. COL. ELIAS NATHANIEL-[6] **BOWKER,** son of Nathaniel-[5] BOWKER (Elias-[4]; John-[3]; Edmund-[2, 1]) and Alice LOVELAND, was born 28 Feb 1790 at Leicester, MA. He married Asenath HOTCHKISS on 18 Apr 1825 at Georgia, VT. She was the daughter of _____ HOTCHKISS and _____; and was born ca 1804; died 1886. Elias-[6] BOWKER , who served in the War of 1812 and was a Supervisor in the Town of Bombay, NY twice, died 22 Oct 1868 at Hogansburg, Franklin, NY.

BOWKER
The Sixth American Generation

Children of Elias[6] BOWKER and Asenath HOTCHKISS:
Surname **BOWKER**

2351. Harriet	born 21 Jan 1826; died 21 Oct 1829 Georgia Plains, VT.		
2352. Nathaniel	born ca 1830 VT; died ____	2354. Charlotte	born ca 1837 NY; died ____
2353. James	born ca 1832 VT; died ___	2355. Henry	born ca 1840 NY; died ____

1282. JOHN[6] BOWKER, son of John-[5] BOWKER (Elias-[4]; John-[3]; Edmund-[2,1]) and Sybil LOOMIS, was born ca 1805 at Georgia Springs, Franklin County, Vermont. He married first to Elvira WHITE 29 Jan 1828. He married second to Sarah M. LEACH on 19 Oct 1842. She was the daughter of ____ LEACH and ____; and was born ca 1819; died 1856 VT. John[6] BOWKER died 26 Nov 1853 at Georgia, VT.

Children of John-[6] BOWKER and Elvira WHITE:
Surname **BOWKER**   (all children born Georgia, VT)

2356. Asenath	born 9 Sep 1829; died 18 July 1869 (in childbirth) Georgia, VT.
	married Elliott L.DARLING 2 Apr 1853 Georgia, VT
	Child: Mary-[8] born ca 1859; Etta B-[8] born ca 1866; and Carrie-[8] DARLING born ca 1869
2357. Jackson	born ca 1832; died ____; married Martha E. REYNOLDS ca ____
	(she dau/o Rev Tertius REYNOLDS and Eliza TALBOT) (she born 31 May 1831 NY)
	Child: Libbie-[8] BOWKER born ca 1867
2358. Nathaniel	born ca 1834; died ____

Children of John-[6] BOWKER and Sarah M. LEACH:
Surname **BOWKER**

2359. Sybill	born ca 1840; died _____
2360. Walter K.	born ca 1843; died 8 Sept 1890; married Lucy _____
2361. Elvira	born 15 Oct 1846; died 19 July 1865 (18-10-5) EOL
2362. Herbert Leach	born 5 Jan 1849; died ____; married Harriet Lucinda HOAGLAND ca ____
	Child: Eugene Herbert-[8] BOWKER born 10 Dec 1879 CA; died 10 Nov 1957 CA; married Mary Elvira ROBINSON
2363. John H.	born ca 1851; died ____; married Adelia HUNT 14 Nov 1870 VT.
	Children: Louisa-[8] born 1871, died 1925; and John Hunt-[8] BOWKER born ca 1882; died 1942
2364. Marion Estella	born ca 1854; died ca 1886; married Chlorus Cornelius BLISS ca ____
	Child: Bertha Alma-[8] BLISS born ca 1874

1284. MARY[6] WILLISON, daughter of Esther-[5] BOWKER (Silas Day-[4] BOWKER; John-[3]; Edmund-[2,1]) and William WILLISON, was born 23 June 1797 at ____, NY. She married Jesse HAMPTON on 19 Dec 1809 at Genoa, Cayuga County, NY. He was the son of John HAMPTON and Martha BENEDICT, and was born 23 Apr 1789 Orange County, NY.; died 11 Nov 1871 Barry, MI. Mary-[6] WILLISON died 19 Apr 1844 at Barry Twsp., Barry County, MI

Children of Mary-[6] WILLISON and Jesse HAMPTON:
Surname **HAMPTON**

2365. Lois Ann	born July 1810; died ____	2366. Joseph Benedict	born 27 Nov 1812; died ___
2367. James Wood	born 20 Dec 1814; died ____		
2368. Almerie	born 30 Jan 1818 Hamburg, Erie, NY; married Nathaniel IDE ca ____		
2369. William Willison	born 12 Jan 1821 Williamsville, Erie, NY; died 18 Mar 1910 BC City, Calhoun, MI		
	married Laura Rosilla COLTON ca ____		
2370. Alvah Phelps	born 22 Apr 1823; died _____		
2371. Julia	born ca 1827; died 31 Dec 1876 Ross, Kalamazoo, MI		

1285. JAMES-[6] WILLISON, brother of above, was born 10 Nov 1790 at Chemung County, NY. He married first to Betsey WILLIAMS ca 1810 at Genoa, NY. She was the daughter of ____ WILLIAMS and ____, and was born ca ____; died 1821 OH. He married second to Margaret BORTHWICK on 5 June 1825 at Allen Township, Allegany County, NY. She was the daughter of John BORTHWICK and Rebecca BRICE, and was born 20 Jan 1798 Schoharie County, NY; died 5 Feb 1884 Barry Twsp, MI. James-[6] died 9 Sep 1866. Note: James-[6] WILLISON served in the War of 1812, in Capt. James MACK"S Co. NY Militia.

Children of James-[6] WILLISON and Martha BORTHWICK:
Surname **WILLISON**

+	**2372. JOHN**	born 1 Apr 1826 NY; died 22 May 1904
	BORTHWICK	married Candace-[6] BOWKER (# 1341) 26 Mar 1848 Barry, MI
		(she dau/o Noah-[5] BOWKER and Mary Polly BECKWITH)
		(she born 31 Aug 1829 NY; died 16 Oct 1902 Caldwell, Massaukee, MI)

Children of James[-6] WILLISON and Margaret BORTHWICK, continued:
Surname **WILLISON**

+	**2373. EDWIN A.**	born ca 1828 NY; died 25 June 1881; married Mary M. ____ ca _____
	2374. Samuel T.	born 7 July 1830 Allegany, NY; died ca 15 June 1899 Mitchell, SD
	2375. Wing Tabor	born 25 Aug 1832 NY; died _____; never married EOL
	2376. Martin Van Buren	born 2 Feb 1835 OH; died 15 Apr 1916; never married EOL
+	**2377. ELIZABETH JANE**	born 25 June 1837 OH; died 15 Nov 1921 MI
		married John Harvey GUTCHESS ca 1856 (he born ca 1832; died 1913)
	2378. Zaphira Barnes	born 14 Nov 1840 MI; died _____
	2379. H. Victor	born 6 Jan 1844; died 9 Aug 1846

1286. ESTHER[-6] WILLISON, sister of above , was born ca 1794 NY. She married John G. COY ca ___. He was the son of Elisha COY and Mary GRAY, and was born 7 Aug 1793 VT ; died 23 April 1877 OH. Esther[-6] WILLISON died ca 1843. John G. COY married second to Mary Ann REY on 11 March 1854.

Children of Esther[-6] WILLISON and John COY:
Surname **COY**

	2380. Mary Polly	born 2 May 1816 NY; died 9 April 1895 IN
	2381. Levi	born 28 Oct 1819 IN; died 9 July 1907 MO
+	**2382. WILLIAM MURL**	born ca 1835 Tompkins County, NY; died 26 Aug 1888
		married Mary DUGAN ca ____ (she born ca 1838; died 1892)

1289. CYNTHIA[-6] WILLISON, sister of above, was born 24 Aug 1807 at Genoa, Cayuga County, NY. She married Isaac ARMSTRONG on Jan 1829 at Genoa. He was the son of _____ ARMSTRONG and ____, and was born 2 Dec 1801 Genoa; died 2 Mar 1883 Genoa, NY. Cynthia[-6] WILLISON died 19 Jan 1873 Genoa, Cayuga, NY.

Children of Cynthia[-6] WILLISON and Isaac ARMSTRONG:
Surname **ARMSTRONG**

+	**2383. WILLIAM**	born 29 Nov 1830 Genoa, NY; died 16 Mar 1903 Unionville, MO		
		married Sarah Jane CONREY (she dau/o John CONREY and Almira ____)		
		(she born 11 July 1834 NY; died 8 Apr 1923 MO)		
	2384. Ambrose	born Sept 1832; died ____	2385. Julia	born ca 1834

1290. ORSEMUS[-6] WILLISON, brother of above, was born 8 Dec 1810 at Genoa, Cayuga County, NY. He married Eunice PETTEE ca 1830 at Genoa, NY. She was the daughter of _____ PETTEE and ____, and was born ca 1815 NY; died 15 Sep 1881 at Barry County, MI. Orsemus[-6] WILLISON died 2 Nov 1867 at Johnstown Township, Barry County, MI.

Children of Orsemus[-6] WILLISON and Eunice PETTEE:
Surname **WILLISON**

2386. George W.	born ca 1832 NY		2390. Orsemus, Jr.	born ca 1848 MI
2387. Hannah	born 5 Dec 1836 NY		2391. Seymour	born 5 Sep 1851
2388. William W.	born 5 Dec 1839 NY; died 7 Apr 1898 MI			
2389. Esther Jane	born ca 1845 MI; died ____		2392. Mary Etta	born ca 1855 MI

1291. MEHITABLE[-6] BOWKER, daughter of Silas Day[-5] BOWKER (Silas Day[-4]; John[-3]; Edmund-2,1) and Amy HARDING, was born 1 Sep 1787 at Big Flats, Chemung County, NY. She married Honorable Wing[-6] TABER ** on 24 March 1807 at Cayuga County, NY. He was the son of Amaziah[-5] TABER (William[-4] (Mary WING); Joseph[-3] (Elizabeth SPOONER); Thomas[-2] (Mary-3 THOMPSON ***) ; Philip[-1](Lydia MASTERS) and Silence BABCOCK, and was born 13 Feb 1782 at New Bedford, MA; died 19 Jan 1865 at Moravia, Cayuga, NY. Mehitable[-6] BOWKER died 27 Nov 1864 at Moravia.

** Wing[-6] TABER was an Assemblyman in 1829, and a Cayuga County Judge for 10 years beginning 2 Mar 1833.
*** Mary[-3] THOMPSON was the daughter of John THOMPSON and Mary[-3] COOKE. Mary[-2] COOKE was the daughter of Francis[-1] COOKE, a Pilgrim on the Mayflower.

Children of Mehitable[-6] BOWKER and Wing[-6] TABER:
Surname **TABER**

2393. Doris Doriah	born 2 Jan 1808 Scipio, Cayuga, NY; died 5 Oct 1891 Cayuga Co., NY
	married Jacob SHARP ca ____ Child: George -8 SHARP born ca 1829

Children of Mehitable-[6] BOWKER and Wing-[6] TABER, continued:

Surname **TABER**

+	**2394. SILAS DAY**	born 15 June 1812 Scipio; died 20 May 1865 Elkland, PA	
		married Harriet CLOSE 21 Dec 1837 Scipio	
	2395. Archibald	born 18 Sep 1813; died 10 Aug 1814	EOL
	2396. Aurelia	born 9 Apr 1815 Scipio; died 1 Feb 1839 Locke, NY	
		married Pliny Hall TUCKER ca 1838 (he born 7 Apr 1804 VT; died 6 Dec 1880 IL)	
		(he s/o Perley Milton TUCKER and Rebecca LYON)	
+	**2397. AMAZIAH**	born 1 July 1818 Scipio; died 13 May 1891 Moravia, NY	
		married Laura C. MORSE 31 May 1841 Moravia , Cayuga, NY	
		(she dau/o Gershom MORSE (Peter) and Rachel LITTLE (Moses)	
		(she born 18 May 1816 Moravia, NY; died 23 Aug 1904 Moravia)	
+	**2398. WILLIAM**	born 2 July 1820 Scipio; died 15 May 1873 Milwaukee, WI	
		married Cordelia M. THOMPSON 1 July 1844 Locke, Cayuga, NY	
		(she born 30 Jun 1824 Nunda Valley, NY; died 29 June 1882 Racine, WI)	
		(she dau/o Joseph THOMPON and Hannah _____)	
	2399. Amy	born 2 July 1820 Scipio; died 3 July 1843; married James BISSELL ca 1838	
	2400. Ann Louisa	born 29 May 1822 Scipio, NY; died in childbirth 16 Aug 1842 Moravia, NY	
		married Orson M. WELCH 1841 Moravia, NY	
		(he born ca 1817 Chenango Co., NY; died ca 1857)	
		Child: Daniel M-[8] WELCH born 16 Aug 1842; died 1889 Moravia)	
	2401. Samuel	born 29 Nov 1823 Moravia, NY; died 19 Nov 1859 Stockton, CA	
+	**2402. JOHN QUINCY**	born 2 Jan 1826 Moravia; died ___ ; married Elizabeth R. SMITH ca 1849 Moravia, NY	
+	**2403. MARY**	born 8 Sep 1827; died 23 April 1896 Auburn, Cayuga, NY	
		married John Locke PARKER 13 Dec 1848	
		(he s/o John H. PARKER and Esther LOCKE) (he born 28 Mar 1825 Moravia, NY)	

1293. ARCHIBALD-[6] BOWKER, brother of above, was born 16 Mar 1790 at Big Flats, Chemung, NY. He married Rebecca V. DRAKE ca 1810 at Cayuga County, NY. She was the daughter of Jasper DRAKE and Mary ____, and was born 7 Dec 1784; died 2 Feb 1872 Summer Hill, Cayuga Co., NY. Archibald-[6] BOWKER died 8 June 1832. They are both buried at Hathaway Cemetery, Summer Hill, NY.

Children of Archibald-[6] BOWKER and Rebecca V. DRAKE:

Surname **BOWKER**

+	**2404. JASPER DRAKE**	born Jan 1812 Cayuga, NY; died 3 Apr 1854; married Ann HINCKLEY
+	**2405. WILLIAM D.**	born Jan 1812 Cayuga Co., NY; died ____ ; married Alma S. POWERS
+	**2406. SILAS III**	born 10 Mar 1815; died 18 Feb 1877 Homer, Cortland, NY
		married Harriet ROGERS 5 Apr 1837
	2407. Mary Ann	born ca 1822; died _____; married William D. HINKLEY
	2408. Elmer	born 8 Dec 1824/ 2 June 1825 Cayuga Co., NY; died 19 June 1859
		married Ann HINKLEY (widow of his brother Jasper # 2404)
+	**2409. ERI**	born ca 1829 Summer Hill, Cayuga, NY; died 16 March 1894
		married Roseanna WIGGINS 2 Nov 1856

1294. LISA-[6] BOWKER, sister of above, was born 30 May 1794 at Locke, Cayuga, NY. She married Nathan-3 DRAKE ca 1809 at ____. He was the son of Jasper DRAKE and Mary ____, and the younger brother of Rebecca above. He was born 10 Dec 1786 Westchester Co., NY; died 13 March 1852 at Boston, Summit, OH. Lisa-[6] BOWKER died 14 Aug 1859 at Boston, OH. They are buried at Fairview Cemetery, Boston Township, Summit Co., OH.

Childen of Lisa-[6] BOWKER and Nathan DRAKE:

Surname **DRAKE**

	2410. David	born ca 1810 Cayuga Co., NY; died 4 Oct 1850; married Ester V. LILLIBRIDGE
		Children: Mary Ann-[8] DRAKE ; and Silas-[8] DRAKE; and Amy-[8] DRAKE
+	**2411. SILAS**	born ca 1813 Cayuga ,Co.; died ____
		1 married Sally ____ (she born ca 1819 NY; died before 1860)
		2 married Emily SKINNER 30 April 1851
+	**2412. MARY ANN**	born 1 Oct 1814 Cayuga Co,; died 28 Oct 1878 Hudson, Summit, OH
		1 married Luther COOK ca 1834; 2 married John DOUDS ca 1845 OH

Children of Lisa-6 BOWKER and Nathan DRAKE, continued:
Surname **DRAKE**

+	**2413. AMY MARY**	born ca 1817 Cayuga Co.; died 3 March 1861; married Leland COOK 21 Oct 1835 OH
	2414. Aurelia	born ca 1818 Cayuga; died 4 April 1901 Boston, Summit, OH
		married Jacob OZMUN (he born ca 1815 OH; died 5 Jan 1873 OH)
+	**2415. JASPER B.**	born 7 May 1820 Summit Co., OH; died 8Sept 1899
		married Caroline HARDY ca ____ (int pub 11 Aug 1844)
		(she dau/o Nathaniel HARDY, Sr. and Rebecca REED)
	2416. James N.	born 18 May 1822 Summit Co., OH; died 19 Sep 1889
		married Emeline W CRANNEZ ca ___ (she born ca 1820 OH)

Children: Hattie-8 DRAKE born ca 1852 IA; and William-8 DRAKE born ca 1855 OH

	2417. Emily	born born 23 Feb 1824 OH; died 19 May 1890 Boston, Summit, OH
		married Augustus H. WARRINER ca ___ (he born ca 1822; died 1854)

Child: Rosalia Augusta-8 WARRINER born ca 1855; died 1917

	2418. John D.	born ca 1826 OH; died 1852
	2419. Joseph	born 19 March 1830 Summit, OH; died 5 Mar 1905 Boston, Summit, OH
+	**2420. BENJAMIN**	born 1 Apr 1832 Boston , OH; died 10 Mar 1903 Porter, Van Buren, MI
		married Elizabeth Emily CUNNINGHAM 4 July 1855
+	**2421. NATHAN**	born 9 July 1834 Summit, OH; died 16 May 1902
		married Lucy M. RHODENBAUGH 13 Oct 1859
+	**2422. MEHITABLE**	born 29 Feb 1836 Summit, OH; died 17 Sep 1888 Portage, OH
		married Joseph HILL ca _____ (he born Nov 1824 VT; died 29 June 1913 OH)
+	**2423. MARIANNE**	born 13 Jan 1839 Summit, OH; died 25 Feb 1920 Summit, OH
		married Thomas Wesley CARTER ca 1858

1296. AURELIA-6 BOWKER, sister of above, was born ca 1804 Cayuga County, NY. She married Levi HENRY ca 1825. He was born 11 Apr 1800; died 11 Oct 1860 at Cayuga County, NY. Aurelia-6 BOWKER died there 21 Feb 1882.

Children of Aurelia-6 BOWKER and Levi HENRY:
Surname **HENRY**

	2424. Sarah M.	born ca 1824 Locke, Cayuga, NY; died _____
		married John Willett BOUTON 28 Oct 1849 Groton, Tompkins, NY
		(he s/o Stephen BOUTON and Almira HARRIS of Virgil)

Child: Jay-8 BOUTON born 28 Dec 1849 Moravia; died 5 Dec 1928 Fort Collins, CO;
married Celestia Amanda NIXON

	2425. Wing	born ca 1826 NY ; died ____
	2426. William	born 7 June 1832 Cayuga, NY; died 15 Dec 1861
	2427. Elvira/Eliza	born ca 1834 NY; died _____ 2428. Olive born ca 1836 Cayuga, NY
	2429. Amanda	born 8 Nov 1838 Cayuga Co., NY; died ____
		married Henry BOSTWICK 2 Aug 1857 Cortland, NY (he born ca 1817; died 1900)

Child: Fay-8 BOSTWICK born ca 1860; died ca 1930

	2430. Charlotte	born ca 1840 NY; died 23 Dec 1866 Cayuga County, NY
+	**2431. ROSETTA**	born ca 1844 Cayuga County, NY; died ca 1910
		married Bert/Burt Delay LOOMIS ca ____ (he born 4 Apr 1844; died ca 1905)
		(he s/o Thomas Elderkin LOOMIS and Anna Luna MURPHY)

1297. WILLIAM-6 ROSE, son of Lisa-5 BOWKER (Silas Day-4 John-3; Edmund-2,1) and Jacob ROSE, was born 27 Apr 1785 Marbletown, Ulster County, NY. He married first to Elizabeth Sally CURTIS on 12 Jan 1806 at Locke, NY. She was the daughter of Joseph CURTIS and Elizabeth Betsey STORY, and was born ca 1786; died ____. His 2nd marriage was to Hannah WATERS on 19 Feb 1849 at Delaware County, NY. She was born ca 1800, died ____. William-6 ROSE died ca 1861.

Children of William-6 ROSE and Sally CURTIS:
Surname **ROSE**

	2432. Joseph	born ca ____ ; died _____
+	**2433. SETH CURTIS**	born ca 1813; died 1893; married Jemima GAYLORD ca ____
		(she dau/o George A. GAYLORD and Lydia ____)
		(she born ca 1833 OH; died 14 Oct 1906 Delaware County, OH
	2434. Minerva	born ca 1816; died _____
+	**2435. WILLIAM HENRY**	born ca 1819; married Eunice N. ____ (she born ca 1821 OH)

1298. CYNTHIA-6 ROSE, sister of above, was born 9 July 1786 at Milton, Cayuga County, NY. She married Eber Andrus HOWE on 17 Oct 1802 at Milton. He was the son of Timothy HOWE and Elsie ____, and was born 26 May 1784; died 6 Mar 1862. Cynthia-6 ROSE died 7 May 1862.

Children of Cynthia-6 ROSE and Eber HOWE:
Surname **HOWE**

	2436. Lathan/Lathron	born 15 Oct 1803	2437. Andalucia	born 9 Aug 1805
	2438. Mark	born 26 Aug 1807		
+	**2439. AARON**	born 10 Aug 1809; died 27 Sept 1898; married Sarah HALSEY ca 1828 OH		
		(she born 24 Sept 1810 OH; died 13 Jan 1865 Taylor City, IA		
		(she dau/o David HALSEY and _____)		
	2440. Frances	born 8 Jan 1811; died ____		
+	**2441. ELIZABETH**	born 13 June 1812; died 22 Feb 1852 Harlem Delaware County, OH		
		married James COCKRELL (as his 2nd wife) ca 1830 Delaware Co., OH		
		(he married first to Nancy LINNABARRY)		
		(he s/o Edward COCKRELL and Elizabeth DAWSON)		
+	**2442. PHILETUS**	born 22 July 1814; married Eliza LAYCOCK ca _____; resided Nankin, Wayne, MI		
	2443. Elsie	born 22 May 1816	2447. John R.	born 24 Jan 1819
	2444. William R.	born 24 May 1821	2448. Francis	born 8 July 1827
	2445. Cynthia	born 24 Oct 1823	2449. Mary Ann	born 27 Apr 1829
	2446. Eber	born 27 Feb 1825; died Aug 1880 OH		

1300. ISAAC HOBBS-6 ROSE, brother of above, was born 31 March 1790 at Tioga, Chenango, NY. He married Anna YOUNG on 10 Aug 1813 at Genoa, Cayuga, NY. She was the daughter of Christian YOUNG and Sarah LINDERMAN, and was born 12 Jan 1795 NY; died 26 Jan 1876 IN. Isaac Hobbs-6 ROSE died 25 Dec 1874 at St. Mary's, Indiana.

Children of Isaac H-6 ROSE and Anna YOUNG :
Surname **ROSE**

	2450. Lisa	born 31 Oct 1814 OH; died 18 June IN
	2451. Eliza	born ca 1815; died 18 June 1885 IN
	2452. Sarah	born Dec 1816 NY; died 17 Feb 1895 IN
	2453. George Evans	born June 1819; died 16 Feb 1871
	2454. Adoniram Judson	born 23 June 1822 OH; died 12 Feb 1911 CA
+	**2455. HORATIO GATES**	born 29 Oct 1826 OH; died 27 Aug 1864 Andersonville Prison, Ft. Sumter, GA
		married Margaret YOUNG 22 Apr 1849 Adams, IN; (she born ca 1830 OH)

1301. SAMUEL HOBBS-6 ROSE, brother of above, was born 5 March 1792 at Tioga, Chenango, NY. He married Delana COLLINS ca 1817 at Groton, Tompkins County, NY. She was the daughter of Joseph L. COLLINS and Tamesin RICE, and was born ca March 1799 at Groton; died ____. Samuel Hobbs-6 ROSE died 10 May 1877 at Belding, MI, and is buried there.

Children of Samuel Hobbs-6 ROSE and Delana COLLINS:
Surname **ROSE**

2456. Stephen	born ca 1818, NY; died ___	2458. Jacob L. born 19 April 1826 NY
2457. Marilla	born 12 Dec 1823 Tompkins Co., NY; died 8 Jan 1893 Orleans, MI	
	married John HOUSEMAN 26 Jan 1843 (he born 16 May 1821; died _____)	
	(he s/o John HOUSEMAN and Charity VEDDER)	
	Children: twins Julius-8 born 9 Mar 1844; died 19 Apr 1844 and Julia-8 ROSE, born 9 Mar 1844; died 14 Mar 1844 MI	

1302. SILAS-6 ROSE, brother of above, was born 2 Sept 1794 Chenango County, NY. He married Nancy YOUNG on 18 June 1818. She was the daughter of Christian John YOUNG and Sarah LINDERMAN, and sister of Anna YOUNG who married Isaac-6 ROSE (# 1300). She was born ca 1799 NY ; died 4 Dec 1882. Silas-6 ROSE died ____.

Children of Silas-6 ROSE and Nancy YOUNG:
Surname **ROSE**

	2459. Warren	born ca 1820; died ____; married Hannah ____		
+	**2460. JEFFERSON**	born ca 1822; died ____; married Sarah A. ca ____		
	2461. Orville	born ca 1826 OH; died ____	2463. Alexander Hamilton	born ca 1834 OH
	2462. Harriet	born ca 1831 OH; died _____	2464. Rebecca	born ca 1838 OH

1303. JOHN[-6] ROSE, brother of above, was born 24 Oct 1796 Locke/Groton Tompkins, NY. He married Mary Eliza CRANS ca ____. She was the daughter of Andrew CRANS and Rebecca JOHNSON, and was born 6 Nov 1811 PA; died 3 March 1884 OH. John-[6] ROSE died 18 Aug 1865 Trenton, OH.

Children of John[-6] ROSE and Mary Eliza CRANS:
Surname **ROSE**

2465. Abigail	born 18 Jan 1836 Trenton, OH; died ____	2467. Salmon J. born 16 June 1840 OH
2466. Eunice H.	born 5 Mar 1838 Trenton, OH; died ____	

1306. JACOB SCHOOLCRAFT[-6] ROSE, brother of above, was born 17 Feb 1802 at Locke, Tompkins ,NY. He married Deborah Ann HEAD on 8 Jan 1824 at Lansing, Tompkins, NY. She was the daughter of _____ HEAD and ____, and was born ca 1802; died ____ (living 1880). Jacob S-[6] ROSE died _____. 1860 resided at Green, Adams Co., OH

Children of Jacob[-6] ROSE and Deborah HEAD:
Surname **ROSE**

+ **2468. SMITH**	born ca 1827 PA; died ca 1870; married Susan STOUT ca ____	
2469. Jeremiah	born ca 1828 PA; died ____	
2470. John	born ca 1831/3 PA; died ____	2472. Mary Ann born ca 1838 OH
2471. Joseph A.	born ca 1833 PA; died ____	
	married Jane/Jenny _____ ca _____ (she born ca 1843; died _____)	
	Children: Jerusha-[8] ROSE born ca 1867; Stella-[8] ROSE born ca 1873; Charles-[8] ROSE born ca 1875;	
	and Deborah-[8] ROSE born ca 1879	

1309. ORSEMUS[-6] BOWKER, son of Daniel-[5] BOWKER (Silas Day[-4]; John [-3]; Edmund[-2,1]) and Azubah GREGORY, was born ca 1800 at Delaware County, NY. He married Sally BOGART ca ____. She was the daughter of ____ BOGART and ____, and was born ca 1809; died 1 Feb 1850 at Hancock, NY. Orsemus[-6] BOWKER died 24 Sept 1877 at Walton, NY.

Children of Orsemus[-6] BOWKER and Sally BOGART:
Surname **BOWKER**

2473. Cynthia	born ca 1829 Hancock, Delaware, NY; died ____
2474. Esther A.	born ca 1830 Delaware Co., NY; died ca 1901 Oberlin, Lorain,OH
	married Willis Gaylord MERRIAM ca 1857 · no issue EOL
	(he ss/o Daniel MERRIAM and Eunice CADY) (he born 18 Apr 1822 NY)
2475. Sally A.	born ca ____; poss. married _____ STALKER ca ____
2476. Mary Ann	born ca 184; died ___; married George KIRSCHNER 27 March 1853 Walton, Del., NY
2477. Silas W. ***	born ca 1839 Delaware Co., NY; died 25 Oct 1863 Folly Island, SC

*** Note: Silas-[7] BOWKER served a a Private in Company B, 144th NY Infantry Regiment in the Civil War., and died at Folly Island, SC 25 Oct 1863. He is buried at the Beaufort National Cemetery, SC with 88 other men from Company B. They are buried in Section 28. His grave is # 2666. His company was formed at Walton, NY.

1310. CYNTHIA[-6] BOWKER, sister of above, was born 17 Aug 1804 at Harvard, Delaware County, NY. She married Samuel B. CURREY ca ___. He was the son of Stephen CURREY and Anna VAIL, and was born 12 March 1801 at Grahamsville, Sullivan Co., NY; died 6 March 1872 at Grahamsville, NY. Cynthia-[6] BOWKER died 6 Mar 1880 at Grahamsville.

Children of Cynthia[-6] BOWKER and Samuel CURREY:
Surname **CURREY**   (all children born Neversink, Sullivan County, NY)

+ **2478. ANDREW B.**	born 8 Dec 1826; died ca 1906
	married Mary M. BURTON ca 1850
2479. Melissa M.	born 29 Dec 1828; died 11 Oct 1847 EOL
2480. Catherine	born 5 April 1831; married James HALL
	Children: Frank -8 HALL born ca ___; and James-8 HALL born ca 1849 NY
2481. Anna E.	born 10 Aug 1838; died 16 Nov 1841 EOL
2482. Alfred H.	born 12 Nov 1840; married Amelia Jeanette _____ ca ____
	Children: Archie-[8] CURREY born 1878, and Alice-[8] CURREY born 1882
+ **2483. GABRIEL FRANCIS**	born 4 July 1844 ; died 1 Nov 1934; married Jennie R. BYERS 3 Oct 1867
2484. Charity A.	born 17 Aug 1847 NY; died July 1886 NY
	married Neal J. BENSON ca ____ (he born ca 1847 NY, a stonemason)
	Children: Rotha-[8] BENSON born ca Aug 1881, and Myra E-[8] BENSON born ca Dec 1883 NY
2485. James R.	born ca 1849; died ___ 2486. Sarah Esther born 17 Aug 1851

1311. ANSON[-6] BOWKER, brother of above, was born April 1810 at Colchester, Delaware County, NY. He married Elizabeth (Betsey) JONES ca ____. She was the daughter of ____ JONES and ____, and was born ca 1815 at Franklin, Delaware Co., NY; died __. Anson[-6] BOWKER died 8 Aug 1898 at Tompkins County, NY. They are buried Walton Town/ Village Cemetery.

Children of Anson[-6] BOWKER and Betsey JONES:
Surname **BOWKER**   (all children born Delaware County, NY)

+	**2487. DANIEL T.**	born 9 May 1837 /40; died 25 May 1916 Stamford, Delaware, NY
		married Hannah <u>Susan</u> SACKRIDER 31 Oct 1860
		(she born 19 July 1843/51; died 20 Nov 1918)
		(she daughter of Timothy SACKRIDER and Nancy GOODENOUGH)

Note: Daniel-[6] BOWKER enlisted in the Civil War on Company C, 114th NY Infantry Regiment on 16 Sep 1864

	2488. Azuba Ann	born ca 1841; married Charles CLARK

Child: Emma Rebecca-[8] CLARK born 31 Dec 1863 Deposit , NY; married Luther F. WATSON; died Dec 1925

+	**2489. ORRIN L.**	born ca 1843; married Olive FRINK ca 1862 Delaware Co., NY
	2490. Hannah J.	born ca 1847; died 20 Nov 1918
	2491. Levi D.	born March 1850; married Stella H. _____ ca 1878 (she born ca 1862)

Child: Lizzie-[8] BOWKER born ca 1879

+	**2492. ORSEMUS**	born ca 1854; married Susan Adelaide SHERMAN
		(she born 9 March 1857; died 26 Oct 1931 Beerston, Delaware Co., NY)
	2493. Silas J.	born Feb 1857; married Sarah J. LANDON 12 Jan 1878

Children: Guy-[8] born May 1883 NY; and Mabel-[8] BOWKER born Sept 1885 NY

+	**2494. ANNIS A.**	born ca 1859; married Charles H. MAY; died 3 Feb 1935

1313. JONATHAN[-6] BOWKER, son of John-[5] BOWKER (Silas Day-[4]; John-[3]; Edmund-[2,1]) and Jerusha ROBINSON, was born 18 Feb 1797 at Lansing, Tompkins County, NY. He married first to Nancy FOOTE ca 1816. She was the daughter of David FOOTE and Irene LANE, and was born 19 May 1797; died 5 Dec 1823 (probably as a result of childbirth) at Groton, NY. He married second to Emeline POWERS ca 1824. She was the daughter of Frederick POWERS (Jacob) and Ruth PENNOYER, and was born 5 Feb 1806 at Dutchess County, NY; died 21 Nov 1888 Groton, Tompkins, NY. Jonathan-[6] BOWKER died 23 Feb 1891. They are both buried at the Groton Rural Cemetery, Tompkins , NY

Children of Jonathan-[6] BOWKER and Nancy FOOTE:
Surname **BOWKER**

	2495. Irene	born ca 1817 Groton, NY; died ca 1835
+	**2496. ALBERT**	born 11 Oct 1821 Groton, NY; died 12 Nov 1902 Dewitt, Clinton, MI (Death Certificate)
		1 married Lucinda KEYES 23 Feb 1845 Sheridan Twsp. Calhoun, MI
		2 married Eunice Lucretia BALLARD ca 20 Dec 1869 Union, Isabella, MI

Children of Jonathan-[6] BOWKER and Emeline POWERS:
Surname **BOWKER**

+	**2497. HARRISON**	born ca 1824; married H. Maria(h) ____ before 1848; died 1875
+	**2498. JOHN HENRY**	born ca 1826 NY; died _____
	POWERS	married Sarah _____ ca ____
	2499. Nelson	born ca 1828 Tompkins Co. NY; died 1907 KS; married Mary J. FLEMING ca ____

Children: Acllia-[8] born ca 1852; and James Dennison -[8] BOWKER born ca 1854, died 1926

+	**2500. ARVILLA**	born 31 Aug 1833 Summer Hill, Cayuga, NY; died 9 Apr 1918 Kingsley, IA
		married George Washington MC COUN 13 Jan 1850 North Lansing, NY
		(he s/o Nelson MC COUN and Selinda BURGESS)
		(he born Apr 1828; died 14 March 1908 Kingsley, Plymouth, IA)
+	**2501. MARTIN**	born ca 1836; died 28 March 1904
	VAN BUREN	married Jane R. _____; resided Groton, Tompkins, NY
	2502. Juliann	born ca 1842; died 6 July 1917 2503. Sarah D. born ca 1847 NY

1314. ESTHER[-6] BOWKER, sister of above, was born ca 1800 at Cayuga County, NY. She married Robert BOTHWELL before 1825. He was the son of Alexander BOTHWELL and Martha WILSON, and was born ca 1801 Cayuga County, NY; died before 1880. Esther-[6] BOWKER died 21 Nov 1888 at Groton, Tompkins, NY.

Children of Esther-[6] BOWKER and Robert BOTHWELL:
Surname **BOTHWELL**

2504. Alex	born ca 1826	2506. Hannah	born ca 1831
2505. Emeline	born ca 1827	2507. James	born ca 1834

Children of Esther[-6] BOWKER and Robert BOTHWELL, continued:
Surname **BOTHWELL**

2508. Sally	born ca 1836		2509. Sophronia	born ca 1838
2510. Esther Ann	born 13 Aug 1839; died 21 July 1926 Groton, Tompkins, NY			

married Marcus Albert AVERY ca ____   (he born ca 1832; died ca 1920)
Children: Delta A-[8] AVERY born ca 1863; died 1924 married ____ WHITMAN;
and Alta F-[8] AVERY born ca 1865; died 1925; married ____ TOWNLEY

1315. HANNAH-[6] BOWKER, sister of above, was born 11 May 1802 at Lansing, Tompkins County, NY. She married William WALKER ca ____. He was the son of ____ WALKER and ____; and was born ca 1799; died ____. Hannah-[6] BOWKER died 14 June 1871. In 1850 they lived in Moravia, Cayuga, NY

Children of Hannah-[6] BOWKER and William WALKER.
Surname **WALKER**

2511. Caleb	born ca 1834; died ____		2513. John	born ca 1844; died ____
2512. Helen A.	born ca 1840; died ____; married John WOODRUFF ca ___ (he born ca 1841 NY)			

Children: Gilbert-[8] born ca 1860 IL; and Frank-[8] WOODRUFF born ca 1866 IL

1316. JEFFERSON T-[6] BOWKER ,brother of above, was born 18 March 1804 at Lansing, Tompkins County, NY.He married Sophronia HENDERSON on 21 April 1824. She was the daughter of Thomas HENDERSON and ___, and was born 30 April 1809 Cayuga County, NY; died 1889 Tioga, PA. Jefferson T-[6] BOWKER died 24 May 1856 , in a logging accident, at Locke, Cayuga County, NY. He is buried in the Howell Cemetery, East of Chapman's Corners on Howell Road, Town of Summerhill, Cayuga County, NY.

Children of Jefferson T-[6] BOWKER and Sophronia HENDERSON:
Surname **BOWKER**

+	**2514. CALVIN**	born 2 Mar 1826; married Eunice JOHNSON 4 July 1846
	2515. Amanda	born 10 July 1827; married Robert F. RYDER ca 1843; died 1908
	2516. Alford/Alfred	born 8 Oct 1829; died 15 April 1866; married Philena/Philinda LOWE 21 Dec 1853
		(she born 13 July 1832 Tompkins Co., NY; died _____)

Child: Eva-[8] BOWKER born ca 1856 NY

+	**2517. MARTHA J.**	born 29 Jan 1832 NY; died 4 Jan 1901 Tioga County, PA
		1 married Jacob CONLEY 1 Jan 1850
		(he s/o Jacob CONLEY and Polly HARVARD/HOWARD)
		(he born 23 Nov 1827 Locke, Cayuga, NY; died 2 Dec 1867)
		2 married Silas STAPLES 20 July 1870 Middlebury, Tioga, PA
		(he born 26 Oct 1808 VT; died 3 June 1888 PA)
+	**2518. PHILINDA**	born 31 Jan 1834 NY; married Chauncey C. TRUMBLE 22 Dec 1853 Locke, NY
	2519. Jefferson T., Jr.	born 19 Feb 1836; died 22 Jan 1901
	(twin)	married Adelia COLBY 22 Sep 1856 (she born ca 1837; died ca 1919)

Children: Ernest-[8] BOWKER born ca 1858; Emma-[8] born ca ___; and Eliza-[8] born ca ___

	2520. Madison (twin)	born 19 Feb 1836; died 4 March 1836	EOL
	2521. Mary	born 1 March 1838 Tompkins Co., NY; died _____	
	2522. Roxanna	born 18 June 1840; married _____ 20 Mar 1856	
	2523. Julia Ann	born 2 Apr 1842; died _____	
+	**2524. WILLIAM HENRY**	born 11 March 1844 Tompkins Co., NY; died ca 1919	
		1 married Jennie May CONLEY 13 Nov 1861 Groton, Tompkins, NY	
		2 married Elizabeth HOURIGAN 26 June 1873	
+	**2525. SYLVESTER**	born 4 Feb 1847 Cayuga Co., NY; died 19 May 1900 Rose Lake, Osceola, MI	
		married Carrie Marianda BROGDEN 6 Feb 1867 Cayuga Co., NY	
		(she dau/o Abraham BROGDEN and Catherine GAY)	
		(she born 16 July 1842 Cortland Co., NY; died 12 Sep 1896 Rose Lake)	
+	**2526. AMAZIAH CHESTER**	born 3 April 1849 Cayuga Co., NY; died 17 July 1940 Dryden, Tompkins, NY	
		married Mary Clara SMITH 10 May 1870	

1317. MADISON-[6] BOWKER, brother of above, was born 23 March 1808 Tompkins County, NY. He married Sarah/Sally DAVIS ca ___. She was the daughter of ____ DAVIS and ___, and was born 3 Aug 1809 NY; died 27 Nov 1883 Lansing, Tompkins, NY. Madison-[6] BOWKER died 17 March 1838 Lansing. Madison-[6] BOWKER, when a young man bought a farm of 40 acres at Beardsley Corners (later North Lansing, NY) where he kept a hotel for several years, and also had a grocery store.

BOWKER
The Sixth American Generation

Children of Madison-⁶ BOWKER and Sally DAVIS:
Surname **BOWKER**

	2527. William H.	born 20 Oct 1828 Tompkins Co., NY; died 8 Feb 1879; married Cornelia ___ bef.1860
+	**2528. MARGARET**	born 3 July 1832 Lansing, Tompkins, NY; died ____
	JERUSHA	married John Henry INGERSOLL 31 Dec 1854 North Lansing
		(he s/o Johnson INGERSOLL and Susanna BULL)
		(he born 25 May 1828 Richland, Oswego, NY; died _____)
	2529. Sarah	born Jan 1838; died 1883; married Johnson FRENCH ca 1853
		(he s/o Thomas FRENCH and Polly BULL of Canada)
		(he born ca 1832 Oswego Co., NY; died Feb 1863 from a fever contracted on a trip to PA)

Children: Ida-⁸ FRENCH born 26 Oct 1859, died 12 Mar 1883; and Edward-⁸ FRENCH born 14 Mar 1861

1320. JAMES M.-⁶ BOWKER, brother of above, was born 30 May 1816 at Tompkins County, NY. He married Elizabeth MILLER ca ____. She was the daughter of _____ MILLER and ___, and was born 18 Feb 1812 Tompkins County, NY; died 1 April 1849. James M.-⁶ BOWKER was a farmer and innkeeper. He died 24 March 1904 at Lansing, Tompkins, NY and is buried in the MILLER Cemetery there.

Children of James M-⁶ BOWKER and Elizabeth MILLER:
Surname **BOWKER**

	2530. Jackson	born ca 1835 Tompkins Co., NY; died ____
		married Margaret E. _____ ca ____

Children: Rhoda L-⁸ BOWKER born ca 1855 NY; and Alice A-⁸ BOWKER born ca 1859

	2531. Henry M.	born 12 Apr 1838; died 27 Apr 1848	EOL
	2532. Mariah	born ca 1841; died _____	
	2533. Isadora	born ca 1842; possibly died young	
+	**2534. JAMES**	born ca 1843 NY; died 21 March 1900; married Frank L. RHODES ca 1868	

1321. POLLY-⁶ BOWKER, sister of above, was born ca 1818 Tompkins County, NY. She married John GOWER ca _____. He was the son of _____ GOWER and ___, and was born ca 1816 ; died ca 1885. Polly-⁶ BOWKER died ca 1898 and is buried at the MILLER Cemetery, Lansing, Tompkins County, NY.

Children of Polly-⁶ BOWKER and John GOWER:
Surname **GOWER**

	2535. Mary	born ca 1838 NY; died _____	
	2536. Madison	born ca 1840; died 28 Dec 1901; never married	EOL
		buried at Bath National Cemetery, Bath, NY (Section G, Row 20)	

Note: Served as a Private in the 14ᵗʰ NY Infantry in the Civil War from 13 May 1863 – 2 June 1863 at Auburn, NY. Served in the 6ᵗʰ Ohio Cavalry; and then in Company K, 3ʳᵈ NY Light Artillery from 21 March 1865 – 3 July 1865. He applied for a pension 26 July 1880 MI

+	**2537. DANIEL**	born 1 Sept 1843 Tompkins County, NY; died 9 June 1901 Greenbush, MI (heart failure		
		married Mary A. ALLEN ca 1868 (she dau/o John ALLEN and Elizabeth CHESTER)		
	2538. Louisa	born ca 1845; died _____		
	2539. Dennison R.	born ca 1849; died _____	2541. Simeon	born ca 1857; died ____
	2540. Lyman	born ca 1856; died 1878	2542. Adelaide	born ca 1859; died _____

1322. JOHN-⁶ BOWKER, brother of above, was born 26 April 1822 at Tompkins County, NY. He married Eliza Ann LEARN on 31 Oct 1838 ____, NY. She was the daughter of John LEARN and Elizabeth ____, and was born 21 Sep 1821 NY; died 14 Sep 1888. John-⁶ BOWKER died 19 July 1879 at Tompkins County, NY.

Children of John-⁶ BOWKER and Eliza Ann LEARN:
Surname **BOWKER** (all children born Tompkins County, NY)

	2543. Madison	born 1 Dec 1839; died 18 Feb 1856 Lansing, Tompkins, NY	EOL
	2544. Martha J.	born 28 Nov 1841; died _____	
	2545. Jefferson	born 28 May 1843; died 18 April 1869; married Eliza WHITEHEAD	
		(she dau/o John WHITEHEAD and Juliann DRAKE) (she born ca 1841 NY)	
	2546. Catherine	born 5 Jan 1845; died 19 April 1866 Lansing	
	2547. Margaret	born 19 June 1846; died 23 June 1864	EOL
+	**2548. JACKSON M.**	born 25 March 1849 Lansing; died Sep 1877	
		married Harriet E. PECK 9 Feb 1870; (she born 3 Nov1846; died 24 Sep 1899)	

Note: Jackson M. BOWKER served as a Private in the 9ᵗʰ NY Heavy Artillery during the Civil War

Children of John-[6] BOWKER and Eliza Ann LEARN, continued:
Surname **BOWKER**

2549. William H.	born 25 Jan 1850; died 15 May 1851	EOL
2550. Clinton	born 1 Aug 1852; married Mary _____; died 9 Aug 1883	
	Children: Lena-[8] BOWKER born ca 1873; and Frances-[8] BOWKER born ca 1878	
2551. Clara/Clarrie	born 12 May 1857; died 9 Aug 1875	EOL
2552. John	born 13 June 1858; died ____	2554. Nora D. born 1 Oct 1868; died 2 Apr 1869
2553. Viola E.	born 23 May 1865; died 19 Jan 1926	2555. Cora B. born 1 Oct 1868; died 2 Oct 1869

1326. LUCINDA-[6] BOWKER, daughter of Joseph-[5] (Silas Day-[4]; John-[3]; Edmund-[2,1]) and Silva RUDI, was born 24 June 1801 at Milton, Cayuga County, NY. She married Derrick (Dernville) Richard SNEDAKER ca 1817. He was the son of Jacobus/ James SNEDAKER and Nancy Ann COX, and was born 8 Jan 1795 Lansing, Tompkins County, NY; died 18 Sept 1838 Tompkins County, NY. Lucinda-[6] BOWKER died 23 Aug 1876 at Allegan, Allegan County, MI.

Children of Lucinda-[6] BOWKER and Derrick SNEDAKER:
Surname **SNEDAKER**

+	**2556. MORRIS JACKSON**	born 16 Dec 1818 Lansing, Tompkins, NY; died 12 Dec 1882 Salt Lake City, UT
		1 married Ann EARL 7 April 1844 Kalamazoo, MI
		(she dau/o Jesse EARL and Jenetta __)
		(she born 22 Feb 1818 Seneca, Ontario, NY; died 18 Oct 1879 Salt Lake City)
		2 married Elizabeth Hannah MOBBS 3 April 1853 Salt Lake City
		(she dau/o William MOBBS and Elizabeth JEWSTER)
		(she born 3 Apr 1838 England; died 16 Mar 1868 Salt Lake City, UT)
		3 married Polly Tryphena FAIRCHILD 15 Feb 1862 (she born 11 Dec 1846)
		(she dau/o John FAIRCHILD and Tryphena Pomeroy LEWIS)
		4 married Lucy RINGROSE 31 Jan 1863 (she born ca 1846; died 1930)
+	**2557. BRADFORD CLINTON**	born 9 Sept 1820 Lansing, NY; died 1880 Salt Lake City, UT
		married Mary Ann BLACKWELL ca ____
		(she dau/o Robert Preston BLACKWELL, Jr. and Nancy Ann CRUTCHER)
		(she born 16 Dec 1827 KY; died 22 Oct 1918 KY)
	2558. Sylvina	born 14 Mar 1822 North Lansing, NY; died 22 Nov 1900 Allegan, MI
		married Lyman W. WATKINS ca ____ (he was a druggist)
		(he s/o _____ WATKINS and _____) (he born ca 1822; died _____)
	2559. Preston	born ca 1823 North Lansing, NY; died _____
	2560. Joseph Warren	born 8 Feb 1826 Lansing, NY; died 20 May 1883 Allegan, MI
		1 married Louisa _____ before 1850; (she born ca 1834 NY)
		2 married Ellen C. _____ before 1870 (she born ca 1836 England)
	2561. Ellen S.	born 29 Nov 1829 Lansing; died 13 March 1876 Lansing EOL

1328. CHESTER-[6] BOWKER, brother of above, was born ca 1807 NY. He married Eliza Louise _____ ca ____. She was born ca 1814 NY; died ____. Chester-[6] BOWKER died ____. In 1863 they resided in Genoa, NY, later moved to Iowa.

Children of Chester-[6] BOWKER and Eliza ____:
Surname **BOWKER**

	2562. Freeman	born ca 1833 NY; died ____
	2563. Louisa	born ca 1835 NY; died ____
	2564. Sara A.	born ca 1837 NY; died ____
+	**2565. OSCAR**	born 22 Sept 1841 NY; died 16 Feb 1911 IA
		1 married Louisa E. LABAR 15 Dec 1861 Genoa, New York
		(she dau/o Theodore LABAR and Louisa _____)
		(she born 8 Dec 1842 NY; died 31 Dec 1882 IA)
		2 married Lydia " Liddie " HOLT 9 Feb 1884
		3 married Mary Anna BREECE 12 March 1891 IA
	2566. Napoleon B.	born 1 June 1848 Morrow Co.,OH; died ca 1874 OH; married Margaret Frances STEEN

Child: Ora Clayton-[8] BOWKER born 20 Aug 1871 OH; married Alice E. MURDOCK ca 1896 MI
Note: Napoleon B. BOWKER enlisted in the Civil War on 9 Aug 1862 in Company H, 81st Ohio Infantry regiment. He was promoted to Corporal on 1 Nov 1864; and mustered out of service on 13 July 1865 at Louisville, KY. (Source: US Civil War Soldiers 1861-65)

1330. IRA-[6] BOWKER, brother of above, was born 23 July 1810 NY. He married Rebecca BORTHWICK ca 1830. She was the daughter of _____ BORTHWICK and ____, and was born 28 Aug 1811; died ____. Ira-[6] BOWKER, who went to California for the " Gold Rush ", died 9 July 1852 at Green County, Wisconsin, while en route back to his home in Rush Township, IL. He is buried at the Ladies Union Cemetery, Stockton, IL. His widow married second to Thomas HAMILTON.

Children of Ira-[6] BOWKER and Rebecca BORTHWICK:
Surname **BOWKER**

+	**2567. GEORGE CLAYTON**	born 29 July 1832 Allen Twsp, Allegany Co., NY; died 7 Apr 1916 Mitchell, KS married Olive HAMILTON 23 Dec 1858 Jo Daviess County, IL (she was the dau/o _____ HAMILTON and _____)
	2568. William Orrin	born 30 Sept 1836 Allen Twsp; died 26 Mar 1862 married Sarah Ann TEFFT 23 Feb 1859 IL
	2569. Joseph S.	born 8 Feb 1839 Rush Twsp; died 1863
+	**2570. JAMES T.**	born ca 1842 Rush; died _____ married Caroline BRICKLER 11 Oct 1866 IL; (she born 8 Sep 1839; died _____)
+	**2571. SYLVIA A.**	born 3 Feb 1844; died _____; married John DRANE 5 Feb 1863
+	**2572. ZACHARY TAYLOR**	born ca 1846; died 10 Sep 1919 Linn, Oregon married Hannah M. GATES ca _____
+	**2573. SYLVINA P.**	born 22 Feb 1849 Rush Twsp, IL ; died ___; married John WILLIAMS ca ____

1332. ASA-[6] BOWKER, half-brother of above, son of Joseph-[5] BOWKER (Silas Day-[4]; John-[3]; Edmund-[2,1]) and Peninah RUDI, was born 28 April 1818 at Tompkins County, NY. He married Hester PIPER on 14 April 1842 at Alamo, MI. She was the daughter of George PIPER and Sarah Ann SPRATT, and was born 29 Dec 1824 Exeter, Devon, England ; died 11 April 1867 at Alamo, Kalamazoo, MI.; died _____. Asa-[6] BOWKER died ca 1861 MI.

Children of Asa-[6] BOWKER and Hester PIPER:
Surname **BOWKER**

2574. Norman L.	born ca 1843 MI; died ___; married Mary E. STAFFORD 14 Apr 1866 MI
	Children: George-[8] BOWKER born ca 1867; and William-[8] BOWKER born ca 1870
2575. Albertus	born ca 1846 MI; died 22 Feb 1908 MI; married Dora W. _____
	Child: Albert-[8] BOWKER born ca _____
2576. Leona Emily	born ca 1851 Kalamazoo, MI

1333. VIOLETTA-[6] BOWKER, daughter of Noah-[5] BOWKER (Silas Day-[4]; John-[3]; Edmund-[2,1]) and Mary Polly BECKWITH, was born 23 Aug 1806 Cayuga County, NY. She married Augustus WOODWORTH ca 1834 Allegany, NY. He was the son of Asa WOODWORTH and Sally BOYNTON, and was born 1 Nov 1812 NY, died April 1893 NE.

Children of Violetta-[6] BOWKER and Augustus WOODWORTH:
Surname **WOODWORTH**

+	**2577. JASPER H.**	born 9 Dec 1834 Allegany, NY; died 2 Nov 1917 Lyons, Cook, IL married Emeline B. STANLEY ca ____
+	**2578. WARREN AUGUSTUS**	born 25 May 1836 Allegany, NY; died 9 June 1922 Saugatuck, Allegan, MI. 1 married Mary A. MILLER ca ____; (she born ca 1839; died ca 1891) 2 married Alice C. REDWAY ca _____

1334. SILAS-[6] BOWKER, brother of above, was born 1 April 1808 at Genoa, Cayuga County, NY. He married Margaret ARDREY ca 1833 at ____, NY. She was the daughter of William ARDREY and Mary BRONG, and was born 20 Feb 1815 NY; died 21 March 1876 MI. Silas-[6] BOWKER died 27 Sept 1888 at Hastings, Barry, MI

Children of Silas-[6] BOWKER and Margaret ARDREY:
Surname **BOWKER**

+	**2579. SUSAN JANE**	born Oct 1833 NY; died ca 1920; 1 married Peter M. RUSSELL ca 1855 2 married John C. RUSSELL 18 Mar 1886 Hastings, Barry , MI
+	**2580. NOAH J.**	born 1 May 1835 Allegany County, NY; died 3 July 1900 Newago County, MI married Aschah Mary ARDREY 24 May 1868 Allegan, MI
+	**2581. DAVID A.**	born April 1837 Potter County, PA; died 10 April 1911 MI 1 married Elmira MOORE 6 Dec 1860/61 Barry County, MI 2 married Nancy Jane MOORE 6 Nov 1872 Ganges, Allegan, MI

Children of Silas-[6] BOWKER and Margaret ARDREY, continued:
Surname **BOWKER**

> 2582. Margaret (Maggie) born ca 1841; died 2 July 1875; married Matthew BAIRD 4 March 1866 Barry Co., MI
> Child: Willis-[8] BAIRD born ca 1871
> 2583. Silas born 4 Oct 1848 Barry County, MI; died 26 May 1850 Barry County, MI   EOL

1335. ESTHER-[6] BOWKER, sister of above, was born 20 May 1810 at Genoa, Cayuga, NY. She married Joseph MUNSON ca 1831 at Genoa, NY. He was the son of Caleb T. MUNSON (John) and Sally COSTON, and was born 28 Oct 1809 at Locke, Cayuga, NY; died ____. Esther-[6] BOWKER, who suffered from postpartum depression, was taken by her husband to live with her parents in Michigan. Her children were raised by aunts, but as adults they went to Michigan to visit their mother. Esther-[6] BOWKER died ca 1878 at Barry County, MI.

Children of Esther-[6] BOWKER and Joseph MUNSON:
Surname **MUNSON**

+	**2584. JOHN N.**	born 10 June 1832 Genoa, Cayuga, NY; died ____
		1 married Sylvia AINSWORTH ca ____; 2 married Sarah HAVENS ca 1867 NY
+	**2585. ORANGE**	born 24 Aug 1834 NY; died ____; 1 married Mary A. WEST 18 Feb 1855
		(she dau/o Lyman WEST and Jerusha HILL)(she born 1 July 1835; died 5 Oct 1879)
		2 married Johanna Ada RICHARDSON ca 1880 (she born ca 1846; died 1919)
		(she dau/o Jacob Mills RICHARDSON and Caroline MERRITT)
	2586. Moses	born 3 Oct 1837; died ____; married Eliza A. BULL 8 Feb 1860
		Children: Ella-[8] born 24 Nov 1860; Lydia-[8] born ca 1863; Grant-[8] MUNSON born ca 1865
	2587. Jane Lucy	born 23 July 1839 NY; died ____; married George WILLIAMS 25 Dec 1858
		Child: Mary -[8] WILLIAMS born ca ___

1340. WELLINGTON-[6] BOWKER, brother of above, was born ca 1827 Genoa, Cayuga, NY. He married Lucy S. COOPER ca 1859. She was the daughter of ____ COOPER and ____, and was born ca 1841 OH; died ca 1874 MI. Wellington-[6] BOWKER died 12 Aug 1896 at Ross Township, Kalamazoo, MI.

Children of Wellington-[6] BOWKER and Lucy S. COOPER:
Surname **BOWKER**

	2588. DeWitt Clinton	born 5 Apr 1862 Hope, Barry, MI; died 5 Aug 1871 Hope, MI	EOL
	2589. Lewis J.	born ca 1864 Hope Twsp, Barry, MI; died ____	
	2590. Caleb E.	born 17 Sept 1867 Hope, MI; died ____	
	2591. Mary J.	born 29 June 1869 Hope, MI; died 26 Sept 1889 Hope, MI	EOL
+	**2592. CANDACE**	born 1 Aug 1871 Hope, MI; died 3 July 1942 Traverse City, MI	
	ESTELLA	married John Clifford FISH 24 Jan 1889 Alba, MI	
		(he s/o John H. FISH and Caroline G. LUDLOW)	
		(he born 22 July 1859 MI; died 2 June 1913 MI)	

1341. CANDACE-[6] BOWKER, sister of above, was born 31 Aug 1829 at Genoa, Cayuga, NY. She married John Borthwick-7 WILLISON (# 2372) on 26 March 1848 at Barry Township, Barry, MI. He was the son of James-[6] WILLISON (# 1285) (William) and Margaret BORTHWICK, and was born 1 April 1826; died 22 May 1904. Candace-[6] BOWKER died 16 Oct 1902 at Caldwell, Massaukee, MI.

Children of Candace-[6] BOWKER and John Borthwick-7 WILLISON:
Surname **WILLISON**

	2593. Edwin P.	born 6 June 1849; died 16 Sept 1919
		married Charlotte M. SPENCER 26 Aug 1871 (she born ca 1852 NY)
		Child: Charles O.-[8] WILLISON born 6 July 1872 Belt, Barry, MI
+	**2594. MARY JANE**	born 5 Sept 1853 Hickory Corners , MI; died 6 Sept 1917 Battle Creek, MI
		married Frederick Tressler SHOUP 1 June 1873 Barry Twsp, Barry MI
		(he s/o Jacob SHOUP and Mary TRESSLER)
		(he born 25 Feb 1840 Franklin Co., PA; died 4 Apr 1918 Battle Creek, MI)
+	**2595. ADELBERT**	born 15 Sept 1857 MI; died 14 April 1929
	WAYNE	married Mary A. CURTIS ca 1878 (she born Nov 1855 Canada; died _____)
	2596. Harriet E.	born 23 Aug 1862; died 3 Feb 1904 MI; married _____ CROSS
+	**2597. NORA A.**	born ca 1865 MI; died ca 1895 Wexford County, MI
		married George HARRISON 29 July 1885

Children of Candace-[6] BOWKER and John Borthwick WILLISON, continued:
Surname **WILLISON**

+   2597. Nora A., continued: (he s/o John HARRISON and Mary ROBERTSON)

                                                 (he born ca 1854; died 1916 Wexford County, MI)

1342. ADAM-[6] FAIRBANKS, son of Moses-[5] FAIRBANKS (Jonathan-[4]; Lydia-[3] HOLBROOK; Mary-[2] BOWKER; Edmund-[1]) and Betsey MATTHEWS, was born 30 May 1790 at Colerain, MA. H married first to Cynthia WILBOR ca.____. She was the daughter of ____ WILBOR and _____, and was born 25 Dec 1801 at Morristown, VT; died 25 May 1844. His second marriage was to Gracia MILLS ca ____. She was the daughter of ____ MILLS of Hadley , MA and ____, and was born ____; died ____. Adam-[6] FAIRBANKS died at Cass, Iowa Sept 1873.

Children of Adam-[6] FAIRBANKS and Cynthia WILBOR:
Surname **FAIRBANKS**

2598. Victor Monroe	born 1 June 1819; died _____	
2599. Caroline	born 26 July 1821; died 15 Feb 1845; married Henry S. LANE	
	(he s/o Seymour LANE and Hettie ROBINSON)	
	(he born ____; died 10 June 1885)	
	Children: Edward Hiram-[8] born 12 May 1840, died 13 Jan 1885; George Monroe-[8] born	
	12 Aug 1842; and Wilbur-[8] LANE born 12 June 1844; died 3 May 1866	
2600. Volney Wilbor	born 11 Nov 1823; died _____	
2601. Lorinda	born 27 July 1826; died 2 Aug 1853; married Alpheus CHESLEY	
2602. Carlo Truman	born 12 July 1829; died ____	
2603. Allen Leonard	born 28 Feb 1832; died ____	2604. Cynthia J. born 5 Aug 1842; died 13 Feb 1850

1350. RICHMOND-[6] FAIRBANKS, brother of above, was born 9 May 1814 at Colerain, MA. He married Louisa GATES ca 1832. She was the daughter of Lovell GATES and HANNAH COATES, and was born ca 1816 at Morristown, VT.; died 3 April 1883. Richmond-[6] FAIRBANKS died 11 July 1881 Hyde Park, VT.

Children of Richmond-[6] FAIRBANBKS and Louisa GATES;
Surname **FAIRBANKS**

2605. Rominor L.	born 30 June 1843; died ____ no issue EOL	
	married Mary M. GODFREY 31 March 1867	
	(she dau/o James GODFREY and Mary M. LANE)	
	(she born 23 July 1848 Waterbury, VT; died ____)	
2606. Irvine A.	born 10 Aug 1845; died ____; farmer at Mansonville, Quebec, Canada	
2607. Truman F.	born 15 June 1848; died ____; farmer at Mansonville, Quebec	
2608. Anna B.	born 17 Mar 1855; died 25 Oct 1860 2609. Lysander L. born 11 July 1858	

1353. JOHN-[6] FAIRBANKS, son of Daniel-[5] FAIRBANKS (Jonathan-[4]; Lydia-[3] HOLBROOK; Mary-[2] BOWKER; Edmund-[1]) and Keziah CLARK, was born 3 Feb 1796 at Colerain, MA. He married Sally BURRINGTON of Colerain ca ____. She was the daughter of ____ BURRINGTON and ____, and was born14 April 1801 Colerain; died 29 May 1842 at Heath , MA. John-[6] FAIRBANKS died 11 Dec 1853 at Whitingham, VT.

Children of John-[6] FAIRBANKS and Sally BURRINGTON:
Surname **FAIRBANKS**

+	**2610. JANE**	born 18 Sept 1826; died ca 1873 Jacksonville, VT.
		married James M. ROBERTS ca 1851
	2611. Daniel Newton	born 21 July 1828; died ____
+	**2612. SARAH ANN**	born 3 July 1831; died 4 July 1858 Hardwick, MA
		married Isaac PIERCE Oct 1853 Greenwich, MA
	2613. John Henry	born 7 July 1833; died ____
	2614. Hiram	born 14 May 1837; died ____
	2615. Mary	born 15 April 1842; died __; married Wolsey B. MC CULLOCH 10 Dec 1857 Paris , IL

1354. KEZIAH-[6] FAIRBANKS, half-sister of above, daughter of Daniel-[5] FAIRBANKS (Jonathan-[4] FAIRBANKS; Lydia-[3] HOLBROOK; Mary-[2] BOWKER; Edmund-[1]) and his second wife Ruth FAULKNER, was born 22 Sept 1818 MA. She married Green NICHOLS on 10 May 1837. He was the son of ____ NICHOLS and ____, and was born 21 Jan 1815 Colerain, Franklin County, MA; died 19 Feb 1888 Stamford, VT. Keziah-[6] FAIRBANKS died 25 Sept 1897 at Stamford.

Children of Keziah-[6] FAIRBANKS and Green NICHOLS:
Surname **NICHOLS**

2616. Daniel Green	born 28 Feb 1838; died 11 Sept 1867		
2617. Gilbert Rominor	born ca 1840/41; died 18 Aug 1864 Stamford, VT.		
2618. Levi Henry	born 29 Aug 1843; died ca 1911		
	1 married Cynthia Miriam JILLSON 31 Dec 1868; married Jennie PRENTICE ca ____		
2619. Acelia Keziah	born 28 May 1850; died _____	2620. Ruth Ann	born 27 Aug 1853 VT

1356. MARY-[6] FAIRBANKS, sister of above, was born 22 Feb 1821 at Shutebury, MA. She married Arad NICHOLS 2 Dec 1840. He was the son of Arad NICHOLS, of Colrain, MA, and Matilda ____, and was born 31 Dec 1811; died 2 Sept 1891.

Children of Mary-[6] FAIRBANKS and Arad NICHOLS:
Surname **NICHOLS**

2621. Mary Caroline	born 21 Feb 1842; died 9 Sept 1893	
	married Henry FAIRBANKS 4 April 1858 North Heath, MA	
2622. Charles Walter	born 20 Dec 1844; married Carrie R. FAIRBANKS 16 Aug 1867 Templeton, VT	
	(she dau/o Sardis FAIRBANKS and Caroline _____)	
	Children: Walter C-[8] born ca 1868; Harry L-[8] born ca 1874; and Edith M-[8] NICHOLS born ca 1877	
2623. Jennie R.	born 13 Aug 1847; died ____; married Horace Lester FISH 28 July 1872	
	(he born 30 Oct 1840; died 26 Feb 1923 Bennington, VT)	
	Children: Lilly J-[8] born ca 1877; and Austin-[8] FISH born ca 1879	
+ **2624. MILLARD ORLIN**	born 10 Jan 1850; died 7 Feb 1929 MA	
	married Prudence Olive NILES 22 Nov 1881 (she born 26 Jan 1859; died 19 Apr 1936)	
+ **2625. LUCY**	born 10 Nov 1852; died 18 Nov 1930 Shelburne, MA	
	married Richard SCHACK 1 Dec 1884	
+ **2626. EMMA ROSANNA**	born 20 Sept 1856/9 ; died ____	
	married James MC CLELLAN 8 April 1883; resided Colrain	
2627. Addie Eliza	born 8 June 1862; died 4 April 1880	

1357. ROMINOR SMITH -[6] FAIRBANKS, brother of above, was born 2 July 1822 at Colerain, MA. He married Prusia/ Prussia Angelia SPRAGUE on 16 Nov 1854. She was the daughter of Levi SPRAGUE and Louisa ELMER of Buckland, MA, and was born 2 Sept 1832; died ____. Rominor-[6] FAIRBANKS died Colerain MA on 18 Sept 1892.

Children of Rominor-[6] FAIRBANKS and Prusia Angelia SPRAGUE:
Surname **FAIRBANKS**   (children all born Vermont)

2628. Levi Daniel	born1 Sept 1855 Colerain, MA; died ____	
2629. Della Olivia	born 18 Oct 1857; died 23 Feb 1935 Whitingham, VT	
	married Frank Humes CUTTING 15 Oct 1884 Greenfield, MA	
	(he s/o James CUTTING and Asenath ROGERS of Whitingham, VT	
	Children: Musa Adelia-[8] born 6 Juner 1886; and Blanche Asenath-[8] CUTTING born 23 Sept 1888	
2630. Charles Merwin	born 11 May 1860; died _____; unmarried EOL	
2631. William Prosper	born 6 Sept 1862; died ____;	
	married Louise M. WILSON 5 Aug 1890; no issue EOL	
2632. Prilla Duverna	born 31 Dec 1864; died 2 Feb 1897 Colrain, Franklin, MA	
2633. Jennie Ruth	born 9 June 1867; died _____; a school teacher	
2634. Gertie Angelia	born 13 June 1870; died ____	
2635. Bertie Rominor	born 13 June 1870; died 14 June 1870	
2636. Oscar Rominor	born 20 June 1873; died _____; married Nellie E. BROWN 10 Dec 1894 Colerain, MA	

1358. RUTH-[6] FAIRBANKS, sister of above, was born 2 Jan 1824. She married John HAGAR ca ____. He was the son of ____ HAGAR and ____, and was born ca ____; died 7 Fen 1852. Ruth-[6] FAIRBANKS died 24 Feb 1852.

Children of Ruth-[6] FAIRBANKS and John HAGAR:
Surname **HAGAR**

2637. Ormond	born 17 June 1848; died 20 Jan 1904
2638. Jeremiah	born 16 March 1850; died 17 June 1873
2639. Patty	born 27 Nov 1851; died 24 Jan 1852

1363. HIRAM-⁶ FAIRBANKS, son of Jonathan -⁵ FAIRBANKS (Jonathan-⁴; Lydia-³ HOLBROOK; Mary-² BOWKER; Edmund-¹) and Sally AYERS, was born 6 Nov 1801 at Heath, MA.. He married Effie CASWELL 4 June 1826. She was the daughter of Gilbert CASWELL and Hannah FOSTER, and was born ca 1806; died 1881. Hiram-⁶ FAIRBANKS died 2 March 1885 at Newburg, Wisconsin.

Children of Hiram⁻⁶ FAIRBANKS and Effie CASWELL:
Surname **FAIRBANKS**

2640. William	born 14 June 1827; died 1 Sept 1828 Antwerp, NY
2641. Laura Ann	born 23 Dec 1829 Antwerp. NY; died ____; married Ralph Douglas KENDALL

Children: Eugene Ralph-⁸; William Herbert-⁸; and Houghton Fairbanks-⁸ KENDALL

2642. Erwin	born 22 Sept 1832 Antwerp, NY; died 22 Feb 1903 Baldwinsville, NY

1 married Julia BROWN June 1852   (she born ca 1835; died 18 Mar 1888)
Child: Frederick-⁸ FAIRBANKS born ca 1853; died at age 10
2 married Sarah JOHNSON 18 Sept 1889 (she from Baldwinsville, NY)

2643. Caswell	born 25 July 1835 Antwerp; died 1897 MN; married Miranda TYLER ca ____
2644. Cornelia	born 29 Sept 1838 Antwerp, died 16 Jan 1882
	married Samuel A. NASH 19 July 1863 Dane, WI. (he born ca 1834 Antwerp, NY)

Child: Annette-⁸ NASH born ca 1860/64 WI

2645. Byron	born 23 Jan 1847 Antwerp, NY; died ____; married Anna CAIN 16 Jan 1874

1364. ROYAL-⁶ FAIRBANKS, brother of above, was born 18 Aug 1803 at Heath, MA. He married first to Miranda WILLIAMS of Clinton, NY ca 1823. She was the daughter of ___ WILLIAMS and ____, and was born March 1804; died 1845. His second marriage was to Jane Freelove KINNE on 26 Oct 1845. She was the daughter of Jacob KINNE and Mercy COVELL, and was born 24 May 1823; died ___. She married second to an Adin PHELPS, and resided in Camden, NJ.

Children of Royal-⁶ FAIRBANKS and Miranda WILLIAMS:
Surname **FAIRBANKS**

2646. William Kenton	born March 1833 Heuvelton, NY; died ____
	Note: He was a ship's captain, unknown if on the Great Lakes or at sea
2647. Sarah	born May 1837 NY; died ____; married Rev. S W WHITFIELD ca ____
2648. Elizabeth	born ca 1838; died ____
2649. George L:yman	born 27 Mar 1842; died ____
2650. Harriet	born 27 Mar 1844; died ca 1859 (age 15) EOL

Child of Royal-⁶ FAIRBANKS and Jane Freelove KINNE:
Surname **FAIRBANKS**

2651. Emma/ Emeline	born 7 July 1846 NY; died 24 Jan 1879 Rome, NY; married Alfred BURNHAM ca ____
	(he s/o Asa BURNHAM and Chloe ____) (he born ca 1842 NY)

Children: Ida M-⁸ born ca 1869; Artie J.-⁸ born ca 1871; and Roy C-⁸ BURNHAM born ca 1873

1365. ANNA-⁶ FAIRBANKS, sister of above, was born 15 Nov 1804 at Heath, MA. She married John BARBER ca ___. He was the son of ____ BARBER and ____, and was born ca 1797; died ca 1843. Anna -⁶ FAIRBANKS died ____.

Children of Anna-⁶ FAIRBANKS and John BARBER:
Surname **BARBER**   (all children born Heath, MA)

2652. Royal F.	born 19 May 1824 ; died ____
2653. Laura Ann	born 19 Aug 1826; died 2 July 1885
2654. Sarah Emeline	born 29 Oct 1828; died 2 July 1900 MA; married Robert M. STETSON ca ____
2655. Joseph Emerson	born 29 Oct 1829; died 13 Dec 1852
2656. Jonathan	born 16 Jan 1832; died 22 Feb 1890 Oswego, NY; married Celestine Jeanette CLEMONS
2657. Levi W.	born 15 Feb 1837; died 20 Sept 1917

1368. DAVID-⁶ FAIRBANKS, brother of above, was born 2 July 1811/13 at Heath, MA. He married Sybil SMITH ca ____. She was born 17 Sept 1809 at Ashfield, NY; died 22 Aug 1890. David-⁶ died 25 Jan 1853 at Antwerp, Jefferson County, NY.

Children of David-⁶ FAIRBANKS and Sybil SMITH:
Surname **FAIRBANKS**   (all children born Antwerp, NY)

2658. John Wallace	born 3 July 1836; died 1877

Children of David-[6] FAIRBANKS and Sybil SMITH, continued:
Surnamw **FAIRBANKS**

2659. David Orville	born 1 June 1839; died 28 June 1905; married Angelia Marie BLODGETT ca ____	
	(she dau/o Jared Hoyt BLODGETT and Adelia INGLES)	
	(she born 26 July 1845 Antwerp, NY; died 29 Aug 1934 Prague, OK	
	Children: Cassius Marcellus-[8] born 4 Ap 1863 Antwerp; died 29 July 1933 OK; and Rozelle Hiram-[8]	
	FAIRBANKS born 16 Sept 1869 KS; died 12 Dec 1943 San Antonio, TX	
2660. Orrin Dempster	born 2 Sept 1844; died before 2 April 1917 (living 1910)	
	married Adda/ Addie/ Adelaide TAFT 15 April 1878 Dundee, MI	
	(she dau/o Hiram TAFT and Elizabeth M. _____)(she born ca 1855, resided Adrian, MI	

1371. ASA-[6] FAIRBANKS, son of Asa-[5] FAIRBANKS (Jonathan-[4]; Lydia-[3] HOLBROOK; Mary-[2] BOWKER; Edmund-[1]) and Lucy SAUNDERS, was born 27 June 1800 at Whitingham , VT. He married Sally STACY ca 1828 . She was the daughter of John R. STACY and Chloe SMITH, and was born 13 April 1805 at Halifax, VT; died 10 Jan 1894. Asa-[6] died 21 Jan 1861 at Whitingham, VT.

Children of Asa-[6] FAIRBANKS and Sally STACY:
Surname **FAIRBANKS**

	2661. Freeman Leroy	born 15 Dec 1829; died 18 Aug 1831	EOL
	2662. Sandford Smith	born 8 Dec 1831; died ____	
	2663. Emery Greenleaf	born 28 Feb 1835; died 1 Feb 1861	EOL
	2664. Lyman Webster	born 24 March 1836; died ____	
+	**2665. SARAH LOVINA**	born 21 Jan 1838; died _____	
		1 married Charles CUTTING 19 March 1857; divorced	
		(he born 17 Aug 1830 Whitingham, VT; died 1 Dec 1888 Halifax, VT)	
		2 married Simeon DUDLEY 30 Jan 1896 (he from Greenfield, MA)	
		(he born 8 Sept 1829 Petersham, MA; died ____) resided Greenfield, MA	
	2666. Chloe Minerva	born 18 March 1840; died 30 May 1883	
	2667. Asa Freeman	born 8 Mar 1842; died 1864.	
		Note: he enlisted in the Civil War at age 22. He was taken sick and died at New Orleans, LA 1864	
	2668. Chester Willard	born 15 Aug 1844; died ____	
	2669. Laura L.	born Oct 1846; died ___; married Charles Parker WILLIAMS ca 1865	
		(he born 16 Oct 1841 Leyden, MA; died ____) resided at Hartford, CT.	
		Children: Malva B-[8] born 27 Nov 1872, died 24 Nov 1875; Lura M-[8] born 27 Aug 1874, died 3 Dec 1895;	
		and Cora B-[8] WILLIAMS born 14 Sept 1879	

1373. EZRA-[6] FAIRBANKS, brother of above, was born 4 Feb 1804 Whitingham, VT. He married Cynthia STACY 23 Sept 1830. She was the sister of Sally STACY, above , who married Asa-[6] FAIRBANKS. Cynthia was born 10 June 1807; died 14 June 1891. Ezra-[6] FAIRBANKS, a farmer, died 11 Oct 1874.

Children of Ezra-[6] FAIRBANKS and Cynthia STACY:
Surname **FAIRBANKS**

+	**2670. ELVIRAH (twin)**	born 29 July 1831; died 9 June 1891	
		married Duane STIMPSON 22 March 1848	
		(he s/o Duane STIMPSON and Sarah STICKNEY)(he born 5 May 1828 Whitingham)	
	2671. Delilah (twin)	born 29 July 1831; died 25 Apr 1884	
		married W S ALLAND 27 Aug 1851 Colrain, MA	
+	**2672. MARANDA**	born 8 Sept 1833; died ____	
		married Dudley W. BURRINGTON 15 Nov 1852 ; resided North Heath, MA	
	2673. Henry	born 28 Aug 1835; died ____	
	2674. Oded	born 5 April 1837; died ____	
	2675. Edwin	born 23 Aug 1840; died ____; married Etta May ____ ; no issue EOL	
	2676. Luzerne	born 29 July 1843; died 7 Feb 1864	
+	**2677. FLORINDA (twin)**	born 28 June 1846; died _____	
		married Rufus PORTER 27 Nov 1867 Halifax, VT	
		(he s/o Barnabas PORTER and Pamelia DAVENPORT of Colrain, MA)	
+	**2678. FLORILLA (twin)**	born 28 June 1846; died _____	
		married George CARPENTER 5 Dec 1869 (he born 21 Feb 1844 Rowe, MA)	
	2679. Herbert John	born 6 Jan 1851; died ____	

1375. ABRAHAM-⁶ FAIRBANKS, brother of above, was born 3 May 1808 at Whitingham, VT. He married Olive COOK ca 1831. She was the daughter of ____ COOK and ____, and was born ca 1813 ; died ____. Abraham-⁶ FAIRBANKS died 20 Dec 1891 at Whitingham.

Children of Abraham-⁶ FAIRBANKS and Olive COOK:
Surname **FAIRBANKS**

2680. Francis	born ca 1832 Whitingham, VT; died by drowning 11 Sept 1890 CA	
	married Cynthia Susan CUTTING ca ____	
2681. Ella	born ca 1836; died before 1897; married Joel Arial LOMBARD of Colrain, MA	
	Children: Gertie A.-⁸ born ca 1874; and Minnie L.-⁸ LOMBARD born ca 1876	
2682. Lavilla	born ca1838; died ____; 1 married Edward BURRINGTON	
	(he s/o William BURRINGTON and Elizabeth ____ of Heath, MA)	
	2 married Charles ESTY	
+ **2683. FRANCESCA**	born ca 1840; died ____	
	1 married Elmer CUTTING 14 Sept 1862; 2 married Faxon CADY ca _____	

1376. LUCY-⁶ FAIRBANKS, sister of above , was born 11 June 1810 at Whitingham, VT. She married Levi LAMB ca ____. He was the son of Levi LAMB (Israel)and Effie MC CARTER, and was born ca 1806 Whitingham, VT , died March 1887 Reedsboro, VT. Lucy-⁶ FAIRBANKS died 12 Aug 1864 Fitchburg, MA.

Children of Lucy-⁶ FAIRBANKS and Levi LAMB:
Surname **LAMB**

2684. Edwin	born ca 1832 ; died from drowning	
2685. Caroline	born ca 1834 ; died ____; married _____LOVELL	
2686. Sarah Maria	born ca 1836; died ____; married Amos UNDERWOOD of Rowe, MA	
2687. Levi Lysander	born 22 July 1841; died 21 May 1921 Chicago, IL	
	married Emma Augusta PRATT 25 Dec 1866	
	(she born 21 May 1839; died 30 Sept 1870 Fitchburg, MA	
2688. Chester	born ca 1845; died ____	2689. Leafy born ca 1849; died ____

1377. ANNA-⁶ FAIRBANKS, sister of above, was born 2 Feb 1813 at Whitingham, VT. She married Warren CHASE ca ____. He was the son of ____ CHASE and ____, and was born30 Nov 1805; died ____. Anna-⁶ FAIRBANKS died 23 Dec 1858.

Children of Anna-⁶ FAIRBANKS and Warren CHASE:
Surname **CHASE**

2690. Diantha	born 21 Oct 1832; died ____	2692. Wilber F.	born 5 Jan 1841
2691. Albert W.	born 26 Jan 1834; died 11 May 1857		

1395. DANIEL-⁶ FAIRBANKS, son of Jonathan-⁵ FAIRBANKS (Daniel-⁴; Lucy-³ HOLBROOK; Mary-² BOWKER; Edmund-¹) and Hannah MORSE, was born 28 Oct 1781 at Holliston, MA. He married Elizabeth BLACKMAN of Dorchester, MA on 8 April 1812. She was the daughter of _____ BLACKMAN and ____, and was born ____; died 11 Nov 1855. Daniel-⁶ FAIRBANKS died 5 Aug 1821 at Holliston, MA

Children of Daniel-⁶ FAIRBANKS and Elizabeth BLACKMAN:
Surname **FAIRBANKS**

2693. George	born ca 1813; died 20 Aug 1815	EOL
2694. Eliza	born 1815; died before 1840; married Royal DOUGLAS of Cambridge, MA ca ____	
	(he 2 married Sarah F. POND 3 April 1840)	
	(he born ca 1811 Cambridge, MA; died ca 1879)	
	Child: Royal-⁸ DOUGLAS, Jr. born ca 1837 ; died ____	
2695. George C. (2)	born ca 1817; died 17 July 1892; a cigar maker	
	married Lucilla HATSTAT ca ___; res. Rockland, ME (she born ca 1821 Rockland)	
2696. Daniel Hiram	born 11 March 1819; died ____	

1396. HANNAH-⁶ FAIRBANKS, sister of above, was born 13 Nov 1783 at Sudbury, MA. She married Martin HAGAR of Marlboro, MA on ____. He was the son of ____ HAGAR and ____, and was born ____; died 21 Sept 1855. Hannah-⁶ FAIRBANKS died 23 Oct 1848. Note: She and her husband joined the Mormons in 1843, and went with them to Nauvoo (IL) then to Utah. Both died in Salt Lake City.

Children of Hannah-6 FAIRBANKS and Martin HAGAR:
Surname **HAGAR**

	2697. Martin, Jr.	born 21 April 1808; died 9 Mar 1880; married Catherine LANGMAID
+	**2698. CHARLES**	born 9 Oct 1809; died 31 July 1890; married Myra Holden FELTON 6 June 1838
	2699. Otis	born 8 Mar 1811; died 12 Nov 1833
	2700. Elizabeth	born 11 June 1814; died 2 Jan 1895
	2701. Hannah Morse	born 21 Nov 1815; died 11 April 1849; married Silas BULLARD ca 1839
		Child: Mark-8 BULLARD born ca _____; resided Greenfield, MA
	2702. Lydia Caroline	born 31 Oct 1817; died ____; married Isaac FLEMING ca 1839

1397. ELIZABETH-6 FAIRBANKS, half sister of above, daughter of Jonathan-5 FAIRBANKS (Daniel-4; Lydia-3 HOLBROOK; Mary-2 BOWKER; Edmund-1) and his second wife Bridget PARMENTER, and was born 16 Sept 1785. She married John CUTLER ca ___ He was the son of __ CUTLER and ___, and was born 31 July 1786 Waltham, MA; died __. They moved to Lima, NY ca 1823, where Elizabeth-6 died 18 Dec 1831 (aged 46).

Children of Elizabeth-6 FAIRBANKS and John CUTLER:
Surname **CUTLER**

	2703. Eliza	born 16 May 1809; died _____
		married John I. KELSEY 12 Oct 1836; resided Riga, NY
	2704. John M.	born 26 Feb 1813; died 20 Aug 1880 Ypsilanti, MI
		married Frances BISHOP 5 Oct 1837 (she from Lima, NY)
	2705. Harriet	born ca 1810; died 29 Sept 886; resided Chicago, IL; unmarried EOL
+	**2706. GEORGE D.**	born 9 April 1822; died ca _____
		1 married Martha BROOKS 19 Sept 1848 (she from West Avon, NY)
		2 married Gertrude BOUGHTON 10 Sept 1861; resided Albion, NY
+	**2707. SUSAN**	born 16 Dec 1823; died 3 Sept 1865
		married Dr. Caleb Holton HAMMOND, Jr. 10 Oct 1848; resided Ionia, MI
	2708. Mary A.	born 11 Feb 1821; died ____; married Rev. J. H. PHELPS ca ___; resided Flushing, MI
	2709. Sarah N.	born 17 May 1825; died 17 Nov 1852
	2710. Henry C.	born Nov 1830; died 2 June 1831

1398. JONATHAN-6 FAIRBANKS, brother of above, was born 7 April 1787 at Sudbury, MA. He married Augusta HADDEN ca ___. She was the daughter of ____HADDEN and ____, and was born ca ___ at Hawack, Scotland; died____. Jonathan-6 FAIRBANKS, a cabinet maker and painter, died 30 Dec 1865 at Cochituate, MA.

Children of Jobnathan-6 FAIRBANKS and Augusta HADDEN:
Surname **FAIRBANKS**

	2711. Jonathan	born ca ____; died ____; married _____
+	**2712. MARGARET ANN**	born 8 Dec 1836 Lexington, MA; died ____; married Edward Payson BOND Nov 1852
		(he born 10 Mar 1830 Lexington; died 7 Aug 1885 at Soldiers Home, Togus, ME)
		Note: He served in the 20th Regt MA Volunteers during the Civil War
	2713. .Nellie Augusta	born ca ___; died ___; married Dr. William Henry BRADLEY of Lowell, MA EOL
	2714. George W.	born 6 July 1844 Concord, MA; died ____; married Abbie B. BENT ca _____
		Child: Thaddeus-8 FAIRBANKS born ca ___; died young

1400. DRURY-6 FAIRBANKS, brother of above, was born 17 July 1793 at Sudbury, MA. He married Mary SPRING 26 Oct 1817. She was the daughter of ____ SPRING and ____, and was born ___; died 15 Feb 1864. He lived in Sudbury until his death on 25 May 1864 of heart disease.

Children of Drury-6 FAIRBANKS and Mary SPRING:
Surname **FAIRBANKS**

	2715. Nelson	born 10 Nov 181; died _____		
+	**2716. NANCY**	born 9 Mar 1821 Sudbury, MA; died 28 Mar 1888 Waltham, MA		
		married James Harvey WRIGHT of Hardwick, MA on 27 Nov 1845		
		(he born ____; died 4 Sept 1896)		
		Note: he was the superintendent of streets and sidewalks in Waltham, MA		
	2717.Winthrop	born 7 April 1823; died _____	2718. Jonathan Parker	born 22 May 1826

Children of Drury-⁶ FAIRBANKS and Mary SPRING, continued:
Surname **FAIRBANKS**

	2719. Hannah	born 9 May 1828; died ____; married Aaron M. GOODNOW 19 July 1848 (he born ca ____; died 19 April 1854 Sudbury, MA)	

Child: Ella-⁸ GOODNOW born 2 May 1849; married Frank WHITNEY 27 May 1879

+ **2720. MARY**   born 22 July 1830; died ____ 20 Oct 1863 Williamsburg, NY
married Joseph T. SPEER 25 Dec 1853
(he s/o Henry SPEER and Rachel ____) (he born 19 Feb 1829 NYC; died _____)

1401. EDDY⁻⁶ FAIRBANKS, brother of above, was born ca 1795 at Sudbury, MA. He married Nancy SIMMS 30 April 1822 at Boston, MA. She was the daughter of Samuel SIMMS and ____ of North Reading, MA. She was born ca 1800 , died 29 Jan 1850. Captain Eddy⁻⁶ FAIRBANKS, as he was called, died 31 July 1862 at North Readding, MA. He was a member of the Ancient & Honorable Artillery Company of Boston.

Children of Eddy⁻⁶ FAIRBANKS and Nancy SIMMS:
Surname **FAIRBANKS**

2721. **ELIZABETH**	born 18 July 1825; died _____; 1 married Lysander E. UPTON ca ____ (he born ca 1823; died 9 Jan 1865) 2 married Benjamin EAMES ca _____; (he born ____; died 19 Aug 1888)	
2722. John B.	born 4 Aug 1827; died ca 1862 CA; never married	EOL
2723. Jonathan	born 28 April 1832; died ____	
2724. James Eddy	born 14 June 1834; died ____	
2725. Samuel S.	born 28 May 1836; died ____; resided NV and CA	
2726. George Varnum	born 15 March 1838; died 7 Jan 1880 Las Vegas, NV	
2727. Luman B. (twin)	born 31 March 1839; died ____NV ; never married	EOL
2728. Christiana (twin)	born 31 March 1839 ; died ____; no issue married Charles CARSWELL ca ___; resided CA.	EOL
2729. Dexter	born 22 Feb 1841; died 23 June 1864; unmarried	EOL

1402. GEORGE⁻⁶ FAIRBANKS, brother of above, was born 15 Sept 1797 at Sudbury, MA. He married Susan SMITH ca 1819. She was the daughter of Brown SMITH and Mary KING, and was born ca ____ at Johnston, RI; died 26 June 1891. George⁻⁶ FAIRBANKS, was a successful businessman, and died 31 Aug 1873.

Children of George⁻⁶ FAIRBANKS and Susan SMITH:
Surname **FAIRBANKS**

2730. Susan Brown (1)	born 11 Aug 1820; died 11 Sept 1827	EOL
2731. George Washington	born 3 Mar 1822; died 23 Nov 1843	
2732. Mary King	born 26 July 1823; died 9 Jan 1869	
2733. Elbridge Gerry	born 25 Feb 1825; died ____; married ____	
2734. Brown Smith	born 10 March 1827; died ____; married _____	
2735. Susan Brown (2)	born 15 Nov 1828; died 15 Oct 1830	EOL
2736. James Waterman	born 4 June 1830; died ____; moved West – family had no contact with him	
2737. Alfred	born 6 July 1831; died ____; married _____	
+ **2738. SUSAN MARIA**	born 24 May 1833; died 27 Jan 1894 NYC, NY married William WYLIE Nov 1857 (as his 2ⁿᵈ wife)(he from Scotland)(resided NYC)	
2739. William Borden King	born 20 May 1835; died 14 Sept 1838	EOL
2740. Anna Washington	born 3 March 1844; died 11 Aug 1880 married George Olney BLACKMAR May 1869; he from Foster, RI	

Child: Ralph William-⁸ BLACKMAR born 6 May 1872; married Katherine LIEBRICH

1403. DEXTER⁻⁶ FAIRBANKS, brother of above, was born 19 July 1799 at Sudbury, MA. He married Lucretia WHEELER ca _____. She was the daughter of _____ WHEELER and ____, and was born 23 June 1802; died 15 July 1879. Dexter⁻⁶ FAIRBANKS died 11 Aug 1879.

Note: In the FAIRBANKS Genealogy, published 1897, is the following: " He spent the greater part of his life in the interests of the insane, and for that reason was called Doctor although he was not a physician. He moved to NY for the express purpose of giving the imbecile son of John Jacob ASTOR (John Jacob, Jr.) his exclusive care and treatment, and had charge of him for over thirty years."

Children of Dexter-6 FAIRBANKS and Lucretia WHEELER:
Surname **FAIRBANKS**

2741. Franklin Dexter	born 9 Nov 1821; died 18 Oct 1863 at his fathers' home in NYC	
	married Anna Maria MEACHAM ca ____	EOL
	(she dau/o Jeremiah MEACHAM and Prudence DUNTON of Boothbay, ME)	
2742. James Prescott	born 14 May 1829; died 1 Feb 1856	EOL
2743. Jane Elizabeth	born ____; died ____; married Dr. F. Willis FISHER ca 1855 NYC	

Children: James Fairbank-8 born 9 July 1861; Mary E-8 born 21 Jan 1863, died 16 May 1870; and Marion Carlotta-8 FISHER born 6 Aug 1865

1404. MARY-6 FAIRBANKS, sister of above, was born 5 Mar 1803 Sudbury, MA. She married Jonas PIERCE on 9 Nov 1824. He was the son of Capt. Jonas PIERCE ++ and ____, and was born 25 Sept 1797 Weston, MA; died 25 Mar 1870 Holliston, MA. Mary-6 FAIRBANKS died 13 Mar 1879.

++ Captain Jonas PIERCE served in the Revolutionary War when he was just 16 years of age.

Children of Mary-6 FAIRBANKS and Jonas PIERCE:
Surname **PIERCE**

2744. Elbridge Fairbank	born 10 July 1828; died 4 April 1886; married Martha DOVE Feb 1840 Skowhegan, ME	
2745. Mary Jane	born 10 April 1829/30 ; died ____; married Samuel Henry DICKINSON 17 Aug 1848	
	(he born ____; died Aug 1860)	
2746. Daniel Webster	born 26 Jan 1830; did ____	
2747. Charles Edward	born 13 Dec 1832; died ____; married Viola M. CAMPBELL ca 1860 Fayette, ME.	
2748. Eliza Douglass	born 1 Jan 1838; died ____; married George M. FRENCH 17 June 1862	

1405. JOSEPH BRADLEY VARNUM-6 FAIRBANKS, brother of above, was born 3 Oct 1804 at Sudbury, MA. He married Margaret HADDEN ca ____. She was the daughter of James HADDEN and ____, and was born 25 Feb 1803 in Scotland; died 19 Oct 1865 at Worcester, MA. Joseph-6 FAIRBANKS died 20 May 1833 at Monroe, NY

Children of Joseph-6 FAIRBANKS and Margaret HADDEN:
Surname **FAIRBANKS**

+	2749. Jonathan	born 7 Jan 1828 Andover, MA; died ____	
	(for children see # 2287)	married Angie-7 BOWKER Sep 1854 Springfield. MO	
		(she dau/o Samuel Noyes-6 BOWKER and Mary EARLE)	
	2750. James Dexter	born 19 Aug 1830 Monroe, NY; died ca 1912)	
	2751. Joseph B. Varnum	born 29 Aug 1833 Sudbury, MA; died 31 Oct 1833	EOL

1406. ELBRIDGE GERRY-6 FAIRBANKS, brother of above, was born 9 Jan 1809 Sudbury, MA. He married Annie C. REMIE ca ____. She was the daughter of Marcus REMIE and Anna C. ALLBRINK, and was born 22 Jan 1811; died 8 Nov 1886. Elbridge-6 FAIRBANKS died 10 July 1842 Cambridge, MA.

Children of Elbridge Gerry-6 FAIRBANKS and Annie C. REMIE:
Surname **FAIRBANKS**

2752. George Elbridge	born 20 May 1832; died 4 April 1887 Cambridge, MA	EOL
2753. Marcus Remie	born Mar 1834; died 23 Mar 1842	EOL
2754. Joseph Bradley	born 26 Feb 1836; died Dec 1887; married Sophia PORTER ca 1859.	
Varnum	(she born Dec 1836 Brighton, MA; died ____)	

Child: Annie M-8 FAIRBANKS born ca ___; married H. S. BROCK

2755. Annie C.	born 18 March 1838; died ____; resided Cambridge, MA	

1408. DANIEL-6 TWITCHELL, son of Nathan-5 TWITCHELL (Keziah-4 HOLBROOK; Samuel-3; Mary-2 BOWKER; Edmund-1; John A,B) and Hannah KEMPTON / KIMPTON, and was born 12 Jan 1742/43 MA. He married Eunice WRIGHT ca ____. She was the daughter of ____ WRIGHT and ____, and was born ca 1772; died ____. Daniel-6 TWITCHELL died 22 Dec 1811.

Children of Daniel-6 TWITCHELL and Eunice WRIGHT:
Surname **TWITCHELL**

2756. Henry	born ca 1797 NH; died ____; married Betsey WHITCOMB ca ____	
2757. Daniel	born ca 1799; died ____	

Children of Daniel-[6] TWITCHELL and Eunice WRIGHT, continued:
Surname **TWITCHELL**

	2758. Hannah	born ca 1801; died ____	
+	**2759. JONAS**	born 4 Mar 1803; died 7 Jan 1878	
		1 married Eliza ROBBINS ca _____;	2 married Lucy O. FELTON
+	**2760. HARVEY DANIEL**	born 31 Mar 1808; died 21 Sept 1864; married Elizabeth SCOTT ca _____	

1411. LUCY G-[6] BURNETT, daughter of Reuben-[5] BURNETT (Lucy-[4] GLEASON; Thankful-[3] HOLBROOK; Mary-[2] BOWKER; Edmund-[1]) and Polly BENJAMIN, was born 23 Jan 1814 Ogdensburg, St. Lawrence, NY. She married John HULETT/HEWLITT, Sr. ca _____. He was the son of Samuel HULETT/HEWLITT and Sarah CLARK , and was born 23 Feb 1805 Canton, St. Lawrence, NY; died 11 Sep 1906 Kingsley, MI. Lucy G-[6] BURNETT died 1840 in childbirth.

Children of Lucy G-[6] BURNETT and John HULETT/HEWLITT, Sr:
Surname **HULETT/HEWLITT**

2761. Clarissa Artimassa	born 20 Mar 1827; died 14 Sep 1902; married William Rice GARDNER ca 1846
2762. Sally	born ca 1833; died ____; married Clark FRASIER ca ____
2763. Alvira Corinthea	born ca 1834; died 1902 MI; 1 married ____ TERRILL;
	2 married _____RICE; 3 married _____ STEELE; 4 married ____ HARTMAN
2764. Phoebe	born ca ____; died young
2765. Polly/Mary	born ca ____; died young
2766. John, Jr.	born ca 15 May 18__; died 9 Dec 1924 Hasting, MI
2767. Henry	born ca 1840; died 5 Apr 1863 at Stone Mtn., VA (Civil War) malaria

Note: Reportedly, his mother died in childbirth and he was taken by her sister to raise, and that his name was changed to BARNES

1412. EVALINE-[6] BURNETT, sister of above, was born 29 Oct 1814 at St. Lawrence County, NY. She married Philander George TAYLOR 27 Oct 1829 NY. He was the son of Noah TAYLOR and Polly BENJAMIN Hulett, and was born 17 Jan 1810 Grand Isle, VT; died 16 Feb 1877 Plainfield, Iowa. Evaline-[6] BURNETT died 29 July 1856 Tomah, WI.

Children of Evaline-[6] BURNETT and Philander George TAYLOR:
Surname **TAYLOR**   (first 10 children born St. Lawrence County, NY; last 2 IL)

2768. Philomen	born 24 Jan 1832 NY; died 24 Mar 1904
2769. George	born 26 Aug 1833; died 2 Feb 1905 MI
2770. Josiah	born 12 Aug 1835; died 4 Oct 1905 IA
	married Francelia Elizabeth GARDNER Wood 18 May 1864 Sycamore, De KALB, IL
	(she dau/o Clarissa HULETT and William GARDNER)
	Children: Llewelyn Francis-[8]; Marie-[8]; Leslie-[8]; William-[8]; and Edward-[8] TAYLOR
2771. Charlotte Elizabeth	born born 30 May 1837; died 1913 WA; married Byron W. HELMER ca ____
	Children: Ella Rouletta-[8] (1858-1942); Byron-[8],Jr. (1864-1929); Horace Eugene-[8] (1869- 1891); and James Spencer-[8] HELMER (1872-1893)
2772. William Noah	born 22 June 1839; died Jan 1862 (Civil War) Fort Holt, KY
2773. Daniel	born 10 May 1841; died 27 Nov 1929 Nebraska
	married Phoebe MERWIN ca 1868
2774. Philanda/Polly	born 16 Apr 1843; died 29 Dec 1883; married Reuben E. FASSETT 8 June 1862 IL
2775. Sylvanus	born 18 Apr 1845; died 20 Mar 1926
2776. Emaline	born 10 June 1849; died 1856 EOL
2777. Evaline	born 10 June 1849; died 29 July 1873
	married John TALBOTT 6 Sep 1866 DeKalb, IL
2778. Harriet	born 27 Nov 1851 IL; died 27 Jan 1931; married Hiram Seth SCOTT 5 Oct 1871
2779. Philander Lee	born 13 May 1853 IL; died 3 June 1925; married Eliza May SANDERS ca ____

1436. IRA[-7] BRUCE, son of John[-6] BRUCE, Jr (John[-5] BRUCE; Bathsheba[-4] BOWKER; John[-3;2]; Edmund-[1]) and Prudence PRIEST, was born 30 March 1814 Princeton, Worcester, MA. He married Phebe SAWIN on 7 Dec 1836 . She was the daughter of Joel SAWIN and Zilpha JONES, and was born ca 1811; died ____. Ira[-7] BRUCE died 4 Aug 1884.

Children of Ira[-7] BRUCE and Phebe SAWIN:
Surname **BRUCE**

2780. Olive	born 28 Apr 1839 Princeton; died ____	
	married Henry K. HAGER 14 Sep 1866 Boyleston, MA	
	(he s/o Elisha HAGER and Mary K. KEYES)	
	(he born ca 1842; died _____)	
2781. Ellen P.	born 19 Dec 1840 MA; died 18 Feb 1861	
2782. Bruce	born 8 Feb 1844; died ____	
2783. Myron Ira	born ca 1844; died 10 Sep 1845	EOL
2784. Abbie Zilpha Frances	born 20 July 1848; died 3 Sep 1907; married George M. HOUGHTON 27 Nov 1884	

1450. GEORGE HENRY[-7] BRUCE, son of Sylvanus[-6] BRUCE (John-[5]; Bathsheba[-4] BOWKER; John[-3;2]; Edmund[-1]) and Hannah READ/REED, was born 7 Aug 1837 MA. He married Vilena Augusta GODDARD ca 1862. She was the daughter of Ephraim GODDARD and ____, and was born ca 1844; died 1885. George Henry-[7] BRUCE died 11 Jan 1919 at Berlin, MA.

Children of George H[-7] BRUCE and Vilena Augusta GODDARD:
Surname **BRUCE**

2785. Lillie/Lelia Grace	born 20 Sep 1864 Berlin, MA; died _____	
	married O. Porter MORSE ca ____ (he born ca 1862; died ____)	
	Children: George V-[9] born ca 1893; Frances-[9] born 1899; and Walter P-[9] MORSE born ca 1903	
2786. Minnie M.	born ca 1874 NH; died ____	
2787. Charles H.	born ca 1877; died young	EOL
2788. Henry Mason	born 9 July 1881; died same day	EOL

1452. DANFORD-[7] BRUCE, son of Abraham[-6] BRUCE (Daniel[-5]; Bathsheba[-4] BOWKER; John-[3;2]; Edmund[-1]) and Mary Polly BRIGGS, was born ca 1818/19 NY. He married Jane Anne BUTTON ca ____ . She was the daughter of Guinette BUTTON and Nancy BAKER, and was born ____, died ____. Danford-[7] served in the 152nd NY Infantry during the Civil War and died at Washington, DC on 14 March 1863 of smallpox. He is buried at Arlington National Cemetery (grave 23, Range 10, 2F)

Children of Danford-[7] BRUCE and Jane Anne BUTTON:
Surname **BRUCE**

2789. Frances M.	born ca 1846; died ____	
2790. Morris L.	born ca 1847; died ____	
2791. Robert B.	born ca 1850; died ____	
2792. Emily I.	born ca 1852; died ____	
2793. George	born 24 Aug 1854; died 24 Aug 1925 Toyah, Reeves, TX.	
	married Marion Belle HUTCHISON Wheat ca 1908	
	(she dau/o William Henry HUTCHISON and Catherine Elizabeth WHITE)	
	Children: George, Jr.-[9] born ca 1896; Albert-[9] born ca 1898; Mattie-[9] born ca 1900; and Anna Helena-[9] BRUCE born ca 1909/10	

1453. JANE-[7] BRUCE, sister of above, was born ca 1822 NY. She married David Fairchild GOODRICH ca 1838 NY. He was the son of Alpheus GOODRICH and ____; and was born ca 1817 NY; died _____. Jane-[7] BRUCE died 16 Feb 1852 Otsego, NY

Children of Jane[7] BRUCE and David GOODRICH:
Surname **GOODRICH**

	2794. Marion	born 13 Mar 1839; died ____; married H B NORTON 30 Jan 1863
+	**2795. ELLEN G.**	born 20 April 1842 NY; died ____; married Lorenzo D. BOVEE 2 Sep 1863
	2796. George	born 5 July 1844; died 20 Feb 1864 of a disease contracted in the Civil War

Note: he enlisted in the 8th NY Cavalry Nov 1863; died at Agina Creek Landing

+	**2797. LA FAYETTE BRUCE** "Lafe"	born 13 Feb 1847; died 15 Sep 1933; 1 married Elizabeth "Lizzie" RICKABAUGH (she born ca 1848 PA; died 20 Sep 1898 KS 2 married Altha Jane LEAVITT 5 March 1900 Emporia, KS (she dau/o Harlow W. LEAVITT and Janett ____) (she born 12 May 1853 NY; died 21 Nov 1944 KS)

1454. HARRIETT[7] BRUCE, sister of above, was born June 1823 NY. She married Truman SPAFFORD ca 1850. He as the son of Asa SPAFFORD and ____, and was born Mar 1832 NY; died ____. Harriett-[7] BRUCE died ____.

Children of Hariett-[7] BRUCE and Truman SPAFFORD:
Surname **SPAFFORD**

	2798. Charles		born Dec 1853; died 23 May 1919 New Berlin,NY; married Julia Matilda BARBER 1880 (she born Jan 1862 NY; died 1 Nov 1925) Children: Florence-[9] Jessie SPAFFORD born 22 Oct 1888, died 14 Sept 1950, married George Henry DULEY 23 Dec 1903 (age 15); and Albert SPAFFORD born July 1882 NY; died 6 Apr 1955 NY
	2799. William	(1)	born ca 1855; died young
	2800. Ida		born ca 1858; died ____; married Henry MILLS 1875 (he born Feb 1853)
	2801. Willis		born ca 1862; died ____
+	**2802. JENNIE**		born Aug 1866; died ____ 2803. William (2) born Jan 1872; died _____

1456. DIANA[7] BRUCE, sister of above, was born 6 Nov 1827/30 NY. She married David Fairchild GOODRICH, as his second wife, ca 1853. He was the son of Alpheus GOODRICH and ____, and was born ca 1817 NY; died ____ KS. He was married first to her older sister Jane (above). Diana-[7] BRUCE died 7 Dec 1885 Emporia, KS

Children of Diana-[7] BRUCE and David Fairchild GOODRICH:
Surname **GOODRICH**

2804. Anna M.	born ca 1854/55; died ____
2805. Anna Amelia	born 15 Aug 1856 NY; died 18 Mar 1921 IL; a Homeopathic physician married Alexander STENHOUSE ca _____
2806. Alpheus C.	born 29 Jan 1860 NY; died 19 Nov 1925 OK married Margret POLING ca 1887 (she born 4 June 1869 OH; died 11 Mar 1928 OK) (she dau/o William POLING and Caroline SLISHER)
2807. Jesse David	born 27 Jan 1865 KS; died 18 June 1941 KS
2808. Jennie D.	born 14 Jan 1870 KS; died 7 Dec 1932; married Horace C. CATLIN ca 1899 (he born 1 July 1851 IL; died 28 Feb 1933)

1463. STEPHEN[7] BOWKER, son of Samuel Ward[6] BOWKER (Silas[5]; John[4,3,2]; Edmund[1]) and Sarah LOCKE, was born 15 Oct 1794 at Royalston, MA. He married Prudence RAND Dec 1814. She was the daughter of ____ RAND and ____; and was born 14 Jan 1795; died ____. Stephen[7] BOWKER died ____.

Children of Stephen[7] BOWKER and Prudence RAND:
Surname **BOWKER**

2809. L.	born ca ____; died ____
2810. Milton R.	born 26 Nov 1815 Walpole, MA; died ____; married Ann/Anna ___ (she born ca 1819)
2811. Edmund C.	born 24 July 1817 Dummerston, VT; died ____
2812. Emily A.	born 1 Sep 1819 Dummerston, VT; died ____
2813. Mary	born 18 Jan 1822 Dummerston, VT; died ____
2814. Samuel P.	born 16 Mar 1824; died ____
2815. Celestia Lucy	born 1 Aug 1826 Townsend, VT; died 24 July 1902 Rutland, VT married _____ CHANNELL ca _____
2816. Stephen	born 4 Feb 1828 Shefford, Quebec, CA; died ____

Children of Stephen-[7] BOWKER and Prudence RAND:
Surname **BOWKER**

+	**2817. WALTER LEONARD**	born 15 Aug 1831 Quebec; died ____ married Julia A. SHIPMAN 23 Oct 1853 Rockingham, VT. (she dau/o Edmond SHIPMAN, IV and Elizabeth / Betsey NICHOLAS) (she born 19 Dec 1825; died ____)
	2818. Sarah R.	born 13 Mar 1834; died ____

1465. SAMUEL-[7] BOWKER, brother of above, was born 28 Dec 1798 at Royalston, MA. He married Mary-[7] GIBSON on 21 Dec 1826 (int pub 5 Nov 1826). She was the daughter of Joseph Barker-[6] GIBSON (Samuel-[5]; Stephen-[4]; Timothy-[3]; John-[2]; [1]) and Submit WARREN, and was born 8 Feb 1800 Ashburnham, MA; died 20 Jan 1890. Samuel-[7] died 5 Nov 1861.

Children of Samuel-[7] BOWKER and Mary GIBSON:
Surname **BOWKER**

+	**2819. MARY CAROLINE**	born 30 May 1829 Westminster, MA; died ____ married Henry B. HOUGHTON 15 Apr 1858 (he of Harvard and Stow, MA) (he born 10 Dec 1827; died 16 July 1861 Stow, MA)
	2820. Abbie F.	born 11 Nov 1830 Westminster; died____ married Charles BROWN 27 Nov 1855(no issue) EOL
+	**2821. SAMUEL**	born 4 May 1832 Westminster; died 10 Mar 1888 Ashby, MA married Harriet ALDRICH 4 May 1856 (she dau/o Timothy ALDRICH and Rebecca WEAVER) (she born 14 Mar 1832; died 21 Dec 1914)
	2822. George T.	born 8 Dec 1840 Ashby, MA; died 6 June 1845 EOL

Reference: John GIBSON of Cambridge, MA and his descendants 1634-1899 , (Family 136) pages 294, 295

1467. ELIZABETH / BETSEY-[7] BOWKER, daughter of Samuel Ward-[6] BOWKER (Silas-[5]; John-[4,3,2]; Edmund-[1]) and Charlotte LOCKE, was born 25 Feb 1804 Royalston, MA. She married Benjamin BOSWORTH 1 Nov 1828, as his second wife. He was the son of Jonathan BOSWORTH and Mary _____; and was born ca 1794; died 21 May 1866. He was married first to Esther BALLOU ca 1826. Elizabeth/Betsey-[7] BOWKER died before 1850.

Children of Elizabeth/Betsey-[7] BOWKER and Benjamin BOSWORTH:
Surname **BOSWORTH**

	2823. Esther Belle	born 7 July 1829 Royalston, MA; died ____
	2824. Matthew Walker (twin)	born 23 Dec 1831 Royalston; died ____; married _____ PHILLIPS ca _____
+	**2825. MARTHA WALKER**	(twin) born 23 Dec 1831 Royalston, MA; died 25 Apr 1903 WI married Austin PHILLIPS on 13 Jan 1849 Royalston (he born ca 1827 MA; died 22 July 1893 WI)

1471. NATHANIEL-[7] BOWKER, son of Stephen Bigelow-[6] BOWKER (Silas-[5]; John-[5]; John-[4,3,2]; Edmund-[1]) and Submit GROVER, was born 26 July 1808 Royalston, MA. He married Philena WHEELER on 9 Nov 1830. She was the daughter of _____ WHEELER and ____; and was born ca 1805; died ____. Nathaniel-[7] BOWKER died _____.

Children of Nathaniel-[7] BOWKER and Philena WHEELER:
Surname **BOWKER**

	2826. Silas W.	born ca 1835; died 1835 EOL
	2827. Lucia A.	born ca 1838; died 1890
+	**2828. CHARLES WATSON**	born ca 1842/43; died ____ 1 married Nancy A. SIBLEY 1 Jan 1863 (she dau/o Joel SIBLEY and Rhoda ALGER) (she born ca 1843; died 20 Aug 1870 2 married Susan B. UPHAM 12 Sep 1871 (she dau/o ____ UPHAM and _____) (she born Sep 1844; died 1922)

1472. LIBERTY-[7] LEAVITT, son of Celia Winslow-[6] TURNER (Betty-[5] BOWKER; John-[4,3,2]; Edmund-[1]) and Laban LEAVITT, was born 20 Oct 1806 at Pembroke, Plymouth, MA. He married Chloe BELCHER 18 Nov 1824. She was the daughter of Friend BELCHER and Chloe MORSE; and was born 10 Sep 1808 Foxboro, MA; died ____. Liberty-[7] LEAVITT died 29 June 1841.

Children of Liberty-[7] LEAVITT and Chloe BELCHER:
Surname **LEAVITT**

2829. Hiram Liberty	born 5 April 1825; died ____	
2830. Catherine Chloe	born 27 May 1826; died ____	
	married William Sanford HOLMES of Easton, MA 27 Apr 1848	
	(he s/o William HOLMES and Melancy _____) (he born ca 1829; died ____)	
2831. George Sumner	born 4 Sep 1827; died 5 Mar 1882 Foxborough, MA	
	married Charlotte E. PAINE of Winslow, ME 2 May 1851	
	(she dau/o Frederick PAINE and _____)	
	Children: Frederic S-[9] born 1852; and Charles P-[9] LEAVITT born ca 1853	
2832. Celia Ann Winslow	born 4 Nov 1830; died ____	
2833. Laurenza L.	born 23 Apr 1832; died 1 March 1894 Norton, MA	
	married Renu WILBON 23 Apr 1848	
2834. John Quincy Adams	born 18 Apr 1834; died Oct 1916	
	1 married Mary E. THRASHER 2 July 1854; 2 married Mattie S. SNOW ca 1886	
2835. James Leprelet.	born 6 Sep 1836; died ____	
2836. Joseph Sanford	born 29 June 1838; died 13 Oct 1917	
	married Sophronia LEAVITT (his cousin) 28 March 1858	
	(she dau/o Nahum-[7] LEAVITT (below) and Eunice EVERSON)	
	(she born 11 Oct 1839; died 26 Feb 1864)	
2837. Frederic Perry.	(twin) born 27 July 1840; died 2 May 1917	
2838. Francis William	(twin) born 27 July 1840; died 24 Jan 1929	
	married Georgiette Augusta PIERCE ca 1861	
2839. Charles Edward A	born 18 Dec 1841; died ca 1909	

1473. SUMNER-[7] LEAVITT, brother of above, was born 3 Jan 1808 at Pembroke, MA. He married Betsey WITHERELL, of Pembroke, on 23 Oct 1831. She was the daughter of Jabez WITHERELL and Lucy PERRY; and was born 11 Dec 1804; died ____. Sumner-[7] LEAVITT died 2 Sep 1857.

Children of Sumner-[7] LEAVITT and Betsey WITHERELL:
Surname **LEAVITT**

2840. Sumner, Jr.	born March 1833; died ____	
	married Mercy F. CARTER 2 Feb 1855 Quincy, Norfolk, MA	
	(she dau/o Samuel CARTER and Abagail ____)	
	Child: Carrie H-[9] LEAVITT born ca 1865; married George H. MORGAN ca 1885	
	2 ch.: Aline-[10] born Nov 1888 MA; and Evelyn C-[10] MORGAN born June 1881 MA	
2841. Samuel	born Dec 1841; died ____	

1474. QUINCY-[7] LEAVITT, brother of above, was born 8 Feb 1809 at Pembroke, MA. He married Clymenia/Climenia SOPER on 22 Dec 1839. She was the daughter of _____ SOPER and ____; and was born ____; died 1 Jan 1887. Quincy-[7] LEAVITT died 12 Dec 1851. Note: Clymneia SOPER Leavitt married 2nd to Bradford BRALEY

Child of Quincy-[7] LEAVITT and Clymenia SOPER:
Surname **LEAVITT**

2842. Clinton Brewster	born 8 Mar 1844; died 16 March 1860	EOL

1475. WINSLOW-[7] LEAVITT, brother of above, was born 17 May 1811 Pembroke, MA. He married Mehitable KEENE of Hanson ,MA. on 4 July 1841. She was the daughter of _____ KEENE and ____; and was born ____; died ____. Winslow-[7] LEAVITT died 1895 at Whitman, MA.

Child of Winslow-[7] LEAVITT and Mehitable KEENE:
Surname **LEAVITT**

2843. Mehitable W.	born 15 Feb 1847 Pembroke; died 28 Mar 1887
	married Hiram L. JENKINS 4 July 1866 (he of Whitman, MA)(had 1 son)

1476. NAHUM-[7] LEAVITT, brother of above, was born 21 Dec 1815 Pembroke, MA. He married Eunice Sprague EVERSON of Hanson, MA ca Sep 1837. She was the daughter of ____ EVERSON and ____; and was born 3 Feb 1819; died 1 Sep 1903. Nahum-[7] LEAVITT died 19 May 1859 at Pembroke, MA.

Children of Nahum-[7] LEAVITT and Eunice EVERSON:
Surname **LEAVITT**   (all children born Pembroke, Plymouth, MA)

2844.	Kimball C.	born 20 Aug 1838; died ____
2845.	Sophronia	born 11 Oct 1839; died 28 Feb 1864; married Joseph LEAVITT (her cousin, above)
2846.	Hiram	born 25 Mar 1841; died 22 Dec 1925 MA
2847.	Un-naamed male	born 5 Jan 1843; died 1843
2848.	Mary Ann	born 10 Jan 1844; died ____
2849.	**ADELIA/DELIA ALICE**	born 26 Jan 1845; died 14 Dec 1909 Whitman, MA
		married Horace LITTLEFIELD 24 Dec 1861
		(he s/o Horace LITTLEFIELD and Delia A. SHAW)
		(he born ca 1834 Berwick, ME; died 3 Apr 1892 Whitman, MA.
2850.	Emma Albertina	born 23 Feb 1847; died ____
2851.	Julius	born ca 1849; died ____
2852.	George Elliott	born 15 May 1850; died ____
2853.	Charlotte Howard	born 11 Oct 1852; died ____

1479. ALEXANDER-[7] BOWKER, son of Jomathan-[6] BOWKER (Solomon-[5]; John-[4,3,2]; Edmund-[1]) and Abigail BEAMAN, was born March 1810 Canada. He married Louisa WHEELER on 2 Apr 1832 at Stanstead, Quebec, Canada. She was the daughter of (poss.) Lemuel WHEELER and ____; and was born ____; died ____. Alexander-[7] BOWKER died 14 Aug 1881 Canada.

Children of Alexander-[7] BOWKER and Louisa WHEELER:
Surname **BOWKER**

	2854. Burnside	born ____; died ____
	2855. Nancy	born ____; died ____
	2856. Ursula P.	born 9 Oct 1834; died 3 Feb 1915/18
+	**2857. VALESTA DRUSCILLA**	born 17 Jul 1841 Stanstead, Quebec, CAN; died 21 June 1897 Stanstead
		married Thomas William LANE 13 May 1867 (as his 2nd wife)
		(he s/o John LANE and Susan BOWERS)
		(he born 25 Jul 1836 **; died 21 May 1917 Stanstead Quebec, CAN
		Note: ** (he was born aboard the Ship ARDWELL enroute from England to Quebec)

1482. NATHANIEL BEAMAN-[7] BOWKER, brother of above, was born 9 Feb 1821 at Dalton, NH. He married Mary Ann PARNELL on 9 May 1853 at Melburne, Quebec, Canada. She was the daughter of Lawrence PARNELL and ____; and was born ca 1827; died 28 Aug 1902 at Lancaster, NH. Nathaniel-[7] BOWKER died 26 March 1889 at Bloomfield, VT.

Children of Nathaniel Beaman-[7] BOWKER and Mary Ann PARNELL:
Surname **BOWKER**

	2858. John E.	born 24 Nov 1860 VT; died Feb 1913 Belfast, ME.
		married Anna SCHOFF 25 Oct 1884 Colebrook, NH
		(she dau/o Oscar H. SCHOFF and Ellen _____)
		(she born ca 1867; died ca 1910)
		Child: Ina O-[9] BOWKER born 4 Mar 1891 VT; died Aug 1975 Concord, NH; married Walter JELLISON 4 June 1913 (he born ca 1890 ME; died ca 1930)
	2859. Harry R/S.	born ca 1863 Bloomfield, VT; died 23 Oct 1894 Groveton, NH
		married Annie J. HOPKINS 29 Dec 1891
		(she born ca 1871; died ___) (she dau/o Frank HOPKINS and _____)
+	**2860. EDWIN S.**	born ca 1865 VT; died 1936 Belfast, Waldo, Maine
		married Cora J. _____ ca 1890
	2861. Jessie L. (male)	born ca 1868 Bloomfield, VT; died 6 Oct 1886 Bloomfield

1484. MARY B-[7] BOWKER, daughter of George-[6] BOWKER (Jotham-[5]; John-[4;3;2]; Edmund-[1]) and Betsey UNDERWOOD, was born 2 June 1823 Barre, Worcester, MA. She married first to William W. HINCKLEY on 4 Dec 1849 Barre. He was the son of Timothy HINCKLEY and Roxanna ____, and was born ca 1826; died 13 Feb 1864. She married second to Ebenezer FOSTER on 7 March 1872. He was the son of Ebenezer FOSTER and Miriam ____, and was born ____; died ____. Mary B-[7] BOWKER died ____.

Children of Mary B-[7] BOWKER and William W. HINCKLEY:
Surname **HINCKLEY**

	2862. Alma Maria	born ca 1851 MA; died 24 Sep 1904 Barre, MA.
		married Hiram MARSH ca ____ Child: William H-[9] MARSH born ca 1868
	2863. Eliza Ruggles	born 8 Feb 1856; died ____; married ____ BARTLETT ca no issue
+	**2864. MARY ELIZABETH**	born May 1857; died ca 1919 Hardwick, MA married Harrison Orcutt THRASHER ca 1880

1487. LUKE FREEMAN-[7] BOWKER, brother of above, was born 22 May 1828 Barre, Worcester, MA. He married Eliza Jane WILSON on 31 Mar 1855 . She was the daughter of Charles WILSON and ___; and was born ca 1832 NY; died ____. Luke Freeman-7 BOWKER died 17 July 1864 at Dinwiddie, VA during a Civil War battle. He was a Pvt. in Co. E, of the 27th MA Infantry . He is buried at City Point National Cemetery in Hopewell, VA.

Children of Luke Freeman-[7] BOWKER and Eliza Jane WILSON:
Surname **BOWKER**

+	**2865. HARRIET ELIZA**	born 11 Feb 1856 MA; died 12 July 1919 married Maxwell Osmer/Osman SCOTT ca 1881
+	**2866. CORA JANE**	born 25 Apr 1858 MA; died 7 Feb 1952 SC 1 married Levi S. HUNTOON 22 Mar 1870 MA 2 married Willard E. DAWSON ca 1884

1493. LEVI-[7] BOWKER, son of Gideon-[6] BOWKER (Antipas-[5]; Josiah-[4]; John-[3,2]; Edmund-[1]) and Hannah FLETCHER, was born 14 March 1783 at Chesterfield, NH. He married Betsey/Betsie SILSBY ca Nov 1806. She was the daughter of Mitchell SILSBY and ____, and was born 16 April 1783 Charlestown, NH ; died ____. He married 2nd to Fanny MARSHALL ca 1832. She was the daughter of ____ MARSHALL and ____, and was born ____; died ____. Levi-[7] BOWKER died 23 March 1863.

Children of Levi-[7] BOWKER and Betsey SILSBY:
Surname **BOWKER**

	2867. John	born ca 1810; died 25 June 1825	EOL	
	2868. Gideon	born 6 March 1810; died ____		
	2869. Hannah Silsby	born 27 March 1812; died ____		
+	**2870. LYMAN HOWE**	born 11 Feb 1814; died ____; married Elizabeth B. SMITH 11 June 1835 (she born 13 Sep 1814; died 13 Apr 1898 IA)		
+	**2871. LEVI GOODELL**	born 2 Jan 1816; died Jan 1874 married Parthena HARTSHORN 10 May 1839 VT (she born ca 1821 Canada; died ____)		
+	**2872. ROSWELL**	born 26 Aug 1817 Lunenburg, VT; died 6 May 1898 Whitefield, NH married Jane BLAKESLEE 2 Feb 1841 (she born ca 1817 Dalton, NH; died Oct 1867) (she dau/o John BLAKESLEE and Bathsheba BLAKE)		
	2873. Laura H.	born 25 Jan 1819; died ____	2875. Lydia	born ca 1825
	2874. Mitchell	born 27 Dec 1821; died ____	2876. James G.	born 27 March 1828

Children of Levi-[7] BOWKER and Fanny MARSHALL:
Surname **BOWKER**

	2877. Betsey	born 20 Oct 1833; died ____ 2878. Mary Helen born 2 Nov 1837

1495. RICE-[7] BOWKER, brother of above, was born 3 Feb 1789 at Guilford, Windham, VT. He married Elizabeth/Betsey CLARK on 3 July 1814. She was the daughter of ____ CLARK and ____, and was born ca 1792 VT; died 28 Feb 1861 Sullivan, OH. Rice-[7] BOWKER died 15 Nov 1843 at Sullivan, Ashland, Ohio.

Children of Rice-[7] BOWKER and Betsey CLARK:
Surname **BOWKER**

	2879. Hazen (male)	born ca 1814/15 Lunenburg, VT; died 1839
+	**2880. FRANKLIN**	born 12 June 1816 Lunenburg, Essex, VT; died Aug 1895 Baxter Springs, MO married Nancy Ann HUMISTON 24 June 1840 Rochester, OH (she born 16 Aug 1814 Colesville, NY; died 25 Jan 1889 Fitchville, OH)
+	**2881. MARTHA J.**	born 21 Mar 1819 Lunenburg; died 1 Apr 1869 Sullivan, Ashland, OH married Anson D. PERSONS 22 Nov 1838 Lorain, OH

Children of Rice-[7] BOWKER and Betsey CLARK, continued:
Surname **BOWKER**

2882. Julius C.	born 25 Oct 1821 VT; died 3 Apr 1887	
	married Eunice Muriel ROSS ca 1843 (she born ca 1821; died 1884)	
	Children: Elbert M-[9] BOWKER born 12 July 1844 OH, died 30 Apr 1912 MO; and Florence C-[9]	
	BOWKER born 17 Feb 1851 OH; died 1 May 1927 MO	
2883. Gideon R.	born ca 1827 VT; died ____; 1 married Lavina JOHNSON 18 Nov 1846	
	Child: Harriet M-[9] BOWKER born ca 1849 OH	
	2 married Adda S. BOWKER 17 Oct 1877 (she born ca 1843 NY; died ____)	
	Child: Hiram J-[9] BOWKER born July 1879 MI	

1497. LYMAN JAMES-[7] BOWKER, brother of above, was born 12 Jan 1794 at Guilford, VT. He married Betsey MERRIAM ca Nov 1818 at Newport, Quebec, Canada. She was the daughter of Isaac MERRIAM and Betsey WAITE and was born ca 1794; died ca 1867. Lyman James-[7] BOWKER died 1 Dec 1867 at Newport, Quebec, Canada.

Children of Lyman James-[7] BOWKER and Betsey MERRIAM:
Surname **BOWKER** (all children born Lunenburg, VT)

2884. Louisa Adeline	born 11 May 1820; died ca 1893	
+ **2885. LEWIS LEANDER**	born 29 Oct 1821; died 16 Feb 1905	
	married Lucy Minerva HEARD 21 Oct 1845 Newport, Que. Canada	
2886. William Hubbard	born 19 June 1824; died 21 Jan 1895; married Julia Ann COATS ca ____	
2887. Charles Brigham	born 22 Mar 1826 2888. Sarah Jane	born 12 Feb 1834; died 6 Mar 1893

1499. LEONARD-[7] BOWKER, brother of above, was born 20 Feb 1799 at Lunenburg, Essex, VT. He married Phoebe CURTISS ca 1821. She was the daughter of _____ CURTISS and ____; and was born ca 1798 NH; died ____. Leonard-[7] BOWKER possibly married second to Cordelia JENNINGS 3 Feb 1853 Coldwater, MI. She was the daughter of Elisha JENNINGS and ____; and was born 14 Aug 1822; died 17 Dec 1877 MI. Leonard-[7] BOWKER died 27 Sep 1869 MI.

Children of Leonard-[7] BOWKER and Phoebe CURTISS;
Surname **BOWKER**

+ **2889. MILO**	born Apr 1822 VT; died 188_ Carson City, Nevada	
ANDERSON	1 married Delinda Thilisama MILLS on 2 Dec 1847 VT	
	(she dau/o Daniel Comstock MILLS and Dorothy Ann FARRAND)	
	(she born 16 June 1828 VT; died 1860 Coldwater, Branch, MI)	
	2 married Mary Ann CASE ca 1867 (she born ca 1834 NY; died ____)	
2890. Henry Curtiss	born ca 1823; died ____	
2891. Gideon R.	born ca 1826 VT; died ____ ; married Lovina ____ ca ____	
	Child: Harriet-[9] BOWKER born ca 1849 OH	
2892. Chester	born ca 1828; died ____	
2893. L. F.	born ca 1829; died ____ 2896. Mary Jane	born ca 1836; died ____
2894. Foster	born ca 1830; died ____	
2895. George Wesley	born 30 June 1830; died 14 Nov 1908 Coldwater, Branch, MI	

1502. JOHN PIERSON-[7] BOWKER, son of Oliver-[6] BOWKER (Ephraim-[5]; Josiah-[4]; John-[3,2]; Edmund-[1]) and Hannah PIERSON/PEARSON, and was born 9 Sep 1787. He married first to Polly BAKER on 18 July 1812 at Rutland, MA. She was the daughter of Ziba BAKER and Mildred CLEVELAND; and was born 2 June 1794 , MA; died 19 Dec 1820, MA. He married second to Patty BAKER Fales Belcher, as her 3rd husband, on 24 July 1822. She was the sister of Polly, and had been married first on 30 May 1811 to Lewis FALES, and second on 6 Jan 1821 to Eleazer BELCHER. Patty BAKER was born 1 Oct 1787; died 25 Nov 1873 Walpole, MA. John P-[7] BOWKER died 24 Jan 1862 at Walpole, MA.

Children of John P-[7] BOWKER and Polly BAKER:
Surname **BOWKER**

+ **2897. JOHN PIERSON, JR**	born 12 Apr 1814; died 14 May 1885; married Sarah P. PETERS 10 Jan 1838	
+ **2898. LEWIS FALES**	born 1 July 1818; died 1867	
2899. Lyman Tyler	born 15 Jan 1820; died 2 Nov 1839 Walpole, MA	EOL

Children of John P-[7] BOWKER and Patty BAKER Fales Belcher:
Surname **BOWKER**

2900. Mary Polly	born 24 Feb 1823; died 13 Dec 1893; marr. Loring JOHNSON 3 Sept 1851 Norfolk, MA	
	(he s/o Comfort JOHNSON and S _____) (he born ca 1812; died 1891)	

Children of John P-7 BOWKER and Patty BAKER Fales Belcher, continued:
Surname **BOWKER**

    2901. Martha Patty   born 28 May 1824; died ____; married Nathaniel LAMSON 7 June 1852
                                       (he s/o Nathaniel LAMSON and _____)

1507. AZUBAH-7 HAGER, daughter of Dolly-6 NEWTON (Tabitha-5 BOWKER; Josiah-4; John-3,2; Edmund-1) and Abraham HAGER. She married Ichabod FARRER on 4 Aug 1804 Westminster, MA. He was the son of ____ FARRER and ____. and was born____, died ____. She married second to Micah GRAVES on 23 Aug 1808. He was the som of Jonathan GRAVES and Elizabeth LEWIS, and was born ca 1787; died 13 June 1823 . Azubah-7 HAGER died ____.

Children of Azubah-7 HAGER and Micah GRAVES:
Surname **GRAVES**   (all children born Westminster < MA)

    2902. Charles Newton   born 28 Apr 1809; died 29 Dec 1885 MA
                             married Laura ____ ca _____ (12 ch)
    2903. Abraham   born 27 Feb 1811; died 27 Dec 1834 MA
    2904. Jonathan   born 14 Aug 1812; died ____
    2905. Micah Jr.   born 22 June 1815; died ____; married Sirena BARNES ca ____
    2906. Persis   born 2 Aug 1817; died 3 Dec 1819   EOL
    2907. Sally/ Sarah   born 11 Sep 1819; died ____
    2908. Marvin Augustus   born 11 Aug 1821; died ____   2909. George Gore   born 18 Sep 1823

1512. LYDIA CHURCH-7 NEWTON, daughter of Ezra-6 NEWTON (Tabitha-5 BOWKER; Josiah-4; John-3,2; Edmund-1) and Lucy HOWE, was born 28 July 1816 MA. She married Elbridge T. CLARK on 12 Sep 1835 at Medway, Norfolk, MA. He was the son of Lemuel CLARK and ____; and was born 11 Sep 1812 Medway, MA; died 6 Feb 1896 at Millis, Norfolk, MA. Lydia Church-7 NEWTON died 31 May 1869.

Children of Lydia Church-7 NEWTON and Elbridge CLARK:
Surname **CLARK**

+   **2910. EDMUND NEWTON** born 6 June 1841 Medway, MA; died 2 Feb 1935 Millis, MA
                                married Tryphena Richardson FISHER ca _____
                                (born 17 Jan 1841 Medway, MA; died 17 July 1832)
    2911. Harriet Lydia   born ca 1842; died ____
    2912. Lucy Jane   born ca ____; died ____
    2913. Mary Ophelia   born ca ____; died ____
    2914. Martha G   born ca 1847; died ____
    2915. Elbridge William   born ca 1850; died 2 Jan 1851
    2916. Lemuel   born 6 Feb 1858; died ____; married Bertha Josephine SWETT 17 Jan 1894
                    Children: Dorothy Newton-9 born 23 Nov 1894, married Walter William HOAR ; and Elbridge
                    Theodore -9 CLARK born 20 Jul 1901 Millis, MA; died Apr 1967 MA

1513. EZRA-7 NEWTON, Jr., a clergyman, and brother of above, was born 30 Sep 1818 MA. He married Martha T. PATTEN on 24 July 1846 at Medway, Norfolk, MA. She was the daughter of ____ PATTEN and ____; and was born ca 1821 NH; died 2 Nov 1906 Seattle, WA. Ezra-7 NEWTON, Jr. died 4 Nov 1897 at Seattle, King, WA.

Children of Ezra-7 NEWTON, Jr. and Martha Brown PATTEN:
Surname **NEWTON**

    2917. Charles Ezra   born Sep 1847 Shutesbury, Franklin, MA; diedf 20 Feb 1921 Seattle, WA
    2918. Henrietta Louise   born 30 July 1851 Kingston, MA; died 1928
    2919. Ella Frances   born 17 Oct 1853 Dighton, Bristol, MA; died ____
    2920. Ezekiel   born 1859 Little Falls, Morrison, MN; died ____

1532. DEWITT CLINTON-7 BOWKER, son of Obediah-6 BOWKER (Ithamar-5; Josiah-4; John-3,2; Edmund-1) and Catherine ANDERSON, was born Aug 1836 NY/NJ. He married Sarah Gertrude DRAKE on ____. She was the daughter of Benjamin DRAKE and Elizabeth ____; and was born ca 1847 NJ; died 26 July 1933. Dewitt Clinton-7 BOWKER died 20 Apr 1906.

Children of Dewitt Clinton-7 BOWKER and Sarah DRAKE:
Surname **BOWKER**

    2921. Lutetia / Lutecia   born ca 1862; died ____

Children of DeWitt Clinton-7 BOWKER and Sarah DRAKE, continued:
Surname **BOWKER**

+   **2922. DEWITT CLINTON,** born 1867; died ____; 1 married _____
          JR.   2 married Imogene _____ ca 1904 (she born ca 1884; died ____)
    2923. John   born ca 1868; died ____; married Lavinia _____ ca 1902 (she born ca 1881; died____)
          Children: Richard-9 born ca 1903; and Dewitt-9 BOWKER born ca 1907
    2924. Ellen/Nellie   born ca 1871; died 1961
    2925. Franklin   born 16 Oct 1874; died 1930; married Alice Curtis BEDELL 1894 Rockville Ctr., NY
          Children: Mildred-9 born 28 Mar 1895 NY, died 23 June 1980 MA; and Norma Bedell-9 BOWKER born
          8 June 1902 NY; died June 1983 Kemosha, WI
+   **2926. OBEDIAH (Obey)** born 24 Feb 1877; died ____; married Caroline SCHROEDER ca 1906
          (she dau/o Charles F. SCHROEDER and Matilda F _____) (she born ca 1887)
    2927. Edward   born ca 1881; died ____
    2928. Bertha   born ca 1885; died ____; married Roscoe LANGDON ca ____
          Children: Roscoe-9 Jr. born May 1909; and Dalton-9 LANGDON born ca ____

1547. JANNETTE/ JEANETTE-7 BOWKER, daughter of Windsor-6 BOWKER (Asa-5; Josiah-4; John-3;2; Edmund-1) and Sarah OSGOOD, was born ca 1828 Hinsdale, Cheshire, NH. She married the Rev. William Horace MARBLE ca 1851 at Hinsdale, NH. He was the son of Elijah MARBLE and Marian B. GIFFORD; and was born13 Feb 1822 ; died 14 Sep 1903 Boulder, CO. Jannette-7 BOWKER died 31 Mar 1876 at Hinsdale, NH.

Children of Jannette-7 BOWKER and Rev. William H. MARBLE:
Surname **MARBLE**
    2929. Mathilda "Mattie"   born ca 1853 Columbus, OH; died ca 1917 Washington, IA
    2930. William Osgood   born May 1854 OH; died ca 1930 Sarasota, FL
          married Adrienne M KAPSY ca ____, OH (her 2nd marriage)
          (she born May 1858 Hungary; died 1930 Sarasota, FL)
          (she dau/o Francis Pepsy KAPSY and Mary Anna KRANZ)
    2931. Florence Clara "Flora" born Apr 1856 WI; died 21 May 1941 (a teacher) single   EOL
    2932. Caroline Sophia " Carrie" born ca 1861 WI; died 30 Mar 1929 Two Harbors, Lake County, MN
    2933. Walter E.   born Jan 1864 WI; died ca 1936 St. Louis, MO
    2934. Frederick J.   born ca 1866 IA; died 1903
+   **2935. JESSIE**   born May 1871 IA; died 21 Feb 1951 Two Harbors, Lake County, MN
          married George Washington WATTS ca 1899
          (he born ca 1868; died 5 Sep 1957 Two Harbors, Lake County, MN)

1553. OLIVE-7 WHEELER, daughter of Mary Hosmer-6 FORBUSH (David-5;4; Martha-3 BOWKER; John-2; Edmund-1) and Daniel WHEELER, was born 16 Jan 1803 Acton, MA. She married Bryant KAY, Jr. ca 1828. He was the son of Bryant KAY born Yorkshire, England) and Ella MCCONNELL (born Ireland), and was born ca 1803 Haverhill, Grafton, NH; died 29 Apr 1857 at Sisterville, WV. Olive-7 WHEELER died 27 April 1858 WV.

Children of Olive-7 WHEELER and Bryant KAY:
Surname **KAY**
+   **2936. MARY**   born 12 Feb 1829 Jamestown, NY; died 27 Dec 1910 CA
        HAYWARD   married William DYE on 9 Jan 1850 Sisterville, WV (he born ca 1817; died 1883)
+   **2937. HANNAH**   born 20 June 1832; died 6 Dec 1906
          married Hervey/Harvey Dale DYE ca 1852   (he born ca 1831; died 1921)
    2938. Harriet   born ca 1837 NY

1557. PARTHENIA-7 DAVIS, daughter of Mary/Polly-6 FORBUSH (James-5; David-4; Martha-3 BOWKER; John-2; Edmund-1) and Elihu DAVIS, was born 12 May 175 Bennington, VT. She married Benjamin GREENSLET on 24 Oct 1813 at Benning-ton. He was the son of James GREENSLET, and ____, and was born ____; died ____. Parthenia-7 DAVIS died 30 July 1880 at Readsboro, VT and is buried at the Bennington Village Cemetery.

Children of Parthenia-7 DAVIS and Benjamin GREENSLET:
Surname **GREENSLET**
    2939. Henry   born 30 Jan 1814; died 28 Jan 1896 West Monroe, Oswego, NY
          married Abigail W. BIGELOW ca 1845 Windham, VT
          Children: Henrietta-9 born (Dec 1849, died 3 Feb 1874; and Elizabeth-9 GREENSLET born 24 June 1854, died 7 June 1937/47

Children of Parthenia[7] DAVIS and Benjamin GREENSLET, continued:

Surname **GREENSLET**

    2940. Charles   born 9 June 1817; died ____; married Sybil DARLING 24 Apr 1837

                           (she dau/o Reuben DARLING and Hannah SCRIPTURE)

                           Children: Harriet M-[9] born ca ___; George W-[9] born ca ____; (killed 3 Nov 1866 by runaway horses);
and Mary E-[9] GREENSLET born ca ____, married E D HICKS

    2941. Amos   born 19 Dec 1819; died ____

    2942. Maryette   born ca _____; died _____

    2943. Norman   born 25 Feb 1824; died ____;

    2944. Elihu   born 5 Apr 1825; died 10 May 1906

                           married Harriet Witum SIMPSON 4 Nov 1847 Bennington, VT

                           Children: Jeanette-[9] born ca 1850; and Eugene-[9] GREENSLET born ca 1852

    2945. Margaret   born ca 1831; died 1899

    2946. Truman   born 6 Feb 1832; died ____; married Lucinda BISHOP ca ____

                           Child: Lois Parthenia-[9] GREENSLET born 5 July 1876, married Hubert Elwood TURNER 24 Dec 1894,
died 7 Nov 1959

1559. POLLY / MARY[7] DAVIS, sister of above, was born 22 March 1802 Bennington, VT. She married Almon / Almeron CRAWFORD ca 1823. He was the son of Thomas CRAWFORD and Sophia ____, and was born ca 1799; died 7 Oct 1870.

Children of Polly/Mary[7] DAVIS and Almon/Almeron CRAWFORD:

Surname **CRAWFORD**

    2947. Mary   born ca 1824; died ____

    2948. Charles   born ca ____; died ____

+   **2949. AUSTIN H.**   born ca 1825; died 13 June 1886 Bennington, VT; married Ann GARDINIER ca ____

                           (she born ca 1826 England; died ____)

    2950. Martha   born ca 1827; died ____

    2951. Caroline   born ca 1832; died ____   2954. Laura   born ca 1841; died ____

    2952. Henry   born ca 1834; died ____

+   **2953. RANDALL J.**   born 5 Dec 1835; died 12 Jan 1895; a builder

                           married Alida HOLLENBECK ca ____

                           (she dau/o William HOLLENBECK and Ann BAISLEY)

                           (she born ca 1844 VT; died 21 Apr 1889)

1560. ALMIRA[7] DAVIS, sister of above, was born 2 July 1806 Bennington, VT. She married Almon/Almeron POTTER on 19 Oct 1834. He was the son of William POTTER and Cynthia BURGESS, and was born 30 Mar 1811; died 10 Mar 1848. Almira[7] DAVIS died 24 Dec 1891 at Union Settlement, Oswego County, New York.

Children of Almira[7] DAVIS and Almon/Almeron POTTER:

Surname **POTTER**

    2955. Eugene B.   born 13 July 1835 Bennington, VT; died ca 1923

    2956. Amos Newell   born 2 July 1837 West Monroe, NY; died 1891

    2957. William Henry born 26 Jukly 1842 West Monroe, NY; died ca 1928

1574. GEORGE WASHINGTON[7] FORBUSH, son of Daniel[6] FORBUSH (James[5]; David[4]; Martha[3] BOWKER; John[2]; Edmund[1]) and his first wife, Nancy GRAPES, was born 19 May 1820 NH. He married Marina WHEELER on 3 July 1843 Dummer, Coos, NH. She was the daughter of _____ WHEELER and _____, and was born 13 Oct 1825 Coos, NH; died ca 1859 Dummer, Coos, NH. George W-[7] FORBUSH died 13 June 1899.

Children of George W-[7] FORBUSH and Marina WHEELER:

Surname **FORBUSH**   (all children born Dummer, Coos, NH)

    2958. Eunice S.   born 14 June 1845; died ____

    2959. Ellen   born 1 Apr 1847; died _____

    2960. Matilda   born 23 June 1848; died 1909; married Hiram COLE ca 1876

                           Child: Osmar Thomas-[9] COLE born ca 1879; died 1972

    2961. Marian   born 13 June 851; died _____

    2962. Amos   born 16 Oct 1853; died ____

    2963. Zenas W.   born 12 Apr 1855; died _____;   married Anna R. CORKUM 6 Mar 1875

                           Children: Zilpha[9] born 12 Apr 1875; Roy H-[9] born 11 Mar 1889; and Dana Z-[9] FORBUSH born 11 Nov 1889

Children of George Washington[-7] FORBUSH and Marina WHEELER, continued:
Surname **FORBUSH**

2964. George Melville   born 9 Jan 1857; died ____
1 married Annie Lovina NAY 30 Mar 1881 Dummer, Coos, NH
(she dau/o Ormsby Henry NAY (Anthony) and Sarah Jane HORN)
(she born 2 July 1865; died 7 July 1889) probably childbirth
Child: Melville-[9] FORBUSH born 1889; died 1889
2 married Emma Maria BYRD ca ____
Children: Zenas-[9] born 4 Jan 1897, died 23 May 1978; and Dallas-[9] FORBUSH born 28 Sep 1902,
died 28 Feb 1960; married Marjorie G S SMITH ca 1936 (she born ca 1906; diede 1991)

1575. CATHERINE[-7] **FORBUSH,** sister of above, was born 12 Apr 1822 Dummer, Coos, NH. She married John M.
BICKFORD on 13 Oct 1839 at Dummer. He was the son of Charles BICKFORD and Elizabeth/ Betsey DURGIN, and
was born 12 July 1818; died 21 Apr 1887. Catherine[-7] FORBUSH died 21 Aug 1900 at Dummer, NH.

Children of Catherine[-7] FORBUSH and John M. BICKFORD:
Surname **BICKFORD**   (all children born Dummer, Coos, NH)

2965. Cyrus E.   born 12 Aug 1840; died 17 July 1896 Lancaster, NH
2966. John Horace   born 22 Apr 1842; died 5 Oct 1862 Dummer, NH
2967. Charles N.   born 26 Aug 1844; died ____
2968. Lucinda E.   born 30 Aug 1846; died 10 Oct 1902 Percy, NH
2969. Caroline Leighton   born 2 Oct 1848; died 4 Nov 1907 Dummer, NH
2970. Runa P.   born 8 Oct 1852; died ____
2971. Hulda Miles   born 22 Mar 1855; died 8 Dec 1940
2972. Willie H.   born 19 June 1858; ____
2973. Lillie V.   born 25 Oct 1860; died ____
2974. Walter E.   born 21 Dec 1865; died 21 June 1934 Vilonia, Arkansas
married Caroline Matilda LEIGHTON ca 1895
(she born 7 Mar 1872 Milan, NH; died 17 Oct 1958 Gardiner, ME.
Children: Mona-[9] born ca 1895; and Harold Charles-[9] BICKFORD born 1898, died 1977

1576 . CAROLINE[-7] **FORBUSH,** sister of above, was born 2 Apr 1824 at Dummer, Coos, NH. She married George Hubbard
LEAVITT on 24 July 1849 at Stark, Coos, NH. He was the son of Peter LEAVITT and Sarah SPAULDING, and was born 30
Mar 1824; died ca 1905 Nebraska. Caroline[-7] FORBUSH died ca 1905.

Children of Caroline[-7] FORBUSH and George LEAVITT:
Surname **LEAVITT**   (all children born Dummer, Coos, NH)

+ **2975. ADDIE H.**   born 29 May 1850; died ____; married Orlando S. BLODGETT Mar 1867
(he s/o James S. BLODGETT and Hersey MYERS)
(he born ca 1849 IL; died 4 June 1885 WI)
2976. Etta   born 22 Oct 1852; died ____; married ____ CRAMER ca 1873
+ **2977. ELLA CLARA**   born 22 Mar 1855; died ____; married Albert SWART June 1871
(he born 4 Feb 1847 IL; died 10 Oct 1925 Chicago, IL)
2978. George Sullivan   born 12 Sep 1858; died ____ Nebraska
2979. Mary   born 15 Aug 1860; died ___ Nebraska; married ____ LLOYD 4 July 1881
2980. Jerome H (Romie)   born 12 July 1866; died 1940; married Jennie R. WEBSTER 17 Sep 1889
(she dau/o David G. WEBSTER and Harriet DANIEL)
(she born ca 1870 Denver, CO; died 1959)
Children: Milo-[9] born Aug 1891 IL; and Hazel-[9] LEAVITT born Aug 1896 IL

1577. JERUSHA[-7] **FORBUSH,** sister of above, was born ca 1826 at Dummer, Coos, NH. She married John L. BICKFORD ca
1846. He was the son of _____ BICKFORD and ____, and was born 1822; died 1866. Jerusha[-8] FORBUSH died ____.

Children of Jerusha[-7] FORBUSH and John L. BICKFORD:
Surname **BICKFORD**

2981. Mary A.   born ca 1847; died ____
2982. Erastus   born ca 1849; died 26 Jan 1925 Crystal, NH; married Elmira C. ____ ca ____
Child: Annie M-[9] BICKFORD born ca 1871

Children of Jerusha-[7] FORBUSH and John L. BICKFORD, continued:
Surname **BICKFORD**

2983. Ephraim	born ca 1851; died ____	2985. Perley	born ca 1859; died ____
2984. Maria H.	born ca 1857; died ____	2986. Adaline	born ca 1862; died ____

2987. Idella   born 3 Aug 1865; died 1 Dec 1928; married Luville JACKSON 21 Sep 1885 Stark, NH
(he s/o Warren JACKSON and Fanny I. NICHOLS)
(he born ca 1863 Stark, NH; died ____)

1578. LEVI-[7] FORBUSH, brother of above, was born 10 May 1828 at Dummer, Coos, NH. He married Mary A. JACKSON on 18 July 1856 at Stark, NH. She was the daughter of _____ JACKSON and _____, and was born Mar 1839 NH; died 1923. Levi-[7] FORBUSH died 13 June 1899 at Oshkosh, WI.

Children of Levi-[7] FORBUSH and Mary A. JACKSON:
Surname **FORBUSH**

2988. Porter	born 19 Apr 1859 Dummer, Coos, NH; died ____
2989. Isabella	born ca ____; died ____
2990. Henry	born ca ____; died ____
2991. Hortense	born 11 Aug 1863 NH; died 1911 Winnebago, WI
	married Charles A. BUCKSTAFF ca 1884
	(he s/o James R. BUCKSTAFF and Sarah B. CHASE)
	(he born 2 Mar 1858; died 1913 Oshkosh, WI)

Children: Mable-[9] born ca 1885, died 1930 ; and Milo-[9] BUCKSTAFF born ca 1889, died 1970

2992. Thirza	born Nov 1864 NH; died ____		
2993. Charles	born Oct 1869 WI; died ____	2994. Pearl A.	born July 1881 WI

Note: According to the 1900 Federal Census, Mary Forbush had 10 children – with only 4 living at that time

1579. EPHRAIM R-[7] FORBUSH, brother of above, was born 17 March 1831 at Dummer, Coos, NH. He married Louisa P. MILES ca ____. She was the daughter of Josiah MILES and Abigail ____, and was born 7 Mar 1831 Dummer, NH; died 14 June 1917.. Ephrain-[7] FORBUSH died 14 June 1917.

Children of Ephraim-[7] FORBUSH and Louisa P. MILES:
Surname **FORBUSH**

+   **2995. CLARA B.**   born ca 1859/60; died _____
married Charles Hosea WENTWORTH 28 Sep 1878 Lancaster, NH
(he s/o Joseph WENTWORTH and Lavina _____)
(he born 11 Sep 1852 Dummer, NH ; died 30 Jan 1935)

2996. Daisy M.   born 9 Oct 1870 WI ; died _____
1 married Sherman M. CARTER ca 1897   (divorced)
(he s/o Matthew CARTER and Bridget WEILER)
Child: Floyd D-[9] CARTER born ca 1901
2 married Ernest E. MUNROE 15 Sep 1926
(he s/o William MUNROE and Maria SHIPLEY)

1580. JAMES HENRY-[7] FORBUSH, half-brother of above, son of Daniel-[6] FORBUSH (James-[5]; David-[4]; Martha-[3] BOWKER; John-2; Edmund-[1]) and his second wife Betsey LEIGHTON, was born 1836, NH. He married first to Betsey Demerrit NICHOLS ca 1852. She was the daughter of Jonathan NICHOLS and Fanny LEAVITT, and was born 6 Sep 1837; died Jan 1855. He married second to Mary A. HORN(E) on 18 Aug 1861 at Dummer, Coos, NH. She was the daughter of William HORN(E) and ____, and was born ca 1845 Milan, NH; died ____. James Henry-[7] FORBUSH died 14 Feb 1910 at Dummer, NH

Child of James Henry-[7] FORBUSH and Betsey NICHOLS:
Surname **FORBUSH**

2997. Mary H.   born July 1846 Stark, NH; died ____;   married Andrew JACKSON 6 Sept 1884
(he s/o Moses JACKSON and Lucy FORBUSH)

Children of James Henry-[7] FORBUSH and Mary A. HORN:
Surname **FORBUSH**   (all children born Dummer, NH)

2998. Elmer	born ca 1863; died ____	3001. Perley	born Feb 1871; died ____
2999. Eliza	born ca 1866; died ____	3002. Nellie	born Feb 1871; died ____
3000. Llewellyn	born June 1869; died ____	3003. Willie U.	born ca 1875; died ____

1581. NANCY M-⁷ FORBUSH, sister of above, was born 25 May 1837 at Crystal, Coos, New Hampshire. She married John N. HOWLAND, as his second wife, on 11 May 1859 at Coos, NH. He was the son of Dorcas Spooner HOWLAND and Mary Ann STREETER, and was born 12 Oct 1820, and died 2 Jan 1882 Whitefield, Coos, NH. Nancy M-⁷ FORBUSH died 9 Apr 1920 at Berlin, Coos, NH.

Children of Nancy M-⁷ FORBUSH and John N. HOWLAND:
Surname **HOWLAND**   (all children born Crystal, Coos, NH)

	3004. Avilda	born 19 Feb 1860; died 20 Dec 1936 Dummer, Coos, NH
	3005. George	born 1860; died _____
	3006. Leonard W.	born 15 Aug 1862; died 18 June 1916 Berlin, Coos, NH
		married Ada M DENNIS Woodrow 26 Apr 1893 (as her 3rd husband)
		(she dau/o Silas DENNIS and Emily MASTERS/MASIO)
		(she born 6 Jan 1861; died 30 Apr 1944)
		Child: Clara M-⁹ HOWLAND born ca 1901
	Note:	She married 4th to Sherman CARTER on 22 Oct 1919; he divorced from Daisy FORBUSH (# 2996 above)
+	**3007. ALMA B.**	born 25 Apr 1865; died _____
		married Charles W. HOLT ca 1888
+	**3008. ELDIN HAZEN**	born 28 Apr 1868; died 28 Feb 1941 Dummer, Coos, NH
		married Saloma Dulcena LEIGHTON ca 1906
	3009. Fred M.	born 15 Apr 1871; died 25 May 1931
		1 married widow Sadie HALL 25 Feb 1892 Dummer, NH (her 3rd marriage)
		2 married Emma Rose WALKER 18 May 1895 Berlin, NH
		(she born Mar 1881 Milan, Coos, NH; died 1970 NH)
		(she dau/o John Henry WALKER and Abbie L. _____)
		Child: Addie Isabel-⁹ HOWLAND born Dec 1898; died Oct 1974; married Ward Burton ROUNDS ca ___; he s/o Burt Leon ROUNDS, born 7 Dec 1897 ME; died 15 Apr 1967 Berlin, Coos, NH
	3010. Edward / Myron	born 2 Dec 1874; died 15 Oct 1887 EOL
	3011. Robert C.	born 19 June 1877; died 29 Apr 1879 Crystal, Coos, NH EOL

1598. JACOB-⁷ POWERS, son of William-⁶ POWERS, II (Elizabeth-⁵ GATES; Ephraim-⁴; Mary-³ BOWKER; John-²; Edmund-¹) and Mary THOMPSON, was born 15 May 1798 at Groton, Grafton, NH. He married first to Lydia MERRIAM ca 1828 . She was the daughter of Jonathan MERRIAM and Sarah CONANT, and was born ca 1798 Ashburnham, MA; died 1829 Rutland, VT. as a result of childbirth. He poss. married second to Sarah EVERTS ca 1830. She was born ca 1811 VT; died ca 1832. He married third to Amelia CONANT ca 1833. She was the daughter of _____ CONANT and ____; and was born ca 1812 VT; died ca 1860. Jacob-⁷ POWERS died ca 1882 at Brandon, Rutland, VT.

Child of Jacob-⁷ POWERS and Lydia MERRIAM:
Surname **POWERS**

3012. William	born June 1829; died ca 1910
	married Mary E. _____ ca ____ (she born ca 1837; died 1910)
	Children: Abel Seward -⁹ POWERS born Aug 1859; and William J-⁹ POWERS born ca 1864

Children of Jacob-⁷ POWERS and Amelia CONANT:
Surname **POWERS**   (all children born Brandon, VT)

3013. Luther C.	born 1834; died ____		
3014. Ruth L.	born 1835; died 1855; married Elias Moulton SMITH ca ____		
3015. Amanda C.	born 1838; died ____	3016. Charles J.	born 1841; died ____

1625. LEONARD MOSMAN -⁷ GATES, son of Phoebe-⁶ MOSMAN (Anna D-⁵ KEYES; Martha -⁴ BOWKER; Asa-³; John-²; Edmund-¹) and Daniel GATES, was born 28 July 1810 at Gardner, MA. He married first to Martha J. LELAND on 24 Dec 1837 at Gardner. She was the daughter of Amasa LELAND and Martha SEAVER, and was born ____; died 2 Jan 1852. He married second to Eliza Ann PEABODY of Nashua, NH. ca ____. She was the daughter of _____ PEABODY and ____; and was born Aug 1827 NH; died ____. Leonard-⁷ GATES died ____. They resided Westminster, MA

Children of Leonard-⁷ GATES and Martha J. LELAND:
Surname **GATES**   (all children born Westminster, Worcester, MA)

+	**3017. EUGENE**	born 2 Jan 1839; died ____
		married Helen RAY 2/5 Sep 1862
		(she daughter of Anson RAY and Emily JACKSON) (she born 3 Apr 1845; 4 Oct 1932
	3018. Leonard	born 30 Oct 1845; died ____; removed to Marshalltown, IA

BOWKER
The Seventh American Generation

Children of Leonard⁻⁷ GATES and Eliza PEABODY:
Surname **GATES**   (all children born Westminster, MA)
    3019. Eldora J.   born 5 March 1856; died 7 Nov 1897 Fitchburg, MA
                                 married Cecil Calvin WHITNEY 10 June 1879
                                 (he s/o Calvin WHITNEY and Huldah BROWN) (he born 5 Jan 1848)
                          Child: Stanley H⁻⁹ WHITNEY born 28 Apr 1881 MA; died ____
    3020. Lauretta   born 27 Dec 1860; died ____; married Josiah MAINS 27 Jan 1895 Templeton, MA
                                 (he s/o Benjamin MAINS and Mary KNIGHT)(he born June 1846 ME; died 22 Feb 1907 MA)
                          Child: Harland Benjamin⁻⁹ MAINS born 29 Apr 1896 Fitchburg, MA; died 20 Jul 1900
    3021. Mary E.   born 2 Jan 1864; died ____; 1 married Chauncey L. SMITH 2 Jan 1882
                                 (he s/o George W. SMITH and Betsey Foster GAY)(he born 5 Mar 1860 Natick, MA)
                                 2 married E. James STEVENS 5 Nov 1892
                                 (he s/o Thomas STEVENS and Caroline Almira BAKER)
                                 (he born 5 Nov 1857 Hollis, NH; died 24 Jan 1899 Worcester, MA
                        References: The WHITNEY Genealogy – page 475; and The WHITNEY Family – pages 924-5;
                        Genealogy of the GATES Family- pages 121, 212

1627. PHEBE DIANTHA⁻⁷ GATES, sister of above, was born 23 Aug 1815 at Gardner, MA. She married Gamaliel Sawyer BEAMAN ca ____. He was the son of ____ BEAMAN and ____, and was born ca 1809; died July 1883 Fitchburg, MA. __.

Children of Phebe⁻⁷ GATES and Gamaliel BEAMAN:
Surname **BEAMAN**
+   **3022. LAURA**   born 13 Mar 1839; died ____
                         married Charles May KNOWLTON 14 Feb 1856; resided Utica, NY
                         (he s/o Walter KNOWLTON and Harriet CARTER)(he born 3 May 1835; died ____)
+   **3023. GAMALIEL**   born 4 Sep 1852; died ca 1937 Princeton, MA.
         WALDO   1 married Mary Priest STEARNS 22 Oct 1885
                         (she dau/o Albert Dinsmore STEARNS and Sarah Minerva PRIEST)
                         (she born 15 Sep 1859; died 12 June 1892)
                         2 married Eileen Marie RAND Sherman 20 June 1894
                         (she dau/o Lucius Clark RAND and Caroline Finetta SIBLEY)(she born 31 Mar 1858)

1656. ELI T.⁻⁷ RICHARDSON, son of Edward⁻⁶ RICHARDSON (Martha⁻⁵ FORBUSH; Lucy⁻⁴ BOWKER; Asa⁻³; John⁻²; Edmund⁻¹) and Cynthia ____, was born ca 1831 at Gilead, Oxford, Maine. he married Hannah Abbott TWITCHELL ca 1855. She was the daughter of Andrew TWITCHWLL and Lydia LITTLEHALE, and was born 12 July 1829 Gilead, ME; died ____.

Children of Eli T⁻⁷ RICHARDSON and Hannah TWITCHELL:
Surname **RICHARDSON**   (children born Gilead, Oxford, Maine)

    3024. Freeman   born ca 1856; died ____
+   **3025. JOHN E.**   born May 1866; died ____
                         married Elizabeth/Lizzie NOLAN 28 Nov 1894 Laconia, NH
                         (she dau/o D F NOLAN and Ellen MAHAN) (she born March 1872 MA)
    3026. George Newton   born ca 1869; died 13 Dec 1942 Derry, NH
                         married Minnie A. CUMMINGS 12 July 1901
                         (she dau/o Randall CUMMINGS and Hannah ____)
                      Child: Ruth E⁻⁹ RICHARDSON born ca 1900 ME

1661. FRANCES ADELINE⁻⁷ TUTTLE, daughter of Lucretia⁻⁶ HAPGOOD (Solomon⁻⁵; Lydia⁻⁴ BOWKER; Asa⁻³; John⁻²; Edmund-1) and Daniel TUTTLE, was born 15 Mar 1811 at Grafton, Windham, VT. She married first to Holland WHEELER on 27 Nov 1835. He was the son of ____ WHEELER and ___, and was born 3 Apr 1796 at Westmoreland, NH; died 10 Oct 1842. She married second to Edward HALL on 12 May 1846. He was the son of Atherton HALL and Olive HALLETT, and was born 20 Dec 1795; died 13 March 1889. Frances A⁻⁷ TUTTLE died 1 Feb 1905.

Children of Frances A⁻⁷ TUTTLE and Holland WHEELER:
Surname **WHEELER**
    3027. Kirke Warren.   born 15 Aug 1835 VT; died 25 June 1904
    3028. Holland, Jr.   born 19 Apr 1837; died 6 June 1902; married Sarah GREIG ca 1868

Children of Frances A-7 TUTTLE and Edward HALL:
Surname **HALL**

3029. Alfred Stevens	born 14 Apr 1850; died ___; 1 married Martha Annette HITCHCOCK 18 Oct 1876	

(she dau/o Josiah Hubbard HITCHCOCK and Martha Ann CHAMBERLIN)
(she born 3 Nov 1849; died 26 Sep 1887)
2 married Delia Rebecca RANNEY 10 Apr 1895 (she born 21 Dec 1854; died ____)
(she dau/o Henry Porteus RANNEY and Augusta HAMBLEN)

3030. Solon Goodridge   born 11 Sep 1852; died ___; married Libbie Fowler CLARKSON 23 Sep 1884
(she dau/o David CLARKSON and Jeanette CRICHTON)
(she born 2 Apr 1860 Dundee, IL; died ____)

1700. HENRY ASA-7 WHEELER, son of Asa Bowker-6 WHEELER (Asa-5; Abigail-4 BOWKER; Ezekiel-3; John-2; Edmund-1) and Persis BURKE, was born 8 Feb 1834 VT. He married Harriet Eliza WILLISTON ca 1856. She was the daughter of Josiah WILLISTON and Eliza FARNHAM, and was born 13 Dec 1835 Rockingham, VT; died 14 April 1910. Henry Asa-7 WHEELER died 22 Apr 1915 at Bennington, VT.

Children of Henry Asa-7 WHEELER and Harriet WILLISTON:
Surname **WHEELER**

+   **3031. NATHANIEL A.**   born 4 July 1869 Bellows Falls, VT; died 13 Aug 1945 Royalton, VT
married Florence F. WETHERBEE 7 June 1893 at Rockingham, VT.
(she born ca 1875; died 1921)

1705. FINETTA-7 WHEELER, daughter of Lorenzo Dow-6 WHEELER (Asa-5; Abigail-4 BOWKER; Ezekiel-3; John-2; Edmund-1) and Finetta LEWIS, was born 29 Dec 1835. She married Enoch WOOD on 12 Feb 1856. He was possibly the son of William WOOD and Rebecca BRADBURY, and was born ca 1832 England; died 27 July 1903. He was a potter, and was possibly related to the famous English potter also named Enoch WOOD. Finetta-7 WHEELER died 26 Aug 1917.

Children of Finetta-7 WHEELER and Enoch WOOD:
Surname **WOOD**

3032. Sarah Finetta   born 16 Oct 1856; died 19 Sep 1932 CT
married Charles Henry LOOMIS (as his 2nd wife) on 2 July 1879
(he born 19 June 1851; died 1 Dec 1911)
(he s/o Clark Merrick LOOMIS and Harriet B. DOWNS)

3033. Lucy E.   born ca 1862 CT; died ____; married Henry W. RUSSELL ca ____
3034. Enoch Leroy   born ca 1877 NJ; died 1 Aug 1902

1728. LUCY JANETTE-7 GARFIELD, daughter of Lucinda-6 LUND (Willard-5; Phineas-4; Thomas-3; Elizabeth-2 BOWKER; Edmund-1) and Ira GARFIELD, was born 5 May 1841 VT. She married John L. Mc CULLOCH 21 Dec 1858. He was the son of ____ MC CULLOCH and ____, and was born ca ____; died ____. Lucy Janette-7 GARFIELD died 15 Nov 1901 Kent, Oregon.

Children of Lucy Janette-7 GARFIELD and John MC CULLOCH :
Surname **MC CULLOCH**

3035. .Mary Adelle   born 27 March 1860 IA; died 26 Dec 1863 IA   EOL
3036. Alice Lucinda   born ca 1862; died 28 Dec 1863 IA   EOL
3037. Alice Adella   born 7 April 1865 Iowa City, IA; died 12 Dec 1940 MN
married George Isaac DAILY
3038. Mary Lucinda   born 20 Feb 1868 IA; died 13 May 1955 MN
married William L. YARWOOD ca ____
Children : Lucy-9 born ca 1904; and Ray-9 YARWOOD born ca 1906
3039. William Henry   born 23 May 1870 Calmar, IA; died 18 Mar 1951
3040. Daisy Luella   born 24 Feb 1876; died ____; married Horace Hawley RICHARDSON
Children: Janette-9 born ca 1904 OR; Lillian-9 born ca 1905 OR; Earl W-9 born ca 1908 OR, died 31 Dec 1981
Eugene , OR; and Roy-9 RICHARDSON born ca 1909 MN.

1735. ABIJAH-7 SPAULDING. son of Samuel-6 SPAULDING (Samuel-5; Henry-4; Elizabeth-3 LUND; Edmund-2,1 BOWKER) and _____, was born 18 March 1787 at Merrimack, NH. He married Hannah Goodrich EASTMAN September 1814. She was the daughter of Nicholas EASTMAN and Olive BARNES, and was born 4 Sept 1792 at Francestown, NH; died 6 April 1877 at Nashua, NH. Abijah-7 SPAULDING died 21 Sep 1867 at Nashua, NH.

Children of Abijah[7] SPAULDING and Hannah EASTMAN:
Surname **SPAULDING**

3041. Eleanor Meriel	born 15 Nov 1816 Litchfield,NH ; died ____
3042. Sarah Heald	born 2 Sep 1818 Merrimack, NH
	married William STANLEY 26 Nov 1835
	(he born 1805 Oshkosh, WI; died _____)
3043. Samuel Jones	born 11 Dec 1820 Lyndeborough, NH; died ____
3044. Elizabeth Goodrich	born 27 March 1824 Lyndeborough, NH; died 31 Jan 1896 St. Louis, MO
	married Rogers Moses SARGENT ca ____
	(he born 7 Sep 1824 Barton, VT)
3045. Mary Bowers	born 16 June 1827 Nashua, NH; married William WHEELER ca
	(he born ca 1815; died _____)
3046. Josiah	born 5 July 1829 Nashua, NH; died ____
3047. Gershom	born 1 Feb 1831 Nashua, NH; died ____

1739. IRA[7] **SPAULDING,** brother of above, was born 30 Nov 1794 at Merrimack, NH. He married first to Nancy MOORE on 17 May 1821. She was the daughter of ____MOORE and ___ of Bedford, NH, and was born 23 Oct 1794; died 7 April 1829. He married second to Eliza Jane ATWOOD on 7 May 1829. She was the daughter of ____ ATWOOD and ____,and was born 25 June 1805 Merrimack, NH; died 1856 Beloit, WI. Ira-[7] SPAULDING died 18 June 1855.

Children of Ira-[7] SPAULDING and Eliza ATWOOD:
Surname **SPAULDING**

3048. Ira	born 8 May 1822 Bedford, NH; died 30 July 1832 Bedford	
3049. William Moore	born 10 Nov 1823 Merrimack; died _____	
3050. Ephraim Heald	born 7 Dec 1824; died 20 Feb 1890	EOL
3051. Nancy Isabella	born 28 Jan 1827; died ____ ; married William KIMBALL 8 May 1851	
3052. Eliza Jane	born ____; died young	
3053. George Washington	born ca ____; died young	
3054. George Franklin	born 12 Feb 1833 Merrimack, NH; died 13 Dec 1912 Merrimack, NH	
3055. Betsey Chandler	born ca 1836; died ____; married John Gardner KIMBALL 19 Nov 1857	
3056. Ellen Maria	born 5 May 1840 Merrimack, NH ; died 28 Sept 1925	
	married Albert GAY 26 Nov 1863 Boston , MA	
	(he s/o Timothy Gay and Mehitabel PEABODY)	
	(he born 5 Aug 1822 Francestown, NH; died 20 July 1902)	

Children: Charles Albert[9] born 30 Apr 1865, married Edna Moore TAFT; Alice Marion-[9] born 2 Mar 1867; and Helen F[9] GAY born 8 Jan 1871 Boston, MA.

3057. Catherina Mears	born ca 1837/38 Merrimack, NH; died ___
	married Chauncey KEELER/KULER ca 1860
3058. Henry Harrison	born ca ___; died young

1746. OLIVER[7] **SPAULDING, Jr.,** son of Oliver[6] SPAULDING (Samuel[5]; Henry[4]; Elizabeth-[3] LUND; Edmund-[2,1] BOWKER) and _____, was born 23 May 1791 at Merrimack, NH. he married Asenath DANFORTH on 28 Dec 1817 at Merrimack. She was the daughter of Solomon DANFORTH and ____ , and was born ca 1796; died ____. Oliver-[7] SPAULDING died ca 1875.

Children of Oliver-[7] SPAULDING, Jr. and Asenath DANFORTH:
Surname **SPAULDING**

3059. Abigail Nourse	born 15 Dec 1817; died ____; married William T. PARKER 1 Aug 1846	
3060. John Lund	born 19 Jan 1821; died ____	
3061. Hosea Ballou	born 22 Serp 1824 Merrimack, NH; died 18 Apr 1894 Somerville, MA	
	married Dorcas MARSHALL 10 June 1848	
	(she born 5 Dec 1820 Turnbridge, VT; died ____)	
3062. Oliver	born 11 Jan 1828; died 28 Jan 1828	EOL

1747. ISAAC[7] **SPAULDING,** son of Isaac[6] SPAULDING (Samuel[5]; Henry[4]; Elizabeth[3] LUND; Edmund-[2,1] BOWKER) and _____, was born 1 Feb 1796 at New Ipswich, NH. He married Lucy KENDALL on 1 May 1828. She was the daughter of Nathan KENDALL of Amherst, NH and _____, and was born 13 Dec 1796; died ____. Isaac-[7] SPAULDING died 14 May 1876. At the time of his death he was said to be the wealthiest man in the state.

Children of Isaac[-7] SPAULDING and Lucy KENDALL:
Surname **SPAULDING**

3063. Edward Francis	born 5 May 1831; died 30 Aug 1837	EOL
3064. Isaac Henry	born 13 May 1840; died 30 Aug 1844	EOL

1748. MOSES[-7] SPAULDING, brother of above, was born 10 March 1797 at Ipswich, NH. He married Anna Hunt KIMBALL on 29 May 1823. She was the daughter of John KIMBALL of Wilton, NH. and ____, and was born 4 Aug 1800 Temple, NH; died 16 May 1864. He was a tanner, and died ca 1879.

Children of Moses-[7] SPAULDING and Anna KIMBALL:
Surname **SPAULDING**

3065. Edward Henry	born 12 March 1825; died ____; 1 married Lucy Ann FLETCHER ca ____
	2 married Anna/Emma HOLT of Lyndeborough, NH
3066. Isaac Kimball	born 21 July 1826; died ____
3067. William Ritter	born 8 April 1828; died ____; married Mary A. HAM
3068. John Augustine	born 29 May 1837; died ____
	1 married Josephine Estelle EASTMAN (she dau/o Joseph EASTMAN and Abigail ___)
	2 married Martha LEARNED Noyes ca ____
	(she dau/o Dr. LEARNED of Fall River, MA and _____)

1749. CHARLES[-7] SPAULDING, brother of above, was born 4 Nov 1798. He married Lydia Jones BURNS on 25 Dec 1827. She was the daughter of Samuel BURNS and ____ of Milford, NH and was born 13 Jan 1806; died 23 March 1861. Charles[-7] SPAULDING died 15 Feb 1880.

Children of Charles-[7] SPAULDING and Lydia BURNS:
Surname **SPAULDING**

3069. Harriet	born 18 Feb 1829; died ____; married Corydon D. KEYES ca ____ NH
3070. Abby Frances	born 28 Aug 1834; died ____; married Charles H. WHITE ca ___, NH
3071. Elias Herrick	born 5 July 1836; died _____ EOL
3072. Charles Carroll	born 4 May 1838; died ____; married Emma Caroline PARKHURST ca ____
	(she dau/o Jonathan PARKHURST and Sarah W. ____)
3073. Lucy Kimball	born 12 March 1840; died ____; married Gardner BLANCHARD ca _____
3074. Mary Ritter	born 3 Jan 1842; died ____; married Asa BLANCHARD of Lyndeboro, NH ca ____

1763. ASA[-7] SPAULDING, son of Asa[-6] SPAULDING (Samuel-[5]; Henry[-4]; Elizabeth[-3] LUND; Edmund-[2,1] BOWKER) and _____, was born 21 April 1794 at Merrimack, NH. He married Sarah GILMORE ca ____. She was the daughter of ____ GILMORE and ___, and was born ca 1797; died ____. Asa-[7] SPAULDING died ____.

Children of Asa-[7] SPAULDING and Sarah GILMORE:
Surname **SPAULDING**

3075. Samuel	born March 1818 Merrimack, NH; died 19 Sep 1894 Danvers, MA
	married Julia S. CROSS 7 Nov 1870 Lawrence, MA
	Children: Samuel Albert-[9] born ca 1873; Chester Cross-[9] born ca 1877; and Julia Stinson-[9] SPAULDING born ca 1878
3076. Joanna	born 1 May 1819; died ____; married William LYON 8 Nov 1848 Danvers, MA
3077. Steven	born ca 1820; died 20 July 1838
3078. Asa Langdon	born 27 Dec 1821 Merrimack, NH; died ____;
	married Martha E. WALLACE 17 Oct 1848
	(she born 3 Apr 1829; died 19 Aug 1850)
	Child: Allen Francis-[9] SPAULDING born ca ____
3079. Albert Jefferson	born 5 Oct 1824 Merrimack, NH; died 14 Dec 1882
	married Sarah DODGE 7 Oct 1850
	Children: Abel Dodge-[9] born ca 1851; and Caroline-[9] SPAULDING born ca 1855

1768. CYNTHIA[-7] SPAULDING, sister of above, was born 3 March 1804. She married Gilbert S. COLBURN/COBURN ca 13 Nov 1828. He was the son of Gilbert COLBURN/COBURN and Cynthia ____, and was born ca 1797 Hillsborough, NH; died ____. Cynthia-[7] SPAULDING died ____.

Children of Cynthia-7 SPAULDING and Gilbert COLBURN/COBURN:
Surname **COLBURN/COBURN**

3080. Gilbert S.	born ca 1830 NH; died ____	3085. Eliza C.H.	born ca 1846 NH; died ____
3081. Maria	born ca 1832 NH; died ____	3086. Silas R.	born ca 1849 NH; died ____
3082. George D.	born ca 1839 NH; died ____	3087. Flora M.	born ca 1856 NH; died ____
3083. Clara J.	born ca 1840 NH; died ____		
3084. Emma D.	born ca 1844 NH; died ____		

1773. MARY-7 FLETCHER, daughter of Sherebiah-6 FLETCHER (Sarah-5 SPAULDING;Henry-4; Elizabeth-3 LUND; Edmund-2,1 BOWKER) and Martha ELLENWOOD, was born ____. VT. She married David IRWIN on 1Aug 1810. He was the son of John IRWIN and ___, and was born 1 July 1778 Ireland; died 22 March 1848 OH. Mary-7 FLETCHER died 6 June 1846.

Children of Mary-7 FLETCHER and David IRWIN:
Surname **IRWIN**

3088. Mary Jane	born 2 Aug 1811; died 12 July 1885
3089. Lucinda	born 23 May 1814; died ____; married _____ CLARK
3090. James F.	born 24 Feb 1817; died 23 July 1892
3091. John	born 8 Aug 1819
3092. David	born 9 Sept 1822; died 3 May 1894
3093. Ann	born 25 Nov 1824; died 28 Nov 1886 KY; married Henry HARTING 8 Jan 1848
3094. Edward Scull	born 4 June 1827; died 20 Feb 1892; married _?__ 2 Apr 1874
3095. Kate	born 17 Feb 1834; died ____; married Edward N. RIDGEWAY 19 Sept 1894

1794. SOLOMON-7 SPAULDING, son of Solomon-6 SPAULDING (Daniel-5; Henry-4; Elizabeth-3 LUND; Edmund-2,1 BOWKER) and _____, was born 20 July 1811 at Merrimack, NH. He married Sarah Darling EDSON on 16 Feb 1834. She was the daughter of Asa EDSON and Theodosia ____, and was born 1 March 1811 at Springfield, VT; died 25 June 1883.

Children of Solomon-7 SPAULDING and Sarah EDSON
Surname **SPAULDING**   (all children born Nashua, NH)

3096. Solomon Warren	born 13 May 1837; died ____		
3097. John Andrew	born 24 July 1841; died ____		
3098. Charles Warren	born 11 June 1843; died ____		
3099. Sarah Greeley	born 19 Sep 1845; died ____; married John Jacob WHITTEMORE ca ____		
3100. Mary Elizabeth	born 31 May 1847; died ____		
3101. Edward Clarence	born 30 Aug 1851; died ____	3102. Everett Sargent	born 30 Aug 1851

1810. MORRIS SMITH-7 LOVEWELL, son of Hephzibah-6 LOVEWELL (John-5 LOVEWELL; Rachel-4 LUND; William-3; Elizabeth-2 BOWKER; Edmund-1) and Laban LASELL/LAZELL, was born 5 May 1822 at St. Albans, Franklin, Vermont. He married Sarah Ann SKINNER on 27 Nov 1845 at St. Albans. She was the daughter of Alvah SKINNER and Betsey SANBORN, and was born 16 Jan 1824 St. Albans, VT; died 21 April 1901 at Ellenburg, Clinton, NY. Smith-7 LOVEWELL died 4 Nov 1878 at Ellenburg, NY.

Children of Smith-7 LOVEWELL and Sarah SKINNER:
Surname **LOVEWELL**   (all children, except Sarah, were born St. Albans, VT)

3103. Merrill Gilbert	born 10 Jan 1847; died 17 Jan 1917 Moers, Clinton, NY
	married Sarah Marie WHITE 30 Jan 1872
3104. Haskell Smith	born 15 Aug 1848/49; died 27 Sep 1936; married Sarah Jane SARGENT 13 Sep 1870
3105. Loren Marcellus	born 12 Apr 1850; died ____; married Sadie D. ____; resided CA
3106. Marshall Milo	born 7 June 1852; died 3 June 1934 Ellenburg, NY
3107. Frederick Alfonzo	born ca 1854; died ____; married Ellen "Nellie" DUGAN ca 1883
3108. Alvah S.	born 26 Oct 1856; died 8 Jan 1917
	married Alice Elvira NORTON 1 Jan 1885 Lodi, CA
3109. Henry Robert	born 2 July 1858; died ___(living 1930) buried Ellenburg, NY
	married Gertrude M. WELSH ca 1890
3110. Erastus Perkins	born 7 May 1860; died ____; married Hattie Belle PAUL ca 1883
	(she born Jan 1861 IA; died ca 1959)
3111. Sarah Jane	born 13 Dec 1862 Ellenburg, NY; died 21 Feb 1930
	married George Clement WHITE ca 1883 (he born 31 Jan 1857 NY; died 4 July 1933)

1818. ALBERT GALLATIN[7] UNDERWOOD, son of Joseph Hall-[6] UNDERWOOD (Thomas-[5]; Mary-[4] LUND; William-[3]; Elizabeth-[2] BOWKER; Edmund-[1]) and Jane AIKEN, was born 16 Sept 1831 at Fayette, ME. He married Eliza TUCK on 6 Nov 1856. She was the daughter of Samuel TUCK and Didamia STIMPSON, and was born 23 Aug 1834; died ____. Albert-[7] UNDERWOOD died 21 July 1906.

Children of Albert Gallatin-[7] UNDERWOOD and Eliza TUCK:
Surname **UNDERWOOD**

3112. William Parker	born 9 Aug 1857; died 2 July 1899; married Annabel MILLER 17 Nov 1886		
	(she dau/o Wallis MILLER and Annie _____)		EOL
3113. Albert Walter	born 7 Sept 1860		
3114. Clara Alberta	31 Jan 1863	3115. Jane Aiken	born 22 Dec 1864

1824. THOMAS UNDERWOOD[7] GAGE, son of Sally-[6] UNDERWOOD (Thomas-[5;] Mary-[4] LUND; William-[3]; Elizabeth-[2] BOWKER; Edmund-[1]) and Isaac GAGE, was born 30 Sept 1819. He married Dolly Adeline FRENCH on 12 June 1845. She was the daughter of Ebenezer FRENCH and Rhoda COBURN, and was born 26 Jan 1826; died 8 Feb 1896. Thomas-[7] GAGE died 20 Jan 1867 NH.

Children of Thomas Underwood-[7] GAGE and Dolly FRENCH:
Surname **GAGE**

3116. Eugene French	born 15 Dec 1850 NH; died 20 March 1885 NH
3117. Edward A.	born 2 Jan 1854 NH; died 9 March 1939 MA
3118. Clara E.	born ca 1860; died ca 1880

1841. LUCY[7] TOWNSEND, daughter of Reuben-[6] TOWNSEND (Margaret-[5] METCALF; Margaret-[4] SHATTUCK; Margaret-[3] LUND; Edward-[2,1] BOWKER) and Sultina HILL, was born 20 July 1818. She married Samuel Sawin COOLIDGE on 24 Aug 1842. He was the son of James COOLIDGE and Annis SAWIN, and was born 24 Aug 1813 Gardner, MA; died ____ VT. Lucy-[7] TOWNSEND died ____.

Children of Lucy-[7] TOWNSEND and Samuel COOLIDGE:
Surname **COOLIDGE**

3119. Arthur	born ca 1845 MA; died ____
3120. Clement	born ca 1849 Ma; died ____

1847. LYMAN[7] LAWS, son of David-[6] LAWS (Thankful-[5] METCALF; Margaret-[4] SHATTUCK; Margaret-[3] LUND; Edmund-[2,1] BOWKER) and Nancy WILDER, was born 30 Sept 1830. He married Eliza Jane FAY ca ____. She was the daughter of ____ FAY and ____, and was born ____; died ___. They resided Boston, MA. Lyman-[7] LAWS died 16 June 1890.

Children of Lyman-[7] LAWS and Eliza FAY:
Surname **LAWS**

3121. David Fay	born 8 Jan 1862; died ca 1910 Spokane, WA
	married Halycon B. " Hallie " SODEN 16 Sept 1891
	Children: Katheryn-[9] born ca ___ ; and Jane Soden-[9] LAWS born ca ____

1853. HIRAM[7] LAWS, son of James Hervey-[6] LAWS (Thankful-[5] METCALF; Margaret-[4] SHATTUCK; Margaret-[3] LUND; Edmund-[2,1] BOWKER) and Julia HASTINGS, was born 27 June 1844 MA. He married Mary Elizabeth DUTTON on 15 Oct 1871. She was the daughter of Hildreth P. DUTTON and Abigail ____, and was born 15 Oct 1849; died ____. Hiram-[7] LAWS died 17 May 1913. They resided Bedford, MA.

Children of Hiram-[7] LAWS and Mary Elizabeth DUTTON:
Surname **LAWS**

3122. Eugene Hiram	born 20 Sept 1873 MA; died _____; graduate of MIT 1896
3123. Frederick Adams	born 4 April 1876 MA; died ____
3124. Julia Ellen	born 8 Jan 1886; died ____; married Kenneth ROGERS 3 May 1883

1859. NANCY[7] WITHERELL, daughter of Roxanna-[6] SIMPSON (Sarah-[5] SHATTUCK; Job-[4]; Mary-[3] LUND; Edmund-[2;1] BOWKER) and John Longley WITHERELL, was born 7 Apr 1800 Groton, MA. She married Alexander BUZZELL on 31 Dec 1818 at Winslow, Kennebec, Maine. Nancy-[7] WITHERELL died 7 Nov 1884.

Children of Nancy[7] WITHERELL and Alexander BUZZELL:
Surname **BUZZELL**

3125. Benjamin Franklin	born ca 1825; died 1897	3131. Ezekiel	born ca 1840; died 1841	EOL
3126. John L.	born ca 1826; died 1847	3132. Loezar O.	born ca 1842; died 1853	EOL
3127. Charles Carlton	born ca 1828; died 1881	3133. Louisa O.	born ca 1843; died 1876	
3128. Harriet	born ca 1831; died ____	3134. George W.	born ca 1844; died 1922	
3129. Hannah	born ca 1833; died 1909	3135. Joseph L	born ca 1846; died 1926	
3130. Roxanna	born ca 1837; died 1921	3136. John W.	born ca 1850; died 1881	

1864. LIBERTY SHATTUCK[7] FOSS, half brother of above, son of Roxanna[6] SIMPSON, and her second husband Joseph FOSS, Jr. was born May 1823 at Clinton, Kennebec, Maine. He married first to Tenny BUTTERFIELD on 5 Dec 1842. She was the daughter of William BUTTERFIELD and Tenny LOVELAND, and was born 3 Feb 1828 Weston, ME; died 1863 at Northport, Waupaca, WI.. He married second to Abbie FARNHAM on 8 Dec 1868. She was the daughter of ____ FARNHAM and _____; and was born ____, died ____. Liberty[7] FOSS died 30 Apr 1903/10 at Danforth, Maine.

Children of Liberty[7] FOSS and Tenny BUTTERFIELD:
Surname **FOSS**

3137 . Matilda	born June 1844 ME; died ____ (single 1900)		
3138. Ellen	born ca 1845; died ____		
3139. John R.	born ca 1847; died ____		
3140. Daniel H.	born ca 1849; died ____	3142. Orington	born ca 1854; died ____
3141. Georgianna	born ca 1852; died ____	3143. Harriet	born ca 1856; died ____
		3144. Betsey	born ca 1858; died ____

1872. ANDREW JACKSON[7] SIMPSON, son of Daniel[6] SIMPSON (Sarah[5] SHATTUCK; Job[4]; Margaret[3] LUND; Edmund[2;1] BOWKER) and Harriet STIMPSON, was born 20 July 1834. He married first to Clara A. MASON Holt 24 Apr 1858. She was the daughter of Ezekiel MASON and Nancy ____, and was born ca 1830; died 12 July 1877 Worcester, MA. He married second to Zurella Jane RICHARDSON ca _____. She was the daughter of ____ RICHARDSON and ____; and was born 16 June 1843; died 30 Apr 1929 OH. Andrew Jackson[7] SIMPSON died 23 Apr 1915 OH.

Children of Andrew J[7] SIMPSON and Clara MASON;
Surname **SIMPSON**

3145. Harriet R.	born ca 1862; died ____	3147. Eliza	born ca 1875; died ____
3146. Delia	born ca 1873; died ____		

Children of Andrew J[7] SIMPSON and Zurella RICHARDSON:
Surname **SIMPSON**

3148. Daniel	born ca 1878; died ____
3149. Caroline " Carrie "	born Aug 1879; died 6 Sep 1936 San Francisco, CA
	married Ernest L. JEFFRIES May 1878 OH
	Children: Clara L-[9] born 1906; Augusta O-[9] born ca 1909 OH; and Vivian Jean-[9] JEFFRIES born 12 Mar 1918 OH; died 5 Dec 2001 OH, married Irvin K. SPANGLER
3150. Henrietta " Etta "	born 20 Nov 1882; died 2 June 1936 OH; married John A. COATE ca ____

1993. GEORGE STEARNS[7] BOWKER, son of Ira[6] BOWKER (Edmund[5]; Micah[4]; Edmund[3]; John[2]; Edmund[1]) and Julia EVERETT, was born 2 June 1818 at Hopkinton, MA. He married Chloe Ann SAUNDERS on 28 Nov 1838. She was the daughter of Nathaniel SAUNDERS of Milford, MA and Hannah HAWKS; and was born ca 1819; died 30 Jan 1892. George S[7] died ___.

Child of George[7] BOWKER and Chloe SAUNDERS:
Surname **BOWKER**

+ **3151. IRA EVERETT**	born 8 Dec 1840; died 21 Aug 1901 Natick, MA
	married Theoda BACON of Natick, MA on 19 March 1863
3152. George W.	born 31 Aug 1850; died 24 Oct 1851

2004. SULLIVAN[7] BOWKER, son of William[6] BOWKER (Asa[5]; Samuel[4]; Edmund[3;2;1]) and Sally HARWOOD, was born 28 Mar 1808 MA. He married Eunice ADAMS 11 Oct 1835 at Winchendon, Worcester, MA. She was the daughter of Benjamin ADAMS and Chloe ALGER , and was born 22 Mar 1818; died 6 Oct 1895 Winchendon. Sullivan[7] BOWKER died 11 Dec 1870 Winchendon.

Children of Sullivan-[7] BOWKER and Eunice ADAMS:
Surname **BOWKER**

	3153. Laura	born ca 1837; died 1838	EOL
+	**3154. JOSEPH**	born Mar 1841; died 2 April 1908; 1 married Evelyn V. SLEEPER 30 Mar 1864 MA	
		(she born ca 1841; died before 1874)	
		2 married Frances Alzina BARNARD Newell 12 Apr 1874 Cavendish, Windsor, VT	
		(she born ca 150 Cavendish, VT; died 19 Dec 1912 Chester, Windsor, VT)	
	3155. William James	born 1 April 1845; died 9 Nov 1931; married Ann Elizabeth HICKS	
		(she born ca 1850; died 1936)	

Child: Fred-[9] born ca 1887, died 1929; and Clarence-[9] BOWKER born 1899

	3156. Benjamin	born ca 1848; died 1849	EOL
	3157. Chloe Ann	born 14 Sep 1855; died ____; married Clarence E. JACKSON 1 Nov 1872 Winchendon	
+	**3158. MARCELLUS SCOTT**	born Oct 1859; died 16 Oct 1933 Gardner, MA	
		married Hattie M. TATRO 4 July 1882	
		(she dau/o Charles TATRO and Orilla BURBY)	
		(she born 8/11 June 1864 Winchendon; died 20 May 1940 Gardner, MA)	

2006. LUTHER-[7] BOWKER, Jr., son of Luther-[6] BOWKER (Asa-[5]; Samuel-[4]; Edmund-[3; 2;1]) and Betsey WALKER, was born 22 Jan 1826. He married Charlotte Newton MAYNARD on 2 Sep 1850. She was the daughter of Oren MAYNARD and Huldah ALGER; and was born 3 Sep 1834 Templeton, MA; died 3 July 1888 Springfield, VT. Luther-[7] BOWKER, Jr. died 1 Feb 1884 Royalston, MA

Children of Luther-[7] BOWKER, Jr. and Charlotte MAYNARD:
Surname **BOWKER**

	3159. Cora H.	born ca 1852; died ____; married Charles H. EVANS 7 Dec 1874 Royalston, MA
+	**3160. EDWIN LUTHER**	born 11 Dec 1854; died 18 July 1928
		1 married Lucy F. WOOD 18 Feb 1882
		(she dau/o George WOOD and Smith _____)
		2 married Mary E. DARRAH 28 May 1892
		(she born 5 Jan 1864 New Brunswick, Canada; died 28 May 1918)
	3161. Albert M.	born ca 1859; died ____; married Kate S. BISHOP 5 Feb 1881
		(she dau/o Franklin BISHOP and Kate DOUGHERTY)

Child: Cola L-[9] BOWKER born Aug 1881

2013. DAVID-[7] WYMAN, son of Hannah-[6] BOWKER (Asa-[5]; Samuel-[4]; Edmund-[3,2,1]) and Silas WYMAN, was born 14 Nov 1812 at Winchendon, Worcester, MA. He married Lucinda OLIN ca 1840. She was the daughter of Reuben OLIN and Hannah NICHOLS; and was born June 1820 Guilford, VT; died 11 July 1886 Eau Claire, Wisconsin. David-[7] died 12 Jan 1883 at Eau Claire, WI.

Children of of David-[7] WYMAN and Lucinda OLIN:
Surname **WYMAN**

	3162. David Earl	born ____; died ____
	3163. Milo Barron, Sr.	born 8 June 1842 Meredith, NY; died 3 Dec 1906 WI
		married Martha E. KERSHNER 19 Sept 1869 Eau Claire, WI
		(she born 2 Sept 1843 NY; died 9 July 1940 Lewiston, Maine)

Children: Milo-[9] Jr. born 1871, died 1871; and Anna Main-[9] WYMAN born 16 June 1872; died Oct 1969 MA; married Rev Arthur Cramp KEMPTON 29 Dec 1897 Eau Claire, WI

+	**3164. ASIGAL D.**	born 31 May 1844 Meredith, NY; died 8 July1911WI; Civil War veteran
		married Agnes Jane " Jennie " HOBBS 11 Sept 1867
		(she dau/o John HOBBS and Georgiana WALL)
	3165. Alice Fredonia	born ca 1852 Eau Claire, WI; died ____
	3166. George Milton	born ca 1855 Eau Claire, WI; died ____; married Ella HODGE ca _____

2028. JAMES MADISON-[7] BOWKER, son of Abiather-[6] BOWKER, Jr. (Abiather-[5]; Samuel-[4]; Edmund-[3; 2; 1]) and Polly FUZZE, was born 21 Dec 1829 at Hopkinton, MA. He married Martha J. NEWTON on 3 July 1862. She was the daughter of Benjamin NEWTON and Lucy ____, and was born ca 1845; died ____. James Madison-[7] BOWKER died 25 March 1894 at Upton, MA.

BOWKER
The Seventh American Generation

Children of James Madison-⁷ BOWKER and Martha J. NEWTON:
Surname **BOWKER**

	3167. William A " Willie"	born ca 1863; died ____; married Mary HOMER ca ___ (she born ca 1855)
+	**3168. STONEWALL JACKSON**	born 11 Jan 1863/64; died 11 June 1945 Milford, MA married Cora Lucy YOUNG 29 Sep 1886/87 (she dau/o Harrison B. YOUNG and Mary J WHITE) (she born ca 1866/67 VT)
	3169. Antonio Abiather	born 22 Mar 1865; died 13 Sep 1946; married Gertrude C. SADLER 30 Apr 1891 (she dau/o Henry SADLER and Laura A. COPELAND) (she born Feb 1868 CT; died 30 Apr 1891 Upton, MA)
	3170. Martha Edna	born 17 Nov 1866 Upton, MA; died ____ married Perley Winslow ROCKWOOD 1 Apr 1896 (he born 6 June 1865 Upton, MA) (he s/o Pardius N. ROCKWOOD and Susan Ann G. TAYLOR)
	3171. John Leavitt	born 20 Mar 1868; died ____; married Mary ____ ca ____ Children: Martha-⁹ born ca 1897 MA; and Mary-⁹ BOWKER born ca 1900
	3172. Dwight Russell	born 19 July 1873; died ___; married Mary G BORDEN 6 July 1903 Boston, MA (she born ca 1865-7 CT)(she dau/o Edward P. BORDEN and Jennie NICHOLS)

2029. LOWELL LELAND-⁷ FROST, son of Harriet-⁶ BOWKER (Abiather-⁵ BOWKER; Samuel-⁴; Edmund-³ ;² ;¹) and Leland FROST, was born 2 July 1799 at Hopkinton, Middlesex, MA. He married first to Sophrona CHASE on 12 May 1850 at Bath, NH. She was the daughter of ___ CHASE and ___; and was born ca 1825 VT; died ___. He married second to Anna Maria JACOBS ca 1887 CA. She was the daughter of ____ JACOBS and ____; and was born 27 Jan 1839 at Woodstock, New Brunswick, Canada; died 16 Dec 1928 Willows, Glen, California. Lowell Leland-⁷ FROST died 3 Jan 1899 at Susanville, Lassen, CA.

Child of Lowell Leland-⁷ FROST and Anna Maria JACOBS:
Surname **FROST**

+	**3173. LOWELLA LELAND**	born 9 Feb 1888 CA; died 23 Dec 1948 CA.(from burns suffered in a house fire) 1 married 1 married Frank Wilbert HUTCHISON ca 1901 (he born ca 1874) 2 married George McLeod CARR 18 May 1919) (he born 7 Mar 1882 Gordon, Berwickshire, England; died 4 June 1977 Chico, CA (he s/o Thomas CARR and Margaret STOUT)

2034. AARON BOWKER-⁷ WHEELOCK, son of Charlotte-⁶ BOWKER (John-⁵; Uriah-⁴; Edmund-³; John-²; Edmund-¹) and Ephraim WHEELOCK, was born 21 Oct 1826 MA. He married Mrs. Ruth CONVERSE Sibley on 17 Nov 1851 at Spencer, MA. She was the daughter of Willard-⁷ CONVERSE and Sarah ____, and was born 10 Aug 1824 Spencer, MA; died there 4 Oct 1883. Aaron Bowker-⁷ WHEELOCK died 20 Oct 1909, and is buried at Charlton, MA.

Children of Aaron B-⁷ WHEELOCK and Ruth CONVERSE Sibley:
Surname **WHEELOCK**

	3174. Edward Aaron	born 17 July 1852 Spencer, MA; died 20 Oct 1909; an undertaker (funeral director) married Ida L. MOREY ca 1876 (she dau/o Edwin MOREY and Lucinda ALLEN) (she born Jan 1860 MA; died 8 July 1917 Oxford, MA) Child: Ethel Ruth-⁹ WHEELOCK born 19 Sep 1889; married Harry B. TUCK 19 Oct 1908 (he s/o Ara J. TUCK and Lillian C. LAMB)
+	**3175. ADA SOPHIA** " Addie "	born 8 Sep 1854 Spencer, MA; died _____ married Frank Adelbert RICE 10 June 1875 Spencer, MA (he s/o Henry T. RICE and Elizabeth A. ____) (he born ca 1855 Walpole, MA)

2035. ALMIRA E-⁷ BOWKER, daughter of Uriah-⁶ BOWKER (Elijah-⁵; Uriah-⁴; Edmund-³; John-²; Edmund-¹) and Lois EAMES, was born 19 Dec 1822 Milford, Worcester, MA. She married Amasa-⁸ CHAPIN 30 Aug 1845 Milford. He was the son of Captain Rufus CHAPIN and Lydia TUFTS, and was born 28 May 1821 Milford; died ____. Almira E-⁷ BOWKER died 23 April 1859 Chicago, IL. Buried Hopkinton, MA.

Children of Almira E-⁷ BOWKER and Amasa CHAPIN:
Surname **CHAPIN**   Reference: History of the Town of Milford, Worcester County, MA

	3176. Edgar H.	born 11 Oct 1847; died ____; resided Chicago, IL
	3177. Annie E.	born 6 Oct 1849 Cincinnati, OH; died 10 Nov 1866 Chicago, IL EOL
	3178. Mary C.	born 31 Mar 1854 Hopkinton, MA; died ____ married Nelson L. LITTEN ca ____ Chicago, IL Children: Annie-⁹; Mira L-⁹; and Gertrude-⁹ LITTEN

2038. CHARLES[-7] **BOWKER**, brother of above, was born 10 Feb 1833 Hopkinton, MA. He married first to Helen R. STACY 25 Feb 1858. She was the daughter of Abel STACY and ____ of Concord, VT; and was born ___; died 26 July 1859. He married second to Elvira PHIPPS of Hopkinton on 22 Feb 1863. She was the daughter of Sylvester PHIPPS and ____; and was born ____; died ____. Charles[-7] BOWKER died ____.

Child of Charles-[7] BOWKER and Helen STACY:
Surname **BOWKER**

3179. Irving	born 23 Dec 1858; died 5 Sept 1859		EOL

Children of Charles[-7] BOWKER and Elvira PHIPPS:
Surname **BOWKER**   (children all born Hopkinton, MA)

3180. Frank P.	born 19 Aug 1863	3182. Lovett H.	born 18 Feb 1873; died 6 Nov 1876
3181. Atherton B.	born 8 May 1865; died 10 Nov 1876		

2051. MARILLA F[-7] **PHIPPS**, daughter of Sarah-[6] BOWKER (Elijah-[5;] Uriah-[4]; Edmund-[3]; John-[2]; Edmund-[1]) and Dr. William Adams PHIPPS, was born 29 Aug 1835. She married John Quincy ADAMS on 26 Jan 1859. He was the son of John ADAMS and Joanna ADAMS, and was born13 Dec 1826 Norfolk, MA; died 1872 at Livingston, NY. Marilla-[7] died 4 July 1874.

Children of Marilla F[-7] PHIPPS and John QUINCY adams:
Surname **ADAMS**

3183. Katherine " Kitti" S.   born 21 May 1860 Chicago, IL; died 15 Nov 1942 Elmhurst, IL
        married Frederick Latimer WELLS ca ____
        (he son of Frederick C. WELLS and Clara LATIMER)
        (he born 9 July 1860; died 9 Dec 1929)
        Note: Mr. WELLS was the President of the DUNER Company in Chicago, Il. They provided railroad supplies and machinery to companies in America and abroad
3184. William Phipps   born 4 Feb 1863 Chicago, IL; died 24 Mar 1937 Miami, FL
        married Nettie Elizabeth MOORE ca 1885   (she born 8 Jan 1863 Hopkinton, MA)
        Children: John Quincy [9] born 23 Aug 1885 ND; married Corinne H. HELSELL; and Robert Brooks-[9] ADAMS born 14 Apr 1887 Hopkinton, MA, married Jessie Mae HELSELL

2052. WALDO-[7] **PHIPPS**, brother of above, was born 9 Oct 1836 MA. He married Margaret H. CLAFLIN on 17 Aug 1862. She was the daughter of William H. CLAFLIN and Margaret Railton THOMPSON, and was born 2 Mar 1842 Holliston, MA; died ____. Waldo-[7] PHIPPS died 10 Feb 1919.

Child of Waldo-[7] PHIPPS and Margaret CLAFLIN:
Surname **PHIPPS**

3185. Jennie L.   born ca 1865; died ___; married Thomas Daniel PARSONS Nov 1892 Boston, MA
        (he born 23 Dec 1860 MN; died 1936 Los Angeles, CA)
        Children: Robert A-[9] born 1897; and Mary M-[9] PARSONS born ca 1900

2053. FREDERICK S[-7] **PHIPPS**, brother of above, was born Aug 1840 Hopkinton, MA. He married Emma Augusta CROCKER on 5 April 1863 at Milford, MA. She was the daughter of William CROCKER and Eleanor DARLING, and was born 5 Apr 1843; died ____. Frederick S[-7] PHIPPS died 13 May 1886 Hopkinton, MA

Children of Frederick-[7] PHIPPS and Emma CROCKER:
Sutrname **PHIPPS**

3186. Hattie A.	born 8 Mar 1866 Hopkinton; died 3 Feb 1936 MA. married Wilbur Fiske ADAMS 31 Oct 1888
3187. Arthur Alphalet	born 22 Aug 1876 Hopkinton, MA; died 12 Oct 1882 Hopkinton EOL
3188. Gertrude E.	born 6 Mar 1880 Hopkinton, MA; died 18 Mar 1961 Alameda, CA

2056. JOSEPH BOWKER[-7] **PHIPPS**, brother of above, was born 27 June 1848 Hopkinton, MA. He married Mary Wheeler WALKER on 10 June 1869 at Milford, MA. She was the daughter of William WALKER and Susan WHEELER, and was born ca 1850; died ____. Joseph B-[7] PHIPPS died ca 1930.

Children of Joseph B-[7] PHIPPS and Mary WALKER:
Surname **PHIPPS**

3189. William Walker	born Jan 1870; died ____; married Marie R ___ ca 1897 (divorced)
3190. Frank Gifford	born ca 1872; died 29 Aug 1893

Children of Joseph B-7 PHIPPS and Mary WALKER, continued:
Surname **PHIPPS**

3191. George Vernon	born 28 May 1874; died 1940	
	married Maude Lavina GRAY 10 June 1905	(she dau/o Cyrus GRAY and _____)
	Children: Lorraine-9 born 1910, died 1984; and Vernon-9 PHIPPS born 1916, died 2002	

2057. NORMAN B-7 PHIPPS, brother of above, was born Oct 1856 at Hopkinton, MA. He married Nellie B. HANSON on 24 Feb 1878 at Marlborough, MA. She was the daughter of Sylvester HANSON and Lucretia A. MILES, and was born Feb 1853; died _____. Norman B-7 PHIPPS died ca 1910 at Waltham, MA.

Children of Norman B-7 PHIPPS and Nellie B. HANSON:
Surname **PHIPPS**

3192. Blanche Sarah	born 14 Apr 1878; died ____; married Perleston QUINN ca 1897	
	(he born Apr 1880 ME; died ____; a mariner)	
	Children: Ethel M-9 born 1898 ME; and Stanley Perleston-9 QUINN born 24 June 1908;	
	died Sept 1979; married Viola ____ ca ____ (ch: Stanley-10 born ca 1931)	
3193. Nettie Marilla	born 4 Sep 1882 MA; died ____	

2072. LUTHER-7 HOSMER, Jr., son of Luther-6 HOSMER (Abigail-5 BARRETT; Abigail-4 BOWKER; Edmund-3;2;1) and Abiah BLISS, was born 21 Aug 1821. He married Nancy Judson HALL on 7 July 1846. She was the daughter of _____ HALL and _____, and was born 26 Nov 1823; died 11 Mar 1878. Luther-7 HOSMER, Jr. died 23 Nov 1866

Children of Luther-7 HOSMER, Jr. and Nancy HALL:
Surname **HOSMER**   (all children born Worcester, MA)

3194. Charles Luther	born 20 Oct 1847; died 28 Nov 1852 Worcester, MA EOL	
3195. Edward Pomeroy	born 23 Sep 1849; died ca 1919 Paxton, MA; married Emma Mabel ORITT ca _____	
	(she dau/o George Uriah ORITT and Emily Susan BAGLEY)	
	(she born 14 Jan 1850; died _____)	
	Children: Charles Edward-9 born 20 Dec 1872 Worcester, MA; and Effie Mabel-9 HOSMER born 3 July 1883	
	Paxton, MA; married Arthur F. STEVENS 26 Sep 1901 (he s/o Hiram STEVENS and Nancy M. TAFT)	
3196. George Henry	born 12 Feb 1853; died 10 Oct 1863 Worcester, MA EOL	
+ **3197. CHARLES ALBERT**	born 23 Apr 1855; died Oct 1920; married Mary Etta HALLETT 18 June 1880	
	(she born 18 Dec 1855 Yarmouth, MA; died 9 Feb 1929 Holden, MA)	

2078. STILLMAN SNOW-7 BARRETT, son of Thornton-6 BARRETT, III; Thornton-5, II; Abigail-4 BOWKER; Edmund-3;2;1) and Rebecca Stanton BREWER, was born 7 May 1835 McKean County, PA. He married Hannah Eliza COOLEY ca 1863. She was the daughter of Aretus COOLEY and Elvira _____; and was born 20 Sep 1829. Stillman Snow-7 BARRETT died ca 1882.

Children of Stillman Snow-7 BARRETT and Hannah Eliza COOLEY:
Surname **BARRETT**

3198. Mary Elida	born ca 1866; died ____		
+ **3199. ANNIE JENNY**	born 31 Jan 1867 Port Alleghany, McKean, PA; died 31 Mar 1933 same place		
	married John Gerard ROBBINS 26 Mar 1884 Lycoming Co., PA		
	(he s/o Madison M. ROBBINS and Justina Elizabeth HALL)		
	(he born 15 Dec 1862 PA; died 7 Aug 1948 McKean, PA		
3200. Fanny I	born 1867 MN; died ____		
3201. Myrtie A.	born 1867 MN; died ____; married Hubert BURGHER ca ____		
	(he born ca 1842 NY; died _____) (he s/o Ephraim BURGHER and _____)		
	Child: Lee Coo-9 BURGHER born Apr 1904; died 17 Aug 1977 OR		
3202. Lettie A.	born ca 1872; died ____	3203. N. Lizzie	born ca 1875; died ____

2087. JULIA MADORA-7 BARRETT, sister of above, was born Oct 1853. She married Rufus Llewellyn WOODARD ca 1873. He was the son of _____ WOODARD and _____; and was born May 1846 VT; died 14 Apr 1925 Rice, MN. Julia -7 died ca 1909.

Children of Julia M-7 BARRETT and Rufus WOODARD:
Surname **WOODARD**

3204. Rufus	born 1873; died 1950	3207. Lucinda M.	born 1884; died ____
3205. Mary J.	born 1875; died 1950	3208. Florence A.	born 1889; died 1976
3206. Adelia Madora	born 1879; died 1957		

2088. GEORGE WARREN-7 BARRETT, son of James Johnson-6 BARRETT (Joseph-5; Abigail-4 BOWKER; Edmund-3;2;1) and Lydia SMITH, was born 13 July 1846. He married Ella Maria TAYLOR on 22 June 1871. She was the daughter of Pliny White TAYLOR and ____; and was born 10 July 1850 at Springfield, VT; died ____. George -7 BARRETT died ____.

Children of George W-7 BARRETT and Ella Maria TAYLOR:
Surname **BARRETT**

3209. Edward Warren	born 10 Aug 1872; died ____; resided Waltham, MA
3210. Alice Marie	born 7 Jan 1874; died 24 July 1897; resided Waltham
3211. Charles Howard	born 24 June 1877; died ____; resided Waltham

2095. AURELIA-7 LEWIS, daughter of Sarah-6 SCRIPTURE (Abigail-5 BRIGHAM; John-4; Elizabeth-3 BOWKER, Edmund-2,1) and Abisha LEWIS, was born 5 April 1795 MA. She married Lyman HINMAN on 16 August 1819 at West Stockbridge, MA. He was the son of _____ HINMAN and _____, and was born 10 May 1794 West Stockbridge, MA; died ca 1864. Aurelia-7 LEWIS died 5 Feb 1861 at Farmington, CT.

Children of Aurelia-7 LEWIS and Lyman HINMAN:
Surname **HINMAN**   (all children born West Stockbridge, Berkshire, MA)

3212. Morgan Lewis (1)	born 3 July 1823; died 16 Feb 1828
3213. Evalina Maria	born 8 Aug 1825 ; died 11 Mar 1903
3214. Edna Sarah	born 28 Feb 1828; died 25 Feb 1897
	married William RICHARDS ca ___; (he born ca 1801; died ca 1861)

+   **3215. MORGAN   (2)**   born 7 Oct 1831; died 3 July 1891 Cardston, Alberta, Canada
          LEWIS   married Harriet HESS 22 Dec 1853 Farmington, Davis, Utah Territory
                  (she dau/o Jacob HESS and Elizabeth FOUTZ)
                  (she born 18 Aug 1833 OH; died 12 Jun 1921)
                  married Rhoda CHASE 4 Apr 1870 Salt Lake City, UT
                  (she dau/o Isaac CHASE and Phoebe OGDEN)
                  (she born 29 Sept 1830 Sparta, Livingston, NY; died 1 Feb 1920 UT)

+   **3216. HENRY LYMAN**   born 6 March 1837 MA; died 2 Jan 1921 Cardston, Alberta, Canada
                  1 married Elizabeth Harriet Chaney COMPTON 17 Mar 1861
                  (she born 8 Oct 1840 TN; died 1 Dec 1912 UT)
                  2 married Mary Jane WHITE 18 Nov 1874   (she born ca 1837; died _____)

          3217. Helen Aurelia   born 20 Sept 1840; died 12 Nov 1911

2102. NANCY ABIGAIL-7 LEWIS, sister of above, was born 1 March 1808 ____ MA. She married Frederick FITCH 20 May 1827 MA. He was the son of _____ FITCH and ____, and was born ca 1806; died 1892. Nancy-8 LEWIS died 20 Apr 1881 at Alford, Berkshire, MA.

Children of Nancy-7 LEWIS and Frederick FITCH:
Surname **FITCH**

3218. Horace Sanford	born ca 1828 MA ; died ca 1914
	married Celestia B. _____ ca _____; (she born ca 1832; died _____)
	Child: Ella S-9 FITCH born ca 1854
3219. Sarah Abigail	born ca 1830 MA; died ca 1913	3220. Nancy born ca 1836 MA

2120. CLARISSA B-7 BRIGHAM, daughter of Abijah-6 BRIGHAM (John-5; Lt. Abijah-4; Elizabetth-3 BOWKER, Edmund-2,1) and Melissa STRATTON, was born 13 March 1818. She married Daniel HITCHINGS ca ____. He was the son of ____ HITCHINGS and ____, and was born ____; died ____. Clarissa-7 BRIGHAM died ____.

Children of Clarissa-7 BRIGHAM and Daniel HITCHINGS:
Surname **HITCHINGS**

3221.Henry	born ca ____; died ____	3224. Frank	born ca ____; died ____
3222. Lucy	born ca ____; died ____	3225. George	born ca ____; died ____
3223. Charles B	born ca ____; died ____	3226. Martha	born ca ____; died ____
	married ____ JONES ca ____		

2122. LAVINIA MOORE-7 BRIGHAM, sister of above, was born 1 Dec 1820/21. She married Robert Lewis GODDARD of Petersham, MA ca _____. He was the son of _____ GODDARD and ____, and was born 21 May 1822; died 15 Jan 1887 Palmer, MA. Lavinia-7 BRIGHAM died _____.   **171**

Children of Lavinia-[7] BRIGHAM and Robert GODDARD:
Surname **GODDARD**

3227. William Lewis	born 1 Aug 1846; died 1 Aug 1873	
3228. Frank Ballard	born 6 Oct 1851; died 9 Nov 1858	EOL
3229. Lisette Martha	born 15 Nov 1861; died 12 Jan 1877	

2123. JOHN WARREN-[7] **BRIGHAM**, brother of above, was born 19 Dec 1822. He married Martha Eliza BRIGHAM ca 1845.She was the daughter of Dr. Luther BRIGHAM and Eunice HAWLEY, and was born ___; died ___. John-[7] BRIGHAM died ____

Children of John Warren-[7] BRIGHAM and Martha BRIGHAM:
Surname **BRIGHAM**

+ **3230. WARREN LUTHER** born 25 Jan 1846 Oakum, MA; died 13 Mar 1880
married Susan Frances ADAMS 25 June 1868
(she dau/o Sylvanus ADAMS and Caroline WESSON)
(she born 3 June 1843 Chicopee, MA; died 4 Oct 1920 Brookline, MA)

3231. Ella	born ca 1851; died ____		
3232. Frank	born ca 1853	3233. Lura	born ca 1855

2124. WILLIAM -[7] **BRIGHAM**, son of John-[6] BRIGHAM (John-[5]; Lt. Abijah-[4]; Elizabeth-[3] BOWKER; Edmun-[2,1]) and Mary LEVERITT, was born 19 July 1819 GA. He married Caroline M.T. WHITE on 10 April 1844 GA. She was the daughter of ____ WHITE and ____, and was born ____; died 24 Feb 1883. William-[7] BRIGHAM died 2 June 1893 at Girard, GA. on the plantation which had originally belonged to his father.

Children of William-[7] BRIGHAM and Caroline WHITE:
Surname **BRIGHAM**   (children all born Girard, GA)

3234. John Christopher	born 16 June 1846; died ____	3240. Clarence Russell	born 6 Sept 1856
3235. William Henry	born 23 July 1848; died ____	3241. Charles	born 3 Oct 1860
3236. Thaddeus Rudolf	born 25 Aug 1849		
+ 3237. Mary Ann Elizabeth	born 12 April 1851; died ____; married Matthew M. DANIEL 30 June 1873 GA		
+ 3238. Sarah Martha	born 10 Nov 1853; died ____; married Howard S. ROYAL April 1886 GA.		
3239. Erasmus Horatio	born 17 April 1854; died 14 May 1864 EOL		

2125. ELIZABETH ANN EUNICE -[7] **BRIGHAM**, sister of above , was born 15 Jan 1824 at Girard, Georgia. She married Artemus B. ROGERS on 6 May 1846 at Watertown, MA. He was the son of ____ ROGERS and ____, and was born 19 April 1817 at Newton, MA; died 17 July 1901 at Watertown, MA. Elizabeth-[7] BRIGHAM died 20 March 1857 at Watertown.

Children of Elizabeth-[7] BRIGHAM and Artemus ROGERS:
]Surname **ROGERS**   (all children born Watertown, MA)

3242. Frank	born 3 April 1847; died 14 Nov 1873
3243. George Leveritt	born 24 April 1849; died 15 dec 1875
3244. Frederick W.	born 15 Sept 1851; died ____; married Ella L. FROST 18 Aug 1874
	Child: Artemus Bixby-[9] ROGERS born 8 Feb 1876
3245. John Brigham	born 25 April 1854; died _____; res. Watertown; unmarried EOL
3246. Lucy Maria	born 17 April 1756; died _____; married Albert C. WRIGHT 24 Aug 1885
	(he born 13 Aug 1857; died 19 June 1888 Waltham, MA)

2126. JOHN-[7] **BRIGHAM**, brother of above, was born 13 Feb 1827 at Burke County, Georgia. He married Mary Elizabeth TAINTER 5 Jan 1852. She was the daughter of Capt. William C. TAINTER and ____, and was born 3 Jan 1830. John-[7] BRIGHAM was a lumber merchant in Watertown, MA with his father, and died there on 20 Dec 1871.

Children Of John-[7] BRIGHAM and Mary Elizabeth TAINTER:
Surname **BRIGHAM**

3247. Cora E.	born 7 Oct 1860; died ____	
3248. Nellie Maria	born 11 Oct 1857; died 27 Sept 1858	EOL
3249. Harry Webster	born 12 Jan 1869; died ____; married Ellen May LEAVITT 12 March 1894	
	(she born 21 March 1869 Newtonville, MA; died _____)	

2128. WILLIAM THEODORE[-7] **BRIGHAM**, son of William[-6] BRIGHAM (John-[5]; Lt. Abijah[-4]; Elizabeth-[3] BOWKER: Edmund-[2,1]) and Adeline COLE, was born 12 Sept 1835 at Watertown, MA. He married Marion Billings COLE on 2 Feb 1864. She was the daughter of _____ COLE and ____, and was born ____, died ____. William[-7] BRIGHAM moved to Baltimore, MD and worked for his uncle , a prominent hat manufacturer. Later he became President of the Brigham-Hopkins Company, retiring in 1899. He then resided at Shelter Island, Suffolk, NY. He died ____

Children of William Theodore-[7] BRIGHAM and Marion COLE:
Surname **BRIGHAM**

3250. Charles Pliny	born 3 Feb 1867; died ____; married Mary Lapham WALKER 11 July 1900 graduated Johns Hopkins University (BA 1888; PhD 1891)
3251. Walter Cole	born 11 Jan 1870; died ____; graduate of Johns Hopkins University; unmarried
3252. Theodore William	born 5 Jan 1876; died ____; unmarried; a naval architect

2132. REBECCA BRIGHAM-[7] HARRIS, daughter of Nancy-[6] BRIGHAM (Joseph-[5]; Lt. Abijah[-4]; Elizabeth-[3] BOWKER; Edmund-[2,1]) and Benjamin HARRIS, was born 17 Jan 1842 at Franklin County, AL. She married Harvey Gholsen SARGENT on 7 April 1868 at Russellville, AL. He was the son of Oran SARGENT and May Ann GHOLSEN, and was born Jan 1841/42 AL; died 16 July 1913 AL. Rebecca-[7] HARRIS died 11 June 1914 Pocahontas, AL.

Children of Rebecca-[7] HARRIS and Harvey SARGENT:
Surname **SARGENT**

3253. Benjamin Harris	born 9 June 1869; died 18 Apr 1935; married Annie Dillard STEADMAN ca ____
3254. Lucy T.	born April 1873; died ca 1910; married Earnest A, WILLIAMS ca ____
3255. Harvey Owen	born 24 Oct 1875 AL; died 12 Feb 1936 Baton Rouge, LA. married Minnie Mack PIERCE 17 Oct 1906 AL (she born 21 Feb 1885 AL; died 20 Dec 1978 Norfolk, VA)
	Child: Harvey Owen-[9] SARGENT, Jr. born 16 Sept 1917 AL; died 1999 (Source: National Society SAR, VA)
3256. Bessie B.	born ca 1879; died ____; married Robert E. TIDWELL ca ___
3257. Rebecca B.	born ca March 1882 AL; died ____; married _____ STEADHAM ca ___

2139. SARAH FRANCES[-7] **PARKER,** daughter of Eunice-[6] BRIGHAM; Joseph-[5]; Lt. Abijah[-4]; Elizabeth-[3] BOWKER; Edmund-[2,1]) and Rev. Addison PARKER, Sr, was born 26 July 1837 Methuen, MA. She married Elias Cornelius ATKINS, as his 3rd wife, on 17 Aug 1865 IN. He was the son of _____ ATKINS and ____, and was born 28 June 1833; died 18 April 1901 Indiana. Sarah F-[7] PARKER died ____.

Note: Elias ATKINS was the founder of the E C ATKINS Co. of Indianapolis IN, which manufactured high grade saws. It was said that he would not let a saw go out of the factory unless it was " perfect ". Another source stated that it was one of the " greatest industries for the manufacture of saws.

Children of Sarah Frances-[7] PARKER and Elias C. ATKINS:
Surname **ATKINS**

3258. Mary Dolbear	born ca 1867; died ____; married Nelson GLADDING ca ____ (he s/o Elias GLADDING and Sarah _____)
	Children: Frances M-[9] born ca ___; and Mary Elizabeth-[9] GLADDING born ca ____
3259. Henry Cornelius	born 27 Nov 1868 ID; died ____; married Sue WINTER 7 Jan 1896 (she dau/o Ferdinand WINTER and Mary KEYES (he graduated Yale University Class of 1899)
	Children: Elias C-[9] born ca ___; Keyes W-[9] born ca ___; and Henry C-[9] Jr. ATKINS born ca ____
3260. Sarah Frances	born ca 1870 ID; died ____; married Thomas Reed KACKLEY ca ____
	Children: Sarah Frances-[9] and Thomas Reed-[9] KACKLEY, Jr
3261. Emma Louise	born ca 1873 IN; died ____; married Edward B. DAVIS ca ____
	Child: Emma Louise-[9] DAVIS born ca ____
3262. Carra Isabel	born May 1874 IN; died ___; 1 married Arthur D. GATES 15 June 1892 2 married Major/Dr. Sandford Hosea WADHAMS 4 Aug 1906 Marion, IN (surgeon) Source: Indiana and Indianans Page 1854-57 Vol. IV

2140. REVEREND ADDISON-[7] PARKER, brother of above, was born 12 November 1839 at Danbury, CT. he married Mary Louisa BOYDEN ca ____. She was the daughter of ____ BOYDEN and ____, and was born ca 1845 MA; died ____. Rev. Addison-[7] PARKER died ____ NY.

Children of Rev. Addison-[7] PARKER and Mary BOYDEN:
Surname **PARKER**

3263. Wilson B.	born ca 1867 MA; died ____ IN		
3264. Edith M.	born ca 1871 MA; died ____	3265. Irving A.	born ca 1877

2144. JOSEPH NICHOLAS-[7] THOMPSON, brother of above, was born ca 1844 AL. He married Lucie Blackwell MALONE ca 1869. She was the daughter of Goodloe Warren MALONE and Mary Spivey BATES, and was born 6 Feb 1847; died ca 1930. Joseph-[7] MALONE died 14 Nov 1926. They resided Alabama.

Children of Joseph-7 THOMPSON and Lucie MALONE:
Surname **THOMPSON**

3266. Dr. Humphrey Bates	born 7 July 1870; died 21 Nov 1936 ; single	EOL
3267. Lawrence K.	born 14 Nov 1871; died 15 Jan 1948 TN	
3268. Joseph Nicholas (Jr)	born 28 April 1877; died 15 Oct 1890 TN	EOL
3269. Lucien Malone	born 7 Jan 1883; died 14 Oct 1972 AL	
3270. Henry	born 1 Oct 1887; died 3 Oct 1887	EOL

2145. REBECCA-[7] THOMPSON, daughter of Rebecca-[6] BRIGHAM (Joseph-[5]; Lt. Abijah-[4]; Elizabeth-[3] BOWKER; Edmund-[2,1]) and Lawrence THOMPSON, was born ca 1846 AL. She married Capt. William Wilkins BAYLESS ca Dec 1866 at Florence, Alabama. He was the son of William Barclay BAYLESS and Ann M. TANNEHILL, and was born ca 1841 Nashville, TN; died ca 1889 AL. Capt. BAYLESS served in Company B; 1st TN Regiment of Confederate Troops during the Civil War. Rebecca-[7] THOMPSON died ca 1918.

Children of Rebecca-[7] THOMPSON and William BAYLESS:
Surname **BAYLESS**

3271. William Barclay	born 6 Oct 1869 AL
3272. Mary	born ca 1873; died ____; married _____ ASHBRIDGE

2167. JOHN-[7] JOYNER, son of James-[6] JOYNER (John-[5]; Hannah-[4] BOWKER; John-[3]; Edmund-[2,1]) and Maria NESBITT, was born ca 1812 MA. He married Mary M. BENTLEY ca 1831. She was the daughter of ____ BENTLEY and _____, and was born ca 1814; died _____. John-[7] JOYNER died ____ Harford, Cortland County, NY.

Children of John-[7] JOYNER and Mary BENTLEY:
Surname **JOYNER**   (all children born Cortland County, NY)

3273. Janette	born ca 1838; died _____		
+ **3274. NELSON**	born ca 1840 NY; died 10 Jan 1894 NY		
	married Elizabeth C. KEYES ca _____;	(she born ca 1846; died ca 1904)	
3275. Helen E.	born ca 1841 ; died _____		
3276. Eugene	born ca 1845 ; died _____		
3277. Emma Lurane	born 11 June 1847; died _____	3280. Mary Frances	born ca 1855; died _____
3278. Catherine A.	born ca 1850; died _____	3281. Hannah	born ca 1857; died _____
3279. Martin	born ca 1851; died _____		

2162. DAVID STOWELL-[7] FLETCHER, son of Caleb-[6] FLETCHER (Sarah-[5] JOYNER; Hannah-[4] BOWKER; John-[3]; Edmund-[2,1]) and Elizabeth STOWELL, was born 17 July 1817 NY. He married Caroline FLEMMING on 21 Oct 1857. She was the daughter of ____ FLEMMING and ____, and was born March 1828 OH; died _____. David S-[7] FLETCHER died _____.

Children of David-[7] FLETCHER and Caroline FLEMMING:
Surname **FLETCHER**

3282. Caleb Remington	born 10 Sept 1858 Solon, OH; died ____		
3283. George Washington	born 21 Oct 1860; died 5 Feb 1930 IA; married Orpha N. RIDDLE 2 April 1884		
	(she dau/o Hiram RIDDLE and Mary BOYER) (she born 31 Mar 1860; died 1942 IA)		
3284. Wallace Crawford	born 13 Apr 1863 IN; died ____	3285. Emma Emeline	born Oct 1868 IN

2183. HUBBARD-[7] JOYNER, son of Francis-[6] JOYNER (Sarah-[5]; Hannah-[4] BOWKER; John-[3]; Edmund-[2,1]) and Lydia LESTER, was born 31 March 1836 at ____. He married Olive RITTER ca 1859. She was the daughter of ____ RITTER and ____, and was born Feb 1844; died _____. Hubbard-[7] JOYNER died ca 1904.

Children of Hubbard-[7] JOYNER and Olive RITTER:
Surname **JOYNER**

3286. Merritt	born 18 May 1861; died 5 Sept 1917 NY; married Martha Lovina COTTRELL ca 1883		
	Children: Samuel -[9] born June 1886 NY; Luella Belle-[9] born 27 Aug 1887, died 3 Mar 1949 NY;		
	and Edith-[9] JOYNER born Sept 1889		
3287. Jasper	born 20 Feb 1863; died 24 July 1927 Sandy Creek, Oswego, NY		
	married Annie Geddes GRINOLS (she born ca 1858 NY)		
3288. Orissa	born ca 1865; married ___ BERRY		
3289. Laura	born ca 1870; married ___ BINGHAM	3292. Myrtle	born ca 1878/1879
3290. Elva	born ca 1872; married ___ BERRY		married _____ La CLAIR
3291. Arthur Alvah	born 21 Aug 1874; died 12 Oct 1930 Fayetteville, Onondaga, NY		

2186. FRANKLIN NOAH-[7] BOWKER, son of Willard-[6] BOWKER (Noah-[5,4]; John-[3]; Edmund-[2,1]) and Sally GREEN, was born 22 July 1809 West Springfield, MA. He married E. Jane CREEKER ca 1837. She was the daughter of ____ and ___; and was born 23 May 1814; died 31 May 1868 Maine, Broome, NY. Franklin N-[7] BOWKER died 28 Mar 1884 Maine, NY.

Children of Franklin Noah-[7] BOWKER and Jane CREEKER:
Surname **BOWKER**

3293. George Willard	born 28 Nov 1837; died 30 Sep 1909 Binghamton, Broome, NY	
	married Hattie L. _____ (she born ca 1838; died ____)	
	Children: May/Mary E-[9] born 1862; married Russell STRINGHAM ca 1888; and Minnie-[9] BOWKER born 1862.	
3294. Lucy A.	born ca 1839; died ____	
3295. Clarissa	born Feb 1844; died ____	
+ 3296. **ROSALIA AUGUSTA**	born Apr 1846 NY; died 28 Mar 1910	
	married Marsden Altonia DURFEE ca 1867	
	(he s/o Amasa DURFEE and Hannah B. SWIFT)	
	(he born 17 Feb 1843 Maine, NY; died 4 Mar 1915)	

2187. AMOS GREEN-[7] BOWKER, brother of above, was born 20 Nov 1810 at West Springfield, MA. He married first Serilla ____ ca ____. She was born ___; died ____ Blandford, MA. His second marriage was to Lovina Adeline WILBUR ca 1840 . She was born ca 1822 NY; died ____. Amos Green-[7] BOWKER died _____

Children of Amos Green-[7] BOWKER and Serilla _____:
Surname **BOWKER**

3297. Samantha J.	born ca 1833 MA; died ____; married Charles F. SIZER 12 June 1851

Children of Amos Green-[7] BOWKER and Lovina Adeline WILBUR:
Surname **BOWKER**

3298. Wilbur F.	born ca 1841 MA; died 27 May 1863 Port Hudson, LA
	Note: Wilbur F-[8] BOWKER enlisted at Peru, VT , as a Private in Company H of the 8th Vermont Infantry,
	and was killed in action at the siege of Port Hudson battle, Louisiana.
3299. Addie M	born Sep 1850; died ____
	married Horace Edgell ROBERTS 17 Apr 1875
	(he s/o LEAVITT ROBERTS and Lucy AGEE) (he born 16 Mar 1836 VT)
	Children: Leavitt-[9] born ca ___; and Ada May-[9] ROBERTS born ca 1876; died 1979;
	married Walter S. UNDERWOOD

2188. WILLIAM MINOR-[7] BOWKER, brother of above, was born 24 May 1816 at Union, Broome County, New York. He married first to a Betsey BEERS 8 Feb 1844 at Litchfield, CT. She was the daughter of _____ BEERS and ____, and was born a 1814 Litchfield, CT; died 14 Jan 1848. His second marriage was to Millicent Parthenia-[5] SKILTON Beers on 4 Feb 1850 at Owego, Tioga County, NY. She was the daughter of James Avery-[4] SKILTON (James Avery-[3]; Henry-[2]; John-[1]) and Chloe STEELE, and was born 24 Dec 1816 at Watertown, CT; died 1 March 1904 Herrick, Bradford, PA. She married first to Rev. Ebenezer Osborne BEERS, brother of Betsey BEERS. William Minor-[7] BOWKER died 17 Feb 1886 at Herrick, Bradford, PA.

Child of William Minor-[7] BOWKER and Betsey BEERS:
Surname **BOWKER**

3300. Nelson Osborne	born 7 March 1845 PA; died ca 1910 WV; married Mary S. FLEMING ca 1872
	(she born 30 Apr 1844 PA; died 22 June 1921 WV)
	(she dau/o David FLEMING and Jane BLAINE)
	Child: Albert Osborne -[9] BOWKER born June 1872 WV; died ____)

Children of William Minor-[7] BOWKER and Mellicent Parthenia-[5] SKILTON Beers :
Surname **BOWKER**

+   **3301. JULIUS AVERY**   born 17 March 1851 Pike, PA; died 23 April 1925 Binghamton, NY
                                               married Harriet/Hattie Asenath WOOD 15 Oct 1873 PA
                                             (she dau/o David Carpenter WOOD and Avilda Evelyne HOLMAN)
                                             (she born 29 Aug 1851 Rush, PA; died 13 Dec 1946 Binghamton, NY)

+   **3302. MILLICENT**   born 6 July 1852 E. Herrick, Bradford, PA; died 5 Feb 1943 E. Herrick, PA
        BETSEY   married Arthur Warren WOOD 25 Dec 1879
                                             (he born 9 Sep 1855 Rush, PA; died 1955 E. Herrick, Bradford, PA)

2207. ELVIRA-[7] BEEBE, daughter of Lathrop-[6] BEEBE (Rebecca-[5] BOWKER; Joseph-[4]; John-[3]; Edmund-[2,1]) and Sally BEMIS, was born 17 Jan 1840 NY. She married Jehiel Delos WHITNEY, a blacksmith, 14 Sep 1864 Concord, Erie, NY. He was the son of _____WHITNEY and ____, and was born 23 Sept 1841 NY; died after 1915. Elvira-[7] BOWKER died _____NY.

Children of Elvira-[7] BEEBE and Jehiel WHITNEY:
Surname **WHITNEY**

    3303. Irving Silas   born ca 1870 NY; died _____
    3304. Bertha Delos   born July 1878 NY; died ____
    3305. Gertrude Beebe   born 27 May 1880 NY; died 3 June 1963; married Ralph Otto WHITNEY 30 June 1914

2210. EZEKIEL BEEBE-[7] HALSTEAD, son of Sally-[6] BEEBE (Sarah-[5] BOWKER; Joseph-[4]; John-[3]; Edmund-[2,1]) and Cornelius HALSTEAD, was born 7 June 1806 NY. He married Sarah Ann BURDICK 21 Dec 1830. She was the daughter of Robert BURDICK and Daisy BOSTWICK, and was born 4 July 1811 NY; died 13 Dec 1908 MI. Ezekiel-[7] died 1 Apr 1897 MI.

Children of Ezekiel Beebe-[7] HALSTEAD and Sarah ANN BURDICK:
Surname **HALSTEAD**

3306. Milo	born Dec 1830 NY; died 21 Jun 1907	3314. William H.	born 28 Jan 1846 MI
3307. Morris	born 3 May 1833 NY; died 1833	3315. Lorenzo	born 5 June 1848 MI
3308. Melissa D.	born ca 1835 NY; died _____	3316. Merritt	born 2 Aug 1850 MI
3309. Myron	born 5 Apr 1836; died 1862, killed in the Civil War	EOL	
3310. Mary Eliza	born 4 July 1838 NY; died 1907		
3311. Martin N.	born 2 May 1840 MI; died 1862, killed in the Civil War EOL		
3312. Oscar F.	born 31 March 1842 MI; died 1914	3317. Royaletta Artimecia born 22 March 1853 MI	
3313.Alvin	born 18 Feb 1844 MI; died 1866	died 29 Jan 1937, married Eli HENRY	

2218. AURORA DWIGHT-[7] MORTON, son of Luna-[6] BEEBE (Rebecca-[5] BOWKER; Joseph-[4]; John-[3]; Edmund-[2;1]) and Asa MORTON, was born 15 June 1815 at Mexico, Oswego County, NY. He married Patience HARDY ca ____. She was the daughter of ___ HARDY and ____; and was born ca 1822; died ____. Aurora Dwight-[7] MORTON died 16 Feb 1877 Evart, MI.

Children of Aurora-[7] MORTON and Patience HARDY:
Surname **MORTON**

    3318. Azer D../ Asa/ Orso   born Sept 1842 MI; died 16 Mar 1915 Evart, MI
                                     married Rosilla SHURTS ca 1866 MI   (she born Apr 1845 MI; died 1920 Evart, MI)
                          Children: Minnie-[9] born ca 1867; Charity-[9] born ca 1868; Lillie-[9] born ca 1870; and
                          William F-[9] MORTON born March 1881
    3319. Polly A.   born ca 1844 MI   3320. Mary A.   born ca 1849 MI

2222. DANIEL P-[7] BEEBE, son of Aurora-[6] BEEBE (Sarah-[5] BOWKER; Joseph-[4;] John-[3]; Edmund-[2;1]) and Sarah COLTON, was born 26 Sept 1809 at ____, NY. He married Eliza Jane GREEN on 10 March 1829. She was the daughter of _____ GREEN and ____, and was born 25 Sep 1814 NY; died 24 June 1887 IA. Daniel P-[7] BEEBE died Dec 1881 at Kankakee, IL.

Children of Daniel-[7] BEEBE and Eliza GREEN:
Surname **BEEBE**

    3321. Catherine   born 22 June 1831; died ____
    3322. Aurora Bowen   born 5 July 1833; died _____
+   **3323. CYNTHIA**   born 29 July 1835 MI; died ca 1915; married Charles Eben BOSWELL 16 Feb 1853 IL
                                   (he born May 1829 England; died 1918)
    3324. Orrin Giles   born 13 July 1838 OH; died ___; married Emma I. _____ ca ___ (she born ca 1854)

Children of Daniel-[7] BEEBE and Eliza GREEN, continued:
Surname **BEEBE**

+   **3325. WILLIAM**   born 17 May 1841 MI; died 4 May 1924 Paulina, O'Brien County, IA
           WALLACE   1 married Ellen Amelia WINNERSTRAND 21 Dec 1887
                       (she dau of William WINNERSTRAND and Bertha _____ (born Sweden)
                       (she born July 1855 MN; died 15 Feb 1908 IA)
                       2 married Mary B. ADAMS 24 Nov 1909

           3326. Rachel Ann   born 7 Aug 1843 MI; died ____
           3327. Mary Abigail   born 19 Nov 1845 MI; died ____

+   **3328. DR. ADDISON J.**   born 7 July 1848 MI; died 30 Oct 1934 West Bend, IA (a minister)
           (Adoniram James)   married Ida Elizabeth HAMBLIN 22 Jan 1879 WI
                       (she dau/o Alvah HAMBLIN and Almira S. EGGLESTON)
                       (she born 21 Feb 1859 WI; died 22 Nov 1932 IA)

           3329. Clark Warren   born 29 Mar 1851 MI; died 9 Feb 1884 IA; married _____ BRAGEL; res. Herschel, IL
           3330. Phebe Jane   born 5 Sep 1853 ; died ____   331. Hulda M.   born 29 Nov 1855

2230. ISAAC WINDSOR-[7] BEEBE, son of Asa-[6] BEEBE (Sarah-[5] BOWKER; Joseph-[4]; John-[3], Edmund-[2,1]) and Mary WHIPPLE, was born 20 May 1830 NY. He married first to Wealthy Arvilla WHEELER ca 1856. She was the daughter of ____ WHEELER and ____, and was born 12 July 1827; died 1 July 1870. Isaac-[7] married second to Esther S. ____ ca 1871. She was born ca May 1833; died ____. Isaac-[7] BEEBE died 4 Feb 1903.

Children of Isaac-[7] BEEBE and Wealthy WHEELER:
Surname **BEEBE**

+   **3332. CHARLES**   born Aug 1857 NY; died _____   3333. Cady   born ca 1858; died 1859 EOL
                       1 married Helen Frances MORRIS   3334. Perley   born ca 1868
                       (she born ca 1859; died _____) 2 married Anna B. _____ ca March 1875

2239. CHARLES-[7] BEEBE, son of Clark-[6] BEEBE (Sarah-[5] BOWKER; Joseph-[4]; John-[3]; Edmund-[2,1]) and Dolly SAVAGE, was born 21 August 1838 Franklin Township, Lenawee County, MI. He married Hannah E. BUNN on 4 July 1863 MI. She was the daughter of James BUNN and Ann MOORE, and was born ca 1841 at Newtown, Somersetshire, England; died ca 1887. Charles-[7] BEEBE died 9 Feb 1892 MI.

Children of Charles-[7] BEEBE and Hannah E. BUNN:
Surname **BEEBE**

+   **3335. NELLIE CECELIA**   born 27 Feb 1873 Franklin, MI; died 15 Jan 1947 South Bend, IN
                          married Emery Artie WEBBER 6 April 1891 Niles, MI
                          (he born 11 Sep 1868 Niles, MI; died 31 Aug 1942 South Bend, IN

2241. EDWARD SEYMOUR-[7] HOLCOMB, son of Catherine-[6] BEEBE (Sarah-[5] BOWKER; Joseph-[4]; John-[3]; Edmund-[2,1]) and Chester HOLCOMB, was born July 1827 at Oswego, NY. He married Ann/Anna E. ____ ca 1849 . She was born ca Apr 1827; died 29 June 1902 Cone, Monroe, MI. Edward-[7] HOLCOMB died ____.

Children of Edward Seymour-[7] HOLCOMB and Ann/Anna E. ____:
Surname **HOLCOMB**

+   **3336. ALBERT NEWELL**   born June 1850 MI; died 4 June 1909 Cone, Monroe, MI
                          married Sarah _____ ca 1871   (she born Apr 1853; died _____)
           3337. Alvin W.   born Nov 1851 MI; died ____

2270. HARRIET-[7] SPENCER, daughter of Polly May-[6] WHITNEY (Eunice-[5] BOWKER; Daniel-[4]; John-[3]; Edmund-[2,1]) and Ezra SPENCER, and was born 9 March 1816 at ____. She married Junia SARGENT ca 27 Nov 1838. He was the son of Junia SARGENT and Sally CLARK, and was born 26 May 1809; died 16 April 1896 Pittsford, VT. Harriet-[7] SPENCER died 17 April 1859 at Pittsford, VT. Junia SARGENT married 2nd to Mary Ann RICHARDSON (1824-1896).

Children of Harriet-[7] SPENCER and Junia SARGENT:
Surname **SARGENT**

           3338. Adelaide S   born ca 1841 ; died _____; married Austin A. DICKERMAN
                          (he born 29 Sep 1841/41; died 6 Dec 1925 Pittsford, VT.)
                 Children: Hattie-[9] born ca 1861; Minnie-[9] born ca 1864 ; and Edward W-[9] DICKERMAN born ca 1869;

Children of Harriet-[7] SPENCER and Junia SARGENT, continued:
Surname **SARGENT**

3339. Adelizza	born ca 1846		
3340. Frank Alvernice	born ca 1849; died ca 1926	3341. Fred	born ca 1849; died 1896

2285. ELIZA ANN-[7] BOWKER, daughter of Samuel Noyes-[6] BOWKER (Daniel-[5,4]; John-[3]; Edmund-[2,1]) and Mary EARLE, was born 15 May 1829 at ____. She married Thomas Andrew HUTCHINS 28 Dec 1852. He was the son of _____ HUTCHINS and was born ca 1824; died 1893. Eliza Ann-[7] BOWKER died 22 July 1901 MO..

Children of Eliza Ann-[7] BOWKER and Thomas Andrew HUTCHINS:
Surname **HUTCHINS**

	3342. Elizabeth Maybin	born 31 Dec 1853 MA; died 18 Oct 1865	EOL
	3343. Howard Bowker	born 1 Feb 1856 MA; died 4 June 1885	
	3344. Mary Earle	born 17 Mar 1858 MA; died Oct 1941 WA	
	3345. Edward William	born 10 May 1860 Sudbury, MA; died 21 Nov 1943	
	3346. Angelina	born 14 Sep 1862 IL; died 29 Nov 1864 IL	EOL
	3347. Flora Luella	born 5 Mar 1867 MO; died 17 May 1936	
+	**3348. CLARA ELSA**	born 26 Oct 1869 MO; died 2 April 1932	
		married John Eddy PIERCE 24 Aug 1893 Oregon City, OR	
		(he born 10 June 1860 MA ; died 9 July 1934 HHyde Park, OR)	
	3349. Francis Samuel	born 19 Dec 1871 MO; died 1 July 1940	
	3350. Morton Weymouth	born 1 Oct 1875 Springfield, MO; died 22 Oct 1875	EOL

2287. ANGELINA / ANGIE-[7] BOWKER, sister of above, was born 13 June 1832 at Sudbury, MA. She married Jonathan -[8] FAIRBANKS ++ on 3 Sep 1856 at Sudbury, MA. He was the son of Joseph Bradley Varnum-[7] FAIRBANKS and Margaret HADDEN, and was born 7 Jan 1828 at Andover, Essex, MA; died Sept 1917 at Springfield, MO. Angie-[7] BOWKER died 29 Dec 1912 at Springfield, MO. Jonathan-[8] FAIRBANKS was a Professor, and taught for many years in Springfield.

Children of Angie-[7] BOWKER and Professor Jonathan FAIRBANKS:
Surname **FAIRBANKS**   (1st 4 children born at St, Mary's, Auglaize County, OH)

	3351. Grace Ida	born 4 June 1857; married George A. STEWART 2 June 1889 Cuyahoga County, OH
	3352. Joseph Maybin	born 12 March 1859; died 19 May 1865
+	**3353. MARY CAROLINE**	born 7 April 1860; died _____; married Silas Erastus JAMES ca ____
		(he s/o Abner JAMES and Catherine WILER)
		(he born 24 Mar 1855 Springfield, OH; died 6 Dec 1930 Zanesville, OH)
	3354. Alben Bradley	born 22 June 1862; died July 1910 Springfield, MO
	3355. Harry Earl	born 18 Feb 1864 Piqua, Miami, OH; died 31 July 1878 Springfield, MO EOL
	3356. Annie	born 20 Mar 1866 Piqua, MO; died 1899
	3357. George Bowker	born 16 April 1868 MO; died Aug 1924 Springfield, MO
		married Sarah DAVIS 21 July 1910 Red Top, Dallas, MO
	3358. John Wilbur	born 13 Nov 1870 MO; died 26 Dec 1943 Springfield, MO
		married Anna INGRAM 3 June 1902 Springfield, Greene Co., MO (she born ca 1871)
		Child: John Howard-[9] FAIRBANKS born ca 1904 MO
	3359. James Otis	born 30 Oct 1873 MO; died 29 Dec 1963 Springfield, MO
		married Golden SANDS 13 Jan 1913 Carthage, Jasper, MO
		(she dau/o Edward L. SANDS and Mary _____) (she born ca 1884 KS ; died _____)
		Child: James-[9] FAIRBANKS born ca 1924

Ancestry of Jonathan-[8] FAIRBANKS:

Jonathan-[1] FAIRBANKS, the immigrant, was born ca 1595 at Soweby, Yorkshire, England. He was the son of John -[A] FAIRBANKS and Isabella STANCLIFFE. He immigrated to this country ca ___, and married Grace SMITH (Samuel SMITH and Grace GAWKROGER). He died 5 Dec 1868 at Dedham , MA.

George-[2] FAIRBANKS, son of Jonathan-1, was born 28 Nov 1619 in England, and came to this country with his parents ca ___. He married Mary ADAMS ca ___. He died 10 Jan 1682 at Dedham, Norfolk, MA. His son, Jonathan-[3] FAIRBANKS, was born ca ____; married Sarah ____, and died 18 Dec 1719.

Jonathan-[4] FAIRBANKS was born on 21 March 1689 Sherborn, Middlesex County, MA . He married Lydia HOLBROOK, and died 26 Nov 1754 at Dedham.   Daniel-[5] FAIRBANKS, son of Jonathan-[4], was born 5 Nov 1723 at Sherborn, MA; married Submit ____; and died ca 1771 at Holliston, Middlesex, MA.

Jonathan^{-6} FAIRBANKS, born 29 Mar 1755 at Holliston, married Bridget PARMENTER. He died 28 Feb 1840 Sudbury, MA. Joseph Bradley Varnum^{-7} FAIRBANKS, born 3 Oct 1804 at Sudbury, married Margaret HADDEN (James) , and died 20 May 1833 at Monroe , NY. Jonathan^{-8} married Angeline/Angie^{-7} BOWKER, above.

2289. HARRIET MATILDA^{-7} BOWKER, sister of above, was born 11 Jan 1839 MA. She married first to Charles Phineas WEBSTER on 4 June 1862 Sudbury, MA. He was the son of James A. WEBSTER and Maria EAYRS/AYRES, and was born 25 June 1833 Derry, NH; died 31 Dec 1865 NH. She married second to Henry Stowe HAPGOOD on 23 Sept 1869. He was the son of John Henry HAPGOOD and Almira Elizabeth STOW, and was born Oct 1841 MA; died ____. Harriet^{-7} died ____.

Child of Harriet-^{7} BOWKER and Charles WEBSTER:
Surname **WEBSTER**
     3360. Nellie Maria   born ca 1863; died ____
Children of Harriet-^{7} BOWKER and Henry Stow HAPGOOD:
Surname **HAPGOOD**
     3361. Charles   born ca 1871 MA; died ____
     3362. Frank Webber   born 6 June 1874; died ____; married Blanche Alice SCHOFIELD 18 Oct 1897
            (she dau/o Chandler P. SCHOFIELD and Jane A. VAN HORN)
            (she born May 1873 MA; died ____)
            Child: Warren Chandler^{-9} HAPGOOD born 23 Sept 1898 MA; died 24 Sept 1963 VT.

2290. FRANCIS/ FRANK MAYBIN^{-7} BOWKER, brother of above, was born 13 Jan 1850. He married first to Anna_____ ca ____ at Sudbury, MA. She was born ca 1854 in England. He married second to Caroline / Carrie Mary CONLEY ca 1881. She was the daughter of William CONLEY and Elizabeth HADLEY, and was born 25 Mar 1853 Halifax, NS; died 15 Aug 1937 Sudbury. Frank^{-7} BOWKER died 12 Feb 1904 Maynard, MA. His widow married second to Lewis DILLMAN on 25 Dec 1906.

Children of Frank Maybin^{-7} BOWKER and Anna _____:
Surname **BOWKER**
     3363. Amy   born ca 1876 Sudbury, MA   3364. Arthur   born ca Mar 1879 Sudbury
Children of Frank-^{7} BOWKER and Caroline/Carrie CONLEY:
Surname **BOWKER**
+   **3365. EVERETT**   born 9 Nov 1882 MA; died ____; married Eva Leslie SANBORN 9 June 1907 Canada
         WILLIAM   (she dau/o Rupert R. SANBORN and Eunice L. NEWCOMB)
                  (she born 28 Dec 1886 MA; died Feb 1974 TX)
     3366. Edith   born Jan 1885 Sudbury, MA; died _____
+   **3367. INA ADELLA**   born 20 Dec 1889 Sudbury, MA; died 4 Jan 1969 Wellesley, MA
                 married Stanley Stearns GRANT 8 June 1911 Newton, MA
                 (he s/o Alonzo GRANT and Catherine DILLMAN)
                 (he born 3 Oct 1889 Halifax, Nova Scotia, Canada; died 2 Mar 1969 Newton, MA

2292. ELLEN L^{-7} HAYNES, daughter of Sarah-^{6} BOWKER (Daniel-$^{5;4;}$ John-^{3}; Edmund-^{2,1}) and John HAYNES, Jr., was born July 1836 at Sudbury, Middlesex, MA. She married Samuel S. WOOD on 1 April 1860 at Sudbury. He was the son of Josiah WOOD and Hannah A. _____, and was born July 1836 VT; died _____. Ellen L^{-7} HAYNES died ____. According to the 1920 Federal Census for Carbon County, Ia, she was living (aged 83) with her son " Shelly " WOOD.

Children of Ellen L-^{7} HAYNES and Samuel WOOD:
Surname **WOOD**
     3368. Herman S.   born ca 1861 MA; died ____; 1920 resided in WY; single
+   **3369. SAMUEL SHELDON** born ca 1870 MA; died ca 1929
         "Shelly "   1 married Harriet J. _____   (she born ca 1863; died _____)
                 2 married Zula May HULL (she born 2 Jan 1889 CO; died 9 May 1944 Saratoga, CO)
                 (she dau/o Lucious G. HULL and Sarah Louise SWALLOW)
     3370. Ralph Waldo   born 19 Feb 1875; died ____; married Sylvia _____ ca _____
            Note: Owned a ranch at Saratoga, Carbon County, Wyoming

2295. JOHN NEWTON^{-7} HAYNES, brother of above, was born 7 July 1843 at Sudbury, Middlesex, MA. He married Susan Norton GODING on 4 Nov 1870 at Sudbury, MA. She was the daughter of Elbrit GODING (Jonas) and Susanna Mayhew NORTON (Jethro), and was born 26 Feb 1854 Sudbury, MA.; died ____. She possibly married 2nd to a George ROBERTS and had a son, Oscar ROBERTS, by him. John^{-7} HAYNES served from Massachusetts in the Civil War. He enlisted 20 Sep 1861 in Co., E, of the 26th MA Infantry Regiment. Promoted to Sgt. on 1 Jan 1865, was mustered out on 28 Aug 1865 at Savannah, GA.

Children of John N-[7] HAYNES and Susan Norton GODING:
Surname **HAYNES**   (all children born MA)

3371. Elizabeth Frances	born 12 Oct 1871; died _____	3372. Carrie Bell	born 17 Feb 1874
3373. John Norton	born 7 March 1876; died _____		
3374. Robert Chester	born 3 May 1877 MA; married Minerva Estelle _____ ca 1903		

Child: Lorene-[9] HAYNES born ca 1904; married John C. BLACKBURN ca ____; 2 daus –
Frances-[10] born ca 1923, and Georgia-[10] BLACKBURN born ca 1928

3375. Florence Agnes	born 31 Jan 1881; died _____
3376. Waldo Foster	born 8 Sept 1886; died May 1965 FL
	married Annie A. _____ Child: Ruth B-9 HAYNES born ca 1921

2311. JOHN AVERY-[7] BUSH, son of Lydia-[6] BOWKER (Joseph-[5]; Daniel-[4]; John-[3:] Edmund-[2,1]) and Avery BUSH, was born 23 June 1832 at Spencer, MA. He married Hannah Matilda CUMMINGS on 1 Oct 1868 at Orion, MN. She was the daughter of Francis H. CUMMINGS and Hannah Carlton WALDO, and was born 28 Aug 1847 at Boston, Suffolk, MA; died 17 Dec 1816 at Eyota, Olmsted, MN. John Avery-[7] BUSH died 17 Dec 1916 at Eyota, MN.

Children of John Avery-[7] BUSH and Hannah CUMMINGS:
Surname **BUSH**

	3377. George Henry	born 26 Dec 1869; died 26 Sept 1930 Eyota, MN
+	**3378. LEWIS**	born 22 Aug 1871 Eyota, MN; died 1 June 1928 Stockton, CA
		married Sarah Olive DURGIN ca 1911/12
		(she dau/o David DURGIN and Caroline May WILMOT)
		(she born 26 Aug 1894; died 17 Nov 1975 Hart, MN)
	3379. Addie Luella	born 8 Jan 1873; died 11 Nov 1919 Abbotsford, Clark, WI
		married Samuel LEWIS ca _____ (he born 10 May 1873 NY; died Apr 1949 WI.)
		(he s/o ____ LEWIS and Nancy Anne Mc CARTNEY)

Child: George -[9] LEWIS born 15 Dec 1910 Westboro, WI.

+	**3380. ELIZABETH**	born 2 Oct 1874 Eyota, MN; died 16 Dec 1927 Monroe Co., WI
		married George Victor HOBSON 17 Nov 1903
		(he born 21 Aug 1871; died 11 Dec 1949 Leon, WI)
	3381. Edna	born 8 Dec 1877; died 22 April 1956 MN
		married Charles Lewis KIRKWOOD 22 June 1916
	3382. John Avery, Jr.	born 26 Nov 1881; died 18 May 1944 Wells, Fairbault , MN; married Helen ___ ca ___
	3383. Eva	born 14 June 1883; died 10 May 1945 Eyota, MN
	3384. Martha	born 7 Mar 1885; died 2 May 1950 Rush, MN
	3385. Lawrence	born 14 May 1889; died 16 Aug 1961 Eyota, Olmsted, MN
		married Marjorie CHERMAK 12 Oct 1916
		(she born 22 July 1896 Chatfield, MN; died 0 Nov 1962 Rochester, MN
		(she dau/o Joseph CHERMAK and Nora E. CASE)
	3386. Howard	born 5 Sep 1892; died 5 Jul;y 1965 MN; married Lillian MOLKE 18 Nov 1915

Child: Walter Howard-[9] BUSH born 27 July 1916, died 29 July 1995

2321. PROCTOR F-[7] BOWKER, son of Amos-[6] BOWKER (Joseph-[5]; Daniel-[4]; John-[3]; Edmund-[2,1]) and Lucy SNOW, was born 7 July 1840 VT. He married Emerett " Emma" SHERMAN on 18 July 1866 MA. She was the daughter of Henry SHERMAN and Cynthia ___; and was born ca 1848 NY; died ___ TX. Proctor-[7] BOWKER died 6 July 1923 San Antonio, TX

Children of Proctor F-[7] BOWKER and " Emma" SHERMAN:
Surname **BOWKER**

3387. Etta May	born 3 May 1867 MA; died 28 Feb 1901 MA	single	EOL
3388. Medora	born 3 Apr 1870; died 5 Jul 1944 San Antonio, TX		
	married George E. CUTLER ca ____ (he born ____; died 6 Sep 1941 TX)		

2337. SEELEY-[7] OWEN, son of Hannah-[6] SEELEY (Deborah-[5] BOWKER; Elias-[4]; John-[3]; Edmund-[2,1]) and Ethan OWEN, was born 20 March 1805 Milton, Chittenden, VT. He was a Mormon and a polygamist. He married first to Lydia Adeline OWEN on 27 Nov 1834 Schuyler, IL. She was the daughter of ____ OWEN and ____, and was born 1 July 1811 Perry, Ohio, died 19 Sept 1846. He took a second wife , Elizabeth Betsey PICKLE/ PICKELL 22 March 1847 OH. She was the daughter of Minard J. PICKLE/ PICKELL and Barbara Mellick FARLEY, and was born May 1826 OH , died after 1900. He married third to Helen Louisa FREDERICK Jefferds ca 1853 (age 14). She was the daughter of David Ira FREDERICK and Martha INGERSOLL, and was born 19 June 1839. Her mother died and she was given to Oren JEFFERDS and his wife to raise .

They adopted her ca 1845. She died ca 1876. Seeley[7] OWEN was a member of the 1847 Mormon Pioneer Vanguard Co. (Lore tells us that Helen received permission to leave Seeley on 25 March 1857, due to the fact that another wife abused her by pounding her with clubs and chairs.. However, she never divorced him)

Children of Seeley[7] OWEN and Lydia OWEN:
Surname **OWEN**

+	**3389. LYDIA ANN**	born 8 Jan 1837 IL; died 26 Nov 1895 Provo, UT	
		married Abraham Golden CONOVER 26 Feb 1857 Salt Lake City, UT	
		(he s/o Col. Peter Wilson CONOVER and Evaline B. GOLDEN)	
		(he born 18 May 1830 ; died _____)	

Children of Seeley[7] OWEN and Elizabeth PICKLE/ PICKELL:
Surname **OWEN**

	3390. Samuel Pickle/Pickell	born 25 Jan 1850; died 3 Oct 1852 Great Salt Lake Desert, UT	EOL
+	**3391. BARBARA ELIZABETH**	born 28 Sep 1853; died 7 May 1919 Park City, Summit, UT	
		married John McClelland BUTTREY 17 Nov 1870 Provo, UT	
		(he s/o John Thompson BUTTREY and Winnie Matilda WILES)	
		(he born 9 Mar 1843 NC; died 25 Feb 1917 Salt Lake City, UT	
	3392. Hannah	born ca 1855; died ___; possibly married John GILSON ca ____	
		(he s/o John William GILSON and Hannah OWEN)	
		Child: John E[9] GILSON born Aug 1875 Utah	
	3393. Seeley, Jr.	born ca 1858; died ____	
+	**3394. JULIA ANN**	born 9 May 1860; died 23 June 1931 UT; married Jerome KEMPTON 10 May 1876;	
		(he born 2 Sep 1851 UT; died 11 Feb 1927 UT)	
	3395. Joseph	born 18 Oct 1861 UT 3396. Miner/ Minard Pickle born Jan 1865 UT	

2347. NATHANIEL B-[7] SEELEY, son of Luke[6] SEELEY (Deborah[5] BOWKER; Elias[4]; John[3]; Edmund[2,1]) and Electra/Electa OWEN, was born ca 1824/25 VT. He married Elizabeth CAMPBELL ca 1844. She was the daughter of John Finley CAMPBELL and Mary SLEETH, and was born ca 1827 OH; died 1906 KS. Nathaniel-[7] SEELEY died ca 1895 IL.

Children of Nathaniel B-[7] SEELEY and Elizabeth CAMPBELL;
Surname **SEELEY**

3397. Edward	born 3 May 1845; died 13 Jan 1928 IL
3398. Electa Anna	born ca 1848 IL; died ____
3399. Margaret Mary	born 13 March 1853 Rushville, IL; died ____; married Alexander TRIMBLE ca 1877
	(he born Jan 1853 IL; died 28 Sep 1927 Rushville, IL)
	Children: Walter Warren[9] born 7 Sep 1881, died 2 June 1940, married Mabel B. WRIGHT;
	Dwight E[9] born Aug 1886 IL ; and Roy A[9] TRIMBLE born Oct 1889 IL
3400. Stephen A. Douglas	born ca 1854 IL; died ____
3401. Luke	born 2 Aug 1857 IL; died 10 Nov 1929 IL; married Izarah Freelove BOWMAN
	Children: Bert -[9]; Everett-[9]; and Violet-[9] SEELEY
3402. William Alfred	born 29 Mar 1861; died 1 Nov 1933 IL; married Flora BODENHAMER
3403. Alice	born 29 Mar 1861 IL; died 13 Oct 1919 IL; married Joseph HODGES

2372. JOHN BORTHWICK-[7] WILLISON   (see # 1341 CANDACE-[6] BOWKER)

2373. EDWIN A -[7] WILLISON, son of James A-[6] WILLISON (Esther[5] BOWKER; Silas Day[4]; John[3]; Edmund-[2,1]) and Margaret BORTHWICK, was born 10 March 1828 NY. He married Mary Maria RICHARDS on 6 Aug 1855 at Barry, MI. She was the daughter of William RICHARDS and Elizabeth Betsey ____, and was born 21 May 1836 OH; died 2 March 1895 at Barry, MI. . Edwin-[7] WILLISON died 25 June 1881 Barry, MI..

Children of Edwin A-[7] WILLISON and Mary M. RICHARDS:
Surname **WILLISON**

3404. John Edwin	born Sept 1856; died 1936; married Lydia Izadora KELLOGG 4 Mar 1887 MI.
	(she born 17 Feb 1865 Barry, MI; died 20 March 1934 MI)
3405. William Emmett	born Nov 1861; died 23 Nov 1924
3406. Sarah Eliza	born 16 Oct 1866; died 14 Mar 1924 Barry, MI
3407. Clarence	born 15 June 1870; died 25 Nov 1934 Barry, MI
3408. Sanford Sidney	born 27 Sept 1872; died 27 Dec 1945 Barry, MI
3409. Epaphroditus R.	born 24 June 1875; died 13 July 1949 Barry, MI

2377. ELIZABETH JANE⁻⁷ WILLISON, sister of above, was born 25 June 1837 OH. She married John Harvey GUTCHESS ca 1857. He was the son of David GUTCHESS and Sally Marie EMERSON, and was born10 Aug 1832; died 12 March 1913 MI. Elizabeth⁻⁷ WILLISON died 15 Nov 1921 MI.

Children of Elizabeth⁻⁷ WILLISON and John Harvey GUTCHESS;
Surname **GUTCHESS**

	3410. Olive	born ca 1858 MI; died _____
	3411. Cinderella	born ca 1864 MI; died ____
+	**3412. SAMUEL VICTOR**	born 13 May 1867 Barry, MI; died 14 Mar 1955 Barry, MI
		married Mariam Helena SHELDON ca ____
	3413. Emma	born 14 Sept 1872; died _____; married Harry PATTERSON ca _____
	3414. Charles Emerson	born 25 Apr 1874 MI; died 23 Jan 1929
		1 married Lena FRANK ca ____; 2 married Dora WILKINSON ca ___
	3415. Dora E.	born 26 June 1875; died 23 July 963 MI
	3416. Ina Lewis	born 4 Oct 1878; died _____; married William OFFLEY ca _____

2382. WILLIAM MURL⁻⁷ COY, son of Esther⁻⁶ WILLISON (Esther⁻⁵ BOWKER; Silas Day⁻⁴; John⁻³; Edmund⁻²,¹) and John G. COY, was born ca 1835 at Tompkins County, NY. He married Mary Ann DUGAN on 26 Jan 1856 at Coshocton, OH. She was the daughter of _____ DUGAN and ____, and was born 7 Apr 1838 OH; died 7 Aug 1892 IA. William Murl⁻⁷ COY died 26 Aug 1888 at Villisca, Montgomery, IA.

Children of William M⁻⁷ COY and Mary Ann DUGAN
Surname **COY**

3417. John Francis	born 30 July 1857; died 28 Aug 1928 NE	3420. Rebecca Minnie	born June 1865 OH
3418. Edward Edwin	born 1 Sept 1858; died 31 March 1947 CA	3421. Carrie	born 3 Feb 1870 OH
3419. Lorenzo Dow	born March 1860 OH	3422. William Clarence	born July 1872 IL
3423. Bert/Bertie	born 5 Dec 1875 IL; died 3 Nov 1903 NE		

2383. WILLIAM⁻⁷ ARMSTRONG, son of Cynthia⁻⁶ WILLISON (Esther⁻⁵ BOWKER; Silas Day⁻⁴; John⁻³; Edmund⁻²,¹) and Isaac ARMSTRONG, and was born 29 Nov 1830 Genoa, Cayuga, NY. He married Sarah Jane CONREY ca _____. She was the daughter of John A. CONREY and Almira _____, and was born 11 July 1834 NY; died 8 April 1923 MO. William⁻⁷ ARMSTRONG died 16 March 1903 Unionville, MO.

Children of William⁻⁷ ARMSTRONG and Sarah Jane CONREY:
Surname **ARMSTRONG**

+	**3424. FREDERICK**	born 15 April 1857 Genoa, NY; died 24 May 1934 Unionville, MO
		married Helen TOWNSEND 23 May 1877 (she born ca 1858; died ca 1940)
	3425. Ida	born 11 May 1858 NY; died 5 March 1940

2394. SILAS DAY⁻⁷ TABER, son of Mehitable⁻⁶ BOWKER (Esther ⁵;Silas Day ⁻⁴; John⁻³; Edmund⁻²,¹) and Wing TABER, was born 15 June 1812 at Scipio, Oswego County, NY. He married Harriet CLOSE on 21 Dec 1837 at Scipio. She was the daughter of Abel CLOSE and Sarah W. ADAMS (Caleb), and was born ca 1814; died 26 April 1887 Moravia, NY. Silas Day⁻⁷ TABER died 20 May 1865 at Elkland, PA

Children of Silas Day⁻⁷ TABER and Harriet CLOSE:
Surname **TABER**

	3426. Wing	born 18 Sep 1841 NY; died 15 Feb 1912 Auburn, Cayuga, NY
		married Jane Menaugh HATHAWAY ca ____
		(she born 25 May 1840 NJ; died 18 Dec 1917 Auburn, NY)
		Child: Charles F⁻⁹ TABER born ca 1870; married Phebe Anna STYER 11 Aug 1917 Sitka, AK
+	**3427. FRANKLIN PIERCE**	born 16 Jan/ June 1853 Cayuga Co., NY; died 27 May 1914 Auburn, NY; an attorney married Mary Kittie⁻⁸ PARKER ca 1880 (# 3443)

2397. AMAZIAH⁻⁷ TABER, brother of above, was born 1 July 1818 at Scipio, Oswego County, NY. He married Laura C. MORSE on 31 May 1841. She was the daughter of Gershom MORSE (Peter) and Rachel LITTLE (Moses), and was born 18 May 1816 at Moravia, Cayuga, NY; died 23 Aug 1904 at Moravia. Amaziah⁻⁷ TABER died 13 May 1891 at Moravia, NY, just a few days before his 50ᵗʰ wedding anniversary.

Children of Amaziah[7] TABER and Laura C. MORSE:
Surname **TABER**

3428.	Jane Davis	born 5 July 1843 Locke, Cayuga, NY; died 1 March 1916 Moravia, NY
		married George Zadock LESTER 21 Feb 1866
		(he born 21 June 1845 Sempronius, NY; died ___)
		(he s/o Thomas LESTER and Eliza RHODES)

Child: Charles-[9] LESTER born 5 June 1867, NY

3429.	Julia	born 7 Aug 1845 Locke, Cayuga, NY; died ____; married Volney ODELL 2 Nov 1867
		(he born 5 Mar 1846 Niles, NY; died 15 Feb 1876 Moravia, NY)
		(he s/o John C. ODELL (Levi) and Anna WESTFALL)

Children: Anna Laura-[9] ODELL born 6 Dec 1868, died 11 June 1894; and Volney[9] ODELL born 26 Oct 1876,
married Flora Luella (Lulu) PARSELL 22 Sep 1897 Niles, NY; died 13 Nov 1959

2398. WILLIAM[7] TABER, brother of above, was born 2 July 1820 at Scipio, Cayuga County, NY. He married Cordelia THOMPSON on 1 July 1844 at Locke, Cayuga County, NY. She was the daughter of Joseph THOMPSON and Hannah WHITE, and was born 20 June 1824 NY; died 29 June 1882 WI. William[7] TABER died 15 May 1873 Milwaukee, WI.

Children of William[7] TABER and Cordelia THOMPSON:
Surname **TABER**

	3430. Charlotte	born 9 June 1845 Fleming, Cayuga, NY; died ____
	3431. Margaret Mehitable	born 23 Nov 1850 NY/PA; died ____
+	**3432. CHARLES WILLIAM**	born 9 June 1867 Elkland, PA; died 16 Sept/Nov 1936 Los Angeles, CA
		married Emily Thornton BREESE Hawkes 12 Nov 1891 Milwaukee
		(she dau/o James Thomas BREESE and Eliza BABCOCK) (she born 8 Sept 1870 CAN.)

2402. JOHN QUINCY[7] TABER, brother of above, was born 2 Jan 1826 at Moravia, NY. He married Elizabeth R. SMITH ca ____. She was the daughter of Enoch SMITH and Hulda BAIRD, and was 6 June 1818 NY; died _____. John Quincy-[7] TABER died 2 Feb 1891 at Garden City, Mississippi.

Children of John Quincy[7] TABER and Elizabeth SMITH:
Surname **TABER**

+	**3433. ELLA ARVILLA**	born 9 Feb 1850 Moravia, NY; died 17 Oct 1895 Kansas City
		married William Henry FARNEY 11 Mar 1875 IL
		(he born 17 May 1851 KY; died 11 Dec 1927 CA)
		(he s/o David Radcliffe FARNEY and Melinda DUNCAN)
	3434. Edward	born 15 May 1851; died 16 Mar 1867 Racine, WI
	3435. Emma	born 23 Sep 1852 Yorkville, Racine, WI; died ____
		1 married F. Washington DOWNING 23 Sep 1869 ; 2 married Louis Howard ROSE Oct 1882
	3436. Mary	born 24 July 1856 WI; died _____
+	**3437. HENRY R.**	born 10 Apr 1858 WI; died ____; lumberman
		married Elizabeth Theresa WEBSTER 8 Apr 1881 (she born 30 June 1858 WI)
	3438. Mehitable A.	born 30 Mar 1860 WI; died ____
	3439. Doris Ann	born 18 Jan 1862 Union Grove, Racine, WI; died 10 Jan 1940 Los Angeles, CA
		1 married Warren Bennett WOOD 26 Nov 1888 Portage, WI

Child: Viola-[9] WOOD born 18 Dec 1891

2 married George Albert SARLES 1 Nov 1910

2403. MARY[7] TABER, sister of above, was born 8 Sept 1827 at Scipio, Cayuga, NY. She married John Locke PARKER on 13 Dec 1848 at ___, Cayuga County, NY. He was the son of John H. PARKER (Caleb) and Esther LOCKE (John), and was born 28 Mar 1825 Moravia; died ___ Auburn, Cayuga, NY. Mary[7] TABER died 23 April 1896 at Auburn, Cayuga, NY.

Children of Mary[7] TABER and John Locke PARKER:
Surname **PARKER**

	3440. Wing Taber, Esq.	born 13 Dec 1849 Moravia, Cayuga, NY; died 23 Mar 1916 Moravia
		1 married Mary JOHNSON ca ____ (she born ____; died 1874)
		2 married Margaret E. " Nellie " KINDRED 1 Oct 1875 Manhattan, NY
		(she born ___; died 1876)
		married Eleanor L. SMITH 1 April 1878 (she born ca 1847; died _____)
		(she dau/o Sullivan SMITH and ___ of Jamesville, WI)

183

Children of Mary[7] TABER and John Locke PARKER, continued:
Surname **PARKER**

3441. William John H.	born 23 Nov 1851 NY; died _____;	married Estelle TALLMAN ca ____
3442. Joseph	born 4 June 1853 NY; died _____;	married Josephine Olive SMITH ca ____
+ **3443. MARY KITTIE**	born 10 Feb 1855 NY; married Franklin P[8] TABER 4 June 1879 Moravia, NY (# 3427)	
	(he born 16 June 1853 Cayuga Co., NY; died 27 May 1914 Auburn, NY	

2404. JASPER DRAKE[7] BOWKER, son of Archibald[6] BOWKER (Silas Day[5,4]; John-[3]; Edmund-[2,1]) and Rebecca V. DRAKE, was born Jan 1812 Cayuga County, NY. He married Ann HINKLEY ca ____. She was the daughter of ____ HINKLEY and ____, and was born ____; died ____. Jasper Drake[7] BOWKER died 3 April 1854.

Children of Jasper Drake-[7] BOWKER and Ann HINKLEY:
Surname **BOWKER**

3444. Archibald	born 15 May 1847 NY ; died 2 Aug 1864 (age 17-2-17)
	Note: he was killed in the Civil War. He served in Company C, 11th Regiment of NY Volunteers
3445. Francis	born 8 July 1849 NY

2405. WILLIAM D[7] BOWKER, twin brother of above, was born Jan 1812 Cayuga County, NY. He married Alma S. POWERS ca ___. She was the daughter of Jacob POWERS and Ruth ROBERTS, and was born ca 1810 NY; died ____. William D[7] BOWKER died _____.

Children of William D[7] BOWKER and Alma POWERS:
Surname **BOWKER**

3446. Jasper	born 6 Nov 1838 Cayuga Co., NY; died 20 April 1932 Superior, NE		
3447. Irene	born 25 Feb 1840 Cayuga Co.		
3448. Ruth P.	born 30 Oct 1841 Cayuga Co.	3450. Almira A.	born 15 Nov 1844 NY
3449. Alma Jane	born 12 July 1842 NY	3451. Louisa Lida	born 19 Aug 1846 NY
3452. Euphemia N.	born 12 Dec 1847 NY; died ____		
3453. Eri	born 10 July 1849 Cayuga Co., ; died ____; married Sarah MORGAN ca ____		
	Child: Niles[9] BOWKER born 4 July 1893 Nebraska		
+ **3454. WILLIAM HENRY**	born 4 Oct 1850 Cayuga Co., NY; died 8 June 1917 West Liberty, IA		
	1 married Almina C. MALICK 12 Jan 1872 Seward County, Nebraska		
	(she dau/o Uriah MALICK and Cloe POWELL)(she born __; died 1890 Milford, NE)		
	2 married Elizabeth VERRY 30 Nov 1892		
3455. Samuel +++	born ca 1856; died Mar 1880 Milford, Seward, Nebraska		
	married Sara C. GRANGER Dec 1879		
	(she dau/o Benjamin Doughty GRANGER and Clarinda L. SPENCER)		
	(she born 1866 OH; died 18 Aug 1880 Seward, NE) (childbirth) EOL		

+++ Source: History of Seward County, Nebraska, Chapter 3

" In March 1880, a bloody tragedy occurred at East Milford, which terminated in the murder of Samuel BOWKER, by two brothers, Milton and John GRANGER. This difficulty grew out of a quarrel between the elder GRANGER and BOWKER, in which BOWKER knocked GRANGER down. Somehow, Mr. GRANGER was dissatisfied with the marriage of his young daughter Sara to Samuel BOWKER some months before. This is supposed to have been the beginning of the trouble . Mr. BOWKER was quite a pugilist and was at all times ready to resent what he considered an insult or an injury, with his fist. He was, some days after this fracas, passing the store of the young GRANGERS, and was invited to alight from his wagon, which he promptly did, and pulled off his coat and announced himself ready for the two GRANGERS.

Some hot words followed with blows, when Milton (GRANGER) drew a revolver and shot twice at BOWKER, when his antagonist knocked the revolver from his hands. John (GRANGER) opened fire. He fired 5 or 6 shots, two of which took effect, one striking near the shoulder blade and passing down the spine, which caused his (BOWKER'S) death. The GRANGER brothers were arrested and put on trial where they pleaded guilty to manslaughter and received a sentence of ten years in State Prison ."

Note: The subject of the dispute ,Sara GRANGER, was only 14 years old when she died in childbirth – some months after her husband, Samuel BOWKER, was murdered by her siblings. A tragic ending for this young couple.

2400. SILAS III[7] BOWKER, brother of above, was born 10 March 1815 at Locke, Cayuga County, NY. He married Harriet ROGERS on 5 April 1837 Cayuga Co., NY. She was the daughter of Samuel ROGERS and Nancy REYNOLDS, and was born 22 Sep 1814 at Summer Hill, Cayuga, NY; died 3 Nov 1886 at Homer, NY. Silas III-[7] BOWKER died 18 Feb 1877 at Homer.

Children of Silas III-7 BOWKER and Harriet ROGERS:
Surname **BOWKER**

<table>
<tr><td></td><td>3456. Lura Jane</td><td>born 7 Nov 1837 Cayuga Co., NY; died _____
1 married Joseph MC CARTNEY ca ____;   2 married John ROGERS ca ____</td></tr>
<tr><td></td><td>3457. Mary Ann</td><td>born ca 1839 NY; died _____;   married Robert Mc CARTNEY ca ____</td></tr>
<tr><td>+</td><td>**3458. GEORGE <u>OSCAR</u>**</td><td>born 22 Sept 1840 Springport, Cayuga, NY; died 16 Feb 1911 Oxford Mills, IA
1 married Louisa E. LABAR 15 Dec 1861 Five Corners, NY
(she born 8 Dec 1842; died 31 Dec 1882)
(she dau/o Theodore LE BAR and Louisa Harriet ST. GERMAIN)
2 married Lydia " Liddie " HOLT 9 Feb 1884
3 married Mary Anna BREESE / BREECE 21 March 1891</td></tr>
<tr><td>+</td><td>**3459. FREDERICK ERI**</td><td>born 19 Sept 1842 Springport, NY; died
married Sarah Ellen WOODARD 19 Sep 1867 Skaneateles, Onondaga , NY
(she born 23 Jan 1847; died 23 Feb 1889)
(she dau/o Horace WOODARD and Chloe Hinckley HAMBLIN)</td></tr>
<tr><td></td><td>3460. Harriet A.</td><td>born 13 June 1844 Homer, NY; died ____; married Albert MOSHER ca _____</td></tr>
<tr><td></td><td>3461. Aurelia</td><td>born 13 May 1845 NY; died ca 1849</td></tr>
<tr><td></td><td>3462. William Dwight</td><td>born ca 1849 NY; died ca 1874; married Dell TANNER ca ____
Children: Hattie-9 BOWKER born ca ___; and Clara-9 BOWKER born ca ___</td></tr>
<tr><td></td><td>3463. Un-named child</td><td>born ca 1853; died young   EOL</td></tr>
<tr><td>+</td><td>**3464. ROSA**</td><td>born 20 Feb 1858 Lysander, NY; died 15 March 1934 Memphis, NY
married William Jefferson RYDER 10 March 1880
(he born June 1860; died 15 April 1945)</td></tr>
</table>

2409. ERI-7 BOWKER, brother of above, was born ca 1829 at Summer Hill, Cayuga County, NY. He married Roseanna WIGGINS ** on 2 Nov 1856 at the Mansion House in Homer, Cortland County, NY. by the Rev. T. E. THURSTON. She was the daughter of Owen WIGGINS (he born ca 1803 Dublin, Ireland ; died ca 1852 Ireland) and Molly ____, and was born ca 1830 in Ireland, died 2 Oct 1893 at Summer Hill, Cayuga , NY. Eri-7 BOWKER died 14 March 1894 at Homer, Cortland, NY.

The following was an article from the Homer, NY Newspaper – dated 15 March 1894

" Eri BOWKER Hangs Himself in a Fit of Depression "

" Eri BOWKER, who has recently moved from his farm in Summer Hill to live with his son, committed suicide yesterday between twelve and one o'clock PM. He had just been moving into his son's house, and while his son was away he went to the barn and hung himself from a beam, and was found not long after.

Coroner BRADFORD was called to his son's home on the Summer Hill Road, about four miles west of this village, to examine into the case. Dr.BRADFORD informs us that Mr. BOWKER, who was sixty-four years old, was afflicted with melancholia since his wife's death about a year ago and it was thought that he had once before attempted to take his life, while staying with a son in Auburn (NY), by taking camphor. He was very despondent and his mind was somewhat unbalanced. His family had watched him to see that he did himself no harm, but this time he eluded them and succeeded in his design. No inquest was deemed necessary by the coroner as the facts were easily ascertained.".

**   Roseanna WIGGINS, born ca 1830 in Ireland, left her home there on 14 April 1848 during the infamous " potato famine " and journeyed to America aboard the ship ATLANTA with a ticket which had been sent to her by her grandmother. Arriving in New York on 10 Oct 1848, she immediately went to her uncle's (Frank THOMPSON) home where she discovered that her grandmother had passed away. She stayed with her uncle until she was able to find employment. In Nov 1849 she secured a position as a housekeeper with a Mr. A. Y. BENSON of Brooklyn, and was charged with caring for the seven BENSON children.

Roseanna worked for the BENSON family for nearly 4 ½ years, but had to return to Dublin to care for her elderly, ailing parents. When she arrived in Ireland she found that her parents had already passed away, and so she returned to America and her position with the BENSON family. Her sister Mary returned with her and was also employed by the BENSONS. After sometime, her sister Mary left the BENSON household and Roseanna did not see her for many years after that.

The BENSON family spent summers at their farm on Long Island, near Islip. Roseanna would go there with them. Mrs. BENSON was not fond of that place and wished to return to her old home which was Summer Hill, Cayuga County, NY. She got her wish, and that was where Roseanna would meet her future husband, Eri BOWKER. At that time he was one of the BENSONS " hired hands ".

Children of Eri-[7] BOWKER and Roseanna WIGGINS:
Surname **BOWKER**

+	**3465. FRANK DRAKE**	born 13 Feb 1858 Summer Hill, NY; died 6 Jan 1933
		married Helen Townley HALL 18 Aug 1877
		(she dau/o Ezra Russell HALL and Clarinda LANTERMAN)
		(she born 3 Oct 1859; died _____)
+	**3466. MARY R.**	born Dec 1860; died _____
		married John E. LOOMIS of Moravia, NY on 2 Nov 1881
+	**3467. FRED**	born 27 Dec 1861 Summer Hill; died ____
+	**3468. EUGENE WIGGINS**	born 23 May 1864 Summer Hill; died 28 Mar 1932 Cortland, NY
		married Mary Ann REED 28 Dec 1887
		(she dau/o Samuel Sanford REED and Clara HENDERSON)
		(she born 19 March 1869 Otisco, NY; died 1 Jan 1945 Cortland, NY)

2411. SILAS-[7] DRAKE, son of Lisa-[6] BOWKER (Silas-[5,4]; John-[3]; Edmund-[2,1]) and Nathan DRAKE, was born ca 1813 Cayuga County, NY. He married first to Sally ___. She was born ca 1819 NY; died before 1860. His second marriage was to Emily Emma SKINNER on 30 April 1851 OH. She was the daughter of ____ SKINNER and ____, and was born ca 1827/30 OH; died ca 1912 . Silas-[7] DRAKE died ca 1864 Concord, Delaware County, Ohio.

Children of Silas-[7] DRAKE and Sally ____:
Surname **DRAKE**   (all children born Ohio)

3469. Miranda	born ca 1845; died ____	
3470. Laura Mehitable	born 29 May 1848; die 22 Sept 1917 Prospect, OH	
	married Willis WEEKS 25 July 1865 (he born ca 1842; died 1917)	

Children: Charles-[9] WEEKS born ca 1867; died 1944; Cora E-[9] WEEKS born ca 1873; and Bessie-[9] WEEKS born ca 1880

Children of Silas-[7] DRAKE and Emily SKINNER:
Surname **DRAKE**   (all children born OH)

3471. Sarah	born ca 1850; died before 1860	
3472. Joseph	born ca 1851/52; died 5 Apr 1876	
3473. Frances	born ca 1853; died ca 1931	3476. Elizabeth Ella born ca 1861; died 3 July 1937 OH
3474. William B.	born ca 1855; died ca 1860	3477. Benjamin E. born 11 Oct 1863; died 5 Dec 1943
3475. Jackson D.	born ca 1858; died 1928 OH married Ida B. JONES ca _____	

2412. MARY ANN-[7] DRAKE, sister of above, was born 1 Oct 1814 at Cayuga County, NY She married first to Luther COOK ca 1834. He was the son of ____ COOK and ____, and was born ca 1810, died ca 1843. Her second marriage was to John DOUDS ca 1845. He was the son of ____ DOUDS and ____, and was born ca 1828; died 1885. Mary Ann-[7] DRAKE died 8 Oct 1878 at Hudson, Summit, OH.

Children of Mary Ann-[7] DRAKE and Luther COOK
Surname **COOK**

3478. Edward	born 9 Aug 1835; died 21 Sept 1843 OH	
3479. Julia	born ca 1836 OH; died _____	
3480. Rufus	born ca 1839 OH; died 18 Feb 1863 TN	

Note: He served in the Civil War as a member of Co. K, 19th Ohio Infantry Regiment, and died of disease (inflammation of the lungs) at the Regimental Hospital in Murfreesville, TN

+	**3481. SIMON L.**	born Apr 1843/44 OH; died 19 Jan 1910 Chattanooga, TN
		married Adaline THOMPSON 23 March 1865 Summit, OH
		(she dau/o Mills THOMPSON and Katherine ALLEN)
		(she born 26 Sept 1841 OH; died _____Chattanooga, TN)

Note; Simon also served in Co. K, 19th Ohio Infantry Regiment during the Civil War

Children of Mary Ann-[7] DRAKE and John DOUDS:
Surname **DOUDS**

3482. William	born ca 1844 OH; died _____	3485. Anna Monita	born ca 1857 OH
3483 James	born ca 1849 OH; died ____		
3484. Caroline / Carrie E	born May 1853 OH; died ca 1914; married Charles Albert VIERS ca ____		

2413. AMY MARY-[7] DRAKE, sister of above, was born ca 1817 NY. She married Leland/Lelon COOK on 21 Oct 1835 OH. He was the son of Rufus COOK and Sarah ____, and was born Feb 1812 MA; died 5 Nov 1876 OH. Amy M-[7] DRAKE died 3 March 1864 at Boston, Summit, Ohio.

Children of Amy-7 DRAKE and Leland COOK:
Surname **COOK**

3486. Orrin/Orson	born Sep 1836 OH; died 16 Aug 1904 Summit, OH	
	married Ann S. CHRISMAN ca 1858	
	Children: Albert Perry-9 (1859-1929); Sidney-9 (1860-1934); and Amy C-9 COOK (1870-1936)	
3487. Orpha	born ca 1838 OH; died _____; married George W. MC KISSON ca ____	
	Children: Amy Catherine-9 born ca 1871, died ca 1951 CA; Ethel Adeline-9 born 20 Nov 1876,	
	died 5 Nov 1949; and George-9 MC KISSON born 1879, died 1900	

2415. JASPER B-7 DRAKE, brother of above, was born 5 July 1820 at Summer Hill, Cayuga County, NY. He married Caroline HARDY 18 Aug 1844. She was the daughter of Nathaniel HARDY, Sr. and Rebecca REED and was born ca 1824, died ___. Jasper B-7 DRAKE died 9 Aug 1899 at Ness City, Kansas.

Children of Jasper B-7 DRAKE and Caroline HARDY:
Surname **DRAKE**

3488. William James	born 4 June 1845 Summit OH; died 8 Sep 1919; married Margaret A. JONES ca ____	
	Children: Ambrose-9 DRAKE born 18 Sep 1870 and William W-9 DRAKE born 2 Aug 1873	
	Note: Served in the Civil War in Company C, 59th Ohio Infantry	
+ **3489. ANDREW TODD**	born 22 Nov 1848 OH; died 14 May 1935	
	1 married Sarah Jane BENBROOK (she born Feb 1849 IL ; died ca 1932)	
	2 married Olive LEACH 20 July 1868 (she born ca 1853; died 1880)	
3490. Orville L.	born 2 Nov 1852 OH; died 13 Jan 1933 Seattle, WA.	
	married S. Mary JACKSON _____ca ____ (she born Feb 1859 IA; died ____)	
3491. Daniel/Denzil	born 26 Apr 1859 OH; died 18 Jan 1933 OK	
	Child: Dora-9 DRAKE born 10 March 1888; died 3 June 1890)	
+ **3492. JOHN BRUFF**	born 4 Sep 1860 OH; died 16 Aug 1931 Ness City, Kansas	
	1 married Mary BURRIS ca 1887 (she born Dec 1861 OH)	
	(she dau/o Jacob BURRIS and Martha H. ____)	
	2 married Nancy Jane WELLS ca ___; 3 married Sadie Leote LARKINS 13 June 1907	
	(she born 16 Oct 1871; died 25 Dec 1932 KS)	
	(she dau/o Reuben LARKIINS and Sarah FREDERICKS)	
+ **3493. HOWARD MILTON**	born 2 Feb 1862 OH; died 29 Sep 1925 KS	
	married Lydia F. ____ ca 1883 (she born ca 1868 IL)	
3494. Harriet E.	born 25 Feb 1864 IA; died 3 July 1922 WA.; married Sylvester William WELLS ca ___	
3495. Mary C.	born ca 1867 IA; died _____ 3496 . James B. born ca 1869 OH; died ____	

2420. BENJAMIN-7 DRAKE, brother of above, was born 1 April 1832 at Boston, Summit Co., IL. He married Elizabeth Emily CUNNINGHAM 4 July 1855. She was the daughter of _____ CUNNINGHAM and _____, and was born 5 Dec 1837 KY; died 3 Jan 1907 at Porter, Van Buren, Michigan. Benjamin-7 DRAKE died 10 March 1903 at Porter. MI.

Children of Benjamin-7 DRAKE and Elizabeth E. CUNNINGHAM:
Surname **DRAKE** (all children born MI)

3497. William A.	born Dec 1856; died 4 March 1915	
3498. Albert Salvans	born 30 March 1859; died 27 Nov 1916	
	1 married Ida May BERRY 3 May 1891; (she born ca 1874; died 1947)	
	2 married Nancy Ann HUDSON	
3499. James Edward	born 9 March 1861; died _____	
3500. Elmer Wilson	born ca 1863; died 8 Feb 1919 Porter, VB, MI.	
3501. Orpha Jane	born ca 1867; died 1930 Kalamazoo, MI; married Sarah Elizabeth MAXHAM	
3502. Bertha May	born 1 Dec 1868 MI; married _____ JAMES ca ____; resided Watervliet, MI	
3503. Mary Agnes	born 15 May 1871 MI; died ____	
3504. Isaac Newton	born 7 April 1877 MI; died 9 Aug 1921 SD *; married Florence ASHWORTH ca ___ *	

Newton DRAKE served in the Spanish American War in Co. K, 33rd MI Infantry from 16 May 1898 to 4 Jan 1899. He contracted several diseases. He was a patient at several hospitals and died at the Battle Mountain Sanatarium in Hot Springs, South Dakota.

3505. Clyde Irwin	born 22 April 1879 MI; died ca 1907	

2421. NATHAN-7 DRAKE, brother of above, was born 9 June 1834 at Summit County, Ohio. He married Lucy Mariah RHODENBAUGH on 15 October 1859 at Summit County, Ohio. She was the daughter of Isaac RHODENBAUGH and Sarah (Katie) _____, and was born July 1843 OH; died 29 March 1921 Cuyahoga, OH. Nathan-7 DRAKE died 16 May 1902 OH.

Children of Nathan-[7] DRAKE and Lucy RHODENBAUGH:
Surname **DRAKE**

	3506. Sylvia/Libbie	born ca 1865 OH; died 19 Dec 1960 OH
+	**3507. HARLEY J.**	born 28 July 1872 OH; died ____
		married Ettie Jennie GREEN 3 June 1896 (she born ca July 1868 PA ; died ___)
	3508. Sadie/Sada	born 6 June 1876 OH; died 3 June 1966 Lakewood, OH EOL

2422. MEHITABLE-[7] DRAKE, sister of above, was born 29 Feb 1836 at Summit County, Ohio. She married Joseph HILL ca ____. He was the son of ___ HILL and ____, and was born ca 1824 VT; died 29 June 1913 OH. Mehitable-[7] DRAKE died 17 Sept 1888 at Portage, OH. Joseph HILL married second to Rosalia Augusta WARRINER on 1 March 1889 at Akron, Ohio.

Children of Mehitable-[7] DRAKE and Joseph HILL:
Surname **HILL**

	3509. Lilly	born 6 Mar 1856 OH; died 5 Dec 1862
	3510. child	born ca 1859 OH; died ____
	3511. Charles Grant	born 30 Sep 1864 OH; died 7 Apr 1933
	3512. Jessie	born Mar 1867 OH; died ____
	3513. Isa May	born 8 Feb 1870; died 21 July 1933 Akron, OH
		married Frank Wilmer MORRIS ca 1888
+	**3514. JOITA JUBA**	born 30 Nov 1871; died 22 July 1949; married Emily Henrietta SPANG ca 1895
	3515. Acquilla	born ca 1874; died ___
	3516. Schuyler James	born 1 Nov 1875; died 15 Aug 1955; married Rhoda May FASIG 20 Sept 1950
	3517. George M.	born ca 1879/80; died ____

2423. MARIANNE-[7] DRAKE, sister of above, was born 13 Jan 1839 at Summit County, Ohio. She married Thomas Wesley CARTER ca 1858. He was the son of ____ CARTER and ____, and was born ca 1839; died before 1910. Marianne-[7] DRAKE died 25 Feb 1920 at Summit Co., Ohio.

Children of Marianne-[7] DRAKE and Thomas Wesley CARTER:
Surname **CARTER**

3518. Ada	born ca 1859 Boston Summit, OH	3521. Thomas Wesley, Jr.	born 18 Mar 1872
3519. William	born 6 Aug 1864; died 7 July 1895		marr. Myrta Emma WETMORE 1920
3520. Mary L.	born 9 Aug 1870 Summit		

2431. ROSETTA-[7] HENRY, daughter of Aurelia-[6] BOWKER (Silas Day-[5,4]; John-[3]; Edmund-[2,1]) and Levi HENRY, was born ca 1844 Cayuga County, NY. She married Bert/ Burt Delay LOOMIS ca _____. He was the son of Thomas Elderkin LOOMIS and Anna Luna MURPHY, and was born 4 April 1844; died ca 1905. Rosetta-[7] HENRY died ca 1910.

Children of Rosetta-[7] HENRY and Burt LOOMIS:
Surname **LOOMIS**

	3522. Ralph Delay	born ca 1867; died ____	3524. Henry	born June 1869; died ____
	3523. Claude	born ca ____; died _____		
+	**3525. INA**	born ca 1876; died May 1941 Cortland, Cortland, NY		
		married George S. WRIGHT 24 Nov 1896		
		(he s/o Charles E. WRIGHT and Sarah L. FOSTER) (he born ca 1877; died Aug 1941)		

2433. SETH CURTIS-[7] ROSE, son of William-[6] ROSE (Lisa-[5] BOWKER; Silas Day-[4;] John-[3;] Edmund-[2,1]) and Elizabeth (Sally) CURTIS, and was born ca 1813 NY. He married Jemima GAYLORD ca ___. She was the daughter of George A. GAYLORD and Lydia ____, and was born ca 1833 OH; died 14 Oct 1906 Delaware County, Ohio. Seth Curtis-[7] died ca 1893 OH.

Children of Seth Curtis-[7] ROSE and Jemima GAYLORD:
Surname **ROSE**

3526. Jessie	born ca 1861 Delaware Co., OH; died ca 1885
3527. Edna	born ca 1863; died 1875 OH
3528. Charles Gaylord	born 26 Apr 1865; died 4 June 1933
3529. James Curtis	born 7 July 1866; died 23 Jan 1942; married Cora Esther POTTER
	(she born 13 Dec 1871; died 26 May 1957)
3530. Edson	born ca 1876; died ____; married Olive KOBELSPERGER ca ___

2435. WILLIAM HENRY[-7] ROSE, brother of above, was born ca 1819 __. He married Eunice N. JOHNSON ca _____. She was born ca 1821 OH, died ca 1900. William Henry[-7] ROSE died ____.

Children of William Henry[-7] ROSE and Eunice N.JOHNSON:
Surname **ROSE**   (all born Trenton Twsp., Delaware County, Ohio

3531. Mary	born ca 1842 OH; died _____	
3532. Thankful C.	born ca 1846 OH; died _____	
	married Albert C. BAILEY 20 Nov 1866 ; (he born ca 1840 OH; died 1912)	
	Children: Grace-[9] BAILEY born ca 1867; and Bertha L-[9] BAILEY born 3 Oct 1870 OH	
	Note: Albert C. BAILEY served in the 32nd Regiment Ohio Infantry during the Civil War. He enlisted as a Private, and was promoted to Sgt.	
3533. Lyman H.	born 1 July 1847 OH; died 30 Oct 1916 Franklin, OH	
+ **3534. ELIZA**	born June/Sep 1849; died 25 Jan 1885 Waco, NE	
	married Edwin T. WILCOX ca ____ ; (he born ca 1852; died 1927)	
3535. Azelia	born ca 1854 OH; died ____; married Alonzo BARRETT ca _____	
+ **3536. WILLIAM ALBERT**	born 1 July 1856 Delaware Co., OH; died 13 Sep 1934 Boulder, CO	
	married Minnie Helen ATTEBERRY ca _____; (she born ca 1865; died 1944)	

2439. AARON[-7] HOWE, son of Cynthia-[6] ROSE (Lisa-[5] BOWKER; Silas Day-[4]; John-[3]; Edmund-[2,1]) and Eber Andrus HOWE, was born 10 Aug 1809 NY. He married Sarah HALSEY ca 1828 OH. She was the daughter of David HALSEY and ____, and was born 24 Sep 1810 OH; died 13 Jan 1865 Taylor City, IA. Aaron-[7] HOWE died 27 Sep 1898.

Children of Aaron-[7] HOWE and Sarah HALSEY:
Surname **HOWE**

3537. Silas R.	born 31 Aug 1829 OH; died 2 Nov 1864
3538. Cynthia	born 23 Oct 1830 OH; died ____
3539. Joshua A.	born 9 Aug 1832 OH; died 17 March 1900
3540. Charles	born 17 Sep 1834 OH; died 10 Nov 1917
3541. Ann	born 15 Jan 1836 OH; died _____
3542. Luther A.	born 17 Aug 1838 OH; died 3 June 1923 IL
	married Narcissus ROUNDTREE 19 Feb 1861 Knoxville, IL
	(she born 16 Jan 1839 IL; died 26 Mar 1929 IL
	(she dau/o John ROUNDTREE and Dosha FUQUA)
	Child: George A-[9] HOWE born ca ____
3543. William H.	born 23 Nov 1840 IL; died 13 Sept 1863
3544. George Washington	born 31 July 1843 IL; died 3 Oct 1920 NE; married Orilla P. WALKER
3545. Jerusha A.	born ca 1845 IL; died ____
3546. Marilla Jane	born 9 Apr 1849 IL; died 13 Mar 1929 IA; married Robert Johnson SALEN

2441. ELIZABETH ROSE [-7] HOWE, sister of above, was born 13 June 1812 NY. She married James Monroe COCKRELL (as his 2nd wife) ca 1830 at Delaware County, Ohio. He was the son of Edward COCKRELL and Elizabeth DAWSON, and was born 5 Jan 1810 VA; died ca 1880 in Delaware County, Ohio. Elizabeth-[7] HOWE died 22 Feb 1852 at Harlem Township, Delaware County, OH.

Children of Elizabeth-[7] HOWE and James Monroe COCKRELL:
Surname **COCKRELL**   (children born Harlem Twsp, Delaware, OH)

3547. Ann M.	born 16 Apr 1831; died 30 Nov 1831	EOL
3548. Peter	born 16 Aug 1832 OH; died 17 Mar 1904 NE	
3549. Emmanuel M.	born 20 Feb 1834; died 12 Dec 1898	
3550. Cynthia	born 30 Oct 1835; died _____	
3551. Hiram	born 15 July 1837; died _____	
3552. John D.	born 9 May 1839; died 1883	
3553. Clarinda	born 9 Dec 1841; died 8 Oct 1866	
3554. Elizabeth	born 15 Oct 1842; died 1900	
3555. George	born 23 Oct 1844; died 23 Aug 1851	EOL
3556. Nathan	born ca 1846; died Apr 1851	EOL
3557. James Jr.	born 22 Aug 1848; died 1942/48 OH	
3558. William Riley	born 28 June 1850; died 4 Feb 1940 OH	

2442. PHILETUS SWIFT/SMITH [7] **HOWE**, brother of above, was born 11 July 1813 at Barlow, NY. He married Eliza LAYCOCK on 29 Dec 1836 at Penn, Knox, OH. She was the daughter of Joseph LAYCOCK and Elizabeth TURNER, and was born 30 Aug 1816 NJ; died 4 May 1900 at Shepherd, Isabella, MI. Philetus[7] HOWE died 8 Jan 1899 at Shepherd, MI.

Children of Philetus[7] HOWE and Eliza LAYCOCK:
Surname **HOWE**

	3559. Joseph	born ca 1838 Knox Co., OH; died 9 Aug 1862 New Orleans, LA	EOL
		He was serving his country in the Civil War when he was killed at New Orleans.	
+	**3560. MARY ANN**	born 2 Sep 1839 OH; died 11 April 1866 MI; married James Dillon CHUBB ca _____	
		(he born 25 Dec 1837 Nankin, MI; died 16 Nov 1920	
	3561. John Robert	born 2 Feb 1841 OH; died 12 March 1894	
+	**3562. HULDAH**	born Oct 1844 OH; died _____	
		married Curtis BRACE (of Detroit, MI) 4 Apr 1861 Wayne, MI	
	3563. Absalom T.	born ca 1845 OH; died ____; married Elizabeth GRAHAM 28 Nov 1868	
		(she born ca 1850 NY; died _____) Child: Bertie[9] HOWE born ca 1869 MI	
	3564. Zorada	born Jan 1848 Wayne, MI; died 2 Nov 1905; married William SWIX ca 1863	
		(he born Aug 1837 MI; died 1904 MI)	

Children: Philetus[9] born ca 1867; John[9] born 1869 (possibly died young); Eliza[9] born ca 1870; and Cora[9] SWIX born 23 June 1882 MI (possibly married James G. FAUNCE)

3565. Elizabetth	born Oct 1849 OH; died _____; married _____ VANDEE ca ____
3566. Julius R.	born Oct 1849 OH ; died _____
	married Rhoda A. GEESEMAN ca 1890; (she born Oct 1860 OH; died _____)

Child: Ruth A[9] HOWE born 11 Sep 1894; and Leah K[9] HOWE born 15 Feb 1895 Toledo, OH

3567. William	born ca 1852; died ____
3568. Emma / Emily	born ca 1854 Wayne, MI; died _____; married _____ BENNETT ca _____

2455. HORATIO GATES[7] **ROSE**, son of Isaac Hobbs [6] ROSE (Lisa[5] BOWKER; Silas Day[4]; John[3]; Edmund[2,1]) and Anna YOUNG, was born 29 Oct 1826 OH. He married Margaret YOUNG 22 Apr 1849 at Adams, IN. She was the daughter of ____ YOUNG and Charity _____, and was born ca 1830 OH; died _____ . Horatio[7] ROSE, a cooper, served in the Civil War and died 27 Aug 1864 at Andersonville Prison, Ft. Sumter, GA.

Children of Horatio[7] ROSE and Margaret YOUNG:
Surname **ROSE**

3569. Julianna / Julia A.	born 6 Jan 1850 IN; died _____	3571. Mary Elizabeth	born 8 Sept 1856
3570. Charles I.	born 20 Feb 1852; died ____	3572. Edgar Alonzo	born 7 Mar 1861

2460. JEFFERSON[7] **ROSE**, son of Silas[6] ROSE (Lisa[5] BOWKER; Silas Day[4]; John[3]; Edmund[2,1]) and Nancy YOUNG, was born ca 1822. He married Sarah A. ___. She was born ca 1828 England; died _____. Jefferson[7] ROSE died ___.

Children of Jefferson[7] ROSE and Sarah A. ____:
Surname **ROSE**

3573. Jerusha	born ca 1847 OH; died ____	3576. Thomas	born ca 1858 OH; died ____
3574. Nancy	born ca 1849 OH; died ____	3577. Charles	born Dec 1859 OH
3575. John	born ca 1856 OH; died ____		

2468. SMITH[7] **ROSE**, son of Jacob Schoolcraft[6] ROSE (Lisa[5] BOWKER; Silas Day[4]; John[3]; Edmund[2,1]) and Deborah Ann HEAD, was born ca 1827 PA. He married Susan STOUT ca ____. She was the daughter of Seneca STOUT and Rachel CLEVENGER, and was born ca 1834; died 1901. Smith[7] ROSE died ca 1870.

Children of Smith[7] ROSE and Susan STOUT:
Surname **ROSE**

	3578. Mary E.	born ca 1853 OH; died ____
	3579. James Stout	born 5 June 1854 OH; died 2 Oct 1924; married Margaret Alice McFARLAND ca 1880
	3580. Jesse	born Oct 1856 OH; died ____; married Ellen Jane WHITE ca ____
		(she born ca 1859; died ca 1916)
	3581. Robert B.	born Dec 1857 OH; died _____; married Elizabeth H. _____ ca ____
		Children: Luella[9] ROSE born ca 1886; and Mary R.[9] ROSE born ca 1899
+	**3582. SARAH DEBORAH**	born Oct 1858; died _____; married Horace Greeley WEST ca ____
		(he s/o _____ WEST and _____) (he born ca 1856; died 1903)

2478. ANDREW B-⁷ CURREY, son of Cynthia-⁶ BOWKER (Daniel-⁵; Silas Day-⁴; John-³; Edmund-²,¹) and Samuel B. CURREY, was born 8 Dec 1826 at Grahamsville, Neversink Twsp., Sullivan County, NY. He married Mary M. BURTON ca 1850. She was the daughter of Edmund BURTON and Huldah PORTER; and was born ca 1832 NY; died 11 Apr 1885 Grahamsville, NY.

Children of Andrew B-⁷ CURREY and Mary M. BURTON:
Surname **CURREY**

3583. Marshall N.	born ca 1851; died 1 March 1864		EOL
3584. Myra A.	born 15 Nov 1852; died 24 Dec 1949		
	married Andrew T. WICKHAM 24 Sept 1876		

Children: Burton Ennis⁹ WICKHAM born ca 1877; Dorothy M⁹ WICKHAM born ca 1879 NY, died 1986, married Dwight Curry DECKER; and Frederick Currey-⁹ WICKHAM born ca 1881

3585. Carrie	born July 1854; died _____ ; married Charles DARTT ca ___

Child: Ida H-⁹ DARTT born ca 1879

3586. Ida J.	born Jan 1856; died ____ ; married Burr W. MOORE ca ____
3587. Herbert Hart	born Apr 1858 NY; died 11 May 1918 Grahamsville, Sullivan, NY
	married Bessie INGRAHAM 8 June 1909
	(she dau/o Manasseh INGRAHAM and Almeda SMITH)
3588. Edmund Stephen	born 27 Aug 1859; died ca 1944 NY
	1 married Frances DuBOIS before 1881; 2 married Caroline "Carrie" HILL
+ **3589. MARIA DOLLIE**	born 14 Jan 1861; died 25 May 1932
	married Charles MORLEY 9 Aug 1882 Grahamsville, Sullivan, NY
	(he s/o John MORLEY and Anna E. CARSON) (he born ca 1855; died 1898)
3590. Janet	born ca 1862; died 1863 EOL
3591. Eva Janet	born ca 1864; died 30 Dec 1900
3592. Gabriel S.	born Apr 1866; died 26 March 1942
	married Bessie INGRAHAM Currey ca 1919 (his brothers' widow)
3593. Harriet " Hattie "	born Sept 1867/71; died _____ ; married Charles L. De VOE

2483. GABRIEL FRANCIS -⁷ CURREY, brother of above, was born 4 July 1844 NY. He married Jennie R. BYERS on 3 Oct 1867. She was the daughter of ____ BYERS and ____, and was born July 1847; died 1920. Gabriel-⁷ CURREY served in Company C, 25ᵗʰ NY Cavalry during the Civil War, including the battles at Winchester, Fort Stephens and Cedar Creek. Gabriel-⁷ CURREY died 1 Nov 1934.

Children of Gabriel-⁷ CURREY and Jennie BYERS:
Surname **CURREY**

+ **3594. LILLIE B.**	born 20 Dec 1869 NY; died ca 1950 Sullivan Co., NY	
	married Orrin R. SHEELEY 26 Feb 1890 (he born 27 Dec 1869; died 1954)	
3595. Emma	born 26 April 1872 NY; died ca 1949 Liberty, Sullivan, NY	
3596. Neal Childs	born 9 July 1875 Grahamsville, NY; died 15 Mar 1930	
	married Linda HORN 11 Dec 1901	
3597. Nettie May	born Dec 1877; died ____	
+ **3598. ALICE J.**	born 11 Nov 1881 Neversink, NY; died ____; married John M/W. GRANT 3 June 1903	

2487. DANIEL T-⁷ BOWKER, son of Anson-⁶ BOWKER (Daniel-⁵; Silas Day-⁴; John-³; Edmund-²,¹) and Elizabeth " Betsey " JONES, was born 8 May 1840 NY. He married Hannah Susan SACKRIDER on 31 Oct 1860/62. She was the daughter of Timothy SACKRIDER and Nancy GOODENOUGH, and was born 19 July 1841; died ca 1918 . Daniel-⁷ BOWKER died 25 May 1916 at Stamford, Delaware County, NY.

Children of Daniel T-⁷ BOWKER and Susan SACKRIDER:
Surname **BOWKER**

+ **3599. WILLIAM HENRY**	born ca 1864; died ____ ; married Vida M. PATCHEN ca 1893
	(she born Feb 1876; died 22 Feb 1915 NY)
	(she dau/o Willis PATCHEN and Jeanette ____)
3600. Burton E.	born 23 June 1870; died 20 Oct 1920 Walton, Delaware, NY
3601. Merton E.	born 23 June 1870; died ____ ; married Irene LONG ca ____
+ **3602. HERBERT/ BERT**	born 12 June 1875 NY; died 24 July 1950 Squaw Grove, DeKalb, IL
	married Sarah Jane SMITH ca 1896

2489. ORRIN L.[7] BOWKER, son of Anson[6] BOWKER (Daniel[5]; Silas Day[4]; John[3]; Edmund[2,1]) and Elizabeth " Betsey " JONES, was born ca 1843 Delaware County, NY. He married Olive FRINK ca 1862 at Delaware County, NY. She was the daughter of John FRINK and Catherine ____, and was born ca 1841; died 24 July 1901 at Shinhopple, Delaware County, NY. Orrin L.[7] BOWKER died ca 1908 at Delaware County, NY.

Note: Orrin L.[7] BOWKER served , as a Private, in the 101st NY Infantry Regiment during the Civil War. He enlisted on 24 Dec 1862. He transferred to Company E, 40th NY Infantry Regiment, and deserted 6 Feb 1864 at NY, NY.

Children of Orrin L.[7] BOWKER and Olive FRINK:
Surname **BOWKER**

+	**3603. HARRIET A.**	born Feb 1864; died ___ ; married William George GRAY 14 Jun 1879 Hamden, NY (he s/o Erastus Root GRAY and Hannah DYER)
+	**3604. JAMES H.**	born 3 Jan 1867; died 28 Apr 1906 Rock Rift, Delaware, NY 1 married Mary VAN PELT ca 1889 2 married Rebecca HAMMOND ca 1897 NY (she born June 1876 NY; died 1 Nov 1904 Rock Rift) 3 married Alice GORTON 15 March 1905
+	**3605. FANNY / FANNIE**	born 26 Jan 1870 Walton, Delaware, NY; died _____ married Oscar W. ORR ca 1888 (he born June 1861; died ____)
+	**3606. CHARLES WALTER**	born 6 July 1874 Pine Brook, Delaware, NY; died 20 June 1958 married Bertha M. MILLER ca 1895 Delaware County, NY
+	**3607. CORA LILY**	born 2 Apr 1877 Walton; died 12 Feb 1967; married Henry Newell TRIPP 24 Feb 1895
	3608. Un-named infant	born 15 Dec 1882; died young EOL
+	**3609. NORA E.**	born 14 March 1884; died Oct 1973 Milford, Otsego, NY 1 married Fred WRIGHT ca 1901; divorced 4 Sep 1909 Delhi, Delaware, NY 2 married Charles HAMMOND 14 Jan 1910 Walton, Delaware, NY (he s/o Delos R. HAMMOND and Margaret BROCK) (he born Dec 1887; died 21 Sep 1953 Norwich, NY)
	3610. George A.	born 14 Aug 1887; died _____

2492. ORSEMUS WHITE [7] BOWKER, brother of above, was born ca 1854 Delaware County, NY. He married Susan Adelaide SHERMAN ca ____. She was the daughter of Spencer Samuel SHERMAN and Adelia Jane BROWN, and was born 9 March 1857; died 26 Oct 1931 at Franklin, Delaware Co., NY. Orsemus[7] BOWKER died 22 Feb 1897 Delaware County, NY.

Children of Orsemus[7] BOWKER and Susan Adelaide SHERMAN:
Surname **BOWKER**

+	**3611. SPENCER HENRY PENN**	born 1 May 1876 Delaware Co., NY; died 29 July 1949 Walton, Delaware, NY married Mabel A. WOODS ca 1901 (she dau/o _____ WOODS and _____) (she born ca 1886/87 NY; died 1927)
+	**3612. DANIEL T.**	born 11 Oct 1877 Franklin, NY; died 21 Oct 1931 married Ona Margaret MOSHER 15 Jan 1903 Trout Creek, Delaware, NY
+	**3613. MYRTLE FRANCES**	born 29 June 1879 NY; died 23 May 1960 PA married Sheridan WATSON ca 1900
+	**3614. HANNAH MAUDE**	born 3 Dec 1883; died 4 Apr 1981 Winter Park, FL 1 married John Wesley " Wes " CRAWFORD 28 Dec 1899 Trout Creek , Delaware, NY 2 married Frederick S. CUYLE 8 Sep 1942 Altoona, PA (he born ca 1868; died 1943)
+	**3615. ERNEST SYLVESTER**	born 26 Sep 1885 NY; died Feb 1967 MI married Vera Etta SILVERNAIL ca ____ (she born 27 Dec 1889 MI; died 6 May 1977 Pontiac, MI) (she dau/o Richard Perry SILVERNAIL and Mary Lillian CLEVELAND)

2494. ANNIS A.[7] BOWKER, sister of above, was born ca 1859 NY. She married Charles H. MAY. He was the son of _____ MAY and ___, and was born ca 1863 NY; died 20 Oct 1928. Annis[7] died 3 Feb 1935. She and her husband are buried at the Walton Town and Village Cemetery, Walton, Delaware, NY.

Children of Annis-[7] BOWKER and Charles H. MAY:
Surname **MAY**

3616. Viola	born ca 1891; died 5 Aug 1948, buried Walton Cemetery	
	married Otto Erastus LAMBERT ca ____	
	(he s/o George D. LAMBERT and Henrietta M. GILSON)	
	(he born 24 Oct 1888; died 5 Oct 1956)	
	Children: Leona B-[9] born ca 1912; Leland A-[9] LAMBERT born 7 Sep 1915;, died Mar 1958	
3617. Hazel B.	born 12 March 1893; died July 1977; she was a nurse	

2496. ALBERT-[7] BOWKER, son of Jonathan-[6] BOWKER (John-[5]; Silas Day-[4]; John-[3]; Edmund-[2,1]) and his first wife Nancy FOOTE, was born 11 Oct 1821 at Groton, Tompkins County, NY. He married first to Lucinda KEYES on 23 Feb 1845. She was the daughter of James KEYES and Casedona ____; and was born 12 April 1825 Royalton, Niagara, NY; died 21 July 1868 at Lincoln, Isabella, MI. He married second to Eunice Lucretia BALLARD on 20 Dec 1869. She was the daughter of ____ BALLARD and ____; and was born ca 1842 OH; died 28 June 1873 MI. Albert-[7] BOWKER died 12 Nov 1902 at Dewitt, Cliinton, MI   Reference: Death Certificate , Dewitt, MI

Children of Albert-[7] BOWKER and Lucinda KEYES:
Surname **BOWKER**

3618. Lucy Ellen	born July 1847 Tompkins Co., NY; died ____	
+ **3619. ELLA AMELIA**	born July 1859 NY; died ____; married Winfield Scott DILLS 20 Feb 1878	
	(he born Jan 1847; died ca 1923)	

Children of Albert-[7] BOWKER and Eunice Lucretia BALLARD:
Surname **BOWKER**

3620. Alonzo	born ca ____; died ____	3622. Ernie R.	born ca 1874 MI
3621. un-named	born 5 Nov 1870 MI; died young		

2497. HARRISON-[7] BOWKER, half brother of above, son of Jonathan-[6] BOWKER and his second wife, Emeline POWERS, was born ca 1823 at Tompkins County, NY. He married Helen Maria(h) SCOFFIELD ca 1847. She was the daughter of ____ SCOFFIELD and ____, and was born ca 1828 NY; died ____. Harrison-[7] BOWKER, a carriage maker, died ca 1870 IN.

Children of Harrison-[7] BOWKER and Helen SCOFFIELD:
Surname **BOWKER**

3623. Caroline (twin)	born ca 1848; died
3624. Clarence (twin)	born ca 1848; died ca 1910; married Sarah Edna MILLER ca ____
3625. Willis L.	born ca 1851; died ____
	married Rachel A ____ (she born ca 1852; died ____)
	Child: Ida M-[9] BOWKER born ca 1873 KS; died ____
3626. Dana D.	born ca 1856 IN; died ____; married Jessie ____ ca ____
	Children: Roy-[9] BOWKER born ca 1884; Harold-[9] BOWKER born ca 1895 ; and Gladys-[9] BOWKER born ca 1896
3627. Frank	born ca 1859; died ____
3628. Newell DeEtte	born 30 July 1869 IN; died 7 Sep 1933 Monmouth, IL
	married Clara C. OLSON ca ____ (she born ca 1872 IL; died ____)
	Child: Lewis Dell-[9] BOWKER born ca 1904

2498. JOHN HENRY POWERS-[7] BOWKER, son of Jonathan-[6] BOWKER (John-[5]; Silas Day-[4]; John-[3]; Edmund-[2,1]) and Emeline POWERS, was born ca 1826 Groton, Tompkins, NY. He 1 married Sarah H. ____ ca ____. She was born ca 1831 NY; died ____. He married 2nd to Ann YOUNG ca ____. She was the daughter of ____ YOUNG and ____; and was born ca ____ NY; died ____.

Child of John Henry Powers-[7] BOWKER and Ann YOUNG:
Surname **BOWKER**

3629. Daniel Nelson	born 2 Nov 1863 Janesville, WI; died 12 Nov 1941 Lee Co., IL
	married Cecelia Antoinette Reed SOUTHARD ca ____
	(she dau/o Henry Haight SOUTHARD and Esther Susan REED)
	(she born 13 Aug 1862; died 5 Feb 1941 IL)
	Children: Margaret Leona-[9] born 1 Aug 1899; married Thomas CROSS; died 5 Dec 1944 IL; and
	Marvene C-[9] BOWKER born 30 Oct 1903; married William Burton LICHTY; died 6 Apr 1931

2500. ARVILLA-[7] BOWKER, sister of above, was born 31 Aug 1833 at Summer Hill, Cayuga County, NY. She married

George Washington MC COUN on 13 Jan 1850 at North Lansing, Tompkins County, NY. He was the son of Nelson MC COUN and Selinda BURGESS, and was born 3 Apr 1828 Cayuga County, NY; died 14 March 1908 at Kingsley, IA. Arvilla-7 BOWKER died 9 April at Kingsley, IA.

Note: George Washington MC COUN served in the Civil War. He was a member of Company A of the 29th Iowa Infantry. His pension record lists him as having filed for a pension on 10 Oct 1863 (Certificate # 24981). He must have received some type of wound or disability before that time. His widow later received a pension (# 666988) .

Children of Arvilla-7 BOWKER and George Washington MC COUN:
Surname **MC COUN**

3630. Nelson J.	born 18 Dec 1850 NY; died 14 March 1915		
	married Margaret TOBIN ca 1875	(she born July 1849 Canada; died ca 1934)	

Children: Mary Jane-9 MC COUN born July 1876 IA; Margaret Mary M-9 MC COUN born Aug 1878

3631. Vinetta	born 9 Feb 1853; died 9 Feb 1853 EOL
3632. George Leslie	born 10 July 1854; died 1 Aug 1854 EOL
3633. John Daniel	born 31 Mar 1858; died 9 Apr 1938; married Rebecca C. ____ (born 1858; died 1925)

Child: Sarah Elsie C-9 MC COUN born ca 1891 IA

3634. George Henry	born 5 Feb 1860; died 2 July 1914
	married Theresa KUNSH 3 Feb 1884 IA (she born 5 Feb 1860; died ____)

+ **3635. IDA MAY** born 10 July 1862 Council Bluffs, IA; died 7 Sep 1946 Kalispell, MT.
1 married Silas GOULD 24 Dec 1876 Iowa
2 married Jasper Lloyd JEWELL ca 1895 at Kalispell, MT.
(he s/o Francis JEWELL and Eliza Alline SHIPMAN)
(he born ca Dec 1859; died 2 Dec 1945 Spokane, WA)

+ **3636. EMMA ETTA** born 10 Aug 1865; died 28 Feb 1947
1 married Reuben Otto RUSCO 14 March 1883; divorced 1895
2 married Patrick H. WARREN ca 1897

3637. Charles Albert	born 20 Apr 1868; died 9 Aug 1950
	married Lizzie ____ ca ____ (she born ca 1869 England; died _____)

Children: Mary-9 MC COUN born ca 1891 NE; and Grace-9 MC COUN born ca 1894 NE

3638. Arvilla " Villa "	born 7 Sep 1870
3639. Lester B.	born 13 March 1875 Cherokee, IA; died 2 Dec 1963 Omaha, NE
	married Margaret ____ ca ____ (she born ca 1878; died _____)

Children: Leonard P-9 MC COUN born ca 1900; and Catherine L-9 MC COUN born ca 1907
Note: he was listed as a Christian Science practitioner

3640. Ernest Truth	born 12 Dec 1877; died 11 Sep 1945 San Antonio, TX
	married Augusta " Gussie " GANS 12 Dec 1900 San Antonio, TX
	(she dau/o Simon GANS and __) (she born 17 Nov 1879; died 9 July 1961 San Antonio

Children: Lucille-9 MC COUN born ca 1903; and Ernest T-9 MC COUN, Jr. born 22 May 1911 TX; died 8 July 1978 Bexar, TX

2501. MARTIN VAN BUREN-7 BOWKER, son of Jonathan-6 BOWKER (John-5; Silas Day-4; John-3; Edmund-2,1) and Emeline POWERS, was born ca 1836, NY. He married Jane R. ____ ca ____. She was born ca 1841; died ____. Martin VB-7 BOWKER died 28 March 1904 NY.

Children of Martin Van Buren-7 BOWKER and Jane R. ____:
Surname **BOWKER**

+ **3641. ERNEST VERNON** born ca 1863 Groton, Tompkins, NY; died between 1920-30
married Addie M. _____ ca _____; (she born ca 1869; died _____)

3642. Carl P.	born ca 1869 ; died _____
3643. May L.	born ca 1871 NY; died ____
3644. Carrie G.	born ca 1874; died 22 Oct 1889 EOL
3645. Coral Glen (m)	born 30 Oct 1878 NY; died _____; married Nancy M. _____
3646. Eri	born 30 Oct 1878; died _____

2514. CALVIN-7 BOWKER, son of Jefferson-6 BOWKER (John-5; Silas Day-4; John-3; Edmund-2,1) and Sophronia HENDERSON, was born 2 March 1826 NY. He married Eunice JOHNSON 4 July 1846 . She was the daughter of _____ JOHNSON and ____, and was born ca 1828 NY; died ____. Calvin-7 BOWKER possibly died 27 Jan 1883 Niagara Co., NY

BOWKER
The Seventh American Generation

Children of Calvin[7] BOWKER and Eunice JOHNSON:
Surname **BOWKER**

+	**3647. ELIZABETH**	born 12 May 1849 IN; died ____; married Frederick Nelson DAVIS ca 1868 (he s/o Joseph DAVIS and Elizabeth BARGER) (he born 10 Apr 1846; died 9 Nov 1908 Arthur, Clare, MI)
	3648. Elmira	born ca 1855 IN; died _____

2517. MARTHA J[7] BOWKER, sister of above, was born 29 Jan 1832 NY. She married first to Jacob CONLEY 1 Jan 1850 at ____. He was the son of Jacob CONLEY and Polly HARVARD/HOWARD, and was born 23 Nov 1827 Locke, Cayuga, NY; died 2 Dec 1867 PA. Jacob CONLEY was a logger and lost his life when a pile of logs began to roll and passed over him. Martha[7] married second to Silas STAPLES on 20 July 1870 at Middlebury, Tioga, PA. He was the son of ____ STAPLES and ____, and was born 26 Oct 1808 VT; died 3 June 1888 PA. Martha[7] BOWKER died 4 Jan 1901 at Tioga County, PA.

Children of Martha[7] BOWKER and Jacob CONLEY:
Surname **CONLEY**

	3649. Cornelia/Amelia	born ca 1851; married Charles CORKINS ca ____ CO
+	**3650. ERMINA**	born ca 1852 PA; died _____ married Ira BRIGGS ca _____ Keeneyville, Tioga, PA (he born ca 1829 NY; died __)
	3651. Jefferson	born ca 1855 PA; died _____
	3652. Sophronia	born ca 1860 PA; died _____; married Alvin RICE

2518. PHILINDA[7] BOWKER, sister of above, was born 31 Jan 1834 NY. She married first Chauncey C. TRUMBLE on 22 Dec 1853 at Locke, Cayuga County, NY. He was the son of Chauncey TRUMBLE and Lois GOODRICH, and was born 7 Sep 1830 Groton, Tompkins, NY; died 27 Mar 1896 Chatham, Tioga, PA. Philinda married second to ____ RICE; and died ca 1917.

Children of Philinda[7] BOWKER and Chauncey TRUMBLE:
Surname **TRUMBLE**   (children born Little Marsh, Tioga County, PA)

+	**3653. MILO ERWIN**	born 6 Feb 1855 ; died 23 July 1947 Pierre, Hughes, South Dakota married Viola Elizabeth SHERMAN 7 Nov 1883 Chatham, Tioga, PA
	3654.Linus Willie	born 3 Oct 1856; died 22 Aug 1911 Petaluma, CA. married Elizabeth JONES June 1884
		Children: Edwin[9] born 1885, died 1905; and John William[9] TRUMBLE born 1898, died 1916
	3655. Charles Sumner	born 13 Dec 1857; died 5 Dec 1867 EOL
	3656. Delta May	born 11 Apr 1866; died 22 Jan 1871

2524. WILLIAM H[7] BOWKER, brother of above, was born 11 March 1844 at Groton, Tompkins, NY. He married first to Jennie May CONLEY on 13 Nov 1861 at Groton, NY. She was the daughter of Charles Chester CONLEY and Rowena May DICKENS, and was born ca 1845 Groton, died 1897 Kansas City, MO. His second marriage was to Elizabeth HOURIGAN 26 June 1873 at Lancaster County, Nebraska. She was the daughter of ____ HOURIGAN and ____, and was born 13 May 1855 Worcester, MA ; died ca 1927 NE. William H[7] BOWKER died 14 March 1919.

Children of William H[7] BOWKER and Jennie May CONLEY:
Surname **BOWKER**

+	**3657. CHARLES ADDISON**	born 17 Oct 1864 NY; died 5 Mar 1903 Jamestown, CA married Elizabeth TOLAND ca ____ at St. John , KS (she dau/o James W. TOLAND and Mary YOUNG) (she born 12 Dec 1868 MI; died 2 Jan 1924)
+	**3658. AMAZIAH CHESTER**	born 7 Feb 1868 Groton, NY; died 7 Feb 1962 St. John, Stafford, KS 1 married Lois Irene ADAMS 21 Feb 1888 2 married Clarinda " Clare " Blanch TEITSWORTH 20 Dec 1904 (she dau/o John Murray TEITSWORTH and Laura Josephine BOUGHNER)

Children of William H[7] BOWKER and Elizabeth HOURIGAN:
Surname **BOWKER**

	3659. Franklin/Frank	born 14 Jan 1874 NE; died 29 Oct 1922 OR
	3660. Jennie L.	born Oct 1876 NE; died _____ married Joseph George ROY ca ____
		Children: Lavinia[9] ROY born ca 1901; and Joseph Harley[9] ROY, Jr. born ca 1908
+	**3661. ALBERT BENJAMIN**	born 14 Jan 1879 NE; died 30 June 1971 San Diego, CA 1 married Minnie A. GIESE ca 1906; 2 married Katherine Harriet BATES after 1920

Children of William H[-7] BOWKER and Elizabeth HOURIGAN, continued:
Surname **BOWKER**

3662. Pearl Mary   born Jan 1882 NE; died ____; married Robert J. FORSYTH ca _____
     Children: Thelma[-9] FORSYTH born ca 1905 NE; and Robert[-9] FORSYTH born ca 1922

+ **3663. EDWARD JAMES**   born 23 Feb 1884 NE; died 23 Aug 1961
     married Lillian B. THOMAS 7 Apr 1902   (she born ca 1883)

3664. Harry William   born 13 May 1888 Neligh, NE; died May 1976 Portland, OR
     married Sue M. CRELLIN ca _____
     Child: Harriet[-9] BOWKER born ca 1915 NE

+ **3665. LEROY S.**   born 25 Oct 1891 Neligh, Antelope, NE; died March 1957
"Roy"   married Eugenia DAVISON ca 1911
     (she born 12 Mar 1891 NE; died March 1985 Neligh)
     (she dau/o _____ DAVISON and Mary L._____ (born England)

2525. SYLVESTER[-7] **BOWKER,** brother of above, was born 4 Feb 1847 at Cayuga County, NY. He married Carrie Marinda BROGDEN ca ____. She was the daughter of Abraham BROGDEN and Catherine GAY, and was born 16 July 1842 Cayuga County, NY; died 12 Sept 1896 at Rose Lake, Osceola, Michigan. Sylvester[-7] BOWKER died 19 May 1900 at Rose Lake, MI.

Children of Sylvester[-7] BOWKER and Carrie BROGDEN:
Surname **BOWKER**

3666. Katie S.   born 9 Oct 1868 Lincoln, MI; died 22 June 1896 Rose Lake, MI

+ **3667. CLIFTON**   born 4 July 1871 MI; died 12 March 1944 Los Angeles, CA
     married Nellie MONAGHAN 21 Aug 1896 Big Rapids, MI

3668. Crystal   born ____; died ____   3670. Kenneth   born ____; died ____
3669. Wesley   born ____; died ____   3671. Harold   born ca 1903; died ____

2526. AMAZIAH[-7] **BOWKER,** brother of above, was born 3 April 1849 Cayuga County, NY. He married Mary Clara SMITH on 10 May 1870. She was the daughter of Joel SMITH and Betsey COVERT, and was born 8 Jan 1850 at Summer Hill, Cayuga County, NY; died 5 Feb 1893 after giving birth to twins who also died. Amaziah Chester[-7] died 17 July 1940 at Dryden, Tompkins, NY.

Children of Amaziah Chester[-7] BOWKER and Mary Clara SMITH:
Surname **BOWKER**

3672. Orrin Smith   born ca 1868 Tompkins Co., ; died ____
3673. Myrtie   born ca 1870 NY; died 23 April 1936; married James Otis SEARLES
3674. Minnie Samantha   born 22 Aug 1872 Groton, NY; died 22 Nov 1919; married Earl BRANCH ca _____

+ **3675. CHARLES E.**   born 10 Sept 1873 Groton; died 14 Jan 1936
     married Linnie GOODALE 14 Dec 1893

3676. Joseph   born 2 Mar 1879 Groton; died 30 Oct 1957 Virgil, NY

+ **3677. FRANK SENECA**   born 22 Oct 1882 Tompkins Co., NY; died 6 Dec 1933
     married Edith Louella SHERMAN Greenfield (as her 2nd husband) ca 1911
     (she born 2 Sept 1886 Dresserville, NY; died _____)
     (she dau/o Fred SHERMAN and Cora CUYKENDALL)

3678. Lydia Jane   born 5 July 1884 Summer Hill, NY; died 16 Aug 1954
     married Orville A. MILES ca 1902
     (he born 20 Jan 1872; died 16 Dec 1950)

+ **3679. HORACE LEWIS**   born 14 June 1887 Sempronius, Cayuga, NY; died 23 Sep 1956 Dryden, Tompkins, NY
     married Frances Emma CRANE ca 1909
     (she born 21 Oct 1884; died 18 Apr 1964 Cortland, NY)

3680. Lewis   born 17 Jun 1889; died _____
3681. Adah   (twin)   born 9 Jan 1893; died 1893   EOL
3682. Mary C. (twin)   born 9 Jan 1893; died 1893   EOL

2528. MARGARET[-7] **BOWKER,** daughter of Madison[-6] BOWKER (John[-5]; Silas Day[-4]; John[-3]; Edmund[-2,1]) and Sarah/Sally DAVIS, was born 3 July 1832 at Lansing, Tompkins County, NY. She married John H. INGERSOLL on 31 Dec 1854 at Lansing. He was the son of Johnson INGERSOLL and Susanna BULL, and was born 25 May 1828 Richland, Oswego County, NY; died ____. Margaret-7 BOWKER died ____. Note: According to the 1860 Census, John H INGERSOLL was residing in Placerville, CA and gave his occupation as a miner.

Children of Margaret[7] BOWKER and John H. INGERSOLL:
Surname **INGERSOLL**

| 3683. Walter Bowker | born 20 Apr 1855 Richland, NY; died ca 1936 Clayton, NY |
| | married Iona M. PEET ca 1877   (she born ca 1853 IA; died 1917) |

Children: Lee L-[9] INGERSOLL born ca ____; and Regina Claire[9] INGERSOLL born ca ____

| 3684. Clara Ada | born 16 Aug 1865 Delaware, IA; died 23 Sep 1867 |
| 3685. Clarence Jesse | born 17 Mar 1870 IA ; died ____ |

2534. JAMES[7] BOWKER, son of James M[6] BOWKER (John[5]; Silas Day[4]; John[3]; Edmund-[2,1]) and Elizabeth MILLER, was born ca 1843 NY. He married Frank L. RHODES ca 1868. She was the daughter of _____ RHODES and ____, and was born ca 1844; died 1915. James[7] BOWKER died 21 March 1900 at Groton, Tompkins, NY. He and his wife, and some children, are buried at Groton Rural Cemetery. There is a monument there with their names, dates and those of three children.

Children of James[7] BOWKER and Frank RHODES:
Surname **BOWKER**

3686. Glenn James	born ca 1869; died 5 Jan 1911 Groton; married Maggie ____ ca _____
	(she born ca 1872 Canada; died ____)
3687. AURILLA " RILLA"	born Mar 1871; died _____:
BELLE	married Nelson LARKIN ca 1891-92 (he an architect)
	(he born Aug 1867 NY; died _____)
3688. E. Pearl	born Jan 1881 NY; died ca 1914
3689. Leona E.	born ca 1883; died 1885 EOL

2537. DANIEL[7] GOWER, son of Polly[6] BOWKER (John[5]; Silas Day[4]; John[3]; Edmund-[2,1]) and John GOWER, was born 1 Sept 1843 at Tompkins County, NY. He married Mary ALLEN ca 1868. She was the daughter of John ALLEN and Elizabeth CHESTER, and was born ca _____; died ____. Daniel[7] GOWER died June 1901 at Greenbush, MI

Source: Portrait and Biographical Album of Gratiot County, Michigan
" (Daniel) leaving home in the second year of the war, he enlisted 1 Sept 1862, in Company K,3rd NY Artillery, and was first sent to New Bern, NC. He then served in South Carolina for 3 months, and then returned to New Bern. In March 1864, he went home on furlough ------- He was in the battle at Ross' Mill, NC 2 Nov 1862; Kingston 14 Dec 1862; White Hall 16 Dec 1862. In the latter engagement he was wounded in the chest by a shell. He was mustered out at Richmond 1 June 1865, and was finally discharged at Syracuse, NY. "

Children of Daniel[7] GOWER and Mary ALLEN:
Surname **GOWER**

| 3690. Edward W. | born ca _____ | 3692. Bertha I. | born ca _____ |
| 3691. Henry A. | born ca ____ | | |

2548. JACKSON M[7] BOWKER, son of John[6] BOWKER (John[5]; Silas Day[4]; John[3]; Edmund-[2,1]) and Eliza LEARN, was born 25 March 1849 at Lansing, Tompkins County, NY. He married Harriet E. PECK ca ____. She was the daughter of ____ PECK and ____, and was born 3 Nov 1846 ; died 24 Sep 1899. Jackson[7] BOWKER died Sept 1877.

Children of Jackson M[7] BOWKER and Harriet PECK:
Surname **BOWKER**

3693. Nellie E.	born June 1871; died 7 July 1872
3694. Jennie E.	born 7 Feb 1874; died 7 July 1872; married Jay BOYER 18 Dec 1890
	(he born 25 Apr 1864; died 23 July 1949)
3695. Ida May	born 7 May 1877; died Oct 1958 Genoa, NY
	married Sidney REEVES 15 Apr 1894 (he born 23 Apr 1871; died 7 Oct 1948)

2556. MORRIS JACKSON[7] SNEDAKER, son of Lucinda[6] BOWKER (Joseph[5]; Silas Day[4]; John[3]; Edmund-[2,1]) and Derrick SNEDAKER, was born 16 Dec 1878 at Lansing, Tompkins County, NY. He married first to Ann EARL 17 April 1844, MI. She was the daughter of Jesse EARL and Jenetta____, and was born 22 Feb 1818 Seneca, Ontario County, NY; died 18 Oct 1879 Salt Lake City, UT.

As a young couple, Morris and Ann joined the Mormon settlement at Nauvoo, IL before they moved from that site in 1846. They were among about 2000 Saints who in the Spring of 1847 , bade farewell to Brigham YOUNG when he departed for the West. At Elkhorn, Nebraska the SNEDAKERS joined a company of Mormons commanded by Daniel SPENCER, when he set out to follow YOUNG West. On 21 Sept 1847 they arrived at Salt Lake City, and before winter had set in, they had erected a log cabin on what was then 4th Street South. It was the first log cabin built in the 9th Ward.

In Sept 1855, age 37, SNEDAKER was selected by his church to go on a "mission" to Texas. He kept a diary of his activity while he was there. He was the 1st salt manufacturer in Salt Lake City, and was also a miner. He died 12 Dec 1882.

Morris-7 SNEDAKER, a polygamist , married his second wife, Elizabeth Hannah MOBBS on 3 April 1853 SLC. She was born ca 1838; died 1868 He married third to Polly Tryphena FAIRCHILD, on 15 Feb 1862. She was the daughter of John FAIRCHILD and Tryphena Pomeroy LEWIS, and was born 11 Dec 1846; died ____.. He took as his fourth wife, Lucy RINGROSE 31 Jan 1863. She was the daughter of _____ RINGROSE and _____, and was born ca 1846; died ca 1930.

Children of Morris-7 SNEDAKER and Elizabeth Hannah MOBBS:
Surname **SNEDAKER**

+	**3696. ELLEN LUCINDA**	born 2 Nov 1860 Salt Lake City, UT; died 3 Aug 1895 Salt Lake (consumption) married Lee Clinton-8 SNEDAKER ca 1883/84
+	**3697. LAURA ANN**	born 27 Nov 1864 Salt Lake City; died 1 Jan 1910 Salt Lake married Lee Clinton SNEDAKER 2 Oct 1883
	3698. Elizabeth Permelda Mobbs	born 16 March 1868 ; died ca 1945 1 married George PLAYTER; 2 married Fred B. GILLETT

2557. BRADFORD CLINTON-7 SNEDAKER, brother of above, was born 9 Sep 1820 at Lansing, Tompkins, NY. He married Mary Ann BLACKWELL 23 April 1846 KY. She was the daughter of Robert Preston BLACKWELL and Nancy Ann CRUTCHER, and was born 16 Dec 1827 KY; died 22 Oct 1918. Clinton-7 SNEDAKER died ca 1880 at Salt Lake City, UT.

Children of Bradford Clinton-7 SNEDAKER and Mary Ann BLACKWELL:
Surname **SNEDAKER**

	3699. Preston Blackwell	born 19 July 1847 KY; died 21 July 1871	
	3700. Alonzo Preston	born 14 Sep 1849 KY; died 28 Sep 1849 KY	EOL
	3701. Flora Lucinda	born 9 Feb 1852 KY; died 12 Feb 1862	EOL
+	**3702. Dr. JOSEPH BRYAN**	born 20 Nov 1854 Woodford, KY; died 10 Apr 1889 Lexington, KY married Sarah Sallie CLARK ca 1874 (she born March 1859 KY; died _____)	
	3703. Martha/Mattie	born 30 March 1857 KY; died 14 Jan 1862	EOL
	3704. Laura Ann	born 4 May 1859 KY; died 8 Jan 1946 Los Angeles, CA 1 married R. BLACKWELL; 2 married Rev. William Ross LLOYD	
		Child: Brilla May-9 LLOYD born ca 1889; died ____	
+	**3705. LEE CLINTON**	born 11/18 March 1862 KY; died 13 Feb 1936 1 married Laura Ann-8 SNEDAKER 2 Oct 1883 Salt Lake City 2 married Ellen Lucinda -8 SNEDAKER ca 1884 3 married Georgia WHEELER 18 June 1913 Salt Lake City, UT	

2565. OSCAR-7 BOWKER, son of Chester-6 BOWKER (Joseph-5; Silas Day-4; John-3; Edward-2,1) and Eliza Louise _____, was born 22 Sept 1840 at Cayuga County, NY. He married first to Louise C. LABAR on 15 Dec 1861 at Genoa, NY. She was the daughter of Theodore LABAR and Louise ___, and was born 8 Dec 1842 NY; died 31 Dec 1882 IA. He married second to Lydia "Liddie" HOLT on 9 Feb 1884. She was the daughter of ____ HOLT and ____, and was born ____, died ____. He married third to Mary Anna BREECE on 12 March 1891 IA. She was the daughter of ____ BREECE and ____, and was born May 1852 PA.

Children of Oscar-7 BOWKER and Louise C. LABAR:
Surname **BOWKER**

3706. Minnie Jane	born 25 Dec 1864 NY; died 1 Nov 1920 IA
3707. William	born ca 1866-69 NY; died ____
3708. Ada	born ca 1870 IA; died ____
3709. Eva L./ Evalyn	born 5 Sep 1872 IA; died 30 Sep 1965 IA 1 married _____ RICKOFF; 2 married Hubert C. UNDERHILL ca ____
	Child: Rhetta L.-9 UNDERHILL born ca 1897
3710. Corella/Louella	born 14 July 1875 IA; died 14 June 1898 IA
3711. Charles E.	born 29 Aug 1878 IA; died 15 Oct 1939 IA
3712. Charlotte Lotta	born ca 1882 IA; died ____

Child of Chester-7 BOWKER and Mary Anna BREECE:
Surname **BOWKER**

3713. Oscar E.	born July 1892 IA; died _____

BOWKER
The Seventh American Generation

2567. GEORGE CLAYTON[-7] **BOWKER,** son of Ira-[6] BOWKER (Joseph-[5]; Silas Day-[4]; John-[3]; Edmund-[2,1]) and Rebecca BORTHWICK, was born 29 July 1832 at Allen Township, Allegany County, NY. He married Olive HAMILTON on 23 Dec 1858 at ___, Jo Daviess County, IL. She was the daughter of Thomas HAMILTON and Melinda WILLEY, and was born ca March 1842 at ___, IN; died 9 Aug 1911 at Mitchell, Kansas. George Clayton-[7] BOWKER died 17 Aug 1911 Mitchell, KS.

Children of George Clayton-[7] BOWKER and Olive HAMILTON:
Surname **BOWKER**

3714. Orren	(1)	born ca 1859 IL; died young		EOL
3715. Relief Rebecca		born 4 Mar 1860 IL; died 29 Nov 1946 MT		
+ **3716. ORREN VALORIS**		born 25 Oct 1861 IL; died 25 Dec 1910 Longdale , OK		
	(2)	married Frances Jane CADY ca 1883		
		(she dau/o ____ CADY and ____) (she born ca 1868; died ca 1950)		
3717. Leroy		born ca 1863 IL; died ____		
3718. Candice J.		born Nov 1864 IL; died 10 Dec 1947		
3719. Blanche		born ca 1867 IL; died ____	3723. Ava C.	born ca Feb 1889 KS
3720. Permina		born ca 1869 IL; died ____		
3721. Chester B.		born 17 Oct 1873 KS; died 29 Mar 1947 CA		
3722. Ethel Edna		born ca 1879 KS; died 24 Feb 1955 Mitchell, KS		

2570. JAMES T[-7] **BOWKER,** brother of above, was born ca 1842 at Rush Township, Jo Daviess County, IL. He married Catherine/Caroline BRICKLER on 11 Oct 1866 t Jo Daviess County, IL. She was the daughter of ____ BRICKLER and ____, and was born 18 Sep 1839 Jo Daviess County IL; died 24 Feb 1908 at Newcastle, WY. James T-[7] BOWKER died ____.

Children of James T-[7] BOWKER and Catherine/Caroline BRICKLER:
Surname **BOWKER**

3724. Ira S.   born ca 1868 IL; died ____
            married Laura S. HOLWELL 4 Jan 1898 WY   (she born ca ____ Canada)
            Children: Edgar D.-[9] BOWKER born ca 1899; Bernice-[9] BOWKER born ca 1905; Doris S.-[9] BOWKER born ca 1906; and Millie-[9] BOWKER born ca ____
3725. Ernest A.   born ca 1872 KS; died ____
3726. Nellie A.   born 3 July 1876 IL; died 26 Oct 1877 San Diego, CA
            married Jefferson DAVIS ca 1897   (a rancher; he born ca 1867; died ____)
            Child: Clifford-[9] DAVIS born ca 1900 WY

2571. SYLVIA[-7] **BOWKER,** sister of above, was born 3 Feb 844 at Rush Township, Jo Daviess County, IL. She married John DRANE on 5 Feb 1863 at Jo Daviess Co., IL. He was the son of John DRANE and Rhoda FLETCHER, and was born 22 Nov 1840; died 1 July 1927. Sylvia-[7] BOWKER died 11 April 1924 at Stockton, Jo Daviess, IL.

Children of Sylvia-[7] BOWKER and John DRANE:
Surname **DRANE**

3727. Rhoda   born ca 1864 Jo Daviess Co., IL; died ____
3728. Leona   born ca 1866 IL; died 1947 Jo Daviess, IL.
3729. Joseph Ira   born 27 Aug 1871, IL; died April 1945
            1 married Nellie Mae PULFREY 5 Sep 1900 IL
            Child: Leslie J.-[9] DRANE born 16 July 1901, died Sep 1981
            2 married Loree Edith LONG ca ____   (she born ca 1913; died ca 2001)
3730. Oran John   born 23 Jan 1880 IL; died 16 Oct 1958 Jo Daviess Co., IL

2572. ZACHARY TAYLOR[-7] **BOWKER,** brother of above, was born ca 1846 at Jo Daviess County, IL. He married first to Hannah M. GATES ca 1875. She was the daughter of ____ GATES and ____, and was born April 1840 MI, died ____ (living Modesto, CA in 1920). Zachary Taylor-[7] BOWKER married second to ____ on 4 Aug 1907 OR. Zachary-[7] died ca 1919.

Children of Zachary Taylor-[7] BOWKER and Hannah GATES:
Surname **BOWKER**

+ **3731. NELLIE E.**   born ca 1877 IL; died ____ (1930 resided Potlatch, ID)
            married Harry Llewellyn Morton GLEAVE 18 Dec 1899 NY (he born ca 1872 England)
   3732. Clinton Bruce   born 10 Oct 1878 Rush Twsp, Jo Daviess, IL; died 30 Oct 1941 Stanislaus, CA
            married Laura E. WILLIAMS 17 Dec 1902 Warren, Jo Daviess, IL
            Children: Robert W-[9] BOWKER born ca 1905, died 1987; and Mable Ellen-[9] BOWKER born ca 1903, died 1970

2573. SYLVINA " VINA"-[7] BOWKER, sister of above, was born 22 Feb 1849 at Rush Township, Jo Daviess, IL. She married John WILLIAMS ca _____. He was the son of William WILLIAMS and ____, and was born 4 May 1846 Wales; died 10 June 1925 Wysox, IL. Sylvina-[7] BOWKER died ca 1893 in IL.

Children of Sylvina-[7] BOWKER and John WILLIAMS:
Surname **WILLIAMS**

3733. Leola	(twin)	born 6 Nov 1876 IL ; died 18 Jan 1963 Jo Daviess Co., IL	
		married Henry Sherman ENDRISS 17 Dec 1895	
		Children: Maurice E-[9] ENDRISS born ca 1899, died 1900; Mildred V-[9] ENDRISS	
		born 9 Jan 1902, died 7 June 1969	
3734. Leanna	(twin)	born ca 1876 IL; died _____	
3735. Minnie S.	(twin)	born 25 Mar 1877 Rush, IL; died 23 Apr 1877	EOL
3736. Mina S.	(twin)	born 25 Mar 1877 Rush, IL; died 27 Apr 1877	EOL

2577. JASPER H-[7] WOODWORTH, son of Violetta-[6] BOWKER (Noah-[5] ; Silas Day-[4]; John-[3]; Edmund-[2; 1]) and Augustus WOODWORTH, was born 9 Dec 1834 at Allegany, NY. He married Emeline B. STANLEY ca _____. She was the daughter of _____ STANLEY and ____, and was born 17 Mar 1841; died 6 Jan 1879. Jasper-[7] WOODWORTH died 2 Nov 1917 Lyons, IL.

Children of Jasper-[7] WOODWORTH and Emeline STANLEY:
Surname **WOODWORTH**

+	**3737. AUGUSTUS**	born 17 June 1867; died 25 Mar 1947 Allegan, MI	
	WARREN	married Effie Mable CHANDLER ca ____; (she born ____; died 1939)	
	3738. Ralph	born ca 1868 MI; died ____	
	3739. Un-named Infant	born 9 Apr 1874; died 9 Apr 1874 Barry, MI	EOL
	3740. Lottie D.	born July 1875 MI; died ca ____; married Charles CHANDLER ca ____	

2578. WARREN AUGUSTUS-[7] WOODWORTH, brother of above, was born 25 May 1836 Allegany, NY. He married first to Mary A. MILLER 24 Oct 1864 Allegan, MI. She was the daughter of ____ MILLER and ____, and was born ca 1839; died 1891. His second marriage was to Alice C. REDWAY on 3 Nov 1894. She was born ca 1848; died 1930. Warren-[7] WOOD-WORTH died 9 June 1922 at Saugatuck, Allegan, MI.

Children of Warren-[7] WOODWORTH and Mary MILLER:
Surname **WOODWORTH**

3741. Charles H.	born 1865 MI; died 1875 MI
3742. Nellie S.	born 22 Oct 1867 Ganges, Allegan, MI; died 13 Mar 1955
	married William L. NAUGHTON ca _____ (he born ca 1864; died 1894)
3743. Saburna J.	born 25 June 1875 ; died 9 Feb 1949
	married Joseph Benjamin ZWEMER ca ____ (he born ca 1879; died ca 1945)

2579. SUSAN JANE -[7] BOWKER, daughter of Silas-[6] BOWKER (Noah-[5]; Silas Day [4]; John-[3]; Edmund-[2,1]) and Margaret ARDREY, was born Oct 1832/33 at ____, NY. She married first to Peter M. RUSSELL (as his 2nd wife 18 March 1854. Identity of his first wife is unknown. He was the son of Peter RUSSELL and Mary ____, and was born 30 Aug 1813 NY; died 20 June 1885 at Croton, Newaygo, MI. Susan-[7] BOWKER married second to John C. RUSSELL, possibly a brother to Peter, on 18 March 1886 at Hastings, Barry, MI. He was born 5 June 1814; died 20 Nov 1894. Susan-[7] BOWKER died ca 1920.

Children of Susan-[7] BOWKER and Peter M. RUSSELL, Jr.:
Surname **RUSSELL**

	3744. Mary C.	born 16 Sept 1855 MI; died 17 Dec 1857 Newaygo, MI	EOL
	3745 Alice Jane	born Nov 1858 Croton, Newaygo, MI; died _____	
	3746. Peter J.	born 16 May 1860 MI; died 28 July 1863	EOL
	3747. Silas B.	born ca 1862 Croton; died 23 Jan 1875 Newaygo, IL	EOL
	3748. Clara/Clarry	born ca 1862; died 1864 MI	EOL
	3749. Peter M (III)	born ca 1866 MI; died before 1900	
+	**3750. HUGH**	born 23 Sept 1869 MI; died _____; married Lydia O. AMES ca 1894	

2580. NOAH J-[7] BOWKER, brother of above, was born 1 May 1835 at Allegany County, NY. He married Aschah Mary ARDREY on 24 May 1868. She was the daughter of James Adra ARDREY and Olive DANIELS, and was born ca 1849 PA; died 12 Aug 1880. Noah J-[7] BOWKER died 3 July 1900 at Newaygo, County, IL.

BOWKER
The Seventh American Generation

Children of Noah-[7] BOWKER and Aschah Mary ARDREY :
Surname **BOWKER**

+	**3751. IDA MAE**	born 25 March 1869 MI; died 15 July 1959 Morley, MI
		1 married Arthur B. TRACEY 11 Aug 1889 Croton, MI (he born 1860 MI; died _____)
		2 married Melvin Leslie GRIFFIS 15 Nov 1893 Big Rapids, MI
		(he born 9 Mar 1854 Canada, died 25 Dec 1935 Croton, MI)
		(he s/o William A. GRIFFIS and Catherine STROWBRIDGE)
	3752. Alma Eugenia	born 12 Aug 1871 Ganges, Allegan, MI; died 20 Mar 1955 MI
		married Lewis A. NORWOOD 4 July 1891 Newaygo, MI
		(he s/o Albert NORWOOD and Arabella PENNOCK)
	3753. Newton Franklin	born 24 Jan 1878 Ganges, Allegan, MI; died 3 Oct 1878 EOL
	3754. Silas Elijah	born 25 Oct 1880 Ganges; died 21 Jan 1881 Croton, MI EOL

2581. DAVID A.-[7] BOWKER, brother of above, was born April 1837 Allegany County, NY. He married first to Almira MOORE on 6 Dec 1860 at Johnstown, Barry, MI. She was the daughter of William B. MOORE and Serafina S. ROGERS, and was probably born 1839 at Hastings, Barry, MI; died 5 Mar 1871 at Hope, Barry, MI. He married second to her sister , Nancy Jane MOORE. Nancy was born Nov 1829 NY, and died 4 Dec 1910. David A.-[7] BOWKER died 11 April 1911 at Barry County, MI. Note: David A. BOWKER served in the Civil War as a member of Company L, 11th Michigan Cavalry Regiment. He enlisted on 11 Nov 1863 (age 26) as a Private and was promoted to Sgt. He was mustered out on 16 May 1865 at Knoxville, TN.

Children of David-[7] BOWKER and Almira MOORE:
Surname **BOWKER**

3755. Cora S.	born 19 Aug 1864/65 MI; died 23 Aug 1958 CA; 1 married __ WITHAM ca 1890
	Children: Clare Augustus-[9] WITHAM born 3 May 1891 Clare, MI, died 23 Aug 1958 CA;
	Grace E-[9] WITHAM born Aug 1892, married Frank SMITH ca 1910
	2 married James G. GRISWOLD ca 1900; 3 married _____ ROGERS
3756. Bertha A.	born ca 1866 MI; died 1888

Child of David A.-[7] BOWKER and Nancy Jane MOORE:
Surname **BOWKER**

3757. Harry A.	born ca 1875 MI; died _____

2584. JOHN N.[7] MUNSON, son of Esther-[6] BOWKER (Noah-[5]; Silas Day-[4]; John-[3]; Edmund-[2,1]) and Joseph MUNSON, was born 10 June 1832 at Genoa, Cayuga County, NY. He married first to Sylvia AINSWORTH/ AYNSWORTH ca ___. She was the daughter of ___ AINSWORTH/ AYNSWORTH and ___, and was born ca 1830; died 1866. His second marriage was to Sarah HAVENS ca 1867 NY. She was the daughter of ____ HAVENS and ____, and was born 3 May 1833 NJ; died ___. John N.[7] MUNSON died ca ____.

Children of John N.[7] MUNSON and Sylvia AINSWORTH/AYNSWORTH:
Surname **MUNSON**

+	**3758. FRANK A.**	born 7 May 1854 NY; died 11 Mar 1938 Syracuse, Onondaga, NY
		married Matilda "Tillie" June OGDEN 7 June 1874
	3759. Joseph Orange	born 6 Sep 1857 NY; died _____
+	**3760. ESTHER E.**	born 19 Oct 1859 NY; died 1938
		married Samuel BABCOCK 11 July 1875
	3761. Willie E.	born 9 May 1862 Chemung, NY; died ____
	3762. Sylvia C.	born 27 June 1866 NY; died 10 Sept 1949 Horseheads, NY
		1 married Elmer E. PERSONIUS 25 Dec 1883 Elmira, NY
		Children: Mabel M-[9] PERSONIUS born ca 1889; Maude-[9] PERSONIUS born ca 1893, died 1924; and
		Hazel-[9] PERSONIUS born ca 1896
		2 married Albert WIXON ca ____ ; (he born ca 1846; died 1922)

Children of John N.[7] MUNSON and Sarah HAVENS:
Surname **MUNSON**

+	**3763. LUCY A.**	born 23 Jan 1869; died 28 Nov 1957
		married Frank E. JONES 9 Feb 1898
+	**3764. JOHN CALEB**	born 24 Sep 1870; died 29 Mar 1946 Almond, Allegany, NY
		married Theodora Harriet " Hattie" NEWELL ca 1914
	3765. Sarah Belle	born 24 Sept 1872; never married

2585. ORANGE-[7] MUNSON, brother of above, was born 24 Aug 1834 at Genoa, Cayuga, NY. He married first to Mary A WEST (his cousin) on 18 Feb 1855. She was the daughter of Lyman WEST and Jerusha HILL, and was born 1 July 1835; died Oct 1879 of cancer. Orange-[7] MUNSON married second to Johanna Ada RICHARDSON ca 1880. She was the daughter of Jacob Mills RICHARDSON and Caroline MERRITT, and was born ca 1846; died 1919.

Children of Orange-[7] MUNSON and Mary A. WEST:
Surname **MUNSON**

+   **3766. WEST**   born 14 Jan 1856 NY; died _____ (still living 1930 Caroline, Tompkins, NY)
        1 married Harriet PERSONIUS 18 Mar 1877
        (she born a 1859 NY; died 26 Sep 1884)
        (she dau/o William Krum PERSONIUS and Julia Almira VOORHIS)
        2 married Lillian A. SLATER 18 Nov 1885
        (she born ca 1861; died before 1910)
        (she dau/o Sharrad SLATER and Clarissa HEFFRON)
        3 married Marion _____ ca 1910 (she born ca 1870 PA)
        1910 resided Chambersburg, Franklin, PA

2592. CANDACE/CANDICE ESTELLA-[7] BOWKER, daughter of Wellington-[6] BOWKER (Noah-[5]; Silas Day-[4]; John-[3]; Edmund-[2,1]) and Lucy S. COOPER, and was born 1 Aug 1871 at Hope, Barry County, MI. She married John Clifford FISH on 24 Jan 1889 at Alba, MI. He was the son of John H. FISH and Caroline G. LUDLOW, and was born 22 July 1859; died 2 June 1913 MI. Candace-[7] BOWKER died 3 July 1942 at Traverse City, MI.

Children of Candace-[7] BOWKER and John Clifford FISH:
Surname **FISH**

    3767. Percy C.   born 8 Dec 1889 MI; died Dec 1966 MI
        married Eloise C. ADAMS 1 June 1914 Otsego, Allegan, MI
        (she born 23 Oct 1891 MI; died Aug 1977 MI)
        Child: Geraldine L-[9] FISH born ca 1916 Kalamazoo, MI; married Maynard Fred BROWN.
        He was born 14 Feb 1909 MI; died 16 June 1993 OH
    3768. James Horton   born 16 June 1891; died ca 1961 MI
+   **3769. MAMIE**   born 19 Nov 1893 Alba, MI; died 11 Feb 1945 Battle Creek, MI
        CAROLINE **   1 married Clifford Edgar LYTTON 22 Feb 1915; divorced ca 1920
        2 married Harry L. GREEN ca _____
        (he born 20 Sep 1893 MI; died 1949 Battle Creek, MI)
        ** Note: Mamie Caroline-[9] FISH was "indentured " on 12 Oct 1898 (at 5 years of age) to Joseph and
        Rose SCHWARK. She was officially adopted , by them, on 16 Nov 1905 at Marshall, Calhoun, MI

    3770. Harry W. ***   born 15 Aug 1895 MI; died 15 May 1958 MI
        *** Note: His last name was changed to SHANNON , he was adopted by George H. and
        Anna E. SHANNON
    3771. Marguerite E. ****   born 3 Sept 1897 MI; died 12 Aug 1973
        married Herbert W. BARKER ca ___
        (he born 24 Jan 1891 NY; died 22 March 1969 MI)
        **** Note: Her last name was changed to SHANNON, probably also adopted by
        George H. and Anna SHANNON
    3772. Milton J. *****   born ca 1899; died Oct 1958
        married Harriet Pearl LINTON   (she born ca 1901)
        *****Note: He was adopted , before he was a year old, by Thomas and Mary HARTWELL,
        changing his surname to HARTWELL

2594. MARY JANE-[7] WILLISON, daughter of Candace-[6] BOWKER (Noah-[5]; Silas Day-[4]; John-[3]; Edmund-[2,1]) and John Borthwick WILLISON, was born 5 Sep 1853 Hickory Corners, Barry County, MI. She married Frederick Tressler SHOUP on June 1873 Barry County, MI. He was the son of Jacob SHOUP and Mary TRESSLER, and was born 5 Feb 1840 Franklin County, PA; died 4 April 1918 Battle Creek, Calhoun, MI. Mary Jane-[7] WILLISON died 6 Sep 1917 Battle Creek, MI.

Children of Mary Jane-[7] WILLISON and Frederick Tressler SHOUP:
Surname **SHOUP**   (all children born Maple Grove, Barry County, MI)
    3773. Candace   born 30 May 1874 ; died _____
        married Byron KETCHAM ca _____

Children of Mary Jane-[7] WILLISON and Frederick Tessler SHOUP, continued:
Surname **SHOUP**

+   **3774. MARGARET G.**   born 10 Aug 1878; died 18 Nov 1971 Battle Creek, MI
                     married Carl Fuller EVANS 15 Jan 1894 Morgan Corners, MI
                     Children: Mary Alice-[9] born ____; married _____ WARD res. Battle Creek, MI; and Gola-9 EVANS
                     born ca ____, married _____ RENCH; res. Kalamazoo, MI

        3775. Orson Frederick.   born 14 Mar 1884 Barry, MI; died 27 June 1917 Kalamazoo, MI
                     married Lora Lee PRESTON 20 June 1906
                     (she dau/o Seymour Blair PRESTON and Mary Ellen WHITE)
                     Child: Orson Leroy-[9] SHOUP born 20 Aug 1915; died 6 Nov 1995 Tucson, AZ;
                     married Norma Evelyn MARTIN (1915-1996)

+   **3776. HATTIE**   born 3 May 1886; died 1968 Augusta , MI
                     married O. Glenn MARSHALL 2 Nov 1907; (he born 11 Sep 1882 MI; died ____)

        3777. Susan E.   born 4 June 1889; died _____; married Henry DREW ca ____
        3778. Zolah Dell   born 6 Mar 1892; died 3 April 1924 Kalamazoo, MI   EOL

2595. ADELBERT WAYNE -[7] **WILLISON,** brother of above, was born 15 Sept 1857 MI. He married Mary A CURTIS ca 1878. She was the daughter of ____ CURTIS and ____, and was born ca Nov 1855; died ____. Adelbert-[7] WILLISON died 14 April 1929.

Children of Adelbert-[7] WILLIISON and Mary CURTIS:
Surname **WILLISON**

+   **3779. MERTON EMMETT** born 25 May 1879 Grand Rapids, MI; died 13 Nov 1953 Cato, MI
                     married Pearl Elizabeth LENT 23 Dec 1910 Allegan, MI
                     (she dau/o Daniel J. LENT and Susanna Caroline LOSINGER)
                     (she born ca 1890; died 1971)

        3780. Ray   born 17 May 1881 MI; died _____

2597. NORA -[7] **WILLISON,** sister of above, was born ca 1865 MI. She married George HARRISON on 29 July 1885. He was the son of John HARRISON and Mary ROBERTSON, and was born ca 1854 England, died ca 1916 Wexford County, MI. Nora-[7] WILLISON died ca 1895 Wexford Co., MI.

Children of Nora-[7] WILLISON and George HARRISON:
Surname **HARRISON**

+   **3781. JOHN VERNON**   born ca 1886; died 1956
                     married Ida F. MC QUILL 24 June 1909 Cedar Creek, Wexford, MI
                     (she dau/o Hosea MC QUILL and Amelia ___) (she born ca 1879 IL; died ___)

+   **3782. MARY ESTHER**   born 1 Sept 1887 Wexford Co., MI; died 20 Sep 1947 Adams, IN
                     married Hiram Clayton WALL 23 Aug 1914 Cadillac, MI   (as his 2nd wife)
                     (he s/o _____ WALL and _____) (he born 10 Apr 1863 IN; died 6 Aug 1954 IN)

        3783. Mason Willison   born ca 1889; died _____

2610. JANE-[7] **FAIRBANKS,** daughter of John-[6] FAIRBANKS (Daniel-[5]; Jonathan-[4]; Lydia-[3] HOLBROOK; Mary-[2] BOWKER; Edmund-[1]) and Sally BURRINGTON, was born18 Sept 1826 VT. She married James Madison ROBERTS ca 1849. He was the son of _____ ROBERTS and ____, and was born ca ___, died ____. Jane-[7] FAIRBANKS died 12 Dec 1870 VT.

Children of Jane-[7] FAIRBANKS and James ROBERTS:
Surname **ROBERTS**

        3784. Andrew Jackson   born Oct 1851/53 MA; died ___; married Della Sylvia WHEELER ca 1885
        3785. Eunice Minerva   born ca 1858 VT; died 7 Dec 1933 VT; married Alfred Orlando PIKE ca ___
                     (he s/o Deliverance PIKE and Marietta PARKER)
                     (he born 29 Apr 1859 VT; died 15 Jan 1926 VT)
        3786. George F.   born 21 Dec 1860; died 1 Dec 1942 VT; married Gertrude Lucy HICKS 29 June 1887
        3787. John   born ca 1863 IL; died _____

2612. SARAH-[7] **FAIRBANKS,** sister of above, was born 3 July 1831. She married Isaac PIERCE on __ Oct 1853 at Greenwich, MA. He was the son of ____ PIERCE and ____, and was bornnca 1827, died ___. Sarah-[7] FAIRBANKS died 4 July 1858.

Children of Sarah[7] FAIRBANKS and Isaac PIERCE:
Surname **PIERCE**

3788. William	born Oct 1855; died ____; married Etta GILBERT

Children: Fred-9 born ca 1881; Alta-9 born ca 1883; and Gerald-9 PIERCE born ca 1885

3789. James	born July 1857; died May 1874

2624. MILLARD ORLIN[7] NICHOLS, son of Mary[6] FAIRBANKS (Daniel[5]; Jonathan[4]; Lydia[3] HOLBROOK; Mary[2] BOWKER; Edmund[1]) and Arad NICHOLS, was born 10 Jan 1850 MA. He married Prudence Olive NILES 22 Nov 1881. She was the daughter of _ _ NILES and __, and was born 26 Jan 1859; died 19 Apr 1936. Millard[7] NICHOLS died 7 Feb 1829 MA.

Children of Millard Orlin[7] NICHOLS and Olive NILES:
Surname **NICHOLS**

3790. Earl Millard	born 7 Nov 1882; died 7 May 1947
	married Ethel Lena CARY ca ____ (she born ___; died 11 Dec 1964)
3791. Royal Edgar	born Oct 1885; died 5 April 1951; married Katherine M. GALVIN ca ___
3792. Roscoe Conklin	born 8 July 1890; died 6 Sept 1916; married Mollie Teresa CROWLEY
3793. William Russell	born 9 Sept 1892; died 3 Sept 1933; married Louisa E. DIMOND
3794. Frank Aaron	born 3 July 1896; died ca 1917

2625. LUCY[7] NICHOLS, sister of above, was born 10 Nov 1852 MA. She married Richard SHACK 1 Dec 1884. He was the son of ____ SHACK and ____, and was born ____, died ____. Lucy[7] NICHOLS died 18 Nov 1930 at Shelburne, MA.

Children of Lucy[7] NICHOLS and Richard SHACK:
Surname **SHACK**

3795. Henry Reynold	born 1 April 1887; died ____; married Genevieve B. _____ ca ____
3796. Vivian H.	born 16 Jan 1890 Colrain, MA; died 13 Aug 1973 MA
3797. Edith	born ca ____; died 21 Oct 1894
3798. Rollo Holland	born 2 May 1892 Colrain, MA; died 10 Aug 1973

2626. EMMA ROSANNA[7] NICHOLS, sister of above, was born 20 Sept 1856 at ____, MA. She married James F. MC CLELLAN on 18 April 1883. He was the son of ____ MC CLELLAN and ____, and was born ___; died ____. Emma Rosanna[7] NICHOLS died ____.

Children of Emma Rosanna-[7] NICHOLS and James MC CLELLAN:
Surname **MC CLELLAN**

3799. Laura Geneva	born 4 June 1885; died ____; married _____ COLE ca ___
3800. Florence Edith	born 17 May 1894; died 19 Dec 1986 MA
	married Wallace Edwin TEMPLE ca ____; (he born ca 1905; died 1971)

2665. SARAH LOVINA[7] FAIRBANKS, daughter of Asa[6] FAIRBANKS (Asa[5]; Jonathan[4]; Lydia[3] HOLBROOK; Mary[2] BOWKER; Edmund[1]) and Sally STACY, was born 21 Jan 1838 VT. She married First to Charles CUTTING on 19 March 1857. He was the son of ____ CUTTING and ___, and was born ca 1831; died ___. They later divorced. She married second to Simeon DUDLEY on 30 Jan 1896. Sarah Lovina[7] FAIRBANKS died ca ____.

Children of Sarah[7] FAIRBANKS and Charles CUTTING:
Surname **CUTTING**

3801. Charles M.	born ca 1858; died ____
3802. James C.	born ca 1859; died ____
3803. Addison F.	born May 1866 VT; died ____
3804. Morris Franklin	born May 1868; died ____; married Elizabeth WORTH Howard 1 Apr 1912
3805. Nettie Lovina	born ca 1871; died ____

2670. ELVIRAH[7] FAIRBANKS, daughter of Ezra[6] FAIRBANKS (Asa[5]; Jonathan[4]; Lydia[3] HOLBROOK; Mary[2] BOWKER; Edmund[1]) and Cynthia STACY, was born 29 July 1831 VT. She married Martin Duane STIMPSON on 22 March 1848. He was the son of _____ STIMPSON and ____; and was born 5 May 1828, died ___. Elvirah[7] FAIRBANKS died 9 June 1891.

Children of Elvirah⁻⁷ FAIRBANKS and Martin Duane STIMPSON:
Surname **STIMPSON**

3806. Addie C.	born 29 May 1851; died ____; married Eugene LOOMIS	
3807. Joel Eugene	born ca 1853; died 10 Feb 1864	EOL
3808. Nellie J.	born 13 May 1861; died ____; married E J CARRIER	
3809. Leafy E.	born 26 Oct 1863; died 29 June 1882; married Fred KNOWLTON	
3810. Elsie V.	born 9 Sep 1865; died ____	

married 28 Mar 1887 Charles Henry ⁻⁹ FAIRBANKS (Henry⁻⁸; Ezra⁻⁷; Asa⁻⁶; Moses⁻⁵; Jonathan⁻⁴; Lydia⁻³ HOLBROOK; Mary⁻² BOWKER; Edmund⁻¹) (he born 4 Mar 1866 North Heath, MA; died _____) Child: Gladys Mary⁻⁹ᐟ FAIRBANKS born 24 Aug 1891

3811. Inez A.	born 26 July 1874; died ____; married Leon P. HAWKES

2672. MARANDA⁻⁷ FAIRBANKS, sister of above, was born 8 Sept 1833 VT. She married Dudley W. BURRINGTON on 15 Nov 1852. He was the son of ___ BURRINGTON and ____; and was born____, died ____. Maranda⁻⁷ died ___.

Children of Maranda⁻⁷ FAIRBANKS and Dudley BURRINGTON:
Surname **BURRINGTON**

3812. Jane E.	born 2 Dec 1852	3816. Bert G.	born 8 Mar 1873
3813. Mary C.	born 29 Sep 1857	3817. Alice R.	born ca ____
3814. Marion W.	born 1 Nov 1859; died 25 Sept 1886		
3815. Fred L.	born 7 May 1865		

2677. FLORINDA⁻⁷ FAIRBANKS, sister of above, twin to Florilla (below), was born 28 June 1846. She married Rufus C. PORTER on 27 Nov 1867. He was the son of Barnabas PORTER and Pamelia DAVENPORT, and was born ____, died ____.

Children of Florinda⁻⁷ FAIRBANKS and Rufus PORTER:
Surname **PORTER**

3818. Anna G.	born 31 May 1869	3822. Clarence W.	born 19 Feb 1878; died 22 May 1886
3819. Henry L.	born 7 Apr 1871	3823. Roy H.	born 13 Sep 1883
3820. George R.	born 14 Feb 1874	3824. Myron A.	born 6 Aug 1887
3821. Myrtie L.	born 3 June 1875		

2678. FLORILLA⁻⁷ FAIRBANKS, twin sister of above, was born 28 June 1846. She married George CARPENTER of North Heath, MA on 5 Dec 1869. He was the son of _____ CARPENTER and ____, and was born 21 Feb 1844; died ____.

Children of Florilla⁻⁷ FAIRBANKS and George CARPENTER:
Surname **CARPENTER**

3825. Myron	born 21 May 1877; died young	3827. Hallie	born 6 Jan 2885
3826. Wayne	born 7 May 1882	3828. Ella	born 19 Feb 1889

2682. FRANCESCA⁻⁷ FAIRBANKS, daughter of Abraham⁻⁶ FAIRBANKS (Asa⁻⁵; Jonathan⁻⁴; Lydia⁻³ HOLBROOK; Mary⁻² BOWKER; Edmund⁻¹) and Olive COOK, was born Aug 1843 MA. She married first to Elmer CUTTING on 14 Sept 1862. He was the son of ___ CUTTING and ____, and was born ____, died ____. She married second to Charles Faxon CADY ca ____. He was the son of ____ CADY and ___, and was born 5 Oct 1832; died 16 Jan 1912 Heath, MA. Francesca⁻⁷ FAIRBANKS died ____.

Children of Francesca⁻⁷ FAIRBANKS and Elmer CUTTING:
Surname **CUTTING**

3829. Edward Thomas	born 19 May 1863; died ____; married Rose FISH ca ___; resided Colrain, MA
3830. Elmer	born Aug 1864 MA; died ____; married Lena GARNER/GATNER ca 1896

Children of Francesca⁻⁷ FAIRBANKS and Faxon CADY:
Surname **CADY**

3831. Willie F.	born ca 1880; died ____	3833. Millie E.	born Aug 1885; died 16 May 1903
3832. Charles/Charlie	born Nov 1882; died ___	3834. Lizzie M.	born ____; died 2 Feb 1961

2698. CHARLES⁻⁷ HAGAR, son of Hannah⁻⁶ FAIRBANKS (Jonathan⁻⁵; Daniel⁻⁴; Lucy⁻³ HOLBROOK; Mary⁻²

BOWKER; Edmund-1) and Martin HAGAR, was born 9 Oct 1809. He married Myra Holden FELTON on 6 June 1838. She was the daughter of ____ FELTON and ____, and was born ___; died ____. Charles-7 HAGAR died 31 July 1890.

Children of Charles-7 HAGAR and Myra FELTON:
Surname **HAGAR**

     3835. Dexter F.   born ca 1840; died ____; married Abbie W. PERRY 27 May 1869
                                 Children: Charles S-9 born ca 1873; William B-9 born ca 1875; Myra I-9 born ca 1878;
                                 and Mary W-9 HAGAR born ca 1879
     3836. Fanny Felton   born ca ____; died 4 Jan 1866
     3837. Lydia Caroline   born ca ____; died ____
     3838. Otis   born ca ____; died ____
     3839. Martin   born ca 1854; died ____; married Ida ____ ca ____
                                 Children: Martin A-9 born ca 1877; and Harry D-9 HAGAR born ca 1879

2706. GEORGE DEXTER-7 CUTLER, son of Elizabeth-6 FAIRBANKS (Jonathan-5; Daniel-4; Lydia-3 HOLBROOK; Mary-2 BOWKER; Edmund-1) and John CUTLER, was born 9 April 1822. He married first to Martha BROOKS on 18 Sept 1848. She was the daughter of David BROOKS and ____; and was born ____; died ____. He married second to Gertrude BOUGHTON on 10 Sept 1861. She was the daughter of Charles Stone BOUGHTON and Caroline Lettice MARKHAM, an was born 20 Sept 1837; died 11 Jan 1876. George D-7 CUTLER died between 1895 and 1900 MI.

Child of George Dexter-7 CUTLER and Martha BROOKS:
Surname **CUTLER**
     3840. Catherine   born 15 June 1849; died ____; married Charles HEDENBURY ca 1871 NY
Children of George Dexter-7 CUTLER and Gertrude BOUGHTON:
Surname **CUTLER**
     3841. Horace   born 15 Dec 1863   3842. Nerna Minerva   born 29 Sep 1867

2707. SUSAN-7 CUTLER, sister of above, was born 16 Dec 1823. She married Dr. Caleb Holton HAMMOND, Jr. on 10 Oct 1848. He was the son of Caleb Holton HAMMOND, Sr. and Joanna STILSON, and was born 14 Aug 1821 at Rochester, NY; died 22 April 1883 at Ionia, MI. Susan-7 CUTLER died 3 Sept 1865.

Children of Susan-7 CUTLER and Caleb HAMMOND:
Surname **HAMMOND**   (children all born NY)
     3843. Joanna Dean   born ca 1851; died 1862   3845. Caleb S.   born ca 1863; died ____
     3844. Susan /Susie   born ca 1856; died ____   3846. Charles B.   born ca 1865; died ____

2712. MARGARET ANN-7 FAIRBANKS, daughter of Jonathan-6 FAIRBANKS (Jonathan-5; Daniel-4; Lydia-3 HOLBROOK; Mary-2 BOWKER; Edmund-1) and Augusta HADDEN, was born 8 Dec 1836 at Lexington, MA. She married Edward Payson BOND ca 1852. He was the son of Artemus BOND and Emily ____, and was born 10 March 1830 Lexington; died 7 Aug 1885 at The Soldiers Home in Togus, Maine. Margaret-7 FAIRBANKS died ____.

Children of Margaret Ann-7 FAIRBANKS and Edward Payson BOND:
Surname **BOND**
     3847. Isabelle/Belle Damon born 25 April 1853; died ____; married Ralph BENT ca 1871
     3848. Nellie   born 28 July 1856; died ____; married Wesley R. PLACE ca 1877
                           (he born ca 1852; died ____)
     3849. Albert   born 30 April 1859; died ____; married Mary E. HARE ca 1880
     3850. Harry   born 5 Sept 1866; died ____; married Elizabeth MONTCRIEF ca 1888

2716. NANCY-7 FAIRBANKS, daughter of Drury-6 FAIRBANKS (Jonathan-5; Daniel-4; Lydia-3 HOLBROOK; Mary-2 BOWKER; Edmund-1) and Mary SPRING, was born 9 March 1821 at Sudbury, MA. She married James Harvey WRIGHT on 27 Nov 1845. He was the son of ____ WRIGHT and ____, and was born 6 April 1816 MA., died 4 Sep 1896 MA. Nancy-7 FAIRBANKS died 28 March 1888 at Waltham, MA.

Children of Nancy-7 FAIRBANKS and James Harvey WRIGHT:
Surname **WRIGHT**
     3851. Frank Drury   born 5 Jan 1851; died 5 Sept 1851 Waltham
     3852. Mary Frances   born 12 Dec 1852; died ____
     3853. Charles Augustus   born 5 Mar 1854 Waltham; died 25 Jan 1893 Waltham

2720. MARY⁻⁷ FAIRBANKS, sister of above, was born 22 July 1830 at Sudbury, MA. She married Joseph T. SPEER on 25 Dec 1853. He was the son of _____ SPEER and _____, and was born 19 Feb 1829 Sudbury; died _____. Mary⁻⁷ FAIRBANKS died 29 Oct 1863.

Children of Mary-⁷ FAIRBANKS and Joseph SPEER:
Surname **SPEER**

3854. Theodore V.		born 2 Nov 1854; died _____; married Sarah B. RANKIN on 11 Feb 1880
3855. Minnie	(1)	born 18 July 1858 NY; died 3 June 1860 NY
3856. Minnie F.	(2)	born 13 Jan 1861 NY; died _____; married Warren S. COLEGROVE

2721. ELIZABETH CUTTER⁻⁷ FAIRBANKS, daughter of Captain Eddy⁻⁶ FAIRBANKS (Jonathan⁻⁵; Daniel⁻⁴; Lydia⁻³ HOLBROOK; Mary⁻² BOWKER; Edmund-¹) and was born 18 July 1825. She married first to Lysander UPTON ca _____. He was the son of Aaron UPTON and Abigail Nabby DAMON, and was born 20 Feb 1823; died 9 Jan 1865. She married second to Benjamin EAMES Jan 1865. He was the son of _____ EAMES and _____, and was born _____, died 19 Aug 1888.

Children of Elizabeth⁻⁷ FAIRBANKS and Lysander UPTON:
Surname **UPTON**

3857. Francis	born 10 Oct 1851; died 9 Nov 1867
3858. Elizabeth Ann	born 1 Mar 1853; died 18 April 1871
3859. Ella	born May 1856; died 5 Dec 1864
3860. Eddy Lysander	born Nov 1860; died ca 1897 Reading, MA
3861. Bertha	born 6 June 1863; died 14 July 1925 MA.

2738. SUSAN MARIA-⁷ FAIRBANKS, daughter of George⁻⁶ FAIRBANKS (Jonathan⁻⁵; Daniel⁻⁴; Lydia-³ HOLBROOK; Mary⁻² BOWKER; Edmund-¹) and Susan _____; was born 24 May 1833 RI. She married William WYLIE Nov 1957. He was born ca 1829 at Glasgow, Scotland; died _____. Susan Maria-⁷ FAIRBANKS died 27 Jan 1894 New York City, NY

Children of Susan Maria-7 FAIRBANKS and William WYLIE:
Surname **WYLIE**

3862. Mary Jane	born 4 Aug 1859 RI; died 1917
	married George Olney BLACKMAR ca 1888 (as his 2ⁿᵈ wife)
	(he born 24 Apr 848 RI; died 13 June 1906 Foster, Providence, RI)
	(he s/o William Sheldon BLACKMAR and Rachel M. ADAMS)
	(he 1 m. her sister Anna Washington-⁷ FAIRBANKS (1844-1880)
3863. Anna Maria	born 9 Nov 1861; died 6 July 1947 Foster, RI (never married)
3864. William Henry	born 6 Apr 1868 RI; died _____
	married Emma B. WERTHER 1897
3865. Agnes Florence	born 15 Aug 1869 Cranston, RI; died _____
	married George Gale SMITH ca _____
	(he s/o George William SMITH and Mary Louisa _____)
	(he born June 1869 NY; died _____)

2759. JONAS⁻⁷ TWITCHELL, son of Daniel⁻⁶ TWITCHELL (Nathan-⁵; Keziah⁻⁴ HOLBROOK; Samuel⁻³; Mary-² BOWKER; Edmund-¹) and Eunice WRIGHT, was born 4 March 1803 VT. He married first to Eliza ROBBINS ca 1828. She was the daughter of _____ ROBBINS and _____, and was born ca 1803, died 1839. He married second to Lucy D. FELTON on 21 July 1841. She was the daughter of _____ FELTON and _____, and was born ca 1807; died _____. Jonas-⁷ TWITCHELL died 7 Jan 1878.

Children of Jonas-⁷ TWITCHELL and Eliza ROBBINS;
Surname **TWITCHELL**

3866. Emily R.	born 4 March 1829 VT; died _____
3867. Lucius N.	born 13 Aug 1832 VT; died _____
3868. Caroline E.	born 5 Aug 1834 VT; died ca 1927
3869. Hannah E.	born 19 June 1836 VT; died _____
3870. Antoinette	born 16 Oct 1839 VT; died _____

Children of Jonas-⁷ TWITCHELL and Lucy D. FELTON:
Surname **TWITCHELL**

3871. Ellen M.	born 18 Oct 1844 VT; died 20 Sept 1885
3872. Fred Felton	born 10 Aug 1849 VT; died ca 1938

2760. HARVEY DANIEL[-7] **TWITCHELL,** brother of above, was born 31 March 1808 VT. He married Elizabeth SCOTT ca
____. She was the daughter of ____ SCOTT and ____, and was born ca 1819; died 27 Mar 1899 Ontario, Canada. Harvey
Daniel[-7] TWITCHELL died 21 Sept 1864.

Children of Harvey-[7] TWITCHELL and Elizabeth SCOTT:
Surname **TWITCHELL**

3873. Marshall Harvey	born 29 Feb 1840 VT; died 21 Aug 1905 Canada; married Adele COLEMAN	
3874. Jonas Monroe	born 20 Mar 1843 VT; died 20 April 1844 VT	
3875. Helen Elizabeth	born 20 Mar 1845 VT; died 12 July 1876	
3876. Isabelle Hannah	born 12 Oct 1848 VT; died 8 Nov 1874; married George A. KING 2 May 1869	
3877. Kate Frances	born 20 Apr 1854 VT; died 14 Nov 1875; married Clark HOLLAND	
	(he born ca 1850; died ca 1874)	

Child: Bert Twitchell[-9] HOLLAND born ca 1870; died ca 1950

2795. ELLEN G-⁸ GOODRICH, daughter of Jane-⁷ BRUCE (Abraham-⁶; Daniel-⁵; Bathsheba-⁴ BOWKER; John-³;²; Edmund-¹) and David Fairchild GOODRICH, was born April 1843/44 NY She married Lorenzo D. BOVEE ca 1841. He was the son of ____ BOVEE and ____; and was born Jan 1834 NY; died ____. Ellen G-⁸ GOODRICH died ____.

Children of Ellen G-⁸ GOODRICH and Lorenzo BOVEE:
Surname **BOVEE**

3878. Floyd D.	born Dec 1864 IL; died ____	
3879. Fred Nicholas	born 26 Oct 1869 KS; died 28 Sep 1949 OK; a Locomotive Engineer	
3880. Nellie	born 4 June 1873 KS; died ____; married Alfred STRAWN ca 1893	

Children: Paul L-¹⁰ born July 1895 CO, died 24 May 1958; and James L-⁸ STRAWN born June 1897 CO

3881. Vida	born ca 1874/75 KS; died ____	
3882. Zone L. (male)	born Dec 1876 KS; died ____	

Reference: Descendants of Edward GRISWOLD of NY; and Landmarks of Tompkins Co., NY

2797. LA FAYETTE BRUCE " Lafe"-⁸ GOODRICH, brother of above, was born 13 Feb 1847 Otsego, NY. He married first to Elizabeth " Lizzie " RICKABAUGH on 20 Nov 1870 at Emporia, KA. She was the daughter of ____ RICKABAUGH and ____, and was born ca 1848 PA; died 20 Sep 1898 Emporia, KS. He married Second to Altha Jane LEAVITT on 5 March 1900 at Emporia, KA. She was the daughter of Harlow LEAVITT and Janett ____, and was born 12 May 1853 NY; died 21 Nov 1944 KS. LaFayette-⁸ GOODRICH served in the 45ᵗʰ WI Infantry during the Civil War and was discharged from the Cumberland Hospital at Nashville, TN for disability on 29 July 1865. He died 15 Sep 1933 KS.

Children of LaFayette-⁸ GOODRICH and Elizabeth RICKABAUGH:
Surname **GOODRICH**

+   **3883. GRACE**   born 2 Dec 1878 KS; died 1 Dec 1973 Wichita, KS.
married Bruce Manley SMITH ca ____ (he s/o Otho SMITH and Jane ____)
(he born ca 1878; died 1948 Wichita, KS)
    3884. Edith Estelle   born ca 1885; died 1937

2802. JENNIE-⁸ SPAFFORD, daughter of Harriett-⁷ BRUCE (Abraham-⁶; Daniel-⁵; Bathsheba-⁴ BOWKER; John-³;²; Edmund-¹) and Truman SPAFFORD, was born Aug 1866 NY. She had no spouse of record, but on various statistics her son was listed as Ethiopian (WW1 draft registration), black and mulatto (Census). Jennie-⁸ SPAFFORD died ____.

Child of Jennie-⁸ SPAFFORD and _____:
Surname **SPAFFORD**

+   **3885. ODELL TRUMAN**   born 29 Oct 1886/88 Pittsfield, NY; died 8 Nov 1963 New Berlin, Chenango, NY
married Elizabeth " Lizzie " May HOLMES ca ____
(she dau/o Clarence HOLMES and Sarah Lizzie DANA)
(she born 1 June 1887 MA; died 6 June 1940 New Berlin, Chenango, NY)

2817. WALTER LEONARD-⁸ BOWKER, son of Stephen-⁷ BOWKER (Samuel Ward-⁶; Silas-⁵; John-⁴;³;²; Edmund-¹) and Prudence RAND, was born 15 Aug 1831/34 Shefford, Quebec, Canada. He married Julia A. SHIPMAN on 23 Oct 1853 at Rockingham, VT. She was the daughter of Edmond SHIPMAN, IV and Elizabeth/ Betsey NICHOLAS, and was born 19 Dec 1825; died before 1881. Walter Leonard-⁸ BOWKER died ____.

Children of Walter Leonard-⁸ BOWKER and Julia A. SHIPMAN:
Surname **BOWKER**   (born Shefford, Quebec, Canada)

3886. Milton Charles	born ca 1855/56; died ____	

married Mary Ella STREETER 16 June 1880 Quebec, Canada
(she dau/o Wilderness STREETER and Mary WARREN) (she born 12 Feb 1857)

3887. Clark	born ca 1859; died ____	3888. Mary	born ca 1864; died ____

2819. MARY CAROLINE-[8] BOWKER, daughter of Samuel-[7] BOWKER (Samuel Ward-[6]; Silas-[5]; John-[4,3,2]; Edmund-[1]) and Mary GIBSON, was born 30 May 1829 at Westminster, MA. She married Henry B. HOUGHTON on 15 April 1858. He was the son of _____ HOUGHTON and _____ of Harvard and Stow, MA; and was born 10 Dec 1827; died 16 July 1861 Stow, MA . Mary Caroline-[8] BOWKER died _____.

Child of Mary Caroline-[8] BOWKER and Henry HOUGHTON:
Surname **HOUGHTON**

3889. Henry B., Jr.	born 19 July 1861 Stow, MA; died _____
	married Lizzie PAGE 6 Aug 1884
	(she born 23 May 1859 Tyngsboro, MA; died 1902 Ashby, MA)
	(she dau/o James PAGE and Almira _____)

Children: Carl Henry -[10] born 30 June 1885 Ashby, MA; died 1952; and Doris Bertha-[10] HOUGHTON born 26 Sep 1887; died 1902 EOL
Reference: John GIBSON of Cambridge, MA and his Descendants 1634-1899 , pages 289-90

2821. SAMUEL-[8] BOWKER, brother of above, was born 4 May 1832 at Westminster, MA. He married Harriet ALDRICH on 4 May 1856. She was the daughter of Timothy ALDRICH and Rebecca WEAVER; and was born 14 Mar 1832; died 21 Dec 1914. Samuel-[8] BOWKER died 10 Mar 1888 at Ashby, MA.

Children of Samuel-[8] BOWKER and Harriet ALDRICH:
Surname **BOWKER**

3890.Charles W.	born 25 May 1857 Ashby, MA; died 6 May 1882 (single)	EOL
3891. Clara E.	born 3 Feb 1859; died Mar 1869	EOL
3892. Mary Louise	born 13 Aug 1861 Ashby; died _____	
	married Frank / Francis Isaac BILLINGS of Fitchburg, MA on 1 Jan 1885	
	(he born Apr 1861 Fitchburg, MA; died _____)	
	(he s/o Francis R. BILLINGS and Hannah Elizabeth KINSMAN)	

Child: Helen-[10] BILLINGS born June 1888 Fitchburg, MA

+ **3893. ABBIE JEANETTE**	born 5 Mar 1863 Ashby; died _____	
	married John DAMON 1 Jan 1885 (he of Fitchburg, MA)	
	(he s/o George DAMON and Rosina PROCTOR)	
	(he born 5 Oct 1858 NH; died 24 Oct 1909 Ashby, MA) (Bright's disease)	
3894. Samuel Warren	born 16 July 1865 Ashby; died 8 Aug 1926 Reading, MA	
	married Nellie BROWN 1 May 1894	
	(she dau/o Lewis C. BROWN and Addie C. DIX) (she born ca 1869)	
3895. Alfred E.	born 25 Feb 1867 Ashby; died Apr 1869	EOL
3896. Frank +	born 17 Apr 1869; died _____ Fitchburg, MA (single)	EOL

    + Note: Frank BOWKER was an amateur actor and wrote and produced local productions, sometimes with his sister Jeanette Damon ; sometimes taking a role himself

3897. Walter	born 12 Aug 1871 Ashby; died 11 Sep 1899 (single)	EOL
3898. Aldrich Alfred ++	born 1 Jan 1875 Ashby; died 21 Mar 1947 San Bernardino, CA	EOL

++ Note: Aldrich BOWKER was a character actor, appearing in 26 movies between 1939-42. He usually played the role of a Judge, a Priest, a Doctor, a JOP, Newspaper editor, etc. He played the role of Father Dunn in the Warner Bros. production of " Waterfront " in 1939. Some other movies were " The Major and the Minor " in 1942, " Ball of Fire ", " Abe Lincoln in Illinois " and " Pride of the Blue Grass " – to name a few. He also appeared on stage in " You Can't Take it With You ", and was the "presenter" when George S. KAUFMAN won the 1937 Pullitzer Prize for that play.

2825. MARTHA WALKER-[8] BOSWORTH, daughter of Elizabeth/Betsey-[7] BOWKER (Samuel Ward-[6;] Silas-[5]; John-[4,3;2]; Edmund-[1]) and Benjamin BOSWORTH, was born 23 Dec 1831 at Royalston, Worcester, MA. She married Austin PHILLIPS on 13 Jan 1849 at Royalston, MA. He was the son of John PHILLIPS and Olive H. FRY; and was born ca 1827 MA; died 22 July 1893 WI. Martha-[8] BOSWORTH died 25 Apr 1903 WI.

Chjildren of Martha-[8] BOSWORTH and Austin PHILLIPS:
Surname **PHILLIPS**

3899. Edwin	born June 1849 IL; died 17 July 1910 WI		
3900. George H. (1)	born ca 1850; died 1853 WI	3903. George H (2)	born ca 1853 WI; died 1863
3901. Ada Elmira "Adele"	born ca 1852 WI; died 8 Oct 1871 WI	3904. Edward	born ca 1855 WI; died 1910
3902. Benjamin (1)	born ca 1852; died young	3905. Esther	born ca 1857; died 1860

Children of Martha Walker-8 BOSWORTH and Austin PHILLIPS, continued:
Surname **PHILLIPS**

+	**3906. JAMES**	born ca 1858 WI; died 6 July 1928; married Jennie Franklin COOPER ca 1879		
	3907. Bert	born ca 1860; died _____		
	3908. Benjamin Franklin (2)	born ca 1861; died 1931		
+	**3909. ALBERT WESLEY**	born July 1864; died 27 May 1935 WI		
		married Emma Lucy LANG 31 Mar 1894 Milwaukee, WI		
	3910. Emily	born ca 1867; died 1870	3912. Betsey	born 1873 WI; died 1930
	3911. Martha Ann	born ca 1870; died 1933	3913. William	born ca 1874; died 1950

2828. CHARLES WATSON-8 BOWKER, son of Nathaniel-7 BOWKER (Stephen Bigelow-6; Silas-5; John-4;3;2; Edmund-1) and Philena WHEELER, was born 15 June 1841 at Royalston, MA. He married first to Nancy A. SIBLEY on 1 Jan 1863 at Worcester, MA. She was the daughter of Joel SIBLEY and Rhoda ALGER, and was born ca 1843; died 20 Aug 1870. He married second to Susan B. UPHAM on 12 Sep 1871 at Winchendon, MA. She was the daughter of ____ UPHAM and ____; and was born Sep 1844; died 1922. Charles Watson-8 BOWKER died _____.

Children of Charles Watson-8 BOWKER and Nancy A. SIBLEY:
Surname **BOWKER**

3914. John Bradley	born 12 Mar 1865; died 14 Nov 1945; married Martha A. THAYER ca 1886 (she born 12 Oct 1866) (dau/o Ethan THAYER and Mary Ann ____)
	Children: Marion Thayer-10 born ca 1887, died 1988; and Harold Sawyer-10 BOWKER born 7 Dec 1888, died 24 Feb 1971; married Susie Mae UPHAM (1890-1983)
3915. Charles Alfred	born 24 Feb 1867 Royalston, MA; died ____

Children of Charles Watson-8 BOWKER and Susan B. UPHAM:
Surname **BOWKER**

3916. Harrison Winthrop	born 10 June 1877 MA; drowned 12 July 1927, MA
	Note: In 1900 he was a student at Harvard University. He was a lawyer (1910 census) in general practice. He drowned when " he fell from the hurricane deck of the Steamer Rose Standish which was sailing from Pemberton to Nantucket ". Source: Bridgeport Telegram 12 July 1927
3917. George Arthur	born 4 June 1881; died ____
3918. Lena M.	born July 1885; died ____
3919. Charles Watson, Jr.	born 11 Sep 1888; p died 15 Sep 1961, a Realtor married Dorothy WHITE 12 Sep 1914 Yonkers, Westchester, NY (she born 24 Mar 1892 Brattleboro, VT; died 24 June 1980 Worcester, MA)
	Child: Charles Watson-10, III born ca 1918 MA; died ____

2849. ADELIA/DELIA-8 LEAVITT, daughter of Nahum-7 LEAVITT (Celia-6 TURNER; Betty-5 BOWKER; John-4, 3, 2; Edmund-1) and Eunice EVERSON, was born 26 Jan 1845 at Pembroke, Plymouth, MA. She married Horace LITTLEFIELD on 24 Dec 1861. He was the son of Horace LITTLEFIELD and Delia A. SHAW; and was born ca 1834 Berwick, Maine; died 3 April 1892 Whitman, MA. Adelia-8 LEAVITT died 14 Dec 1909 Whitman, MA.

Children of Adelia-8 LEAVITT and Horace LITTLEFIELD:
Surname **LITTLEFIELD**

3920. George Ellsworth	born 14 Aug 1864; died ____
3921. Benjamin Everett	born 28 Sep 1866; died ____
3922. Bradford L.	born 29 Mar 1869; died ca 1934; married Minnie WHITING ca 1894
3923. Edward L.	born 21 Jan 1873; died ____; married Florence M. FITZGERALD Chase 18 May 1913 (she dau/o John FITZGERALD and Mary J. CHURCHILL)(she born ca 1877 MA) (she 1 married James C. CHASE 25 Apr 1896)
	Child: Chester J-10 LITTLEFIELD born 5 May 1913; died 15 Jan 2000 ME
3924. Henry W.	born Oct 1875; died ____
3925. Nahum Franklin "Frank"	born 21 July 1881; died ____ married Ida May BELL 4 June 1902 Whitman, Plymouth, MA
	Children: Lloyd B-10 born 1903/04 Whitman, MA; and Vernon C-10 LITTLEFIELD born 23 Dec 1910 Whitman, MA

2857. VALESTA DRUSCILLA-8 BOWKER, daughter of Alexander-7 BOWKER (Jonathan-6; Solomon-5; John-4, 3, 2; Edmund-1) was born 17 July 1841 at Stanstead, Quebec, Canada. She married Thomas William LANE, as his 2nd wife, on 13 May 1867 at Stanstead. He was the son of John LANE and Susan BOWERS, and was born, at sea aboard the Ship

BOWKER
The Eighth American Generation

ARDWELL, on 25 July 1836; died 21 May 1917 Stanstead. Valesta-[8] BOWKER died 21 June 1897 Stanstead.

Children of Valesta-[8] BOWKER and Thomas W. LANE:
Surname **LANE**   (all children born Barnston, Stanstead, Quebec, Canada)
    3926. Elmer Adwill   born 19 July 1867; die 28 May 1921 Stanstead
           Child: Arton Harold-[10] LANE born July 1901; died ____; married Grace Carolyn MILLER on 28 Sep 1927 VT
    3927. Elizabeth A.   born ca 1873; died 23 Nov 1883 Barnston   EOL
    3928. Gertrude Josephine   born 21 July 1877; died 27 Nov 1957
+   **3929. MINNIE MABLE**   born 28 Oct 1885; died 24 June 1952 Verdun, Montreal, Ontario, Canada
           married Oral Charles SMITH ca 1905   (he born 6 July 1882; died 12 Oct 1918)

2860. EDWIN SHERMAN-[8] BOWKER, son of Nathaniel Beaman-[7] BOWKER (Jonathan-[6]; Solomon-[5]; John-[4, 3, 2]; Edmund-[1]) and Mary Ann PARNELL, was born ca 1865 VT. He married Cora Hatch JELLISON 29 June 1890. She was the daughter of Thomas JELLISON and Elizabeth Jane BUZZELL; and was born ca 1864/66 ME, died 1934. Edwin S-[8] BOWKER died ca 1936 Belfast, Waldo, Maine.   Reference: History of the City of Belfast in the State of Maine; page 331

Children of Edwin S-[8] BOWKER and Cora Hatch JELLISON:
Surname **BOWKER**
+   **3930. THOMAS EDWIN**   born 25 Apr 1891 Belfast, Maine; died ____; married Martha Hazel SHAW 20 Jan 1914
    3931. Harry Elmer   born 27 Apr 1896 Belfast, Maine,; died _____
           married Helen ____ ca 1920   (she born Canada ca 1899)
           Children: Claude-[10] born ca 1922 ME; Cecil-[10] born ca 1924 ME; Merle-[10] born ca 1926 ME; Eugene-[10] born ca 1927 ME; and Floyd-[10] BOWKER born ca 1929 ME.

2864. MARY ELIZABETH "Lizzy"-[8] HINCKLEY, daughter of Mary-[7] BOWKER (George-[6]; Jotham-[5]; John-[4,3,2]; Edmund-[1]) and William W. HINCKLEY, was born May 1857 Barre, MA. She married Harrison Orcutt THRASHER 14 Apr 1880. He was the son of David THRASHER and Nancy ROBBINS; and was born 12 June 1855/56 MA; died 2 May 1907. Mary Elizabeth-[8] HINCKLEY died 1919 at Hardwick, MA.

Children of Mary-[8] HINCKLEY and Harrison Orcutt THRASHER:
Surname **THRASHER**
    3932. Austin Millard   born 1 May 1882 Hardwick, MA; died 20 Aug 1963 North Bedford, MA
           married Lena May HOWARD 18 Oct 1905 at West Springfield, MA
           (she dau/o Fred L. HOWARD and Josie R. BATES)
           Child: Irene Margaret-[10] THRASHER born 19 Oct 1910; died 12 Nov 1997; married Frederick MARTIN
           ca 1934 (ch: Diana Margaret-[11] MARTIN born ca 1939 MA)
++   3933. Leon Chester   born 19 Sep 1883 Hardwick, MA; died 28 Mar 1915 and is buried at Hardwick, MA
    On his gravestone it reads " lost his life on the British ship FALABA which was sunk by a torpedo from a German submarine "
++ Note: Reference is from Wikipedia and states " The "THRASHER INCIDENT " as it became known in US Media, nearly became the start of America's Involvement in WW1 on 28 March 1915. The British steamship RMS FALABA was torpedoed and sunk by German U-Boat U-28. In the incident 104 people were killed including one American passenger Leon Chester THRASHER, a 31 year old mining engineer from MA.

+   **3934. HOWARD ROY/RAY** born 30 Apr 1886; died ____
           married Mabel Sumner BARNES 4 May 1910 Hardwick, MA
           (she dau/o Willard BARNES and Clariette ____)
    3935. Ruth Alma   born 8 July 1888 Hardwick, MA; died 13 Jan 1976 MA
           married John D. NEYLON / NAYLON ca ca 1913
    Children: Elizabeth-[10] born 12 Jul 1914, died 27 Jan 1985 Boston, MA; and Harrison Leon-[10] NEYLON / NAYLON born 21 July 1925

2865. HARRIET ELIZA-[8] BOWKER, daughter of Luke Freeman-[7] BOWKER (George-[6;] Jotham-[5]; John-[4;3;2]; Edmund-[1]) and Eliza Jane WILSON, was born 11 Feb 1856 MA. She married Maxwell Osmer SCOTT 13 July 1881 Fitchburg, MA. He was the son of Salmon Maynard SCOTT and Mary Malvina SPAULDING, and was born 14 Feb 1858, died 24 June 1911 Worcester (peritonitis). Harriet-[8] BOWKER died 12 July 1919 SC.

Children of Harriet-[8] BOWKER and Maxwell SCOTT:
Surname **SCOTT**
    3936. Mary Laura   born 24 July 1882; died 8 Feb 1965; married Frank ABBOTT ca ____
+   **3937. ROBERT**   born 3 June 1887; died 10 Dec 1973; married Annie LAYTON 3 June 1912
      WALLACE   (she dau of William Irvin LAYTON and Mary E. _____)

Children of Harriet[8] BOWKER and Maxwell SCOTT, continued:
Surname **SCOTT**

3938. Ernest Maxwell	born 27 Jan 1896 MA; died 28 May 1971 MA; married Alice A. ALDRICH
	(she dau/o George A. ALDRICH and Cora EMERSON) (born 1888; died 1962)
	1 married Walter B. DODGE 29 Dec 1909
3939. Stanley W.	born 30 Oct 1901; died 21 Aug 1971 OH
	married Irene Gladys ____ (she born 3 Feb 1903; died Aug/Sep 1967)

Children: Thelma Irene[10] born ca 1922; and Stanley W.[10] SCOTT, Jr. born ca 1924

2866. CORA JANE[8] BOWKER, sister of above, was born 25 April 1858 MA. She married first to Levi S. HUNTOON on 22 March 1870 MA. He was the son of Horace HUNTOON and Ruth ____; and was born ca 1845; died 1904. They may have divorced, since she married second to Willard E. DAWSON c a1884. He was the son of _____ DAWSON and ____; and was born ca 1864 Ny; died 1930. Cora Jane[8] BOWKER died 7 Feb 1952 SC.

Child of Cora Jane[8] BOWKER and Willard DAWSON:
Surname **DAWSON**

3940. Maude E.	born 25 Apr 1885 Ayer, ME; died ____
	married Clifford Milo PORTER 3 May 1904 Erving, MA
	(he s/o Lucius PORTER and Lavilla CARMEL/CORNELL)
	(he born 8 Nov 1875 MA; died ____)

Children: Evelyn Sadie[10] born 11 July 1905; and Roger W[10] PORTER born ca 1908

2870. LYMAN HOWE[8] BOWKER, son of Levi[7] BOWKER (Gideon[6]; Antipas[5]; Josiah[4]; John[3,2]; Edmund[1]) and Betsey SILSBY, was born 11 Feb 1814 at Chesterfield, NH. He married Elizabeth B. SMITH on 11 June 1835. She was the daughter of ____ SMITH and ___, and was born 13 Sep 1814; died 13 April 1898 IA. Lyman Howe[8] BOWKER died 9/11 March 1899 at Eldora, Hardin, Iowa.

Children of Lyman Howe[8] BOWKER and Elizabeth SMITH:
Surname **BOWKER**   (all but last 2 children born NH)

3941. Levi D.	born 1837; died 4 Oct 1863 Little Rock, AR; married Sarah M. JAMESON 3 Aug 1861
	Child: Levi[10] BOWKER born ca 1863
3942. Desenna/Dephina	born 1840; died ____
+ **3943. FANNIE L.**	born May 1842; died ____; married Martin LARUE 9 Sep 186_ Rock Island, IL
+ **3944. CHARLES WILSON**	born 3 Oct 1845; died 21 Oct 1928 Mansonville, Quebec, Canada
	married Mary Jane PICKLE ca 1870
	(she born 17 June 1849 Potton, QUE; died 4 Feb 1924 Mansonville, QUE
3945. Augustus	born 1846; died ____
+ **3946. ADELAIDE**	born 18 Apr 1848; died 1908; married George Henry ADDISON ca ___
3947. Eugene	born 1850; died ____
3948. Chloe Ann	born 1852; died ____
3949. Prentiss/Prentice	born Apr 1855 IA; died _____; a saloon keeper
	married Ida May ADAMS 11 Apr 1876 IL (she dau/o Alfred ADAMS and Louisa ____)
3950. Frank	born 1860 IL; died ____

2871. LEVI GOODELL[8] BOWKER, brother of above, was born 2 Jan 1816 at Chesterfield, NH. He married Parthena HARTSHORN on 10 May 1840 T. She was the daughter of HARTSHORN and ____, and was born ca 1821 Canada; died ____. Levi[8] BOWKER died Jan 1874.

Children of Levi[8] BOWKER and Parthena HARTSHORN:
Surname **BOWKER**

3951. Barbara A.	born 27 July 1842; died 24 Aug 1913 Chicago, IL		
	married Charles W. FOGG ca ____	(he born ca 1837 Maine; died ____)	
	Children: Charles-B-[10] born ca 1862; and Benton R-[10] FOGG born ca 1869		
3952. Luanna	born ca 1841; died 31 Jan 1849	EOL	
3953. Malvena	born ca 1844; died 12 Apr 1847	EOL	
3954. Madison	born ca 1847; died ____	3956. Luretta	born ca 1851; died ____
3955. Millard F.	born ca 1848; died ____	3957. Effie	born ca 1856; died ____
+ **3958. CLAUDINE W.**	born 3 Dec 1859 IL; died 8 Oct 1936 IL		
	married John L. CURRY 2 Oct 1886 Chicago, IL (he born ca 1853 Chicago, Il)		

2872. ROSWELL[-8] BOWKER, brother of above, was born 26 Aug 1817 at Lunenburg, VT. He married Jane BLAKESLEE on 2 Feb 1841. She was the daughter of John BLAKESLEE and Bathsheba LAKE, and was born ca 1818 at Daltoon, NH; died ____. Roswell[-8] BOWKER died 6 May 1898 at Whitefield, NH.

Children of Roswell[-8] BOWKER and Jane BLAKESLEE:
Surname **BOWKER** (all children born Lunenburg, VT)

	3959. Adrian	born ca 1843 VT; died ____		
+	**3960. MITCHELL HARVEY**	born 24 Nov 1845; died 9 Oct 1935 Whitefield, NH		
		1 married Laura Permelia BROOKS 1 Nov 1867 Lunenburg, VT		
		2 married Annie WHITTAKER 9 Nov 1899 Whitefield, NH		
	3961. Laura A.	born ca 1846; died ____		
	3962. Ellen H.	born Oct 1849; died ____	3964. Flora	born ca 1855; died ____
	3963. Clara	born ca 1853; died ____	3965. Lizzie	born 7 Dec 1858; died ____

2880. FRANKLIN[-8] BOWKER, son of Rice[-7] BOWKER (Gideon[-6]; Antipas[-5]; Josiah[-4]; John[-3, 2]; Edmund[-1]) and Betsey CLARKE, was born 2 June 1816 at Lunenburg, Essex, VT. He married Nancy Anne HUMISTON on 24 June 1840 at Rochester, Ohio. She was the daughter of Isaac HUMISTON and Susannah DICKSON; and was born 16 Aug 1814 at Colesville, NY; died 25 Jan 1889 at Fitchville, Ohio. Franklin[-8] BOWKER died Aug 1895 at Baxter Springs, MO.

Children of Franklin[-8] BOWKER and Nancy HUMISTON:
Surname **BOWKER**

+	**3966. HUBERT/ HUGH DEMAREST**	born 14 Aug 1842 Sullivan, OH; died 14 Jan 1927 Chicago, OL
		married Susie GORDON Smith 25 Nov 1867 Piscataway, NJ
		(she born 5 Dec 1849 Piscataway, NJ; died 31 Mar 1932 Chicago, IL)
	3967. Evaline/ Eva A.	born 16 Aug 1845; died 10 May 1924; married Emery Willard HAKES 25 Dec 1871
		Child: Juanita-[10] HAKES born 19 Dec 1880; married Frederick Penn WEAVER, Sr. on 5 Nov 1904
	3968. Norris/Harris	born ca 1850; died ____

2881. MARTHA J[-8] BOWKER, sister of above, was born 21 March 1819 Lunenburg, VT. Sher married Anson D. PERSONS on 24 Nov 1838 at Lorain, Ohio. He was the son of David PARSONS/ PERSONS and Lucretia EDDY; and was born 13 Nov 1806 Montpelier, VT; died 3 Jan 1875 Sullivan, Ashland, Ohio. . Martha J-[8] BOWKER died 1 April 1869 at Sullivan, Ashland, Ohio.

Children of Martha[-8] BOWKER and Anson PERSONS:
Surname **PERSONS**

	3969. Ransom	born 25 May 1840 Huntington, OH; died 9 Sep 1863 Sullivan, Ashland, OH
+	**3970. HERBERT ALVIN**	born 5 Nov 1841 Sullivan, OH; died 2 Dec 1916 Homerville, Medina, OH
		married Laura Jane NEWTON 4 Feb 1866
		(she dau/o Isaac Luther NEWTON and Sarah Ann LAVANWAY)
		(she born 1 Mar 1848; died 5 Jan 1929)
	3971. Helen	born 6 Nov 1843; died 7 Jan 1877
	3972. Charles C.	born 22 July 1846; died 16 Jan 1901 Lodi, Athens, OH
	3973. Josephine	born 18 Aug 1851; died 25 Apr 1908 OH
	3974. Dr. Willis Fremont	born 9 Jan 1857; died 24 Aug 1932 Mogadore, Portage, OH
		1 married Lucinda Ellen COOPER 27 Nov 1878
		(she born ca 1856; died 1896)
		Children: Jessie H-[10] born ca 1880; Paul Fisk-[10] born ca 1892; and Arthur W-[10] PERSONS born ca 1895
		2 married Elva ____ 23 April 1901 (divorced)

2885. LEWIS LEANDER[-8] BOWKER, son of Lyman James[-7] BOWKER (Gideon[-6]; Antipas[-5]; Josiah[-4] ; John-[3,2]; Edmund[-1]) and Betsey MERRIAM, was born 29 Oct 1821 at Lunenburg, VT. He married Lucy Minerva HEARD on 21 Oct 1845 at Newport, Quebec, Canada. She was the daughter of Edmund HEARD and Mary WILLARD, and was born 5 Dec 1824 Newport, QC; died 4 Aug 1897 QC. Lewis L-[8] BOWKER died 16 Feb 1905 at Sawyerville, Quebec, Canada.

Children of Lewis L-[8] BOWKER and Lucy HEARD:
Surname **BOWKER**

+	**3975. EDMUND HEARD**	born 27 June 1849 QC; died 9 Apr 1929 Corinth, NY
		married Lucy M. FERGUSON ca ____

Children of Lewis L-8 BOWKER and Lucy HEARD, continued:
Surname **BOWKER**

+	**3976. LYMAN JAMES**	born 5 July 1853 QC; died 22 Mar 1924 Sawyerville, QC
		married Clarinda Lenora HARVEY ca 1874
	3977. Luvia/Lucia	born 2 Sep 1855 QC; died 25 June 1944
		married Artemus FARNSWORTH ca ____
+	**3978. HERBERT RICE**	born 1 Dec 1857 QC; died 16 May 1950
		1 married Ormesinda " Sinda " Cornelia FARNSWORTH ca ____
		(she dau/o David FARNSWORTH and Nancy Sophia STEVENS) ---.
		(she born 30 May 1861; died 17 Jan 1897 Sawyerville, QC
		2 married Jennie DRAPER 29 Dec 1897 (she born ca 1862; died 1929)

2889. MILO ANDERSON-8 BOWKER, son of Leonard-7 BOWKER (Gideon-6; Antipas-5; Josiah-4; John-3;2; Edmund-1) and Phebe CURTISS, was born Apr 1822 VT. He married first to Delinda Thilisama MILLS on 2 Dec 1847 VT. She was the daughter of Daniel Comstock MILLS and Dorothy Ann FARRAND, and was born 16 June 1828 VT; died ca 1860 Coldwater, Branch, MI. He married second to Mary Ann CHASE ca 1867. She was the daughter of ____ CHASE and ____, and was born ca 1834 NY; died ____. Milo A-8 BOWKER died ca 1880's at Carson City, Nevada.

Children of Milo-8 BOWKER and Delinda MILLS:
Surname **BOWKER**

	3979. Cordelia	born ca 1849 MI; died ____
	3980. Emma	born July 1851 MI; died ____
		1 married David E. DAVIS 4 Jan 1869 (he born ca 1843; died 1873)
		2 married Elijah Thompson CROSON ca 1874 (he born ca 1833)
	3981. William Frederick	born ca 1853; died 1931

Child of Milo-8 BOWKER and Mary Ann CHASE:
Surname **BOWKER**

	3982. Ella A.	born 13 Nov 1868 CA; died 11 Oct 1936 Portland, OR
		married Gustus Charles MORRIS ca ____
		(he born 10 Aug 1864; died 3 June 1929 Portland, OR)

2897. JOHN PIERSON-8 BOWKER, Jr., son of John Pierson-7 BOWKER, Sr. (Oliver-6; Ephraim-5; Josiah-4; John-3;2; Edmund-1) and Polly BAKER, was born 12 April 1814. He married Sarah P. PETERS on 10 Jan 1838. She was the daughter of ____ PETERS and ____; and was born ca ____; died ____. John Pierson-8 BOWKER, Jr. died 14 May 1885.

Children of John P-8 BOWKER, Jr. and Sarah PETERS:
Surname **BOWKER**

	3983. Sarah Peters	born 28 Feb 1839; died ____; married Richard BLISS 15 Oct 1888
	3984. John W.	born 11 May 1850; died ____
	3985. Edward	born 15 Mar 1854; died 23 Apr 1854 EOL

2898. LEWIS FALES-8 BOWKER, brother of above, was born 1 June 1818 at Walpole, Norfolk, MA. He married first to Ann DARROW ca 1839. She was born ____; died before 1848. He married 2nd to Sarah Ann MELCHER on 30 Nov 1848 at Boston, MA. She was the daughter of Benjamin F. MELCHER and Sarah JEFFREY; and was born Sept 1824 Maine; died 14 Nov 1891 Newton, MA. Lewis Fales-8 BOWKER died 23 Oct 1867 Houston, TX.

Children of Lewis F-8 BOWKER and Ann DARROW:
Surname **BOWKER**

+	**3986. LEWIS / LOUIS L.**	born 31 Oct 1840 NYC, NY; died 1923; married Mary J. TURNER ca 1867
		(she born 22 Apr 1847 Walpole, MA; died ____)
	3987. George	born ca 1841 NY; died ____

Children of Lewis F-8 BOWKER and Sarah Ann MELCHER:
Surname **BOWKER**

	3988. Ella	born ca 1852; died ____
+	**3989. JESSIE LYMAN**	born 14 Apr 1856; died 29 Jan 1915
		married Walter Hunnewell STEARNS, Jr. 30 June 1875

2910. EDMUND NEWTON-8 CLARK, son of Lydia Church-7 NEWTON (Ezra-6; Tabitha-5 BOWKER; Josiah-4; John-3;2;

Edmund[-1]) and Deacon Elbridge T. CLARK, was born 6 June 1841 at Medway, Norfolk, MA. He married Tryphena Richardson FISHER on 8 Jan 1867 at Braintree, MA. She was the daughter of Lewis FISHER and Betsey RICHARDSON, and was born 17 Jan 1841 Medway, MA; died 17 July 1932 Medway. Edmund Newton-[8] CLARK died 2 Feb 1935 at Millis, Norfolk, MA.

Children of Edmund Newton-[8] CLARK and Tryphena FISHER:
Surname **CLARK**   (all children born Medway, MA)

3990. Ernest Newton	born 8 Oct 1868; died _____ CO	
3991. Elsie Lydia	born 28 Jan 1870; died ____MA; married Perry S. NEWCOMB 22 Dec 1892	
3992. Betsey Fisher	born 26 Aug 1871; died 9 Aug 1960	
3993. Arthur Lewis	born 19 Feb 1873; died 8 June 1873	
3994. Irving Richardson	born 24 Oct 1874; died 26 Oct 1953 Millis, MA	
	married Nellie WAMBOLT 16 Feb 1920	
3995. Fannie Louise	born 23 Oct 1876; died ___; married Wainer Howard HOLBROOK 27 Oct 1908	

2922. DEWITT CLINTON-[8] BOWKER, Jr., son of Dewitt Clinton-[7] BOWKER, Sr., (Obediah-[6]; Ithamar-[5]; Josiah-[4]; John-[3;2]; Edmund-[1]) and Sarah Gertrude DRAKE, was born ca 1867/68. He married first to _____ca 1892. He married second to Imogene ____ ca 1904.

Children of Dewitt-[8] Clinton BOWKER, Jr. and _____:
Surname **BOWKER**

3996. Maud	born ca 1893; died ____	3998. Wilbur	born ca 1900; died ____
3997. Clinton	born ca 1895; died ____	3999. Grace	born ca 1905; died ____

Children of Dewitt Clinton-[8] BOWKER, Jr. and Imogene ____:
Surname **BOWKER**

4000. Caroline	born 1908; died ____	4001. Olive	born ca 1909; died ____

2926. OBEDIAH-[8] " OBEY " BOWKER, brother of above, was born 24 Feb 1877. He married Caroline SCHROEDER ca 1906/07. She was the daughter of Charles F. SCHROEDER (German immigrant) and Matilda F. _, and was born ca 1887 NY. .

Children of Obediah-[8] BOWKER and Caroline SCHROEDER:
Surname **BOWKER**

4002. Helen	born 1907 NY; died ____	4005. Alice	born ca 1913
4003. Everett	born ca 1908; died ___	4006. Frank	born ca 1916; died ____
4004. Lawrence	born ca 1909; died ____	4007. James	born ca 1919; died ____

2935. JESSIE-[8] MARBLE, daughter of Jannette/Jeanette-[7] BOWKER (Windsor-[6;] Asa-[5]; Josiah-[4]; John-[3;2]; Edmund-[1]) and the Rev. William Horace MARBLE, and was born ca 1871 IA. She married George Washington WATTS ca 1899. He was the son of ___ WATTS and ___; and was born ca 1868; died 5 Sep 1957 at Lake County, MN. Jessie-[8] MARBLE died 21 Feb 1951.

Children of Jessie-[8] MARBLE and George Washington WATTS:
Surname **WATTS**

4008. Florence	born ca 1901; died 2003; married John Edwin JOHNSON ca ____
	(he born ca 1899; died 1975)
4009. Marion K.	born ca 1901; died 1902 EOL
4010. John	born ca 1909 MN; died ____
4011. Dorothy Marjorie	born 20 Mar 1911 MN; died 6 Oct 2007 Bothwell, WA.

2936. MARY HAYWARD/ HEYWOOD-[8] KAY, daughter of Olive-[7] WHEELER (Mary Hosmer-[6] FORBUSH; David-[5;4]; Martha-[3] BOWKER; John-[2]; Edmund-[1]) and Bryant KAY, was born 12 Feb 1829 at Jamestown, Chatauqua, NY. She married William DYE on 9 Jan 1850 at Sisterville, Tyler, West Virginia. He was the son of Daniel S. DYE, Jr. and Teresa UNDER-WOOD, and was born 15 Feb 1817 OH; died 9 Nov 1883 CA. Mary H-[8] KAY died 27 Dec 1910 at Orosi, Tulare, CA.

Children of Mary H-[8] KAY and William DYE:
Surname **DYE**

4012. Hervey Elbridge	born ca 1850; died 1912
4013. Adoniram Judson	born Mar 1853; died 1933
	married Alice ____ ca 1875 (she born ca Nov 1853 Ireland)

Children: Arthur-[10] born ca 1875; Harry-[10] DYE born Sept 1878 NY

Children of Mary H[8] KAY and William DYE, continued:
Surname **DYE**

4014. Harriet Lorilla "Hattie"	born ca 1858; died 1855
4015. James Monroe	born 10 July 1859; died 8 Aug 1922 CA
4016. Sorella Ella	born ca 1865; died 1944

2937. HANNAH[8] KAY, sister of above, was born 20 June 1832 at Carroll, Chatauqua, NY. She married Hervey/Harvey Dale DYE on 21 Apr 1852 at Tyler, Charles, West Virginia. He was the son of Enoch DYE and Elizabeth " Betsey " BROWN; and was born 18 Mar 1831 OH; died 22 April 1921 Wayne Co., Iowa. Hannah[8] KAY died 6 Dec 1905/06 Wayne, IA.

Children of Hannah[8] KAY and Hervey/ Harvey DYE:
Surname **DYE**

4017. Luella Catherine	born May 1853 OH; died 1920; married John WINLAND ca 1873 (he born ca 1850)
4018. Franklin T.	born ca 1854/55 VA; died 1863 EOL
4019. Olive Elizabeth	born 22 July 1857; died 20 Oct 1942 IA
	married Robert Carter HUTCHISON ca 1875
	(he born Jan 1849; died 28 Jan 1929 IA)
	Children: Bertha-[10] born ca 1876 and Clyde-[10] HUTCHISON born Oct 1881 IA
4020. Cora B. (1)	born ca 1858; died young
4021. Charles Clinton	born Nov 1860 IA; died 1926; married Adella " Della" De MOTTE ca ____
	(she born 12 May 1873 OH)(she dau/o Frank H. De MOTTE and Cevilida KUMLER)
4022. Mary Eva	born Dec 1864; died ____
4023. Harriet Leticia "Lettie"	born Jan 1867; died ____; married Milford W. HAMILTON ca ____
4024. Cora Belle (2)	born ca 1871; died ____
4025. Laura Melvina	born ca 1872; died ____; married Novia Sanford BEAVERS ca 1906 ++
	(he born 28 Aug 1872; died 1945)
	(he s/o Isaac Newton BEAVERS and Nancy Maria HUTCHINSON)

++ Note: Novia S. BEAVERS invented and had patented a "gasoline pressure-lamp" on 22 Oct 1907 (# 868,962)
He was a successful merchant and later worked in real estate

2949. AUSTIN H[8] CRAWFORD, son of Polly/Mary[7] DAVIS (Mary/Polly[6] FORBUSH; James[5]; David[4]; Martha[3] BOWKER; John-[2]; Edmund[1]) and Almon/Almeron CRAWFORD, was born ca 1825 Bennington, VT. He married Ann GARDINIER ca ____ . She was the daughter of ____ GARDINIER and ____; and was born ca 1826 England; died ____ . Austin[8] CRAWFORD died 13 June 1886 Bennington, VT.

Children of Austin[8] CRAWFORD and Ann GARDINIER:
Surname **CRAWFORD**

4026. Romeyn / "Ronnie "	born 18 Aug 1854; died 5 May 1917
4027. Mary A. (1)	born ca ____
4028. Emma/Emily	born ca 1861 NY; died 2 Jan 1924 Bennington, VT; married Eugene F. MOON ca ___
	Child: Leah Arline-[10] born 7 Nov 1891; died 16 Oct 1971; married ____ COOK ca ____
4029. Mary (2)	born 1867 NY; died 1924 VT; married William HOLT ca ____

2953. RANDALL J[8] CRAWFORD, brother of above, was born 5 Dec 1835 Hoosick, NY. He married Alida HOLLENBECK ca 1862. She was the daughter of William HOLLENBECK and Ann BAISLEY, and was born ca 1844 VT; died 21 April 1889. Randall[8] CRAWFORD, a builder, died 12 Jan 1895.

Children of Randall[8] CRAWFORD and Alida HOLLENBECK:
Surname **CRAWFORD**

4030. Frank(lin) Henry	born 6 June 1862 VT; died ____; carpenter
	married Theresa Rogers ALBRO 17 Apr 1884 Bennington, VT
	Children: Buell Albro-[10] born 3 Aug 1887; died 13 Dec 1958 Burlington, VT; and Alida-[10] CRAWFORD born ca 1889
4031. Edward A	born 25 June 1865 VT; died 2 Oct 1940 Oak Park, IL
	married Emma L. CHAUVIN 17 Oct 1889 Bennington, VT
4032. Eliza B/ Lizzie B	born Dec 1868; died ____; married Archie E. NORTON 25 Sep 1889 Bennington
	(he s/o Albert A. NORTON and Helen L. ___) (he born 20 July 1867 VT; died 1906)
4033. Elmer R.	born ca 1873 VT; died ____ married Ellen B. WATTS 16 June 1915 Chicago, IL

BOWKER
The Eighth American Generation

2975. ADDIE H-[8] LEAVITT, daughter of Caroline-[7] FORBUSH (Daniel-[6]; James-[5]; David-[4]; Martha-[3] BOWKER; John-[2]; Edmund-[1]) and George Hubbard LEAVITT, was born 2 Apr 1824 at Dummer, Coos, NH. She married Orlando S. BLODGETT on 24 July 1849 at Stark, Cooc=s, NH. He was the son of James S. BLODGETT and Hersey MYERS, and was born ca 1849 Il; died 1905 Nebraska. Addie H-[8] LEAVITT died ca 1905.

Children of Addie H-[8] LEAVITT and Orlando BLODGETT:
Surname **BLODGETT**

4034. Nettie M.	born ca 1869 IL; died ____	
4035. Sadie E.	born Oct 1870; died ____; married Marion R. STOREY 25 Dec 1881 WI	
4036. Manzo	born ca 1876 IL; died ____ 4037. Addie	born 29 Aug 1879 Leroy, IL

2977. ELLA CLARA-[8] LEAVITT, sister of above, was born 22 Mar 1855 Dummer, Coos, NH. She married Albert C. SWART June 1871. He was the son of ____ SWART and ____, and was born 3 Feb 1847 IL; died 10 Oct 1925 Chicago, IL. Ella C-[8] LEAVITT died ____.

Child of Ella Clara-[8] LEAVITT and Albert SWART:
Surname **SWART**

> 4038. Esther Ella   born 4 Mar 1881 Boone, IL; died 2 Aug 1980 San Bernardino, CA
> 1 married Leslie Henry JONES ca ____
> 2 married Ernest Francis VREELAND ca ____ (he born 1886; died 1964)
> Children: Stanley-[10] born ca 1921; Ralph W.-[10] born ca 1927 and Charlene-[10] VREELAND born ca 1930

2995. CLARA B-[8] FORBUSH, daughter of Ephraim-[7] FORBUSH (Daniel-[6]; James-[5]; Martha-[3] BOWKER; John-[2]; Edmund-[1]) and Louisa P. MILES, was born ca 1859. She married Charles Hosea WENTWORTH on 28 Sep 1878 at Lancaster, NH. He was the son of Joseph WENTWORTH and Lavina ____; and was born 11 Sep 1852 NH; died 30 Jan 1935 Dummer, NH. Clara-[8] FORBUSH died ____.

Children of Clara-[8] FORBUSH and Charles Hosea WENTWORTH:
Surname **WENTWORTH**

4039. Lena M.	born Jan 1880; died _____
4040. Harriet Belle	born Sept 1881 Stark, Coos, NH; died ____
" Hattie "	married Henry Lee ABBOTT 15 Feb 1911
	(he s/o Anthony ABBOTT and Hettie COOPER of Lancaster, NH)
+ **4041 . GLADYS E.**	born Feb 1890 NH; died ____; married Elijah H. FOGG 16 Oct 1911 Lancaster, NH
	(he s/o Lester Delmont FOGG and Emma F. RIMS/RINES
4042. Dorothy Rea	born 2 Jan 1899 Guildhall, VT; died _____
4043. Robert Ephraim	born 25 Aug 1900 VT; died 4 Mar 1975 Hartford, VT.
	married Laversa F. JOHNSON 11 June 1934
	(she dau/o Clinton JOHNSON and Cherlus _____)

3007. ALMA B-[8] HOWLAND, daughter of Nancy-[7] FORBUSH (Daniel-[6]; James-[5]; David-[4]; Martha-[3] BOWKER; John-[2]; Edmund-[1]) and John N. HOWLAND, was born 25 Apr 1865 at Crystal, Coos, NH. She married Charles W. HOLT ca 1888. He was the son of Jones Wesley HOLT and Casilla C. MURCH; and was born ____; died __. He served as a Private in the US Army during World War 1. Alma B-[8] HOWLAND died ca 1859 Ellsworth, Hancock, ME.

Children of Alma B-[8] HOWLAND and Charles W. HOLT:
Surname **HOLT**

4044. Infant	born 23 June 1889; died same day
4045. Harry Warren	born 23 Aug 1891 Berlin, Coos, NH; died 14 Aug 1973 St. Johnsbury, Caledonia, VT
	married Amy Little NASH 28 July 1920
	(she dau/o Charles K. NASH and Myra DELANO)
4046. Paul Hammond	born 29 Dec 1893; died Dec 1963 NH
	married Eva M. ____ ca 1923 (she born ca 1901 NH; died _____)
	Children: Ruth-[10] born ca 1924; Marion-[10] born ca 1929; and Norman-[10] HOLT born ca 1933
4047. Howland Emmons	born 5 Apr 1897; died 8 Feb 1961 San Bruno, CA
	married Ethel F. ARMSTRONG 3 Dec 1921 Berlin, NH
	(she dau/o Thomas ARMSTRONG and Helen EMERY)
	Child: Maurice-[10] HOLT born ca 1922

3008. ELDIN/ ELDON HAZEN-8 HOWLAND, brother of above, was born 20 Apr 1868 Crystal, Coos, NH. He married Saloma Dulcena LEIGHTON 24 Oct 1898. She was the daughter of E F LEIGHTON and Eliza SPREDBURY, and was born 25 Mar 1883; died 8 June 1965. Eldin-8 HOWLAND died 28 Feb 1941 at Dummer, NH.

Children of Eldin/Eldon-8 HOWLAND and Saloma LEIGHTON:
Surname **HOWLAND**

	4048. Melvin George	born 15 Aug 1907; died 6 Jan 1997 Berlin, Coos, NH
	4049. Alvin George	born 25 June 1911; died 26 Sep 1989
	4050. Kermit J.	born 30 June 1913; died 30 July 1990
	4051. Jesse Eldin	born 24 June 1916; died 6 Jan 1984 Lancaster, Coos, NH
	4052. Paul Harvey	born 10 Sep 1918; died 18 Apr 1997 NH
	4053. Irene E.	born 3 Mar 1920; died 4 Jan 2009 VT
+	**4054. ERNESTINE BARBARA** (twin)	born 3 Jan 1924; died _____ married Joseph Frank COMEAU 9 Sep 1952 (his 2nd marriage) (he s/o David COMEAU and Ida Adella MICHAUD) (he born 17 May 1914 Van Buren, VT; died 2 Dec 1991 Lyndonville, VT)
	4055. Ernest Bazel (twin)	born 3 Jan 1924; died 13 Mar 2005

3017. EUGENE-8 GATES, son of Leonard Mosman-7 GATES (Phoebe-6 MOSMAN; Anna D-5 KEYES; Martha-4 BOWKER; Asa-3; John-2; Edmund-1) and Martha J. LELAND, was born 2 Jan 1839 Westminster, MA. He married Helen RAY on 2/5 Sept 1862. She was the daughter of Anson RAY and Emily JACKSON, and was born 3 Apr 1845; died 4 Oct 1932.

Children of Eugene-8 GATES and Helen RAY:
Surname **GATES**

4056. Luella Frances	born 18 Sep 1864 Westminster, MA; died _____
	married George Arthur SARGENT ca _____
	Child: Chester Eugene-10 SARGENT born 15 May 1894 Westminster, MA
4057. Albert Eugene	born 9 Jan 1871 Westminster, MA; died _____
	married Janette FORSYTHE on 16 June 1892
	(she dau/o George FORSYTHE and Ellen Mc LAINE) (she born ca 1869)
	Child: Esther Helen-10 GATES born 10 Aug 1893 Westminster, MA

3022. LAURA-8 BEAMAN, daughter of Phebe Diantha-7 GATES (Phebe-6 MOSMAN; Anna-5 KEYES; Martha-4 BOWKER; Asa-3; John-2; Edmund-1) and Gamaliel BEAMAN, was born 13 Mar 1839 at Westminster, MA. She married Charles May KNOWLTON ca _____. He was the son of Walter KNOWLTON and Harriet CARTER, and was born 3 May 1835; died _____.

Children of Laura-8 BEAMAN and Charles KNOWLTON:
Surname **KNOWLTON**

4058. George W.	born 17 June 1862; died _____; married Harriet RAND 15 Feb 19887
4059. Esther M.	born 15 Aug 1874 NY; died young
4060. James	born Oct 1877 NY; died _____

3023. GAMALIEL WALDO-8 BEAMAN, brother of above, was born 4 Sep 1852 Westminster, MA. He married first to Mary Priest STEARNS on 22 Oct 1885. She was the daughter of Albert Dinsmore STEARNS and Sarah Minerva PRIEST; and was born 15 Sep 1859; died 12 June 1892. He married second to Eileen Maria RAND Sherman on 20 Jan 1894. She was the daughter of Lucius Clark RAND and Caroline Finetta SIBLEY, and was born 31 Mar 1856; died 18 Nov 1935 at East Princeton, MA. Gamaliel Waldo-8 BEAMAN was a well-known landscape artist who studied in Boston and later in Paris, France. Three of his largest paintings were " The Battlefield From Lookout Mountain in TN; "Niagara Falls in Winter", "and Eagle Head, Manchester, MA". He died ca 1937 at East Princeton, MA.

Children of Gamaliel Waldo-8 BEAMAN and Mary Priest STEARNS:
Surname **BEAMAN**

4061. Madeline	born 16 July 1886 Cambridge, Middlesex, MA; died 15 Oct 1972 Brookline, MA
4062. Helen Louise	born 25 Aug 1890; died 15 Oct 1891

3025. JOHN E-8 RICHARDSON, son of Eli T-7 RICHARDSON (Edward-6; Martha-5 FORBUSH; Lucy-4 BOWKER; Asa-3; John-2; Edmund-1) and Hannah TWITCHELL, was born May 1866 at Gilead, Oxford, Maine. He married Elizabeth/ Lizzie NOLAN on 28 Nov 1894 at Laconia, NH. She was the daughter of D F NOLAN and Ellen MAHAN, and was born ca 1872 MA.

Children of John E-[8] RICHARDSON and Lizzie NOLAN:
Surname **RICHARDSON**

4063. Florence M.	born Feb 1896 ME; died poss. 20 Dec 1971	

          married Alva R. BRYANT 1 May 1913 Gilead, ME (he was born 1868) divorced ____

        Child: Clayton-[10] BRYANT born 31 Aug 1921 Bethel, Oxford, ME; married Dorothy Florence MACHIA
        20 Sep 1947 Gilead. She born 6 Aug 1918; died 24 Jan 2005

    4064. Carl C.   born ca 1903; died ____

3031. NATHANIEL A-[8] WHEELER, son of Henry Asa-[7] WHEELER (Asa Bowker-[6]; Asa-[5]; Abigail-[4] BOWKER; Ezekiel-[3]; John-[2]; Edmund-[1]) and Harriet WILLISTON, was born 4 July 1869 at Bellows Falls, VT. He married Florence F. WETHER-BEE on 7 June 1893 at Rockingham, VT. She was the daughter of _____ WETHERBEE and _____, and was born ____; died _____. Nathaniel A-[8] WHEELER died 13 Aug 1945 at Royalton, VT.

Children of Nathaniel A-[8] WHEELER and Florence WETHERBEE:
Surname **WHEELER**

    4065. Henry Nathaniel   born 4 Nov 1894 VT; died 12 Dec 1981
                       1 married Gladys Alberta CHURCHILL 15 Aug 1917 Burlington, VT
                       (she dau/o Herbert CHURCHILL and Kate RANKIN)
                       (she born 18 Sep 1895; died ____)
        Child: Deane Everett-[10] WHEELER born 11 June 1925 ME; died 9 July 1975 CA
                       2 married Maude BARNUM ca _____

    4066. Dorothy Frances   born 4 June 1902; died Apr 1984 So. Royalton, VT
                       married Elwin Alba BROWNELL ca _____   (no issue)   EOL
                       (he s/o Herbert BROWNELL and Louisa CROWELL)
                       (he born 29 Aug 1895 Barnard, VT; died 14 July 1974)

+   **4067. MARJORIE**   born 13 Nov 1903 Waterbury, VT; died 26 Jan 1992 Farmington, CT.
         LAURA   married Harold Andrew PINNEY 6 Aug 1925 Rutland, VT
                       (he s/o Clarence A. PINNEY and Carrie Medina WILSON)
                       (he born 18 May 1894; died 4 Jan 1964)

3151. IRA EVERETT-[8] BOWKER, son of George Stearns-[7] BOWKER (Ira-[6]; Edmund-[5]; Micah-[4]; Edmund-[3]; John-[2]; Edmund-[1]) and Chloe Ann SAUNDERS, was born 8 Dec 1840 at Hopkinton, MA. He married Theoda BACON on 19 March 1863. She was the daughter of Austin BACON and Nancy COOLIDGE of Natick, MA; and was born 22 Aug 1840; died 1 Feb 1904

Children of Ira E-8 BOWKER and Theoda BACON:
Surname **BOWKER**

    4068. Ada Louisa   born 29 Sep 1864; died ____; married Charles Welcome HOLDEN 31 Jan 1900
                       (he s/o Orange C. HOLDEN and Emeline E. ____)

    4069. Dana Everett   born 16 March 1866; died 1 June 1904 Natick, MA
                       married Ada Mabel DAMON 31 Oct 1888
                       (she dau/o George DAMON and Aurelia ___) (she born July 1866 MA; died 1926)
        Child: Helen Gertrude-[10] BOWKER born 7 June 1890; spent life at the MA. School for the Feeble Minded; died 1952

    4070. Harry E.   born Sept 1872; died young

3154. JOSEPH-[8] BOWKER, son of Sullivan-[7] BOWKER (William-[6]; Asa-[5]; Samuel-[4]; Edmund-[3;2;1]) and Eunice ADAMS, was born March 1841 at Winchendon, Worcester, MA. He married first to Evalyn V. SLEEPER on 30 March 1864 at Winchendon. She was the daughter of Samuel SLEEPER and Lucy E. ___, and was born c 1841 Munson, MA; died ____. He married second to Frances Alzina BARNARD Newell on 12 Apr 1874. She was the daughter of ___ BARNARD and ____, and was born ca 1845-1850 Cavendish, Windsor, VT; died 19 Dec 1912 at Chester, VT. Joseph-[8] BOWKER died 2 April 1908 at Winchendon, MA.
Note: Frances BARNARD had a son by her first marriage to Cyrus NEWELL. His name was Leon Barnard NEWELL (born 1 Jan 1870) – and is often listed as Leon BOWKER. He may have used the name BOWKER but was not the son of Joseph. Leon died from syphillus and chronic intestinal nephritis

Child of Joseph-[8] BOWKER and Evalyn SLEEPER:
Surname **BOWKER**

    4071. Ashley V.   born ca 1866 MA; died 1941 MA; married May E. HOWE 21 Feb 1890 Athol, MA
                      (she dau/o Lucius HOWE and Emeline ___) (she born ca 1871)
        Child: Clifford A-[10] BOWKER born 12 Feb 1891 Athol; died 1966

Children of Joseph[8] BOWKER and Frances A. BARNARD Newell:
Surname **BOWKER**

4072. .Austin Joseph	born 24 Mar 1875 VT; died 1944 MA	
	married Carrie M. BELCHER 24 Nov 24 Nov 1897 VT	
	Child: Gerald[10] BOWKER born 23 Apr 1914 VT; died 25 May 1968	
4073. Anna Josephine	born 21 July 1880 Reading,VT; died 14 Oct 1884 Reading, VT (spinal meningitis)	
4074. Ryland Hardy	born 29 Sep 1883; died 18 Aug 1853	
	married Mabel/ Maybelle NELSON 31 Dec 1905 Chester, VT.	
	(she dau/o Charles Nelson and Clara KELLEY)	
	(she born 14 Sep 1886; died 29 Sep 1963)	
	Children: Verna M[10] born ca 1910; Ivan A[10] born ca 1912; and Alberta R[10] BOWKER born ca 1913	
4075. Sidney Albert ++	born 15 Aug 1887 Cavendish, VT; died 23 July 1916 Springfield, MA	
	married Bertha Blanche NELSON ca 1911 Child: Virginia Mary[10] BOWKER born ca 1913/14	
	++ Cause of death for Sidney: " he fell from a 3rd floor window and died instantly "	

3158. MARCELLUS SCOTT[8] BOWKER, brother of above, was born Oct 1859 at Winchendon, MA. He married Hattie M. TATRO on 4 July 1872. She was the daughter of Charles TATRO and Orilla BURBY, and was born 8/11 June 1864 Winchendon, MA; died 20 May 1940 at Gardner, MA. Marcellus[8] BOWKER died 16 Oct 1933 Gardner, MA.

Children of Marcellus[8] BOWKER and Hattie TATRO:
Surname **BOWKER**

4076. Frederick Marcellus	born 27 Aug 1883 Winchendon, Ma; died 1957 Gardner, MA (chair maker)
	married Lillian GATES ca ____ (she dau/o Eugene C. GATES and _____)
4077. Eva B.	born 15 Mar 1886 MA; died 13 Mar 1973
	1 married Herbert PEASE 12 Sep 1901; 2 married William Gardner HALEY ca ____
4078. Etta V.	born June 1892; died ____; 1 married George E. MONTVILLE 9 Sep 1908
	(he s/o Fred MONTVILLE and Tilda BLANCHARD) (he born ca 1887)
	2 married Thomas J. RIVARD 24 April 1931
	(he s/o William RIVARD and Elsa CLOUTIER)
4079. Freda Mabel	born 6 July 1899; died 1934

3160. EDWIN LUTHER[8] BOWKER, son of Luther[7] BOWKER, Jr. (Luther[6]; Asa[5]; Samuel[4]; Edmund[3;2;1]) and Charlotte Newton MAYNARD, was born 11 Dec 1854. He married first to Lucy F. WOOD on 18 Feb 1882 ar Royalston, MA. She was the daughter of George WOOD and Smith ____, and was born ca ___, died ____. He married second to Mary E. DARRAH ca 1892. She was the daughter of ____ DARRAH and ____; and was born 5 Jan 1864 at New Brunswick, Canada, died 28 May 1918. Edwin Luther[8] BOWKER died 18 July 1928.

Child of Edwin Luther[8] BOWKER and Lucy Wood:
Surname **BOWKER**

4080. Floyd Luther	born 13 Oct 1883; died June 1963 FL

Children of Edwin Luther[8] BOWKER and Mary E. DARRAH:
Surname **BOWKER**

+	**4081. ROY CLEMENT**	born 15 May 1893 Athol, Worcester, MA; died 13 Mar 1969 Washington, DC
		married Kathleen Sanders HOSMER 24 Feb 1918
		(she dau/o Asa HOSMER and Belle SANDERS) (she born 24 Aug 1893)
	4082. Ann F.	born ca 1928; died ____

3164. ASIGAL D[8] WYMAN, son of David[7] WYMAN (Hannah[6] BOWKER; Asa[5]; Samuel[4]; Edmund[3,2,1]) and Lucinda OLIN, was born 31 May 1844 at Meredith, NY. He married Agnes Jane " Jennie " HOBBS on 11 Sept 1867. She was the daughter of John HOBBS and Georgiana WALL, and was born __; died __. Asigal D[8] WYMAN, a logger, died 8 July 1911 WI.

Children of ASIGAL[8] WYMAN and " Jennie" HOBBS:
Surname **WYMAN** (children all born Eau Claire, Wisconson)

4083. Frederick Albert	born 6 Feb 1870; died 18 Sep 1956 Los Angeles, CA
	married Catherine " Kate" _____ ca ____
4084. John Sidney	born 17 June 1874 ; died 7 Sept 1947 Knoxville, TN
	married Ruby Irene BREWEN 30 Nov 1904 Missoula, MT.
4085. Jessie C.	born 3 Apr 1882; died 29 Mar 1973 Alhambra, CA

3168. STONEWALL JACKSON-8 BOWKER, son of James Madison-7 BOWKER (Abiather-6;5; Samuel-4; Edmund-3;2;1) and Martha J. NEWTON, was born 11 Jan 1863 at Upton, Worcester, MA. He married first to Cora Lucy YOUNG on 29 Sep 1886 at Upton. She was the daughter of Harrison B. YOUNG and Mary J. WHITE, and was born ca 1866 VT; died 23 Mar 1900 in childbirth. Stonewall-8 BOWKER married second to Mary E. " Mame" LOWE ca 1900. She was the daughter of ____ LOWE and ____; and was born ca 1871; died 4 Nov 1912 Johnson City, Broome, NY. Stonewall-8 BOWKER died 11 June 1945 at Binghamton, Broome, NY.

Childen of Stonewall-8 BOWKER and Cora Lucy YOUNG:
Surname **BOWKER**

4086. Clarence Jackson	born 19 Feb 1889 Ashland, MA; died 22 June 1957 Johnson City, NY married Christine KROM ca ____	
4087. Eugene Madison	born 25 Nov 1894 Framingham, MA; died 20 June 1967 Binghamton, NY	
4088. Lillian Edna	born 22 Nov 1896 Framingham, MA; died 7 Dec 1966 Toronto, Canada married Howard CANFIELD ca ____	
4089. Cora Louise	born 23 Mar 1900; died 1 July 1900	EOL

Children of Stonewall-8 BOWKER and Mary LOWE:
Surname **BOWKER**

4090. Henry Leonard	born 13 July 1901 Johnson City, NY; died 28 Feb 1903	EOL
4091. Emma May	born 30 Mar 1905 Johnson City, NY; died 28 Mar 1996 Southbridge, MA married Halmer Victor TORNWALL 23 June 1930 Brattleboro, VT	
4092. Erma	born 4 Mar 1908 Johnson City; died 14 Mar 1913	EOL

3173. LOWELLA LELAND-8 FROST, daughter of Lowell Leland-7 BOWKER (Harriet-6 BOWKER (Abiather-5; Samuel-4; Edmund-3-2-1) and Anna Maria JACOBS, was born 9 Feb 1888 California. She married first to Frank Wilbert " Bert " HUTCHISON 9 Feb 1908 . He was the son of James Linley HUTCHISON and Ada S. FLINT; and was born 9 Feb 1874; died 2 Mar 1923. She married second ca 1924 to George " Joss " McLeod CARR. He was the son of Thomas CARR and Margaret Brotherston McLeod STOUT, and was born 7 March 1882 at Gordon, Berwickshire, Northumberland, England; died 4 June 1977 at Chico, CA. Lowella-8 FROST died 22 Dec 1948 at Chico, Butte, CA, from burns suffered in a house fire two days earlier.

Children of Lowella-8 FROST and Frank Wilbert HUTCHISON:
Surname **HUTCHISON**

4093. Lola Alberta	born 27 Nov 1908 CA; died 18 Sep 1961	
4094. Beryl Elaine	born 29 Aug 1910 CA; died 18 Dec 2003 CA married Albert Otto WILLIAMS 28 Feb 1932 CA	
4095. Maxine Faye	born 21 Sep 1912; died 7 Oct 1996 CA; married ____ HENSEN ca ____	
4096. Christine Z.	born 26 Dec 1917 CA; died 15 Jan 1965 Walnut Creek, CA	
4097. Etta Mable	born 19 May 1920 CA; died 24 Nov 1963 Oakland, CA.	

Child of Lowella-8 FROST and George CARR:
Surname **CARR**

4098. George McLeod, Jr.	born 17 Dec 1925 ; died 4 June 1977 Chico, CA

3175. ADA SOPHIA " Addie" -8 WHEELOCK, daughter of Aaron Bowker-7 WHEELOCK (Charlotte-6 BOWKER; John-5; Uriah-4; Edmund-3; John-2; Edmund-1) and Ruth CONVERSE Sibley, was born 8 Sept 1854 Spencer, MA. She married Frank Adelbert RICE on 10 June 1875 at Spencer. He was the son of Henry T. RICE and Elizabeth A ____; and was born ca 1855 Walpole, MA; died ____. Ada Sophia-8 WHEELOCK died ____.

Children of Ada Sophia-8 WHEELOCK and Frank Adelbert RICE:
Surname **RICE**

4099. Hallie Adelbert	born 29 May 1878 Spencer, MA; died ____ married Maude Elsie OLNEY 12 Sep 1911 Charlton, MA (she dau/o Frank L. OLNEY and Julia E. ____) (she born 25 July 1885; died Feb 1968 Worcester, MA) Child: Marcia Elizabeth-10 RICE born ca 1916
4100. Myron Frank	born 17 July 1887 Spencer, MA; died Jan 1967 Auburn, MA (candy shop owner) married Sarah ____ ca ____ (she born ca 1886 MA) Children: Raymond-10 born ca 1907 MA; and Robert W-10 RICE born ca 1915 MA

3197. CHARLES ALBERT-[8] HOSMER, son of Luther-[7] HOSMER, Jr (Luther-[6,] Sr.; Abigail -[5] BARRETT; Abigail[4] BOWKER Edmund-[3;2;1]) and Nancy Judson HALL, was born 23 April 1855 at Worcester, MA. He married Mary Etta HALLETT on 18 June 1880. She was the daughter of _____ HALLETT and _____; and was born 18 Dec 1855 Yarmouthport, MA; died 9 Feb 1929 at Holden, MA. Charles Albert-[8] HOSMER died Oct 1920.

Children of Charles Albert-[8] HOSMER and Mary Etta HALLETT:
Surname **HOSMER**   Reference: Ancestors and Descendants of Josiah HOSMER 1600-1902 , page 65

4101. Charles May	born 23 Apr 1881 Boston; died 4 Sep 1963 Worcester; married Rosena BERRY ca _____
4102. Albert Edward	born 3 Jan 1884 Boston; died 2 Aug 1908 Worcester
4103. Sophronia Hallett	born 22 Oct 1890 Somerville, MA; died 24 May 1957 Worcester
4104. George Henry	born 23 Apr 1894 Malden, MA; died _____

3199. ANNIE JENNY-[8] BARRETT, daughter of Stillman Snow-[7] BARRETT (Thornton-[6,] III; Thornton-[5] II; Abigail-[4] BOWKER; Edmund-[3;2;1]) and Hannah Elizabeth COOLEY, was born 31 Jan 1867 at Port Alleghany, McKean County, PA. She married John Gerard ROBBINS on 26 Mar 1884 at McKean, PA. He was the son of Madison M. ROBBINS and Justina Elizabeth HALL, and was born 15 Dec 1862 PA; died 7 Aug 19448 McKean, PA. Annie Jenny-[8] BARRETT died 31 March 1933 at Port Alleghany, PA.

Children of Annie Jenny-[8] BARRETT and John ROBBINS:
Surname **ROBBINS**

4105. Pearle Violet	born 17 Jan 1885; died May 1975; married Milford Leroy NELSON 26 Mar 1908
4106. Alpha Leroy	born 4 May 1886; died 18 Nov 1886	EOL
4107. Lula Mable	born 4 Jan 1888; died 31 Mar 1966; married Guy Morgan NELSON 26 Mar 1914
4108. Orlo Eugene	born 13 Apr 1890; died 11 Apr 1911; married Ruth Turner SHEPARD 30 Oct 1918
4109. Alton John	born 1 Jan 1893; died Oct 1973; married Lena TOWNSEN(D) ca _____
4110. Aneta/Anita Fae	born 15 Aug 1905; died 23 Feb 1971; married Hilding Julius WINTERQUIST ca _____
	(she born 15 Dec 1870 England; died 1 Apr 1960 Los Angeles, CA)

3215. MORGAN LEWIS-[8] HINMAN, son of Aurelia-[7] LEWIS (Sarah-[6] SCRIPTURE; Abigail-[5] BRIGHAM; John-[4;] Elizabeth-[3] BOWKER, Edmund-[2,1]) and Lyman HINMAN, was born 1 Oct 1831 at Berkshire County, MA. He married first to Harriet HESS ca _____. She was the daughter of Jacob HESS and Elizabeth FOUTZ, and was born 18 Aug 1833; died 12 July 1921. He was a Mormon , and took a second wife , Rhoda CHASE, on 4 April 1870 at Farmington, Utah Territory.. She was the daughter of Isaac CHASE and Phebe OGDEN, and was born 29 Sept 1830 Sparta, NY; died 3 July 1891 Cardston, Alberta, Canada.. Rhoda was previously married to Judson STODDARD.

Children of Morgan Lewis-[8] HINMAN and Harriet HESS:
Surname **HINMAN**   (all children born Farmington, Davis, Utah)

4111. Florence Aurelia	born 3 Jan 1855; died 13 July 1855		EOL
4112. Elizabeth Aurelia	born 10 March 1859; stillborn		EOL
+ **4113. EVA MARIA**	born 20 Oct 1862 UT; died 27 Feb 1934 UT		
	married Robert S.FULTON ca _____		
4114. Nancy Helen	born 31 May 1863; died _____		
4115. Alice Edna	born 20 Feb 1865; died 14 Mar 1865		EOL
4116. Morgan	born 11 Dec 1867; died 8 May 1869		EOL

Children of Morgan Lewis-[8] HINMAN and Rhoda CHASE:
Surname **HINMAN**

4117. Frank Henry	born 5 Feb 1871; died 26 Sep 1892 Cardston, Alberta, Canada
	married Sarah HOCHSTRASSER 2 Sept 1890
+ **4118. NELLIE**	born 4 July 1877; died 14 July 1950 Cardston
	married Walter Edward PITCHER 26 Oct 1895 CA
	(he Bishop of Cardston : ordained 31 July 1925 LDS)
	(he born 13 July 1871 Davis Co., UT; died 4 Jan 1946 Alberta, Canada
	(he s/o Edward PITCHER ans Susan EVERETT)

Child: Nellie-[10] PITCHER born 12 July 1906; died 10 Jan 1998; married Frank M. BROWN

4119. Clara May	born 1 Jan 1874 Salt Lake City, UT	4119a. Rhoda	born ca 1879; died _____

3216. HENRY LYMAN-[8] HINMAN, brother of above, was born 6 March 1837 West Stockbridge, Berkshire, MA. He was also a Mormon, and married first to Elizabeth Harriet Chaney COMPTON on 17 March 1861 at Farmington, Davis, Utah. She was the daughter of _____ COMPTON and ____; and was born 8 Oct 1840 TN; died Dec 1912 UT. His second marriage was to Mary Jane WHITE on 18 Oct 1874 UT. She was the daughter of _____ WHITE and _____, and was born ca 1837, died ____. Henry Lyman-[8] died 27 Jan 1921 Cardston, Alberta, Canada.

Children of Henry Lyman-[8] HINMAN and Elizabeth COMPTON:
Surname **HINMAN**

4120. Henry Lyman, Jr.	born 10 Sep 1862 UT; died 13 Sep 1863	EOL	
4121. Catherine Aurelia	born 25 Aug 1864 UT; died 19 April 1928 Canada		
	1 married Benjamin Franklin KNOWLTON ca ____		
	2 married Josiah Austin HAMMER ca _____		
4122. John Howard	born 24 Dec 1866 UT; died ca 1934		
4123. Kate	born ca 1867 ; died _____		
+ **4124. MORGAN LEWIS**	born 4 Nov 1868 UT; died 4 Feb 1931 Box Elder, UT		
	married Cynthia Ann BROWN ca ____		
	(she born 7 Sep 1875 UT; died 2 Apr 1930 UT)		
4125. Mary Emma	born 18 Sep 1872 UT; died 29 Dec 1957 Salt Lake City; married Joseph SEAL ca ____		
4126. Robert Paul	born 12 May 1877 UT; died 17 Aug 1951 UT		

3230. WARREN LUTHER-[8] BRIGHAM, son of John Warren-[7] BRIGHAM (Abijah-[6;] John-[5]; Lt. Abijah-[4]; Elizabeth-[3] BOWKER; Edmund-[2,1]) and Martha BRIGHAM, was born 25 Jan 1846 at Oakum, MA. He married Susan Frances ADAMS 25 June 1868. She was the daughter of Sylvanus ADAMS and Caroline WESSON, and was born 3 June 1843 Chicopee, MA; died 4 Oct 1920 at Brookline, MA. Warren Luther-[8] BRIGHAM died 13 March 1880.

Children of Warren Luther-[8] BRIGHAM and Susan ADAMS:
Surname **BRIGHAM**

+ **4127. EDITH**	born 6 June 1870; died _____; married Walter WEBLING 30 Jan 1895
	(she s/o Edward H. WEBLING (of England) and Anna SAGE of Canada)
4128. Ethel	born 30 April 1872; died _____; married Walter Briggs FOX 5 Dec 1900
	(he s/o Robert L.B. FOX and Katherine CARLETON)
4129. Enid	born 20 March 1874; died _____

3274. NELSON-[8] JOYNER, son of John-[7] JOYNER (James-[6]; John-[5]; Hannah-[4] BOWKER; John-[3]; Edmund-[2,1]) and Mary M. BENTLEY, was born ca 1840 Cortland, NY. He married Elizabeth C. KEYES ca ____. She was the daughter of ____ KEYES and ____, and was born ca 1846; died 1904. Nelson-[8] JOYNER died 0 Jan 1894 NY.

Children of Nelson-[8] JOYNER and Elizabeth KEYES:
Surname **JOYNER**

4130. Jessie	born 14 Aug 1867; died 26 Feb 1925 McLean, NY; married Fred TRAPP ca _____	
	Child: Ruth J-[10] TRAPP born ca 1897; died 1987	
4131. Edwin	born 3 Jan 1870; died 1 May 1922; married Jessie ELLIOTT	
4132. Martha	born 14 Jan 1874; died 13 April 1879	EOL
4133. Lucy	born 23 Sep 1876; died 20 March 1942; married Bert ENSIGN	
4134. Luna	born 23 Sept 1876; died 20 Dec 1910; married George RUSSELL	

3296. ROSALIA " ROSE " AUGUSTA-[8] BOWKER, daughter of Franklin Noah-[7] BOWKER (Willard-[6]; Noah-[5,4]; John-[3]; Edmund-[2;1]) and Jane CREEKER, was born April 1846 Maine, Broome, NY. She married Marsden Altonia DURFEE ca 1867. He was the son of Amasa DURFEE and Hannah B. SWIFT, and was born 17 Feb 1843 Maine, NY; died 4 Mar 1915. Rosalia " Rose"-[8] BOWKER died 28 March 1910 NY.

Children of Rosalia-[8] BOWKER and Marsden DURFEE:
Surname **DURFEE**   (all children born Maine, Broome, NY)

4135. Winnie B.	born ca 1868; died ____
4136. Myrtie J.	born ca 1869/70; died 25 May 1948 Newark Valley, Tioga, NY
	married Chauncey Mc INTYRE ca 1887 (he born ca 1862 NY)
	Children: Wellington-[10] born ca 1890; and Luella-[10] Mc INTYRE born ca 1892
4137. George J.	born ca 1872; died _____
4138. Herbert Marsden	born 16 May 1875; died 1964 4139. Clara/Clarie E. born Mar 1880; died ____

3301. JULIUS AVERY-8 BOWKER, son of William Minor-7 BOWKER (Noah-5,4; John-3; Edmund-2,1) and his second wife, Melicent Parthenia SKILTON Beers was born 17 March 1851 at Pike, PA. He married Hattie Asenath WOOD 15 Oct 1873 PA. She was the daughter of David Carpenter WOOD and Avilda Evelyne HOLMAN, and was born Aug 1851 PA; died ____. Julius Avery-8 BOWKER died 1 Feb 1989 Bradford County, PA..

Children of Julius Avery-8 BOWKER and Hattie WOOD:
Surname **BOWKER**

4140. Rosa Avilda	born 24 July 1874 Herrick, PA; died 8 Nov 1966 St. Petersburg, FL	
	married William Lester-6 ATWOOD 12 Aug 1896 Herrick, PA	
	(he s/o George Charles-5 ATWOOD and Henrietta TAYLOR)	
4141. May	born 6 Jan 1879 Middletown, PA; died 10 Aug 1951 Northampton, MA	
	married Melvin Jesse COOK 5 July 1912 LeRaysville, PA	
	(he s/o Ellis William COOK and Martha HARRIS) (he born 25 July 1877)	
	Child: Donald Bowker-10 COOK born 14 Jan 1917 PA	
4142. Edith Millicent	born 24 Aug 1882 PA; died 2 Nov 1970 Johnson City, Broome, NY	
	(she was a piano teacher)	
4143. Gladys Julia	born 14 Nov 1894 PA; died 1 Feb 1989 Binghamton, NY	

3302. MILLICENT BETSEY-8 BOWKER, sister of above, a piano teacher, was born 6 July 1852 at East Herrick, PA. She married Arthur Warren WOOD 25 Dec 1879 Orwell, PA. He was the son of ____ WOOD and ____, and was born 9 Sep 1855 Rush, PA, died 1955 E. Herrick, Bradford, PA. Millicent-8 BOWKER died 1943 E. Herrick, PA..

Children of Millicent-8 BOWKER and Arthur WOOD:
Surname **WOOD**

4144. William Arthur	born 21 July 1886 Herrick, PA; died 12 June 1978 Okemos, Ingham, MI
	married Mildred Leona BAKER 10 April 1912
	(she d/o George Nichols BAKER and Ida Amanda OVERPECK)
	(she born 3 April 1889; died)
4145. Ernest Bowker	born 17 Oct 1888 Herrick, PA; died 27 July 1970 Dade County, FL; an engineer
	married Sara Frances COOK 11 May 1918
	(she dau/o Rev. Milton Lewis COOK and _____) (she born ca 1892 PA)
	Children: Mary Thomas-10 WOOD born 16 March 1919 Easton, PA; Darwin Lewis-10 WOOD born 21 July 1921 East Orange, NJ; and Philip Warren-10 WOOD born 29 Dec 1924 Chatham, NJ

3323. CYNTHIA-8 BEEBE, daughter of Daniel P-7 BEEBE (Aurora-6; Sarah-5 BOWKER; Joseph-4; John-3; Edmund-2,1) and Sarah COLTON, was born 29 July 1835 MI. She married Charles Eben BOSWELL on 16 Feb 1853 at Will, IL. He was the son of _____ BOSWELL and ____, and was born 6 May 1829 England; died ca 1918. Cynthia-8 BEEBE died ca 1915.

Children of Cynthia-8 BEEBE and Charles BOSWELL:
Surname **BOSWELL**

4146. Ellen Elizabeth	born ca _____	
4147. Frances J.	born ca 1857 IL; died _____	
	married Abraham J. YOUNG ca ____	(Child: Dawson B-10 YOUNG 1893-1968)
+ **4148. ARTHUR HENRY**	born 3 Jan 1859 Wilmington, IL; died ___; married Lillian Matilda HILLS ca 1885	
4149. Andrew	born ca 1866	
4150. Mary Abbie	born March 1870 IL; married _____ ALLEN Child: Luella F-10 ALLEN born Aug 1890 IL	

3325. WILLIAM WALLACE-8 BEEBE, brother of above, was born 17 May 1841 MI. He married first to Ellen Amelia WINNERSTRAND on 21 Dec 1887 MN. She was the daughter of William WINNERSTRAND and Bertha _____, and was born 27 July 1855 MN; died 15 Feb 1908. He married second to Mary B. ADAMS on 24 Nov 1909. She was the daughter of John E. ADAMS and Melinda Bell _____, and was born ___, died ____ William Wallace-8 BEEBE died 4 May 1924 at Paulina, IA.

Children of William Wallace-8 BEEBE and Ellen WINNERSTRAND:
Surname **BEEBE**

4151. Frank Wallace	born 13 May 1889 IA; died ___; married Inez Charlotte YOUNG 23 Dec 1909
	(she born 15 Jan 1881 IA; died _____)
4152. Bertha Amelia	born 14 Feb 1892 IA; died ____; married _____ Mc CAULEY
4153. Gladys	born Oct 1895 IA ; died _____; married Glen FANNING
4154. Fredanna	born ca ____; died _____

Note: Source: Old Soldiers of O'Brien Co., Iowa, published privately 1909.

William Wallce[-8] BEEBE enlisted 5 Aug 1862 at Essex, IL in Company B, 113th IL Volunteer Infantry. He served at Hollow Springs, the first attack at Vicksburg, Arkansas Post, and all through the siege of Vicksburg and Jackson, Mississippi. He was shot and then taken prisoner. He was in Libby Prison, and hospitals in Richmond for 4 months. He was paroled and returned to Chicago 1 Jan 1864. He returned to his regiment on 19 May at Memphis, TN. Afterwards, at a fight in Guntown, MS, he was taken prisoner again and was held at Andersonville and other prisons for 9 months. He was discharged at Springfield, IL 1 July 1865. He settled in O'Brien County March 1883, living in Parker Township.

3228. DR. ADDISON J[-8] BEEBE, brother of above was born 7 July 1848 MI. He married Ida Elizabeth HAMBLIN on 22 Jan 1879 at _____, Wisconsin. She was the daughter of Alvah HAMBLIN and Almira S. EGGLESTON, and was born 21 Feb 1859 WI; died 9 Feb 1884 IA. Dr. Addison[-8] BEEBE, a medical doctor and a minister, died 30 Oct 1934 at West Bed, Iowa.

Children of Dr. Addison J-[8] BEEBE and Ida HAMBLIN:
Surname **BEEBE**

4155. Vincent Roland	born March 1882 IA; died ____	
4156. Caro	born ca 1887 IA; died ____	
4157. Divida	born March 1889 IA; died ____	
4158. Brig. General Lewis Charles	born 7 Dec 1891; died 17 Feb 1951, buried Arlington National Cemetery	
	1 married Beatrice _____ ca _____; Child: William Wallace-[10] BEEBE born ca 1918	
	2 married Dorothy Mc RAE ca _____	
	Children: James McRae-[10] BEEBE born ca 1926; and John-[10] BEEBE born ca 1928	

3332. MARSHALL CHARLES[-8] BEEBE, son of Isaac Windsor[-7] BEEBE (Asa[-6]; Sarah[-5] BOWKER; Joseph[-4]-; John[-3]; Edmund-[2,1]) and Wealthy Arvilla WHEELER, was born Aug 1857 NY. He married first to Helen Frances MORRIS ca 1877. She was the daughter of ____ MORRIS and _____, and was born ca 1859; died ____. His second wife was Anna B. ____. She was born ca March 1875; died ____.

Children of Charles[-8] BEEBE and Helen Frances MORRIS:
Surname **BEEBE**

4159. Daisy Arvilla	born 14 Oct 1878	
4160. Asa	born 24 May 1881; died 24 Feb 1897	
+ **4161. JOSEPHINE EUGENIA**	born 7 Mar 1883; died ____; married Nathan FISK ca 1904 (he s/o Frank G. FISK and Nettie A. YATES) (he born ca 1877)	
4162. Grace F.	born 26 Aug 1886; married Milton SWANN Nov 1972 Frrankfort, Clinton, IN	

Children of Charles[-8] BEEBE and Anna B. ____:
Surname **BEEBE**

4163. Polyanthus	born ca 1894 IN; died ____	4164. Rebecca P. born Oct 1897 IN

3335. NELLIE CECELIA[-8] BEEBE, daughter of Charles[-7] BEEBE (Clarke[-6]; Sarah[-5] BOWKER; Joseph[-4]; John[-3]; Edmund-[2,1]) and Hannah BUNN, was born 27 Feb 1873 at Franklin, Lenawee, Michigan. She married Emery Artie WEBBER on 6 April 1891. He was the son of Henry Clay WEBBER and Elizabeth Dorcas DAILEY;, and was born 11 Sep 1868 MI; died 3 Aug 1942 South Bend, IN.. Nellie[-8] BEEBE died 15 Jan 1947 South Bend, IN.

Children of Nellie[-8] BEEBE and Emery WEBBER:
Surname **WEBBER**   (all children born Niles, Michigan)

4165. Grace Emerald	born 1 Feb 1892 MI; died 24 March 1975 Grand Rapids, MI
	1 married James Grover LEACH
	(he born 21 Jan 1889 Columbus, IN ; died _____
	Children: Lester R[-10] born 2 Feb 1912; died 2 Jan 1982 Grand Rapids, MI and Katherine Nellie-[10] LEACH born 16 Sep 1914; died 21 Feb 1980 Lansing, MI; married __ VROLAND (Child: Terrell Lee[11] VROLAND)
	2 married W C ROBINSON ca _____
4166. Orrin Clay	born 13 Sep 1893 MI; died 14 April 1957 Niles, MI
	married Hazel E. FISHER 1 Dec 1914
	(she dau/o Bert Riley FISHER and Lulu Elizabeth CADE
	(she born 14 April 1897 MI; died ____)
	Children: Betty Lou -[10] born ca 1919; and Carlton F[10] WEBBER born 20 May 1923; died 21 Oct 2006 FL
+ **4167. LYLE ARTHUR**	born 18 Aug 1902; died 2 July 1966 Niles, MI
	married Helen Elizabeth MOORE ca ____
	(she dau/o Fred Mordecai MOORE and Bessie Winnie ORR)
	(she born 16 Mar 1904; died 22 April 1975 MI)

Children of Nellie-8 BEEBE and Emery WEBBER, continued:
Surname **WEBBER**

4168.Olive Marie	born 16 Aug 1904; died 16 July 1973 IN; married Oral J. TRENT 10 Jan 1933
	(he born 1 Oct 1902; died 23 May 1965 IN)
4169. Irma Belle	born 2 Nov 1906; died 19 May 2000 South Bend, IN
	married Lester C. HETH/ HEPH 31 Dec 1933
	(he s/o Alvin C. HETH/HEPH and Lillian GROOM)
	(he born 7 Nov 1904; died 22 Sept 1956 IN)
4170. Raymond Beebe	born 29 May 1910; died 21 Oct 1955 South Bend, IN

3336. ALBERT NEWELL-8 HOLCOMB, son of Edward Seymour-7 HOLCOMB (Catherine-6 BEEBE; Sarah-5 BOWKER; Joseph-4; John-3; Edmund-2,1) and Anna Anna E ____, was born June 1850 Michigan. He married Sarah ____ ca 1871. He died 4 June 1909 at Cone, Monroe, MI.

Children of Albert Newell-8 HOLCOMB abd Sarah ____:
Surname **HOLCOMB**

4171. Olive	born Feb 1887; died ____	4173. Harry	born Feb 1893; died ____
4172. Leona	born Jan 1891; died ____		

3348. CLARA ELSA-8 HUTCHINS, daughter of Eliza Ann-7 BOWKER (Samuel Noyes-6; Daniel-5,4; John-3; Edmund-2,1) and Thomas Andrew HUTCHINS, was born 26 Oct 1869 . She married John Eddy PIERCE 24 August 1893 at Oregon City, OR. He was the son of John PIERCE and Elizabeth Jane FLAGG, and was born 10 June 1860 MA; died 9 July 1934 Hyde Park, Suffolk County, MA. Clara Elsa-8 HUTCHINS died 21 April 1932 MA.

Children of Clara Elsa-8 HUTCHINS and John PIERCE:
Surname **PIERCE**

4174. Stanford Irving	born 12 June 1894; died 24 June 1894 Oregon City EOL
4175. Lucile Edna	born 29 May 1895; died 29 June 1989 Nantucket, MA
	1 married William Hadwen BARNEY 24 Sept 1919 Logan, OR
	2 married Charles Kunkle BELL 2 Oct 1951
4176. Marie Elizabeth	born 11 Oct 1897; died 22 March 1922; married Albert STONESTREET 23 Nov 1920
4177. Lawrence Jonathan	born 3 June 1900 MA; died 14 Nov 2002 Seattle, WA
	married Isabel Susan COLEMAN
4178. Theodore Hutchins	born 12 Aug 1902; died 8 Nov 1948 Seattle, WA.; married Marion Edith GILMORE
4179. Emerson Bowker	born 19 May 1911 Hyde Park, MA; died 9 June 1997 Seattle, WA.

3353. MARY CAROLINE-8 FAIRBANKS, daughter of Angeline/Angie-7 BOWKER (Samuel Noyes-6; Daniel-5,4; John-3; Edmund-2,1) and Jonathan FAIRBANKS, was born 7 April 1860. She married Silas Erastus JAMES ca ____. He was the son of Abner JAMES and Catherine WILER, and was born 24 Mar 1855 Springfield, OH; died 6 Dec 1930 Zanesville, OH. Mary Caroline-8 FAIRBANKS died ____.

Children of Mary Caroline-8 FAIRBANKS and Silas JAMES:
Surname **JAMES**

4180. Euphemia	born 19 Sept 1879 Springfield, OH; died ____
4181. Della C.	born 23 Sept 1882 Springfield; died 11 Jan 1969 OH
	married Edward L.KINNEY ca ____ (he born ca 1881 KS)
	Child: Paul-10 JAMES born ca 1910 OH

3365. EVERETT WILLIAM-8 BOWKER, son of Frank Maybin-7 BOWKER (Samuel Noyes-6; Daniel-5,4; John-3; Edmund-2,1) and Caroline/Carrie CONLEY, was born 9 Nov 1882 MA. He married Eva Leslie SANBORN on 9 June 1907 Nova Scotia, Canada. She was the daughter of Rupert SANBORN and Eunice L. NEWCOMB, and was born 28 Dec 1886 MA; died Feb 1974 TX. Everett-8 BOWKER died Sept 1965.

Children of Everett-8 BOWKER and Eva L. SANBORN:
Surname **BOWKER**

4182. Frank Roderick	born 6 June 1908; died Jan 1964
	married Stephanie MARSINIK 20 Nov 1931 Salem , NH
	(she dau/o John MARSINIK and Justine MILWICZ)

Children of Everett[8] BOWKER and Eva L. SANBORN, continued:
Surname **BOWKER**

+	**4183. ELINOR B.**	born 15 Dec 1912 MA; died 1998 Peoria, AZ		
		married Robert Stottler FIERY ca 1932		
		(he s/o Albert Tice FIERY and Malinda G. GAVER)		
		(he born 22 June 1909; died 6 July 1974)		
	4184. Clifford Alden	born June 1915; died 29 June 2008 MO; married __?__ 1938		
	4185. Caroline L.	born ca 1927 MA	4187. Janet C.	born ca 1932 MA
	4186. James L.	born ca 1930 MA	4188. Martha	born ca 1934 MA

3367. INA ADELLA[8] BOWKER, sister of above, was born 20 Dec 1889 at Sudbury, MA. She married Donald Stanley Stearns GRANT 8 June 1911 Newton, MA. He was the son of Alonzo GRANT and Catherine DILLMAN; and was born 3 Oct 1889 Halifax, Nova Scotia, Canada; died ____. Ina Adella[8] BOWKER died 4 Jan 1969 at Wellesley, MA.

Children of Ina Adella[8] BOWKER and Stanley Stearns GRANT:
Surname **GRANT**

4189. Lloyd Ernest	born 13 Jan 1912; died 20 Dec 1990 poss. Bath, Maine
4190. Katherine C.	born 5 Feb 1917; died 2 Mar 1993 Clearwater, FL
	married Harry Gustav OLSON 4 Feb 1940 Wellesley, MA
	(he born 3 May 1901 MA; died 15 Oct 1981 FL)
4191. Muriel Edith	born 19 Oct 1919 Natick, MA; died 15 July 1984; married _____ HURST ca _____

3369. SAMUEL SHELDON " SHELLEY " [8] WOOD, son of Ellen L[7] HAYNES (Sarah[6] BOWKER; Daniel[5,4]; John[3]; Edmund[2,1]) and Samuel S. WOOD, was born ca 1869/70 MA. He married first to Harriet J. BURGESS ca 1899. She was the daughter of Silas Randolph BURGESS and Mary Ann RHEA; and was born 27 Oct 1857 IA; died ___. He married second to Zula Mae HULL ca ____. She was the daughter of Lucious G. HULL and Sarah Louise SWALLOW; and was born 2 Jan 1889 CO; died 9 May 1944 Saratoga, Carbon County, WY. Shelley[8] WOOD died ca 1929.

Children of Shelley[8] WOOD and his 2nd wife Zula Mae HULL:
Surname **WOOD**

4192. L. Sheldon	born ca 1915 WY; died ca 1929 Saratoga, Carbon County, WY
4193. William Samuel	born 1 Sept 1916 WY; died 4 Jan 1992 Carbon C., WY
	married Sarah Valentina CRUZ ca (she born 2 June 1916 WY; died 29 Oct 2010)
	Children: Rebecca-[10] born ca 1932 WY; Sheldon-[10] born ca 1939 CO; and
	William-[10] WOOD born ca 1940 WY
4194. Rita Harriet	born 23 Apr 1918 WY; died 18 Aug 2010 Casper, WY; married Gerald O'CONNELL
	Children: Gerry-[10] born ca 1940; Robby-[10] born ca ___; David-[10] born ca ___; and
	Kathy-[10] O'CONNELL born ca ____
4195. Kent/Kenneth	born ca 1921 WY, died ____
4196. Ralph Neil	born 29 July 1923 WY; died 2 Jan 2001 CA
4197. Robert L.	born 13 Dec 1926; died 16 Feb 2001 Saratoga, Carbon, WY

3378. LEWIS[8] BUSH, son of John Avery-[7] BUSH (Lydia[6] BOWKER; Joseph[5]; Daniel[4]; John[3]; Edmund[2,1]) and Hannah Matilda CUMMINGS, was born 22 Aug 1871 at Eyota, MN. He married Sarah Olive DURGIN ca 1911. She was the daughter of David DURGIN and Caroline May WILMOT, and was born 26 Aug 1894; died 17 Nov 1975 at Hart, MN. Lewis[8] BUSH died 1 June 1928 at Stockton, CA.

Children of Lewis[8] BUSH and Sarah DURGIN:
Surname **BUSH**

4198. Franklin O.	born 10 Nov 1912 MN; died 21 Apr 1975 Rochester, MN
4199. Marvel Avery	born 1 Apr 1916 MN; died 18 Jan 1966 MN.
	married Mae Verne Virginia JOSLIN 28 Feb 1935
	(she born 9 Aug 1917; died Sept 1988 MN)
Child:	Sarah Marie-[10] BUSH born 18 Jan 1938; died Apr 2001 MN
4200. John	born 2 May 1918; died 15 July 1969 MN.
4201. Paul E.	born 28 Oct 1920; died 17 Nov 1974 MN

3380. ELIZABETH[8] BUSH, sister of above, was born Oct 1874 at Eyota, Olmsted, Minnesota. She married George Victor HOBSON on 19 Nov 1903. He was the son of _____ HOBSON and ____, and was born 21 Aug 1871; died 11 Dec 1949 at Leon, WI. Elizabeth[-8] BUSH died 16 Dec 1927 at Monroe County, WI.

Children of Elizabeth[-8] BUSH and George V. HOBSON:
Surname **HOBSON**

4202. Harry Howard	born 10 July 1903 WI; died Nov 1954; married Gladys Marie H. JOHNSON ca ____
4203. John Thomas	born 8 Dec 1905; died May 1941 WI
4204. Fred Lee	born 14 May 1907; died 20 Nov 1992; married Nellie S. _____ ca ____
4205. Hannah B.	born 17 May 1908 WI; died 10 Sept 1989
	married John E. FILTER ca ____ (he born ca 1901; died 1971)
4206. Sarah	born 15 Sep 1909 WI; died 1 Mar 1967 OH; married Theodosis CHAMIS ca ____
4207. William	born 26 Mar 1911 WI; died May 1911 WI EOL
4208. Forest Gerald	born 14 Aug 1912 WI; died 9 Nov 1997 OH; married Lois _____
4209. Erie Dewitt	born 9 Sep 1913 WI; died 4 Apr 1998 OH; married Elizabeth Mary BRENNAN

3389. LYDIA ANN[-8] OWEN, daughter of Seeley[-7] OWEN (Hannah[-6] SEELEY; Deborah-[5] BOWKER; Elias[-4]; John[-3]; Edmund-[2,1]) and Lydia OWEN, was born 8 Jan 1839 Schuyler, IL. She married Abraham Golden CONOVER on 26 Feb 1857 at Salt Lake City, Utah. He was the son of Col. Peter Wilson CONOVER and Evaline B. GOLDEN, and was born 18 May 1830.

Children of Lydia Ann[-8] OWEN and Abraham CONOVER:
Surname **CONOVER**   (all children born Provo, Utah)

+	**4210. ABRAHAM/ABRAM JR.**	born 26 July 1858; died 18 Oct 1940 Ferron, Emery,UT
		married Elizabeth Juliet LOVELESS 4 Dec 1879
	4211. Lydia Ann	born 20 Nov 1859; died 14 Sept 1949 Provo, UT; married James C. LEETHAM
		Child: Kitty-[10] LEETHAM born ca ___, married Karl Fairbanks KEELER 14 Sept 1910
	4212. Alta Evaline	born 16 Jan 1862; died 31 Dec 1933 Provo, UT
	4213. Seeley Francis	born 23 Oct 1864; died 4 Nov 1907 Provo; married Ida SMITH
	4214. Wilbur Wallace	born 31 Oct 1867; died 19 Sept 1948
	4215. Don Wilson	born 30 Oct 1871; died 3 Jan 1942 Provo, UT
		married Harriet Ann HARRISON ca _____ (she born ca 1877; died 1964)
	4216. Lois Orenia	born 23 Mar 1874; died 26 Nov 1897
	4217. Alpheus	born 13 Oct 1876; died 11 Dec 1888 EOL
	4218. Hugh	born 26 Feb 1879; died 6 March 1902 Provo, UT

3391. BARBARA ELIZABETH[-8] OWEN, half sister of above, daughter of Seeley[-7] OWEN and Elizabeth PICKLE, was born 28 Sept 1853 at Salt Lake City, Utah. She married John McClelland BUTTREY on 17 Nov 1870 at Provo, Utah. He was the son of John Thompson BUTTREY and Winnie Matilda WILES, and was born 9 March 1843 NC; died 25 Feb 1917 Salt Lake. Barbara[-8] OWEN died 7 May 1919 at Park City, Summit, Utah.

Children of Barbara E[-8] OWEN and John M. BUTTREY
Surname **BUTTREY**

	4219. Abraham	born 12 Nov 1871; died 12 Nov 1871 EOL
	4220. Matilda Elizabeth	born 28 Nov 1872 Provo, UT; died 1 Jan 1907; married John Joseph BROWN ca ____
	4221. Hannah Jane	born 7 Oct 1874 Provo; died 13 April 1967 Salt Lake, UT
		married Edward Llewellyn THOMAS ca ____
	4222. Lodemia Evelyn	born 18 Sept 1876 UT; died 29 Oct 1940
		1 married Thomas Mark HEWITSON 16 Jan 1899; divorced ca 1911
		2 married Peter JACOBSEN ca 1925
	4223. Rachel A.	born 2 Nov 1878 Wasatch, UT; died 24 April 1964 Los Angeles, CA
		married Michael Mark MURPHY ca ____
	4224. John Seal	born 12 July 1881 Wasatch, UT; died 12 Dec 1947; married Minnie Alvin MILLER
	4225. Sidney Lee	born 20 Feb 1883 Bench Creek, UT; died 2 June 1888 EOL
	4226. Joseph Vance	born 7 Sept 1885 UT; died 21 May 1959 Salt Lake
		1 married Louise _____; 2 married Caroline WEBB; 3 married Verna YOUNG
+	**4227. MINNIE PEARL**	born 1 April 1887 Wasatch, UT; died 21 May 1959 Salt Lake
		married James Franklin DALTON ca 1907
	4228. Florence Gertrude	born 8 March 1889 Wasatch, UT; died June 1959
		married Frederick James NEWMAN 27 Jan 1908
	4229. Thomas Richard	born 7 Feb 1891 UT; died Dec 1973; married Alma May JOHNSON ca ____

Children of Barbara Elizabeth[-8] OWEN and John BUTTREY, continued:
Surname **BUTTREY**

4230. Flossie Ethel	born 18 Dec 1892 Wasatch, UT; died 29 Sept 1978
	married Lorenzo Vernal EWELL 31 Aug 1910
4231. Elisha	born 20 Jan 1896 Wasatch, UT; died 4 Nov 1970

3394. JULIA ANN[-8] OWEN, sister of above, was born 9 May 1860 Utah. She married Jerome Sargt KEMPTON on 10 May 1876. He was the son of Jerome Bonaparte KEMPTON and Rosetta Anise CHAPMAN (Mormons), and was born 2 Sept 1851 UT; died 11 Feb 1927 UT. Julia Ann[-8] OWEN died 23 June 1931 Utah.

Child of Julia Ann[-8] OWEN and Jerome KEMPTON:
Surname **KEMPTON**

4232. ANNIE ELIZABETH	born 9 June 1877; died 5 May 1962
	1 married Albert Sidney PERRY 1 Jan 1900
	(he born ____; died 19 Aug 1914)
	2 married Arthur LOTZ ca ____

3412. SAMUEL VICTOR[-8] GUTCHESS, son of Elizabeth Jane[7] WILLISON (James[-6]; Esther[-5] BOWKER; Silas Day[-4]; John-[3]; Edmund[-2,1]) and John Harvey GUTCHESS, was born 13 May 1867 at Barry, Michigan. He married Miriam/Marion Helena SHELDON 22 Nov 1894. She was the daughter of ____ SHELDON and ____, and was born ca ____, died ____. Samuel Victor[-8] GUTCHESS died 15 March 1955 at Barry, MI.

Children of Samuel V[-8] GUTCHESS and Miriam SHELDON:
Surname **GUTCHESS**

4233. Grace Ina	born March 1896; died 1992 Barry, MI
	married Alfred Franklin JONES ca ____ (he born ca 1893; died ____)
4234. Alice C.	born 10 June 1902 MI; died 14 Feb 1941 IL
	married Carl Theron HAWES ca ____ (he born ca 1897; died ____)
4235. Vesta	born 6 Aug 1903 MI; died 18 June 1988 Largo, FL
	married Emerson William LINDSAY 14 Feb 1931 IN
	(he s/o Robert LINDSAY and Ruby Mc CULLOUGH)
	he born 2 July 1904 MI; died Feb 2010 Brandon, Pinellas, FL)
4236. Victor	born 26 Jan 1905; died Aug 1964
4237. Vern L.	born 7 June 1908 MI; died 8 April 1991 MI; married Gladys ROGERS ca ____
4238. Velma Marion	born 19 July 1914 MI; died 23 March 1958 MI; married Herbert E. SPENCE ca ____
4239. Raymond	born 11 April 1917 MI; died 23 July 1987 MI
4240. Von E.	born 19 June 1921 MI; died 20 July 1992
4241. Donald H.	born 4 March 1922 MI; died 29 April 1997 MI

3424. FREDERICK[-8] ARMSTRONG, son of William[-7] ARMSTRONG (Cynthia[-6] WILLISON; Esther[-5] BOWKER; Silas Day[-4]; John-[3]; Edmund[-2,1]) and Sarah Jane CONREY, was born 15 April 1857 Genoa, NY. He married Helen TOWNSEND on 23 May 1877. She was the daughter of ____ TOWNSEND and ____, and was born ca 1858; died ca 1940 . Frederick-[8] ARMSTRONG died 24 May 1934 Unionville, MO.

Children of Frederick[-8] ARMSTRONG and Helen TOWNSEND:
Surname **ARMSTRONG**

4242. Wilmer Kendall	born 12 March 1878 MO; died March 1965; married Golda Willa PROBASCO ca ____
4243. Ethel	born May 1882 MO; died ____
4244. Hattie/Hallie	born April 1887 MO; died ____; married Fred Harper DRURY ca ____
4245. George Wood	born 27 Nov 1892 Unionville, MO; died ____
4246. Norma	born 16 Feb 1900; died 27 Oct 1945 MO

3427. FRANKLIN PIERCE[-8] TABER, son of Silas Day[-7] TABER (Mehitable[-6] BOWKER; Silas Day[-5,4]; John-[3]; Edmund[-2,1]) and Harriet CLOSE, was born 16 Jan 1853 at Cayuga County, NY. He married Mary Kittie[-8] PARKER 4 June 1879 at Moravia, Cayuga, NY. She was the daughter o f Mary[-7] TABER and John Locke PARKER, and was born 10 Feb 1855; died ____. Franklin[-8] TABER, an attorney, died 27 May 1914 at Auburn, Cayuga, NY.

Children of Franklin[8] TABER and Kittie[8] PARKER:
Surname **TABER**

4247. John	born 5 May 1880 NY; died 1 Nov 1965 Auburn, Cayuga, NY	
	married Gertrude J _____ ca ___	
	Child: Charles[10] TABER born ca 1920	
4248. Silas	born 19 Sep 1881 Moravia, Cayuga, NY; died March 1965; a mechanical engineer	
	married Isabel Helen NAGEL 11 Aug 1915 Elmira, NY	
	(she born 22 Aug 1885 Montour Falls, NY; died ____)	
	(she dau/o John NAGEL and Margaret KNIGHT)	
	Children: Mary[10] born 22 Sep 1918; and William[10] TABER born 11 July 1920	
4249. Mary	born 30 May 1884 Auburn, NY; died ____; had an AB from Wellesley College	
	married Amos Bateman THATCHER 17 Oct 1911 Auburn, NY	
	Child: John Taber[10] THATCHER born 20 Dec 1912 Syracuse, NY	
4250. Emily	born 3 Sep 1887 Auburn, NY; died Jan 1967 Auburn	

3432. CHARLES WILLIAM[8] TABER, son of William[7] TABER (Mehitable[6] BOWKER; Esther[5]; Silas Day[4]; John[3]; Edmund[2,1]) and Cordelia THOMPSON, was born 9 June 1867 at Elkland, PA. He married Emily Thornton BREESE Hawkes 12 Nov 1891 at Milwaukee, Wisconsin. She was the daughter of James Thomas BREESE ++++ and ____, and was born born in Canada on 8 Sept 1870. She was a musician and composer. Charles William[8] TABER died 16 Sep/Nov 1936 at Los Angeles.

Children of Charles Wm[8] TABER and Emily/ Emma BREESE:
Surname **TABER**

+ **4251. RUTH JEAN**	born 18 July 1893 Milwaukee, WI; died ca 1983	
	married Nathan Mills WHITTLESEY, Sr. 9 June 1915 Pasadena, CA.	
	(he born 15 Aug 1891 New Preston, CT; died 15 July 1957 CA)	
	(he s/o Robert C. WHITTLESEY and Nora Belle HATCH)	
4252. Vera C.	born ca 1895 WI ; died ____	
4253. Rush W.	born ca 1899 WI; died _____	4254. Kenneth W. born 15 Aug 1901 WI

++++ James Thomas BREESE, father of Emily, had A.M., D.D., and M.D. degrees. He was born in England and was a medical missionary to the hills of Kentucky. His father was Dr. J. BREESE, a Congregational minister and his mother was Lady Ann ROBERTS.

3433. ELLA ARVILLA[8] TABER, daughter of John Quincy[7] TABER (Mehitable[6] BOWKER; Silas Day[5,4]; John[3]; Edmund[2,1]) and Elizabeth R. SMITH, was born 9 Feb 1850 Moravia, Cayuga, NY. She married William Henry FARNEY March 1875 at Bloomington, IL. He was the son of David Radcliffe FARNEY and Malinda DUNCAN, and was born 17 May 1851 Grayson, IL; died 11 Dec 1927 Los Angeles, CA. Ella Arvilla[8] TABER died 17 Oct 1895 Kansas City.

Children of Ella Arvilla[8] TABER and William FARNEY:
Surname **FARNEY**

4255. Bessie Garner	born 6 Feb 1876 Racine, WI; died ____
	1 married Claude S. PECK 9 Mar 1896 (he born Aug 1868 KY; died ____)
	2 married Frank D. GILL ca ____
4256. Doris Ann	born 21 Sept 1879; died ____; married Harry E. COFFIN 2 Sept 1928
	(he born ca 1879 TN; died ____)
4257. Daisy Ellen	born 11 May 1882; died 19 June 1911
	1 married Walter S. SWICKHAMER 2 Dec 1899 Jackson, MO
	(he s/o G B SCHWECHEIMER and Julia ____) (he born June 1877 MO)
	2 married Henry Henderson HART 3 Mar 1904 Louisville, KY

3437. HENRY R/T[8] TABER, brother of above, was born 10 April 1858 at Albion Grove, Wisconsin. He married Elizabeth Theresa WEBSTER 8 Apr 1881 Grand Forks, ND. She was the daughter of Sylvester Monroe WEBSTER and Elizabeth TAYLOR, and was born 29/30 June 1858 Mayville, WI; died 10 Oct 1930 Cowlitz, WA.. Henry[8] TABER died 28 Sep 1924 at Longview, Cowlitz, WA.

Children of Henry[8] TABER and Elizabeth WEBSTER:
Surname **TABER**

+ **4258. FRANK WENDELL**	born 18 Mar 1882 MN; died 24 Sep 1937 Seattle, WA
	married Ethel Parmeter BLANCHARD 9 March 1908

BOWKER
The Eighth American Generation

Children of Henry-[8] TABER and Elizabeth WEBSTER, continued:
Surname **TABER**

4259. Charles Norman	born 20 Aug 1884 Auburn, Walsh County, ND; died 28 Jan 1943 OR	
	married Hulda M. THOM 3 May 1910 ND	
	Child: Charles William-[10] TABER born 23 July 1920 Fargo, ND; died 6 Feb 2005 OR	

+   **4260. FLORENCE**   born 23 Feb 1887 Buxton, Traill Co., ND; died _____
             LEOTA   married Ernest Manley ELLIOTT 9 July 1914 ND

     4261. Henry Webster   born 7 Sep 1888 Buxton, ND; died _____
                                married Bessie Celia DUNTLEY 17 June 1914 ND
                                (she dau/o Aldred S. DUNTLEY and Mary THOM)
                                (she born 11 March 1888; died ____)
                                Children: Harriet Isabella-[10] born 12 Nov 1916 ; Mary Elizabeth-[10] born 23 July 1918 ;
         and Betty Rose-[10] TABER born 21 Aug 1929 (all born Saskatchewan, Canada)

     4262. Warren Robert   born 11 Jan 1894 Kelso, Trail, ND; died 13 Nov 1959 Sonoma, CA; US Navy WW 1
     4263. Russell James   born 8 Mar 1898 Buxton, ND; died 1 Feb 1964 OR
                                married Mildred S. _____ ca _____
         Children: Russell J-[10] born ca 1931 WA; Lina E-[10] born ca 1935 WA; and Harry W-[10] TABER born ca 1936 WA

3443. MARY KITTIE-[8] PARKER, see # 3427 Franklin Pierce-[8] TABER for children

3454. WILLIAM HENRY-[8] BOWKER, son of William D-[7] BOWKER (Archibald-[6]; Silas Day-[5,4]; John[3]; Edmund-[2,1]) and Alma S. POWERS, was born 4 Oct 1850 at Cayuga County, NY. He married first to Almina MALICK on 12 Jan 1872 at Milton, Seward, Nebraska. She was the daughter of Uriah MALICK and Chloe POWELL, and was born 30 March 1854 OH; died ca 1890. His second marriage, on 30 Nov 1892, was to Elizabeth VERRY. She was the daughter of William M. VERRY and Sarah Jane WATKINS, and was born 12 July 1870 IA; died 12 May 1935 Saskatchewan, Canada. William Henry-[8] BOWKER died 8 June 1917 at West Liberty, Muscatine County, Iowa.

Children of William H-[8] BOWKER and Almina MALICK:
Surname **BOWKER**

     4264. Isma Almerian   born 19 Sept 1872 NE; died 23 Oct 1957 Lincoln, NE; married Edna O. CADY ca ___
                                (she dau/o Willis CADY and Margaret June FRANKLIN)
                                (she born 4 June 1876 IA; died Dec 1954)
     4265. Jesse   born 20 Aug 1875 NE; died 13 Dec 1951 Unity, Saskatchewan, Canada
     4266. Henry Harry   born 12 May 1880 NE; died 8 Sep 1963 Unity, Saskatchewan, Canada
                                married Jennie Pearl Eliza MARTIN ca ____
                                (she born ca 1889; died ca 1965)
     4267. Alma Chloe   born 20 June 1885 NE; died 11 Sept 1944 Wauneta, Seward, Alaska
                                married H. Edward KRAUSNICK 26 Jan 1910 Seward, Alaska
     4268. Leroy   born 20 Oct 1887 Benkleman, Dundy, NE; died 15 Nov 1978 Walla Walla, WA.
                                married Violet Verna OSBORN ca 5 Mar 1910 Seward (she born 11 Mar 1882, NE)
                                (she dau/o Marion Wright OSBORN and Victoria E. HULSE)
         Children: Norman Leroy-[10] born 31 Mar 1917 San Francisco, CA; married Joey MILLER ca 1940 Caldwell, ID.
                        and Garnet-[10] BOWKER born ca 1921

Children of William H-[8] BOWKER and Elizabeth VERRY:
Surname **BOWKER**

4269. Madge R.	born Sept 1894 NE; died _____	4271. Mildred Vera	born ca 1909 IA; died ____
4270. Lloyd Roman	born Sept 1897 NE; died _____		

3458. GEORGE OSCAR-[8] BOWKER, son of Silas-[7] BOWKER (Archibald-[6]; Silas Day-[5,4]; John[3]; Edmund-[2,1]) and Harriet ROGERS, was born 22 Sept 1840 at Springport, Cayuga County, NY. He married first to Louisa LABAR on 15 Dec 1861 at Five Corners, Genoa, Cayuga, NY. She was the daughter of Theodore LE BARE/ LABAR and Louisa Harriet ST. GERMAIN, and was born 8 Dec 1842; died 31 Dec 1882 at Oxford Mills, Jones County, IA. It is believed that he married second to Lydia HOLT VanVoltenburg on 9 Feb 1884 at Jones County, IA (Reference: Book D – Jones Co. Marriages 1877-84) She was the daughter of William HOLT and Mary TURNER, and was born ca 1842 OH; died 12 March 1891. George Oscar-[8] BOWKER married third to Mary Ann (Anna) BREECE. She was the daughter of Henry BREECE and Emeline ABELL, and was born ca 1856 PA; died 11 Feb 1913 at Oxford Mills. (Reference: Mayflower Cemetery Jones Co., IA Gravestone Records) George Oscar-[8] BOWKER ran the BOWKER HOUSE HOTEL in Oxford Mills for many years. He died 16 Feb 1911. His body was found in the Wapsie River near the wagon bridge. His shoes were found on the bank of the river and there was no water in his lungs. Another unsolved mystery !!!

Children of George Oscar-[8] BOWKER and Louisa LABAR:
Surname **BOWKER**

	4272. R.S.	born ca _____ ; died ____
	4273. C.	born ca ____ ; died ____
+	**4274. MINNIE JANE**	born 25 Dec 1864 Cayuga Co., NY; died 1 Nov 1920
		married Richard Henry JONES 31 Dec 1882 Oxford Mills, IA
		(he born ca 1854 VA ; died ____)
	4275. William A.	born ca 1868/69; died 4 July 1948
	4276. Ada	born ca 1870 IA; died ____
+	**4277. EVELYN/EVA**	born 5 Sep 1872; died 30 Sept 1965 IA
	LOUISA	1 married Christian Martin RICKHOFF 3 June 1888 Jones County, IA
		(he born ca 1859; died 1892)
		2 married Hubert Charles UNDERHILL 13 Aug 1897 Cedar Rapids, IA
	4278. Louella May	born 19 July 1875; died 14 June 1898 Oxford Mills, IA
	4279. Charles E.	born 24 Aug 1878 IA; died 15 Oct 1938 Oxford Mills, IA
		married Elizabeth ELLIOTT ca 1911

Children: Charles W-[10] born ca 1912; and Alvin-[10] BOWKER born ca 1913

Child of George Oscar-[8] BOWKER and Mary Ann BREECE:
Surname **BOWKER**

	4280. Oscar Bruce	born 23 July 1892 Oxford Mills, IA; died 8 Apr 1920 IA
		married Helva V. SCHROEDER ca _____

Child: Oscar Wilbert -[10] BOWKER born 27 Aug 1914; died 16 Dec 1996 Alexandria, VA; married Inez DELANEY 10 June 1939. She dau/o Andrew DELANEY and Marie ____ . She born ca 1920 IA; died _____

3459. FREDERICK ERI-[8] BOWKER, brother of above, was born 19 Sept 1842 at Springport, Cayuga, NY. He married Sarah Ellen WOODARD on 19 Sept 1867 at Skaneateles, Onondaga, NY. She was the daughter of Horace WOODARD and Chloe Hinckley HAMBLIN, and was born 23 Jan 1847 at SummerHill, Cayuga, NY; died 23 Feb 1889, probably from complications after childbirth at Mandana, Onondaga, NY. Frederick Eri-[8] BOWKER died 27 Jan 1925 at Skaneateles, NY.

Children of Frederick Eri-[8] BOWKER and Sarah WOODARD:
Surname **BOWKER**   (all children born Cayuga County, NY)

+	**4281. EVA ALVENA**	born 16 April 1869; died 21 Jan 1926
		married Ludovico SICKLES 23 Feb 1898 Skaneateles, NY
		(he s/o Eugene L. SICKLES and Elizabeth _____)
	4282. Una Alberta	born 25 Aug 1871; died 30 June 1889 Mandana, NY
+	**4283. HORACE**	born 30 Oct 1873; died 5 Jan 1963 Deland, FL
	FREDERICK	married Grace Millicent EDWARDS 19 Jan 1902
		(she born 28 Jan 1882 Skaneateles; died 1 June 1926 Batavia, NY)
+	**4284. JAY HINCKLEY**	born 22 March 1876; died Jan 19532 Bethesda, MD.
		married Cornelia Theodora EDWARDS 30 Oct 1901
	4285. Lulu Albertine	born 25 Aug 1878; died March 1954 Skaneateles, NY
	4286. Etta Irene	born 7 Jan 1883; died Dec 1960 Skaneateles
	4287. Myrtle Ina	born 13 Aug 1885; died 10 March 1933; married Stephen Fort BURT 23 Feb 1921

Child: Marietta-[10] BURT born ca 1922 NY (1930 resided Lysander, Onondaga, NY)

+	**4288. ELLEN ALBERTA**	born 31 Jan 1889; died 5 May 1980 Yakima, WA.
		married Edward Sumner PRENTICE ca 1915
		(he s/o Fred Miles PRENTICE and Mary AUSTIN)
		(he born 1 Nov 1892/93; died 11 Feb 1967 CA)

3464. ROSA-[8] BOWKER, sister of above, was born 20 Feb 1858 Lysander, Onondaga, NY. She married William Jefferson RYDER on 10 May 1880. He was the son of Robert T. RYDER and Manda ___, and was born June 1860; died 15 April 1945. Rosa-[8] BOWKER died 15 March 1934 at Memphis, NY.

Children of Rosa-[8] BOWKER and William RYDER:
Surname **RYDER**

+	**4289. ALBERT EUGENE**	born 14 Apr 1883; died 17 Feb 1927; married Elizabeth FITZPATRICK
	4290. Letha V.	born ca 1889
	4291. Clair	(male) born ca 1902; died ____ ; married Ruth ____ (she born ca 1902)

Child: Donald-[10] RYDER born ca 1920

3465. FRANK DRAKE[8] BOWKER, son of Eri-[7] BOWKER (Archibald[-6]; Silas Day[-5,4]; John[-3]; Edmund[-2,1]) and Roseanna WIGGINS, was born 13 Feb 1858 at Summer Hill, Cayuga County, NY. He married Helen Townley HALL on 18 Aug 1877. She was the daughter of Ezra Russell HALL and Clarinda LANTERMAN, and was born 3 Oct 1859; died 21 Jun 1934 at Cortland, Cortland, NY. Frank-[8] BOWKER died 6 June 1933 at Homer, Cortland, NY.

Children of Frank Drake-[8] BOWKER and Helen HALL:
Surname **BOWKER**

	4292. Clara Rose/ Carrie	born 12 April 1878; died 6 Sept 1896	EOL
+	**4293. MABEL ROSE**	born 22 Sept 1879; died 17 Dec 1913 Homer, Cortland, NY	
		married Clarence E. HOPKINS 16 Dec 1896 Blodgett Manor, NY	
+	**4294. FRANK DRAKE (Jr)**	born 15 March 1882; died ____; married Clara CONWAY 5 July 1922	
	4295. Arthur	born 6 Feb 1884; died Dec 1976 Syracuse, Onondaga, NY	
+	**4296. HELEN JENNIE**	born 20 Apr 1885; died 4 Oct 1974 Avoca, Steuben, NY	
		married Lee Nellis SHULTS 15 Dec 1914	
+	**4297. MARY MATTIE**	born 7 March 1887; died 21 Dec 1973 Plainwell, MI	
		married Earl Dale SMITH 1 Jan 1914	
	4298. E. Russell	born 18 July 1889; died 22 April 1958	

1 married Florence Floretta ALBRO ca 1890 Cortland, NY
2 married Helen E. BOYD 21 April 1917
3 married Mildred Helen SASSMAN 15 July 1927
Note: He was a horse dealer and farmer; his business was named BOWKER & BACON, Cortland, NY

	4299. Eri	born 9 Feb 1891; died 17 Aug 1903	EOL
	4300. Ruth	born 26 Jan 1893; died 16 May 1961 Long Beach, CA	
		married Edward J. GARNES ca ____ (he born ca 1893 LA; died 1955 LA)	

Children: Doris-[10] born ca 1915 WI; Jane-[10] born ca 1918 WI; Jack-[10] born ca 1922 WI; and May-[10] GARNES born ca 1926 WI

4301. Walter	born 25 Dec 1894; died 10 April 1958; married Edith WALRAD 7 Dec 1910
	(she dau/o Fred WALRAD and Charlotte ELLSWORTH)
	(she born 29 Dec 1894; died 7 Feb 1990 Cortland, NY)

Child: George-[10] BOWKER born 5 Nov 1912; died 18 Jan 1990

4302. John Hall	born 8 March 1897; died Feb 1988; graduated Cornell University 1922
	married Frances H. RINCH Feb 1920 (she born ca 1897 OH, died ____)

Children: Barbara A-[10] born ca 1922 NY; and John H-[10] BOWKER , Jr. born ca 1928 MA

4303. Irene Florence	born 8 May 1903; died Nov 1985

3466. MARY R-[8] BOWKER, sister of above, was born Dec 1860 at Summer Hill, Cayuga, NY. She married John E. LOOMIS 2 Nov 1881. He was the son of Levi W. LOOMIS and Louise E. ____, and was born July 1861; died ____. They res. Waterloo, Seneca County, NY. where he was a foreman in a wagon factory, and she was a music teacher. Mary R-[8] BOWKER died _____.

Children of Mary R-[8] BOWKER and John LOOMIS:
Surname **LOOMIS**

4304. John E. (Jr.)	born Dec 1887; died ____	4305. Charles Eugene B.	born ca 1901 Waterloo, NY

3467. FRED-[8] BOWKER, brother of above, was born 27 Dec 861 at SummerHill, Cayuga County, NY. He married Julia C. HONEYWELL ca 1879. She was the daughter of Gilbert H. HONEYWELL and Sarah ____, and was born 23 Oct 1861 at Summer Hill; died 14 Dec 1937 at Cortland, Cortland, NY. Fred-[8] BOWKER was Chief of Police in the City of Cortland for 14 years, and after retiring from that position, was an auctioneer. He died 26 Jan 1945 at Cortland, NY.

Children of Fred-[8] BOWKER and Julia HONEYWELL:
Surname **BOWKER**

4306. F. Grenville	born 2 May 1880; died ____; married Margaret A. Mc GRAW ca 1902
	(she born ca 1879/80 NY; died 10 Feb 1924)(buried Camillus, Onondaga, NY)
4307. Sarah Augusta	born 28 Dec 1885; died 1972; married Daniel Meredith CURTIS 12 June 1912 Cortland
	(he s/o Daniel H. CURTIS and Kate O'BRIEN)
	(he born 5 Apr 1884 Worcester, MA; died 28 Apr 1956 Cortland, NY)

Children: Daniel F-[10] born ca 1914; and Marion J-[10] CURTIS born ca 1917

4308. Ethel Julia/Grace	born 6 Dec 1899 Cortland; died 16 Jan 1916 Cortland	EOL

3468. EUGENE WIGGINS -[8] BOWKER, brother of above, was born 23 May 1864 at Summer Hill, Cayuga County, NY.

He married Mary Ann " Mame" REED ++ on 28 Dec 1887. She was the daughter of Samuel Sanford REED and Clarissa Clark " Clara " HENDERSON, and was born 19 March 1869 at Otisco, NY; died 11 Jan 1945. Eugene-[8] BOWKER died of acute myocarditis and chronic bronchitis on 28 March 1932 at Cortland, NY. He and his wife are buried at the Cortland Rural Cemetery.

Children of Eugene Wiggins-[8] BOWKER and Mary Ann REED:
Surname **BOWKER**

4309. HAROLD EUGENE	born 5 Feb 1889; died 7 Jan 1969 Cortland, NY
	married Jessie BAIRD 14 April 1913 (she dau/o Robert BAIRD and Ruttie IVES)
	(she born 10 June 1893 Plattsville, Ontario, Canada; died _____)
4310. GERTRUDE BELLE	born 14 May 1894 Cortland; died 3 April 1978 Cortland
	married Clarence Darwin STEVENS 20 April 1913
4311. HOWARD EDWARD	born 28 Apr 1900 Cortland; died 9 Sept 1939 Bath, NY
	married Dorothy May Mc KINNEY 30 May 1920 Cortland, NY
	(she dau/o George Mc KINNEY and Susie Belle FOX)
	(she born 15 Aug 1901 McLean, Tompkins, NY; died 15 Dec 2003 , age 102)
4312. HERBERT RAYMOND	born 24 Oct 1903/04; died Oct 1970 Rockland, NY (SSDI)
	1 married Bernice May DORAN ca _____; divorced ca _____
	(she dau/o Edward C. DORAN and Grace A. ____) (she born ca 1905; died _____)
	2 married Dorothy F. EHLIG ca _____
	(she dau/o Harry EHLIG and Eunice A. _____) (she born ca 1907; died _____)
4313. Clara Mildred	born 2 July 1907; died 19 July 1924 EOL

++ Ancestry of Mary Ann " Mame"-[7] REED

The immigrant, William-[1] READE, was born ca 1605 England. It is unknown as to whom his wife was, or just when he came to America. It is known that he died ca 1663 at MA. James-[2] REED, his son, was born ca 1657 MA. William-[3] REED was born 1 May 1685 MA. William-[3] married an Elizabeth ____and, they were the parents of Samuel W-[4] REED born 17 Sept 1750 who married Rebecca KNOWLTON and died 9 March 1822. Rebecca KNOWLTON was the daughter of John KNOWLTON and Prudernce THOMAS, and was born 12 Nov 1759; died 19 Sep 1831. Their son Watson-[5] REED, born 19 April 1804; married Sylvia SAMSON ca ____. Sylvia was the daughter of Elnathan SAMSON and Polly ___, and was born ca 1815; died ca 1880. They resided at Union, Broome County, NY and later moved to Cortland County. Samuel Sanford-[6] REED, son of Watson-[5], was born 9 March 1841in Virgil (VR of Homer, Cortland, NY) He died 26 Nov 1921 (aged 80 years 8 months and 17 days).

Samuel Sanford-[6] REED served as a Private in Company I, 75th Regiment, NYS Volunteers during the Civil War. His military record shows that he enlisted at Auburn, Cayuga County, NY on 9 Oct 1861. His unit was called the "Auburn Regt. " and was under the command of Captain Lansing PORTER. His enlistement was for a term of 3 years. He was described as 5'71/2 " tall, with sandy complexion, blue eyes and red hair. He was a farmer and tinsmith by trade.

He was discharged from the service under a medical disability due to the loss of his left hand and the amputation of his left arm below the elbow. It was caused by an accidental discharge of his gun while he was on duty at Camp Kearney, Carrolton, LA on 10 Nov 1862. It is reported that he always wore a beard, red in color, and therefore was called " Sandy " . He wore a hook on his left arm. He received a pension of $ 30. per month for his disability. After moving to SummerHill he served as the Postmaster there.

He married Clarissa " Clara " HENDERSON +++ on the 4th of July 1861 (before going into the service) at Otisco, NY. She was the daughter of Colonel William H. HENDERSON and Dyeretta NORTON (Elon; Daniel) and was born 17 Sep 1841 at Otisco, Onondaga, NY; died 8/18 Feb 1918. They were the parents of 13 Children, including Mary Ann " Mame"-7 REED who married Eugene Wiggins BOWKER.

Samuel Sanford-[6] REED and his wife celebrated their 50th wedding anniversary on 4 July 1911 at their home in Cortland, NY. He died 26 Nov 1921. He and his wife are buried at the Homer Cemetery, Homer, NY.

+++ Ancestry of Clarissa-[4] HENDERSON

Edward-[1] HENDERSON, probably of Scottish heritage, was born ca 1735; died ca 1819. He immigrated to America sometime before 1773, when he is known to have placed an ad in the Philadelphia Gazette seeking the location of a runaway servant girl. At that time he was residing in Bethlehem Twsp., Hunterdon Co., NJ. It is believed that he had two wives. One child from the first marriage to a Susannah ____; and nine children from his second marriage to a Rachel ____, including Phineas-[2] HENDERSON who was born 8 May 1773 at Bethlehem, NJ. Phineas-[2] HENDERSON married an Elizabeth MILLER ca 1792. She was born ____; died 18 May 1824 at Tully, Onondaga County, NY, and is buried in the Cardiff Cemetery at LaFayette, Onondaga County, NY.

Phineas-[2] HENDERSON was one of the early settlers in the Tully Valley, going there in 1796 from Hunterdon Co., NJ. He was the father of Colonel William H-[3] HENDERSON, who was born ca 1808 at Tully, married Dyeretta NORTON, and died 20 April 1875. He is buried at Hilldale Cemetery, Otisco, Onondaga, NY. Dyeretta NORTON was the daughter of Elon NORTON (Daniel) and Thursia JONES, and was born Aug 1809 Schoharie County, NY; died ca 1898.

An epitaph to the HENDERSON family monument in the Otisco Cemetery Otisco, NY reads as follows:

" Colonel William[-3] HENDERSON was born in the Town of Tully, NY in AD 1808. His parents Phineas and Elizabeth HENDERSON were the first settlers of the town. He resided in the Town of Otisco for 50 years, a man of sterling character, honored by his fellow citizens with civil offices, from the first step of the ladder, to that of member of the Legislature, and the military from that of Private to Colonel. He was also a member of the IOOF. In his death a void was created that cannot well be filled. "   Colonel[-3] William HENDERSON was the father of **Clarissa Clark[-4]** HENDERSON (above) who married Samuel Sanford[-6] REED.

3481. SIMON L[-8] COOK, son of Mary Ann[-7] DRAKE (Lisa-[6] BOWKER; Silas Day-[5,4]; John-[3]; Edmund-[2,1]) and Luther COOK, and was born April 1844 OH. He married Adaline THOMPSON 23 March 1865 Summit, OH. She was the daughter of Mills THOMPSON and Katherine ALLEN, and was born 26 Sept 1841 OH; died 15 Dec 1921 at Chattanooga, TN. Simon L[-8] COOK died 19 Jan 1910 Chattanooga.

Children of Simon L[-8] COOK and Adaline THOMPSON:
Surname **COOK**

4314. John A.	born ca 1867; died ____	
4315. Frank H.	born Sept 1868 MI; died ____	
4316. Mae D.	born Feb 1871 KS; died ____; married ____ HERBERT ca ____; divorced	
	Children: Carrie[10] born Nov 1888 KS; Addie F[10] born Mar 1890 WI; and Lyle[-10] HERBERT born Mar 1891 WI	
4317. Jessie B.	born 1 Jan 1877 KS; died 4 May 1959 FL; married Wyley Griffin SEALS	
4318. Pearl J.	born Dec 1878/79 KS; died ____	
4319. George A.	born 30 Mar 1882 KS; died 30 Sept 1865 FL	
	married Orpha Gertrude GANO (she born 1886; died 1942)	

3489. ANDREW TODD[-8] DRAKE, son of Jasper B-[7] DRAKE (Lisa-[6] BOWKER; Silas Day-[5,4]; John-[3]; Edmund-[2,1]) and Caroline HARDY, was born 22 Nov 1848 OH. He married first to Olive LEACH 20 July 1868. She was the daughter of ____ LEACH and ____, and was born 22 Aug 1853 WI, died 8 Apr 1880 Ness, KS. He married second to Sarah Jane BENBROOK ca 1890. She was the daughter of Ratcliffe Marion BENBROOK and Eliza Louisa HALL; and was born Feb 1849; died 1932. Andrew Todd-[8] DRAKE died 14 May 1935.

Children of Andrew Todd-[8] DRAKE and _____:
Surname **DRAKE**

4320. Olive Amey	born ca 1869; died ____		
4321. Orlando	born 21 June 1871 KS; died 19 Jan 1943 MN		
	married Sarah Frances " Frankie" BENBROOK (she born ca 1879, died 1957)		
4322. Mary Edith	born 3 July 1875; died 9 July 1954	4323. Mina Alice	born 12 Aug 1878

3492. JOHN BRUFF[-8] DRAKE, brother of above, was born 4 Sep 1860. He married first to Mary BURRIS ca 1887. She was the daughter of Jacob BURRIS and Martha H. ____, and was born Dec 1861 OH; died ____. His second wife was Nancy WELLS. She was the daughter of ____ WELLS and ____, and was born ____; died ____. His third wife was Sadie Leote LARKINS. She was the daughter of Reuben LARKINS and Sarah FREDERICKS , and was born 16 Oct 1871 IL; died 25 Dec 1932. John Bruff[-8] DRAKE died 16 Aug 1931.

Children of John Bruff[-8] DRAKE and _____
Surname **DRAKE**

4324. Enoch Perdue	born 25 March 1882; died 25 March 1882	EOL
4325. Hardy I.	born Sept 1887; died 5 Oct 1907	

Child of John B-[8] DRAKE and Sadie LARKINS:
Surname **DRAKE**

4326. Ralph Rothwell	born 8 Mar 1898 KS; died 5 Oct 1931 Ness, KS
	married Sophrona Therina TALLEY 4 Sept 1921
	(she dau/o Elby Clifford "Alvie" TALLEY and Hattie RAND)
	(she born 17 Sept 1898 MO; died 26 July 1990 KS)
	Children: Earl R-[10] born ca 1923; Merrill Clayton-[10] born 19 June 1925 KS, died 9 Mar 1963 MO, married Bettie Eileen WALKER 18 Apr 1946 MO (1925-2004); and Laveta M-[10] DRAKE born ca 1927/28

3493 HOWARD MILTON[-8] DRAKE, brother of above, was born 21 Feb 1862 OH. He married Lydia Frances WHITMER ca 1883. She was the daughter of ____ WHITMER and ____, and was born ca 1868 IL; died ____. They resided at Nabisco, Beaver, OK. Howard Milton-[8] DRAKE died 29 Sept 1925 Liberal, Seward, KS.

Children of Howard Milton[-8] DRAKE and Lydia WHITMER:
Surname **DRAKE**

4327. Hazel M.	born ca 1888 KS; died ____; married Burton F. MANNING ca ____	
	(he born ca 1886 MO; died ____)	
	Children: Howard E[-10] born Aug 1908 OK; Audrey R[-10] MANNING born ca 1912 OK	
4328. Lila Belle	born Mar 1894 KS; died 25 July 1941; married Ranie Henry PETERS	
	(he born 25 July 1885 TX; died 7 Dec 1958 KS)	
	Children: Dale Claude[-10] born 6 June 1918 OK, died 10 Nov 1993 OK; and Laveta M[-10] PETERS	
	born ca 1923, died 1959 OK	
4329. Glenn W.	born ca 1897 KS; died ____	

3507. HARLEY J[-8] DRAKE, son of Nathan[-7] DRAKE (Lisa[-6] BOWKER; Silas Day[-5,4]; John[-3]; Edmund[-2,1]) and Lucy RHODENBURGH, was born 28 July 1872 at Richfield, Summit, Ohio. He married Etta Jennie GREEN on 3 June 1896 at Cuyahoga County, Ohio. She was the daughter of _____ GREEN and ____, and was born ca July 1868 Pa; died _____.

Children of Harley[-8] DRAKE and Etta GREEN:
Surname **DRAKE**

4330. Gaylord	born ca 1897 OH; died _____; married Hazel M _____ ca ____
	Children: Chester[-10] born ca 1927 OH; and Willis[-10] DRAKE born ca 1929 OH
4331. Paul A.	born ca 1902 OH; died 13 Nov 1981
	married Margaret Vernard BUTCHER ca ____
4332. Florence May	born 2 Aug 1905 OH; died 24 Sept 2002 Riverside, CA
	married George T. EBERT 24 Oct 1925 Cuyahoga, OH (he born ca 1904)
4333. Margaret A.	born 26 Oct 1910 Lakewood, OH; died 30 Jan 2001 Cleveland, OH
	married Thomas M. HUGHES 29 June 1936
	(he born 26 Sep 1909 Westmeath, Ireland; died 4 July 1975 Cleveland, OH)
	(he s/o Thomas HUGHES and Theresa DUNN)

3514. JOITA JUBA[-8] HILL, son of Mehitable[-7] DRAKE (Lisa[-6] BOWKER; Silas Day[-5,4]; John[-3]; Edmund[-2,1]) and Joseph HIL, was born 30 Nov 1871 OH. he married Emily Henrietta SPANG ca 1895. She was the daughter of _____ SPANG and ____, and was born ca 1877; died 1966. Joita Juba[-8] HILL died 22 July 1933 Akron, Ohio.

Children of Joita Juba[-8] HILL and Emily SPANG:
Surname **HILL**

4334. Floyd	born 18 March 1896; died 17 Apr 1922 Portage, OH	
4335. Maude Josephine	born ca 1902; died 3 Dec 1917	EOL
4336. Orrin Frederick	born 17 April 1906; died 2 June 1973	4337. Joseph T. born ca 1911

3525. INA[-8] LOOMIS, daughter of Rosetta[-7] HENRY (Aurelia[-6] BOWKER; Silas Day[-5,4]; John[-3]; Edmund[-2,1]) and Burt LOOMIS, was born ca 1876 NY. She married George S. WRIGHT 24 Nov 1896. He was the son of Charles E. WRIGHT and Sarah L. FOSTER, and was born ca 1877; died Aug 1941. Ina[-8] LOOMIS died May 1941 Cortland, Cortland, NY.

Children of Ina[-8] LOOMIS and George S. WRIGHT:
Surname **WRIGHT**

4338. Carlton Lewis	born 8 Aug 1897; died 27 Apr 1969	
	married Dorothy Irene KREIDER ca -___	(she born ca 1913; died 1982)
4339. Margery	born 23 June 1900; died 30 Dec 1902	EOL
4340. Raymond	born 25 Nov 1901; died 31 March 1963 FL	
	married Rose Mary PEOPLES ca ____	
4341. Ruth E.	born 6 May 1905 Fleming, NY; died 18 Oct 1989 Cortland, NY	
	married Arthur FOX ca ____	
4342. Mildred	born ca 1907; died 21 May 1917	EOL
4343. Richard H.	born 6 Feb 1910 Moravia, NY; died 9 June 1968 Rochester, Monroe, NY	
	married Ruth C. WINANS ca ____	
4344. Wilbur S.	born 18 July 1912; died June 1972 Syracuse, NY	
4345. Winifred Stella	born 18 July 1912; died 27 March 2001 Lockport, NY	
	married Clifford Claude BENNETT ca ____	
4346. George Bernard	born 25 Nov 1918; died 4 May 2002	
4347. Rosemary	born 12 May 192 Montville, NY; died 27 Sep 1993 FL; married Walter COFFIN	

3534. ELIZA-⁸ ROSE, daughter of William Henry-⁷ ROSE (William-⁶; Lisa-⁵ BOWKER; Silas Day-⁴; John-³; Edmund-²,¹) and Eunice N. JOHNSON, was born June/Sept 1849. She married Edwin Twin WILCOX ca ____. Ge was the son of ____ WILCOX and _____, and was born ca 1852; died ca 1927. Eliza A-⁸ ROSE died 25 Jan 1885 at Waco, NE.

Cjhildren of Eliza A-⁸ ROSE and Edwin T. WILCOX:
Surname **WILCOX**

4348. Traverse Craig	born ca 1874; died 1963	4350. William Edgar	born ca 1879; died 1966
4349. Albert Clare	born ca 1876; died 1904	4351. Harold Martin	born ca 1883; died

3536. WILLIAM ALBERT-⁸ ROSE, brother of above, was born 1 July 1856 Delaware County, OH. He married Minnie Helen ATTEBERRY ca _____. She was the daughter of Henry Thomas ATTEBERRY and Margaret NEET, and was born 10 May 1865 IA; died 5 Oct 1944 at Boulder, CO. William Albert-⁸ ROSE died 13 Sept 1934 at Boulder, Colorado.

Children of William Albert-⁸ ROSE and Minnie ATTEBERRY:
Surname **ROSE**

4352. Verdon Benjamin	born 11 Jan 1889 KS; died 12 June 1983 ID; married Mary Ethel HOYT ca ____
4353. Florence	born 29 May 1890; died _____; married Charles F. ROSE ca ____; (he born ca 1889)
4354. Forest E.	born 2 March 1892; died 20 Jan 1993 KS
4355. Georgia	born 7 Oct 1894; died 4 Sep 1979 Los Angeles, CA
	married Frank T D BAUGUESS ca ____
4356. Charles Orville	born 29 Oct 1897 KS; died 8 Jan 1979; married Grace Alice COLVIN ca ____
	(she born ca 1905; died 2002)

3560. MARY ANN-⁸ HOWE, daughter of Philetus-⁷ HOWE (Cynthia-⁶ ROSE; Lisa-⁵ BOWKER; Silas Day-⁴; John-³; Edmund-²,¹) and Eliza E. LAYCOCK, was born 2 Sept 1839 OH. She married James Dillon CHUBB ca _____. He was the son of ___ CHUBB and ___, and was born 25 Dec 1837 Nankin, MI; died 16 Nov 1920. Mary Ann-⁸ HOWE died 11 April 1866 MI.

Children of Mary Ann-⁸ HOWE and James D. CHUBB:
Surname **CHUBB**

4357. Irving/Erving Lyle	born 30 Oct 1863; died 4 May 1942 CA.
	married Harriet Ann " Hattie " BRIDGE 18 June 1888 MN
	(she dau/o George Amos BRIDGE and Eliza WARREN)
	(she born 5 July 1862 IL; died 26 aug 1950 CA)
	Children: Myrtle Ella-¹⁰ CHUBB born Mar 1889, died ca 1971; and Flora May-¹⁰ CHUBB born 13 Feb 1894 ;
	died 15 Sep 1973 CA; 1 married Pearl Elgin REED 10 Aug 1910; 2 married Harland MARTIN ca 1938
4358. Gilbert F.	born 24 Sept 1865 MI; died 13 April 1866 MI

3562. HULDAH-⁸ HOWE, sister of above, was born Oct 1844 OH. She married Curtis BRACE on 4 April 1861 at Wayne, MI. He was the son of Willis BRACE and Harriet CURTIS, and was born Aug 1840 NY; died _____ (still living in 1920)

Children of Huldah-⁸ HOWE and Curtis BRACE:
Surname **BRACE**

4359. William	born ca 1866; died ____
4360. Charles D.	born June 1866 MI; died _____; married Mary HARGER
	Child: Romaine Harger-¹⁰ BRACE born July 1894 NY
4361. Josie	born ca 1870; died ____
4362. Nellie	born ca 1874 MI; died ____; married Joseph SCOTT ca ____
	Children: Margery-¹⁰ born ca 1898; Eugene-¹⁰ born ca 1901; and Margaret-¹⁰ SCOTT born ca 1913
4363. George C.	born ca 1878; died _____

3582. SARAH DEBORAH-⁸ ROSE, daughter of Smith-⁷ ROSE (Jacob Schoolcraft-⁶; Lisa-⁵ BOWKER; Silas-⁴; John-³; Edmund-²,¹) and Susan STOUT, was born Oct 1858 Ohio. She married Horace Greeley WEST ca 1876 OH. He was the son of ____ WEST and ____, and was born ca 1856, died 1903. Sarah Deborah-⁸ ROSE died _____.

Children of Sarah Deborah-⁸ ROSE and Horace WEST
Surname **WEST**

4364. Nellie G.	born Nov 1877 OH; died ____
4365. Gordon Robert	born 26 Sept 1881; died 15 Jan 1976 OH; married Helen Lucinda JEFFERS ca ____
	Children : Jeanne-¹⁰ born ca 1920; Betty-¹⁰ born ca 1922; and June-¹⁰ WEST born ca 1926 OH

Childrten of Sarah Deborah-8 ROSE and Horace WEST, continued:
Surname **WEST**

4366. Jay Thomas	born24 Jan 1884 OH; died ____		
	1 married Cora Isabella MORGAN ca ____; 2 married Carolyn ARTMAN ca _____		
4367. Ruby L.	born March 1885 OH	4370. Fred Max	born 14 Oct 1891 OH
4368. Marjorie N.	born Oct 1888 OH	4371. Esther H.	born Apr 1893 OH
4369. Nina R.	born May 1890 OH	4372. Charles Dana	born 26 May 1895 OH

3589. MARIA DOLLIE-8 CURREY, daughter of Andrew B-7 CURREY (Cynthia-6 BOWKER; Daniel-5; Silas Day-4; John-3; Edmund-2,1) and Mary M. BURTON, was born 14 Jan 1866. She married Charles O. MORLEY on 9 Aug 1882 at Grahamsville, Sullivan County, NY. He was the son of John MORLEY and Anna E. CARSON, and was born ca 1855; died ca 1898. Maria Dollie-8 CURREY died 25 May 1932.

Children of Maria Dollie-8 CURREY and Charles MORLEY:
Surname **MORLEY**

4373. Ethel	born April 1883; died 1932; married Mark M. SLATER (he born ca 1872 NY)
4374. Ida Maude	born 25 July 1885 Liberty, NY; died 24 May 1977
	married George E. MITTEER 14 Jan 1909
	(he s/o Edward B. MITTEER and Fannie GILLETT)
	(he born 24 May 1884 Ellenville, NY; died April 1976 Ellenville, Ulster, NY
4375. Leah A.	born May 1887 Liberty, NY; died ____
	married Orville Warren COLLINS 15 June 1910; he was an undertaker
	(he s/o Warren N. COLLINS and Nora Marie WELLER)
	(he born 15 July 1886; died Dec 1978 Glens Falls, NY)
	Child: Katherine-10 COLLINS born ca 1911

3594. LILLIE / LILLIAN B-8 CURREY, daughter of Gabriel Francis-7 CURREY (Cynthia-6 BOWKER; Daniel-5; Silas Day-4; John-3; Edmund-2,1) and Jennie BYERS, was born 20 Dec 1869 NY. She married Orrin R. SHEELEY on 26 Feb 1890. He was the son of _____ SHEELEY and ____, and was born 27 Dec 1869; died 1954. Lillie-8 CURREY died ca 1950 Sullivan Co., NY.

Children of Lillie-8 CURREY and Ralph SHEELEY:
Surname **SHEELEY**

4376. Florence Ray	born 30 Oct 1890; died ____; a nurse
4377. Ralph Eli	born 10 Oct 1892; died March 1970 Camarillo, Ventura, CA
4378. Louisa May	born 16 Feb 1895; died ____
	1 married Edward HYDE ca ____; 2 married Harold GENSLER
	Child: Harold-10 GENSLER born ca 1916

3598. ALICE J-8 CURREY, sister of above, was born ca 1882 at Neversink, NY. She married John M/W GRANT on 3 June 1903. He was the son of ____ GRANT and ___, and was born ca 1882; died ____. Alice-8 CURREY died ____.

Children of Alice-8 CURREY and John GRANT:
Surname **GRANT**

4379. Victor C.	born ca 1905/06; died ____; married Dorothy L. ____ ca ____
	Child: Dorothy Lois-10 GRANT born ca 1932 NY
4380. Douglas John O.	born 16 Sept 1909 NY; died 1 April 1989 FL
4381. Donald Gerald	born ca 1915; died 3 Aug 1963; married Veronica Theresa LOBUS ca ____

3599. WILLIAM HENRY-8 BOWKER, son of Daniel T-7 BOWKER (Anson-6; Daniel-5; Silas Day-4; John-3; Edmund-2,1) and Hannah Susan SACKRIDER, was born ca 1864 NY. He married Vida M. PATCHEN ca 1893. She was the daughter of Willis PATCHEN and Jeanette ___, and was born ca Feb 1876; died 22 Feb 1915 NY. William Henry-8 BOWKER died 1918.

Children of William Henry-8 BOWKER and Vida M. PATCHEN:
Surname **BOWKER**

+ **4382. EDITH M.**	born 11 July 1893/4 NY Hobart, NY; died 29 Jan 1952
	1 married William NICHOLS 28 Oct 1912 Del. Co., NY
	(he s/o Chester NICHOLS and Ella _____)
	2 married Willard O. MADDEN ca 1925 (he born Jan 1894 NY; died 1964 NY

Children of William Henry[-8] BOWKER and Vida M. PATCHEN, continued:
Surname **BOWKER**

	4383. Leslie S.	born July 1896 NY; died ____	4384. Arthur W.	born Sept 1897NY
+	**4385. ROLAND S.**	born 20 March 1904 NY; died Dec 1979 Walton, Delaware, NY		

married Bessie DIETRICH 6 April 1928 NY
(she dau/o Jacob DIETRICH and Effie Adelaide WHITE)

3602. BERT[-8] / HERBERT BOWKER, brother of above, was born 12 June 1875 IL. He married Sarah Jane SMITH ca 1896. She was the daughter of Israel SMITH and Mary Margaret THOMAS, and was born 22 July 1875 IL; died 25 July 1941 DeKalb, IL. Bert[-8] BOWKER died 24 July 1950 DeKalb, IL..

Children of Bert[-8] BOWKER and Sarah Jane SMITH:
Surname **BOWKER**

+	**4386. LESTRAL**	born 27 Nov 1897 IL; died Nov 1975 IL
	HERBERT	married Mabel E. THIELEN 8 Feb 1921
+	**4387. LUETTA**	born 2 Aug 1899 IL; died May 1978 Rockford, IL; married Earl L. HART ca _____
		(he s/o George Sherman HART and Petra Cody REESE)
	4388. Ross	born 26 Mar 1904 IL; died May 1981 DuPage, IL
		married Lorraine Elenor GILLIS 5 Oct 1929 (she born Nov 1912 Creston, Ogle, IL)
		(she dau/o Merritt Edward GILLIS and Eda Gorgina QUITNO)
	4389. Honnor/Honner	born 23 Apr 1906 IL; died 3 Jan 1988 Los Angeles, CA
	Winifred	married Milton Carl PETERSON ca ____ (he born 30 Oct 1901 Sweden; died 2001)

Children: James [10] born ca ____; and Sandra[-10] PETERSON born ca ____

3603. HARRIET-[8] BOWKER, daughter of Orrin L[-7] BOWKER (Anson-[6]; Daniel-[5]; Silas Day[-4]; John[-3]; Edmund-[2,1]) and Olive FRINK, as born 1 Feb 1864. She married William George GRAY on 14 June 1879 aqt Hamden, NY. He was the son of Erastus Robert GRAY and Hannah DYER, and was born 1859 NY; died 9 Apr 1926 PA. Harriet-[8] BOWKER died ____.

Children of Harriet-[8] BOWKER and William GRAY:
Surname **GRAY**

4390. Seymour	born 19 March 1882; died 17 Feb 1951; married Juliette DODDS ca ____
4391. Mary June	born Dec 1884; died _____

3604. JAMES H-[8] BOWKER, brother of above, was born 3 Jan 1867 Delaware County, NY. He married first to Mary VAN PELT ca 1889. She was the daughter of ____ VAN PELT and ____; and was born ___; died ____. He married second to Rebecca HAMMOND ca 1896 NY. She was the daughter of Delos R. HAMMOND and Margaret/Maggie BROCK, and was born June 1876 NY; died 11 Nov 1904 at Rock Rift, Delaware, NY. He married third to Alice GORTON on 15 March 1905. She was the daughter of ____ GORTON and ____, and was born ____; died ____. James H-[8] BOWKER died 28 Apr 1906 at Rock Rift, Delaware, NY.

Child of James H-[8] BOWKER and Mary VAN PELT:
Surname **BOWKER**

4392. ELSIE	born 19 Sep 1890; died June 1977 Otsego, NY
	1 married Arlington TUBBS ca _____ (he born ca 1873; died 1937)
	(he s/o Chester TUBBS and Finetta GAGE)
	2 married Ernest C. BLENCOE 21 Jan 1958

Children of James H-[8] BOWKER and Rebecca HAMMOND:
Surname **BOWKER**

4393. Ralph D.	born 13 Nov 1897 ; died 2 Apr 1950; married Marie Agnes COVERT 16 Apr 1917
	(she born ca 1899/1900; died ____)
	Child: Donald-[10] BOWKER born 11 Sep 1917/18 Little Falls, Herkimer, NY; died 10 Nov 2010
4394. Elizabeth Margaret	born 30 May 1900; died 27 Sep 1985
	married Henry Carlyle GILLETTE 11 June 1920 Delaware Co., NY
	(he s/o James J. GILLETTE and Emma J. SCOVILLE)
	(he born 15 Oct 1898 NY; died Feb 1982 Endwell, Broome, NY
	Child: Ronald-[10] GILLETTE born ca 1928
4395. Jeanette	born ca 1903; died ____; married Clifford S. PALMER 10 Oct 1921
	(he s/o Seymour PALMER and Anna ___) (he born 27 Mar 1899 NY; died 12 Sep 1955)

3605. FANNY / FANNIE E-⁸ BOWKER, sister of above, was born 26 June 1870 Delaware County, NY. She married Oscar W. ORR ca 1888. He was the son of James ORR and Clara ____ ; and was born June 1861; died __KS. Fanny-⁸ BOWKER died __.

Children of Fanny-⁸ BOWKER and Oscar ORR:
Surname **ORR**

4396. Willie James	born 20 Apr 1889; died Aug 1983 NC	
4397. Roy Sylvester	born 28 Nov 1890 KS; died 17 June 1949 Lawrence, KS.	
	married Marie R. _____ ca ____ (she born ca 1899 IA; died _____)	
	Child: Augereta-¹⁰ ORR born ca 1925 KS	
4398. Hazel Irene	born ca 1902; died ____; married ____ SMITH (divorced)	

3606. CHARLES WALTER-⁸ BOWKER, brother of above, was born 6 July 1874 at Pine Brook, Delaware County, NY. He married Bertha M. MILLER 1894-97. She was the daughter of Fields MILLER and Rebecca M. ____, and was born July 1879; died 31 Oct 1938 at Walton, Delaware, NY

Children of Charles W-⁸ BOWKER and Bertha MILLER:
Surname **BOWKER**

4399. Bessie J.	born ca 1901 Colchester, NY; died 1969 Clayville, Oneida, NY
	married Thomas Lavern LENOX 7 Dec 1922 no issue
4400. Mary Kate	born Apr 1910 Colchester; died ____; 1 married Harold FRANKLIN ca 1927
	Children: Bertha-¹⁰ born ca 1928 NY; and Charles-¹⁰ FRANKLIN born ca 1929 NY
	2 married George COOK ca ____

3607. CORA LILLIAN/ LILLY-⁸ BOWKER, sister of above, was born 2 April 1877 at Walton, Delaware, NY. She married Henry N. TRIPP on _ Feb 1895. He was the son of Ephraim TRIPP and Sally ____, and was born Dec 1869; died ____.

Children of Cora Lily-⁸ BOWKER and Henry TRIPP:
Surname **TRIPP**

4401. Lelah L.	born Sept 1899; died ____; married _____ JACOBS ca ____		
4402. Eva M.	born ca 1902; died ____; married ____ GREVELING ca ____		
4403. Morris	born ca 1907; died ____	4404. Harold	born ca 1910; died ____

3609. NORA E-⁸ BOWKER, sister of above, was born 14 March 1884 NY. She married first to Fred WRIGHT ca 1901. He was the son of _____ WRIGHT and __; and was born __; died __. They divorced 4 Sep 1909 at Delhi, Delaware, NY. She married second to Charles HAMMOND on 14 Jan 1910 Walton, Delaware, NY. He was the son of Delos HAMMOND and Margaret BROCK, and was born Dec 1887; died 21 Sep 1953 at Norwell, NY. Nora E-⁸ died Oct 1973 Milford, Otsego, NY

Child of Nora E-⁸ BOWKER and Fred WRIGHT:
Surname **WRIGHT**

4405. Letha	born 20 Sep 1902 Bear Springs Mtn., Walton, Delaware, NY; died 31 Aug 1994 Otsego
	married Archie PECK 17 Sep 1921 Asbury Park, NJ (he born __; died 24 Mar 1985)
	Children: DeVillo-¹⁰ born 27 April 1924, married Irene COLLINS; Norma-¹⁰ born ca ___, married Walter OLMSTEAD; and Wanda-¹⁰ PECK born ca ____, married Lloyd JESTER

3611. SPENCER HENRY PENN-⁸ BOWKER, son of Orsemus-⁷ BOWKER (Anson-⁶; Daniel-⁵; Silas-⁴; John-³; Edmund-²,¹) and Susan Adelaide SHERMAN, was born 1 May 1876 Delaware County, NY. He married Mabel A. WOODS ca _____. She was born ca 1886 NY; died 23 Nov 1927 at Walton, Delaware County, NY. Spencer-⁸ BOWKER died 29 July 1949.

Children of Spencer-⁸ BOWKER and Mabel WOODS:
Surname **BOWKER**

+	**4406. MAUDE E.**	born 10 Aug 1902; died Oct 1954; married Arthur KILMER 22 July 1919 NY
+	**4407. SUSAN RUTH**	born 7 Aug 1904; died 18 Nov 1964; married Olin Northrup Mc CLENNON 5 Aug 1922
	4408. Howard Spencer	born 4 March 1906 NY; died 9 July1972 Walton, NY
	4409. Vera A.	born 21 Oct 1908 ; died 23 Feb 1982; married Wesley Henry GRANSBURY 3 Dec 1925
	4410. Bessie	born 6 May 1914; died 2 Feb 1990 Walton, NY
		married Marvin Jay DARLING 4 Mar 1931; divorced 25 Apr 1953
		(he s/o Jubel DARLING and Caroline DUREY) (he born 20 Nov 1884; died 17 Aug 1964 Walton, NY)
		Children: George-¹⁰ ; Robert-¹⁰; Patrick-¹⁰; and Joyce-¹⁰ DARLING (married ____ SEWARD)
	4411. George Franklin	born 22 Apr 1917 Walton, NY; died 19 Nov 1963; married ___?___ 28 April 1947

3612. DANIEL TRACY-8 " Dode" BOWKER, brother of above, was born 11 Oct 1877 at Franklin, Delaware County, NY. He married Ona Margaret MOSHER on 19 Jan 1903 at Trout Creek, Delaware County, NY. She was the daughter of James MOSHER and Sarah ALLENTONG, and was born 15 Dec 1888 NY; died 8 Feb 1963 Walton, NY. Daniel-8 BOWKER, a dairy farmer, died 21 Oct 1931. Resided Walton, Delaware County, NY

Children of Daniel T-8 BOWKER and Ona Margaret MOSHER:
Surname **BOWKER**   (children born Walton, Delaware, NY)

4412. Joseph Edward	born 19 Feb 1905; died 21 Sept 1966 Highland Falls, NY	
	1 married Daisy Iona BEISMER 14 Apr 1923 Delaware Co., NY	
	(she born Sep 1906; died 30 July 1932)	
	Child: Paul William " Pete"-10 BOWKER born 6 Jan 1927; died 18 Aug 1992	
	2 married Belle NEER 27 May 1966 (she born ca 1897; died 1981)	
4413. James Toledo	born 28 Mar 1907 NY; died 12 May 1976; married __?__ 27 May 1966	
4414. Daniel Clayton.	born 14 Sep 1908 NY; died 31 Jan 1957 Walton, NY	
	married Iva THOMAS 10 Aug 1931 Deposit, Delaware, NY	
	Children: David-10; Thomas-10; and Alana Sue-10 BOWKER	
4415. William	born 3 Feb 1911; died 1914	EOL
4416. Gladys	born 9 Feb 1913; died 25 July 1922	EOL
4417. Alice M.	born 21 Sep 1915 Rock Rift, NY; died 11 Oct 2011 Walton, NY (obit)	
	1 married Bernard O. WOOD ca ____1933	
	(he born 19 Oct 1911; died May 1969 Walton, NY)	
	(he s/o Theron WOOD and Celia KITTLE)	
	Children: Bernard O.-10 Jr. born ca 1934; William A-10 WOOD born ca 1936	
	2 married Jesse WOOD (bro/o Bernard) 27 Jan 1949 Lanesboro, PA (obit)	
	(he born ca 1911; died ca 1993)	
4418. Jesse B.	born 27 Nov 1917; died 2006 NY	
	married Florence Gransbury ROOD 9 Jan 1942; (she born ca 1922; died 1977)	
4419. Glenn R.	born 1 June 1919 NY; died 17 Jan 1998 Walton, NY; married _?_	
	Child: Glenn R.-10 BOWKER, Jr.born 22 July 1948; died 18 July 2003 Walton, NY	
4420. Otto L.	born 16 Oct 1921 NY; died 25 Jan 1944; killed in action WW2 (US Air Corps)	
4421. Orson O.	born 12 Apr 1926 NY; died 19 Feb 2001 Walton, NY; married Barbara O'HARA ca ____	
4422. Donald Francis	born 16 Feb 1933 NY; died 22 Aug 2009 Walton, NY; married _?_ 11 Aug 1956	

3613. MYRTLE FRANCES-8 (Myrtie) BOWKER, sister of above, was born 29 June 1879 NY. She married 1st to Sheridan WATSON ca 1899. He was the son of Harvey WATSON and ____, and was born July 1877 Hancock, Delaware, NY, died ____. Myrtle-8 married 2nd to Frank E. DARLING ca 1910. He was the son of ____ DARLING and ___, and was born 19 June 1886 PA; died May 1969 PA. Myrtle-8 BOWKER died 23 May 1960 PA.

Children of Myrtle Frances-8 BOWKER and Sheridan WATSON:
Surname **WATSON**

4423. Orson " Orsie "	born 7 Nov 1900 NY; died 2 Sept 1963
4424. Everett	born ca 1902; died ____
4425. Kenneth	born 13 Sept 1903; died Sept 1983 Honesdale, PA
	married Viola De REAMER ca ____ (she born ca 1906; died 1984)
4426. Mildred	born ca 1906; died ____
4427. Evelyn/ Eveline	born 1 May 1907 NY; died ____
	married Charles De REAMER ca ____ (he born ca 1905; died ____)
4428. Ernest/ Earnest	born 2 June 1909; died April 1981 Wayne Co., PA

Children of Myrtle Frances-8 BOWKER and Frank E. DARLING:
Surname **DARLING**

4429. Ona	born 26 Mar 1911; died 8 Feb 1990 Honesdale, PA
4430. Frank E. Jr.	born 23 Feb 1913; died 12 July 1925
	Death was caused by his clothing accidentally catching on fire
4431. James H.	born 11 Dec 1916 Honesdale, PA; died 27 May 1935
	Died as a result of an automobile accident which fractured the base of his skull

3614. HANNAH MAUDE-8 BOWKER, sister of above, ws born 3 Dec 1883 NY. She married first to Frederick " Bubby" CUYLE on 28 Dec 1899 at Trout Creek, Delaware, NY. He was the son of William Henry CUYLE and Maria MAYES, and was born 12 Feb 1868 Trout Creek, NY; died 24 Nov 1943 Johnson City, NY. She married 2nd to John Wesley " Wes " CRAWFORD ca ____. Hannah Maude-8 BOWKER died 4 April 1981 FL. **242**

Children of Hannah-8 BOWKER and Frederick CUYLE::
Surname **CUYLE**

+	**4432. NORA LEOLA**	born 12 Feb 1902 ; died 22 June 1993; married Harold Andrew PRUYN ca 1922
	4433. Dena Belle	born 14 June 1904; died 18 Nov 1958; married William ROOD ca 1922
		(he born 27 Feb 1904; died 27 May 1966) (s/o Linus ROOD and Mary M ____)
+	**4434. WILLIAM HENRY**	born 2 Feb 1907 NY; died 28 March 1985 NY; married Margaret LEWIS 27 Aug 1938

3615. ERNEST SYLVESTER-8 BOWKER, brother of above, was born 26 Sep 1885/6 NY. He married Vera Etta SILVER-NAIL on 25 Oct 1908 MI. She was the daughter of Perry R. SILVERNAIL and Mary Lillian CLEVELAND; and was born 27 Dec 1889 MI; died 6 May 1977. Ernest-8 BOWKER died 27 Feb 1967 MI.

Children of Ernest S-8 BOWKER and Vera SILVERNAIL:
Surname **BOWKER**   (all children born MI)

4435. Perry V.	born 29 Jan 1906 MI; died 22 Sep 1960
	married Leona M. FISHER 2 Oct 1925; divorced ca ____
	Children: Harold E-10 born ca 1929; Ruth E-10 born ca 1932 and Russell-10 BOWKER born ca 1934
4436. Chester D.	born 28 Apr 1911; died 5 Oct 1946; married Alpha _?_ Oct 1930
4437. Laverne Ernest "Vern"	born 17 Feb 1914; died 10 Jan 1970 MI
4438. Daniel Lester	born 23 Feb 1917; died 3 Oct 1974 Pontiac, MI
4439. Amos Stephen	born 14 Feb 1920; died 18 Jan 2007 Lapeer, MI
4440. Ward F.	born ca 1923; died ____
4441. Lillian A.	born 26 Mar 1929; died 4 May 2010; married __?___ 30 Oct 1948

3619. ELLA AMELIA-8 BOWKER, daughter of Albert-7 BOWKER (Jonathan-6; John-5; Silas Day-4; John-3; Edmund-2;1) and his first wife Lucinda KEYES, was born July 1859 Groton, Tompkins, NY. She married Winfield Scott DILLS on 20 Feb 1878 NY. He was the son of William DILLS and Phoebe Maria HILLIKER; and was born 30 Jan 1847; died ca 1923. Ella Amelia-8 BOWKER died 1949 at Dewitt, Clinton, MI.

Children of Ella Amelia8 BOWKER and Winfield Scott DILLS:
Surname **DILLS**

4442. Clair Bowker	born 9 July 1879 MI; died 5 June 1959 MI; married Carrie Bertha NELLER ca 1900
	Children: Ernest Ray-10 born ca 1901, died 1989; and Ella C-10 DILLS born ca 1907
4443. William Scott	born ca ____; died ____

3635. IDA MAY-8 MC COUN, daughter of Arvilla-7 BOWKER (Jonathan-6; John-5; Silas Day-4; John-3; Edmund-2,1) and George Washington McCOUN, was born 10 July 1862 at Council Bluffs, IA. She married first to Silas L. GOULD on 24 Dec 1876 IA. He was the son of ____ GOULD and ____, and was born 1854, died 1908 SD. She married second to Jasper Lloyd JEWELL 11 March 1895 at Kalispell, MT. He was the son of Francis JEWELL and Eliza Alline SHIPMAN, and was born 4 Dec 1857 NY; died 2 Dec 1945 Spokane, WA. They divorced 1905 Kalispell, MT. Ida May-8 MC COUN died 7 Sept 1946.

Children of Ida May-8 MC COUN and Silas L. GOULD:
Surname **GOULD**

4444. Silas Lee	born 14 Dec 1877 IA; died ____28 Nov 1962 Fresno, CA (a ship joiner)
	married Mabel Louise HUBBART ca ____
	(she dau/o Henry HUBBART and Alice ____)(she born 1880 MT; died ____)
	Children: Julius L-10 born ca 1809 MT; and Henry-10 GOULD born ca 1908 MT
4445. Estella M.	born March 1880; died _____ (1930 res. Weston, Marshall, SD)
	married John KUNST ca 1898 (he born ca 1871 LA)
4446. Clara E.	born ca Aug 1886 SD (1920 res. Coalinga, Fresno, CA)
	married R C KIRKLAND 11 March 1895 Kalispell, MT

Children of Ida May-8 MC COUN and Jasper JEWELL:
Surname **JEWELL**

	4447. Marshall Shipman	born Aug 1896 MT; died Nov 1983 Deer Park, WA; married Edna PALMER ca ____
+	**4448. MABEL LOUISE**	born 2 Oct 1897; died 4 March 1997 Salt Lake City, UT
		1 married Hugh Barr ELLIOT 2 Dec 1917 Kalispell, Flathead, MT. (he born ca 1887)
		2 married Ernest Dainey BROONER 14 July 1923 Missoula, MT
		(he s/o Hiran Butler BROONER and Millie Ann MEDCALF (E)
		(he born 8 May 1887 Dale , Spencer, IN; died ____)

Children of Ida May-[8] MC COUN and Jasper JEWELL, continued:
Surname **JEWELL**

4449. Lester Emerald	born 9 Aug 1899; died 15 May 1983 Spokane, WA.; married Eva Chalyce KRATZER	
	Children: Eva M-[10] born ca 1925 MT; and Lester-[10] JEWELL born ca 1927 MT	
4450. Edith	born 13 Nov 1905; died 31 Dec 1994; married Orville MC ELEVEE	
	(he born ca 1903; died -____)	
	Children: Frederick-[10] born ca 1928 CA; and Louis E.-[10] MC ELEVEE born ca ____	
4451. Henry Lee	born 15 Sept 1908; died ____	

3636. EMMA ETTA-[8] MC COUN, sister of above, was born 10 Aug 1865 IA. She married first to Reuben Otto RUSCO on 14 March 1883. He was the son of ____ RUSCO and ____, and was born ___, died ___. They divorced in 1895 and she married 2nd to Patrick H. WARREN ca 1897. He was the son of___ WARREN and ___, and was born___ died ____.

Children of Emma Etta-[8] MC COUN and Reuben RUSCO:
Surname **RUSCO**

4452. Sarah Arvilla	born 10 Feb 1884 SD; died 16 July 1970/78 ID		
	1 married George Eldridge RASMUSSEN Sept 1899		
	2 married George B. MERRILL ca ___	4454. Delta Luella	born 16 March 1888
4453. Ora	born ca 1886; possibly died young	4455. Alta Mae	born 15 June 1892

3641. ERNEST VERNON-[8] BOWKER, son of Martin VanBuren-[7] BOWKER (Jonathan-[6]; John-[5]; Silas Day-[4]; John-[3]; Edmund-[2,1]) and Jane ____, was born ca 1863/64 at Groton, Tompkins County, NY. He married Addie M ____ ca ____. She was born ca 1869 NY. Ernest-[8] BOWKER died between 1920-30.

Children of Ernest Vernon-[8] BOWKER and Addie M ____:
Surname **BOWKER**

4456. Fletcher Vernon	born 5 June 1891; died March 1977
	married Mabel Katherine COATS ca ____ (she born Nov 1889 PA)
	(she dau/o Charles Sumner COATS and Elizabeth SLOMINSKE)
	Child: Fletcher V-[10] born 28 Aug 1918 PA, died 18 Feb 2001; and Dorothy-[10] BOWKER born ca 1926 PA
4457. Jesse Lee	born 20 March 1900 NY; died ___; married Stella R. ____ ca ____
4458. Ruth M.	born ca 1903; died ____; married Guy B. COOLEY ca 1928
	(he born ca 1882; died ____) (he Supt. of Steam RR Mc Kean Rock, Allegheny, PA)

3647. ELIZABETH-[8] BOWKER, sister of above, was born 12 May 1849 at ____. She married Frederick Nelson DAVIS ca 1864/ 65. He was the son of Joseph DAVIS and Elizabeth BARGER , and was born 10 April 1846; died 9 Nov 1908 at Arthur, Clare, MI. Elizabeth-[8] BOWKER died ____. She suffered from chronic diabetes.

Children of Elizabeth-[8] BOWKER and Frederick DAVIS:
Surname **DAVIS**

4459. Frederick Acel	born 30 Mar 1866 OH; died 28 Sept 1913 MI; married Sarah Rose WOOD 4 Oct 1892
4460. Charles Emerson	born 29 Oct 1870 OH; died 20 Aug 1944 MI;
	married Myra Adessa ROBINETTE ca 1899
4461. Bertha M.	born 21 Aug 1871 OH; died 23 Jan 1914 MI
	married William Thomas CRAWFORD ca 1886 (she 15 years old)
4462. Edith E	born 8 Sep 1875; died ____; married Thomas Walter JOHNSON ca 1892
4463. Luella/ Louella B	born 9 Oct 1878 OH; died 30 Dec 1901 MI ; married Harvey Marion WRIGHT
4464.Cora Bell	born 6 May 1881 OH; died 13 March 1959 MI
	1 married Sylvanus MATHERSON ca 1894 MI (she 13 years old)
	2 married Earl Richard WINTERS 9 Sept 1912
4465. Alice Marie	born 9 June 1882 OH; died 12 July 1973 MI;
	married James Henry JOSLIN 19 April 1898
+ **4466. NORA**	born Dec 1886 OH; died 13 Mar 1959 MI
	1 married Frank FOSTER 15 Apr 1902 MI (he born ca 1884; died ____)
	2 married Valentine AMBURGEY 15 Dec 1913 MI
	(he born 26 April 1883 KY; died 23 Mar 1959 MI)
	(he s/o Robert AMBURGEY and Nancy Ann PUCKETT)
4467. Minnie	born 3 June 1888 MI; died 28 June 1939 MI; married Frank ROBERTS ca ____

3650. ERMINA-8 CONLEY, daughter of Martha J-7 BOWKER (Jefferson-6; John-5; Silas-4; John-3; Edmund-2,1) and Jacob CONLEY, was born ca 1852 PA. She married Ira BRIGGS of Keeneyville, Tioga County, PA on _____. He was the son of ____BRIGGS and _____, and was born ca 1829; died ____. Ermina-8 CONLEY died ca 1897.

Children of Ermina-8 CONLEY and Ira BRIGGS:
Surname **BRIGGS**

4468. Burt J.	born Aug 1872 PA; died 21 Nov 1938 PA; married Sadie E. SHAW ca 1897
	Child: Mortimer-10 BRIGGS born ca
4469. Rosa Nell	born Aug 1875 PA; died 25 Dec 1955; married Homer Phillip CLOOS 3 Jan 1896
4470. Esther May	born 1875 PA; died ____
4471. Mattie	born 25 Dec 1886; died 3 Jan 1965;
	married Ray Phillip ERWAY 19 Sep 1907 Wellsboro, PA
	(he s/o Rutsor P. ERWAY and Martha OWLETT)
	(he born 7 Mar 1881; died 5 Feb 1957 Blossburg, PA)
	Child: Milton B-10 ERWAY born 4 July 1908 PA; died June 1975

3653. MILO ERWIN-8 TRUMBLE, son of Philinda-7 BOWKER (Jefferson-6; John-5; Silas Day-4; John-3; Edmund-2,1) and Chauncey TRUMBLE, was born 6 Feb 1855 at Little Marsh, Tioga County, PA. He married Viola Elizabeth SHERMAN on 7 Nov 1833 at Chatham, Tioga, PA. She was the daughter of Charles SHERMAN and Mercy____, and was born 29 Dec 1861 Prince George, VA, died 15 Dec 1936 Pierre, So. Dakota. Milo-8 TRUMBLE died 23 July ____ at Pierre, Hughes, South Dakota.

Children of Milo Erwin-7 TRUMBLE and Viola SHERMAN:
Surname **TRUMBLE**

4472. George Chauncey	born 10 Apr 1885 Little Marsh, PA; died 12 Mar 1964
	married Marian Adell BENSON ca ____
	(she born 4 Aug 1896 NY; died Mar 1984 Pierre, SD)
4473. Charles Erwin	born 13 Dec 1887 Okbojo, SD; died 5 Feb 1915
4474. Albert Curry/Curie	born 25 Aug 1889 SD; died 31 Aug 1979
4475. Frederick William	born 1893 Okbojo, SD ; died young EOL
4476. Delta Elizabeth	born 14 Feb 1895 Okbojo,SD; died 1 Dec 1986
	married William H. FIEDLER 12 Apr 1922 Hayes, SD
	(he s/o Fred FIEDLER and Caroline R ____) (he born 10 July 1889 SD)
4477. Nora Otelia	born 19 Aug 1897Okbojo, SD; died 9 July 1969

3657. CHARLES ADDISON-8 BOWKER, son of William Henry-7 BOWKER (Jefferson-6; John-5; Silas Day-4; John-3; Edmund-2,1) and Jennie May CONLEY, was born 17 Oct 1864 NY. He married Isabelle TOLAND ca 1882 at St. John's, Stafford County, KA. She was the daughter of James W. TOLAND and Mary YOUNG, and was born 12 Dec 1866 MI; died 16 Mar 1923. Charles A-8 BOWKER died 5 March 1903 at Jamestown, Calaveras Co., CA. He is buried at San Francisco, CA.

Children of Charles Addison-8 BOWKER and Isabelle TOLAND;
Surname **BOWKER**

	4478. Mary J.	born 20 Nov 1882/83; died 17 Jan 1884 St. John's, KS EOL
+	**4479. JOSIE M.**	born 15 Mar 1884; died 23 Nov 1905 St. John's KS
		married Forbes M. MORGAN ca 1897 (she age 13)
		(he born 25 Dec 1870 MO; died 24 Feb 1949 KS)
		(he s/o Ebba C. MORGAN and Florella ___)
+	**4480. CHARLES**	born 6 Oct 1886 KS; died 17 Feb 1939 OK
	ADDISON, Jr	married Josie GOWENS 14 Aug 1906
+	**4481. WILLIAM**	born 6 July 1887 KS; died 2 Aug 1962 CO; married Mabel Ophelia JUDSON ca 1914
	HENRY	(she born 1896 OK; died _____)
+	**4482. JENNIE ROWENA**	born 18 Dec 1888 KS; died Apr 1973 KS; married John Browning STIMATZE
+	**4483. JAMES**	born 7 June 1892 KS; died 14 July 1950 KS
	ADDISON	married Anna Belle ROBERTS 31 July 1909 OK (she born 9 Jan 1892; died 5 Jan 1942)

3658. AMAZIAH CHESTER-8 BOWKER, brother of above, was born 7 Feb 1868 Groton, Tompkins, NY. He married first to Lois Irene ADAMS on 21 Feb 1888. She was the daughter of John Quincy ADAMS and Bettie Marion WHEELER; and was born 19 Mar 1868 Cooper, Kalamazoo, MI; died 12 Jan 1900 St. John, Stafford, MI. He married second Clarinda " Clare" Blanche TEITSWORTH, on 20 Dec 1904. She was the daughter of John Murray TEITSWORTH and Laura Josephine

BOUGHNER; and was born 3 Aug 1882 KS; died 25 Aug 1952. Amaziah[-8] BOWKER died 7 Feb 1962 Stafford, KS.. There is an epitaph on the monument of Amaziah and Clarinda which reads " For those whom they loved, they did their best ".

Children of Amaziah[-8] BOWKER and Lois Irene ADAMS:
Surname **BOWKER**

+	**4484. AMAZIAH ALVIN**	born 31 Oct 1888 KS, died 30 June 1987 Houston, TX
	"Ammie"	married Martha BALCEROWICZ ca _____
		(she born 21 Apr 1887 IL; died 30 June 1987 Houston, TX)
		(she dau/o _____ BALCEROWICZ and Mary DROZYNSKA)
	4485. Dulcie Mae	born 29 Sept 1890 KS; died 19 Feb 1975 St. John, KS
		married Harley Ray TURNER 17 Apr 1911 Emporia, KS (a Pharmacist)
		(he s/o Hamilton J. TURNER and Anna R. _____)
		(he born 21 June 1888; died 3 Sep 1966 St. John, KS)

Children: Duomo Bowker[-10] born 3 Feb 1912 KS, died 19 Mar 1919; and Kanza Rae[-10] BOWKER born 24 Sep 1920

	4486. Hubert Chester	born 23 Mar 1893 KS; died 20 Dec 1965 St. John, Stafford, KS (never married)
	4487. Elsie	born ca 1898 KS; died _____

Children of Amaziah Chester[-8] BOWKER and " Clare" TEITSWORTH:
Surname **BOWKER**

4488. Hinda Bernadean	born ca 1908 KS; died 2001		4491. Laura	born ca 1924 KS; died _____
4489. Helen Clare	born ca 1919/20 KS; died 1993			
4490. Warren	born ca 1922 KS; died _____; poss. married _____ TITTEL (dau/o Frederick TITTEL)			

3663. ALBERT BENJAMIN[-8] BOWKER, half brother of above, son of William Henry[-7] (Jefferson[-6]; John[-5]; Silas Day[-4]; John[-3]; Edward[-2,1]) and his second wife Elizabeth HOURIGAN, and was born 14 Jan 1879 NE. He married first to Minnie Almienie GIESE ca 1906. She was the daughter of Joachim GIESE and Susanna Elvienie KOLP, and was born 29 Jan 1886 at Chapman, NE; died 17 Feb 1911 at Chapman, NE (probably as the result of childbirth). He married second to Katherine Harriet BATES after 1920. She was the daughter of _____ BATES and _____; and was born ca 1886; died 1969. Albert B[8] BOWKER died 30 Jan 1971 San Diego, CA.

Chjildren of Albert B[-8] BOWKER and Minnie GIESE:
Surname **BOWKER**

4492. Arthur Donald	born 22 June 1907 Hardman, OR; died 15 Dec 1974 San Diego, CA
	married Esther M. JOHNSTON on 7 Jan 1949 San Diego
	(she born 21 Sept 1906 WA; died 22 July 1996)
	(she dasu/o Norman JOHNSTON and _____ ANDERSON)
4493. Margaret Elizabeth	born 12 Jan 1911 Hardman, OR; died 5 May 2012 Neligh, NE
	married William Fred DUEMLING ca _____
	(he s/o George Andrew DUEMLING and Rose Clara SCHMIDT)
	(he born 20 July 1900 NH; died 15 May 1988 Kitsap, WA)

Children: had 3 daus and 1 son, including Linda June[-10] DUEMLING born 23 June 1944 Bremerton, WA

3664. EDWARD JAMES[-8] BOWKER, brother of above, son of William Henry-[7] BOWKER and Elizabeth HOURIGAN, was born 23 Feb 1884 Nebraska. He married Lillian B. THOMAS ca __. She was born 3 Aug 1882 IA ; died 1 June 1961. Edward James[-8] BOWKER died 23 Aug 1961.

Children of Edward James[-8] BOWKER and Lillian B. _____:
Surname **BOWKER**

	4494. Vaunita Glen	born 7 Oct 1902 SD; died 6 Oct 1995 Hot Springs, SD
		married Daniel Jerome LARSEN 24 Dec 1921 SD (3 dau)
+	**4495. LYLE W.**	born 18 Nov 1904 NE; died June 1986 Fall River, SD
		married Marie PERREAULT 4 Oct 1926 Fall River, SD

Child: Valmore Eugene-[10] BOWKER born ca 1927; died 2004

4496. Gerald I.	born ca 1907 NE; died _____
4497. James E.	born ca 1910 SD; died ___
4498. Lawrence Stewart	born 31 May 1912 SD; died 28 Nov 1998 Medford, OR

3665. LEROY S[-8] " Roy " BOWKER, brother of above, was born 25 Oct 1891. He married Eugenia DAVISON ca 1911 at Neligh, NE. She was the daughter of _____ DAVISON and ___, and was born ca 1892 MO; died _____. Leroy S.[-8] died Mar 1957.

Children of Leroy S-8 BOWKER and Eugenia DAVISON:
Surname **BOWKER**

4499. Marjorie L.	born ca 1914	
4500. George D.	born ca 1916/17 NE; died 3 Sep 1946 Hot Springs, SD	
	married Annie May ROSSKNECHT ca _____	
	(she dau/o Gustav ROSSKNECHT and Marie/Mary Eliza MARION)	
	(she born 13 May 1910 Ft. Totten, ND; died 3 Jan 1969 Hot Springs, SD)	
	Child: Georgia Ann-10 BOWKER born ca 1943	
4501. William H.	born 24 April 1920; died July 1983 NE	
4502. Howard C.	born 2 Feb 1922; died 29 Oct 2009 AZ	
4503. Glen L.	born 13 Sep 1927; died 11 Aug 2013 Neligh, NE	

3667. CLIFTON-8 BOWKER, son of Sylvester-7 BOWKER (Jefferson-6; John-5; Silas Day-4; John-3; Edmund-2,1) and Marianda Carrie BROGDEN, was born 4 July 1871 MI. He married Eleanor " Nellie " MONAGHAN on 21 Aug 1896 at Big Rapids, MI. She was the daughter of _____ MONAGHAN and ____; and was born ____; died ____. Clifton-8 BOWKER died 12 March 1944 at Los Angeles, CA.

Children of Clifton-8 BOWKER and Nellie MONAGHAN:
Surname **BOWKER**

4504. C. Bruce	born 14 June 1897 MI; died 22 June 1978 Los Angeles, CA (single)	
+ **4505. CRYSTAL ELEANOR**	born 27 Sep 1898 MI; died 24 Oct 1984 Orange, CA.	
	1 married Edward M. OLSON ca 1920 MI (he born ca 1892 MI) (divorced)	
	2 married James C. CONWAY 20 Nov 1953	
	(he born 24 Dec 1894 CA; died 27 Apr 1975 CA)	
4506. Wesley	born 16 Sep 1899 MI; died 13 Apr 1974 Jackson, MI	
	married Anna Beulah ____ ca 1925 (she born ca 1906; died 1998)	
	Child: Audrey Jean-10 BOWKER born 25 Ma 1926; died 29 Nov 1972; married Richard Curtis ALT 25 May 1950	
4507. Kenneth	born 21 Sep 1900; died July 1981 Las Vegas, NV	
	married Martha ____ ca 1935	
	Children: Paul-10 born ca 1936; and Jay-10 BOWKER born ca 1939	
4508. Harold	born 17 May 1902; died 17 Mar 1990 CA	
	married Mary J. REID / BURROUGHS ca 1927	
	Children: Jack Leon-10 born 17 Jan 1928 CA, died 1 Apr 2010, married Bernice M. BRIDLE 1 May 1954 Los Angeles, CA; and Donald-10 BOWKER born 2 Dec 1931 CA.	

3675. CHARLES E-8 BOWKER, son of Amaziah Chester-7 BOWKER (Jefferson-6; John-5; Silas Day-4; John-3; Edmund-2,1) and Mary Clara SMITH, was born 10 Sept 1873 at Groton, Tompkins, NY. He married Linnie GOODALE on 14 Dec 1893. She was the daughter of Asaph GOODALE and Celia HALL, and was born 5/15 Jan 1877 at Lapeer, Cortland County, NY; died 13 Sep 1955 at Locke, NY. Charles E-8 BOWKER died 14 Jan 1936 at Dryden, Tompkins, NY.

Children of Charles E-8 BOWKER and Linnie GOODALE:
Surname **BOWKER**

+ **4509. MARY CELIA**	born 8 Jan 1897 NY; died 1967; married Gilbert T. FRANCIS ca ____	
	(he born ca 1893; died ca 1949)	
+ **4510. JAMES CLAYTON**	born 28 Aug 1899; died 3 April 1982	
	married Frances Marion McKINNEY 28 April 1923	
4511. Asaph	born 19/29 Dec 1901; died Aug 1972 Cortland, NY	
	1 married Mabel WYLIE 28 April 1923; 2 married Agnes M. SEELEY 14 Sep 1935	
4512. Mildred	born ca ____; died ____; married _____ CALALE of Cortland, NY	

3677. FRANK SENECA-8 BOWKER, brother of above, was born 22 Oct 1822 Sempronius, Cayuga Co., NY. He married Edith Luella SHERMAN Greenfield (as her 2nd husband) ca 1911. She was the daughter of Fred SHERMAN and Cora CUYKENDALL, and was born 2 Sep 1886 at Dresserville, NY; died _____. Frank S-8 BOWKER died 6 Dec 1933.

Children of Frank Seneca-8 BOWKER and Edith SHERMAN:
Surname **BOWKER**

4513. Gerald Edison	born 19 June 1912 NY; died Feb 1977 KY	

Children of Frank Seneca-[8] BOWKER and Edith SHERMAN, continued:
Surname **BOWKER**

4514. Winifred J.	born 23 May 1917; died 10 May 1992 Rochester, NY	
	married John <u>Kemsey</u> MACKEY ca _____ Rochester, NY (a railroad mail clerk)	
	(he s/o James E. MACKEY and Ada E. ___) (he born 13 June 1900 NY)	
4515. Marian Esther	born ca 1920; died 2006; married Mario DIEGO 30 March 1940 Auburn, NY	
	(he son of James DIEGO and Lillian SANTORO)	
	(he born 29 Nov 1919 NY; died 2 May 1994 Auburn, NY)	

3679. HORACE LEWIS-[8] BOWKER, brother of above, was born 14 June 1887 Sempronius, Cayuga, NY. He married Emma Frances CRANE ca 1909. She was the daughter of Uzal Newton-[5] CRANE (Charles Briant-[4]; Uzal-[3,2] Jonathan-[1]) and Anna Cornelia WOODHULL, and was born 21 Oct 1884 Dover, Ocean, NJ; died 18 April 1964 at Cortland, NY. Horace Lewis-[8] BOWKER died 23 Sep 1956 at Dryden, Tompkins, NY.

Children of Horace-[8] BOWKER and Frances Emma CRANE:
Surname **BOWKER**

+	**4516. ALWYN BERNADINE**	born 22 March 1912 Cayuga, NY; died 10 Oct 1978 NY
		married Clayton Jay STETSON ca _____
		(he s/o Oliver Jay STETSON and Edith May JOHNSON)
		(he born 28 Dec 1907; died Feb 1975 Freeville, Tompkins, NY)
+	**4517. LORRAINE D.**	born 29 Aug 1914 NY; died May 1983 Clark, Union, NJ
	4518. Jean F.	born 19 Oct 1917 NY; died 4 Nov 1992; married _____ SHERMAN ca ____

3687. AURILLA " RILLA" BELLE-[8] BOWKER, daughter of James-[7] BOWKER (James M-[6]; John-[5]; Silas Day-[4]; John-[3]; Edmund-[2,1]) and Frank L. RHODES, was born March 1871 NY. She married Nelson LARKIN ca 1891/92 NY. He was the son of _____ LARKIN and ____, and was born Aug 1867 NY; died ____. Aurilla Belle-[8] BOWKER died ca ____.

Childen of Aurilla-[8] BOWKER and Nelson LARKIN:
Surname **LARKIN**

4519. Leslie Glenn	born 2 Dec 1892 NY; died ____
	married Margaret/Mary Elizabeth McCLUNE ca ____ (she born May 1896 Canada)
	(she dau/o Hugh McCLUNE and Catherine ____)
	Children: Howard Lester-[10] born 12 Mar 1922 MI, died 14 Apr 1999 MO; Duane-[10] LARKIN born 1 June
	1923, died July 1976 MI

3696. ELLEN LUCINDA-[8] SNEDAKER, daughter of Morris Jackson-[7] SNEDAKER (Lucinda-[6] BOWKER; Joseph-[5]; Silas Day-[4]; John-[3]; Edmund-[2,1]) and Elizabeth Hannah MOBBS . See children (below)

3697. LAURA ANN-[8] SNEDAKER, sister of above. See children below

3691. DR. JOSEPH BRYAN-[8] SNEDAKER, son of Bradford-[7] SNEDAKER (Lucinda-[6] BOWKER; Joseph-[5]; Silas Day-[4]; John-[3]; Edmund-[2,1]) and _____, was born 20 Nov 1854 Woodford, KY. He married Sarah Sallie CLARK 2 Dec 1874. She was the daughter of _____ CLARK and ____, and was born ca March 1859 KY; died ____. Joseph-[8] SNEDAKER died 10 April 1889 at Lexington, KY.

Children of Dr. Joseph-[8] SNEDAKER and Sallie CLARK:
Surname **SNEDAKER**

4520. Sue Clark	born 27 Sep 1876; died 28 May 1942
	1 married Phillip BENNETT ca 1909 (he born ca 1841; died 1914)
	2 married Robert W. ALEXANDER ca 1914 (he born ca 1868; died ____)
4521. Bradford Clinton	born 3 April 1879 KY ; died April 1941 NY
4522. Samuel	born 28 Dec 1882; died Jan 1965 ; married Bessie ____ ca ____
	Child: Bessie May-[10] SNEDAKER born ca 1906 KY
4523. Claude Alexander	born 25 Nov 1886 KY; died 30 Aug 1956 San Francisco, CA
	1 married Mattie Frances PETTY 11 Jan 1910 (she born ca 1887; died 1951)
	Children: Edson Edgar Clark-[10] born ca 1910; and Francis Frank-[10] SNEDAKER born ca 1911; died 1913
	2 married Mabel HICKEY 13 April 1918 (she born ca 1893)
	Child: Marian Lere-[10] SNEDAKER born 11 June 1921 SLC
	3 married Fannie May MENEFEE 25 Dec 1927 (she born ca 1889)

3705. LEE CLINTON-8 SNEDAKER, son of Bradford Clinton[-7] SNEDAKER (Lucinda[-6] BOWKER; Joseph[-5;] Silas Day-[4]; John-[3]; Edmund-[2,1]) and Mary Ann BLACKWELL, was born 1 March 1862. He married first to Laura Ann[-8] SNEDAKER 2 Oct 1883 . She was the daughter of Maurice[-7] SNEDAKER and Elizabeth Hannah MOBBS; and was born 3 Nov 1860 SLC, died 3 Aug 1896 of consumption. He married second to Ellen Lucinda[-8] SNEDAKER ca 1883. His third wife was Georgia WHEELER. She was the daughter of _____ WHEELER and ____, and was born____, died ___. They married ca 1884. Lee Clinton[-8] SNEDAKER died 13 Feb 1936 at Salt Lake City, UT.

Children of Lee Clinton-[8] SNEDAKER and Laura Ann-[8] SNEDAKER:
Surname **SNEDAKER**

	4524. Maurice Clinton	born ca 1884; died 1885	EOL	
+	**4525. ERMA VENICE**	born 21 July 1886; died 13 Feb 1936 SLC		
		married Edwin Rush REEVES ca _____		

Children of Lee Clinton-[8] SNEDAKER and Ellen Lucinda-[8] SNEDAKER:
Surname **SNEDAKER**

4526-. Earl Mobbs	born ca 1886; died ca 1888	EOL	
4527. Laura Jean	born June 1889; died 30 Dec 1895	EOL	
4528. Mary	born ca 1890; died ca 1890	EOL	
4529. Bradford Clinton IIII	born ca 1893; died 1896	4531. Julius Lee	born Nov 1897; died 1906
4530. Wesley Jean	born ca 1895; died 1897	4532. Helen Claire	born ca 1901; died 1903

Child of Lee Clinton-[8] SNEDAKER and Georgia WHEELER:
Surname **SNEDAKER**

4533. Ross Lloyd	born 19 Dec 1906 Salt Lake; died 1 Aug 1989 SL; married Dorothy PROCTOR ca ____

3716. ORREN VALORIS-8 BOWKER, son of George Clayton[-7] BOWKER (Ira[-6]; Joseph-[5]; Silas Day-[4]; John-[3]; Edmund-[2,1]) and Olive HAMILTON, was born 25 Oct 1861 IL. He married Frances Jane CADY ca 1883 . She was the daughter of James Abner CADY and Margaret CORNELL, and was born 10 June 1868 Delta, MI; died 12 Dec 1950 Phillipsburg, KS. Orren V-[8] BOWKER died 25 Dec 1910 at Longdale, OK.

Children of Orren Valoris-[8] BOWKER and Frances CADY:
Surname **BOWKER**

4534. Homer Andrew	born 29 July 1885 KS; died 4 Aug 1943 Colorado
4535. Leroy Lionel	born 4 Sep 1888 NE; died 27 Oct 1979 KS
	married Lucinda WILSON Custer ca 1910 (her 2nd marriage)
4536. Herbert Lee	born 25 Nov 1894 TX; died 19 May 1980
	married Pearl E _____ ca ____
	Children: Helen M[-10] born 1918 KS; Lillian C[-10] born ca 1921 KS; Ralph L[-10] born ca 1924;
	and Herbert[-10] BOWKER born ca 1930
4537. Lillian May	born ca 1895; died 1900 EOL
4538. Cassie Naomi	born 18 Apr 1898 KS; died 23 May 1980 KS; married Jesse R. CRAWFORD ca 1915
	(he born ca 1893 OK; died _____)
	Children Esther E[-10] born ca 1916; Opal M[-10] born ca 1918; Jesse-[10] Jr. born 1925/6;
	Donald[-10] born ca 1932; and Harold[-10] CRAWFORD born ca 1935 (all born KS)
4539. Thomas Horatio	born 8 Oct 1900/02 OK; died Nov 1980 MO
4540. Clara Christina	born 3 Dec 1903 OK; died 30 June 1974 MT
	married Stacey Thompson WOOLSTON 23 Aug 1923
	(he s/o Jay I. WOOLSTON and Gerdie ___)
	(he born 8 July 1895; died 22 July 1959 Butte, MT)
4541. Francis Drew	born 10 Jan 1907 OK; died 6 June 1997 CO
	married Velma Mae BROCKETT 30 Mar 1929
	(she born 28 May 1912 KS; died 7 Jan 2002 Greeley, CO)
	(she dau/o George L. BROCKETT and Mary A. ____)
	Children: Dean I[-10] born 5 Dec 1932; died 15 Nov 1987 KA; and Donna Rae-[10] BROCKETT
	born 24 Nov 1937; died 27 Nov 1959 KA, married Merlin L. FOSTER

3731. NELLIE E-8 BOWKER, daughter of Zachary Taylor-[7] BOWKER (Ira-[6]; Joseph-[5]; Silas Day-[4]; John-[3]; Edmund-[2,1]) and Hannah GATES, was born 3 July 1876 at ___, IL. She married Harry Llewellyn Morton GLEAVE on 18 Dec 1899. He was the son of Samuel GLEAVE and ___; and was born 18 Dec 1872 at Manchester, Lancashire, England; died 5 Jan 1934 at Potlatch. Latah, Idaho. Harry GLEAVE immigrated to America ca 1892. Nellie-[8] BOWKER died 26 Oct 1977 San Diego, CA.

Children of Nellie[8] BOWKER and Harry GLEAVE:
Surname **GLEAVE**

4542. Katherine Alice	born 22 Dec 1901 WY; died ____	
4543. James	born 10 July 1904 WY; died 30 Dec 19__ Moscow, Latah, ID	
4544. N. Inez	born 7 Apr 1909; died ____; married Rudolph NELSON 9 Oct 1930 ID	
	(he s/o Samuel O. NELSON and Rosa SCHAUFFELBERGER)(he born ca 1906/8 ID)	
4545. Frederick "Fred" R.	born 18 Aug 1913 ID; died 28 June 2006 WA; married Janice Nell LEMON ca 1945	

3737. AUGUSTUS-WARREN[8] WOODWORTH, son of Jasper[7] WOODWORTH (Violetta[6] BOWKER; Noah[5]; Silas Day[4]; John[3]; Edward[2,1]) and Emeline STANLEY, was born 17 June 1867. He married Effie Mable CHANDLER ca ____. She was the daughter of ___ CHANDLER and ___, and was born ___, died ca 1939. Augustus[8] WOODWORTH died 25 March 1947 MI

Children of Augustus[8] WOODWORTH and Effie CHANDLER:
Surname **WOODWORTH**

4546. Mabel Violetta	born 15 July 1896; died 22 Feb 1971	
	1 married Edward PRESTON before 1920/ divorced before 1930	
	2 married Walter W. MAYERS	
4547. Chandler A.	born 27 June 1899; died 20 Oct 1904 EOL	
4548. Grace Endora	born 25 March 1902; died 16 July 1957	

3750. HUGH[8] RUSSELL, son of Susan Jane[7] BOWKER (Silas[6]; Noah[5]; Silas Day[4]; John[3]; Edmund[2,1]) and Peter M. RUSSELL, was born 23 Sep 1869 at Croton, Newaygo, MI. He married Lydia O. AMES on ! May 1894. She was the daughter of George L. AMES (William) and Susan Anne HILL, and was born ca Feb 1877; died 29 March 1962 Contra Costa, CA.

Children of Hugh[8] RUSSELL and Lydia AMES:
Surname **RUSSELL**

4549. Charles Eugene	born 10 Oct 1895; died 27 Dec 1964 MI; married Esther E. ___ ca ____	
4550. Archie G.	born 4 June 1901; died 13 Apr 1961 Contra Costa CA.	
4551. Winifred Helen	born 11 May 1903 MI; died 25 Apr 1958 Los Angeles, CA	
	married Elmer JACOBS ca 1920 (he born ca 1894 NY; died ____)	
	Child: Robert[10] JACOBS born ca 1921 MI	
4552. James Richard	born 22 May 1907 MI; died ____	

3751. IDA MAE[8] BOWKER, daughter of Noah[7] BOWKER (Silas[6]; Noah[5]; Silas Day[4] John[3]; Edmund[2,1]) and Aschah Mary ARDREY, was born 25 March 1869 MI. She married first to Arthur TRACEY on 1 Aug 1889 at Croton MI. He was the son of ____ TRACEY and ____, and was born ca 1860; died ____. She married second to Melvin Leslie GRIFFES on 15 Nov 1893, as his second wife, at Big Rapids, MI. He ws the son of William A. GRIFFES and Catherine STROWBRIDGE, and was born 9 Mar 1854 Canada; died 25 Dec 1935 Croton, MI. Ida May[8] BOWKER died 15 July 1959 at Morley, Mecosta, MI.

Children of Ida Mae[8] BOWKER and Melvin Leslie GRIFFES:
Surname **GRIFFES**

4553. Mildred	born 11 April 1894 Croton, MI; died ____	
4554. Ray	born 2 Feb 1896 Croton; died 8 Dec 1972 Croton	
+ **4555. WALLACE**	born 14 Apr 1898; died 1 Jan 1972 Lakeview, MI.	
	married Bertha M. ____ (she born 1908; died 1996 gs)	
4556. Ruby Bell	born 17 Sep 1899; died ____	
4557. Viola June	born 29 June 1902 Croton, died ____	
4558. Musetta Bobbe	born 4 May 1905 Newago, MI; died 6 Apr 1937 MI	
	1 married Carl G. MAY ca 1921 (he born 1901)	
	Child: Donald Maurice[10] MAY born 10 Sept 1922; died 2 Feb 1992 Deltona, FL	
	2 married Fred Richerson BOYD 5 Oct 1925	
	(he born 5 Jan 1893 MI; died 18 May 1960 Newaygo, MI)	
	(he s/o Levi BOYD and Frances MANLEY)	
	Child: George L[10] BOYD born 11 June 1926; died 13 Nov 1987 Detroit, MI	
4559. Lurene Beatrice	born 20 Mar 1908 Croton, died Feb 1988 Muskegon, MI	
	1 married Norman ENGELBRETSEN 31 Dec 1925, divorced	
	2 married Theodore (Ted) Sanford YOUNG 19 Apr 1931 MI	
	(he born 10 July 1903; died 9 July 1973 MI)	

Children of Ida Mae[8] BOWKER and Melvin Leslie GRIFFES, continued;
Surname **GRIFFES**

> 4560. Leo Arnold   born 6 May 1912 ; died 6 Mar 1989 Flint, MI
> married Thornita GRIFFES ca 1937   (she born 7 Mar 1915; died 6 June 2005 MI)
> Children: Judith A[10] born 8 Mar 1938; married Dovie F. RAYE 19 Feb 1981; and Kathleen[10] GRIFFES born ca 1940 MI

3758. FRANK A[8] MUNSON, son of John[7] MUNSON (Esther[6] BOWKER; Noah[5]; Silas Day[4]; John[3]; Edmund[2;1]) and his first wife Sylvia AINSWORTH, was born 7 May 1854 NY. He married Matilda " Tillie " June OGDEN June 1874. She was the daughter of ____ OGDEN and ____; and was born 24 Feb 1853 NY; died 21 July 1909 NY. Frank A[8] MUNSON died ____

Children of Frank A[8] MUNSON and Tillie OGDEN:
Surname **MUNSON**

> 4561. Jessie   born ca 1877 MI; married Willard S. VAN VLIET ca ___ (he born ca 1882 NY)
> Child: Lawrence[10] VAN VLIET born ca 1907
> 4562. Cora M.   born Oct 1884 NY; died ____
> 4563. Frank Warren   born 29 Aug 1888 NY; died 1932 Binghamton, Broome, NY

3760. ESTHER E[8] MUNSON, sister of above, 18 Oct 1859 NY. She married Samuel BABCOCK on __ July 1875. He was the son of ____ BABCOCK and ____; and was born ____, died ____. Esther[8] MUNSON died 1938 Groton, Tompkins, NY.

Child of Esther[8] MUNSON and Samuel BABCOCK:
Surname **BABCOCK**

> 4564. Floyd W.   born 21 Aug 1888 Tompkins, NY; died Nov 1985 Ithaca, NY

3763. LUCY A[8] MUNSON, daughter of John[7] MUNSON (Esther[6] BOWKER: Noah[5]; Silas Day[4]; John[3]; Edmund[2;1]) and his second wife Sarah HAVENS, was born 23 Jan 1869. She married Frank E. JONES on 9 Feb 1898.

Child of Lucy A[8] MUNSON and Frank E. JONES:
Surname **JONES**

> 4565. Fred E.   born ca 1901; died ____; married Leona ____ ca ___ (she born ca 1908)
> Children: Robert[10] born ca 1926; Mary[10] born ca 1928; William[10] JONES born ca 1930

3764. JOHN CALEB[8] MUNSON, brother of above, was born 24 Sep 1870. He married Harriet " Hattie " Theodora NEWELL ca 1914. John C[8] MUNSON died 29 Mar 1946 at Almond, Allegany, NY.

Children of John Caleb[8] MUNSON and Hattie NEWELL:
Surname **MUNSON**

> 4566. Ida M.   born 27 May 1916 Erin, Chemung, NY; died 15 June 2003 Arkport, Steuben, NY
> married Elton Raymond AMIDON ca ____
> 4567. Joseph L.   born 17 Oct 1918 Erin; died Oct 1997 Arkport; married Luna Edith HENRY ca ____
> 4568. Anna B.   born 25 May 1921 Erin; died 6 Oct 1995 Phoenix, AZ; married Willis A. HARVEY

3766. WEST[8] MUNSON, son of Orange[7] MUNSON (Esther[6] BOWKER; Noah[5]; Silas Day[4]; John[3]; Edmund[2,1]) and Mary A. WEST, was born 14 Jan 1856 NY. He married first to Harriet PERSONIUS on 18 March 1877. She was the daughter of ____ PERSONIUS and ____; and was born ____; died 26 Sept 1884.

He married second to Lillian A. SLATER on 18 Nov 1885. She was the daughter of Sharrad SLATER and Clarissa HEFFRON, and was born___; died ____. His third wife was Marion ____. West[8] MUNSON, a farmer and carpenter, resided on Snyder Hill (Dryden) Tompkins County, NY and died ____.

Children of West[8] MUNSON and Harriet PERSONIUS:
Surname **MUNSON**

> +   **4569. ALICE MAY**   born 31 Jan 1878; died 20 March 1944; married Victor VIELE ca ____
>   " Allie "   (he s/o Nicholas VAN VIELE and Ursula KEACH)
>   (he born 7 May 1876; died 30 Apr 1922 Elmira, NY)
> Child: Herbert N[10] VIELE born ca 1901; died 1908
> 4570. Amy H.   born 24 July 1880; died ____; never married
> 4571. Charles Clayton   born 16 Oct 1882; died ____; married Evelyn ____ (she born ca 1889 PA)
> Child: Ella[10] MUNSON born ca 1911

Child of West[8] MUNSON and Lillian SLATER:
Surname **MUNSON**

4572. Harry D.   born 15 Oct 1888; died ____ ; 1 married Mary E. ___ (she born ca 1890)
               Child: Ernest A[10] MUNSON born 11 Feb 1917; died 17 Dec 1994 FL
               2 married Emma E. _____ ca 1922   (she born ca 1900)

Children of West[8] MUNSON and Marion _____:
Surtname **MUNSON**

4573. Bernard   born ca ____

3769. MAMIE CAROLINE[8] FISH, daughter of Candace[7] Estella BOWKER (Wellington[6]; Noah[5]; Silas Day[4]; John[3]; Edmund [2,1]) and John Clifford FISH, was born 9 Nov 1893 at Alba, Michigan. At the age of 5 she was indentured to Joseph and Rose SCHWARKwho adopted her on 16 Nov 1905 MI. Her name was changed to SCHWARK. She married first to Clifford Edgar LYTTON on 22 Feb 1915 at Battle Creek, MI. He was the son of Jessie LITTEN and Annetta Jane TORRENCE, and was born 24 April 1886 OH , died 29 Dec 1937 OH. They divorced. Her second marriage was to Harry L. GREEN on _____. He was born 20 Sept 1893; died 1949 Battle Creek, MI. Mamie Caroline[8] FISH Schwark died 11 Feb 1945 at Battle Creek.

Child of Mamie[8] FISH-Schwark and Clifford LYTTON:
Surname **LYTTON**

4574. Rita Violet   born 8 Oct 1915 MI; died 10 Mar 1982 MI; married Elwood Grant PERRY 10 Aug 1933
               (he s/o Willard Grant PERRY and Kate Alberta CLINE)
               (he born 17 Apr 1910; died 1 June 1983 AZ)
4575. Bernitta R.   born 11 Oct 1922 MI; died 4 Nov 2002 FL; married John R. ADCOCK ca ____
4576. Harry L.   born 12 Oct 1926 MI; died 27 July 1993 FL

3774. MARGARET G[8] SHOUP, daughter of Mary Jane[7] WILLISON (Candace[6] BOWKER; Noah[5]; Silas Day[4]; John[3]; Edmund[2,1]) and Frederick Tressler SHOUP, was born 10 Aug 1878 at Maple Grove, Barry, Michigan. She married Carl Fuller EVANS 15 Jan 1894 at Morgans Corners, MI. He was the son of Levi EVANS and Mary Milenthia BARNES, and was born 15 Nov 1874; died 1957. Margaret[8] SHOUP died 18 Nov 1971 at Battle Creek, MI.

Children of Margaret[8] SHOUP and Carl EVANS:
Surname **EVANS**

4577. Mary Alice   born 17 Jan 1895 Eaton Co., MI; died ca 1990 Battle Creek, MI
               married Clyde WARD ca 1915 Battle Creek   (he born 18 Aug 1894; died _____)
               Children: Clyde[10] born ca 1918; and John[10] WARD born ca 1925; died 16 Oct 1941 BC
4578. Sherman Orson   born 20 Jan 1900; died June 1967 Battle Creek, MI
               married Violet ____ ca 1928   (she born ca 1910)
4579. Elsie June   born 24 Apr 1902 Battle Creek, MI; died 13 June 1937
               married Harley Everett CARTER 1 Nov 1924   (he born ca 1893; died 1967)

4580. Gola Belle   born 15 Jan 1906; died 25 Sep 1990 Plainwell, MI
               married Raymond RENCH 9 Oct 1926
               (he s/o Daniel RENCH and Ida M. TAYLOR)
               (he born 21 Jan 1895/98 MI; died 9 July 1973 Kalamazoo, MI)
               Children: Raymond[10], Jr. born ca 1927, married Katherine HILL; and Thomas[10] RENCH born ca 1929

4581. Marcille Ruth   born 10 Oct 1910 ; died 2 Sept 1968 MI; married Claude E. LAMER

3776. HATTIE M[8] SHOUP, sister of above, was born 3 May 1886, MI. She married O. Glenn MARSHALL ca ____ . He was the son of Samuel MARSHALL and Mary S. ____ , and was born 11 Sept 1882 MI; died ____ . Hattie[8] died _____ .

Children of Hattie[8] SHOUP and Glenn MARSHALL:
Surname **MARSHALL**

4582. Doyle B.   born ca 1908/09 MI; died ____ ; married Neva/Nina _____ ca 1931
               Children: Dawn[10] born ca 1932; Barbara[10] born ca 1935; Garth[10] born ca 1937; and Union[10] MARSHALL born ca 1939
4583. Lona /Lena M.   born ca 1910
4584. Sophia   born ca 1916/17 MI; died _____
4585. Rachel M.   born ca 1920
4586. Marvel J.   born ca 1930

3779. MERTON EMMETT-8 WILLISON, son of Adelbert-7 WILLISON (Candace-6 BOWKER; Noah-5; Silas Day-4; John-3; Edmund-2,1) and Mary CURTIS, was born 25 May 1879. He married Pearl Elizabeth LENT on 23 Dec 1910 at Allegan, MI. She was the daughter of Daniel J. LENT and Susanna Caroline LOSINGER, and was born 28 Jan 1890; died 30 Nov 1971 MI. Merton-8 WILLISON died 13 Nov 1953 MI.

Children of Merton-8 WILLISON and Pearl LENT:
Surname **WILLISON**

4587. Eldridge	born 13 Apr 1911 Thompsonville, MI; died 4 Feb 1962
	married Arvilla BENTSEN 31 Mar 1934 (she born ca 1913)
	(she dau/o Marius BENTSEN and Mary LINDSAY)
4588. Mary	born 1 July 1914; died ____; married John AVRAM ca 1934
	Child: John-10 AVRAM, Jr. born ca 1935
4589. Alice D.	born 8 Jan 1917; died 22 Apr 2009; married Clarence CASTLE ca 1934
	Children: Betty-10 born ca 1935; Arlene-10 born ca 1937; and Robert-10 CASTLE born ca 1939
4589. Delbert Wayne	born 30 Nov 1918 MI; died 9 Apr 1979 MI; married Eva Almira HARTWELL
4590. Merton Forest	born 31 Jan 1920 Kent MI; died 16 Apr 1991 Reynolds, MI
4591. Kenneth	born ca 1921; died ____
4592. Eleanor P.	born 24 Nov 1925; died 23 Oct 2003 Rockford, MI; married _____ BROWN

3781. JOHN VERNON-8 HARRISON, son of Nora-7 WILLISON (Candace-6 BOWKER; Noah-5; Silas Day-4; John-3; Edmund-2,1) and George HARRISON, was born ca 1886. He married Ida F. MC QUILL on 24 June 1909 at Cedar Creek, Wexford County, Michigan. She was the daughter of Hosea MC QUILL and was born ca 1879/80 IL. John V-8 died ca 1956.

Children of John V-8 HARRISON and Ida F. MC QUILL:
Surname **HARRISON**

4593. Alva/Alvah M.	born ca 1911 MI; died _____
4594. Everett V.	born 27 May 1912 MI; died 17 Feb 2002 FL
	married Beatrix Alyce PATTERSON 8 Nov 1940 MI
4595. Ivan D.	born 7 Feb 1914 MI; died Aug 1981 CA; married Etta _____ ca ____
4596. Russell L.	born 20 June 1915 MI; died 4 June 2006 MI; married Marie ____ ca _____

3782. MARY ESTHER-8 HARRISON, sister of above, was born 1 Sep 1887 at Wexford County, MI. She married Hiram Clayton WALL on 23 Aug 1914 at Cadillac, MI. He was the son of ____ WALL and ____ , and was born 10 April 1863 IN; died 16 Aug 1954 IN. Mary Esther-8 HARRISON died 20 Sep 1947 at Adams County, Indiana .

Children of Mary Esther-8 HARRISON and Hiram WALL:
Surname **WALL**

4597. Virgil Bectol	born 24 July 1909 MI; died 29 Sep 2000 GA; married Ruby HARRISON
4598. Royce Elwon	born 17 Sept 1915 Adams Co., IN; died 13 Dec 2003 IN
	married Roberta Jeane SCOTT 27 Oct 1940
	(she dau/o Robert SCOTT and Mabel WOLFE)
	(she born 13 Mar 1922; died 26 Feb 2013 Leesburg, FL)
	Children: Alice-10 born ca ___; married Larry ORR; and Joanne (Jodi)-10 WALL born ca ___, married Bill SMITH
4599. Claudie Twylo	born 10 Sept 1921 IN; died 14 Sept 1931 EOL

BOWKER

3883. GRACE[-9] GOODRICH, daughter of LaFayette[-8] GOODRICH (Jane[-7] BRUCE; Abraham-[6]; Daniel[-5]; Bathsheba[-4] BOWKER; John-[3;2]; Edmund[-1]) and Elizabeth RICKABAUGH, and was 2 Dec 1878 KS. She married Bruce Manley SMITH ca 1897. He was the son of Otho SMITH and Janett ____; and was born ca 1878; died 1948 Wichita, KS. Grace[-9] GOODRICH died 1 Dec 1973 at Wichita, KS.

Child of Grace[-9] GOODRICH and Bruce Manley SMITH:
Surname **SMITH**

4600. George Barley	born 4 June 1898 Wichita, KS; died 27 June 1974 Kansas City, KS
	married Edith Rose LEAVITT 4 Aug 1920
	(she dau/o Ransom A. LEAVITT and Lillian MAYES)
	(she born 2 Mar 1904; died 6 Dec 1975 St. Louis, MO)
	Children: Gilbert Ransom-[11] born 12 Oct 1920, died 7 Sep 2006; and George Howard-[11] SMITH
	born 29 Nov 1926, died 23 Jan 2008 St. Louis, MO

3885. ODELL TRUMAN[-9] SPAFFORD, son of Jennie-[8] SPAFFORD (Harriett-[7] BRUCE; Abraham-[6]; David[-5]; Bathsheba[-4] BOWKER; John-[3;2]; Edmund[-1]) and unknown, was born 29 Oct 1886/88 at Pittsfield Chenango, NY. He married Lizzie May HOLMES ca ____. She was the daughter of Clarence HOLMES and Sarah Lizzie DANA, and was born 16 June 1887 MA; died 6 June 1940 at New Berlin, Chenango, NY. Odell[-9] SPAFFORD died 8 Nov 1963 New Berlin, Chenango, NY

Children of Odell[-9] SPAFFORD and Lizzie HOLMES:
Surname **SPAFFORD**

4601. Lyle	born ca 1917; died ____
4602. Lila H	born 29 Dec 1918; died 4 Sep 2000 Syracuse, NY
	married Johnson Jack MOOREHAND 3 July 1947 (his 2nd marriage)
	(he s/o Fred George MOOREHAND and Edna ____)
	(he born 6 Jan 1906; died 17 Nov 1978) (1940 Census lists him as negro/black)
4603. Lola J.	born 21 Dec 1920; died 2 Feb 2008 Syracuse, Onondaga, NY

3893. ABBIE JANETTE / JEANETTE[-9] BOWKER, daughter of Samuel-[8] BOWKER (Samuel-[7]; Samuel Ward-[6]; Silas-[5]; John-[4;3;2]; Edmund[-1]) and Harriet ALDRICH, was born 5 March 1863 at Ashby, MA. She married John DAMON of Fitchburg, MA on 1 Jan 1885. He was the son of ____ DAMON and ____; and was born Oct 1858 NH; died ca 1909. Abbie Jeanette[-9] BOWKER, an amateur actress, was active in the League of Women Voters; and at one time was in charge of the Unitarian Alliance School of NC; and died ____.

Children of Abbie Jeanette[-9] BOWKER and John DAMON:
Surname **DAMON** (children born Fitchburg, MA)

4604. Rodney Locke	born 18 Jan 1886; died 1928 Hopedale, Worcester, MA
	married Edna T. MARTIN ca ____
	(she dau/o John W. MARTIN and Harriet S. ____)
	(she born ca 1890; died ____) (she was a nurse)
4605. Clarence Elmer	born 6 July 1887; died 28 Aug 1942 ; married Mary Jane ____ ca ____
4606. Richard A/B	born Sep 1889; died 1 June 1953 Boston, MA
	married Mildred Arlene USHER 12 Feb 1914 Hopedale, Worcester, MA
4607. Harold Bowker.	born 24 Feb 1893; died 16 Mar 1900 Fitchburg, MA EOL

3906. JAMES[-9] PHILLIPS, son of Martha-[8] BOSWORTH (Elizabeth-[7] BOWKER; Samuel Ward-[6]; Silas-[5]; John-[4;3;2]; Edmund-[1]) and Austin PHILLIPS, was born ca 1858 Wisconsin. He married Jennie Franklin COOPER ca 1879. She was the daughter of George E. COOPER and Elizabeth L. ____, and was born May 1862 WI; died ____. James[-9] PHILLIPS died ____.

Children of James[-9] PHILLIPS and Jennie COOPER:
Surname **PHILLIPS** (all children born Marinette County, WI)

4608. Emma	born Jan 1880; died ____	4611. Stella	born July 1885; died ____
4609. William Benjamin	born 19 Aug 1881; died ____	4612. Wesley	born Nov 1891; died ____
4610. Charles Henry	born 2 Nov 1883; died ____	4613. Dewey Allen	born 26 June 1893/94; died ____

3909. ALBERT WESLEY-⁹ PHILLIPS, son of Martha Walker-⁸ BOSWORTH (Elizabeth/Betsey-⁷ BOWKER; Samuel-⁶; Silas-⁵; John-⁴ˀ³ˀ²; Edmund-¹) and Austin PHILLIPS, was born July 1864 at Marinette, Wisconsin. He married Emma Lucy LANE on 31 March 1894 at Milwaukee, WI. She was the daughter of William Hancock LANE and Aurelia M. LISCOE, and was born 29 June 1866 Oshkosh, WI; died 2 Feb 1933 LaPort, TX. Albert W-⁹ PHILLIPS died 27 May 1935 at Peshtigo, Marinette, I

Children of Albert W-⁹ PHILLIPS and Emma LANE:
Surname **PHILLIPS**   (all children born Wisconsin)

4614. Clarence Elmo	born 24 Aug 1894 Peshtigo, WI ; died 29 Apr 1958 Houston, TX; married Ida J. GIBBS	
4615. Harry Kyle	born 13 Oct 1895; died 17 Feb 1976 IL; married Opal Alvah CASSETTY 7 Apr 1926 IL	
	(she dau/o Charles Bruce CASSETTY and Harriet B.PHILLIPS)	
	(she born 15 Oct 1907; died 23 July 1970 IL)	
4616. Kenneth A.	born 5 Sep 1897; died 24 Jan 1933 IL; married Alice S. PHILLIPS ca ____	
4617. Gladys Anna	born 2 Sep 1898; died 1 June 1994 Los Angeles, CA	
4618. Harold	born 12 May 1901; died 18 Apr 1975 Sweet Home, OR	
4619. Doris Susie	born 19 Apr 1903; died 1993 Tacoma , WA	
	1 married Clifford A. SEARL ca ____ ; 2 married Ivan SMITH ca ____	
4620. Avis M.	born 24 Jan 1905; died 8 Oct 1997 Tacoma, WA	

3929. MINNIE MABLE-⁹ LANE, daughter of Valesta Druscilla-⁸ BOWKER (Alexander-⁷; Jonathan-⁶; Solomon-⁵; John-⁴ˀ ³ˀ ²; Edmund-¹) and Thomas William LANE, was born 28 Oct 1885 at Barnston, Stanstead, Quebec, Canada. She married Oral Charles SMITH ca 1905. He was the son of ____ SMITH and ____; and was born 6 July 1882 Stanstead; died 12 Oct 1918 Stanstead. Minnie-⁹ LANE died 24 June 1952 at Verdun, Montreal, Quebec, Canada.

Children of Minnie-⁹ LANE and Oral Charles SMITH:
Surname **SMITH**   (children born Stanstead, Quebec, Canada)

4621. Harold E.	born 21 Sep 1906; died 29 May 1981 Stanstead
	married Florence MAJOR ca ____ (she born ca 1909; died 2003)
4622. Homer Ellsworth	born 7 June 1910; died 15 Mar 1978; married Beatrice Muriel MAJOR ca _____
	(she dau/o Walter James MAJOR and Lillian Dell McDOWELL)
	(she born 25 Nov 1918; died 15 Feb 1989 Stanstead)

3930. THOMAS EDWIN-⁹ BOWKER, son of Edwin S-⁸ BOWKER (Nathaniel Beaman-⁷; Jonathan-⁶; Solomon-⁵; John-⁴ˀ³ˀ²; Edmund-¹) and Cora H. ____, was born 25 Apr 1891 at Belfast, Maine. He married Martha Hazel SHAW on 20 Jan 1914 at Belfast. She was the daughter of Chester H. SHAW and Rose B. JACKSON, and was born ca 1888; died 3 Feb 1947 Gardiner, ME. Thomas Edwin-⁹ BOWKER died ____ .

Child of Thomas Edwin-⁹ BOWKER and Martha SHAW:
Surname **BOWKER**

4623. Martha Elizabeth	born 21 Apr 1917 Belfast; died ____	Child: Joanne -¹¹ HUGHES born ca ____
	married Clifton L. HUGHES 17 Mar 1939 Belfast, Maine	
	(he born ca 1906; died 4 Aug 1976 Augusta, ME)	

3934. HOWARD RAY/ROY-⁹ THRASHER, son of Mary Elizabeth-⁸ HINCKLEY (Mary-⁷ BOWKER; George-⁶; Jotham-⁵; John-⁴ˀ³ˀ²; Edmund-¹) and Harrison Orcutt THRASHER, was born 30 Apr 1886 MA. He married Mabel Sumner BARNES on 4 May 1910 ar Hardwick, MA. She was the daughter of Willard BARNES and Clariette ____; and was born ca 1890; died ____ .

Children of Howard-⁹ THRASHER and Mabel BARNES;
Surname **THRASHER**

4625. Mary Clariette	born 2 Feb 1911; died 8 June 1993; married Joseph Berry ROBINSON ca 1936
	(he born ca 1911; died 24 Feb 1984 Dennisport, MA)
	(he s/o Joseph S. ROBINSON and Ora Miranda BERRY)
	Child: Joseph H-¹¹ ROBINSON born ca 1938
4626. Alice/Alyce	born 5 Dec 1912 MA; died 27 Aug 1989 W. Springfield, MA
	married _____ GODDARD ca ____
4627. Edith Lucinda	born 9 Aug 1915 MA; died 19 Aug 2001
	married John Warner ROBINSON (brother of above) ca ____ (he born ca 1913)
	Children: John H-¹¹ born ca 1936; and William R-¹¹ ROBINSON born va 1938
4628. Leon C.	born 30 Apr 1926 MA; died 26 June 2008 MA.

BOWKER
The Ninth American Generation

3937. ROBERT WALLACE[-9] SCOTT, son of Harriet[-8] BOWKER (Luke Freeman[-7]; George[-6]; Jotham[-5]; John[-4;3;2]; Edmund[-1]) and Maxwell Osmer/Osman SCOTT, was born 3 June 1887 MA. He married Annie LAYTON on 3 June 1912 MA. She was the daughter of William Irvin LAYTON and Mary E ___, and was born ____FL; died ____. Robert W[-9] SCOTT died 10 Dec 1973.

Children of Robert W[-9] SCOTT and Annie LAYTON:
Surname **SCOTT**

4629. David (?)	born ca 1913; died ____	
4630. Harold	born ca 1914; died ____	
4631. Robert W., Jr.	born ca 1915; died ____	
4632. Mildred	born 1 Jan 1916 MA; died 12 June 1998 FL	
	married Arnold HARWOOD ca _____	Child: Sylvia[-11] HARWOOD born ca 1933

3943. FANNIE L[-9] BOWKER, daughter of Lyman Howe[-8] BOWKER (Levi[-7]; Gideon[-6]; Antipas[-5]; Josiah[-4]; John[-3;2]; Edmund[-1]) and Elizabeth SMITH, was born May 1842 NH. She married Martin LARUE on 16 Feb 1865 at Rock Island, IL. He was the son of ___ LARUE and ____; and was bornnca 1838 NY; died ____. Fannie L[-9] BOWKER died 0 Mar 1928 Eldora, Hardin, IA.

Children of Fannie L[-9] BOWKER and Martin LARUE:
Surname **LARUE**

	4633. Edward	born 1868; died ____
+	4634. **MAUDE E.**	born ca 1869 Eldora, Hardin, IA; died 1 Dec 1946 Eldora, IA
		married Christopher Nicholas SCHWARCK ca ____
		(he s/o John Peter SCHWARCK and Hannah Mary Christine FREDVORST)
		(he born ca 1862; died 1945)
	4635. Elizabeth " Lizzie "	born 3 Aug 1873 DeKalb, IL; died 8 Sep 1915 Eldora, IA
		marred Arthur HUEN 1 Dec 1895 (he born 1869; died 1965)
	Children: Inez Estelle[-11] (1896-1990) and Ralph Glen[-11] HUEN (1901-1979)	
	4636. Burton	born 9 Oct 1873 Port Byron, IL; died ____; married Cordelia HECKMAN ca 1900
	4637. Cora	born ca 1878 IL; died ____ 4638. Forest born ca 1880 IL; died ____

3944. CHARLES WILSON[-9] BOWKER, brother of above, was born 3 Oct 1845 NH. He married Mary Jane PICKLE 14 Aug 1869 at Swanton, VT. She was the daughter of Abraham PICKLE and Fanny SWEETSBURGH, and was born 17 June 1849 Potton, Quebec, Canada; died 14 Feb 1924 Mansonville, Quebec, Canada. Charles W[-9] died 21 Oct 1928 at Mansonville, QUE.

Children of Charles W[-9] BOWKER and Mary Jane PICKLE:
Surname **BOWKER**   (children born Quebec, Canada)

	4639. Blanche Aurora	born 9 Nov 1870; 17 April 1953
		married Harry Leon GALE 18 Sep 1895 (he born ca 1871; died 1962)
	4640. Archibald W.	born ca 1874; died ____
	4641. Annie Louise Winifred	born 17 Dec 1875; died ____
	4642. Charles Edward	born Sep 1880; died ____
+	4643. **HARRY MILTON**	born 1 Mar 1886; died 6 June 1925 Montreal, Quebec
		married Marion Monroe SAFFORD on 25 June 1919 at Brome, Quebec
		(she was born ca 1891; died 1944)
	4644. Larry/Lawrence	born ca 1890; died ____
	Reference: The PICKLE Family of VT, Across the Border, Vol. 1	

3946. ADELAIDE[-9] BOWKER, sister of abvove, was born 18 Apr 1848 VT/NH. She married George Henry ADDISON on 16 July 1865. He was the son of George ADDISON and Esther MILLER, and was born 10 Feb 1836 at Greenfield, Erie, PA; died 2 Mar 1922 Oakland, IA. Adelaide[-9] BOWKER died 20 June 1908 at Minden, Pottawattamie, Iowa.

Children of Adelaide[-9] BOWKER and George Henry ADDISON:
Surname **ADDISON**

4645. William Durfee	born 24 July1866; died 25 Oct 1935 Manning, IA
4646. Kitty Clyde	born 12 Mar 1868 IA; died 3 Aug 1888 Oakland, IA
4647. Mary Ellen	born ca 1870 IA; died 1958 Waterloo, IA
4648. Cordelia	born 12 Feb 1871 Nevada, IA; died 8 May 1956
	married Isaac Oliver SMITH 19 Feb 1888 IA
4649. Chester S.	born 15 Nov 1872 IA; died 2 Apr 1930

Children of Adelaide-[9] BOWKER and George Henry ADDISON, continued:
Surname **ADDISON**

4650.	Fannie Eliza	born ca 1875 IA; died 2 July 1959 Colorado Springs, CO
4651.	George Harrison	born 8 Aug 1878 IA; died 15 Oct 1956 Oakland, Pottawattamie, IA
4652.	Desvenia Darrell (m)	born 3 May 1881; died 18 Feb 1970 Council Bluffs, IA
4653.	LeRoy R.	born 5 May 1883; died 14 Sep 1905
4654.	Charles Lyman	born 16 Mar 1889 Walnut, IA; died 13 Aug 1981 Omaha, Nebraska

3958. CLAUDINE-[9] BOWKER, daughter of Levi-[8] BOWKER (Levi-[7]; Gideon-[6]; Antipas-[5]; Josiah-[4]; John-[3;2]; Edmund-[1]) and Parthena HARTSHORN, was born 3 Dec 1859 IL. She married John L. CURRY 2 Oct 1886 Chicago, IL. He was the son of ____ CURRY and ____, and was born ca 1853 Chicago, IL; died ____. Claudine-[9] BOWKER died 8 Oct 1936 IL.

Children of Claudine-[9] BOWKER and John L. CURRY:
Surname **CURRY**

4655.	Charles Burton	born 18 Aug 1887 IL; died ____; married Lillian ____ ca ____
4656.	Laura M.	born May 1890; died ____
4657.	Alice L.	born Sept 1891; died ____
4658.	William Bradley	born 3 Sep 1893; died 26 July 1959 Los Angeles, CA
4659.	Catherine P.	born Jan 1897 IL; died ____

3960. MITCHELL HARVEY-[9] BOWKER, son of Roswell-[8] BOWKER (Levi-[7]; Gideon-[6]; Antipas-[5]; Josiah-[4]; John-[3,2;] Edmund-[1]) and Jane BLAKESLEE, was born 24 Nov 1845 at Lunenburg, VT. He married first to Laura Permelia BROOKS on 1 Nov 1867 at Lunenburg. She was the daughter of Jonah BROOKS and Sophronia BRADFORD, and was born 12 Apr 1841 Lunenburg, VT; died 7 Oct 1895 Whitefield, Coos County, NH. He married second to Annie WHITTAKER on 9 Nov 1899 at Whitefield. She was the daughter of _____ WHITTAKER and ____; and was born ca 1866 Durham, Province of Quebec, Canada; died ____. Mitchell-[9] BOWKER died of apoplexy on 9 Oct 1935 at Whitefield, NH.

Childreen of Mitchell-[9] BOWKER and Laura BROOKS:
Surname **BOWKER**

4660.	Charles Harvey	born 20 March 1870 Lisbon, NH; died ____; married Bertha A. LIBBEY 24 Sep 1891
4661.	Edgar Marshall	born 18 Apr 1876 Lisbon, NH; died 19 Apr 1958

                  1 married Marie H. HALLIGAN 30 Aug 1904 Boston, MA
        Children: Bradford Mitchell-[11] born 27 Jan 1906, died 15 Nov 1996, married Henriette JEANERET
            21 Apr 1934; and Robert E-[11] BOWKER born ca 1913, died 1989
                  2 married Ernestine DOMENICO 11 Oct 1953

3966. CAPT. HUGH / HUBERT DEMAREST-[9] BOWKER, son of Franklin-[8] BOWKER (Rice-[7]; Gideon-[6]; Antipas-[5]; Josiah-[4;] John-[3,2]; Edmund-[1]) was born 14 Aug 1843 Sullivan, OH. He married Susan GORDON Smith on 25 Nov 1867 Piscataway, NJ. She was the daughter of _____ and ____; and was born 5 Dec 1849 Piscataway, NJ; died 31 Mar 1932 at Chicago, IL. Hugh-[9] BOWKER died 14 Jan 1927 Chicago, IL.

Children of Hugh-[9] BOWKER and " Susie " GORDON:
Surname **BOWKER**

4662.	Madge	born ____; died 6 Nov 1900 Chicago, IL ***
		married Clarence Buckley BEARDSLEY ca _____
4663-.	Hugh, Jr.	born ca 1869; died ____
4664.	Randolph E.	born 24 Aug 1872 IL; died 7 Dec 1936 Chicago, IL
		married Katherine S _____ ca _____ (she born Mar 1876 IL)

        Children: Virginia-[11] born July 1898 IL; Dorothy-[11] born ca 1901 IL, married ____ NELSON; and
                Ruth-[11] born ca 1902, married ____ GRACE

+	**4665. CORINNE LADD**	born 7 Feb 1874 Cleveland, OH.,; died 29 Mar 1967 Chicago
		married Herbert Alexander HULLIGAN 26 Apr 1897 Chicago, IL
		(he s/o William HULLIGAN and Fannie Elizabeth LORD)
		(he born ca 1867; died 16 Mar 1906)
	4666. Ernest G.	born ca 1880; died ____ Child: Corinne-[11] BOWKER born ca 1909
		married Laura C. PAETZOLD/PATZOLD 13 Oct 1906 Chicago, IL
		(she dau/o Carl Herman PAETZOLD and Bertha WOLF)
		she born 16 Jan 1881; died Jan 1973)

BOWKER
The Ninth American Generation

*** Article in the 7 Nov 1900 Davenport Republican (Davenport, Iowa)
SHOT WIFE BY ACCIDENT
Clarence Buckley BEARDSLEY,
a Wealthy Chicago Man, Kills His Wife

" Chicago, Nov 6 – By the accidental discharge of a revolver last night, Clarence Buckley BEARDSLEY, a man of wealth and well known in the city's business circles, shot and killed his wife, Madge BOWKER Beardsley. The accident occurred in the family apartment at the MACKINTOSH, 370 Superior St. The victim, on receiving the shot, fell to the floor with a scream, and was dragged up by her husband to die in his arms.

In handling the revolver from which the bullet made the fatal wound, Mr. BEARDSLEY was endeavoring to instruct her how to frighten away any burglars who might prowl about the house during his absence on a business trip which he was on the point of making to the Pacific slope. He had removed the cartridges, had showed her how to hold the weapon, then replaced the bullets, and had started across the room to put the revolver in a bedroom closet, when there was a click, flash of fire, and his wife fell to the floor with the cry: *Oh, my back* ! As was found later, the bullet had lodged just above the heart, and within ten minutes death came. "

3970. HERBERT ALVIN-[9] PERSONS, son of Martha J-[8] BOWKER (Rice-[7]; Gideon-[6]; Antipas-[5]; Josiah-[4]; John-[3,2]; Edmund-[1]) and Anson D. PERSONS, was born 5 Nov 1841 at Sullivan, Ashland, Ohio. He married Laura Jane NEWTON on 4 Feb 1866. She was the daughter of Isaac Luther NEWTON and Sarah Ann LAVANWAY, and was born 1 March 1848; died 5 Jan 1929. Herbert Alvin-[9] PERSONS died 2 Dec 1916 at Homerville, Medina, OH.

Children of Herbert Alvin-[9] PERSONS and Laura Jane NEWTON:
Surname **PERSONS**

4667. Walter Laverne	born 28 Feb 1868 Sullivan, OH; died 3 Nov 1943 Oberlin, OH	
	married Emma BEHR ca ____	
4668. Charles William	born 5 Nov 1869; died 31 Dec 1952 OH	
	married Mary Julia HATHAWAY 19 Oct 1899	
4669. Harland G.	born 26 July 1871; died 25 Aug 1871	EOL
4670. Flora E.	born 25 Aug 1875; died 30 Nov 1961;	
	married Bert R. MAYES 23 Oct 1901 OH	
4671. Orvis Allen	born 13 Apr 1878 Oberlin, OH; died Dec 1945 Washington, DC	
	married Rozzie Lois BRAINARD 25 Jan 1896	
4672. Luella Jeanette	born 7 Oct 1880; died 6 Feb 1951	
	married Winfred/Winferd Randolph DALZELL 2 Jan 1907	
+ **4673. MARTHA A.**	born Jan 1887; died 8 June 1958; married Orva Otho GARVER ca 1916	

3975. EDMUND HEARD-[9] BOWKER, son of Lewis Leander-[8] BOWKER (Lyman James-[7]; Gideon-[6]; Antipas-[5]; Josiah-[4]; John-[3,2]; Edmund-[1]) and Lucy HEARD, was born 27 June 1849, Sawyerville, Quebec, Canada. He married Lucy M. FERGUSON ca 1870. She was the daughter of ____ FERGUSON and ____, and was born ____, died ____. Edmund Heard-[9] BOWKER died 9 Apr 1929 Corinth, NY.

Children of Edmund-[9] BOWKER and Lucy FERGUSON:
Surname **BOWKER**

+ **4674. CORA LOUISE**	born 25 Dec 1871 East Springfield, NY; died 5 Oct 1968	
	married Mark Abram HOLLISTER ca 1891	(he born ca 1864 NY)
4675. Frederick	born 1886 Springfield, NY; died 1888 Springfield	

3976. LYMAN JAMES-[9] BOWKER, brother of above, was born 5 July 1853 Quebec, Canada.. He married Clarinda Lenora HARVEY ca 1874. She was the daughter of ____ HARVEY and ____; and was born 9 Apr 1853; died 6 Nov 1919. Lyman James-[9] BOWKER died 22 Mar 1924 Sawyerville, Quebec, Canada.

Children of Lyman James-[9] BOWKER and Clarinda HARVEY:
Surname **BOWKER**

4676. Esther A. J.	born Sept 1875; died 12 Aug 1889 Sawyerville, QC
4677. Lucy Minerva	born 3 Apr 1880; died 28 Aug 1951; married Walter W. SHERMAN 23 Dec 1900 QC
Child: Marion-[11] SHERMAN born June 1907	
+ **4678. ELWIN LEWIS**	born 27 June 1884; died 25 Nov 1959; married Minnie Arletta SMITH ca ____
	(she born ca 1885; died 1941)

BOWKER
The Ninth American Generation

3978. HERBERT RICE-9 BOWKER, brother of above, was born 1 Dec 1857 QC. He married first to Ormesinda " Sinda " Cornelia FARNSWORTH on 9 Oct 1888 at Sawyerville, QC. She was the daughter of David Albert FARNSWORTH and Nancy Sophia STEVENS, and was born 30 May 1861; died 17 Jan 1897 QC. He married second to Jennie DRAPER on 29 Dec 1897 QC. She was the daughter of Alfred DRAPER and Mary GLIDDEN; and was born 26 Dec 1862 Compton, QC; died 1929. Herbert Rice9 BOWKER died 16 May 1950.

Children of Herbert Rice-9 BOWKER and Ormesinda FARNSWORTH:
Surname **BOWKER**

    4679. Edmund Heard   born 13 Sep 1891; died 23 Oct 1973; married Naomi Mabel GILMAN 6 Sep 1917
                                (she dau/o Lewis Eugene GILMAN and Mary Ann CAMPBELL)
                                (she born 31 Aug 1897 NH; died 7 Dec 1985 Belleville, Ontario, Canada)
                        Child: Evelyn Erma-11 born 1 May 1923 Canada

+   **4680. AUSTIN STEVENS**   born 10 Aug 1896 Sawyerville, QC; died 30 July 1990 North Hatley, QC
                                married Ruth Ethel GILMAN 8 Mar 1922   (sister of above)
                                (she born 11 Dec 1899; died 11 Nov 1989)

Child of Herbert Rice-9 BOWKER and Jennie DRAPER:
Surname **BOWKER**

    4681. Edna Mary   born 8 Jan 1899 QC; died 24 Mar 1993 Huntingville
                                married Ernest Gilbert MIDDLEMISS ca ____   (he born ca 1889; died 1965)

3986. LEWIS / LOUIS L-9 BOWKER, son of Lewis Fales-8 BOWKER (John Pierson-7; Oliver-6; Ephraim-5; Josiah-4; John-3,2; Edmund-1) and his first wife, Ann DARROW, was born 31 Oct 1840 NY. He married Mary J. TURNER ca 1867. She was the daughter of ____ TURNER and ____; and was born 22 Apr 1847 Walpole, MA; died ____. Louis-9 BOWKER died ca 1923.

Children of Louis9 BOWKER and Mary J. TURNER:
Surname **BOWKER**

    4682. Willard L.   born 2 Oct 1867 Walpole, MA; died ca 1932
                                married Rose BELLINGHAM ca 1901
                                (she dau/o Robert BELLINGHAM and Hannah) (she born Jan 1880 WI; died 1942)
                        Child: Louis L-11 BOWKER born 6 Aug 1902 NH, died 10 Feb 1998 Shrewsbury, MA, married Elizabeth
                                MORSE ca 1924

3989. JESSIE LYMAN-9 BOWKER, brother of above, daughter of Lewis Fales-8 BOWKER (John Pierson-7; Oliver-6; Ephraim-5; Josiah-4; John-3,2; Edmund-1) and Sarah Ann MELCHER, was born 14 Apr 1856 MA. She married Walter Hunnewell STEARNS, Jr. on 30 June 1875. Jessie Lyman-9 BOWKER died 29 Jan 1915.

Children of Jessie Lyman-9 BOWKER and Walter STEARNS, Jr.
Surname **STEARNS**

    4683. Herbert Chester   born 1876; died 1933   4685. Ella Bowker born ca 1879; died ____
    4684. Walter Alston   born 1878; died ___   4686. Roger Ernest born 1883; died 1913

4041. GLADYS E-9 WENTWORTH, daughter of Clara B-8 FORBUSH (Ephraim-7; Daniel-6; James-5; David-4; Martha-3 BOWKER; John-2; Edmund-1) and Charles Hosea WENTWORTH, was born Feb 1890 NH. She married Elijah H. FOGG on 16 Oct 1911 at Lancaster, NH. He was the son of Lester Delmont FOGG and Emma F. RIMS/RINES; and was born 1881 NH; died June 1971 Guildhall, VT. Gladys-9 WENTWORTH died ____.

Children of Gladys-9 WENTWORTH and Elijah FOGG:
Surname **FOGG**

    4687. Winston Clyde   born ca 1913; died ____
                                married Marcia Elmira TUTTLE 30 Jan 1937 Jefferson, NH
                                (she dau/o Irving A. TUTTLE and Jeanette Ida LANTON)
    4688. Ruth F.   born ca 1915; died ____
    4689. Pierson Rines   born 25 Jan 1916; died 21 Nov 1991
                                married Dorothy Alyce SMITH 10 June 1976   (she born 22 Jan 1928; died ____)
                                (she dau/o Omlah R. SMITH, Sr. and Grace R. HAMBLET)
    4690. Bernard Delmont   born 14 May 1918; died 31 July 1935 congenital idiocy
    4691. Emily G.   born ca 1920; died ____
    4692. Joanne Estelle   born 1 Oct 1927 Coos, NH; died 9 Feb 1995 Tacoma, WA; married _?_ 29 Jan 1955 FL.

4054. ERNESTINE BARBARA[-9] HOWLAND, daughter of Eldin-[8] Howland (Nancy-[7] FORBUSH; Daniel-[6]; James-[5]; David-[4]; Martha-[3] BOWKER; John-[2]; Edmund-[1]) and Saloma LEIGHTON, was born 3 Jan 1924 NH. She married Joseph Frank COMEAU on 9 Sep 1952, as his second wife. He was the son of David COMEAU and Ida Adella MICHAUD, and was born 17 May 1914 Van Buren VT; died 2 Dec 1991 Lyndonville, VT. Ernestine-[9] HOWLAND died _____.

Children of Ernestine-[9] HOWLAND and Joseph Frank COMEAU:
Surname **COMEAU**

4693. Linda Sue	born 12 Aug 1952 Concord, Essex, VT; married Patrick Herbert BROWN 30 July 1971 St. Johnsbury, VT (he s/o Patrick BROWN and Virginia ____)
4694. Barbara Joan	born 31 Aug 1953 Concord, VT;
4695. David Kermit	born 7 Feb 1955 Concord, VT; died 5 May 1975 (automobile accident)
4696. Donna Marie	born 25 Oct 1956 Concord, VT; married Robin Stacy CARPENTER 5 Nov 1972 (he s/o Leslie Maurice CARPENTER and Joyce Evelyn SILVER) (he born 28 Mar 1954 El Paso, TX)

4067. MARJORIE LAURA[-9] WHEELER, daughter of daughter of Nathaniel-[8] WHEELER (Henry Asa-[7;] Asa Bowker-[6]; Asa-[5]; Abigail-[4] BOWKER; Ezekiel-[3]; John-[2]; Edmund-[1]) and Florence F. WETHERBEE, was born 13 Nov 1903 at Waterbury, Washington, VT. She married Harold Andrew PINNEY, a violin maker, on 6 Aug 1925 at Rutland, VT. He was the son of Clarence E. PINNEY and Carrie Medina WILSON; and was born 18 May 1894 Plymouth, VT; died ca 1964. Marjorie-[9] WHEELER died 26 Jan 1992 at Farmington, CT.

Children of Marjorie Laura-[9] WHEELER and Harold Andrew PINNEY:
Surname **PINNEY**

4697. Florence Mae	born 5 Apr 1926 Windsor, VT; died _____; married _____ CARRICK ca ____
4698. Harold Andrew, Jr. " Sonny "	born 16 May 1931 Plymouth, VT; died Mar 1975 married _____
4699. Natalie Frances	born 22 June 1932; died ____; married Robert L. GAY (he born ca 1928; died 1999)
4700. Leta Caroline	born 4 Aug 1934; died ____; married _____ HILL ca ____
4701. Norma Eileen	born 3 Apr 1936; died _____ married Bernard Anthony THIBODEAU 13 Aug 1955 (he s/o Arthur THIBODEAU and Blanche LAMBERT) (he born ca 1934)
4702. Nelson Ellsworth	born 16 Sep 1938; died 16 Dec 2009 Durham, NC 1 married Shirley _____ ca _____ Children: Jay-[11]; Michael-[11]; and Curtis-[11] PINNEY 2 married Carol Ann BRIDGES Dichard 1 May 1994
4703. Robert Gordon	born 14 Mar 1943; died ____
4704. Terry Bruce	born 24 Nov 1945; died ____
4705. Lorraine Linda	born 11 June 1947; died ____; married Steven GLEASON ca 1965

4081. ROY CLEMENT[-9] BOWKER, son of Edwin Luther-[8] BOWKER (Luther-[7;6]; Asa-[5]; Samuel-[4]; Edmund-[3;2;1]) and Mary E. DARRAH, was born 15 May 1893 at Athol, Worcester, MA. He married Kathleen Sanders HOSMER on 24 Feb 1918. She was the daughter of Asa HOSMER and Belle SANDERS, and was born 24 Aug 1893; died ____. Roy Clement-[9] BOWKER died 13 March 1969 at Washington, DC.

Children of Roy Clement-[9] BOWKER and Kathleen HOSMER:
Surname **BOWKER**   Reference: History of Royalston, MA by Lilley B. CASWELL, page 383

4706. Albert Hosmer, PhD	born 8 Sep 1919; died 20 Jan 2008 married Rosedith SITGREAVES on 26 Sep 1964 NY (she born 30 Jan 1915; died Feb 1992) He was Chancellor of City University of NY; Dean of Grad School at Stanford U., Chancellor of U of CA, at Berkeley
4707. Ann F.	born ca 1927; died ____

4113. EVA MARIA[-9] HINMAN, daughter of Morgan Lewis-[8] HINMAN(Aurelia-[7] LEWIS; Sarah-[6] SCRIPTURE; Abigail-[5] BRIGHAM; John-[4]; Elizabeth-[3] BOWKER, Edmund-[2,1]) and his first wife, Harriet HESS, was born 20 Oct 1862 UT. She married Robert S. FULTON before 1877. He was the son of ____ FULTON and ____, and was born ____; died ___. Eva Maria-[9] HINMAN died 27 Feb 1934 Utah.

Child of Eva Maria[-9] HINMAN and Robert FULTON:
Surname **FULTON**

4708. Claude Owen   born 4 Feb 1877 UT; died 1944
                               married Maud HIBBARD 14 Nov 1901 Morgan, Utah
                               Children: Norman L[-11] born ca 1904; Nina M[-11] born ca 1906; Charles O[-11] born ca 1910;
                               and Ken H[-11] FULTON born ca 1914; all born Utah

4118. NELLIE[-9] HINMAN, half-sister of above, daughter of Morgan Lewis[-8] HINMAN and his second wife, Rhoda CHASE, was born 4 July 1877. She married Walter Edward PITCHER 29 Oct 1895. He was the son of Edward PITCHER and Susan EVERETT, and was born 13 July 1871 UT; died 4 Jan 1946 Alberta, Canada. Nellie[-9] HINMAN died 14 July 1950 at Cardston, Alberta, Canada.

Children of Nellie[9] HINMAN and Walter PITCHER:
Surname **PITCHER**

4709. Susan/Susie S.   born Aug 1896 Alberta, Canada; died 19 Apr 1966; married Warren SMITH ca ___

4710. Rhoda A.   born Nov 1898/99 Alberta; died 17 Jan 1928

4711. Morgan Hinman   born 15 Dec 1901; died 10 Nov 1981Provo, UT; married Mary F. JACOBSON ca ____

4712. Frank Hinman   born 10 Dec 1903 Alberta; died 15 Sep 1989 Alberta, Canada
                               married Caroline Willey LEE ca ____

4713. Nellie H.   born 12 July 1906 Alberta; died 10 Jan 1998; married Frank M. BROWN ca ____

4714. Everett H.   born 8 Dec 1908 Alberta; died 16 May 1921 Cardston, Alberta

4715. June / Jane   born 19 June 1910 Alberta; died 2 Mar 203 married Marion Beal NOYES II ca ____
                               (he born ca 1907; died 1965)

4716. Walter   born 15 Apr 1915; died 3 Feb 1981 Alberta, Canada

4717. Callis   born 3 Oct 1915; died 29 Apr 1973 Toronto, Ontario, Canada
                               married Ina MINER ca ____

4718. Katie   born 23 Sep 1919 Cardston; died 6 Apr 2006 Calgary, Alberta, Canada

4124. MORGAN LEWIS[-9] HINMAN, son of Henry Lyman[-8] HINMAN (Aurelia[-7] LEWIS; Sarah[-6] SCRIPTURE; Abigail[-5] BRIGHAM; John[-4]; Elizabeth[-3] BOWKER, Edmund[-2,1]) and Elizabeth COMPTON, was born 4 Nov1868 Utah. He married Cynthia Ann BROWN ca 1890. She was the daughter of ____ BROWN and ____, and was born 7 Sept 1875 UT; died 2 Apr 1930 UT. They lived at Alberta, the Territories of Canada, Idaho and Utah. Morgan Lewis[-9] HINMAN died 4 Feb 1931 at Box Elder , Utah.

Children of Morgan[-9] HINMAN and Cynthia Ann BROWN:
Surname **HINMAN**

4719. Estella   born 15 June 1891 Alberta, Canada; died _____

4720. Mary Elizabeth "Beth" born 7 July 1892 Alberta; died ____

4721. Frank L.   born 9 May 1894 Alberta; died ____

4722. Kate   born 1 Dec 1896 Alberta; died ____; married ____ FARYWEATHER

4723. Delbert   born 23 Sept 1897 Alberta; died ____
                               married Orra Elizabeth SILVERS 3 May 1938 Twin Falls, ID

4724. Dora   born 28 Dec 1898; died ____

4725. Adelaide   born 28 Nov 1900; died 12 Nov 1981; 1 married Leo A. CLAYTON ca 1920
                               Children: Dewayne L[-11] born ca 1921; Leola H[-11] born ca 1923; Jerold A[-11] born ca 1926 ID;
                                       Ona[-11] born ca 1927; and Gene[-11] CLAYTON born ca 1936
                               2 married _____ BURLEY ca ____ ID

4726. Orvel D.   born 3 Nov 1901 Alberta; died 19 Sep 1945 Garland, Utah
                               married Gay McNEIL ca 1936

4727. Viola   born ca 1906 Canada; died ____; married _____ PORITTE

4728. Ruby   born 7 Sept 1908 Canada; died 8 Oct 2001 Box Elder, Utah
                               married Rudy E. SCHOLER ca 1925
                               Children: Norma[-11] SCHOLER born ca 1926; and Robert Emil[-11] SCHOLER
                                       born 22 Nov 1927 UT, died 14 May 1999 NY

4729. Melvin   born ca 1913 Idaho; died ____

4730. Roy   born ca 1914 Idaho; died ____

4731. Ralph   born ca 1915 Idaho; died ____

4127. EDITH-9 BRIGHAM, daughter of Warren Luther-8 BRIGHAM (John Warren-7; Abijah-6; John-5; Lt. Abijah-4; Elizabeth-3 BOWKER; Edmund-2,1) and Susan ADAMS, was born 6 June 1870 at Boston, MA. She married Walter WEBLING on 30 Jan 1895. He was the son of Edward H. WEBLING (born London , England) and Anna SAGE (of Brantford, Canada), and was born ____; died ____. Edith-9 BRIGHAM ____. They resided Brookline, MA

Children of Edith-9 BRIGHAM and Walter WEBLING:
Surname **WEBLING**

4732. Dorothy	born 21 May 1896; died ____
4733. Constance	born 11 Mar 1898; died ____; married Malcolm JENNEY
	(he s/o Walter JENNEY and Elizabeth B. HEDGE of So. Boston, MA)
	Children: Barbara-11 JENNEY born 1 Dec 1923
4734. Walter, Jr.	born 15 Jan 1905

4148. ARTHUR HENRY-9 BOSWELL, son of Cynthia-8 BEEBE (Daniel-7; Aurota-6; Sarah-5 BOWKER; Joseph-4; John-3; Edmund-2,1) and Charles Eben BOSWELL, was born 3 Jan 1859 at Wilmington, IL. He married Lillian Matilda HILLS ca 1885. She was the daughter of Eban HILLS and Phila B. ____, and was born 3 Nov 1867 IL; died 12 Aug 1919. Arthur-9 BOSWELL died ____.

Children of Arthur Henry-9 BOSWELL and Lillian HILLS:
Surname **BOSWELL**

4735. Edna Mabel	born 5 Oct 1886 IA; died 20 Sept 1965 CO
4736. Emma Bell	born 10 July 1890 NE; died 12 June 1959 LA
4737. Evelyn Phila	born 10 July 1890 NE; died 20 Mar 1969 NE
4738. Abraham Andrew	born 4 Jan 1892 NE; died Oct 1967 NE
4739. Elmer Hubert	born 14 Oct 1894 NE; died Oct 1953
4740. Floyd Glen S.	born 23 Oct 1900 NE; died 14 April 1963 IL
4741. Clarence E.	born 29 Oct 1904 NE; died Sept 1964
4742. Levi Charles	born 27 Sept 1906; died 25 Nov 1977 OK
	married Charlotte Marcia VINCK ca ____ (she born ca 1912; died ca 1982)
	Child: John Charles-11 BOSWELL born ca 1934; died 2003 KS
4743. Cynthia G.	born ca 1910; died ____

4161. JOSEPHINE EUGENIA-9 BEEBE, daughter of Charles-8 BEEBE (Isaac-7; Asa-6; Sarah-5 BOWKER; Joseph-4; John-3; Edmund-2,1) and Helen Frances MORRIS, was born 7 Mar 1883 NY. She married Nathan FISK ca 1904. He was the son of Frank G. FISK and Nettie A YATES, and was born ca 1877.

Children of Josephine E-9 BEEBE and Nathan FISK:
Surname FISK

4744. William Francisco	born 13 Sep 1905 IN; died 28 Marc 1965 Los Angeles, CA
4745. Josephine	born 11 Oct 1908 IN; died 29 Sep 1984 Chicago, IL
4746. Nathan B.	born 3 June 1911 OH; died 4 June 1988 Tucson, AZ

4167. LYLE ARTHUR-9 WEBBER, son of Nellie Cecelia-8 BEEBE (Charles-7; Clarke-6; Sarah-5 BOWKER; Joseph-4; John-3; Edmund-2,1) and Emery WEBBER, was born 18 Aug 1902. He married Helen Elizabeth MOORE 1 Oct 1922. She was the daughter of Fred Mordecai MOORE and Bessie Winnie ORR, and was born 6 March 1904; died 22 April 1975 MI. Lyle Arthur-9 WEBBER died 2 July 1966 Niles, MI.

Children of Lyle Arthur-9 WEBBER and Helen Elizabeth MOORE:
Surname **WEBBER**

4747. Roderick Moore	born 6 June 1926; died 14 June 1982
4748. Thayne (female)	born 31 Jan 1928 IN; died ____; married John R. OPPELT ca 1947
4749. Lois D.	born ca 1930 IN; died ____
4750. Arthur	born ca 1933 IN; died ____

4183. ELINOR B-9 BOWKER, daughter of Everett William-8 BOWKER (Frank Maybin-7; Samuel Noyes-6; Daniel-5,4; John-3; Edmund-2,1) and Eva L. SANBORN, was born 15 Dec 1912 MA. She married Robert Stottler FIERY ca 1932. He was the son of Albert Tice FIERY and Malinda G. GAVER, and was born 22 June 1909; died 6 July 1974. Elinor-9 BOWKER died 1998 Peoria, AZ

BOWKER
The Ninth American Generation

Children of Elinor[-9] BOWKER and Robert FIERY:
Surname **FIERY**

4751. Everett Earle	born 24 March 1933 MO; died 11 Nov 2007
4752. Jean	born 15 July 1935; married Charles P. SMITH, Jr. ca ____

Child: Cynthia Dale-[11] SMITH born 17 Apr 1959

4210. ABRAHAM/ABRAM-[9] CONOVER, Jr., son of Lydia Ann-[8] OWEN (Seeley-[7]; Hannah-[6] SEELEY; Deborah-[5] BOWKER; Elias-[4]; John-[3]; Edmund-[2,1]) and Abraham/Abram CONOVER, Sr., was born 24 July 1858 UT. He married Elizabeth LOVELESS on 4 Dec 1879. She was the daughter of ____ LOVELESS and ____, and was born March 1862; died ____. Abraham-[9] CONOVER, Jr., a Mormon, died 18 Oct 1940 at Ferron, Emery, Utah.

Children of Abraham-[9] CONOVER, Jr. and Elizabeth LOVELESS:
Surname **CONOVER**   (all children born Emery County, UT)

	4753. Anna M.	born Aug 1881; died ____
+	**4754. ALTA JEANETTE**	born 15 April 1883; died 13 Feb 1956 Orange, CA
		married Mark Anthony TUTTLE 3 Dec 1901
		(he born 14 Jan 1880; died 10 June 1949, Orangeville, CA) (he was a CA. state auditor)
		(he s/o Azariah TUTTLE ++ and Mary Elizabeth WILKINS)

++ Note: Azariah TUTTLE, a Mormon, was a noted Sheriff of Emery County, Utah, and supposedly, on 24 March 1897 formed a posse to follow the bank robbers known as Joe WALKER and George LEE, part of the Robbers Roost Gang. They were involved with Butch Cassidy and the Sundance Kid. Azariah was shot in the left thigh by Joe WALKER and suffered problems from that wound for the rest of his life.

4755. Abraham/Abram	born 6 Aug 1884; died 26 Aug 1959
Seeley (Seel)	married Emma Ethel JENSEN 13 May 1902
	Children: Elden Kenneth-[11] born 15 Nov 1902, died 16 Mar 1982; Ray-[11] born 20 May 1906, died 8 June 1954 UT; and Harry Linden-[11] CONOVER born 5 Nov1908, died 24 May 1976 UT
4756. Clyda (f)	born Feb 1886; died ____
4757. Milburn	born ca Aug 1889; died ____
4758. Jesse Maurice	born 30 Oct 1892; died 23 Feb 1978; married Ione STEVENS ca 1912
4759. Challmer Glen (Chall)	born 15 May 1898; died 30 Sept 1955 UT; married Esther CARLSON 5 Mar 1919
4760. Reta	born ca 1901; died ____
4761. Golden Reed	born 26 July 1903; died 7 Sept 1984; married Louisa PETTY Nov 1942

4227. MINNIE PEARL-[9] BUTTREY, daughter of Barbara Elizabeth-[8] OWEN (Seeley-[7]; Hannah-[6] SEELEY; Deborah-[5] BOWKER; Elias-[4]; John-[3]; Edmund-[2,1]) and John Mc Clelland BUTTREY, was born 1 April 1887 at Wasatch, Utah. She married James Franklin DALTON ca 1907. He was the son of John William DALTON and Isabella HUNTSMAN, and was born 11 June 1881 UT; died 4 Dec 1945 Salt Lake City, UT. Minnie Pearl-[9] BUTTREY died 21 May 1959.

Children of Minnie Pearl-[9] BUTTREY and James Franklin DALTON
Surname **DALTON**   (all children born Utah)

4762. John Franklin	born 16 May 1907; died 13 Dec 1936 UT
4763. Barbara Isabel	born 14 Mar 1909; died 7 May 1978 ID
4764. Alfred Alfonzo	born 3 Apr 1911 UT; died 20 Mar 1995 ID
	married Clara F. THURMAN 30 May 1929
4765. Marvin Reed	born 1 Jan 1914; died 3 April 1976 Contra Costa, CA
4766. Belva Katherine	born 11 Nov 1915; died 31 Jul 2006 WA; married Olin Temple OLIVER 13 Jan 1948
4767. Joseph Elmer	born 3 Aug 1917; died 2 Apr 1996 Salt Lake City, UT
4768. Russell Iven	born 15 Sept 1919 UT; died 9 Feb 2009 ID
	married Marguerite Naomi. PICKENS 23 Sep 1940
4769. Riley Orvell	born 18 Oct 1921; died Oct 1969 SLC; married _____ 12 Sept 1953
	Child: John Franklin-[11] DALTON born 9 June 1954; died 23 Oct 2000 SLC
4770. Marlin Clyde	born 6 Feb 1923; died 10 Aug 1943 killed in action WW2 (Manila)
4771. David Isaac	born 5 Jan 1929; died 25 Apr 2000; married Georgia Ruth POWELL 5 Mar 1953

4232.   ANNIE ELIZABETH-[9] KEMPTON, daughter of Julia Ann-[8] OWEN (Seeley-[7]; Hannah-[6] SEELEY; Deborah-[5] BOWKER; Elias-[4]; John-[3]; Edmund-[2,1]) and Jerome KEMPTON, was born 9 June 1877 Utah. She married first to Albert Sidney PERRY on 1 Jan 1900. He was the son of ____ PERRY and ____; and was born 16 Aug 1873 Bristol, ME; died 19 Aug 1914. She married second to Arthur LOTZ ca ____. Annie-[9] KEMPTON died 5 May 1962.

Children of Annie[9] KEMPTON and Albert PERRY:
]Surname **PERRY**

4772. Walter Sidney	born ca 1900; died 1901
4773. Robert	born ca 1902; died 1968
4774. Irene Elizabeth	born 30 Dec 1903; died 1983; married Arthur Daniel FRENCH ca 1921
	(he s/o Amos Jerome FRENCH and Myrtle ROGERS)
	(he born 27 Apr 1897 WI; died 9 Aug 1929 Portland, OR)
	Children: Eugene Orville-[11] born 9 Oct 1922 OR, died 23 Nov 2003 Lilliwauf, WA; and Marjorie Arlene-[11] FRENCH born ca 1927, died 24 July 1986 Vancouver, WA

4251. RUTH JEAN[9] TABER, daughter of Charles William-[8] TABER (William[7]; Mehitable[6] BOWKER; Esther[5]; Silas Day-[4]; John[3]; Edmund-[2,1]) and Emily Thornton BREESE, was born 18 June 1893 at Milwaukee, Wisconsin. She married Nathan Mills WHITTLESEY on 9 June 1915 at Pasadena, CA. He was the son of Robert C. WHITTLESEY and Nora Belle HATCH, and was born 15 Aug 1891 at New Prestyon, CT; died ____. He was a Friends minister, a graduate of the Pilgrim Bible College in Pasadena. Ruth[9] TABER died ca 1983.

Children of Ruth[9] TABER and Nathan WHITTLESEY:
Surname **WHITTLESEY**

4775. Taber Hart	born 5 Apr 1917 Los Angeles, CA; died 28 Dec 2008 Nevada City, CA
	married Isabel Lena BARKER 2 June 1944
	(she dau/o Frederick Nicholas BARKER and Lena WINGER)
	(she born 24 May 1920; died 6 Sept 2010)
4776. Faith Vera Ruth	born 14 Sept 1918 Pasadena, CA; died ____
4777. Rev. Wellington Wheatcroft	born 17 Mar 1920 Pasadena; died 20 Dec 2010 St. Petersburg, FL
4778. Nathan Mills, Jr.	born 30 Dec 1921 Pasadena; died 4 Oct 2010 Newburg, OR
	married Margaret GOLDENSTEIN 5 Sep 1949 OR

4258. FRANK WENDELL[9] TABER, son of Henry R-[8] TABER (John Quincy[7]; Mehitable[6]; Silas Day-[5,4]; John[3]; Edmund-[2,1]) and Elizabeth R. SMITH, was born 18 March 1882 at ____ Minnesota. He married Ethel BLANCHARD Parmenter on 9 March 1908, as her second husband. She was the daughter of Addison BLANCHARD and Elosia Ann Matilda HADLOCK, and was born 13 Jan 1886 Canada, died 2 April 1968. She married first to Walter Harvey PARMENTER on 8 Sept 1902. They had 4 children. Frank Wendell[9] TABER died 10 Dec 1949 Los Angeles, CA.

Children of Frank Wendell[9] TABER and Ethel BLANCHARD Parmenter :
Surname **TABER**

4779. Henry Blanchard	born 26 Nov 1916 Canada; died 23 June 1983 WA
4780. Elosia Victory	born 11 Nov 1918 Saskatchewan, Canada; died 23 Sept 1995 Canada
	married Cedric Hugh BAILEY 23 Dec 1937 Quebec, Canada
4781. Lawretta E.	born 26 Aug 1920 Saskatchewan; died 10 July 2005 Canada
	married John DALKE 10 Sept 1943
4782. Norma Rosalie	born 3 Oct 1922 Saskatchewan; died 19 Oct 2003 Montana
	1 married Austin BAKER ca ____; 2 married Charles Lansing EICHORN ca ____

4260. FLORENCE LEOTA[9] TABER, sister of above, was born 23 Feb 1887 at Buxton Township, Traill County, North Dakota. She married Ernest Manley ELLIOTT on 9 June 1914 ND. He was the son of John M. ELLIOTT and Mary ____; and was born 9 April 1889 ND; died ____. Florence Leotta[9] TABER died ____.

Children of Florence Leotta[9] TABER and Ernest Manley ELLIOTT:
Surname **ELLIOTT**

4783. John Taber	born 4 Sept 1916 Cass, ND; died 1 Feb 2002 Cass, ND		
4784. Donald	born ca 1920; died ___		
4785. McLain	born ca 1922; died ___	4786. Elizabeth	born ca 1926; died ____

4274. MINNIE JANE[9] BOWKER, daughter of George Oscar-[8] BOWKER (Silas[7]; Archibald[6]; Silas Day-[5,4]; John[3]; Edmund-[2,1]) and Louisa LABAR was born 25 Dec 1864 Cayuga County, NY. She married Richard Henry JONES on 31 Dec 1882 at Oxford Mills, Iowa. He was the son of ____ JONES and ____, and was born ca 1854 VA; died ____. Minnie Jane[9] BOWKER died 1 Nov 1920.

BOWKER
The Ninth American Generation

Children of Minnie Jane[-9] BOWKER and Richard Henry JONES:
Surname **JONES**

4787. Addie May	born 30 May 1884 Richland, IA	4789. Chester H.	born ca 1889; died ____
4788. Clarence Leroy	born ca 1887; died _____	4790. Laura R.	born ca 1891; died ____

4277. EVA LOUISA[-9] BOWKER, sister of above, was born 5 Sept 1872. She married first to Christian Martin RICKHOFF on 3 June 1888 at Jones County, IA. He was the son of Frederick Fritz RICKHOFF and Louisa CHASE-SCHARR, and was born 27 July1859 in Hamburg, Germany; died 25 Dec 1892, Jones County, IA. Chrisitian died from injuries suffered in an accident in which he became entangled in the machinery at a flour mill where he was employed. Eva[-9] BOWKER married second to Hubert Charles UNDERHILL on 13 Aug 1897 at Cedar Rapids, IA. He was the son of John B.UNDERHILL and Rebecca STUTSMAN, and was born ca 1870 IL, died ca1954 IA. Eva[-9] BOWKER died 30 Sept 1965 IA.

Children of Eva [-9] BOWKER and Christian RICKHOFF:
Surname **RICKHOFF**

4791. Clarence Coy	born 25 Aug 1890 IA; died July 1984 IA; married Mabelle Elsie PAYN
4792. Glenn Martin	born 4 Aug 1892 IA; died 26 Apr 1959 Los Angeles, CA
	married Maude Beulah JEFFREY ca ____
	Child: Robert Charles[-11] RICKHOFF born ca 1921; died 1998

Children of Eva/Evelyn[-9] BOWKER and Hubert UNDERHILL:
Surname **UNDERHILL**

4793. Retha Loella	born 9 Jan 1898; died 29 Aug 1971 IA; married Walter WOLGEMUTH
4794. Alta Bowker	born 1 Sept 1901 IA; died 11 April 1903
4795. Forest Hubert	born 1 Sept 1904 IA; died 20 Feb 1944
	1 married Helen CRUIKSHANK ca ___ ; 2 married Fae D. McCREIGHT ca ____

4281. EVA ALVENA[-9] BOWKER, daughter of Frederick Eri[-8] BOWKER (Silas[-7]; Archibald[-6]; Silas Day [5,4]; John[-3]; Edmund[-2,1]) and Sarah Ellen WOODARD, was born 16 April 1869 Cayuga County, NY. She married Ludovico SICKLES on 23 Feb 1898 at Skaneateles, Onondaga County, NY. He was the son of Eugene L. SICKLES and Elizabeth ____, and was born ca 1871 NY; died ___. He was a farmer. Eva Alvena[-9] BOWKER died 21 Jan 1926. They resided at Venice and Niles in Cayuga Co., NY.

Children of Eva Alvena-[9] BOWKER and Ludovico SICKLES:
Surname **SICKLES**

4796. Herbert	born 8 Dec 1898 Cayuga Co., NY; died 10 Nov 1913 Onondaga Co., NY
4797. Eri Frederick	born 7 July 1900; died 2 July 1979 Auburn, NY.
	married Margaret _____ (she born 22 Dec 1909 NY; died 9 Nov 2006 NY)
4798. Virginia	born ca 1904 Cayuga County, NY; died ____

4283. HORACE FREDERICK[-9] BOWKER, brother of above, was born 30 Oct 1873 Cayuga County, NY. He married Grace Millicent EDWARDS on 19 Jan 1902. She was the daughter of ____ EDWARDS and ____, an was born 8 Jan 1882 Skaneateles, Onondaga, NY; died 1 June 1926 Batavia, NY. Horace[-9] BOWKER died 5 Jan 1963 at Deland, FL.

Children of Horace[-9] BOWKER and Grace EDWARDS:
Surname **BOWKER**

4799. Grace Cora	born 1 Apr 1903 ; died 3 Aug 1937; married Perle Frampton FISHER ca ____
	Children: Frank B[-11] born ca ____; and Edward F[-11] FISHER born ca ____ NY
	(he born ca 1895; died 1981)
4800. Lula May (RN)	born 19 July 1905 Summer Hill, Cayuga, NY; died 25 July 1953 NY, NY
4801. Frieda Bernice	born 10 Feb 1908 Summer Hill; died 7 Jan 1987 Willard, NY
4802. Hazel	born 16 May 1910 Summer Hill; died ca ____ Volusia, FL
4803. Herbert Frederick	born 12 Mar 1913 Summer Hill; died 24 Oct 1985 Canandaigua, NY
	married Dorothy JOHNCOX ca ___
	(she dau/o Alfred JOHNCOX and Edith SWEET)(she born ca 1914 ; died ____)
	Children: Lois[-11] born ca 1931, married Walter ATKINSON 8 Dec 1951 Rushville, NY- Child: David Bruce[-12] ATKINSON born 17 Jan 1953; and Richard[-11] BOWKER born ca 1936 (Cornell Univ. grad)
4804. Eleanor	born 20 Aug 1914 SummerHill; died 24 Nov 2000 Baltimore, MD
	married Milton REIZENSTEIN, Jr. 3 March 1941
	(he born 10 July 1911 NY; died 16 July 2006)
	(he s/o Milton REIZENSTEIN and Rose HOLLANDER)

Children of Horace⁻⁹ BOWKER and Grace EDWARDS, continued:
Surname **BOWKER**

4805. Harold Edwards	born 22 Feb 1916 SummerHill; died 5 Nov 1991 Canandaigua, NY
	married Geraldine JAMES 15 July 1935
	(she born 8 Mar 1917 Ontario Center, NY; died 21 Mar 1990 Canandaigua, NY)
	Child: Harold Frederick⁻¹¹BOWKER born 11 July 1937; died 27 Oct 1991 Rochester, NY

4284. JAY HINCKLEY⁻⁹ BOWKER, brother of above, was born 22 March 1876 at Skaneateles, Onondaga, NY. He married Cornelia Theodora EDWARDS on 30 Oct 1901 at Skaneateles. She was the daughter of William R. EDWARDS and Cora Jane HALL, and was born 3 Oct 1878 at Skaneateles, died 16 Aug 1966 at Washington, DC. Jay⁻⁹ BOWKER died Jan 1953 at Bethesda, MD.

Children of Jay⁻⁹ BOWKER and Cornelia EDWARDS:
Surname **BOWKER**

4806. Marian	born 27 Jan 1903 Owasco, Cayuga, NY; died 27 Feb 1987 Silver Spring, MD	
	married John Rundell BROMELL 26 Dec 1928 Washington, DC	
	(he s/o Joseph G. BROMELL and Philena RUNDELL)	
	(he born 3 Nov 1895 VA; died 20 Aug 1960 Cherokee, NC)	
	Child: John⁻¹¹ BOWKER born ca 1931 Washington, DC	
4807. Ellen Mabel	born 11 Aug 1905 NY; died 10 Nov 2002 (age 97)	
	married Howard Elmore WAY 30 Oct 1928; a researcher for the US Dept. of Commerce	
	(he s/o Harry P. WAY and Jennie PROUGH)	
	(he born 10 Mar 1898 Altoona, PA; died 29 Jan 1882 Silver Spring, MD)	
	Children: Margaret-¹¹ born ca 1931 DC; Alice-¹¹ born ca 1932 DC; and	
	Stanley-¹¹ WAY born 2 Apr 1938 DC	
4808. Irving Edwards	born 11 Jan 1911 Newburgh, NY; died 24 Feb 1927 DC	EOL
4809. Jay Paul	born 5 Jan 1913; died 13 May 2009 MD; married Lois HUFFMAN ca ____	
	Children: Anne Louise-¹¹ born ca 1944 MD; James Alan-¹¹born ca 1946; and	
	Janet Elaine⁻¹¹ BOWKER born 5 Jan 1947, married ____ MILLER	
4810. Lucile	born 9 Dec 1914; died 2 Dec 2005 **; married Edwin Austin DAVIS	
	(he s/o ____ DAVIS and Helen Leonore BARNETT) (he born 1914; died 1995)	
	Children: Nancy⁻¹¹ born ca , married ____ BABB; William⁻¹¹ born ca ___; and Bruce-¹¹ DAVIS born ca ____	

** Lucile⁻¹⁰ BOWKER was a graduate of the University of MD; resided Bethesda; was the author of a book entitled " Of Prayer and Praise " ; was a Presbyterian; and was survived by 7 grandchildren and 15 great grandchildren

+   **4811. JOHN ERNEST**   born ca 1924; died ____; married Edith Marie PAULS ca ____

4288. ELLEN ALBERTA⁻⁹ BOWKER, sister of above, was born 31 January 1889 at Cayuga County, NY. She married Edward Sumner PRENTICE on 6 January 1915. He was the son of Fred Miles PRENTICE and Mary AUSTIN, and was born 1 Nov 1892 NY; died 11 Feb 1967 at Riverside, CA (Ref: CA Death Index 1940-97) They resided most of their married life in Yakima, Washington. He was a fruit shipper and manager of a cold storage company. Ellen-⁹ BOWKER died _____.

Children of Ellen Albverta⁻⁹ BOWKER and Edward PRENTICE:
Surname **PRENTICE**

4812. Helen Alberta	born 5 Apr 1916 Yakima, WA; died 2 Nov 1991
4813. Fred Austin	born 2 Apr 1917 Yakima; possibly died young
4814. Phyllis E.	born ca 1922 WA; died ____
4815. Janith A.	born ca 1925 WA; died ____

4289. ALBERT EUGENE⁻⁹ RYDER, son of Rosa⁻⁸ BOWKER (Silas⁻⁷; Archibald⁻⁶; Silas Day ⁵,⁴; John⁻³; Edmund⁻²,¹) and William Jefferson RYDER, was born 14 April 1883. He married Elizabeth " Lizzie " FITZPATRICK ca ____. She was the daughter of James FITZPATRICK and Clara CHAPPELL, and was born ca 1886; died ____. Albert Eugene⁻⁹ RYDER died 17 Feb 1927 Onondaga County, NY.

Children of Albert Eugene⁻⁹ RYDER and Elizabeth FITZPATRICK:
Surname **RYDER**

4816. Ruth Violet	born ca 1907; died 14 Aug 1999 NY
4817. Bessie Alberta	born 30 March 1910 NY; died 26 March 1997 NY
	married Daniel Andrew MILLER 3 Oct 1929

Children of Albert Eugene[-9] RYDER and Elizabeth FITZPATRICK, continued:
Surname **RYDER**

4818. George W.	born ca 1912; died 1981
4819. Marion J.	born ca 1915; died ____
4820. Velma S.	born ca 1918; died ____
4821. Ralph Eugene	born 24 Feb 1925; died 21 Jan 2009 Greenwood, IN
	married Dorothy Judith PINEGAR ca _____
	(she born ca 1924; died 2004) Child: William Jeffrey[-11] RYDER born ca ____
4822. Luella E.	born ca 1927; died ____

4293. MABEL ROSE[-9] BOWKER, daughter of Frank Drake[-8] BOWKER (Eri-[7]; Archibald-[6]; Silas Day [5,4]; John-[3]; Edmund-[2,1]) and Helen Townley HALL, was born 22 Sep 1879 at SummerHill, Cayuga County, NY. She married Clarence E. HOPKINS on 16 Dec 1896 at Blodgett Manor, NY. H was the son of Adolphus HOPKINS and Sarah BROWN, and was born April 1874 Virgil, Cortland, NY; died 17 Aug 1923 at ____ WI. Mabel Rose-[9] BOWKER died 17 Dec 1913 at Homer, Cortland, NY.

Children of Mabel Rose[-9] BOWKER and Clarence HOPKINS:
Surname **HOPKINS**   (all children born Summer Hill, NY)

4823. Clayton Bowker	born 14 Mar 1900; died 19 Mar 1969 Contra Costa, CA
	married Gladys SNYDER 25 Oct 1919
4824. Ernest Wilfred	born 20 May 1906; died ca 1975 KS; married Dorothy YOUNG 13 Apr 1936
4825. Marian Rose	born 25 July 1908; died 21 Mar 1996 NJ; married Howard William WHITE ca 1973
	(he born ____; died 1976 Cortland, NY)
4826. Gladys Irene	born 8 April 1911 Homer, NY; died 18 Sep 1994 Perth Amboy, NJ
	married LaFayette William LIVINGSTON 2 Aug 1931 Avoca, NY
	(he born 1 Dec 1905 Hornell, NY; died 31 Aug 1973 Avoca

4294. FRANK DRAKE[-9] BOWKER, brother of above, was born 15 March 1882 at SummerHill, Cayuga, NY. He married first to Jennie ____, possibly on 14 Jan 1909 at ___, NY. According to the draft records for WW1 (1917-18) he resided at RD # 4 Cortland, NY, and listed his nearest relative as Jennie R. BOWKER. No children were listed. Jennie was born ca 1886.

On the 1920 Census he and his wife Jennie are listed with a nephew Ernest HOPKINS (13) # 4824 above, and no children of their own. It is believed that Jennie died ca 22 May 1921. He married second to Clara CONWAY on 5 July 1922. She was the daughter of John CONWAY and Ursula LOOMIS, and was born 12 Nov 1892; died 20 July 1975 Cortland, NY. Frank-[9] BOWKER died ____.

Children of Frank D[-9] BOWKER and Clara CONWAY:
Surname **BOWKER**

4827. Gerald John	born10 Sep 1923; died 8 Nov 2000 Syracuse, Onondaga, NY
4828. Frances Helen	born 28 April 1926; died ____
4829. Jane Irene	born 18 May 1930; died ____
4830. Dorothy Marie	born 1 Feb 1933

4296. HELEN JENNIE[-9] BOWKER, sister of above, was born 20 April 1885 at Summer Hill, Cayuga, NY. She married Lee Nellis SHULTS on 15 Dec 1914 at ____. He was the son of ____ SHULTS and Rebecca ___; and was born 20 Sep 1881 at Avoca, Steuben, NY; died 1954. Helen-[9] BOWKER died 4 Oct 1974 at Avoca, Steuben, NY.

Children of Helen Jennie[-9] BOWKER and Lee SHULTS:
Surname **SHULTS**

4831. Dorothy Rebecca	born 2 Jan 1917; died ____; married Albert Lee BARTLETT ca ____
	(he poss born 31 Jan 1913; died 11 July 1978 Collier County, FL)
	Children: Kelly Lynn [11] born ca ____; Jay Lee-[11] BARTLETT born ca ____, married Karen SPICER
4832. Laura	born ca _____; died ____
4833. Grace Mary	b[11]orn 21 Feb 1925 Avoca; died ____; married Roscoe S. FOX ca ____

4297. MARY MATTIE[-9] BOWKER, sister of above, was born 7 March 11887 at SummerHill, Cayuga, NY. She married Earl Dale SMITH on 1 Jan 1914. He was the son of ____ SMITH and ____, and was born ca 1888; died ____. Mary M[-9] BOWKER died 21 Dec 1973 at Plainwell, Michigan.

BOWKER
The Ninth American Generation

Children of Mary M[-9] BOWKER and Earl SMITH:
Surname **SMITH**

4834. Helen Josephine	born 3 Sept 1914; died ____; married Charles SCHOFF ca ____	
4835. Hilda Bernice	born 10 Feb 1916; died ____; married Harvey FISHEL ca ____	
4836. Lois Jane	born 11 Aug 1922; died 1958	
	1 married Maxwell SCHUYLER ca ___; 2 married Neil JOHNSON ca ____	
4837. Phyllis Mary	born 13 Sep 1926; died ____; married Clair LEWIS ca ____	
4838. Joyce Elaine	born 28 July 1928; died ____; married Clifton H. SCHNEIDER ca ____	

4309. HAROLD EUGENE[-9] BOWKER, son of Eugene Wiggins[-8] BOWKER (Eri-[7]; Archibald-[6]; Silas Day [5,4]; John-[3]; Edmund-[2,1]) and Mary Ann REED, was born 5 Feb 1889. He married Jessie M. BAIRD on 14 April 1913 Montclair, NJ. She was the daughter of Robert BAIRD and Ruthie/Ruttie IVES, and was born 10 June 1893 at Plattsville, Ontario, Canada; died 17 Jan 1996 Cortland, NY. She immigrated from Canada in 1898 and was naturalized in 1913. Harold-[9] BOWKER died 7 Jan 1969 at Cortland, NY.

Children of Harold-[9] BOWKER and Jessie BAIRD:
Surname **BOWKER**

	4839. Kenneth Eugene	born 22 Mar 1914 DeRuyter, NY; died 22 Dec 1925 Cortland, NY. EOL
+	**4840. GORDON ROBERT**	born 3 Sep 1927 Cortland, NY; died ____; married Patricia BENTON 20 June 1953 (she born 4 Oct 1931 Monson, MA;)

4310. GERTRUDE BELLE[-9] BOWKER, sister of above, was born 14 May 1894 at Homer, Cortland, NY. She married Clarence Darwin STEVENS on 20 April 1913 at Tully, NY. He was the son of Fred I. STEVENS and Nettie E. ____, and was born 3 Feb 1895 at Scott, NY; died Sep 1935. Gertrude-[9] BOWKER died 3 April 1978 at Gortland, NY.

Children of Gertrude Belle-[9] BOWKER and Clarence D. STEVENS
Surname **STEVENS**

4841. Bernice Gertrude	born 23 April 1914 Homer, NY; died 5 Aug 1949
	married Harold Vance COMERFORD ca _____
	(he s/o Neil D. COMERFORD (born NY) and Florence L. ____ (born KS)
	(he born ca 1913 NY; died _____)
4842. Robert Darwin	born ca 1921/22; died _____
	1 married Ann AUCHMOODY ca ____; 2 married Rita ELLIS ca ____
4843. Richard Kenneth	born ca 1924/25; died ____; married Shirley DICKINSON

4311. HOWARD EDWARD[-9] BOWKER, brother of above, was born 28 April 1900 at Cortland, NY. He married Dorothy May Mc KINNEY on 20 May 1920 at Cortland. She was the daughter of George-[3] Mc KINNEY Alexander-[2,1]) and Susie Belle FOX, and was born 15 Aug 1901 at McLean, Tompkins County, NY; died 15 Dec 2003 at the age of 102.

Howard Edward-[9] BOWKER served in WW 1 as a member of the 4th Division Supply Company, 77th Field Artillery, American Expeditionary Forces. He died 7 Sep 1939 at Bath (NY)Veterans Hospital and is buried at the Bath National Cemetery there.

Children of Howard Edward-[9] BOWKER and Dorothy May Mc KINNEY:
Surname **BOWKER**

+	**4844. GERALDINE MARIE**	born 22 June 1921 NY ; married Gerald Glenn HEILMAN 8 June 1946 (he s/o John Elias HEILMAN and Mary Jane DETWEILER) (he born 17 May 1922;)
+	**4845. GENEVIEVE MAE**	born 6 Feb 1924 NY; married Robert August THERRE 238 Oct 1945 (he s/o Augustus W. THERRE and Helen/Nellie TRUAX) (he born 24 Mar 1911; died 1999)
+	**4846. PAUL EDWARD**	born 14 May 1926 NY
		1 married Norman Jean VOORHEES 10 July 1948 North Syracuse, NY
		(she born 13 Sept 1928; died 25 April 2000)
		(she dau/o Clarence VOORHEES and Erma HOWELL)
		2 married Fances Jean STERLING Drisko 29 March 2003 Cary, NC
		(she dau/o Charles Lee STERLING and Hazel Frances DOTY)
		(she wid/o George Dolbey DRISKO) (she born 3 June 1927 Syracuse, NY,)
	4847. George Eugene	born 23 Nov 1933; died 16 Feb 2002, unmarried , cancer

4312. HERBERT RAYMOND-9 **BOWKER**, brother of above, was born 24 Oct 1903 (SSDI records) NY. He married first to Bernice May DORAN ca ___. They divorced ca ___. She was the daughter of Edward C. DORAN and Grace A. ___, and was born ca 1905; died ____. He married second to _____ (unknown). He married third to Dorothy F. EHLIG ca ___. She was the daughter of _____ EHLIG and ____, and was born 10 Sept 1906 Orangetown, Rockland, NY.; died 20 Oct 2000 Bergen, NJ. Herbert Raymond-9 (Ray) BOWKER died Oct 1970 at Rockland, NY.

Child of H. Raymond/Ray-9 BOWKER and Bernice DORAN:
Surname **BOWKER**

4848. Eileen Grace	born 12 Dec 1922; died ____; married Wendell C. WARD ca ____	
	(he s/o Frederick J. WARD and Lulu M. _____)	
	(he born ca 1921; died _____ Baldwinsville, NY)	
	Child: Gary C-11 WARD born ca ____	

4382. EDITH M-9 **BOWKER**, daughter of William Henry-8 BOWKER (Daniel-7; Anson-6; Daniel-5; Silas Day-4; John-3; Edmund-2,1) and Vida M. PATCHEN, was born 11 July 1893/4 Hobart, NY. She married first to William NICHOLS on 28 Oct 1912 Delaware County, NY. He was the son of Chester NICHOLS and Ella ____; and was born 1886; died ____. She married second to Willard O. MADDEN ca 1924. He was the son of John H. MADDEN and Dora M. ___; and was born Jan 1894 NY; died 1964 Worcester, Otsego, NY

Children of Edith M-9 BOWKER and William NICHOLS:
Surname **NICHOLS**

	4849. Elsie V.	born ca 1915 NY; died _____
+	**4850. HAZEL L.**	born 11 Nov 1916 NY; died 10 June 2001
		1 married Henry K. BEAGLE ca ___
		(he s/o George BEAGLE and Lulu RIFENBURG)
		(he born 10 Aug 1910; died Sep 1990) (probably divorced)
		2 married George W. HIBBERT 3rd ca _____ (before 1960)
	4851. William Chester	born ca 1919 NY; died ____

Children of Edith M-9 BOWKER and Willard O. MADDEN:
Surname **MADDEN**

4852. Leigh / Lee W.	born 2 Apr 1929; died 7 Feb 2011 Charlottesville, NY	
	married Margaret HENDERSON ca _____ (she born 11 June 1931; died 3 Dec 2009)	
4853. Mary	born ca ____; died ____; married Norman IVES ca _____	

4385. ROLAND S-9 **BOWKER**, son of William Henry-8 BOWKER (Daniel-7; Anson-6; Daniel-5; Silas Day-4; John-3; Edmund-2,1) and Vida M. PATCHEN, was born 20 March 1904 NY. He married Bessie DIETRICH on 6 April 1928 at Walton, NY. She was the daughter of Jacob DIETRICH and Effie Adelaide WHITE, and was born ____; died ____. Roland-9 BOWKER died Dec 1979 at Walton, Delaware, NY.

Children of Roland S-9 BOWKER and Bessie DIETRICH:
Surname **BOWKER** (all children born Walton, Delaware, NY)

4854. Dorothy I.	born 16 Nov 1928 ; died _____; married _____ BARNHART	
4855. Carlton L.	born 13 June 1930; died 15 Jan 2005; married _____	
	Child: Timothy M-11 BOWKER born ca ____	
4856. Ruth A.	born 2 Nov 1933; died 7 Feb 2005 Walton; married Irven G. BARTLETT 26 Apr 1958	
	(he born 1 May 1933; died 15 June 1977)	
4857. Marian	born 7 Dec 1935; died _____; married _____ HODGE	

4386. LESTRAL HERBERT-9 **BOWKER,** son of Bert-8 BOWKER (Daniel T-7; Anson-6; Daniel-5; Silas Day-4; John-3; Edmund-2;1) and Sarah Jane SMITH, was born 27 Nov 1897 IL. He married Mabel E. THIELEN ca 1920. She was the daughter of Barney THIELEN and Elizabeth ___; and was born 1901-02; died ____. Lestral-9 BOWKER died Nov 1975 IL.

Children of Lestral Herbert-9 BOWKER and Mabel THIELEN:
Surname **BOWKER**

4858. Ivan B.	born 20 Dec 1921 IL; died 1995 Aurora, Kane, IL		
	married Bernice A. Des LAURIERS ____ (she born ca 1923, died 2009)		
4859. Earl R.	born 1928/29; died _____		
4860. Leroy L.	born ca 1934; died _____	4861. Jerry R.	born ca 1937; died ____

4387. LUETTA-9 BOWKER, sister of above, as born 2 Aug 1899 IL. She married Earl L. HART ca 1918. He was the son of George Sherman HART and Petra Cody REESE, and was born 14 Apr 1897 IL; died May 1967 Rockford, IL. Luetta-9 BOWKER died May 1978 Rockford, IL.

Children of Luetta-9 BOWKER and Earl L. HART:
Surname **HART**

4862. Wayne E.	born 5 Oct 1919; died 14 Sep 2009 Janesville, IL	
	married Bernice E. FISHER Meske 15 Apr 1983	
	Children: Charles-11 born ca ____; and William-11 HART born ca ____	
4863-. Donald	born ca ____; died ____	

4392. ELSIE-9 BOWKER, daughter of James H-8 BOWKER (Orrin L-7; Anson-6; Daniel-5; Silas Day-4; John-3; Edmund-2,1) and Mary VAN PELT, was born 19 Sep 1890. She married first to Arlington John TUBBS 27 Jan 1909. He was the son of Chester TUBBS and Finetta GAGE, and was born ca 1873; died 1937. She married second to Ernest C. BLENCOE of Maryland , Oswego County, NY, on 21 Jan 1958 Oneonta, NY. He was the son of ____ BLENCOE and ____, and was born 15 Jan 1887; died 19 Nov 1963. Elsie 9 BOWKER died June 1977 Oswego, NY.

Children of Elsie-9 BOWKER and Arlington TUBBS:
Surname **TUBBS**

4864. Ralph C.	born 22 Feb 1910 Colliersville, NY; died 17 July 1970	
	married Bessie NORTH ca ____	(she born ____; died Nov 1964)
	Children: Wendell-10 TUBBS ; and Janice-10 TUBBS	
4865. Kenneth James	born 15 March 1913; died July 1981 Maryland, NY	
4866. Francis	born 18 Feb 1926	

4406. MAUDE E-9 BOWKER, daughter of Spencer Henry-8 BOWKER (Orsemus-7; Anson-6; Daniel-5; Silas-4; John-3; Edmund-2,1) and Mabel WOODS, was born 10 Aug 1902 NY. She married Arthur KILMER on 22 July 1919 NY. He was the son of Eugene KILMER and Mary Bridget FOLEY, and was born 19 July 1893/5; died June 1978 Walton, Delaware, NY. Maude-9 BOWKER died Oct 1954.

Children of Maude-9 BOWKER and Arthur KILMER:
Surname **KILMER**

4867. Arthur	born ca 1920; married Ruby ____ ca 1939	(Child: Marion-11 KILMER born ca 1940)	
4868. William	born ca 1921		
4869. Jack	born ca 1922	4872. Kenneth	born ca 1931
4870. Roy	born ca 1923	4873. Theodore	born ca 1933
4871. Betty	born ca 1930	4874. Roger	born ca 1939

4407. SUSAN RUTH-9 BOWKER, sister of above, was born 7 Aug 1904 NY. She married Olin Northrup Mc CLENNON on 5 Aug 1922. He was the son of Herbert Mc CLENNON and Flora NORTHRUP, and was born 27 Apr 1902; died 22 May 1960 ** Walton, Delaware, NY . Susan Ruth-9 BOWKER died ca 1964.

Children of Susan Ruth-9 BOWKER and Olin Mc CLENNON:
Surname **Mc CLENNON**

4875. Olin S.	born ca 1923/24; died ____		
4876. Margaret	born ca 1925; died ____	4879. Arnold	born ca ____; died ____
4877. Marion I.	born ca 1927/28; died ____		
4878. Arlene Louise	born 23 Sep/Nov 1934; died 22 Apr 2002		

** Troy (NY) Record newspaper 24 May 1960
Walton Man Kills Brother-in-law

Walton (UPI) Howard Spencer BOWKER, 54, was charged yesterday with first
degree murder in the shotgun killing of his brother-in-law.
State troopers said BOWKER shot Olin Mc CLENNON, 54, with a deer slug or
a ball shot from a 12 gauge shotgun, apparently after a family argument.
They said Mc CLENNON's wife Susan (sister of Howard) witnessed the shooting.
Authorities said BOWKER surrendered quietly at the scene.

BOWKER
The Ninth American Generation

Excerpts from another article on 6 July 1960 in the Oneonta (NY) Star newspaper
Prosecution Seeks Mental Test for Murder Defendant
Move Approved by Counsel for BOWKER

" BOWKER a Walton bachelor faces second degree murder charges in the alleged killing
of his brother-in-law, Olin Northrup Mc CLENNON in Walton earlier this year'
"District Attorney Richard FARLEY requested that BOWKER be sent to the Binghamton State Hospital
for an 'inquiry as to his sanity' "
"- members of the defendants family (stated) that after he had been wounded in the North Africa
campaign, he was returned to the US and was given additional treatment in a mental institution – "

4432. NORA LEOLA[-9] CUYLE, daughter of Hannah Maude[-8] BOWKER (Orsemus[-7]; Anson[-6]; Daniel[-5]; Silas[-4]; John[-3]; Edmund[-2,1]) and Frederick " Bubby " CUYLE, was born 12 Feb 1902 NY. She married first to the Rev. Harold Andrew PRUYN ca 1922. He was the son of Wayne Merton PRUYN and Mable STRAIT; and was born 5 July 1901; died 13 July 1961 at Ocean Isle, Brunswick, NC. Nora Leola[-9] CUYLE married second to Wayne Nathan NORRIS . Nora-[9] died 22 June 1993.

Children of Nora Leola[-9] CUYLE and Harold PRUYN:
Surname **PRUYN**

4880. Jack Wayne	born 26 July 1923 NY; died May 1963 Chenango Forks, NY	
4881. Mary Elaine	born ca 1930 PA; died 2013	
4882. William Dennis	born 1936; died 1936	
4883. Judith L.	born 5 Aug 1939; married Larry QUISTGAARD 13 Sep 1957	

4434. WILLIAM HENRY[-9] CUYLE, brother of above, was born 2 Feb 1907 NY. He married Margaret A. LEWIS on 27 Aug 1933 at Johnson City, NY. She was the daughter of Paul Guy LEWIS and Arlene Blanche SAXE, and was born ca 1909; died 1991. William Henry[-9] CUYLE died 28 March 1985 NY.

Children of William Henry[-9] CUYLE and Margaret LEWIS:
Surname **CUYLE**

4884. Barbara Joan	born 21 May 34 Binghamton, NY; died 10 Mar 2012 Binghamton (single)
4885. Megan Evan	born 12 Apr 1938 Binghamton, NY; died 15 June 2009 Binghamton
	married Walter NOREIKA, Jr. 17 June 1961 (he born ca 1936)

4448. MABEL LOUISE[-9] JEWELL, daughter of Ida May[-8] McCOUN (Arvilla-[7] BOWKER; Jonathan-[6]; John-[5;] Silas Day-[4]; John-[3]; Edmund-[2,1]) and Jasper Lloyd JEWELL, was born 12 Oct 1897 at Kalispell, Montana. She married first to Hugh Barr ELLIOTT on 2 Dec 1917. He was the son of George Seth ELLIOTT and Mary PATTERSON, and was born 14 Dec 1884 +; died Dec 1968. They probably divorced. Mabel-[9] married second to Ernest Dainey ++ BROONER on 14 July 1923. He was the son of Herman Butler BROONER and Millie Ann MEDCALF, and was born 8 May 1887 Dale, Spencer, Indiana; died 12 March 1948 Los Angeles, CA. He was a printer on a daily newspaper. He served on World War 1, enlisting on 18 Sept 1917. He was attached to Company L, 33rd Infantry (Ohio), and rose to the rank of Cpl. He was in the American Expeditionary Forces from 5 June 1918 to 26 Jan 1919. He was honorably discharged on 8 Feb 1919. Mabel-[9] JEWELL died ca 1991 at Salt Lake City, Utah.

Source of info: + World War 1 Draft registration card; ++ Registration card (in his own handwriting) plainly written as middle name being Dainey, not Dana.

Child of Mabel Louise[-9] JEWELL and Hugh Barr ELLIOTT:
Surname **ELLIOTT**

4886. JEWELL LOUISE born 6 Nov 1919 Kalispell, MT; died ____; married Edward French SHANNON ca ____
Note: She used the name Jewell Louise Elliot Brooner; and was possibly legally adopted by her step-father

Children of Mabel Louise[-9] JEWELL and Ernest Dainey BROONER:
Surname **BROONER**

4887. Ernest Carl	born ca 1923 MT; died ____; married Mary Caroline WILKE ca ____
	Child: Barbara Jean-[11] BROONER born ca ___; married Alan MORRIS ca ____
4888. Jean Ammie	born ca 1926 MT; died ____; married Phillip COWLEY ca ____
	2 married Donald TYLER ca ____ Child: Paul Donald-[11] TYLER born ca ___

4466. NORA[-9] DAVIS, daughter of Elizabeth[-8] BOWKER (Martin VanBuren[-7]; Jonathan[-6]; John[-5]; Silas Day[-4]; John[-3]; Edmund[-2,1]) and Frederick DAVIS, was born Dec 1866 OH. She married first to Frank A. FOSTER on 15 April 1902 MI. He was the son of ____ FOSTER and ____, and was born ca 1884; died ____. She married Second to Valentine AMBURGEY on 15 Dec 1913 MI. He was the son of Robert AMBURGEY and Nancy Ann PUCKETT; and was born 26 April 1883 KY; died 23 March 1959 MI. Nora[-9] DAVIS died 13 March 1959 MI.

Children of Nora[-9] DAVIS and Frank FOSTER:
Surname **FOSTER**

4889. Ward Avery	born 16 June 1902; died 1 May 1966 Clare, MI.	
	married Christine R. ____ ca ____	(Child: Rolland E[-11] FOSTER born ca 1925)
4890. Sidney	born ca 1904 MI; died ____	

Child of Nora[-9] DAVIS and Valentine AMBURGEY:
Surname **AMBURGEY**

4891. Ethel	born ca 1918 WI; died ____; married Jacob SANFRO ca ____
	Child: John[-11] SANFRO born ca 1937 WI

4479. JOSIE M[-9] BOWKER, daughter of Charles Addison [-8] BOWKER (William H[-7]; Jefferson[-6]; John[-5]; Silas Day[-4]; John[-3]; Edmund[-2,1]) and Isabelle TOLAND, was born 15 Mar 1884 KS. She married Forbes M. MORGAN ca 1897 at age 13. He was the son of Ebba C.MORGAN and Flora/ Florella ____; and was born 25 Dec 1870 MO; died 24 Feb 1949 KS. Josie M[-9] BOWKER died 23 Nov 1905 (age 21) at St. John, KS.

Children of Josie M[-9] BOWKER and Forbes MORGAN:
Surname **MORGAN**

4892. Florella May	born Oct 1898; died 1974		
4893. Ebba	born 1901; died 1901	4894. Joyce Paul	born 1903; died 1966

4480. CHARLES[-9] ADDISON BOWKER, JR, brother of above, was born 6 Oct 1885 KS. He married Josephine " Josie " GOWEN(S) on 14 Aug 1906 at Stafford, KS. She was the daughter of Coleman Bruce GOWEN(S) and Nancy Ellen CALVERT; and was born 18 Nov 1892; died 1 May 1982 Woodward, OK. Charles Addison[-9] BOWKER, Jr. died 17 Feb 1939 OK.

Note: Josie GOWEN married three more times. Husband #2 was Percy Winnum THATCHER whom she married 28 Apr 1940. # 3 was Ernest BAALHORN; they married July 1954. And her 4th husband, whom she married 23 June 1972, was Earl Bennin RINNER/RENNER. (She had a son by her 3rd marriage. His name was Ernest W. BAALHORN, born ___; died 1958)

Children of Charles Addison[-9] BOWKER, Jr. and Josie GOWEN(S):
Surname **BOWKER**

4895. Charles Coleman	born 9 Feb 1907; died 23 July 1909	EOL
4896. Forney Bruce	born 29 Oct 1909; died May 1973 OK; married Clara Martha SECREST 14 Sep 1931	
	(she dau/o George SECREST and Edna WARREN)	
	(she born 19 Mar 1912; died 21 July 2007 OK)	
	Children: Donnie B[-11] born ___; and Clarice Elaine-[11] BOWKER born 31 July 1938 Buffalo, OK; died 1993 Oklahoma City, OK; 1 married Ernest William DEEDS ca ____ (he born ca 1931;died 1956); 2 married Calvin LAUGHERY, Jr. 2 May 1959 OK	
4897. Cecil	born 21 Dec 1911; died 27 Dec 1911	EOL
4898. Lillie Ellen	born 21 July 1913; died 1 Dec 1945 OK	
	married James Hugh FLEMING 11 Aug 1930 Buffalo, OK	
	(he born 7 Sep 1911; died 16 Aug 1997 Rosston, Harper, OK)	
	(he s/o James William FLEMING and Georgia Edith WILSON)	
	Children: Leslie E-[11] born ca 1930; Joe G[-11] born Oct 1934; Mary E-[11] born ca 1936; and Calvin E-[11] FLEMING born ca 1938	
4899. Claude Arnold	born 7 July 1915; died 25 Nov 2004 Beaver, OK	
	married Edith SMITH 14 Sep 1932 Buffalo, OK	
	(she born ____; died 28 Apr 1998)	
	Children: C A (Chuck)[-11]; James Aaron-[11]; and Ramona Jean-[11] BOWKER Coats	
4900. Esta L.	born ca 1917; died ____; married EDMONDS ca ____	
4901. J. Basil	born 29 July 1919; died 23 Oct 1988 Woodward, OK	
	married Audrey Mae BUSS Hurst 20 Jan 1956 (divorced before 1965)	
4902. Joe Galen	born 29 Aug 1921; died 31 Aug 1922	EOL
4903. Joy Dale (m)	born 21 Dec 1923; died 12 Dec 1999 Oklahoma City, OK	
4904. Mareta Belle	born 8 Jan 1926; died 17 Aug 1940 (ruptured appendix)	
	married Percy Lee HATCHER 14 June 1940 (she 14 yrs. old)	

4481. WILLIAM HENRY-⁹ BOWKER, brother of above, was born 6 July 1887 KS. He married Mabel Ophelia JUDSON ca 1914. She was the daughter of _____ JUDSON and _____, and was born ca 1896 OK; died _____. William Henry-⁹ BOWKER died 2 Aug 1962 CO.

Children of William Henry-⁹ BOWKER and Mabel JUDSON:
Surname **BOWKER**

4905. Lois I.	born ca 1915; died ____	
4906. Charles R.	born 12 Nov 1916 OK; died June 1974 CA; married Olive _____ ca ____	
4907. Klein P (Cline)	born 22 June 1919; died May 1971 CO; married Lucille M. ____ ca ____	
	Child: Elsie L-¹¹ BOWKER born ca ____	
4908. William H.	born ca 1922 KS; died ____	
4909. Gerald A.	born ca 1927 KS; died ____	
4910. Harry J.	born ca 1929/30 KS; died ____; married Margaret P. STANTON 27 Apr 1968 CA (she born ca 1933; died ____)	
4911. Neona (?)	born ca 1934 NE; died _____	4912. Roy born ca 1937 CO; died ____

4482. JENNIE ROWENA-⁹ BOWKER, sister of above, was born 18 Dec 1888 KS. She married John Browning STIMATZE ca 1905. He was the son of Joachim W. STIMATZE and Sarah _____; and was born 27 Oct 1886; died 3 Feb 1969 St. John, KS. Jennie Rowena-⁹ BOWKER died April 1973 KS.

Children of Jennie Rowena-⁹ BOWKER and John STIMATZE:
Surname **STIMATZE**

4913. Wauneta Audine	born 7 Feb 1906; died 29 Aug 1991 Bird City, Cheyenne, KS married _____ COMPTON ca
4914. Conway John	born 10 Mar 1909 KS; died 9 Mar 2000 ID; married Norma Beatrice LITZ ca _____
4915. Roy E.	born 17 Oct 1911; died 19 Feb 1990 Wichita, KS
4916. Charles Addison	born 30 Nov 1913; died 30 Apr 2001 KS.; buried Syracuse, Hamilton, KS
4917. Melvin Elmer	born 25 Oct 1915 KS; died 8 Mar 1994 St. John, KS
4918. Emmett Ray	born 29 Nov 1919; died 16 Mar 1920
4919. Rowena Elizabeth	born 5 Dec 1920; died 20 Apr 1999; 1 married George Shelby EAKIN (he born 28 Jan 1914; died 30 Mar 1984 KS)
	Child: Robert L-¹¹ EAKIN born ca 1938; Shirley B-¹¹ EAKINS born 1945,died 2003
	2 married Emil W REHMERS 4 Oct 1960 (he born 1921; died !990)

4483. JAMES ADDISON-⁹ BOWKER, brother of above, was born 7 June 1892 Stafford County, KS. He married Anna Belle ROBERTS on 31 July 1909 OK. She was the daughter of _____ ROBERTS and _____; and was born 9 Jan 1892; died 5 Jan 1942. James A-⁹ BOWKER died 31 July 1950 Yuma, CO.

Children of James Addison-⁹ BOWKER and Anna Belle ROBERTS:
Surname **BOWKER**

+	4920. **WILMA BLENNE**	born 5 Nov 1910; died 10 Nov 1985 Cimarron, KS married John Rex TOOTHAKER 29 Nov 1929
+	4921. **CELIA MAY/MAE**	born 2 Sep 1912 KS; died 28 Nov 1994 KS married James William DUNSWORTH 22 Dec 1930 (he born 31 Mar 1909 KS; died 10 Nov 1974 Garden City, KS) (he s/o Frank Hatfield DUNSWORTH and Hazel Mary MOORE)
	4922. Lulu Esther	born 24 Dec 1914 KS; died July 1982 married June A. HARMON ca 1936 (he born 9 May 1907; died 12 Mar 1993 El Dorado, Arkansas)
		Child: Gwendolyn-¹¹ HARMON ca 1937 KS
	4923. Stewart J.	born 8 Feb 1917 KS; died June 1985 OK married Ethel Alice BEATTY ca _____ (she born 16 Oct 1918 KS; died 16 Dec 1974)
	4924. James Arden	born ca 1926 KS; died ____
	4925. Richard A.	born 11 Mar 1928 KS; died 23 June 2010 Oxnard, CA 4926. Dean E. born ca 1930

4484. AMAZIAH ALVIN-⁹ " Ammie" BOWKER, son of Amaziah Chester-⁸ BOWKER (William Henry-⁷; Jefferson-⁶; John-⁵; Silas-⁴; John-³; Edmund-²,¹) and Lois Irene ADAMS, was born 31 Oct 1888 KS. He married Martha BALCEROWICZ ca 1909. She was the daughter of _____ BALCEROWICZ and Mary DROZYNSKA; and was born 21 Apr 1887 IL; died 30 June 1987 Houston, TX. Amaziah-⁹ BOWKER died 30 June 1987 Houston, TX.

Child of Amaziah[9] BOWKER and Martha BALCEROWICZ:
Surname **BOWKER**

4927. Alvin Joseph	born 10 Sep 1910 Seward, KS; died 10 June 1997 Temple, TX
	married Pearl BEDNAREK ca 1943
	(she born 11 July 1908 Claburne, TX; died 7 Apr 1975 McAllen, TX)
	Child: Delano Vernon[11] BOWKER born 25 Dec 1944 McAllen, TX; died 31 Mar 1995 Victoria, TX)

4495. LYLE W[9] BOWKER, son of Edward James[8] BOWKER (William Henry[7]; Jefferson[6]; John[5]; Silas[4]; John[3]; Edmund[2,1]) was born 18 Nov 1904 NE. He married Marie PERREAULT on 4 Oct 1926 at Fall River, SD. She was the daughter of _____ PERREAULT and ____; and was born ca 1906; died 1983. Lyle W[9] BOWKER died

Children of Lyle[9] BOWKER and Marie PERREAULT:
Surname **BOWKER**

4928. Valmore Eugene	born 14 Feb 1927; died 21 Aug 2004 at the Fort Meade Veterans Hospital, SD
	married Ida M. _____ ca ____ (she born 15 July 1931)
4929. Donald James	born ca 1938; died 18 Oct 2009 Hot Springs, SD
4930. Dennis	born ca 1943; died ____
4931. Robert Wayne	born 9 Nov 1944; died 21 Sep 2010 Sturgis, SD
4932. Gary M.	born ca ____; died ____ 4933. Steven L. born 14 July 1949

4505. CRYSTAL ELEANOR[9] BOWKER, daughter of Clifton[8] BOWKER (Sylvester[7]; Jefferson[6]; John[5]; Silas Day[4]; John[3]; Edmund[2,1]) and Eleanor " Nellie " MONAGHAN, was born 27 Sep 1898 MI. She married first to Edward M. OLSON ca 1920 MI. He was the son of _____ OLSON and ____, and was born ca 1892 MI. They divorced and she married second to James C. CONWAY on 20 Nov 1953. He was the son of ____ CONWAY and ____, and was born 24 Dec 1894 CA; died 27 Apr 1975 CA. Crystal[9] BOWKER died 24 Oct 1984 Orange, CA.

Children of Crystal[9] BOWKER and Edward OLSON:
Surname **OLSON**

4934. Walter Harold	born 1 Jan 1921 MI; died 7 Jan 1994 Evart, MI
4935. Lawrence Arvene	born 16 Apr 1923 MI; died 21 Dec 1989 Taylor, MI
4936. Dorland Robert " Oley "	born 2 Nov 1927 MI; died ____; married Virginia M. PLONT 1955

4509. MARY CELIA[9] BOWKER daughter of Charles E[8] BOWKER (Amaziah Chester[7]; Jefferson[6]; John[5]; Silas Day[4]; John[3]; Edmund[2,1]) and Linnie GOODALE, was born 8 Jan 1897 NY. She married Gilbert T. FRANCIS 28 Dec 1913 NY. He was the son of ____ FRANCIS and Lucinda A. TYLER, and was born 12 March 1893; died 9 Feb 1949. Mary Cecelia[9] BOWKER died ca 1967.

Children of Mary C[9] BOWKER and Gilbert FRANCIS:
Surname **FRANCIS**

4937. Charles B.	born 9 Aug 1914 NY; died Nov 1975
	married Castella WILLIAMS 30 Dec 1939 (4 ch)
4938. Lucinda L.	born 22 Oct 1915; died 7 May 1982; married Hollis W. BELL ca ____
	(he s/o Clarence H. BELL and Pearl Martha ROSS)
	(he born 16 June 1912; died 17 Dec 2006 King Ferry, Cayuga, NY)
4939. Emmett F.	born 4 Feb 1917; died 15 Sept 1931 EOL
4940. Carl Albert	born 10 Apr 1918; died 3 Jan 1998 FL; married Gladys LOOMIS 27 Sep 1940
4941. Clayton Gilbert	born 28 Aug 1919; died 2 June 1995 Moravia, Cayuga, NY
	married Ethel Frances TERWILLIGER Campbell 12 May 1951
	(she dau/o George TERWILLIGER and Jenny TOMPKINS)
4942. Asaph/ Asa L.	born 7 May 1921; died March 1985 NY; married Beatrice HEATH 23 Jan 1942
4943. Vivian	born 1 Jan 1924; died 1 Jan 1941 EOL
4944. Leslie Ralph	born 25 Aug 1925; died 19 Aug 1997; 1 married Renee' GEEVES 23 June 1945
	(she born ___; died 1 Sept 1947) 1 son
	2 married Virginia SIGNOR 23 Nov 1949 (3 sons, 1 dau)
	(she dau/o George Osborne SIGNOR and Grace L. MERRY)
	(she born 5 Feb 1932 Genoa, NY; died Dec 1991 Locke, Cayuga, NY)
4945. Rowland L.(Tuffy)	born 21 Jan 1928; died 2 Feb 2007 MO
4946. Bertha L.	born 12 Aug 1929; died 22 Nov 2011 Norwich, NY
4947. Celia May	born ca _____

4510. JAMES CLAYTON[-9] **BOWKER,** brother of above, was born 28 Aug 1899 NY. He married Frances Marion[-4] McKINNEY on 10 June 1922 at Dryden, Tompkins, NY. She was the daughter of George-[3] Mc KINNEY (Alexander-[2,1]) and Susie Belle FOX, and was born 10 June 1903 at McLean, Tompkins County, NY; died 3 April 1982 at Cortland, NY. Note: According to a diary handed down to her daughter , Frances wrote " was married at Dryden, Mabel and Burrell stood up with us. We went to Groton at night. Terrible storm."

Chjildren of James Clayton-[9] BOWKER and Frances Marion-4 Mc KINNEY:
Surname **BOWKER**

+	**4948. EDITH MAY**	born 6 June 1923; died 30 May1984; married Edward J. CARPENTER 18 Apr 1942 (he s/o Fred S. CARPENTER and Ruth H. WOODCOCK) (he born 1 Jan 1920 Dryden, NY; died 3 March 996 Dryden)
+	**4949. ESTHER MARY**	born 9 Feb 1925; died 2000) 1 married Arthur CARPENTER 27 June 1944; divorced 1953 2 married John WEIN 19 Mar 1955 (he born 28 Aug 1914; died 31 Nov 1972) 3 married Almon A. MERRIWEATHER 10 Mar 1976 (he born __; died 10 Dec 1981)
+	**4950. CLAYTON, Jr.**	born 13 March 1926; died 22 Feb 2011 Phoenix, AZ married Geraldine Emma WEBB 4 May 1946 (she born 27 Sep 1926; 23 May 2014 AZ
+	**4951. CARLTON GENE**	born 21 July 1930; married Margaret Chilton DURKEE 18 June 1955 Homer, NY (she dau/o Albert J. DURKEE and Florence FOSTER) (she born 6 Feb 1935; died 3 July 2014 NC)
+	**4952. ROBERT FAY**	born 6 Sep 1932; married Jeanne Marie MILLER 10 July 1954 (she born 8 Dec 1932;)
+	**4953. SUSIE BELLE**	born 12 Feb 1937; married Douglas Edmund Mac KECKNIE 2 June 1956 (he born 2 April 1932;)
+	**4954. KAREN RUTH**	born 25 Dec 1939; married John GALEOTTI, Jr. 14 Feb 1959 (he born 29 Jan 1938; died 20 May 2000)
+	**4955. JO ANNE**	born 16 May 1945; married Richard WILLIAMS 30 Jan 1965 (he born 26 Apr 1944;)

4516. ALWYN BERNADINE[-9] **BOWKER,** daughter of Horace Lewis[-8] BOWKER (Amaziah Chester[-7]; Jefferson[-6]; John[-5]; Silas Day[-4]; John[-3]; Edmund-[2,1]) and Frances Emma CRANE, was born 22 March 1912 Cayuga Co., NY. She married Clayton Jay STETSON ca 1932. He was the son of Oliver Jay STETSON and Edith May JOHNSON, and was born 28 Dec 1907; died Feb 1975 Freeville, Tompkins, NY. Alwyn[-9] BOWKER died 10 Oct 1978.

Children of Alwyn-[9] BOWKER and Clayton Jay STETSON:
Surname **STETSON**

4956. . George Clayton, Sr.	born 7 Oct 1933; died 13 June 2000 Dryden, NY	
4957. Irene	born 13 Aug 1936; died 6 Feb 2000 Ithaca, Tompkins, NY married Donald Earl LITTLE ca _____ (he s/o Amos Foster LITTLE and _____) (he born ____; died 2000)	
4958. Carlos Eugene	born 13 Sep 1940 Tompkins Co., NY; died 2 Dec 2012 Ithaca, Tompkins, NY married Linda SPAULDING ca ____ Children: Joyce Louise-[11]; Dawn Marie-[11]; and Jeffrey[-11] STETSON	
4959. Alton	born ca ____; died ____; married Marilou REUSCH ca ____ (she born 28 Feb 1948; died 4 Mar 2013 Ithaca, NY) Children: Jodi K-[11] born ca ____, married Timothy BRAZO ca ___; and Victoria-[11] STETSON	
4960. Ervin	born ca _____; died ____	
4961. Marilyn	born 22 Jan 1944; died ____; married _____ HUNSINGER ca ____	

4517. LORRAINE D[-9] **BOWKER,** sister of above, was born 29 Aug 1914 NY. She married Russell Samuel CURRAN ca 1940. He was the daughter of Jeremiah J. CURRAN and Florence CULBERT, and was born 20 Oct 1911 NJ; died 20 May 1995 Ocean City, NJ. Lorraine-[9] BOWKER died May 1983 Clark, Union, NJ.

Children of Lorraine-[9] BOWKER and Russell CURRAN:
Surname **CURRAN**

4962. Gale F.	born 24 Jan 1941; died 4 Aug 2001 NJ; married Leslie B. HENRICH, Jr.
4963. Geraldine	born 23 Apr 1944; died 1 Apr 2006 Galloway, NJ

4525. ERMA VENICE[-9] SNEDAKER, daughter of Lee Clinton[-8] SNEDAKER (Bradford Clinton[-7]; Lucinda[-6] BOWKER; Joseph[-5]; Silas Day[-4]; John[-3]; Edmund[-2,1]) and Ellen Lucinda[-8] SNEDAKER, was born 21 July 1886 Salt Lake City, UT. She married Edwin Rush REEVES ca 1921 Salt Lake. He was the son of ____ REEVES and ____, and was born 21 Sept 1883; died 3 June 1953. Erma Venice[-9] SNEDAKER died 13 Feb 1936 Salt Lake.

Children of Erma Venice[-9] SNEDAKER and Edwin REEVES:
Surname **REEVES**

4964. Edwin Lee	born 9 Aug 1922; died 7 May 2006 ID	
4965. Mary Ellen	born 26 Nov 1923; died 12 April 2001 ID; married ____ NELSON	
4966. Betty Jean	born 19 Feb 1926; died 7 May 2010 UT	
	married Donald E. FARNSWORTH June 1946	

Children: Darrell-[11]; Sharon-[11]; Debra-[11]; KaLynn-[11]; and Richard[-11] FARNSWORTH

4967. Georgia Anna	born 23 Feb1930 UT; died 30 Nov 2010Salt Lake City, Utah
	married Robert YATES 21 June 1950 (he s/o David Leroy YATES and Rhea ___)

Children: David-[11]; Rhea-[11] ; Steven-[11] YATES

4555. WALLACE[-9] GRIFFES, son of Ida Mae[8] BOWKER (Noah[-7]; Silas[-6]; Noah[-5]; Silas[-4]; John[-3]; Edmund[-2,1]) and Melvin Leslie GRIFFES, was born 14 April 1898 MI. He married Berttha M. _____ ca 1926. She was the daughter of ___ and ____, and was born ca 1908; died 1996 (gs). Wallace[-9] GRIFFES died 1 Jan 1972 at Lakeview, MI.

Children of Wallace-[9] GRIFFES and Bertha M. _____:
Surname **GRIFFES**   (children bornCroton, Newaygo, MI)

4968. Mervin J.	born 25 Aug 1927; died 30 Dec 1989 MI		
4969. Doreen C.	born ca 1929;		
4970. Harry	born ca 1932	4972. Richard	born ca 1938
4971. Norman J.	born 1 July 1936	4973. Clifford	born 4 Dec 1939

4569. ALICE MAY[-9] MUNSON, daughter of West[-8] MUNSON (Orange-[7]; Esther[-6] BOWKER; Noah[-5]; Silas Day[-4]; John[-3]; Edmund[-2,1]) and Harriet PERSONIUS, was born 31 Jan 1878 at ____. She married Victor Van VIELE ca ____. He was the son of Nicholas Van VIELE and Ursula KEACH, and was born 7 May 1876 Montour Falls, NY; died 30 April 1922 at Elmira, NY. Alice May-[9] MUNSON died 20 March 1944.

Children of Alice May-[9] MUNSON and Victor VIELE:
Surname **VIELE**

+	**4974. AMY URSULA**	born May 1897 Elmira, Chemung, NY; died 25 Mar 1974 Elmira, NY	
		married Harry William RICE ca 1922	
	4975. Charles Munson	born 10 July 1899; died 1 Feb 1981 Virginia Beach, VA	
		married Ethel _____ ca 1920 (she born ca 1899 PA; died ____)	

Child: Thelma-[11] VIELE born ca 1921 NY

	4976. Herbert N.	born ca 1901; died 1908	EOL
+	**4977. MARY WEST**	born 18 Dec 1903 NY; did 28 Aug 1985 MA	
		married Victor Francis GEORGE 1 Dec 1921	
	4978. Lawrence V.	born 9 Sep 1905; died Feb 1985 Elmira, NY; 1 married Catherine ____ before 1930	
		2 married Agnes BERTHOD Garrison ca ___(she born 6 Aug 1899; died 25 June 1969)	

Children: Lawrence-[11] born ca 1937, died 2 Apr 2010 Boulder, CO; and Louise-[11] VIELE born ca 1939, married ____ LYNCH

4979. Ada Alberta	born 30 Nov 1906; died 25/29 March 1961 Elmira, NY
	1 married William Randall COMPTON, Jr. 28 March 1922
	(he born 9 July 1902; died 18 May 1974)
	(he s/o William Randall COMPTON, Sr. and Helen Rosamond TUBBS)

Child: John Robinson-[11] COMPTON born 24 Feb 1923 Elmira, NY

2 married Harold Franklin WOOD ca _____   (he born 1899; died 1984)

Child: Margaret E-[11] WOOD born 6 Jan 1936 Elmira, died 29 April 2011 Elmira Hgts, NY; 1 married Richard BRINK; 2 married John B. EMMICK 26 Dec 1985

4980. Alice Harriet	born 8 Oct 1912; died ca 1938
4981. Elizabeth Phebe	born 2 Jan 1915; died 15 Nov 1983 Hampden, MA
	married Walter W. SNOW (Walter Wladyslaw SUSONOWSKI) ca 1937
	(he s/o Wladyslaw SOSNOWSKI and Anastasia ____)(born Poland)
	(he born ca 1915 Westfield, MA; died ____) Child: Richard J-[11] SOSNOWSKI born ca 1938

4634. MAUDE E[-10] LARUE, daughter of Fannie L[-9] BOWKER (Lyman Howe[-8]; Levi[-7]; Gideon[-6]; Antipas[-5]; Josiah[-4]; John[-3;2]; Edmund[-1]) and Martin LARUE, was born ca 1869 at Eldora, Hardin, Iowa. She married Christopher Nicholas SCHWARCK ca 1892. He was the son of John Peter SCHWARCK and Hannah Mary Christine FREDVORST, and was born ca 1862; died 1945. Maude E-[10] LARUE died 1 Dec 1946 at Eldora, Iowa.

Children of Maude[-10] LARUE and Christopher SCHWARCK:
Surname **SCHWARCK**

4982. Fannie Louella	born 14 Sep 1892; died June 1980 ; married Clayton J. SCHENCK ca ____	
4983. Alonzo Lyman	born 23 Aug 1894; died 5 Dec 1934 Grundy, IA	
4984. Martin Wallace	born 2 Aug 1899 IA; died Oct 1977 Eldora, IA; married Mildred _____ ca 1922	
	Children: Martin-[12] born ca 1923; and Harold[-12] SCHWARCK born ca 1924	
4985. Ila J.	born 16 Sep 1902 IA; died 21 Aug 1994 IA	
	married Delbert KIRKDORFFER 27 Aug 1925 Eldora, IA	
	(he s/o Jacob KIRKDORFFER and Sarah Alice FORD)	
4986. Irma F.	born 28 Feb 1905 Eldora, IA; died 4 Aug 2003, single	
4987. Mildred	born 17 Oct 1908 IA; died ____; Robert Kenneth KINNEY 9 Aug 1934 Eldora, IA	
4988. Floyd John	born 4 Apr 1911 Eldora, IA; died 29 Mar 1998 Eldora, IA	
	married Alice C. WARE 31 Aug 1930 (he s/o Charles H. WARE and Susan E. HESS)	

4643. HARRY MILTON[-10] BOWKER, son of Charles Wilson[-9] BOWKER (Lyman[-8]; Levi[-7]; Gideon[-6]; Antipas[-5]; Josiah[-4]; John[-3;2]; Edmund[-1]) and Mary Jane PICKLE, was born 1 March 1886 at Mansonville, Quebec, Canada. He married Marion Monroe SAFFORD on 25 June 1919 at Brome, Quebec. She was the daughter of Myron Garrett SAFFORD and Penelope Thorburn HAMILTON; and was born ca 1891; died Sep 1944. Harry Milton[-10] BOWKER died 6 June 1925, a bookkeeper, Montreal, Quebec, Canada.

Children of Harry M[-10] BOWKER and Marion SAFFORD:
Surname **BOWKER**

4989. Dorothy Elizabeth	born 9 July 1920; died Sep 1991 Quebec
4990. Pauline Safford	born 9 Feb 1923; died 24 Apr 1972
4991. Mary Hamilton	born 23 Mar 1924; died 5 June 1966
4992. Harriet Milton	born 27 Aug 1925; died 1988

4465. CORINNE LADD[-10] BOWKER, daughter of Captain Hugh Demarest[-9] BOWKER (Franklin[-7]; Rice[-7]; Gideon[-6]; Antipas[-5]; Josiah[-4]; John[-3;2]; Edmund[-1]) and Susie GORDON, was born 7 Feb 1874 at Cleveland, Ohio. She married Herbert Alexander HULLIGAN ca 1898. He was the son of William HULLIGAN and Fannie Elizabeth LORD, and was born ca 1867; died 16 Mar 1906. Corinne-[10] BOWKER died 29 Mar 1967 at Chicago, IL.

Child of Corinne[-10] BOWKER and Herbert HULLIGAN:
Surname **BOWKER** *****

+	**4993. HERBERT** *****	born 22 July 1899; died 20 Dec 1968
	HUMISTON	married Frances Katherine DOCKER ca _____ (she born ca 1900; died ca 1992)

***** After Mr. HULLIGAN'S death in 1906 Corinne[-10] changed her name back to her maiden name of BOWKER; and also changed that of her son. He was known as Herbert Humiston BOWKER thereafter.

4673. MARTHA A[-10] PERSONS , daughter of Herbert Alvin[-9] PERSONS (Martha[-8] BOWKER; Rice[-7]; Gideon[-6]; Antipas[-5]; Josiah[-4]; John[-3;2]; Edmund[-1]) and Laura Jane NEWTON, was born Jan 1887. She married Arva Otho GARVER ca 1916. He was the son of ____ GARVER and _____, and was born ca 1891 OH; died ____. Martha[-10] PERSONS died 8 June 1956.

Children of Martha[-10] PERSONS and Orva Otho GARVER:
Surname **GARVER**

4994. Harold Alvin/Arva	born 24 June 1917 OH; died 13 Feb 1990 FL
4995. Howard Russell	born 8Aug 1919; died 28 Mar 1987 FL
4996. Arthur <u>Wesley</u>	born 20 Apr 1922; died 23 Mar 2002; married Marjorie G._____
	(she born 23 Feb 1923; died 15 Mar 2003 St. Petersburg, FL)

BOWKER
The Tenth American Generation

4674. CORA LOUISE[10] **BOWKER,** daughter of Edmund Heard[9] BOWKER (Lewis Leander[8]; Lyman James [7]; Gideon[6]; Antipas[5]; Josiah[4]; John[3,2]; Edmund[1]) and Lucy M. FERGUSON, was born 25 Dec 1871 East Springfield, NY. She married Mark Abram HOLLISTER ca 1891. He was the son of _____ HOLLISTER and ____; and was born ca 1864 NY. Cora Louise[10] BOWKER died 5 Oct 1968. Dr. HOLLISTER was a teacher, and later a Supt. of Schools at Corinth, Saratoga Springs, NY

Children of Cora Louise[10] BOWKER and Dr. Mark Abram HOLLISTER, PhD:
Surname **HOLLISTER**
+   **4997. MADELEINE H.**   born ca 1893; died ____; married Harold DAVIS ca 1919
+   **4998. HAROLD EDMUND** born ca 1896; died _____
                              married Christine Houghton WHITE ca 1923
                              (she born ca 1892 NY; died ____)
     4999. Adelaide Irene.   born 12 Jan 1907; died 10 Feb 2000 PA.
                              married Dr. Frank Reid STANSEL ca _____   (2 sons and a daughter)
                              (he s/o of Numa Reid STANSEL and Frances Moen MASSEY)
                              (he born 7 Aug 1904 NC; died 2 Dec 1999 MA)

4678. ELWIN LEWIS[10] **BOWKER,** son of Lyman James[9] BOWKER (Lewis Leander[8]; Lyman James[7]; Gideon[6]; Antipas[5]; Josiah[4]; John[3,2]; Edmund[1]) and Clarinda HARVEY, was born 27 June 1884 Canada. He married Minnie Arletta SMITH ca 1915. She was the daughter of __ SMITH and _; and was born ca 1885; died 1941. Elwin Lewis[10] BOWKER died 25 Nov 1959.

Children of Elwin Lewis[10] BOWKER and Minnie Arletta SMITH:
Surname **BOWKER**
     5000. Mabel Irene   born 25 June 1916; died 29 May 1989; married Wilfrid Jeffrey GRAPES 14 Sep 1940
                             (he born ca 1915; died 1998)
                             Child: Warren Wilfrid[12] GRAPES born ca 1944; died 1994
     5001. Douglas Lyman   born 24 Oct 1925; died 1925 Sawyerville, QC

4680. AUSTIN STEVENS[10] **BOWKER,** son of Herbert Rice[9] BOWKER (Lewis Leander[8]; Lyman James[7]; Gideon[6]; Antipas[5]; Josiah[4]; John[3,2]; Edmund[1]) and Ormesinda FARNSWORTH; and was born 10 Aug 1896 at Sawyerville, QC. He married Ruth Ethel GILMAN on 8 Mar 1922. She was the daughter of Lewis Eugene GILMAN and Mary Ann CAMPBELL, and was born 11 Dec 1899; died 1 Nov 1989. Austin Stevens[10] BOWKER died 30 July 1990 at North Hatley, QC.

Children of Austin Stevens[10] BOWKER and Ruth GILMAN:
Surname **BOWKER**   (all children born Sawyerville, QC)
     5002. Agnes Mary   born 24 May 1923; died ____; married Theodore Munn BUCK 10 Aug 1946
                            (he s/o Thomas Munn BUCK and Phyllis Rebecca TRAVER)
                            (he born 11 Feb 1918 Sawyerville, QC; died 26 Jan 1995 Sawyerville)
     5003. Gordon Lewis   born 4 Sep 1925; died _____; married Audrey ____ ca ____
     5004. Hazel Ruth   born 27 Feb 1928; died ____; married Gene DROUIN ca ____
     5005. Florence Verna   born 15 Aug 1932; died ____; married James " Jim " VETTY ca ____
     5006. Elsie Irene   born 2 Jan 1936; died ____; married Lynford Clayton LOWRY ca ____
                            (he s/o Clayton Thomas LOWRY and Pansy Viola PARKER)
                            (he born 28 Mar 1935 Sawyerville, QC; died _____)
     5007. Norman B.   born ca ____; died _____; married Betty _____ ca ____

4754. ALTA JEANETTE[10] **CONOVER,** daughter of Abraham[9] CONOVER, Jr. (Lydia Ann[8] OWEN; Seeley[7]; Hannah[6] SEELEY; Deborah[5] BOWKER; Elias[4]; John[3]; Edmund[2,1]) and Elizabeth LOVELESS, was born 15 April 1883 UT. She married Mark Anthony TUTTLE 3 Dec 1901. He was the son of Azariah TUTTLE and Mary Elizabeth WILKINS, and was born 14 Jan 1880; died 10 June 1949 CA.. Alta Jenette[10] CONOVER died 13 Feb 1956 at Orange, CA.

Children of Alta[10] CONOVER and Mark TUTTLE:
Surname **TUTTLE**
+   **5008. HUGH MARK**   born 9 March 1903 UT; died 10 Oct 1966 Los Angeles, CA
                            1 married Laurel Mae POULSON 10 Dec 1923 Cache, UT; divorced
                            2 married Ruth FISHER ca 1943; divorced
                            (she dau/o William George FISHER and Margaret ALLISON)
                            (she born 19 Jan 1908 UT; died 22 Nov 1981 Salt Lake City, UT
                            3 married Dolores GARCIA Swenson ca 1958

Children of Alta Jeanette[10] CONOVER and Mark Anthony TUTTLE, continued:
Surname **TUTTLE**

5009. Howard Milton	born 7 Jan 1906; died 1 Jan 1996 Salty Lake City, UT
	married Emily Louise NELSON 19 Sept 1930 San Francisco, CA
	(she dau/o Carl NELSON and Mary LAWRENCEN) (she born 9 Sep 1908 UT)
5010. David <u>Ward</u>	born 8 Nov 1908 UT; died 30 Nov 1952 SLC
	married Jewel Elizabeth PITTS ca ____
	(she born 29 May 1911; died 8 Jan 1986 NM)
5011. Alta Irene	born 12 Sept 1914; died 25 Nov 2000 Pasadena, CA
	married Richard Weldon BUNNELL ca 1930
	(he s/o Clarence Fritche BUNNELL and Bessie Caroline JACKSON)
	(he born 2 Apr 1906 UT; died 17 Feb 1985 Orange, CA

4811. JOHN ERNEST[10] BOWKER, son of Jay Hinckley[9] BOWKER (Frederick Eri[8]; Silas[7] Archibald [6]; Silas Day[5,4]; John[3]; Edmund[2,1]) and Cornelia Theodora EDWARDS, was born 6 July 1924 at Washington, DC. He married Edith Marie PAULS ca ____. She was the daughter of Gustave PAULS AND Mary ____; and was born ca 1926 DC; died ____. Ernest[10] BOWKER died 18 May 2013. Alexandria, VA. Note: John Ernest[10] BOWKER served as a 1st Lt. in the US Army Air Force during WW 2. He entered the service on 17 Feb 1943, and was discharged 28 Jan 1946. He was a graduate of the University of Maryland; a Protestant; and in 2007 resided at 79 Oak St., Bath, Maine. Reference: Young American Patriots: District of Columbia, page 166.

Children of John Ernest[10] BOWKER and Edith PAULS:
Surname **BOWKER**

5012. John Michael	born ca ____	5016. Diane Edwards	born ____
5013. Tersea Jane	born ____	5017. Virginia Ann	born ____
5014. Amy Jean	born ____	5018. Christine Mary	born Sept 1955
5015. Maureen Ellen	born ____	5019. Judith Marie	born ____

4840. GORDON ROBERT[10] BOWKER, son of Harold Eugene[9] BOWKER (Eugene Wiggins[8]; Eri[7]; Archibald[6]; Silas Day[5,4]; John[3]; Edmund[2,1]) and Jessie BAIRD, was born 3 Sept 1912 at Cortland, NY. He married Mary Patricia BENTON on 20 June 1953 at ____. She was the daughter of ____ BENTON and ____; and was born 4 Oct 1931 at Monson, MA.

Children of Gordon[10] BOWKER and Patricia BENTON:
Surname **BOWKER**

5020. Sarah Baird	born 22 June 1954 Worcester, MA; married Niles J. FRANTZ 17 April 1993
5021. Susan Wesley	born 28 Sep 1955 Albany, NY; married Richard P. CLARENDON 19 Nov 1978
	Children: Henry Benton[12] born 14 Nov 1983 Bradenton, FL; and Daniel Patton[12] CLARENDON born 19 May 1987 Bradenton, FL
5022. Benton Teachout	born 14 May 1957 Schenectday, NY; died 10 Apr 1974 (drowned)
5023. Anthony Schuyler	born 28 Oct 1963 Albany, NY; unmarried
	Child: Robert Anthony[12] BOWKER born 7 Apr 1995 Miami, FL

4844. GERALDINE MARIE[10] BOWKER, daughter of Howard Edward[9] BOWKER(Eugene Wiggins[8]; Eri[7]; Archibald[6]; Silas Day[5,4]; John[3]; Edmund[2,1]) and Dorothy May[4] Mc KINNEY (George B[3]; Alexander[2,1]) , was born 22 June 1921 at Cortland, New York. She married the Reverend Gerald Glenn HEILMAN on 8 June 1946 at Mattydale, Onondaga, NY. He was an ordained Methodist minister, and was the son of John E. HEILMAN and Mary J. ____, and was born 17 May 1922.

Children of Geraldine Marie[10] BOWKER and Gerald HEILMAN:
Surname **HEILMAN**

	5024. Suzanne Kathryn	born 17 May 1948; single
+	**5025. PETER SCOTT**	born 22 June 1950
		married Nancy Marie HOPEWELL 31 May 1969
		(she dau/o ___ HOPEWELL and Esther Marie BENJAMIN) (she born18 Sep 1949)
+	**5026. ELIZABETH ANN**	born 17 Feb 1952; married William Charles DINCHER 25 Aiug 1973
		(he s/o Paul A. DINCHER and _____) (he born 4 Nov 1950)
+	**5027. PAUL DAVID**	born 14 Jan 1955; married Mary Elizabeth PAULHAMUS Colcino 22 Aug 1980
		(she born 3 Apr 1951; divorced 1997/98)
+	**5028. REBECCA LEE**	born 4 Feb 1957
		married Dale Kenneth HEFFNER 31 May 1982 Central Oak Hts, W. Milton, PA
		(he s/o of Kenneth Aaron HEFFNER and Mabel Ann HOCK) (he born 29 Jan 1958)

4845. GENEVIEVE MAE[-10] BOWKER, sister of above, was born 6 Feb 1924 at Syracuse, Onondaga County, NY. She married Robert A. THERRE, as his 2nd wife, on 28 Aug 1945 at Cavalry Evangelical Church, Mattydale, NY. He was the son of Augustus THERRE and Helen TRUAX, and was born 24 Mar 1911; died 15 Aug 1999. Robert had two daughters from his first marriage to Evelyn M. CROUSE . Evelyn was the daughter of John J. CROUSE and Frances F. MAHONEY, and was born ca 1911 NY; married 2 July 1932; died 20 July 1944 as a result of fatal burns received at her home. The daughters were: Mary Ann born 15 Apr 1935, and Patricia Louise THERRE born 7 March 1942. Genevieve raised the girls as though they were her own.

Child of Genevieve[-10] BOWKER and Robert THERRE:
Surname **THERRE**

5029. MARGARET JEANNE	born 13 Sept 1947 Syracuse, NY
	married Daniel Royal KIRKBY 28 Dec 1968

4846. PAUL EDWARD[-10] BOWKER, brother of above, was born 14 May 1926 at Syracuse, Onondaga, NY. He married first to Norma Jean VOORHEES on 10 July 1948 at Andrews Memorial Methodist Church, North Syracuse, NY. She was the daughter of Clarence VOORHEES AND Erma HOWELL, and was born 13 Sep 1928; died 25 April 2000 at Syracuse, NY. His second wife was Frances Jean-[10] STERLING Drisko. They married on 29 March 2003 at Cary, NC. She was the daughter of Charles Lee STERLING (Fred J; Charles; Charles) and Hazel Frances[-9] DOTY (John C.Jr.[-8]; John C.Sr.[-7]; Britain[-6]; William[-5]; William[-4]; Joseph[-3]; Isaac[-2]; Edward[-1]of the MAYFLOWER). She was born 3 June 1927 Syracuse, NY; and was the widow of George Dolbey DRISKO.

Children of Paul Edward[10] BOWKER and Norma Jean VOORHEES:
Surname **BOWKER**

5030. LINDA DIANE	born 19 April 1950 Syracuse, NY
	married Louis Paul BREGOU 8 May 1969
	(he son of Paul BREGOU and Loretta TONNA) (he born 9 Oct 1950)
5031. CATHY LEE	born 17 Sep 1954 Syracuse, NY
	1 married Donald GRIFFIN 14 Oct 1972; divorced; no issue
	2 married John (Jack) Raymond BECKER ca 1976; divorced (he born 1 Mar 1948)

4850. HAZEL LENA[-10] NICHOLS, daughter of Edith M[-9] BOWKER (William Henry[-8]; Daniel[-7]; Anson[-6]; Daniel[-5]; Silas Day[-4]; John[-3]; Edmund[-2,1]) and William NICHOLS, was born 11 Nov 1916 NY. She married first to Henry BEAGLE ca 1934. He was the son of George BEAGLE and Lulu RIFENBURG; and was born 10 Aug 1910; died Sep 1990. They were divorced. She married second to George W. HIBBERT, III ca ____. He was the son of George HIBBERT, II and ____, and was born 10 Sep 1926; died 12 Feb 2004 Saratoga Springs, NY. Hazel Lena[-10] NICHOLS died 10 June 2001 NY.

Child of Hazel L[-10] NICHOLS and Henry BEAGLE:
Surname **BEAGLE**

5032. Arline	born ca 1935; married Richard SILVERNAIL Dec 1955 NY
	(he born 4 June 1936; died 20 Nov 2002 Brant Lake, NY)
	he s/o Fred SILVERNAIL and _____)

Note: Possibly other children of this marriage – but have been unable to verify any names and dates

Child of Hazel L[-10] NICHOLS and George W. HIBBERT, III:
Surname **HIBBERT**

5033. George, IV	born 25 Oct 1960 Saratoga Springs, NY; died 26 Feb 2012 Saratoga

4886. JEWELL LOUISE[-10] ELLIOTT (Brooner), daughter of Mabel Louise[-9] JEWELL (Ida May[-8] McCOUN; Arvilla[-7] BOWKER; Jonathan[-6]; John[-5]; Silas Day[-4]; John[-3]; Edmund[-2,1]) and Hugh Barr ELLIOTT, was born 6 Nov 1919 at Kalispell, Montana. (Note: Her mother divorced Hugh ELLIOTT and married Ernest Dainey BROONER, and she Jewell used his name. It is not known whether or not she was formally adopted by him). Jewell[-10] married Edward French SHANNON ca ____. He was the son of ____ SHANNON and ____; and was born 18 Dec 1917 at Walnut Grove, MN; died 13 July 1997 at Mankato, MN. Jewell-[10] ELLIOTT (Brooner) died ____.

Children of Jewell[-10] ELLIOT (Brooner) and Edward French SHANNON:
Surname **SHANNON**

5034. Robert Gregory	born 25 June 1949 Hennepin Co., MN
5035. Ronald Douglas	born 22 Mar 1951 Hennepin Co., MN
5036. Kathleen Louise	born 14 Dec 1952 Meeker Co., MN
5037. Kevin Michael	born 22 Nov 1956 Meeker CO., MN

4920. WILMA BLENNE-[10] BOWKER, daughter of James Addison-[9] BOWKER (Charles Addison-[8]; William H-[7]; Jefferson-[6]; John-[5]; Silas Day-[4]; John-[3]; Edmund-[2,1]) and Anna Belle ROBERTS, was born 5 Nov 1910 KS. She married John Rex TOOTHAKER on 29 Nov 1929. He was the son of Thomas B. TOOTHAKER and Hannah Nora FITZGERALD, and was born ca 1904; died 1992. Wilma-[10] BOWKER died 10 Nov 1985 Cimarron, KS.

Children of Wilma-[10] BOWKER and John Rex TOOTHAKER:
Srname **TOOTHAKER**

5038. John Rex, Jr.	born 29 Sep 1930; died 30 July 1962 CA	
5039. Dean	born 3 May 1933; died same day	
5040. Eugene	born ca 1934; died ____; married Elsie ____ ca ____	
5041. Ray Vernon	born 6 May 1935 KS; died 14 Dec 2011 Cimarron, Gray, KS	
	married Barbara Kay HOUK 26 Oct 1957	
	Children: Sandra-[12]; Monica-[12]; Tammy-[12]; and William-[12] TOOTHAKER	
5042. Robert	born ____; died ____; married Bonnie ____ ca ____	

4921. CELIA MAY-[10] BOWKER, sister of above, was born 2 Sep 1912 KS. She married James William DUNSWORTH on 22 Dec 1930. He was the son of Frank Hatfield DUNSWORTH and Hazel Mary MOORE, and was born ca 1909 KS; died 10 Nov 1974 Garden City, KS.Celia May-[10] BOWKER died 28 Nov 1994 KS.

Children of Celia May-[10] BOWKER and James William DUNSWORTH:
Surname **DUNSWORTH**

5043. Loretta Faye	born 5 Nov 1931 KS; died 17 Nov 1988; married ____ CLARK ca ____	
5044. William Laverne	born 31 Aug 1934; died 12 Aug 1936	EOL
5045. Esther J. (twin)	born 11 June 1939; died ____; married Donald FRENCH ca ____	
5046. Lester Gene	born 11 June 1939; died 15 Apr 1942 Garden City, KS.	
5047. James William, Jr.	born 2 Apr 1946 Deerfield, KS; died 26 Dec 2010 Hutchinson, KS	
	married Bobbie Hall GLASS 15 Sep 1994	
5048. Arthur Ray	born 30 Oct 1947 Garden City; died 31 Oct 2002 Wichita, KS	

4948. EDITH MAY-[10] BOWKER, daughter of James Clayton-[9] BOWKER (Charles E-[8]; Amaziah-[7]; Jefferson-[6]; John-[5]; Silas Day-[4]; John-[3]; Edmund-[2,1]) and Frances Marion-[4] McKINNEY (George B-[3]; Alexander-[2,1]) was born 6 June 1923 at McLean, Tompkins Co., NY. She married Edward CARPENTER on 18 April 1942. He was the son of Fred S-[4] CARPENTER (John-[3]; Stephen-[2;] Abner-[1]) and Ruth Helen WOODCOCK, and was born 1 Jan 1920; died 3 Mar 1996 NY. Edith-[10] BOWKER died 30 May 1984 at Dryden, Tompkins, NY. She and her husband are buried at Willow Glen Cemetery there.

Children of Edith May-[10] BOWKER and Edward CARPENTER:
Surname **CARPENTER**

+	**5049. LAWRENCE**	born 29 May 1943; died ____	
	EDWARD	married Linda WAINWRIGHT 20 April 1974	(she born 2 May 1949)
+	**5050. VIRGINIA ANNE**	born 21 June 1944 Dryden , Tompkins, NY	
		married Douglas STAIRS 22 July 1966	(he born 19 Nov 1943)
	5051. STEVEN	born 30 June 1947	
		married Donna BROOKHOUSE 14 Mar 1966	(she born 4 Oct 1946)
+	**5052. JEAN**	born	
		married Robert L. EATON 20 July 1970	(he born 2 July 1949)

4949. ESTHER MARY-[10] BOWKER, sister of above, was born 9 Feb 1925 at McLean, NY. She married three times. Her first marriage was to Arthur CARPENTER on 27 June 1944. He was the son of ____ CARPENTER and ____; and was born ca 1919; died ____. They divorced in 1953, and she married second to John WEIN on 19 March 1955. He was the son of Samuel WEIN and Anna ____, and was born 28 Aug 1914; died 31 Nov 1972. She married third to Almon A. MERRIWEATHER, Jr. on 10 Mar 1976   . He was the son of Almon MERRIWEATHER and Mary ____, and was born 10 Dec 1911; died 28 Sep 1992 at Mexico, NY. Esther Mary-[10] BOWKER died 21 Oct 2006 at Emeryville, Alameda, CA.

Children of Esther Mary-[10] BOWKER and Arthur CARPENTER:
Surname **CARPENTER**

+	**5053. JAMES RUSSELL**	born 18 June 1945; married Madeline ZEABEAU 17 Jan 1967 (she born 9 Feb 1950)
	5054. Bonnie Louise	born 16 Sep 1946 NY;

4950. CLAYTON JUNIOR-[10] BOWKER, brother of above, was born 13 March 1926 NY. He married Geraldine " Gerri " Erma WEBB on 4 May 1946. She was the daughter of _____ WEBB and ____, and was born 27 Sep 1926; died 23 Nov 2014 AZ. Junior-[10] BOWKER died 22 Feb 2011 at Phoenix, AZ. They are buried in the family plot at McLean, Tompkins, NY.

Children of Clayton Junior-[10] BOWKER and Geraldine WEBB:
Surname **BOWKER**

+	**5055. CAROL JEAN**	born 6 Jan 1947 NY; 1 married Joseph E. LAPHAM ca ____ ; divorced
		2 married John Joseph O'KEEFE ca ____ (he born 10 Mar 1940)
+	**5056. CLAYTON**	born 16 Jan 1949 NY
	WILLIAM	1 married Elaine BURCHEL 16 Nov 1968; divorced
		2 married Krystyna BARINOWSKI 11 Oct 1984 (she born 5 Dec 1949)
+	**5057. MARION/MARY**	born 17 Oct 1951 NY
	ELIZABETH	married Russell Robert FELLOWS 7 Aug 1970 Dryden, NY
		(he bborn 11 Oct 1948)
+	**5058. DOROTHY ANNE**	born 5 May 1955 NY
	"Deedie"	1 married Gary Dell NASH 25 Aug 1979 (he born 16 Sep 1946)
		2 married Michael " Mike " FENNER ca ____
+	**5059. GLORIA KAY**	born 1 Mar 1970 NY; married Roger Mark RUUSPAKKA ca 1995

4951. CARLTON-[10] " Pete " BOWKER, brother of above, was born 21 July 1930 NY. He married Margaret DURKEE on 18 June 1955. She was the daughter of Albert DURKEE and Florence FOSTER, and was born 6 Feb 1935; died 13 July 2014.

Children of Carleton-[10] BOWKER and Margaret DURKEE:
Surname **BOWKER**

+	**5060. CYNTHIA ANN**	born 6 Aug 1957; married Matthew AREMIA 11 Dec 1982 (he born 2 Apr 1958)
	5061. Diane Louise	born 28 Dec 1958
	5062. Thomas Andrew	born 2 June 1963; married Shari JONES 11 Oct 2003
		Child: Sean Thomas-[12] BOWKER born 29 Sep 2005

4952. ROBERT FAY-[10] BOWKER, brother of above, was born 6 Sep 1932 NY. He married Jeanne Marie MILLER on 10 July 1954. She was the daughter of _____ MILLER and ____, and was born 8 Dec 1932.

Children of Robert-[10] BOWKER and Jeanne MILLER:
Surname **BOWKER**

+	**5063. DEBORAH ANNE**	born 24 May 1955; married Douglas DICKERSON 26 Aug 1978 (he born 12 Dec 1952)
	5064. William Bradley	born 8 Nov 1956; married Melody Diane HALL ca 1984 (she born 7 July 1951)
		Child: David Kristopher-[12] BOWKER born 15 Jan 19__
	5065. Laura Lynn	born 21 Nov 1958; married Randy Arthur KIETH 30 June 1979 (he born 19 Apr 1956)
		Children: Chelsea Lynn-[12] born 30 Oct 1988; and Logan-[12] KIETH born 26 Nov 1994
	5066. Robert Aaron	born 14 Dec 1960; married Nancy STOUT 20 Sep 1986 (she born 30 Dec 1965
		Children: Matthew-[12] born 24 Sep 1990; Sarah-[12] born 23 Mar 2000; and
		Abigail Elizabeth-[12] BOWKER born 9 Nov 2001

4953. SUSIE BELLE-[10] BOWKER, sister of above, was born 12 Feb 1937 at ____ NY. She married Douglas Edmund MAC KECKNIE on 2 June 1956. He was the son of _____ MAC KECKNIE and ____, and was born 2 Apr 1933; died 8 Mar 2004 at Locke, Cayuga, NY.

Children of Susie Belle-[10] BOWKER and Douglas MAC KECKNIE:
Surname **MAC KECKNIE**

	5067. Michelle Susan	born 6 Mar 1960 Tupper Lake, NY; married Brian KWARTA 1 Aug 1981 Moravia, NY
		(he born 28 July 1960 Rochester,NY) (he s/o Robert "Bob" KWARTA and Cecile _)
		Children: Bethany Nicole-[12] born 4 Apr 1991; Bradley Jordan-[12] born 31 July 1993;
		and Brielle Mariah-[12] KWARTA born 4 July 1997
	5068. Carol Lynne	born 20 Dec 1962 Tupper Lake, NY; married Patrick BARRY 2 Oct 1999 Moravia, NY
		Children: Nicholas Patrick-[12] born 10 July 2003; David James-[12] born 24 Nov 2005;
		and Neva Anne-[12] BARRY born 29 Jan 2008
	5069. James Douglas	born 19 Nov 1964 Cortland, NY
		married Bonnie Diane NAST 15 Aug 1987 Auburn, NY (she born 8 June 1966)
		Children: Jacob Clayton-[12] born 30 Mar 1996 Penfield, NY; and Joshua Douglas-[12] Mac KECKNIE born 5 Dec 1999

Children of Susie Belle[-10] BOWKER and Douglas MAC KECKNIE, continued:
Surname **MAC KECKNIE**

    5070. Barbara Jeanne   born 13 Dec 1966 Cortland, NY
                             married Karl M. NORRIS 2 May 1992 Moravia, NY   (he born 6 Aug 1967)
                  Children: Maria Antoinette[-12] born 21 Oct 1994; Emily MacKecknie[-12] born 7 Sep 1998;
                  and James Joseph[-12] NORRIS born 9 Jan 2003

4954. KAREN RUTH[-10] BOWKER, ister of above, was born 25 Dec 1939 at ____ NY. She married John GALEOTTI, Jr. on 14 Feb 1959. He was the son of John GALEOTTI (born 1 Apr 1910; died 2 Jan 1966 Homer, Cortland, NY) and ____; and was born 29 Jan 1938; died 20 May 2001.

Children of Karen Ruth[-10] BOWKER and John GALEOTTI, Jr.:
Surname **GALEOTTI**

+   **5071. MICHAEL TRENT**   born 15 Mar 1960 NY
                               1 married Kathy Mc KANE 28 July 1979; divorced 1987 (she born 20 Dec 1959)
                               2 married Tammy MARSHALL ca 1990
    5072. Christopher John   born 4 Jan 1963; 1 married Deborah MILLER 1991; divorced 1992
                               2 married Wanda RODRIQUEZ May 2001
                  Children: Brenden[-12] born 6 Dec 1997; Anna Gabriella[-12] born 7 Oct 1999; John Carlos[-12]
                  born 17 Aug 2003; and Maia Cafriella[-12] GALEOTTI born 5 Feb 2005
    5073. David Noel   born 27 Dec 1963 Cortland, NY
                               married Deborah Marie PRANTE 20 Sep 1986   Garden Grove, CA
                               (she born 3 Feb 1961) (she dau/o Walter PRANTE and _____)
                  Children: Kyle Anthony[-12] born 7 Oct 1989; and Nicholas John[-12] GALEOTTI born 13 Nov 1992
    5074. Timothy John   born 2 Aug 1968;   married Stella VIDAL 6 June 1992; divorced 1997

4955. JO ANNE[-10] BOWKER, sister of above, was born 16 May 1945 at ____ NY. She married Richard P. WILLIAMS on 30 Jan 1965. He was the son of _____ WILLIAMS and ____, and was born 26 Apr 1944; died 4 Feb 2008 NY.

Children of JoAnne[-10] BOWKER and Richard WILLIAMS:
Surname **WILLIAMS**

    5075. Anthony Michael   born 24 Dec 1965; married Hollis THOMASES 12 June 1993
    5076. Kimberlee Annette   born 3 Apr 1967;   married John L. ECKHARDT ca 1993
                  Children: Madysen Leigh[-12] born 31 May 1997; and Nicholas Clay[-12] ECKHARDT born 9 June 1999

4974. AMY URSULA[-10] VIELE, daughter of Alice May[-9] MUNSON (West[-8] MUNSON; Orange[-7]; Esther[-6] BOWKER; Noah[-5]; Silas Day[-4]; John[-3]; Edmund[-2;1]) and Victor Van VIELE, was born May 1897 at Elmira, Chemung, NY. She married Harry William RICE ca 1922. He was the son of Harry John RICE and Elizabeth Sarah SHARP,, and was born 17 May 1894 at Lambeth, London, England; died 3 Aug 1962 Elmira, NY. In 1930 they resided at Big Flats, Chemung County, NY. The US Federal Census that year listed him as a toolmaker in an automobile factory. Amy Ursula[-10] VIELE died 25 Mar 1974 Elmira.

Children of Amy Ursula-[10] VIELE and Harry RICE:
Surname **RICE**

    5077. Harry Jr.   born 12 Apr 1923; died 15 Oct 2010 Montour Falls, Schuyler, NY
    5078. Anna Mae   born ca 1925; died ____
    5079. Phyllis   born ca 1926; died ____
    5080. James   born 19 Aug 1930; died 30 Dec 2004 Montour Falls, NY
    5081. Doris / Denise (f)   born ca 1935; died ____

4977. MARY WEST[-10] VIELE, sister of above, was born 18 Dec 1903 at Rochester, Monroe, NY. She married Victor Francis GEORGE 1 Dec 1921 at Erin, Chemung, NY. He was the son of William Charles GEORGE and Amy Beatrice CROSS, and was born 18 Dec 1903; died 29 Dec 1946 Westfield, MA. Mary West[-10] VIELE died 28 Aug 1985 at Westfield, MA.

Children of Mary West[-10] VIELE and Victor GEORGE:
Surname **GEORGE**

    5082. Robert William   born ca 1922 Elmira, NY; died 1989 Elmira
    5083. Alice May   born 26 Oct 1923 Elmira, NY; died 26 Oct 2012
                               married Michael C. DEVENO ca _____ (he born 19 Dec 1920 MA; died 24 Aug 1993)
                  Children: Michael[-12] Jr; Phillip [-12]; Paul[-12]; Tina[-12]; and Debra [-12] DEVENO

Children of Mary West-[10] VIELE and Victor GEORGE, continued:
Surname **GEORGE**

5084. Leo Victor	born ca 1925 CT; died 2001 Westfield, MA	
	married Barbara Leigh TRYON ca _____	(2 sons, 1 dau)
5085 Elizabeth Jane /"Betty"	born ca 1928 MA; died ____; married ____ LECLAIRE	
5086. James	born ca 1929; died ____	
5087. David West	born ca 1931 MA; died 1993	
5088. Rose Mary/Rosemary	born 30 Dec 1932 Westfield, MA; died 24 Feb 2012 Sandisfield, MA	
	married Willard PLATT ca _____	

Child: Barbara-[12] PLATT born ca ____

5089. Charles Albert	born ca 1935 Westfield, MA; died 1935	EOL
5090. Donald Ernest	born ca 1937 Westfield, MA; died 1981 CA	
5091. Harold "Skip" Louis	born 1939 Westfield, MA; died ____	
5092. Roger Laurence	born 1940 Westfield, MA; died ____	

4993. HERBERT HUMISTON[-11](HULLIGAN) BOWKER, son of Corinne Ladd[-10] BOWKER (Capt Hugh D[-9] BOWKER; Franklin[-8]; Rice-[7;] Gideon[-6]; Antipas[-5]; Josiah[-4]; John-[3;2]; Edmund-[1]) and Herbert HULLIGAN, was born 22 July 1899 IL. He married Frances Katherine DOCKER 29 April 1925. She was the daughter of Joseph George DOCKER and Katherine THORNLEY; and was born 3 May 1900; died 19 Jan 1992 Burlington, Ontario. Herbert Humiston[-11] BOWKER died 20 Dec 1968.

Children of Herbert Humiston[-11] (Hulligan) BOWKER:
Surname **BOWKER**

5093. Herbert H. Jr.	born 19 Dec 1926 IL; died _____; graduate of US Military Academy at West Point, MD	
	married Marjorie A.DRUMM 18 Oct 1950 San Francisco, CA	
	Children: Herbert, III[-13] born 30 Apr 1951 Oakland, CA; David Michael[-13] born 22 Apr 1954 Chicago, IL; and Julia-[13] BOWKER born 8 Nov 1957 Chicago,IL	
5094. Nancy Ann	born 10 Mar 1929; died ____	
	married Major John Love GERRITY, Jr. 26 Nov 1952 Fort Knox, KY	
	Children: John Love[-13], Jr. born 29 Jan 1954 Chicago, IL; and Kathleen F[-13] GERRITY born 18 Feb 1956 Fort Monroe VA	

4997. MADELEINE[-11] L. HOLLISTER, daughter of Cora Louise[-10] BOWKER (Edmund Heard[-9]; Lewis Leander[-8]; Lyman James[-7]; Gideon[-6]; Antipas[-5]; Josiah[-4]; John-[3;2]; Edmund-[1]) and Mark Abram HOLLISTER, was born ca 1893 NY. She married Harold DAVIS 11 May 1918. He was the son of ____ DAVIS and ____, and was born 2 Dec 1893; died Oct 1980 Corinth, NY.

Children of Madeleine[-11] HOLLISTER and Harold DAVIS:
Surname **DAVIS**

5095. Robert E.	born ca 1920	5098. Douglas H.	born ca 1927
5096. Ruth L.	born ca 1924		
5097. Marjorie J.	born ca 1925; died 7 June 2007 Langhorne, PA		

4998. HAROLD EDMUND[-11] HOLLISTER, brother of above, was born ca 1896 NY. He married Christie Houghton WHITE ca 1916. She was the daughter of Walter H. WHITE and Saisy HOUGHTON; and was born 30 Sep 1897 Corinth, Saratoga, NY; died 18 Jan 1986 Wilmington, OH. Buried Corinth, NY.

Children of Harold E[-11] HOLLISTER and Christie WHITE:
Surname **HOLLISTER**

5099. Harold H.	born ca 1924 NY	5101. Walter Mark	born 22 Nov 1930 VT
5100. Richard Parker	born 29 Sep 1926 VT	5102. Jane C.	born ca 1937 NY

5008. HUGH MARK[-11] TUTTLE, son of Alta Jeanette[-10] CONOVER (Abraham-[9], Jr; Lydia Ann[-8] OWEN; Seeley[-7]; Hannah[-6] SEELEY; Deborah-[5] BOWKER; Elias[-4]; John-[3]; Edmund-[2,1]) and Mark TUTTLE, was born 9 March 1903 UT. He married first to Laurel Mae PAULSEN on 10 Dec 1923 at Cache, UT. They divorced and he married second to Ruth FISHER ca 1943. She was the daughter of William George FISHER and Margaret ALLISON, and was born19 Jan 1908 UT; died 22 Nov 1981 Salt Lake City, UT. They also divorced, and he married third to Dolores GARCIA Swenson ca 1958.

Children of Hugh Mark[-11] TUTTLE and Laurel PAULSEN:
Surname **TUTTLE**

5103. Jean	born ca 1925; died ____; married _____ STEVENS ca ____ Denver, CO		
5104.Hugh, Jr.	bornca 1928; died ____		
5105. Timothy (Tim)	born ca _____	5106. Theodore (Ted)	born ca ____

5025. PETER SCOTT[-11] HEILMAN, son of Geraldine Marie[-10] BOWKER (Howard Edward[-9]; Eugene Wiggins[-8]; Eri-[7]; Archibald[-6]; Silas Day-[5;4]; John-[3]; Edmund-[2;1]) and Gerald Glenn HEILMAN, was born 22 June 1950 at ____. He married Nancy Marie HOPEWELL on 3 May 1969 at Trinity United Methodist Church, Williamsport, PA. She was the daughter of _____ HOPEWELL and ____; and was born 18 Sep 1949.

Children of Peter Scott[-11] HEILMAN and Nancy Marie HOPEWELL:
Surname **HEILMAN**
>5107. Anastasia Marie   born 14 Nov 1970; married John LOHR 11 July 1992
>>Children: Jacob Peter[-12] born 8 Oct 2002; and Faith Marie[-12] LOHR born 22 Apr 2004
>5108. Zachariah Scott   born 25 Aug 1974

5026. ELIZABETH ANN[-11] HEILMAN, sister of above, was born Feb 1952 at ____. She married William Charles DINCHER on 25 Aug 1973 at Trinity United Methodist Church, Williamsport, PA. He was the son of ____ DINCHER and ____; and was born 4 Nov 1950 at ___.

Children of Elizabeth Ann[-11] HEILMAN and William Charles DINCHER:
Surname **DINCHER**
>5109. Gerald Paul Joseph   born 28 Dec 1975 Stuttgart, Germany
>>married Nathalie Ann JOHNSON 18 June 2005 Lumberton, NC
>5110. Andrew Michael   born 4 Nov 1977; married Elizabeth MAMMINA 26 Feb 2005

5027. PAUL DAVID [-11] HEILMAN, brother of above, was born 14 Jan 1955 at ____. He married Mary Elizabeth PAULHAMUS Colocino , as her second husband, on 22 Aug 1980 at _____. She was the daughter of _____ PAULHAMUS and ____; and was born 3 Apr 1951. She had a son, Todd COLOCINO, by a previous marriage. Paul[-11] divorced Mary ca 1998/99.

Children of Paul David[-11] HEILMAN and Mary Elizabeth PAULHAMUS Colocino:
Surname **HEILMAN**

5111. Amanda Joye	born 1 Aug 1982	5113. Ivy Rose	born 21 Feb 1986
5112. Lance Isaac	born 25 Mar 1984		

5028. REBECCA LEE[-11] HEILMAN, sister of above, was born 4 Feb 1957 at ____. She married Dale Kenneth HEFFNER on 31 May 1982 at Sylvan Chapel, Central Oak Hts., West Milton, PA. He was the son of Kenneth Aaron HEFFNER and Mabel Ann HOCK, and was born 29 Jan 1958.

Children of Rebecca Lee[-11] HEILMAN and Dale HEFFNER:
Surname **HEFFNER**   (children all born Allentown, PA)

5114. Jessica Elizabeth	born 29 Dec 1984	5116. Sarah Anna	born 3 Nov 1989
5115. Joshua Bartla	born 15 July 1986	5117. Jacqueline Marie	born 2 July 1993

5029. MARGARET JEANNE[-11] THERRE, daughter of Genevieve Mae[-10] BOWKER (Howard Edward[-9]; Eugene Wiggins[-8]; Eri-[7]; Archibald[-6]; Silas Day[-5;4]; John[-3]; Edmund-[2;1]) and Robert August THERRE, was born 13 Sep 1947 at Syracuse, Onondaga, NY. She married Daniel Royal KIRKBY on 28 Dec 1968 at Sacred Heart Catholic Church, Cicero, Onondaga, NY. He was the son of Kenneth KIRKBY and Jean GAUDET, and was born _____.

Children of Margaret Jeanne[-11] THERRE and Daniel KIRKBY:
Surname **KIRKBY**
>5118. Michelin Noel   born 4 Apr 1969 St. Mary's Hospital, Syracuse, NY
>>married Daniel John KELEHER 9 Oct 1993 Sacred Heart Church, Cicero, NY
>>Children: Madelyn Elise[-12] born 23 Feb 2006; and Daniel-[12] KELEHER born 24 Mar 2008
>5119. Daniel Robert Kenneth born 9 Aug 1982

5030. LINDA DIANE[-11] BOWKER, daughter of Paul Edward[-10] BOWKER (Howard Edward[-9]; Eugene Wiggins[-8]; Eri-[7]; Archibald[-6]; Silas Day[-5;4]; John[-3]; Edmund-[2;1]) and Norman Jean VOORHEES, was born 19 Apr 1950 at Syracuse, Onondaga, NY. She married Louis Paul BREGOU on 8 May 1969. He was the son of Paul BREGOU and Loretta TONA, and was born 9 Oct 1950 NY.

Children of Linda Diane[-11] BOWKER and Louis BREGOU:
Surname **BREGOU**
>5120. Paul James   born 24 Oct 1969; died 27 Oct 1969
>5121. Christina Ellen   born 27 May 1971; married Timothy Todd BURTIS 7 Aug 1993
>>(he born 13 Nov 1965) (he s/o _____ BURTIS and _____)
>>Children: Theodore[-13] born 11 June 1999; and Alex[13] BURTIS born 14 July 2002

Children of Linda Diane[-11] BOWKER and Louis BREGOU, continued:
Surnmae **BREGOU**

> 5122. Jacquelyn Elizabeth   born 18 Nov 1973;
> married Scott Lawrence CONOVER 8 July 1995
> (he s/o Robert CONOVER and Ida May ____) (he born 30 Nov 1966 NY)
> Children: Carolyn Elizabeth-[13] born 22 Aug 1996; Madelyn Diane[13] born 9 July 1998; and Scott
> Lawrence13 CONOVER, Jr. born 20 Feb 2006 England
>
> 5123. Adam Paul   born 20 Nov 1982 NY
> married Christina SIMON 21 July 2005 Hilton Head, NC
> (she born 5 Aug 1983) (she dau/o ____ SIMON and _____)
> Children: Landon Grey[13] born 3 Feb 2008; Karter Louis-[13] born 25 Mar 2010; and
> Maisy[13] BREGOU born 27 Sep 2012
>
> 5124. Elizabeth Katherine   born 4 Aug 1984 NY
> married Ryan SCOTTRON 15 April 2012 San Juan, Puerto Rico
> Child: Miles Anthony[12] SCOTTRON born 27 March 2013 MA

5031. CATHY LEE[-11] BOWKER, sister of above, was born 17 Sep 1954 at Syracuse, Onondaga, NY. She married first to Donald GRIFFIN on 14 Oct 1972 at ____. They divorced ca ____; no issue. She married second to John (Jack) Raymond BECKER ca ____ 1976. He was the son of _____ BECKER and _____; and was born 1 Mar 1948.

Children of Cathy Lee-[11] BOWKER and " Jack " BECKER:
Surname **BECKER**

> 5125. Sara Elizabeth   born 4 Mar 1977
> 5126. Jennifer Mary   born 13 Mar 1982
> married Drue HOLDEMAN _ Oct 2006, Jacksonville, FL
> Child: Hannah Emily-[13] HOLDEMAN born 20 Aug 2007 FL
> 5127. Anthony Joseph   born 13 Aug 1987

5049. LAWRENCE EDWARD[-11] CARPENTER, son of Edith[-10] BOWKER (James Clayton[-9]; Charles E[-8]; Amaziah-[7]; Jefferson-[6]; John[-5]; Silas Day[-4]; John[-3]; Edmund-[2;1]) and Edward CARPENTER, was born 29 May 1943. He married Linda WAINWRIGHT on 20 Apr 1974 . She was the daughter of _____ WAINWRIGHT and ____; and was born 2 May 1949.

Children of Lawrence-[11] CARPENTER and Linda WAINWRIGHT:
Surname **CARPENTER**

> 5128. John Edward   born 6 Feb 1975   5129. Benjamin Fitz   born 30 June 1977

5050. VIRGINIA ANNE[-11] CARPENTER, sister of above, was born 21 June 1944 at Dryden, Tompkins, NY. She married Douglas STAIRS on 22 July 1996. He was the son of ____ STAIRS and ____; and was born 19 Nov 1943.

Children of Virginia-[11] CARPENTER and Douglas STAIRS:
Surname **STAIRS**

> 5130. Scott Leslie   born 6 Mar 1968; married Kimberlee HOLMES 24 Mar 1990
> Children: Joshua Holmes-[13] born 22 Feb 1991; Heidi Elizabeth-[13] born 19 July 1993;
> and Gregory Scott-[13] STAIRS born 4 Sep 1994
> 5131. Jennifer Jean   born 5 April 1970

5051. STEVEN[-11] CARPENTER, brother of above, was born 30 June 1947 at Dryden, Tompkins, NY. He married Donna BROOKHOUSE on 16 March 1966. She was the daughter of _____ BROOKHOUSE and ____; and was born 4 Oct 1946.

Children of Steven-[11] CARPENTER and Donna BROOKHOUSE:
Surname **CARPENTER**

> 5132. Susan Elizabeth   born 8 Aug 1966
> 1 married Jeffery SIMMONS 30 Aug 1988   (he born 25 Mar 1963)
> 2 married Randy KILTS ca _____   (Child: Jason-[13] KILTS born Aug 1996)
> 5133. Fred James   born _____

5052. JEAN[-11] CARPENTER, sister of above, was born _____. She married Robert L. EATON on 20 July 1970. He was the son of ____ EATON and ____, and was born 2 July 1949.

Children of Jean-[11] CARPENTER and Robert EATON:
Surname **EATON**

5134. Traci Rochelle	born 5 Dec 1974	5135. Joseph Clayton	born 16 June 1979

5053. JAMES RUSSELL-[11] CARPENTER, son of Esther MARY-[10] BOWKER (James Clayton-[9]; Charles E-[8]; Amaziah-[7]; Jefferson-[6]; John-[5]; Silas Day-[4]; John-[3]; Edmund-[2;1]) and Arthur CARPENTER, was born 18 June 1945 at Cortland, Cortland, NY. He married Madeline ZEABEAU on 17 Jan 1967. She was born 9 Feb 1950.

Children of James-[11] CARPENTER and Madeline ZEABEAU:
Surname **CARPENTER**

5136. Patti Ann   born 7 Oct 1967
                    married Christopher SMITH 17 Jan 1986   (he born 24 Aug 1966)
          Child: Brandon Lee-[13] SMITH born 14 Jan 1987
5137. Jo Ann   born 23 Oct 1968 married Duane OLSON 5 Apr 1986 (he born 19 June 1964)
          Children: Brandi Nicole-[13] born 18 Oct 1986; and Amanda Lyn-[13] OLSON born 29 Nov 1990
5138. Christie Ann   born 11 Dec 1973; married Ryan KEITH 20 Mar 1993
          Child: Brittany Alice-[13] CARPENTER born 18 Apr 1991; also adopted Joshua ____

5055. CAROL JEAN-[11] BOWKER, daughter of Clayton Junior-[10] BOWKER (James Clayton-[9]; Charles E-[8]; Amaziah-[7]; Jefferson-[6]; John-[5]; Silas Day-[4]; John-[3]; Edmund-[2;1]) and Geraldine WEBB, was born 6 Jan 1947. She married first to Joseph E. LAPHAM on 20 May 1973. They divorced and she married second to Joseph O'KEEFE on _____ . He was the son of _____ O'KEEFE and ____, and was born 10 March 1940.

Children of Carol Jean-[11] BOWKER and Joseph LAPHAM:
Surname **LAPHAM**

5139. Brian Keith   (twin)   born 17 Feb 1968; married Christina Lynn PARNELL 15 July 2000
          Child: Clayton Wayne-[13] LAPHAM born 9 Jan 2003
5140. Barbara Kay (twin)   born 17 Feb 1968;
5141. Scott Edward   born 28 Sep 1974; married Julie _____ 13 Nov 1993
          Child: Katelyn Renee-[13] LAPHAM born 3 June 1994

5056. CLAYTON WILLIAM "Bill" -[11] BOWKER, brother of above, was born 16 Jan 1949. He married first to Elaine BURCHEL ca 1972. They divorced, and he married second to Krystyna " Krys " BARINOWSKI on 11 Oct 1984. She was the daughter of _____ BARINOWSKI and _____, and was born 5 Dec 1949.

Children of Clayton-[11] BOWKER and Elaine BURCHEL:
Surname **BOWKER**

5142. Carlen Renee   born 17 Oct 1973
                    married Lenny/ Leonard BRUENWILER ca _____
          Children. Jace Leonard-[13] born 6 Aug 2000, died 8 Jan 2002, and Ava Renee-[13] BRUENWILER born 30 Mar 2002
5142. Kyle Morgan   born 26 Oct 1979

5057. MARION ELIZABETH (Mary Beth) -[11] BOWKER, sister of above, was born 17 Oct 1951. She married Russell Robert FELLOWS on 7 Aug 1970 at Dryden, Tompkins, NY. He was the son of __ FELLOWS and ?; and was born 11 Oct 1948.

Children of Marion-[11] BOWKER and Russell FELLOWS:
Surname **FELLOWS**

5143. James Douglas   born 7 April 1971; married Suzanne ____ 30 June 1994 Washington, DC
          Children: Nicholas Clayton-[13] born 9 Nov 1999; and Louisa Marion-[13] FELLOWS born 30 Aug 2002
5144. Angela Celeste   born 17 Sep 1973; married Scott ORME 23 May 1992
          Child: Tanis Scott-[13] ORME born 3 May 1995
5145. Ammon David   born 3 Dec 1979; married Victoria ____ 3 July 2000
          Child: Jeremy Nicholas-[13] FELLOWS born 15 Jan 2003
5146. Lisa Virginia   born 27 July 1984; married Keith McCURDY ca ____
          Child: Keith-[13] McCURDY born 2 July 2004

5058. DOROTHY ANNE-[11] BOWKER, sister of above, was born 5 May 1955. She married Gary Dell NASH on 25 Aug 1979. He was the son of _____ NASH and ____; and was born 11 Oct 1948.

Children of Dorothy[-11] BOWKER and Gary NASH:
Surname **NASH**

5147. JoAnne Marie	born 30 June 1982	5148. Cindy Anne	born 3 Aug 1986

5059. GLORIA KAY[-11] BOWKER, sister of above, was born 1 Mar 1970. She married Roger Mark RUUSPAKKA on 20 May 1995. He was the son of _____ RUUSPAKKA and ____, and was born 22 Nov 1960.

Children of Gloria[-11] BOWKER and Roger RUUSPAKKA:
Surname **RUUSPAKKA**

5149. Trevor Logan	born 18 June 2002	5151. Connor Dylan	born 24 Mar 2005
5150. Tyler Mark Fellows	born 12 Apr 2002		

5060. CYNTHIA ANNE[-11] BOWKER, daughter of Carleton[-10] BOWKER (James Clayton[-9]; Charles E[-8]; Amaziah Chester[-7]; Jefferson[-6]; John[-5]; Silas Day[-4]; John[-3]; Edmund[-2;1]) and Margaret DURKEE, was born 6 Aug 1957. She married Matthew AREMIA on 11 Dec 1982. He was the son of _____AREMIA and ____; and was born 2 Apr 1958.

Children of Cynthia[-11] BOWKER and Matthew AREMIA:
Surname **AREMIA**

5152.Michael   born 29 May 1983; married Kristen SILGUERO ca ____
          Children: Kadence Ilise[-13] born 16 Jan 2009; and Daliyah Cassidy[-13] AREMIA born 12 Mar 2011
5153. Michelle   born 22 May 1986; married Luke MITCHELL ca _____
          Child: Griffin Scott[-13] AREMIA born 25 July 2014
5154. Nicholas   born 24 Dec 1992

5063. DEBORAH ANN[-11] BOWKER, daughter of Robert Fay[-10] BOWKER (James Clayton[-9]; Charles E[-8]; Amaziah Chester-7; Jefferson[-6]; John[-5]; Silas Day[-4]; John[-3]; Edmund[-2;1]) and Jeanne Marie MILLER, was born 24 May 1955 NY. She married Douglas DICKERSON on 26 Aug 1978. He was the son of _____ DICKERSON and ____; and was born 12 Dec 1952.

Children of Deborah[-11] BOWKER and Douglas DICKERSON:
Surname **DICKERSON**

5155. Jedediah Earl (twin)	born 19 July 1979	5157. Deven Michael	born 27 June 1987
5156. Jeremiah Errol (twin)	born 19 July 1979		

5071. MICHAEL TRENT[-11] GALEOTTI, son of Karen Ruth[-10] BOWKER (James Clayton[-9]; Charles E-[8]; Amaziah Chester[-7]; Jefferson[-6]; John[-5]; Silas Day[-4]; John[-3]; Edmund[-2;1]) and John GALEOTTI, was born 15 March 1960 at Ft. Sam Houston, TX. He married first to Kathy Lynn McKANE on 21 July 1979. She was the daughter of Richard McKANE and Janet ____; and was born 20 Dec 1959. They divorced, and Michael[-11] married second to Tammy MARSHALL on 13 Jan 1990.

Children of Michael[-11] GALEOTTI and Kathy McKANE:
Surname **GALEOTTI**

5158. Michael Trent, Jr.	born 2 July 1980	5159. Joseph Michael	born 23 Jan 1982

Children of Michael[-11] GALEOTTI and Tammy MARSHALL:
Surname **GALEOTTI**

5160. Jonathan William	born 16 Oct 1989	5162. Jenna Marie	born 5 Feb 1999
5161. Emillie J.	born 3 Dec 1994		

BOWKER

INDEX - BOWKER SURNAMES

293

INDEX - BOWKER SURNAMES

294

295

INDEX - BOWKER SURNAMES

BOWKER,

, James Alan	267
, James Alfred	83
, James Arden	274
, James Clayton	247, 276
, James Dennison	132
, James H	197, 240
, James M	134
, James Madison	108, 167, 168
, James T	136, 199, 242
, Janet	228, 267
, Jannette	87
Jasper	128, 184
, Jay	247
, Jay Hinckley	233, 267
, Jay Paul	267
, Jean F	248
, Jeanette	155, 240
, Jefferson	75, 133, 134
, Jennie	18, 46, 195, 197
, Jennie Rowena	245, 274
, Jerry R	270
, Jerusha	75
, Jesse	232, 242, 244
, Jessie	151
, Jessie Lyman	215, 260
, Joanna	87, 107
, JoAnne	276, 285
, Joe Galen	273
, John	1, 4, 5, 10, 11, 13, 32, 33, 34, 62, 63, 66, 71, 74, 75, 83,126, 134, 135, 155, 267
, John Anderson	86
, John Antipierce	5, 13
, John Bradley	211
, John E	151, 152
, John Ernest	267, 281
, John H	126, 234
, John Henry Powers	132, 193
, John Hunt	126
, John Leavitt	168
, John Michael	281
, John Pierson	85, 153, 154, 215
, John Starkweather	62, 108
, John S	87
, John W	215
, Jonathan	14, 39, 41, 61, 74, 84, 106, 132
, Joseph	4, 10, 32, 33, 34, 66, 70, 71, 72,75, 167, 196, 220, 221
, Joseph Edward	242
, Joseph Proctor	70, 124
, Joseph S	136
, Joseph W	124
, Josiah	5, 9, 14, 29, 40
, Josie M	245, 273
, Jotham	39
, Jotham Liberty	84
, Joy Dale	273
, Judith Marie	281
, Julia	133, 287
, Juliann	132
, Julius Avery	176, 225
, Julius C	153
, June Irene	268
, Kanza Rae	246
, Karen Ruth	276, 285

BOWKER,

, Katie S	196
, Kenneth	196, 247, 269
, Kyle Morgan	290
, Klein P	274
, L.	148, 153
, Laura	152, 167, 214, 246, 284
, Laverne Ernest	243
, Lawrence	216, 246, 257
, Lemuel	62
, Lena	135, 211
, Leon	220
, Leona	136, 197
, Leonard	85, 153
, Leroy	199, 232
, Leroy L	196, 249, 270
, Leroy S	246, 247
, Leslie S	240
, Lestral Herbert	240, 270
, Levi	85, 87, 107, 152
, Levi D	132, 213
, Levi Goodell	152, 213
, Lewis	137, 193, 196
, Lewis Fales	153, 215
, Lewis Leander	153, 214, 215
, Lewis Warren	124
, Lillian	222, 243, 249
, Lillie Ellen	273
, Linda Diane	282, 288
, Lisa	34, 72, 73, 74, 128, 129
, Lizzie	132, 214
, Lloyd Roman	232
, Lois	30, 33, 69, 266, 274
, Lorena	87
, Lorraine D	248, 276
, Louella May	233
, Louis L	260
, Louisa	126, 135
, Louisa Adeline	153
, Louisa Lida	184
, Lovett H	63, 169
, Lovice	61, 106
, Luanna	213
, Lucena	40
, Lucia A	149
, Lucille	267
, Lucinda	75, 135
, Lucy	6, 18, 30, 41, 85, 175
, Lucy Ellen	193
, Lucy M	122
, Lucy Minerva	259
, Luetta	240, 271
, Luke	39
, Luke Freeman	84, 152
, Lulu	233, 266, 274
, Lura Jane	185
, Lutetia	154
, Luther	62, 107, 167
, Lydia	6, 19, 40, 41, 61, 62, 70 106, 107, 123, 152, 196
, Lyle W	246, 275
, Lyman Howe	152, 213
, Lyman James	85, 152, 213
, Lyman Tyler	153
, Lysander	41
, Mabel	132, 280
, Mabel Rose	234, 268

296

BOWKER,

, Mable Ellen	199
, Madge	232, 258, 259
, Madison	74, 75, 133, 134, 213
, Maggie F	124
, Malvena	213
, Marcellus Scott	167, 221
, Mareta Belle	273
, Margaret	87, 134, 137, 197
, Margaret Elizabeth	246
, Margaret Jerusha	134
, Margaret Leona	193, 196
, Mariah	134
, Marian	267, 270
, Marian Esther	248
, Marion Elizabeth	284, 290
, Marion Estella	126
, Marion Thayer	211
, Marjorie L	247
, Martha	3, 5, 6, 17, 29, 87, 228
, Martha A	109
, Martha Edna	168
, Martha Elizabeth	256
, Martha J	133, 134, 152, 195, 214
, Martha Patty	154
, Martha R	124
, Martin VanBuren	132, 194
, Marvene C	193
, Mary	2 ,3 ,4, 5 ,6, 10, 29, 32,
	70, 72, 76, 108, 122, 123,
	148, 168, 175, 205, 209
, Mary Ann	117, 128, 131, 133, 185
, Mary B	84, 151, 152
, Mary C	196
, Mary Caroline	149, 210
, Mary Catherine	124
, Mary Celia	247, 275
, Mary Gage	63, 109
, Mary H	124, 152, 279
, Mary J	137, 245
, Mary Jane	153
, Mary Kate	241
, Mary Louise	210
, Mary M	122
, Mary Mattie	234, 268, 269
, Mary Polly	34, 75, 153
, Mary R	186, 234
, Matilda	69, 122
, Matthew	284
, Maud/Maude	216, 241, 271
, Maureen Ellen	281
, May	175, 194, 225
, Medora	124, 180
, Mehitable	72, 127, 128
, Merton E	91
, Micah	9, 29
, Mildred	155, 232, 247
, Millard F	213
, Millicent Betsey	176, 225
, Millie	199
, Milo Anderson	153, 215
, Milton Charles	209
, Milton R	148
, Minnie	175
, Minnie Jane	198, 233, 265, 266
, Minnie Samantha	196
, Miranda	106

BOWKER,

, Mitchell	152
, Mitchell Harvey	214, 258
, Myrtie	196
, Myrtle Frances	192, 242
, Myrtle Ina	233
, Nahum	63
, Nancy	39, 62, 151
, Nancy Ann	287
, Napoleon B	135
, Nathaniel	33, 39, 70, 71, 83, 86,
	126, 149
, Nathaniel Beaman	84, 151
, Nellie	197, 199, 249, 250
, Nelson	132, 175
, Neona	274
, Nerlie E	199
, Newell DeEtte	193
, Newton Franklin	201
, Niles	184
, Noah	10, 32, 34, 67, 76, 136, 200,
	201
, Nora D	135
, Nora E	192, 241
, Norma Bedell	155
, Norman	136, 232, 280
, Norris/Harris	214
, Noyes	18
, Obadiah/Obediah	41, 86, 87, 155, 216
, Olive	216
, Oliver	40, 85
, Ora Clayton	135
, Orren/Orrin	199
, Orren Valoris	199, 249
, Orrin L	132, 192
Orrin Smith	196
, Orsimas/Orsemus	34, 74, 131, 132
, Orsemus White	192
, Orson O	242
, Oscar	135, 198
, Oscar Bruce	233
, Oscar Wilbert	233
, Otto L 242	
, Patience	63, 110
, Paul Edward	269, 282
, Paul William	242, 247
, Pauline Safford	29
, Pearl Mary	196
, Peninah	75
, Permina	199
, Perry V	243
, Persis	14, 31, 33, 62
, Phebe	14
, Philinda	133, 195
, Phoebe	85
, Polly	41, 61, 75, 134
, Prentiss/Prentice	213
, Proctor F	124, 180
, Prudence	14, 18, 40
, R S	233
, Rachel	3
, Ralph	63, 240
, Ralph Wheelock	108
, Ramona Jean	273
, Randolph E	258
, Rebecca	32, 67
, Relief Rebecca	199

297

INDEX - BOWKER SURNAMES

INDEX – SURNAMES OTHER THAN BOWKER

INDEX – SURNAMES OTHER THAN BOWKER

312

INDEX – SURNAMES OTHER THAN BOWKER

313

INDEX – SURNAMES OTHER THAN BOWKER

FLYNN, Mary 52, 96
FOGG, Benron 213
, Bernard Delmont 260
, Charles W 213
, Elijah H 218, 260
, Emily 260
, Joanne Estelle 260
, Lester Delmont 218, 260
, Pierson Rines 260
, Ruth F 260
, Winston Clyde 260
FOLEY, Mary Bridget 271
FOLLETT, Roxalana 87
FOLSOM, Hattie Belle 112
, Ira 112
FOOTE, David 132
, Nancy 74, 132
FORBES, Phineas 15
FORBUSH, Abel 19, 42
, Abner 19
, Abraham 15
, Adaline 89
, Almira 43
, Amos 156
, Anna 19, 43
, Asa 19
, Benjamin Franklin 19
, Betsey 42, 88, 89
, Caroline 88, 157
, Catey 19
, Catherine 88, 157
, Charles 158
, Chebar 43, 89
, Chloe 19
, Clara B 158, 218
, Daisy M 158, 159
, Daniel 3, 15, 42, 88, 89
, Dallas 157
, Dana Z 156
, David 5, 14, 15, 42
, Dea. Thomas 6, 18
, Dolly 42
, Ebenezer 6, 18, 19
, Eliza 158
, Elizabeth 5, 13, 19
, Ellen 156
, Elmer 158
, Emily 89
, Ephraim 15, 42, 89, 158
, Eunice 42, 89, 156
, Evaline 89
, George 88, 89, 157
, George Washington 156, 157
, Hannah 5, 19
, Harriet Ann 89
, Henry 158
, Hortense 158
, Isabella 158
, James 15, 42, 43, 89, 158
, Jerusha 89, 158
, John 3, 5
, Lavina 89
, Levi 89, 158
, Llewellyn 158
, Lois 42
, Lucy 15, 19, 42, 43
, Marian 156

FORBUSH, Martha 5, 19, 47
, Mary H 42, 87, 158
, Matilda 156
, Mary/ Molly 42, 87
, Melville 157
, Miranda 89
, Miriam 15, 42
, Molly 15
, Nancy 89, 159
, Nellie 158
, Patience 89
, Paul 42
, Pearl A 158
, Perley 158
, Phineas 15
, Rebecca 15, 42
, Roxey 43
, Roy H 156
, Ruth 15, 42
, Sally 42, 121
, Samuel 42
, Sarah 15
, Silas 42
, Simeon 42
, Thirza 158
, William Harrison 89
, Willie U 158
, Zenas W 156, 157
, Zilpha 156
FORD,, Sarah Alice 279
FORSYTH, Robert J 196
, Thelma 196
FORSYTHE, George 219
, Janette 219
FOSS, Betsey 166
, Daniel H 166
, Ellen 166
, Harriet 166
, John R 166
, Joseph 58, 101
, Liberty Shattuck 166
, Matilda 166
, Orington 166
, Georgianna 166
FOSTER, Ahigail 27, 55
, Alexander 97
, Ebenezer 84, 151
, Frank 244, 272, 273
, Hannah 140
, Mary Elizabeth 97
, Merlin I 249
, Rolland E 273
, Sarah L 188, 237
, Sidney 273
, Ward Avery 273
FOUTZ, Elizabeth 171, 223
FOX, Arthur 237
, Robert L B 224
, Roscoe S 268
, Susie Belle 235, 269, 276
, Walter Briggs 224
FRANCIS, Asaph / Asa L 275
, Bertha L 275
, Carl Albert 275
, Celia May 275
, Charles B 275
, Clayton Gilbert 275

318

INDEX – SURNAMES OTHER THAN BOWKER

INDEX – SURNAMES OTHER THAN BOWKER

HARTWELL, Eva Almira	253	
, Ira	59	
, Jacob	59	
, Margaret	59	
, Margaret Shattuck	102, 103	
, Mary	202	
, Nancy	59	
, Oliver	28, 59	
, Rachel	59, 102	
, Ruth Farnsworth	59	
, Samuel	9, 28	
, Sarah	9, 28, 59	
, Thomas	202	
HARVARD, Polly	133	
HARVEY, Clarinda Lenora	215, 259	
, Willis	251	
HARWOOD, Andrew	42, 88	
, Arnold	257	
, Asahel	88	
, Betsey Eliza	88	
, Clarissa	88	
, Eunice	88	
, Hannah	29, 33, 61, 62	
, James	29, 61, 88	
, John	10, 33, 42, 88	
, Martha	88	
, Mary	88	
, Rachel	7	
, Sally	62	
, Sarah	10, 33, 107	
, Sylvia	257	
, William	88	
HASKELL, Catherine A	125	
HASKINS, Lucinda	70, 124	
HASLEY, Josephine Maria	103	
, Luther	103	
HASTINGS, Elizabeth	47	
, John	57, 85, 100	
, Julia Augusta	57, 100	
, Ruth	18, 40, 46, 85	
HATCH, Nora Belle	231, 265	
, Sarah	51	
HATCHER, Percy Lee	273	
HATHAWAY, Jane Menaugh	182	
, Mary Julia	259	
HATSTAT, Lucilla	142	
HAVEN, Amelia Caroline	110	
, Elisha	110	
, Eliza	110	
, Ellen Maria	110	
, Geoorge Edwin	110	
, Josephus Sanford	110	
, Josiah Stone	110	
, Margaret Phipps	110	
HAVENS, Sarah	137, 201	
HAWES, Carl Theron	230	
HAWKS / HAWKES, Hannah	106, 166	
HAWLEY, Eunice	113, 172	
HAYDEN, Edmund	29	
, Sarah	9, 29, 30	
HAYES, Mariah C	107	
HAYNES, Abigail	10, 32	
, Addison	122	
, Adeline	121	
, Caroline	121	
, Carrie Bell	180	
, Charles	31, 66	

HAYNES, Clarence Edwin	122	
, David	84	
, Elbridge	121	
, Elias E	122	
, Elizabeth Frances	180	
, Ellen L	122, 179	
, Florence Agnes	180	
, Frederick	121	
, George	121	
, Georgianna	121	
, Harriet/ Hattie	122	
, John	69, 121, 122	
, John Newton	122, 179, 180	
, John Norton	180	
, Lorene	180	
, Mary	3, 84	
, Rebecca	31, 66, 70	
, Robert Chester	180	
, Ruth B	180	
, Sarah Frances	122	
, Susan Emily	121	
, Waldo Foster	180	
HAYWARD, Adam	63	
, Joel	44	
, Josiah Hartwell	15, 42	
, Lucy	30	
, Mary	87	
, Sarah	15, 42	
, Semira	109	
HEAD, Deborah Ann	74, 131	
HEALD, Elizabeth	17, 44	
, Ephraim	52, 95	
, Sarah / Sally	52, 95	
HEARD, Edmund	214	
, Lucy Minerva	153, 214, 215	
HEATH, Beatrice	275	
HECKMAN, Cordelia	257	
HEDENBURY, Charles	206	
HEDGE, Elizabeth B	263	
HEFFNER, Dale Kenneth	281	
, Jacqueline Marie	288	
, Jessica Elizabeth	288	
, Joshua Bartla	288	
, Kenneth Aaron	288	
, Sarah Anna	288	
HEFFRON, Clarissa	202, 251	
HEILMAN, Amanda Joyce	288	
, Anastasia Marie	288	
, Elizabeth Ann	281, 288	
, Gerald Glenn	269, 281	
, Ivy Rose	288	
, John Elias	269, 281	
, Lance Isaac	288	
, Paul David	281, 288	
, Peter Scott	281, 287	
, Rebecca Lee	281, 288	
, Suzanne Kathryn	281	
, Zachariah Scott	288	
HELMER, Byron W	146	
, Ella Rouletta	146	
, Horace Eugene	146	
, James Spencer	1446	
HELSELL, Corinne H	169	
, Jessie Mae	169	
HEMENWAY, Abigail	27	
, Elizabeth	18, 45	
HEMINGWAY, Abigail	27, 55	

324

INDEX – SURNAMES OTHER THAN BOWKER

INDEX – SURNAMES OTHER THAN BOWKER

INDEX – SURNAMES OTHER THAN BOWKER

INDEX – SURNAMES OTHER THAN BOWKER

MOSMAN, Mary	45
, Moses	45
, Phebe	90
, Phoebe	45, 90, 91
, Samuel	17, 45
, Silas	90
MOWER, Abigail	32, 68
MUNROE, Ernest E	158
, William	158
MUNSON, Alice May	251, 277
, Amy H	251
, Anna B	251
, Bernard	252
, Caleb	76, 137
, Charles Clayton	251
, Cora M	251
, Ella	137, 251
, Ernest A	252
, Esther E	201, 251
, Frank A	201, 251
, Frank Warren	251
, Grant	137
, Harry D	252
, Ida M	251
, Jane Lucy	137
, Jessie	251
, John	137, 201
, John Caleb	201, 251
, Joseph	76, 137, 201, 251
, Lucy A	201, 251
, Lydia	137
, Orange	137, 202
. Sarah Belle	201
, Sylvia C	201
, West	251, 251
, Willie E	201
MURCH, Casilla C	218
MURDOCK, Ada M	120
, Alice E	135
, John Franklin	70, 122, 123
, Joshua	122
, Louis J	123
, Mary L	123
, Robert	122
, Walter C	123
, William	122
MURPHY, Anna Luna	129, 188
, Michael Mark	229
MUSON, Moses	137
MUSSEY, John	54
, Reuben Diamond	54
MUZZEY, Sarah	14
MYERS, Hersey	157, 218
MYRICK, Caleb	46
, Sally	18, 46
NAGEL, Isabel Helen	231
, John	231
NASH, Amy Little	218
, Annette	140
, Caroline	99
, Charles K	218
, Cindy Anne	291
, Gary Dell	284, 290
, JoAnne Marie	291
, Samuel A	140
NAST, Bonnie Diane	284
NAUGHTON, William L	200

337

NAY, Ormsby Henry	157
, Annie L	157
NAYLON/NEYLON, Elizabeth	212
, Harrison Leon	212
, John D	212
NEER, Belle	242
NEET, Margaret	238
NEILL, Amelia	75
NELLER, Carrie Bertha	243
NELSON,	258
, Bertha Blanche	221
, Carl	281
, Charles	221
, Emily Louise	281
, Guy Morgan	223
, Mabel/Maybelle	221
, Mary	67, 117
, Milford Leroy	223
, Rudolph	250
, Samuel	250
NESBITT, Maria	66
NEWCOMB, Eunice L	179, 227
, Perry S	216
NEWCOWS, Lizzie	164
NEWELL, Cyrus	220
, Harriet Theodora	251
, Leon Barnard	220
, Theodora Harriet	201
NEWMAN, Frederick James	229
NEWTON, Abraham Howe	86
, Azubah	40
, Benjamin	167
, Beulah	38
, Charles	14, 40, 86, 154
, Dolly	40, 85
, Elisha	14, 40
, Ella Frances	154
, Ezra	40, 85, 154
, Genevieve Alleta	86
, Henrietta Louise	154
, Isaac Luther	214, 259
, Kezia	46
, Laura Jane	214, 259
, Lucy	86
, Lydia Church	86, 154
, Martha J	108, 168
, Mary	40
, Miriam	39
, Phebe/Phoebe	10, 32
, Sally Hastings	85
, Tabitha	40, 86
NICHOLAS, Elizabeth	209
NICHOLS, Acelia	139
, Addie Eliza	139
, Arad	77, 139
, Betsey DeMerritt	89, 158
, Charles Walter	139
, Chester	239, 270
, Daniel Green	139
, Earl Millard	204
, Edith M	139
, Elsie V	270
, Emma Rosanna	139, 204
, Fanny I	158
, Frank Aaron	204
, Gilbert Rominor	139
, Green	77, 138, 139

INDEX – SURNAMES OTHER THAN BOWKER

INDEX – SURNAMES OTHER THAN BOWKER

INDEX – SURNAMES OTHER THAN BOWKER

PART TWO

Descendants of James-1 BOWKER

BOWKER Descendants of James-1
The First American Generation

1. **JAMES⁻¹ BOWKER,** the immigrant, his parentage uncertain, was born ca 1645 at Lancashire, England. He was possibly christened at the Manchester Cathedral on 4 Oct 1646. (Ref. England, Births and Christenings 1538 – 1975) Folklore tales that relate he was a "Swede" are erroneous. As the story goes, he was taken, as an infant, to Sweden by an older relative, possibly a sister. He presumably lived with her until her death in 1667 and then immigrated to America from Sweden ca 1680. He was thought to be the youngest of three brothers (Edmund, John and James). This seems highly unlikely as Edmund was 35 years older than James, and it is more reasonable that both James and John were sons of Edmund⁻¹. However, since there is no definite proof regarding James, this researcher has chosen to present his line of descendants separately.

James⁻¹ BOWKER came to America ca 1680, and resided at Bryants Corners (now Norwell, MA) on 7 acres of land he purchased from Thomas INGHAM. He married Mary HINKLEY ca 1683 at Scituate, Plymouth, MA. She was the daughter of Samuel HINKLEY and Sarah SOOLE/SOULE, and was born ca 1665 at Scituate, MA.; died there ca 1733. James⁻¹ BOWKER died at Scituate on 14 Oct 1724.

Children of James ⁻¹ BOWKER/BUCAR/BOUCHER/BUKER and Mary HINKLEY:
Surname **BOWKER**   (all children born Scituate, MA.)

+	**2. MARTHA**	born 8 July 1684; died 9 April 1750 Pembroke, MA
		married Samuel ⁻⁴ RAMSDEN/RAMSDELL 24 Dec 1712 Scituate, MA
		(he s/o Daniel⁻³ RAMSDEN/RAMSDELL and Hannah CASWELL)
		(he born 6 Jan 1690; died 2 Dec 1759 Pembroke, MA
	3. Lazarus	born 3 Nov 1686; died ____; no further info
+	**4. MARY**	born 20 Feb 1688; died 20 July 1766 Hanover, MA
		married Joseph RAMSDEN/RAMSDELL 10 Dec 1718 Scituate
		(he born 15 Aug 1693; died Nov 1770)
		(he brother of above)
	5. Elizabeth	born 19 May 1691; died 5 Oct 1711; no further info
+	**6. DEBORAH**	born 13 Aug 1693; died 20 Oct 1758
		married Timothy CASWELL 15 Apr 1723 Scituate, MA
		(he s/o Thomas CASWELL and Mary RAMSDEN)
+	**7. JAMES**	born 6 Aug 1695; died 17 July 1761 Scituate, MA
		married Hannah LAMBERT 23 July 1717 Scituate, MA
	8. Abigail (1)	born 27 Oct 1697; died Nov 1699 EOL
+	**9. ABIGAIL (2)**	born 13 April 1700; died ____; married William BARRELL 20 Feb 1723
+	**10. RICHARD**	born 24 June 1702; died 17 July 1763 Scituate, MA
		1 married Mary BATES ca 1725
		(she dau/o Joseph BATES and Esther HILLIARD)
		(she born 13 March 1700; died Oct 1729)
		2 married Sarah PALMER 4 Aug 1731
		(she dau/o Elnathan PALMER and Marcy CLARKE)
		(she born ____; died 10 Nov 1750)
		3 married Phoebe HILL 12 July 1753

BOWKER Descendants of James-1
The First American Generation

Children of James[-1] BOWKER and Mary HINKLEY, continued:
Surname **BOWKER**

	11. Edmund	born 15 Aug 1704; died 2 May 1729
		married Elizabeth HOLT ca ____
		(she dau/o _____ HOLT and _____)
		(she born ca 1700 Scituate, MA; died _____)
	12. Rebekah	born 3 March 1705/6; died 18 May 1785
		married John HOUSE 9 Jan 1739/40 Hanover, MA
		(he s/o Samuel HOUSE and Sarah PINSON)
		(he born 27 Dec 1708 Scituate, MA; died ____)
+	**13. BENJAMIN**	born 11 Jan 1709/10; died 7 May 1754 Scituate
		married Hannah PROUTY 24 Feb 1735/36

Source: Town Records of Maine 1620-1988
History of the BRIGHAM Family
Vital Records of Massachusetts

2. MARTHA⁻² **BOWKER**, daughter of James-[1] BOWKER and Mary HINKLEY, was born 8 July 1684 at Scituate, MA. She married Samuel[-4] RAMSDEN on 24 Dec 1712 at Scituate, MA. He was the son of Daniel[-3] RAMSDEN/RAMSDELL (Joseph-[2]; John-[1]++) and Hannah CASWELL, and was born 6 Jan 1690; died 3 Dec 1759 Pembroke, MA. Martha[-2] BOWKER died 9 April 1750 at Pembroke:

Ancestry of Samuel[-4] RAMSDEN/RAMSDELL

++ John[-1] RAMSDEN/RAMSDELL was born ca 1601 Halifax, Yorkshire, England. He married Priscilla CHASE ca ____. She was born ca 1607 England; died 23 Jan 1675 at Lynn, Essex, MA. She was the daughter of Aquila Benjamin CHASE and Martha Sarah JELLIMAN. John[-1] RAMSDEN/RAMSDELL died 27 Oct 1688 Lynn, MA.

Joseph[-2] RAMSDEN/RAMSDELL was born ca 1620 England. Possibly, he and his parents came to America ca 1641. He married Rachel-[2] EATON on 2 Mar 1645 Plymouth, MA. Rachel[-2] was the daughter of Francis[-1] EATON and his 3rd wife Christian(a) PENN, and was born ca 1625; died ca 1659. Joseph[-2] married second to Mary SAVERY/ SAVORY on 16 Oct 1661. Joseph[-2] RAMSDEN/RAMSDELL died 25 May 1674 Plymouth, MA.

Daniel[-3] RAMSDEN/RAMSDELL, possibly an only child, was born 14 Sep 1649 MA. He married Hannah CASWELL on 12 Mar 1672. She was the daughter of Thomas CASWELL and Mary SANDERSON, and was born 14 July 1651; died _____. Daniel[-3] RAMSDEN/RAMSDELL died ca 1722 Taunton, MA.

Children of Martha[-2] BOWKER and Samuel[-4] RAMSDEN/RAMSDELL:
Surname **RAMSDEN/RAMSDELL**

+	**14. SAMUEL, JR.**	born 4 Jan 1714; died ca 1801; married Dorothy BISHOP 26 Jan 1734
+	**15. MARY**	born May 1715; died 1776; married Daniel CROCKER/CROOKER ca 1734
	16. Content	born 3 Apr 1720; died 1721 EOL
+	**17. SUSANNA**	born ca 1721; died 1 July 1791 Nova Scotia, Canada
		married David Daniel HERSEY 20 May 1743
		(he s/o David HERSEY and Elizabeth JOYCE)
		(he born 24 Jan 1721 Pembroke; died ____)

Note: this family moved from Plymouth, MA to Chebogue, Nova Scotia ca 1763

4. MARY⁻² **BOWKER,** sister of above, was born 20 Feb 1687 at Scituate, Plymouth, MA. She married Joseph[-4] RAMSDEN/RAMSDELL on 10 Dec 1718 at Scituate. He was the son of Daniel[-3] RAMSDELL/RAMSDEN and Hannah CASWELL, and was born 5 Aug 1693 Plymouth, MA; died Nov 1770 Hanover, MA. He was the brother of Samuel[-4] RAMSDEN/RAMSDELL (above) who married Martha[-2] BOWKER. Mary[-2] BOWKER died 20 July 1766.

Children of Mary[-2] BOWKER and Joseph [-4] RAMSDELL:
Surname **RAMSDEN**   (all but last child born Pembroke, Plymouth, MA)

+	**18. JOSEPH, JR**	born 22 Sep 1719 ; died 24 Oct 1778; married Mary DAWES 30 Dec 1741
+	**19. BENJAMIN**	born 1 Oct 1721; died 5 Oct 1804; married Lusanna BISHOP ca ____
	20. Daniel	born 20 Sept 1723; died ____; married Mary DILLINGHAM 18 May 1749
+	**21. SIMEON**	born 24 Dec 1726; died 13 Oct 1799
		1 married Mary TURNER 4 June 1757
		2 married Sarah TURNER 18 July 1790
+	**22. NATHANIEL**	born 30 Mar 1730; died ___ Bridgewater, MA; married Mary PRATT ca ____
+	**23. NEHEMIAH**	born 13 Nov 1734 Hanover, MA; died 30 Sep 1800 Harvard, Worcester, MA
		married Rebecca CHAMBERLAIN 17 Nov 1757 Hanover, MA
		(she born ca 1736; died 1818)

6. DEBORAH⁻² **BOWKER**, daughter of James[-1] BOWKER and Mary HINKLEY, was born 13 Aug 1693 at Scituate, MA. She married Timothy CASWELL on 15 April 1723 Scituate. He was the son of Thomas CASWELL and Mary RAMSDEN, and was born 1692 Bristol, MA; died June 1757. Deborah[-2] BOWKER died 20 Oct 1758.

Children of Deborah-² BOWKER and Timothy CASWELL:
Surname **CASWELL**

24. Job		born ca 1723 Hanover, MA; died 18 April 1809 Leeds, Androscoggin, Maine
		married Mercy PERRY ca _____
	Children: John-⁴ born ca ____; Mercy⁴ born ca ___; and Levi⁴ CASWELL born ca ___	
25. Ezekiel		born 17 Oct 1725 Hanover, MA; died _____

7. JAMES-² **BOWKER**, brother of above, was born 6 Aug 1695 at Scituate, Plymouth, MA. He married Hannah LAMBERT on 23 July 1717 at Scituate. She was the daughter of John LAMBERT and Hannah HOLMES, and was born 10 April 1697 Scituate, died ca 1725 at Scituate. James-² BOWKER died 17 July 1763 at Scituate.

Children of James-² BOWKER and Hannah LAMBERT:
Surname **BOWKER**   (all children born Scituate, Plymouth, MA)

+	**26. LAZARUS**	born 26 April 1718; bpt. 28 June 1719; died 20 Aug 1798 Scituate, MA
		married Abigail BUCK 7 July 1739 Scituate
		(she dau/o Thomas BUCK and Hannah TAYLOR)
		(she born 20 Oct 1723; died 16 July 1768)
	27. Mary (1)	born 10 Aug 1719; died 30 Dec 1723 Scituate, MA EOL
+	**28. JAMES**	born 7 Aug 1721; died ca 1784; married Mary ELMES 20 Jan 1743
		(she dau/o John ELMES and Mary VINAL)
		(she born 3 Jan 1724; died ca 1773)
+	**29. JOHN**	born 3 Oct 1724; died 17 Feb 1807; married Anna WRIGHT 13 Oct 1746
		(she dau/o John WRIGHT and _____)
+	**30. HANNAH**	born 9 Aug 1726; died ___;1 married Ebenezer LANE, Jr. 24 Sep 1744 Scituate
		(he s/o Ebenezer LANE, Sr. and Mary LEAVITT) (he born ca 1722)
		2 married Daniel DAMON, Jr. 28 May 1761
		(he s/o Daniel DAMON and Judith LITCHFIELD) (he born ca 1742)
+	**31. LYDIA**	born 5 Sep 1728; died ca 1763
		married Luke BISHOP Oct 1746 (he born ca 1720; died _____)
+	**32. DEBORAH**	born 4 Nov 1730; died 10 May 1813
		married James BARRELL 7 April 1750 Scituate, MA (he # 39)
+	**33. EDMUND**	born 20 Aug 1732; died 9 Feb 1827 (age 94) Scituate
		married Lydia LAMBERT 2 Dec 1756 Scituate
		(she dau/o James LAMBERT and Sarah BRIDGES)
		(she born ca 1735; died 24 July 1824 Scituate)
	34. Mary (2)	born 13 Sep 1734; died _____; married Isaiah STODDER on 5 Dec 1754
		(he born ca 1730; died _____)
	35. Ruth	born 1 Aug 1736; died _____; married Peleg SIMMONS 6 July 1758
		(he s/o Ebenezer SIMMONS and Lydia KENT)
		(he born Sep 1728 Scituate, MA; died 5 Oct 1817 Scituate)
	Child: Ruth⁴ SIMMONS born 8 Feb 1760 Scituate, MA	
+	**36. JOSEPH**	born 5 March 1739 (gs); died 4 March 1802
		married Elizabeth Deborow COWING 26 May 1760
		(she born 14 April 1740 Scituate, MA; died 31 Nov 1831 Phippsburg, ME
+	**37. DESIRE**	born 14 April 1741; died ca 1821 Hartford, NY
		married Colburn BARRELL 28 May 1761 (# 43)
		(he s/o William BARRELL and Abigail BOWKER)
		(he born 7 May 1738; died 30 Nov 1777 Quebec, Canada)

9. ABIGAIL-² **BOWKER**, daughter of James-¹ BOWKER, was born 13 April 1700 at Scituate, Plymouth, MA. She married William BARRELL II on 20 Feb 1723 at Scituate. He was the son of William BARRELL and Lydia TURNER; and was born ca 1683; died 1752. Abigail-² BOWKER died _____.

Children of Abigail-² BOWKER and William BARRELL:
Surname **BARRELL**   (all children born Scituate, Plymouth, MA)

	38. Abigail	born 5 May 1728; died before 1742 EOL
+	**39. JAMES**	born 29 Dec 1729; died 17 April 1827
		married Deborah-³ BOWKER (# 32 above) on 7 Apr 1750 Scituate, MA

Children of Abigail-[2] BOWKER and William BARRELL, continued:
Surname **BARRELL**

40. Mary	born 1 Aug 1731; died ____	
41. JOHN	born 31 March 1734; died 20 July 1804	
	married Judith SNOW 20 April 1756 Bridgewater, MA	
42. Elisha	born 28 Sep 1735; died 21 May 1829 Hanover, Plymouth, MA	
	married Mary COLLAMORE 6 Jan 1774 Scituate, MA	
	(she born ca 1736; died 8 Jan 1831)	

Children: Mary-[4] born 21 Sep 1774, died 1852; Elisha-[4] born 7 Mar 1777; and Sarah-[4] BARRELL born 4 Feb 1779, died ca 1845

+ **43. COLBURN**   born 7 May 1738; died 20/30 Nov 1777 Quebec, Canada
     married Desire-[2] BOWKER 28 May 1761 (she # 37)

Child: Colburn-[4] BARRELL born 4 Oct 1763/4; died 23 Oct 1842, married Esther VIDETO 2 Nov 1786 Canaan, NY

Note: Colburn-[3] BARRELL served in the Revolutionary War, beginning at Lexington, then Boston, etc., until he was captured by the British during the Ticonderoga campaign. He had reached the rank of Sgt. He died on a British prison ship off the shore of Quebec, Canada. His widow moved, with her children, to Columbia County, NY. Later they moved to Hartford, Washington, NY where she died ca 1821.

44. Abigail   born 18 July 1742; died 5 June 1816 Norwell, MA
     married Nehemiah PALMER 14 July 1768

Child: Nathaniel-[4] PALMER born ca 1778; died ca 1862

10. RICHARD-[2] BOWKER, brother of above, was born 24 June 1702. He married first to Mary BATES on 2 Nov 1725. She was the daughter of Joseph BATES and Esther HILLIARD , and was born 13 March 1700 ; died Oct 1729. He married second to Sarah PALMER on 4 Aug 1731. She was the daughter of Elnathan PALMER and Marcy CLARKE, and was born ___, died 10 Nov 1750. He married third to Phoebe HILL on 12 July 1753. Richard-[2] BOWKER died 17 July 1763 Scituate, MA.

Children of Richard-[2] BOWKER and Mary BATES:
Surname **BOWKER**

+ **45. MARY**   born ca 1726; died 1797
     married Jesse TORREY 6 Dec 1744 Hanover, Plymouth, MA
     (he s/o Nathaniel TORREY and Hannah TILDEN)
     (he born ca 1725; died 16 July 1793 Hanover, MA)
+ **46. RICHARD**   born ca 1727; died ____; married Mary PRATT 21 April 1751
+ **47. LUKE**   born ca 1729; died ca 1790; married Joanna DUNBAR 11 Nov 1752

Child of Richard-[2] BOWKER and Sarah PALMER:
Surname **BOWKER**

48. Sarah   born 5 Jan 1733 Pembroke, MA; died ____

Child of Richard-[2] BOWKER and Phoebe HILL:
Surname **BOWKER**

49. Phoebe   born ca 1754; died 30 Aug 1824 Cheshire, NH
     married Hiram PRESCOTT 27 Oct 1770 Lancaster, Worcester, MA
     (s/o Jonathan PRESCOTT and Vashti HOUGHTON)
     (he born ca 1752; died 24 Mar 1824 Cheshire, NH)

13. BENJAMIN-[2] BOWKER, brother of above, was born 11 Jan 1709/10 at Scituate, Plymouth, MA. He married Hannah PROUTY on 24 Feb 1735/36 at Scituate. She was the daughter of Edward PROUTY, Sr. and Elizabeth HOWE, and was born 15 May 1714; died ca 1785 Scituate. Benjamin-[2] BOWKER died 7 May 1754 Scituate.

Children of Benjamin-[2] BOWKER and Hannah PROUTY:
Surname **BOWKER**   (children born Scituate, MA)

+ **50. BENJAMIN, Jr.**   born 14 Feb 1738/39; died ca 1806; married Hannah SPARHAWK(E) 10 Nov 1763
  51. Hannah   born 25 Nov 1740; died 1771
+ **52. EUNICE**   born 7 Dec 1744; died 1834; married John DAMON 11 Apr 1771
     (he s/o Daniel DAMON and Judith LITCHFIELD)
     (he born 26 Mar 1744 Scituate; died ca 1815)

53. Joshua (1)	born 1 May 1747; died ca 1754		EOL	
54. Margaret/ Margret	born 27 May 1749; died 1800			
55. Elisha	born 20 Sep 1751; died Jan 1754	56. Joshua	(2)	born 29 Jan 1755

14. SAMUEL-³ RAMSDEN/RAMSDELL, JR. , son of Martha-² BOWKER (James-¹) and Samuel RAMSDELL/ RAMSDEN, was born 4 June 1714, baptized 2 Sep 1716, at Pembroke, Plymouth, MA. He married Dorothy BISHOP on 26 Jan 1744 at Pembroke. She was the daughter of John BISHOP and Elizabeth KEEN, and was born 28 Jan 1715 Plymouth, MA; died 31 March 1801 Pembroke, MA. Samuel-³ RAMSDEN, Jr. died 28 March 1801.

Children of Samuel-³ RAMSDEN, Jr. and Dorothy BISHOP
Surname **RAMSDEN**   (all children born Pembroke, Plymouth, MA)

57. Content	born 23 Sept 1744; died ca 1750	EOL
58. Samuel III	born 23 June 1746; died 22 Apr 1830 Hanson, Plymouth, MA	
59. Elizabeth	born 16 Nov 1747; died ____	
60. Gershom	born 16 June 1750; died ____; 1 married Mary CAREY ca ____	

Children: Gershom-⁵ born ca 1776; and Betsey-⁵ RAMSDELL born ca 1778, died 1790
2 married Sarah DELANO ca ___   Child: William-⁵ RAMSDELL born ca 1791
3 married Lydia BOWKER

61. Martha	born 7 Apr 1754; died ____	
62. Content (2)	born 21/25 May 1755; died ____; married Michael RAMSDELL ca _____	

Child: Lydia-⁵ RAMSDELL born ca 1775, died ca 1850

63. Abigail	born 28 Jan 1757; died 7 Apr 1757	EOL
64. John	born 15 Jan 1759; died 23 May 1807 Rutland, VT.	

15. MARY-³ RAMSDEN, sister of above, was born May 1715 at Pembroke, MA. She married Daniel CROOKER/CROCKER on 28 April 1736. He was the son of Daniel CROOKER and ____; and was born 20 April 1716 Pembroke; died 6 Nov 1773 Pembroke, MA. Mary-³ RAMSDEN died 19 Jan 1776.

Children of Mary-³ RAMSDEN and Daniel CROOKER/CROCKER:
Surname **CROOKER**   (children born Hanover, MA)

	65. Lemuel	born 30 July 1736; died ____	
	66. Betta	born 30 Oct 1738; died ____	
+	**67. DANIEL**	born 5 June 1740; died 6 Feb 1818; 1 married Abigail STUDLEY 17 Dec 1763	
		(she born ca 1741; died 25 Sept 1775 Pembroke, MA)	
		2 married Hannah WHITE 14 Dec 1776	
		(she born 7 Sep 1754 MA; died 22 Aug 1828 Hanson, Plymouth, MA)	
	68. Ensign	born 6 Feb 1742; died 28 Feb 1743	69. Lazarus born 6 Feb 1744

17. SUSANNA-³ RAMSDEN, sister of above, was born ca 1721. She married David HERSEY, Jr. on 20 May 1743 at Pemroke, MA. He was the son of David Daniel HERSEY and Elizabeth JOYCE, and was born 24 Jan 1721 Pembroke; died ca 1797 Nova Scotia. This family moved to Nova Scotia in 1763. Susanna-³ RAMSDEN died ca 1791 Nova Scotia.

Children of Susanna-³ RAMSDEN and David HERSEY, Jr. :
Surname **HERSEY** (children born Pembroke, MA)

+	**70. DANIEL**	born ca 1745; died ____; married Desire WESTON 5 Jan 1774 NS	
	71. Mercy	born ca 1746; died ____	72. Elizabeth born ca 1747; died ____
+	**73. SAMUEL T.**	born ca 1750; died ca 1850; 1 married Susan Elizabeth TIDD ca _____	
		2 married Lydia CLARKE 21 April 1774	
	74. Martha	born ca 1752; died 1852; married Joshua GARDNER 5 Jan 1774	

Children: Judah-⁵ born 24 July 1775; Elizabeth-⁵ born 25 Aug 1776; Susanna-⁵ born 15 Oct 1778, died
7 Apr 1784; and Mary-⁵ GARDNER born 13 Feb 1781
(he s/o David GARDNER and Mary ____)

75. LEVI	born Jan 1754; died 8 Feb 1842	
	1 married Chloe DAY 8 Mar 1780 St John, New Brunswick, Canada	
	2 married Leah WAGNER of Bear River ca 1821	
76. Deborah	born ca 1756; died ____; married Charles O'NEIL 24 July 1758	

18. JOSEPH⁻³ RAMSDEN/ RAMSDELL, Jr., son of Mary⁻² BOWKER (James⁻¹) and Joseph RAMSDEN, was born 22 Sept 1719 Plymouth, MA . He married Mary DAW(E)S on 20 Dec 1741at Pembroke, MA. She was the daughter of _____ DAW(E)S and _____, and was born ca 1719 at Bridgewater, Plymouth, MA; died 20 July 1766 at Hanover, Plymouth, MA. Joseph⁻³ RAMSDELL died 24 Oct 1778 at Hanover, MA.

Children of Joseph⁻³ RAMSDELL and Mary DAW(E)S:
Surname **RAMSDELL**   (children born Pembroke, Plymouth, MA)

77. John	born 21 Jan 1742; died 17 Aug 1743	EOL
78. Hannah	born 28 July 1743; died ____	
79. Lydia	born 30 Jan 1745; died 1846 (101)	
80. Lot	born 17 Jan 1747; died 9 Nov 1822 Hanson, MA; married Rachel TORREY 21 Nov 1771	
81. Simeon	born 11 May 1752; died ____	
82. Olive	born 14 April 1754; died ____	
83. Mary	born 6 Oct 1758; died ____	
84. Ruth	born ca 1761; died ____	
85. Joseph III	born 6 April 1764; died 13 May 1807; married Eunice NASH 29 Nov 1787 Hanover, MA	

19. BENJAMIN⁻³ RAMSDEN, brother of above, was born Oct 1721 at Pembroke, Plymouth, MA. He married Lusanna BISHOP on 8 Dec 1743 at Pembroke. She was the daughter of Hudson BISHOP and Abigail KEEN, and was born 17 Nov 1717 Hanover, Plymouth, MA; died Jan 1807 at Hanover. Benjamin⁻³ RAMSDELL died 5 Oct 1804 at Hanover, MA.

Children of Benjamin⁻³ RAMSDELL and Lusanna BISHOP:
Surname **RAMSDELL**   (children born Pembroke, MA)

86. Benjamin, Jr.	born 21 Nov 1744; died ____	
87. Lusanna	born 11 Dec 1746; died ca 1820 Camden, Maine	
	married Benjamin BARNES ca ____ (he born 1746; died 1816)	
	Children: Benjamin-⁵ born ca 1774, died ca 1816; and Abel-⁵ RAMSDELL born ca 1781, died ca 1858	
88. Deborah	born 29 Nov 1748; died ____	
89. Content	born 6 Nov 1752; died 6 Jan 1804 Hanover, MA	
90. Edmond	born 9 July 1754; died ____	91. Charles born 6 Mar 1756; died ____

21. SIMEON⁻³ RAMSDEN/RAMSDELL, brother of above, was born 24 Dec 1726 at Pembroke, Plymouth, MA. He married first to Mary TURNER on 4 June 1757. She was the daughter of JoshuaTURNER and Elizabeth ____,and was born 12 Nov 1732 Scituate, MA; died 22 Mar 1781 East Bridgewater, MA. He married second to Sarah TURNER on 18 July 1790. She was the daughter of ___ TURNER and ____; and was born 27 Jan 1733 Pembroke; died 29 April 1796 MA. Simeon⁻³ died 13 Oct 1799.

Children of Simeon-³ RAMSDELL and Mary TURNER:
Surname **RAMSDELL**

+	**92. JOHN**	born 5 May 1758; died ___
	STOCKBRIDGE	married Hannah ALLEN 30 Sept 184 Plymouth, MA
		(she dau/o Samuel ALLEN and Hannah PRATT) (she born 17 May 1761 Bridgewater)
	93. Mercy Munroe	born 4 July 1760; died 15 Nov 1817 Pembroke, MA
	94. Anne Stockbridge	born ca 1764; died 18 Dec 1824 MA
		married Seth FOLGER 15 Feb 1770 Nantucket, MA
	95. Abner Turner	born 19 May 1765; died 1779 EOL

22. NATHANIEL⁻³ RAMSDEN/RAMSDELL, brother of above, was born 30 March 1730 at Pembroke, Plymouth, MA. He married Mary PRATT 10 Jan 1753. She was the daughter of ____ PRATT and ____; and was born ____, died 18 April 1821 at Bridgewater, MA. Nathaniel⁻³ RAMSDEN died 6 Dec 1762 at Bridgewater, MA.

Children of Nathaniel⁻³ RAMSDELL and Mary PRATT:
Surname **RAMSDELL**

96. Daniel	born 21 Aug 1754; died 10 Dec 1779 East Bridgewater, MA
	married Betty SOULE 22 Aug 1776 Bridgewater
	(she dau/o Isaac SOULE and Agatha PERRY)
	(she born 14 Apr 1756 Pembroke, MA; died ____)

Children of Nathaniel[-3] RAMSDELL and Mary PRATT, continued:
Surname **RAMSDELL**

97. Matthew	born 19 March 1756; died ____; married Mary ALLEN 20 Dec 1779	
98. James	born 26 July 1758; died ____; married Eunice ALLEN 17 Nov 1785	
	(she born ca 1766; died 1792)	
99. Margaret	born ca 1759/60; died ____	
100. Joseph	born 3 Oct 1761; died 13 June 1830 MA; married Lydia GLOYD 10 Oct 1787	
	(she dau/o James GLOYD and Isabel DERNON)	
	(she born 30 Mar 1767; died 19 July 1846 MA)	

23. NEHEMIAH[-3] RAMSDEN, brother of above, was born 13 Nov 1734 at Hanover, Plymouth, MA. He married Rebecca CHAMBERLAIN on 17 Nov 1757 at Hanover, MA. She was the daughter of Freedom CHAMBERLAIN and Mary SOULE; and was born 28 Feb 1735/36 Pembroke; died 15 Sep 1818 at Harvard, Middlesex, MA. Nehemiah[-3] RAMSDEN died 30 Sep 1800 at Harvard, MA.

Children of Nehemiah[-3] RAMSDEN and Rebecca CHAMBERLAIN:
Surname **RAMSDEN**   (children born Pembroke, Plymouth, MA)

101. Freedom	born 4 Mar 1759; died 29 Dec 1764
102. Nehemiah, Jr.	born 25 Oct 1761; died ____
103. Nathaniel	born 1 May 1763; died ____
104. Seth	born 13 June 1768; died 1792 Waterford, Oxford, ME
+ **105. BARTLETT**	born 18 Feb 1770; died 25 Jan 1832
	married Emma BEAN 14 April 1796
106. Rebecca	born 1 April 1771; died 14 Nov 1812
107. Ezekiel	born 16 Aug 1772; died Apr 1850 NY
	married Charity POST 19 May 1796 Greenville, Greene, NY
108. Betty	born 19 Feb 1775; died ____
109. Nabby	born 16 May 1779

26. LAZARUS-3 BOWKER, son of James[-2] BOWKER (James-1) and Hannah LAMBERT, was born 2 April 1718 at Scituate, Plymouth, MA. He married Abigail BUCK on 7 July 1739 at Scituate. She was the daughter of Thomas BUCK and Hannah TAYLOR, and was born 20 Oct 1723; died 16 July 1768. Lazarus[-3] BOWKER died 20 Aug 1798 Scituate.

Children of Lazarus[-3] BOWKER and Abigail BUCK:
Surname **BOWKER**   (all children born Scituate, MA)

+ **110. LAZARUS, Jr.**	born ca 1742; bpt. 11 Mar 1743; died 26 May 1832	
	married Mary[-5] COLLIER 12 Nov 1768 Scituate, MA	
	(she dau/o Thomas[-4] COLLIER and Bridget SOUTHWORTH)	
	(she born 22 April 1746; died 18 Oct 1786)	
111. Abigail	born 30 Nov 1745; died ____	
+ **112. GERSHOM**	born ca 1747; bpt. 4 Oct 1747; died 1796; married Elizabeth STETSON 18 Feb 1773	
	(she dau/o Isaac STETSON and Ruth PROUTY)	
	(she born 7 Jan 1754; died 19 Feb 1842)	
113. Dimmick	born 1 April 1750; died 1756	EOL
+ **114. ZEBULON**	born 23 Oct 1751; died ca 1839 Cambridge, VT	
	married Deborah RANDALL 5 Sep 1773	
115. Jonathan	born 7 June 1752/3; bpt. 30 Mar 1754; died ____	
116. Lemuel	born/bpt. 16 Feb 1755 117. Nabby born/bpt 26 March 1757	

28. JAMES-3 BOWKER, brother of above, was born 7 Aug 1721 at Scituate, Plymouth, MA. He married Mary ELMES on 20 Jan 1743 at Scituate (int pub 9 Oct 1742). She was the daughter of John ELMES and Mary VINAL, and was born 3 Jan 1724; died ca 1773. James[-3] BOWKER died ca 1810 at Lincoln, Maine.

Children of James[-3] BOWKER and Mary ELMES:
Surname **BOWKER**

+ **118. JAMES IV**	born ca 1743 Scituate, MA; died ca 1830 Durham, Cumberland, ME
	married Ruth SARGENT 22 Oct 1767 Georgetown, Maine
	(she dau/o Jonathan SARGENT and Mercy GRAY) (she born 14 Feb 1745/46)

Children of James⁻³ BOWKER and Mary ELMES, continued:
Surname **BOWKER**

	119. Rhoda	born ca 1744 ; bpt. 17 June 1744 Scituate; died ____
	120. Cornelius	born 7 Sep 1746 Scituate ; bpt. 28 Sep 1746; died ____
	121. Job	born ca 1755 Scituate; died ca 1811; married Anne ADAMS 24 Apr 1774
	122. Joseph	born ca 1758; died ____
	123. David	born 12 May 1761 Bowdoinham, ME; died 12 May 1838 Bowdoinham, ME
		married Bethia SPARKS 26 Dec 1782 Bowdoin, ME
		Child: Isaac⁻⁵ BOWKER born 26 Mar 1799 ME, died 18 Nov 1885; married Roxanna SIMPSON ca ____
	124. Dimmick	born ca 1763; died ___
+	**125. WILLIAM**	born ca 1765 Georgetown, Sagadahoc, ME; died ____
	126. Mary	born ca 1766 Georgetown, ME; died ____
	127. Zaccheus	born ca 1770 Bowdoin, ME; died Aug 1837 Bowdoin
+	**128. ELIHU**	born ca 1773 Lincoln Co., ME; died 1 Oct 1844
		married Elizabeth PARKS 20 July 1801 Bowdoinham, Maine

29. JOHN⁻³ BOWKER, son of James⁻² BOWKER (James⁻¹) and Hannah LAMBERT, was born 3 Oct 1724 Scituate, Plymouth, MA. He married Anna/Ann Jemima WRIGHT on 13 Oct 1746 at Scituate. She was the daughter of ____ WRIGHT and ____, and was born 30 Apr 1726 Hanover, Plymouth, MA; died 12 July 1816 Scituate, MA. John⁻³ BOWKER died 17 Feb 1807.

Children of John⁻³ BOWKER and Anna WRIGHT:
Surname **BOWKER**

	129. Rebecca	born 27 Aug 1747; died 10 March 1804
+	**130. BARTLETT**	born 22 Jan 1749 MA ; died 16 Jan 1829 VT
		1 married Christina Webb HOLMES 27 Sep/ 9 Dec 1779 Scituate, MA
		(she born ca 1750; died 1793)
		2 married Susanna WITHINGTON 7 Sep 1794 (she born ____; died 1797)
		3 married Jemima KNOWLTON 1 Oct 1798
		(she dau/o Ezekiel KNOWLTON and Anna MILES)
		(she born 28 Feb 1770 Templeton, MA; died 4 Apr 1847 Fitzwilliam NH
	131. Lucy	born 7 March 1751; died Nov 1815 MA
	132. Anna	born 13 Sep 1752; died 4 May 1813 VT
+	**133. CAPT. JOHN, Jr.**	born 22/28 Aug 1754; died ____
		1 married Faith HOLMES 25 Mar 1779 Scituate, MA
		(she born 10 Feb 1753; died 20 July 1788)
		(she dau/o Thomas HOLMES and Lydia WHITE)
		2 married Annis MARSHALL 10 Dec 1789 Fitzwilliam Cheshire, NH
+	**134. HANNAH**	born 2 Feb 1756 Scituate; died 2 Jan 1821 Cummington, MA
		married Stephen TOWER 21 April 1776 Scituate, MA
+	**135. CHARLES**	born 18 Nov 1757 Plymouth, MA; died 21 July 1839 Fitzwilliam, NH
		married Beulah STONE 19 Apr 1787
	136. Ruth	born 29 Sept 1759; died ____
	137. Delight	born 25 July 1761; died 27 July 1793
+	**138. CAPT. STEPHEN**	born 17 Feb 1763 Scituate, MA; died 17 March 1802 NH
		married Lucy CUSHING 30 April 1789 Scituate, MA
		(she dau/o Ensign Pickles CUSHING and Abigail HATCH)
		(she born 6 July 1771 Scituate; died 11 Feb 1852 Fitzwilliam, NH)
+	**139. ELIJAH**	born 18 Nov 1764; died 14 June 1812 MA
		married Anna R. SYLVESTER 25 March 1788
		(she born 1 Apr 1768; died 17 Aug 1816)
	140. Relief	born 13 Sept 1766; died May 1845 MA
+	**141. DESIRE**	born 12 Oct 1769; died ____; married Joseph CUSHING 19 June 1790

30. HANNAH⁻³ BOWKER, sister of above, was born 9 Aug 1726 at Scituate, MA. She married first to Ebenezer LANE, Jr. on 24 Sept 1744 at Scituate. He was the son of Ebenezer LANE and Mary LEAVITT, and was born ca 1722; died ____. She married second to Daniel DAMON, Jr. on 28 May 1761. He was the son of Daniel DAMON and Judith LITCHFIELD, and was born ca 1742; died ____. Hannah⁻³ BOWKER died ____.

Children of Hannah-[3] BOWKER and Ebenezer LANE:
Surname **LANE**

142. Hannah   born ____; bpt. 24 Oct 1745; died July 1827 Cohasset, MA
                               married Hezekiah WORRICK 18 Nov 1764 Cohasset, Norfolk, MA
                               (he s/o Chasling WORRICK and Susanna/Susan TOWER)
                               (he born 9 Aug 1740 Hingham, MA; died 16 May 1813 Cohasset)
                   Child: Laban-[5] WORRICK born 2 May 1773, died 13 Nov 1850 Cohasset ; married Sally LINCOLN ca 1793

143. Ebenezer III   (1)   born 13 Nov 1748 Hingham, MA; died 28 Nov 1748   EOL
144. Ebenezer   (2)   born 23 Sep 1750 Hingham; died _____
                               1 married Lucy GRAY 31 July 1774
                               2 married Susanna NICHOLS 22 July 1801
145. Eli   born 8 Aug 1755 Hingham; died 22 Jan 1818 Cohasset, MA
146. Gorham   born 29 Feb 1756 Hingham; died 14 Nov 1832
                               married Rebecca JONES 2 Jan 1776   (she born ca 1758; died ca 1825)
           Children: Hannah-[5] born 12 Mar 1777; Gorham[5] Jr. born 25 July 1779; Rebecca-[5] born 11 Mar 1781; John Hancock[5]
           born ca 1793, died 1862 and Benjamin Randall[5] LANE born 19 Oct 1802; died 1880, married Rebecca ROSE
147. Luther (1)   born 7 Apr 1760 Hingham; died 1761   EOL
148. Luther (2)   born 18 Feb 1768 Hingham; died 1 July 1829 Union, OH
                               married Lodica GREENE ca _____
                               (she dau/o Joseph GREENE and Jerusha UTLEY)
                               (she born 1 Oct 1782 CT; died 18 June 1823 Union, OH)
           Children: Eliza-[5]; Elizabeth[5]; Hannah-[5]; Lodica-[5]; Fannie-[5] born ca 1802, died 1847; Luther-[5] Jr.;
           Austin-[5] born ca 1819; and David[5] LANE born ca 1820

31. LYDIA-[3] **BOWKER,** sister of above, was born 5 Sep 1728 MA. She married Luke BISHOP 2 Oct 1746 Scituate, MA. He was the son of Hudson BISHOP and Abigail KEEN, and was born 8 June 1720 MA; died NJ. Lydia-[4] BOWKER died ca 1763.

Child of Lydia-[3] BOWKER and Luke BISHOP:
Surname **BISHOP**
+   **149. LYDIA**   born 20 Aug 1749 Scituate, MA; died 4 May 1815 Durham Androscoggin, ME
                               married Caleb ESTES 24 June 1769 (he s/o Edward ESTES and Patience CARR)

32. DEBORAH-[3] **BOWKER,** sister of above, was born 4 Nov 1730 at Scituate, MA. She married James [3] BARRELL (# 39) (Abigail-[2] BOWKER; James-[1]) on 7 Apr 1750 Scituate. He was the son of William BARRELL and Abigail BOWKER, and was born 29 Dec 1729; died 17 April 1827 Scituate, MA.. Deborah-[3] BOWKER died 10 May 1813.

Children of Deborah-[3] BOWKER and James BARRELL:
Surname **BARRELL**
+   **150. JAMES, Jr.**   born 1751; bpt. 30 June 1751; died 1795
                               married Martha FARROW 10 Dec 1772 Scituate, MA
151. William   born ____; bpt. 14 Oct 1753
152. Noah   born ca 1755: died ___
                   Child: Noah-[5] BARRELL born ___; died 10 April 1859 Norwell, MA
153. Bartlett   born ca 1758; died Sep 1855
                               married Relief/Leafy NASH 6 July 1794 Scituate, MA
                               (she dau/o Thomas NASH and Eunice STETSON)
           Children: Bartlett-[5] Jr. born 16 Aug 1799, died 12 Mar 1832 Scituate; Mary-[5] born ca 1808,
           married Abraham BURBANK; Benjamin-[5] BARRELL born ca 1814, died 7 Mar 1895

33. EDMUND/EDMOND-[3] **BOWKER,** son of James-[2] BOWKER (James-[1]) and Hannah LAMBERT, was born 20 Aug 1732 at Scituate, MA. He married Lydia LAMBERT on 2 Dec 1756 at Scituate. She was the daughter of James LAMBERT and Sarah BRIDGES, and was born ca 1735; died 24 July 1824 Scituate. Edmund-[3] BOWKER died 19 Feb 1827 at Scituate.

Children of Edmund-[3] BOWKER and Lydia LAMBERT:
Surname **BOWKER**   (children born Scituate, MA)
+   **154. LYDIA**   born 26 Mar 1757; died 17 Jan 1852 Hanover, Plymouth, MA
                               married Abner CURTIS 25 May 1775 Scituate, MA
                               (he s/o Abner CURTIS and Deborah MANN)
                               (he born ca 1754 Hanover, MA; died 2 Feb 1838)

Children of Edmund-[3] BOWKER and Lydia LAMBERT, continued:
Surname **BOWKER**

	155. Desire	born 16 May 1760; died ____
+	**156. EDMUND**	born 16 Sep 1762; died 30 April 1812 Hebron, Oxford, ME
		married Patience BARROWS ca 1785
		(she dau/o Deacon William BARROWS and _____)
+	**157. CAPT. JAMES**	born 9 June 1765; died 1 June 1827 Buckfield, Oxford, ME
		married Judith CHASE 15 Nov 1787 at Buckfield, Maine
		(she dau/o Thomas CHASE and Hannah HASKINS) (she born 4 Apr 1766; died ____)
	158. Phillip	born 6 Nov 1767; died ____
	159. Sarah	born 16 June 1770; died ____
	160. Paul	born 21 April 1773; died 11 Feb 1795 EOL
+	**161. ALLEN**	born 1 May 1775; died 21 Aug 1822 Scituate, MA
		married Eunice O. VINAL 6 Jan 1805 Boston, MA
		(she born 20 Oct 1777 Scituate, MA; died 16 March 1821)
+	**162. WARREN**	born 14 July 1777 Scituate, MA; died 19 Aug 1855 Boston, MA
		married Rebecca Holmes CROSWELL 4 Mar 1799 (she born ca 1777; died 1853)

36. JOSEPH[3] **BOWKER**, brother of above, was born 16 March 1739 (gs) at Scituate, Plymouth, MA. He married Elizabeth Deborow Cowing on 26 May 1760 at Scituate. She was the daughter of Job COWING and Deborah GANNETT, and was born 14 April 1740 at Scituate, MA; died 1 Nov 1831 at Phippsburg, Sagadahoc, Maine. Joseph-[3] BOWKER died 4 March 1802 Georgetown, ME (now Phippsburg).

Children of Joseph-[3] BOWKER and Elizabeth COWING:
Surname **BOWKER**

+	**163. DEBORAH**	born 20 Aug 1762 Scituate; died 20 April 1855 Augusta, Kennebec, ME
		married John SOULE ca ____ (he born ca 1759; died 1834)
+	**164. LEVI**	born 25 July 1763 Scituate; died 28 July 1850 Machias, Washington, ME
		married Elizabeth " Betsey " WATTS 24 Dec 1789 Jonesborough, ME
		(she dau/o Samuel WATTS and Elsie BEAN
		(she born May 1765 Haverhill, MA; died 23 Feb 1854 Machias, ME
	165. Desire	born 8 Apr 1764 Georgetown, Sagadahoc, ME; married Joseph HALL 23 Sep 1788
+	**166. JOSEPH**	born 5 Mar 1766; died 5 April 1817; married Elizabeth HALL 11 Dec 1787
		(she born ca 1770; died 31 July 1853 Phippsburg, ME
	167. John	born 25 June 1768; died ____
+	**168. NANCY**	born 18 July 1770; died 2 Aug 1856
		married David FARRIN 12 March 1791 Georgetown , Sagadahoc, ME
		(he s/o John FARRIN and Hannah NEWMAN)
		(he born 8 Feb 1767 Brunswick, ME; died 5 Feb 1847 Brunswick)
		Child: Thomas-[5] FARRIN born 1793 Brunswick, ME; died ca 1827; married Lucy SNOWMAN ca ___
		(she 1793-1852 ME) Child: Charles David-[6] FARRIN born ca 1823, died 1855 at sea nr. Indonesia
+	**169. RACHEL**	born 25 July 1772; died 9 Sep 1856 Augusta, ME
		married Thomas DICKMAN 26 Aug 1797 (he born ____; died 1820 ME)
+	**170. HANNAH**	born 8 Jan 1775; died ___; married Abel WRIGHT 29 April 1804 Bowdoinham, ME
		(he s/o Jesse WRIGHT and Abigail COOK)
		(he born 23 Apr 1784 Androscoggin, ME; died March 1829 Oxford, Maine)
+	**171. LAZARUS**	born 13 Oct 1776; died 7 Jan 1858 ME.
		married Agnes LENNAN/LENNIN/LENNING 5 Jan 1805
+	**172. JAMES**	born 3 March 1779; died 13 Oct 1852 Phippsburg, ME.
		married Eunice BATCHELDER 4 April 1804
+	**173. WASHINGTON**	born 15 May 1781 ME; died 9 Aug 1858 Brunswick, ME
		1 married Sally LAMONT 24 May 1804 (she born ca 1785; died 1806)
		2 married Jane SPEAR 25 Jan 1806 (int pub) (she born 1785, died 1811)
		3 married Elizabeth " Lettie " MINOT 26 June 1812 Georgetown, ME.
		(she dau/o John MINOT and Jemima ____) (she born 1783; died 1845)
		4 married Lettice ORR 1 Dec 1849
+	**174. REBECCA**	born 4 Oct 1783; died 8 Oct 1858; married M. John TUCKER ca 1804

37. DESIRE-³ BOWKER, sister of above, was born 14 April 1841 Scituate, MA. She married Colburn BARRELL on 28 May1861 (# 43). He was the son of William BARRELL and Abigail BOWKER, and was born 7 May 1738 Scituate; died 30 Nov 1777. He served in the Revolutionary War and was captured by the British during the Ticonderoga Campaign, and died on a prisoner of war ship in the St. Lawrence River near Quebec, Canada. Desire-³ BOWKER died ca 1821.

Child of Desire-³ BOWKER and Colburn BARRELL:
Surname **BARRELL**

    175. Colburn, Jr.   born ca 1763 MA; died ca 1840; married Esther VIDETO ca 1786
                                 (she born ca 1766; died 1846)
                    Child: Lydia-⁵ BARRELL born ca 1798, died 1874; married Moses ROWLEY ca 1819

39. JAMES-³ BARRELL – for descendants see # 150 (4th generation)

41. JOHN-³ BARRELL, brother of above, was born 31 March 1734. He married Judith SNOW on 20 April 1756 at Bridgewater, MA. She was the daughter of Isaac SNOW and Hannah SHAW, and was born 7 Dec 1736; died 26 May 1807 Hartland, Windsor, VT.. John-³ BARRELL died 20 July 1804.

Children of John-³ BARRELL and Judith SNOW:
Surname **BARRELL**

176. Molly	born ca 1757; died 1758	179. Abigail	born ca 1765; died ____
177. Edmund	born ca 1760; died ____	180. John	born ca 1767; died 1836
178. Judith	born ca 1763; died ____		

43. COLBURN-3 BARRELL, son of Abigail-² BOWKER and William BARRELL (see # 37 above)

45. MARY-³ BOWKER, daughter of Richard-² BOWKER (James-¹) and Mary BATES, was born ca 1726 MA. She married Jesse TORREY on 6 Dec 1744 at Hanover, Plymouth, MA. He was the son of Nathaniel TORREY and Hannah TILDEN, and was born ca 1725 Hanover, MA; died 16 July 1793 at Hanover. Mary-³ BOWKER died ca 1777.

Children of Mary-³ BOWKER and Jesse TORREY:
Surname **TORREY**   (all children born Hanover, MA)

    181. Ruth   born 18 July 1745; died ____
    182. Hannah   born ca 1747; died 12 May 1807 Hanover, MA
    183. James   born 5 Aug 1750; died ca 1784
    184. Nathaniel   born 23 Jan 1753; died ____ Fowlerville, NY
    185. Jesse, Jr.   born 1 March 1755; died 18 March 1777
    186. Mary   born 12 Mar 1757; died 29 May 1838 Chesterfield, NH
    187. Elizabeth   born 20 April 1760; died ca 1799; married Samuel GROSS ca ____
                         (he born ca 1749; died ca 1817)
                Child: Ruth Ann-⁵ GROSS born ca 1783; died 1828
    188. Job   born 10 Sept 1762
    189. Elihab   born 1 Sep 1765; died 23 Aug 1812

46. RICHARD-³ BOWKER, brother of above, was born ca 1727 MA. He married Mary PRATT 21 April 1751. She was the daughter of ____ PRATT and ____, and was born ____, died ____. Richard-⁴ BOWKER died ___.

Children of Richard-³ BOWKER and Mary PRATT:
Surname **BOWKER**   (all children born Pembroke, Plymouth, MA)

    190. Nelson   born 12 Feb 1752 ; died ____; married Alice AUSTIN 19 Nov 1795
    191. Rebecca   born 25 May 1754; died ____; married Lindes TOWER 24 Nov 1774
                         (he s/o James TOWER and Mary Day) (he born 11 Dec 1749; died 21 Apr 1805 VT)
            Child: Gad Hitchcock-⁴ TOWER born 1 June 1776 MA; died 1839; married Martha COOK on 27 Feb 1806 PA
    192. Richard   born 14 Aug 1756; died ____;
+   **193. BENJAMIN**   born 9 Aug 1758; died ____; married Jemima HILL 14 Jan 1787
    194. Lydia   born 7 Apr/Oct 1760; died 14 Nov 1847
                         married Gershom RAMSDELL ca 1797 (his 3rd wife)
                         (he s/o Samuel RAMSDELL and Dorothy BISHOP)
                         (he born 12 Aug 1750; died 14 Oct 1836 Leeds, Maine

47. LUKE-³ BOWKER, brother of above, was born ca 1729/30, MA. He married Joanna DUNBAR on 14 Dec 1752 at Scituate, MA. She was the daughter of _____ DUNBAR and ____, and was born ____; died ____. Luke⁻⁴ BOWKER died ca 1790.

Children of Luke-³ BOWKER and Joanna DUNBAR:
Surname **BOWKER**

	195. Anne	born 13 Sept 1753; died __
+	**196. BATHSHEBA /**	born 20 Mar 1755 Scituate, MA; died 8 Feb 1838 Pomfret, VT
	BARSHABA	married John DOTEN 19 Aug 1779 Plympton, MA
		(he s/o Edward DOTEN/DOTY and Joanna WHITING/ WHITTON, Dunham)
		(he born 3 Sep 1750 MA; died 30 Mar 1812 Pomfret, VT)
+	**197. DAVID**	born 24 Sept 1756; died ca 1824; married Huldah HARDEN ca 1780
	198. Mary	born 8 Nov 1758; died young
	199. Calvin	born 2 Sep 1760; died ____
	200. Mary (2)	born 2 Sept 1764
	201. Ruth	born 18 Sep 1767
+	**202. LIBERTY**	born 13 May 1775; died 21 May 1846 Savoy, Berkshire, MA
		1 married Sarah GURNEY 20 June 1796 Abington, Plymouth, MA
		(she born 5 May 1770; died 8 March 1826)
		2 married Katy WEEKS 28 Aug 1826 (she born 4 Jan 1781; died 6 Sep 1852)

50. BENJAMIN⁻³ BOWKER, Jr., son of Benjamin⁻² BOWKER (James⁻¹) and Hannah PROUTY, was born 16 Feb 1738 at Scituate, MA. He married Hannah SPARHAWKE on 10 Nov 1763 at Scituate, MA. She was the daughter of Joseph SPARHAWKE and Elizabeth ____, and was born 2 April 1738; died 20 Dec 1778. He married second, ca 1780, to Mrs. Anne/Anna _____ Sylvester. Benjamin⁻³ BOWKER, Jr. died ca 1806 at Scituate.

Children of Benjamin-³ BOWKER, Jr. and Hannah SPARHAWKE/ SPARROWHAWK:
Surname **BOWKER**

+	**203. BENJAMIN III**	born 21 Dec 1764 Scituate; died ____
		married Chloe STETSON on 30 Jan 1791 Scituate, Plymouth, MA
+	**204. ELISHA**	born 21 Sept 1767 Scituate; died ca 1840 VT
		married Sarah/Sally SPEAR 9 Jan 1793 Quincy, ME.
		(she born ca 1768 MA; died ____)
	205. Hannah	born 29 July 1770; died ____
	206. Esther	born 26 Oct 1773; died ____
+	**207. JOEL**	born 4 July 1775; died 1858 Salem, MA
		1 married Eunice PEARSON 23 Dec 1802
		(she born 7 March 1780 Salem, MA; died 20 Apr 1808 a result of childbirth)
		2 married Margaret ROGERS 4 Oct 1808 (she born 3 April 1780, died ____)
		3 married Lucretia ROGERS 26 April 1819 Ipswich, Essex, MA
		(she born 3 March 1786; died ____)
		(she dau/o Daniel ROGERS and Mary APPLETON)
	208. Polly	born ca 1781; died ____

Children of Benjamin-³ BOWKER and Anne/Anna ____ Sylvester:
Surname **BOWKER**   (all children born Scituate, MA)

+	**209. CAPT. JOSHUA**	born 8 Oct 1783; died ____ (living 1860)
		married Nancy Ann CUSHING 25 Dec 1813 Scituate, MA.
		(she born ca 1781; died 1838)
	210. Charlotte	born 4 June 1785; died 11 Mar 1843; married Allen CLAPP 20 Jan 1807
	211. Sylvester	born 3 Dec 1788 ; died _____

52. EUNICE⁻³ BOWKER, sister of above, was born ----- 1744 at Scituate, Plymouth, MA. She married John DAMON on 11 April 1771 at Scituate. He was the son of Daniel DAMON and Judith LITCHFIELD, and was born 26 Mar 1744 at Scituate; died ca 1815. Eunice⁻³ BOWKER died ca 1834.

Children of Eunice-[3] BOWKER and John DAMON:
Surname **DAMON** (all children born Scituate, MA)

212. Eunice B.	born 23 Feb 1772; died 18 Sep 1835 Scituate
213. John, Jr.	born 26 July 1774; died 10 Sep 1834 Scituate
214. Melzar	born 4 Apr 1776; died 31 May 1822 Scituate
	married Bathsheba E. JONES 16 Apr 1809
	(she born 14 Sep 1781 Hingham, MA; died Nov 1833 Scituate, MA

Children: Melzar[5], Jr. born 21 Feb 1810 Scituate, died 21 Aug 1825; Joan/Joanna[5] born 13 Feb 1815; and Lydia Thomas-[5] DAMON born 4/6 June 1816

215. Abigail " Nabby "	born 22 Apr 1778; died 22 Apr 1862 Scituate
216. Polly	born 20 Aug 1780; died 1835 Scituate
217. Jacob	born 19 Aug 1783; died 2 Jan 1857 Scituate

67. DANIEL[-4] **CROCKER/CROOKER,** son of Mary[-3] RAMSDELL (Martha[-2] BOWKER; James[-1]) was born 5 June 1740 at Hanover, Plymouth, MA. He married first to Abigail STUDLEY ca 1763 at Hanover. She was the daughter of Joshua STUDLEY and Lydia PRATT, and was born 28 June 1741; died 25 Sept 1775 at Pembroke, Plymouth, MA. He married second to Hannah WHITE on 17 Dec 1776. She was the daughter of Benjamin WHITE and Hannah DECROW; and was born ca 1754; died 22 Aug 1828 Hanson, Plymouth, MA. Daniel[-4] CROCKER/CROOKER died 6 Feb 1818 at Pembroke.

Children of Daniel[-4] CROCKER and Abigail STUDLEY:
Surname **CROCKER/CROOKER**

	218. Nabby	born ca 1765; died ____
+	**219. BETTY**	born ca 1766/67; died 13 Jan 1816
		married Barzillai / Barze STURTEVANT 18 Mar 1790
		(he born ca 1763; died 1842)
	220. Lydia	born ca 1768; died ____
+	**221. ENSIGN**	born 25 Oct 1770 Pembroke; died 7 Jan 1853 Hanover, MA
		married Hannah MONROE ca 1801 (she born ca 1775; died ____)
	222. Daniel	born 3 Sept 1773; died 1 Oct 1843; married Silviana HARDEN ca ____

Children of Daniel[-4] CROCKER/CROOKER and Hannah WHITE:
Surname **CROCKER/CROOKER**   (all children born at Pembroke, Plymouth, MA)

223. Hannah	born 15 Aug 1777; died ____	
224. Mollie	born 7 Sep 1778; died ____	
225. Peniah	born 24 Dec 1780; died 12 June 1789	
226. Martilla	born 11 Nov 1782; died ____	
227. Sally	born 12 March 1784; died ____	230. Deborah born 1 Nov 1788
228. Judith	born 20 June 1785; died ____	231. Salome born 25 June 1790; died 13 Jun 1791
229. Joanna	born 8 Nov 1787; died ____	232. Zoa born 21 Apr 1794

70. DANIEL[-4] **HERSEY,** son of Susanna[-3] RAMSDELL (Martha-[2] BOWKER; James[-1]) and David Daniel HERSEY, was born ca 1745 at Pembroke, Plymouth, MA. He married Desire WESTON on 5 Jan 1774 Nova Scotia, Canada. She was the daughter of Nathan WESTON and Hannah EVERSON, and was born ____, died ____. Daniel[-4] HERSEY died ____.

Children of Daniel[-4] HERSEY and Desire WESTON:
Surname **HERSEY**   (children all born Nova Scotia, Canada)

	233. Desire	born 18 Mar 1775; died ____	
	234. Jesse	born 3 Oct 1777; died 29 Oct 1859 ; married Elizabeth COFFRAN ca ___	
		(she dau/o William-[2] COFFRAN and _____)	
	235. David	born 7 Sep 1779; died 15 Oct 1865; never married	EOL
	236. Rebecca	born 7 Sep 1783; died ___; never married	EOL
	237. Phoebe	born 7 July 1784; died ____	
	238. Lydia	born 5 Jan 1786; died ____; married George BRIDGEO	
		(he s/o Francis BRIDGEO and _____)	
+	**239. ZADOC**	born 20 Aug 1791; died ____; married Desire DOANE 1 Jan 1824	
		(she dau/o Israel -[2] DOANE and _____)	
+	**240. ZENAS**	born 7 Nov 1794; died ___; married Elizabeth RING ca ____	
		(she dau/o Capt. George-[2] RING and _____)	
+	**241. RICHARD**	born 17 Dec 1799; died ____; married Elizabeth HALL 19 Dec 1822	
		(she dau/o Thomas HALL and _____)	

73. SAMUEL YARMOUTH⁻⁴ HERSEY, brother of above, was born ca 1755 Pembroke, Plymouth, MA. He married first to Susan Elizabeth TIDD on ____. She was the daughter of ____ TIDD and ____, and was born ____, died ____. He married second to Lydia CLARKE on 21 Apr 1774. She was the daughter of ____ CLARKE and ____, and was born ca 1755, died ca 1804. Samuel-⁴ HERSEY died ca 1850.

Children of Samuel⁻⁴ HERSEY and Lydia CLARKE:
Surname **HERSEY**

+	**242. SAMUEL, Jr.**	born ca 1776 New Brunswick, Canada; died ca 1851 New Brunswick
		married Elizabeth MAYES on 13 June 1802
		(she born ca 1780; died 25 Oct 1825 Hampstead, NB, Canada
+	**243. HANNAH**	born ca 1778 NB; died ___; married Daniel SLOCUM, Sr ca 1794
		(he s/o Ebenezer SLOCUM and Esther COREY)
		(he born ca 1774 RI; died 1797 Hampstead, NB, Canada
	244. Solomon	born ca 1783 NB; died ____
	245. Elizabeth	born 13 Dec 1786 NB; died _____
	246. Levi	born ca 1789 NB; died ____
	247. Elijah J.	born 24 Mar 1790 NB; died 10 Feb 1873 Linneus, Aroostock, Maine
	248. David	born ca 1799 NB; died ____
	249. Daniel	born ca 1800 Nova Scotia; died 3 Dec 1882 Gagetown, NB, Canada
	250. Jesse	born ca 1807; died ____

75. LEVI⁻⁴ HERSEY, brother of above, was born ca Jan 1754 Pembroke, Plymouth, MA. He married first to Chloe DAY on 8 March 1780 at St. John, New Brunswick, Canada. She was the daughter of ____ DAY and ____; and was born 17 June 1758; died ca 1820 Yarmouth, Nova Scotia. He married second to Leah WAGNER ca 1821. She was the daughter of ____ WAGNER and ____; and was born ca 1800; died ____. Levi⁻⁴ HERSEY died 8 Feb 1842 at Little River, Digby County, Nova Scotia.

Children of Levi⁻⁴ HERSEY and Chloe DAY:
Surname **HERSEY**(children born Nova Scotia)

+	**251. LEVI**	born 30 Dec 1780; died ca 1820; married Mary RICHARDSON ca ___
		(she dau/o Reuben RICHARDSON and ____)
	252. John Irish	born 27 Mar 1783 Falmouth, NS; died 1 Nov 1868 NS
		married Mary ELDRIDGE ca ____
		(she dau/o Capt. Barnabas ELDRIDGE and _____)
	253. Susanna	born 5 Dec 1785; died 14 July 1867; married Jacob KILLAM ca 1808
		(he born 4 May 1774; died 3 Sept 1843) (he s/o John KILLAM and ____)
		(he s/o John KILLAM and Joanna PARROT)
	254. Ezra	born 10 Apr 1788; died 1800; went abroad EOL
	255. Abigail	born 17 June 1791; died Sept 1856; married John DAKIN ca ____
		Child: Levi Hersey⁻⁶ DAKIN born 25 Dec 1830 NS, died 22 July 1922 OR; married Clara Jane SMITH 29 Sep 1861
	256. Jedidiah	born 23 July 1793; died ____ ; married _____ ERB ca ____
	257. Chloe	born 17 Nov 1795; died ca 1850; married Samuel TIDD
	258. Pamelia	born 1 July 1797; died before 1881; married Noah BROWN of Little River
	259. Freeman	born 17 June 1800; died ____
		married Rachel SAUNDERS ca ____; and moved to Ontario, Canada
	260. Samuel	born 3 June 1802; died Jan 1888 NS; married Martha DENTON ca ____
	261. Jeremiah	born 27 Nov 1804; died 1887; married Sarah TIDD (sister of Samuel)
	262. Cynthia	born 3 Sept 1806; died Apr 1897
		married Deacon George CHUTE March 1830
		(he s/o Thomas CHUTE and ____) (he born ____; died April 1897)
		Children: Deacon⁻⁶ born ca 1831, died 1878; Louise Jane-⁶ born ca 1834; Susan Amelia⁻⁶ CHUTE born ca 1841

Children of Levi⁻⁴ HERSEY and Leah WAGNER:
Surname **HERSEY**

	263. Matilda	born 1 March 1821; died ____
		1 married Andrew HARRIS ca ____ (he s/o John⁻² HARRIS)
		2 married Thomas Benjamin TREFRY ca ____ (he s/o William TREFRY)
	264. Jesse	born 1823; died 1868; married Jerusha FROST ca _____ (dau/o Stephen FROST)
		Child: Bernard⁻⁶ HERSEY born ca 1866
	265. Annie	born ____; died at age 4

Children of Levi-[4] HERSEY and Leah WAGNER, continued:
Surname **HERSEY**

+	**266. DANIEL**	born 1826/27; died ____; married Eliza WHITENECT/WHITENECK ca ____ (she born ca 1823; died 1901)
	267. William	born ____; died ____ (lost at sea aged 17)
	268. Mary	born ____; died ____ (age 4 months)
	269. David	born ____; died ____; married Isabella HERSEY (dau/o of Zenas HERSEY)
	270. Charles W.	born ----; died ____; married Georgiana SAUNDERS ca ____ (she dau/o Watson SAUNDERS)
	271. Elizabeth	born 1835; died 1923; married William BUCKMAN ca ____

92. JOHN STOCKBRIDGE-[4] RAMSDELL, son of Simeon-[3] RAMSDELL (Mary-[2] BOWKER; James-[1]) and Mary TURNER, was born 5 May 1758 at Pembroke, MA. He married Hannah ALLEN on 30 Sept 1784 at Plymouth, MA. She as the daughter of Samuel ALLEN and Hannah PRATT, and was born 17 May 1761 at Bridgewater, Plymouth, MA; died ____.

Children of John Stockbridge-[4] RAMSDELL and Hannah ALLEN:
Surname **RAMSDELL**

+	**272. HANNAH PRATT**	born 7 Aug 1785; died 4 Sept 1831 married Benjamin -[5] BOWKER, Jr. 4 Sep 1831 (he s/o Benjamin-[4] BOWKER and Jemima HILL)
	273. John	born 17 June 1787; died Apr 1821 Leeds
	274. Bartlett	born ca 1789; died ____; married Emily STURTEVANT ca ____

Children: Elbridge Bartlett-[6] born 1826, died 28 Oct 1897; Joseph W-[6] born 14 Apr 1830; Maria S-[6] born 14 Apr 1830; and Levi S-[6] RAMSDELL born 18 Apr 1840

+	**275. CLARISSA**	born 15 Feb 1791; died 1845; married Gad -[5] BOWKER 20 Nov 1823 (he brother of Benjamin, Jr. above)		
+	**276. MARTIN**	born 23 Sep 1793; died ____; married Bethiah Ames ROBINSON 3 Apr 1825		
	277. Oren	born 26 Sep 1796; died ____		
	278. Mary Munro	born 22 May 1799; died ____	280. Huldah Allen	born 5 May 1805
	279. Rosella	born 23 Apr 1801; died 23 Oct 1867 Hanover, MA		

105. BARTLETT-[4] RAMSDEN/RAMSDELL, son of Nehemiah-[3] (Mary-[2] BOWKER; James-[1]) and Rebecca CHAMBER-LAIN, was born 18 Feb 1770. He married Emma BEAN on 14 April 1796. She was the daughter of ____ BEAN and ____; and was born 6 Dec 1773; died 22 July 1814. Bartlett-[4] RAMSDEN died 25 Jan 1832.

Children of Bartlett-[4] RAMSDEN and Emma BEAN:
Surname **RAMSDEN**

	281. Betsey	born 11 Sep 1802; died 10 Jan 1897 married Reuben MAKER 22 Mar 1819 (he born ____; died 10 Nov 1875)

Child: Lovicy-[6] MAKER born ____; married Theodore H. MUNSON

110. LAZARUS-[4] BOWKER, Jr., son of Lazarus-[3] BOWKER (James-[2,1]) and Abigail BUCK, was born ca 1742 at Scituate, Plymouth, MA. He married Mary-[5] COLLIER on 12 Nov 1768 at Scituate. She was the daughter of Thomas -[4] (Gershom-[3]; Thomas-[2,1]) COLLIER and Bridget SOUTHWORTH, and was born 22 April 1746 Scituate; died 18 Oct 1786. Lazarus-[4] BOWKER married second to Sarah TURNER on 18 May 1794. He died 26 May 1832 at Scituate.

Children of Lazarus-[4] BOWKER, Jr. and Mary COLLIER:
Surname **BOWKER**

+	**282. DIMMICK**	born 10 Dec 1769; died ca 1860 Scituate, MA; married Margaret WHITTON 10 Feb 1799
	283. Jennie/Jenne	born 11 June 1771; died 15 Sep 1839
	284. Abigail	born 26 Nov 1772; died 10 Oct 1833 Hingham, MA
	285. Susanna	born 21 Jan 1776; died ____
+	**286. HOWARD**	born 25 May 1778; died 7 Oct 1858 Scituate, MA 1 married Nancy GARDNER ca 1803 (she born ca 1785; died ca 1815) 2 married Eveline TILDEN 23 Sep 1816 Marshfield, MA (she dau/o Samuel TILDEN and Margaret FOSTER) (she born 19 Mar 1796 Marshfield; died 22 June 1874)

Children of Lazarus⁻⁴ BOWKER and Mary COLLIER, continued:
Surname **BOWKER**

287. Sally	born ca 1780; died young		291 Huldah	born 20 Aug 1786
288. Sally (2)	born 12 June 1782; died 16 Jan 1851			
	1 married Aaron CURTIS ca ____		(he born ca 1766; died ca 1818)	
	2 married Isaac STEVENS 20 Jan 1819			
289. Mary	born 12 June 1782; died ____			

+   **290. LAZARUS III**   born 12 May 1784; died 28 Dec 1867; married Martha CUSHING ca 1807

112. GERSHOM⁻⁴ BOWKER, brother of above, was born ca ____; bpt. 4 Oct 1747 Scituate, MA. He married Elizabeth STETSON on 18 Feb 1771 at Scituate. She was the daughter of Isaac STETSON and Ruth PROUTY, and was born 7 Jan 1754; died 19 Feb 1842. Gershom⁻⁴ BOWKER died ca 1796.

Children of Gershom⁻⁴ BOWKER and Elizabeth STETSON:
Surname **BOWKER**   (all children born Scituate, MA)

292. Gershom, Jr.	born 21 Jan 1775; died ____; married Elizabeth CALEF 22 Nov 1801 Boston			
293. Isaac Stetson	born 1 March 1778; died ____			
294. Lemuel	born 28 Jan 1781; died ____			
295. Nathaniel	born 25 May 1783; died ____			

+   **296. HOMER**   born 19 Sep 1785; died 1864; married Tryphena SYLVESTER 7 Apr 1811
         (she born 25 Sep 1790; died 20 Oct 1864 Scituate, MA)

297. Mary	born 19 Apr 1788; died ____		299. Abigail	born 22 Sept 1793
298. Harris	born ____; bpt. 29 July 1792; dy		300. Harris (2)	born 24 Dec 17

114. ZEBULON⁻⁴ BOWKER, brother of above, was born 23 Oct 1751 at Scituate, MA. He married Deborah RANDALL 5 Sep 1773. She was the daughter of Job RANDALL, Jr. and Mary JENNI(NGS, and was born 6 Oct 1751 Pembroke, MA; died Mar 1782. Zebulon⁻⁴ BOWKER died 23 Oct 1839 at Cambridge, VT.

Children of Zebulon⁻⁴ BOWKER and Deborah RANDALL:
Surname **BOWKER**

301. Abigail	born 3 March 1774; died 22 Oct 1856; married Jacob HUNTLEY ca ____

+   **302. JOSEPH**   born 24 Oct 1780 Rutland, VT; died 6 Oct 1868 Bennington, VT
         married Rhoda HAMILTON ca ____
         (she born 28 July 1780 ARK.; died 1 Sep 1855 Sandgate, VT)

118. JAMES⁻⁴ BOWKER, IV, son of James⁻³ BOWKER (James⁻²;¹) and Mary ELMES, was born ca 1743 at Scituate, MA. He married Ruth SARGENT on 22 Oct 1767 at Georgetown, Maine. She was the daughter of Jonathan SARGENT and Mercy GRAY; and was born 14 Feb 1746 York, ME; died ____. James⁴ BOWKER died ca 1830 Durham, Cumberland, ME.

Children of James⁻⁴ BOWKER, IV and Ruth SARGENT:
Surname **BOWKER**   (children born Bowdoinham, Maine)

+   **303. JAMES-V**   born 22 Feb 1768; died 3 Aug 1837 Bowdoin, ME; married Jane WRIGHT 21 Oct 1790

304. Ruth Rogers	born 22 Mar 1770; died ____

+   **305. RHODA**   born ca 1772; died 14 July 1851 Bowdoinham, ME
         married Nicholas WEYMOUTH ca 1799

306. Mercy	born ca 1774; died ____
307. Mary	born ca 1779; died 4 Feb 1852
308. Sarah	born ca 1783; died 11 Oct 1830 Durham, Androscoggin, ME

125. WILLIAM⁻⁴ BOWKER, brother of above, was born ca 1763/ 65 at Sagadahoc, Maine. He married _____ ca ____. It is believed that he moved to New Jersey. This researcher cannot find any info regarding a wife.

Child of William-⁴ BOWKER and _____?? :
Surname **BOWKER**

309. SAMUEL	born 2 Mar 1785 Stafford, NJ; died 1861 Monmouth, NJ
MICHAEL	married Lucretia APPLEGATE 17 Nov 1805
	(she dau/o Bartholomew APPLEGATE and Mary MILLER)
	(she born ca 1788 Dover, Monmouth, NJ; died there ca 1845)

128. ELIHU-⁴ BOWKER, brother of above   son of James-³ BOWKER (James-²;¹) and _____, was born ca 1773 at Lincoln, Maine. He married Elizabeth PARKS on 20 July 1801 at Bowdoinham, ME. She was the daughter of ____ PARKS and ____, and was born 27 July 1773 London, England; died 20 Aug 1865 at Richmond, Sagadahoc, Maine. Elihu-⁴ BOWKER died 1 Oct 1844 at Richmond, ME.

Children of Elihu-⁴ BOWKER and Elizabeth PARKS:
Surname **BOWKER**   (children born Richmond, Sagadahoc, Maine)

310. Captain Charles	born 9 Dec 1801; died 13 June 1883; married Louisa PREBLE ca ____	
	Children: Ella-⁶ born ca 1836; and Margaret-⁶ BOWKER born ca 1839	
311. Lavina	born 8 Apr 1804; died ____	
312. Edward C.	born 27 Mar 1807; died 29 May 1870 Richmond, ME	
313. Daniel	born 9 Nov 1809; died 18 Dec 1882 Bowdoin, ME	
314. Cordelia	born 30 Sep 814; died 22 Oct 1890 Bowdoin, ME	

130. BARTLETT-⁴ BOWKER, son of John-³ BOWKER (James-²,¹) and Anna WRIGHT, was born 2 Feb 1749 at Scituate, Plymouth, MA. He married first to Christina HOLMES ca 27 Sep 1779 at Scituate. She was the daughter of Thomas HOLMES and Lydia WHITE, and was born 27 April 1755 Scituate; died ca 1793. He married second to Susanna WITHINGTON on 7 Sep 1794 at Fitzwilliam, Cheshire, MA. She was born ca ____; died 1797. He married third to Jemima KNOWLTON Wright on 1 Feb 1798 at Fitzwilliam, MA. She was the daughter of Ezekiel KNOWLTON and Anna MILES, and the widow of Thomas WRIGHT, and was born 28 Feb 1770 Templeton, Worcester, MA; died 4 April 1847 at Fitzwilliam, Cheshire, NH. Bartlett-⁴ BOWKER died 16 Jan 1829 at Fitzwilliam.

Children of Bartlett-⁴ BOWKER and Christina HOLMES:
Surname **BOWKER**

	315. Christina	born 20 Feb 1781; died 21 Feb 1781	EOL
+	**316. REBECCA**	born 30 May 1782; died ___; married David STOWELL 14 Apr 1803 NH	
+	**317. BARTLETT, Jr.**	born 6 Dec 1784 NH; died 10 Sept 1865 St .Johnsbury, VT	
		married Hannah CARPENTER 27 Jan 1809	
		(she born 5 Oct 1787; died 14 Nov 1857 St. Johnsbury, VT	
		(she dau/ Davis B. CARPENTER and Miriam MANNING)	
	318. STEPHEN	born 8 Dec 1788 Fitzwilliam, NH; died 11 July 1860 Newfane, VT	
		married Sarah/ Sally WHITNEY 7 Apr 1814	
	319. Anna (twin)	born 22 Jan 1792 NH; died ____; married Ezekiel COLLINS ca ____	
	320. Samuel (twin)	born 22 Jan 1792; died 23 Jan 1792	EOL

Child of Bartlett-⁴ BOWKER and Susanna WITHINGTON:
Surname **BOWKER**

321. Daniel	born 12 Jan 1795 Fitzwilliam; died ____;married Phila ____ ca ____	
	Children: Mary F-⁶ born ca 1828; Daniel K-⁶ born ca 1835 ; and Sophie F-⁶ BOWKER born ca 1837	

Children of Bartlett-⁴ BOWKER and Jemima KNOWLTON Wright:
Surname **BOWKER**

	322. Wright	born 28 Nov 1798 NH; died ca 1821 EOL
+	**323. LUKE**	born 28 Apr 1800; died 23 March 1887
		1 married Rhoda HARWOOD/ HURD 13 Apr 1828
		2 married Sarah HOWE ca 1830
		3 married Rebecca BALLARD Simonds 28 Nov 1844 (2 daus)
		(she dau/o Eliphaz BALLARD and ____ of Lancaster, MA)
+	**324. CAPT. ELIJAH**	born 8 Jan 1803 Fitzwilliam; died 12 Feb 1878 Fitzwilliam, NH
		married Dorothy CROMBIE 18 Nov 1830 NH (she born ca 1807; died 1884)
	325. Lucy	born ca 1804; died ca 1827
+	**326. CYNTHIA**	born 12 Feb 1807; died 27 July 1856 Topeka, KS
		1 married Dexter B. ROLLINS 5 Oct 1831 ; 2 married Rev. Jesse STONE 6 Sep 1840
		(he born 8 Sep 1806 Fitzwilliam; died 19 Feb 1893 Topeka, KS)
		(he s/o Deacon Artemus STONE and _____)
	327. Roxanna	born 28 July 1809; died 29 Aug 1863 St. Johnsbury, VT
		married Leander Holmes STOWELL 26 Dec 1831
+	**328. HANNAH**	born 25 Mar 1815 Fitzwilliam; died 24 April 1901 Fitchburg, MA
		married James COREY 2 April 1835
		(he born 12 Nov 1805 Richmond, NH; died 12 July 1889 Fitchburg, MA)

133. CAPTAIN JOHN⁻⁴ BOWKER, brother of above, was born 22/28 Aug 1754 MA. He married first to Faith HOLMES on 12 Dec 1778. She was the daughter of Thomas HOLMES and Lydia WHITE, and sister to Christina HOLMES (above) was born 10 Feb 1753, died 20 July 1788. He married second to Annis MARSHALL on 10 Dec 1789 at Fitzwilliam, Cheshire, NH. She was the daughter of _____ MARSHALL and ____, and was born ____, died ____. Capt. John⁻⁴ BOWKER died ____.

Children of Captain John⁻⁴ BOWKER and Faith HOLMES:
Surname **BOWKER**

329. Lydia	born 11 Oct 1779 Scituate, MA; died ____	
330. John	born 1 Aug 1781 Fitzwilliam, Cheshire, NH; died _____	
331. Thomas	born 17 Mar 1783 Fitzwilliam; died 2 Apr 1863	
	married Lydia BANNISTER ca 1811	
	(she dau/o Timothy BANNISTER and Prudence STEWART)	
	(she born 10 Sep 1783; died 26 Nov 1857)	
	Child: Charles C-⁶ BOWKER born 27 Feb 1812 NY; died 3 Feb 1871; married Lurana BUTLER ca ___; she born 16 Dec 1814; died 13 Mar 1908	
332. Relief	(1) born 14 Feb 1785; died 17 Feb 1785	EOL
333. Hannah	(1) born 26 Apr 1788; died 7 Sep 1788	EOL

Children of Captain John⁻⁴ BOWKER and Annis MARSHALL:
Surname **BOWKER** (all children born Fitzwilliam, Cheshire, NH)

334. Warren		born 16 June 1792	338. Lucinda	born 18 Jan 1803
335. Relief	(2)	born 27 Oct 1793	339. Rebecca	born 27 Aug 1805
336. Hannah	(2)	born 26 Aug 1795	340. Benjamin Marshall	born 12 Jan 1808
337. Salome		born 9 Nov 1798		

134. HANNAH / ANNA⁻⁴ BOWKER, sister of above, was born 2 Feb 1756 at Scituate, MA. She married Stephen⁻⁶ TOWER ** on 21 April 1778 at Scituate. He was the son of Peter⁻⁵ TOWER (Peter⁻⁴; Jeremiah⁻³·²; John⁻¹) and Deborah STOWELL, and was born 24 May 1755 at Hingham, Plymouth, MA; died 25 April 1826 Cummington, MA. Hannah⁻⁴ BOWKER died 2 Jan 1821 at Cummington, MA.   ** Reference: TOWER Genealogy: an account of the descendants of John TOWER of Hingham, MA

Children of Hannah⁻⁴ BOWKER and Stephen⁻⁶ TOWER:
Surname **TOWER** (all children born Cummington, Hampshire, MA)

+	**341. ANNA**	born 15 Sep 1776; died 17 Nov 1871 Harmony, NY
		married Samuel ROBINSON 13 Sep 1801 Cummington, MA
+	**342. STEPHEN, Jr.**	born 8 March 1778; died 1856 Cummington, MA
		(he born ca 1773; died 1856 Batavia, NY)
		married Meletiah " Millie " BARTLETT 15 Dec 1803
	343. Luke	born 7 May 1780; died 11 Sep 1804 Cummington, MA
+	**344. JOHN**	born 8 July 1781; died 30 Sep 1827 Youngstown, NY
		married Ruth REED 1 Mar 1809 Charlemont, MA
		(she dau/o Rev. Jesse REED and Ruth WHITMAN)
		(she born 29 Mar 1785 Charlemont, MA; died ____)
+	**345. DAVID**	born 11 Dec 1782; died 13 Mar 1870 Wilson, NY
+	**346. JOANNA**	born 27 Sep 1784; died 6 Mar 1885 Batavia, NY
+	**347. DEBORAH**	born 16 July 1786; died 1 Aug 1869 Fayette, Fulton, OH
+	**348. CLARISSA**	born 3 May 1788; died 29 May 1876 Porter, NY
+	**349. PETER**	born 10 July 1790; died ca 1886
		1 married Hannah BAILEY; 2 married Olive BALDWIN Smith
+	**350. OTIS**	born 28 Oct 1791; died 11 Oct 1870 Bethel, MI
	351. Salome	born 27 Jan 1793; died 3 Mar 1811 Cummington, MA EOL
	352. Galen	born 1 March 1794; died 10 March 1794 EOL
+	**353. RHODA BOWKER**	born 26 Nov 1795; died 23 Aug 1833 Cummington, MA

135. CHARLES⁻⁴ BOWKER, brother of above, was born 18 Nov 1757 at Plymouth, MA. He married Beulah STONE on 19 Apr 1787 at Fitzwilliam, NH. She was the daughter of _____ STONE and ____; and was born 22 Feb 1767; died ____. Charles⁻⁴ BOWKER died 21 July 1839 at Fitzwilliam, NH.

Children of Charles⁻⁴ BOWKER and Beulah STONE:
Surname **BOWKER**   (all children born Fitzwilliam, Cheshire, NH)

354. Charles, Jr.	born 24 July 1787; died ____			
355. Sylvester (1)	born 13 Nov 1789; died 25 Mar 1793		EOL	
356. Betsey	born 29 Aug 1793; died ____	359. Mallama	born 7 Sept 1803	
357. Sylvester (2)	born 17 May 1798; died ____	360. Loring	born 9 Dec 1805	
358. Leonard	born 13 May 1801; died ____	361. Christany	born 27 Sep 1808	

138. CAPTAIN STEPHEN⁻⁴ BOWKER, brother of above, was born 17 Feb 1763 at Scituate, MA. He married Lucy CUSHING 30 April 1789 at Scituate, MA. She was the daughter of Ensign Pickles CUSHING and Abigail HATCH, and was born 6 July 1771 Scituate; died 11 Dec 1852 Fitzwilliam, Cheshire, NH. Stephen⁻⁴ BOWKER died 17 March 1802 at Walpole, NH. Lucy CUSHING Bowker married second to Capt. Davis B. CARPENTER on 7 Feb 1804 (as his 2ⁿᵈ wife) at Walpole, NH.

Children of Stephen⁻⁴ BOWKER and Lucy CUSHING:
Surname **BOWKER**

	362. Lucy Cushing (1)	born 16 Sep 1792 Scituate, MA; died young	EOL
+	**363. ABIGAIL**	born 5 Oct 1794; died ____	
	" Nabby "	married Walter CARPENTER 18 Oct 1812	
		(he s/o Davis CARPENTER and Miriam MANNING)	
		(he born 3 Aug 1874 Walpole, NH; died 1862 NH)	
+	**364. CUSHING**	born 23 Apr 1795 Fitzwilliam, NH; died 13 Sep 1870 Quebec, Canada	
		1 married Sarah Van DOORN 13 Feb 1817 NH	
		2 married Abigail Worcester RIDER on 20 Dec 1827 Quebec, Canada	
		3 married Sarah MARSTON Allard 15 Nov 1842 Quebec, Canada	
	365. Lucy (2)	born 6 Apr 1798; died 21 Oct 1876 Cleveland, OH	
		married Charles Ebenezer CREHORE, Sr. 9 Apr 1826	
		(he s/o Ebenezer CREHORE and Hannah DAVENPORT)	
		Child: John Davenport⁻⁶ CREHORE born 23 Nov 1826 Walpole, NH; died 7 Oct 1884;	
		married Lucy WILLIAMS 30 Dec 1862	
+	**366. SARAH/SALLY**	born 9 June 1800; died 8 Jan 1891; married Orren Lathrop BENNETT 14 Sep 1820	
+	**367. SAMUEL GRIFFIN**	born ca 1802 Fitzwilliam, NH ; died 30 Sept 1839 Fitzwilliam, NH	
		married Orpha FAY 16 Nov 1826	
		(she dau/o John Thomas FAY and Levinah BRIGHAM)	
		(she born 9 Nov 1804; died 17 Sept 1851)	

139. ELIJAH-⁴ BOWKER, brother of above, was born 18 Nov 1764 at Scituate, MA. He married Anna R. SYLVESTER on 25 March 1788. She was the daughter of ____ SYLVESTER and ____, and was born ____; died ____. Elijah-⁴ BOWKER died 14 June 1812 Norwell, MA.

Children of Elijah-⁴ BOWKER and Anna SYLVESTER:
Surname **BOWKER**

+	**368. ELIJAH, Jr.**	born 14 July 1788; died 19 May 1827; married Hannah BENSON 14 July 1811
	369. Sally	born 15 Oct 1790; died 13 June 1811
	370. John	born 11 Sep 1792; died 3 Sep 1823; married Abigail BENSON 11 Sep 1814
	371. James Sylvester	born 28 Sep 1794; died 9 Feb 1858 Scituate, MA
		married Abigail BENSON (int pub 9 Oct 1824) (widow of his brother John)
+	**372. DELIGHT**	born 11 Oct 1796; died 15 Jan 1849 Scituate
		married Stephen CLAPP 14 Apr 1814
		(he s/o Sylvanus CLAPP and Elizabeth BROOKS)
		(he born 20 July 1787; died 13 Feb 1825 MA)
+	**373. CHARLES**	born 21 Oct 1798; died ____
		married Martha WHITTEN/WHITON 24 Nov 1816 Boston, MA
+	**374. CHARLOTTE**	born 26 Jan 1800; died ___; married Joshua B. YOUNG of Hull, MA 8 Apr 1824
		(he s/o Job YOUNG and Mary ____)
		(he born 31 Dec 1797 MA; died 24 May 1888 Auburn, ME.)
	375. Rebecca	born 26 Feb 1802; died ____
	376. Dorcassina	born 21 Mar 1804; died ____; married Charles HARLOW 13 May 1826 Boston
	377. Ruth	born 26 April 1808; died ____

141. DESIRE-4 BOWKER, sister of above, was born 12 Oct 1769 at Scituate, Plymouth, MA. She married Joseph-6 CUSHING on 19 June 1790. He was the son of Pickles-5 CUSHING (Joseph-4,3; John-2; Matthew-1) and ____, and was born 12 March 1768; died 10 May 1844. Desire-4 BOWKER died 19 Sep 1867. They resided Scituate.

Children of Desire-4 BOWKER and Joseph-6 CUSHING:
Surname **CUSHING**

378. Relief / Leafy	born 16 Nov 1791; died 31 Oct 1864; never married	EOL
379. Lucy	born 12 Aug 1793; died 29 Oct 1864	
	married William H. BEAN ca _____	
	Children: Elizabeth-6 born ca 1819, died 1902; and Rebecca-6 BEAN born ca 1825, died 1907	

+   **380. JOSEPH**   born 19 Dec 1794; died 24 Nov 1883 Scituate, MA
married Betsey REED 4 Aug 1812 Marblehead, MA

+   **381 STEPHEN**   born 17 Jan 1797; died 1 Dec 1871
1 married Ethalinda EDWARDS 20 Dec 1823
2 married Catherine PHILIPS 23 Aug 1859
(she dau/o Simon PHILIPS and Nancy ____) (she born ca 1800; died ___)

   382. Rebecca   born 31 Jan 1799; died ____; married Jefferson HEALY (he born ca 1805)
Children: Stephen L-6 born ca 1842 MA; and John C-6 HEALY born ____; died ____; married Adeline D. KOHN 28 July 1863 (she dau/o William KOHN and Martha ____)

+   **383. MATILDA**   born 29 Nov 1801; died 18 Aug 1884; married David BURR 7 Nov 1824
(he s/o David BURR and Mary FEARING)
(he born 7 Nov 1778; died 21 June 1852 Scituate, MA)

   384. John   born 31 Dec 1804; died ____

+   **385. ANNA / ANNE**   born 20 Jan 1809; died 5 Oct 1905; married Nichols LITCHFIELD 10 Dec 1828
(he born ca 1805-07 MA; died _____)

+   **386. MARTIN**   born 9 July 1810; died 15 Feb 1883; married Laura A. HOLT 1 Jan 1840 Lowell
(she born 31 May 1817 Lowell, MA; died 3 Nov 1891)

+   **387. ALLYNE**   born 9 Dec 1811; died 14 Aug 1884; 1 married Sarah DAMON 21 Dec 1834
(she born 15 Oct 1814; died 20 Mar 1872)
2 married Mary B. NICHELS (Gilman) 30 Aug 1874
(she born ca 1819; died 1913)
(she dau/o Samuel S. NICHELS and Abigail MASON)

Reference: The TOWER Genealogy, an account of the descendants of John TOWER of Hingham, MA , pages 413-418

149. LYDIA-4 BISHOP, daughter of Lydia-3 BOWKER (James-2,1) and Luke BISHOP, was born 20 Aug 1749 at Scituate, Plymouth, MA. She married Caleb ESTES 24 June 1769 at Scituate, MA. He was the son of Edward ESTES and Patience CARR, and was born 26 Nov 1747; died 11 Mar 1822 at Durham, Androscoggin, ME. Lydia-4 BISHOP died 4 May 1815 at Durham, Androscoggin, Maine.

Children of Lydia-4 BISHOP and Caleb ESTES:
Surname **ESTES**   (children all born Durham, ME)

   388. Lydia   born 8 May 1770; died ca 1850/55; married William P. STORY 28 June 1794

   389. Sarah   born 4 Mar 1772; died 15 Jan 1857 Sanford, ME; married Elisha TUTTLE

   390. Simeon   born 17 Feb 1774; died 6 July 1863 Durham
married Sarah DAVIS 9 March 1797
(she dau/o Daniel DAVIS and Mary COLLINS)

   391. Patience   born 29 Jan 1776; died 20 Mar 1805
married James ESTES (int pub 19 June 1794)

   392. Caleb, Jr.   born 6 Apr 1778; died 25 May 1864 China, Kennebec, ME
1 married Charlotte DAY ca ___
(she dauo Josiah DAY and Thankful BLETHEN)
2 married Sarah ROBINSON 2 Sep 1823

   393. Joseph   born 5 Sep 1780; died 16 Nov 1851; married Mary JONES 1 Oct 1801
(she dau/o Noah JONES and ____)

   394. Israel   born 25 Aug 1782; died 25 Mar 1875
1 married Sarah BOOK (int pub 19 Oct 1803)
2 married Mrs. Charlotte BLAKE Johnson 20 Feb 1840

Children of Lydia-⁴ BISHOP and Caleb ESTES, continued:
Surname **ESTES**

395. Thomas	born 27 Aug 1784; died 16 Aug 1870	
	married Betsey/ Betty Hayford ALDEN Dec 1871	
	(she born 19 Oct 1786; died 23 Jan 1857)	
396. John	born 19 Oct 1786; died 1787	EOL
397. Desire	born 15 Oct 1788; died ____; married Isaac COX	
398. Mary	born 15 Feb 1792; died 22 Feb 1865 Brunswick, Cumberland, ME	

150. JAMES-⁴ BARRELL, Jr. , son of Deborah⁻³ BOWKER (James-²;¹) and James BARRELL, was born 17 Feb 1747 Scituate, MA;, bpt. 30 June 1751 at Scituate, MA. He married Martha FARROW 10 Dec 1772 Scituate. She was the daughter of Thomas FARROW and Jemima DAMON; and was born 19 May 1754; died ca 1849. James⁻⁴ BARRELL, Jr. died ca 1795/96.

Children of James⁻⁴ BARRELL, Jr. and Martha FARROW:
Surname **BARRELL**　　　(children born Scituate, MA)

	399. James	born 5 Aug 1773; died 8 July 1850 Scituate, MA
	400. Benjamin	born 27 Mar 1775; died ____; married Hannah ROGERS 10 June 1802
		(she dau/o Israel ROGERS and Hannah ___)
		(she born ca 1779 Charlestown, MA)
	Child: Benjamin⁻⁶ BARRELL born ca 1803; died 27 Oct 1858 (pauper)	
+	**401. MARTHA**	born 3 Oct 1777; died 11 Apr 1848; married Elisha HAYDEN 1803 Scituate
		(he s/o Elisha HAYDEN and Deborah PIERCE)(he born ca 1790; died 1854)
	402. Jemima	born 5 Dec 1779; died 21 Mar 1850 Worth, Jefferson, NY
		married Richard PROUTY 1 Mar 1801 Worcester, MA
	403. Colburn	born 25 Apr 1781; died 30 Apr 1859
		married Susan TAYLOR 3 Nov 1822 Charlestown, MA
+	**404. ABEL**	born 28 Jan 1784; died ___; married Mary ALDEN 8 Aug 1810
		(she dau/o Jonathan ALDEN and Experience WASHBURN)
		(she born 31 Dec 1786 Bridgewater, MA; died 5 Sep 1874 Bridgewater)
	405. Lydia	born 18 May 1789; died ____; married Benjamin STUDLEY 26 Nov 1809
		(he s/o John STUDLEY and Sarah C. GANNETT)
		(he born 1787 Scituate, MA; died 4 Apr 1867
	406. Elias	born 8 June 1791; died 23 Oct 1870 Old Saybrook, CT; married Lydia ____
+	**407. DESIRE**	born 4 Dec 1793; died 6 Jan 1872
		married James Newton SPARRELL 6 Oct 1822
	408. Thomas	born 21 Jan 1796; died Nov 1879; married Hulda _____ ca ____

154. LYDIA⁻⁴ BOWKER, daughter of Edmund⁻³ BOWKER (James -²;¹) and Lydia LAMBERT; and was born 26 March 1757 Scituate, MA. She married Abner CURTIS on 25 May 1775. He was the son of Abner CURTIS and Deborah MANN, and was born ca 1754; died 2 Feb 1838. Lydia⁻⁴ BOWKER died 17 Jan 1752 Hanover, MA.

Children of Lydia⁻⁴ BOWKER and Abner CURTIS:
Surname **CURTIS** (children born Hanover, Plymouth, MA)

+	**409. DAVIS**	born 13 Oct 1776 Hanover, MA; died 15 Feb 1862 Liberty, Waldo, ME
	COLLAMORE	1 married Charlotte LOVICE on 1 Nov 1794 Hanover, MA
		(she born ca 1774; died ca 1862)
		2 married Mary OLIVER 26 Dec 1799
	410. Desire	born 1 Feb 1778; died 15 June Quebec , Canada
		married Thomas Farrow FARRAR, Jr. 25 Mar 1798
	Child: Rufus-⁶ FARRAR born ca 1828; died ____	
	411. Job	born ca 1780; died Feb 1843 Scituate, MA
	412. Deborah	born ca 1782; died 29 Dec 1884
	413. Mary	born ca 1784; died ____
	414. Sarah Lambert	born 5 Aug 1789; died 29 Dec 1884 Hanover, MA
		married Levi NASH 5 Aug 1819

156. EDMUND⁻⁴ BOWKER, son of Edmund⁻³ BOWKER (James⁻²,¹) and Lydia LAMBERT, was born 16 Sept 1762 at Scituate, Plymouth, MA. He married Patience BARROWS ca ____. She was the daughter of Ichabod BARROWS and Rebecca

CARPENTER of Hebron, Maine, and was born ca 1758; died 1840 in Blanchard, Maine. Edmund[4] BOWKER died 30 April 1812 at Hebron, Oxford, Maine.

Children of Edmund-[4] BOWKER and Patience BARROWS:
Surname **BOWKER**

	415. Silva	born 11 Mar 1786 Paris, ME; died 2 Feb 1813
	416. Mary	born 12 Aug 1788 Paris, ME; died ____; married Daniel MACOMBER ca ____
	417. Patience	born 28 March 1791 Hebron, ME; died 7 Oct 1872 Blanchard, NE
		married Ruel K. PACKARD ca ____ (resided Blanchard, ME)
	418. Lydia	born 19 Jan 1793 Hebron; died ___; married Dea. ____ MARTIN; resided Bangor, ME
	419. Sarah	born 9 Dec 1794 Hebron; died 1815
+	**420. PAUL**	born 4 Mar 1797 Hebron; died 26 Jan 1874 Cumberland, ME
		married Mary KING Bearce ca ____ (she wid/o Gideon BEARCE)
	421. William	born 18 Feb 1799 Hebron; died ____
		married Betsey CRAFTS ca ____ (resided Monson, Maine)
	422. Parlin/ Partin	born ca 1801; died ___
	423. Keziah	born 15 Dec 1803 Hebron; died ____
		married James C. WHITING ca ____ (resided Monson, Maine)

157. JAMES[4] BOWKER, brother of above, was born 9 June 1765 at Scituate, Plymouth, MA. He married Judith CHASE on 15 Nov 1787. She was the daughter of Thomas CHASE and Hannah HASKINS, and was born 4 April 1766; died ____. James[4] BOWKER, a blacksmith, died 1 June 1827 at Buckfield, Oxford, Maine.

Children of James-[4] BOWKER and Judith CHASE:
Surname **BOWKER**

+	**424. CAPT. JAMES, Jr.**	born 10 May 1788; died ____; married Abagail BICKNELL ca ____
		(she dau/o John BICKNELL and ____ of Buckfield) (she born ___; died Nov 1879)
	425. Tryphosa	born 18 Aug 1789; died ____; married Simeon HOWARD ca ____
		(he from Woodstock, Maine)
	426. Anson	born 7 June 1792; died in the War of 1812
+	**427. CYPRIAN**	born 1 Dec 1793; died ____
		1 married Rachel MAYHEW ca _____ (she born ca 1795; died 1837)
		2 married Mary MAYHEW Cole ca ____
	428. Sally	born 22 Jan 1796; died 25 Sep 1880 Buckfield, ME
+	**429. EDMUND**	born 3 Oct 1798; died ____
		married Mary Ann CHASE ca (resided Woodstock, ME)
		(she dau/o Merrill CHASE and Sally TUCKER) (she born 5 Aug 1803)
	430. Judith	born 13 July 1800; died 30 Nov 1801
+	**431. JUDITH (2)**	born 18 May 1802; died 16 Nov 1885
		married James BICKNELL ca ____ (resided Buckfield, ME)
		(he born 9 Mar 1802; died 27 Oct 1869)
+	**432. HARVEY**	born 4 May 1804; died 26 May 1868
		1 married Phebe PROCTOR 4 July 1824; (she born ca 1805; died 1825)
		2 married Diana CURTIS 21 Oct 1827 (she born ca 1808; died 1899)
	433. Alonzo	born 16 April 1806; died ___; married Phebe ANDREWS ca ____
	434. Elvira	born 16 April 1806; died ___; married William CROCKETT ca ____
+	**435. LAURA J.**	born 29 March 1808; died 29 Nov 1873
		1 married William Plummer BRACKETT ca 1831
		2 married Edmund C. BOWKER ca ____ (he # 931)

161. ALLEN[4] BOWKER, brother of above, was born 1 May 1775 at Scituate, MA. He married Eunice O. VINAL 6 Jan 1805 Boston, Suffolk, MA. She was the daughter of _____ VINAL and ____; and was born 20 Oct 1777; died 6 March 1821. Allen[4] BOWKER died 21 Aug 1822 Scituate.

Child of Allen-[4] BOWKER and Eunice O. VINAL:
Surname **BOWKER**

436. Mary	born ca 1809 MA; died 22 Jan 1855 MA
	married James DENNISON ca 1853 MA (he s/o Isaac DENNISON and Sarah ____)

Children of Allen[-4] BOWKER and Eunice O. VINAL, continued:
Surname **BOWKER**

437. Harriet	born 16 Apr 1811 MA; died 26 Dec 1875 Boston, MA	
	married John BRYANT 20 Oct 1846 (as his 2nd wife)	
	(he s/o Peleg BRYANT and Patience STEVENS)	
	(he born 13 Jan 1797 Plymouth, MA; died 2 June 1879 New Bedford, MA)	
438. Eunice Vinal	born ca 1812; died 14 Sep 1890 Newburyport, MA	
	married William BRICHER *** ca ____; int pub 28 July 1843 (as his 2nd wife)	
	(he born 21 March 1813 England; died 15 June 1886 Newburyport, MA)	
	(he served in Co. A, 48th Regt. MA. Infantry – Civil War)	

*** Note: William BRICHER was married 1st to Elizabeth Dame MUIR, and was the father of the noted Hudson River style artist Alfred Thompson BRICHER who was born 10 Apr 1837 NH, died 1908 Staten Island, NY. He had a studio on West 14th Street, NY. He was a marine watercolor artist and some of his paintings are titled "Low Tide at Grand Manan ", " The Grotto at Orr's Island", and " Surf at Conanicut". His art was in galleries in New York and Boston, and owned by private parties.

439. Martha V.	born ca 1814/15 MA; died ____	
	married Alfred C. GARRATT 13 Apr 1854	

162. WARREN-[4] BOWKER, brother of above, was born 14 July 1777 at Scituate, MA. He married Rebecca Holmes CROSWELL on 4 March 1799. She was the daughter of Nathaniel CROSWELL (Andrew CROSSWELL and Rebecca HOLMES) and Polly/Mary WHITMAN, and was born 1777/79 Suffolk, MA.; died 27 Dec 1853. Warren-[4] BOWKER died 19 Aug 1855 at Boston, MA.

Children of Warren[-4] BOWKER and Rebecca CROSWELL:
Surname **BOWKER**

440. Caroline	born ____; bpt. 18 Oct 1801 Scituate, MA; died ____	
441. Warren Thatcher	born 24 Nov 1799 Scituate, MA; died ___	
	married Elizabeth F ____ca _____ (she born ____; died 26 Dec 1816)	
442. Edmund	born ca 1804; died ____	
+ **443. LUCY**	born 11 Feb 1810 Scituate, MA; died 5 Jan 1897 Boston, MA.	
	married True Glidden[-7] WHITTIER 1 May 1837	
	(he s/o Nathaniel[-6] WHITTIER and Nancy MERRILL)	
	(he born 20 Aug 1805; died 3 Mar 1892 Boston, MA)	

163. DEBORAH-[4] BOWKER, daughter of Joseph[-3] BOWKER (James [-2,1]) and Elizabeth Deborow COWING, was born 20 Aug 1762 at Scituate, Plymouth, MA. She married John SOULE ca ___. He was the son of Abisha SOULE and Abigail DELANO, and was born 19 Jan 1759; died 31 Aug 1834 Augusta, ME. Deborah[-4] BOWKER died 20 April 1855 at Augusta, Kennebec, Maine.

Children of Deborah[-4] BOWKER and John SOULE:
Surname **SOULE**

444. Abigail	born ca 1784; died 13 Dec 1850	
	married Jonathan PERKINS 21 Sep 1805 Hallowell, Kennebec, Maine	
445. Elizabeth	born ca 1784; died ____	
446. Capt. John Bowker	born 30 Dec 1790 ME; died 1 Dec 1832 Bath, Sagadahoc, ME	
	married Nancy NORCROSS ca ____	
	(she born ca 1793; died ca 1860) Child: Eliza Gale[-6] SOULE born ca 1827; died 1910	
447. Abisha	born ca 1791; died ____	
448. Althea	born 28 May 1795; died 12 May 1863 ME	
449. Deborah	born 1 July 1798; died ____	
450. Charlotte	born 24 June 1801; died ____; married Moses SAFFORD ca ____	
	Children: Augustus A-[6] born ca 1826; Augusta C-[6] born ca 1836; and Charlotte-[6] SAFFORD born ca 1836	
451. Dunesbury	born 24 June 1801	

164. MAJOR LEVI-[4] BOWKER, brother of above, was born 25 July 1763 at Scituate, Plymouth, MA. He married Elizabeth "Betsey " WATTS on 24 Dec 1789 at Jonesborough, Washington County, Maine. She was the daughter of Samuel WATTS and Elsie BEAN, and was born May 1765 at Haverhill, Essex, MA; died 23 Feb 1854 at Machias, Washington, ME. Levi-[4] BOWKER died 28 July 1850 at Machias, ME.

It is not known exactly when he moved from MA to Maine, but was probably after 1783, as he enlisted in the Revolutionary War at Scituate in March 1781. He served under Captain KING and Colonel TUPPER until 18 Dec 1783. He applied , and was granted a pension on 3 May 1818. He was then residing in Machias. In the " History of Machias " by George W. DRISKO, he is referred to as Major Levi BOWKER, although other records indicate that he was a private in the Army.

Children of Levi-4 BOWKER and Betsey WATTS:
Surname **BOWKER**   (all children born Machias, Maine)

+	**452. WATTS**	born 12 Dec 1790; died ca 1850 Shelbourne, Nova Scotia
		married Lydia Lockwood STICKNEY ca ____
+	**453. LYDIA**	born 1 Nov 1793; died 1874; married Otis P. HANSCOM ca ____
+	**454. LEVI(Jr)**	born 26 Aug 1795; died 19 June 1887; married Martha CROCKER ca ____
+	**455. BETSEY**	born 2 Sep 1797; died ____ ; married Simeon GETCHELL 1 Sept 1818
	456. Hannah	born 9 Feb 1800; died ____
		married Stephen BOYNTON ca 1843 (as his 3rd wife)(he was married 4 times)
		(he s/o Amos BOYNTON and Lucy LORING) (he born 10 June 1787)

Child: Mary-6 BOYNTON born ca 1844

+	**457 SARAH/SALLY**	born 10 Apr 1802; died ____ ; married Ellis HANSCOM ca ____
+	**458. DEBORAH**	born 19 July 1805; died ____ ; 1 married James Mc KELLAR ca ___
		2 married William BUGBEE ca ___
+	**459. FREDERICK**	born 25 June 1808 Machias, ME; died 25 Oct 1888 buried Wilmington, DE
		1 married Rachel Anna DUTTON 3 July 1851
		(she dau/o James DUTTON and Mary GOULD) (she born 19 July 1825; died 16 Nov 1886)
		2 married Mary SMITH ca ____
	460. Mary	born 28 Feb 1810; died ____ ; unmarried EOL

166. JOSEPH-4 BOWKER, brother of above, was born 5 March 1766 at Scituate, MA. He married Elizabeth HALL on 11 Dec 1787. She was the daughter of ____ HALL and ____, and was born ca 1770, died 31 July 1853 at Phippsburg, ME. Joseph-4 BOWKER died 5 April 1817.

Children of Joseph-4 BOWKER and Elizabeth HALL"
Surname **BOWKER**   (all children born Georgetown, Sagadahoc, Maine)

	461. Edward	born 31 May 1788; died ____
	462. Levi	born 25 April 1790; died ____
		married Mary Ann JONES 27 Sep 1812 Portland, Cumberland, ME
	463. Jacob	born 17 Nov 1792; died ____ ; married Elizabeth WILLIAMS ca ____
	Child: Eleanor Lee-6 born 2 Apr 1813, died 5 Jan 1902; married Samuel Lincoln Webb GAHAN on 6 March 1830 Dresden, ME	
	464. Mary	born 1 April 1795; died ____ ; married Sebastian ANTHONY 10 Apr 1827
	465. Sarah	born ca 1797; died ____ ; married Robert CROCKER 14 Dec 1818
	466. Elizabeth	born ca 1800; died ____ ; married William BROWN 14 Apr 1822 Lincoln, ME

168. NANCY-4 BOWKER, sister of above, was born 18 July 1770 ME. She married David FARRIN on 12 March 1791 at Georgetown, Sagadahoc, Maine. He was the son of John FARRIN and Hannah NEWMAN, and was born 8 Feb 1767 Brunswick, Maine; died 5 Feb 1847 Brunswick. Nancy-4 BOWKER died 2 Aug 1856.

Child of Nancy-4 BOWKER and David FARRIN:
Surname **FARRIN**

+	**467. THOMAS**	born ca 1793 Brunswick, ME; died 1827; married Lucy SNOWMAN ca _____
		(she born ca 1793; died 1829)

169. RACHEL-4 BOWKER, sister of above, born 25 July 1772 Sagadahoc, Maine. She married first to Thomas DICKMAN on 26 Aug 1797. He was the son of ____ DICKMAN and _____, and was born ___, died ca 1820, ME. She married second to Alexander ORROCK ca ____. He born ca ___; died 1815. Rachel-4 BOWKER died 9 Sep 1856 at Augusta, Kennebec, Maine.

Children of Rachel-4 BOWKER and Thomas DICKMAN:
Surname **DICKMAN**

	468. Thomas Bell	born 12 Apr 1796; died ____ ; married Helen Maria ADAMS 24 Jan 1866
+	**469. GUSTAVUS**	born ca 1804 Augusta; died 1866 Brooklyn, Kings, NY
	ADOLPHUS	married Abigail BURBANK 15 Jan 1830

Children of Rachel⁻⁴ BOWKER and Thomas DICKMAN, continued:
Surname **DICKMAN**

	470. Hannah	born ca 1805; died ____
+	**471. CONSTANTINE**	born ca 1807 Gardiner, Kennebec, Maine; died 18 Dec 1892
		married Pauline FIELD 5 Apr 1832 Gardiner. Maine
		(she dau/o Benjamin FIELD and Anna _____)
		(she born 30 Mar 1814 Gardiner, ME; died 1899 Gardiner)
	472. James	born ca 1808; died ____

170. HANNAH⁻⁴ BOWKER/BUKER, sister of above, was born 8 Jan 1775 ME. She married Abel WRIGHT on 29 April 1804 at Bowdoinham, ME. He was the son of Jesse WRIGHT and Abigail COOK, and was born 23 Apr 1784 Androscoggin, ME; died March 1829 Oxford, Maine. Hannah-⁴ BOWKER died ____.

Children of Hannah⁻⁴ BOWKER and Abel WRIGHT:
Surname **WRIGHT**

	473. Thursa/Thursey	born ca 1806; died 8 Jan 1896 Dexter, ME; married Josiah SHEPARD ca ____
+	**474. DELANE**	born 14 Apr 1810 Lewiston, ME; died 1865 Middleton, WI
		married Cotton A. DURGIN ca 1831
		(he s/o Andrew DURGIN and Sarah/Sally SARGENT)
		(he born Aug 1802 NH; died 4 Oct 1871 Greenfield, Monroe, WI)
+	**475. LORENZO DOW**	born 3 Aug 1812 Lewiston, ME; died 11 Nov 1884 Nashua, NH
		married Nancy A. ROBBINS ca 1857 (possibly his 2ⁿᵈ wife)
		(she born ca 1823/24 NH; died ____ Nashua, NH)
	476. Daniel Dimmick B	born 10 Oct 1814; died ____; married Martha J. DILLINER ca ___ (she born ca 1820)
	477. Hannah Bowker/Buker	born 10 May 1817; died ____; married Jesse E. ROWELL (he born ca 1815 ME)
	478. Mary	born 27 Mar 1819; died ca 1903; married Abiel WALKER (he born ca 1815)
	479. Abel, Jr.	born 10 Jan 1822; died ____; married Sarah Cousins CHAOTE (she born ca 1828)
		Children: Lorenzo Dow⁻⁶ born ca 1852; and Constantine⁻⁶ WRIGHT born ca 1867
	480. Benjamin Russell	born 10 June 1825 ME; died ____

171. LAZARUS⁻⁴ BOWKER, brother of above, was born 13 Oct 1776 Scituate, MA. He married Agnes LENNAN/ LENNIN/ LENNING on 5 Jan 1805. She was the daughter of Thomas LENNAN/ LENNIN and Mary OLIVER; and was born 4 June 1785; died 23 April 1858 Phippsburg, Maine. Lazarus⁻⁴ died 7 Jan 1858 ME.

Children of Lazarus⁻⁴ BOWKER and Agnes LENNAN:
Surname **BOWKER**

	481. Thomas	born 20 Dec 1805; died 20 June 1806 Georgetown, ME.
+	**482. ISAAC HALL**	born 4 June 1807 Georgetown, ME; died 21 March 1859 Phippsburg, ME.
		married Eliza ____ 5 Jan 1836 Phippsburg, ME
	483. Joseph	born 4 Jan 1810 Georgetown, ME; died 3 May 1882 Phippsburg
		1 married Hannah Almira LARRABEE 14 Feb 1837
		2 married Mary-⁵ BOWKER 13 Nov 1838 (she # 490)
		(she dau/o James⁻⁴ BOWKER and Eunice BATCHELDER)
	484. George Washington	born 12 Mar 1812 Georgetown, ME; died 31 Aug 1812 Georgetown
	485. Samuel	born 20 Sept 1814; died ____
		married Elizabeth E. EATON 21 March 1848 ME. (she born ca 1822; died ____)
		Children: Charles J-⁶ born ca 1850; Samuel W-⁶ born ca 1854; Elizabeth A⁻⁶ born ca 1856;
		Heber Durgin⁻⁶ BOWKER born 11 Feb 1858, died 1940 Putnam FL

172. JAMES⁻⁴ BOWKER, brother of above, was born 3 Mar 1779 at Scituate, MA. He married Eunice BATCHELDER on 4 April 1804. She was the daughter of ____ BATCHELDER and ____; and was born 24 Oct 1777; died 31 Dec 1862 at Phippsburg, ME. James⁻⁴ BOWKER died 13 Oct 1852 at Phippsburg, Maine.

Children of James⁻⁴ BOWKER and Eunice BATCHELDER:
Surname **BOWKER**

	486. Beulah Bisby	born 20 May 1806 Phippsburg; died ca 1880

Children of James-⁴ BOWKER and Eunice BATCHELDER, continued:
Surname **BOWKER**

+	**487. FLAVEL**	born 7 July 1808; died 17 Nov 1891 Georgetown, ME
		married Angeline REED 9 Dec 1835 ME
		(she born 9 Oct 1808 ME; died 19 May 1888 Brunswick, ME)
		(she dau/o Col. Andrew REED and Beatrice Mc COBB)
	488. Eliza	born 7 July 1809 Georgetown; died 22 April 1888
+	**489. ELBRIDGE**	born 5 April 1811 Georgetown; died 19 June 1884
	490. Mary	born 6 May 1813; died 7 June 1901 Bath, ME
		married Joseph-⁵ BOWKER (# 483) 13 Nov 1838 (he s/o Lazarus-⁴ BOWKER
	491. Rachel Ann	born 30 Dec 1814 Phippsburg; died ____
+	**492. TIMOTHY**	born 1 Nov 1816; died 11 March 1902 Phippsburg, Maine
	BATCHELDER	married Elizabeth Percy MORRISON ca 1841 (she born ca 1817; died ca 1920)
	493. Priscilla	born ca 1821; died 3 March 1864
+	**494. NANCY**	born ca 1823; died ca 1910; married Charles SYLVESTER on 4 May 1848
	495. John A.	born ca 1832 Phippsburg; died 10 June 1856 Bath, ME

173. WASHINGTON-⁴ BOWKER, brother of above, was born 15 May 1781 Maine. He married first to Sally LAMONT on 24 May 1804. She was the daughter of ____ LAMONT and ____, and was born ca 1785, died before 1806. He married second to Jane SPEAR (int pub) 25 Jan 1806 at Georgetown, Maine. She was the daughter of ____ SPEAR and ____, and was born ca 1785; died 1811(possibly childbirth). He married third to Elizabeth " Lizzie" MINOT on 26 July 1812. She was the daughter of John MINOT and Jemima ___, and was born 2 Aug 1783 Brunswick, ME; died 22 Sept 1845 Brunswick. His 4ᵗʰ wife was Lettice ORR. She was born ca 1793; died 18 Apr 1864. They married on 1 Dec 1849 at Brunswick. Washington-⁴ BOWKER died 9 Aug 1858 at Brunswick.

Children of Washington-⁴ BOWKER and 2ⁿᵈ wife Jane SPEAR:
Surname **BOWKER**

496. Robert	born 29 Nov 1809 Brunswick, ME; died 22 Feb 1883 Brunswick, ME
	married Martha DUNNING ca ____
497. Jane	born 8 Nov 1811; died 29 Sep 1841; married Redford D. TALLMAN 18 Sept 1830

Children of Washington-⁴ BOWKER and 3ʳᵈ wife Lizzie MINOT:
Surname **BOWKER**

498. John Minot	born 20 July 1813; died 17 March 1900 Brunswick, ME
	1 married Charlotte M. WALKER 28 Feb 1846 Brunswick, ME
	2 married Almora MITCHELL 23 July 1862
499. Frances M.	born 28 Nov 1815 Brunswick; died 15 Nov 1901
	married Thomas STREET 20 Sep 1864 (he born 28 Oct 1807; died 28 Jul 1898 ME)
500. Elizabeth A.	born 5 July 1818; died ____ ;married George W. GARLAND 7 Oct 1840 Brunswick
501. Henry M.	born 23 July 1820; died 17 Sep 1896 Brunswick, ME
	1 married Rachel R. DONNELL 18 Sep 1849
	2 married Hannah Frances SIMPSON 15 Nov 1864
	3 married Hattie WOODARD 22 Oct 1895

174. REBECCA-⁴ BOWKER, sister of above, was born Oct 1783 Maine. She married John TUCKER ca 1804. He was the son of ____TUCKER and ____; and was born ca 1778; died 8 Mar 1856. Rebecca-⁴ BOWKER died 23 Sep 1812 at Hanover, ME.

Children of Rebecca-⁴ BOWKER and John TUCKER:
Surname **TUCKER**   (all children born Bath, Maine)

502. Irene	born ca 1805; died 17 Nov 1887; married Benjamin LANE 8 May 1825
503. Betsey	born ca 1807; died 20 Feb 1882; married Jeremiah COTTON 25 Nov 1848 ME
504. Cornelia	born 30 Jun 1810; died 11 Dec 1893; married James G. GETCHELL
505. Nancy	born 5 Aug 1812; died ____
506. Zobida	born 1 Aug 1815; died 10 Dec 1875; married Charles Henry AMES ca ____
507. John Adams	born Mar 1818; died ____ ; married Mary E. GOODWIN ca 1862 (she born 1838)
508. George Washington	born 20 Apr 1821; died 1 Apr 1879; married Mary Ann REED 29 Aug 1843
509. Thomas Jefferson	born 2 Sep 1823; died 1870; married Sarah E. WHITE ca ____
	(she born ca 1824; died 1908)
510. Rebecca Madison	born 2 Aug 1828; died 5 July 1832 EOL

193. BENJAMIN[-4] BOWKER, son of Richard-[3] BOWKER (Richard-[2]; James-[1]) and Mary PRATT, and was born 9 Aug 1758 at Hanson, Plymouth, MA. He married Jemima HILL on 14 Jan 1787. She was the daughter of ____ HILL and ____; and was born 7 July 1757; died 31 March 1820. Benjamin[-4] BOWKER died ____ .

Children of Benjamin[-4] BOWKER and Jemima HILL:
Surname **BOWKER**

	511. Rebecca/Becca	born ca 1787; died 10 Oct 1883 Hanson
		married Thomas MACOMBER (2nd wife) 3 March 1808 Hanson, MA
		(he born ____; died 13 Jan 1840)
		Children: George[-6] born 22 Feb 1809, died 5 Feb 1901 Hanson, MA; and Betsey[-6] MACOMBER
		born 19 Apr 1812; died 14 Mar 1904; married ____ PERRY ca ____
		Note: Records indicate that Becca BOWKER may have had an illegitimate son named Lebbeus BOWKER
		who was born 18 Feb 1803; and died 15 Aug 1822 at Hanson, MA
+	**512. BENJAMIN, Jr.**	born 19 Apr 1789 Hanson, MA; died 16 May 1849
		married Hannah Pratt RAMSDELL 29 Sep 1811
	513. Richard	born 13 May 1791; died 16 April 1873 Hanson
		married Mary JOSSELYN 26 Aug 1818
		Children: Benjamin[-6] born ca 1818; William M[-6] born ca 1820; and Abigail[-6] BOWKER born ca 1822
+	**514. GAD/GARD**	born 30 May 1795 Hanson, MA; died July 1876 Hanson, Plymouth, MA
		married Clarissa RAMSDELL ON 20 Nov 1823
		(she dau/o John Stockbridge RAMSDELL and Hannah ALLEN)
		(she born 15 Feb 1791; died ca 1845)

196. BATHSHEBA / BARSHABA[-4] BOWKER, sister of above, was born 20 March 1755 at Scituate, MA. She married John DOTEN/DOTY on 19 Aug 1779 MA. He was the son of Edward DOTEN/DOTY (a Mayflower descendant of Edward[-1] DOTEN/DOTY) and Joannah WHITING/WHITTON Dunham, and was born 9 Aug 1750 MA; died 20 Mar 1812 Pomfret, VT. Bathsheba[-4] BOWKER died 8 Feb 1838 at Pomfret, VT.

Child of Bathsheba[-4] BOWKER and John DOTEN/ DOTY:
Surname **DOTEN/DOTY**

515. JOHN EDWARD	born 3 July 1780 Pembroke, MA; died 8 Apr 1863 Pomfret, VT.
	married Elizabeth[-7] VOSE 6 Sep 1804 (she dau/o Thomas[-6] VOSE and _____)
	(she born 14 Mar 1783 Goffstown, NH; died 7 Aug 1865 Pomfret, VT)

197. DAVID[-4] BOWKER, son of Luke-[3] BOWKER (Richard-[2]; James-[1]) and Joanna DUNBAR, was born 24 Sep 1756. He married Huldah HARDEN 9 Jan 1780 Abington, Plymouth, MA. She was the daughter of Nathaniel HARDEN and Rebecca TAYLOR, and was born 16 Jan 1757; died ca 1828. David[-4] BOWKER died ca 1824.

Child of David[-4] BOWKER and Huldah HARDEN:
Surname **BOWKER**

516. Agnes	born 23 Dec 1780 Pomfret, VT;

Children of David-[4] BOWKER and Huldah HARDEN, continued:
Surname **BOWKER**

+	**517. DAVID, Jr.**	born 28 Dec 1781 ; died 15 April 1842 Scituate; married Eunice CLAPP 18 Oct 1807
		(she dau/o Michael CLAPP and Eunice ____)
		(she born 18 Dec 1790; died 30 June 1865)
	518. Becca	born 16 Oct 1782 Pomfret, VT.

202. LIBERTY[-4] BOWKER, brother of above, was born 13 May 1775 at Scituate, Plymouth, MA. He married first to Sarah GURNEY on 20 June 1796 at Abington, Plymouth, MA. She was the daughter of Joseph GURNEY and Sarah ___ ; and was born 5 May 1770; died 8 March 1826. Liberty[-5] BOWKER married second to Katy WEEKS on 28 Aug 1826. She was the daughter of__ WEEKS and __; and was born 4 Jan 1781; died 6 Sep 1852. Liberty[-4] BOWKER died 21 May 1846 at Savoy, MA.

Children of Liberty[4] BOWKER and Sarah GURNEY:
Surname **BOWKER**

+	**519. MELVIN**	born 14 March 1798; died 9 Sept 1874 Savoy, MA
		married Betsey WILLET 26 May 1822 Hanson, Plymouth, MA
	520. Sarah	born 2 March 1800; died ____
	521. David	born 31 Jan 1802; died ____

Children of Liberty⁻⁴ BOWKER and Sarah GURNEY, continued:
Surname **BOWKER**

	522. Mary	born 16 Jan 1804 Abington, MA; died ____
+	523. **CALVIN**	born 5 Sep 1806; died 8 Sep 1896 Adams, MA (Innkeeper; postmaster)
		married Eliza BELDING ca ____
	524. James Madison	born 7 Dec 1808 Pembroke, MA; died ____
		married Deborah Elizabeth BARNEY 22 April 1832

Child: George Madison Barney ⁻⁶ BOWKER born ca 1833

	525. Joanna	born 4 May 1811; died 1815	EOL

203. BENJAMIN⁻⁴ BOWKER, III, son of Benjamin⁻³ BOWKER, JR (Benjamin⁻²; James⁻¹) and Hannah SPARHAWKE, was born 21 Dec 1764 at Scituate, MA. He married Chloe STETSON on 30 Jan 1791 at Scituate. She was the daughter of Isaac STETSON and Ruth PROUTY, and was born 21 Aug 1767; died 18 Dec 1850 at Charlestown, Sullivan, NH.

Children of Benjamin⁻⁴ BOWKER III and Chloe STETSON:
Surname **BOWKER**   (all children born Scituate, MA)

	526. Benjamin	born ____; died 16 Dec 1868
	527. Chloe	born ca 1791; died 4 April 1860 Keene, NH
		married David MARSH 8 Mar 1814 Charlestown, MA

Children: David⁻⁶ , Jr. born ca 1817; Chloe⁻⁶ born ca 1817; and Hannah ⁻⁶ MARSH born 1820/21; died 1835

	528. Eunice	born ____; died ____; married Dan SHEPLEY
	529. Hannah Sparhawke	born ____; bpt. 15 Mar 1798; died ____
	530. Ruth	born ____; died ____
	531. Stephen Curtis	born ca 1803; died 16 Feb 1847; married Elenor ROBERTS ca ____

Child: George⁻⁶ BOWKER born ca 1849; died 1933

	532. Joshua	born 13 Nov 1805; died 15 July 1869 Charlestown, MA
		married Elizabeth DUNSMOOR ca ____
	533. Isaac	born ca 1809/10; died 1 June 1844 Scituate

204. ELISHA-⁴ BOWKER, brother of above, was born 21 Sep 1767 at Scituate, MA. He married Sarah/Sally SPEAR on 9/21 Jan/June 1793 at Quincy, MA. She was the daughter of William SPEAR, Jr. and Anna/Hannah BRACKETT; and was born 6 Oct 1769 Quincy, MA ; died ____. Elisha-⁴ BOWKER died ca 1840 at Springfield, VT.

Children of Elisha-⁴ BOWKER and Sally SPEAR:
Surname **BOWKER**

	534. Hannah S.	born 15 Dec 1795 VT; died 1 Dec 1862
		married George NEWCOMB 18 Feb 1814 Springfield, VT (he born 1787, died 1824)
	535. Elizabeth	born 20 Nov 1806 Springfield, VT; died 30 Dec 1889
+	**536. PIERPONT FAY**	born ca 1809 Springfield, VT; died 19 May 1887 Keene, NH; stone mason
		married Mary Ann RANDALL ca (she born NH)

207. JOEL-⁴ BOWKER, brother of above, was born 4 July 1775 at Scituate, MA. He married first to Eunice PEARSON on 23 Dec 1802. She was the daughter of ____ PEARSON and ____, and was born 7 March 1780 Salem, MA; and died 20 April 1808 (two weeks after giving birth to her 4th child). He married second (int pub 27 Aug 1808) to Margaret ROGERS. She was the daughter of ____ ROGERS and ____, and was born 3 April 1780; died ___ (probably before 1819). He married third to Lucretia ROGERS (int pub 3 April 1819). She was the daughter of __ ROGERS and ___, and was born 3 March 1786 Salem, MA.

Children of Joel⁻⁴ BOWKER and Eunice PEARSON;
Surname **BOWKER**

	537. Eunice	born 16 May 1803 Salem, MA; died 8 Jan 1839 Ross Twsp., MI.
		married George TORREY, Sr. (int pub Feb 1826)
		(he born ca 1801; died ca 1854)
	538. Nancy	born 30 Oct 1804 Salem, Essex, MA; died 18 Jan 1887 MA
		married George CURTIS 11 Nov 1834
		(he born 23 Sep 1807 Ma; died 16 Feb 1875)
		(he s/o Consider CURTIS and Mary HOUSE)
	539. Joel, Jr.	born 8 May 1806 Salem; died ____; married Leafy CURTIS int pub 2 Aug 1828
	540. Mary	born 6 April 1808; died ____

Children of Joel-[4] and Lucretia ROGERS:
Surname **BOWKER**

      541. Daniel Rogers born 24 Feb 1820; died ____   542. George   born 4 Sept 1824

209. CAPTAIN JOSHUA-[4] **BOWKER,** half-brother of above, son of Benjamin-[3] BOWKER (Benjamin-[2]; James-[1]) and Anne/Anna SYLVESTER, was born 8 Oct 1783 at Scituate, MA. He married Nancy Ann CUSHING on 25 Dec 1813 at Scituate. She was the daughter of Benjamin CUSHING and his 2nd wife Mary COLESWORTHY, and was born 8 Aug 1781; died ca 1838. Captain Joshua-[4] BOWKER died ____.

Children of Captain Joshua [4] BOWKER and Nancy Ann CUSHING:
Surname **BOWKER**   (children all born Scituate, MA)

      543. Joshua   born 20 Feb 1816; died ____
      544. Benjamin Cushing   born 18 July 1818; died ____
      545. Mary Ann Brooks   born 31 Jan 1821; died ____
      546. Stephen Cushing   born 25 July 1826; died ___; a shoemaker
                                married Mandana FARROW 5 Mar 1860 Scituate
                                (she dau/o Rufus FARROW and Deborah Richmond CUSHING)
                                (she born 29 Sept 1830 Scituate, MA; died ____)
                  Children: Milfred-[6] born ca 1866; and Amos-[6] BOWKER born ca 1868
                                2 married Mary Etta GARDNER 7 Dec 1883
                                (she born ca 1834) (she dau/o Charles G. GARDNER and Hannah ____)

219. BETTY⁻⁵ CROCKER/ CROOKER, daughter of Daniel⁻⁴ CROCKER/CROOKER (Mary⁻³ RAMSDELL; Martha⁻² BOWKER; James⁻¹) and Abigail STUDLEY, was born ca 1766/67 at Pembroke, Plymouth, MA. She married Barzillai / Barze STURTEVANT on 18 Mar 1790. He was the son of Lemuel STURTEVANT and Deborah BRYANT, and was born 16 Nov 1763 MA; died 28 Dec 1842 Wakefield, MA. Betty⁻⁵ CROCKER/ CROOKER died ____.

Children of Betty⁻⁵ CROCKER and Barze STURTEVANT:
Surname **STURTEVANT**

547. Nancy	born 22 Jan 1791; died 16 Nov 1791	
548. Heman	born 31 July 1792; died 1862; married Sarah GREEN ca ____	
	Child: John Quincy Adams⁻⁷ STURTEVANT born ca 1825 Woburn, MA; died 22 Oct 1903	
+ **549. LEWIS**	born 7 Feb 1795 Halifax, Plymouth, MA; died 19 Oct 1952	
	married Rebecca EVANS 5 Apr 1821 Stoneham, MA	
550. Barzillai / Barze	born 24 Mar 1797; died 9 Aug 1884 Woburn, MA	
551. Betsey	born ca 1799; died 10 July 1828; married Henry GREEN 27 May 1817	
	Children: Elizabeth Thompson⁻⁷ born 1819, died 1839; and Elvira V⁻⁷ GREEN born ca 1822	

221. ENSIGN⁻⁵ CROCKER, brother of above, was born 25 Oct 1770 at Pembroke, Plymouth, MA. He married Hannah MONROE ca 1801. She was the daughter of Henry MONROE, Jr. and Mary MILLER; and was born 18 Dec 1774 died 13 April 1853. Ensign⁻⁵ CROCKER died 1 Oct 1843/53.

Children of Ensign⁻⁵ CROCKER and Hannah MONROE:
Surname **CROCKER**

552. Betsey	born 23 Aug 1802; died ____	
553. Ensign Daniel	born 4 Feb 1807; died 10 Jan 1869; married Mary BAILEY(she born 1808, died 21 Nov 1841) ; 2 married Sylvia FOSTER ca ___ (she born ca 1818; died 1885)	
	Children: Mary E⁻⁷ born ca 1835, died 1845; James Francis⁻⁷ born 1 Aug 1842; and Arthur⁻⁷ CROCKER born 11 May 1857	
554. Mary Miller	born 2 Aug 1810; died ____	
555. Hannah	born 28 Aug 1812; died ____	
556. Deborah	born 1 July 1815; died ____; married Joseph POOL ca ____	
	Children: Joseph W⁻⁷ born ca 1839; and Deborah A⁻⁷ POOL born May 1843	
557. Elijah	born 13 Sep 1817	558. Nabby Studley	born 11 Oct 1824

239. ZADOC⁻⁵ HERSEY, son of Daniel⁻⁴ HERSEY (Susanna⁻³ RAMSDELL; Martha⁻² BOWKER; James⁻¹) and Desire WESTON, was born 20 Aug 1791 Yarmouth, Nova Scotia. He married Desire DOANE 1 Jan 1824. She was the daughter of Israel DOANE and Mehetabel KENNEY, and was born 19 Apr 1798; died 28 Nov 1881 NS. Zadoc⁻⁵ HERSEY died ____.

Children of Zadoc⁻⁵ HERSEY and Desire DOANE:
Surname **HERSEY**

559. Olivia Jane	born 14 Apr 1826; died 20 Feb 1901; marr. Capt. Francis G. COOK 6 Mar 1850 (he s/o Capt. Francis COOK and _____)
560. Lydia Anne	born 25 Aug 1828; died 27 Mar 1876; married John Ellis ROGERS 6 Feb 1853 (he born 14 Apr 1827; s/o James ROGERS and _____)
561. Daniel M.	born 19 June 1833; married Harriet PERRY ca 1855 (he lost at sea by shipwreck 13 Sep 1866) (she dau/o Capt. Leonard PERRY)
562. Orinda	born 28 Nov 1835; died 22 Sep 1920 Melbourne, Yarmouth, NS married Alexander ANDREWS, Jr. 23 Jan 1855 (he s/o Alexander ANDREWS, Sr. and Hannah KINNEY) (he born 15 Sep 1829; died 1907 Yarmouth)
563. Israel	born 27 Dec 1837 ; died 18 Apr 1901; married Louisa R. COOK ca 1860 (she dau /o John⁻² COOK and Ruth MAGRAY) (she born ____; died 22 Sep 1900)
564. Rosanna	born 11 Jan 1839; died ____; married Whitman COFFRAN 10 Nov 1861 (he s/o William COFFRAN and ____)

BOWKER Descendants of James-1
The Fifth American Generation

Children of Zadoc[5] HERSEY and Desire DOANE, continued:
Surname **HERSEY**   Reference: Yarmouth, Nova Scotia Genealogies (HERSEY), page 687-689
    565. Theresa   born 9 Oct 1846; died 12 Mar 1889; married Cornelius ROGERS 14 Mar 1870
        (he s/o James ROGERS and _____)

240. ZENAS[5] HERSEY, brother of above, was born 7 Nov 1794 at Yarmouth, NS. He married Elizabeth RING ca 1824. She was the daughter of Captain George-[2] RING and Lydia CHURCHILL; and was born ca 1798, died ____.

Children of Zenas[5] HERSEY and Elizabeth RING:
Surname **HERSEY**
    566. Milford   born ca 1825; died 8 June 1894 married Hannah KINNEY Coldwell ca ____
        Children: Mary Hannah[7] born ____, married James R. WYMAN; Heman Rogers[7] born ____,
        married Margaret WILSON; and Georgiana[7] HERSEY born ____, married James P. WHITMAN
    567. Mary Jane   born ____; died ____
        married William TURNBULL of St. John, NB on 18 July 1847
    568. Isabella   born ____; died ____; married David HERSEY (son of Levi HERSEY)(# 269)
    569. Margaret Hall   born ca 1834; died 20 July 1856; married John W. TREFRY 28 Dec 1854
        (he s/o William TREFRY and ____)
    570. Lois Anne   born ____; died ____
        1 married John PARRY 28 Dec 1854   (he s/o Captain Ebenezer PARRY and _____)
        2 married Thomas W. JONES 1 Nov 1862
    571. Alice   born 1837; died 28 Aug 1856; unmarried   EOL
    572. George   born ____; died ____ age 17 (lost at sea)   573. Francis   born ____

241. RICHARD[5] HERSEY, brother of above, was born 17 Dec 1799 at Yarmouth, Nova Scotia. He married Elizabeth HALL on 9 Dec 1822. She was the daughter of Thomas HALL and ____; and was born ____; died ____. Richard[5] HERSEY died ___.

Children of Richard[5] HERSEY and Elizabeth HALL:
Surname **HERSEY**
    574. Thomas   born 6 Dec 1823; died ____
    575. Desire   born 14 Feb 1827; died 25 March 1866; married Edward REEVES 11 Nov 1851
    576. Lydia Anne   born 20 Dec 1828; died ____; married Nelson GRAY 28 Apr 1861
    577. Jacob N.   born 4 March 1831; died 7 Nov 1861 St. John NB
    578. John Wentworth   born 22 Aug 1833; died ____
        1 married Mary L. GRACE 11 Mar 1860 (she dau/o Crocker P. GRACE and _____)
        2 married Henrietta MURPHY ca ____ (she dau/o Martin MURPHY and ___)
        3 married ____ SMITH ca ____
    579. William Freeman   born 19 Aug 1836; died ____; married ____ GULLISON ca ____
    580. David Oram   born 17 Jan 1840; died ca 1861; unmarried   EOL
    581. Emily Hannah   born 10 Apr 1842; died ___; married Hervey D. ELLIS 6 Sep 1862
        (he s/o Joseph Alden ELLIS and _____)
    582. Lois A.   born 28 Sep 1844; died ____
        1 married William FREEMAN ca _____; 2 married _____ NICKERSON ca ____
    583. Benjamin F.   born 10 Aug 1847; died ____; married Elizabeth L. FLOYD of Digby, NS

242. SAMUEL[5] HERSEY, Jr., son of Samuel[4] HERSEY (Susanna[3] RAMSDELL; Martha[2] BOWKER; James[1]) and Lydia CLARKE, was born ca 1776 New Brunswick, Canada. He married Elizabeth MAYES on 13 June 1802. She was the daughter of James MAYES and Hannah JACKSON, and was born ca 1780; died 25 Oct 1825 Hampstead, NB, Canada. Samuel[5] HERSEY, Jr. died ca 1851 NB.

Children of Samuel[5] HERSEY, Jr. and Elizabeth MAYES:
Surname **HERSEY**
    584. Lydia   born Aug 1803 Hampstead, NB; died ____
    585. Samuel Jackson   born Aug 1808; died 28 Jan 1888 Ontario, Canada
        married Sarah Ann _____ ca ____
    586. Nancy   born Feb 1814 Wickham, NB, Canada; died ____
    587. Leverett Hughes.   born June 1816; died 18 Feb 1904   588. Deborah Ann born 3 Oct 1819
        married Catherine CHASE ca 1832 (age 15)

243. HANNAH-5 HERSEY, sister of above, was born ca 1778 New Brunswick, Canada. She married Daniel SLOCUM, Sr. 1 Jan 1795. He was the son of Ebenezer SLOCUM and Esther COREY, and was born ca 1774; died 1797. Hannah-5 died ____.

Children of Hannah-5 HERSEY and Daniel SLOCUM:
Surname **SLOCUM**

589. Esther	born 1794 NBV; died ____ ; married Henry WORT 10 Nov 1816
	(he born 1786 NB; died 8 Dec 1839)
	Children: David Mansfield-7 born 1815, died 1881; and Daniel-7 WORT born ca ____
590. Daniel, Jr.	born 1797; died 1885

251. LEVI-5 HERSEY, Jr., son of Levi-4 HERSEY (Susanna-3 RAMSDELL; Martha-2 BOWKER; James-1) and Chloe DAY, was born 30 Dec 1780 at Digby Nova Scotia, Canada. He married Mary RICHARDSON ca 1804. She was the daughter of Reuben RICHARDSON and ____, and was born 11 Oct 1778, died ____. Levi-5 HERSEY died ca 1820.

Children of Levi-5 HERSEY and Mary RICHARDSON:
Surname **HERSEY**

591. Sarah	born 1803; died 1878; married Samuel BEALS ca ____ (he born 1802; died 1844)
592. Susanna	born 28 Oct 1805; died 28 Jan 1887; married William FRANKLAND ca ____
593. Reuben ***	born 24 Apr 1808; died ____ (lost in the Brig BILLOW 10 Apr 1831)

*** Reuben HERSEY was a seaman on the Brig BILLOW travelling from Bermuda to Halifax carrying discharged troops, and passengers, including about 68 children, and a crew of eight (a total of 137). The vessel encountered gale force winds and was dashed onto the rocks off Lockeport, then called the Ragged Islands. No one survived – although some bodies were washed ashore and were recovered.

594. Mary	born 27 Nov 1812; died ____; 1 married John ELWELL 13 Apr 1836
	(he born ___; died 15 Mar 1848)
	Child: John G-7 ELWELL born ca ___; married Martha HOBB ca 1867
	2 married Matthew JEFFERY 2nd ca ____ (he s/o Matthew JEFFERY and _____)
595. Eliza	born ca 1815; died ____, unmarried 596. Levi born ca 1818; died young

266. DANIEL-5 HERSEY, half-brother of above, son of Levi-4 HERSEY and his second wife Leah WAGNER, was born ca 1826/27 Nova Scotia, Canada. He married Eliza WHITENECT/WHITENECK ca 1850. She was the daughter of John WHITENECT/WHITENECK and Louisa F ____, and was born ca 1822; died 1901. Daniel-5 HERSEY died 1901 at Freeport, Digby, Nova Scotia, Canada.

Children of Daniel-5 HERSEY and Eliza WHITENECT/WHITENECK:
Surname **HERSEY**

597. Charles Minard/Miner	born ca 1851; died ____ married Henrietta LARKIN 25 Dec 1875
598. William	born 24 Nov 12853; died ____; married Matilda Ann SULLIVAN 8 May 1881
	(she dau/o Joseph SULLIVAN and Elizabeth ____)
599. Louisa	born ca 1855; died ____ 600. Mary E. born ca 1857; died ____
601. Waitsell	born ca 1858; died 7 Mar 1914 Freeport, NS; married Ophelia STORY 20 Apr 1888
602. Ira	born 8 Nov 1860 Freeport, NS; died 12 Dec 1943 Freeport
	married Edith Augusta BUCKMAN 25 July 1885 (9 ch)
603. Ora Lee	born 16 Mar 1866; died ____; married Webster C. TITUS 7 Jan 1893 Freeport

272. HANNAH PRATT-5 RAMSDELL (for children see # 512 Benjamin-5 BOWKER)

275. CLARISSA-5 RAMSDELL, sister of above (for children see # 514 Gad-5 BOWKER)

276. MARTIN-5 RAMSDELL, brother of above, was born 23 Sep 1793. He married Bethiah Ames ROBINSON on 3 Apr 1825 at Bridgewater, MA. She was the daughter of Benjamin ROBINSON and Keziah AMES; and was born 20 June 1802; died ____.

Children of Martin-5 RAMSDELL and Bethiah ROBINSON:
Surname **RAMSDELL**

604. Martin, Jr.	born 10 Dec 1825; died ____; married Mary W. LAPHAM 14 Mar 1852
605. Theodore	born ca 1828; died 3 Apr 1900 Boston, MA
606. Marshall L.	born ca 1831; died 18 Sep 1908 Andover, MA
	married Georgette RUSSELL 15 Apr 1863
	(she dau/o Moody RUSSELL and Frances ____)
607. Abba Lazell	born 21 Sep 1833; died ____

Children of Martin[-5] RAMSDELL and Bethiah ROBINSON, continued:
Surname **RAMSDELL**

608. Fannie Kingman	born 12 Jan 1837; died 22 May 1904; married Charles SWEETSER 14 Oct 1860	
609. Osiel Ames	born 11 July 1840; died ____	
610. Benjamin	born 21 July 1843; died 24 Mar 1848	EOL

282 . DIMMICK[-5] BOWKER, son of Lazarus[-4] BOWKER (Lazarus[-3]; James[-2, 1]) and Mary[-5] COLLIER, was born 10 Dec 1769 at Scituate, Plymouth, MA. He married Margaret WHITTON / WHITON on 10 Feb 1799. She was the daughter of ____ WHITTON / WHITON and ____; and was born ca ____; died ____. Dimmick-[5] BOWKER died ca 1860 Scituate, MA.

Children of Dimmick[-5] BOWKER and Margaret WHITTON:
Surname **BOWKER**   (all children born Scituate, MA) Reference: COLLIER Genealogy; Scituate, MA VR

611. Elias	born 25 March 1802; died ____
612. Louisa	born 10 May 1805; died ____
613. Elvira	born ca 1806/7; died ____
614. Henry	born 27 July 1810; died ____ ; married Mary MERRITT ca ____
615. Thirza	born 16 Jan 1813; died ____
+ **616. LAZARUS**	born 13 Nov 1817; died 20 Nov 1867 ; painter
	married Margaret Cornelia Forbes VALENTINE 30 May 1835 Scituate, MA
	Note: His obit listed his address as 1 Revere Place, Boston, MA

286. HOWARD[-5] BOWKER, brother of above, was born 25 May 1778 at Scituate, MA. He married first to Nancy GARDNER 13 July 1803. She was the daughter of Moses GARDNER and Agatha HAMMOND; and was born ca 1785; died 25 April 1815. He married second to Eveline TILDEN on 3 Sep 1816 at Marshfield. She was the daughter of Samuel TILDEN and Margaret FOSTER; and was born 19 March 1796 Marshfield; died 22 June 1874. Howard[-5] BOWKER died 7 Oct 1858 at Scituate, MA.

Child of Howard-[5] BOWKER and Nancy GARDNER:
Surname **BOWKER**

+ **617. CLARISSA**	born 23 Sep 1807 Boston, MA; died 15 Sep 1857
GARDNER	married Henry LEARNED 10 Dec 1826 Scituate, MA
	(he s/o Grant LEARNED and Martha GARFIELD)
	(he born 6 May 1803 Roxbury, MA; died 8 Feb 1887 Boston, MA
618. Horatio Nelson	born 27 Sep 1809 Boston; died 22 Oct 1891 Weymouth, MA (a carpenter)
	married Susan Matilda RICHARDSON 28 Jan 1828 (she born ca 1809; died 1894)
	Children: Andrew Gardner-[7] born 1828; Susan Matilda-[7] born 1830, died 1858; Ann E-[7] born ca 1833; Eveline A-[7] born ca 1838; Helen Adeline[-7] born ca 1842, died 1844; George Richardson[-7] born ca 1844; and Horatio Nelson[-7] BOWKER , Jr. born ca 1852, died 1859
619. Henry H.	born 16 Dec 1811 Boston; died 18 Dec 1885 Scituate, MA
	married Mary Cole MERRITT 19 Apr 1872 Scituate
620. Gustavus G.	born 2 Apr 1813/15 ; died _____ (he a Police Officer in NYC)
	1 married Henriette/a (poss.) SAUNDERS ca 1838
	Children: Henry[-7] born ca 1839 NY; Gustavus-[7] Jr. born ca 1841 NY; and Lucy[-7] BOWKER born ca 1847 NY
	2 married Elizabeth ____ ca ____ (she born ca 1825 England; died ____)

Children of Howard[-5] BOWKER and Eveline TILDEN:
Surname **BOWKER**

621. Eveline Tilden	born 1 July 1821; died 30 May 1905; married David TORREY 30 Nov 1854
	(he born ca 1821; died 1884) (he s/o David TORREY, Sr. and Vesta HOWARD)
	Child: Emma Howard[-7] born 5 Mar 1856, died 19 Sep 1935; married George Edgar BATES 26 Sep 1882
	(he born 12 May 1860); and Edwin[-7] BOWKER born 13 Apr 1864
622. Howard, Jr.	born 12 May 1824 Boston, MA; died 29Jan 1892 Malden, MA
	1 married Sophia N. CONNER 13 July 1850
	(she dau/o John CONNER and _____) (she born ca 1827; died ____
	Child: Frank H/K-[7] BOWKER born ca 1851/53 Boston, MA
	2 married Marietta MAYO 25 Dec 1862
	(she dau/o Watson G. MAYO and Elizabeth CAMBRIDGE) (she born ca 1839 MA)
	Child: Watson T-[7] BOWKER born ca 1864; died ____)
+ **623. DAVIS WHITING**	born 4 Dec 1831; died 18 Oct 1907; married Lucia Drew FAUNCE 26 Nov 1857
	(she dau/o Nathaniel FAUNCE and Marcia WASHBURN)
	(she born 2 July 1831; died 27 Dec 1936 Plymouth, MA)

290. LAZARUS[-5] BOWKER , III, brother of above, was born 12 May 1784 Scituate, MA. He married Martha CUSHING 18 Oct 1807 Boston, MA. She was the daughter of ___ CUSHING and ___, and was born ca 1787; died 15 Aug 1868 Cambridge, MA. Lazarus[-5] BOWKER died 28 Dec 1867.

Children of Lazarus[-5] BOWKER, III and Martha CUSHING:
Surname **BOWKER**

624. Desire	born ca 1808; died ____; married James VINAL ca _____ (he born ca 1804)	
625. Perez Gill	born ca 1809 Boston, MA; died 28 April 1881 Hingham, MA	
	married Eunice Jacobs CUSHING 12 April 1835 (she born 29 Sep 1806)	
	(she dau/o Charles Whiting CUSHING and Deborah RICHMOND)	
	Children: George R[-7] born ca 1838; and Clementine[-7] BOWKER born ca 1844 Scituate, MA, married George R. RIPLEY 28 June 1864 (he s/o Henry RIPLEY and Clarissa CUSHING)	
626. Almira C.	born Sept 1813; died 30 Aug 1878; married John Henry JONES 21 Apr 1838	
627. Abbie	born ca 1815; died _____	
628. Martha	born ca 1817; died ____; married William GREEN ca _____	
629. Joseph	born ca 1819; died young	
+ **630.WINSLOW LEWIS**	born 25 Oct 1825; died 15 Dec 1904; 1 married Maria/Marcia H. ____ ca 1849	
	2 married Susan E. SWAIN ca Apr 1860 Chichester, NH	

296. HOMER[-5] BOWKER, son of Gershom[-4] BOWKER (Lazarus[-3]; James-[2;1]) and Elizabeth STETSON, was born 19 Sep 1785 Scituate, Plymouth, MA. He married Tryphena SYLVESTER on 7 Apr 1811 at Scituate. She was the daughter of Thomas SYLVESTER and Relief JORDAN, and was born 25 Sep 1790; died 20 Oct 1864 at Scituate, MA. Homer[-5] BOWKER died 15 Apr 1864 Scituate.

Children of Homer[-5] BOWKER and Tryphena SYLVESTER:
Surname **BOWKER**

631. Harriet Thomas		born 1 June 1811, died _____
632. Nathaniel Homer	(1)	born 13 June 1814; died 17 Apr 1824 Scituate
633. Evelina		born 5 Aug 1816; died ____
634. Henry Warren		born 6 Oct 1819; died _____
635. Parsons		born 15 May 1822; died ____; married Deborah H. DYER 11 Nov 1844
636. Nathaniel	(2)	born 5 Oct 1824; died ____
637. Eliza Ann (1)		born 14 Dec 1827; died 6 Mar 1830
638. Eliza Ann (2)		born 5 Nov 1830; died ____; married David TENNEY ca ____
		(he s/o Robert G. TENNEY and _____)
639. Nancy West		born 19 Dec 1833; died 3 Oct 1895 640. Emelina born Aug 1834; died ____

302. JOSEPH-[5] BOWKER, son of Zebulon[-4] BOWKER (Lazarus[-3]; James-[2;1]) and Deborah RANDALL, was born 24 Oct 1780 at Rutland, VT. He married Rhoda HAMILTON 17 Jan 1805. She was the daughter of James HAMILTON and Rhoda MOREHOUSE; and was born 28 July 1780 Newton, Fairfield, CT; died 1 Sep 1855 Sandgate, VT. Joseph-[5] BOWKER died 6 Oct 1868 Bennington, VT.

Children of Joseph-[5] BOWKER and Rhoda HAMILTON:
Surname **BOWKER**   (children born Sandgate, Bennington, VT)

641. William	born 5 Dec 1805; died 21 Aug 1876 VT
642. Polly	born 14 Oct 1807 VT; died 12 June 1888 TN
643. Rhoda	born 23 Feb 1810 VT; died 28 Mar 1890 ; married Reuben WEBB (8 ch)
+ **644. CLARKE**	born 22 Apr 1812 Bennington, VT.; died 24 June 1887 Dallas City, IL
	married Lovina PERRY 1 July 1838 NY
	(she dau/o Asa PERRY and Ruhanna WAITE)
	(she born Oct 1816 Onondaga Co., NY; died 30 Sep 1904 Hancock, IL)
645. Eleanor	born 19 Mar 1814; died 6 Aug 1871 VT
646. Abigail	born ca 1818 VT; died 1918
647. Fanny	born 3 Mar 1819 VT; died 1900 648. Catherine born 28 Jan 1822; died 17 Dec 1844 VT

303. JAMES[-5] BOWKER-V (BUKER), son of James[-4] BOWKER, IV (James-[3;2;1]) and Ruth SARGENT, was born 22 Feb 1768 at Bowdoinham, Maine. He married Jane WRIGHT 21 Oct 1790. She was the daughter of John WRIGHT and Mary BOWEN; and was born 29 Aug 1764; died ____. James[-5] BOWKER/BUKER died ____.

Children of James-5 BOWKER/BUKER and Jane WRIGHT:
Surname **BOWKER/BUKER**

	649. William	born 10 Mar1791; died ____ ; married Abigail ALLEN 21 Mar 1814
	650. Caleb	born Sept 1792; died 16 Nov 1832; married Lydia COOMBS 9 Apr 1813
	651. Mary Polly	born 29 Nov 1793; died 1824; married Ebenezer BEAL
	652. John	born 12 June 1795 ME; died 23 Sept 1854
		married Mary Belcher HENSHAW 28 June 1816
+	**653. THOMAS**	born ca 1797; died 9 Apr 1877; 1 married Rhoda-6 WEYMOUTH 15 Oct 1820
		2 married Nancy HALL 7 Jan 1827; 3 married Lydia HUNTINGTON 21 Jan 1866
	654. Abigail	born July 1798; died 1850; married Joshua BEAL 9 Mar 1818
+	**655. RUFUS**	born ca 1799; died 3 Jan 1830; married Betsey-6 WEYMOUTH 25 Dec 1823
		(she dau/o Rhoda-5 BOWKER and Nicholas WEYMOUTH)(she born 1806; died 1838
	656. Betsey	born ca 1800; died ____ 657. Joseph born ca 1805; died 1862

305. RHODA-5 BOWKER/BUKER, sister of above, was born ca 1772 at Bowdoinham, Maine. She married Nicholas WEYMOUTH ca 1799. He was the son of _____ WEYMOUTH and _____; and was born ____, died 17 Aug 1849 ME. Rhoda-5 BOWKER/BUKER died 14 July 1851 Bowdoinham.

Children of Rhoda-5 BOWKER/BUKER and Nicholas WEYMOUTH:
Surname **WEYMOUTH**

+	**658. RHODA**	born 30 Jan 1800; died 29 Dec 1825 Bowdoinham, ME
		married Thomas-6 BOWKER/BUKER ca 1822 (# 653)
+	**659. BETSEY**	born ca 1806; died 1835
		1 married Rufus-6 BOWKER/BUKER ca 1822/23 (# 655)
		2 married James SEDGLEY 1 July 1835

309. SAMUEL MICHAEL-5 BOWKER, son of William-4 BOWKER (James-3;2;1) amd _____; was born 2 Mar 1785 at Stafford, NJ. He married Lucretia APPLEGATE on 17 Nov 1805. (Marriage records give Michael BOWKER and Lucretia APPLEGATE) She was the daughter of Bartholomew APPLEGATE and Mary MILLER, and was born ca 1788 Dover, Monmouth, NJ; died ca 1845 at Monmouth, NJ. Samuel Michael-5 BOWKER died 1861 Monmouth, NJ.

Children of Samuel Michael-5 BOWKER and Lucretia APPLEGATE:
Surname **BOWKER**

	660. Michael	born ca 1808; died ____
+	**661. JOSEPH**	born 27 Oct 1810 Barnegat, NJ; died 1 Nov 1889 Barnegat, Ocean, NJ
		married Nancy Ann PAUL ca 1829
+	**662. SAMUEL**	born ca 1811/12 Monmouth, NJ; died 1873 Lebanon, Ohio
		married Malinda HUTCHINSON ca ____
		(she dau/o William T. HUTCHINSON and Clarissa B. MOORE)
		(she born ca 1819 IL; died ca 1860)

316. REBECCA-5 BOWKER, daughter of Bartlett-4 BOWKER (John-3; James-2;1) and his first wife Christina HOLMES, was born 30 May 1782 at Fitzwilliam, Cheshire, NH. She married David STOWELL on 14 April 1803 NH. He was the son of Abijah STOWELL and ____, and was born 30 May 1779; died 25 Oct 1849 VT. Rebecca-5 BOWKER died _____.

Children of Rebecca-5 BOWKER and David STOWELL:
Surname **STOWELL**

	663. David	born 29 Dec 1804; died 29 Mar 1854
		1 married Lydia Emeline PORTER 16 May 1830 (she born ____; died 1836)
		2 married Emily Caroline STARRETT 26 Oct 1837 (she born ___; died 1845)
		3 married Caroline Augusta WING ca ____ (she born ca 1822, died 1871)
+	**664. REBECCA**	born 19 Oct 1807 VT; died 11 Dec 1878
		married John WHITTEMORE ca 1830 Fitzwilliam, NH
	665. Leander Holmes	born ca 1809; died 1875

317. BARTLETT-5 BOWKER, Jr. brother of above, was born 6 Dec 1784 at Fitzwilliam, NH. He married Hannah CARPENTER on 27 July 1809. She was the daughter of Davis B. CARPENTER ++ (Jesse) and Miriam/Mariam MANNING, and was born 7 Oct 1787/8; died _____. Bartlett-5 BOWKER, Jr. died 10 Sep 1865 at St. Johnsbury, VT.

++ Note: Davis B CARPENTER married second to Lucy CUSHING Bowker of Scituate, MA on 7 Feb 1804. He moved to Walpole, NH. and died 23 Aug 1824 . He was a farmer and inn keeper.

Children of Bartlett-5 BOWKER, Jr. and Hannah CARPENTER:
Surname **BOWKER**

666. George	born ca 1809; died 1858	Child: George Morse-7 BOWKER born ca 1841; died 1924
667. Miriam/Meriam	born 19 Dec 1810; died ____
668. Roxana A.	born 17 Jan 1812; died ____

+   **669. DAVIS C.**   born 13 May 1815 VT; died 1875; married Fanny Almira CUSHING ca 1841
(she dau/o Matthew CUSHING and ____) (she born 24 June 1821; died _____)
Child: Rosetta Emily-7 BOWKER born ca 1842 VT; married George Nathan CASS of Boston 1 July 1871 (as his 2nd wife) (he born ca 1831-35; died 1882) (he s/o Nathan CASS and Sarah CURRIER) He was a well-known landscape artist. Two of his more well-known paintings were " Evening on the Kennebec River ", and " View in Medway , MA "

670. Lucy C.	born 7 May 1817; died ____; married James FLACK 12 Nov 1860 St Johnsbury, VT.
671. Harriet F.	born 17 Aug 1820; died ____
672. Sybel/ Sybill	born 27 Feb 1822; died ____
673. Calvin	born 27 Aug 1823; died 30 Nov 1902 St. Johnsbury, VT
	married Malvina E. SHOREY 13 July 1863 St. Johnsbury, VT

Child: Rosa Mabel-7 BOWKER born 1875

674. Hannah J.	born 14 June 1826; died 14 May 1860
675. Charles J.	born 30 May 1830; died ___; married Susan H. FAY 27 Oct 1886 (she born ca 1830)

318. STEPHEN-5 BOWKER, brother of above, was born 8 Dec 1788 Fitzwilliam, NH. He married Sarah / Sally WHITNEY on 7 Apr 1814. She was born ca 1783 NH; died ____. Stephen-5 BOWKER died 11 July 1860 at Newfane, VT.

Children of Stephen-5 BOWKER and Sally WHITNEY:
Surname **BOWKER**

+   **676. STEPHEN WRIGHT**   born 4 Nov 1821; died 12 Apr 1878 Newfane, VT.; Hotel keeper
married Henrietta / Harriet _____ ca _____

323. LUKE-5 BOWKER, son of Bartlett-4 BOWKER (John-3; James-2,1) and Jemima KNOWLTON Wright, was born 28 April 1800 at Fitzwilliam, Cheshire, NH. He married first to Rhoda HARWOOD on 13 Apr 1828. She was born 10 Apr 1807, died 17 June 1844. He married second to Sarah HOWE 28 Nov 1844. She was born ca 1808; died 1877 Fitzwilliam, NH. He married third to Rebecca BALLARD Simonds ca 1878. She was the daughter of Eliphaz BALLARD and ____ of Lancaster, MA, and the widow of Reuben SIMONDS, and was born 1820; died ____. Luke-5 BOWKER died 23 Mar 1887.

Children of Luke-5 BOWKER and Rhoda HARWOOD/ HURD:
Surname **BOWKER**

677. Charles	born 15 Nov 1831 Fitzwilliam, NH; died _____
	married Sarah _____ ca 1861

Children: Alice E-7 born ca 1862; and Louisa-7 BOWKER born ca 1867

678. Milton	born 3 Aug 1834 Fitzwilliam, NH; died 14 July 1874 Fitchburg, MA
	married Maria M. LAMB 20 Feb 1867 (she dau/o Nathan LAMB and Rhoda ____)
679. Emeline (1)	born ca 1837; died 30 July 1843 EOL

Children of Luke-5 BOWKER and Sarah HOWE:
Surname **BOWKER**

680. Emeline (2)	born ca 1846; died ____
+ **681. SARAH**	born 3 Aug 1849; died 19 Jan 1933; married Samuel Stillman STONE 4 Oct 1882

324. CAPTAIN ELIJAH-5 BOWKER, brother of above, was born 8 Jan 1803 Fitzwilliam, NH. He married Dorothy CROMBIE on 18 Nov 1830. She was the daughter of ____ CROMBIE and ____; and was born 9 June 1807; died 19 Oct 1884. Capt. Elijah-5 BOWKER was a prominent resident of Cheshire County, NH, and the Town of Bowkerville, NH was named after him. He died 12 Feb 1878 at Fitzwilliam (Bowkerville), NH.

Children of Capt. Elijah-5 BOWKER and Dorothy CROMBIE:
Surname **BOWKER**

682. Lucy	born Dec 1831; died ____; married George DAMON ca ____

Children: Minnie M-7 born ca 1867 NH, married James Wilmer WRIGHT 31 Dec 1890 (s/o George WRIGHT and Jane SMITH); and James-7 DAMON born ca 169 NH, died 13 Feb 1914

Children of Captain Elijah⁻⁵ BOWKER and Dorothy CROMBIE, continued:
Surname **BOWKER**

683. Lyman W.	born 23 Oct 1833 Fitzwilliam, NH; died 24 May 1909 Portsmouth, NH	

683. Lyman W.   born 23 Oct 1833 Fitzwilliam, NH; died 24 May 1909 Portsmouth, NH
married Clara Ann BROCKWAY ca ____
(she dau/o Lockhart Willard BROCKWAY and Mary Ann WHITTEMORE)
(she born 1 Dec 1834 Hinsdale, NH; died 9 June 1881 Fitzwilliam)
684. James B.   born ca 1839; died ____; married Clara ____
685. Daniel French   born ca 1842; died ____;   married Mary Elizabeth EVERETT ca _____
(she born 23 Dec 1844 Fitzwilliam; died 15 May 1928 Fitzwilliam)
Children: Leo Elijah-⁷ born 9 Apr 1863; Arthur⁻⁷; George D⁻⁷ born ca 1872; and Robert M-⁷ BOWKER
686. Mary A.   born ca 1851; died ____

326. CYNTHIA⁻⁵ BOWKER, sister of above, was born 1 Feb 1807 Fitzwilliam, NH. She married first to Dexter B. ROLLINS on 5 Oct 1831. He was the son of ____ ROLLINS and ____; and was born ____; died ____. She married second to the Rev. Jesse Artemus STONE on 6 Sept 1840, as his 1ˢᵗ wife. He was the son of Deacon Artemus STONE and Isabel ____; and was born 8 Sep 1806 at Fitzwilliam, NH; died 19 Feb 1893 Topeka, KS. Cynthia⁻⁵ BOWKER died 27 July 1856 at Topeka, KS. Rev. Jesse STONE married second to Sarah Caroline PACKARD 8 Jan 1857.

Children of Cynthia⁻⁵ BOWKER and Rev. Jesse STONE:
Surname **STONE**

687. William Henry   born 21 June 1841 Fitzwilliam, NH; died ca 1910 Titusville, PA
married Frances GENEVRA Oct 1866 Titusville, PA; 2 married Clara ____ ca 1888
Children: George-⁷ born 2 Feb 1868, dy; Herbert W⁻⁷ born 12 Jan 1870; and Ada Lorena⁻⁷ STONE born 30 Dec 1871, dy

+   **688. CYNTHIA E.**   born 16 Jul 1843 Fitzwilliam; died _____
married Capt. Henry L. BARKER 25 July 1863 Topeka, KS
(he born 23 June 1835 NY, son of John BARKER and _____)
689. Lyndes Ballard   born 25 June 1845 Fitzwilliam, NH; died ____
690. Ann Hazelton Judson   born 6 May 1848 Fitzwilliam; died 3 Oct 1892 Topeka, KA   EOL
married T D BRAGUNIER Mar 1866 KS; divorced 1882

+   **691. MARY LOUISA**   born 2 June 1850 Boston, MA; died   (living 1916)
1 married William Spencer JEWELL 7 July 1868; divorced
(s/o Thomas JEWELL and ___ WILLIS)
2 married Charles Alfred BLISS 20 Sep 1883 Topeka, KS
(he s/o Dea. James BLISS and Joanna BREWSTER)
(he born 21 Nov 1831; died 12 Oct 1898)
692. Jesse Bartlett   born 28 Mar 1852 Medford, MA; died May 1903 Topeka, KS; unmarried

Reference: Ancestors and Descendants of Deacon Gregory STONE of Cambridge, MA 1320-1917

328. HANNAH⁻⁵ BOWKER, sister of above, was born 25 March 1815 at Fitzwilliam, Cheshire, NH. She married James COREY on 2 April 1835 at Fitzwilliam. He was the son of Anthony COREY and Lovice/Lovisa BOOM, and was born 12 Nov 1805 at Richmond, Cheshire, NH; died 12 July 1889 at Fitchburg, MA. Hannah-⁵ BOWKER died 24 April 1901 Fitchburg, MA.

Children of Hannah⁻⁵ BOWKER and James COREY:
Surname **COREY** (all children born Fitzwilliam, Cheshire, NH)

693. Lucy Ann   born 5 May 1836 ; died 14 March 1910 Fitzwilliam
married David SOLMAN 23 Sept 1857 (he born ca 1830)
694. Antoinette   born 1 Aug 1837; died 27 Nov 1885 Fitchburg, MA
married Jeremiah GREENWOOD 30 Nov 1854

695. Helen Louise   born 20 Mar 1840; married Albertt C. HARRIS ca 1876
696. Mary Frances   born 5 June 1842; died 11 Oct 1901 Wichendon, MA
married Henry PECK 31 Jan 1861
697. James Warren   born 11 Nov 1848; died 3 April 1899 Fitchburg, MA
married Laura TYLER ca ____   (he born ca 1850)
698. Charles Austin   born 7 Sep 1851; died _____
married Hattie Frances FOSS 12 Aug 1875 (she born ca 1853)

341. ANNA-⁵ TOWER, daughter of Hannah⁻⁴ BOWKER (John⁻³; James⁻²,¹) and Stephen TOWER, Sr., was born 15 Sep 1776 at Cummington, MA. She married Samuel ROBINSON of Cummington, on 13 Sep 1801. He was the son of ____ ROBIN-SON and ____, and was born ca 1773; died ca 1856 at Batavia, NY. Anna-⁵ TOWER died 17 Nov 1871 at Harmony, NY.

Children of Anna-⁵ TOWER and Samuel ROBINSON:
Surname **ROBINSON**

699. Galen	born 30 July 1802; died ____	703. Melissa Jane	born ca 1809/10
700. Anna Alvira	born 29 Sep 1804; died ____	704. Samuel, Jr.	born 17 Aug 1811
701. Robert Clark	born 17 Aug 1806; died 1891 Harmony, Chatauqua, NY		
	married Jane/ Janet BLOSSOM ca ____	705. Nahum	born ca __ ; dy
702. Stephen	born 28 Sep 1808; died ____	706. Fidelia	born 24 Dec 1817

342. STEPHEN⁻⁵ TOWER, Jr., brother of above, was born 8 March 1778 at Cummington, MA. He married Meletiah " Millie " BARTLETT on 15 Dec 1803. She was the daughter of Edward BARTLETT and Zilpha SYLVESTER, and was born 14 Dec 1783 Stoughton, MA; died 18 Aug 1864 Cummington, MA. Stephen⁻⁵ TOWER, ,Jr. died 7 June 1856 Cummington, MA.

Children of Stephen⁻⁵ TOWER, Jr. and Meletiah BARTLETT:
Surname **TOWER**

+	**707. WEALTHY T.**	born 18 Jan 1805; died 31 Aug 1887 MA
		1 married Peter BARTLETT 1 July 1823
		2 married William GIDDINGS 1 Jul 1842
	708. Permelia (1)	born 20 Oct 1806; died before 1811
+	**709. CALVIN BOWKER**	born 4 Nov 1808; died 13 Oct 1885 Worthington, Hampshire, MA
		married Amanda M. HIGGINS 28 May 1835 Worthinghton, MA
		(she dau/o Luther HIGGINS and Lydia RING)
	710. Permelia (2)	born 24 Nov 1811; died 25 Sep 1867; married Tillson BARTLETT ca ____
	711. Zilpha	born 5 May 1814; died 5 May 1814 EOL
	712. Anna Almina	born 11 Oct 1816; died 5 Jan 1820 EOL
+	**713. LUTHER**	born 13 Dec 1819; died 6 Nov 1898; married Sabrina TOWER 25 Nov 1841
	BARTLETT	(she born 29 May 1820 MA; died 6 Oct 1908 Cummington, MA)

344. JOHN⁻⁵ TOWER, brother of above, was born 8 July 1781Cummington, MA. He married to Ruth REED on 1 Mar 1809. She was the daughter of Rev. Jesse REED and Ruth WHITMAN, and was born 29 Mar 1785 Charlemont, MA; died 17 Nov 1833 Cummington, MA. John⁻⁵ TOWER died 30 Sep 1827 at Youngstown, NY.

Children of John-⁵ TOWER and Ruth REED:
Surname **TOWER**

	714. John Madison	born 5 Apr 1810; died ____
	715. Salome	born 14 Mar 1812; died 3 June 1816 EOL
	716. Celemna	born 5 May 1815; died 26 Oct 1853
		married Hiram BARTLETT 6 May 1835 Worthington, MA
+	**717. DEXTER**	born 12 Mar 1817; died 13 Jan 1896 Williamsburg, MA
		1 married Bertia Irena PIERCE 30 Nov 1847 Windsor, MA
		(she born ca 1825; died Aug 1886) (she dau/o Isaac PIERCE and ____)
		2 married Mrs. Evaline Rogers Sep 1888
	718. Laura	born 13 May 1819; died 1890; married Cephas THAYER ca ____
	719. Roswell	born 4 Sep 1821; died 15 July 1881 Windsor, MA
		married Elizabeth BRYANT 8 Apr 1851
		Children: Ada-⁷ born ca 1854; John-⁷ born ca 1855; George-7 born ca 1857;
		Clifford⁷ born ca 1859; and Fanny A⁻⁷ TOWER born ca 1864
	720. Russell	born 31 May 1826; died 14 Jan 1909 Holyoke, MA
		married Rebecca S. GRANGER 2 July 1865 Worthington, MA
		(she dau/o Abraham GRANGER and Jane ____)
		Children: Celemna Edith -⁷ born ca 1867; Mary Etta-⁷ born ca 1869 and Ruth Winifred⁻⁷ TOWER
		born ca 1870, died 1876

345. DAVID⁻⁵ TOWER, brother of above, was born 11 Dec 1782 at Cummington, MA. He married first to Elsie Mason DEAN , int pub, 12 Dec 1812. She was the daughter of Dr. ___ DEAN and ____of Adams, MA; and was born 26 Mar 1792; died 6 Apr

1833. David⁻⁵ TOWER married second to Mary BASSETT of Adams, int pub 26 Apr 1834. David⁻⁵ TOWER died 13 Mar 1870 Wilson, Niagara County, NY.

Children of David⁻⁵ TOWER and Elsie Mason DEAN:
Surname **TOWER**

721. David Dean	born 14 Nov 1814; died ____		
722. Peter G.	born 26 Nov 1816; died ____	727. Levi Lincoln	born 15 Oct 1826; died ____
723. Christopher Mason	born 20 Sep 1818; died ____	728. John W.	born 20 Oct 1828; died ____
724. Luke Bowker	born 21 May 1820; died ____	729. Daniel Timothy	born 13 Aug 1831
725. Anna	born 26 May 1822; died 24 Sep 1838		
726. Stephen Asa	born 27 Sep 1824; died ____		

346. JOANNA⁻⁵ TOWER, sister of above, was born 27 Sep 1784 Cummington, MA. She married Lemon MINER of Windsor, MA on 21 Jan 1807. He was the son of Ephraim MINER and Elizabeth ___; and was born 23 June 1785; died 12 May 1836 Batavia, NY. Joanna⁻⁵ TOWER died 6 Mar 1885 at Batavia, NY (aged 100 yr., 5mo, 9 da)

Children of Joanna⁻⁵ TOWER and Lemon MINER:
Surname **MINER**

730. Emmeretta	born 30 July 1809; died _____	737. LaFayette	born 12 Aug 1825; died ____
731. Austin T.	born 9 Feb 1811; died _____	738. Julia A.	born 1 June 1828; died ____
732. Ephraim Harrison	born 5 Dec 1813; died ____		
733. John Tower	born 3 Jan 1815; died ____		
734. Stephen Tower	born 30 Dec 1816; died ____		
735. Norman F.	born 12 Jan 1819; died 28 June 1845		
736. Elizabeth Ann	born 22 Mar 1822; died ____; married Jerome THOMPSON ca ____		

347. DEBORAH⁻⁵ TOWER, sister of above, was born 16 July 1786 Cummington, MA. She married Anselm FORD of Cummington , on 7 June 1807. He was the son of Hezekiah FORD and Huldah ____; and was born on 27 June 1788. Deborah⁻⁵ TOWER died _____.

Children of Deborah⁻⁵ TOWER and Anselm FORD:
Surname **FORD**

739. Deborah	(1)	born and died 15 Aug 1807	745. Deborah Elmina (2)	born 11 Mar 1818
740. Charles		born 22 Jan 1809; died ____	746. Anna	born ____
741. Hosea		born 4 Apr 1810; died ____	747. Cyrus	born ____
742. Otis		born 5 Jan 1812; died ____	748. Delia	born ____
743. Amos		born 6 Dec 1813; died ____	749. Frank	born ____
744. Lucius		born 9 Nov 1815; died ____		

348. CLARISSA⁻⁵ TOWER, sister of above, was born 3 May 1788 Cummington, MA. She married Elkanah TIMOTHY on 16 Aug 1807. He was the son of Daniel TIMOTHY and Anna BOYD, and was born 8 Apr 1789; died 30 Nov 1850 at Porter, NY. Clarissa⁻⁵ TOWER died 29 May 1876 at Porter, Niagara County, NY.

Children of Clarissa⁻⁵ TOWER and Elkanah TIMOTHY:
Surname **TIMOTHY**

750. Hiram	born 16 Feb 1809; died 3 Mar 1809	754. Frances	born 1 Aug 1815
751. Mary Ann	born 9 Apr 1810; died ____	755. Clarissa Ann	born 16 Jul y 1817
752. Helen B.	born 25 Nov 1811; died ____	756. Charles Dewey	born 14 Sep 1819
753. Otis	born 30 Aug 1813; died ____	757. John Henry	born 17 Nov 1821

349. PETER⁻⁵ TOWER, brother of above, was born 10 July 1790 at Cummington, MA. He married Hannah BAILEY on 5 April 1819. She was the daughter of John BAILEY and Lucy TOWER, and was born ca 1798; died 27 Dec 1831 at Porter, NY. He married second to Olive BALDWIN Smith on 13 June 1833. She was the daughter of Guy BALDWIN and Tryphena HARMON, and was born 22 May 1803; died 17 Mar 1886 at Porter, Niagara County, NY.

Children of Peter⁻⁵ TOWER and Hannah BAILEY:
Surname **TOWER**   (Children born at Porter, NY)

758. Lyanda	born 19 Oct 1819; died ____	759. John Edwin	born 3 Jan 1821; died ____

Children of Peter[5] TOWER and Hannah BAILEY, continued:
Surname **TOWER**

760. William	born 1 Oct 1822	762. Octavia	born 18 Jan 1827; died 18 Oct 1830
761. James Monroe	born 1 Oct 1824	763. Elizabeth Ann	born 16 July 1829; died 31 Aug 1854

Children of Peter[5] TOWER and Olive BALDWIN Smith:
Surname **TOWER**

764. Luke	born 24 May 1834 NY	768. Eugene (twin)	born 9 Oct 1840; died 2 Nov 1849
765. George Pearce	born 19 May 1836	769. Peter Smith	born 22 Mar 1843
766. Harmon Baldwin	born 28 Aug 1838	770. Olive Almina	born 15 June 1846
767. Emugene (twin)	born 9 Oct 1840		

350. OTIS[5] TOWER, brother of above, was born 28 Oct 1791 at Cummington, MA. He married Susanna BOWKER 10 Feb 1817 at Granville, NY. She was the daughter of Liberty BOWKER and ____, and was born 26 Oct 1792 at Rutland Co., VT. died 22 Jan 1869 at Bethel, MI. Otis[5] TOWER died 11 Oct 1870 at Bethel, MI.

Children of Otis[5] TOWER and Susanna BOWKER:
Surname **TOWER** (all children born Niagara County, NY; either at Porter or Wilson)

771. Mary	born 19 Dec 1821; died ____
772. Anna	born 15 Oct 1823; died ____
773. Otis Franklin	born 10 Aug 1825; died 12 Sep 1847
774. John	born 23 Sep 1827; died ____
775. Caroline	born 6 April 1830; died 9 Oct 1893 Bronson, MI
	married John Quincy ADAMS ca 1853
	(he s/o Myron ADAMS and Sarah T. ____) (he born ca 1832; died 1916 IA)

Children: Susie[7] born ca 1854; Joanna[7] born ca 1857; and Carrie[7] ADAMS born ca 1860

776. Adeline Sophia	born 16 July 1832; died ____

353. RHODA BOWKER[5] TOWER, sister of above, was born 26 Nov 1795 at Cummington, MA. She married Warren E. TOWER 1 Apr 1817. He was the son of Nathaniel TOWER and Leah ____, and was born 9 Jan 1789 Cummington, died 26 May 1834. Rhoda Bowker[5] TOWER died 23 Aug 1833.

Children of Rhoda Bowker[5] TOWER and Warren TOWER:
Surname **TOWER**

+	**777. SALOME**	born 9 Oct 1817; died 21 July 1895 Cummington
		married Ephraim Tillson BARTLETT int pub 12 May 1837
		(he s/o Ephraim BARTLETT and Elizabeth TILLSON)
		(he born 13 Aug 1813; died 16 Sep 1857 Cummington, NH/MA
	778. Mariam/ Miriam	born 5 Jan 1819; died ____
	779. Sabrina	born 29 May 1820; died 6 Oct1908 Worthington, MA
+	**780. ALMINA /**	born 6 Oct 1822; died 24 May 1889
	ELMINA	married Otis Boise[7] BARTLETT 1 May 1851 (he # 1158)
		(he born 15 May 1826 Cummington; died _____)
		(he s/o Peter BARTLETT and Wealthy T[6] TOWER # 698)
	781. Warren E.	born 5 Apr 1824; died 2 Dec 1901 Cummington
		1 married Agnes L. LYMAN 27 Nov 1852
		(she dau/o Benjamin B. LYMAN and Roxana PACKARD)
		(she born 30 May 1834 Cummington; died ____)

Child: Edith Marion[7] TOWER born 22 Apr 1857; died 8 Sep 1894; married Alfred C. STEVENS 14 Feb 1877
2 married Margaret Jane LAVERY 3 June 1893

	782. Lorenzo H	born 14 Aug 830; died 4 Mar 1910 Cummington
		married Vesta A. BARTLETT 27 Nov 1856
		(she dau/o Ephraim BARTLETT and Betsey MARSHALL)
		(she born 16 Oct 1830; died _____)

Children: Theodore P-[7] born 18 July 1860, married Lottie WALLACE 1 Aug 1901, no issue;
Arthur-[7] born 1 Mar 1858, died 8 Oct 1859; Bessie[7] BARTLETT born 9 Apr 1867, died 22 Sep 1867

363. ABIGAIL " Nabby "[5] BOWKER, son of Captain Stephen[4] BOWKER (John[3; 2]; James[-1]) and Lucy CUSHING, was born 3 Oct 1794 at Scituate, Plymouth, MA. She married Walter CARPENTER on 18 Oct 1812. He was the son of Davis B. CARPENTER and Miriam MANNING, and was born 22 Sep 1782 at Walpole, NH; died _____Union, Monroe, NY.

Children of Abigail[5] BOWKER and Walter CARPENTER
Surname **CARPENTER**   (children born Walpole, NH)
    783. Stephen B.   born 7 July 1819; died 5 Nov 1869
    784. Edwin C.   born 5 Nov 1820; died _____
                    married Mary ROBIN 15 Feb 1744   (she born 1818 NY; died 1895)
             Children: Herbert W[7] born June 1852; Cecil[7] born 1854 NY; and Edwin[7] Jr. CARPENTER born ca 1858
    785. George   born ca 1823; died 27 Oct 1887
    786. Eliza Ann   born 9 Jan 125; died 8 May 1866
    787. Henry M.   born 31 July 1826; died ____   789. Harriet L. born 21 Mar 1830; died 9 Mar 1861
    788. Samuel G.   born 14 Oct 1827; died ____   790. Nancy L. born 31 July 1833; died 18 Sep 1886

364. CUSHING[5] BOWKER, brother of above, was born 23 April 1795 at Walpole, Cheshire, NH. He married first to Sarah Van DOORN on 13 Feb 1817 NH. She was the daughter of Moses Van DOORN and Sarah____, and was born 23 Apr 1795; died 10 Apr 1827 Quebec, Canada. He married second to Abigail Worcester RIDER on 20 Dec 1827 at Shefford Co., Quebec, Canada. She was the daughter of ____ RIDER and ____, and was born ca 1803; died 1841. He married third to Sarah MARSTON Allard on 15 Nov 1842 Quebec, Canada. She was the daughter of ____ MARSTON; and the widow of Steven ALLARD, and was born 1 April 1809 England; died 17 April 1888. Cushimg[5] BOWKER died 13 Sep 1870 at Warden, Quebec.

Children of Cushing[5] BOWKER and Sarah Van DOORN:
Surname **BOWKER**
    791. Sarah Elizabeth   born 22 Aug 1819; died 24 Sep 1819   EOL
    792. Stephen Cushing   born 30 Oct 1820 NY; died 20 June 1901 Quebec, Canada
                    1 married Maria Phoebe BROWN 6 Jan 1847
Children: Charles Adna[7] BOWKER born 22 Mar 1862; died ca 1931 Warden, Quebec, Canada, and George Edwin[7] BOWKER born ca ___
                    2 married Elvira L. MACK 17 Mar 1884
    793. William Short   born 30 June 1823; died 13 Sep 1897
    794. Sarah Sophia   born 23 June 1825; died 5 Feb 1897
Children of Cushing[5] BOWKER and Abigail RIDER :
Surname **BOWKER**
+   **795. RENSSALAER**   born 6 April 1829 at sea; died 11 Jan 1914 Melvin, Ford, IL
         SYLVENDER   married Mary Batchelder SPAULDING ca 1858 (she born ca 1829; died 1876)
    796. Christina   born 17 June 1830; died 19 Nov 1920
+   **797. LAURA RIDER**   · born 21 June 1832; died 6 Aug 1899
                    married Samuel MARSTON 22 Apr 1850 Shefford, Quebec, Canada
                    (he born 31 Aug 1828 NH; died 24 June 1895)
    798. Sylvender   born 16 Feb 1834; died 11 Jan 1911 IL
    799. Lucy Cushing   born 7 Nov 1835; died 13 Sep 1870
+   **800. ABIGAIL RIDER**   born 20 Oct 1837 Canada; died 19 July 1915 / 1925 Philadelphia, PA
                    married Jacob SPACKMAN Apr 1862 Montreal, Quebec, Canada
                    (he born 24 Aug 1823 Wiltshire, England; died 18 Nov 1901 Philadelphia, PA)
    801. Harriet Rider.   born 12 Aug 1839; died 20 July 1930
Children of Cushing[5] BOWKER and Sarah MARSTON Allard:
Surname **BOWKER**
+   **802. MARY LOUISA**   born 24 Feb 1845; died 8 Aug 1932; married George MARSTON 1 Feb 1865
    803. Martha Jane   born 24 Sep 1847; died 12 / 17 Nov 1873; married John A. MARTIN
    804. Griffin Samuel   born ca 1850; died 8 Apr 1933 Quebec, Canada
    805. Myron Proctor   born 4 June 1852; died ____

366. SARAH[5] BOWKER, sister of above, was born 9 June 1800 at Westmoreland, Cheshire, NH. She married Orren Lathrop BENNETT on 14 Sept 1820 NH. He was the s/o Steven BENNETT and Ruth FELLOWS, and was born 15 Sep 1792 Dummerston, VT; died 26 Feb 1886. Sarah-5 BOWKER died 8 Jan 1891 at Dummerston, Windham; VT

Children of Sarah[5] BOWKER and Orren BENNETT:
Surname **BENNETT**
    806. Stephen Bowker   born 2 Aug 1821 VT; died 14 Jan 1900 Carroll, NY
                    married Jane Loisa/Louisa NORCROSS 18 Jan 1848   (8 ch)
                    (she dau/o Luke NORCROSS and Louisa FRENCH)
                    (she born 18 Jan 1830; died 20 Sep 1900 Carroll, Chatauqua, NY)

Children of Sarah-5 BOWKER and Orren BENNETT, continued:
Surname **BENNETT**

807. Oscar La Fayette	born 19 Jan 1823 VT; died 1 Dec 1899	
808. Henry Clay	born 1 Mar 1825 VT; died 20 Dec 1861 Carroll, NY	
809. Lucyann	born ca 1826; died 17 Apr 1848	
810 George Rodney	born 12 May 1836 VT; died 7 Apr 1905 Marlboro, VT	
811. Sarah Jane	born 18 Nov 1839 VT; died ____	

367. SAMUEL GRIFFIN-5 BOWKER, brother of above , was born ca 1802 Fitzwilliam Cheshire, NH. He married Orpha FAY on 16 Nov 1826. She was the daughter of John Thomas FAY and Levinah BRIGHAM, and was born 9 Nov 1804; died 17 Sep 1851. Samuel Griffin-5 BOWKER died ____ca 1839.

Children of Samuel-5 BOWKER and Orpha FAY:
Surname **BOWKER**

	812. Charles	born ca 1830; died 24 March 1832	EOL
+	**813. SAMUEL FRANCIS**	born 23 Apr 1833 Fitzwilliam, NH; died 18 May 1900 Crystal Lake, IA	
		1 married Rosanna Lovinga ANGIER ca ____	
		(she born 4 March 1837 IL; died 23 July 1861 Fitzwilliam, NH)	
		2 married Mary Amanda CHASE ca 1862	
		(she born 12 June 1838 MA; died 9 Jan 1917 Davenport, IA)	
	814. Sarah Jane	born 1835; died 22 Jan 1838	EOL

368. ELIJAH-5 BOWKER, JR., son of Elijah-4 BOWKER (John-3; James-2;1) and Anna SYLVESTER, was born 14 July 1788 at Scituate, MA. He married Hannah BENSON on 14 July 1811. She was the daughter of ____ BENSON and ____, and was born ____; died ____. Elijah-5 BOWKER, Jr. died 19 May 1827.

Children of Elijah-5 BOWKER, Jr. and Hannah BENSON:
Surname **BOWKER**

815. Stephen	born 14 Sep 1811		818. Sally/Sarah	born 30 Sep 1814
816. Susanna	born ____; died 12 Nov 1875			
+ **817. WILLIAM**	born ca 1819/20; died 24 Sep 1889.			
	married Eliza Brooks RICHARDS 24 Aug 1844 Weymouth, MA			

372. DELIGHT-5 BOWKER, sister of above was born 11 Oct 1796 at Scituate, MA. She married Stephen CLAPP on 14 April 1814. He was the son of Sylvanus CLAPP and Elizabeth BROOKS, and was born 20 July 1787; died 13 Feb 1825 MA. Delight-5 BOWKER died 15 Jan 1849 at Scituate, MA.

Children of Delight-5 BOWKER and Stephen CLAPP:
Surname **CLAPP**

819. Melatiah	born 13 Feb 1815; died 4 May 1890		
820. Stephen Gorham (1)	born 27 Aug 1816; died 1824	EOL	
821. Otis Parsons	born 12 Mar 1818; died 18 Dec 1887		
	married Margaret Charlotte FLAGG 22 Oct 1843		
	(she born 11 Aug 1821 ME; died 22 Oct 1885 MA)		
822. Elizabeth Brooks	born 12 Sep 1819; died 7 Mar 1898		
823. Hannah Stone	born 8 Mar 1821; died ____		
824. Temperance	born 26 Aug 1822; died 13 June 1857; married Hanson Merry SLEEPER 14 Apr 1850		
	(he s/o Samuel T W SLEEPER and Bethana ____)		
	(he born 21 Jan 1827 Bristol, NH; died 12 June 1857)		
825. Stephen (2)	born 5 Oct 1824; died before 1 Dec 1882; married Rachel J. SHERMAN		
	(he was a Civil War veteran , having served in Co. G, 18th MA Infantry; and Co. C. 32nd MA Infantry		

373. CHARLES-5 BOWKER, brother of above, was born 21 Oct 1798 MA. He married Martha WHITTEN/ WHITON 24 Nov 1816 MA. She was the daughter of ___ WHITTEN/WHITON and __; and was born ___; died __. Charles-5 BOWKER died ___.

Children of Charles-5 BOWKER and Martha WHITTEN:
Surname **BOWKER**

826. Matthew H.	born ca 1822; died ____

Children of Charles-5 BOWKER and Martha WHITTEN, continued:
Surname **BOWKER**

	827. Elizabeth	born ca 1823; died 1 Dec 1909; married _____ FADEN ca ____
+	**828. ELLIS**	born ca 1824; died ____; married Harriet _____ ca ____
	829. Leonard	born ca 1825; died 26 May 1894 Somerville, MA

1 married Catherine E. COMERY Wildes 16 Jan 1859 Boston, MA
(she born ca 1826 Maine; died ____)(she dau/o Joseph COMERY and Sarah ____)
2 married Laura Louisa FARR ca ____ (she born ca 1842 NH)
Children: Edwin Leonard-7 born 13 July 1878; died 1948; and Ella W-7 BOWKER born 6 Jan 1883;
died 15 Oct 1970; married George A. FLAGG (he born 13 Dec 1870 Wakefield, MA)

	830. Franklin	born ca 1829; died ____; married Eliza J. ____ ca ____

Children: Georgianna-7 born ca 1854; and Edward W-7 BOWKER born ca 1866

+	**831. HENRY**	born ca 1833; died ____
		married Mary Ada MIERS 16 Aug 1865 Boston, MA (she born Sep 1843 MA)

374. CHARLOTTE-5 BOWKER, sister of above, was born 26 Jan 1800 at Scituate, MA. She married Joshua B. YOUNG ca ____. He was the son of Job YOUNG and Mary ____; and was born 31 Dec 1797 MA; died 24 May 1888 at Auburn, Maine.

Children of Charlotte-5 BOWKER and Joshua YOUNG:
Surname **YOUNG**

832. Ruth B.	born ca 1830; died ____		
833. Charles B.	born ca 1832; died ____	836. William A.	born ca 1835; died ____
834. Albert	born ca 1832; Hotel Keeper	837. Lucy B.	born ca 1839; died ____
835. Rebecca	born ca 1837; died ____	838. Mary	born ca 1841; died ____

380. JOSEPH-5 CUSHING, son of Desire-4 BOWKER (John-3; James-2, 1) and Joseph CUSHING, was born 19 Dec 1794 at Scituate, Plymouth, MA. He married Betsey REED on 4 Aug 1812 at Marblehead, Essex, MA. She was the daughter of ____ REED and _____, and was born ca 1798 Baldwin County, Alabama, died ____. Joseph-5 CUSHING died 24 Nov 1883.

Children of Joseph-5 CUSHING and Betsey REED:
Surname **CUSHING**   (all children born Baldwin County, Alabama

839. Cynthia Harriet	born ca 1821; died ____		
840. Alline/Allyne	born ca 1829; died ____; married Elizabeth ENFINGER		
	(she dau/o Francis Edward ENFINGER and Elizabeth ____)		
	(she born ca 1840 AL; died 1898 FL)		
841. Clayton W.	born ca 1831; died _____		
842. Joseph	born ca 1832; died ____	845. Rebecca	born ca 1840; died ____
843. Eliza	born ca 1835; died ____	846. Henry	born ca 1842; died ____
844. William	born ca 1838; died ____		
847. Louis B "Lewis"	born Jan 1843; died ____ (poss. before 1920)		
	married Susan MADDOX 11 June 1871	(she born ca 1847; died ca 1880)	
848. Benjamin Franklin	born March 1848; died 1914 FL (blind)		
" Frank "	married Nancy Ann SWEENEY ca 1873	(she born Dec 1853 GA)	

381. STEPHEN-5 CUSHING, brother of above, was born 17 Jan 1797 at Scituate, MA. He married first to Ethalinda EDWARDS on 1 Feb 1824. She was the daughter of Oliver EDWARDS and Sarah HOWLETT, and was born 1801; died 1858. He married second to Catherine PHILIPS on 23 Aug 1859. She was the daughter of Simon PHILIPS and Nancy ____, and was born ca 1800; died ____. Stephen-5 CUSHING died 1 Dec 1871.

Children of Stephen-5 CUSHING and Ethalinda EDWARDS:
Surname **CUSHING**

	849. Minerva	born 16 Nov 1824; died 1921; married Alvah CROCKER 20 Nov 1872 (as his 3rd wife)
		(he s/o Samuel CROCKER and Comfort Adams JONES)
		(he born14 Oct 1801; died 26 Dec 1874)
+	**850. OLIVER**	born 12 March 1829; died 17 Jan 1890;
	EDWARDS	married Mary EDSON 7 Sept 1853
	851. Angeline	born 10 Jan 1832; died 12 Sept 1860 (childbirth)
		married Artemus S. TYLER 12 Oct 1854 (he s/o Silas TYLER and Fanny ____)

Children: Stanley Cushing-7 born 4 June 1857; and Artemus Lawrence-7 TYLER born 12 Sept 1860

Children of Stephen-5 CUSHING and Ethalinda EDWARDS, continued:
Surname **CUSHING**

852. Ethalinda   born 14 Aug 1834; married Artemus S. TYLER (as his 2nd wife) on 17 July 1862
         Children: Fannie Maria-7 born 11 June 1867; and Ethalinda-7 TYLER born 10 Sept 1871, died 19 July 1872
853. Desire <u>Helen.</u>   born ca 1846; died 2 July 1855   EOL

383. MATILDA-5 CUSHING, sister of above, was born 29 Nov 1801 at Scituate, MA. She married David BURR, Jr. on 7 Nov 1824. He was the son of David BURR, Sr. and Mary FEARING, and was born 7 Nov 1778; died 21 June 1852 Scituate, MA. Matilda-5 CUSHING died 18 Aug 1884.

Children of Matilda-5 CUSHING and David BURR:
Surname **BURR**

854. Job   born ca 1828; died ____   855. Matilda Cushing   born 4 Nov 1831
856. Elisha   born 15 May 1839; did 10 Nov 1909; married Mary Jane PRATT ca _____
         Children: Carl-7 born ca 1884, died ca 1961; and Russ Pratt-7 BURR born ca 1887

385. ANNA / ANNE-5 CUSHING, sister of above, was born 20 Jan 1809 at Scituate, MA. She married Nichols LITCHFIELD, a shipwright, on 10 Dec 1828. He was the son of ____ LITCHFIELD and ____, and was born 18 July 1805; died 23 April 1879 MA. Anna-5 CUSHING died 5 Oct 1905.

Children of Anna-5 CUSHING and Nichols LITCHFIELD:
Surname **LITCHFIELD**

857. Lawrence   born 26 Dec 1829; died ____; married Sarah Minot LINCOLN 17 Nov 1852
858. Mary E.   born 30 Sept 1831; died ____; married Donald McKAY
859. Abigail   born ca 1833; died 1834
860. Allyne Cushing   born 15 July 1835; died ____; married Susan CARVER
         Child: Almira-7 LITCHFIELD born ca 1876
861. Almira Howe   born 17 Oct 1843; died 1922
    "Myra"   married George Sullivan MERRILL ca ___   (he born 19 Nov 1831; died 1907)

386. MARTIN-5 CUSHING, brother of above, was born 9 July 1810 at Scituate, MA. He married Laura Ann HOLT on 1 Jan 1840 at Lowell, MA. She was the daughter of ____HOLT and ____, and was born 31 May 1817 Lowell, died 3 Nov 1891 . Martin-5 CUSHING died 15 Feb 1883.

Children of Martin-5 CUSHING and Laura HOLT:
Surname **CUSHING**

862. Laura Ann   born 3 Nov 1841 Lowell; married Henry Turner JENKINS 27 Apr 1862
         (he s/o Turner Hatch JENKINS and Sarah L. WOODWARD)
         (he born 29 July 1836 Scituate; died 8 Feb 1893 Plymouth, MA)
863. Susan C.   born 3 Nov 1845; died 1 Jan 1846
864. Leafy M.   born 2 Mar 1848; died 14 July 1850 Scituate, MA.

387. ALLYNE-5 CUSHING, brother of above, was born 9 Dec 1811 at Scituate, MA. He married first to Sarah DAMON on 21 Dec 1834. She was the daughter of Elijah DAMON and Sally SEARS, and was born 15 Oct 1814; died 20 Mar 1872. He married second to Mary B. NICHELS (Gilman) on 30 Aug 1874. She was the daughter of Samuel S. NICHELS and Abigail MASON, and was born ca 1819; died ca 1913. Allyne-5 CUSHING died 14 Aug 1884.

Children of Allyne-5 CUSHING and Sarah DAMON:
Surname **CUSHING**

865. Sarah E.   born 27 Oct 1836; died 1910; married William H. SEARLES 1 Nov 1869
         (he s/o James SEARLES and Hannah ____)
866. Maria   born 24 Jan 1838; died 24 June 1924 Hingham, MA
867. Henry   born 14 Feb 1839; died 20 Apr 1854
868. Ellen   born 17 March 1840; died ____; married William FILLEBROWN 19 Dec 1877
869. Abbie L.   born 6 July 1842; died ____; married Samuel Lincoln GROSS
870. Irene   born 14 April 1845; died 14 May 1872
871. Hosea   born 21 Dec 1847; died ____
872. Elijah   born 30 Sep 1850; died 5 Oct 1888; married Abbie F. KING 18 June 1874

Children of Allyne-5 CUSHING and Sarah DAMON, continued:
Surname **CUSHING**

873. Martin	born 24 Feb 1852; died ____; married Elizabeth S " Lizzie " HUDSON 10 Nov 1880 (she dau/o Daniel HUDSON and Sarah PRAY)	

Children: Euylla-7 born 13 Sep 1881; George Henry-7 born 1 June 1884; Harold Martin-7 born 30 June 1887; Grace Burr-7 born ca 1888; and Charles Howe-7 CUSHING born ca 1891

874. Joseph	born 18 Jan 1854; died 11 Oct 1854	EOL
875. Josephine	born 7 Mar 1855; died 5 Sep 1855	EOL
876. Euylla Josephine	born 7 Mar 1856; died 1 Apr 1857	EOL
877. Euylla Josephine (2)	born 21 July 1858; died 18 Jan 1877 Somerville, MA	

401. MARTHA-5 BARRELL, daughter of James-4 BARRELL, Jr. (Deborah-3 BOWKER; James-2;1) and Martha FARROW, was born 3 Oct 1777 at Scituate, MA. She married Elisha HAYDEN, Jr. ca 1804. He was the son of Elisha HAYDEN and Deborah PIERCE, and was born ca 1790 Scituate, MA; died 1854. Martha-5 BARRELL died 11 April 1848 Scituate, MA.

Children of Martha-5 BARRELL and Elisha HAYDEN:
Surname **HAYDEN**

878. Elisha	born ca 1805 Scituate, MA	880. William (1) born ca 1809; died 1816
879. Deborah	born 1807; died ___; married Joel CURTIS ca ____	
881. Mary Ann	born ca 1811; died ___	
882. Martha	born 23 Sep 1814; died 1 Feb 1891; married Amos Hatch TILDEN, Sr. 22 Nov 1833	
883. un-named infant	born and died 1816	EOL
884. William (2)	born 1817; died ____	
885. Charles Walters	born ca 1822; died ___; married Deborah W. HUNT ca 1846	

404. ABEL-5 BARRELL, brother of above, was born 28 Jan 1784 Scituate, MA. He married Mary ALDEN on 8 Aug 1810. She was the daughter of Jonathan ALDEN and Experience WASHBURN, and was born 31 Dec 1786 Bridgewater, MA; died 5 Sep 1874 at Bridgewater. Abel-5 BARRELL died ____.

Children of Abel-5 BARRELL and Mary ALDEN:
Surname **BARRELL**

886. Hannah G.	born 8 Sep 1812; died 28 Feb 1879 MA; married John REED 28 Nov 1833	
887. Marianne	born 1 July 1820; died 15 Apr 1854	
888. Martha	born 26 Apr 1823; died ____	
889. George Whitfield	born 27 Dec 1825; died 1841	890. Thomas born 10 Apr 1829

407. DESIRE-5 BARRELL, sister of above, was born 4 Dec 1793 MA. She married James Newton SPARRELL, Jr. on 6 Oct 1822. He was the son of James N. SPARRELL, Sr. and Rachel TURNER, and was born 5 Mar/May 1798; died 1 Mar 1859 Norwell, Plymouth, MA. Desire-5 BARRELL died 6 Jan 1872

Children of Desire-5 BARRELL and James Newton SPARRELL, Jr. :
Surname **SPARRELL**

891. Martha James	born 16 Feb 1823; died ____
892. James Newton, III	born 18 Feb 1825; died 1877 Norwell, MA
	married Emeline GLEASON 6 July 1846 New Bedford, MA
	(she born ca 1823; died 28 June ____ New Bedford, MA)
893. Mary Turner	born 29 Jan 1827; died _____
894. Debbie Cushing Nash	born 11 May 1829; died ____; married Stephen B. SKIFF 30 Nov 1848
895. George Henry	born 10 May 1831; died ____
+ **896. CHARLES WARREN**	born 30 Dec 1835; died 6 May 1906 Norwell, MA; married Susan M. EWELL ca 1859
897. Desire L.	born 11 Oct 1837; died 1 Nov 1864 Scituate; married _____ WILLIAMSON ca ____

409. DAVIS -5 COLLAMORE CURTIS, son of Lydia-4 BOWKER (Edmund-3; James-2,1) and Abner CURTIS, was born 13 Oct 1776 at Hanover, Plymouth, MA. He married first to Charlotte LOVICE on 1 Nov 1795 at Hanover, MA. She was the daughter of ____ LOVICE and ____; and was born ca 1774; died 15 Feb 1862. He married second to Mary OLIVER 26 Dec 1799. He married third to Margaret STANLEY 13 July 1843. She was born ca 1797; died 1842. Davis -5 CURTIS died 15 Feb 1862 at Liberty, Waldo, Maine.

Children of Davis -5 CURTIS and Charlotte LOVICE:
Surname **CURTIS**

898. Hiram	born ____; died ____	902. Charlotte	born 1795; died 1876
899. John O.	born ____; died ____	903. Mary	born 1804; died ____
900. Lydia	born ____; died 1853	904. James Madison	born 1814; died 1868
901. Polly (1)	born____; died young		

Child of Davis-5 CURTIS and Mary OLIVER:
Surname **CURTIS**   905. Polly (2)   born ____; died ____

420. PAUL-5 BOWKER, son of Edmund-4 BOWKER (Edmund-3; James-2,1) and Patience BARROWS, was born 4 March 1797 at Hebron, Oxford, Maine. He married Mary KING Bearce , as her 2nd husband, on 6 Oct 1826 at Hebron. She was the daughter of ____ KING and ____, and was born ca 1796; died 1876. She was the widow of Gideon BEARCE. Paul-5 BOWKER died 26 Jan 1874 at Otisfield, Cumberland, Maine.

Children of Paul-5 BOWKER and Mary KING Bearce:
Surname **BOWKER**

+	**906. GIDEON B.**	born ca 1824; died 15 July 1865 Hilton Head, SC (Civil War)		
		married Avis E. ALLEN ca ____ (she born ca 1828; died ____)		
		(she dau/o Micah ALLEN and Elizabeth DUNHAM)		
	907. Cyrus King	born ca 1828; died 1865	908. Susan	born ca 1830; died ____
+	**909. JOSEPH HENRY**	born 17 June 1835; died 8/9 Dec 1917; 1 married Mary Jane IRISH 25 July 1854		
		2 married Rosamund C. KNIGHT 26 Mar 1870		

424. CAPTAIN JAMES-5 BOWKER, Jr., son of James-4 BOWKER (Edmund-3; James-2,1) and Judith CHASE, was born 10 May 1788 at Paris, Maine. He married Abigail BICKNELL ca ____. She was the daughter of John BICKNELL and his first wife Rebecca ____, and was born ____, died ____. Captain James-5 BOWKER, Jr. died Nov 1879.

Children of Captain James-5 BOWKER, Jr. and Abigail BICKNELL:
Surname **BOWKER**

	910. Whitmore Warhop	born 18 Nov 1817 Buckfield, ME; died ____
		married Mary CUMMINGS ca ____ (as her 2nd husband)
		(she dau /o Isaac CUMMINGS and ____) (she wid/o Col. Simon H. CUMMINGS)
		Children: Delphinus S-7 born 3 Dec 1859; and Charles W-7 BOWKER born 19 July 1861
	911. Abigail Bicknell	born 12 March 1819 Buckfield; died ____
	912. Caroline Augusta	born 1 Dec 1820 Buckfield; died ____; married Horatio DOWNER ca ____
+	**913. MARY TRACY**	born 29 Sep 1822 Buckfield, ME; died ____
		married Thomas Jones HILBORN 30 Oct 1853 Paris, Maine
		(he s/o Thomas HILBORN and Esther SMITH)
		(he born 16 Oct 1825; died 1870)
	914. Ordessa Marion	born 13 Feb 1828 Buckfield; died ____; married Mary JORDAN ca ____
		(she dau/o Noah JORDAN and ____ of Norway, Maine)
		Children: Cora Ellen-7 born 27 May 1858, married Sidney SANBORN; James E-7 born 8 Oct 1859;
		and Fannie Emma-7 BOWKER born 7 July 1862, married Gilbert P. ABBOTT
	915. Aravesta Delphina	born 23 Feb 1831 Buckfield; died ____
		married Prentiss Mellen COLBURN ca ____
	916. Delphinus Parris	born 7 Oct 1835 Paris, ME; died 28 April 1841

427. CYPRIAN-5 BOWKER, brother of above, was born 1 Dec 1793 at Paris, Maine. He married first to Rachel MAYHEW on 10 Mar 1815 Oxford, ME. She was the daughter of William MAYHEW and Joanne FARROW, and was born ca 1795, died ca 1837. He married second to Mary MAYHEW Cole 30 Oct 1838, as her second husband. She was the daughter of William MAYHEW and Joanna FARROW, and was born 22 Mar 1784, died ____. Cyrprian-5 BOWKER died 12 June 1872 Paris, ME .

Children of Cyprian-5 BOWKER and Rachel MAYHEW:
Surname **BOWKER**

+	**917. JOHN M.**	born ca 1816 Fairfax, ME; died 8 Nov 1894 Winnebago, WI
		married Dorothy " Dolly " STARBIRD ca 1838
		(she dau/o John STARBIRD and Sarah TOBEY)

Children of Cyprian-5 BOWKER and Rachel MAYHEW, continued:
Surname **BOWKER**

+	**918. CYPRIAN, Jr.**	born ca 1817 Woodstock, ME; died 8 Nov 1894 Winnebago, WI.
		married Abigail ROBBINS 30 Oct 1841 Woodstock, Oxford, ME
	919. James	born 25 Jan1822 Woodstock; died ____
	920. Rachel	born 28 May 1825 Woodstock; died 1830
	921. Joanna Mayhew Curtis	born 3 July 1827; died _____

429. EDMUND-5 BOWKER, brother of above, was born 3 Oct 1798. He married Mary Ann CHASE ca ____. She was the daughter of Merrill CHASE and Sally TUCKER, and was born 5 Aug 1803; died ____. Edmund-5 died ____.

Children of Edmund-5 BOWKER and Mary Ann CHASE:
Surname **BOWKER**   (children born Woodstock, Oxford, Maine)

	922. Esther	born 11 July 1827; died _____
	923. Anson W.	born 5 June 1828; died 24 Aug 1900 spinal meningitis
	924. Albion	born 17 May 1830; died 26 Mar 1909; married Angelina DUDLEY 24 July 1853
		(she dau/o Perrin DUDLEY and Paulina FELT) (she born 20 July 1833 Woodstock)
		Children: Oscar Fitzalan-7 born ca 1856; and Stella May-7 BOWKER born ca 1867
	925. George W.	born 7 Sep 1831; died 1913; single; lumberman in Washington state EOL
	926. Henry J.	born 29 Apr 1833; died 26 Feb 1838 EOL
+	**927. COLISTA/**	born 11 Aug 1836; died ____
	CALISTA	married Ambrose Shurtliff CURTIS ca ____
	928. Charles Henry	born 24 Oct 1838; died 1875
	929. Galen G.	born 1 Nov 1841; died ____ MD.
	930. Chauncey Whitman	born 29 Aug 1843; died 1 Nov 1849 EOL
	931. JAMES LORING	born 13 Aug 1845 Woodstock, Oxford, ME; died 30 Dec 1925 Woodstock
		married Ellen E. DAVIS 1 Jan 1866 (she born Dec 1849; died ____)
	932. Winfield	born ca 1855; died _____ 933. Ida M. W. born ca 1857; died ____

431. JUDITH CHASE-5 BOWKER, sister of above, was born 18 May 1802 Paris, Maine. She married James BICKNELL 11 July 1824. He was the son of John BICKNELL and Shuah SMALL, and was born 9 March 1802; died 27 Oct 1869. Judith-5 BOWKER died 6 Nov 1885.

Children of Judith Chase-5 BOWKER and James BICKNELL:
Surname **BICKNELL**

	934. Arabella	born 2 Oct 1825; died ____; married Merritt FARRAR ca _____
	935. James F.	born 7 May 1828; died ____; 1 married Rebecca S. FLETCHER.
		Children: Everett F-7 born 4 Apr 1854; married Lizzie BENNETT ; and Isabel-7 BICKNELL
		born 7 June 1859; died 7 Jan 1884
		2 married Emily C. TURNER Mason 15 Sep 1906 (she born ca 1842; died ____)
	936. Rosetta J.	born 10 Sept 1829; died 22 May 1906
		1 married Charles B. HALL ca ___; 2 married Joseph BICKNELL ca ____
+	**937. VIRGIL D P**	born 24 March 1833; died ____; married Frances WARREN ca ____
	938. Columbia P	born 30 May 1835; died ____; married Levi TURNER ca ____
	939. Levi P.	born 24 Aug 1837; died ca 1889
		moved to CA and was killed in a mine cave–in.
		Child: Fannie S-7 BICKNELL born 1 April 1864; married Warren LOTHROP
	940. Georgianna	born 15 Feb 1843; died ____; married James A. WARREN ca ____
		(he s/o Tristam WARREN and Jumalier FOSTER)(he born 2 July 1842; died ca 1901)
		Children: Charles A-7 born 10 Feb 1862, married Rosetta J. TURNER; and James W-7 WARREN
		born 5 May 1856; died 13 Feb 1871 – killed while in the woods)
+	**941. ISABELLA R.**	born 24 Feb 1845; died ca 1926 Buckfield, ME; married Cyrus De COSTER ca ____
		(he s/o Chandler Phinney De COSTER, Jr. and Tryphena HALL)
	942. Juliette	born 27 Feb 1847 Buckfield, ME; married Edwin Charles MAYHEW 20 Jan 1868
		(he s/o Deering MAYHEW and Polly HARLOW)(he born 31 Aug 1848; died 5 June 1914 Auburn, ME)

432. HARVEY-5 BOWKER, brother of above, was born 4 May 1804 Paris, Maine. He married first to Phoebe PROCTOR on 4 July 1824. She was the daughter of ____ PROCTOR and ____; and was born ca 1805; died 1825, possibly as a result of child-birth. He married second to Diana CURTIS on 21 Oct 1827. She was the daughter of Oliver CURTIS and Joanna MAYHEW;

and was born ca 1808; died 1899. Harvey⁻⁵ BOWKER died 26 May 1868.

Child of Harvey⁻⁵ BOWKER and Phoebe PROCTOR:
Surname **BOWKER**

943 Levi	born ca 1825; died ____; 1 married Ann Maria KEENE ca ____
	2 married Hannah L. HASEY ca 1863

Children of Harvey⁻⁵ BOWKER and Diana CURTIS:
Surname **BOWKER**   (children all born Woodstock, Oxford, Maine)

	944. Phebe	born ca 1829; died ____
	945. William Curtis	born 6 July1830; died ca 1850/51
+	**946. EDMUND**	born 31 Aug 1832; died 2 Sept 1902; 1 married Sarah B. KENDRICK ca 1853
		2 married Julia M⁻⁶ BRACKETT Jackson 22 Dec 1865 (# 937)
	947. Addison F.	born 10 Aug 1834; died 25 Apr 1918; married Judith Ann FARRAR ca 1859
		(she dau/o Nathan FARRAR and Susannah BROCK) (she born 1840; died 1930)
	948. Orin	born ca 1838; died ____
	949. Delphinus P.	born ca 1840/42; died 25 Feb 1875 Norway, Maine
		married Sarah P. HOPKINS 9 Dec 1862
+	**950. KILBOURN P.**	born Oct 1841; died ____; married Vesta Heath DOBLE Abbott ca 1868
+	**951. MARTHA ELLEN**	born 22 Apr 1846; died 24 Oct 1911 Worcester, MA (cancer of the uterus)
		married Charles Augustus GOWELL ca ____
		(he s/o Charles GOWELL and Emeline ____) (he born 23 June 1842 Abington, MA)

435. LAURA J⁻⁵ BOWKER, sister of above, was born 29 Mar 1808 at Scituate, MA. She married William Plummer BRACKETT ca 1831. He was the son of William P. BRACKETT and ____, and was born 27 Feb 1808 Westboro, Cumberland, ME; died 22 May 1878. Laura J⁻⁵ BOWKER died 29 Nov 1873.

Children of Laura J⁻⁵ BOWKER and William P. BRACKETT:
Surname **BRACKETT**   (all children born Maine)

+	**952. JULIA M.**	born 19 Dec 1832; died ____; 1 married Luther JACKSON ca ____
		2 married Edmund⁻⁶ BOWKER 22 Dec 1865 (# 931)
	953. Helen M.	born 6 Aug 1835; died 10 Aug 1935
	954. William P.	born 5 Apr 1838; died ____
	955. Laura (1)	born 14 Mar 1841; died 12 Aug 1842
+	**956. LAURA JANE (2)**	born 24 Dec 1842; died ____; married Adelbert BARTLETT ca ____
	957. Jeremiah C	born Aug 1845; died 7 Apr 1917 Lewiston, ME
	958. Lionel Orin.	born 22 Aug 1847; died 9 Jan 1914 Auburn, ME; married Sarah J ____ ca 1881
		Children: Velma G-⁷ born Sept 1876 Auburn, ME; and Hattie E-⁷ BOWKER born Feb 1889 Auburn, ME

443. LUCY⁻⁵ BOWKER, daughter of Warren⁻⁴ BOWKER (Edmund-³; James-²; ¹) and Rebecca Holmes CROSWELL, was born 11 Feb 1810 at Scituate, MA. She married True Glidden-⁷ WHITTIER 1 May 1837 at Boston, MA. He was the son of Nathaniel-⁶ WHITTIER (Nathaniel-⁵;⁴; Reuben-³; Nathaniel-²; Thomas-¹) and Nancy MERRILL, and was born 20 Aug 1805; died 3 Mar 1892 Boston Lucy⁻⁵ BOWKER died 5 Jan 1897 Boston.

Children of Lucy⁻⁵ BOWKER and True-⁷ WHITTIER:
Surname **WHITTIER**

	959. Caroline Rebecca	born 3 Feb 1838 Vienna, ME; died ____
+	**960. MOZART**	born 16 Dec 1839 Vienna, ME; died 1927 Boston, MA
		1 married Anna Ann TRIPP ca ____ (she born ca 1837; died 30 June 1913)
		2 married Matilda YOUNG Thayer 3 June 1894 (born ca 1852)
	961. Cornelia Corinna	born 21 June 1843 Vienna, ME; died 27 Mar 1893 Boston, MA
	962. Henry Croswell	born 24 Apr 1845 / 46 Farmington, ME; died ___
		1 married Harriet M. GLIDDEN 18 Jan 1865 Child: Ira G-⁷ WHITTIER born ca 1866
		(she dau/o Ira F. GLIDDEN and Harriet ____) (she born ca 1847)
		2 married Frances / Fannie NORTHRUP ca 1878
		Children: May B-⁷ WHITTIER born Apr 1879 RI; F. Millie-⁷ born Sep 1881RI; and Hope L C-⁷ WHITTIER born Mar 1892 RI
+	**963. NATHANIEL** **BOWKER**	born 17 Apr 1847 Farmington, ME; died 4 Dec 1911 Adel, GA.
		1 married Cynthia Frances BECKLER 2 Apr 1868 Boston, MA
		2 married Eva Mary ANDREWS 15 Oct 1883 (born 1851; died 1933)

Children of Lucy-⁵ BOWKER and True-⁷ WHITTIER, continued:
Surname **WHITTIER**

964. Frances Allen	born 3 Oct 1848 Farmington, ME; died 5 Aug 1896 Boston, MA
	married Eugene Barnes NELSON 20 Nov 1872
	(he s/o George NELSON and Elizabeth ____)
	(he born Nov 1847 Hillsboro, NH; died 13 Oct 1918 Hillsboro)
	Children: Henry E-⁷ born 1874; Mabel W-⁷ born 1877; and Edith W-⁷ NELSON born 1879
965. Charles Collyer	born 4 Oct 1851 Farmington, ME; died 24 Oct 1924 unmarried

452. WATTS-⁵ BOWKER, son of Major Levi-⁴ BOWKER (Joseph-³; James-²,¹) and Betsey WATTS, was born 12 Dec 1790 Machias, Washington, Maine. He married Lydia Lockwood STICKNEY ca ____ . She was the daughter of Samuel STICKNEY and Elizabeth JAMES ; and was born 20 May 1794; died ____ . Watts-⁵ BOWKER died ca 1850 Shelbourne, Nova Scotia, CA. .

Children of Watts-⁵ BOWKER and Lydia STICKNEY:
Surname **BOWKER**   (all children born Machias, Washington Co., ME)

+	**966. SARAH ANN**	born ca 1814; died ca 1880; married James A. GETCHELL
		(he s/o Marshall GETCHELL and Mary HOLMES)
		(he born 25 Oct 1814; died 25 Feb 1887)
	967. Elizabeth	born ca 1816; died ca 1852; married James FERRIS EOL
	968. Margaret	born 8 Aug 1818; died 30 May 1896; married Jacob FOSTER(as his 2ⁿᵈ wife)
		(he s/o Deacon Samuel FOSTER and Comfort SCOTT)
		(he born 6 Dec 1818; died 4 March 1901)(1 m. Deborah SMITH)
+	**969. WINSLOW**	born ca 1824-25; died 2 Feb 1894; married Hannah Jewett BOYNTON
+	**970. WILLIAM CLARK**	born ca 1830; died ca 1896; married Ruth H. WATTS ca 1850
		(she dau/o Samuel WATTS and Comfort SCOTT)
		(she born 27 April 1839; died 29 Jan 1917 Machias, ME)
+	**971. WATTS HENRY**	born 29 Dec 1836; died 20 Jan 1912 ; married Julia M. LYON 3 May 1858
		(she dau/o James LYON and Susan LONGFELLOW)

453. LYDIA-⁵ BOWKER, sister of above, was born 1 Nov 1793 Machias, Maine. She married Otis P. HANSCOM 11 May 1817. He was the son of Isaac HANSCOM and Betsey PINEO, and was born 30 May 1795; died 19 June 1873. Lydia-⁵ BOWKER died 19 May 1874.

Children of Lydia-⁵ BOWKER and Otis HANSCOM:
Surname **HANSCOM**

	972. Betsey Anna	born 1 Oct 1818; died 1847; married Marshall HARMON 21 Sept 1836
		(he s/o Japhet HARMON and Sarah GETCHELL) (he born 13 April 1810 Machias)
+	**973. SIMON OTIS**	born 20 Nov 1820/23; died 2 Feb 1899
		married Julia Raymond WHITE 2 May 1846 Machias, ME
	974. Laura	born 6 Feb 1824; died 1899; married Nathaniel CROCKER 3 June 1855
	975. Mary	born ca 1826; died 1827
+	**976. WATTS BOWKER**	born 14 June 1829; died 27 Apr 1900; married Sarah Perkins ROBINSON 19 Dec 1852
		(she born 12 Oct 1833; died 16 Feb 1920)
	977. Deborah	born ca 1832; died 1905; married William STONE
	978. Isabella " Belle "	born 16 Nov 1834; died 19 Sep 1902 Machias, ME
		married John INGLEE(as his 2ⁿᵈ wife) ca 1859
		(he born April 1817; died 25 Oct 1909)
		(he s/o Ebenezer INGLEE and Elizabeth SMITH)
	979. Lucinda	born Aug 1838 ; died 1931
		1 married Joseph Whitney LONGFELLOW 27 Sept 1858; div Oct 1880
		(he born 8 Feb 1836 Machias; died ca 1926)
		2 married Elisha F BLACKMAN ca 1883
		(he s/o Eben BLACKMAN and Hannah FOLSOM)
		(he born Apr 1833 East Machias, ME; died 10 Dec 1900 Augusta, ME

454. LEVI-⁵ BOWKER, Jr., brother of above, was born 26 Aug 1795 at Machias, Washington, ME. He married Martha G. CROCKER on 22 May 1822 at Machias. She was the daughter of Simeon CROCKER and Katherine WATERHOUSE, and was born 2 July 1803; died 24 May 1886. Levi-⁵ BOWKER, Jr. died 19 June 1887.

Children of Levi-5 BOWKER, Jr. and Martha G. CROCKER:
Surname **BOWKER**

	980. Simeon	born Nov 1823; died ____ (living 1900) WA
	981. Wellington	born 2 Dec 1824; died 11 Aug 1825 Marshfield, Washington, ME
+	**982. NATHAN**	born 15 May 1826; died 18 July 1910 ; married Mary Abigail BERRY ca 1850
	STEPHEN	(she dau/o Stephen BERRY and ____)
		(she born 2 Nov 1827 ME; died 11 April 1911)
+	**983. FERDINAND**	born ca 1830; died ca 1852; married Lucy-3 BOYNTON 2 Oct 1850 Machias
		(she dau/o Stephen-2 BOYNTON and Hannah JEWETT)
		(she married 2nd to Albert MOORS)
	984. Warren	born 8 Mar 1832; died 24 Feb 1834
	985. George William	born ca 1834; died between 1900-1910
		married Lucinda N ___ ca ___ (she born Feb 1846 ME; died ____)

Child: Harold George-7 BOWKER born ca 1889; died ca 1964)

	986. Enoch E.	born ca 1835/6; died 9 Nov 1868 Machias, ME
	987. Martha A.	born 4 April 1837/40; died 12 Sep 1902 Machias
		married Roscoe G. BOYNTON ca ____
		(he s/o Stephen BOYNTON and Hannah JEWETT) (he born July 1836)

Children : Elmira-7 born ca 1863; Annie-7 born ca 1865; Emily -7 born ca 1868,
married Bradford ESTEY ca ____; and George-7 BOYNTON born Oct 1870

	988. Hannah	born ca 184_; died ____

455. BETSEY-5 BOWKER, sister of above, was born 2 Sept 1797 at Machias, ME. She married Simeon GETCHELL on 1 Sep 1818. He was the son of Joseph GETCHELL, JR. and Sally BERRY, and was born May 1795; died ____.

Children of Betsey-5 BOWKER and Simeon GETCHELL:
Surname **GETCHELL**

	989. Levi B.	born ca____; died Oct 1900 Machias; married Julia A CROCKER ca ____
	990. Willard	born 8 Apr 1822; died 5 Dec 1899 MI
		married Susanna Rebecca CHASE 7 Nov 1848
		(she dau/o Henry CHASE and Rebecca SCOTT) (she born Sept 1824; died 1901)

Children: Frederick W-7 born ca 1849; Rebecca-7 born May 1851, married Fred SMITH;
and Nellie T-7 GETCHELL born ca 1856

	991. Frederick Warren	born 31 Aug 1825; died 1 Nov 1906 ND; married Martha HANSCOM 2 Oct 1852
		(she dau/o Moses HANSCOM and Martha Lyon KELLY)
		(she born 14 Dec 1832 East Machias; died 14 July 1911 Barnes, ND

Children: Judson Ray-7 born June 1855 ME; died 3 Feb 1934 Eugene, OR, married
Sarah S. WADSWORTH; and Simeon S-7 GETCHELL born ca 1860 MN

+	**992. SARAH**	born 14 Aug 1827; died 20 July 1864 Marshfield, ME;
		married William P. LYON ca 1847
		(he born 25 Jan 1818; died 21 Nov 1862)(he s/o Henry LYON and Betsey CROCKER)
	993. John Randolph	born 20 Dec 1829; died 18 Sep 1910 MN
		married Rebecca HOLMES ca 1860 (she born ca 1825; died ca 1860)
	994. Lucinda	born 16 July 1833; died 1911; married Daniel S. CHASE 19 Nov 1853
		(he born 13 June 1826; died 22 Feb 1909 East Machias, ME)

Children: Laura F-7 born June 1858; Walter F-7 born 1859; and George C-7 CHASE born 1860

	995. Andrew Mc K.	born 13 May 1835; died 17 Oct 1889 Franklin, MI
		married Emily J. HAGUE ca 1861
		(she dau/o Thomas HAGUE and Charlotte __) (she born ca 1831 England)

Children: Morton-7 born ca 1872; and Frank H-7 GETCHELL born ca 1874

	996. Agnes Bowker	born 17 Feb 1839; died 6 March 1925 Auburn, Maine
		1 married Joshua D. WATTS 17 Jan 1863
		(he s/o Thomas Greenleaf WATTS and Ruth MARSTON)
		2 married Thomas Thompson MERRY (as his 3rd wife) 8 Oct 1874

457. SARAH / SALLY-5 BOWKER, sister of above, was born 10 April 1802 at Machias, Maine. She married Ellis HANSCOM ca ____. He was the son of Isaac HANSCOM and Betsey PINEO, and brother of Otis P. HANSCOM (above), and was born ____; died ____. Sarah-5 BOWKER died ca ____.

Children of Sarah/Sally-5 BOWKER and Ellis HANSCOM:
Surname **HANSCOM**

997. Fred B.	born Aug 1829 ME; died ____; 1 married Susan BURNHAM ca _____	
	2 married Mary A. BASLEY ca ____ (she born ca 1836 ME)	
998. James O.	born ca 1831 ; died ____; married Mary/ May G. SMITH (she born ca 1837)	
999. George Edward	born Feb 1840; died ____	
	married Martha H. PEACH Crocker (as her 2nd husband) ca ____	
	(she born Sept 1832 ; died 1908)	
1000. Hannah B.	born ca 1833; died ____; unmarried	EOL
1001. Mary E.	born ca 1836; died ____; married George A. PARLIN	
+ **1002. LADWICK HOLWAY**	born ca1844; died ____; married Ida Ann SMITH ca 1864 Machias (she born 2 Jul 1845 Nova Scotia)	
1003. Leverett	born ca 1847; died ____; unmarried	EOL
1004. Horace	born Aug 1848; died 21 July 1909; unmarried	EOL

458. DEBORAH-5 BOWKER, was born July 1805 at Machias, Washington, Maine. She married first to James Mc KELLAR ca ____. He was the son of John Mc KELLAR and Martha Mc CARTER, and was born 27 Dec 1775 at St. Georges, Lincoln, Maine; died ____ probably Machias, ME. She married second to William BUGBEE 25 Nov 1846. He was the son of _____ BUGBEE and ____; and was born 9 Apr 1798; died 4 March 1853.

Children of Deborah-5 BOWKER and James Mc KELLAR:
Surname **Mc KELLAR**   (children born Machias, Maine)

1005. Eben	born 28 Mar 1830/31; died _____; married Sarah M. COLLINS ca _____
	Children: Deborah Mary-7 born May 1870 MA; and James M-7 Mc KELLAR born May 1873 MA,
	married Marian WHITE (children: James8, and twins Percy8 and Harold8 Mc KELLAR)
1006. Mary B.	born 5 June 1833; died 18 June 1920 Machias; never married EOL
1007. William	born ____; died ____

459. FREDERICK-5 BOWKER, brother of above, was born 25 June 1808 Machias, Washington, Maine. He married Rachel Ann DUTTON on 3 July 1851. She was the daughter of James DUTTON and Mary GOULD, and was born 19 July 1825 Delaware; died 16 Nov 1885. Frederick-5 BOWKER died 25 Oct 1888 at Camden, NJ, and is buried at Wilmington, Delaware.
Children of Frederick-5 BOWKER and Rachel Anna DUTTON:
Surname **BOWKER**   (children born Delaware)

1008. Mary Gould	born 19 April 1852; died 3 June 1924;
	married Rev. Thomas Love SPRINGER 9 Nov 1875
	(he born 25 Aug 1849; died 5 Apr 1928)
	Child: Courtland Bowker-7 SPRINGER born 15 May 1878
1009. Emily B.	born June 1857; died ____; married Dr. Robert SHIMMELL/SHIMWELL ca 1881
	(he born April 1851 PA; parents born England)
	Children: Georgia B-7 born Feb 1883 PA; and Emily-7 SHIMMELL born June 1892; neither one ever married
1010. Levi Watts	born 9 May 1858; died 5 Dec 1898 Philadelphia, PA; ship carpenter
1011. George McClellan	born 14 Dec 1861; died ____; never married EOL
1012. Harry	born ca 1865; died ____ 1013. Frank born ca 1867; died ____

467. THOMAS-5 FARRIN, son of Nancy-4 BOWKER (Joseph-3; James-2,1) and Elizabeth COWING, was born ca 1793 at Brunswick, Maine. He married Lucy SNOWMAN ca 1822. She was the daughter of ____ SNOWMAN and ___; and was born ca 1793; died 1829. Thomas-5 FARRIN died ca 1827.

Child of Thomas-5 FARRIN and Lucy SNOWMAN:
Surname **FARRIN**

1014. Charles David	born ca 1823; died ca 1855 at sea near Indonesia
	1 married Mary Ann SAVAGE ca 1838 (she born ____; died 1839)
	Child: Susan-7 FARRIN born ca 1839; died 1852 ME
	2 married Mary WALKER ca 1843 Child: Charles A-7 FARRIN born ca 1844; died 1930

469. GUSTAVUS ADOLPHUS-5 DICKMAN, son of Rachel-4 BOWKER (Joseph-3; James-2,1) and Thomas DICKMAN, was born ca 1805/06 Augusta, Kennebec, Maine. He married Abigail BURBANK 15 June 1830 at Augusta. She was the daughter of _____ BURBANK and ____, and was born 21 April 1810; died 8 Dec 182 at Augusta, ME. Gustavus-5 DICKMAN died 11 Feb 1865 (obit notice) in Brooklyn, Kings, NY. He was a ship's captain.

Children of Gustavus[-5] DICKMAN and Abigail BURBANK:
Surname **DICKMAN**   (children born Augusta, Maine)

1015. Helen Parlin	born ca 1831; died 3 Feb 1912 Brooklyn, NY	
1016. Mary Augusta	born ca 1834; died 19 June 1905	
1017. Gustavus Franklin	born ca 1835; died 17 Nov 1881 Brooklyn, NY; a ship broker	
	married Louisa C. FORBES 4 Oct 1860(she born ca 1839 NY)	

Children: Mary B-[7] born ca 1862 NY; and Fred[-7] DICKMAN born 6 Apr 1864 NY

1018. Charles Burbank	born Apr 1841; died 18 Feb 1901 Philadelphia, PA; Sea Captain/ US Navy
	1 married Emma M. STAYLEY/STANLEY 13 Feb 1864
	(she dau/o George STAYLEY/STANLEY and _____)
	2 married Elizabeth "Lizzie" B. SNYDER Tice ca 188/90
1019. Thomas	born ca 1842; died 20 Aug 1888 Brooklyn, NY
1020. George	born 29 Apr 1846; died 15 Nov 1898 London, England (while on a trip)
1021. William Adriance	born ca 1852; died 3 July 1881 Brooklyn, NY; single EOL

471. CONSTANTINE[-5] DICKMAN, brother of above, was born ca 1807 Augusta, Maine. He married Pauline FIELD on 5 April 1832 at Gardiner, Maine. She was the daughter of Benjamin FIELD and Anna _____, and was born 30 March 1814 Gardiner, ME; died ca 1899 Gardiner, ME. Constantine[-5] DICKMAN died 18 Dec 1892.

Children of Constantine-[5] DICKMAN and Pauline FIELD:
Surname **DICKMAN**   (children born Maine)

1022. Frances A.	born ca 1833; died ___	1024. Harriet M. "Hattie"	born ca 1840; died ca 1870
1023. Julia P.	born ca 1835; died ___		

474. DELANE[-5] WRIGHT, daughter of Hannah[-4] BOWKER/BUKER (Joseph[-3]; James-[2,1]) and Abel WRIGHT, was born 14 Apr 1810 at Lewiston, Maine. She married Cotton A. DURGIN ca 1831. He was the son of Andrew DURGIN and Sarah/Sally SARGENT, and was born Aug 1802 at Stafford, NH; died 4 Oct 1871 at Greenfield, WI. Delane[-5] WRIGHT died ca 1865 Middleton, WI. Cotton DURGIN married second to Eliza AMES on 14 June 1868 WI.

Children of Delane-[5] WRIGHT and Cotton A. DURGIN:
Surname **DURGIN**   (all children born Newburgh , Maine)

	1025. Sarah A.	born ca 1832; died 21 Aug 1865 Belfast, Waldo, ME; married Charles A BROWN
	1026. Lorenzo Wright	born Nov 1833; died 18 Nov 1914 Butte, CA.
	1027. Isaac Allard	born 23 Jan 1836; died 17 May 1897 Yreka, CA
		married Esther AMO ca _____ (she born ca 1854; died 1918)
	1028. Josiah L.	born 30 Nov 1838; died 29 Oct 1919 Salt Lake City, UT
+	**1029. JOHN VARNEY**	born 20 Jan 1840; died 10 Jan 1915; married Ellen FITZPATRICK 20 Oct 1865 WI
	1030. Andrew E.	born ca 1841; died 23 Aug 1894 Tunnel City, WI
	1031. William	born ca 1849; died _____

475. LORENZO DOW[-5] WRIGHT, brother of above, was born 3 Aug 1812 at Lewiston, Maine. He married Nancy A. ROBBINS ca 1857. She may have been his 2nd wife. She was the daughter of _____ ROBBINS and _____; and was born 1823/24 NH; died _____ Nashua, NH. Lorenzo Dow [-5] WRIGHT died 11 Nov 1884 Nashua, NH.

Children of Lorenzo Dow[-5] WRIGHT and Nancy ROBBINS:
Surname **WRIGHT**

1032. Nancy	born ca 1858 NH; died _____
1033. Eunice R.	born ca 1861 NH; died 6 Aug 1899 Upton, MA
	married Daniel Mc QUESTEN 7 June 1882 (his 2nd marriage)
	(he s/o Simon Mc QUESTEN and Rhoda ___; he born ca 1850)
1034. Josephine	born ca 1865 NH; died ___; 1 married George E. WATSON 25 Dec 1882 Nashua, NH
	(he s/o Elijah WATSON and Philinda ____)
	(he born ca 1854; killed 9 Jan 1892 by railroad cars at Dunstable, MA) buried NH
	2 married James Monroe FRANKLIN 20 Apr 1892 Gardner, MA
	(marriage and census forms state that he was black/ colored)
	(he was the s/o Benjamin FRANKLIN and Laura ROGERS)
	(he born 19 Mar 1863 Fitchburg, MA; died ____)
1035. Helen L.	born 1870; died 28 June 1927; married _____ BENNETT ca ____

BOWKER Descendants of James-1
The Fifth American Generation

482. ISAAC HALL-5 BOWKER, son of Lazarus-4 BOWKER (Joseph-3; James-2,1) and Agnes LENNIN/ LENNAN, and was born 4 June 1807 at Georgetown, Maine. He married Eliza _____ 5 Jan 1836 at Phippsburg, Maine. She was the daughter of _____ and ____, and was born ____; died ____. Isaac Hall-5 BOWKER died 21 March 1859 at Phippsburg, Sagahadoc, Maine

Children of Isaac Hall-5 BOWKER and Eliza ____:
Surname **BOWKER**

1036. Edward Payson	born 12 Oct 1836 Bangor, ME; died 17 Feb 1865 Phippsburg married Bertha A. LEONARD 3 March 1864 Bath, ME	
1037. John James	born 28 Mar 1838 Bangor; died 15 June 1840 Phippsburg	EOL
1038. Eliza Ann	born 23 May 1840; died ____; married Alonzo Parsons WILDES 30 Nov 1865 (he born 8 Dec 1840; died 14 March 1886 Bath, ME) (he s/o John WILDES and Prudence BLAISDELL)	

Children: Annie P-7 born ca 1861, died ca 1925; and Alonzo F-7 WILDES born 4 Mar 1872, died 30 June 1944; married Mary B. SAFFORD 26 Aug 1916 Bath, ME

+ 1039. **ISAAC NEWTON**	born 15 Aug 1842 Phippsburg; died 22 Feb 1924 Bath, ME; ship pilot married Maria Jane BROWN ca 1872 (she born Dec 1841)	
1040. Harriet Emeline	born 29 Aug 1844; died 30 June 1859 Phippsburg	EOL
1041. Ella Jane Porter	born 17 May 1849 Phippsburg; died ____ married Daniel K. FOSTER 24 Oct 1872 Bath, ME	
1042. Cyrus Augustus	born Nov 1852 Phippsburg; died 2 Feb 1854 Phippsburg, ME	EOL

487. FLAVEL-5 BOWKER. son of James-4 BOWKER (Joseph-3; James-2,1) and Eunice BATCHELDER, was born 7 July 1808 at Phippsburg, ME. He married Angeline REED 9 Dec 1835 ME. She was the daughter of Col. Andrew REED and Beatrice Mc COBB, and was born 9 Oct 1808 Phippsburg; died 19 May 1888 Brunswick. Flavel-6 BOWKER died 17 Nov 1891 Brunswick.

Children of Flavel-5 BOWKER and Angeline REED:
Surname **BOWKER** (all children born Phippsburg, Maine)

1043. Ann Mary — born 12 Nov 1836; died 16 Jan 1915 Brunswick, ME
married Capt. Stephen Collins MORRISON ca ____
(he born 9 Sep 1828 ME; died 1913 Brunswick, ME)
(he s/o Moses MORRISON and Elizabeth LOWELL)
1044. Hannah Augusta — born 3 April 1839; died ____
1045. Abbie Angier — born ca 1842; died ___; married Walter Leavitt CLIFT ca 1870
Children: Abbie L-7 born 7 Aug 1871; James W-7 born 25 Sep 1878; and Thomas Reed-7 CLIFT born 13 June 1880
1046. Caroline Reed — born ca 1844/45; died _____; married Charles Davis THYNG ca 1869
Children: Herbert M-7 born 15 May 1875; Arthur Davis-7 born Feb 1876; and Cora H-7 THYNG born July 1878
1047. Edwin Tewksbury — born ca 1847/48; died ____; married Mary Alice PENNELL ca 1872
Children: Frederick T-7 born 4 Mar 1873 ME ; and Julia F-7 BOWKER born 20 Nov 1878
1048. Frederick McCobb — born 5 June 1853; died 6 Aug 1872
1049. Frances Drummond — born 3 Nov 1855; died ____; married Dr. Robert G. STANWOOD ca ____
Child: Edna G-7 STANWOOD born Sept 1883

489. ELBRIDGE-5 BOWKER, brother of above, was born 5 April 1811 at Georgetown, Maine. He married first to Elizabeth D. PERCY on 18 Dec 1838. She was the daughter of James PERCY and Sarah ___, and was born 10 June 1812; died 1 May 1856. He married second to Angeline R. MARR on 5 March 1861 at Phippsburg, Maine. She was the daughter of John MARR and Louisa Lois TIBBETTS, and was born ca 1830/31; died 9 Dec 1885.

Children of Elbridge-5 BOWKER and Elizabeth PERCY:
Surname **BOWKER** (all children born Phippsburg, Maine)

1050. Elizabeth Eunice — born 23 July 1841; died ____
1051. Isaiah — born 13 May 1843; died 16 May 1864 Phippsburg
+ 1052. **CUTLER ELBRIDGE** — born 27 Oct 1845; died 21 Apr 1922 Bath, Maine
married Mary Ann BLACK 9 March 1873 (she born June 1846; died 1931)
+ 1053. **ADELIA LORING** — born 24 June 1848; died 1913 Harpswell, Maine
married John R. EASTMAN 25 Nov 1869
1054. James Percy — born 26 April 1852; died ca 1904 Bath, ME; married Lucretia HEALD 24 Feb 1885
Child: Eveline-7 BOWKER born ca 1885

Child of Elbridge[-5] BOWKER and Angeline MARR:
Surname **BOWKER**
> 1055. Lucretia Nichols.   born ca 1865 ME; died ____; married Milford C. OLIVER 7 Aug 1912

492. TIMOTHY BATCHELDER[-5] BOWKER, son of James[-4] BOWKER (Joseph[-3]; James[-2,1]) and Eunice BATCHELDER, was born 1 Nov 1816 Maine. He married Elizabeth Percy MORRISON ca 1841. She was the daughter of ___ MORRISON and ___; and was born 29 Dec 1817; died ca 1920. Timothy[-5] BOWKER died 1920.

Children of Timothy[-5] BOWKER and Elizabeth MORRISON:
Surname **BOWKER**   (children all born Phippsburg, Sagadahoc, Maine

1056. Anna Maria	born ca 1842; died ____	
1057. Beulah Percy	born 6 May 1844; died 22 Nov 1859	EOL
1058. Emma Jane	born ca 1847; died 1920; married John H. CAMPBELL (he born ca 1835 ME)	

+ **1059. FREEMAN CLARK**   born 27 April 1850; died 1933 Bath, Maine
married Annie L. SPRAGUE 2 March 1874

> 1060. George Morrison   born 23 June 1853; died 1928; married Olive Ann SPINNEY ca 1892
> 1061. Charlotte Amelia   born 6 March 1855; died ____; married Dr. Frank Alvin ROGERS 30 Nov 1876
> (he s/o John Alvin ROGERS and Julia Ann NEALLY) (he born Oct 1855 ME
> Children: Amabel[-7] born Sept 1881 NE, married Horatio Perkins PARKER; Frank L[-7] born Feb 1884 MA;
> and Alice M[-7] ROGERS born Oct 30 !888 Ma; died ___ NY
> 1062. Sewall B.   born 14 May 1857; died 15 Sep 1857   EOL

+ **1063. WILLIAM RICHARDSON**   born 30 March 1860; died 15 Dec 1932 Phippsburg, ME
1 married Abbie E WALLACE ca 1891
2 married Hattie/Hallie Mc PHEE 21 Dec 1918
(she dau/o James Mc PHEE and Myra ____) (she born ca 1879; died ____)

> 1064. Mary Morse   born 5 Dec 1862; died 5 Jan 1863   1065. Lena P.   born ca 1866; died ____

494. NANCY[-5] BOWKER, sister of above, was born ca 1823 at Phippsburg, Maine. She married Charles SYLVESTER on 4 May 1848 at ____. He was the son of ____ SYLVESTER and ____, and was born 19 June 1798; died 5 Dec 1858. Nancy[-5] BOWKER died ca 1910.

Children of Nancy[-5] BOWKER and Charles SYLVESTER:
Surname **SYLVESTER**
> 1066. Sarah E.   born 31 Aug 1849 ME; died 29 April 1879; married Charles MASDEN 20 Mar 1870
> 1067. Della   born 22 Aug 1852; died after 1910; married Oscar M. TITUS
> 1068. Charles O.   born 31 March 1857; died 1920; married Mary EDGECOMB ca 1889

512. BENJAMIN[-5] BOWKER, Jr., son of Benjamin[-4] BOWKER (Richard-[3,2]; James[-1]) and Jemima HILL, was born 19 Apr 1789 Hanson, MA. He married Hannah Pratt RAMSDELL on 29 Sep 1811. She was the daughter of John Stockbridge RAMSDELL and Hannah ALLEN, and was born 15 Feb 1791; died 28 Sep 1845 Hanson, Plymouth, MA. Benjamin[-5] BOWKER, Jr. died 16 May 1849.

Children of Benjamin[-5] BOWKER, Jr. and Hannah Pratt RAMSDELL:
Surname **BOWKER**
> 1069. Mary Jane   born 15 June 1812; died ____

+ **1070. TURNER**   born 5 May 1813; died ca 1855
married Harriet TILDEN 20 Dec 1835 Marshfield, MA

514. GAD/ GARD[-5] BOWKER, brother of above, was born 30 May 1795 at Hanson, Plymouth, MA. He married Clarissa RAMSDELL on 20 Nov 1823. She was the daughter of John Stockbridge RAMSDELL and Hannah ALLEN, and was born 15 Feb 1791; died ca 1845. Gad[-5] BOWKER died July 1876 Hanson, MA.

Children of Gad[-5] BOWKER and Clarissa RAMSDELL:
Surname **BOWKER**   (children born Hanson, Plymouth, MA)

+ **1071. JOHN ADAMS**   born 4 Sept 1824; died _____
married Mary Ann WILLIS 28 Sep 1856 Hanson, MA.
(she dau/o John WILLIS and Adelia YOUNG)

Children of Gad[-5] BOWKER and Clarissa RAMSDELL, continued:
Surname **BOWKER**

	1072. Rosella W.	born 28 Jan 1827; died 19 Apr 1874
+	**1073. ANDREW**	born 12 Dec 1828; died 26 Apr 1891 Hanson, MA
	CLARENCE	1 married Sarah Jane HOUSE; 2 married Betsey BARKER 15 June 1855
	1074. Luther	born 4 Jan 1831; died 5 Sep 1875 Hanson, MA
+	**1075. GEORGE T.**	born ca 1833/34; died 31 Oct 1881
		1 married Miranda C. WALKER; 2 married Alice S. HARDING
+	**1076. HANNAH**	born Nov 1836; died 21 March 1909 Springfield, MA
		married M. Nymphus CHANDLER 28 Apr 1866 (as his 2nd wife)
		(he s/o Stetson CHANDLER and Eliza ____) (he born May 1821)

515. JOHN EDWARD[-5] **DOTEN / DOTY,** son of Bathsheba[-4] BOWKER (Luke[-3]; Richard[-2]; James-1) and John DOTEN / DOTY, was born 3 July 1780 at Pembroke, MA. He married Elizabeth[-7] VOSE on 6 Sep 1804 at Bridgewater, VT. She was the daughter of Thomas V[-6] VOSE (Lt. Samuel[-5]; Lt. Robert[-4]; Lt. Henry[-3]; Capt. Thomas[-2]; Robert[-1]) and _____, and was born 14 Mar 1783 Goffstown, NH; died 7 Aug 1865 Pomfret, VT.. John Edward[-5] DOTEN / DOTY a teacher and civil engineer, died 8 April 1863 at Pomfret, VT.

Children of John Edward[-5] DOTEN/DOTY and Elizabeth VOSE:
Surname **DOTEN / DOTY**   (all children born Pomfret, VT)

	1077. Calvin	born 30 Aug 1805; died 14 Jan 1834

Children of John Edward[-5] DOTEN/DOTY and Elizabeth VOSE, continued:
Surname **DOTY/DOTEN**

+	**1078. SARAH MATILDA**	born 12 Feb 1808; died 22 Aug 1892 Pomfret, VT
		married Henry Little PAGE 14 Mar 1830 Woodstock, VT
		(he born 27 Dec 1801 Salem, NH; died 13 May 1844)
		(he s/o Abner PAGE and Jane LITTLE)
	1079. Hosea	born 29 Nov 1809;died 17 Jan 1886 Woodstock, VT
		1 married Lois PADDOCK 9 Dec 1834 Pomfret, VT
		(she dau/o John PADDOCK and Lucy VAUGHN)
		(she born 27 May 1809 Woodstock, VT; died 2 Feb 1857 Woodstock)
		Child: Abby Murdock[-7] DOTEN / DOTY born 1 Aug 1840
		2 married Harriet Frances WARE 27 May 1858 Pomfret, VT
		(she born 23 Jan 1829; died 18 Nov 1858)
		(she dau/o Leonard WARE and Nancy Ann THOMAS)
		3 married Julia Elvira WOOD 4 July 1868 Pomfret, VT
		(she born 3 Nov 1840 Hartwell, VT; died _____)
		(she dau/o Joshua WOOD and Belinda LATIMER)
	1080. Samuel Spencer	born 23 Oct 1811; died 5 Jan 1891
		1 married Charlotte WINN 17 July 1843 Pomfret, VT
		(she dau/o Otis WINN and Rebecca MARCY)
		(she born 29 Mar 1819 Windsor, VT; died 2 Nov 1859 Pomfret, VT)

Children: Edward Otis[-7] born 3 Mar 1844; Elizabeth Rebecca[-7] born 24 May 1846, died 26 Oct 1865; William Emery[-7] born 3 Mar 1850, died 29 Jan 1853; and Fred Ware[-7] DOTEN/DOTY born 30 Jan 1855

		2 married Cynthia Irene WOOD 26 June 1861
		(she dau/o Amos WOOD and Eunice VAIL)
		(she born 25 Feb 1824 Pomfret, VT; died 22 Mar 1874 Pomfret, VT)
	1081. Electa	born 19 July 1813; died 26 Oct 1895 Pomfret, VT
		married Henry Warren LEACH 23 Jan 1873 (as his 2nd wife)
		(he born 12 Mar 1812 No. Bridgewater, VT; died 21 Sep 1898)
		(he s/o John LEACH and Lavinia SNOW) no issue EOL
	1082. Abigail Evarts	born 7 Oct 1817; died 5 Oct 1900 single EOL
	1083. Louisa	born 19 Oct 1819; died 28 Feb 1871 No. Bridgewater, VT
		married Henry W. LEACH 6 Sep 1865 (as his 1st wife) EOL
	1084. Joanna	born 21 Aug 1823; died ____ single EOL
	1085. John Quincy	born 24 Nov 1825; died 22 Mar 1827 EOL

517.   DAVID⁻⁵ BOWKER, son of David ⁻⁴ BOWKER (Luke⁻³; Richard⁻²; James⁻¹) and Huldah HARDEN, was born 28 Dec 1781 Scituate, MA. He married Eunice CLAPP 18 Oct 1807. She was the daughter of Michael CLAPP and Eunice ____; and was born 18 Dec 1790; died 30 June 1865. David⁻⁵ BOWKER died 15 April 1842 at Scituate.

Children of David⁻⁵ BOWKER and Eunice CLAPP:
Surname **BOWKER**

+	**1086. DAVID**	born 16 June 1808; died 12 Dec 1890 VA.;
		1 married Hannah S. CARSWELL 6 July 1830
		2 married Sylvania GORDON 4 July 1849 (she born 22 Sep 1824; died 12 May 1897)
	1087. Theodore Persons	born 13 Jan 1811; died 25 Sep 1875
		married Lydia Brooks TOTMAN 27 Nov 1833 Boston, Suffolk, MA.
		(she dau/o Isaac TOTMAN and Mary CLAPP) (she born 13 Apr 1815 Scituate)

Child: Theodore P-⁷ BOWKER, Jr. born ca 1841 MA; died 12 Nov 1862 Antietam, MD
Note: he a member of Co A., MA 13ᵗʰ Infantry Regt, Civil War, wounded 17 Sep 1862 at Antietam, MD on 17 Sep 1862 (age 21)

	1088. JOHN HILLIARD	born 11 Feb 1813; died ____; married Sarah DUNCAN
	1089. Eunice	born 14 March 1815; died ____
	1090. Catharina Whiting	born 17 Aug 1817; died 20 May 1892; married _____ HARLOW ca ____
	1091. James Clapp	born 24 Sep 1818; died ____
	1092. Helen Clapp	born 14 Feb 1821; died 18 Nov 1889 Cambridge, MA
	1093. Edwin L.	born 4 Jan 1824; died 5 Sep 1901; married Charlotte NOTTAGE ca ____
	1094. Laurinda	born 22 July 1828 Scituate; died 15 May 1909 Milwaukee, WI
		married Timothy Appleton CHAPMAN 15 May 1850
		(he s/o George W. CHAPMAN and Mary_____) (he born ca 1825; died ____)
	1095. Charles H.	born 2 Oct 1830; died 26 July 1877 OR
		married Harriet May CHAPMAN 6 Sep 1865
	1096. Lyman Dean	born 7 Dec 1833; died 20 Feb 1868 Cambridge, MA

519. MELVIN⁻⁵ BOWKER, son of Liberty-⁴ BOWKER (Luke⁻³; Richard-²; James⁻¹) and Sarah GURNEY, was born 14 March 1798 at Pembroke, Plymouth, MA. He married Betsey WILLET on 26 May 1822 at Hanson, Plymouth, MA. She was the daughter of ____ WILLET and ____; and was born ca 1801; died 23 April 1829 (probably as a result of childbirth) at Savoy, Berkshire, MA.

Children of Melvin⁻⁵ BOWKER and Betsey WILLET:
Surname **BOWKER**

+	**1097. ALONZO MELVIN**	born 14 Mar 1823; died 15 March 1865
		married Ruth F. HUNT 18 July 1847 Savoy, MA
+	**1098. CHARLES**	born 16 Sep 1824; died 10 Dec 1906 Bernardston, Franklin, MA
		1 married Delcy Derry DUNHAM ca 1847
		(born ca 1829; died 1852)
		2 married Harriet P. DAWES 23 March 1853
		(she dau/o Samuel DAWES and ____)
	1099. Calvin	born 29 Dec 1826; died 16 Feb 1827 Savoy, MA EOL
	1100. Betsey Willet	born 7 Apr 1829; died 23 Aug 1830 Savoy, MA EOL

523. CALVIN⁻⁵ BOWKER, brother of above, was born 5 Sep 1806 MA. He married Eliza BELDING ca ___. She was the daughter of ____ BELDING and ____, and was born ca 1809 MA; died ____. Calvin-⁵ BOWKER, an Innkeeper and Postmaster in Adams, MA, died 8 Sep 1896 at Adams.

Children of Calvin-⁵ BOWKER and Eliza BELDING:
Surname **BOWKER**

	1101. Catherine E (Kate)	born ca July 1841; died ____
		1 married Zelotus WOOD on 8 March 1860.
		(he s/o Mason B. WOOD and ____) (he born 6 Aug 1835; died ____)

Child: Lillian-⁷ WOOD born Apr 1865; died ___; married Arthur A. ANDREWS
2 married _____ HALL ca ____

	1102 . Calvin Liberty	born ca 1845; died 29 Apr 1846.
	1103. Addie D.	born June 1856; died ____; 1 married Levi HATHAWAY ca 1874

Child: Cora Lillian-⁷ HATHAWAY born 1 Jan 1875, married Fred MILLER 22 Sep 1903
(he s/o James V. MILLER and Hannah WHEELOCK)

536. PIERPONT FAY⁻⁵ BOWKER, son of Elisha⁻⁴ BOWKER (Benjamin-³,²; James⁻¹) and Sally SPEAR, was born ca 1809 at Springfield, VT. He married Mary Ann RANDALL She was the daughter of ____RANDALL and ____; and was born ____; died ____. Pierpont F⁻⁵ BOWKER, a stone mason , died 19 May 1887 Keene, NH

Children of Pierpont-⁵ BOWKER and Mary A. ____
Surname **BOWKER**

1104. George F.	born ca 1833; died ____	
1105. Harris H.	born 5 July1837 Rockingham, VT; died ca 1902 (age 65)	
	married Nancy BINGHAM 16 May 1868 (she born 1849 VT)	
1106. Bryant W.	born 29 May 1842; died 5 Feb 1863 (20-7-17) Chester VT	
1107. Laura B.	born ca ____ died 9 Apr 1848 Chester, VT.	
1108. Mary Alice	born ca 1850; died ____	

married Oramel Waist FLETCHER 1 Jan 1875 Keene, NH as his 2ⁿᵈ wife
(he son of Jonas FLETCHER and Lucinda SAWTELL)
(he born 30 Jan 1834 Windsor, VT; died 11 Oct 1911)
Children: Minnie Evelyn-⁷ FLETCHER born 29 June 1879 Keene, NH

549. LEWIS⁻⁶ STURTEVANT, son of Betty⁻⁵ CROCKER/CROOKER (Daniel⁻⁴; Mary⁻³ RAMSDELL; Martha-² BOWKER; James⁻¹) and Barzillai / Barze STURTEVANT was born 7 Feb 1795 Halifax, Plymouth, MA. He married Rebecca EVANS on 5 April 1821 at Stoneham, Middlesex, MA. She was the daughter of Asaph EVANS and Rhoda HUTCHINSON, and was born 19 July 1802 Petersborough, NH; died _____. Lewis⁻⁶ STURTEVANT died 19 Oct 1852 at Pepperell, Middlesex, MA.

Children of Lewis⁻⁶ STURTEVANT and Rebecca EVANS:
Surname **STURTEVANT**

1109.	Asaph E.	born ca 1824; died 11 Dec 1893 MA (he was a cooper)
		married Mary Ann RICHARDSON int pub 17 Nov 1864 MA
		(she dau/o Daniel RICHARDSON (a basket maker) and Mariah _____)
1110.	Barzillai	born Mar 1827; died 30 Jan 1903 Malden, MA
		married Rosilla WOODS 7 June 1854
		(she born ca 1827)(she dau/o Levi WOODS and _____)

Child: Frank A⁻⁸ STURTEVANT born ca 1859

1111.	Horace E	born ca 1829; died ____; married Almina RICHARDSON 30 June 1852
		(she born ca 1830; died ____)
1112.	Thomas Hutchinson	born 16 Oct 1840; died 5 Oct 1893; married Sara Ellen GAY 8 May 1859
		(she born 15 Oct 1839 Milbury, MA; died ____)
		(she dau/o John C. Gay and Margaret GOWAN

Child: Frank Edward⁻⁸ STURTEVANT born ca 1861

1113.	Rebecca C.	born 10 Jan 1841; died ____; married Nathan Allen COLE 17 Feb 1864

Child: Lelia/Leila⁻⁸ COLE born 31 Jan 1865; died ____

1114.	Henry Clay	born ca 1843; died ____

616. LAZARUS⁻⁶ BOWKER, son of Dimmick⁻⁵ BOWKER (Lazarus⁻⁴,³; James⁻²,¹) and Margaret WHITTON, was born 13 Nov 1817 at Scituate, MA. He married Margaret Cornelia Forbes VALENTINE on 21 June 1835 at Scituate, MA. She was the daughter of _____ VALENTINE and ____; and was born ca 1820, died ____. Lazarus⁻⁶ BOWKER died 20 Nov 1867.

Children of Lazarus⁻⁶ BOWKER and Margaret VALENTINE:
Surname **BOWKER**   (children all born Scituate, MA)

	1115. George F.	born 28 March 1836; died ____
	1116. Arabel	born 13 May 1838; died ____
	1117. Almina	born 16 Sept 1841; died ____
+	**1118. HELEN DALLAS**	born 17/18 June 1844; died July 1920
		married James W. WEEKS III on 21 July 1872 (as his 2ⁿᵈ wife)
		(he s/o James W. WEEKS, Jr. and Sarah Place SHERIFF)
		(he born 4 Sept 1827; died 1920 MA)

617. CLARISSA GARDNER⁻⁶ BOWKER, daughter of Howard⁻⁵ BOWKER (Lazarus-⁴ Jr; Lazarus-³; James-² Jr., James-¹) and his first wife Nancy GARDNER, was born 23 Sep 1807 at Boston, Suffolk, MA. She married Henry LEARNED on 10 Dec 1826 at Scituate, MA. He was the son of Grant LEARNED and Martha GARFIELD, and was born 6 May 1803 Roxbury, MA; died 8 Feb 1887 Boston, MA. Clarissa-⁶ BOWKER died 15 Sep1857.

Children of Clarissa⁻⁶ BOWKER and Henry LEARNED:
Surname **LEARNED**   (children born NY)

1119.	Howard Bowker	born 7 Nov 1827; died 7 May 1849
1120.	Clarissa G. B.	born 13 April 1829; died ____; 1 married _____ BRONSON 24 June 1852
		2 married Elijah Dunham HENRY 11 June 1863 (he born ca 1836; died 1895)

Child: Mattie B.-⁸ HENRY born ca 1867; died ____; married Frank C. THOMPSON ca 1889

1121.	Henry Gustavus	born 7 Nov 1830; died ____
1122.	Albert Woodman	born 27 Aug 1832; died 9 Dec 1885 Boston, Suffolk, MA (single)

Children of Clarissa Gardner-6 BOWKER and Henry LEARNED, continued:
Surname **LEARNED**

	1123. Martha Garfield	born 11 Apr 1837; died ___; married Charles S. CLARK 14 Feb 1856 St. Louis, MO
		Child: Mattie G-8 CLARK born ca 1855; died ___
+	**1124. GRANT**	born 10 Mar 1840; died 10 Apr 1879
	BARSTOW	1 married Mary LARNED ca ____ (she born 1843; died 1884)
		2 married Antoinette C_____ 26 June 1861
	1125. Daniel Dearborn	born 10 Nov 1841; died 24 Apr 1861 St. Louis, MO
+	**1126. GEORGE**	born 4 Mar 1846; died ____
	WASHINGTON	married Kezia Eliza Adelaide STACEY 28 Apr 1873
		(she born 29 Dec 1851; died 9 May 1934 Barnhart, MO)

623. DAVIS WHITING-6 BOWKER, son of Howard-5 BOWKER (Lazarus-4 Jr; Lazarus-3; James-2 Jr; James-1) and his second wife Eveline TILDEN, and half-brother of Clarissa (above), was born 4 Dec 1831 at South Scituate, MA. He married Lucia Drew FAUNCE on 26 Nov 1857. She was the daughter of Nathaniel FAUNCE and Marcia WASHBURN, and was born 2 July 1831; died 27 Dec 1899. Davis Whiting-6 BOWKER died 18 Oct 1907 at Kingston, MA.

Children of Davis W-6 BOWKER and Lucia FAUNCE:
Surname **BOWKER**

	1127. **JULIA EVELINE**	born 29 Aug 1858; died 5 Nov 1936 Plymouth, MA	
+		married Elwin Nicholas STRANGER 9 Nov 1879	
		(he s/o Andrew R. STRANGER and Helen ____)	
		(he born 15 Mar 1849; died 3 May 1925)	
	1128. Jennie Louise	born 1 Jan 1860; died 15 Aug 1922	
	1129. Eliza Waterman	born 26 Aug 1861; died 24 Mar 1935	
	1130. Maynard Ellsworth	born 23 Feb 1864; died 7 July 1865	EOL
	1131. Quincy Davis	born 4/19 July 1865; died ca 1957	
		married Grace Hamilton WADSWORTH 9 Nov 1899 Kingston, MA	
		(she dau/o Hamilton WADSWORTH and Lucy E. PETERSON)	
		(she born 21 Jan 1876; died ____)	
		Children: Howard Stanley-8 born ca 1901; died 1956; Miriam-8 BOWKER born ca 1908	
	1132. Ella Faunce	born 28 Mar 1867; died 2 Jan 1957 MA	

630. WINSLOW LEWIS-6 BOWKER, son of Lazarus-5 BOWKER (Lazarus-4;3; James-2;1) and Martha CUSHING, was born 25 Oct 1825 Boston, MA. He married first to Maria/Marcia ____ ca 1850. She was born __; died ____. He married 2nd to Susan E. SWAIN ca Apr 1860 at Chichester, NH. She was the daughter of William SWAIN and Sally ____; and was born ca 1838 NH; died ____. Winslow-6 BOWKER died 15 Dec 1903 at Cambridge, MA.

Children of Winslow Lewis-6 BOWKER and Maria/Marcia ____:
Surname **BOWKER**

	1133. Frank Fay	born 7 June 1850 Boston, MA; died 12 Nov 1867 Cambridge, MA
+	**1134. JOSEPHINE**	born 6 Feb 1852 Cambridge, MA; died 5 Jan 1875 Cambridge, MA (childbirth)
	CORA	married John Edmund THURSTON 4 Nov 1873/74 Cambridge

Child of Winslow-6 BOWKER and Susan E. SWAIN:
Surname **BOWKER**

	1135. Arthur L.	born 2 Oct 1861; died 4 June 1908 Cambridge, MA
		married Gertrude Elizabeth " Lizzie" COOK 17 Jan 1889
		(she dau/o George H. COOK and Augusta ____) Child: Helen-8 BOWKER born ca 1892

641. CLARKE-6 BOWKER, son of Joseph-5 BOWKER (Zebulon-4; Lazarus-3; James-2;1) and Rhoda HAMILTON, was born 22 April 1812 VT. He married Lovina PERRY on 1 July 1838 NY. She was the daughter of Asa PERRY and Ruhanna WAITE; and was born Oct 1816 Onondaga County, NY; died 30 Sep 1904 at Hancock, IL. Clarke 6 BOWKER died 24 June 1887 at Dallas City, IL.

Children of Clarke-6 BOWKER and Lovina PERRY:
Surname **BOWKER**

	1136. **MARQUIS**	born 24 Aug 1839 NY; died 27 June 1917 Nevada, Vernon, MO
+	**LATHRAM**	married Frances DUSHER ca 1864 (she born 13 Oct 1841; died 18 May Nevada, MO)

Children of Clarke[-6] BOWKER and Lovina PERRY, continued:
Surname **BOWKER**

+	**1137. FRANKLIN W.**	born 23 May 1842 NY; died 14 Feb 1927; married Catherine LAUGHLIN ca 1863 (she born ca 1845 MO; died 14 Dec 1921 Dallas City, IL
	1138. Harriet/Hattie	born 14 May 1844 OH; died 27 Sep 1934 Hancock, IL; married Nathan ROSS ca ____
	1139. Ellen	born 19 Nov 1848 OH; died ____
	1140. Mary	born 27 Sep 1854 IL; died 23 Feb 1918

646. THOMAS[-6] BOWKER/BUKER, son of James[-5] BOWKER/BUKER (James[-4] BOWKER; James [3; 2 ;1]) and Jane WRIGHT, was born ca 1797 Maine. He married Rhoda[-6] WEYMOUTH (# 651) ca 1820. She was the daughter of Rhoda[-5] BOWKER/ BUKER and Nicholas WEYMOUTH, and was born 30 Jan 1800 Milford, MA; died 29 Dec 1825 Bowdoinham, ME. Thomas[-6] BOWKER/ BUKER died 1877.

Children of Thomas[-6] BOWKER/BUKER and Rhoda[-6] WEYMOUTH:
Surname **BOWKER/.BUKER**

1141. Hamilton	born ca 1821; died 1897	1143. Albion K.	born ca 1825; died 1896
1142. Orren	born ca 1823; died 1894		

648. RUFUS[-6] BOWKER/BUKER, brother of above, was born 6 Aug 1799 Maine. He married Betsey[-6] WEYMOUTH (# 652) 25 Dec 1823. She was the daughter of Rhoda[-5] BOWKER/BUKER and Nicholas WEYMOUTH, and was born 21 June 1806 Littlefield, ME ; died 23 Nov 1835/39. Rufus[-6] BOWKER/BUKER died 3 Jan 1830 Bowdoinham, ME.

Children of Rufus[-6] BOWKER/BUKER and Betsey[-6] WEYMOUTH:
Surname **BOWKER/BUKER**

	1144. Polly	born 28 Sep 1824 Bowdoinham, ME: died ____
+	**1145. SIMS / SYMS**	born 9 July 1826; died 24 Sep 1894 Braintree, Norfolk, MA
	GARDNER	married Mary Ann SPEAR 3 July 1856 Weymouth, MA. (she dau/o John B. SPEAR and Wealthy RICHARDS) (she born ca 1831; died 1925)
	1146. Noble M.	born ca 1829; died 3 May 1895; married Sarah A. WOOD 2 Jan 1856

651. RHODA[-6] WEYMOUTH, for children see # 646 above

652. BETSEY[-6] WEYMOUTH, for children see # 648 above

654. JOSEPH [6] BOWKER, son of Samuel Michael[-5] BOWKER (William[-4]; James-[3;2;1]) and Lucretia APPLEGATE, was born 2 Oct 1810 at Barnegat, NJ. He married Nancy Ann PAUL ca 1829. She was the daughter of Benjamin PAUL and Elizabeth CRANE, and was born 27 Oct 1810 Manahawkin, NJ; died 8 May 1869 at Barnegat, NJ. Joseph[6] died 1 Nov 1889.

Children of Joseph Michael[-6] BOWKER and Nancy Ann PAUL:
Surname **BOWKER**

1147. William W.	born 19 Jan 1830; died 16 Jan 1903
1148. Mary Ann	born ca 1831; died ____
1149. Earl Pointset	born 29 Aug 1833 Manahawkin, NJ; died 2 May 1917 Staten Island, NY married Eliza Jane LETTS ca ____ (she dau/o Alex LETTS and Frances KING) (she born ca 1844 Barnegat, NJ)

Children: Sarah-[8] born 1867, died 1869; Benjamin[8] born 1870, died 1870; and Octavia L-[8] BOWKER born 1873, died 1947

1150. Carlton P.	born ca 1834 Manahawkin, NJ; died 3 May 1917 Staten Island, NY
1151. Elizabeth	born ca 1835 Barnegat; died Feb 1902 Barnegat, NJ
1152. Emeline	born ca 1837 Barnegat; died 1870 Barnegat, NJ

655. SAMUEL[-6] BOWKER, brother of above, was born ca 1811/12 at Monmouth, NJ. He married Malinda HUTCHINSON ca 1836. She was the daughter of William T. HUTCHINSON and Clarissa B. MOORE, and was born ca 1819 IL; died ca 1860 OH. Samuel[-6] BOWKER died ca 1873 Lebanon, Ohio.

BOWKER   Descendants of James-1
The Sixth American Generation

Children of Samuel[6] BOWKER and Malinda HUTCHINSON:
Surname **BOWKER**

1153. Fred Hutchinson	born ca 1837; died 31 Dec 1895 Warren Co., Ohio	
	married Mary Elizabeth SIMONTON ca 1862 Child: Fred-[8] born ca 1863; died 1865	
1154. Elizabeth	born ca 1842; died ____	
1155. Michael	born ca 1844; died ____	
+ **1156. WILLIAM T.**	born 14 July 1848 OH; died 8 Jan 1935 Lebanon, OH	
	married Emma " Emily " KEEVER ca 1871/72	
	(she born 22 Oct 1850 OH; died 19 Mar 1927 Lebanon, OH)	
1157. Brandon	born ca 1860 OH; died 1883	

656. REBECCA[6] STOWELL, daughter of Rebecca[5] BOWKER (Bartlett[4] BOWKER; John[3]; James[2,1]; and David STOW-
ELL, was born 19 Oct 1807 VT. She married John B. WHITTEMORE 6 Oct 1829 at Fitzwilliam NH. He was the son of John
WHITTEMORE and Hannah STONE; and was born 22 Oct 1806; died 12 Feb 1879. Rebecca[6] STOWELL died 11 Dec 1878.

Children of Rebecca[6] STOWELL and John WHITTEMORE:
Surname **WHITTEMORE**

1158. Abbie Tower	born 20 Aug 1830; died 16 Jan 1877
	married Otis Taft RUGGLES 16 Oct 1851 Cambridge, MA
1159. George Albin/Alben	born 13 Mar 1834; died ____; married Mary Louise BLOOD 31 Mar 1875
1160. David Stowell	born 11 June 1837; died 6 Mar 1838
1161. Emma Maria	born 30 Mar 1843 NH; died ____
	married Frank Marion HOWE 3 Sep 1872 (he s/o Ira HOWE and ____)
	Children: Don Whittemore-[8] born 6 Dec 1876 Lansing, MI; and Harry H-[8] HOWE born ca 1880

660. DAVIS C[6] BOWKER, son of Bartlett[5] BOWKER (Bartlett[4]; John-[3]; James-[2,1]) and Hannah CARPENTER, was born
13 May 1815 VT. He married Fannie Almira CUSHING ca 1841. She was the daughter of Matthew CUSHING and ____; and
was born ____; died ____. Davis[6] BOWKER, a Railroad Foreman, died ca 1875.

Child of Davis C[6] BOWKER and Fannie Almira CUSHING:
Surname **BOWKER**

+ **1162. ROSETTA EMILY**	born Jan 1842 VT; died ____
	married George Nelson/Nason CASS 1 July 1871 (his 2nd marriage)
	(he s/o Nathan CASS ++ and Sarah CURRIER)
	(he born ca 1832 Canaan, NH; died 17 Mar 1882 Boston, MA)
	++ Nathan CASS, was the son of Theophilus CASS and Susanna LIBBEE. Theophilus CASS served in the
	Revolutionary War.

667. STEPHEN WRIGHT[6] BOWKER, son of Stephen-[5] BOWKER (Bartlett[4]; John-[3]; James-[2,1]) and Sarah WHITNEY, was
born 4 Nov 1821 at Fitzwilliam, NH. He married Henrietta A. HALLADAY ca 1847. She was born ca 1826; died ____. Stephen
Wright-[6] BOWKER died 12 April 1878 at Newfane, VT.

Children of Stephen W[6] BOWKER and Henrietta HALLADAY:
Surname **BOWKER**

+ **1163. EMMA D.**	born ca 1848; died ____
	married William K. WOOD 4 Nov 1868 Newfane, VT.
	(he born ca 1834; died ____) Child: Julius Wright-[8] WOOD born 16 Feb 1870 NY
1164. Charles L.	born ca 1850; died ____
1165. Henry O.	born Mar 1854 VT; died ____
	married Ada Frances PERRY ca 1880 (she born ca 1861 NY)
	Children: Eva N-[8] born ca 1889, married ____ KIMBALL; and Henry W-[8] BOWKER born ca 1883
1166. Eva Henrietta	born ca 1856 Newfane, VT; died ____
	married Charles Haynes DAVENPORT 1 Dec 1877 Brattleboro, VT
1167. Edgar Wright	born 27 July 1858 Newfane, VT; died ____
	married Rosa Mabel DUNCKLEE 13 Nov 1878
	(she born 3 Mar 1860 Manchester, NH; died ____)
	(she dau/o Henry DUNCKLEE and Roxana WHITING)

672 . SARAH-6 BOWKER, daughter of Luke-5 BOWKER (Bartlett-4; John-3; James-2,1) and Sarah HOWE, was born 3 Aug 1849 Fitzwilliam, NH. She married Samuel Stillman STONE on 4 Oct 1882, as his 2nd wife. He was the son of Artemus STONE, Jr. and Ann L. SIMONDS, and was born 27 Nov 1841; died 11 Aug 1929. Sarah-6 BOWKER died 19 Jan 1933 at Fitzwilliam.

Children of Sarah-6 BOWKER and Samuel S. STONE:
Surname **STONE**

1168. Arthur E	born 20 Oct 1886; died 2 Nov 1967; married Margaret E. PHILLIPS ca ____ (she born ____; died 1958)	
	Children: Stillman P-8 born ca ____; and Jessie M-8 STONE born ca ___; married ____ BROWN	
1169. Walter Milton	born ca 1889/90 NH; died ____ 1 married Beulah May LATTRELL 1 Dec 1910 2 married Helen J. OBER 17 Sep 1921 Troy, NH	

679. CYNTHIA E-6 STONE, daughter of Cynthia-5 BOWKER (Bartlett-4; John-3; James-2,1) and the Rev. Jesse STONE, was born 16 July 1843 at Fitzwilliam, NH. She married Capt. Henry L. BARKER on 25 July 1863 at Topeka, KS. He was the son of John G. BARKER and Sarah ____, and was born June 1835 NY; died ____. Cynthia-6 STONE died ____.

Children of Cynthia-6 STONE and Capt. Henry BARKER:
Surname **BARKER**

1170. Frank H.	born ca 1865 KS	1173. Marian E.	born ca 1875
1171. Hattie M.	born ca 1867	1174. Viola	born July 1891
1172. Cora L.	born ca 1872		

682. MARY LOUISE-6 STONE, sister of above, was born 2 June 1850 at Boston, MA. She married fist to William Spencer JEWELL on 7 July 1868. They divorced, and she married second to Charles Alfred BLISS on 20 Sep 1883 at Topeka, KS. He was the son of Deacon James BLISS and Joanna BREWSTER, and was born 21 Nov 1831; died 12 Oct 1898.

Children of Mary Louisa-6 STONE and Charles Alfred BLISS:
Surname **BLISS**

1175. George C.	born ca 1887
1176. Leila May/Maud	born 1889 TX; died ca 1959; married Frederick Arthur COOK ca ____ (he born ca 1892; died 1940)
	Children: Clarence F-8 born ca 1916, died 1987; and Dorothy L-8 COOK born ca 1917, died 1976
1177. Arthur	born ca 1892

698. WEALTHY T-6 TOWER, daughter of Stephen-5 TOWER, Jr. (Hannah-4 BOWKER; John-3; James-2,1) and Meletiah BARTLETT, was born 18 Jan 1805 Cummington, MA. She married first to Peter BARTLETT on 1 July 1823. He was the son of Peter BARTLETT and Bethia MORSE, and was born ca 1800 Boston, MA, died 30 July 1837.

Wealthy-6 TOWER married second to William GIDDINGS on 6 Apr 1842, as his second wife.. He was the son of Joseph GIDDINGS and Mary BUTTON, and was born 25 Sep 1802 New London, CT; died ca 1874 Lisbon, ct. Wealthy-6 TOWER died 31 Aug 1887.

Children of Wealthy-6 TOWER and Peter BARTLETT:
Surname **BARTLETT**

	1178. William Eustice	born 5 Feb 1825; died _____ 1 married Rebecca KYLE ca ____; 2 married Corinth WINCHING ca ____	
	1179. Horace Ames	born 20 Oct 1826; died 19 June 1896 Worthington, MA	
+	**1180. OTIS BOYD**	born 1 May 1828 Cummington, MA; died _____ married Elmina/Almina-6 TOWER 1 May 1851 (she # 771)	
	1181. Angelina B.	born 6 Feb 1835; died 20 July 1835	EOL

Child of Wealthy-6 TOWER and William GIDDINGS:
Surname **GIDDINGS**

1182. Charles Bartlett	born ca 1843; died 1847	EOL

700. CALVIN BOWKER-6 TOWER, brother of above, was born 4 Nov 1808 at Cummington, MA. He married Amanda M. HIGGINS on 28 May 1845 at Worthington, Hampshire, MA. She was the daughter of Luther HIGGINS and Lydia KING/ RING, and was born 28 Aug 1815; died 27 June 1889. Calvin-6 TOWER died 13 Oct 1885 at Worthington Center, MA.

Children of Calvin Bowker[-6] TOWER and Amanda HIGGINS:
Surname **TOWER**

1183. Lydia Amanda	born 20 July 1836; died 10 Aug 1899 Worthington, MA	
	1 married Sumner Wick STONE ca ____	
	(he s/o Oren STONE and Jane BRYANT) (he born ca 1829; died 5 Apr 1904)	
1184. Elvira Nancy	born 17 Sep 1839; died 7 Aug 1907 Springfield, MA	
1185. Angelina D.	born 3 May 1843; died ____; married Milo Joel HASKINS 10 Apr 1865 (1842- ___)	
1186. Grace I.	born 14 July 1849; died ____	

704. LUTHER BARTLETT[-6] BOWKER, brother of above, was born 13 Dec 1819 MA. He married Sabrina TOWER 25 Nov 1841. She was the daughter of Warren TOWER and Rhoda TOWER, and was born 29 May 1820 MA; died 6 Oct 1908 Cummington, MA. Luther B[-6] TOWER died 6 Nov 1898.

Children of Luther B[-6] TOWER and Sabrina TOWER:
Surname **TOWER**

1187. Mary A.	born ca 1843	1191. Herbert	born ca 1855
1188. Henry L.	born ca 1845; died 9 May 1936	1192. Julia	born ca 1858
1189. Eunice	born ca 1848; died ____	1193. Maria E.	born ca 1859/60
1190. Charles W.	born ca 1852	1194. Adella/Della	born ca 1861

708. DEXTER[-6] TOWER, son of John M[-5] TOWER (Hannah[-4] BOWKER; John[-3]; James[-2,1]) and Ruth REED, was born 12 March 1817 Cummington, MA. He married first to Irene Bertia PIERCE on 30 Nov 1847 Windsor, MA. She was the daughter of Isaac P. PIERCE, of Windsor, Berkshire, MA, and ____; and was born ca 1825; died Aug 1886. He married second Sept 1888 to Mrs. Evaline R Rogers, a widow. Dexter[-6] TOWER was a successful landowner and carpenter, and died 13 Jan 1896 Williamsburg, MA.

Children of Dexter[-6] TOWER and Irene PIERCE:
Surname **TOWER**

1195. Clinton T.	born ca 1855; died _____; 1 married Ida BARTLETT
	(she born ca 1859; died Apr 1888)
	Children: Arthur Clinton[-8] born ca ____; George H-[8] TOWER born ca ___
	2 married Lucy L. ALLEN of Florence, MA on 31 July 1889
	(she dau/o Bennett ALLEN and Cordelia WARREN)
	Children: Clara A[-8] born 22 June 1890; and Bertrand[-8] TOWER born 22 Sep 1893
1196. Climena Belle	born ca ____; died ____; **married Alfred D. SWEET of Wilmington, VT**
	Children: Lizzie Tower[-8] born ____; married Caleb HILL; Elgin Austin[-8] born 19 July 1880, died 1896
	and Perley D-[8] SWEET born ca ____ (single)

768. SALOME[-6] TOWER, daughter of Rhoda Bowker[-5] TOWER (Hannah[-4] BOWKER ; John[-3]; James[-2,1]) and Warren TOWER, was born 9 Oct 1817 at Cummington, Hampshire, MA. She married Ephraim Tilson BARTLETT (int pub 12 May 1837) at Cummington. He was the son of Ephraim BARTLETT and Elizabeth TILSON, and was born 12 Aug 1813 Cummington, died 16 Sep 1857 Cummington. Salome[-6] TOWER died there on 21 July 1895.

Children of Salome[-6] TOWER and Ephraim BARTLETT:
Surname **BARTLETT**   (children all born Cummington, Hampshire, MA)

	1197. Rhoda Eliza (1)	born 11 April 1838; died 10 Nov 1842	EOL
	1198. Arline Pratt	born 19 Sep 1839; died 11 Nov 1842	EOL
	1199. Rhoda Eliza (2)	born 5 July 1840; died ____	
+	**1200. LUCIUS WARREN**	born 3 Apr 1841; died 5 Mar 1928 Hartford, CT	
		1 married Mary Monroe CHALMERS 11 May 1871	
		(she born ca 1845; died 1890) buried Cedar Hill Cemetery, Hartford, CT	
		2 married Zilpha J. BARTLETT Crozier ca _____	
		(she born ca 1843; died 1918) buried Cedar Hill Cemetery, Hartford, CT	
	1201. Ermina D.	born 1 Sep 1844; died 19____	
		married Joseph SUHANEK 27 Feb 1889 (he from So. Hadley, MA)	
		(he born ____; died 18 July 1895 Hartford, CT)	
+	**1202. ALICE PRATT**	born 1 July 1847; died ____; married William E. BURDICK 22 Feb 1875	
		(he born 15 Feb 1851 Westbrook, CT; died 28 Jan 1898 Hartford, CT)	

Children of Salome[6] TOWER and Ephraim BARTLETT, continued:
Surname **BARTLETT**

1203. Vesta E	born 16 Oct 1849; married Joseph THRALL of Windsor, CT on 8 Sep 1875	
	(he born 31 Aug 1831; died 31 May 1910 (78-9-0) Windsor, CT)	

Children: Oliver Joseph[8] born 23 April 1882; and Alice May[8] THRALL born 29 July 1886

1204. Ann Eliza	born 24 May 1855; died 29 Aug 1867	EOL
1205. Flora L	born 6 Dec 1856; died ___	
	married Arthur ULRICH of E. Hartford, CT on 25 Oct 1882	

Children: William Leroy-[8] born ca 1885 Buffalo, NY, married Gladdis HUBBARD 26 Oct 1909 Hartford, CT;
and Olive Ermina-[8] ULRICH born ca 1888
Reference: The TILSON Genealogy from Edmond TILSON at Plymouth (1638-1911), pages 369-72; and Census records

771. ALMINA/ELMINA[6] TOWER, see # 1158 Otis Boise/Boyd[7] BARTLETT for children

786. RENSSALAER[6] SYLVENDER BOWKER, son of Cushing[5] BOWKER (Captain Stephen[4]; John[3,2]; James[1]) and
Abigail Worcester RIDER, was born 6 April 1829. He married Mary Batchelder SPAULDING 23 Apr 1855 IN. She was the
daughter of David SPAULDING and Abigail SMITH; and was born 25 Feb 1829; died 8 Jan 1876. Rensselaer[6] BOWKER,
a carpenter, died 11 Jan 1914.

Children of Rensselaer[6] BOWKER and Mary SPAULDING:
Surname **BOWKER**

+	**1206. ALBERT**	born Aug 1859 IL; died 9 Dec 1907 Chicago. IL
	RENSSALAER	married Elizabeth FRANKLIN ca 1885
+	**1207. CHELLIS IRWIN**	born 1 Nov 1860; died 9 Feb 1959 Alameda, CA
		married Mary E. __ ca 1883
		(she born May 1867 Micronesia (Caroline Islands); died ___
+	**1208. ELLA SPAULDING**	born 20 Mar 1863; died 10 Nov 1935; married George W. THACKERAY
		(he born 16 Nov 1866; died 6 Dec 1944)(he s/o John THACKERAY and Catherine)
+	**1209. LUCY ELVIRA**	born 1863/64; died 1950; married Albert H. EMINGER ca ___
+	**1210. ERNEST**	born July 1865; died ___; married Haidee S. TAIT 6 June 1895
	SYLVENDER	(she born 13 Oct 1873 KS; died 16 Dec 1944 Chicago, IL)
		(she dau/o George TAIT and Mildred TERRILL)
+	**1211.WILLIAM CUSHING**	born 21 Oct 1866; died 2 July 1938 Sacramento, CA
	SHORT	1 married Mame/Mamie DUNN; 2 married Leona TAYLOR
	1212. Abigail Spaulding	born 14 Apr 1869; died Oct 1928 IL; married _____ VADKIN ca _____

788. LAURA RIDER[6] BOWKER, sister of above, was born 21 June 1832 NH. She married Samuel MARSTON on 22 Apr
1850 at Shefford, Quebec, Canada. He was the son of Jeremiah MARSTON and ____, and was born 31 Aug 1828 NH; died
24 June 1895. Laura Rider[6] BOWKER died 13 Sep 1870.

Children of Laura Rider[6] BOWKER and Samuel MARSTON:
Surname **MARSTON**

	1213. Amanda/Miranda	born 8 April 1851 Quebec; died ___
+	**1214. SAMUEL**	born 25 Jul 1853 Quebec; died 20 Jan 1925 Waterloo, Quebec
	CUSHING	married Charlotte " Shallie " May WESTOVER ca 1888 (she born 5 Sep 1866)
		(she dau/o Daniel WESTOVER and Lydia Roxanna WOODWARD)
	1215. Rueben Sylvester	born 27 Oct 1855 Canada; died 10 Aug 1940 Waterloo, Quebec, Canada
		married Charlotte SOLOMON ca 1877 Roxton, Quebec, Canada

Children: Ethel Maude-[8] born 6 Jan 1881, died 16 Oct 1958, married Edson Andrew BLANE 17 July 1907; and
Albert E-[8] MARSTON born ca 1888

	1216. Charlotte .	born 23 Feb 1858 Canada; died 24 Apr 1928 Manchester, NH
		1 married Nelson BANGS 12 June 1873 Waterloo, Quebec, Canada
		(he born Jan 1852; died ____)
		(divorced granted in NH 5 Apr 1887 due to abandonment of Nelson BANGS)

Children: Charles S-[8] born ca 1875; William Henry-[8] born ca 1877, died 1940; and Una Mae-[8]
BANGS born ca 1882

	2 married Edwin A. COLBY 29 Nov 1900 NH
	(he born ca 1866 NH; died 2 Nov 1940 Manchester, NH)
	(he s/o Francis W. COLBY and Paulina WHEELER)

Children of Laura Rider⁻⁶ BOWKER and Samuel MARSTON, continued:
Surname **MARSTON**

1217. Almon Proctor	born 11 May 1867 Shefford; died 14 Feb 1936 Warden, Shefford, Quebec, CA	
	married Carrie L. FARLEY ca ____	
	(she born ca 1865; died 1939)	
	Child: Gladys Eva-⁸ MARSTON born ca 1897; died 1971 Quebec	
1218. Ettie/Etta	born 2 Sep 1871Canada; died ____	
1219. Hattie Elsie	born 2 Sep 1871 Canada; died 1909 Danville, Quebec	
1220. Alvin Wilson	born 9 Apr 1875 Quebec, CA; died 21 Mar 1905 NH	
	married Ida M. CLOUGH 10 June 1903 Manchester, NH	
1221. S D	born ca 1880 Canada; poss. died young	

791. ABIGAIL RIDER⁻⁶ BOWKER, sister of above, was born 20 Oct 1837 Quebec, Canada. She married Jacob SPACKMAN April 1862 at Montreal, Quebec, Canada. He was the son of ____ SPACKMAN and ____; and was born 24 Aug 1823 Wiltshire, England; died 18 Nov 1901 Philadelphia, PA. Abigail R⁻⁶ BOWKER died 19 July 1915/25 at Philadelphia.

Children of Abigail R⁻⁶ BOWKER and Jacob SPACKMAN:
Surname **SPACKMAN**

1222. John A.	born ca 1865 Canada; died ____
1223. Gertrude	born May 1866 MD; died ____
1224. Frederick Arthur	born Jan 1869 PA; died 21 Mar 1949; married Mary Hanna PECK ca ____
	(she born ca 1873; died 1948)
	Child: Winifred-⁸ SPACKMAN born ca 1904; died 1999
1225. Ella L.	born 8 Aug 1871 Philadelphia, PA; died 11 Dec 1948 Philadelphia
1226. Edgar W.	born Oct 1875 PA; died ____; married Anita W. ____ ca ____
	(she born ca 1878; died 1900)

793. MARY LOUISA⁻⁶ BOWKER, sister of above, was born 24 Feb 1845, Quebec, Canada. She married George MARSTON 1 Feb 1865. He was the son of ____ MARSTON and ____; and was born April 1841 Quebec; died ____. Mary Louisa⁻⁶ BOWKER died 8 Aug 1932.

Children of Mary Louisa⁻⁶ BOWKER and George MARSTON:
Surname **MARSTON**

	1227. Carrie Emma	born ca 1870; died 1939
+	**1228. GARDNER**	born 11 Oct 1874 Hillsborough, NH; died 5 Jan 1944 NH
	ERNEST	married Elizabeth/Lizabell SAVORY 16 Sep 1905
		(she dau/o Charles A. SAVORY and Ellen J. PIPER) (she born ca 1873)

813. SAMUEL FRANCIS⁻⁶ BOWKER, son of Samuel Griffin⁻⁵ BOWKER (Stephen⁻⁴; John ^{3,2}; James⁻¹) and Orpha FAY. He married first to Rosanna Lovina ANGIER ca ____. She was the daughter of ____ ANGIER and ____, and was born 4 March 1837 IL; died 23 July 1861 at Fitzwilliam, Cheshire, NH. He married second to Mary Amanda CHASE on ____. She was the daughter of Daniel Webster CHASE and Mary Martha HALE, and was born 2 June 1838 MA; died 9 Jan 1917 Davenport, IA. Samuel F⁻⁵ BOWKER died 18 May 1900 Crystal Lake, IA.

Child of Samuel Francis⁻⁶ BOWKER and Rosanna ANGIER:
Surname **BOWKER**

+	**1229. ELLIOTT**	born 10 Nov 1859 Fitzwilliam, NH; died 17 Feb 1945 Garner, IA
	FRANCIS	married Ella Adelle BURDICK 5 April 1895
		(she born 24 Aug 1863 Pittstown, NY; died Feb 1953 IA)
		(she dau/o John BURDICK and Ann ____)

Children of Samuel Francis ⁶ BOWKER and Mary Amanda CHASE:
Surname **BOWKER**

	1230. Julia	born 10 Oct 1863 NH; died ____
+	**1231. HENRY FAY**	born 16 Mar 1864 NH; died 17 Aug 1941 Davenport, Scott, IA
		married Flora Emma HARDIE ca 1891
		(she dau/o Josiah J. HARDIE and Harriet Elizabeth CHASE
		(she born 17 Dec 1871 Crystal Lake, Hancock, IA, died 27 Mar 1916 Davenport, IA)

Children of Samuel Francis-6 BOWKER and Rosanna ANGIER, continued:
Surname **BOWKER**

	1232. Wallace H.	born Oct 1868 NH; died 2 Jan 1935	
		married Emma S. NIELSON 5 Jan 1890 IL (she born ca 1872 WI; died 1940)	
		Child: Mervin S-8 BOWKER born Jan 1891/2 Rock Island, IL; died 15 Nov 1964; married Mildred O ___	
		(she born ca 1898 MN) and had child: Lois-9 BOWKER born ca 1932	
+	**1233. MINNIE**	born 13 July 1870 NH; died 8 July 1940 Harvey, Wells, ND	
	ROSE	married Orton N. EMERY ca 1889	
	1234. Daniel W.	born 24 Feb 1872 Crystal Lake, Hancock, IA; died 1953 Minot, ND	
		married Clara Matilda KLUVER ca 1894	
		(she born Apr 1872 IA; died ____) (she dau/o C F KLUVER and Dora _____)	
+	**1235. LESLIE**	born 9 Feb 1874 Crystal Lake; died 23 Oct 1925 Cherokee Co., IA	
	EUGENE	married Melvina Millie GILLSTRAP/ GILKTRAP ca Dec 1899 IA	
	1236. Grace	born 9 Feb 1874; died 23 Oct 1877 IA	EOL
+	**1237. MAMIE**	born 29 Sep 1879 IA; died 4 June 1963 Fairbault, MN	
	ESTELLA	1 married Roscoe Conklin ROBERTS ca 1896 ND (prob divorced)	
		2 married Charles Amos ALMY ca 1918 Minot, ND	

817.   WILLIAM-6 BOWKER, son of Elijah-5 BOWKER, Jr. (Elijah-4; John-3; James-2;1) and Anna SYLVESTER, was born ca 1819/20. He married Eliza Brooks RICHARDS on 24 Aug 1844 at Weymouth, Norfolk, MA. She was the daughter of Minot RICHARDS and Eliza THAYER, and was born 24 Aug 1824 Weymouth; died 3 Nov 1896 Weymouth, MA. William-6 BOWKER died 24 Sep 1889.

Children of William-6 BOWKER and Eliza RICHARDS:
Surname **BOWKER**

	1238. James K. Polk	born 15 Aug 1844; died ____
	1239. Mary Adelaide	born 26 Sep 1846; died ____
+	**1240. ANN ESTELLE**	born 20 Dec 1848; died 3 Mar 1894
		married Samuel Joseph ROSS 13 Mar 1865
		(he born 1 June 1844; died 18 Oct 1934 Weymouth, MA)
		(he s/o ____ ROSS and Mehitable HOLBROOK)
	1241. Emma	born ca 1851; died ____
+	**1242. MARIA ELIZA**	born Dec 1852; died 6 Sep 1928; married Henry Franklin ROWELL ca 1869
		(he born May 1849/52 ME; died 26 Apr 1906 Weymouth, MA.)
	1243. William H.	born ca 1856; died ____
	1244. George Frederic	born Oct 1861/62; died ____; married Mary E. GILL ca 1889
		(she dau/o Hugh GILL and ____)

828. ELLIS-6 BOWKER, son of Charles-5 BOWKER (Elijah-4; John-3; James-2,1) and Martha WHITTEN, was born ca 1824 MA. He married Harriet ____ ca ____. She was the daughter of _____ and _____; and was born ____; died ____. Ellis-6 BOWKER died ____.

Child of Ellis-6 BOWKER and Harriet ____:
Surname **BOWKER**

	1245. Adeline M.	born ca 1848; died ____; married Davis P. HOWARD 6 Dec 1879
		(he s/o Apollos HOWARD and Beliah/Beulah PORTER)
		(he born ca 1846; died ____)

832. HENRY-6 BOWKER, brother of above, was born ca 1833. He married Mary Ada MIERS on 16 Aug 1865. She was the daughter of James A. MIERS and Deborah H ___; and was born ca 1843/46; died ____. Henry-6 BOWKER died ____.

Children of Henry-6 BOWKER and Mary Ada MIERS:
Surname **BOWKER**

1246. Walter/Wallace H.	born May 1866; died ____		
	married Ella F. LEAVITT on 11 Nov 1902 Boston, MA		
	Children: Harold-8 born Oct 1889; and Marian L-8 BOWKER born Nov 1891		
1247. Martha E.	born Mar 1868 MA; died ____		
1248. Ada	born ca 1870; died ____	1249. Anna G.	born Nov 1876

850. OLIVER EDWARDS⁻⁶ CUSHING, son of Stephen⁻⁵ CUSHING (Desire⁻⁴ BOWKER; John-³; James-²,¹) and Ethalinda EDWARDS, was born 12 March 1829 MA. He married Mary Bass EDSON on 7 Sep 1853. She was the daughter of John EDSON and Mary BASS, and was born 21 Jan 1829 Bridgewater, Plymouth, MA; died 30 Oct 1917 at Lowell, MA. Oliver E⁻⁵ CUSHING, an engineer, died 17 Jan 1890 at Lowell, MA.

Children of Oliver Edwards⁻⁶ CUSHING and Mary EDSON:
Surname **CUSHING**

+	**1250. MARY**	born 1 Jan 1855 MA.; died ____
		married Martin Ellsworth HALL 2 Oct 1878
		(he born 19 Sept 1847 DC; died 21 Feb 1904)
		(he s/o David Aiken HALL and Abigail Wolcott ELLSWORTH)
+	**1251. MARGARET DAISY**	born 23 July 1857 ; died ____ ; married Edward Thayer ABBOTT 6 April 1883
		(he born ____; died 15 Sep 1895)
	1252. Angeline	born 5 Aug 1860; died ____
	1253. Edith	born 14 July 1864; died 28 Sept 1865

896. CHARLES WARREN⁻⁶ SPARRELL, son of Desire-⁵ BARRELL (James-⁴, Jr; Deborah-³ BOWKER; James-²,¹) and James Newton SPARRELL, Jr. was born 30 Dec 1835 at South Scituate, Plymouth, MA. He married Susan M. EWELL ca 1859. She was the daughter of Allen EWELL and Althea OAKMAN; and was born ca 1839 Scituate, MA; died 2 May 1929 Scituate. Charles Warren⁻⁶ SPARRELL died 6 May 1906 at Norwell, MA.

Children of Charles Warren⁻⁶ SPARRELL and Susan EWELL:
Surname **SPARRELL**

1254. Mary E.	born ca 1862		1257. Ernest H.	born ca 1873
1255. Albert L.	born ca 1865		1258. Helen J.	born ca 1877
1256. Charles Walter	born ca 1866; died 1896		1259. John Henry	born ca 1880

906. GIDEON⁻⁶ BOWKER, son of Paul⁻⁵ BOWKER (Edmund-⁴,³; James-²,¹) and Mary ___ Bearce, was born 4 March 1797 at ____, ME. He married Avis E. ALLEN ca 1848. She was the daughter of Micah ALLEN and Elizabeth DUNHAM, and was born ca 1824; died ____. Gideon⁻⁶ BOWKER served as a Pvt. in Co. K. 12th Maine Volunteer Regt. and died at Hilton Head, SC on 15 July 1865 from a fever.

Children of Gideon⁻⁶ BOWKER and Avis ALLEN:
Surname **BOWKER**   Reference: History of Paris, Maine pages 529-31

1260. Mary Eliza	born 6 Feb 1849; died ____; unmarried	EOL
1261. Anna Coleman	born 26 Aug 1853; died ____; unmarried	EOL
	Note: Mary and Anna resided together in Lewiston, Maine	
1262. Edward/Everett Forest	born 28 Dec 1856; married Ada YOUNG ca ____ (she born ca 1863; died 1903 Bath, Maine)	
1263. Alanson Southworth	born 27 Aug 1862; died ____; married Della W. DALEY ca ____	

909. JOSEPH HENRY⁶ BOWKER, brother of above, was born 17 June 1835 at Gardner, Maine. He married first to Mary Jane IRISH on 25 July 1854. She was the daughter of ____ IRISH and ____; and was born ca 1835; died 1870. He married second to Rosamund C. KNIGHT on 26 Mar 1870. She was the daughter of ____ KNIGHT and ____; and was born 16 May 1841; died 17 Oct 1923. Joseph Henry⁻⁶ BOWKER died 8/9 Dec 1917 Pittsfield, Cumberland, Maine.

Children of Joseph Henry⁻⁶ BOWKER and Mary Jane IRISH:
Surname **BOWKER**

1264. Rufus K.	born 8 Sep 1857 Minot, ME; died ____; married Nellie SPILLER 4 Sep 1880 (dau/o Moses SPILLER and Elizabeth WHITNEY) (she born 2 Jan 1861)
1265. Frank E.	born ca 1860 Otisfield, ME; died 29 May 1936 married Clara Belle WHITTEMORE 1 Nov 1879 Minot, Androscoggin, ME (she dau/o Orrin WHITTEMORE and Sarah L. ___) (she born Feb 1862 Minot, ME)

Child of Joseph Henry⁻⁶ BOWKER and Rosamund KNIGHT:
Surname **BOWKER**

1266. Maurice	born 15 Jan 1871; died 1944; married Alberta B. WHITTIER 14 Dec 1892 (she born 1869 ME; died 11 June 1895 ME)
	Child: Guy F⁻⁸ BOWKER born 16 Sept 1893; died 1949

913. MARY TRACY⁻⁶ BOWKER, daughter of Captain James⁻⁵ BOWKER (James⁻⁴; Edmund⁻³; James⁻²,¹) and Abigail BICKNELL, was born 29 Sep 1822 at Buckfield, Maine. She married Thomas Jones HILBORN on 30 Oct 1853 at Woodstock, Oxford, Maine. He was the son of Thomas HILBORN and Esther SMITH, and was born 16 Oct 1825 ME; died ca 1870.

Children of Mary Tracy⁻⁶ BOWKER and Thomas HILBORN:
Surname **HILBORN**   (children born Paris, Oxford, Maine)
        1267. Allaris Melcher   born 18 Jan 1860 ; died ____
        1268. George Beauregard   born 16 May 1862; died ____; married Nellie B. INGERSON ca 1881
                                     (she dau/o George S. INGERSON and Kate E. SIMONDS)
                                     (she born June 1865; died 19 Aug 1937)
                            Children: Luther Alberto⁻⁸ born 17 May 1882; Elizabeth Melissa⁻⁸ born 12 Sep 1883; Jennie M⁻⁸
                            born 17 Apr 1885; and James⁻⁸ HILBORN born 21 Apr 1887, died 11 May 1906. All born NH
        1269. Thomas Forrest   born 4 April 1864; died ____
                                     married Nellie F. TRIPP 3 Feb 1893 Brockton, MA
                                     (she dau/o Nathaniel TRIPP and Alpha TUKESBURY)
                                     (she born ca 1865 Dennisport, MA; died ____)

917. JOHN M⁻⁶ BOWKER, son of Cyprian⁻⁵ BOWKER (James⁻⁴; Edmund⁻³; James⁻²,¹) and Rachel MAYHEW, was born ca 1816 at Fairfax, Maine. He married Dorothy T. " Dolly " STARBIRD 27 Oct 1837 . She was the daughter of John STARBIRD and Sarah TOBEY, and was born 11 Sept 1815 ; died 18 May 1853. John M⁻⁶ BOWKER died 6 Aug 1895.

Children of John⁻⁶ BOWKER and Dorothy STARBIRD:
Surname **BOWKER**
+   **1270. GILMAN ROE**   born Apr 1838 ME; died 1922
                                     married Hannah Sabra LYON(S) 1 Jan 1862 (she born ca 1847; died ____)
        1271. James Greenleaf   born ca 1841; died 29 Aug 1895; married Katherine BOWKER ca ____
                    Children: James A⁻⁸ born 1865; Ann⁻⁸ born 1868; Mary E⁻⁸ born 1870; Martha L⁻⁸ born 1875; and Nellie⁻⁸ born 1878
        1272. Rachel Erman   born 29 Sep 1845; died 2 May 1931
        1273. Levi Starbird   born ca 1846; died ____
        1274. Sally Edwina   born 20 Feb 1848; died 28 May 1895
        1275. Celia Ann   born 6 Jul 1850; died 4 Apr 1905; married John ADAMS ca (born 14 Jan 1856 ME)
        1276. Angela   born ca 1852; died ____
        1277. George Washington   born 26 Oct 1853/54; died 1 Oct 1926; married Arabella _____ ca ____
                            Child: Ralph⁻⁸ BOWKER born ca 1879
        1278. John Adams   born 14 Jan 1856 ME; died 26 Apr 1919 ME
        1279. Dolly A.   born ca 1858

918. CYPRIAN⁻⁶ BOWKER, Jr., brother of above, was born ca 1817 at Woodstock, Oxford, Maine. He married Abigail ROBBINS on 30 Oct 1841 at Woodstock. She was the daughter of Nathaniel ROBBINS and Nancy ____, and was born ca 1824; died ca 1896. Cyprian⁻⁶ BOWKER, Jr. died 8 Nov 1894 at Winnebago, Wisconsin.

Children of Cyprian⁻⁶ BOWKER, Jr. and Abigail ROBBINS:
Surname **BOWKER**
        1280. Arabelle   born ca 1844 ME; died 2 Sep 1928 Oshkosh, Winnebago, WI
        1281. Nancy Anna   born 22 Apr 1847 Oxford, ME; died 10 May 1929 WI
+   **1282. NATHANIEL**   born Nov 1850/1 Oxford, ME; died 29 March 1917 WI
                                     married Ettie/Etta M. LAKE 10 Sept 1874   (she born ca 1854; died 1882)
        1283. Harriet F.   born 6 Aug 1852; died 22 July 1926 Marietta, MN
                                     married Leonardus L. THORNBURG ca _____
        1284. Ella Frances   born ca 1856 WI; died ca 1930
        1285. Ida   born 25 Oct 1858; died 31 March 1931 Oshkosh, WI
        1286. Estella Mary   born Feb 1860; died 18 Aug 1860   EOL
        1287. Onella Abigail   born Feb 1860; died ca 1930 Seattle, WA
        1288. James   born 20 Oct 1862; died 28 Aug 1867   EOL
        1289. Rose Marie   born 1866 WI; died 1932 Seattle, WA

927. COLISTA/CALISTA M⁻⁶ BOWKER, daughter of Edmund⁻⁵ BOWKER (James⁻⁴; Edmund⁻³; James⁻²,¹) and Mary Ann CHASE, was born 11 Aug1836 at Woodstock, Oxford, Maine. She married Ambrose Shurtliff CURTIS 24 Nov 1859. He was the son of Crosby CURTIS and Mary PAINE, and was born July 1839, died 2 Jan 1915. Colista/Calista⁻⁶ BOWKER died ____.

Children of Colista/Calista-6 BOWKER and Ambrose CURTIS:
Surname **CURTIS**
1290. Galen B.	born ca 1864; died 18 Oct 1950 Tacoma, WA
	married Bertha HICKS ca _____
	(she dau/o Henry HICKS and Margaret E. SLATER)
	(she born ca 1865 Clinton, IA; died 8 Jan 1951 Tacoma, WA)
	Child: Gail-8 CURTIS born ca 1902)

\+   **1291. ERNEST/EARNEST**   born 18 Apr 1867; died 4 Jan 1952
RUPERT   married Lucy Ida SWAN 3 Dec 1899 Woodstock, ME
(she dau/o Oliver G. SWAN and Louisa ____)
(she born ca 1883; died _____)
1292. Otis D.   born ca 1872; died _____

931. JAMES LORING-6 BOWKER, brother of above, was born 13 Aug 1845 Woodstock, Oxford, Maine. He married Ellen E. DAVIS on 1 Jan 1866. She was the daughter of ____ DAVIS and ____; and was born Dec 1849; died 15 Mar 1913. James L-6 BOWKER, a postmaster, died 30 Dec 1925 at Woodstock, Maine.

Children of James L-6 BOWKER and Ellen DAVIS:
Surname **BOWKER**   (all children born Woodstock, Oxford, ME)
1293. Irving L.	born ca 1867; died 7 Feb 1951 Portland, ME
	1 married Minnie Ella DORR 21 July 1894
	2 married Lulie/Lulu TRULL 14 Sept 1904
	(she dau Roscoe TRULL and Esther A. WALKER)
	(she born ca 1870 Me; died ____)
1294. James P.	born ca 1869; died ____
1295. Albert Lawrence	born 27 Sep 1871; died 13 May 1962 West Paris, Maine
	married Nellie Louise STILWELL 8 June 1904 ME
	(she dau/o Edwin R. STILWELL and Fannie L. ____)
	(she born ca 1885; died 1984)
1296. Wilford Franklin	born ca 1875; died 12 June 1963
	married Fannie F. CURTIS 20 Oct 1894 Woodstock
	(she dau/o Daniel H. CURTIS and Cynthia E. ____)

Child: Curtis W-8 BOWKER born 14 Feb 1911; died 25 Jan 1990; married Norine E. ____.
Two children: Fay-9 born ca 1933 and Betty-9 BOWKER born ca 1936

1297. Mary Pearl	born 20 Sep 1878; died ____)
	married Hans Johansen MULLER 2 Oct 1901

Children: Bessie K-8 born ca 1905; died ca 1989; and Frederick J-8 MULLER born ca 1907
1298. Esther M.	born May 1886; died ____
	married Edward R. " Ted " STANLEY ca 1907; poss. NH
	(he born ca 1882/83 NH; died ____)

Children: Margaret-8 born ca 1908; Robert-8 born ca 1911; Edward-8 STANLEY born ca 1918
1299. Elmer Roy	born 6 Aug 1890; died 19 Aug 1983 Pinellas, FL
	married Martha R. _____ ca _____

Children: Elinor-8 born ca 1918; and Olive-8 BOWKER born ca 1919

937. VIRGIL D. P-6 BICKNELL, son of Judith-5 BOWKER (James-4; Edmund-3; James-2,1) and James BICKNELL, was born 24 March 1833. He married Frances M. WARREN 22 Jan 1858. She was the daughter of Tristam WARREN and Jumalier FOSTER; and was born 19 Jan 1838, died ____. Virgil-6 BICKNELL died ____.

Children of Virgil-6 BICKNELL and Frances WARREN:
Surname **BICKNELL**
1300. Frances Eudora	born 20 Apr 1858; died ____; married Emerson AMES ca ____
1301. James Elmer	born 27 Apr 1860; died ____
	married Amy K. BONNEY 20 Jan 1906 Buckfield, ME
1302. Florence W.	born 1 Feb 1862; died _____ unmarried EOL
1303. Nellie	born 18 Feb 1864; died 27 Dec 1946; married George RECORD ca ____
13041. Minnie	born 17 July 1868; died ____; married Selden BARRETT ca _____

941. ISABELLA[-6] BICKNELL, sister of above, was born 24 Feb 1845 ME. She married Cyrus De COSTER ca 1873. He was the son of Chandler Phinney De COSTER, Jr. and Tryphena HALL, and was born 18 May 1842; died Nov 1916 ME. Isabella[-6] BICKNELL died ca 1926 at Buckfield, ME.   Note: Cyrus De COSTER served in the 32nd ME Regt, Co. E during the Civil War

Children of Isabella[-6] BICKNELL and Cyrus De COSTER:
Surname **De COSTER**

1305. Lillian D.	born ca 1874; died ____; married Oakley STOUT ca ____	
1306. Cyrus, Jr.	born ca 1879; died ____; married Jeanne WORKMAN ca ____	

946. EDMUND[-6] BOWKER, son of Harvey[-5] BOWKER (James[-4]; Edmund[-3]; James[-2,1]) and Phoebe PROCTOR, was born 31 Aug 1832 Maine. He married first to Sarah KENDRICK 7 Dec 1852. She was the daughter of ____ KENDRICK and ____, and was born ca 1835; died ____. He married second to Julia M. BRACKETT Johnson on 22 Dec 1865. She was the daughter of William Plummer BRACKETT and Laura Jane[-6] BOWKER, and was born 19 Dec 1832; died ____. Edmund[-6] BOWKER died 2 Sep 1902.   Note: Julia M. BRACKETT was married first to Luther JACKSON (see #952 below)

Children of Edmund[-6] BOWKER and Sarah KENDRICK:
Surname **BOWKER**   (children born Franklin Plantation, Oxford, Maine)

1307. Franklin C.	born ca 1854; died 7 Nov 1898 Newton, MA		
1308. Sarah E.	born ca 1856; died ____	1309. William C.	born ca 1859; died young

Child of Edmund[-6] and Julia BRACKETT Jackson:
Surname **BOWKER**

1310. Willie E.	born Oct 1866; died ____; married Tressie E. NOYES 29 Dec 1891
	(she dau/o Joseph A. NOYES and Sylvina FARWELL (?))

950. KILBOURN P[-6] BOWKER, brother of above, was born Oct 1841 ME. He married Vesta Heath DOBLE Abbott (as her 2nd husband) ca 1868. She was the daughter of Willard DOBLE and Bethia ROWE, and was born May 1836; died 4 May 1910. She was married 1st to George P. ABBOTT on 23 Apr 1859 at Sumner, ME, and had a child named Harry A. ABBOTT.

Children of Kilbourn[-6] BOWKER and Vesta DOBLE Abbott:
Surname **BOWKER**

1311. Minnie S.	born ca 1869; died ____
1312. Martha D.	born 2 Feb 1872 Sumner, Oxford, ME; died ____

951. MARTHA ELLEN[-6] BOWKER, sister of above,   was born 22 April 1846 at Woodstock, Maine. She married Charles Augustus GOWELL ca ____. He was the son of Charles GOWELL and Emeline ____; and was born 23 June 1842 Abington, MA; died ____. Martha[-6] BOWKER died of cancer of the uterus on 24 Oct 1911 at Worcester, MA.

Children of Martha-[6] BOWKER and Charles GOWELL:
Surname **GOWELL**

1313. Ellen Emma	born Sept 1865; died 1907 MA; married George M. GEYER ca 1892
	(he born Nov 1852 MA; died ____)
	Children: Harry[-8] born ca 1887; Lizzie E.[-8] born ca 1893; Blanch I.[-8] born ca 1897; and Edith C.[-8] GEYER born ca 1899
1314. Lizzie A.	born ca 1867; died ____
1315. Charles H.	born ca 1868; died ____

952. JULIA M[-6] BRACKETT, daughter of Laura Jane[-5] BOWKER (James[-4]; Edmund[-3]; James-[2,1]) and William Plummer BRACKETT, was born 19 Dec 1832 ME. She married first to Luther JACKSON (as his 2nd wife) ca 1850. He was the son of Nathaniel JACKSON and Nancy GOODWIN and was born ca 1820 ME; died 15 May 1864. She married 2nd to Edmund C[-6] BOWKER (# 946) on 22 Dec 1865. He was the son of Harvey[-5] BOWKER and Phoebe PROCTOR, and was born 31 Aug 1832; died 2 Sep 1902. Julia-[6] BRACKETT Jackson died ____. Note: Child of Edmund[-6] BOWKER and Julia-[6] BRACKETT listed above (# 1310)

Children of Julia M[-6] BRACKETT and Luther JACKSON:
Surname **JACKSON**

1316. Luther Henry	born 23 Aug 1851 Oxford, ME; died ____
1317. Seth W.	born ca 1854; died ____; married Anna M. ____ ca 1894 (she born Dec 1867 PA)
	Children: Ralph M[-8] born Dec 1895 Pa; and Florence B[-8] JACKSON born Mar 1898 PA
1318. Helen M.	born ca 1857; died ____
1319. Hattie M.	born ca 1858; died ____

956. LAURA JANE⁻⁶ BRACKETT, sister of above, was born 24 Dec 1842 ME. She married Josiah Adelbert BARTLETT 1 Jan 1863. He was the son of Joseph BARTLETT and Fannie TILSON, and was born 23 Nov 1841; died 20 Jan 1916 Mexico, Maine. Laura-⁶ BRACKETT died ____.

Children of Laura J⁻⁶ BRACKETT and Adelbert BARTLETT:
Surname **BARTLETT**   Reference: Anthony BRACKETT, Jr. of Stroudwater Parish and his Descendants, P. 171

1320. Emerson P.	born 2 Dec 1870; died ____; 1 married Alice COOK ca _____ (she born ca 1873)
	2 married Hattie M. COOK/CORK 2 Jan 1900
	(she dau/o Osman COOK/CORK and Sarah J. BARTON) (she born ca 1879/80)
1321. Alice J.	born ca 1903; died ____
1322. Lionel E.	born ca 1906; died ____
1323. Irving C.	born ca 1905; died ____
1324. Jeremiah L. (Jerry)	born ca 1910; died ____
1325. Grace E.	born ca 1917; died ____
1326. Gertrude M.	born ca 1920; died ____; married ____ REDDING ca ____
	Child: Eugenia H⁻⁸ REDDING born ca 1939

960. MOZART⁻⁶ WHITTIER, son of Lucy⁻⁵ BOWKER (Warren⁻⁴; Edmund⁻³; James⁻²;¹) and True⁻⁷ Glidden WHITTIER, was born 16 Dec 1839 at Vienna, Maine. He married first to Anna Ann TRIPP ca 1865. She was the daughter of Russell TRIPP and Diadama NICKERSON; and was born ca 1837; died ca 1893. He married second to Matilda YOUNG Thayer on 3 June 1894. She was the daughter of ____ YOUNG and ____; and the widow of ____ THAYER. She was born ca 1852; died ____. Mozart⁻⁶ WHITTIER died ca 1927 at Boston, MA.

Children of Mozart⁻⁶ WHITTIER and Anna Ann TRIPP:
Surname **WHITTIER**

1327. Maud B.	born 6 May 1866 MA; died 30 June 1913
	married William " Will" Herbert WORTH 5 Oct 1887
	(he born Feb 1856 MA) Child: Marjorie W· ⁸ WORTH born Sept 1888 IL
1328. Albert Brown	born 8 Mar 1868 MA; died 13 Sep 1919
1329. Lila Frances	born 27 Sep 1874 Boston, MA; died 10 June 1939 Seattle, WA
	married Fred STIRMELL ca ____

963. NATHANIEL BOWKER⁻⁶ WHITTIER, son of Lucy⁻⁵ BOWKER (Warren⁻⁴; Edmund⁻³; James⁻²;¹) and True Glidden⁷ WHITTIER, was born 17 April 1847 at Farmington, Maine. He married first to Cynthia Frances BECKLER 2 April 1868 at Boston, MA. She was the daughter of Charles M. BECKLER and Cornelia Lavinia LORING, and was born 18 Jan 1850 Boston; died 4 June 1883 at Somerville, MA. He married second to Eva Mary ANDREWS on 15 Oct 1883 at Lynn, MA. She was the daughter of Richard Edward ANDREWS and Sarah Stone DRAKE, and was born 14 Dec 1851 at Boston; died ____. Nathaniel Bowker⁻⁶ WHITTIER died 4 Dec 1911 at Adel, GA.

Children of Nathaniel Bowker⁻⁶ WHITTIER and Cynthia BECKLER:
Surname **WHITTIER**

1330. Francis True	born 1 Feb 1869 Chelsea, MA; died _____	EOL
	married Annie L. Pinkham TORREY 16 Sep 1908 Lynn, MA	
	(she dau/o Albert H. TORREY and Louisa RINDS)(she born ca 1866 Wicasset, ME;)	

Two adopted children: Fred Perkins WHITTIER (name changed from Herbert Raymond JONES); and Dorothy Alice WHITTIER (name changed from Harriet A. HOOK) (for information only)

1331. Cornelia Corrinna	born 26 Nov 1870 Boston, MA; died 14 Nov 1876	EOL
1332. Cordelia Malvina	born 29 Apr 1872 Boston; died __ ; never married	EOL
1333. Lucy Bowker	born 5 Sep 1873 Boston; died ____	
	married Olen Lecton/Leston CARTER ca ____ (as his second wife)	
	(he s/o Nathaniel CARTER and Polima ____)	
	(he born ca 1853; died _____)	
1334. Carrie Henrietta	born 3 Aug 1874 Boston; died 11 Oct 1874	EOL
1335. Cynthia Hope	born 28 Jan 1876; died ____	
	married Charles L. ANDREWS 17 Feb 1896 Lynn, MA	
	(he s/o Richard Edward ANDREWS and Sarah Stone DRAKE)	
	(he born 18 Mar 1874 Suffolk, MA; died ____)	
	Child: Charles S⁻⁸ ANDREWS born ca 1897	
1336. Grace Helen	born 27 Oct 1881; died 27 Sep 1882 Boston	

Children of Nathaniel Bowker⁻⁶ WHITTIER and Eva ANDREWS:
Surname **WHITTIER**

1337. Nathalia Andrews	born 29 Jul 1884 Lynn, MA; died ____; married Chester A. VITTUM 14 April 1903	

(he s/o Charles Horace VITTUM and Abigail " Abbie " DOW)
(he born 20 Oct 1882 NH; died 25 Sep 1965 Cook Co., GA)
Children: Elmer-⁸ born ca 1904 NH, died 13 June 1973 FL; and Alpheus⁻⁸ VITTUM
born ca 1907 NH, died Dec 1962

+   **1338. NATHANIEL**   born 19 Nov 1885 Lynn, MA; died _____
            BOWKER   married Catherine/ Katie Julia SHEPPARD 28 June 1908 Tifton, GA
                    (she dau/o Oscar Fitzallen SHEPPARD and Carrie Lee GREEN)
                    (she born 27 May 1892 Tifton, GA; died _____)
        1339. Amy Stone   born 1 Jan 1892 Lynn, MA; died 14 May 1908 Tifton, GA
        1340. Mary Agua   born 10 June 1897 Lawrence, MA; died ____

966. SARAH ANN⁻⁶ BOWKER, daughter of Watts⁻⁵ BOWKER (Major Levi⁻⁴; Joseph⁻³; James-²,¹) and Lydia Lockwood STICKNEY, was born 1814 Machias, Washington, Maine. She married James A. GETCHELL ca 1836. He was the son of Marshall GETCHELL and Mary HOLMES, and was born 28 Oct 1814; died 25 Feb 1887. Sarah Ann⁻⁶ BOWKER died ca 1880.

Children of Sarah Ann⁻⁶ BOWKER and James GETCHELL:
Surname **GETCHELL**

+   **1341. FRANCIS MARION**   born 22 Apr 1837; died _____
            "Frank "   married Almeda Frances PERRY ca 1858
                    (she dau/o Stephen PERRY and Martha DIXON)
        1342. Henry   born May 1840 Marshfield, ME; died 12 Dec 1909 Orling, Pierce, WA
                    married Sarah Elizabeth ELWELL ca 1888
        1343. Simon Gilbert   born Feb 1843 ME; died _____ WI
                    married Eliza Ann _____ ca 1871   (she born ca 1853; died 1920)
                    Child: Evander Plummer-⁸ GETCHELL born 28 Jan 1874; died 1925; married Anna Mildred ____;
                    she born 1882 OH; died 1925
        1344. Jeremiah S.   born ca 1845; died 11 June 1864 WV

969. WINSLOW⁻⁶ BOWKER, brother of above, was born ca 1824/25 Machias, Maine. He married Hannah Jewett BOYNTON 16 Dec 1850. She was the daughter of Stephen BOYNTON and Hannah JEWETT, and was born 12 July 1832; died ____. Winslow⁻⁶ BOWKER died 2 Feb 1894.

Children of Winslow-⁶ BOWKER and Hannah BOYNTON:
Surname **BOWKER**

        1345. Lucy   born 29 Sep 1851; died ____; married Clarence DELANO ca ____
                    Child: Margaret⁸ DELANO born ca _____
        1346. Elizabeth "Lizzie"   born 26 July 1854; died ____; married H. Lester GROVER ca ____   EOL
        1347. Frederic W.   born 1 Jan 1862; died ____; 1 married Lucy B. McCABE ca ____
                    2 married Mary H. FARRAR ca ____   EOL

970. WILLIAM CLARK⁻⁶ BOWKER, brother of above, was born ca 1830 Machias, Maine. He married Ruth H. WATTS ca 1863. She was the daughter of Samuel WATTS and Esther WHITNEY, and was born 27 April 1839; died 29 Jan 1917. William C⁻⁶ died ca 1896.

Children of William C⁻⁶ BOWKER and Ruth H. WATTS:
Surname **BOWKER**

        1348. Laura E.   born ca 1864 Machias, ME; died 19 Feb 1888 Minneapolis, MN
                    married Frank SCHOPPEE 29 Sep 1885 Brookline, MA
                    (he s/o George Pierpont SCHOPPEE and Adelaide W. CAMPBELL)
                    (he born 4 Apr 1861 MN; died 20 Nov 1945)
        1349. Herbert A.   born 23 Jan 1866 Machias; died ____ (a carpenter, later a druggist)
                    married Sarah Frances CRANE 6 Apr 1892 Brookline MA
                    (she dau/o Leander Hancock CRANE (Capt. Abijah) and Edwina SMITH)
                    (she born ca 1871 ME; died _____)
                    Child: Francis L-⁸ BOWKER born 18 Mar 1893 Brookline, MA; died 1 June 1900 Machias, ME
                    from burns when his night clothes caught on fire (age 7)   EOL

Children of William C-6 BOWKER and Ruth H. WATTS, continued:
Surname **BOWKER**

1350. Samuel Watts	born 31 Oct 1868 Machias; died 12 Oct 1955 NY	
	married Amy Lauretta RANKIN 16 Oct 1893 Brookline, MA	
	(she dau/o James W. RANKIN and Susan POTTER)	
	(she born 17 Oct 1867 Taunton, MA; died ca 1948)	

Child: Barbara-8 BOWKER born ca 1901

971. WATTS HENRY-6 BOWKER, brother of above, was born 20 Dec 1836 at Machias, Washington County, Maine. He married Julia M. LYON 3 May 1858. She was the daughter of James LYON and Susan LONGFELLOW, and was born June 1838; died ____. Watts Henry-6 BOWKER died ca 1912.

Children of Watts Henry-6 BOWKER and Julia LYON:
Surname **BOWKER**

	1351. Edwin P.	born Oct 1858; died ____; married Caroline " Carry " M. HOWE 2 June1888
		(she born Aug 1859 ME) (she dau/o David HOWE and Sarah MEAD)
+	**1352. ARTHUR W.**	born ca 1864; died ca 1920; married Edna Peavy CRANE ca 1891
		(she born Jan 1868; died ____)(she dau/o Rufus CRANE and Angelia GARDNER)

Children: Elizabeth-8 born ca ____; and Julia-8 BOWKER born ca ____

+	**1353. EVERETT M.**	born Nov 1866; died ____; married Lucy GRIGGS ca ___ (she dau/o William GRIGGS)
	1354. Phillip H.	born ca 1869 ME; died ____

973. SIMON OTIS-6 HANSCOM, son of Lydia-5 BOWKER (Major Levi-4 ; Joseph-3; James-2,1) and Otis Pineo HANSCOM, and was born 20 Nov 1820/23 at Machias, Washington, Maine. He married Julia Raymond WHITE on 2 May 1846 at Machias. She was the daughter of Thomas WHITE and Abigail HARMON; and was born 7 Jan 1826; died 18 Dec 1903. Simon-6 HANSCOM died 2 Feb 1899 at East Machias.

Children of Simon-6 HANSCOM and Julia WHITE:
Surname **HANSCOM**

+	**1355. HERBERT**	born 16 Nov 1846; died 14 Aug 1919 East Machias, ME	
	MORTIMER	married Margaret A. MAKER 9 June 1870	
		(she born 16 Jan 1850 Cutler, ME; died 15 Oct 1906 East Machias, ME)	
		(she dau/o Luther MAKER and Margaret A. CARD)	
	1356. Otis	born 31 Jan 1848; died Nov 1848	EOL
	1357. Mary Abby	born 1 April 1850; died 23 March 1853	EOL
	1358. Isabelle "Belle"	born 10 June/ July 1852; died 29 Oct 1927 Ramsey, MN	
		married George Mifflin Dallas JACKMAN ca ____ (he born 1847; died 1892)	

Children: Charles H-8 born ca 1879; and Harry S-8 JACKMAN born ca 1881, died 1940

	1359. Nellie F.	born 14 Oct 1854; died ____	
	1360. Anna I.	born ca 1857; died 14 Sept 1956	
	1361. Fannie Lillian	born 31 Dec 1858; died 27 May 1860	EOL
	1362. James Henry	born 24 Dec 1862; died ____	
	1363. Julia Ermina "Mina"	born 24 April 1867; died 3 Mar 1952 Bowdoin, Maine	
	1364. Flora L.	born 27 March 1869; died 15 March 1936 East Machias, ME	

976. WATTS BOWKER-6 HANSCOM, brother of above, was born 4 June 1829 at Machias, Maine. He married Sarah Perkins ROBINSON 19 Dec 1852. She was the daughter of ____ ROBINSON and ____; and was born 12 Oct 1833; died 16 Feb 1920. Watts B-6 HANSCOM died 27 April 1900.

Children of Watts Bowker-6 HANSCOM and Sarah ROBINSON:
Surname **HANSCOM**

	1365. Charles LaSalle	born ca 1854; died ____; never married
	1366. Arthur	born ca 1856; died ____
	1367. Edward	born ca 1857; died ____; married Abbie WINSLOW

Children: Beatrice-8 born ca ____; and Dean-8 HANSCOM born ca ___; resided Hyde Park, MA

	1368. Lincoln C.	born ca 1860; died ____; married Rose CHIPMAN ca ____ (no issue)
+	**1369. MARY C.**	born 14 Sep 1862; died 12 Oct 1941
		1 married William W. HALE 29 Jan 1880 (he born 1 Jan 1853 MA; died ____)
		2 married Albert J. GRAF ca 1908

Children of Watts Bowker⁻⁶ HANSCOM and Sarah ROBINSON, continued:
Surname **HANSCOM**

1370. Florence R.   born ca 1866; died ____; married George BUCKNAM ca ____
         Children: Austin⁻⁸ born ca ____; Philip⁻⁸ born ca ____; and Louise⁻⁸ BUCKNAM born ca ____
1371. Maude   born ca 1868; died ____; married Harry TOWNSEND ca ____
         Children: George-⁸ born ca ____; and Priscilla-⁸ TOWNSEND born ca ____
1372. Bessie   born ca 1875; died ____; married Charles Munger CHASE ca 1892
         Child: Elton-⁸ CHASE born ca ____

982. NATHAN STEPHEN⁻⁶ BOWKER, son of Levi-⁵ BOWKER, Jr. (Levi⁻⁴; Joseph⁻³; James-²,¹) and Martha G. CROCKER, was born 15 May 1826. He married Mary Abigail BERRY ca 1850. She was the daughter of Stephen BERRY and Rebecca BERRY, and was born 28 Nov 1827; died 16 Sept 1911. Nathan S⁻⁶ BOWKER died 18 July 1910.

Children of Nathan⁻⁶ BOWKER and Mary Abigail BERRY:
Surname **BOWKER**   (all children born Marshfield, Washington, Maine)

1373. Stephen   born ca 1850; died ____; unmarried
+   **1374. SIMEON OSCAR**   born 20 Jan 1851; died 1 May 1907; married Keziah J. HOLMES 2 Mar 1871/72
         (she dau/o Tristam HOLMES and Hannah Knight BERRY)
         (she born 19 April 1851 Marshfield, ME; died ____)
1375. Ferdinand B   born June 1852; died ____; married Lillian PALMER ca 1882 Marshfield
         (she born ca April 1862; died ____)
         Children: Harlan L-⁸ born ca ____; married Eve L. GETCHELL 4 Dec 1909; Samuel-⁸ born ca ____;
             and Horace T-⁸ BOWKER born ca ____
1376. Samuel C   born ca 1855; died ____; unmarried
1377. Ada F.   born Nov 1865; died ____; married Dayton W. SMITH 26 May 1897
         (he born ca Dec 1863; died ____)

983. FERDINAND⁻⁶ BOWKER, brother of above, was born ca 1830 ME. He married Lucy⁻³ BOYNTON on 2 Oct 1850 at Machias, Washington, Maine. She was the daughter of Stephen⁻² BOYNTON and Hannah JEWETT, and was born 15 Mar 1827 Machias, ME; died ____. Ferdinand⁻⁶ BOWKER died ca 1852, and his widow married second to an Albert MOORS.

Children of Ferdinand⁻⁶ BOWKER and Lucy BOYNTON:
Surname **BOWKER**

1378 . Levi F   born 20 May 1851; died 9 Feb 1894 Machias, ME
         married Charlotte MUNSON ca 1873
         (she dau/o Warren MUNSON and Charlotte McCANN/McKAN)
         (she born ca 1850; died ____)
         Child: Mabel-⁸ BOWKER born ca 1874 OH; died 1918; married James R. TAYLOR
1379. Ferdinand F.   born 23 Nov 1852 Machias, ME; died 3 May 1853 Machias EOL

992. SARAH⁻⁶ GETCHELL, daughter of Betsey⁻⁵ BOWKER (Major Levi⁻⁴; Jioseph⁻³; James⁻²,¹) and Simeon GETCHELL, was born 14 Aug 1827 at Machias, Washington, Maine. She married William P. LYON ca 1846/7. He was the son of Henry LYON and Betsey CROCKER, and was born 25 Jan 1818; did 21 Nov 1862. Sarah⁻⁶ GETCHELL died 20 July 1864 at Marshfield, Maine.

Children of Sarah⁻⁶ GETCHELL and William P. LYON:
Surname **LYON**

+   **1380. GEORGE M.**   born 27 Dec 1846/7; died 1927 Marshfield, ME
         married Jane Ann "Jenny" BERRY ca 1866
         (she born July 1849; died 11 Dec 1901 MN)
1381. Willie H.   born 8 Jan 1848; died 7 Mar 1933 MN
         married Josephine LEIGHTON ca ____ (she born May 1854)
         Child: Willie-⁸ LYON born ca ____
1382. Amelia G.   born ca 1850; died ____; no issue
+   **1383. SIMEON GETCHELL**   born 5 May 1852; died ____; 1910 resided Oakland, CA
         married Hannah SEDGLEY ca 1879
         (she born Nov 1857 CA; died ____) (she dau/o John SEDGLEY and Eliza ____)
1384. Sanford P.   born ca 1854; died ____; married Sarah ELLISON ca ____
         Children: Marion-⁸ born ca ____; and George-⁸ LYON born ca ____

Children of Sarah-6 GETCHELL and William P. LYON, continued:
Surname **LYON**

1385. Eliza / Lizzie	born ca 1857; died ____; married Willis A. BLOOD ca ____
	Children: Fred-8 born ca ____; Charles-8 born ca ____; and Leon-8 BLOOD born ca ____

+   **1386. ANDREW M**.   born 2 May 1860 Marshfield, ME; died 8 Jan 1923 Milford, CT; a carpenter
married Catherine Durling Lynn CLARK 24 Nov 1879 Boston, MA
(she dau/o Ralph Robert Clark and Maria Augusta DURLAND)
(she born 26 Aug 1853 Nova Scotia, Canada; died 23 Nov 1916 Milford, CT)

1002. LADWICK HOLWAY-6 HANSCOM, son of Sarah/Sally-5 BOWKER (Major Levi-4; Joseph-3; James-2,1) and Ellis HANSCOM, was born 23 June1844 Machias, Maine. He married Ida Ann SMITH 24 Dec 1864 Machias. ME. She was the daughter of ____ SMITH and ____, and was born 2 July 1844 Nova Scotia; died 2 May 1918. Ladwick-6 HANSCOM died 21 Nov 1912 Machias, Washington, Maine.

Children of Ladwick Holway-6 HANSCOM and Ida SMITH:
Surname **HANSCOM**

1387. Robert Ellis	born 4 Jan 1866; died 28 March 1950; an undertaker
	married Inez Isabella BERRY ca ____
1388. Emily	born 6 Aug 1867; died ____; married Sewall T. CHASE 31 Oct 903
1389. Willis	born 5 Nov 1869; died ____; undertaker (in business with brother Robert)
+ **1390. ARTHUR**	born 29 Jan 1873; died ____; married Naomi C. BERRY 10 Nov 1898
1391. Carroll Lee (m)	born 25 Mar 1876; died 19 Nov 1972 Calais, Maine
	married Bernice F. Mc REAVY 2 Sept 1903
1392. Allen Ray	born 20 Aug 1878; died ____; married Bertha LONG 4 May 1904
1393. Bertha Flora	born 29 Oct 1880; died ____
1394. George Ernest	born 9 July 1884; died ____

1029. JOHN VARNEY-6 DURGIN, son of Delane-5 WRIGHT (Hannah-4 BOWKER/BUKER; Joseph-3; James-2,1) and Cotton A. DURGIN, was born 20 Jan 1840 Newburgh, Penobscot, Maine. He married Ellen " Nelly "FITZPATRICK on 20 Oct 1865 at Crawford, WI. She was the daughter of _____ FITZPATRICK and ____; and was born July 1847 NY; died 15 July 1936 Sanborn, IA. John V-6 DURGIN died 10 Jan 1915 Sanborn, O'Brien, IA.

Children of John V-6 DURGIN and Ellen FITZPATRICK:
Surname **DURGIN**

1395. Lida B	born Jan 1869 IA; died _____; married Walter I. SIMPSON 28 Dec 1889 Sanborn, IA.
	(he born Mar 1863 NY; died ____) (before 1910)
	Child: Donald Walter-8 SIMPSON born 18 Mar 1896 Sheldon, IA
1396. Ethlyn	born ca 1873 ME; died _____; married _____ THOMAS
1397. Lillian D.	born ca 1875 MN; died _____
+ **1398. ALLARD JOHN**	born 24 Nov 1878 SD; died 11 Dec 1938 Albert Lea, Freeborn, MN
	1 married Bessie Jeanette SMITH ca _____
	2 married Annie KALSCHEVER ca _____
1399. Edna Katherine	born 21 May 1884 SD; died ____ (poss. died before 1925)
	married Arthur C. JOHNSON ca 1905 (he born ca 1880 SD)

1039. ISAAC NEWTON-6 BOWKER, son of Isaac Hall-5 BOWKER (James-4; Joseph-3; James-2,1) and Eliza _____, was born 15 Aug 1842 at Phippsburg, Maine. He married Maria Jane BROWN ca 1872. She was the daughter of _____ BROWN and ____; and was born Dec 1841; died ____. Isaac Newton-6 BOWKER , a coastal pilot, died 22 Feb 1924 at Bath, Maine.

Children of Isaac Newton-6 BOWKER and Eliza _____:
Surname **BOWKER**

1400. Ella/Etta P.	born June 1877; died ____; married Eugene W. JOHNSON ca ____
	(he born Nov 1841; died ____) (he a Sea Captain)
+ **1401. EDWARD** **NEWTON**	born 31 Jan 1878/79; died 18 Jan 1966 Sanford, ME.
	married Viena Sarah STIMSON ca ____
	(she born 2 Mar 1881 Laconia, Belknap, NH; died 1 Oct 1953 Portsmouth, NH
	(she dau/o David Samuel STIMSON and Lucy A. GERRY)

1052. CUTLER ELBRIDGE-6 BOWKER, son of Elbridge-5 BOWKER (James-4; Joseph-3; James-2,1) and Elizabeth PERCY, was born 27 Oct 1845 at Phippsburg, Maine. He married Mary Ann BLACK on 9 March 1873. She was the daughter of Thomas BLACK and Sarah ___ ; and was born June 1846; died 1931. Cutler Elbridge-6 BOWKER died 21 Apr 1922 at Bath, Maine.

Children of Cutler E-6 BOWKER and Mary Ann BLACK:
Surname **BOWKER**

+	**1402. THOMAS BLACK**	born 10 July 1874; died ____
		married Florence Mabel NEWCOMB 18 Oct 1902
		(she dau/o Jesse P. NEWCOMB and Hattie M. DUNBAR)
		(she born ca 1883; died _____)
+	**1403. AFTON CUTLER**	born 20 June 1879; died 13 Dec 1962 Bath, Maine
		married Jenniebelle May WILLIS 22 Nov 1901
		(she dau/o Fred Lincoln WILLIS and Isadora MC FADDEN)
		(she born ca 1884; died ____)
	1404. Percy Ray	born 11 Mar 1889/93 Bath, ME; died 10 Sep 1980 Pasco, FL; married Ruth V. _____

Child: Clarence William-8 BOWKER born 28 Feb 1920; died 6 Jan 1978; member of the Coast Guard

1053. ADELIA LORING-6 BOWKER, sister of above, 24 June 1848 Phippsburg, Sagadahoc, Maine. She married John Rich. EASTMAN , a fisherman, on 25 Nov 1869. He was the son of John Dana EASTMAN and Abigail RICH; and was born 10 Sep 1839 Harpswell, ME; died 19 Feb 1923 Portland, ME.. Adelia-6 BOWKER died 5 Aug 1913 South Portland, Maine.

Children of Adelia Loring-6 BOWKER and John R. EASTMAN:
Surname **EASTMAN**

+	**1405. ELIZABETH MAE**	born ca 1870; died ____ ; married William W. RICH ca 1892
+	**1406. EPHRAIM RICH**	born 9 Jan 1875; died 1930
		1 married Lulu M. CATLIN 21 April 1898 (she born ca 1881)
		(she dau/o Stephen W. CATLIN and Philena S. SMALL)
		2 married Marion B. WING Hoffman 26 July 1910 South Portland, ME
		(she dau/o Charles WING and Elizabeth DEXTER of Brunswick, ME)
		(she born ca 1880 ME; died ____)
	1407. Arthur H.	born July 1877; died 11 July 1916 So. Portland, ME (typhoid fever) (he a fisherman)
	1408. John	born _____; died ____
	1409. James P.	born ca 1882; died ____ (before 1930) (a sailor, mate on a steamship)
		married Marietta D. SNOW 27 July 1908
		(she dau/o Frank Oliver SNOW and Delight D. KEMP) (she born ca 1881 ME)
	1410. Blanche Marion	born ca 1887; died ____

1049. FREEMAN CLARK-6 BOWKER, son of Timothy-5 Batchelder BOWKER (James-4; Joseph-3; James-2,1) and Elizabeth Percy MORRISON, was born 27 April 1850 at Phippsburg, Lincoln, Maine. He married Annie L. SPRAGUE on 2 March 1874. She was the daughter of ____ SPRAGUE and ____ , and was born 1854; died 1951. Freeman-6 BOWKER died ca ____ .

Children of Freeman C-6 BOWKER and Annie L. SPRAGUE:
Surname **BOWKER**

	1411. Bertha May	born June 1877; died 1907
		married Sheldon Alvin HOUGHTON, Jr. 28 Nov 1906
		(s/o Sheldon A HOUGHTON, SR. and Mary L. HOLYOKE)
	1412. Jay Kimball	born 23 June 1884; died 1961
		married Ada Maude KIMBALL on 8 Jan 1905
		(she dau/o Charles H. KIMBALL and Flavilla C. HANSON)
		(she born 26 Sep 1884 Woburn, MA; died _____)
	1413. Henry Percy	born 23 Nov 1887; died 19 July 1944 Concord, NH
		married Lena M. HOLLIS ca ____ (she born ca 1894 MA; died ____)

1063. WILLIAM RICHARDSON-6 BOWKER, brother of above, was born 4 May 1859. He married first to Abbie E. WALLACE ca 1891. She was the daughter of Lemuel Goodwin WALLACE and Nancy Dingley EASTMAN, and was born 12 Mar 1870; died 17 Jan 1910. He married second to Hattie/ Hallie Mc PHEE Fogg on 21 Dec 1918. She was the daughter of James Mc PHEE and Myra ____ , and was born ca 1879, died ____ . William R-6 BOWKER died 15 Dec 1932 Phippsburg, ME.

Children of William Richardson[6] BOWKER and Abbie E. WALLACE:
Surname **BOWKER**   (children born Phippsburg, Lincoln, Maine)

1414. Hattie V.	born Sep 1891; died ____	1418. Howard E. born 29 Apr 1907; died 16 Sep 1971
1415. Beatrice M.	born 7 Aug 1893; died ____	
1416. Olive Esther	born 28 Oct 1895; died Apr 1976 ME	
1417. Ada H.	born 15 Apr 1900; died Jan 1966 ME	

1070.TURNER[6] BOWKER, son of Benjamin-[5] BOWKER, Jr (Benjamin-[4]; Richard-[3,2]; James-[1]) and Hannah Pratt RAMSDELL, was born 5 May 1813 at Hanson, Plymouth, MA. He married Harriet TILDEN on 20 Dec 1835 at Marshfield, MA. She was the daughter of Elisha TILDEN and Grace LOVIS; and was born 12 Nov 1808 ; died 27 Oct 1855 Hanson, MA. Turner[6] BOWKER died ca 1855 Hanson.

Children of Turner[6] BOWKER and Harriet TILDEN:
Surname **BOWKER**

	1419. Harriet Tilden	born ca 1838; died ____
+	**1420. MARY JANE**	born 8 Nov 1841 Hanson, MA; died 19 Nov 1883 Hanson
		1 married Calvin Francis BOURNE on 6 April 1856
		(he born Dec 1834; died Nov 1868) (he s/o William BOURNE and Sylvia WHITMAN
		2 married George W. JACKMAN 19 Mar 1870 Hanson, MA
		(he s/o Alfred JACKMAN and Eliza ____)

1071. JOHN ADAMS[6] BOWKER, son of Gad/Gard-[5] BOWKER (Benjamin-[4]; Richard-[3,2]; James-[1]) and Clarissa RAMS-DELL, was born 4 Sep 1824 at Hanson, Plymouth, MA. He possibly married first to (unknown). He married second to Mary Ann WILLIS on 28 Sep 1856 at Hanson. She was the daughter of John WILLIS and Adelia / Fidelia YOUNG, and was born ca 1827; died ____. John Adams[6] BOWKER died ____.

Child of John Adams[6] BOWKER and unknown wife:
Surname **BOWKER**

1421. David W.	born ca 1848

Children of John Adams-[6] BOWKER and Mary Ann WILLIS:
Surname **BOWKER**

1422. Benjamin F.	born ca 1856; died ____	1423. Charles P/F	born ca 1858; died ____
1424. Clarissa A.	born 2 April 1860; died ____		
1425. John Willis/Weston	born 6 July 1864 Hanson, Ma; died ____; married Elva L. ESTES on 15 Aug 1886		
	(she dau/o Stephen H. ESTES and Diana H. ____)		

Children: Ethel-[8] born ca 1889; Lloyd-[8] born ca 1893 and John W.-[8] BOWKER, Jr. born ca 1908

1073. ANDREW [6] BOWKER, brother of above, was born 12 Dec 1828 at Hanson, Plymouth, MA. He possibly married first to Sarah Jane HOUSE ca ____. She born __?_; died 1851. He married second to Betsey BARKER on 15 June 1855. She was the daughter of Daniel BARKER and Betsey ____, and was born ___; died 10 Feb 1918. Andrew C-[6] BOWKER died 26 Apr 1891 .

Children of Andrew-[6] BOWKER and Betsey BARKER:
Surname **BOWKER**

	1426. Francella E.	born ca 1858; died 12 Sep 1940
+	**1427. ANDREW**	born 4 Mar 1861 Hingham, MA; died 11 Mar 1907 Rockland, MA.
	CLARENCE	married Mabel J. JACKSON 7 Sep 1884 Rockland
	1428. Arthur Everett	born 10 June 1863; died ____

1075. GEORGE T-[6] BOWKER, brother of above, was born ca 1833/34 at Hanson, MA. He married first to Miranda C. WALKER on 24 May 1855. She was the daughter of Clarendon WALKER and Ruth ____, and was born ____; died 13 Oct 1895. He married second to Alice S. HARDING on 18 Sep 1877. George T-[7] BOWKER died 31 Oct 1881.

Children of George T[6] BOWKER and Miranda WALKER:
Surname **BOWKER**

1429. George Elliot	born 5 Aug 1856; died 6 Dec 1935
	married Jane Gilman BAILEY 5 Oct 1909
	(she dau/o Stephen W. BAILEY and Emily J. STETSON) (she born ca 1873)
1430. Fred W.	born ____; died 9 July 1940; married Lettie W. BROUNVILLE ca ____

1076. HANNAH-6 BOWKER, sister of above, was born Nov 1836 Hanson, Plymouth, MA. She married Nymphus Marston CHANDLER, as his second wife, on 28 April 1866. He was the son of Stetson CHANDLER and Eliza ____ ; and was born May 1821; died 1909, MA. Hannah-6 BOWKER died ____ .

Children of Hannah-6 BOWKER and Nymphus Marston CHANDLER:
Surname **CHANDLER**

1431. May Florence	born ca 1866; died ____	
1432. Mary	born June 1867; died ____ ; married Clifford HUNT ca ____ ; (he born Aug 1859)	
1433. Ella A.	born Feb 1873	

1078. SARAH MATILDA-6 DOTEN / DOTY, daughter of John Edward-5 DOTEN / DOTY (Bathsheba-4 BOWKER; Luke-3; Richard-2; James-1) and Elizabeth-7 VOSE, was born 12 Feb 1808 at Pomfret, VT. She married Henry Little PAGE on 14 Mar 1830 at Woodstock, VT. He was the son of Abner PAGE and Jane LITTLE, and was born27 Dec 1801 Salem, NH; died 13 May 1844 Pomfret, VT. Sarah Matilda-6 DOTEN / DOTY died 22 Aug 1892 Pomfret, VT.

Children of Sarah Matilda-6 DOTEN / DOTY and Henry PAGE:
Surname **PAGE**

1434. John Quincy	born 24 Oct 1830; died ____	1439. Christiana Electa	born 25 Dec 1838
1435. William Little	born 24 Jan 1832; died ____	1440. Ellen Lucretia	born 23 Aug 1840
1436. Joseph Wright	born 16 Aug 1833; died ____	1441. Sarah Louisa	born 31 Dec 1842
1437. Elizabeth Jane	born12 Mar 1835; died ____	1442. Henry Little	born 27 Aug 1844
1438. Edwin Ruthven	born 21 Nov 1836; died 17 Aug 1856		

1086. DAVID-6 BOWKER, son of David-5 BOWKER (David-4; Luke-3; Richard-2; James-1) and Eunice CLAPP, was born 16 June 1808, MA. He married first to Hannah S. CARSWELL on 6 July 1830. She was the daughter of _____ CARSWELL and ___ , and was born ____ , died ____ . His second wife was Sylvia GORDON. They married on 4 July 1849. She was the daughter of Samuel GORDON and Clarissa SMITH, and was born 22 Sep 1824 Mount Vernon, Maine; died 12 May 1897 Northumberland, VA. David-6 BOWKER died 12 Dec 1890 VA.

Children of David-6 BOWKER and Sylvia GORDON:
Surname **BOWKER**

1443. David E.	born 19 Mar 1851; died 28 Oct 1919
1444. James Llewellyn	born 25 Sep 1853 ME; died 22 Feb 1921 Richmond, VA
	married Alma Virginia ALEXANDER ca 1884
	(she dau/o Thomas B. ALEXANDER and Elizabeth A. HAYNIE)
	(she born 26 Oct 1857 Richmond, VA; died 20 July 1933)
	Children: Helen L.-8 born ca 1885; Laura Mae-8 born ca 1887, died 1965; Alice Cora-8 born ca 1891, died 1984
	and James Leslie-8 BOWKER born ca 1893, died 1966
1445. Charles Davis	born 25 Sep 1856 ME; died 12 Nov 1882 VA
1446. Clarissa Helen/Ellen	born 25 Apr 1857 ME; died 31 Mar 1884 Waltham, MA
1447. Alice Selvina	born 7 Aug 1859 Kennebec, ME; died 1 Dec 1946 Northumberland, VA

1088. JOHN HILLIARD-6 BOWKER, brother of above, was born 1 Feb 1813 Scituate, MA. He married Sarah DUNCAN on 27 Aug 1835. She was the daughter of __ DUNCAN and ___ , and was born 1815; died ___ John Hilliard-6 BOWKER died ____ .

Children of John Hilliard-6 BOWKER and Sarah DUNCAN:
Surname **BOWKER**

1448. John H.	born ca 1839 MA; died 9 Mar 1901 Fall River, MA
	married Georgeanna GIBBS ca 1862
	(she born May 1841; died 1904 Fall River, MA)
	Children: Frederick D-8 born 18 Dec 1868, died 1920, married Genevra M. ALMY; and
	Walter G-8 BOWKER born ca 1871 RI; died 7 May 1992 Fall River, MA
1449. Sarah L.	born ca 1850; died ____ ; married Henry O. LITTLEFIELD 23 Dec 1868
	(he s/o Billings LITTLEFIELD and Thankful ____)
1450. Laura	born ca 1840; died ____

1097. ALONZO MELVIN-6 BOWKER, MD, son of Melvin-5 BOWKER (Liberty-4; Luke-3; Richard-2; James-1) and Betsey WILLETT, was born 14 March 1823 at Cummington, MA. He married " Hepsey " (Hephzibah) Ann Barney STURTEVANT on 4 July 1847 at Savoy, MA. She was the daughter of Daniel Elkins STURTEVANT and Hephzibah BARNEY, and was born

19 July 1822; died 12 July 1909 Plainville, IL. Alonzo Melvin[6] BOWKER, a Physician, died 15 March 1865.

Children of Alonzo Melvin[6] BOWKER and " Hepsey " STURTEVANT:
Surname **BOWKER**

	1451. Betsey Addie	born 13 July 1848 Savoy, MA; died 9 May 1932
		1 married Jarvis W. MILLER 26 Dec 1869
		2 married Joseph ALESHIRE ca 1871
		(he born 29 May 1849 Berkshire, MA; died 24 June 1911 Plainville, IL
+	**1452. FRANCENA MARIE**	born 21 June 1853; died 12 Mar 1905 Salt River, Ralls, MO
		married James Edley CAMPBELL ca 1875 (he born Nov 1850 IL; died ____)
+	**1453. MELVIN WILLET**	born 10 Feb 1860 MA; died 9 June 1926 Quincy, Adams, IL
		married Anna B. ____ ca 1886
		(she born 1 May 1867; died 19 Dec 1915 IL)
	1454. Charles Liberty	born ca 1863/64; died 18 Jan 1946 Seattle, King, WA.

1098. CHARLES H[6] BOWKER, brother of above, was born 16 Sep 1824 MA. He married first to Delcy Derry DUNHAM on 22 Mar 1848. She was the daughter of William DUNHAM and Hannah ____; and was born ca 1829; died 1852. He married second to Harriet Philena DAWES on 23 March 1853. She was the daughter of Samuel DAWES and Philena E. ___, and was born 24 Dec 1830; died 21 Feb 1910. Charles H-[6] BOWKER died 10 Dec 1906 at Bernardston, Franklin, MA.

Children of Charles[6] BOWKER and Harriet P. DAWES:
Surname **BOWKER**

+	**1455. DELCY HARRIET**	born 21 Feb 1854; died 5 June 1935 Raymond, WA
		married George Truman SWAZEY 24 Dec 1881 Bernardston, MA
		(he born 19 Mar 1852 Waterbury, VT; died ___; an attorney)
	1456. Alphonso Varian, MD	born 17 Jan 1857 Savoy, MA; died 9 Oct 1950
		married Ella Louise AMIDON 27 Nov 1884 Montague City, MA
		(she dau/o William AMIDON and Frances _____)
		(she born May 1855; died _____)
	Child: Marion B-[8] BOWKER born ___; died ____; married ____ SIBLEY; she also an MD worked in General Practice	
	1457. Charles Willet	born 10 July 1860; died 22 March 1863
	1458. Samuel Dawes, MD	born ca 1863; died 15 Nov 1912 Cambridge, MA
	1459. Arthur Hume	born 18 Apr 1867; died 1948
		married Carrie F. FENTON 14 Jan 1893 Bernardston, MA
		(she dau/o Ephraim FENTON and Betsey _____)
		(she born 2 Jan 1868 Nova Scotia; died ca 1962)
	1460. Effie Louise	born Sep 1868; died _____
		married Theodore Charles FORBES 4 Aug 1896 Bernardston, MA
		(he s/o Charles P. FORBES and Anna ROOT)
	Children: Charles S-[9] born 1902 MA; and Willet V-[9] FORBES born ca 1905	
	1461. Rosa Evelyn " Rosie "	born 16 Mar 1870; died Nov 1967
		married Francis H. MAXWELL on 25 Aug 1900 Greenfield, MA
		(he s/o Henry F. MAXWELL and Luthera A. PARMENTER)

1118. HELEN DALLAS-⁷ BOWKER, daughter of Lazarus-⁶ BOWKER (Dimmick-⁵; Lazarus-⁴˒³; James-²˒¹) and Margaret Cornelia Forbes VALENTINE, was born 17/18 June 1844 MA. She married James W. WEEKS III on 21 July 1872, as his second wife. He was the son of James W. WEEKS, Jr. and Sarah Place SHERIFF, and was born 4 Sep 1827; died ca 1920 MA.

Child of Helen Dallas-⁷ BOWKER and James WEEKS, III:
Surname **WEEKS**
+   **1462. ALMINA BELL**   born 16 Sep 1875 Boston, MA; died ca 1957 Peabody, MA
                    married William Wallace Mc GREGOR on 25 Dec 1892 at Framingham, MA
                    (he born 30 July 1869 Yonkers, NY; died 25 Feb 1933 at Peabody, Essex, MA.
                    (he s/o Cassino Mc GREGOR and Anna WALDRON)

1124. GRANT BARSTOW-⁷ LEARNED, son of Clarissa Gardner-⁶ BOWKER (Howard-⁵; Lazarus-⁴ Jr.; Lazarus-³; James-² Jr.; James-¹) and Henry LEARNED, was born 10 March 1840 NY. He married first to Mary LARNED ca ____. She was the daughter of ____ LARNED and ____; and was born ca 1843; died 1884 . He married second to Antoinette C GABRILLAC on 26 June 1861. She was born ca 1843, died 1872, and was the daughter of Hippolite GABRILLAC and Eliza HOWARD. Grant-⁷ LEARNED died 10 Apr 1879.

Children of Grant-⁷ LEARNED and Antoinette GABRILLAC:
Surname **LEARNED**
+   **1463. GEORGE HENRY**   born 15 Oct 1861 St. Louis, MO; died 7 Nov 1904 St. Louis
                    married Bertha E. RHEIN 13 Aug 1884 St. Louis, MO
                    (she dau/o John J. RHEIN and Catherine RENZ)
                    (she born ca 1870; died 1951)
      1464. James   born ca 1866; died 1866   EOL   1466. Josephine   born ca 1870; died 1872
      1465. Mary   born ca 1868; died 1870   EOL   1467. Walter   born 1871; died 1871

1126. GEORGE WASHINGTON-⁷ LEARNED, brother of above, was born 4 March 1846. He married Kezia Eliza Adelaide STACEY on 28 Apr 1873. She was the daughter of ____ STACEY and ____; and was born 29 Dec 1851 England; died 9 May 1934 Barnhart, MO. George W-⁷ LEARNED died ____.

Children of George W-⁷ LEARNED and Kezia STACEY:
Surname **LEARNED**
      1468. Harry Grant   born 7 Aug 1875 ST Louis, MO; died ____
                    married Anna C. BLANKE ca ____
                    Children: Caroline Gertrude-⁹ born ca 1906, died 1981; Henry G-⁹ Jr. born ca 1908, died 1966;
                    and George W-⁹ LEARNED born ca 1910

1127. JULIA EVELINE-⁷ BOWKER; daughter of Davis Whiting-⁶ BOWKER (Howard-⁵; Lazarus-⁴ Jr.; Lazarus-³; James-² Jr. ; James-¹) and Eveline TILDEN, was born 29 Aug 1858 MA. She married Elwin Nicholas STRANGER, as his second wife, on 9 Nov 1879. He was the son of Andrew R. STRANGER and Helen ____; and was born 15 Mar 1849; died 3 May 1925. He had been previously married to Lizzie S. HEDGE on 16 Sep 1871. She was the daughter of Barnabas HEDGE and Priscilla ___, and was born ___; died ____. Julia Eveline-⁷ died 5 Nov 1936 at Plymouth, MA.

Children of Julia Eveline-⁷ BOWKER and Elwin STRANGER:
Surname **STRANGER**
      1469. Annie Gertrude   born 9 Jan 1882; died 1976
      1470. Florence Evelyn   born 27 Aug 1885; died 1 Jan 1886   EOL
+   **1471. HELEN DAVIS**   born 5 May 1892; died July 1978 Sedgwick, KS.
                    married Frank Howard MITCHELL on 30 Mar 1921
                    (he s/o Guy Lindsey MITCHELL and Amelia Catherine ECKE)
                    (he born 3 Jan 1896 MO; died 6 Dec 1969 Newton, Harvey, KS)

1134. JOSEPHINE CORA[7] **BOWKER**, daughter of Winslow Lewis-[6] BOWKER (Lazarus-[5;4;3]; James-[2;1]) and Maria H. ____; was born 6 Feb 1852 at Cambridge, MA. She married John Edmund THURSTON (# 5130 in THURSTON Genealogy) on 4 Nov 1874 at Cambridge. He was the son of Daniel Holt THURSTON and Jane Drown SHACKLEY, and was born 1 May 1853 Cambridge; died ____. Josephine-[7] BOWKER died 15 Jan 1875 in childbirth.

Child of Josephine Cora-[7] BOWKER and John Edmund THURSTON:
Surname **THURSTON**

+	**1472. DAVID**	born 15 Jan 1875; died 1946 Somerville, MA.
	WINSLOW	married Grace Emeline ALDEN 29 Oct 1901 Medford, MA
		(she dau/o William Fernald ALDEN and Lucy Ann LESTER) she born ca 1875 Medford, MA)

1136. MARQUIS LATHRAM[7] **BOWKER**, son of Clarke-[6] BOWKER (Joseph-[5]; Zebulon-[4]; Lazarus-[3]; James-[2;1]) and Lovina PERRY/ FERRY, was born 24 Aug 1839 NY. He married Frances DUSHER ca 1862. She was the daughter of ____ DUSHER and ____; and was born 13 Oct 1842; died 18 May 1917 at Nevada, Vernon, MO. Marquis-[7] BOWKER died 27 June 1917 Nevada, MO.

Children of Marquis-[7] BOWKER and Frances DUSHER:
Surname **BOWKER**

+	**1473. WILLIAM M.**	born 2 May 1865 Carthage, Hancock, IL; died 7 Feb 1931 Nevada, MO
	1474. Franklin	born Feb 1865; died ____; married Mary/Marion E FERRY ca 1889
		Child: Pearl Lillian-[9] BOWKER born 1 Oct 1889 Sigourney, Keokuk, IA
	1475. Effie Lee	born 22 Nov 1866 Hancock, IL; died 20 Dec 1908
	1476. Lillie	born ca 1869; died ____
+	**1477. JACOB OSCAR**	born 17 Feb 1873 IL; died 2 May 1943 Burns, ID
+	**1478. FREDERICK GUY**	born 22 Apr 1876 Hancock, IL; died 10 Mar 1929 NE
+	**1479. MARY AGNES**	born 13 July 1878 Il; died ca 1972; married William W. ARBAUGH ca 1897
	1480. Harriet S. " Hattie"	born ca 1881; died 1962
	1481. Robert McClellan	born 2 June 1884 IL; died 7 Apr 1912 Union, Barton, MO
+	**1482. GROVER DUSHER**	born 16 June 1888 IL; died 18 Nov 1922 Nevada, MO

1137. FRANKLIN W[7] **BOWKER**, brother of above, was born 23 May 1842 NY. He married Catherine LAUGHLIN ca 1863 IL. She was the daughter of George LAUGHLIN and Mary RIGDEN, and was born 25 Sep 1844 Scotland Co., MO; died 14 Dec 1921 Dallas City, IL. Franklin W-[7] BOWKER died 14 Feb 1927 at Mt. Sterling, Brown, IL.

Children of Franklin-[7] BOWKER and Catherine LAUGHLIN:
Surname **BOWKER**

+	**1483. MINNIE L.**		born ca 1864 IL; died 13 Sep 1948; married James Henry CLARK ca ____
	1484. Nettie		born 26 Apr 1868 IL; died 23 ____ 1928; married Sidney John COLLISON ca ____
	1485. Maude	(twin)	born 17 Apr 1871; died ____
+	**1486. ROGER**	(twin)	born 17 Apr 1871; died 18 Oct 1954; married Amy Z. LAMB 17 Oct 1891 Hancock, IL
	1487. Kittie		born 10 Nov 1873; died 9 Apr 1929 ; married Ernest P. ROSEWURM ca 1900
+	**1488. INEZ**		born 7 Dec 1879 IL; died ____; married Edward L. HUPFER ca ____
+	**1489. GEORGE WATTS**		born 1 June 1882 IL; died 22 Mar 1961; married Minnie Pearl SHAIN ca ____
	1490. Mable		born 4 Nov 1884 Il; died ____

1145. SIMS GARDNER[7] **BOWKER/ BUKER**, son of Rufus-[6] BOWKER/BUKER (James-[5] BOWKER; [4; 3; 2; 1]) and Betsey-[6] WEYMOUTH, and was born 9 July 1826 at Bowdoinham, ME. He married Mary Ann SPEAR on 3 July 1856 at Weymouth, Norfolk, MA. She was the daughter of John B. SPEAR and Wealthy RICHARDS, and was born ca 1831; died 1925. Sims-[7] BOWKER/BUKER died 24 Sep 1894 at Braintree, Norfolk, MA.

Children of Sims Gardner-[7] BOWKER/BUKER and Mary Ann SPEAR:
Surname **BOWKER/BUKER**

	1491. George C.	born ca 1857 Dorchester, MA; died 13 Oct 1930 Braintree, MA
		1 married Chloe CARY ca ____ ; 2 married Ella COOK ca ____
	1492. Edward Gardner	born 20 Aug 1860 Braintree, MA; died 30 Nov 1920 Braintree
		married Annie Mae WHITEHOUSE ca 1888 Braintree, MA
+	**1493. SARAH B.**	born 4 Jan 1864 Braintree; died 15 Apr 1920 Braintree
		married George Dow NEWCOMB 16 June 1893

Children of Sims Gardner[-7] BOWKER/BUKER and Mary Ann SPEAR, continued:
Surname **BOWKER/BUKER**

1494. Emma Jane	born Aug 1866 Braintree; died 13 Nov 1876	EOL	
1495. Mary Elizabeth	born 2 Mar 1868; died 27 Mar 1903 Braintree, MA		
1496. William Henry	born 13 Sep 1870 Braintree; died 17 Jan 1952 Braintree, MA		
	married Minnie E. ROSS ca _____ (she dau/o Samuel J. ROSS and _____)		

Children: William H-[9], Jr. born ca 1898; died 1966; Harold Sidney-[9] born ca 1900; and Everett Alton[-9] BOWKER/BUKER born 1902; died 1976

1497. Charles F.	born 31 Oct 1872 Bowdoinham, ME; died 13 Feb 1947 Weymouth, MA
	married Annie A. CAESAR ca _____
+ **1498. AMOS STETSON**	born 31 Oct 1874 Braintree; died 31 May 1967
	married Anne Estelle ROSS 19 Aug 1896 Weymouth, MA
	(she dau/o Samuel J. ROSS and Anne Estelle- BOWKER)

1156. WILLIAM T[-7] BOWKER, son of Samuel-[6] BOWKER (Samuel Michael[-5]; William[-4]; James-[3;2;1]) and Malinda HUTCHINSON, was born14 July 1848 OH. He married Emma KEEVER ca 1870/71 Turtle Creek, Warren, Ohio. She was the daughter of Martin KEEVER and Elizabeth STRICKLAND, and was born 22 Oct 1850 OH; died 19 March 1927 at Lebanon, OH. William T[-7] BOWKER, a shoemaker, died 8 Jan 1935 at Lebanon, Ohio.

Children of William T[-7] BOWKER and Emma KEEVER:
Surname **BOWKER**

1499. Cora	born 15 Oct 1872; died 13 Mar 1951
+ **1500. MYRTLE**	born 3 Aug 1874; died 25 Oct 1949; married Walter BIGGS ca ____
1501. Horace	born 30 Oct 1876; died 20 Jan 1957; married Mabel CAMP 2 Mar 1911 OH
	(she dau/o John W. CAMP and Emma Jeanette GRAY) (she born May 1892 OH)

Child: Faye C[-9] BOWKER born 28 Mar 1920

1502. Guy	born 1 Dec 1878; died 8 Mar 1941 (no issue) EOL
+ **1503. CLYDE**	born 11 Nov 1880; died 13 Apr 1960
1504. Jennie	born 21 Aug 1882; died ____ 1479. Earl Edward born 6 July 1884; died 20 May 1951
1505. Frederick Harrison	born 10 Apr 1886; died Apr 1964 Mauteno, IL
	married Pearl KINDER ca ____ (she born ca 1888; died 1941)
+ **1506. WILLIS**	born 3 June 1888; died 21 Jan 1949 Lebanon, Ohio
	married Mary PETERS ca 1909 (she born ca 1891)
+ **1507. CHARLES ANDREW**	born 14 Nov 1890; died 26 July 1962 Milan, Allen, IN
	married Grace Mae RICHARDS 29 April 1911 KY (she born ca 1891)
	(she dau/o Isaac RICHARDS and Mary Jane HIZER)
+ **1508. ORVILLE G.**	born 12 Dec 1894 ; died 20 June 1960 MI
	married Blanche Cora SNELL 12 Aug 1917 (she born ca 1897 KS)
1509. Fern	born ca 1895; died ____

1162. ROSETTA EMILY[-7] BOWKER, daughter of Davis C[-6] BOWKER (Bartlett-[5;4]; John[-3]; James-[2;1]) and Fannie Almira CUSHING, was born Jan 1842 VT. She married George Nelson CASS on 1 July 1871 (as his 2nd wife). He was the son of Nathan CASS and Sarah CURRIER, and was born ca 1832 NH; died 17 March 1882 Boston, MA. He was a well-known artist in the Boston and White Mountain area of NH. His paintings were mainly landscapes and still-life and were done in various medias.

Note: Rosetta[-7] BOWKER was a teacher, before her marriage, at the "prestigious finishing school" known at that time as the Lasell Female Seminary in Auburndale (Newton), MA. The school was founded as the Auburndale Female Seminary, by Edward LASELL, in 1851. He died during the first semester of operation and the school was renamed the Lasell Female Seminary. The curriculum was a " highly scientific approach to domestic work, art and music ", and attracted women from all over the country. In 1932 the name was again changed to Lasell Junior College. In 1943 it began offering Associate Degrees, and in 1989 it became a 4-year college and admitted male students in 1997.

Children of Rosetta[-7] BOWKER and George N. CASS:
Surname **CASS**

1510. William Barrett	born 1 Nov 1874 Medfield, MA; died _____; married Nancy D. ____ ca ____

Child: Barrett B[-9] CASS born ca 1913 NY

1511. Alvin Cushing	born 11 May 1876; died 11 Mar 1950 Kings Co., NY (a lawyer)
	married Mildred _____ ca _____

Children: Margaret C[-9] born ca 1915; and Lewis[-9] CASS born ca 1923

1512. Fannie E.	born Nov 1880 NY; died

1163. EMMA D-7 BOWKER, daughter of Stephen-6 BOWKER (Stephen-5; Bartlett-4; John-3; James-2,1) and Henrietta A. HALLADAY, was born 1848 Newfane, VT. She married William K. WOOD on 4 Nov 1868 . He was the son of Emory WOOD and Sybil ROPER, and was born ca 1834; died ____. Emma D-7 BOWKER died ____.

Child of Emma D-7 BOWKER and William WOOD:
Surname **WOOD**

1513. Julius Wright   born 16 Feb 1870 NY; died ____; a baker

        1 married Susan _____ ca 1899   (she born Mar 1870 NY)

        2 married Gertrude NORCROSS 27 June 1912

        (she dau/o Alonzo NORCROSS and Sarah _____)

        (she born ca 1876; died ____) Child: Paul A-9 WOOD born ca 1917

1180. OTIS BOISE/ BOYD-7 BARTLETT, son of Wealthy-6 TOWER (Stephen, Jr-5; Hannah-4 BOWKER; John-3; James-2,1) and her first husband Peter BARTLETT, was born 15 May 1828 at Cummington, MA. He married Elmina/Almina TOWER on 1 May 1851. She was the daughter of Warren TOWER and Rhoda Bowker-5 TOWER, and was born 6 Oct 1822; died 24 May 1889 Cummington, MA

Children of Otis B-7 BARTLETT and Elmina/Almina TOWER:
Surname **BARTLETT**

1514. Granville Otis   born 15/18 Apr 1852; died 1899 Holyoke, MA

      married Lillian K. FERGUSON May 1894 Springfield, MA

      (she dau/o George FERGUSON and Jane TILLSON) (she born ca 1865 MA)

1515. Elmer Ellsworth   born 27 Feb 1862 MA; died ____

1200. LUCIUS WARREN-7 BARTLETT, son of Salome-6 TOWER (Rhoda Bowker-5 TOWER; Hannah-4 BOWKER; John-3; James-2,1) and Ephraim Tilson BARTLETT, was born 3 April 1841 CT. He married first to Mary Monroe CHALMERS on 11 May 1871. She was the daughter of William CHALMERS and Ann ____, and was born 23 Sep 1845; died 15 Apr 1900 Hartford, CT. He married second to Mrs. Zilpha J. BARTLETT Crozier ca ____. She was born 2 Oct 1843 Cummington, MA; died 1918. She is buried Cedar Hill Cemetery, Hartford. Lucius-7 BARTLETT died 5 Mar 1928 at Hartford, CT.

Children of Lucius-7 BARTLETT and Mary Monroe CHALMERS:
Surname **BARTLETT**   (all children born Hartford, CT)

1516. Anna Elizabeth   born 26 Apr 1872; died ____

1517. Warren Tower   born 9 July 1874; died ____

1518. Mary Alice   born 2 Nov 1876; died 1963; married Frederic H. FORBES 29 Sep 1903

      (he s/o Warren L. FORBES and Annie Hyde PECK)

      (he born Apr 1870; died 1928)

    Children: Barbara Hyde-9 born 14 Nov 1905; George Bartlett-9 born 13 Nov 1909; and Warren P-9 FORBES born ca 1917

1519. Arthur Lucius   born 30 Oct 1878; died ____; a tailor

      married Mildred Leata GRAY 16 Oct 1909

      (she born ca 1887 Springfield, MA; died ____ Hartford, CT)

      (she dau/o George L. GRAY and Martha BARTLETT)

1520. George Chalmers born 1 Sep 1883; died 5 Sep 1883; buried Cedar Hill Cemetery, Hartford, CT

1521. Helen Louise   born 6 Apr 1887; died ____

1202. ALICE PRATT-6 BARTLETT, sister of above, was born 1 July 1847 at Hartford, CT. She married William E. BURDICK, an architect, on 22 Feb 1875. He was the son of ____ BURDICK and ____, and was born 15 Feb 1851 Westbrook, CT; died 28 Jan 1898 at Hartford, CT. Alice Pratt-6 BARTLETT died 1912.

Children of Alice P-6 BARTLETT and William BURDICK:
Surname **BURDICK**

1522. Edwin Parker   born 24 Nov 1875 Grand Rapids, MI; died ____; civil engineer

      married Gertrude KEMP 14 Oct 1902

    Child: Virginia-8 BURDICK born 26 Nov 1909 Staten Island, NY

1523. Harry Elbert   born 29 Apr 1877 Hartford, CT; died 25 Mar 1878   EOL

1524. Herbert Clemens born 11 Oct 1879 Hartford, CT; died 1917

    Note: 1900 Federal Census lists him as residing at the CT. Hospital for the Insane

1525. Irvin Grant   born 24 Apr 1884; Hartford; died 23 Jan 1885   EOL

1206. ALBERT RENSSALAER-[7] BOWKER, son of Renssalaer-[6] BOWKER (Cushing-[5];Captain Stephen-[4]; John-[3;2]; James-[1]) and Mary Batchelder SPAULDING, was born 6 Sep 1859 IL. He married Elizabeth FRANKLIN ca 1885. She was the daughter of ____ FRANKLIN and ____, and was born Mar 1858 IA, died 1930 CA. Albert-[7] BOWKER died 9 Dec 1907 Chicago, IL.

Children of Albert-[7] BOWKER and Elizabeth FRANKLIN :
Surname **BOWKER**

	1526. Renssalaer	born 1886; died 1886	EOL
	1527. Florence	born 1887; died 1895	EOL
+	**1528. HOWARD FRANKLIN**	born 3 Jan 1889 MN; died 8 July 1970 Alameda, CA	
		married Mary Violetta BOWKER ca April 1913 (she # 1521)	
		(she born 29 May 1896 Oakland, CA; died 5 Sep 1972 Alameda, CA	
		(buried with her husband at Arlington National Cemetery, VA)	
+	**1529. ROCKTON ADAM**	born 22 Feb 1891 IL; died 20 Jan 1971 IL; married Ethel L. SUNDBORG ca ____	
		(she born 7 July 1897; died Mar 1973)	
+	**1530. WALLACE JOHN**	born 8 July 1893 IN ; died ____	
		married Frances VAN COTT ca ____	
		(she born 12 Mar 1896 IL; died Jan 1982)	
	1531. Henry George	born 15 Mar 1897; died 28 Sep 1910 CA.	EOL
	1532. Alfred Sumner K.	born 1901; died 1950; married Katherine JAYEN ca 1923 (she born ca 1903 KS)	
		Child: Alfred S K-[9] BOWKER, Jr. born 1925 IL	

1207. CHELLIS ERWIN-[7] BOWKER, brother of above, was born 6 Nov 1860 Memphis, TN. He married Mary E. ____ ca 1883. She was the daughter of ____ and ____; and was born May 1867 Micronesia, Phillipine Islands; died before 1940. Chellis-[7] BOWKER died 9 Feb 1959 Alameda, CA.

Children of Chellis-[7] BOWKER and Mary E ____:
Surname **BOWKER**

1533. Rensselaer	born 24 Apr 1885 Micronesia, Island of Pouape; died ____	
	married Jane TAYLOR ca ____	
	(she dau/o William TAYLOR and Martha ____)	
1534. Bayard Gordon	born Oct 1887 Micronesia; died ____	
1535. Lucy	born May 1891 Micronesia, Island of Reek, died ____	

1208. ELLA SPAULDING-[7] BOWKER, sister of above, was born 20 Mar 1863. She married George W. THACKERAY ca ____. He was the son of John THACKERAY and Catherine ____; and was born 16 Nov 1866; died 6 Dec 1944. Ella-[7] BOWKER died ca 1935.

Children of Ella-[7] BOWKER and George W. THACKERAY:
Surname **THACKERAY**

1536. Arthur Rensselaer	born 7 Dec 1891; died 8 Apr 1953 Melvin, Ford, IL	
	married Winifred Emily NICHOLS ca ____	
	(she born 10 Jan 1895; died 7 Oct 1961 Gibson, IL)	
	(she dau/o William NICHOLS and Lottie ____)	
	Children: George-[9] born ca 1921; and Ella-[9] THACKERAY born 1926	

+	**1537. PAULINE GRACE**	born 22 Apr 1902; died 22 June 1983 CA
		married Francis Eugene PERKINS ca 1925

1209. LUCY ELVIRA-[7] BOWKER, sister of above, was born 16 June 1864. She married Albert H. EMINGER ca ____. He was the son of John EMINGER and Mary ____, and was born 3 June 1856 IL; died 26 Feb 1927 IL. Lucy-[7] BOWKER died ca 1950.

Children of Ella-[7] BOWKER and Albert EMINGER:
Surname **EMINGER**

1538. Evan B.	born Sep 1889; died ____		
1539. Mabel B.	born Mar1893; died ____	1541. Ferna R.	born ca 1901; died ____
1540. Ralph E.	born 21 Aug 1894; died ____; married Angie Bell WRIGHT ca ____		

110. ERNEST SYLVENDER[-7] **BOWKER,** brother of above, was born July 1865. He married Haidee TAIT on 6 June 1895. She was the daughter of George TAIT and Mildred TERRILL, and was born 13 Oct 1873 KS; died 16 Dec 1944 Chicago, IL. Ernest-[7] BOWKER died 1939.

Children of Ernest-[7] BOWKER and Haidee TAIT:
Surname **BOWKER**

1542. Helen M.	born ca 1897; died ____; married Bowen SMITH ca ____
1543. Grace P.	born ca 1899; died ____
1544. Ernest Stuart	born 2 Dec 1902; died 29 July 1938 Holly Springs, NC
1545. Rae Johnson	born ca 1906; died ____

1211. WILLIAM CUSHING SHORT[-7] **BOWKER,** brother of above, was born 21 Oct 1866 IL. He married first to Leona TAYLOR ca ____. She was the daughter of ____ TAYLOR and ____, and was born 8 Oct 1873 IN, died 6 May 1905 IN. He married second to Mame / Mamie DUNN ca 1907. She was the daughter of Michael DUNN and Anna ALLEN, and was born ca 1878 CA; died 1920.

Children of William Cushing-[7] BOWKER and Leona TAYLOR:
Surname **BOWKER**

+   **1546. VIOLETTA MARY**   born 29 Mar 1896 IL; died 5 Sep 1972 Alameda, CA
                               married Howard Franklin-[8] BOWKER ca April 1913 (see # 1528 for children)
          1547. Birdell Estella   born 1 Apr 1898 IL; died 6 Sep 1983 Fresno, CA
                               married Frank Owen COOPER ca ____ (Child: Carter-[9] COOPER born 1921; died 1999)
                               (he s/o Albert Annis COOPER and Emma Rosabelle GOSE) (1897- 1950)
          1548. William Gail   born 2 Aug 1900 IL; died 5 Feb 1976 Portland, OR

1214. SAMUEL CUSHING[-7] **MARSTON,** son of Lucy Rider-[6] BOWKER (Cushing-[5]; Captain Stephen-[4]; John-[3,2]; James-[1]) and Samuel MARSTON, was born 25 July 1853 Shefford, Quebec, Canada. He married Charlotte May " Shallie " WESTOVER ca 1888. She was the daughter of Daniel WESTOVER and Lydia Rosanna WOODWARD, and was born 5 Sep 1866; died _____. Samuel Cushing-[7] MARSTON died 20 Jan 1925 at Waterloo, Quebec, Canada.

Children of Samuel Cushing-[7] MARSTON and Charlotte WESTOVER:
Surname **MARSTON**

1549. Ernest Wellington	born 29 Sep 1888; died ____
	1 married Josie WILLIAMS 11 Sep 1911 Richford, Franklin, VT
	(she dau/o William WILLIAMS and Jane GOODHUE)
	2 married Gertrude Daisy DEUSO/DENSO 15 Dec 1925
	(she born 17 Apr 1904; died 27 Sep 1988)
	(she dau/o Mahlon DEUSO/DENSO and Nora A. ____)

                  Child: Richard W-[9] MARSTON born 11 Sep 1927; died 21 May 2002; married Pauline Frances ALLEN
                            19 May 1951 (she dau/o Guy Levitt ALLEN and Gladys CURTIS)

1550. Pearl Evelyn.	born 19 Dec 1890; died _____
	married Earl Levon Mc LAUGHLIN ca 1922
	(he s/o James Mc LAUGHLIN and Carrie E. MARSTON)
1551. Arthur Clifford	born 1 Oct 1893; died 22 Jan 1978 (gunshot to the head)
	1 married Vernie Emma LEE ca 1927; 2 married Dorothy HALL 5 June 1935
	(she dau/o John HALL and Minerva COLVIN) (she born 16 Apr 1909)
1552. Mildred Laura	born 6 May 1897; died ____
1553. Chester C.	born 27 Oct 1899 Quebec; died 24 Sep 1992 FL
	married Alice May LUNDERVILLE 5 Sep 1927 Richford, VT

                Child: Roland Carmie-[9] MARSTON born ca ___, married Henrietta TETREAULT 29 June 1966

1228. GARDNER ERNEST[-7] **MARSTON,** son of Mary Louisa-[6] BOWKER (Cushing-[5]; Captain Stephen-[4]; John-[3,2]; James-[1]) and George MARSTON, was born 11 Oct 1873 at Hillsborough, NH. He married Lizabell / Elizabeth SAVORY on 16 Sep 1905. She was the daughter of Charles A. SAVORY and Ellen J. PIPER, and was born ca 1873; died ____. Gardner-[7] MARSTON died 5 Jan 1944 NH.

Children of Gardner-[7] MARSTON and Lizabell SAVORY:
Surname **MARSTON**

1554. Lyle S.	born ca 1905 NH; died _____

Children of Gardner⁻⁷ MARSTON and Lizabell SAVORY, continued:
Surname **MARSTON**

1555. Ruth Ernestine	born 3 Sept 1906; died 17 Oct 1989 NH	
	married Gustave Daniel LUND (Goustaff D. BJORKLUND) 22 Aug 1927 NH	
	(he s/o Nils Daniel LUND (BJORKLUND) and Marie ANDERSON)	
	(he born ca 1904 NH; died 5 Nov 1938)	
	Children: Shirley E-⁹ born ca 1932; and Kenneth K-⁹ LUND born ca 1936	
1556. Kenneth Earl	born 10 Apr 1910; died 29 Apr 1957	
	married Dorothy L. DUNLAP 30 Sep 1938 (she born ca 1911; died _____)	
1557. Paul	born Dec 1912; died 11 Dec 1976 NH	

1229. ELLIOTT FRANCIS⁻⁷ BOWKER, son of Samuel Francis⁻⁶ BOWKER (Samuel Griffin⁻⁵; Stephen⁻⁴; John-³,²; James-¹) and Rosa/Rosanna ANGIER, was born 10 Nov 1859 Fitzwilliam, NH. He married Ella Adelle BURDICK ca 1895. She was the daughter of John BURDICK and Ann ___, and was born ____ NY; died Feb 1953 IA. Elliott F⁻⁷ BOWKER died 17 Feb 1945 Garner, Iowa.

Children of Elliott F⁻⁷ BOWKER and Ella A. BURDICK:
Surname **BOWKER**

1558. Edna M	born 29 Mar 1896 Britt, IA; died ____; married William Francis STAPLES 16 Jan 1952
	(he s/o Winslow STAPLES and Ann ____)
	(he born 17 July 1879 Stillwater, MN; died 3 Oct 1953 Britt, IA)
1559. Ethel Eugenia	born 18 Feb 1899; died Sept 1991 IA.; married Homer DOWNS ca ____
	(he born 7 Aug 1896 Cullom, IL; died ____)
	Children: Richard K-⁹ born 6 May 1929 Titonka, IL; and Robert E-⁹ DOWNS born ca 1932 IL.

1231. HENRY FAY⁻⁷ BOWKER, half-brother of above, son of Samuel Francis⁻⁶ BOWKER and, his 2ⁿᵈ wife, Mary Amanda CHASE, and was born 16 Mar 1864 NH. He married Flora Emma HARDIE ca 1891. She was the daughter of Josiah Jerome HARDIE and Harriet Elizabeth CHASE, was born 17 Dec 1871 IA; died 27 Mar 1916 IA. Henry Fay-⁷ BOWKER died 17 Aug 1941 at Davenport, IA

Children of Henry Fay⁻⁷ BOWKER and Flora HARDIE:
Surname **BOWKER**

1560. Floyd Dyer	born 8 Feb 1892 Crystal Lake, IA; died 23 Dec 1947 Davenport, IA	
	married Pearl Melissa COFFELT ca 1917	
	Child: Dorothy Florann-⁹ BOWKER born ca 1918; died 1963	
1561. Alta M.	born 9 May 1893 Rock Island, IL; died Aug 1980 RI	
	married Raymond R. CONKLIN ca _____ (he born ca 1892; died 1947)	
1562. Francis Josiah	born 20 Dec 1896 IA; died June 1972 Osawatamie, KS	
	married Lulu B. SHANNON ca ____ (she born ca 1899; died ____)	
	Children: Frank-⁹ born 1918; died 1992; and Audrey-⁹ BOWKER born ca 1922	
+ **1563. FLORA MARIE**	born 21 June 1901 RI; died 4 Nov 1979 Davenport, Scott, IA	
	married Fred Sailor SMITH ca 1919	
	(he s/o John Kelly SMITH and Susan Jane BEAMISH)	
	(he born 22 Aug 1896; died 3 Nov 1962 Davenport, IA	
1564. FLORENCE AMANDA	born 7 Dec 1905; died 30 July 1986 Davenport, IA	
	married Louis Elijah COFFELT ca 1922	
	(he born 13 Mar 1902; died 27 Feb 1962)	

1233. MINNIE ROSE⁻⁷ BOWKER, sister of above, was born 13 July 1870 NH. She married Orton N. EMERY ca 1889. He was the son of ____ EMERY and ____, and was born Jan 1862 WI, died ____ ND. Minnie Rose-⁷ BOWKER died 8 July 1940 at Harvey, Wells, ND.

Children of Minnie Rose⁻⁷ BOWKER and Orton EMERY:
Surname **EMERY**

1565. Nellie A	born Jan 1890 IA; died ____	1569. Evelyn Viola	born 10 Aug 1910 ND
1566. Melvin Francis	born 14 Dec 1892 IA; died Aug 1983 ND		died 25 Aug 2005 ND
+ **1567. RALPH EUGENE**	born 6 July 1894 IA; died 26 July 1947 ND		
	married Blonda G. ____ ca 1925	(she born 14 Mar 1898; died May 1985 ND)	
1568. Maud Irene	born 26 June 1898 IA; died ____		

Children of Minnie Rose-7 BOWKER and Orton EMERY, continued:
Surname **EMERY**
    1570. Glenwood J.   born ca 1908 ND; died ___; married Sylvia ca 1935
          Child: Wayne-9 EMERY born ca 1936

1235. LESLIE EUGENE-7 BOWKER, brother of above, twin of Grace-7 BOWKER, was born 9 Feb 1874 at Crystal Lake, Hancock, IA. He married Melvina Millie GILLSTRAP 12 Sep 1899. She was the daughter of John Gifford GILLSTRAP and Rachel Ellen LENTZ, and was born 24 Dec 1879; died 21 Oct 1936 IA. Leslie Eugene-7 BOWKER died 23 Oct 1925 IA.

Children of Leslie-7 BOWKER and Melvina GILLSTRAP:
Surname **BOWKER**
    1571. Ada May   born 29 Mar 1900; died 13 Feb 1972; married Henry Nicholas CLARK 20 Nov 1922
              (he s/o N F CLARK and Kate BECKMAN) (he born 1895)
        Children: Mary Kathleen-9 (1923-1923); Howard Francis-9 (1925-2004); and Delores Marie-9 CLARK (1934 - 1976
    1572. Florence Rachel   born 9 Mar 1901 IA; died ____
+   **1573. FRANK L.**   born 1903 MN; married Adeline C. ? ca 1927 (she born ca 1903)
    1574. Sadie Ellen   born 1904 MN; died ____
    1575. Harvey Eugene   born 10 Feb 1907 IA; died 14 July 1956 Crystal Lake, IA
    1576. Charles Albert   born 26 May 1909; died 2 June 1991 IA
    1577. Helen A.   born ca 1913 IA
    1578. Robert Sydney   born 24 May 1917 IA; died 15 Feb 2005 IA
    1579. William Herbert   born 3 Sep 1918 IA; died 16 May 1999 CA

1237. MAMIE ESTELLA-7 BOWKER, sister of above, was born 29 Sep 1879 IA. She married first to Roscoe Conklin ROBERTS ca 1896 ND. He was the son of Daniel M. ROBERTS and Harriet E. ____; and was born 11 Aug 1872 MI; died 9 May 1944 Los Angeles, CA. They were probably divorced. She married 2nd to Charles Amos ALMY ca 1918 Minot, ND. He was the son of Fred ALMY and Betsey ____; and was born 12 Apr 1882; died 9 Jan 1961. Mamie Estella-7 BOWKER died 4 June 1963 at Fairbault, MN.

Child of Mamie Estella-7 BOWKER and Roscoe ROBERTS:
Surname **ROBERTS**
+   **1580. SYLVIA IRENE**   born 29 Mar 1900 Crystal , IA; died 7 May 1985 Walnut Creek, CA
          married William Montgomery BALFOUR ca 1921   (he born ca 1898; died 1964)

1240. ANN ESTELLE-7 BOWKER, daughter of William-6 BOWKER (Elijah-5;4; John-3; James-2;1) and Eliza Brooks RICHARDS, was born 20 Dec 1848 Weymouth, MA. She married Samuel Joseph ROSS on 13 Mar 1865. He was the son of ____ ROSS and Mehitable HOLBROOK, and was born 1 June 1844; died 18 Oct 1934 Weymouth, MA.

Children of Ann Estelle-7 BOWKER and Samuel Joseph ROSS:
Surname **ROSS**   (children all born Weymouth, Norfolk, MA)
    1581. George Augustus   born 6 June 1865; died ____
          married Mary J. LEVANGIE 20 Mar 1905 (as her 2nd husband)(1 marr. to # 1583)
    1582. .Mary Adelaide   born 27 Mar 1867; died ____
          1 married John LYONS 20 July 1884
        Children: Charles Henry-9 born ca 1885; and Annie-9 LYONS born ca 1889
          2 married Henry C. PERRY 30 Apr 1893
        Children: Minnie-9 born ca 1893; Clifford-9 born ca 1895; and Lillian-9 PERRY born ca 1899
    1583. Joseph Alanson   born 27 Apr 1869; died 28 Feb 1904 Weymouth, MA
          married Mary J. LEVANGIE 1 Feb 1896   (she born ca 1872; died ___)
        Child: Samuel Joseph-9 ROSS born ca 1896
    1584. William F.   born 16 Dec 1873; died ____; married Rose R. ____ ca ____
+   **1585. MINNIE ETTA**   born 30 Sep 1875 Braintree, MA; married William H. BOWKER/BUKER 10 Nov 1896
          (he s/o Sims Gardner BUKER and Mary Ann SPEAR # 1470))
          (he born 13 Sep 1870 Braintree; died 17 Jan 1952 Braintree, MA)
    1586. Annie Estella   born 14 Mar 1877; died ____;
          married Amos Stetson BOWKER/BUKER 19 Aug 1896 (he # 1498)
    1587. Ella Mabel   born 20 June 1878; died 28 June 1972
          married Frederick A. ROULSTON ca ___
        Children: Mabel Ella-9 born 1897; and George Archibald-9 ROULSTON born ca 1899

Children of Ann Estelle-[7] BOWKER and Samuel Joseph ROSS, continued:
Surname **ROSS**

> 1588. Louis Sidney   born 5 Apr 1880; died 1941 Weymouth, MA; married Louise H. SMITH 10 Jan 1900
> > Children: Elmer Frederick-[9] born ca 1901, died 1911; and Arthur Louis-[9] ROSS born ca 1903
> 1589. Benjamin Harrison   born 5 Oct 1889   1590. Herbert Lincoln   born 10 Feb 1892

1242. MARIA ELIZA-[7] BOWKER, sister of above, was born Dec 1852 MA. She married Henry Franklin ROWELL ca 1869. He was the son of Benjamin Franklin ROWELL and Sarah BEAN; and was born May 1849/52 ME; died 26 Apr 1906 Weymouth, MA. Maria Eliza-[7] BOWKER died 6 Sep 1928.

Children of Maria Eliza-[7] BOWKER and Henry Franklin ROWELL:
Surname ROWELL   (all children born Weymouth, Norfolk, MA)

> 1591. George Frank   born 13 Aug 1870; died ____;   married Lilla BUZZELL 16 Jul 1893
> > (she dau/o John P. BUZZELL and Arabella BERRY)
> 1592. Fannie May   born 13 Aug 1870; died 27 Nov 1873 Weymouth, MA   EOL
> 1593. Walter A.   born Oct 1871; died ____
> 1594. Ethel May   born ca 1872; died 18 Mar 1923 Marshfield, MA
> > married Edward Wells Spurr ARNOLD ca ____;   (he born ca 1874; died 1914)
> 1595. Albertus Henry   born Sept 1874; died 13 Oct 1955 Middleton, CT; married Cornelia May ARNOLD
> 1596. Lillian " Lillie "   born 4 Aug 1876; died 20 July 1946
> > Eunice   married Solon Waldo TIRRELL 12 Aug 1896 (he born 1851; died ____)
> 1597. Archie Garfield   born ca 1877; died 1882 Weymouth, MA   EOL
> 1598. Arthur Clifford   born 2 Aug 1880; died 1882 Weymouth   EOL
> 1599. Maude Eliza Myra born 1 Apr 1882; died 14 Oct 1964 Marshfield, MA
> > married William Thomas DAMON 29 June 1904
> > (he s/o Silas DAMON and Abba WENTWORTH)
> 1600. John Herbert   born 1883; died 21 Sep 1883 Weymouth   EOL

+   **1601. BENJAMIN**   born 19 Feb 1887; died 3 Dec 1942; married Maria C. SOUSA 31 Dec 1905
          JEFFERSON   (she born ca 1887 Portugal; died ____)
                          (she dau/o Philemon SOUSA and Georgianna NACHADO)

> 1602 Henry F.   born 9 Sep 1888; died 1 Feb 1889   1604. Bessie Evelyn   born 20 July 1891
> 1603. Bertha Louise born 24 Nov 1890; died ____   1605. Frederick   born ca 1896

1250. MARY C-[7] CUSHING, daughter of Oliver Edwards-[6] CUSHING (Stephen-[5]; Desire-[4] BOWKER; John-[3]; James-[2,1]) and Mary Bass EDSON, was born Jan 1855 Lowell, MA. She married Martin Ellsworth HALL on 2 Oct 1878. He was the son of David Aiken HALL and Abigail Wolcott ELLSWORTH, and was born 19 Sep 1847 Washington, DC; died 21 Feb 1904. Mary C-[7] CUSHING died ca 1928.

Children of Mary C-[7] CUSHING and Martin E. HALL:
Surname **HALL**

> 1606. Margaret Woodburn   born 22 Dec 1879; died 16 Jan 1932 NY
> > married Faxton Eugene GARDNER 23 July 1927
> > (he born ca 1878; died ca 1933)
> > Child: May Frances-[9] GARDNER born ca 1908; died 1962)
> 1607. Ann Louise   born 15 Jan 1881 FL; died 20 Apr 1966
> 1608. Wolcott Ellsworth born 3 Jan 1884 RI; died ____   Child: Roger Wolcott-[9] HALL born ca 1919; died 2008
> > married Katrina Howard ROGERS ca ___

1251. MARGARET DAISY-[7] CUSHING, sister of above, was born 23 July 1857. She married Edward Thayer ABBOTT on 4 April 1883. He was the son of Ziba ABBOTT and Elizabeth THAYER; and was born 30 Jan/June 1843; died 15 Sep 1895. Margaret -[7] CUSHING died ca 1938.

Children of Margaret Daisy-[7] CUSHING and Edward ABBOTT:
Surname **ABBOTT**

> 1609. Elizabeth Emma   born ca 1884 MA; died 1884 MA
> 1610. Daisy Odiorne   born 13 Jan 1885 MA; died July 1963 MA
> 1611. Elizabeth Thayer   born May 1887 MA   1612. Gertrude Cushing   born 17 Feb 1889 MA; died

1270. GILMAN ROE[-7] **BOWKER,** son of John M[-6] BOWKER (Cyprian-[5;] Capt. James-[4]; Edmund-[3]; James-[2,1]) and Dorothy STARBIRD, was born Apr 1838 ME. He married Hannah Sabra LYON(S) on 1 Jan 1862. She was the daughter of Reuben LYON(S) and Mary Ann CARLISLE; and was born ca 1847; died ____. Gilman-[7] BOWKER died ca 1922.

Children of Gilman Roe-[7] BOWKER and Hannah LYON(S):
Surname **BOWKER**

	1613. Lilla Armina	born Jan 1864; died 23 Jan 1949	1619. Jinna	born Mar 1880; died 1880
+	**1614. CHARLES R.**	born 24 Jan 1865; died 4 Jan 1955; married Mary Jane HEBB 22 Mar 1889		
		(he s/o George S. HEBB and Catherine GREEN Mc GRAW)		
+	**1615. HATTIE ESTELLA**	born 19 Apr 1868/69; died 1951		
		married Everett Forrest ALDRICH (his 2nd wife) 10 Nov 1886 Penobscot, ME.		
		(he s/o Moses Weston ALDRICH and Hannah COLSON)		
		(he born 1 Sept 1852; died 14 Mar 1914)		
+	**1616. CLOTILDE**	born 17 Nov 1870; died 23 Jan 1961 Penobscot, ME.		
		married James M. SMITH ca 1891 Penobscot, ME		
+	**1617. ADA VELZORA**	born 19 Sep 1874; died 2 July 1950 Carroll, Penobscot, ME.		
	1618. Adelbert / Bert Gilman	born 28 Aug 1878; died 4 Jan 1961 Augusta, Maine married Edith M. SEVERANCE 25 Apr 1904 Topsfield, ME		

1282. NATHANIEL[-7] **BOWKER,** son of Cyprian-[6] BOWKER, Jr. (Cyprian-[5], Sr; James-[4]; Edmund-[3]; James-[2,1]) and Abigail ROBBINS, was born Nov 1850/51 at Oxford County, Maine. He married first to Ettie/Etta M. LAKE on 13 Sept 1874 Winnebago County, WI. She was the daughter of _____ LAKE and ____, and was born ca 1854; died 1882 Oshkosh, WI. He married second to Alma Romina JOHNSON on 20 Sep 1890. She was the daughter of Leroy JOHNSON and Olive EDDY, and was born 10 Nov 1851; died 20 Nov 1945 Kenosha, WI. Nathaniel-[7] BOWKER died 29 Mar 1917 .

Children of Nathaniel-[7] BOWKER and Etta LAKE:
Surname **BOWKER**

+	**1620. JOHN H.**	born 14 Feb 1875 WI; died 23 Aug 1958 Oshkosh, Winnebago, WI
		married Stella A. GILMORE 2 July 1930 Oshkosh
		(she dau/o Duane GILMORE and Maud J. BUCK)
		(she born 25 Jan 1906 Winnebago; died ____)
	1621. Mabel B.	born 1877; died 8 Aug 1949; 1 married Alvin Henry MANTZ ca ____
		2 married John AHLERS ca 1898; 3 married Michael DONOVAN ca 1906

Child of Nathaniel-[7] BOWKER and Alma JOHNSON:
Surname **BOWKER**

+	**1622. GUY WILFORD**	born 24 May 1894 Oshkosh, WI; died 17 Oct 1965 WI
		married Winifred BARTOW ca 1919 WI

1291. ERNEST RUPERT[-7] **CURTIS,** son of Colista/Calista-[6] BOWKER (Edmund-[5]; James-[4]; Edmund-[3]; James-[2;1]) and Ambrose CURTIS, was born 18 Apr 1867 Woodstock, ME. He married Lucy I. SWAN on 3 Dec 1899 at Woodstock. She was the daughter of Oliver Greenleaf SWAN and Lois Eliza BUCK, and was born ca 1883; died ____. Ernest-[7] CURTIS died ____.

Children of Ernest-[7] CURTIS and Lucy SWAN:
Surname **CURTIS**

1623. Annie Maud	born 19 Dec 1904; died June 1981; married Franze MILLS 9 Nov 1934 Rochester, NH	
	(he s/o Lewis MILLS and Agnes FLANDERS) (he born 25 Sep 1905; died June 1979)	
	Child: Dale-[9] MILLS born ca 1939	
1624. Frank Ambrose	(twin) born 28 Jan 1907; died Jan 1987 , single	EOL
1625. Fred Otis.	(twin) born 28 Jan 1907; died 1988	
1626. Colista Mabel	born 4 Aug 1908; died 9 Aug 2004; married Robert Clyde MORGAN ca ___	
1627. Bertha Ellen	born 23 Sep 1912; died 30 Sep 2002; married George Maitland ELWELL ca 1933	
	(he s/o Joseph ELWELL and Delia L _____)	
	(he born 26 Sep 1904; died 15 Jan 1984 ME	
	Children: Edward-[9] born ca 1934; Rena-[9] born ca 1935; Avis-[9] born ca 1937 and Ann-[9] ELWELL born ca 1939	
1628. Galen Jacob.	born 4 Jan 1914; died Sep 1966 ME; married Eva G. MARSHALL 31 Aug 1940 ME	
1629. Leona Belle	born 7 Nov 1916; died ___ ; married Merle WHITMAN ca ____ (he died 1978)	
	Children: Marshall-[9] born ca 1937; Mahlon-[9] born ca 1938; Mona-[9] born ca 1939; Maude-[9]; and Louise-[9] WHITMAN born ca ____	
1630. Ernest James.	born 6 Oct 1918; died 1 Mar 1996 ME	

Children of Ernest Rupert[-7] CURTIS and Lucy SWAN, continued:
Surname **CURTIS**

1631. Lucy Lenora	born 6 Aug 1920; died 3 June 2006; married George A. RIDLEY 9 Nov 1946
	(he s/o Charles H. RIDLEY and Blanche M. HART)
	(he born 17 Sep 1923 ME; died 27 Sep 1985 ME)
Children: George-[9] Jr. born ca ___; Nancy-[9] born ___, married ___ DAMON; and Kay-[9] RIDLEY born ca ___, married ____ HILL	

1338. NATHANIEL BOWKER[-7] WHITTIER, Jr., son of Nathaniel Bowker[-6] WHITTIER (Lucy[-5] BOWKER; Warren[-4]; Edmund[-3]; James[-2;1]) and his second wife Eva ANDREWS, was born 19 Nov 1885 at Lynn, MA. He married Catherine / Katie Julia SHEPPARD 28 Jun 1908 at Tifton, GA. She was the daughter of Oscar Fitzallen SHEPPARD and Carrie Lee GREEN, and was born 27 May 1892 at Tifton, GA; died 1968. Nathaniel Bowker[-7] WHITTIER died ____.

Children of Nathaniel Bowker[-7] WHITTIER and Katie Julia SHEPPARD:
Surname **WHITTIER**

1632. Vernon	born 5 May 1909; died 16 Apr 1984 Leon, FL
	married Cornelia Pearl CONNER ca ____ (she born 8 June 1910 FL; died 16 Dec 1991
1633. Nathaniel Beryl	born 3 Nov 1911; died ____
1634. Robert Julian	born 2 Sep 1913; died 14 June 1974 Vero Beach, FL
" Bob "	married Edna Faye PARK ca 1936 (she born ca 1916; died 1985)
1635. Mary C.	born 23 Jan 1918 GA; died 3 Aug 2006 Gainesville, FL
	married Alfred Lee NEIL, Sr. ca ____ (Child: Robert Curry-[9] NEIL born ca 1940)

1341. FRANCIS MARION " Frank"-[7] GETCHELL, son of Sarah Ann-[6] BOWKER (Watts[-5]; Major Levi[-4]; Joseph[-3]; James-[2;1]) and James A. GETCHELL, was born 23 Apr 1837 ME. He married Almeda Frances PERRY 4 April 1859. She was the daughter of Stephen PERRY and Martha DIXON, and was born 22 April 1837; died 1920.

Children of Francis Marion-[7] GETCHELL and Almeda PERRY:
Surname **GETCHELL**

1636. George born ca 1859; died 1870 1637. Almeda Frances born ca 1861; died 1863	
1638. John Sedgwick	born 18 Oct 1864 Marshfield, ME; died 12 Feb 1944 Vancouver, WA
	1 married May Mary HUGHES ca _____
	(she dau of John HUGHES and Eliza THOMPSON)
	(she born 1 May 1880 England; died 11 Apr 1963 WA)
	2 married Maggie ____ ca ____
Child: Francis Hamiton-[9] GETCHELL born ca 1895; died 1967	
1639. Evander Perry	born 15 Feb 1869; died _____; married Annette WALKER 15 June 1897
Child: Ralph A-[9] GETCHELL, MD, born ca 1899; married Gwendolyn P ____ ca ____; she born ca 1905	

1352. ARTHUR W-[7] BOWKER, son of Watts Henry[-6] BOWKER (Watts[-5]; Major Levi[-4;] Joseph[-3]; James-[2,1]) and Julia LYON, was born ca 1864 Machias, Maine. He married Edna Peavy CRANE ca 1891. She was the daughter of Rufus CRANE and his second wife, Elizabeth PEAVY, and was born Jan 1868 ME; died ____. Arthur-[7] BOWKER died ca 1920.

Children of Arthur-[7] BOWKER and Edna Peavy CRANE:
Surname **BOWKER**

1640. Elizabeth	born Jan 1892 MA; died 9 Feb 1952 Newton, MA
	married Chester Chamberlain BUTTS ca ____
Children: Elizabeth Bowker-[9] born ca 1919, died 1998; and Charles Richard-[9] BUTTS born ca 1925, died 1982	
1641. Julia	born May 1896

1353. DR. EVERETT MURRAY-[7] BOWKER, brother of above, was born 2 Nov 1866/67 Machias, Washington, Maine. He married Lucy Mary N. GRIGGS ca 1897/98. She was the daughter of William GRIGGS and Harriet Mary GIPSON and was born 12 Jan 1871, died 17 June 1955. Dr. Everett M-[7] BOWKER, who was active in civic affairs, was the Norfolk Co. Commissioner at the time of his death on 8 Sep 1923 Brookline, MA

Children of Dr. Everett M-[7] BOWKER and Lucy GRIGGS:
Surname **BOWKER**

1642. Philip Griggs ++	born 17 Apr 1899 Brookline, MA; died 29 Aug 1966 Stavanger, Norway
	married Margit Pauline LUNDE ca July 1948 Brookline, MA
	(she dau/o Peder LUNDE and Gjertine ____) (she born 28 Jan 1910 Norway; died 30 May 1991 FL)

++. Philip Griggs BOWKER , a graduate of the Stone School in Boston and Dartmouth College Class of 1923, was an insurance broker. He served as a MA State Senator from 1933-40. He had previously served on the Brookline, MA Planning Board 1928-29; and was on the Board of Selectman from 1929-34. He was a Republican.   A longtime bachelor he was asked by a reporter why he was still single, to which he replied that he was " looking for the rare girl who combines the faculties of excellent cook, brilliant conversationalist, and pleasant personality – " then added " I want one who will allow me a night out with the boys every now and then."

Children of Dr. Everett M-7 BOWKER and Lucy GRIGGS, continued:
Surname **BOWKER**

+	**1643. WINTHROP HAROLD**	born 20 July 1900; died 1962 (a construction Engineer) married Edith Dorothea HILL 14 June 1928 (she born 12 Nov 1901 MA; died 10 Apr 1994 Falmouth, Maine)
	1644. Everett Murray, Jr.	born 17 Sep 1901 Brookline, MA; died 10 Nov 1981 Chestnut Hill, MA
	1645. Eleanor G.	born ca 1905; died ____
	1646. Helen I.	born 21 Nov 1912; died 23 Sept 1995 Jamaica Plain, Suffolk, MA

1355. HERBERT MORTIMER-7 HANSCOM, son of Simon-6 HANSCOM (Lydia-5 BOWKER; Major Levi-4; Joseph-3; James-2,1) and Julia WHITE, was born 16 Nov 1846 at Machias, Maine. he married Margaret A. MAKER on 9 June 1870 at Cutler, Maine. She was the daughter of Luther MAKER and Margaret A. CARD, and was born16 Jan 1850 Cutler; died 15 Oct 1906 East Machias. ME. Hernert-7 HANSCOM died 11 Aug 1919 at East Machias, ME.

Children of Herbert-7 HANSCOM and Margaret MAKER:
Surname **HANSCOM**

	1647. Alice Julia	born 26 Feb 1871 East Machias; died 20 May 1925 East Machias
	1648. Frances "Fannie" D.	born 6 June 1872 E. Machias; died ____; married Charles W. FORBES 12 Dec 1896
+	**1649. ISABELLE CLIFFORD**	born 26 Dec 1873 East Machias; died 14 Feb 1927 1 married ____ MORTLOCK ca ____ ; 2 married Luther FORBES 11 Sept 1900 (he s/o John FORBES and Ann MULHOLLAND) (he born 1867; died 1924)
	1650. Lila/Lola (f)	born 21 June 1878 E. Machias; died 24 Aug 1895
	1651. Herbert R.	born 25 Aug 1885 East Machias; died 10 March 1887 EOL
	1652. Thomas Harold	born 28 Nov 1888 E. Machias; died 8 Dec 1955 Scarborough, Maine married Marion C KENNEDY ca ____ (she born ca 1889; died ____)

1369. MARY C-7 HANSCOM, daughter of Watts Bowker-6 HANSCOM (Lydia-5 BOWKER; Major Levi-4; Joseph-3; James-2,1) and Sarah ROBINSON, was born 14 Sep 1862 Machias, Maine. (DAR # 136822) She married first to William W. HALE on 29 Jan 1880. He was the s/o ___ HALE and __, and was born 1 Jan 1853 MA; died ___. Mary C-7 HANSCOM died 12 Oct 1941.

Children of Mary-7 HANSCOM and William HALE:
Surname **HALE**   (all children born Maine)

1653. Helen M.	born 13 Nov 1881; died ____; married Charles J. GRAHAM 25 June 1906 (he born 12 May 1881 MA; died ____) (she DAR # 174185) Child: Stanley Keith-9 GRAHAM born 17 Jan 1922 Detroit, Wayne, MI
1654. Arthur W.	born 21 Feb 1884 ; died ____
1655. Margarie	born Sept 1886; died 4 June 1963 OH
1656. Kenneth C.	born 13 July 1889; died 6 Feb 1985 FL; married Marie L. ____ ca ____
1657. Sarah M.	born Jan 1892; died ____ 1658. Dorothy D. born 22 Dec 1893; died ____

1374. SIMEON OSCAR-7 BOWKER, son of Nathan Stephen-6 BOWKER (Levi-5,4; Joseph-3; James-2,1) and Mary Abigail BERRY, was born 20 Jan 1851 at Marshfield, Washington, Maine. He married Keziah J. HOLMES on 2 March 1871. She was the daughter of Tristam HOLMES and Hannah BERRY; and was born 19 April 1851 at Marshfield. Me; died 8 April 1906, " burned to death when clothes caught on fire from a burning grass fire ". Simeon Oscar-7 BOWKER died 1 May 1907.

Children of Simeon O-7 BOWKER and Keziah HOLMES:
Surname **BOWKER**   (all children born Marshfield, Washington County, Maine)

1659. Nathan T.	born 27 July1872; died 22 June 1949 Fairfield, ME 1 married Jennie E. INMAN 3 Oct 1899 (she born ca 1873; died ____) Child: Philip Mullin-9 BOWKER born ca 1900; died 1986 2 married Nina E. JOHNSON 25 Dec 1911 Waterville, ME (she born ca 1884; died ____) (she dau/o Norman JOHNSON and Nellie ____)
1660. Leslie S.	born June 1873; died 26 June4 1949

Children of Simeon[-7] BOWKER and Keziah HOLMES, continued:
Surname **BOWKER**

+   **1661. SEYMOUR**   born 29 Mar 1875; died ___; married Lillian Mabel " Lillie" GETCHELL 8 July 1896
           HARMON   (she dau/o Oscar J. GETCHELL and Josephine M. BERRY (Stillman)
+   **1662. CLARENCE LEVI**   born 3 May 1877; died ____; married Mary C. TURNER ca ___ (she born ca 1885 IRE)
           1663. Gertrude E.   born June 1879; died ____

1380. GEORGE MELLUS[-7] LYON, son of Sarah-[6] GETCHELL (Betsey-[5] BOWKER (Major Levi-[4]; Joseph-[3]; James-[2,1]) and
William P. LYON, was born 27 Dec 1846/7 at Machias, Washington, Maine. He married Jane Ann " Jenny " BERRY ca 1866.
She was the daughter of _____ BERRY and ____; and was born 12 July 1848 Marshfield, ME; died 16 May 1900 NYC, NY.
George M[-7] LYON died ca 1927 Marshfield, Washington, Maine.

Children of George M[-7] LYON and Jenny BERRY:
Surname **LYON**

       1664. Sarah   born ca 1868; died ____
       1665. Phyzannah /   born ca 1869; died ca 1919; married Simon Bushrod ELWELL ca 1892
              Phirannah   (he born 28 Sep 1864; died 3 Dec 1947)
                              (he s/o Stephen Pope ELWELL and Ruth FOSS)
                   Children: George-[9] born ca 1898; and Herbert B[-9] ELWELL born ca 1901
       1666. Irving Charles   born ca 1871; died ___; married Charlotte " Lottie" GOOCH ca ____
                             (she born ca Oct 1879; died _____)
       1667. Roscoe Dolbear   born 27 June 1874; died ____; unmarried
       1668. Willard Getchell.   born 15 Jan 1876; died ____; married Ada M. ANDREWS ca ___
                  Children: Melvin-[9] born Jan 1900 ME; Doris-[9] born 1903 MA; and Vivian-[9] LYON born 1906 MA.
       1669. Effie   born Nov 1877; died ____; married Enoch HOWIE 25 June 1896 Machias, ME
                        (he s/o John HOWIE and Ann HARMON)   (he born Dec 1871; died ____)
                  Children: John Willard-[9] born 30 Jan 1898; Pearl Mellin-[9] " Perley" born 19 Sep 1899; and
                Calista M[-9] HOWIE born 1 Nov 1901
       1670. Anna/Annie   born Sept 1879; died 29 May 1938; married William Elmer ACKLEY 10 Nov 1896
                        (he s/o William W. ACKLEY and Mary Jane SCOFIELD) (he born 1873; died 1960)
                  Child: Marion-[9] ACKLEY born ca 1901, died 21 July 1981 Bangor, ME; married Clinton ALBEE
       1671. Josephine E. "Josie"   born June 1881; died ____; married Ernest Millard ANDREWS 8 June 1903
                  Child: Harry/ Harold Leon-[9] ANDREWS born ca 1909
       1672. Lizzie   born Jan 1883; died ____; married Walter B. CLOW 15 Oct 1902 Machias, ME
       1673. Walter Chase   born 25 Jan 1885; died 12 June 1927
+   **1674. AMELIA L.**   born Sept 1886; died 13 Jan 1967 Calais, Maine
                          married Samuel Hunter THOMPSON 23 Aug 1905
       1675. Mary A.   born May 1888; died ____; married Uriah T. CROSBY 28 Sep 1920
       1676. Carrie Clocker   born 17 Mar 1890; died 17 Feb 1960; married Henry Thaxter MILES 19 May 1906
                        (he born ca 1852; died 1959)
                  Children: Warren-[9:] Elwyn C[-9] born ca 1907; and Elsie May[-9] MILES born ca 1914
       1677. Henry   born 17 Mar 1890; died ____

1383. SIMEON GETCHELL[-7] LYON, brother of above, was born 5 May 1852 Machias, Maine. He married Hannah
SEDGLEY ca 1879 CA. She was the daughter of John SEDGLEY and Eliza ____, and was born Nov 1857 CA; died ____.
Simeon G[-7] LYON died ____.

Children of Simeon[-7] LYON and Hannah SEDGLEY:
Surname **LYON**   (children born Placer, CA)

       1678. James Sedgley   born 2 April 1880 died _____   1683. Edgar   born May 1896
       1679. Frederick William   born 15 April 1882; died 19 Feb 1951 Santa Cruz, CA
                       1 married Bertha _____; 2 married Lillian B ____
       1680. Herbert Simeon   born 14 May 1885; died 19 Feb 1914 Placer, CA
+   **1681. GRACE A.**   born 7 Dec 1887; died March 1974 CA; 1 married Samuel J. DEPENDENER ca _____
                       (he born 1 Nov 1876 OH; died ca 1935 Auburn, Placer, CA)
                       2 married David P. EDWARDS ca ____
                       (he s/o William EDWARDS and Mary POWELL ; born 6 Jan 1875; died 10 May 1942)
       1682. Ethel   born Nov 1890; died ____   1684. Mignonette   born ca 1898; died bef. 1900

1386. ANDREW M-7 LYON, brother of above, was born 2 May 1860 at Marshfield, Washington, Maine. He married Catherine Durling Lynn " Cassie" CLARK on 24 Nov 1879 at Boston, MA. She was the daughter of Ralph Robert CLARK and Maria Augusta DURLAND, and was born 26 Aug 1853 Annapolis, Nova Scotia, Canada, died 23 Nov 1916 Milford, CT. Andrew M-7 LYON died 8 Jan 1923 at Milford, CT.

Children of Andrew-7 LYON and Catherine CLARK:
Surname **LYON**

+	**1685. AVARD**	born 11 Jan 1881 NS; died 16 Feb 1958 West Boxford, MA
	PHINNEY	married Frances Ethna SIAS 6 Nov 1904 Methuen, MA
		(she dau/o John Smith SIAS and Mary Ella GERRY)
		(she born 30 Mar 1888 West Boxford; died ca 1968 Brookfield, MA)
	1686. Leda Clark	born Nov 1882 NS; died 6 June 1963 Methuen, MA
		married Samuel RUSHTON ca 1903/04 Pawling, NY
	1687. Millie L.	born ca 1887 Nova Scotia; died 22 Oct 1937 CT.
+	**1688. SADIE MARIE**	born 23 Oct 1888 Sierra Madre, California; died 4 Feb 1970 Pawling, NY
		married Vernon Velman/Welman BAKER ca 1906
		(he born 16 June 1886 Prince Albert, South Africa; died 10 Jan 1961 NS)
		(he s/o Israel Parker BAKER and Mary Jane WILKINS)
	1689. Bradford Morse	born 15 March 1893 Riverside, California; died 5 March 1947 Georgetown, MA
		married Grace T. NOONAN ca ____; divorced
	1690. Percy Lloyd	born March 1895 NS, Canada; died 7 March 1947 NH
	1691. Ruby Lola	born 17 July 1897 MA; died 9 Aug 1979 Haverhill, MA
	1692. Aubrey E. (m)	born 31 Oct 1900 MA; died Aug 1981 FL

1390. ARTHUR-7 HANSCOM, son of Ladwick Holway-6 HANSCOM (Sarah/Sally-5 BOWKER; Major Levi-4; Joseph-3; James-2,1) and Ida SMITH, was born 29 Jan 1873 Machias, Maine. He married Naomi G. BERRY on 10 Nov 1898. She was the daughter of Thomas Frederick BERRY and Laura FOSS, and was born 5 July 1875 Marshfield, ME; died 26 July 1963 Machias.

Children of Arthur-7 HANSCOM and Naomi BERRY:
Surname **HANSCOM**

1693. Richard Ladwick	born 12 Feb 1900 Machias, ME; died ____	
	married Evelyn C. ____	(she born ca 1905)
	Children: Barbara-9 born ca 1926; Richard-9 born ca 1933; and Ann E-9 HANSCOM born ca 1935	
1694. Olive B.	born ca 1908; died ____ 1695. Gertrude L.	born ca 1915; died ____

1398. ALLARD JOHN-7 DURGIN , son of John Varney-6 DURGIN (Delane-5 WRIGHT; Hannah-4 BOWKER/BUKER; Joseph-3; James-2,1) and Ellen FITZPATRICK, was born 24 Nov 1878 SD. He married first to Bessie Jeanette SMITH ca ____. She was the daughter of Charles Dwight SMITH and Jeanette ____, and was born 18 July 1881; died 30 Jan 1915 St. Cloud, MN. He married second to Annie KALSCHEUER ca ____. She was the daughter of Frank KALSCHEUER and ____, and was born 10 June 1855 SD; died 20 Dec 1961 Albert Lea, MN. Allard John-7 DURGIN, a railroad telegraph operator, died 11 Dec 1938 at Albert Lea, Freeborn, MN.

Children of Allard John-7 DURGIN and Bessie SMITH:
Surname **DURGIN**

1696. Jeanette E.	born ca 1905 MN		1697. Kenneth A.	born ca 1909 MN

Children of Allard John-7 DURGIN and Annie KLASCHEUER:
Surname **DURGIN**

1698. Jean B.	born 2 May 1912 MN; died 6 Feb 1985 Albert Lea, MN; married ____ YOST ca ____
1699. Lawrence John	born 29 May 1920 City, Freeborn, MN; died July 1986 MN

1401. EDWARD NEWTON-7 BOWKER, son of Isaac Newton-6 BOWKER (Isaac Hall-5; Lazarus-4; Joseph-3; James-2,1) and Maria Jane BROWN, was born 31 Jan 1879 ME. He married Viena Sarah STIMSON ca 1905. She was the daughter of David Samuel STIMSON and Lucy A. GERRY, and was born 2 Mar 1881 at Laconia, Belknap, NH; died 11 Oct 1953 Portsmouth, NH. Edward Newton-7 BOWKER, a machinist at the Navy Yard in Portsmouth, died 18 Jan 1966 at Sanford, Maine.

Children of Edward Newton-7 BOWKER and Viena STIMSON:
Surname **BOWKER**

1700. Arthur M.	born 6 Aug 1906 ME; died 8 Feb 1968 Augusta, Maine

Children of Edward Newton[-7] BOWKER and Viena STIMSON, continued:
Surname **STIMSON**

1701. Marshall E.	born 1 May 1909 ME; died 1938
1702. Mildred Evelyn	born 22 Jan 1911; died 1 May 2006 Sanford, ME (a teacher)
	married Everett Leon GROVER 23 Sep 1936 (he born ca 1911 ME)
	(he s/o Otis L. GROVER and Beatrice D. STAPLES)

Child: Robert[-9] BOWKER born ca 1938 ME

1402. THOMAS B-[7] BOWKER, son of Cutler Elbridge[-6] BOWKER (Elbridge[-5]; James[-4]; Joseph[-3]; James[-2,1]) and Mary Ann BLACK, was born 10 July 1874 ME. He married Florence Mabel NEWCOMB on 18 Oct 1902. She was the daughter of Jesse P. NEWCOMB and Hattie M. DUNBAR, and was born ca 1883; died ____. Thomas B[-7] BOWKER died ____.

Children of Thomas-[7] BOWKER and Florence NEWCOMB:
Surname **BOWKER**

1703. Cutler A.	born 27 Nov 1904; died 1976 East Brunswick, NJ
	married Martha WURSTER ca ____
	(she dau/o Albert G. WURSTER and Martha C. RABKE)
1704. Arnold F.	born 5 Apr 1906; died Nov 1972 Milford, NJ
1705. Thomas G.	born 1908/09 Milton, MA; died ____; married E. Irma WURSTER ca ____
	(she sister of above) Child: Dick-[9] BOWKER born ca 1932 MA.
1706. Dorothy	born 10 Oct 1910 Everett, MA; died ____

1403. AFTON CUTLER-[7] BOWKER, brother of above, was born 20/21 June 1879. He married Jenniebelle May WILLIS on 22 Nov 1901. She was the daughter of Fred Lincoln WILLIS and Isadora Mc FADDEN, and was born ca 1884; died ____. Afton Cutler-[7] BOWKER died 13 Dec 1962 at Bath, Maine.

Children of Afton Cutler-[7] BOWKER and Jennie WILLIS:
Surname **BOWKER**

1707. Hazel May	born 16 Mar 1902; died 7 Apr 1988 Bath, ME.
	married Edward James Mc MANN 23 Apr 1921 (div before 1940)
	(he s/o John H. Mc MANN and Mary E CRESSEY)
	(he born 7 Oct 1899 ME; died 31 Jan 1978)
1708. Maud H.	born ca 1904; died _____
1709. Madelyn Louise	born 21 Nov 1907; died 10 Mar 2002; married Maurice R. NADEAU 30 June 1934 ME
	(he s/0 Jean Baptiste NADEAU and Zouel/Zoe Vitaline MATAYER)
	(he born 3 Sep 1911; died Sep 1980)

Child: Robert-[9] NADEAU born ca 1936

1710. Arlene/ Eileen	born ca 1912; died _____	1711. Frederick	born ca 1918

1405. ELIZABETH MAE-[7] EASTMAN, daughter of Adelia Loring[-6] BOWKER (Elbridge[-5]; James[-4]; Joseph[-3]; James[-2,1]) and John R. EASTMAN, was born ca 1870 at South Portland, Maine. She married William W. RICH 10 June 1891. He was the son of ___ RICH and ____, and was born ca 1865 ME; died ____. Elizabeth Mae-[7] EASTMAN died ____.

Children of Elizabeth-[7] EASTMAN and William RICH:
Surname **RICH**

1712. Lewis Elbridge	born 12 Apr 1892; died ____
	married Elna Katherine CHRISTIANSEN 23 Oct 1922 South Portland, ME
	(she dau/o Peter CHRISTIANSEN and Marie JORGENSEN (both born Denmark)
	(she born ca 1900 Fort Edward, NY; died ___)

Children: William-[9] born ca 1926; and Dorothy [9] RICH born ca 1931

1713. Milford E.	born ca 1895; died ____; married Elsie M. _____ ca ___

1406. EPHRAIM RICH-[7] EASTMAN, brother of above, was born 9 Nov 1875 South Portland, Maine. He married first to Lulu/ Luella M. CATLIN on 21 Apr 1898. She was the daughter of Stephen W. CATLIN and Philinda/Philena S.SMALL; and was born ca 1881; died before 1910. He married second to Marion B. WING Hoffman, a divorcee, on 26 July 1910 at South Portland, Maine. She was the daughter of Charles WING and Elizabeth DEXTER, and was born ca 1880 Brunswick, ME; died ____. Ephraim-[7] EASTMAN died 1930.

Note: Marion WING Hoffman had a son named Hoyt HOFFMAN, from her first marriage.

Children of Ephraim-[7] EASTMAN and Lulu CATLIN:
Surname **EASTMAN**

1714. Alfred E.		born ca 1899; died ____; married Alice M. ____ ca ____ (she born 1897)
		Child: Elliott E-[9] EASTMAN born ca 1935
1715. Arthur L.		born ca 1901; died ____
1716. Lena May		born 30 Jan 1902; died 26 Dec 2001 (age 99+); married _____ CROWE ca ____
+	**1717. ELFRA MADELINE**	born 9 June 1903 Harpswell, ME; died ca 1992 East Harpswell
		married Forrest H. JOHNSON 1 Oct 1923
		(he born 16 Oct 1896 Swans Isle, ME; died 20 Oct 1972 Portland, ME)

Children of Ephraim-[7] EASTMAN and Marion B. WING Hoffman:
Surname **EASTMAN**

1718. John	born ca 1913; died ____
1719. Marion Elizabeth	born 16 Sep 1915 South Portland, ME; died ____
1720. Fred Bartlett	born 19 Oct 1916 South Portland, ME; died 12 March 1918 (measles and pneumonia)

1420. MARY JANE-[7] BOWKER, daughter of Turner-[6] BOWKER (Benjamin-[5] Jr; Benjamin-[4]; Richard [3,2]; James-[1]) and Harriet TILDEN, was born ca 1842 Hanson, MA. She married Calvin F. BOURNE on 6 April 1856. He was the son of _____ BOURNE and ____; and was born ca 1840; died ca 1880. Mary Jane-[7] BOWKER died 19 Nov 1883 Hanson, MA.

Children of Mary Jane-[7] BOWKER and Calvin BOURNE:
Surname **BOURNE**

+	**1721. ELLSWORTH T.**	born 11 July 1861; died 28 Aug 1950
		married Arabella F. CHURCHILL 22 Mar 1884 at Hanson, Ma
		(she dau/o Ebenezer A. CHURCHILL and Mary Farrell FORD)
		(she born 20 June 1867 WI; died 16 Aug 1951 Marshfield, MA)
	1722. Harriet J.	born ca 1866; died ____ 1723. Myrtie M. born ca 1871; died ____

1427. ANDREW CLARENCE-[7] BOWKER, son of Andrew-[6] BOWKER (Gad-[5]; Benjamin-[4]; Richard-[3,2]; James-1) and Betsey BARKER, was born 4 Mar 1861 at Hingham, MA. He married Mabel A. JACKSON on 7 Sep 1884 at Abington, MA. She was the daughter of Leander JACKSON and Anna ____; and was born 1865 ME; died ____. Andrew-[7] BOWKER died 11 Mar 1907 Rockland, MA.

Child of Andrew-[7] BOWKER and Mabel JACKSON:
Surname **BOWKER**

1724. Georgia Hazel	born 27 Jan 1888 Rockland, MA; died ____
	1 married Harry Lincoln LANE on 1 June 1907; divorced ca ____
	(he s/o Walter LANE and Harriet MORGAN)
	re-married Harry Lincoln LANE on 24 May 1921 Concord, NH
	Child: Mildred Winslow-[9] LANE born 3 Nov 1912; died 29 May 1998; married Reed Blackinton FULLER

1452. FRANCENIA MARIE-[7] BOWKER, daughter of Alonzo Melvin-[6] BOWKER, MD, (Melvin-[5]; Liberty-[4]; Luke-[3]; Richard-[2]; James-[1]) and Hepsey Ann STURTEVANT, was born 21 June 1853 at Savoy, Berkshire, MA. She married James Edley CAMPBELL 24 Oct 1875. He was the son of Alfred Franklin CAMPBELL and Mary Polly Burton HUDSON; and was born ca Nov 1850 IL; died 14 Dec 1936 Eads, Kiowa, CO. Francenia Marie-[7] BOWKER died 12 Mar 1905 at Salt River, Ralls, MO.

Children of Francena Marie-[7] BOWKER and J Edley CAMPBELL:
Surname **CAMPBELL**

1725. Addie Francenia	born 31 May 1876 IL; died 29 Nov 1967
	married Charles Willis SMITH 5 Jan 1896 MO
1726. Myrtie May	born 18 May 1879 MO; died 1963
1727. Edith Maud	born 22 Nov 1880 MO; died 28 Dec 1963
1728. Ethel Annis/Anise	born 4 Oct 1882 MO; died 10 Jan 1972 Audrain, MO
	married Harvey Weco POPKES 8 Nov 1904
	(he born 23 May 1880; died 31 Aug 1949 Perry, Ralls, MO.
	Children: Pearl-[9] born ca 1907 MO; Opal-[9] born ca 1909 MO; Lyle Harvey-[9] born ca 1913 MO;
	Addie Bernice-[9] born 6 Aug 1917 MO, died Feb 1982 MO; and Earl L-[9] POPKES born ca 1923
1729. William	born June 1883 MO; died ____

Children of Francenia Marie-7 BOWKER and James Edley CAMPBELL, continued:
Surname **CAMPBELL**

1730. Elmer	born 1 July 1885 MO; died 3 Dec 1969
1731. Zella/Zelia Belle	born 23 Oct 1886 MO; died Sep 1960 TX
1732. Iva Lena	born 6 Mar 1892 MO; died 27 Feb 1985 CO
1733. Nola/Nela Bowker	born 8 June 1895; died 10 Jan 1991
	married Lee C. WOMACK ca 1917 (he born ca 1889)

Children: Chester-9 born ca 1918, died 2 Mar 1986 CO; and Maxine V-9 WOMACK born ca 1923

1453. MELVIN WILLETT-7 BOWKER, brother of above, was born 10 Feb 1860 MA. He married Anna B. ____ ca 1886. She was born 1 May 1867; died 19 Dec 1915 IL. Melvin Willett-7 BOWKER died 6 Sep 1926 IL.

Children of Melvin-7 BOWKER and Anna B. ____:
Surname **BOWKER**

1734. Eldon/Elden G.	born 18 June 1889 Plainville, IL; died ____; married Edna L. COCHRAN ca ____
	(she dau/o Frank COCHRAN and Mary L. ____)

Children: Melvin N-9 born 19 May 1911 IL, died Oct 1974; and Dorothy-9 BOWKER born ca 1915 IL

1455. DELCY HARRIET-7 BOWKER, daughter of Charles-6 BOWKER, MD (Melvin-5; Liberty-4; Luke-3; Richard-2; James-1) and Harriet Philena DAWES, was born 21 Feb 1854. She married George Truman SWAZEY 24 Dec 1881 Bernardston, MA.. He was an attorney, the son of ____ SWAZEY and ____; and was born 19 March 1852 Waterbury, VT; died ____. Delcy-8 BOWKER died 9 June 1935 at Raymond, WA.

Children of Delcy-8 BOWKER and George T. SWAZEY:
Surname **SWAZEY**

1735. Harold B	born 1 Jan 1884 Bernardston, MA; died ___
1736. George T., Jr.	born 3 Feb 1885 Wahepton, ND; died ____; graduate of the US Naval Academy
1737. Henrietta	born 6 Feb 1893 Barre, VT; died ____

1462. ALMINA BELL-8 WEEKS, daughter of Helen Dallas-7 BOWKER (Lazarus-6; Dimmick-5; Lazarus-4;3; James-2;1) and James W. WEEKS, III, was born 16 Sep 1875 at Boston, MA. She married William Wallace Mc GREGOR on 25 Dec 1892 at Framingham, MA. He was the son of Cassino Mc GREGOR and Anna WALDRON, and was born 30 July 1869 Yonkers, NY; died 25 Feb 1933 Peabody, MA. Almina Bell-8 WEEKS died ca 1957 at Peabody.

Children of Almina Bell-8 WEEKS and William Wallace Mc GREGOR:
Surname **Mc GREGOR**

1738. Bradford "Bunky"	born ca 1893; died ____	
1739. Helen Dallas	born 30 May 1894 Medford, Ma; died ____	
1740. Effie Belle	born 16 June 1896; died 20 Aug 1892 Peabody, MA	
	married Omer Gideon SOUCY ca 1916	
	(he s/o Joseph Gideon SOUCY and Rosalie Cesaree GUERETTE)	
	(he born 27 Feb 1897 MA; died July 1978 Peabody, MA)	
	Children: William-10 born ca 1917; Jenny-10 born ca 1918; and Helen Roberta-10 SOUCY born ca 1927, married Carroll Snow PAGE ca ____ (had Brian C. PAGE who married Ruth ZEISET)	
1741. Robert Bruce	born 10 March 1899 Woburn, MA; died ____	
1742. Richard I.	born 25 Sep 1900; died 12 May 1986	
1743. Emma Lorinda	born 1 Apr 1907; died 25 Aug 1999	
	1 married Kurt Lennart SEASTRAND ca ____; 2 married Herbert Neal NEWTON	
	3 married George Frederick FLORENCE ca ____	
1744. Amey J.	born ca 1907 MA; died 1910 MA	EOL
1745. Thelma Elizabeth	born 12 July 1909; died ____	
1746. Wallace Bradford	born 5 Dec 1910; died 7 Jan 2001	
1747. Bernice Evelyn	born 21 Aug 1913; died 26 Nov 2012 Peabody, MA	

1463. GEORGE HENRY-8 LEARNED, son of Grant Barstow-7 LEARNED (Clarissa G-6 BOWKER; Howard-5; Lazarus-4 Jr.; Lazarus-3; James-2, Jr.; James-1) and Antoinette C GABRILLAC, was born 15 Oct 1861 at St. Louis , MO. He married Bertha E. RHEIN on 13 Aug 1884. She was the daughter of John J. RHEIN and Catherine RENZ, and was born ca 1870; died 1951. George Henry-8 LEARNED died 7 Nov 1904 St. Louis, MO

Children of George Henry-8 LEARNED and Bertha RHEIN:
Surname **LEARNED**

+ **1748. GEORGE**	born 22 Aug 1887 MO; died 21 Mar 1974 St. Louis, MO	
HENRY, Jr.	married Nellie L. EDWARDS ca ____	
	(she born 9 Dec 1894 IL; died Jan 1969 MO)	
	(she dau/o George Francis EDWARDS and Catherine BRENNAN)	
1749. Albert Carl	born ca 1890; died 1948	

1445. HELEN DAVIS-8 STRANGER, daughter of Julia Eveline-7 BOWKER (Davis Whiting-6; Howard-5; Lazarus-4 Jr; Lazarus-3; James-2 Jr.; James-1) and Elwin Nicholas STRANGER, was born 5 May 1892. She married Frank Howard MITCHELL on 30 March 1921. He was the son of Guy Lindsey MITCHELL and Amelia Catherine ECKE; and was born 3 Jan 1896 MO, died 6 Dec 1969 at Newton, Harvey, KS. Helen Davis-8 STRANGER died July 1978 Sedgwick, KS.

Children of Helen Davis-8 STRANGER and Frank MITCHELL:
Surname **MITCHELL**

1750. Harley Davis	born 22 Jan 1922 Newton, KS ; died 16 Apr 1995 Newton, KS.
	married Violet E. ____ 17 Sep 1950
1751. Alden Wallace	born 18 Dec 1922 Newton, KS; died 12 June 2010 W. Farmington, Maine
	married Marian Starling HALL 18 June 1946
	(she born ca 1924; died 2012)
	Children: son born ca ____ ; dau born ca ____; and John Philip-10 MITCHELL born 11 Aug 1954, died 3 Oct 1994 San Francisco, CA

Children of Helen Davis[-8] STRANGER and Frank MITCHELL, continued:
Surname **MITCHELL**

1752. Guy Elwin	born 14 Mar 1927 Plymouth, MA; died 15 Jan 1999 Apopka, Orange, FL
	married _____ on 21 May 1949

1472. DAVID WINSLOW[-8] THURSTON, son of Josephine Cora[-7] BOWKER (Winslow[-6] BOWKER; Lazarus[-5;4;3]; James-[2;1])
and John Edmund THURSTON, was born 15 Jan 1875 at Cambridge, MA. He married Grace Emeline ALDEN on 29 Oct 1901
at Medford, MA. She was the daughter of William Fernald ALDEN and Lucy Ann LESTER, and was born ca 1875 Medford,
MA; died ____. Daniel Winslow[-8] THURSTON died 1946
at Summerville, MA.

Children of Daniel Winslow[-8] THURSTON and Grace ALDEN:
Surname **THURSTON**

1753. Rev. Daniel Alden	born 4 Dec 1902 Medford, MA; died 4 Dec 1989 Amesbury, MA
	married Ruth E. ____ ca 1931 (she born ca 1907) (he a Methodist preacher)
Children: Ellery Alden[-10] born 31 Mar 1932 MA; died 14 Dec 2012 MA; and Donald Winslow[-10] THURSTON born 4 Mar 1937 MA	
1754. Edmund Winslow	born 3 Dec 1904; died 15 Apr 1888 Concord, NH (a school teacher)
	married Eleanor May NINDE ca 1931
	(she dau/o George F. NINDE and Ellen A. FALES) (she born 20 Aug 1904)
Children: Robert N[-10] born 6 June 1932 NH; died 21 Oct 2007 OH; and Barbara S[-10] THURSTON born ca 1935	
1755. Franklin Bowker	born 18 May 1907 Medford, MA; died 21 May 1997 Medford, MA
	married Amy C _____ ca 1939 Child: John F[-10] THURSTON born ca 1940

1473. WILLIAM M[-8] BOWKER, son of Marquis Lathram[-7] BOWKER (Clarke[-6]; Joseph[-5]; Zebulon[-4]; Lazarus[-3]; James[-2;1])
and Frances DUSHER, was born 2 May 1865 Carthage, Hancock, IL. He married first to Nadine SCOTT ca 1893. She was the
daughter of Charles Robert SCOTT and Mary L. DIXON, and was born ca 1870; died 1910 Nevada. He married 2nd to Emma
May LONGACRE ca 1913. She was the daughter of Andrew Jackson LONGACRE and Sarah Frances CATON, and was born 6
Dec 1885 Drywood, Vernon, MO; died Mar 1945 Nevada, MO. William M[-8] BOWKER, a lawyer in the firm of SCOTT and
BOWKER in Nevada, MO, died there 7 Feb 1931 .

Child of William[-8] BOWKER and Emma LONGACRE:
Surname **BOWKER**

1756. Mary F.	born 15 Mar 1914; died 11 Jan 1944; married Stone Mc FARLAND ca ____
	(he born ca 1910 MO; he a lawyer)

1477. JACOB OSCAR[-8] BOWKER, brother of above, was born 17 Feb 1873 IL. He married Frances " Tot " BARNARD on 19
May 1903, as her second husband. She was the daughter of Alfred Ernest BARNARD and Mary Hannah ALSTON, and was born
ca 1877; died 1961. She married 1st to Isaac LIONBERGER and had a son Albert Leland LIONBERGER born ca 1896 NE, died
1989. Jacob Oscar[-8] BOWKER died 2 May 1943 Burns, ID

Child of Jacob Oscar[-8] BOWKER and Frances BARNARD Lionberger:
Surname **BOWKER**

1757. Thelma Gertrude	born 28 May 1920; died 26 Apr 1997; married _____ Mc CREA ca ____

1478. FREDERICK GUY[-8] BOWKER, brother of above, was born 22 Apr 1876 Burnside, IL. He married Addie Maud
HURTT on 9 June 1897 MO. She was the daughter of William Tallmadge HURTT and Mary Malinda BARNEY, and was
born 10 Dec 1877 Johnson, Shelby, OH; died 1 April 1917 NE. Frederick[-8] BOWKER died 10 Mar 128 Beaver City, NE.

Children of Frederick Guy[-8] BOWKER and Addie HURTT:
Surname **BOWKER**

1758. Frederick Bryan	born 16 Dec 1898 Sheldon, MO; died 28 May 1980 Ponca City, OK
1759. Frank Oscar	born 29 Oct 1900; died 19 Aug 1972 Alexandria, NE
1760. Thomas William	born 29 Jul 1902 Beaver City , NE; died 23 Oct 1983 Herington, KS
1761. Dwight Harold	born July 1904 Beaver City; died Apr 1950 CO
1762. Robert Raymond	born 19 Sep 1906 Beaver City; died 15 Nov 1909 McCook, NE
1763. Marie Madene	born 29 Apr 1908 Beaver City; died 15 Dec 1997 Buffalo, NE

1479. MARY AGNES⁻⁸ BOWKER, sister of above, was born 13 July 1878 IL. She married William W. ARBAUGH ca 1896. He was the son of John ARBAUGH, Jr. and Sarah J.___, and was born Aug 1872 IA. Mary Agnes⁻⁸ BOWKER died 2 Mar 1972.

Children of Mary Agnes⁻⁸ BOWKER and William ARBAUGH:
Surname **ARBAUGH**

1764. Ora	born 23 June 1898; died ____	
1765. Earl M.	born 23 June 1898; died 30 Nov 1982; married Willie Edna ROBERTS	
	(she born ca 1900; died 1991)	
1766. Ernest D.	born 24 July 1904 MO; died 18 Apr 1994 Houston, TX	

1482. GROVER DUSHER⁻⁸ BOWKER, brother of above, was born 16 June 1888/89 IL. He married Mary Edna WELBORN ca 1913. She was the daughter of Joseph T. WELBORN and Ida Florence WILSON, and was born Sep 1893 MO; died Apr 1926 Nevada, MO. Grover⁻⁸ BOWKER died 18 Nov 1922 Nevada, MO.

Children of Grover⁸ BOWKER and Mary Edna WELBORN:
Surname **BOWKER**   (children all born Missouri)

1767. William Welborn	born 19 Nov 1913 MO; died 3 Feb 1989 Nevada, MO
	1 married Eunice ____ ca ____; 2 married Ellen Irene GEORGE Banes after 1961
1768. Lucille	born ca 1916; died ____ 1769. John/Jack born ca 1920

1483. MINNIE LAVINA⁻⁸ BOWKER, daughter of Franklin W⁻⁷ BOWKER (Clarke⁻⁶; Joseph⁻⁵; Zebulon⁻⁴; Lazarus⁻³; James⁻²,¹) and Catherine LAUGHLIN, was born ca 1864 IL. She married James Henry CLARK on 16 Jan 1884 at Schuyler County, IL. He was the son of Nathaniel Henry CLARK and Mercy Jane WELLS, and was born 30 May 1863 Dallas City, IL; died 2 Feb 1958 Dallas City. Minnie L⁻⁸ BOWKER died 13 Sep 1948.

Children of Minnie L⁻⁸ BOWKER and James Henry CLARK:
Surname **CLARK**

+	**1770. ETHEL**	born 29 Mar 1886 Dunham, Hancock, IL; died 9 Jan 1971
	CORINNE	married Walter Mark AVISE 25 Dec 1906
	1771. Henry Ray	born 28 Nov 1888 IL; died 18 Aug 1989 IL;
		married Nellie Margaretha LITTLE 21 Feb 1920
	1772. Kathryn Mercy	born 24 Sep 1896; died 21 Jan 1989 IL
		married Kent Wallace DUNHAM 22 Mar 1919 Dunham, IL
		Child: Beulah⁻¹⁰ DUNHAM born ca 1920, died 2009
	1773. Annice Maud	born 28 Dec 1898; died ____; married Millard Rice MYERS 25 Dec 1919
		Child: Jack M-¹⁰ MYERS born ca 1928; died 2001

1486. ROGER F⁻⁸ BOWKER, brother of above and twin of Maude⁻⁸ (# 1459), was born 17 April 1871 IL. He married Amy Z. LAMB on 17 Oct 1891. She was the daughter of Abraham C. LAMB and Louise KIDSON, and was born 17 Feb 1873; died 10 May 1958. Roger⁻⁸ BOWKER died 18 Oct 1954.

Children of Roger⁻⁸ BOWKER and Amy LAMB:
Surname **BOWKER**

	1774. Bessie Beatrice	born 5 Aug 1892; died Apr 1974; married Carl Preston GRIFFITHS ca ____
		(he s/o Joseph Preston GRIFFITHS, Jr. and Elva Ann AVISE)
		(he born 22 July 1885 Hancock, IL; died Oct 1975 Hancock)
	1775. Ruth Irene	born 27 May 1897; died 2 Nov 1943 Hancock
		(married Ellsworth James SCHENCK 21 June 1918; 2 married ____ RICE
	1776. Pearl Lillian	born 17 Feb 1898; died Oct 1981
+	**1777. THELMA**	born 9 Apr 1904; died 1 July 2001 Dallas City, IL
	NOREEN	married Guy Harold OLLIS 27 Dec 1925 IL
		(he s/o William Mathias OLLIS and Martha Ellen BOWEN)
	1778. Frank Abraham	born 2 July 1906; died 25 Oct 1919 EOL

1488. INEZ⁻⁸ BOWKER, sister of above, was born 7 Dec 1879 IL. She married Edward L. HUPFER ca 1913. He was the son of Conrad HUPFER and Barbara SCHREPFER, and was born ca 1885 IL; died 6 Oct 1979 Hamilton, IL. Inez⁻⁸ BOWKER died __ .

Children of Inez⁻⁸ BOWKER and Edward HUPFER:
Surname **HUPFER**

1779. Wilma	born 3 Aug 1914 Dallas, Hancock, IL; died 15 Feb 1997 Matthews, NC	
	married Robert CARNSHAW, Jr. ca ____ (he born ca 1920 FL; died 1999 NC)	
1780. Edward Bowker	born 1917; died 1917	

1489. GEORGE WATTS⁻⁸ BOWKER, brother of above, was born 1 June 1882 IL. He married Minnie Pearl SHAIN ca 1903. She was the daughter of William D. SHAIN and Olive _____, and was born 25 Sep 1887, died 20 Aug 1971 San Diego, CA. George W⁻⁸ BOWKER died 22 Mar 1961 San Diego, CA.

Children of George Watts⁻⁸ BOWKER and Minnie SHAIN:
Surname **BOWKER**

1781. Vivienne Eileen   born 15 Aug 1904; died 9 Jan 1990 Orange Co., CA;
                         1 married Louis E HASKETT ca 1929; 2 married _____ BOYD ca ____
                         Children: Betty A⁻¹⁰ born ca 1930, and Katherine⁻¹⁰ HASKETT born ca 1938
1782. Clark S.   born ca 1907; died ____
1783. Ned A.   born 8 Mar 1910; died 24 Nov 1966 Orange, CA

1493. SARAH B⁻⁸ BOWKER/BUKER, daughter of Sims Gardner⁻⁷ BOWKER/BUKER (Rufus⁻⁶; James-^{5,4,3,2,1} BOWKER) and Mary Ann SPEAR, was born 4 Jan 1864 at Braintree, MA. She married George Dow NEWCOMB on 16 June 1883. He was the son of George D. NEWCOMB and Mary J ____, and was born Dec 1855; died ____. Sarah-⁸ BOWKER died 15 Apr 1920 Braintree, MA

Children of Sarah B⁻⁸ BOWKER/BUKER and George NEWCOMB:
Surname **NEWCOMB**   (all children born Braintree, MA)

+   **1784. ERNEST**   born 6 Apr 1884 Braintree, MA; died ____
                          married Caroline " Carrie " S. ____ ca ___   (she born Mar 1886)
     1785. Laura May   born 15 Nov 1888; died __   1787. Sarah Florena   born 17 Dec 1893; died ____
     1786. Mary Tinkham   born 1 Aug 1891; died ___   1788. Alice L.   born 1909/10; died ____

1498. AMOS STETSON⁻⁸ BOWKER/BUKER, brother of above, was born 31 Oct 1874 at Braintree, MA. He married Anne Estelle ROSS on 19 Aug 1896 at Weymouth, MA. She was the daughter of Samuel Joseph ROSS and Anne Estelle BOWKER (she # 1586); and was born 14 March 1877; died ____. Amos Stetson-⁸ BOWKER died 31 May 1967.

Children of Amos Stetson⁻⁸ BOWKER/BUKER and Anne ROSS:
Surname **BOWKER/BUKER**

1789. Myrtle Irene   born 8 July 1902; died 28 Feb 1927
                         married George Sheldon CRAIG ca 1922
                         (he s/o Alexander CRAIG and Jemima NORVAL)
                         (he born 20 Mar 1897 Aberdeen, Scotland; died 22 Mar 1978 Norfolk, MA)
                         Children: Alice L⁻¹⁰ born ca 1923; and Pearl C⁻¹⁰ CRAIG born ca 1926
1790. Arthur L.   born ca 1906; died ____
1791. Doris Lillian (twin)   born 8 May 1909; died 5 May 1934 Norfolk, MA
1792. Doris Louise (twin)   born 8 May 1909; died ____

1500. MYRTLE⁻⁸ BOWKER, daughter of William T⁻⁷ BOWKER (Samuel⁻⁶; Samuel Michael⁻⁵; William⁻⁴; James^{-3,2,1}) and Emma KEEVER, was born 3 Aug 1874 OH. She married Walter Edward BIGGS ca 1893. He was the son of James W. BIGGS and Susanna LAUDERBAUGH, and was born Aug 1872 OH; died ca 1944. Myrtle-⁸ BOWKER died 25 Oct 1949.

Children of Myrtle⁻⁸ BOWKER and Walter Edward BIGGS:
Surname **BIGGS**

1793. John Walter   born Jan 1894 OH; died ca 1910
1794. Emma Rena/Reena   born Sept 1899 OH; died 1984
                         married Welton Leroy HIZAR ca _____   (he born ca 1890; died 1972)
                         Children: Edward Leroy⁻¹⁰ ; and Wanda Lorraine-¹⁰ HIZAR
1795. Walter H.   (twin) born 15 Oct 1903 Waynesville, Wayne, OH; died 23 July 1976 OH
                         married Ellen G _____ ca ___   (she born ca 1907; died 1983)
1796. William/Willie (twin) born 15 Oct 1903; died May 1983 OH

Children of Myrtle-8 BOWKER and Walter Edward BIGGS, continued:
Surname **BIGGS**

    1797. Elda   born ca 1908; died ____   1798. Genevieve   born ca 1911; died ____

    1799. Louella M.   born 5 July 1913; died 7 Dec 2006; married John C. HIATT ca 1938 (he born ca 1913
            Child: John-10 HIATT born ca 1940; died 1998

1503. CLYDE K-8 BOWKER, brother of above, was born 11 Nov 1880 OH. He married Ethel L.____ ca 1905. She was born ca 1885 OH; died ca 1957. Clyde-8 BOWKER died 13 April 1960 Hamilton, Butler, OH.

Child of Clyde-8 BOWKER and Ethel __?__:
Surname **BOWKER**

+   **1800. HAROLD CHESTER** born 17 May 1906 OH; died 9 Mar 1990 OH
               married Marie Dorothy GLOMB 18 July 1931

1506. WILLIS-8 BOWKER, son of William T-7 BOWKER (Samuel-6; Samuel Michael-5; William-4; James-3;2;1) and Emma KEEVER, was born 3 June 1888 at Warren County, Ohio. He married Mary PETERS ca 1909. She was the daughter of Francis PETERS and Rosanna Jane RICHARDS, and was born 2 Aug 1890 IN; died 25 Oct 1951 Cincinnati, OH. Willis-8 BOWKER died 21 Jan 1949 Lebanon, Ohio.

Children of Willis-8 BOWKER and Mary PETERS:
Surname **BOWKER**

    1801. Emma J.   born ca 1910 IN; died ____   1804. Milton W.   born 26 June 1916; died 4 Apr 1932

    1802. Ethel   born ca 1912; died ____

+   **1803. WILLIAM EARL**   born 5 Mar 1914 IN ; died 23 Sep 1972 TX; married Helen ____

1507. CHARLES ANDREW-8 BOWKER, brother of above, was born 14 Nov 1890 Clinton County, IN. He married Grace Mae RICHARDS on 29 Apr 1911. She was the daughter of Isaac Monroe RICHARDS and Mary Jane HIZER, and was born 9 Mar 1893, died 3 July 1966 Aurora, IN. Charles Andrew-8 BOWKER died 26 July 1962 at Milan, Allen, IN.

Children of Charles Andrew-8 BOWKER and Grace Mae RICHARDS:
Surname **BOWKER**

    1805. Rachel Mae   born 16 Feb 1912 IN; died Mar 1984 Aurora, IN
                        married George McClellan BUFFINGTON, Jr. ca ____   (he born ca 1901; died 1982)
                        (he s/o George Mc. BUFFINGTON, Sr. and Bridget GALLAGHER)

    1806. Marvin Charles   born 29 July 1914 Aurora, IN; died 1 Dec 1969 FL

    1807. Cecil Edgar   born 20 Apr 1919 Aurora; died 14 May 1997 Colorado Springs, CO
                        married Geneva AGRUE ca 1938   Child: Bonnie S-10 BOWKER born ca 1939 IN
                        (she born 12 Feb 1919 IN; died 26 May 2012 Colorado Springs, CO)

    1808. Monroe William born 29 Sep 1922 Aurora; died 16 Mar 1985 Milan, Ripley, IN
                        1 married Wanda Marie CARTER ca 1940
                        2 married Ruby TAYLOR 13 Feb 1960 (she born ca 1929; died 1988)

1508. ORVILLE G-8 BOWKER, brother of above, was born 12 Dec 1894 Warren County, Ohio. He married Blanche C. SNELL 12 Aug 1917. She was the daughter of George Washington SNELL and Bertha A. HENSEL, and was born Dec 1897; died 20 June 1960. Orville-8 BOWKER died 20 Dec 1960 MI

Children of Orville G-8 BOWKER and Blanche SNELL:
Surname **BOWKER**

    1809. Noel   born 21 May 1918 OH ; died 18 Nov 1991 CA
                        married Mary Margaret KRESS ca ____ (she dau /o Clyde KRESS and Elsie O. ____)
                        (she born 30 Nov 1916; died 10 Dec 1984 Riverside, CA)

    1810. Garnet E.   born 6 Nov 1921 ; died 25 Dec 2004 OH; married Stephen P. CAUDELL, Sr. ca ____
               Children: Stephen-10 Jr. ; and David-10 CAUDELL

    1811. Gladys M. " Toni "   born 8 Jan 1923 Warren Co., OH ; died 11 May 1985 OH

1528. HOWARD FRANKLIN-8 BOWKER, son of Albert-7 BOWKER (Renssalaer-6; Cushing-5; Captain Stephen-4; John-3;2;James-1) and Elizabeth FRANKLIN, was born 3 Jan 1889 MN. He married Violetta Mary-8 BOWKER ca Apr 1913. She was born 29 May 1896 Alameda, CA; died 5 Sep 1972 Alameda, CA. She and her husband are buried at Arlington National

Cemetery, VA. Howard Franklin[8] BOWKER died 8 July 1970 Alameda, CA.

Children of Howard Franklin-[8] BOWKER and Violetta Mary-[8] BOWKER:
Surname **BOWKER**

> 1812. Howard Franklin, Jr.   born 24 Apr 1914 Chicago, IL; died 9 Jun 1943
> > Note: He was a Major in the US Marine Corps, WW 2, and was killed in action 9 June 1943
> 1813. Gordon Albert   born 3 Aug 1917 Norfolk, VA;. died 11 Jan 1944; married Hazel ____ ca ____
> > Note: He was a Lt. in the US Navy , and was reported missing in action 11 Jan 1944. He was awarded a
> > Purple Heart and his name is on the monument at Ft. William McKinley, Manila, Phillipines
> 1814. Irving Allen   born 27 Dec 1922 Manila, Phillipines; died 2 Feb 1995 Salinas, CA
> > married Nancy COZZENS ca ____
> > > Child: Marilyn [-10] BOWKER born ca ___; married Mark DORMAN (child: Elizabeth[-11] DORMAN)

1529. ROCKTON ADAM[-8] BOWKER, brother of above, was born 22 Feb 1891 IL. He married Ethel Linnea SUNDBORG ca 1920. She was the daughter of John P. SUNDBORG and Maria PETERSON, and was born 7 July 1897 Chicago, IL; died March 1973. Rockton[-8] BOWKER died 20 Jan 1971 IL.

Children of Rockton-[8] BOWKER and Ethel SUNDBORG:
Surname **BOWKER**

> 1815. Viola Florence   born 22 May 1921 Chicago, IL; died 23 Oct 2000 New Mexico
> > married James Joseph O'SULLIVAN 16 Sept 1942
> 1816. Nancy   born 15 May 1931; died ____
> 1817. Joyce   born ca 1932; died 29 Dec 1998 CA   1818. Ronald   born 22 Oct 1934; died 1958

1530. WALLACE JOHN[-8] BOWKER, brother of above, was born 8 July 1893 IN. He married Frances VAN COTT / BAN-COTT ca 1919. She was the daughter of ____ VAN COTT/ BANCOTT and ____, and was born 12 Mar 1896 IL; died Jan 1982 IL. Wallace John[-8] BOWKER died 17 June 1929 IN.

Children of Wallace John[-8] BOWKER and Frances VAN COTT:
Surname **BOWKER**   (all born Chicago, Cook County, IL)

> 1819. Warren Howard   born 3 Nov 1919; died 20 May 2001 Chicago Heights,Cook, IL
> > married Jean JANIS 26 May 1951 Cook County, IL
> > (she born 21 June 1915; died 11 Apr 1997)
> 1820. Gerald Wendell   born 5 Sep 1922; died 18 June 2011 Homewood, Cook,IL
> > married Dorothy E. MILLER 8 July 1949 Cook County, IL
> > Note: He was a pilot in WW2, in Italy, with the 451st Bomb Group
> > > Children: Susan Carlsen-[10] born ____, married Dale JOHNSON; Lori-[10] born ca   -   ---;
> > > married James O'BRIEN; and Carol-[10] BOWKER born ca ____
> 1821. Howard   born 13 Sep 1924; died 17 Nov 2010 Flossmoor, Cook, IL

1537. PAULINE GRACE[-8] THACKERAY, daughter of Ella[-8] BOWKER (Albert B-[7]; Rensselaer-[6]; Cushing-[5]; Captain Stephen-[4]; John-[3;2]; James[-1]) and George W. THACKERAY, was born 22 April 1902. She married Francis Eugene. PERKINS ca 1924. He was the son of Addison Fayette PERKINS and Grace Mae MARBLE; and was born 5 June 1900; died 9 Sep 1775 San Bernardino, CA. Pauline-[8] THACKERAY died 22 June 1983 CA.

Children of Pauline-[8] THACKERAY and Francis Eugene PERKINS:
Surname **PERKINS**

> 1822. Francis Addison   born 25 July 1925; died 8 Mar 1993 Marshall, MO.
> 1823. May Ella   born ca 1927; died 2008; married _____ WALKER ca ____
> 1824. Karl William   born 9 Oct 1928 IL.; died 27 Mar 2010
> 1825. Paul Clayton   born 19 Sep 1931 Cook Co., IL; died 18 Mar 1985 Chicago, IL
> > married Beverly Ann JACKSON 12 Sep 1958 Cook Co., IL (she born 29 July 1938)
> 1826. June Rae   born ca 1933; died ____
> 1827. Robert Eugene   born 10 May 1935 IL; died 26 June 2008 CA.   1828. Betty J.   born ca 1937

1563. FLORA MARIE [-8] BOWKER, daughter of Henry Fay[-7] BOWKER (Samuel Francis-[6]; Samuel Griffin-[5]; Stephen-[4]; John-[3,2]; James[-1]) and Flora Emma HARDIE, and was born 21 June 1901 Rock Island, IL. She married Fred Sailor SMITH 16 Jun 1918. He was the son of John Kelly SMITH and Susan Jane BEAISH, and was born 22 Aug 1896; died 3 Nov 1962 Marie-[8] BOWKER died 4 Nov 1979 Davenport, IA

Children of Flora Marie-8 BOWKER and Fred SMITH:
Surname **SMITH**

1829. Fay Kelly	born 25 Sep 1920 Battle Creek, MI; died 3 Aug 1963 Davenport, IA
1830. Flora Dean	born 25 Jan 1923 Davenport; died 1 June 2007 Bettendorf, IA
1831. Richard Edwin	born ca 1924 Davenport, IA; died ____
1832. Louise Marie	born 31 Dec 1926 Davenport, IA; died 26 Jan 1929 Davenport
1833. Eldon L.	born 8 Apr 1929 Davenport; died 11 June 2009 Davenport
	married Mary E. HAGEN 30 July 1948 Davenport, IA
1834. Marvin L.	born 1 Nov 1932 Davenport, IA; died ____
1835. Robert Nielson	born 4 Dec 1933 Davenport; died 26 Oct 1996 Northridge, Los Angeles, CA
1836. Shirley May	born 20 May 1937 Davenport, IA; died 16 June 2007 Blue Grass, Scott, IA
	married Melvin V. WULF ca ____
	(he born 3 Sep 1929; died 6 Mar 1998 Blue Grass, IA
1837. George Edward	born 5 Oct 1941 Davenport; died 9 Sep 2012 Kingsport, TN

1564. FLORENCE AMANDA-8 BOWKER, sister of above, was born 7 Dec 1905 at Davenport, IA. She married Louis Elijah COFFELT ca 1922. He was the son of ____ COFFELT and ____; and was born 13 March 1902; died 27 Feb 1962. Florence-8 BOWKER died 30 July 1986 at Davenport.

Children of Florence Amanda-8 BOWKER and Louis COFFELT:
Surname **COFFELT**

1838. Flora Ann	born 16 Dec 1923; died ____; married Robert N. CARMONY ca ____
	(he born 18 Oct 1924 TN; died 1 Nov 23001 IA)
1839. Lois	born 10 Oct 1925 IA; died 3 July 1981
1840. Louis D.	born 2 Sep 1927; died ___; married Charlotte L. ___ ca ____ (she born 1928)
1841. Beverly Jean	bon 16 Nov 1929; died 28 Oct 1997; married Sherrill D. COX ca ____
	(he born 1930)

1567. RALPH EUGENE-8 EMERY, son of Minnie Rose-7 BOWKER (Samuel Francis-6; Samuel Griffin-5; Stephen-4; John-3,2; James-1) and Orton EMERY, was born 6 July 1894 IA. He married Blonda ____ ca 1925. She was born 14 Mar 1898 ND, died May 1985 ND. Her parents were born in Norway. Ralph-8 EMERY died 26 July 1947. He was a World War 1 veteran, as a Pvt. in the US Army. It is interesting to note that on his WW1 registration card – he asked for exemption to service on the ground that " I am against going out of the US to fight ". Note: Guess they didn't listen to him.

Children of Ralph-8 EMERY and Blonda G. ____:
Surname **EMERY**

1842. Clinton	born ca 1926; died ____	1844. Lorraine	born ca 1930
1843. Dena/Denna Lou	born 14 Jan 1829; died ____	1845. Eugene	born ca 1832

1573. FRANK L-8 BOWKER, son of Leslie Eugene-7 (Samuel Francis-6; Samuel Griffin-5; Stephen-4; John-3,2; James-1) and Melvina GILLSTRAP / GILKTRAP, was born ca 1903. He married Adeline C ____ ca 1927. She was born ca 1903; died ____.

Children of Frank L-8 BOWKER and Adeline C. ____:
Surname **BOWKER**

1846. Dorothy	born ca 1928		
1847. Ronald James	born ca 1934; died 8 June 2009 CA		
1848. Thomas	born 9 Mar 1933	1849. Marion	born ca 1939

1580. SYLVIA IRENE-8 ROBERTS, daughter of Mamie Estella-7 BOWKER (Samuel Francis-6; Samuel Griffin-5; Stephen-4; John 3,2; James-1) and Roscoe Conklin ROBERTS, was born 29 Mar 1900 Crystal, IA. She married William Montgomery BALFOUR ca 1921. He was the son of ____ BALFOUR and ____; and was born ca 1898; died 1964.

Children of Sylvia-8 ROBERTS and William BALFOUR:
Surname **BALFOUR**

1850. Alverna Mae	born 22 June 1922 ND; died 10 Apr 2009 Concord, CA
	married Orville E. SMITH ca ____
	(he born 25 Nov 1920 ND; died 3 Nov 1996 ND)
1851. Monte L.	born 5 Apr 1926 ND; died 1 Apr 2006 Walnut Creek, CA

1585. MINNIE ETTA-8 ROSS, daughter of Anne Estelle-7 BOWKER (William-6; Elijah-5,4; John-3; James-2,1) and Samuel Joseph ROSS, was born 30 Sept 1875 at Braintree, MA. She married William Henry BOWKER / BUKER on 10 Nov 1896 at Weymouth, MA. He was the son of Sims Gardner BOWKER / BUKER and Mary Ann SPEARS, and was born 13 Sep 1870 Braintree; died 17 Jan 1952 Weymouth, MA. Minnie Etta-8 ROSS died ____ .

Children of Minnie Etta-8 ROSS and William Henry BOWKER / BUKER:
Surname **BOWKER / BUKER**   (children born Braintree, Norfolk, MA)

1852. William Henry, Jr.	born 18 Feb 1898; died Aug 1966	
	married Florence E M _____	(she born ca 1907; died ___)
1853. Harold Sidney	born 1 May 1900; died ____; married Ruth McCOY ca ____	
1854. Everett Alton	born 7 Aug 1902; died 3 Oct 1976 Weymouth, MA	

1601. BENJAMIN JEFFERSON-8 ROWELL, son of Maria Eliza-7 BOWKER (William-6; Elijah-5,4; John-3; James-2,1) and Henry Franklin ROWELL, was born 19 Feb 1887 MA. He married Maria C. SOUSA on 31 Dec 1905. She was the daughter of Philemon SOUSA and Georgianna NACHADO, and was born ca 1887 Portugal; died ____ . Benjamin F-8 BOWKER died 3 Dec 1942.

Children of Benjamin J-8 ROWELL and Maria SOUSA:
Surname **ROWELL**

+	**1855. GWENDOLYN**	born 11 June 1909, MA; died 23 Feb 1981 Los Angeles, CA
	IRENE	married Fred W. TAYLOR ca 1928
	1856. Henry	born ca 1912; died ____ 1859. Marjorie C. born ca 1923; died 1995
	1857. Elsie M.	born ca 1916; died ____
	1858. Lillian G.	born 28 Dec 1920 MA; died 11 June 1989 Key Largo, FL

1614. CHARLES R-8 BOWKER, son of Gilman Roe-7 BOWKER (John M-6; Cyprian-5; Capt. James-3; Edmund-3; James-2,1) and Hannah Sabra LYON(S), was born 24 Jan 1865 ME. He married Mary Jane HEBB on 22 Mar 1889 at Springfield, Penobscot, Maine. She was the daughter of George S. HEBB and Catherine GREEN Mc GRAW, and was born 27 July 1872 Carroll, Penobscot, ME; died 25 Jan 1966 Lincoln, ME. Charles R-8 BOWKER died4 Jan 1955.

Children of Charles R-8 BOWKER and Mary Jane HEBB:
Surname **BOWKER**   (children all born Carroll, Penobscot, ME)

	1860. Millie Mae	born 21 Feb 1892; died ____; married Frank Everett YOUNG 14 Sep 1913
+	**1861. ARTHUR LYNN**	born 1 Aug 1894; died 9 Jan 1978 Lincoln, ME
		married Grace Edna JORDAN 1 Oct 1917
		(she dau/o Edwin Hurd JORDAN and Helen "Nellie" PORTER)
		(she born 25 Jul 1901; died 17 Jan 1966 Lincoln, ME)
	1862. Frances Louise	born 24 Feb 1898; died 16 Aug 1975; married Lucy Twombly FLEMING 26 Oct 1918
	1863. Daisy Lillian	born 8 Nov 1899; died 2 Oct 1988; married Leo Lot BEATHAM 10 June 1916
	1864. Agnes Catherine	born 9 Jan 1903; died 10 Jul 1995; married Oland Maurice COLE 25 July 1925
	1865. Leo Elmer	born 7 Aug 1906; died 1 May 1969; married Doris E. ____
	1866. Blaine W.	born 24 Sep 1916; died 24 Sep 1969 Los Angeles, CA
		married Norma H. MERRILL 7 Mar 1938

1615. HATTIE ESTELLA-8 BOWKER, sister of above, was born 19 Apr 1868/69. She married Everett Forrest ALDRICH on 10 Nov 1886 (as his second wife) at Penobscot County, ME. He was the son of Moses Weston ALDRICH and Hannah COLSON, and was born 1 Sept 1852 Penobscot; died 14 March 1914 at Carroll, ME. Hattie Estella-8 BOWKER died ca 1951.

Children of Hattie Estella-8 BOWKER and Everett ALDRICH:
Surname **ALDRICH**

1867. Rosa Hannah	born 11 March 1887; died 2 Apr 1936; married George Columbus DRAKE ca ____
1868. Armina Alberta	born 5 May 1889; died 5 Aug 1917; married Frank Edward SEVERANCE ca ____
1869. Ruth Cleveland	born 15 Mar 1892; died 29 May 1892
1870. Edith Velzora	born 19 Mar 1893; died 15 Jan 1955
1871. Dora Ellen	born 21 Sep 1895; died May 1987 LA.
	1 married Edwin L. WOODARD ca ____; 2 married Joseph THIEBAULT ca ____
1872. Horace Gilman	born 26 June 1898; died 17 Jan 1966
	married Pauline Frances SCHORTMANN ca 1921 (she born ca 1904; died 1969)

Children of Hattie Estella[-8] BOWKER and Everett ALDRICH, continued:
Surname **ALDRICH**

1873. Virginia Lyle	born 18 July 1901; died 27 Dec 1983 LA.
	1 married Vinal J. STEWART ca ____; 2 married _____ HOYLE ca ____
1874. Charles Lynn	born 29 Apr 1905; died 15 Aug 1973 Penobscot, ME
	1 married Eunice Emily ROYAL ca ____ (she born ca 1908; died 1967)
	2 married Ruth Laura ALLEN ca ____ (she born ca 1916; died 2006)

1616. CLOTILDE[-8] BOWKER, sister of above, was born 17 Nov 1870 Penobscot, Maine. She married James M. SMITH ca 1891. He was the son of ___ SMITH and ____, and was born 16 Mar 1868, died 2 Nov 1926 Penobscot, ME. Clotilde[-8] BOWKER died 23 Jan 1961 ME.

Children of Clotilde[-8] BOWKER and James M. SMITH:
Surname **SMITH**

1875. Bertha I.	born Sept 1892; died ____	1881. Bessie A. born 10 Mar 1909; died ____	
1876. James Clarence	born Jan 1895; died ____		
1877. Hannah B.	born Nov 1897; died ____		
1878. Pitt J.	born ca 1901; died ____; married Mildred E. SMITH (she born ca 1899)		
1879. Gilman Roe	born ca 1904; died ____; married Ruth T. SMITH ca ____		
1880. Lavina Burr	born 8 Feb 1907; died 1954; married Earl Leroy DICKER ca 1927		
	(he born 27 Apr 1907; died 4 Aug 1996)		

Children: Hannah[-10] born 1928, died 1997; Earlene[-10] born 1941, died 2012; and
Patricia[-10] DICKER born 1946, died 2009

1617. ADA VELZORA[-8] BOWKER, sister of above, was born 19 Sep 1874 Penobscot, Maine. She married first to George Sumner ALDRICH on 2 July 1896 at Carroll, Penobscot, ME. He was the son of Moses West ALDRICH and Hannah H. COLSON, and was born 22 Apr 1863; died 29 Sep 1919 Carroll, ME of stomach cancer. She married second to Wheeler G. SMITH on 16 Jan 1921 at Lakeville, Penobscot, ME. He was the son of John B. SMITH and Delphina COLE, and was born 27 Nov 1869; died 2 Dec 1940 and is buried at Springfield, ME. Ada V[-8] BOWKER died 2 July 1950 Carroll, ME.

Children of Ada Velzora[-8] BOWKER and George ALDRICH:
Surname **ALDRICH**

1882. Carl Cortland	born 2 May 1897; died 16 June 1964 Lincoln, ME
	married Alice Caroline RANDALL ca ____
	(she born 11 Aug 1916; died 22 Sep 1996)
1883. Reuben Roy	born 18 Apr 1900; died 3 Aug 1962; married Viola Alice CARLL 18 May 1929
1884. Vernon	born Apr 1900; died ____
1885. Albert Gilman " Burt "	born 21 Oct 1902; died 13 June 1974 Bangor, Penobscot, ME
	married Mary Elizabeth PERRY ca _____
1886. Alice Lillian	born 7 July 1905; died 14 Nov 1971
1887. Ethel E.	born 1 July 1908; died 19 Dec 1910 Carroll, ME

1620. JOHN H[-8] BOWKER, son of Nathaniel[-7] BOWKER (Cyprian[-6;5]; James[-4]; Edmund[-3]; James[-2,1]) and his first wife, Etta M. LAKE, was born 14 Feb 1875 at Omre, WI. He married Stella A. GILMORE on 26 July 1930. She was the daughter of Duane GILMORE and Maud J. BUCK, and was born 25 Jan 1906 at Winnebago, WI; died ____. John[-8] BOWKER died 23 Aug 1958 at Wood, WI. He is buried at Riverside Cemetery. John[-8] BOWKER was a veteran of the Spanish-American War.

Note: Stella GILMORE had a daughter Audrey GILMORE born ca 1929 WI. Audrey married Alex Charles RUMBUC 8 Oct 1949. He was the son of Charles R. RUMBUC and Magdalena PONOSKY, and was born 9 Nov 1927; died 29 May 2013.

Child of John-[8] BOWKER and Stella A. GILMORE:
Surname **BOWKER**

1888. Etta F.	born 7 July 1931 WI; died Nov 1976
	married Edward Kermit EATON ca ____ (he s/o Melvin EATON and Ida ____)
	(he born 14 Jan 1921 Oshkosh, WI; died 12 June 1993 Oshkosh)

1622. GUY WILFORD-[8] BOWKER, half-brother of above, son of Nathaniel[-7] BOWKER and his second wife, Alma Romina JOHNSON, was born 24 May 1894 WI. He married Winifred BARTOW 4 Aug 1918 Oshkosh, WI. She was the daughter of Leverett Henderson BARTOW and Helen May CHASE, and was born 26 Dec 1899 Oshkosh, WI; died 1957 Oshkosh.. Guy W[-8] BOWKER died 17 Oct 1965 WI.

Children of Guy[-8] BOWKER and Winifred BARTOW:
Surname **BOWKER**

1889. N. Leroy/ Roy	born 29 Sep 1919 WI; died 2 Mar 1991 Kenosha, WI
1890. Helen	born ca 1922; died ____; married _____ WALKER
1891. Guy W., Jr	born 16 June 1927; died 7 Dec 2003
	married Barbara BAGGERSON 19 June 1950

Children: David[-10] born ca ___; Jeffery[-10] born ca ____; and Michael[-10] BOWKER born ca ____

1892. Ione May.	born 8 Feb 1932; died 1 Sep 2011 La Crosse, WI

Info source: Obituaries of both John[-7] and Guy[-7] BOWKER (Oshkosh Daily Northwestern)

1643. WINTHROP HAROLD[-8] BOWKER, son of Dr. Everett Murray[-7] BOWKER (Watts Henry[-6]; Watts[-5]; Major Levi[-4]; Joseph[-3]; James[-2,1]) and Lucy Mary N. GRIGGS, was born 20 July 1900 ME. He married Edith Dorothea HILL on 14 June 1928. She was the daughter of Willard Converse HILL and Clara A. LAYCOCK, and was born 12 Nov 1901 MA; died 10 Apr 1994 at Falmouth, MA. Winthrop Harold[-8] BOWKER, a construction engineer, died ca 1962 MA.

Children of Winthrop Harold[-8] BOWKER and Edith Dorothea HILL:
Surname **BOWKER**

1893. Sarah Preble +	born 25 May 1930; died ____
	married Dr. Robert Henry GIBBS, Jr. (PhD) 9 June 1951
	(he s/o Robert Henry GIBBS, Sr. and Elizabeth KILGORE)

Child: Elizabeth Dorothea[-10] GIBBS born 4 July 1955

+   Note: Sarah Preble[-9] BOWKER received AB and MS degrees from Cornell University, Ithaca, NY (zoology)
Source: Dinwiddie Family Records, pages 82,83

1894. Anna	born ca 1932; died ____

1649. ISABELLE CLIFFORD[8] HANSCOM, daughter of Herbert Mortimer[-7] HANSCOM (Simon[-6]; Lydia[-5] BOWKER; Major Levi[-4]; Joseph[-3]; James[-2,1]) and Margaret MAKER, was born 26 Dec 1873 at East Machias, Washington, Maine. She married first to ____ MORTLOCK ca ____. She married second to Luther FORBES on 11 Sep 1900. He was the son of John FORBES and Ann MULHOLLAND, and was born ca 1867, died 1924. Isabelle[-8] HANSCOM died 14 Feb 1927.

Children of Isabelle[-8] HANSCOM and Luther FORBES:
Surname **FORBES**

1895. Margaret A	born ca 1904; died 1981	1899. Robert H	born ca 1917; died 1978
1896. Isabelle F	born ca 1908; died 14 July 1967; married Carle E CHURCH, Jr. ca ____		
	(he born ca 1906; died 1969)		
1897. Luther H. Jr.	born ca 1912; died 1912		
1898. Roberta F	born ca 1913; died ca 1990; married Rosario L. LOCICERO ca ____ (1911- 1968)		

1661. SEYMOUR HARMON-[8] BOWKER, son of Simeon[-7] BOWKER (Nathan Stephen[-6]; Levi[-5; 4]; Joseph[-3] ; James[-2,1]) and Keziah J. HOLMES, was born 29 March 1875 at Marshfield, Washington, Maine. He married Lillian Mabel GETCHELL on 8 July 1896 at Machias, Maine. She was the daughter of Oscar GETCHELL and Josephine BERRY (Stillman BERRY) and was born ____; died ____. Seymour[-8] BOWKER died 26 June 1949.

Children of Seymour-[8] BOWKER and Lillian GETCHELL:
Surname **BOWKER**   (all born Marshfield, Washington, Maine)

1900. Esther Lillian	born 28 Sep 1897; died 16 Apr 1969 Bridgewater, MA
	married Lee Martin GETCHELL, Jr. 16 June 1921
1901. Hazel L.	born 10 Mar 1899; died 26 Feb 1993 East Greenwich, RI
	married Carl J. THOMPSON ca ____
	(he born 3 Mar 1898 ME; died Dec 1966 Bridgewater, MA)
1902. Oscar Simson	born 25 Sep 1900; died 25 Feb 1989 Greenfield, MA; married Leona C. COOPER ca ___
1903. Mabel G.	born 16 May 1904; died 29 June 1986 Machias, ME
	married William Isaac HANSCOM 16 June 1925
	(he born 23 Dec 1885 Marshfield, ME; died 23 Feb 1975 Marshfield, ME)
1904. Alvin W.	born ca 1908; died ____; married Etta ____ ca ____

Children: Jean-[10] born ca 1935 CT; and Alvin-[10] BOWKER, Jr. born 25 Jan 1937 CT

1905. Leslie S.	born ca 1909; died ____
1906. Gertrude	born 31 March 1912; died 25 May 1997 ME (Child: E. Eldon-[10] LYONS born ca 1939)
	married Eldon L. LYONS 8 July 1935 (he born ca 1903)

1662. CLARENCE LEVI-8 BOWKER, brother of above, was born 3 May 1877 at Machias, Maine. He married Mary C. TURNER ca ____. She was the daughter of ____ TURNER and ____, and was born ca 1885 Ireland.; died ____. Clarence Levi-8 BOWKER died ____.

Children of Clarence-8 BOWKER and Mary TURNER:
Surname **BOWKER**

1907. Marian Elizabeth	born 2 Feb 1914 MA; died 5 Aug 1989 Brisbane, CA	
1908. Adelaide Mildred	born ca 1916 Bridgewater, MA; died ____	
	married Joseph Gaspar PAIVA 7 Feb 1934 MA	
1909. Katherine R.	born 16 Feb 1917 MA; died 31 Dec 1997 New Bedford, MA	
1910. Clarence R.	born 28 Feb 1918 MA; died Jan 1978 Stoughton, MA	
1911. Frances I.	born ca 1920; died ____	1912. Robert U. born ca 1922; died ____

1674. AMELIA L-8 " Mamie " LYON, daughter of George M-7 LYON (Sarah-6 GETCHELL; Betsey-5 BOWKER; Major Levi-4; Joseph-3; James-2,1) and Jane Ann " Jenny " BERRY, was born Sept 1886 at ____, MA. She married Samuel Hunter THOMPSON on 23 Aug 1905. He was the son of Charles Augustus THOMPSON and Sophia Gleason THAXTER; and was born Jan 1880; died 12 April 1965. Millie-8 LYON died 13 Jan 1967 Calais, ME.

Children of Mamie-8 LYON and Samuel THOMPSON:
Surname **THOMPSON**   (all children born at Northfield, Washington, Maine)

1913. Ralph I.	born ca 1906/07; died _____	
1914. Charles Augustus	born 19 Feb 1908; died 24 July 1981 Stillwater, ME	
1915. Alice B.	born ca 1909; died ____; married Leander F. BAGLEY ca _____	
	(he s/o John Adams BAGLEY and Lucy Mae BERRY)	
1916. Lawrence L.	born 26 May 1912; died ____	
1917. Paul M.	born 10 Sep 1915; died ____	1919. Samuel Hunter, Jr. born 26 Aug 1925
1918. John King	born 14 Sep 1918; died 4 July 1992 Machias, ME	

1681. GRACE A-8 LYON, daughter of Simeon Getchell-7 LYON (Sarah-6 GETCHELL; Betsey-5 BOWKER; Major Levi-4; Joseph-3; James-2,1) and Hannah SEDGLEY, was born 7 Dec 1887 CA. She married first to Samuel Joseph DEPENDENER ca ____. He was the son of ____ DEPENDENER and ____, and was born 1 Nov 1876 OH; died ca 1935 at Auburn, Placer, CA. She married second to David P. EDWARDS ca ____. He was the son of William EDWARDS and Mary POWELL, and was born 6 Jan 1875 WI; died 10 May 1942. Grace-8 LYON died March 1974 Placer, CA.

Children of Grace-8 LYON and Samuel DEPENDENER:
Surname **DEPENDENER**

1920. Hazel Mignonette	born 1908/09; died 1911	EOL
1921. Jack Alden	born 24 April 1910; died ca 1936 Auburn, Placer, CA	
1922. Burt Samuel	born 30 June 1911 Auburn; died 11 Dec 1979 CA	
1923. Raymond Lyon	born 3 Oct 1913; died 1 Aug 1935 Auburn, CA	

1685. AVARD PHINNEY-8 LYON, son of Andrew M-7 LYON (Sarah-6 GETCHELL; Betsey-5 BOWKER; Major Levi-4; Joseph-3; James-2,1) and Catherine CLARK, was born 11 Jan 1881 Nova Scotia, Canada. He married Frances Ethna SIAS on 6 Nov 1904 at Methuen, MA. She was the daughter of John Smith SIAS and Mary Ella GERRY, and was born 30 March 1888 West Boxford, MA; died ca 1968 Brookfield, MA. Avard-8 LYON died 16 Feb 1958 Methuen, MA.

Children of Avard-8 LYON and Frances SIAS:
Surname **LYON**

1924. Grace Frances	born 5 April 1906 Methuen, MA; died 1 Sep 1979 Worcester, MA
	married Henry Warner GIFFORD 16 June 1923 West Boxford, MA
1925. Gladys Ethel	born 9 Dec 1908 W. Boxford; 6 Jan 1985 New London, NH
	married Edward Frothingham EDWARDS, Sr. ca ____ (he born ca 1902; died 1984)
1926. Catherine Durling	born 11 Jan 1913 W. Boxford; died 15 June 1963 Lawrence, MA
1927. Marion Elizabeth	born 24 Feb 1918 W. Boxford; died 6 Feb 2005 Denvers, MA

1688. SADIE MARIE-8 LYON, sister of above, was born 23 Oct 1888 CA. She married Vernon Velman/Welman BAKER ca 1906. He was the son of Israel Parker BAKER and Mary Jane WILKINS, and was born 16 June 1886 Prince Albert, South

Africa, died 10 Jan 1961 Nova Scotia. Sadie Marie-8 LYON died 4 Feb 1970 at Pawling, Dutchess, NY.

Children of Sadie Marie-8 LYON and Vernon BAKER:
Surname **BAKER**

1928. Lloyd	born 4 Oct 1906 Nova Scotia; died 5 March 1924
1929. Hazel Ruby	born 7 Oct 1909 Margaretsville, NS; died 12 Oct 1956 NS
1930. Florence Myrtle	born 14 July 1912 Forest Glade, Annapolis, NS; died 27 Aug 1981 Pawling, NY
	married Ralph Victor HILTON 14 Aug 1933 Margaretsville, NS
	(he born 13 Apr 1909 NS; died March 1980 Pawling, NY)
	Child: Delores Louella-10 HILTON born 21 Oct 1939 Concord, NH
1931. Walter Israel	born 2 Sep 1914 NS; died 30 Sep 1972 NS
1932. Ethel Katherine	born 13 Jan 1917 NS; died 26 Aug 1986 Middleton, Nova Scotia
	married _____ GATES ca ____
1933. Ruby Lola	born 2 Aug 1918 NS; died 2 Feb 1990 NS
1934. John Vernon	born 21 May 1920; died 1926 Middleton, Nova Scotia

1717. ELFRA MADELINE-8 EASTMAN, daughter of Ephraim-7 EASTMAN (Adelia Loring BOWKER-6; Elbridge-5; James-4; Joseph-3; James-2,1) and Lulu/Luella CATLIN, was born 9 June 1903 Harpswell, Maine. She married Forrest H. JOHNSON on 1 Oct 1923. He was the son of ____ JOHNSON and ____; and was born 16 Oct 1896, ME; died 20 Oct 1972 Portland, ME. Elfra-8 EASTMAN died 1992 East Harpswell, ME.

Children of Elfra-8 EASTMAN and Forrest JOHNSON:
Surname **JOHNSON**   (all children born South Portland, Maine)

1935. Luella Mae	born 9 Aug 1924; died 7 Jan 2012 Portland, ME
	married Arnold H. SMITH ca 1946
	Child: Linda-10 SMITH born ca ___; married John FENDERSON; and Arnold-10 SMITH born ca ___ ; died 2011
1936. Forrest H., Jr	born ca 1927; died ____
1937. Dorothy L.	born ca 1929; died ____; married Brenton Richard CROSSMAN 23 July 1949
	(he s/o Cedric CROSSMAN and Charlotte M. GREENLAW) (he born ca 1925/26)
1938. Donald E.	born 18 July 1930; died ____
1939. Willard R.	born 10 Jan 1935; died 2 Aug 1994
1940. Raymond Lee	born 15 May 1938 Portland, ME; died 15 Jan 1987 Portland
1941. Bruce	born ca ____

1721. ELLSWORTH T-8 BOURNE, son of Mary Jane-7 BOWKER (Turner-6; Benjamin-5,4; Richard-3,2; James-1) and Calvin Francis BOURNE, was born 11 July 1861 at Hanson, Plymouth, MA. He married Arabella F. CHURCHILL on 22 March 1884 Hanson. She was the daughter of Ebenezer A. CHURCHILL and Mary Farrell FORD, and was born 20 June 1867 WI; died 16 Aug 1951 Marshfield, MA. Ellsworth-8 BOURNE died 28 August 1950 at Marshfield, Plymouth, MA.

Children of Ellsworth-8 BOURNE and Arabella CHURCHILL:
Surname **BOURNE**   (all children born at Hanson, Plymouth, MA)

1942. Francis L. (Frank)	born 19 Feb 1886; died ____; Clara PERKINS 23 Dec 1905

Children of Ellsworth-8 BOURNE and Arabella CHURCHILL, continued:
Surname **BOURNE**

1943. Ethel	born 5 Jan 1889; died 16 Jan 1892 Hanson EOL
1944. Grace Mildred	born Nov 1892; died ____; married Auburn Sterling HENDERSON ca ____
1945. Carl Merton	born 5 Aug 1895; died 25 Apr 1973 Brockton, MA
	married Hazel Maud HANNA ca ____
	(she born 12 Sep 1903 Canada; died 26 Mar 1992 MA)
1946. Leon Everett	born 1 Aug 1897; died Aug 1966 MA
	married Mary Katherine BARRY ca ____
	(she born 14 Dec 1897; died Jan 1979 MA)
1947. Harold Turner	born 17 Oct 1905; died 12 Apr 1984 MA
	married Phyllis May STUDLEY 5 Nov 1939 Hanover, MA
	(she born 22 April 1913 Hanover; died 23 Mar 2003 Brant Rock, Plymouth, MA)
1948. Gladys Louise	born 4 July 1909 Hanover, MA; died 10 Nov 1986 Hanover, MA
	married Harold Sanford LAWRENCE 2 Feb 1929

1748. GEORGE HENRY⁻⁹ LEARNED, Jr. son of George Henry⁻⁸, Sr. (Grant Bartsow⁻⁷; Clarissa-⁶ BOWKER; Howard-⁵; Lazarus⁻⁴, Jr; Lazarus⁻³; James⁻². Jr., James⁻¹) and Bertha RHEIN, was born 22 Aug 1887 MO. He married Nellie L. EDWARDS ca ____. She was the daughter of George Francis EDWARDS and Catherine BRENNAN, and was born 9 Dec 1894 IL; died Jan 1969 MO. George Henry⁻⁹ LEARNED, Jr. died 21 Mar 1974 at St. Louis, MO.

Children of George Henry-⁹ LEARNED, Jr. and Nellie EDWARDS:
Surname **LEARNED**

1949. Raymond E.	born ca 1916 MO; died 28 Nov 1964 St. Louis, MO	
	married Bernice Victoria MURPHY ca ____	(she born ca 1917; died 2002)
1950. George Henry III	born 14 Feb 1918 MO; died 26 July 1995 St. Louis, MO.	
	married Mary Ann RIORDAN ca ____	(she born ca 1924; died 1990)

1770. ETHEL/ETHYL⁻⁹ CLARK, daughter of Minnie L⁻⁸ BOWKER (Franklin-⁷; Clarke⁻⁶; Joseph⁻⁵; Zebulon⁻⁴; Lazarus⁻³; James⁻²,¹) and James Henry CLARK, was born 29 Mar 1886 Dunham, Hancock, IL. She married Walter Mark AVISE on 25 Dec 1906. He was the son of ____ AVISE and Harriet M. BROWN; and was born 8 April 1887 Valentine, Nebraska ; died May 1964. Ethel⁻⁹ CLARK died 9 Jan 1971.

Children of Ethel-⁹ CLARK and Walter Mark AVISE:
Surname **AVISE**

1951. Minnie Clair	born 27 Oct 1907 IL; died 19 Feb 2011
1952. James Franklin	born 10 May 1910; died 28 July 1998 Mesa, AZ
1953. Walter Rex	born 21 Nov 1913 IL; died 7 Sep 1990 Sarasota, FL

1777. THELMA NOREEN / NORENE⁻⁹ BOWKER, daughter of Roger⁻⁸ BOWKER (Franklin W⁻⁷; Clarke⁻⁶; Joseph⁻⁵; Zebulon⁻⁴; Lazarus⁻³; James⁻²,¹) and Amy Z. LAMB, was born 9 Apr 1904 IL. She married Guy Harold OLLIS on 27 Dec 1925 IL. He was the son of William Mathias OLLIS and Martha Ellen BOWEN, and was born 29 Jan 1902; died 2 July 1995 Dallas City, IL. Thelma N⁻⁹ BOWKER died 1 July 2001 Dallas City, IL.

Children of Thelma-⁹ BOWKER and Guy Harold OLLIS:
Surname **OLLIS**

1954. Martha Jean	born 14 Dec 1927 Madison, IA; died 19 Mar 1971 Gulfport, IL
1955. Joan	born 9 Sep 1932 Madison, Lee, IA; died 15 May 1994 Vancouver, WA.

1784. ERNEST BYRON⁻⁹ NEWCOMB, son of Sarah B⁻⁸ BOWKER/BUKER (Sims Gardner-⁷; Rufus⁻⁶;James⁻⁵,⁴,³,²,¹ BOWKER) and George Dow NEWCOMB, was born 6 May 1883 MA. He married Caroline " Carrie " S. ____ ca 1907. She was born 1886 MA ; died ____. Ernest⁻⁹ NEWCOMB died ____.

Children of Ernest B-⁹ NEWCOMB and Caroline S. __?__:
Surname **NEWCOMB**

1956. Ernest Byron, Jr.	born ca 1908; died ____		
1957. Dorothy M.	born ca 1908; died ____; married Albert JONES ca	(he born ca 1902 MA)	
1958. George T/C	born ca 1912; died ____		
1959. Harold M/A	born ca 1915; died ____		
1960. Sarah Brown	born 2 Mar 1920; died 25 Apr 2000 Weymouth, MA		
1961. Edward Avery	born 6 Mar 1922; died ____		
1962. Alfred Irving	born 9 Feb 1925; died 17 Dec 1998 Weymouth, MA		
1963. Arlene V.	born 3 July 1927; died ____	1964. Barbara A.	born ca 1929; died ____

1800. HAROLD CHESTER⁻⁹ BOWKER, son of Clyde K⁻⁸ BOWKER (William-T⁻⁷; Samuel⁻⁶; Samuel Michael⁻⁵; William⁻⁴; James⁻³,²,¹) and Ethel L ____, was born 17 May 1906 OH. He married Marie Dorothy GLOMB on 18 July 1931 OH. She was the daughter of __ GLOMB and Anna __, and was born ca 1912; died ___. Harold C⁻⁹ BOWKER died 9 March 1990 Hamilton, OH.

Children of Harold C-9 BOWKER and Marie GLOMB:
Surname **BOWKER**

1965. Donald R.	born 27 Nov 1933; died 13 Dec 1933	1968. Thomas	born ca 1939
1966. Sue Ann	born 15 Apr 1936; died 22 June 2005; married William BROWN ca _____		

(he born 18 Nov 1937; died 22 Jan 2013)
(he s/o John BROWN and Marie ECKSTEIN)
Children: Gerald-11 born ca ____; and Sondra-11 BROWN born ca ____, married Roy WESSELMAN

1967. Ronald Clyde   born 17 Feb 1935 OH; died 7 Oct 2011 OH; married Gail Ann SHAW ca ____

1803. WILLIAM EARL-9 BOWKER, son of Willis-8 BOWKER (William T-7; Samuel-6;5; William-4; James-3;2;1) and Mary Isabelle PETERS, was born 5 March 1914 IN. He married Helen Louise MISTLER ca ____. She was the daughter of Nicholas MISTLER and Daisy M. BOLSER, and was born 12 Sep 1915 OH; died 31 Oct 1991 Houston, TX. William Earl-9 BOWKER, Sr. died 23 Sep 1972 Houston, TX.

Children of William E-9 BOWKER and Helen _____:
Surname **BOWKER**

1969. Delores	born 12 April 1934 OH; died 1983 TX; 1 married John DOTSON ca _____		
	2 married Bryan A. FRANK ca ____; 3 married George MARTIN ca _____		
1970. William Earl, Jr.	born ____		
1971. Patricia Ann	born 17 Mar 1938; died 14 Sep 1995 OH; 1 married Donald FARMER ca ____		
	2 married William J. WELLMEIER 19 Feb 1972		
1972. Richard Norman	born 22 Sep 1944; died 15 Mar 1998 Pasadena, TX		
	married Sharon Kaye DENLEY 1 Sep 1965		
1973. Judith Lorraine	born 26 Oct 1946 OH; died 2006 Houston, TX		
1974. Ralph	born ____	1978. Carol Ann	born ____
1975. Milton	born _____		
1976. Sharon Kaye	born 2 May 1950 OH; married Harold Wayne PETERS 27 Aug 1966 Harris, TX		
	divorced 21 Aug 1973 Harris, TX		
1977. Faye A	born 6 Apr 1953 OH; 2 married Steven R. FRENCH 19 July 1984 Harris, TX		

1855. GWENDOLYN IRENE-9 ROWELL, daughter of Benjamin Jefferson-8 ROWELL (Maria Eliza-7 BOWKER; William-6; Elijah-5,4; John-3; James-2,1) and Maria SOUSA, was born 11 June 1909 MA. She married Fred Watson TAYLOR ca 1928. He was the son of William Brundage TAYLOR and Minnie Etta WATSON, and was born 8 Aug 1910 NH, died 25 Mar 1976 Old Saybrook, CT. Gwendolyn-9 ROWELL died 23 Feb 1981 Los Angeles, CA. Note: On the 1940 Census Fred TAYLOR was listed as a patient at the Taunton (MA) State Hospital for the Insane.

Children of Gwendolyn-9 ROWELL and Fred TAYLOR:
Surname **TAYLOR**

1979. Ralph E	born ca 1929 MA	1983. Jacqueline	born ca 1937
1980. Kenneth (twin)	born ca 1933	1984. Gwendolyn	born ca 1939 Weymouth, MA;
1981. William (twin)	born ca 1933; died 14 Aug 2010		
1982. Robert	born 16 Mar 1934; died 8 Feb 2001 Weymouth, MA		

1861 ARTHUR LYNN-9 BOWKER, son of Charles-8 BOWKER (Gilman Roe-7; John M-6; Cyprian-5; Capt. James-4; Edmund-3; James-2,1) and Mary Jane HEBB, was born 1 Aug 1894 at Carroll, Penobscot, Maine. He married Grace Edna JORDAN on 1 Oct 1917. She was the daughter of Edwin Hurd JORDAN and Helen " Nellie " PORTER, and was born 25 July 1901 Eddington, Penobscot, ME; died 17 Jan 1968 Lincoln, ME. Arthur Lynn-9 BOWKER died 9 Jan 1978 Lincoln, ME.

Children of Arthur Lynn-9 BOWKER and Grace JORDAN:
Surname **BOWKER**   (all children born Lincoln, Penobscot, Maine)

1985. Stanley Arthur	born 30 Mar 1919; died 12 Oct 2010 Lincoln, ME
	married Evelyn M. NEAL 27 June 1942
1986. Kenneth Jordan	born 6 Oct 1921; died 1936
1987. Stillborn child	born and died 6 Sep 1922
1988. Halton Lynn	born 26 Jan 1924; died 15 Mar 2002 Lee, ME
	1 married Leah Hope KELLEY 13 June 1948; 2 married Glennis M. GIFFORD 17 June 1951
1989. Betty Jane	born 21 Feb 1937; died 20 July 2008 Lincoln, ME
	married Walter Leamon Mc KINNON ca _____ (he born ca 1932; died 2001)

476

INDEX - BOWKER SURNAMES

478

480

484

490

www.ingramcontent.com/pod-product-compliance
Lightning Source LLC
Chambersburg PA
CBHW080810280326
41926CB00091B/4126